I0817493

"Everyone interested in the Jewish context of New Testament literature will welcome the appearance of the English translation of Strack and Billerbeck's classic commentary that provides myriads of parallels with rabbinic literature. As an added bonus, David Instone-Brewer's introduction very helpfully clarifies the proper use of this valuable tool and at the same time answers the criticisms leveled against it in its original German form. I salute editor Jacob Cerone, translator Joseph Longarino, and Lexham Press for a job well done!"

—**Craig A. Evans,** John Bisagno Distinguished Professor of Christian Origins, Houston Baptist University

"I have long wished for an English translation of Strack-Billerbeck. The person who would use this resource properly must read David Instone-Brewer's introduction. Following his guidelines, this is an unparalleled resource for Old Testament, Second Temple Jewish, and especially rabbinic uses of keywords, phrases, and concepts in the New Testament—book by book and verse by verse. Some books and portions of books are treated in far more detail than others, but what is available here is simply not found together in one given work anywhere else. Many, many thanks to Lexham for completing a project a long time in the works."

—**Craig L. Blomberg,** Distinguished Professor of New Testament, Denver Seminary

"Given the problems with Strack-Billerbeck and (I confess) how slowly I read German, I have always opted to simply read through the rabbinic sources directly. But for the majority of readers who cannot afford the leisure to do so, this work solves the linguistic limitation. It also provides much of the material mined and recycled by generations of commentators subsequent to Strack-Billerbeck. It can thus be highly useful, provided readers heed the important cautions noted by rabbinics scholar David Instone-Brewer in the introduction."

—**Craig S. Keener,** F. M. and Ada Thompson Professor of Biblical Studies, Asbury Theological Seminary

"The appearance of this commentary is a breathtaking achievement. For a century its analysis and full ancient citations were accessible only in German. Plus, we have decades of hindsight to mull over how Strack-Billerbeck has been misunderstood, misapplied, and (unfairly or not) maligned. At long last there is a fully integrated digital and print text, crowned with a fresh and erudite introduction by Dr. Instone-Brewer. It is a version we hope will last another hundred years."

—**Gary S. Shogren,** professor of New Testament, Seminario Escuela de Estudios Pastorales, San José, Costa Rica

"The impulse to investigate the Jewish context for Jesus and the writings of the New Testament has perhaps never been stronger. Recent scholarship has, for good reasons, gravitated toward the Second Temple period that preceded the time of Jesus to contextualize the New Testament. Nevertheless, it would be a profound mistake to presume that rabbinic thought has nothing to contribute merely because it derives from a later period. In many instances, rabbinic teachings find their roots in this older material. To this point, Strack-Billerbeck, the essential tool for rabbinic opinion relative to the New Testament, has been accessible only to scholars or others who could read German. That obstacle has been eliminated with this new English translation, an achievement that will certainly position it as the essential tool in the English language for discovering 'what the rabbis taught' in regard to the content of the New Testament."

—**Michael S. Heiser,** executive director, Awakening School of Theology; host of the Naked Bible Podcast

A COMMENTARY

on the

NEW TESTAMENT

from the

TALMUD & MIDRASH

A COMMENTARY *on the* NEW TESTAMENT *from the* TALMUD & MIDRASH

Volume 3

• • •

HERMANN L. STRACK
& PAUL BILLERBECK

JACOB N. CERONE, GENERAL EDITOR
JOSEPH LONGARINO, TRANSLATOR
WITH AN INTRODUCTION BY DAVID INSTONE-BREWER

LEXHAM PRESS

A Commentary on the New Testament from the Talmud & Midrash, Volume 3
Strack & Billerbeck

Lexham Academic, an imprint of Lexham Press
1313 Commercial St., Bellingham, WA 98225
LexhamPress.com

Print ISBN 9781683595472
Digital ISBN 9781683595489
Library of Congress Control Number 2021939610

General Editor: Jacob N. Cerone
Translator: Joseph Longarino
Lexham Editorial: Derek R. Brown, Abigail Stocker, David Bomar
Cover Design: Brian Hintz, Brittany Schrock
Typesetting: Anna Fejes

CONTENTS

Editor's Preface

Jacob N. Cerone

Strack and Billerbeck's *Commentary on the New Testament from the Talmud and Midrash* has had an enduring effect on New Testament studies and its relationship to Judaism. As a collection of thousands of possible parallels from rabbinic sources that in some way (e.g., linguistically, culturally, theologically) relate to the corpus of canonical New Testament documents, there is simply no work like it. Although this reference work has been criticized for its dating of rabbinic material, its strong Lutheran distinction between the supposed legalism of Judaism and the grace found in Christ, and the legitimacy of the suggested parallels, it continues to function as a sourcebook for an initial investigation into the potential Jewish backgrounds of New Testament texts (see Introduction to the English Translation). It is because of the enduring value of this work that it appears in English translation for the first time, almost one hundred years after its initial publication in German. Accompanying the translation is an introduction by David Instone-Brewer, who details the reception history of Strack-Billerbeck and charts a course for its responsible usage. All who use these volumes should read his introduction before engaging with the work itself.

Characteristics of this Translation

Stack-Billerbeck is a massive work. The original German edition consisted of four volumes and contained 4,102 pages. There is an unevenness to the work as it attempts to avoid redundancies. Volume 1 covers only the Gospel of Matthew but spans 1,055 pages. Volume 2, however, covers Mark, Luke, and John (including three excurses: "The Memra of Jesus," "The Feast of Tabernacles," and "The Day of Jesus' Death") in 867 pages. Volume 3 treats the remainder of the New Testament in 857 pages. The excurses in Volume 4 include important topics on Judaism and the New Testament such as circumcision, the Sermon on the Mount, leprosy and lepers, Elijah, and the resurrection from the dead.

The heart of the work has always been the verse-by-verse commentary and not the excurses in volume 4. For this reason, the publisher of the

English edition has decided to leave the excurses untranslated for the time being. Within the commentary, references to the titles of the excurses have been translated in the event that volume 4 is someday published in English (see page xviii for a list of the excurses included in volume 4).

The translation work followed a number of principles. First, the English translation of Strack-Billerbeck is not a revision or an update of the original German text. Each translator aimed to produce an accurate translation of the German text. The editor and translators made no attempt to return to Strack and Billerbeck's original sources to correct real or perceived errors; Strack-Billerbeck is a historical work that stands and falls on its own merits. Second, the translators attempted to provide a balance between a smooth English idiom and a faithful rendering of a rather wooden German original. The goal was to produce a translation that was immediately understandable without compromising the integrity of the original work. Third, the names of rabbis and places have been translated into English rather than transliterated (e.g., R. Judah b. Tabbai instead of Jehuda b. Ṭabai), using common designations as can be found in many translated editions of rabbinic texts. The spelling has been standardized except in instances where Billerbeck notes unique variants. Finally, Strack and Billerbeck's method of transliterating Hebrew/Aramaic has been maintained, though with some minor changes.[1]

User's Guide

A number of general characteristics of Strack-Billerbeck might be confusing at first. The following is a brief guide to help navigate the unique format of the work.

Typeface

In the main body of the text, Strack and Billerbeck shifted between a larger typeface and a smaller typeface. The larger typeface usually, though not always, consisted of their own comments on the passage or on the rabbinic literature that would be included within that section of the commentary. The smaller typeface was reserved for the many citations from source texts that were intended to illustrate or illuminate a specific word, phrase, or clause.

Citation of the Talmud, Mishnah, and Tosefta

Strack-Billerbeck's manner of citing the rabbinic literature has been largely preserved, though with minor alterations. For example, pHor 3,48^{a},39

1. E.g., ç has been changed to ṣ, sch has been reduced to sh, and ^{e} has been simplified to e.

becomes y. Hor. 3.48A.39; Schab 108[b] becomes b. Šabb. 108B; TSchab 7,23 becomes t. Šabb. 7.23; and Nidda 9,7 becomes m. Nid. 9.7. In their introduction to each of the first three volumes, the authors explain the significance of these abbreviations and the editions used for their work:

Editions and Abbreviations

- Jerusalem Talmud: Krakau 1609; abbreviation = y.
- Babylonian Talmud: Amsterdam 1644ff. (used only in cases of doubt); abbreviation = b.
- Tosefta: M. S. Zuckermandel, Pasewalk 1880; abbreviation = t.

Manner of Citation

- The Mishnah is cited according to chapter and paragraph (e.g., m. Šabb 3.4).
- The Babylonian Talmud is cited according to leaves and pages (e.g., b. Šabb 30B).
- The Jerusalem Talmud is cited according to chapter, sheet, column, and line (e.g., y. Ber. 4.7D.43).

Footnotes

There are three different types of footnotes used in these volumes. The first type contains information that previously was in the main text (e.g., parenthetical discussions or citations of secondary literature). These notes can be identified by the fact that they look like common footnotes. For example:

According to G. Dalman, this passage is a late interpolation (*Die Worte Jesu: Mit Berücksichtigung des nachkanonischen jüdischen Schriftums und der aramäischen Sprache erörtert*, 2nd ed. [Leipzig: Hinrichs, 1930], 1:221).

The second type of footnote begins with the abbreviation "S-B" (Strack-Billerbeck). For example:

S-B: These words can probably be rightly understood only as a question; for a different understanding, see the rendering at § Matt 4:17 B, #2, n. c.

These notes contain material originally presented by Strack-Billerbeck as footnotes. It was necessary to maintain a distinction between these notes and others to aid in locating internal references to footnotes across the work. For instance, in Romans 3:9 A, #1, n. *d* the authors refer the reader to the S-B footnote at § Matt 5:43, #1, n. *g*. Being able to distinguish between the various types of footnotes helps the reader find the note in question.

The third type of footnote, beginning with the abbreviation "TN," is the translator's note. For example:

TN: The German "auf jemand Rücksicht nehmen" is polyvalent in meaning and could mean "show consideration for," "take account of," "make allowances for," all of which come into play in the discussion below.

These notes contain important context for understanding the material, translation difficulties, or relevant information to aid the reader. Although translator notes could have multiplied, they are limited to what was deemed essential.

Navigating Strack-Billerbeck

Strack and Billerbeck used a combination of biblical references and page numbers when making internal references within the commentary. At times, they were inconsistent and/or inaccurate with their references. Maintaining this practice would have been complex and would have had little benefit. Therefore, page references have been eliminated entirely and replaced with references to the work's internal hierarchy. The running headers aid in quickly navigating the volumes. For example:

In the discussion of Romans 5:1, the text reads, "On 'peace' see also 1 En. 105:2 at § Rom 1:3 A, A, #1, n. γ." To find 1 Enoch 105:2, begin by looking for Romans 1:3 in the running headers. You will find that Romans 1:3 has been divided into two discussions. Romans 1:3 A has information about the phrase "Concerning his Son" and Romans 1:3 B has information about the phrase "Who was born from the seed of David." Look for 1:3 A in the headers. Romans 1:3 A is further divided into two large discussions, A and B. Look for Romans 1:3 A A in the headers. Within Romans 1:3 A, A, there are three further divisions, #1, #2, and #3. The headers will contain this information as well. Once you have found Romans 1:3 A A #1 in the header, look for note γ in the main text. There, at the beginning of the note, is the citation of 1 Enoch 105:2. Although the headers do not provide the comprehensive hierarchy used in each section, they provide ample and sufficient information for finding the reference.

In numerous instances, this revised navigational system will make it easier to find the reference. In other instances, it will make it more difficult. In these latter cases, additional information has been supplied in the reference, such as "final paragraph," "toward the beginning," "middle," "toward the end," etc. References to the excurses (excluding those contained in volume 2) have not been changed. The reason for this was simple: the references to numbered or lettered sections simply do not correspond to what is found in the volumes themselves. Although an attempt was made to repair the cross-references, the inaccuracies were too great and citations too difficult to find, and the attempt was ultimately abandoned.

Symbols

Strack and Billerbeck used a number of symbols that require brief explanation. The em-dash *without* spaces on either side (e.g., xxx—xxx) indicates the standard presence of parenthetical information. However, the em-dash *with* spaces on both sides (e.g., xxx — xxx) indicates a break of some kind. Strack and Billerbeck used this symbol most frequently to indicate the presence of their own commentary on a citation.[2] They also used this symbol to signal a general break between the preceding and subsequent material. Context will aid in determining the nature of the break. Like the spaced em-dash, ‖ indicates a break in the preceding material, most often a transition between citations. Mark 14:51, n. *b* provides a prototypical example of how the spaced em-dash and ‖ function:

> ‖ ʾAbot de Rabbi Nathan 25: (Ben Azzai [ca. 110]) said, "It is easier to rule the entire world than to sit and teach in front of people wrapped in linen garments העטופין סדינין." — A parallel passage occurs in Midr. Ps. 18 § 34 (81A). ‖ Babylonian Talmud ʿErubin 54B: "In her love, you like to stagger all the time" (Prov 5:19; according to the Mishnah, in the love of the Torah). Like R. Eleazar b. Pedat (ca. 270), who was said to have sat and occupied himself with the Torah on the lower market of Sepphoris, while his linen garment סדינו lay on the upper market of Sepphoris.

Here, Strack-Billerbeck provides the comment that the content of ʾAbot de Rabbi Nathan 25 has a parallel in Midr. Ps. 18 § 34 (81A). Following this comment is ‖, which signals to the reader that a citation of another source text will follow (in this case, Babylonian Talmud ʿErubin 54B).

Quotation Marks

The use of quotation marks in these volumes is unique. Billerbeck did not use them at all, or rather he limited them to the citation of Scripture and to other exceptional cases. Instead of using quotation marks to introduce a citation or dialogue, Billerbeck used a colon, but he provided no indication of where the citation or dialogue ended. In order to aid in the reading

2. Parentheses or square brackets within or at the end of a citation also serve this function.

process, quotation marks have been added for all dialogue and to mark the beginning and end of citations. The only exception to this rule is the use of opening and closing quotation marks for citations from the Talmud, Mishnah, and Tosefta. The extensive amount of dialogue, dialogue within dialogue, and quotation of Scripture (which itself often contains dialogue) within the Talmud, Mishnah, and Tosefta made the use of quotation marks for the beginning and end of the citation prohibitive. Our hope is that by adding these quotation marks for most of the source texts and for dialogue, the reader will find the text much improved and easier to read.[3]

Abbreviations of Rabbinic Literature and Editions Used[4]

A. Tractates in the Mishnah, Talmud, Tosefta

B. Bat. = Baba Batra
B. Meṣ. = Baba Meṣiʿa
B. Qam. = Baba Qamma
Bek. = Bekorot
Bik. = Bikkurim
Ber. = Berakot
Giṭ = Giṭṭin
Hor. = Horayot
Zebaḥ. = Zebaḥim
Ḥag. = Ḥagigah
Ḥul. = Ḥullin
Ṭehar. = Ṭeharot
Yebam. = Yebamot
Yad. = Yadayim
Kil. = Kilʾayim
Ketub. = Ketubbot
Meg. = Megillah
Mid. = Middot
Moʿed Qaṭ. = Moʿed Qaṭan
Mak. = Makkot
Makš. = Makširin
Menaḥ. = Menaḥot
Maʿaś. = Maʿaśerot
Maʿaś. Š. = Maʿaśer Šeni
Miqw. = Miqwaʾot
Neg. = Negaʿim
Ned. = Nedarim
Soph = Sopherim
Sanh. = Sanhedrin
ʿAbod. Zar. = ʿAbodah Zarah
ʿEd. = ʿEduyyot
ʿErub. = ʿErubin
ʿArak. = ʿArakin
Pesaḥ. = Pesaḥim
Qidd. = Qiddušin
Roš Haš. = Roš Haššanah
Šebu. = Šebuʿot
Šabb. = Šabbat
Šeqal. = Šeqalim
Tem. = Temurah
Taʿan. = Taʿanit
Ter. = Terumot

3. Where the reader finds the addition of quotation marks to be unhelpful, it may be of some assistance to know that the opening quotation mark is almost always reflective of a colon in Strack-Billerbeck, which itself was a signal that a citation or dialogue ensues.

4. The following abbreviations has been adapted and updated from Strack-Billerbeck's list, which was included in each of the volumes of the German text.

B. Midrashim (see *Einleitung in Talmud und Midraš*, 202ff.)

Rab. (Gen., Exod., Lev., Num., Deut.) = Rabbah: Venice 1545

Midr. (Song, Lam.) = Midrash on the Megillot (Song of Songs, Lamentations): Lviv 1861.

Mek. = Mekhilta: Vienna 1865 (Weiß).

SLev = Sifra Leviticus: Bucharest 1860 (Malbim).

SNum = Sifre Numbers: Vilnius 1864 (Friedmann).

SDeut = Sifre Deuteronomy: Vilnius 1864 (Friedmann).

Midr. Sam. = Midrash on Samuel: Kraków 1893 (Buber).

Midr. Ps. = Midrash on the Psalms: Vilnius 1891 (Buber).

Midr. Prov. = Midrash on the Proverbs: Vilnius 1893 (Buber).

Tanḥ. = Tanḥuma: Vienna 1863.

TanḥB.: Vilnius 1885 (Buber).

Pesiq. = Pesiqta: Lyck 1868 (Buber).

Pesiq Rab. = Pesiqta Rabbati: Vienna 1880 (Friedmann).

Pirqe R. El. = Pirqe Rabbi Eliezer: Prague 1784.

S. Eli. Rab. = Seder Eliyahu Rabba: Vienna 1902 (Friedmann).

S. Eli. Zut. = Seder Eliyahu Zuta: Vienna 1902 (Friedmann).

Ag. Ber. =ʾAggadat Berešit: Warsaw 1876.

Abot R. Nat. = Abot de Rabbi Nathan.

Yalquṭ Simeon: Vilinus 1897.

Leqach Tob: Vilnius 1884 (Buber).

Levy: J. Levy, *Neuhebräisches und Chaldäisches Wörterbuch*, 4 vols. (Leipzig 1876–1889).

Bar(aita).

C. Works by H. Strack Cited within Strack-Billerbeck

1. *Einleitung in Talmud und Midraš*, 5th entirely newly revised ed. (Munich: Beck, 1921).
2. *Ausgewählte Mišnatraktate* (nach Handschriften und alten Drucken herausgegeben, Text vokalisiert, Vokabular und mit Berücksichtigung des Neuen Testaments erläutert):

- *Pirqé Aboth. Die Sprüche der Väter*, 4th ed. (Munich: Hinrich, 1915).
- ʿAboda *Zara: Der Mischnatractat "Götzendienst"*, 2nd ed. (Munich: Hinrich, 1909).
- *Sanhedrin-Makkoth. "Gerichtshof, Geißelstrafe"* (Munich: Hinrich, 1910).
- *Pesaḥim. "Passahfest"* (mit Berücksichtigung auch der jetzigen Passahfeier der Juden) (Munich: Hinrich, 1911).
- *Berakhoth. "Lobsagungen"* (Munich: Hinrich, 1915).
- *Joma. "Versöhnungstag"*, 3rd ed. (Munich: Hinrich, 1912).
- *Sabbath. "Sabbat"* (Munich: Hinrich, 1890).
- In preparation: *Neziqin: drei Baboth "Beschädigungen"*.
- In preparation: Prof. H. Laible, *Nedarim "Gelübde"*.

3. *Jesus, die Häretiker und die Christen nach den ältesten jüdischen Angaben. Texte, Übersetzung und Erläuterung* (Leipzig: Hinrichs, 1910).

Translated Titles for Excurses Included in Volume 2

2. The Day of Jesus' Death
5. The Feast of Tabernacles
17. The Memra of Yahweh

Translated Titles for Excurses Included in Volume 4

1. Preliminary Remarks on the Sermon on the Mount
3. Circumcision
4. The Feast of the Passover
6. Fasting
7. The Institution of the Ancient Jewish Synagogue
8. The Ancient Jewish Synagogue Service
9. The Shema
10. The Shemone Esre (Eighteen Benedictions)
11. The Tefillin (Prayer Straps)
12. The Tzitzit (Show Fringes)
13. Excommunication from the Synagogue
14. Pharisees and Sadducees

15. The Stance of Judaism toward the Non-Jewish World
16. The Old Testament Canon and Its Inspiration
18. The 110th Psalm in Ancient Jewish Literature
19. The Good and Evil Inclination
20. The Parable of the Workers in the Vineyard
21. Ancient Jewish Demonology
22. Ancient Jewish Private Charity
23. Works of Love
24. An Ancient Jewish Feast
25. Taxes on Produce from the Soil
26. The Nature of Ancient Jewish Slavery
27. Leprosy and Lepers
28. Elijah
29. This World, the Days of the Messiah, and the Future World
30. Signs and Calculations of the Messianic Time
31. Sheol, Gehenna, and the Garden of Eden
32. General or Partial Resurrection of the Dead?
33. Depictions of Judgment in Ancient Jewish Literature

Introduction to the English Translation

David Instone-Brewer

The work commonly known as "Strack-Billerbeck" is a rich compendium of rabbinic sources that help illustrate the language and thinking of many of the authors and initial readers of the New Testament. It is an invaluable resource that has been underused, partly because it was in German and partly because its aim and character was misunderstood by many scholars.

Hermann Strack's academic life was devoted to combating anti-Semitism based on ignorance of Jewish sources. This involved court battles, pamphlet campaigns against powerful opponents, and academic publications. Despite his Christian convictions about the superiority of the New Testament, he refused to allow Jewish traditions to be denigrated and misrepresented. A recent reappraisal recognizes that Strack and Franz Delitzsch, "despite a theological starting-point inimical to Judaism, their Judaica scholarship, their contacts with Jewish scholars and their opposition to prevailing trends in German Christianity consistently led them in pro-Jewish directions."[1]

The sources amassed to illustrate each New Testament phrase represent Judaism in all its diversity. They are, as much as possible, quoted along with their surrounding context and assigned rough dates—though these need to be assessed intelligently (see below). These quotations are not designed to form a compendium of Jewish theology, though the topic of soteriology (an example explored below) illustrates how caricatures such as "salvation by works" are avoided and a balanced view is presented.

Historical Background

The commentary and accompanying excurses are the product of a collaboration between Hermann L. Strack and Paul Billerbeck. Strack (1848–1922) served as assistant professor of Old Testament exegesis and Semitic languages at the University of Berlin. His expertise in rabbinic literature is clearly seen by the fact that he edited numerous rabbinic tractates, published widely on rabbinic Judaism, and wrote one of the first scholarly in-

1. See Alan Levenson, "Missionary Protestants as Defenders and Detractors of Judaism: Franz Delitzsch and Hermann Strack," *Jewish Quarterly Review* XCII (2002): 383–420, here 384.

troductions to rabbinic literature.[2] Strack developed close ties with Jewish scholars and Jewish communities in Germany and defended Jews in court amid rising anti-Semitism. Strack's interest in rabbinic literature served his commitments to his Protestant faith. While he had an appreciation of rabbinic texts in their own right, his aim was to better understand them in order to demonstrate the inherent Jewishness of the New Testament documents and to demonstrate the fulfillment of the Old Testament and Jewish expectations in the Christian religion.[3]

Although Strack held a professorship and was a distinguished, well-published member of the academic guild, Paul Billerbeck (1853–1932) was an outsider to academia. Billerbeck studied Protestant theology at the Universities of Greifswald and Leipzig, but he did not pursue doctoral studies[4] or the life of the academy. After completing his studies, he entered the ministry as a Lutheran pastor. During his time as a pastor, Billerbeck participated in the mission to the Jews in Berlin (*Institutum Judaicum*), which had been cofounded by Strack, and exerted his efforts toward producing scholarly treatments of and publications on rabbinic literature in the periodical *Nathanael*.

Billerbeck's publications in *Nathanael* and his work for the mission eventually attracted the attention of Strack and led to an invitation in 1906 for Billerbeck to work on the commentary.[5] The forewords to the separate volumes provide conflicted testimony about the various responsibilities of the collaborators. Volume 1 seems to indicate the project was conceived by Strack and executed with Billerbeck's aid. However, after Strack's death in 1922, Billerbeck was pressed by his supporters to disclose the true nature of the work. He writes in the foreword to volume 4:

> Finally, a word of a personal nature. I have been asked several times to clarify the late Professor Doctor Strack's share in the composition of the commentary. In this regard, I refer to the preface of the first volume, in which Strack did not claim any involvement in the writing of the work. As editor, Professor Strack has earned the greatest merit for the publication and dissemination of the work. It is solely due to the efforts of his name and personality that the printing could be started in the time of greatest economic need shortly after the end of the War, and that the work immediately attracted attention not

2. Hermann L. Strack, *Einleitung in Talmud und Midraš* (Munich: C. H. Beck, 1921).

3. See Alan Levenson, "Missionary Protestants," 383–420; Siegfried S. Schatzmann, "Strack, Hermann Leberecht (1848–1922), and Paul Billerbeck (1853–1932)," ed. Donald K. McKim, *Dictionary of Major Biblical Interpreters* (Downers Grove, IL; InterVarsity Press, 2007), 937–41; William Baird, *History of New Testament Research, Volume Two: From Jonathan Edwards to Rudolf Bultmann* (Minneapolis, MN: Fortress Press, 2003), 417–22.

4. Billerbeck, however, indicates in the foreword to volume 2 that the University of Greifswald awarded him a doctorate in recognition of his work on the project.

5. Schatzmann, "Strack," 938.

> only in Germany, but also widely abroad, which made the printing of further volumes economically possible. For this demand of my work, I would like to call upon him, who would not live to see its appearance, now that it is ready, my warm thanks.[6]

If this is indeed accurate, and Joachim Jeremias believes it is,[7] Billerbeck's accomplishment of almost single-handedly assembling this vast collection of parallels is even more impressive.

The Purpose

The overall aim of Strack-Billerbeck is perhaps best expressed by Schoettgen, whose thousand-page work in 1733 had a similar agenda, which he described thus:

> The main use of this volume is that the phrases and sayings of the New Testament are illustrated from the ancient rabbinic writings in far greater light than can ever be expected from heathen writers.[8]

The Greek and Latin classics were part of every gentleman's education and every scholar's foundations, so it was understandable that the New Testament was largely interpreted through them. Looking for linguistic and cultural parallels in classical literature works fairly well in the epistles or Acts, but the world of the Gospels stood apart from the culture of the occupying army in the land. Strack and Billerbeck recognized the value of Schoettgen's work but also highlighted its limitations.

Historical verification of Gospel events was not the aim, though they did not shy away from this. For example, they faced the issue of whether Passover occurred on the night of the Last Supper (as in the Synoptics) or on the eve of the crucifixion (as in John), and this question became the topic of a long excursus.[9] Modern readers also seek historical verifications of this kind, but the Jewish traditions explored here are not well-suited for answering such questions.

Illustrating the sayings, concepts, parables, theological background, and cultural assumptions is the main aim of Strack-Billerbeck. When read with this purpose, it is an unparalleled sourcebook.

---

6. Hermann L. Strack and Paul Billerbeck, *Kommentar zum Neuen Testament aus Talmud und Midrash: Exkurse zu einzelnen Stellen des Neuen Testaments* (München: C. H. Beck, 1928), 4.1:v–vi (English translation by Jacob N. Cerone).

7. Joachim Jeremias, "Billerbeck, Paul (1853–1932)," *Theologische Realenzyklopädie* 4:641.

8. J. C. Schoettgen, *Horae Hebraicae et Talmudicae in universum Novum Testamentum* (Leipzig: Hekel, 1733), xx (preface).

9. Excursus: "The Evidence from the Four Gospels Concerning the Day of Jesus' Death when Considered in Relation to the Halakah," at the end of volume 2.

Potential Misuse

The richness of rabbinic quotations collected in Strack-Billerbeck can save a scholar hours of work with Hebrew concordances and background reading. Almost invariably there are more quotations than necessary, which means that the key text one needs to follow up on is very likely to be found there (or is present in the other sections referred to). Paradoxically, this richness has been criticized, not because of the resource itself but because of the way that it has been used.

Easy access to all these texts can be both a valuable research tool and a source of temptation for lazy scholarship. Almost every phrase and idea in the New Testament that could possibly have an origin in Judaism has been annotated with likely parallels in rabbinic literature. This presents the temptation to assume that all these parallels are significant—as well as the more insidious temptation to regard these sources as the conclusions of one's research rather than a starting point. This can also tempt the lazy reader to use Strack-Billerbeck as a key to New Testament interpretation or a summary of Jewish thought, when it is neither.

The stated aim of this work is to collect excerpts that may illustrate the language and concepts found in the New Testament. To understand any text, it is essential to know how a reader at the time would have understood it. If a modern writer refers to "pork-barrel politics," a reader in two thousand years' time could be forgiven for thinking this relates to pigs. So a list of contemporary quotations using such language would be invaluable to them. Ideally this would be a balanced collection of quotations that include sources from local political debates where pork-barrel deals might be welcomed, and some from government circles where they are condemned. But if the quotations came only from government sources—because perhaps everything else had been destroyed in a devastating war—the future reader would have a very one-sided negative viewpoint.

This is akin to what we often have in rabbinic sources, because most of the Jewish literature from New Testament times was destroyed. We have some of the religious documents of a Jewish sect found in Dead Sea caves, some paraphrases of the Old Testament (a few Targumim and some rewritten Bible stories at Qumran), and the legal discussions of a few rabbis (mostly Hillelites) who survived the destruction of Jerusalem in 70 CE. Because this small group refounded Judaism, it is tempting to regard them as representative of the majority in Jesus' day. However, when they debated their rivals, the Shammaites, they were few enough to meet in a large upper room.[10] So they probably numbered no more than half of the one hundred and twenty early Christians who met in a similar location (Acts 1:13–15).

10. Mishnah Šabbat 1.4: "And these are of the *halachoth* which they stated in the upper room of Hananiah b. Hezekiah b. Garon when they went up to visit him. They took a count, and

Therefore, we have to ask two critical questions when we see the lists of quotations that illustrate a text. First, are they actually parallels, or do they merely use similar language? The "Kingdom" is clearly an important theme for both rabbinic Judaism and Jesus' followers, but the word does not mean the same to both groups. That's why the Gospels spend so much time spelling out what they mean by it. However, it is still necessary to explore the Jewish meaning, because this is what the readers are assumed to know well. By knowing what the Gospels are disagreeing with, we can understand the differences they are asserting.

Second, we have to ask whether the quotations are representative of wider Judaism. Modern Jews and scholars of ancient Judaism were particularly offended to read the supposed parallels to "hate your enemies" (Matt 5:43). Everyone agrees that the listed quotations are not representative of Judaism, then or now. Even Strack and Billerbeck themselves may have been aware of this potential misunderstanding, because they state in the foreword to the first volume: "We strongly oppose the idea that from what we have gathered here (e.g., the Sermon on the Mount), a conclusion can be drawn about the actual or supposedly valid form of Judaism"—with a footnote to the "15 principles of Jewish ethics."

A much closer parallel is now known in the opening page of the Qumran sect's Community Rule: "in order to love all the sons of light ... hate all the sons of darkness" (1QS I, 10). If this had been available, the offending list of quotations could have been omitted as irrelevant. In this instance, the list of supposed parallels fails both of these critical questions, because they are not true parallels of the text and they do not represent Judaism in general. This does not mean they should not have been included, but the reader should beware of making simplistic conclusions.

Scholarly Warnings

Strack-Billerbeck was condemned as unworthy scholarship at the world's largest gathering of scholars for biblical studies in 1961, during the presidential address of the annual meeting of the Society of Biblical Literature and Exegesis. Now known as "SBL," this annual meeting still attracts thousands of scholars, and many of them continue to be influenced by this speech even if they don't realize it. It was given by Samuel Sandmel, a foremost scholar of Jewish background, and published with the memorable title "Parallelomania." It was widely cited, and it cast doubt on any scholarship based on Strack-Billerbeck. Although scholars continued to consult

Beth Shammai outnumbered Beth Hillel; and on that day they enacted eighteen measures."

the work—because it was too useful to ignore—they stopped referring to it, in case doing so might diminish their perceived scholarship.

Actually, Sandmel's criticism consisted of "four major errors in the use of Strack and Billerbeck." To be sure, he blames the layout of the work for these misuses, but he nevertheless acknowledges it as "a useful tool."[11]

First, Sandmel says, there are too many quotations from periods later than the New Testament. This is a serious matter, but only if one ignores the dates of sources. The use of parallels from similar cultures can help us understand language and concepts even if they don't come from exactly the same time. Second, the quotations are presented without any context or discussion. This too is serious, especially when readers are, as Sandmel describes, "devoid of rabbinic learning" and yet "arrogating to themselves a competency they do not possess."

His third complaint is a strange one: the lists of quotations are too long. Clearly, you can never have too many primary sources, because these are the foundations of historical research. He complains instead that the quotes aren't balanced by sources that present a contrary viewpoint. This is often true but necessary. Billerbeck explained in his introduction to volume 3 that "the manuscript had to be abbreviated ... in the economic necessities ... of such a comprehensive work." To include counterpoints at every stage would not only grossly enlarge the work, but would veer away from its aim—which is to illustrate the meanings of phrases and ideas, rather than fairly represent the various competing Jewish theologies.

His fourth complaint is not aimed at those who misuse Strack-Billerbeck, but at the authors themselves: he says they have a Christian bias. He points in particular at the unfortunate list of texts illustrating "hate your enemies" and says, reasonably, that the same kinds of quotations can be found in Christian writings against heretics. Nevertheless, it would be wrong to conclude that hatred of enemies was a defining characteristic of either religion.

Sandmel's warnings are worth heeding by the specialist and nonspecialist alike. His warning is like that of a driving instructor: this powerful tool is so easy to use that one can forget the dangers. It is too easy to come to false conclusions by forgetting to look at dating and context. And this work should not be regarded as a compendium of Jewish beliefs, because its topics are defined by the New Testament. When these warnings are heeded, Strack-Billerbeck becomes an invaluable set of signposts toward fertile areas of exploration for New Testament research.

11. Samuel Sandmel, "Parallelomania," *Journal of Biblical Literature* 81 (1962): 1–13, here 8–10.

Lutheran Bias

E. P. Sanders led a renewed attack against Strack-Billerbeck in his important work on ancient Jewish soteriology.[12] He said the authors showed theological bias in their presentation of Jewish soteriology, as though all Jews believed in "salvation by works." This is what Paul accused them of, according to Luther and other interpreters. Sanders' central thesis was that Jews believed in salvation by covenant membership. This meant either that Paul had been misunderstood or that the "Judaizers" he was attacking had a different theology than most other Jews.

Sanders' conclusions came as no surprise to Jewish scholars, but New Testament scholarship faced upheaval in two directions: some dug in their heels to defend Lutheran interpretations, while some dug deeper to find out what Paul could have meant by "works of the law." The outcome was a rediscovery among Christian scholars of the variety of Jewish soteriology.

Sanders also accused Strack and Billerbeck of selecting rabbinic sources in order to present a specific view that is summarized as "a religion of the most complete self-redemption; it has no room for a redeemer-savior who dies for the sins of the world."[13] This quotation was reused by other authors as proof of this Lutheran bias, based on the fact that Billerbeck was a Lutheran pastor.[14]

However, this quote does not represent the wide variety of soteriology found throughout the work. When one reads Strack-Billerbeck as a whole, it reflects a wide variety of soteriology, and it becomes clear that the authors certainly do not imply that Jews in general believed that salvation came from personal effort.

Soteriology was as varied in ancient Judaism as it is in Christianity today. Most Jews accepted the axiom that "all Israel will be saved,"[15] though this depends on who was a Jew. We now know that those at Qumran regarded those who didn't follow their *halakah* as not truly part of Israel. Paul, of course, had his own views about who was "true Israel," as expounded in Romans 9–11. On this point, as Sanders observed, rabbinic Judaism was more or less in agreement: "All Israel" included everyone who was born

12. E. P. Sanders, *Paul and Palestinian Judaism* (London: SCM Press, 1977).

13. Strack and Billerbeck, *Kommentar zum Neuen Testament*, 4.1:6.

14. E.g., Eugene J. Fisher, "From Polemic to Objectivity? A Short History of the Use and Abuse of Hebrew Sources by Recent Christian New Testament Scholarship," *Hebrew Studies* 20/21 (1979/80): 199–207, here 201; Jörg Frey, "New Testament Scholarship and Ancient Judaism: Problems—Perceptions—Perspectives," in Jörg Frey, *Qumran, Judaism, and New Testament Interpretation: Kleine Schriften III*, ed. Jacob N. Cerone, Wissenschaftliche Untersuchungen zum Neuen Testament 424 (Tübingen: Mohr Siebeck, 2019): 19–44, here 23.

15. "All Israel have a portion in the world to come" (m. Sanh. 10.3, cited at S-B Rom 11:26). This is the start of extensive discussion both in rabbinic literature and in Pauline literature. In Mishnah the discussion includes a list of exceptions that grows with time, while Paul argues that "Israel" is not identical to the Jewish nation.

a Jew, except for a few heretics.[16] They did also expect a few proselytes to be saved, and these were expected to increase in the time of the messiah.[17]

On almost every other matter there was wide disagreement, and a wide variety of Jewish views are presented in Strack-Billerbeck. The authors do not emphasize the concept of salvation by personal merit, as Sanders claims. Indeed, the sources they quote demonstrate that personal merit is generally mentioned in rabbinic discussions in order to point out that it is insufficient for salvation.

The big issue was how a less-than-perfect person could gain heaven. It was clear that everyone was a sinner because everyone died, and death came only from sin.[18] The schools of Hillel and Shammai both believed that there were three paths: the evil go to hell, the perfect go to heaven, and those Jews in-between get to heaven by a third path. Shammai argued that they went to hell for a brief period of suffering ("they squeal and then rise"), whereas Hillel argued that God immediately accepted them by his gracious mercy.[19] Jesus, of course, rejected both views by emphasizing there are only two paths.

R. Yohanan b. Zakkai told a parable of people invited to a king's party, some of whom prepared themselves and others who didn't. When the king saw those in dirty clothing, they were told to stand and watch the feasting—indicating that those in the third group would be admitted to heaven but with diminished status. Jesus, of course, said that those who failed to repent were not admitted.[20]

Many Jews shared the concept of a balance sheet—of good deeds weighed against bad deeds—which determined entrance to heaven.[21] They realized

16. S-B Rom 2:29 A, #2.

17. S-B Rom 3:9 A, #3, B.

18. S-B Rom 3:9 B.

19. Tosefta Sanhedrin 13.3 (cited and discussed at S-B John 1:14, #2): "The House of Shammai says, There are three groups: one for eternal life to come, and one for shame, for eternal contempt. The one for eternal life—these are the perfectly righteous. The one for shame, for eternal contempt—these are the perfectly evil (Dan 12:2). The balanced of them go down to gehenna and squeal and rise from there and are healed. ... And the House of Hillel says, 'And great in mercy' (Exod 34:6) — He inclines toward mercy." The point at which Hillel disagrees with Shammai is only at the conclusion; both groups believed in the three paths.

20. Babylonian Talmud Šabbat 153A (a later version is cited at S-B Matt 22:2–14): "R. Yohanan b. Zakkai said: The matter may be compared to the case of a king who invited his courtiers to a banquet, but he didn't set a time. The wise ones among them got themselves adorned and waited at the gate of the palace, saying, 'Does the palace lack anything?' The foolish ones among them went about their work, saying, 'Is there a banquet without a whole lot of preparation?' Suddenly the king demanded the presence of his courtiers. The wise ones went right before him, adorned, but the fools went before him filthy from their work. The king received the wise ones pleasantly, but showed anger to the fools. He said, 'These, who adorned themselves for the banquet, will sit and eat and drink. Those, who didn't adorn themselves for the banquet, will stand and look on." The Gospels contain three different reinterpretations of this parable (Matt 22:2–15 // Luke 14:12–24; Matt 25:1–13; Luke 13:25–28) but each time, the third path is specifically excluded.

21. S-B Rom 3:21 A.

that most Jews would fail a judgment of this kind, so there were various ideas about how this deficit was made up. Most of these depended on "merits" that were accumulated from the excess good deeds done by others. However, mere obedience was not a "good" deed, because the commands had to be obeyed out of love for God: "If you do not do the words of the Torah for their own sake, the words of the Torah will kill you."[22]

Some rabbis thought that time spent studying Torah would be counted, while others warned against this belief.[23] One's personal sufferings could be counted as good deeds, and this became a source of comfort for those suffering greatly in this lifetime.[24] Merits earned by others through good deeds or suffering also could be allocated to you, and this especially included the sufferings of martyrs.[25]

The concept of a suffering messiah called "ben Joseph" is a persistent thread in rabbinic Judaism that is often ignored but was highlighted by Strack and Billerbeck.[26] They concluded that this theology started in the middle of the second century, but material found at Qumran suggests it was already developed by the first century.[27] The messiah's suffering allowed for enough merits for all of Israel.

The full-blown concept of "merits" cannot be demonstrated in early rabbinic texts, though it was likely already nascent in New Testament times. Similarly in Christian circles, Anselm developed the doctrine that Christ's death provided a payment that was sufficient to redeem all believers. Although this wasn't stated clearly until the eleventh century, it may be regarded as implicit in the concept of redemption in the New Testament. In the same way, the theory of payment of merits may be earlier than its first exponents.

However, this concept of merits was unnecessary for many rabbinic thinkers, because God's mercy could be relied on. As expressed in a beautiful midrash on Song of Songs, God treated Israel like a little child, whom you forgive if they simply say sorry.[28] When people run out of their own goodness, God adds grace.[29] Repentance always tips the balance, because

---

22. Sifre Deuteronomy 32:2 § 306 (131B) cited at S-B Rom 3:1f., D. Also Sifre Deuteronomy 11:13 § 41 (79B) cited at S-B Rom 13:10: "Perhaps you might say, 'Look, I study the Torah so that I may become rich or so I may be called "Rabbi" or so I may receive recompense!' Then Scripture teaches, 'To love Yahweh your God.' Everything that you do you should do only out of love."

23. S-B Rom 2:17 B.

24. S-B Luke 24:26, I, #2.

25. S-B Luke 24:26, I, #2; S-B Rom 9:3, #2.

26. S-B Luke 24:26, II.

27. David C. Mitchell, *Messiah ben Joseph* (Newton Mearns, UK: Campbell, 2016), 79–98.

28. Numbers Rabbah 2 (138B) cited at S-B Rom 3:1f., G.

29. S-B Rom 2:6 explores the paradox in m. ʾAbot 3.15 that judgement is based both on grace and on works. R. Eleazar concludes: "if he does not have (what gives the merits the greater weight over the debt), you give to him from what is yours (from your grace)."

every repented transgression turns into a merit.[30] It is only gentiles who have to earn heaven, and some might actually do so.[31]

Good works are not unnoticed by God; even though they don't earn your entrance to heaven, rewards such as a crown are possible.[32] The only "work" that is required of all Israelites is faith, as exemplified by Abraham.[33] This was the basis of salvation even in the first century, so that Sadducees were excluded from heaven by their lack of faith in the resurrection.[34]

All these varied and sometimes contrary soteriological concepts are found in Strack-Billerbeck. Nevertheless, the purpose of this work was not to catalog Jewish theology but to aid the interpretation of New Testament phrases and ideas. Although it contains a great variety of Jewish theology, this is selected with a specific bias: to illustrate the New Testament. This means that important Jewish ideas and theology may be absent simply because they do not parallel anything found in the New Testament. This is not a failure of the work, but a feature of its aim to provide Jewish background for the New Testament.

Importance of Dating

Paradoxically, one improvement that Strack and Billerbeck wished to make to Schoettgen's work has become the source of their greatest criticism by modern scholarship: their dating of sources. At first glance, the sources are all carefully dated, but modern scholars have concluded that such dates are not reliable. Although this conclusion itself is not reliable (as explained below), the dating of rabbinic sources is less secure than this work implies.

Dating is certainly important, because it can be argued that the Jewish world changed more in the first century than during the millennium before or after. The crux for this change was the revolt against Rome ending with the sack of Jerusalem in 70 CE. This represented not only a military defeat but also the death of almost all the religious establishment. If Josephus is to be believed, the fault lay as much with stubborn and zealous Jews as with the Romans; and if Jewish traditions are to be believed, the Romans helped to save Judaism.

The story is told of Yohanan b. Zakkai being carried out of besieged Jerusalem pretending to be dead in a coffin, then reviving and presenting himself to Vespasian, whom he prophesied would become emperor.

30. Jerusalem Talmud Pe'ah 1.16B.13 (cited at S-B Luke 15:7 B): "If the evil one repents of his wickedness … all transgressions which he has committed will be credited to him as merit."

31. S-B Rom 3:9 A, #1, n. *m*.

32. S-B 1 Cor 9:25 B, #2.

33. S-B Rom 4:2f., #1, n. *d*.

34. "those saying there is no resurrection of the dead" (m. Sanh. 10.1); cited at S-B Rom 2:29 A, #2.

Flattered, or perhaps realizing the value of peaceful Jews, he allowed Yohanan and his followers to set up an academy in Yavneh. There, the great projects that culminated in rabbinic literature got started.

But the Judaism that was rescued and recorded by Yohanan and his followers was not the same as the Judaism of New Testament times. The multitude of factions and sects was replaced by a single authority based on a majority vote by scholarly rabbis. Competing voices such as apocalyptic Jews and Qumran Jews were almost completely forgotten, though some of their literature survived. Details about other groups, such as the Sadducees, Therapeuti, and Zealots, have almost totally disappeared. Even groups similar to Yohanan, such as the followers of Shammai and Gamaliel, are known only by means of their disagreements with those closest to the dominant survivors, the Hillelites.

Clearly the literature of these survivors has to be used with care when describing the multifaceted world of Judaism before 70 CE. After the temple was destroyed, even the topics of conversation changed. In their literature, they still talked about the temple and priesthood, but with a somewhat unrealistic awe—so when they discuss what happened to all the donated gold, instead of noting that the high priests became immensely wealthy, they assumed that the gold plating in the temple got gradually thicker.[35] Discussing table manners became more important than sacrifices, and interest in judicial affairs dropped off, because they had no authority to carry out punishments.

However, these changes can also help to distinguish early traditions from later ones. It is by no means true that all discussions of temple activities originate in temple times, but subject matter and underlying assumptions can certainly be indicative of dating.

Another change is the reliance on Scripture as a foundation for regulations. Although early traditions were based on Torah, proof texts or exegetical explanations were not required. The loss of the temple and of almost every recognized leader necessitated a new source of authority. So after 70 CE, Scripture proofs were added to debates, even to the disputes between Hillelites and Shammaites that happened in the past. Even though proofs were added later, they fit very well and are convincing even for rejected viewpoints, so they may represent the unrecorded exegeses that had actually been used; but there had been no perceived need to record them before.

If Scripture proofs were added to these debates, then what else might have been changed after they were written? Concerns like this make scholars treat dated traditions with caution.

---

35. Mishnah Šeqalim 4.4 (cited at S-B Matt 17:24, #4, n. *d*): "The surplus of the elevation offering [of the shekels]: what did they use to do with it? [They buy with it] hammered gold plate for the House of the Holy of Holies."

Principles of Dating

Jacob Neusner's seminal article in 1978 on dating Jewish traditions[36] has been extremely influential. He concluded that the only safe date for any tradition is the date when it was published within a written collection. This means that no traditions in Mishnah could be safely regarded as earlier than 200 CE, and nothing in the Babylonian Talmud should be regarded as earlier than the start of the sixth century. New Testament scholars took this conclusion seriously. However, Neusner was such a prolific writer that most scholars stopped reading his work. That's a pity, because one thing that made Neusner a great scholar was that he changed his mind when he found new evidence. His conclusions about dating rabbinic material gradually changed as he researched further. This can be traced within the paragraphs and footnotes of his work, but I had clear firsthand experience of the magnitude of this change.

When I sent my PhD thesis[37] to Neusner, he replied: "I tried to like it, but I couldn't." It depended too much on attempts to date some exegetical traditions as early and others as late. Despite my demonstration that the early ones used dramatically different methods and assumptions to the later ones, he wasn't impressed. However, by the time I sent him my initial work on TRENT[38] (which depends even more on dating rabbinic traditions), he had a different viewpoint. He said that I wasn't being adventurous enough in assigning early dates, because he now regarded aspects such as the structure behind Mishnah to originate as far back as the second century BCE.

Some scholars took Neusner's first warning about dating as an excuse to ignore the difficult world of rabbinic literature. Others, like E. P. Sanders, simply ignored him, saying: "I use only passages that are attributed to a pre-70 Pharisee or to the Schools of Hillel and Shammai. Exceptions to this rule will be justified case by case."[39] Wisdom lies, of course, somewhere between the two approaches.

Neuser endorsed TRENT because it dated rabbinic traditions using three principles that are generally recognized among rabbinic scholars. This process validated itself, because the traditions that are found to originate before 70 CE by these methods describe a different cultural world and mindset to the later ones. The methodology is not perfect, but on the other

36. J. Neusner, "The Use of the Later Rabbinic Evidence for the Study of First-Century Pharisaism," in *Approaches to Ancient Judaism: Theory and Practice*, ed. William Scott Green, Brown Judaic Studies 1 (Missoula, MT: Scholars Press for Brown University, 1978), 215–25.

37. *Techniques and Assumptions in Jewish Exegesis Before 70 CE* (Tübingen: Mohr Siebeck, 1992).

38. TRENT—*Traditions of the Rabbis in the Era of the New Testament* (Grand Rapids: Eerdmans, 2004–).

39. E. P. Sanders, *Judaism: Practice & Belief, 63 BCE–66 CE* (London: SCM Press, 1992), 6.

hand it is not difficult, and it can be used for validating the dates assigned within the volumes of Strack-Billerbeck. The three principles are:

(1) Dates can be provisionally assigned according to the named attributions.

That is, if the tradition says so-and-so said something, they likely did—or someone from the same generation did. This traditional approach is what Neusner criticized, but we can track when he changed his mind. During the third of his twenty-two parts analyzing the order of Purities, he suddenly realized that he had only just come across the first instance where he doubted an attribution. Concerning all the attributions that could be verified against their relative order, he noted: "The temporal order of attributions is generally sound … in every instance [in the tractate Kelim], except that just cited [mKel.17.5]."[40]

Mistakes, when they occur, tend to involve rabbis who often debate each other (so they lived at the same time) and occasionally rabbis of the same name. The latter error is more often made by modern scholars who don't know the system of patronyms—that is, the way in which rabbis are identified by their father's name, with a few notable exceptions. For example, "R. Judah HaNasi" (T5; mid-second century) is often called simply "Rabbi" in the Talmuds, but he isn't called "R. Judah." That shortened name is given to R. Judah b. Ilai (i.e., the son of Ilai), except in the Jerusalem Talmud where he is always named in full and the form "R. Judah" refers to Judah b. Pazzi, aka b. Simon (early fourth century) or sometimes to Judah IV (late fourth century).

This confusion isn't as bad as it sounds, because I've picked the worst case. The important point is that each individual corpus is remarkably consistent in naming individuals. The reason is that the date of a ruling or opinion was critically important. Rabbinic law is akin to modern case law—it is built on precedent, so later rulings have to take into account previous ones.

It was especially important to correctly record the sources of rulings that originated in Mishnaic times (i.e., before 200 CE) because these were later regarded with an unassailable status and were often interpreted almost like Scripture.

Traditionally, individuals weren't assigned specific dates but were divided into generations, which were worked out by noting which individuals spoke to each other and who passed on the former sayings of whom.

The table below lists all individuals in the generations of the "Tannaim" (i.e., the rabbis from Mishnaic times) from T1 to T6, plus the pre-Tannaitic individuals labelled T0. The dates assigned to each generation should be

---

40. Jacob Neusner, *A History of the Mishnaic Law of Purities*, 22 vols., Studies in Judaism in Late Antiquity 6 (Leiden: Brill, 1974–1997), 3:239.

regarded merely as guidelines. For example, although R. Eliezer b. Hyrcanus supposedly spans the end of the first century and start of the second, his comments usually refer to the beginning of this period; and because he had a very traditional viewpoint, his opinions normally represented an even earlier time.

Rabbis who created the later debates in the Jerusalem and Babylonian Talmuds are divided into generations of Palestinian Amoraim and Babylonian Amoraim respectively, but these are less important for studying New Testament background.

(2) Traditions develop over time, and later additions depend on the earlier ones.

This fairly obvious fact is significant because the earlier contributions tend to remain unchanged. Occasionally later rabbis show they no longer understand the meaning of an archaic word, or they point out that a saying was attributed to the wrong person. And yet the early traditions remain unedited, even when such issues are identified. Also, helpfully, later additions tend to be added at the end, and rarely within a tradition. This is especially important with regard to lists of exceptions, which can grow with time.

The reason behind these practices is partly the importance of accurately preserving the foundations on which later case law depended, and partly because these traditions were memorized. When a text has been memorized, it is not easy to successfully remember small alterations—as anyone will know if they have tried memorizing a Scripture verse in a new translation. And inserting even a few new words will break up the memory and make it less secure. All this makes it often possible to identify the relative age of different material added to a tradition that has grown during generations of discussion, even when the material is not attributed to any named person.

Neusner realized the importance of these factors when he got to Part 4 of his work on Purities. He noted: "Unattributed sayings are not a great problem ... and most can be assigned to a time period."[41] This should not be regarded as a glib statement that everything is datable, but it is usually possible to decide which bits preceded the others.

Some of the oldest material in Mishnah is anonymous, especially the underlying structure of the tractates, which is almost identical in Mishnah, Tosefta, and both Talmuds. This structure extends even to the level of individual discussions, which are often diverted in surprising directions on the basis of anonymous comments that later generations did not feel they

41. Neusner, *History of the Mishnaic Law*, 4:244.

had the authority to supplant. This suggests that those anonymous sources are very old.

The Mishnah gives prominence to another type of anonymous material that it attributes to a vague body called "the Sages" (*hakamim*). This isn't a particular group of rabbis or those from a specific timeframe. They appear to represent the majority vote that ended a debate, whenever that occurred. Such conclusions are rarely disagreed with at a later stage, except occasionally in Tosefta.

However, the majority of anonymous material occurs within debates, where they appear to represent a common question or conventional wisdom that is stated in order to explain the context of a debate. This material can be dated by the names of those who respond to it.

(3) Non-halakhic traditions (i.e., outside Mishnah, Tosefta, and Talmuds) are undatable.

This early conclusion by Neusner has stood the test of time. This sadly meant that he rejected the conclusions of his own previous books on the life of Yohanan ben Zakkai.[42] He concluded that biographical details about the lives of rabbis and individual sayings that are separate from legal discussions were no more reliable for historical research than Christian hagiography.

Halakah consists of the debates in a classroom or in a court that are recorded carefully because they become the basis for future debates that eventually become fixed rulings. The rest of rabbinic traditions come under the heading of *haggadah*—consisting of Scripture commentaries, wise sayings, and stories. Portions of haggadic material occur within the Talmud just as halakhic excerpts are cited in commentaries.

The reason for the distinction is the carefulness with which they are treated. One way to imagine this is a modern-day speaker who proclaims that "Martin Luther said: I have a dream." If this happened in a classroom, someone would interrupt and say, "You mean, of course, Martin Luther King." But if this happened in a church or an after-dinner speech, no one would bother to interrupt, and there would be no attempt to correct it even if it were being recorded.

Haggadic sources do not include such corrections or doubts, though halakhic debates are often appended with correct attributions or alternate wording. Stories about a rabbi also tend to originate a couple of centuries after his death, when his fame has spread and his memory is venerated. This doesn't mean they don't contain truth, but we should always be wary.

---

42. Jacob Neusner, *A Life of Rabban Yohanan Ben Zakkai, c.1–80 C.E.*, Studia Post-biblica 6 (Leiden: Brill, 1962); idem, *Development of a Legend: Studies on the Traditions Concerning Yohanan Ben Zakkai*, Studia Post-biblica 16 (Leiden: Brill, 1970).

Commentaries do not decide the meaning of a text, but tend to be a collection of competing interpretations, each introduced by a phrase such as "And another [interpretation]: ..."

Strack-Billerbeck makes no distinction between these two different types of sources. Each is quoted, with a date, as if equal certainty applies to legal debates and biographical stories. The diligent reader should be aware of the limitations of dates for haggadic sources.

The Usefulness of Strack-Billerbeck

For scholars studying a passage in the New Testament, Strack-Billerbeck provides an unparalleled introduction to useful background material from the rabbinic world. Given the huge number of volumes of rabbinic material, easy access to this rich world is immeasurably helpful.

However, we should bear in mind the authors' first aim in creating this compendium, as defined so well by their predecessor Schoettgen, cited above: "the phrases and sayings of the New Testament are illustrated" by this material. We can fall into problems when we attempt to go beyond this aim.

If we try to uncover the culture or even history of New Testament times using this rabbinic material, as Strack-Billerbeck tempts us to do, we have to tread carefully. This is not an unworthy task (I attempt this myself in TRENT), but that kind of endeavor requires a much more nuanced effort at dating sources than is presented here.

No New Testament scholar should limit themselves by working without the riches of Strack-Billerbeck, but the benefits of these heights require careful attention to this preflight safety warning.

The Generations of the Tannaim (the Rabbis from Mishnaic Times)

Key

R. = Rabbi ("my great one")
Rn. = Rabban ("our great one")
b. = ben ("son of")

Bold = 10 or more instances in T0–T2 and 50 or more in T3–T6, in Mishnah.

Italics = only one mention in Mishnah or none (i.e., found only in other works)

Name1 (Name2) means Name2 is normally omitted.

Pre-Tannaitic [T0]

Abtalion [BCE 1]

Aqabia b. Mahalalel [BCE 1?]

Antigonos of Soko [BCE 2]

Baba b. Buta [BCE 1]

Ben He He [BCE 1]

Bené Batera [BCE 1]

Eliehoenai b. Hakof [CE 1]

Hanamel the Egyptian [CE 1]
aka (*Hanan*... in Babli)

Hillel (the Elder) [BCE 1]

Huna the Circle Maker [BCE 1]

Yohanan the High Priest
aka John Hyrcanus BCE 2

Yose b. Yoezer [BCE 2]

Yose b. Yohanan [BCE 2]

Joshua b. Gamala [BCE 1?]

Joshua b. Perahiah [BCE 2]

Judah b. Tabbai [BCE 1]

R. Measha [BCE 1]

Menahem [BCE 1]

Nittai (Mittai) of Arbela [BCE 2]

Shammai (the Elder) [BCE 1]

Shemaiah [BCE 1]

Simeon b. Shetah [BCE 1]

Simeon the Pious [BCE 3]
aka Simeon I - Jos.Ant.12.43;
or Simeon II – Jos.Ant.12.224

Tannaim 10-80 CE [T1]

Abba Jose Cholikofri

Admon

Ben Bukri

Dosetai of Kefar Yathmah

R. Eleazar b. Harsom

Rn. Gamaliel (the Elder) I

Hanan b. Abishalom

Hananiah b. Hezekiah b. G.

R. Hanina, Chief of the priests

R. Ishmael b. Phabi (or *Fabi*)

Yoezer of the Birah

R. Yohanan (Nehuniah) b. Gudgeda

Yohanan b. ha-Horanith

Rn./R. Yohanan b. Zakkai

Jonathan b. Uzziel

Judah b. Durtai

Menahem b. Signai

Nahum the Mede

Nahum the Scribe

Rn. Simeon b. Gamaliel I

Simeon b. Hillel

R. Simeon of Mizpah

R. Zechariah b. Kubetal

Tannaim 80–120 CE [T2]

Abba Yose b. Hanin

Abba Saul b. Batnit

(Yohanan) *Ben Bag Bag*

Ben Batera (R. Simeon)

Ben Patura

Boethus b. Zonin

R. Dosa b. Harkinas

R. Eleazar b. ʿArakh

R. Eleazar b. Azariah

R. Eliezer (b. Hyrcanus)

R. Eliezer b. Diglai

R. Eliezer b. Jacob I

R. Eliezer (or Eleazar) b. Zadok I

Rn. Gamaliel II

R. Halapta

R. Hanina b. Dosa

R. Hanina b. Gamaliel II

R. Huspit

R. Hyrcanus in Kefar Etam

R. Yose b. (R.) Honi

R. Yose the Priest

R. Joshua (b. Hananiah)

R. Joshua b. Batera

R. Joshua b. Hyrcanus

R. Judah b. Batera

R. Levitas of Yavneh

Nahum of Gimzo

R. Nehuniah b. Elinathan

R. Nehuniah b. Haqqanneh

Onqelos (Aquila?)

R. Pappias

Samuel the Small

Simeon ha-Pakuli

R. Simeon b. Nathaniel

Simeon brother of Azariah

R. Simeon son of the Chief

R. Yaqim of Hadar

R. Yeshebab

R. Zadok

R. Zechariah b. Abkulas

R. Zechariah b. Haqqassab

Tannaim 120–140 CE [T3]

Abtolemus

R. Aqiba (b. Joseph)

(R. Simeon) Ben Azzai

(Simeon) Ben Nanos

(Simeon) Ben Zoma

R. Eleazar (b.) Hisma

R. Eleazar b. Judah of Bartota

R. Eleazar b. Perata I

R. Eleazar of Modiim

Elisha b. Abbuyah

R. Hananiah b. Hakinai

R. Hananiah b. Teradion

R. Hanina b. Antigonos

R. Ilai or *Ila*

R. Ishmael (b. Elisha)

R. Yohanan b. Beroqah

R. Yohanan b. Joshua

R. Yohanan b. Matthew

R. Yohanan b. Nuri

R. Yose son of the Damascene

R. Yose the Galilean

R. Yose b. Qisma

R. Joshua b. Mathia

R. Judah b. Baba

R. Judah the Priest

R. Matthew b. Heresh

Nehemiah of Bet Deli

R. Simeon b. Aqashya

Simeon of Teman

R. Tarfon

Tannaim 140–165 CE [T4]

Abba Eleazar b. Dulai

Abba Saul

R. Eleazar b. Matthew

R. Eleazar (b. Shammuah in M)

R. Eliezer b. Jacob II

R. Eliezer b. R. Yose the Galilean

R. Eliezer b. Pilai

R. Hananiah b. Aqabia

R. Hananiah b. Aqashia

R. Hanina of Ono

R. Ishmael b. R. Yohanan b. Beroqah

R. Jacob (b. Qorshai)

R. Yohanan the sandal-maker

R. Jonathan (b. Joseph)

R. Joshua b. Qarha

R. Yose (b. Halapta)

R. Yose b. ha-Hotef the Ephrathi

R. Josiah (the Great)

R. Judah (b. Ilai)

R. Meir

R. Menahem (b. R. Jose b. Halapta)

R. Nehemiah

R. Simai

Rn. Simeon b. Gamaliel II

R. Simeon of Shezuri

R. Simeon (b. Yohai)

Tannaim 165–200 CE [T5]

Abba Gorjon of Sidon

R. Dosa

R. Dustai b. Yannai

R. Eleazar b. R. Simeon (b. Yohai)
(= Eliezer b. Simeon in Babli)

R. Eliezer (Eleazar) *Haqqappar*

R. Eliezer (or Eleazar) b. Zadok II

R. Halapta (b. Dosa) *of Kefar Hananiah*

R. Isaac

R. Ishmael b. R. Yose (b. Halapta)

Yadua the Babylonian

R. Yose b. R. Judah (b. Ilai)

R. Yose Ketanta
aka *Yose* (Isi) *b. Aqabia*?
aka *Isi b. Judah*? (b.Pes.113b.)

R. Yose b. Meshullam

R. Judah b. Tema

R. Nathan

R. Nehorai

R. Phinehas b. Yair

Rabbi (Judah, ha Nasi)

R. Simeon b. Eleazar

R. Simeon b. Halapta

R. Simeon b. Menasia (Manasseh)

Symmachus (b. Joseph)

Tannaim 200–220 CE [T6]

Rn. Gamaliel (b. Rabbi) III

Hiyya (bar Abba, the Great)

Bar Qappara

R. Simeon b. Judah (ha-Nasi)
aka R. Simeon b. Rabbi

R. Shela

R. Zakkai

Foreword

Volume 3

The third volume of Strack-Billerbeck's Commentary which appears here for the general public brings the ongoing elucidation of the New Testament from the Talmud and Midrash to an end. To keep the scope and cost of the third volume within reasonable bounds, the manuscript had to be abbreviated belatedly. In the process, one or another passage that was referred to in the earlier volumes may have been eliminated. As regrettable as the irregularities that thus arose are, they may nevertheless find a gracious excuse in the economic necessities that presently confront the printing of such a comprehensive work. If it succeeds in completing this four-volume work despite these difficulties, this is in large part to the credit of the Notgemeinschaft der Deutschen Wissenschaft. To thank this society publicly here is a duty gladly performed by the publisher and the author. — The still outstanding fourth volume shall offer a series of longer discussions (excurses) on individual New Testament passages. It has just begun to be printed.

Paul Billerbeck

Frankfurt (Oder), 6 Mar 1926

The Letter of Paul to the Romans

1:1 A: Paul.

On the name Παῦλος see § Acts 13:9 A, #3. — In accordance with the style of Greek letters at the time, the name of the letter writer comes first; see, for example, Josephus, *Ant.* 16.6.3, 4, 5, 6; 17.5, 7; in the NT, Acts 23:26, and in the apocrypha, 1 Esdras 6:7; 8:9; 1 Macc 11:30, 32; 12:6, 20; 13:36; 14:20; 15:2, 16; 2 Macc 1:10; 11:16, 22, 27, 24. — 2 Maccabees 1:1 is different: here the recipients are named first and then the sender of the letter. The latter form is encountered in rabbinic literature;[a] but here there is no lack of examples of the first form.[b]

a. Tosefta Sanhedrin 2.6 (416): To our brothers, the inhabitants of Upper and Lower Galilee; may your peace be great! לאחנא בני גלילא עילאה ולבני גלילא תחתאה שלמכון יסגא. — For the whole passage, along with parallels, see § Matt 4:12, #2. ‖ Jerusalem Talmud Nedarim 6.40A.31: In the one letter he (supposedly Rabbi)[1] wrote, "To his holiness Hananiah! לקדושת חנניה!" — Similarly in y. Sanh. 1.19A.7; different, however, in b. Ber. 63A.

b. Genesis Rabbah 75 (48C): Our teacher (= Rabbi, † 217?) said to R. Ephes (Aphes), "Write a letter in my name to our lord, king (Caesar) Antoninus." He started and wrote, "From Judah, the patriarch, to our lord, king Antoninus." That one[2] took it, read it, and tore it to pieces. He said to him, "Write, 'From your servant Judah to our lord, king Antoninus! מן עבדך יהודה למרן מלכא אנטונינוס'" He said to him, "Rabbi, why did you scorn your honor?" He answered him, "Am I somehow better than my forefather? Did he not say, 'So says your servant Jacob'? (Gen 32:5)." — The parallel in Tanḥ. וישלה 39A reads: Our holy teacher (= Rabbi) wrote thus, "To Antoninus. Your servant Judah sends you the greeting of peace! לאנטונינוס יהודה עבדך שואל בשלומך" — However, here, as in TanḥB וישלח § 5 (82B), לאנטונינוס can be related to what precedes: "Our holy teacher wrote thus to Antoninus."

1:1 B: Called to be an apostle.

1. κλητός, a verbal adjective, = "called," specifically to an office or for a task. The OT קָרָא corresponds to this meaning of καλεῖν in, for example, the following passages.

a. Exodus 31:2: "I have called Bezalel by name קָרָאתִי בְשֵׁם." — Septuagint: ἀνακέκλημαι ἐξ ὀνόματος. — The sense is changed in Tg. Onk. 31:2: "I have made Bezalel great through

1. See Wilhelm Bacher, *Die Agada der Tannaïten*, 2nd ed. (Strassburg: Trübner, 1902), 1:385.4.
2. TN: The reference is to the teacher.

the name, that is, I have made a great name for him רַבֵּיתִי בְּשׁוּם בצלאל." — Targum Yerušalmi I: "I have made a great name for Bezalel קְרֵיית בְּשׁוּם טַב." ‖ Babylonian Talmud Berakot 55A: R. Yohanan († 279) said, "There are three things God himself calls out openly מַכְרִיז and these are: famine, abundance, and a good steward." On famine, see 2 Kgs 8:1: "Yahweh has proclaimed קָרָא a famine" (Tg.: זַמֵּין = he has determined, set). On abundance, see Ezek 36:29: "I will call to קָרָאתִי the grain and make it abundant." On a good steward, see Exod 31:1f.: "Yahweh said (ויאמר, as cited in the midr.) to Moses, 'Behold, I have called Bezalel by name.'"

b. Exodus 35:40: "Yahweh called Bezalel by name קָרָא בְשֵׁם." — Septuagint: ἀνακέκληκεν ἐξ ὀνόματος. — Targum Onkelos: "Yahweh has made a great name רַבִּי בְּשׁוּם for Bezalel."— Targum Yerušalmi I: "Yahweh has determined a great name מַנֵּי בְּשׁוּם טַב for Bezalel."

c. Numbers 1:16: "Those who are called from the community = those called to be representatives of the community, קְרִיאֵי הָעֵדָה" (so the *kethib*; the *qere*: קְרוּאֵי העדה). — Septuagint: ἐπίκλητοι τῆς συναγωγῆς those called to be representatives of the community. — Targum Onkelos: "The conveners of the community מְעַרְעֵי כְנִשְׁתָּא." — Targum Yerušalmi I: "Those who invite (call) the people of the community מְזַמְּנֵי עַם כְּנִישְׁתָּא."

d. Isaiah 42:6: "I have called you in righteousness קְרָאתִיךָ בְצֶדֶק." — Septuagint: ἐκάλεσά σε ἐν δικαιοσύνῃ. — Targum: "I have made you great (glorified) in truth רַבִּיתָךְ בִּקְשׁוֹט."

e. Isaiah 48:15: "I have also called him (Cyrus) אַף־קְרָאתִיו." — Septuagint: ἐγὼ ἐκάλεσα. — The targum, which interprets the words in relation to Abraham, reads, "I have also made him great רַבִּיתֵיהּ."

f. Isaiah 49:1: "Yahweh called me from the womb קְרָאָנִי." — Septuagint: ἐκάλεσε τὸ ὄνομά μου. — Targum: "Before I was, he designated (appointed) me זַמְּנַנִי."

g. Isaiah 51:2: "For when he was but one I called him (Abraham) קְרָאתִיו." — Septuagint: ἐκάλεσα αὐτὸν. — Targum: "I brought him to my service (to worship me) קָרֵבְתֵּיהּ לְפוּלְחָנִי."

The targum passages above show that the expression קְרָא = "call" in the sense of "to appoint to an office" was not common for the argumists. See also § Rom 1:6.

2. ἀπόστολος = שָׁלִיחַ, with suffixes and in the plural שָׁלוּחַ, Aram. שְׁלוּחָא. In rabbinic literature, this was the name of any "emissary," insofar as he was the appointee, delegate, representative of someone else; hence the legal principle: a person's emissary is as the person himself שְׁלוּחוֹ שֶׁל אָדָם כְּמוֹתוֹ (e.g., m. Ber. 5.5; Mek. Exod. 12:4 [5A]; 12:6 [7A]; b. Qidd. 41B; b. Ḥag. 10B; b. Naz. 12B; b. B. Meṣ. 96A; b. Menaḥ. 93B).

Babylonian Talmud Qiddušin 41B: R. Joshua b. Qarha (ca. 150) said, "From what passage of Scripture can it be shown that someone's emissary is as the person himself? From Exod 12:6, because it says, 'The whole assembly of the community Israel should slaughter between the two evenings.' How then does the whole assembly slaughter together? Does not rather only one slaughter? But one can understand from this that someone's appointee (emissary) is as the person himself." — In y. Qidd. 1.62A.35, R. Eleazar (ca. 270) is the author. ‖ Babylonian Talmud Nedarim 72B: R. Jonathan (ca. 140, student of Ishmael) said, "We find in the whole Torah that someone's emissary is as the person himself." — Parallels can be found in b. B. Meṣ. 96A; b. Naz. 12B.

שָׁלִיחַ is used to designate:

a. The delegate at the finalization of a betrothal.

Mishnah Qiddušin 2.1: The husband can finalize the betrothal himself or do so through his delegate בִּשְׁלוּחוֹ; the wife can put her betrothal into effect herself or do so through her delegate; the husband can either himself give his daughter in marriage when she is still under-age (not yet 12.5 years old) or do so through his delegate. — See also b. Qidd. 41A below at n. *b*.

b. The delegate appointed to deliver or receive divorce papers.

Mishnah Giṭṭin 3.6: If someone from abroad delivers divorce papers and gets sick, he appoints a delegate before the judicial authority (thus according to the reading of Rashi: עושה בבית דין שליח), dispatches him, and explains before them, "In my presence they (the divorce papers) were written and in my presence they were signed." But the one who will be the emissary does not have to explain, "In my presence they were written and in my presence they were signed"; instead he explains, "I am a delegate of the judicial authority שְׁלִיחַ בֵּית דִּין." ‖ Mishnah Giṭṭin 4.1: If someone sends divorce papers to his wife and then overtakes the delegate שָׁלִיחַ or sends another delegate to him and says to him: "The divorce papers which I gave you are void," behold, they are void. If he (the husband) arrived at his wife earlier (than the delegate delivering the divorce papers) or sent a (second) delegate to her with the explanation: "The divorce papers which I sent to you are void," behold, they are void. But if the divorce papers have already reached her hand, then he can no longer declare them to be void. ‖ Babylonian Talmud Qiddušin 41A: From where can the delegation שְׁלִיחוּת (at an engagement) be demonstrated? Because the baraita says: ושלח (in ושלחה in Deut 24:1) teaches that he (the husband) may appoint a delegate שָׁלִיחַ; ושלחה in Deut 24:1 teaches that she (the wife to be dismissed) may appoint a delegate. (שלח and the ושלחה read without the dagesh is not interpreted as = "to dismiss by divorce papers," but rather = "to dispatch a delegate.") ושלח and ושלחה ("'and' he sends," "'and' she sends") teaches that the delegate (in turn) may appoint a delegate (the ו = "and" has inclusive meaning). Hence, it (the proof for the commissioning of a delegate) has been found in the case of divorces; where does (the proof) come from in the case of engagements?… Scripture says: "And she moves out and is granted to another man" (Deut 24:2); it (Scripture) compares marriage to moving out (divorce): as a delegate can be appointed in the case of divorce, so can a delegate be appointed in the case of marriage.

c. The one entrusted with the office of the prayer leader שְׁלִיחַ צִיבּוּר.

Mishnah Berakot 5.5: If someone prays and makes a mistake in the process, it is a bad omen for him; and if it is the communal delegate (the prayer leader), it is a bad omen for those who commission him; for someone's delegate is as the person himself.

d. The one entrusted with a task before the court שְׁלִיחַ בֵּית דִּין.

See m. Giṭ. 3.6 above at n. *b*. ‖ Mishnah Yoma 1.5: The elders of the court (the great Sanhedrin) handed him (the high priest prior to the Day of Atonement) over to the elders of the priesthood. He was led up to the balconies of the family of Abtina (who were renowned for the way they prepared incense [see m. Yoma 3.11]). They would adjure him, say goodbye, and then go away. They would say to him, "My lord high priest, we are delegates of the court, and you are our delegate and a delegate of the court. We adjure you by the one who causes his name to dwell in this house (temple) that you change nothing of what we have said to you (concerning the rite of the Day of Atonement)."

e. One appointed or commissioned as a delegate by God.

α. Moses. Babylonian Talmud Baba Meṣiʿa 86B: Rab Judah († 299) said that Rab († 247) said, "Everything that Abraham himself did for the angels of service God himself did for his (Abraham's) children, and everything that Abraham did through his appointee שליח God also did for his children through an appointee. Abraham 'ran to the cattle' (Gen 18:7), and in Num 11:31 it says, 'A wind broke forth from Yahweh and drove quail over from the sea.' Abraham 'took curds and sweet milk' (Gen 18:8), and in Exod 16:4 it says, 'Behold, I will rain bread from heaven on you.' Furthermore, Abraham 'stood before them under the tree' (Gen 18:8), and in Exod 17:6 it says, 'Behold, I (Yahweh) will stand before you there on the rock at Horeb.' Abraham 'went with them to escort them' (Gen 18:16), and in Exod 13:21 it says, 'Yahweh went before them by day in a pillar of cloud.' '(But) let some water be fetched' (Gen 18:4) (thus Abraham did not fetch it himself), and in Exod 17:6 it says, 'You (Moses as God's appointee) shall strike the rock and water will come out of it and the people will drink.'" ‖ β. Elijah, Elisha, and Ezekiel. Midrash Psalm 78 § 5 (173B): R. Aha (ca. 320) said in the name of R. Jonathan (read: Yohanan, † 279), "There are three keys that God does not hand over to any appointee שליח: the key to the womb (see Gen 29:31), the key to the graves in the case of the resurrection of the dead (see Ezek 37:13), and the key to rainstorms (see Deut 28:12). And if God wants, he gives them to the righteous. The key for a barren woman he handed over to Elisha (see 2 Kgs 4:16 and 17). The key for the resurrection of the dead he gave to Elijah in the case of the son (of the widow) from Zarephath (see 1 Kgs 17:21 and 23), and (in the case of the resurrection) of the son of the Shunammite woman by Elisha (see 2 Kgs 4:34 and 36), and to Ezekiel in the valley of Dura (see Ezek 37:1 and 9). And the key for the rainstorms (he handed over) to Elijah (see 1 Kgs 17:1 and 18:1)." — Compare the parallel in b. Taʿan. 2A at § Matt 6:26, #3. ‖ Babylonian Talmud Sanhedrin 113A: Elijah the Tishbite from among the sojourners of Gilead said, "As Yahweh the God of Israel lives, there will be neither dew nor rain …" (1 Kgs 17:1). He prayed for mercy, and he was given the key for rain, and he headed off and went from there.… "And after these things it happened that the woman's son fell ill …" (1 Kgs 17:17). There he prayed for mercy that he might be given the key for the resurrection of the dead. It was said to him, "Three keys are not handed over to any appointee שליח: that for a woman giving birth (conception), that for rain showers, and that for the resurrection of the dead." It would (now) be said, "Two are in the hands of the student and one in the hands of the master (God). Bring (therefore) that one (for rain showers) and receive this one (for the resurrection of the dead). This is what is written in 1 Kgs 18:1: 'Go, show yourself to Ahab, and I (God, therefore not Elijah) will grant rain.'" ‖ γ. During the presentation of sacrifices, the priest is regarded as an appointee of God, not of the community. Babylonian Talmud Qiddušin 23B: Rab Huna b. Joshua (ca. 350) said, "Behold, the priests are (during the act of sacrifice) delegates (representatives) of the All Merciful One שליחו דרחמנא. For if you thought that they are our delegates שלוחי דידן, would there not then be something that we are not permitted to do, but that they are permitted to do?" (The appointee can of course do only what his commissioner can do. Since the nonpriestly Israelites cannot sacrifice, the priest would also not be able to sacrifice, if he were an appointee of the community. It follows that the sacrificing priests can only be an appointed representative of God.) — The same is found in b. Yoma 19A; see also b. Ned. 35B.

f. In the legend in Jellinek, *Beth ha-Midrash* 5.60 (see § Matt 10:2 B, #2),[3] Peter is explicitly designated as or designates himself as שְׁלוּחוֹ שֶׁל יֵשׁוּ = ἀπόστολος Ἰησοῦ. In the same text, the other disciples are also called "his (Jesus') apostles" שְׁלוּחָיו.

1:1 C: Set apart.

ἀφωρισμένος in the sense = מוּקְדָּשׁ, see הִקְדַּשְׁתִּיךָ (Jer 1:5), targum: זַמֵּנְתָּךְ "I have designated you," with the etymology = פָּרוּשׁ or נִבְדָּל "separated, set apart."

Leviticus 20:26: "You shall be holy קְדֹשִׁים to me, for I, Yahweh, am holy קָדוֹשׁ, and I have set you apart וָאַבְדִּיל from the nations so that you would belong to me." — Septuagint: καὶ ἔσεσθέ μοι ἅγιοι, ὅτι ἐγὼ ἅγιός εἰμι κύριος ὁ θεὸς ὑμῶν, ὁ ἀφορίσας ὑμᾶς ἀπὸ πάντων τῶν ἐθνῶν, εἶναί μοι. — Targum Onkelos: "You are to be holy קַדִּישִׁין before me, for I am holy קַדִּישׁ, and I have set you apart ואפרשית from the nations so that you would serve before me." — Targum Yerušalmi I: "You shall be holy before me, for I, Yahweh, am holy, who chose you and set you apart דבחרית בכון ואפרשית יתכון from the nations so that you would serve before me." — Sifra Leviticus 20:26 (374A): "You shall be holy to me, for I am holy" (Lev 20:26); as I am holy, so you shall be holy; as I am set apart פרוש, so you shall be set apart פרושים. "And I set you apart from the nations so that you would belong to me" (Lev 20:26); since you are set apart מובדלים from the nations, behold, you belong to me (to my name); and if not, behold, you belong to Nebuchadnezzar, the king of Babylon, and his companions. — See SLev 19:2 (342A) and Lev. Rab. 24 (122D). ‖ Isaiah 56:3: "Let no foreigner who has bound himself to Yahweh say, 'Yahweh will certainly set me apart הבדל יבדילני from his people.'" — Septuagint: μὴ λεγέτω ὁ ἀλλογενὴς ὁ προσκείμενος πρὸς κύριον· ἀφοριεῖ με ἄρα κύριος ἀπὸ τοῦ λαοῦ αὐτοῦ. — Targum: "Let the son from the nations who has been added to the people of Yahweh not say, 'Yahweh will certainly separate me אפרשא יפרשנני from his people.'"

1:1 D: For the gospel of God.

1. In the LXX, εὐαγγέλιον means α. "payment for good news" (2 Sam 4:10; 18:22); β. "good news" itself (only in 2 Sam 18:25, "If he [the messenger] is alone, good news εὐαγγέλια is in his mouth"). — The Hebrew equivalent is בְּשׂוֹרָה (Aram. בְּשׂוֹרְתָא or בְּסוֹרְתָא, בְּסוֹרָא). This means α. in general, "news"[a] and therefore can also be used when bad news is in view;[b] then β. specifically, and most of the time, "good news."[c] The latter is more precisely

3. Adolph Jellinek, *Beth ha-Midrash: Sammlung kleiner Midraschim und vermischter Abhanlungen aus der ältern jüdischen Literatur*, 6 vols. (Leipzig: Nies, 1853–1873). The first through fourth volumes were published in Leipzig in 1853 (vols. 1 and 2), 1855 (vol. 3), and 1857 (vol. 4). The fifth and sixth volumes were published by Herzfeld & Bauer in Vienna in 1873 and 1877, respectively.

called בְּשׂוֹרָה טוֹבָה, Aram. בְּסוֹרָא טָבָא, בְּשׂוֹרְתָא טָבָא (טָבְתָא).[d] By contrast, בְּשׂוֹרָה רָעָה = evil, bad news; Aram. בְּשׂוֹרְתָא בִישָׁא.[e]

a. 2 Samuel 18:20: אִישׁ בְּשֹׂרָה "Man with news" = messenger. ‖ Targum 2 Samuel 4:10: "To give him a gift for his news בְּסוֹרְתֵיהּ."

b. Genesis Rabbah 81 (52B): While (Jacob) was still observing sorrow for Deborah (Rebekah's wet nurse [Gen 35:8]), the (sorrowful) news בשורתא came to him that his mother died. ‖ Midrash Lamentations 1:5 (52A): News came and announced בשורה ובשרית that (the emperor) Nero died. ‖ Targum Job 3:26: "I had still not found any friends because of the news מִבְּסוֹרְתָא about the cattle and jennies, and I was still not comforted because of the news about the fire, and I had still not recovered from the news about the camels. Then came the agitation because of the (sorrowful) news מבסורתא about the children."

c. 2 Samuel 18:25: "The king said, 'If he (the messenger) is alone, (good) news בְּשׂוֹרָה is in his mouth.'" ‖ Targum 2 Samuel 18:25 has the same with just בְּסוֹרְתָא.

d. Mishnah Berakot 9.2: Concerning rain and good news בְּשׂוֹרוֹת טוֹבוֹת it is said (as a form of praise), "Blessed be the one who is good and bestows good!" And concerning bad news בְּשׂוֹרוֹת הָרָעוֹת (so the Babylonian Talmud, whereas the versions of the Mishnah read bad messages שְׁמוּעוֹת הרעות) it is said, "Blessed be the true judge!" — The first part of this Mishnah is cited, for example, in Gen. Rab. 13 (10B). ‖ 2 Samuel 18:27: "He comes with good news בשורה טובה." ‖ Targum 2 Samuel 18:27: "And he will bring good news בְּסוֹרָא טָבָא." ‖ Babylonian Talmud Roš Haššanah 19A: Rab Tobi b. Mattenah (ca. 300?) responded, "On the 28th of the month (Adar) the good news בְּשׂוֹרְתָא טָבְתָא came to the Jews that they did not have to deviate from the Torah." — This sentence originates from Meg. Taʿan. 12. ‖ In Midr. Lam. 1:5 (52A), Rabban Yohanan b. Zakkai († ca. 80) said to emperor Vespasian, "Good news has been delivered to you בשורתא טבתא איתבשרת." — In the parallel passage b. Giṭ. 56B, we read "Good news has come to you שמועה טובה אתיא לך."

e. See b. Ber. 9B in n. *d* above. ‖ Targum Lamentations 1:2: "When the people, the house of Israel, heard this bad news בשורתא בישא (which the scouts delivered concerning the land of Israel), … they raised their voice and wept."

2. εὐαγγελίζεσθαι (very rarely εὐαγγελίζειν; see LXX 1 Sam 31:9; 2 Sam 18:19; and in the NT Rev 10:7; 14:6), the verb that is associated with εὐαγγέλιον, corresponds to the OT בִּשֵּׂר. This verb בִּשֵּׂר (Aram. בַּשַּׂר or בַּסַּר) means α. in general: "to deliver news"[a] (therefore it is also used in the case of news concerning misfortune)[b] and β. specifically (and most of the time): "to deliver good news,"[c] which is expressed more fully and precisely as: בִּשֵּׂר טוֹב or בִּשֵּׂר בְּשׂוֹרָה טוֹבָה.[d] — בִּשֵּׂר can be used in a transitive construction with the accusative of the person to whom the news is directed, just as εὐαγγελίζεσθαι can be used (see Luke 3:18; Acts 8:25, 40; 13:32; 14:15, 21; 16:10; Gal 1:9; 1 Pet 1:12);[e] accordingly, both verbs can be used with a personal subject in the passive.[f]

a. Targum 1 Samuel 11:12: "Who is it who brought the news (דִּי מְבַסַּר = who proclaimed), saying, 'Saul is not fit to be king over us?'" ‖ Targum 2 Samuel 18:20: "Joab said to him, 'You are not a man who is fit to deliver news לְבַסָּרָא on this day. You may deliver news תְּבַסַּר on another day, but on this day you should not deliver news תְּבַסַּר.'" ‖ Psalm 40:10, "I have proclaimed בִּשַּׂרְתִּי righteousness in the great assembly." — Targum: "I have proclaimed בַּשְּׂרֵית righteousness in the great community." ‖ Targum Psalms 68:12: "Yahweh gave the words of the Torah to his people, but Moses and Aaron proclaimed מְבַשְּׂרִין the word of God to the great host of Israel."

b. 1 Samuel 4:17: "Then the one who delivered the news הַמְבַשֵּׂר answered and said, 'Israel fled before the Philistines, and there has been a great defeat among the people, and both your sons are dead, Hophni and Phinehas, and the ark of the covenant has been stolen.'" — Targum: "And the one who delivered the news דִּמְבַשֵּׂר answered …." ‖ Targum Yerušalmi I Genesis 41:26f.: "The seven beautiful cows, they proclaim מְבַשְּׂרָן seven years; the seven beautiful ears of corn, they proclaim מְבַשְּׂרָן seven years. This is a dream. (Here בַּשֵּׂר is used in the case of good news.) And the seven lean and ugly cows, which came up after them, they proclaim מְבַשְּׂרָן seven years; the seven puny ears struck by the east wind proclaim מְבַשְּׂרָן that there will be seven years of hunger." (Here בשר is used in the case of bad news.)

c. Nahum 2:1: "Behold, on the mountains the feet of one who delivers (good) news רַגְלֵי מְבַשֵּׂר (about the fall of Nineveh), who proclaims peace." — Targum is similar with just מְבַסַּר. ‖ Psalm 68:12: "The Lord proclaimed; there was a great host of women proclaiming (glad) news הַמְבַשְּׂרוֹת." — See the translation of the targum *ad loc* above at n. *a.* ‖ 2 Samuel 18:26: "Behold, a man comes running alone! And the king said, 'This one too is one who brings (good) news מְבַשֵּׂר.'" — The targum is similar with just מְבַסַּר. ‖ Isaiah 41:27: "As the first (I said it) to Zion — behold, behold, here it is now! And I gave to Jerusalem a proclaimer of (good) news מְבַשֵּׂר (sg. with a collective meaning)." — Targum: "The words of comfort that the prophets prophesied beforehand about Zion, behold, they have arrived, and I will give Jerusalem a proclaimer of (glad) news מבסר." ‖ Targum Yerušalmi I Genesis 21:7: "How trustworthy was the one who proclaimed (good) news, who brought Abraham the (good) news מְבַשְּׂרָא דְּבַשַּׂר and said, 'Sarah will suckle children one day.'" ‖ Babylonian Talmud Pesaḥim 3B.41: Yohanan of Huqqoq (ca. 200)[4] went out into the villages. When he came (back), people said to him, "Did the wheat turn out well?" He answered them, "The barley turned out well." (From this it should be assumed that there was nothing good to say about the wheat.) People said to him, "Go out and bring the (good) news בַּשֵּׂר to the horses and donkeys. For it is written, 'The barley and the straw for the horses and the animals used for riding' (1 Kgs 5:8)."[5] ‖ See further examples in n. *e*; additionally, Tg. Yer. I Gen. 41:26 above in n. *b*; m. Soṭah 9.6 and b. Soṭah 11A at § Luke 2:25 C, #4, n. *b.*

d. Sifre Deuteronomy 32:4 § 307 (133A): You have brought me good news בִּשַּׂרְתַּנִי בְשׂוֹרָה טוֹבָה, tomorrow my portion will be with these ones in the future world (see the whole passage at § Luke 23:43, #1). ‖ Numbers Rabbah 14 (173D): "Much studying is weariness for the body יְגִעַת בָּשָׂר" (Eccl 12:12). If you exert yourself much יגעת in studying the words of the learned, God will proclaim to you good news מבשרך בשורות טובות. This is how בָּשָׂר should

4. According to y. Pes. 1.27C.63 and y. B. Meṣ. 3.9A.61, he was a contemporary of R. Hiyya the Elder, thus around 200 CE.

5. TN: The versification is different in the MT than in translations where the corresponding text is 1 Kgs 14:28.

be interpreted in Eccl 12:12. ‖ In b. Ḥul. 87A, a Sadducee (heretic) says to the Patriarch Judah I († 217?): "Rabbi, I bring you good news מבשר טובות אני לך." ‖ Midrash Lamentations 1:5 (52A) איתבשרת בשורתא טבתא; see #1, *d.* ‖ 1 Kings 1:42: "Come in, for you are a brave man and you will bring good news וְטוֹב תְּבַשֵּׂר." Targum: וְטָב תְּבַסַּר. ‖ Targum Yerušalmi I Genesis 49:21: "Naphtali, a quick messenger, is like the roe which bolts over mountaintops, he who delivers good news מבשר בשורן טבן." — See Tg. Yer. II Gen. 49:21. ‖ Isaiah 52:7: "The one who brings good news מבשר טוב"; Tg.: מְבַסַּר טָב.

e. 1 Samuel 31:9: "They cut off his (Saul's) head and removed his armor and sent (them) throughout the land of the Philistines to bring (good) news to the temple of their idols and to the people לְבַשֵּׂר בית עצביהם ואת העם." — Targum: לְבַסָּרָא בֵּית טַעֲוָתְהוֹן וְיַת עַמָּא. ‖ 2 Samuel 18:19: "Ahimaaz, the son of Zadok, said, 'I will run and deliver the news to the king וַאֲבַשְּׂרָה את המלך.'" Targum: וַאֲבַסַּר ית מלכא. ‖ Isaiah 61:1: "To bring (good) news to the wretched לְבַשֵּׂר עֲנָוִים." Targum: לְבַשָּׂרָא עִנְוְתָנַיָּא. ‖ Genesis Rabbah 30 (18B): R. Judan (ca. 350) said in the name of R. Abba b. Kahana (ca. 310), "'And you will go to your fathers in peace' (Gen 15:15); thereby he brought him (Abraham) the good news בִּשְּׂרוֹ that his father would have a share in the future world." ‖ Tanḥuma שמות 64B: Abraham said before God, "Lord of the world, for all the good works I have amassed in this world, am I to go to my fathers (Gen 15:15)?" Then God brought him the good news בשרו, "Assuredly, by your life! Your father repented (and therefore has a share in the future world)." — See parallels at § Luke 22:31, n. *c.* ‖ Babylonian Talmud Baba Meṣiʿa 86B: Who were those three men (with Abraham in Gen 18)? Michael, Gabriel, and Raphael. Michael, who had come to bring Sarah the good news לבשר את שרה (see Gen 18:10).... — The whole passage can be found at § Luke 1:19 A, #4, n. *i.* — Additionally, see SDeut 32:4 and Num. Rab. 14 above in n. *d.*

f. For the passive εὐαγγελίζεσθαι, see LXX 2 Sam 18:31: εὐαγγελισθήτω ὁ κύριός μου ὁ βασιλεύς = "Let the good news be delivered to my lord king," or, "May my lord king receive the good news." — Septuagint Joel 2:32 (= 3:5 in the Hebrew text), where וּבַשְּׂרִידִים is translated with καὶ εὐαγγελιζόμενοι = those to whom the good news was delivered. In the NT, see Matt 11:5; Luke 7:22; Heb 4:2, 6; 1 Pet 4:6. ‖ For the passive of בִּשֵּׂר, see 2 Sam 18:31: יִתְבַּשֵּׂר אֲדֹנִי הַמֶּלֶךְ; targum: יִתְבַּסַּר רִבּוֹנִי מַלְכָּא = "let the good news by delivered to my lord king." ‖ Targum Yerušalmi I Genesis 22:5: "We want to go there to test whether what has been proclaimed to me as good news מה דאתבשרית is true." ‖ Targum Ruth 1:6: "Then she headed off ... and began to return from the country of Moab, because the good news had been proclaimed אתבשרת to her in the country of Moab by the mouth of an angel...." ‖ Targum Lamentations 1:2: "When the people, the house of Israel, heard this bad news which had been brought דאתבשרו to them concerning the land of Israel." ‖ Genesis Rabbah 47 (29C): R. Nehemiah (ca.150) said, "Could the good news about breastfeeding already be brought נתבשרה בחלב to her (Sarah), since she was not yet pregnant?" ‖ Pesiqta Rabbati 42 (178A): Immediately the good news about offspring was proclaimed (to Abraham) נתבשר בבנים. ‖ Midrash Lamentations 1:5: See above in #1, n. *d.* ‖ TanḥumaB שמות § 15 (5A): Our father Abraham did not die before the good news about his father Terah's conduct was brought to him עד שנתבשר, namely that he repented. ‖ Jerusalem Talmud Šeqalim 3.47C.62: It has been taught in the name of R. Meir (ca. 150): "Whoever clings to the land of Israel (permanently dwells there) and speaks the holy language and enjoys its fruits in purity and recites the Shema morning and evening, to him let the good news be brought יְהֵא מְבוּשָּׂר that he is a son of the future world." — The parallel passage in y. Šabb. 1.3C.23 reads: He may consider himself assured מוּבְטָח לוֹ that he belongs to the life of the future world. — Differently in SDeut 32:43 § 333 (140B). ‖ Jerusalem Talmud Ketubbot 12.35A.26: A voice from heaven came forth and called to them, "Whoever has not slacked in mourning Rabbi, to him let the good news be brought יהא מבושר concerning the life of the future world (namely that he will have a share in it)." — A parallel passage can be found in y. Kil. 9.32B.18. ‖ Jerusalem Talmud Berakot 5.9D.25: R. Samuel b. Nahman (ca. 260) said, "If you incline your heart to prayer (you pray devoutly), let the good news be brought to you תהא מבושר that your prayer is heard. And what basis is there for this in Scripture? 'If you incline your heart, you will listen with your ear' (so Midr. Ps. 10:17)."[6] R. Joshua b. Levi (ca. 250) said, "If a person's lips (in prayer) move (automatically), let the good news be brought יהא מבושר to him that his prayer is heard. What basis is there for this in Scripture? If he achieves the self-movement of the lips, (then there is) 'peace, peace to those far and near, says Yahweh, and I will heal him' (so Midr. Isa. 57:19)." — In the parallel passage of Lev. Rab. 16 (116D), instead of מבושר, one finds מוּבְטָח = he may be assured; additionally, R. Joshua b. Nahmani is the author instead of R. Samuel b. Nahman; in the ed. Ven. 1545 the text is corrupt. — In Midr. Ps. 108 § 1 (232A), only the quotation of R. Samuel b. Nahman is found, but with many additions. ‖ Exodus Rabbah 46 (101B): Moses began grieving over the shattering of the tablets of the Law. God said to him, "Do not grieve because of the earlier tablets, for they contained only the ten commandments; but I will give you the second tablets so that on them will be halakoth, midrash (study, interpretation, explanation of Scripture), and haggadoth (nonhalakic interpretations of Scripture)"; this is what Job 11:6 means: "and that he would make known to you the secrets of wisdom, that it contains true knowledge twice" (that is, the written and the oral Torah). And not only this, but may the good news also be brought אתה מנושר to you that I have forgiven your sins; as it says, "Know that God overlooks your guilt" (Job 11:6). ‖ מְבוּשָּׂר in these passages corresponds to εὐηγγελισμένος in Heb 4:2 and εὐαγγελισθείς in Heb 4:6.

3. In the NT, the content of εὐαγγέλιον refers to the good news about the realization of messianic salvation. This good news can therefore be called α. an εὐαγγέλιον Ἰησοῦ Χριστοῦ (Mark 1:1) or an εὐαγγέλιον τοῦ Χριστοῦ (Rom 15:19; 1 Cor 9:12; 2 Cor 2:12; 9:13; 10:14; Gal 1:7; Phil 1:27; 1 Thess 3:2), because messianic salvation is realized through Jesus, the Christ (Messiah); β. an εὐαγγέλιον τῆς βασιλείας (Matt 4:23; 9:35; 24:14), because with the inbreaking of messianic salvation the kingdom of God has appeared on earth; γ. an εὐαγγέλιον τῆς χάριτος τοῦ θεοῦ (Acts 20:24) or an εὐαγγέλιον τῆς σωτηρίας ἡμῶν (Eph 1:13) or an εὐαγγέλιον τῆς εἰρήνης (Eph 6:15), because the grace of God in Christ and our salvation through Christ and the peace between God and the world constitute the sole content of this good news. — The ancient synagogue also knew of good news which was closely

6. S-B: According to Pesiq. Rab. 195B, Abba Saul (ca. 150) is the author of this explanation; cf. t. Ber. 3.4 (6); b. Ber. 31A.

related to the messianic time. Its substance comprised the redemption and liberation of Israel, the peace and salvation that would come into the world; the day when one would shout to Israel, "The kingdom of God has been revealed, your God has become king!"[a] Either the returning prophet Elijah[b] or the Messiah[c] is hailed as the deliverer of this joyful message. It was Israel's daily prayer that this day would come soon.[d]

a. Targum Isaiah 40:9: "Climb up onto a high mountain, you prophets who bring good news to Zion מְבַסְּרִין לציון; lift up your voice with strength, you who bring good news to Jerusalem מבסרין לירושלם, lift (them) up, do not fear, say to the cities of the house of Judah, 'The kingdom of your God has been revealed אִתְגְּלִיאַת!'" ‖ Targum Isaiah 52:7: "How beautiful on the mountains of the land of Israel are the feet of the one who brings good news מְבַסַּר, who proclaim peace, of the one who brings good news מְבַסַּר טָב, who proclaims redemption פּוּרְקָן, who says to the community of Zion, 'The kingdom of your God has been revealed אתגליאת!'" ‖ Additionally, see the passages in notes *b* and *c*.

b. Targum Yerušalmi I Numbers 25:12: "Behold, I will make my covenant of peace with him (Phinehas = Elijah) and will make him a messenger of the covenant ('angel of the covenant' [Mal 3:1]), and he will live forever to bring the good news of redemption לְמִבַשְּׂרָא גְאוּלְתָא at the end of days." ‖ Pesiqta 51A: "My beloved (= God according to the midr.) arises and speaks to me" (Song 2:10). R. Azariah (ca. 380) said, "Is not then the arising the same thing as the speaking?[7] But this is what is meant: 'he arises with me' through Elijah, and 'he speaks to me' through the king, the Messiah. And what does he say to me? 'Arise, my love, my beautiful one (= the community of Israel) and come here; for behold, the winter הַסְּתָין (*qere*) is past' (Song 2:10f.). This refers to the blasphemous (Roman) empire (which at the time of R. Azariah had become Christian), which misleads מסיתה (haggadic interpretation of הסתין) people; as it says, 'If your brother, your mother's son, misleads you יסיתך' (Deut 13:7). 'The rain is over, is gone' (Song 2:11); this refers to servitude (which is now over). 'The flowers appeared on the earth' (Song 2:12)." R. Eleazar (ca. 270) said, "These are the 'four blacksmiths' (Zech 2:3):[8] Elijah, the king the Messiah, Melchizedek (the high priest at the messianic time) and the one anointed for war (= Messiah b. Joseph; on this interpretation of Zech 2:3 see Num. Rab. 14 [172B] at § Matt 1:21 C, n. *a*, toward end). 'The time of singing הזמור has arrived' (Song 2:12); the time of the foreskin (of the gentiles) has arrived so it may be cut off שתזמר (interpretation of הזמור); the time of the godless has arrived so that they may be shattered ('Yahweh has shattered the staff of the godless, the rod of rulers' [Isa 14:5]); the time of the blasphemous (Roman) empire has arrived so that it may be wiped off the face of the earth; the time of the kingdom of God מלכות שמים has arrived so that it may be revealed שתגלה, for it says, 'Yahweh will be king over the whole earth' (Zech 14:9)." — This is the content of what God has to say to Israel in his "arising" through Elijah. The following (see n. *c*) then brings the news of the Messiah. Parallels can be found

---

7. S-B: These words can probably be rightly understood only as a question; for a different understanding, see the rendering at § Matt 4:17 B, #2, n. *c*.

8. TN: The versification is different in the MT than in translations where the corresponding text is Zech 1:20.

in Midr. Song. 2:13 (100B); Pesiq. Rab. 15 (74B). ‖ Pesiqta Rabbati 35 (161A): "Rejoice and be glad, daughter Zion!" (Zech 2:13). When will this word be fulfilled? At the time when God redeems Israel. Three days before the Messiah comes, Elijah will come and stand on the mountains of Israel and weep and mourn over her and say, "Behold, land of Israel, how long will you stand in barrenness, drought, and desolation? And his voice will be heard from one end of the world to the other." Then he will say to them, "Peace has come into the world," for it says, "Behold, on the mountains the feet of one who brings good news רגלי מבשר, who proclaims peace" (Nah 2:1). When the godless hear this, they will all be glad and say to one another: Peace has come for us! On the second day he will come and stand on the mountains of Israel and say, "Good has come into the world"; for it says, "The one who proclaims good מבשר טוב" (Isa 52:7). On the third day he will come and say, "Salvation ישועה (σωτηρία) has come into the world"; for it says, "The one who proclaims salvation" (Isa 52:7). Then when he sees the godless, they will say just as he will say, "Your God has become king for Zion" (so the midr. interprets the end of Isa 52:7); this teaches you that salvation will come for Zion and its children but not for the godless. In that hour God will make his glory and his kingdom מלכותו appear to all who come into the world, and he will redeem Israel and reveal himself at her head ונגלה; for it says, "He who opens the breach will pull out before them; they will open the breach and come in at the gate and go out through it, and he their king will go before them and Yahweh will be at their head" (Mic 2:13). ‖ Leqach Tob Numbers 24:17 (ed. Buber 2:130A): A seventh voice from heaven will loudly proclaim: "Comfort, comfort my people" (Isa 40:1), and Elijah will bring the good news מבשר to Israel: "Your God has become king!" (Isa 52:7). — See the whole passage at § Luke 24:26, II, #3, n. *b* and § Matt 3:3. ‖ At the beginning of b. ʿErub. 43B, Rashi summarizes the task that Elijah has to complete as forerunner of the Messiah: "Before the arrival of the Son of David (the Messiah) Elijah will come to bring good news לבשר."

c. In the concluding chapter of Der. Er. Zut. we read: R. Yose the Galilean (ca. 110) said, "The peace is great, for when the king, the Messiah, is revealed to Israel נגלה, he will begin only with peace; for it says, 'How lovely on the mountains are the feet of the one who brings good news רגלי מבשר, who proclaims peace' (Isa 52:7)." ‖ Pesiqta 51A.20: (extension of the citation in n. *b*:) "'The voice of the turtledove is heard in our land' (Song 2:12); thereby is meant the king, the Messiah; for it says, 'How lovely on the mountains are the feet of the one who brings good news …' (Isa 52:7)." — See the parallel passages in n. *b*. ‖ Pesiqta Rabbati 36 (162A): Our teachers have taught: In the hour when the king, the Messiah, is revealed נגלה, he will come and stand on the roof of the temple. And he will proclaim to them, the Israelites, and say to them, "You who are bowed down, the time of your redemption גאולתכם has arrived! And if you do not believe it, look at my light which shines over you; for it says, 'Stand up, let there be light; for your light comes and the glory of Yahweh shines over you' (Isa 60:1). It shines over you alone, but not over the gentiles of the world; for it says, 'For behold, gloom covers the earth and darkness the nations, but Yahweh will shine over you and his glory will appear over you' (Isa 60:2). In that hour, God will cause the light of the king, the Messiah, to blaze. And all the gentiles of the world will be in gloom and darkness; and they will all go to the light of the Messiah and Israel; for it says, 'And gentiles (*goyim*) will go to your light, kings to the rising of your shining' (Isa 60:3). And they will come and lick the dust off the feet of the king, the Messiah; for it says, 'And they will lick the dust of your feet' (Isa 49:23). And they will all come and fall on their face before the Messiah and before Israel and say to them, 'We wish to be servants to you and Israel.' And every single person in Israel will have 2800 servants; for it says, 'On that day it will happen (so the midr.) that ten men from all (70) tongues of the gentiles (= 700) will fasten onto the tips (of which there are four) of a Judean's tunic' (so four times 700 = 2800; see b. Šabb. 32B) and say, 'We wish to go with you, for we have heard that God is with you.'" ‖ Targum Lamentations 2:22: "Shout freedom חֵירוּתָא to your people, to the house of Israel, through the Messiah, as you did on the day of Passover through Moses and Aaron; for the young men will be gathered together all around from every place to where they were dispersed on that day because your anger, Yahweh, became powerful. And there was no one among them who escaped or remained. Those whom I had draped in cloths and those I had raised with the delicacies of kings, they have annihilated their enemies." ‖ Sefer Zerubbabel (Jellinek, *Beth ha-Midrash* 2.56.24): Michael said to me (Zerubbabel), "Approach me and incline your heart to what I will say to you, for the word in the name of the living God is truth." And he said to me, "Menaḥem b. Ammiel (a name for the Messiah) will suddenly come in the month of Nisan and stand in the Valley of Arbel, and all the learned of Israel will go out to him. And Ben Ammiel will say to them, "I am the Messiah Yahweh has sent to bring you good news לבשרכם and to redeem you from the hand of your oppressors." And the learned will look at him and scorn him.... ‖ Pirqe Mashiaḥ (Jellinek, *Beth ha-Midrash* 3.73.17): In that hour (after the annihilation of the gentiles of the world by God), God will clothe the Messiah with a crown and put the helmet of salvation כובע ישועה (cf. Isa 59:17) on his head and lay splendor and glory upon him and adorn him with garments of honor and set him on a high mountain to bring good news to Israel לבשר לישראל. And he will proclaim with his voice, "Salvation has drawn near קרבה ישוע!" Then the Israelites will say, "Who are you?" And he will answer, "I am Ephraim!" And the Israelites will say, "Are you the one God has named 'Ephraim, he is my firstborn, Ephraim is my favorite son' (Jer 31:9, 19)?" And he will answer them, "Yes!" Then the Israelites will say to him, "Go and bring good news ובשר to those who sleep in the double cavern so that they may resurrect first." In that hour, he will go up and bring good news ומבשר to those who sleep in the double cavern and will say to them, "Abraham, Isaac, and Jacob, arise, enough with your sleep!" And they will answer him and say, "Who is it who has taken the (grave) dust from us?" And he will say to them, "I am Yahweh's Messiah, salvation has drawn near, the hour has drawn near!" And they will answer him, "If this in fact is the case, go and bring good news (read ובשר) to the first man first so that he may resurrect first." In that hour, it will be said to the first man, "Enough with your sleep!" And he will say, "Who is it who banishes sleep from my eyes?" And he will say, "I am Yahweh's Messiah from your offspring." Immediately the first man will resurrect and his whole generation and Abraham, Isaac, and Jacob and all righteous ones and patriarchs and all generations from one end of the world to the other and they will make heard the voice of rejoicing and of song; for it says, "How lovely on the mountains are the feet of the one who brings good news" (Isa 52:7).... The king, the Messiah, is beautiful as the deliverer of good news to

Israel, and the mountains will skip before him like calves, and the trees of the field will clap their hands concerning the salvation of Israel; for it says, "You will go out with joy and be led in peace ..." (Isa 55:12). — The messenger of joy (Nah 2:4) remains unspecified in Midr. Sam. 19 § 5; see this passage at § Luke 2:25 C, #2, n. *b*.

d. For evidence, see § Acts 1:6.

4. The word εὐαγγέλιον is found in rabbinic writing in the (purposely) corrupted form אָוֶן גִּלָּיוֹן or עֲוֹן גִּלָּיוֹן. The second component in these phrases, גִּלָּיוֹן (pl. גִּלְיוֹנִים), designates a blank scroll or the empty margins on a scroll that has been written on[a] which were used to attach remarks. און גליון means accordingly "scroll of perdition" or "margin of perdition" and עון גליון "scroll of sin" or "margin of sin,"[b] a designation that is supposed to serve to slander the Gospel writings (see similar slanderous terms at § Matt 12:24, #2, n. *c*). אָוֶן by itself is also found in the sense of און גליון;[c] however, it is less likely that the Gospel writings are designated with גִּלְיוֹנִים by itself.[d]

a. Mishnah Yadayim 3.4: The margin גִּלָּיוֹן of a (Torah) scroll which is located at the top and the bottom, at the beginning and the end, makes the hands unclean (thus it is considered to be holy). R. Judah (ca. 150) said, "The margin at the end does not make (the hands) unclean until the stick (around which the scroll was rolled) has been attached to it." ‖ Babylonian Talmud Menaḥot 30A: The measure of the margin גליון at the bottom (on a Torah scroll) amounts to a hand's breadth, at the top three fingers and in between the individual columns as much as the space constituted by the width of two fingers. ‖ Babylonian Talmud Šabbat 116A: The question was raised by them, "Should the margins הגיליונין of a book of the Torah (because of the names of God which may be written on them) be saved from a fire, or should they not be saved from a fire?" ... The margins (blank spaces) on the top and bottom (on a Torah scroll), between the individual sections of writing, between the individual columns, at the beginning of the book and at the end of the book make the hands unclean....

b. Babylonian Talmud Šabbat 116A: R. Meir (ca. 150) named it (the book of the *minim* = Jewish Christians; here are meant the Gospel writings) *ʾaven-gillayon* "margin of perdition" (writing of perdition), R. Yohanan († 279) named it *ʿavōn-gillayon* "margin of sin" (writing of sin).

c. See b. Šabb. 116A at § Matt 5:17 B, #3. In this passage, the ed. Amsterdam 1644ff. gives the simple term און three times, while the Munich manuscript[9] has עון גליון three times. The ed. Frankfurt 1720ff. reads, instead of the first עון גליון, the words אורייתא אחריתי = a different Torah; instead of the second, we read דספרא = of the book; and instead of the third, we read just אנא = I. Apparently this is an intervention of censorship.

d. Tosefta Yadayim 2.13 (683): The *Gilyonim* and the books of the *minim* (heretics, Jewish Christians) do not make the hands unclean (are not considered to be holy writings). ‖ Tosefta Šabbat 13.5 (129): The *Gilyonim* and the books of the *minim* are not saved. Instead, they are left to burn in their place (where they are located), they themselves and the names of God in them. — Bacher, *Die Agada der Tannaïten*, 1:258: "By גליונים we are to understand

---

9. See Hermann Strack, *Jesus, die Häretiker und die Christen: nach den ältesten jüdischen Angaben: Texte, Übersetzung und Erläuterungen* (Leipzig: Hinrichs, 1910), 2.

the Gospels; by ספרי מינים copies of the Bible which are made and used by heretics." — However, the parallel passages m. Yad. 3.4 and b. Šabb. 116A in n. *a* unambiguously show that also in t. Yad. 2.13, by *Gilyonim*, we should understand the margins of the scrolls, and as for t. Šabb. 13.5, it follows clearly from b. Šabb. 116A that only the margins of the books are in mind when the *Gilyonim* are mentioned. Here it is asked whether the margins of a Torah scroll are not meant by the *Gilyonim* in a baraita in t. Šabb., and it is replied that, rather, the margins of the books of the *minim* גליונין דסיפרי מינים are meant; then it is added that the point there is that the books of the *minim* are as margins ספרי מינים הרי הן כגליונין. — The "Gospels" do not fit in this context. — Moriz Friedländer wants us to understand *Gilyonim* as the schema of the Ophites mentioned by Celsus and Origen.[10]

1:2 A: Which he proclaimed beforehand.

ὃ προεπηγγείλατο. — The προ of προεπηγγείλατο indicates that the messianic redemption formed a part of the divine plan for the world from the beginning. A baraita in b. Pesaḥ. 54A expressed this thought as follows: Seven things were created before the world was created: the Torah, repentance, the garden of Eden, gehenna, the throne of glory, the (heavenly) sanctuary, and the name of the Messiah.... The name of the Messiah, as it says in Ps 72:17: "May his name exist forever, before the sun existed his name was 'Yinnon'" (so the midr.). — See the parallels at § John 1:1 A, B, n. *a* and § Matt 25:31 B.

1:2 B: By his prophets.

The rabbinic scholars counted in total 48 prophets and 7 prophetesses whose prophecies are recorded in Holy Scripture.[a] Additionally, they speak of countless other prophets whose prophecies remained unrecorded since they had no significance for the Torah and later generations. But God will one day make their sayings known to everyone.[b] Thus, the concept "prophet" was quite broadly conceived. This is shown, among other ways (see § Luke 2:25 C, #3, notes *d–i*), by the occasional enumeration of the expressions which were considered to be synonymous with "prophet."[c] — A peculiar theory without an easily discernible slant was developed concerning the ancestry and origin of the prophets.[d] — The classification of the prophets into earlier and later prophets נְבִיאִים רִאשׁוֹנִים and נ' אַחֲרוֹנִים was already known in rabbinic literature, although without a sharp temporal boundary separating the two groups.[e] By contrast, these expressions cannot be found in ancient Jewish literature as a way of designating earlier and later prophetic writings in the OT canon.

a. After the time and activity of the prophets mentioned in Scripture are discussed in S. ʿOlam Rab. 17–20, chapter 21 says in connection with what precedes: These are the 48

---

10. Moriz Friedländer, *Der vorchristliche jüdische Gnosticismus* (Göttingen: Vandenhoeck & Ruprecht, 1898), 83.

prophets, along with their prophecies, who prophesied to the Israelites and they were written down in (holy) writings. ‖ Babylonian Talmud Megillah 14A: "Then the king removed his signet ring from his hand (and gave it to Haman)" (Esth 3:10). R. Abba bar Kahana (ca. 310) said, "The removal of the signet ring was more powerful than the 48 prophets and the 7 prophetesses who prophesied to the Israelites; for these all did not bring them back to the good, but the removal of the signet ring brought them back to the good." Our teachers taught: "48 prophets and 7 prophetesses prophesied to the Israelites, without diminishing or augmenting what is written in the Torah, except the reading of the scroll of Esther." ‖ Babylonian Talmud Megillah 14A: Who were the 7 prophetesses? Sarah, Miriam, Deborah, Hannah, Abigail, Hulda, and Esther. – These 7 prophetesses are listed also in S. ʿOlam Rab. 21, but with the addition that all the matriarchs are called prophetesses; see § Luke 2:25 C, #3, n. *d.*

b. Seder ʿOlam Rabbah 21: Furthermore, there were (in addition to the 48 prophets) as many prophets as the number of those who went out of Egypt (= 600,000), but they were not written down.... For there is no single city in the land of Israel where there were no prophets; but every prophecy that was necessary for the Torah was written down. In the Song of Songs there is this interpretation about them: "How beautiful are your caresses, my sister bride, how sweet are your caresses, more than wine, and the scent of your ointments, more than balsam" (Song 4:10f.) ‖ A baraita in b. Meg. 14A: Many prophets arose for the Israelites, twice as many as the number of those who went out of Egypt; but the prophecy which was necessary for the following generations was written down, and that which was not necessary was not written down. ‖ Midrash Song of Songs 4:11 (115A): R. Darosa (4th cent.) and R. Jeremiah (ca. 320) said in the name of R. Samuel b. Isaac (ca. 300), "60 myriads of prophets arose for the Israelites in the days of Elijah." R. Jacob (b. Idi, ca. 280) said in the name of R. Yohanan († 279), "120 myriads.... And why was their prophecy not published? Because it was not necessary for the following generations. Say therefore, 'Every prophecy that was necessary for its time and the following generations was published, and every prophecy which was necessary for its time but not for the following generations was not published. But in the future God will fetch them up (the prophets) and publish their prophecy.' This is what Zech 14:5 means, 'All holy ones will come with you, Yahweh my God' (the midrash text reads אלהים)." R. Berekhiah (ca. 340) said in the name of R. Helbo (ca. 300), "Just as 60 myriads of prophets arose for the Israelites, so also did 60 myriads of prophetesses arise for them, and Solomon came and made them known; for it says, 'Your lips drip like a honeycomb, O bride' (Song 4:11)." – Parallels can be found in Midr. Ruth 1:1 (123A); Midr. Eccl. 1:11 (10A); Midr. Lam. 4:22 (77B).

c. ʾAbot de Rabbi Nathan 34 (9A): A prophet is designated with 10 names; these are: messenger צִיר, entrusted one נֶאֱמָן, servant עֶבֶד, sent one שָׁלִיחַ (= מַלְאָךְ), beholder הוֹזֶה, watcher צוֹפֶה, seer רוֹאֶה, dreamer חוֹלֵם, prophet נביא, and man of God אִישׁ הָאֱלֹהִים. – References are not given. – The end of S. ʿOlam Rab. 20, in discussing Ezekiel and Daniel, gives as an additional name, "child of man" בן אדם.

d. Leviticus Rabbah 6 (109C): R. Yohanan († 279) said, "Every prophet whose own name is stated explicitly along with the name of his father was a prophet and the son of a prophet;

and every prophet whose own name is given but his father's name is not stated explicitly was a prophet but his father was not." R. Eleazar (ca. 270) in the name of R. Yose b. Zimra (ca. 220) adduced for this the following: "'Haggai and Zechariah, the son of Iddo the prophet, prophesied' (this is how Ezra 5:1 is cited); for he was a prophet, son of a prophet." But the rabbis said, "Whether his (the father's) name is explicitly stated or not, he is a prophet and the son of a prophet; for thus Amos spoke to Amaziah, 'I am not a prophet nor the son of a prophet' (Amos 7:14). Just as he was a prophet, even though he says, 'I am not a prophet,' so also was his father a prophet, even though he says, 'I am not the son of a prophet.'" ‖ Midrash Lamentations Introduction 24 (36B): R. Yohanan († 279) opened his talk with the following: "'The oracle concerning the valley of vision (= Jerusalem)' (Isa 22:1); this is the valley about which all seers have prophesied, the valley from which all seers have arisen." For R. Yohanan said, "Every prophet whose city is not explicitly stated was a Jerusalemite." — See the parallel passage to both of the last sayings by R. Yohanan from b. Meg. 15A at § Acts 3:25 A, #3. ‖ Babylonian Talmud Sukkah 27B: R. Eliezer (ca. 90) said, "There is not a single tribe in Israel from which prophets would not have come." ‖ Seder ʿOlam Rabbah 21: There is not a single city in the land of Israel in which there would not have been prophets.

e. Mishnah Soṭah 9.12: After the earlier prophets had died, the Urim and Thummim ceased. — Since, according to b. Soṭah 48B, the cessation of the latter coincided with the destruction of the first temple, we should, at least theoretically, understand the earlier prophets to denote the preexilic prophets. However, it says in b. Soṭah 48B: Who are the earlier prophets? Rab Huna († 297) said, "They are David, Samuel, and Solomon...." Rab Nahman b. Isaac († 356) said, "Who are the earlier prophets? All of them with the exception of Haggai, Zechariah, and Malachi; for these are the later prophets."

1:2 C: In the Holy Scriptures.

1. γραφαὶ ἅγιαι = כִּתְבֵי הַקֹּדֶשׁ; this term designates α. the Holy Scriptures in general which form the OT canon;[a] β. the hagiographa = Ketuvim in particular.[b]

a. Mishnah Yadayim 3.5: All Holy Scriptures כל כתבי הקדש make the hands unclean. — The same without כל in m. Yad. 4.6. ‖ Mishnah Šabbat 16.1: (On the Sabbath) all Holy Scriptures must be saved from a fire, whether it is permitted (on the Sabbath) to read what is contained in them or not (as, e.g., in the hagiographa). And whatever language they are written in, they must still be buried (when they waste away). And why is it not permitted to read what is in them (on the Sabbath)? In order not to neglect the house of learning (cf. the citation in n. *b*). ‖ Mishnah ʿErubin 10.3: If someone (on the Sabbath) is reading at the edge of the Torah scroll and it rolls out of his hand, he may roll it back up again. If he was reading on a rooftop and it rolled out of his hand, he may roll it back up again, provided that it did not get to a length of ten hand-widths (in a public area). However, if it has gotten to ten hand-widths, then he will flip it onto the side with Scripture (and let it lie). R. Judah (ca. 150) said, "If it is still only a pin's breadth from the ground, it may still be rolled back up." R. Simeon b. Yohai (ca. 150) said, "Even if it is already lying on the ground, it may be rolled back up, because no objection can be made on the basis of Sabbath rest when it comes to caring for the Holy Scriptures." – In the discussion about this passage, the expression כתבי הקדש is found four times in b. ʿErub. 97B and 98A. ‖ Mishnah Baba Batra 1.6: The Holy Scriptures (which are the common property of two parties) cannot be separated (in the case that they are written on one scroll), even if both sides wish to do so. ‖ Mishnah Sanhedrin 10.6: "Burn the city (which has let itself be misled to renounce Yahweh) and all its spoil with fire as a whole burnt offering for Yahweh, your God" (Deut 13:17). It says its spoil, not God's spoil. On the basis of these words it has been said, "Whatever is sacred in such a city should be taken out of it. The priestly collections are left to decay, but the second tithe and the Holy Scriptures are covered (buried)."

b. Tosefta Šabbat 13.1 (128): Although it has been said, "The hagiographa בכתבי הקודש may not be read (on the Sabbath) (see Šabb. 16.1 in n. *a*)," they may nevertheless be studied and presented on (or: researched) and, even more so, may something be searched for in them; they may be taken and searched in. R. Nehemiah (ca. 150) said, "Why has it been said, 'The hagiographa בכתבי הקודש may not be read (on the Sabbath)?' Because of the ordinary writings. It should be said, 'The hagiographa may not be read—how much less ordinary (profane) writings!'" – Parallels with variations can be found in Sop. 15 § 3; y. Šabb. 16.15C.6, 19; b. Šabb. 116B. ‖ Jerusalem Talmud Šabbat 16.15B.51: Between the Torah and the Neviʿim (on the one hand) and the hagiographa כתבי הקודש (on the other hand) there is this difference: the latter (the hagiographa) are not saved from a fire (on the Sabbath). – This tradition contradicts the tradition in m. Šabb. 16.1 above in n. *a*. It is then added that this tradition corresponds to the opinion that the hagiographa do not make the hands unclean.

2. That the good news of the messianic time of salvation was proclaimed beforehand in the Holy Scriptures was of course the opinion of the ancient synagogue as well. This is shown by the messianic interpretation of countless OT passages. R. Yohanan († 279) says briefly in b. Ber. 34B: "All prophets prophesied only up until the days of the Messiah. But concerning the future world (which follows the days of the Messiah) it says, 'No eye has seen, O God, except you, what is prepared for the one who awaits' (so Midr. Isa. 64:3)." – Parallel passages can be found in b. Sanh. 99A and b. Šabb. 63A; in the latter R. Hiyya b. Abba, a student of R. Yohanan, is named as the author, whereas in the other two he appears as the tradent of R. Yohanan. – The sense of the saying is not, though, that the prophets prophesied only about the days of Messiah but rather that their prophecies about the eventual reward do not extend beyond the messianic time. The saying, however, also presupposes that all prophets proclaimed the messianic time beforehand.

1:3 A: Concerning his Son.

A. In the figurative or metaphorical sense, God's "son" designates the one who by virtue of his special divine election stands in as close a relationship to God based on love and obedience as a son to his father. In this sense the following are named as God's "son":

1. In the OT, disregarding the designation of the angels as בְּנֵי אֱלֹהִים (Gen 6:2ff.; Job 1:6; 2:1; 32:7); בְּנֵי אֵלִים (Ps 29:1; 89:7); בַּר אֱלָהִין (Dan 3:25) (cf. Jude 7):

α. The people of Israel.

Exodus 4:22f.: "Yahweh has spoken thus, 'My firstborn son בְּנִי בְכֹרִי is Israel. And so, I command you, "Let my son אֶת־בְּנִי go."'" — Targum Onkelos and Yerušalmi I: "My firstborn son is Israel בְּרִי בוּכְרִי יִשְׂרָאֵל.... Let my son go יָת בְּרִי." ‖ Hosea 2:1: "Instead of it having been said to them, 'You are not my people,' it will be said to them, 'Sons of the living God' בְּנֵי אֵל־חָי." — The targum avoids the metaphorical expression: And it will come to pass, instead of them having been led into exile among the gentiles when they transgressed the Torah and it having been said to them: "You are not my people," they will be made great again and it will be said to them: "People of the God who remains forever." ‖ Hosea 11:1: "When Israel was a youth, I came to love him, and out of Egypt I called my son לִבְנִי." — Targum: "... and from Egypt I named them 'sons.'" (So according to Tg. Isa. 1:2; in principle it could also be translated: "Out of Egypt I called them as sons," or "Out of Egypt I called sons for them"; see § Matt 2:15) ‖ Deuteronomy 14:1: "You are sons בָּנִים to Yahweh your God." — Targum Onkelos: "You are sons בְּנִין before Yahweh your God." — Targum Yerušalmi I: "You are as beloved sons before Yahweh your God." ‖ Psalm 73:15: "I would have faithlessly misled the generation of your sons דּוֹר בָּנֶיךָ." — Targum: "I would have acted wickedly toward the generation of your sons על דר בניך." ‖ Psalm 80:16: "You have raised for yourself a son בֵּן." — The targum interprets the words in relation to the Messiah; see further under #3. ‖ Jeremiah 31:9: "I have become Israel's father, and Ephraim, he is my firstborn." — The targum weakens this: "I myself have become like a father כְּאָב to Israel, and Ephraim is precious (valuable, חֲבִיב) before me." ‖ For additional examples, see Isa 1:2, 4; 30:1:9; 43:6; 45:11 (here, instead of בָּנַי found in the targum, there is עַמִּי my people); 63:8; Jer 3:14; 31:20.

β. The king of Israel.

Psalm 2:7: "You are my son בְּנִי, today I have begotten you יְלִדְתִּיךָ." — The targum attenuates this: "You are dear (precious) to me as a son to his father, innocent as if I had created you today (= as a child just born)." See also verse 12: "Kiss the son (?) נַשְּׁקוּ בַר." — Septuagint: δράξασθε (accept) παιδείας. — Targum: "Accept teaching קַבִּילוּ אוּלְפָנָא." On this translation, see Num. Rab. 10 (158C): "What, my son, ..." (Prov 31:2). It does not say, "What, my son בְּנִי," but rather, "what בְּרִי." This refers to the commands and admonitions of the Torah, since the Torah is called בר (= pure, clean), as it says, "Kiss what is pure" (Ps 2:12; accept what is pure = the teaching of the Torah)! — Additionally, see § Heb 1:5 A, #3, S-B footnote. ‖ 2 Samuel 7:14: "I will be a father to him (Solomon), and he is to be a son לְבֵן to me." — Septuagint: ἐγὼ ἔσομαι αὐτῷ εἰς πατέρα, καὶ αὐτὸς ἔσται μοι εἰς υἱόν. — Targum: "I will be like a father כְּאַב to him, and he shall be just like a son כְּבַר to me." ‖ Psalm 89:28: "So, I will also make him the firstborn בְּכוֹר; the highest among the kings of the earth." — Targum: "I will also make him the firstborn among the kings of the house of Judah, the highest over the kings of the earth." ‖ The explanation of Ps 82:6 is controversial. The rabbinic scholars interpreted it in relation to the Israelites and their unjust judges; see further under #3.

2. In the LXX, apocrypha, and pseudepigrapha:

α. The people of Israel.

Septuagint Exodus 4:22f.: υἱὸς πρωτότοκός μου Ἰσραήλ· ειπα δέ σοι· ἐξαπόστειλον τὸν λαόν μου (underlying text: אֶת־בְּנִי). — Septuagint Hosea 1:10: καὶ ἔσται, ἐν τῷ τόπῳ, οὗ ἐρρέθη αὐτοῖς, οὐ λαός μου ὑμεῖς, κληθήσονται καὶ αὐτοὶ υἱοὶ θεοῦ ζῶντος. — Septuagint Deuteronomy 14:1: υἱοί ἐστε κυρίου τοῦ θεοῦ ὑμῶν. — Septuagint Psalm 73:15: τῇ γενεᾷ τῶν υἱῶν σου ἠσυνθέτηκα. — Septuagint Jeremiah 31:9: καὶ Ἐφραῒμ πρωτότοκός μου ἐστίν. ‖ Sirach 36:17 (Hebrew): "Have mercy on the people that is named with your name, (on) Israel, whom you have named 'firstborn' בכור." — (Greek:) ἐλέησον λαὸν, κύριε, κεκλημένον ἐπ' ὀνόματί σου, καὶ Ἰσραήλ, ὃν πρωτογόνῳ ὡμοίωσας. ‖ Judith 9:13: "Make my word and my deception into a wound and bruise for those who have decided upon cruel things against your covenant and your holy house and Mount Zion and the house of the possession of your sons υἱῶν σου." ‖ Wisdom 16:26: "So that your sons οἱ υἱοί σου, whom you loved, O Lord, might learn that it is not growing fruits that nourishes man but rather your word preserves those who believe in you." — Wisdom 18:13: "For those who had disbelieved in everything because of their magic arts confessed when their firstborn children perished that the people was God's son θεοῦ υἱὸν λαὸν εἶναι." See also Wis 9:4, 7; 12:7, 19, 20, 21; 16:21; 19:6. ‖ 3 Maccabees 6:28: "Let go of the sons τοὺς υἱούς of the almighty living God in heaven." ‖ Jubilees 1:24f.: "They will act according to my commandment, and I will be a father to them, and they will be children to me. And they all shall be called children of the living God, and all angels and all spirits will know and will recognize them, that they are my children and I am their father in strength and righteousness, and that I love them." — Jubilees 2:20: "I have chosen the seed of Jacob from what I have seen, and I have written him down for myself as a firstborn son and made him holy for myself for all eternity." ‖ Psalms of Solomon 17:27: "He (the son of David = Messiah) will not allow further injustice to abide in their midst...; for he knows them, that they all are sons of their God υἱοὶ θεοῦ αὐτῶν." See also Pss. Sol. 18:4. ‖ Assumption of Moses 10:3: "The heavenly one will stand up from his seat of power and go out from his holy dwelling on high and wrath because of his children *propter filios suos*." ‖ Testament of Judah 24: "He himself (the heavenly father) will pour out the spirit of grace over you, and you will be his sons ἔσεσθε αὐτῷ εἰς υἱούς in truth and you will walk in his commandments." ‖ 4 Ezra 6:58: "We your people, however, whom you have called your firstborn, your only son (*primogenitum, unigenitum*), your devotee and friend, we are given into their hands (the gentiles of the world)!" ‖ Sibylline Oracles 3:702ff.: "But the sons of the great God υἱοὶ δ' αὖ μεγάλοιο θεοῦ will all dwell in peace around your temple, rejoicing in what the creator and the righteously judging sole ruler will give them." — Sibylline Oracles 5:202: "For they too (the Gauls) have prepared misery for the children of God θεοῦ τέκνοις." — Additionally, see § Matt 5:9, #2.

β. The pious and righteous.

Septuagint Psalm 89:17: "Then you spoke by face to your sons τοῖς υἱοῖς σου" (the word in the text: לַחֲסִידֶךָ "to your pious ones"). ‖ Sirach 4:10 (Hebrew): "May he be as a father to orphans and stand in as a husband to widows; then God will call you 'son' and be gracious to you and save you from the open grave." — The Greek reads as follows: γίνου ὀρφανοῖς ὡς πατὴρ καὶ ἀντὶ ἀνδρὸς τῇ μητρὶ αὐτῶν, καὶ ἔσῃ ὡς υἱὸς ὑψίστου, καὶ ἀγαπήσει σε μᾶλλον ἢ μήτηρ σου. ‖ Wisdom 2:16ff.: "We (men of the world) are considered to be scum by him (the righteous one), and he avoids our ways like impurities; he praises the end of the righteous and boasts that God is his father. Let us see whether his words are true, and test what sort of end he will have. For if the righteous man is God's son υἱὸς θεοῦ, he will attend to him and save him from the hand of his adversaries." — Wisdom 5:4f.: "We fools regarded his (the righteous man's) life as madness and his end as without honor; how he is now (in the divine court) counted among the children of God ἐν υἱοῖς θεοῦ, and how his inheritance is among the holy ones!" — See also Wis 2:13: "He (the righteous one) boasts that he knows God, and calls himself παῖς κυρίου = servant, but also child of the Lord." — Additionally, see § Matt 5:9, #2. ‖ 1 Enoch 62:11: "The angels of punishment will receive them (the ruling powers) to take revenge on them for having mistreated his (God's) children and elect ones." ‖ Psalms of Solomon 13:9: "He (God) warns the righteous as a beloved son ὡς υἱὸν ἀγαπήσεως and his chastisement is as that given to a firstborn." ‖ In particular the patriarch Levi is designated as God's Son in T. Levi 4: "The Lord heard your prayer that he would expel godlessness from you, and that you would become a son υἱόν to him and a helper and servant of his face."

γ. The Messiah.

1 Enoch 105:2: "I and my son (= Messiah) will be united with them always on the ways of truth during their life. You will have peace; rejoice, children of the truth."[11] ‖ 4 Ezra 7:28f.: "For my son the Christ (*filius meus Messiah*), will be revealed with all who are with him and he will give to all who remain peace for 400 years. After these years my son, the Christ, will die along with all who have human breath." (The textual tradition is not unified; other manuscripts have, instead of "*filius meus Messiah*," just "*Messiah meus*" or "*Messiah*" or "*Messiah dei.*") — 4 Ezra 13:32: "Then, when this happens and when the signs arrive which I have told foretold to you, then my son (*filius meus*) will appear whom you have seen as a man rising (from the heart of the sea)." — 4 Ezra 13: 37: "However, he, my son (*filius meus*), will punish the sins of the gentiles who have drawn up against him...." — 4 Ezra 13:52: "Just as no one can explore or know what is in the depths of the sea, so also can none of those who dwell on earth see my son (*filium meum*) nor his companions except at the hour of his day." — 4 Ezra 14:9: "But you (Ezra) are to be removed from men and from now on you will dwell with my son (*cum filio meo*) and his companions until the times are up." (These passages do not have in view a preexistent Messiah; see § John 1:1 A, A, n. *c*.) — Everywhere in these passages the expression "my son" in God's mouth is a designation for the Messiah, synonymous with Χριστός or מָשִׁיחַ. The NT passages also are to be understood accordingly, as in Matt 3:17: οὗτός ἐστιν ὁ υἱός μου ὁ ἀγαπητός (Mark 1:11: σὺ εἶ ὁ υἱός μου ὁ ἀγαπητός, similarly Luke 3:22); Matt 16:16: σὺ εἶ ὁ Χριστὸς ὁ υἱὸς τοῦ θεοῦ τοῦ ζῶντος (Mark 8:29 has only σὺ εἶ ὁ Χριστός, Luke 9:20: τὸν Χριστὸν τοῦ θεοῦ); Matt 17:5 (Mark 9:7; 2 Pet 1:17): οὗτός ἐστιν ὁ υἱός μου ὁ ἀγαπητός (Luke 9:35: ὁ υἱός μου

---

11. According to G. Dalman, this passage is a late interpolation (*Die Worte Jesu: Mit Berücksichtigung des nachkanonischen jüdischen Schriftums und der aramäischen Sprache erörtert*, 2nd ed. [Leipzig: Hinrichs, 1930], 1:221).

ὁ ἐκλελεγμένος); Matt 8:29 (Mark 5:7; Luke 8:28); 26:63: εἰ σὺ εἶ ὁ Χριστὸς ὁ υἱὸς τοῦ θεοῦ (Mark 14:61: σὺ εἶ ὁ Χριστὸς ὁ υἱὸς τοῦ εὐλογητοῦ, Luke 22:66: εἰ σὺ εἶ ὁ Χριστός, cf. verse 70: σὺ οὖν εἶ ὁ υἱὸς τοῦ θεοῦ;); Matt 27:40: εἰ υἱὸς εἶ τοῦ θεοῦ (lacking in Mark 15:30; by contrast, Luke 23:35: εἰ οὗτός ἐστιν ὁ Χριστὸς τοῦ θεοῦ ὁ ἐκλεκτός); Matt 27:54: ἀληθῶς θεοῦ υἱὸς ἦν οὗτος (Mark 15:39: ἀληθῶς οὗτος ὁ ἄνθρωπος υἱὸς ἦν θεοῦ, Luke 23:47: ὄντως ὁ ἄνθρωπος οὗτος δίκαιος ἦν); Mark 3:11: ὅτι σὺ εἶ ὁ υἱὸς τοῦ θεοῦ (similarly, Luke 4:41, but with the addition: ὅτι ᾔδεισαν τὸν Χριστὸν αὐτὸν εἶναι, where the equivalence ὁ υἱὸς τοῦ θεοῦ = ὁ Χριστός is confirmed). Additionally, see John 1:34, 49; 10:36; 11:17; 20:31; 1 John 3:8; 5:5.

3. In rabbinic literature:

α. The people Israel.

See references at § Matt 5:9, #2; special attention should be called to the citation used there from Pesiq. Rab. 5 (14B), in which R. Judah b. Shalom (ca. 370) polemicizes against the claim of Christians that they are the true children of God. — Here reference should be made to the following passages. Sifre Deuteronomy 14:1 § 96 (94A): "You are sons of Yahweh your God" (Deut 14:1). R. Judah (ca. 150) said, "If you conduct yourselves as sons כבנים, behold, you are sons; but if not, you are not sons." R. Meir (ca. 150) said, "Either way, you are sons of Yahweh your God. And, likewise, it says, 'The number of the children of Israel will be as the sand by the sea …' (Hos 2:1)."[12] And it will come to pass, instead of it having been said to them, 'You are not my people,' it will be said to them, 'sons of the living God.'" — For similar statements that are supposed to show that the Israelites remain God's children despite their falling away from God, see SDeut 32:5 § 308 (133A); 32.19 § 320 (137A). ‖ Leviticus Rabbah 18 (118A): R. Yohanan († 279) said in the name of R. Eliezer b. Yose the Galilean (ca. 150), "When the Israelites stood at Mount Sinai and said, 'We want to do and listen to everything that Yahweh has spoken' (Exod 24:7), in that hour God called the Angel of Death (= Satan; see § Matt 4:1 B, #3, C) and said to him, 'Although I have made you lord of the world (קוזמוקרטור = κοσμοκράτωρ) over humanity, you are to have nothing to do with this nation (Israel), for they are my sons 'בני'; this is what Deut 14:1 means, 'You are sons of Yahweh your God.'" — In other dress, TanḥB וארא 9 (13A): (God said,) "If the Angel of Death comes and says to me, 'What have I been created for (if the Israelites are not to die)?,' then I will say to him, 'If I have created you, I have created you for the gentiles of the world, but not for my sons בני; for I have made these gods,' as it says, 'I myself have said, "You are gods and all of you sons of the Most High"' (Ps 82:6)." — For additional parallels with many variations, see Midr. Song. 8:6 (131A); Exod. Rab. 41 (98A); Num. Rab. 16 (181D); Tanḥ. שלח לך 214A; TanḥB שלח Appendix § 1 (38B); see also Exod. Rab. 32 (93D); 51 (103D). ‖ Babylonian Talmud ʿAbodah Zarah 5A: Resh Laqish (ca. 250) said, "Come, we want to thank our fathers; for if they had not sinned (at Mount Sinai, the sexual appetite would not have arisen with

12. S-B: See b. Yoma 22B on this proof text: R. Jonathan (ca. 220) raised the objection, "It says in Hos 2:1, 'The number of the children of Israel will be as the sand by the sea' (thus at least limited), and it says (in the same passage), 'It cannot be measured or counted' (thus unlimited). There is no contradiction. In the latter (it is meant), if they obey God's will; in the former (it is meant), if they do not do God's will. (But even in the latter case God's promise is fulfilled: 'the number will be as the sand by the sea,' a proof that the Israelites are considered to be God's children even in their disobedience.)"

them, and) we would not have come into the world. For it says, 'I myself have said, "You are gods and all of you sons of the Most High'" (Ps 82:6); but you have corrupted your actions, 'indeed you will die as men' (Ps 82:6). This means, 'If they had not sinned, they would have sired no children....'" A baraita: R. Yose (ca.150) said, "The Israelites received the Torah only so that the Angel of Death might have no power over them. For it says, 'I myself have said, "You are gods and all of you sons of the Most High"' (Ps 82:6); but you have corrupted your actions, 'indeed you will die as men.'" — See Num. Rab. 16 (182A): God said to the Israelites, "I said, 'If you do not sin, you will live and keep existing, like me, just as I live and keep existing forever and ever.' I myself have said, 'You are gods and all of you sons of the Most High' (Ps 82:6); as the angels of service who do not die; but after this greatness (majesty) you wanted to die; 'indeed as אדם will you die,' as the first man...." ‖ Midrash Psalm 2 § 9 (14B): "I will speak of a decree: 'Yahweh said to me: You are my son'" (Ps 2:7). That is talked about in a decree of the Torah and in a decree of the prophets and in a decree of the hagiographa. It is written in a decree of the Torah: "My firstborn son is Israel" (Exod 4:22). And it is written in a decree of the prophets: "Behold, my servant will act wisely" (Isa 52:13), and after that (read: before that) it is written: "Behold, my servant, whom I uphold, my chosen one, in whom my soul delights" (Isa 42:1). And it is written in a decree of the hagiographa: "A saying of Yahweh to my lord, 'Sit at my right hand'" (Ps 110:1). Furthermore, it is written, "Yahweh said to me, 'You are my son'" (Ps 2:7), [and another Scripture passage says, "Behold, one like a son of man came with the clouds of heaven" (Dan 7:13)]. — The parenthetical reference to Dan 7:13 is not in Yalquṭ 2 § 621. The first decree is related to Israel, the third to the Messiah, and in the case of the second it remains uncertain whether Israel or the Messiah was understood by the term "servant of Yahweh." ‖ Midrash Psalm 2 § 17 (16B) on the words: "Kiss the son ..." (Ps 2:12): A metaphor. To whom is this likened? To a king who was enraged about the inhabitants of a province (or a city). The inhabitants of the province went and propitiated the king's son so that he might propitiate the king. He went and propitiated his father. After he had let himself be propitiated by his son, the inhabitants of the province came to sing a song of praise to the king. The king said to them, "You want to sing me a song of praise? Go and say a song of praise to my son, for if it were not for him, I would have long ago destroyed the inhabitants of the province." Thus, the gentiles of the world wish to say a song of praise to God; as it says, "All you gentiles, clap your hands" (Ps 47:2). Then God says to them, "You want to sing me a song of praise? Go and say it to Israel, for if it were not for them, the world would not continue to exist for one hour" (older editions: you would not continue to exist for one hour); as it says, "Rejoice, you gentiles (*goyim*), over his people" (Deut 32:43)! — Here Israel is denoted by the parable as God's Son; the passage proves not only that individual rabbis conceived of the בַּר in Ps 2:12 as "son," but also that here and there the whole second psalm is interpreted in relation to the people of Israel. For further interpretations of Ps 2 in relation to the people of Israel, see § Heb 1:5 A, #3.

β. The Messiah b. David.

A baraita in b. Sukkah 52A: Concerning the Messiah b. David—may he soon be revealed in our days—the Holy One, blessed be He!—says, "Ask anything of me, I will give it to you," as it says, "'I will speak of a decree,' Yahweh said to me, 'You are my son, today I have begotten you. Ask of me, and I will give the gentiles as your inheritance'" (Ps 2:7f.). If he (then) sees that the Messiah b. Joseph is killed, he will say before him (God), "Lord of the world, I ask of you only life." Then he (God) will say to him, "Life? Before you said it, your father David prophesied long ago about you, as it says in Ps 21:5, 'He asks life of you, you have granted it to him, life always and forever.'" ‖ See Midr. Ps. 2 § 9 (14B) in the previous n. *a.* ‖ Midrash Psalm 2 § 9 (14B): "Yahweh said to me, 'You are my son'" (Ps 2:7). R. Judan (ca. 350) said, "Are all these comforts which are contained in the decree of the king of kings (i.e., in Ps 2:7) to be fulfilled in the king, the Messiah? And why all this? Because he will occupy himself with the Torah." ‖ Midrash Psalm 2 § 9 (14B): "(You are my son,) today I have begotten you" (Ps 2:7). R. Huna (ca. 350) said, "Sufferings have been divided into three parts: one taken by the fathers of the world and every (other) generation up until then, and another by the generation of religious persecution (at the time of Hadrian), and the other the generation of the king, the Messiah. And when the hour comes, God will say to them, 'It rests on me to create him (the Messiah) into a new creature (after the sufferings which have struck him).' Likewise it says, 'Today I have begotten you.' This hour is a (new) creation for him." — See parallels at § Luke 24:26, I, #4, n. *g.* ‖ Yalquṭ Simeoni on Ps 2:2 (2 § 620): Like a thief who stood there and blurted out blasphemous words against the king's palace and said, "If I find (meet) the king's son, I will seize him and kill him and crucify him and prepare a grievous death for him." And the Holy Spirit (which prevails in the Holy Scripture and speaks from it) will mock him: "The one who is enthroned in heaven laughs" (Ps 2:4). — The "son" in the metaphor is the interpretation of the "anointed" (Messiah) in Ps 2:2. The passage in Yalquṭ is abbreviated from Mek. Exod. 15:9 (48B); see § Heb 1:5 A, #4, n. *b.* ‖ Psalm 80:16: "Shield (? this vine) which your right hand has planted, and the son וְעַל בֵּן, whom you have raised strong for yourself." Targum: "(Remember) the sprig which your right hand has planted, and the king, the Messiah, whom you have made powerful for yourself." — Here the text word בֵּן "son" is explained with מַלְכָּא מְשִׁיחָא. ‖ The targum Ps 2 does not clearly indicate whether it has interpreted the psalm in relation to the Messiah. The interpretation could possibly also be about David. It renders verse 7: "I will tell of a stipulation (decree) of Yahweh: he said, 'You are dear to me as a son to a father, innocent as if I had created you today.'" — See Midr. Ps. 2:7 further below at the end of B. — For a reading that is closer to the messianic interpretation of Ps 2, see the entry at § Heb 1:5 A.

In these rabbinic passages the Messiah is called God's "son" only where a messianically interpreted OT passage explicitly provides reason to do so. As far as we can see, God's "son" is not found in rabbinic literature as a standalone designation for the Messiah independent of a passage of Scripture. This is striking, since in earlier times "my son" in God's mouth is definitely used as a standalone designation for the Messiah, as is shown by the citations from the pseudepigrapha in #2, γ above. It would not be mistaken to assume that the rabbinic scholars purposely avoided the expression "son" of God because in the meantime it had become a common designation for the Messiah by Christians.

B. The ancient synagogue had no conception of the Messiah as God's son in an actual physical sense; they lacked any reason to have such a conception: they know neither about a preexistence of the Messiah (see § John 1:1 A), nor about his supernatural birth without a father (see § Matt 1:18 C, #3); with respect to the latter it is significant that the word about the virgin's son in Isa 7:14 is nowhere interpreted in relation to the Messiah (cf. Matt 1:23). Although the Messiah may be spoken of here and there in rabbinic literature as "son of God" in the actual physical sense, this occurs only in open or oblique polemic against the Christian dogma about Jesus' divine sonship.

Exodus Rabbah 29 (88D): "I am Yahweh your God" (Exod 20:2). R. Abbahu (ca. 300) said, "This is like a king of flesh and blood who reigns while he (at the same time) has a father or a brother or a son. But the Holy One, blessed be He!, says, 'I am not so. "I am the first" (Isa 44:6), for I have no father; "and I am the last," for I have no brother; "and apart from me there is no God," for I have no son.'" ‖ Jerusalem Talmud Šabbat 6.8D.28: (Nebuchadnezzar answered,) "'The appearance of the fourth one is like a son of the gods בר אלהין'" (Dan 3:25). R. Reuben (ca. 300) said, "In that hour an angel came down and struck this blasphemer on his mouth. He said to him, 'Rectify your words! Does he (God) then have a son ובר אית ליה?' Thereupon he said, 'Blessed be the God of Shadrach, Meshach, and Abednego, who sent his "son."' This is not what is written here, but rather 'who sent his "angel" so that he might save his servants who trusted in him' (Dan 3:28)." — Parallel passages can be found in Midr. Song. 7:9 (129B), where the tradent is R. Phineas (ca. 360); the intervening angel is Michael, who is called God's פריטין (read: אפירטין = ὑπηρέτης "servant"); similarly, Midr. Sam. 5 § 7 (30B); in Exod. Rab. 20 (82D), R. Berekhiah (ca. 340) is the author, and Satan is named instead of Michael. ‖ Deuteronomy Rabbah 2 (199C): "Do not get mixed up with the doublers" (so the midr. expresses Prov 24:21); do not get involved with those who say that there are two divinities.... R. Aha (ca. 320) said, "God was enraged at Solomon when he said this verse. He said to him, 'You have said a word concerning the hallowing of my name (read שמי instead of שמא) but only with a suggestive expression (literally: with a notarikon expression):[13] "do not get mixed up with the doublers"!' Immediately he searched his soul and clarified the word: 'There is one and there is no second one; he has neither son nor brother' (Eccl 4:8), neither brother nor son, rather: 'Hear, Israel, Yahweh our God is one Yahweh' (Deut 6:4)." — In Num. Rab. 15 (179B) only the beginning is found. ‖ Midrash Ecclesiastes 4:8 (23B): "There is one and there is no second one" (Eccl 4:8); this is the Holy One, blessed be He!, of whom it says, "Yahweh our God is one Yahweh" (Deut 6:4). "And there is no second one," because he has no companion (partner, associate) in his world. "He has neither son nor brother" (Eccl 4:8); he has no brother, and as for a son—whence would he have one? But because God loves Israel, he calls them "sons" (see Deut 14:1: "You are sons of Yahweh your God"); he calls them brothers (see Ps 122:8: "For the sake

13. TN: Notarikon is a way of using the letters of a Hebrew term or expression to form another word, sentence, or idea.

of my brothers and friends, I will speak for your peace.")[14] ‖ The beginning of ʾAg. Ber. 27: "Thus says Yahweh, 'It will happen in all the land that any mouth that confesses two will be rooted out'" (so Midr. Zech. 13:8). R. Berekhiah (ca. 340) said, "God said, 'Any mouth that says that there are two (divinities) is to be rooted out and perish; "but the third will remain" (Zech 13:8), these are the Israelites,[15] as it says, "On that day Israel will be the third along with Egypt and Assyria" (Isa 19:24).' But the godless Babylonians (code name for Romans = Christians) say that God has a son because it says, 'The appearance of the fourth one is like a son of the gods' (Dan 3:25). God says, 'You blasphemers, is it written about him: "He was like a son of God" בר אלהא?[16] If that were written, you would have an excuse; but it is written only: "He was like a son of the gods" בר אלהין, which are the angels, which are called sons of God. Separate yourself from such a one! Whoever says this does not belong to you (Israelites). Nebuchadnezzar did not belong to you; he was a Babylonian. When he was castigated for this, did he not then say the truth? For it says, "Blessed be the God of Shadrach ..." (Dan 3:28).' God forbid that he would have said, 'The one who sent his "son,"' but rather (he said): 'The one who sent his "angel."'" — Some sentences from this passage are anonymous in Num. Rab. 15 (179B). ‖ ʾAggadat Berešit 31 in Jellinek, *Beth ha-Midrash* 4.46.25: R. Abun (II, ca. 370) said in the name of R. Hilqiah (ca. 320), "Foolish is the heart of the liars who say, 'The Holy One—blessed be He!—has a son.' How could this be, if God could not look at Abraham's son because of pain when he saw that he was on the brink of slaying him, but rather immediately called, 'Do not lay your hand on the boy' (Gen 22:12)? How then if he himself had a son, should he have given him up without destroying the world and turning it to chaos תהו ובהו? Therefore, Solomon says, 'There is one and not two' (Eccl 4:8). But out of love for Israel he calls them sons, as it says, 'My firstborn son is Israel' (Exod 4:22)." — In the edition of ʾAggadat Berešit available to us (Warsaw 1878), the whole passage is suppressed up until the concluding sentence. ‖ Midrash Psalm 2:7, ed. Warsaw 1875 folio 5A: "You are my son" (Ps 2:7). From this passage an answer may be given to those who say, "He (God) has a son יֵשׁ לוֹ בֵּן." And you can respond to them: "(Scripture) does not say, 'You are a son from me' בן לי אתה, but rather, 'You are my son,' as a servant to whom his master wishes to give inner reassurance and says to him, 'I love you as my son כברי.'" — In Buber's edition, the introductory sentence is missing entirely. The conclusion in § 9 (14B) reads: "You are my son" (Ps 2:7). He does not say, "A son from me" בן לי, but rather,

14. S-B: On Ps 122:8, see Mek. Exod. 14:15 (35B): "Why are you crying out to me?" (Exod 14:15). R. Hananiah b. Hakinai (ca. 120) said, "(God says,) 'Did I not write long ago, "He (the true friend) is born as a brother for affliction?" (Prov 17:17). I am a brother to Israel in the hour of her need; the Israelites are brothers (see Ps 122:8).'"

15. S-B: See Deut. Rab. 2 (199C): R. Judah b. Simeon (ca. 320) said, "'Thus says Yahweh, "It will happen in all the land that any mouth that confesses two will be rooted out and perish"' (Zech 13:8). The mouths that say, 'There are two principalities (powers = divinities)' are to be rooted out and perish. Who will remain? 'The third will remain,' these are the Israelites, which are called the 'threefold ones,' because they consist of three parts, the priests, the Levites, and the (ordinary) Israelites; because they stem from three fathers, from Abraham, Isaac, and Jacob." — Similar explanations are found also in Tanḥ. שופטים 16A; TanḥB שופטים § 10 (16B).

16. S-B: So, with the commentary, עץ יוסף should be read instead of בר אלהין.

"You are my son," as a servant to whom his master wishes to give inner reassurance and says, "You are dear to me like my son כבני." See Tg. Ps. 2:7 above at A, #3, β, toward the end.

1:3 B: Who was born from the seed of David.

The apostle Paul expressly attests the Davidic ancestry of Jesus in 2 Tim 2:8 as well. If the adversarial, pharisaical party ever contested the descent of Jesus from David—though the NT contains no trace of this—Paul, the pupil of the Pharisees, would certainly have known about this. The witness of Rom 1:3 and 2 Tim 2:8 is therefore all the weightier. It shows at any rate that, after the assessments he could make about Jesus' genealogy, there was no reason at all for the apostle to doubt his descent from David. — For the assumption at that time that the Messiah would be a Davidite, see § Matt 1:1 C, #1.

1:4: According to the Spirit of holiness.

On πνεῦμα ἁγιωσύνης, see § Luke 2:25 C, #1. — For the alleged identification of the Messiah with the Spirit of God, see § John 1:1 A, D.

1:5: Among all the gentiles.

On the universalism or particularism of the ancient synagogue, see § Matt 23:15 A; § John 10:16; and § Rom 3:9 A.

1:6: Called (κλητοί).

The theology of the ancient synagogue is also familiar with the idea of an "invitation" or "calling" to the salvific goods of the future. This is shown by the rabbinic parables, which are presented at § Matt 22:2–14 as parallels to the NT parable of the wedding garment. Additionally, see the citations at § Matt 22:3 A and § Acts 13:48. See also § Matt 25:34 B and § Rom 1:1 B.

Here reference may be made to the following passages. Babylonian Talmud Baba Batra 75B: What does "Yahweh will create … a cloud by day over their assemblies מִקְרָאֶהָ" (Isa 4:5) mean? Rabbah († 330, perhaps more correctly: Raba, † 352) said that R. Yohanan († 279) said, "The Jerusalem of the future world (= of the messianic time) is not like the Jerusalem of this world: anyone who wants to goes up to the Jerusalem of this world; but only those who are invited (called הַמְזוּמָּנִין) will go up to the Jerusalem of the future world. ‖ Pesiqta Rabbati 41 (174B): Resh Laqish (ca. 250) said in a presentation, "When the Israelites sin here (in this world), Jacob is chastised in the double cavern. Therefore when redemption comes, he will rejoice with them: 'Jacob will rejoice, (the people of) Israel will be glad' (so Midr. Ps. 14:7)." But R. Alexandrai (ca. 270) suggested a different sense, "Why will Jacob rejoice? If a man has to circumcise his son or take a wife, who rejoices? The one who is invited מְזוּמָּן to the meal. Likewise, Jacob is invited (מזומן = called) to God's meal which he will host for the righteous one day in the future: 'Listen to me Israel (= Jacob), my called one מְקוֹרָאִי' (Isa 48:12 is thus cited by the midr.). What does מקוראי mean? My invited one (called one

מזומני). Therefore, when the meal of redemption comes, he will rejoice because he is invited מזומן to the meal, 'Jacob will rejoice' (Ps 14:7)." — In the parallel passage Midr. Ps. 14 § 7 (58A), R. Simeon b. Laqish is the author of the saying of R. Alexandrai; in Midr. Lam. 2:4 (65B), we find only the beginning of the whole explanation, but it is very different.

1:7 A: In Rome.

Ῥώμη in rabbinic writing is most of the time רוֹמֵי, and rarely רוֹמָא; see § Acts 18:2 B. — On the origin of the Jewish community in Rome, see Emil Schürer's work *Geschichte des jüdischen volkes im zeitalter Jesu Christi.*[17] — Of the older rabbinic scholars who were active in Rome, rabbinic literature mentions the following in particular.

1. Theudas תּוֹדוֹס, perhaps at the time when the temple was still standing.

Tosefta Yom Ṭob 2.15 (204): What is a "helmeted (armored) boar" גְּדִי מְקוּלָּס?[18] It is roasted as a whole (unhacked), while its head and its shanks (lie) in its interior (i.e., are bent into the abdominal cavity without being detached). If one has cooked, however much there is, and stewed it, however much there is, it is not "helmeted." A helmeted boar may be prepared on the night (evening) of the last day of Passover, a helmeted calf on the night of the first day of Passover, but no helmeted boar on that day (because the calf can be viewed as a Passover lamb). R. Yose (ca. 150) said, "Theudas in Rom תודוס איש רומי instructed the people of Rome בני רומי (i.e., the members of the Jewish community there) to take lambs and to prepare them as helmeted on the nights of Passover." Then it was said, "He is on the brink of letting people eat what is holy outside [of Jerusalem], because they (the boars prepared in this manner) are called Passover lambs (and the Passover lamb may be eaten only in Jerusalem)." — The parallel y. Pesaḥ. 7.34A.47 in a baraita: R. Yose (ca. 150) said, "Theudas in Rome introduced among the people of Rome (instructed them to do the following) the custom of eating helmeted boars on the nights of Passover." Then the scholars (of the motherland) sent word to him, "If you were not Theudas, would we not ban you?" — What was it about Theudas (what was exceptional about him)? R. Hananiah (which one?) said, "The livelihood of the rabbis came from him. — Are you not being trumped up as one who brings the multitude to eat what is holy outside (of Jerusalem)? For everyone who brings the multitude to eat what is holy outside must be banned." — Parallel passages can be found in y. Moʿed Qaṭ. 3.81D.23; b. Pesaḥ. 53A; b. Beṣah 23A; in b. Ber. 19A.26 instead of תני רב יוסף we read: תניא ר׳ יוסי אמר; furthermore, here the words in the ed. Frankfurt am Main 1720ff. are: "Simeon b. Shetah (ca. 90 BCE) sent word to him," which would make Theudas a contemporary of Simeon b. Shetah; according to the ed. Amsterdam 1644ff., this should be replaced by: "Word was sent to him." ‖ For a further saying of Theudas, see b. Pesaḥ. 53B at § Matt 6:9 C, n. *o*; see also Midr. Ps. 28 § 2 in the following #2.

17. Emil Schürer, *Geschichte des jüdischen Volkes im Zeitalter Jesu Christi*, 4th ed. (Leipzig: Hinrichs, 1909), 3:57–66.

18. S-B: More detail can be found on this point in the excursus "The Ancient Jewish Passover Celebration".

2. פַּלְטוֹן or פַּלְטִיוֹן,[19] perhaps a contemporary of Theudas (see #1), since both men are named alongside each other in:

Midrash Psalm 28 § 2 (115A): Theudas in Rome said, "Hananiah, Mishael, and Azariah undertook studies and said, 'If the frogs (Exod 7:28), which had no merit of the fathers, were saved because they offered themselves for the hallowing of the divine name (see b. Pesaḥ. 53B at § Matt 6:9 C, n. *o*), how much more are we, the sons of Abraham, Isaac, and Jacob, to whom a command is issued for the hallowing of the divine name and to whom he (God) will one day give the full wage, how much more are we obligated to offer our lives for the hallowing of the divine name!'" פלטון in Rome said, "They undertook studies from the Torah, as it is said in Deut 4:29: 'And from there (where you will serve idols) you will serve Yahweh your God, and you will seek him and you will find him when you seek him with all your heart.'" ‖ Midrash Song of Songs 8:5 (130B): פלטיון in Rome openly said in a presentation, "Mount Sinai was (at the giving of the Law) ripped out and placed in the highest heaven so that the Israelites were located under it; for it says in Deut 4:11, 'You drew near and stood under the mountain' (so the midr.)."

3. R. Matthew b. Heresh (Harash) had emigrated to Rome before the Hadrianic War, where he founded his own school. According to m. ʾAbot 4.15, his motto was: "Let everyone come first with a greeting of peace and be the tail of a lion rather than the head of a fox."

He is mentioned in the Mishnah in m. Yoma 8.6: If anyone is ravenously hungry, he may (on the Day of Atonement) eat even what is unclean (forbidden by the Law) until his eyes become bright (cf. 1 Sam 14:27, 29). If anyone has been bitten by a ravenous dog, he may not eat from its liver lobes (because this was not considered to be an actual means of healing). R. Matthew b. Heresh allowed it. ‖ Jerusalem Talmud Megillah 1.71D.30: In the name of R. Matthew b. Heresh it has been said, "(The five letters) מנצפ״ך (with the special writing at the end of a word) are a halakah from Moses from Sinai." ‖ It is reported many times that R. Matthew b. Heresh inquired about the saying of R. Ishmael († ca. 135) concerning the fourfold atonement for sins; see this saying with parallels at § Matt 12:32, #1, at the beginning.

1:7 B: To those beloved of God.

ἀγαπητοί = חֲבִיבִין (sg. חָבִיב, Aram. חַבִּיבָא, indicative חַבִּיב) is a rather common title of honor for Israel.

Mishnah ʾAbot 3.14: (R. Aqiba, † ca. 135) used to say, "… The Israelites are beloved חביבין, for they have been called sons of God. As a special form of love, it was declared to them that they have been called sons of God; for it says, 'You are sons to Yahweh your God' (Deut 14:1). The Israelites are beloved; for a precious instrument was given to them through which the world was created (here the Torah is meant). As a special form of love, it was declared to them that a precious instrument has been given to them through which the world was created; for it says, 'I have given you a good teaching; do not abandon my Torah'

---

19. Bacher thinks of the name Plato (*Die Agada der Tannaïten*, 2nd ed. [Strassburg: Trübner, 1902], 2:561).

(Prov 4:2)." ‖ Babylonian Talmud Yoma 52A: R. Yose (ca. 150) can say to you, "The Israelites are beloved חביבין; for Scripture has not said that they need a representative (appointee שָׁלִיחַ in prayer; each one may pray to God without a mediator)." ‖ A baraita in b. Meg. 29A: R. Simeon b. Yohai (ca. 150) said, "Come and see how beloved חביבין the Israelites are before God! For even in the place where they went into exile the Shekinah (deity) was with them." ‖ A baraita in b. Menaḥ. 43B: The Israelites are beloved חביבין, for God has surrounded them with commandments, with the *tefillin* (prayer straps) on their heads and the tefillin on their arms, with the show fringes (*tzitzit*) on their clothes and the *mezuzah* (inscription post) on their doors, and concerning them David said, "Seven times (2 *tefillin*, 4 *tzitzit*, 1 *mezuzah* = 7) a day do I praise you" (Ps 119:164). ‖ Synonymous with חביב is יָדִיד = darling, beloved. Babylonian Talmud Menaḥot 53A: (R. Ezra [ca. 380] said,) "Let the beloved one ידיד come, the son of the beloved, and let him build the beloved thing for the beloved one in the portion of the beloved one so that thereby the beloved ones יְדִידִים may be atoned for. Let 'the beloved one' come, that is King Solomon (see 2 Sam 12:25: 'He called his name Jedidiah'); the son of 'the beloved one,' that is Abraham (see Jer 11:15: 'What does my beloved ידידי want in my house?'). And let him build 'the beloved thing,' that is the sanctuary (see Ps 84:2: 'How beloved ידידות are your dwelling places, Yahweh Sabaoth!'). For 'the beloved one,' that is God (see Isa 5:1: 'I will sing of my beloved ידידי'); in the portion of 'the beloved one,' that is Benjamin (see Deut 33:12: 'Concerning Benjamin he said, "The beloved ידיד of Yahweh dwells safely with him,"' namely with the temple, which supposedly lay in the region of Benjamin); so that thereby (through the temple) 'the beloved ones' may be atoned for, that is the Israelites (see Jer 12:7: 'I have given the beloved ידידות of my soul into the hand of enemies')."

1:7 C: To those called to be holy (see § Acts 9:13).

1:7 D: Grace to you and peace!

In his letter to the 9 ½ tribes dwelling on the other side of the Euphrates, Baruch son of Neriah similarly opens with the greeting: "Grace and peace to you (*misericordia et pax sit vobis*)!" (2 Bar. 78:2). — For the praise and reward of peace, see § Matt 5:9, #1; in particular for the greeting of peace, see § Matt 5:47 and § John 20:19; on the greeting of peace in letters, see t. Sanh. 2.6 (416) at § Matt 4:12, #2; b. Sanh. 96A at § Luke 1:19 A, #4, n. *g*; Tanḥ. וישלח 93A at § Rom 1:1 A, n. *b*.

1:8 A: First, I thank my God through Jesus Christ.

Just as the relationship and conduct of the Christian is mediated to God through (διά) Christ, so also is his prayer. Different is the idea that the angels bring prayers before God's throne (see § Rev 5:8).

1:8 B: In the whole world.

ἐν ὅλῳ τῷ κόσμῳ a hyperbolic expression גּוּזְמָא, (הֲוַאי) לְשׁוֹן הֲבַאי.

Babylonian Talmud Ḥullin 90B: We have learned there (m. Tamid 2.2): "A pile (for the ashes) was in the middle of the altar (of burnt offering); sometimes there were 300 *homers* (of ashes) on it." Raba († 352) said, "An exaggeration גוזמא! (Furthermore, we have learned in m. Tamid 3.4:) The animal offered for the Tamid was given drink from a golden chalice" (giving the animal something to drink right before the slaughter was supposed to make the skinning easier, see Rashi). Raba said, "An exaggeration גוזמא (it was not a cup of gold)!" R. Ammi (ca. 300) said, "The Torah speaks with an exaggerated expression לשון הואי (literally: an expression of nothingness = it is not to be taken precisely), the prophets speak with an exaggerated expression, the scholars speak with an exaggerated expression. The scholars speak with an exaggerated expression: this is what we have (just) said. The Torah speaks with an exaggerated expression: 'cities great and fortified to the sky' (Deut 1:28). The prophets speak with an exaggerated expression: 'The earth burst at their noise' (1 Kgs 1:40)." R. Isaac b. Nahmani (ca. 280) said and Samuel († 254) said, "In three passages the scholars speak with exaggerated expressions לשון הואי, and these are: The pile of ashes (on the altar of burnt offering), the vine, and the curtain (in the sanctuary). The pile of ashes: this is what we have said. The vine; for we have learned (in m. Mid. 3.8): A golden vine stood at the entrance to the temple building היכל which was extended over a supporting trellis, and if anyone had pledged (a leaf) or a berry or a grape (of gold) as a freewill offering, he brought it and hung it on it." R. Eleazar b. Zadok (probably the elder, ca. 100) said, "Once it happened that 300 priests were ordered for it in order to clean it up" (the last six words are not in the editions of the Mishnah. – The exaggeration lies in the number 300). The curtain; for we have learned (in m. Šeqal. 8.5) that Rabban Simeon b. Gamaliel (ca. 140) said in the name of R. Simeon the chief priest, "The thickness of the curtain amounts to a handbreadth; it was woven from 72 cords and in each cord there were 24 (individual) threads. Its length measured 40 cubits, its width 20 cubits, and it was produced from 82 myriads (of threads). In each year two were made and 300 priests submerged it (in case it became unclean)." (Again, the exaggeration lies in the number 300). – Parallels can be found in b. Tamid 63A; see also y. Šeqal. 8.51B.11 and see § Matt 27:51 A, #3. ‖ Babylonian Talmud ʿArakin 10B: Rabbah bar Shela (ca. 325) said that Rab Mattenah (ca. 275) said in the name of Samuel († 254), "There was a *magrepha* (instrument, type of organ) in the sanctuary in which there were 10 holes each of which produced 10 kinds of sound. This implies that it produced 100 kinds of sound in total." In a baraita it has been taught: It was one cubit tall and its height measured one cubit; for one pipe (literally: shaft) came out from it in which there were 10 holes and each one produced 100 kinds of sound. This implies that it produced 1000 kinds of sound. Rab Nahman b. Isaac († 356) said, "Let your (mnemonic) remark be: The baraita is an exaggeration גוזמא."

1:9 A: God is my witness.

On oaths see § Matt 5:34, #3. It is notable that the apostle does not use one of the rabbinic formulas of assertion but rather follows OT tradition and manner of expression; see Josh 22:27; 1 Sam 12:5; Jer 42:5; Ps 89:38, where the targumim regularly render עֵד = μάρτυς with סָהִיד (determ. סָהֲדָא) = "witness."

1:9 B: Whom I serve in my spirit.

Service in the heart = the service of prayer.

Sifre Deuteronomy 11:13 § 41 (80A): "to serve him" (Deut 11:13), this is prayer תְּפִלָּה. You say: This is prayer; or is it not rather the service of sacrifice עֲבוֹדָה? Scripture teaches: "In your whole heart" (Deut 11:13); how, then, is there a service of sacrifice in the heart? What does Scripture teach with: "to serve him in your whole heart"? This is prayer (see Ps 141:2; Dan 6:11,21). How, then, was there in Babylon a service to God (service of sacrifice) פּוּלְחָן? What therefore does Scripture teach with: "to serve him"? This is prayer: just as the service of the altar is called a "service" עֲבוֹדָה, so also is prayer called a "service" עבודה. ‖ Babylonian Talmud Taʿanit 2A in a baraita: "To love Yahweh your God and to serve him in (with) your whole heart" (Deut 11:13). What sort of a service is it that happens in the heart? Say: this is prayer.

1:9 C: How I ceaselessly make mention of you (think of you).

1 Maccabees 12:11: "Now at all times we think of you unceasingly ἀδιαλείπτως both on the festival days as well as on the other fitting days during the presentation of the sacrifices and in the prayers, as it is right and fitting to think of the brothers μνημονεύειν." ‖ 2 Baruch 86:1,3: "When you receive this letter, read it carefully in your assemblies ... and think of me (Baruch) while you read it, just as I think of you while writing it down and at all times."

1:10: Always in my prayers.

The words πάντοτε ἐπὶ τῶν προσευχῶν μου can be connected both with what precedes (μνείαν ὑμῶν ποιοῦμαι) and with what follows (δεόμενος). Analogous cases of ambiguous constructions are familiar in rabbinic literature as well as in the OT.

Mekilta Exodus 17:9 (61B): Isi b. Judah (ca. 170) said, "There are five words which have no (certain) relation הֶכְרֵעַ: שְׂאֵת (Gen 4:7), אָרוּר (Gen 49:7), מָחָר (Exod 17:9), מְשֻׁקָּדִים (Exod 25:34), and וְקָם (Deut 31:16). — שְׂאֵת whence? (Either:) "Is there not removal שְׂאֵת (of guilt) if you act rightly?" Or: ("Why did your countenance fall? But not if you do the right thing!" [Gen 4:6b-7a]). Bearing (atoning) שְׂאֵת (but it says this) if you do not do the right thing. ("Sin lurks at the door ....") — אָרוּר: "Cursed be their anger, for it is fierce!" Or: "For in their anger they slew the man and in their wantonness they mutilated the cattle of the cursed one."[20] — מָחָר: "Tomorrow I will stand on the top of the hill." Or: "Go out and fight with Amalek tomorrow!" מְשֻׁקָּדִים: "Its calyxes and its flowers are shaped like almond blossoms." Or: "And on the lamp-stand there are four chalices shaped like almond blossoms." — וְקָם: ("Behold, you are lying

20. S-B: The Samaritan text reads this by attenuating אריר to אַהוּר = strong, powerful; cf. Bacher, *Die Agada der Tannaïten*, 2:376; Abraham Geiger, *Urschrift und Übersetzungen der Bibel: In ihrer Abhängigkeit von der innern Entwicklung des Judentums* (Breslau: Julius Hainauer, 1857), 375. The Samaritan targum retained the construction of the Old Testament base text.

down now to go to your fathers) and this people will get up and prostitute itself to strange gods." Or: "Behold, you are lying down now to go to your fathers and you will resurrect."[21] These are the five words in the Torah that have no relationship. — Parallel passages can be found in Tanḥ. בשלח 85B according to the Mekilta; b. Yoma 52A enumerates the five words without more detailed explanation; y. ʿAbod. Zar. 2.41C.62 is anonymous = Mekilta with the addition: R. Tanḥuma (ca. 380) also added Exod 34:7: "Jacob's sons had come from the field when they heard." Or: "When they heard it, the men were pained"; Midr. Song. 1:2 (83B) gives a detailed explanation only for שְׂאֵת and the saying of R. Tanḥuma; Gen. Rab. 80 (51C) with the omission of מָחָר and without explanation for the other four words, but with the addition of R. Tanḥuma's supplement. ‖ Genesis Rabbah 65 (41D): ("Isaac said to Jacob, 'Who are you, my son?'" [Gen 27:18].) "Then Jacob said, 'I (therefore Jacob), Esau (however) is your firstborn'" (so Midr. Gen. 27:19; in order to remove the untruthfulness from Jacob's words אנכי was detached from the following עשו בכורך and made into a standalone part of the answer). R. Levi (ca. 300) said, "It is I אָנֹכִי, who will one day receive your 10 commandments (which begin with אָנֹכִי); but Esau is your firstborn."

1:14: To Greeks as well as to barbarians.

1. Ἕλλησιν. — From the word family to which Ἕλληνες belongs one finds as a loanword in rabbinic literature α. the substantive אֶלַס = Ἕλλας, but only with the meaning "Graecia Magna" = Lower Italy, particularly in connection with טַרְסִיס (טרסוס) = Tartessus;[a] β. the adjective אֶלֵּינִסְטִי, אֶלֵּינִסְתִּי "Greek" or "in Greek."[b] However Ἕλληνες itself was not taken over into rabbinic writing. In the rabbinic writings the Greeks are called (in accordance with the OT יָוָן, really Ionians, thus Greece), in Hebrew יְוָנִים,[c] sg. יְוָנִי, or in Aramaic יַוְנָאֵי,[d] sg. יַוְנָאָה.

a. Jerusalem Talmud Megillah 1.71B.51: "And the sons of Javan: Elishah and Tarshish, Kittim and Dodanim" (Gen 10:4); (these are:) Hellas (Greater Greece), Tartessus אלסטרסס (read: אלס טרסיס), Achaia (read אֲכָיָה instead of אביה) and Dardania (region in Moesia). — Among the parallels are Gen. Rab. 37 (22C): אלסוטרוס (read: אלס טרסיס), Italy and Dardania; Tg. Yer. I Gen. 10:4: "And the sons of Javan: Elishah, אלס (Hellas = Greater Greece) and Tartessus וטרסס, אכזיא (read: אכייא = Achaia) and Dordania." Targum 1 Chronicles 1:7: "And the sons of Muqdon (Macedonians): Hellas (read אלס instead of אלסו) and Tartessus טרסוס, Italion and Dardania."

b. See § Acts 21:37.

c. For example, b. Meg. 11A.19: In the days of the Greeks בימי יוונים; likewise, in the same text line 20. — See also b. Sukkah 56B at § Luke 1:5 A, #1, n. *b*; here "kings of the Greeks" = מלכי יונים and right after that the "Greeks" יונים.

d. Targum Yerušalmi I Deuteronomy 32:24: "And I will provoke (incite) against them the Greeks יַוְנָאֵי, who bite with their teeth like the animals of the field (= like wild animals)." ‖

21. S-B: An example for the latter construction appears in b. Sanh 90B; see this passage at § Matt 22:32, #2, A.

Targum Joel 4:6: "You have sold the sons of Judah and the sons of Jerusalem to the sons of the Greeks בני יונאי, to remove them far from their territory."

2. According to the Greek view, βάρβαροι = בַּרְבָּרִים, בַּרְבְּרִיִּים, ברבריין, בַּרְבָּרַיָּא (sg.: בַּרְבָּר, בַּרְבָּרִי, בַּרְבָּרוֹן, בַּרְבָּרָאָה) designates all non-Greek speakers. However, all the other master races of antiquity likewise called "barbarians" everyone who spoke a language other than their own. Thus, the Jews were barbarians, for example, in the eyes of the Babylonians, Medes, and Romans.[a] Conversely the Jews at that time had no qualms about calling the Egyptians barbarians occasionally.[b] However, the rabbis also commonly understand under the label barbarians either illiterate individuals or crude primitive peoples.[c]

a. Midrash Lamentations Introduction #23 (36B): You will find, when Nebuchadnezzar came down from Jerusalem and the exiles of Zedekiah were in his power, the (earlier) exiles of Jeconiah went to meet them clothed inwardly in black and outwardly in white, and he was praised as the "conqueror of the barbarians" נִקִיטָא ברבריא = νικητὴς βαρβάρων. – In the parallel passage Midr. Eccl. 12:7 (54A) the last sentence is not present. ‖ Midrash Esther 2:21 (94A): "In those days, when Mordecai sat at the king's gate, Bigthan and Teresh, both eunuchs of the king, became enraged" (Esth 2:21). What sort of rage was this? He (Ahasuerus) deposed two and appointed one. He deposed those in charge of executing the punishment (read קוּסְטִינָרִין = *quaestionarii* instead of קלסרוקין), who guarded the threshold, and he appointed this barbarian הברברי הזה, who sat at the king's gate. – Here the Jew Mordecai is designated as a barbarian. – In the parallel passage Abba Gurion, ed. Buber 10B, קלוסנטרין and ברברי are juxtaposed to each other; Krauß regards the first as καλάσιρις = soldier;[22] Buber regards it as καλοὶ (*senatores*); but the word might be corrupted from קְלִיסְטְנָרִין = *quaestionarii*; in Tg. Esth. 2:21: קלוסנתרין and בכין, for the latter, Levy wants to read בַּבַּיִין = "gatekeepers, those who stand at the gate,"[23] and Krauß בריון = φρούριον "soldier";[24] but in that case it might be more obvious to understand בַּרְיוֹן in its otherwise assured meaning = "crude, unrestrained man," so that is would be a replacement word for ברברו. ‖ Leviticus Rabbah 22 (121A): When he (namely Titus after Jerusalem was conquered) came to Rome, all the Romans came to meet him and praised him as a conqueror of the barbarians נקיטא ברברייא = νικητὴς βαρβάρων; see above Midr. Lam. Introduction #23. – The same in Midr. Eccl. 5:8 (26B) with the form נקיטא ב׳.

b. Targum Psalms 114:1: "When Israel came out of Egypt, the house of Jacob from the nations of the barbarians מעמי ברבראי" (text word: מֵעַם לֹעֵז = "from a people speaking a foreign language").

c. Jerusalem Talmud Baba Meṣiʿa 2.8C.18: Simeon b. Shetah (ca. 90 BCE) was employed in (trading) flax. His students said to him, "Rabbi, stop this. We want to buy you a donkey,

---

22. Samuel Krauß, *Griechische und Lateinische Lehnwörter in Talmud, Midrasch und Targum* (Berlin: S. Calvary & Co., 1898), 2:543B.

23. J. Levy, *Neuhebräisches und Chaldäisches Wörterbuch über die Talmudim und Midraschim* (Leipzig: F. A. Brockhaus, 1876), 1:79f.

24. Krauß, *Griechische und Lateinische Lehnwörter in Talmud, Midrasch und Targum*, 2:166A.

then you will not have to labor so much." They went and bought him a donkey from a Saracen,[25] and there was a pearl hanging on it. They came to him and said to him, "From now on you will not have to labor anymore." He answered them, "Why?" They said to him, "We bought a donkey for you from a Saracen and there was a pearl hanging on it." He answered them, "And did its master know about this?" They said, "No!" He said to them, "Take it back, then!" But did Rab Huna († 297) not say that Bibi b. Goslon (Giddel?) said in the name of Rab († 247), "It was replied before Rabbi († 217?), 'Even if one has the same opinion as the one who said that what has been robbed from the *goy* is forbidden, does not the whole world agree that what he has lost is allowed?' (Why then the instruction of R. Simeon b. Shetah to bring back the pearl to the owner?) Do you think then that Simeon b. Shetah was a barbarian ברברון?" Simeon b. Shetah preferred to hear (from the mouth of a pagan), "Blessed be the God of the Jews (because of their honesty), more than he wanted the bounty of this whole world." (Through this behavior, Simeon b. Shetah hallowed God's name, whereas if he had acted alternatively, his behavior perhaps would have given occasion for God's name to be cursed by the pagan and thereby would have desecrated God's name.) See Deut. Rab. 3 (200A). ‖ Genesis Rabbah 42 (25D): R. Samuel b. Nahman said, "... It is like a king's friend who remained in a province, and for his sake the king busied himself (caringly) with the province. But when the barbarians ברברים wanted to set themselves on him (the friend), it was said, 'Woe to us, for the king will not busy himself (any more) with the province if we kill his friend!'" — In the parallel Lev. Rab. 11 (112D) we find the form ברבריים, Midr. Esth. 1:1 (82A) and Midr. Ruth 1:1 (124A) ברבריין. ‖ Exodus Rabbah 20 (83A): R. Simeon b. Laqish (ca. 250) said, "It is like a king's son, who was led captive by the barbarians ביד הברברים, and they oppressed him unduly...." ‖ Jerusalem Talmud Sukkah 5.55B.13: In the days of Trajan טְרוּגְיָינוֹס, the blasphemer, a son was born to him on the 9th of Ab (the day of the destruction of Jerusalem). And they (the Jews) fasted. His daughter died on the feast of Hanukkah (25th of Kislev), and they lit lights (as was prescribed on the feast of the dedication of the temple). Then his wife sent word to him, "Instead of subjugating the barbarians הברבריים (here the Parthians are meant), come (rather) and subjugate the Jews who have risen against you." — The parallel passages Midr. Lam. 1:16 (56B); 4:19 (77A), which are much more elaborate and have טרגיינס (= Trajan) instead of טרכינס, offer the form ברבריין.

3. In the writings of secular authors, Ἕλληνες καὶ βάρβαροι is a designation for the whole human race.[a] Similarly, Jewish literature divided all humanity into two parts: "Israel" and "nations of the world."[b] In Paul the following phrases correspond to this Jewish division of humanity into two parts: Ἰουδαῖοι καὶ ἔθνη (Rom 3:29; 9:24), Ἰουδαῖος καὶ Ἕλλην (Rom 1:16; 2:9, 10; 10:12; Gal 3:28), Ἰουδαῖοι καὶ Ἕλληνες (Rom 3:9; 1 Cor 12:13). However, in the mouth of the apostle Paul, Ἕλληνες καὶ βάρβαροι is not coextensive with the same compound in the secular authors: the apostle counted the Jewish people among neither the Hellenes nor the barbarians;

25. S-B: Saracen = Ishmaelite in, e.g., Tg. Yer. I Gen. 37:25; 39:1.

for him the expression Ἕλληνες καὶ βάρβαροι comprises only humanity outside of Israel or pagan humanity.

a. Even Philo and Josephus use Ἕλληνες καὶ βάρβαροι in this sense. Philo, *Opif.* 43 (Mangey's ed., 1:30): "It (the number seven) is honored also among the most respected of the Hellenes and barbarians who have occupied themselves with mathematics."[26] ‖ Josephus, *Against Apion* 1.11: "I think I have made it sufficiently clear that recording ancient happenings is more at home among the barbarians than among the Hellenes." ‖ *Against Apion* 1.22: "I must now however satisfy the expectation of those who give no credence to the records of the barbarians and want to believe only the Hellenes, and show that many of these are also familiar to our people...."

b. For evidence, see § Luke 12:30.

1:17 A: For the righteousness of God is revealed in it (the gospel).

δικαιοσύνη θεοῦ "righteousness of God" = coming from God (by God's judgment) and as a consequence valid as righteousness before God. — On the expression, see Deut 33:21: "He (Gad) practiced צִדְקַת יהוה 'the righteousness of Yahweh' (= what is right before Yahweh) and his laws with Israel." — Targum Onkelos Deuteronomy 33:21: "What is his (the territory of Gad) will be accepted by God as most excellent; for there in his possession (portion) Moses, the great teacher of Israel, is buried; and this one (Moses) went out and in at the head of the people, he practiced righteous deeds before Yahweh זָכְוָן קֳדָם י״י (= what was right before Yahweh) and his laws with Israel." ‖ Targum Yerušalmi I: "He (Gad) saw a good land for himself and received his portion in the territory of the firstborn; for in that land was a place, full of precious stones and pearls, in which Moses, the teacher of Israel was buried. And just as he (Moses) had gone in and out at the head of the people in this world, he will also go in and out in the future world, because he practiced righteous deeds before Yahweh זָכְוָן קֳדָם י״י (Yer. II: זכוותיה דה׳ = 'the righteousness of Yahweh') and taught his people, the house of Israel, his laws." ‖ The LXX is completely different: δικαιοσύνην κύριος ἐποίησε καὶ κρίσιν αὐτοῦ μετὰ Ἰσραήλ. ‖ See § Rom 3:21 A.

1:17 B: The righteous one will live as a consequence of faith.

On Hab 2:4 see § Gal 3:11, #1.

1:18 A: Wrath of God.

The effort to remove anthropomorphisms on the principle that no evil (bad) resides in God[a] led Jewish teaching about Scripture occasionally

---

26. Philo, *Philōnos tou Ioudaiou Ta Heuriskomena hapanta: Philonis Iudaei Opera quae reperiri potuerunt omnia*, ed. Thomas Mangey (London: Innys, 1742).

to reinterpret the "wrath" or "fury" or "anger" of God as an angel of destruction מַלְאַךְ חַבָּלָה.[b]

a. Tanḥuma תזריע (155B): What does "The evil one does not abide with you" (Ps 5:5) mean? R. Berekhiah (ca. 340) said in the name of R. Tanḥum b. Hanilai (ca. 280; so the names are to be switched) in the name of R. Yohanan († 279), "Only angels of peace stand before God, but angels of wrath מַלְאֲכֵי זַעַף are far from him, for it says in Exod 34:6, 'Yahweh … is אֶרֶךְ אַפַּיִם (longsuffering).' How so? Do we not already know then that he is longsuffering (therefore why is it said here)? Rather what does ארך אפים mean? That angels of wrath are far from him (ארך אפים is thus interpreted= 'keeping away from wrath'); for it says, 'They come from a far land, from the end of heaven, to Yahweh with the tools of his anger, to destroy the whole earth' (Isa 13:5)." — The same is found more briefly in TanḥB תזריע § 11 (20A). ‖ TanḥumaB תזריע § 12 (20B): R. Eleazar b. Pedat (ca. 270) said in the name of R. Yohanan († 279), "The name of God is mentioned (in Scripture) not in the case of something bad but rather in the case of something good." (Then follows an explanatory proof from Scripture.) The same in Tanḥ. תזריע 155B.36; additionally, see 156B.15 and TanḥB תזריע § 13 (21A.10). — In Gen. Rab. 3 (3D.37), the saying is attributed to R. Eleazar (b. Pedat) himself, specifically in the version: God never connects his name to the bad but rather to the good.

b. Jerusalem Talmud Taʿanit 2.65B.43: What does אֶרֶךְ אַפַּיִם in Joel 2:13 mean? (The Midrash understands it = far from wrath.) It is like a king who had two cruel legions. The king said, "If they dwell with me in the city and the inhabitants of the city enrage me, they (the legions) will rise against them (and destroy them). Behold, therefore I prefer to summon them far away. In that case, if the inhabitants of the city enrage me, they will placate me again before I have those angels come, and I will accept their placation." Thus God also said, "*af* (wrath) and *ḥema* (fury) are angels of destruction. Behold I will summon them from far away. In that case, if the Israelites enrage me, they will repent before I have those angels come back, and I will accept their repentance (see Isa 13:5 as above under n. *a*). — Parallels can be found in Pesiq. 161B; Midr. Ps. 5 § 7 (27B); 86 § 7 (187B) is in part anonymous. ‖ Deuteronomy Rabbah 3 (200C): R. Hiyya b. Abba (ca. 280) said, "When God said to Moses in heaven, 'Up, climb up quickly from here' (Deut 9:12), five angels of destruction heard it and wanted to do him harm, and these were: אַף wrath, חֵימָה fury, קֶצֶף anger, מַשְׁחִית destroyer, and מְכַלֶּה exterminator. But when Moses mentioned the merit of the fathers, as it is written, 'Remember Abraham, Isaac, and Israel, your servants' (Exod 32:13), then anger, destroyer, and exterminator fled and the two hard (cruel) ones, wrath and fury, remained. Then Moses said before him, 'Lord of the world, behold, I have mentioned three and then three fled. Now stand also against wrath! For it says, "Arise, Yahweh, against your wrath" (so Midr. Ps 7:7).' Behold, God stood against wrath. How do we know that Moses stood against fury? See Ps 106:23: 'If Moses, his chosen one, had not stepped into the gap before him, to turn away his fury, so that he would not cause destruction.'" — Similar is the anonymous statement in Exod. Rab. 41 (98A); Exod. Rab. 44 (100B) writes in the name of R. Isaac; Midr. Eccl. 4:2f. (22B) writes in the name of R. Joshua b. Levi (ca. 250); in Midr. Ps. 7 § 6 (33A), R. Samuel b. Nahman is mistakenly given as the author instead of R. Joshua b. Levi; the saying is anonymous in TanḥB כי תשא § 13 (57A); Midr. Ps. 18 § 13 (71B). ‖ Pesiqta 45A: R. Phineas (b. Hama [ca. 360]) said in the name of R. Abin (ca. 325) in the name of R. Hanin (ca. 300), "Even the mediator (= Moses) started to feel the force of the sin (the making of the golden calf). It says in Ps 68:13, 'The kings of the armies flee, they flee.'" R. Judan (ca. 350) said in the name of R. Aybo (ca. 320), "It does not say here, the 'angels' of the armies, but rather the 'kings' of the angels (so read with Pesiq. Rab.); for even Michael and Gabriel (the head angels) had not been able to look at the face of Moses. However, when they (Israel) sinned, Moses too was not able to look at the face of the servants of the company, as it says, 'For I dreaded "wrath" and "fury"' (Deut 9:19)." — Parallels can be found in Midr. Song. 3:7 (107A); in Pesiq. Rab. 15 (69A) R. Isaac b. Abin speaks in the name of R. Hanin; in Num. Rab. 11 (162D) R. Phineas b. Abin is given as the tradent; in Midr. Sam. 17 § 4 (49A), R. Phineas speaks in the name of R. Abin b. Hanin; Midr. Eccl. 9:11 (44A) is anonymous. ‖ Babylonian Talmud Šabbat 55A: Who were those six men in Ezek 9:2? Rab Hisda († 309) said, "anger קֶצֶף, wrath אַף, fury חֵימָה, destroyer מַשְׁחִית, smasher מְשַׁבֵּר, and exterminator מְכַלֶּה." — A few lines previously these men are designated as "angels of destruction."

1:18 B: Over all godlessness and unrighteousness of men.

ἀσέβεια is related to ἀδικία approximately as irreligiosity is to immortality. From the rabbinic writings, one can compare the difference between עֲבֵירוֹת שֶׁבֵּין אָדָם לַמָּקוֹם "sins between man and God" = ἀσέβεια and עֲבֵירוֹת שֶׁבֵּין אָדָם לַחֲבֵירוֹ "sins between man and his neighbor" = ἀδικία.

Mishnah Yoma 8.9: R. Eleazar b. Azariah (ca. 100) said in a presentation the following, "'You are to become pure from all your sins before (= against) Yahweh' (so the Midr. construes Lev 16:30). The Day of Atonement atones for the sins between man and God, but not for those between a man and his neighbor (another person), until he reconciles with (placates) his neighbor (another person)." — Additionally, see b. Roš Haš. 17B.28 at § Rom 2:11, #2.

1:20 A: His invisible being.

The invisible being of God was quite often emphasized by the ancient synagogue so strongly that the possibility of seeing God was denied even to the highest angels (see the citations at § Matt 18:10 C). The common opinion was that no man could see God in the present age. Only at the hour of death would every human, good as well as bad, have to appear before God, to greet the face of the Shekinah. But in eternity seeing God, the epitome of all blessedness, would be the privilege of all the pious and righteous (see § Matt 5:8 B, #2). The inability of humanity to see God in this life was often grounded in the experience that no one was able to look at the blazing sun, which was only one of God's servants.[a] Because of his invisible being, God himself is designated many times as the one who sees all things but who himself is seen by no one.[b]

a. Sibylline Oracles Preface 7ff.: "There is one God who alone reigns, immeasurably immense, without beginning, almighty, invisible ἀόρατος, himself alone seeing everything, while he himself is not seen by mortal flesh. For what flesh can see the heavenly and true, immortal God with his eyes, him, who inhabits the vault of heaven? Rather, people cannot even stand in the face of the blazing sun, those who are born mortal men, who are veins and flesh." ‖ Babylonian Talmud Ḥullin 59B: The emperor (Hadrian) said to R. Joshua b. Hananiah (ca. 90), "I would like to see your God!" This one responded, "You cannot see him." That one said, "I tell you, I want to see him!" Then at the time of the summer solstice he went and faced him toward the sun and said to him, "Look at it!" He said, "That I cannot do." He responded to him, "Of the sun, which is one of the servants which stands before God, you say, 'I cannot look at it.' Is that not true above all of the Shekinah (divinity) itself?" ‖ TanḥumaB נשא § 34 (22B): R. Abin the Levite, the son of rabbis (probably Abin II, ca. 370) said, "Joseph had spoken a word of praise, and his master (Potiphar) saw him, how he whispered (prayed softly) with his mouth. He said to him, 'Joseph, what are you saying there?' He answered and said to him, 'I am praising God.' He said to him, 'I would like to see your God!' Joseph answered him, 'Behold, the sun, one of innumerable servants, you cannot look at, so how much less his glory itself!'" — The same in Num. Rab. 14 (173C).

b. Sibylline Oracles 4:12: "(The great God,) who, while seeing all things at once is himself seen by no one." — See Sib. Or. Preface 7ff. in n. *a* above. ‖ Jerusalem Talmud Šeqalim 5.49B.18: R. Hoshaiah the elder (ca. 225) had as a teacher for his son a blind man who used to eat with him daily. Once he had guests and the blind man did not come to eat with him (since he had not been invited). In the evening he (R. Hoshaiah) went to him and said, "Let my lord not be angry with me; but since I had guests today, I thought that the honor of my lord should not be disparaged today (because of unkind remarks). Therefore I did not eat with my lord today." He answered him, "You have placated the one who is seen but does not see. May the one who sees and is not seen (= God) accept your placation (and repay you for it)!" He said to him, "Where did you get that from?" He answered him, "From R. Eliezer b. Jacob (ca. 150). A blind man came into the city of R. Eliezer b. Jacob. R. Eliezer b. Jacob took his place beneath him, so it might be said, 'If this were not a significant person, R. Eliezer b. Jacob would not have taken his place beneath him.' They (therefore) gave him honorable provisions. He said to them, 'Why?' It was said to him, 'R. Eliezer b. Jacob took his place beneath you.' Then he prayed this prayer for him, 'You have shown love to one who is seen but does not see. May the one who sees but is not seen repay love to you.'" — The same is found in y. Pe'ah 8.21B.39. ‖ See b. Ḥag. 5B and Lev. Rab. 4 (108A) at § John 1:18 A. ‖ Pesiqta Rabbati 6 (24A): "How great are your works, Yahweh, how deep are your thoughts!" (Ps 92:6). Come and see the wonders of God! ... He created his world, he shaped the children of men in it and *mazziqin* (wreckers = demons): the *mazziqin* see the children of men but the children of men do not see them. He created *mazziqin* and angels of service, and the angels of service see the *mazziqin* but the *mazziqin* do not see the angels of service. He created the angels of service and the *mazziqin* and the children of men: he (God) sees all but all creatures do not see him. Say: "how deep are your thoughts"! ‖ Deuteronomy Rabbah 1 (196A): Who is the God of the gods? The one who sees but is not seen.

1:20 B: Since the creation of the world.

ἀπὸ κτίσεως κόσμου = לבריאת עולם,[a] or: מיום שברא חקב״ה את העולם,[b] or (and most of the time): משׁשת ימי בראשית[c] "since the 6 days of creation."

a. Babylonian Talmud ʿAbodah Zarah 9B: In a baraita it has been taught: If 4,231 years from the creation of the world לבריאת עולם someone should say to you: "Buy a field worth 1,000 *denars* for 1 *denar*," do not buy it (for then the Messiah can come at any moment; see excursus "Signs and Calculations of the Messianic Time").

b. Babylonian Talmud Berakot 7B: R. Yohanan († 279) said in the name of R. Simeon b. Yohai (ca. 150), "Since the day God created the world, there was no one who called God "Lord" אדון until Abraham came and called him 'Lord' (see Gen 15:8)." ‖ Babylonian Talmud Berakot 31B: R. Eleazar (ca. 270) said, "Since the day God created the world, there was no one who called God "Sabaoth" until Hannah came and called him "Sabaoth" (see 1 Sam 1:11).

c. Babylonian Talmud Sukkah 49A: R. Yohanan († 279) said, "The *shith* (a drain at the southwest corner of the altar of burnt offering) has existed since the six days of creation." ‖ Babylonian Talmud Berakot 34B: What does "No eye has seen ..." (Isa 4:3) mean? R. Joshua b. Levi (ca. 250) said, "Thereby the wine is meant that has been kept in its grapes since the six days of creation (for the meal that the righteous will enjoy in the future)." ‖ The term מִבְּרֵאשִׁית by itself = from the beginning, always; so already Sir 15:14 (Hebrew): "God created man from the beginning."

1:20 C: Through his works.

τοῖς ποιήμασιν = through his works of creation. See in the OT מַעֲשֵׂי יְדֵי יהוה "the works of the hands of Yahweh" = the works of creation in Ps 8:7; 19:2; additionally, the term מַעֲשׂוּם by itself in the same sense in Ps 103:22. For the targum, in every one of these passages, עוֹבָדָא = work. In the rabbinic literature, this means the single work of creation (but also the totality of all works) מַעֲשֵׂה בְרֵאשִׁית.

Babylonian Talmud Roš Haššanah 11A: R. Joshua b. Levi (ca. 250) said, "Every work of creation כל מעשה בראשית was created in its (full) form (size); they were created with their knowledge (with their consent); they were created at their (explicit) request; for it says, 'And so heaven and earth and all צבאם were completed' (Gen 2:1). Do not read צבאם 'the host,' but rather צִבְיוֹנָן 'their request.'" — Parallels can be found in b. Ḥul. 60A. ‖ Babylonian Talmud Šabbat 88A: Resh Laqish (ca. 250) said, "What does 'It was evening and it was morning, the sixth day יום הששי' (Gen 1:31) mean? What is the superfluous ה for (before ששי, which is lacking on days 1–5)? It teaches that God made an arrangement with the works of creation מעשה בראשית and said to them, 'If the Israelites accept the Torah, you will last, but if not, I will let you turn back into chaos (*tohu vabohu*).'" — The same is found in b. ʿAbod. Zar. 3A.16. In the more extended explanation of Tanḥ. בראשית 1B the superfluous ה = 5 is interpreted in relation to the 5 books of the Torah. By contrast, Rashi in commenting on b. Šabb. 88A has יום הששי refer to the sixth day of Sivan, the day on which the law was given.

1:20 D: Perceived (νοούμενα).

The possibility of knowing God from the works of creation is described in most detail in Wis 13:1ff.;[a] 2 Baruch also regards this possibility as beyond dispute.[b] The rabbinic scholars do not go into this question in greater detail. For them, knowledge in paganism of the true God was a given due to the fact that both Adam and the oldest generations of humanity, on the one hand, and Noah and his descendants, on the other, had received from God six or seven commandments which would have been completely sufficient to keep the pre- and extra-Israelite world from sinking into idolatry.[c] The rabbinic scholars occasionally celebrate Abraham as a fully valid proof of the truth that man is certainly able, from himself (i.e., from his own power) to know the true God and creator of the world from his works.[d] According to a later midrashic work, Job, Hezekiah, and the Messiah are further witnesses to this truth.[e]

a. Wisdom 13:1ff.: "All people were futile (foolish) by nature, for whom ignorance of God was suited and who were not able to know the existent one from the visible good, nor did they know the artificer, although they paid attention to the works, but instead they considered as gods ruling the world either fire or wind or swift air or the circle of the stars or powerful water or the lights of heaven. If they, because they were delighted by the beauty of these things, viewed them as gods, they should have known how much better (more beautiful) the Lord of these things is, for the author of beauty had created them. But if they were amazed at their force and power, they should have known from this how much more powerful the one who made them is. For from the magnitude and beauty of created things their author should accordingly be seen (θεωρεῖται; see καθορᾶται in Rom 1:20). However, they are nevertheless little to blame because of these things, for they who seek God and want to find him easily go astray; for they look into these things as they linger among his works, and let themselves be coaxed by the appearance, since the sight of them is indeed beautiful. On the other hand, though, they are not excused (συγγνωστοί, see ἀναπολογήτους in Rom 1:20). For if they were able to know so much that they were able to comprehend the world, why did they not more quickly find its ruler!?"

b. 2 Baruch 54:17f.: "Now, though, turn only to destruction, you who are now wrongdoers; for you will be harshly afflicted, since you formerly neglected the knowledge of the Most High. For his works have not taught you, nor has the skillful arrangement of his creation, which always exists, persuaded you (of this)."

c. See further below at § Rom 1:20 E.

d. Genesis Rabbah 64 (40C): R. Yohanan († 279) and R. Hanina (b. Hama [ca. 225]) both said, "When he was 48 years old, Abraham knew his creator." Resh Laqish (ca. 250) said, "When he was 3 years old, Abraham knew his creator. Where (does the proof for this come from)? 'עֵקֶב, that is, 172 (years) Abraham listened to the voice of his creator' (Gen 26:5)." — The midr. interprets עקב according to its numerical value = 172. Since Abraham lived to be 175 years old according to Gen 25:7, he must have entered into God's service as a three-year old, if he served God for 172 years. — Parallels can be found in Gen. Rab. 30 (18B), where

R. Levi (ca. 300) is named as the tradent of Resh Laqish and no proof text from Scripture is given; 46 (29A); 95 (60B), where there is a detailed interpretation of עקב; Midr. Song. 5:16 (121A); Pesiq. Rab. 21 (105A), where yet a third opinion is given, namely that Abraham knew God when he was 50 years old; TanḥB לך לך § 4 (31A), where R. Hanina is the representative of the opinion of Resh Laqish; חיי שרה § 6 (60A) lacks the opinion of Resh Laqish; בהר § 3 (53A) has only Resh Laqish; in Num. Rab. 18 (184D), the saying of Resh Laqish is anonymous; in b. Ned. 32A, R. Ammi b. Abba is the author instead of Resh Laqish. ‖ Maʿaśe Abraham:[27] When Terah, Abraham's father, saw this (that Nimrod's people wanted to kill the child Abraham), he hid him in a cave underground, where he lived for three years. After three years he pulled him from the cave and brought him outside. When he saw the sun rising, he said in his heart, "This sun created the world, and I want to worship it, for it created me and placed spirit and soul and wisdom in me to serve it." When the sun went down and the moon shone, he said in his heart, "It seems to me that this one created the world, and I want to worship it, for it created both me and the whole world." He stood in prayer the whole night until the morning light. But when the moon went down and the sun came up, he said, "It appears to me as if I prayed in vain." Then he said, "Now I know that this one (moon) and that one (sun) are only two servants who serve the one great and mighty lord, and in truth, he is seen by no man in the world, for he is to be feared and lives and remains forever without changing and he made heaven and earth and all their host." Immediately Abraham said to his father Terah, "My father, who created heaven and earth?" He answered, "Our gods!" Abraham said to him, "Where are they?" He answered him, "They stand on the walls of my house." He said, "Since they are in your house, I will go and sacrifice to them, to see if they will perhaps find pleasure in me as they do in other children of men." Abram went to his mother and wept before her and said to her, "Make me cake from fine-ground flour so that I may make an offering of it to the gods of my father." She made him a cake; he took it and came (with it) to them. And behold, the smallest one was leaned against the others. Then Abraham said, "Woe, woe, how weak you are! Certainly, time has passed and you have eaten nothing. Stand upright and I will give you a beautiful cake that my mother has made me." And it happened, when it did not stand upright, that he went to his mother and said, "This cake was not beautiful; make me another cake which is more beautiful than the one from before." She did. Immediately Abram took it and offered it before the greatest idol among them all. He said to him, "Stretch out your hand and take my gift בִּרְכָתִי (see Gen 33:11) and refresh your heart!" But he gave him no answer, for he was wood. Immediately the spirit of wisdom and of purity alighted on Abram and said, "They have eyes and do not see; they have ears and do not hear" (Ps 115:5f.). What did Abram do? He said in his heart, "If they hold up in the fire, something truly exists in them." Then he took fire and lit it at a distance and said to them, "When it gets (too) hot for you, then get yourselves out of it; but if not, you may burn in the fire!" And it happened, when they all were burned in the fire, that his father Terah came in the evening to pray to his idols. He found them burned and said to

27. The text found is in Chaim Meir Horowitz, *Sammlung kleiner Midraschim* (Berlin: H. Itzkowski, 1881), 43 line 18.

his wife, "Who burned my gods?" She said, "I do not know." Then he asked his son Abram, "I heard that you entered (to see them) and your mother made you a cake and you went in (with it)." Abram answered, "My father, my father, how long they have been in your house without eating, and the smallest one had become weak and lay on the ground. Then I had compassion for him and got him a beautiful cake. But when the largest saw that I gave it to the smallest one, great wrath flared up in him and he burned him and also himself." His father answered and said, "My son is a great fool. This one (idol) can neither speak nor hear nor do good or evil. But you have lied. How can the one burn the other and himself too!" Then Abram said, "My father, my father, let your ear hear what you have let out of your mouth! For you have abandoned the one who created you and heaven and earth and served your idol, in which nothing exists." (Then Abraham is brought by his enraged father before King Nimrod.) Nimrod said to Abram, "Why did you burn the gods of your father?" Abram answered and said, "What should I say to my lord? In truth my father is guilty because he did not give them anything to eat. In truth I saw the smallest one lying on the ground and spoke to my mother that she might make me a really beautiful cake and I brought it before the smallest one. Then the wrath of the largest one flared up and he burned that one and himself with fire." Nimrod said to him, "These idols can do absolutely nothing!" He said to him, "My lord king, see and hear what you have let out of your own mouth, namely that those idols can do absolutely nothing; and you want to abandon the living God and eternal king who created heaven and earth and all their host, and serve idols made of wood?!" Nimrod answered Abram, "I am the one who created heaven and earth and all their host!" Abram said, "Let us now test whether your words are true, my lord. Tell the sun to rise in the west and set in the east! If you can do this, I will serve you my whole life, for you can truly speak and you live and hear." When Nimrod heard his words, which were true and right, he was exceedingly astonished at the three-year old boy that he spoke such words; and he called all astrologers and told them all these words. (Then comes Abraham's condemnation to death by fire and his salvation from the furnace of the Chaldeans (this is the interpretation of אוּר כַּשְׂדִּים in Gen 15:7). ‖ For passages with similar content, see Gen. Rab. 38 (23C); Jellinek, *Beth ha-Midrash* 1.25 (מעשה אברהם); 2.118 (מעשה אברהם); 5.40 (מדרש דאברהם); Tanna Devei Eliyahu Zuṭa 25; Sefer ha-Yashar נח (edition Wilna 1870 folio12A); Midr. ʾAbot, Warsaw 1896 p. 15ff.; Johann Christian Fabricius, *Codex Pseudepigraphus Veteris Testamenti.*[28]

e. Numbers Rabbah 14 (173A.40): "Who has given to me that I should repay him?" (Job 41:3). (The passage) speaks of Abraham, who knew God from himself, as it says in Prov 14:14, "Whoever is of devious heart will be full from his ways" סוּג לֵב (Prov 14:14). What does "Whoever is of devious heart will be full from his ways" mean? R. Abba b. Kahana (ca. 310) said, "The heart that is full of scum סִגִים will one day be full from its ways. 'And whoever is a good man, from himself' (Prov 14:14); this goes for Abraham who knew God from himself מֵעַצְמוֹ (= out of his own self), and there was no one who taught him how he might know God, only he from himself. And this man is one of the four children of men who knew God from himself. Job knew God from himself. How do we know this? For he

28. Johann Christian Fabricius, *Codex Pseudepigraphus Veteris Testamenti* (Hamburg and Leipzig: Liebezeit, 1713), 1:336ff.

says, 'From my bosom (= from my inner self or from myself) I kept the words of his mouth' (Job 23:12). (The midr. reads מֵחֵקִי instead of מֵחֻקִּי; cf. LXX: ἐν δὲ κόλπῳ μου ἔκρυψα ῥήματα αὐτοῦ.) Hezekiah, the king of Judah, he too knew God from himself. Where do we derive this from? For it is written about him, 'He will eat curds and honey by the time he understands to reject what is bad and choose what is good' (Isa 7:15). And the king, the Messiah, knew God from himself." (A proof text is lacking; it should be noted, though, that the Messiah's knowledge of God belongs to the past already. Therefore, a Messiah is presupposed who has already appeared and now dwells somewhere in hiddenness; on this type of messiah, see § John 1:1 A, A, n. *c* and § John 1:1 A, B, n. *c*.)

1:20 E: So that they are without excuse.

Among the apocrypha, Wis 13:1ff. belongs here; see above § Rom 1:20 D, n. *a*. — For the rabbinic scholars, it was similarly a firm conviction that the nations of the world had no excuse before God since they had sunk into paganism. It was generally accepted that from the beginning God gave certain basic commandments[a] to men on their journey, which were supposed to offer them the possibility of adhering to the original knowledge and worship of God. Adam received six basic commandments[b] and Noah along with his descendants received seven.[c] It was further said that on Sinai God had offered the Torah to all the gentiles[d] and gave them the opportunity again on Ebal to accept the knowledge of the Torah.[e] The fact that the pre- and extra-Israelite world neither kept those basic commandments,[f] nor later paid any heed to the Torah and therefore became subject to idolatry, remains their own fault,[g] which cannot be justified by anything.

a. Basic commandments without which the maintenance of human order is inconceivable. Sifra Leviticus 18:4 (338A): "My laws" (Lev 18:4), these are the words in the Torah which, if they were not written, would have to be written with good reason, as, for example, concerning theft, adultery, idolatry, blasphemy, and bloodshed (murder). If these were not written, they would have to be written with good reason (because they are absolutely necessary for the continued existence of humanity). "My statutes" (Lev 18:4), these are those regulations to which the evil inclination and the *ʿakum* (gentiles) take exception, as, for example, concerning eating pork, clothing made of mixed fibers, the removal of the shoe by the sister-in-law (in the case that levirate marriage is refused), the cleansing of the leper, the red heifer, the ram to be sent away into the wilderness, to which the evil inclination and the *ʿakum* (gentiles) take exception (cf. on this the excursus "The Good and Evil Inclination"). This means: "I, Yahweh, have determined you are not authorized to take exception to them." — The same as a baraita in b. Yoma 67B. — The ancient synagogue made the five commandments listed above the foundation of the Adamic and Noachic commandments because they were necessary for the existence of human society.

b. The Adamic commandments. — Deuteronomy Rabbah 2 (198D): How many things was the first man given a commandment about? The scholars (so the baraita) taught the following: "The first man was given a commandment concerning six things: concerning idolatry, blasphemy, judges (= judiciary), bloodshed (murder), adultery, and theft." Rabbi (Judah I [† 217?]) said, "All these commandments are contained in one verse: 'Yahweh Elohim commanded men with the following, "From every tree of the garden you may eat" (Gen 2:16).' (The proof is then given in detail via inference by analogy, according to which when the same word appears in two passages of Scripture, one may draw on the content of the one passage of Scripture to illuminate the other. Scripture reads:) 'He commanded' relates to idolatry, see, 'Because he walked after an (idolatrous) "commandment"' (Hos 5:11). "'Yahweh' relates to idolatry, see, 'Whoever blasphemes the name of "Yahweh"' (Lev 24:16). 'Elohim' related to the judges, see, 'The matter of two should come before "Elohim" (= judge according to the Midr.)' (Exod 22:8). 'Men' is related to bloodshed, see, 'Whoever sheds a "man's" blood' (Gen 9:6). 'With the following' relates to adultery, see, '"With the following": If a man dismisses his wife …' (Jer 3:1). 'From every tree of the garden you may eat,' but not from the one who is robbed, and thereby gave him the prohibition concerning theft." — Parallel passages can be found in Midr. Song. 1:2 (82B), where the author is R. Eleazar (ca. 270), and instead of 6 commandments, 7 commandments are erroneously named; in Gen. Rab. 16 (11C), the author is R. Levi (ca. 300) and the proof text for "judge" comes from Exod 22:27; in Pesiq. 100B, the author is R. Judah b. Simeon (ca. 320), and instead of 6 commandments likewise 7 commandments are named; in Midr. Ps. 1 § 10 (5B), the author is R. Levi, without a proof from Scripture. ‖ A variant tradition about the *mitzvoth* of Adam is found in b. Sanh. 56B: R. Judah (ca. 150) said, "The first man received only one commandment, specifically concerning idolatry, see, 'Yahweh commended the divinity to Adam' (so Midr. Gen. 2:16)." R. Judah b. Batera (ca. 110) said, "Also concerning blasphemy." Some said, "Also concerning the judges (administration of justice)." This follows the opinion of what Rab Judah († 299) said in the name of Rab († 247), "'I am God,' you are not to blaspheme me; 'I am God,' you are not to exchange me (idolatrously for another god); 'I am God,' let the fear of me be upon you (in judicial decisions)? According to whose opinion? According to the opinion of 'some people'" (whose three Adamic commandments: idolatry, blasphemy, and administration of justice, Rab also finds implied in the words: "I am God" in Gen 2:16). ‖ The six commandments laid on Adam were later commanded to the descendants of Noah with the addition of a seventh commandment (not to eat part of an animal while it was still alive). This seventh commandment was irrelevant for Adam, because according to rabbinic understanding he was prohibited from consuming meat. Babylonian Talmud Sanhedrin 59B: Rab Judah († 299) said that Rab († 247) said, "The first man was not allowed to consume flesh; see Gen 1:29f., 'Let this (the plant world) serve to nourish you and every animal of the earth,' but the animals of the earth are not for your nourishment. But when the children of Noah came, he (God) permitted meat for them (see Gen 9:3, 'Everything that moves, that lives there, is to serve for your nourishment. I have given you everything, just as the green of the plants.') Should the member of a living animal not be used? Scripture teaches, 'You are not to eat meat while it still has its soul, its blood.'" — On this interpretation of Gen 9:4, see § Acts 15:20 D, II, #1, n. *a*.

c. The Noachic commandments. — Tosefta ʿAbodah Zarah 8.4, 6 (473.12, 21): Seven commandments were given to the children of Noah, specifically concerning administration of justice, idolatry, blasphemy, adultery, bloodshed, theft ... and the member from a living animal. ‖ Seder ʿOlam Rabbah 5: Seven (of the ten Sinaitic commandments) had been commanded to the children of Noah. (Then comes a proof from Scripture from Gen 2:16 similar to the one brought forth above in n. *b* according to Deut. Rab. 2:) "He commanded" relates to the judges (administration of justice), see, "I have chosen him, that he may 'command' ... to practice righteousness and justice" (Gen 18:19); "Yahweh" relates to blasphemy, see, "Whoever blasphemes the name of 'Yahweh'" (Lev 24:16); "Elohim" relates to idolatry, see, "There is to be no other 'Elohim' except me" (Exod 20:3); "men" relates to bloodshed, see, "Whoever sheds a 'man's' blood" (Gen 9:6); "in the following way" relates to adultery, see, "'In the following way': If a man dismisses his wife ..." (Jer 3:1); "from every מִכֹּל tree of the garden" relates to theft, see, "From every" מִכֹּל, in relation to what one falsely swears by ... (Lev 5:2–4); "you may eat," this relates to the member of a living animal, see, "'You may not eat' meat while it still has its soul, its blood" (Gen 9:4). ‖ A baraita in b. Sanh. 56B.1.13: Seven commandments were given to the children of Noah concerning administration of justice, blasphemy, idolatry, adultery, bloodshed, theft, and the member of a living animal. R. Hanina b. Gamaliel (ca. 120) said, "Also concerning the blood of a living animal (see on this § Acts 15:20 D, II, #1, n. *a*)...." R. Hidqa (ca. 120) said, "Also concerning castration." R. Simeon (ca. 150) said, "Also concerning sorcery. ... Where do we find proof for this?" R. Yohanan († 279) said, "From Gen 2:16." — The itemized proof is then given just as above in S. ʿOlam Rab. 5, except the closing sentence is different: "From every tree of the garden," but not from what is robbed; "you are to eat," but not a member of a living animal. — Then follows: When R. Isaac (ca. 300) came, he taught contrary to the Tannaitic tradition: "He commanded" in Gen 2:16 related to idolatry and "Elohim" to the judges. (The further debate about this then also finds the scriptural proof in Exod 32:8 and Hos 5:11, or in Exod 22:7.) — Parallel passages can be found in Gen. Rab. 34 (20D); Exod. Rab. 30 (89D); Midr. Song. 1:2 (83A); Midr. Prov. 31:29 (55B). ‖ Different traditions about the Noachic commandments. Babylonian Talmud Sanhedrin 56B: In the school of Manasseh (during the tannaitic period) it was taught: Seven commandments were given to the children of Noah: concerning idolatry, adultery, bloodshed, theft, the member of a living animal, castration, and the mixing of two different types. See the additional explanations above in b. Sanh. 56B.1.13. ‖ Babylonian Talmud Ḥullin 92A: "Then they weighed my wage, thirty pieces of silver" (Zech 11:12).... Ulla (ca. 280) said, "This refers to the 30 commandments that the children of Noah took on themselves but of which they kept only three. The one, that they not give males (individuals used for pederasty) a marriage contract; the other, that they not weigh the meat of a killed animal (or also—cf. Rashi ad loc.—of a dead person) in the meat market; the third, that they honor the Torah." ‖ Among texts from an older time, Jub. 7:20 belongs here: "In the 28th Jubilee, Noah began to command his children's children with the ordinances and the commandments and all justice that he knew; and he admonished his children to practice righteousness and to cover the shame of their flesh and to bless the one who created them, and to honor father and mother and to love his neighbor, and to keep themselves from harlotry and all unrighteousness."

d. The Torah offered to the nations on Sinai. Mekilta Exodus 20:2 (74A): (When God revealed himself on Sinai at the giving of the law,) all the kings of the nations of the world gathered together with Balaam, the blasphemer (in order to ask him what God intended). But when they had heard the word from his mouth (that God appeared at the giving of the law [see Mek. Exod. 18:1 (64B)]), they all turned away and each one went to his place. And this is why the nations of the world were called upon (to accept the Torah), so that they would have no excuse in the face of the Shekinah by saying, "If we had been called upon, we would have taken (the Torah) on ourselves long ago." Behold, they were called upon, but they did not take (the Torah) on themselves; for it says, "Yahweh came from Sinai" (Deut 33:2) and revealed himself to the descendants of Esau, the blasphemer, and said to them, "Are you willing to accept the Torah?" They answered him, "What is written in it?" He said to them, "You shall not kill!" They answered, "This is the inheritance that our father bequeathed to us; for it says, 'By your sword you will nourish yourself' (Gen 27:40)." He revealed himself to the children of Ammon and Moab and said to them, "Are you willing to accept the Torah?" They answered him, "What is written in it?" He said to them, "You shall not commit adultery!" They said to him, "We all descend from adultery; for it says, 'Then Lot's two daughters became pregnant by their father' (Gen 19:36); how can we accept it then!" He revealed himself to the children of Ishmael and said to them, "Are you willing to accept the Torah?" They answered him, "What is written in it?" He said, "You shall not steal!" They answered, "Our father was blessed with this blessing; for it says, 'He (Ishmael) will be a wild ass of a man' (Gen 16:12). It also says, 'For stolen, I am stolen' (Gen 40:15)." But when he came to the Israelites with "the fire of the law in his right hand for them" (so the midr. interprets Deut 33:2), then they all opened their mouth and exclaimed, "We want to do and obey everything that the Lord has spoken" (Exod 24:7). — The same is found as a baraita in shorter form in Midr. Lam. 3:1 (69A); a more extended version is found in SDeut 33:2 § 343 (142B) with the conclusion: There was no nation among the nations to which he would not have gone, spoken, and knocked on their door, to see whether they were willing to accept the Torah. And so it says, "All the kings of the earth praised you, Yahweh, when they heard the words of your mouth" (so Midr. Ps. 138:4). Perhaps they heard and accepted! However, it says, "But they do not do the same" (Ezek 33:31 as cited by Yalquṭ; the passage is related by the midr. to the gentiles). It also says, "In wrath and fury I will take revenge on the gentiles, who were not willing to listen" (Mic 5:14). — The same concluding sentences of SDeut 33:2 with some variations are also in Pesiq. 199B; Tanḥ. וזאת הברכה 31B. Here the following explanation comes first: "And he said, 'Yahweh came from Sinai'" (Deut 33:2). This teaches that God circulated the Torah among all nations, but they did not accept it, until he came to the Israelites and they accepted it. For it says in Deut 33:2, "He shone upon them from Seir, these are the sons of Esau, who are the inhabitants of Seir" (this is what בני שעיר appears to mean here; differently, Gen 36:20f.). "He shone from Mount Paran," these are the sons of Ishmael; for it says, "He settled in the wilderness of Paran" (Gen 21:21). It is also written, "He arose and made the earthquake" (Hab 3:6). When God saw that they were not willing to accept the Torah, he made them jump up and skip to gehenna. ‖ Here we should also include passages that claim that at the giving of the law God's voice divided itself into four or seventy voices, in accordance with the number of the four main languages or in accordance with the number of the seventy nations of the earth. This means that God offered his Torah to each of the seventy nations in their own languages. Sifre Deuteronomy 33:2 § 343 (142B): When God revealed himself to give the Torah to Israel, he did not reveal himself in one language but rather in four languages. "And he said, 'Yahweh came from Sinai'" (Deut 33:2): this pertains to the Hebrew language; "he shone upon them from Seir": this pertains to the Roman language (Seir is the location of Esau and Esau = Rome); "he shone from Mount Paran": this pertains to the Arabic language (Paran is the location of Ishmael in Gen 21:21); "and he came וְאָתָא from holy myriads": this pertains to the Aramaic language (because אתא is an Aramaic word). ‖ Babylonian Talmud Šabbat 88B: In the school of R. Ishmael († ca. 135) it was taught: "As a hammer that smashes rocks" (Jer 23:29). As the hammer (blow) is divided into innumerable sparks, so the word that came from the mouth of God (at the giving of the law) divided itself into seventy languages. — In the parallel passage b. Sanh. 34A, the manifold meaning of a passage of Scripture is shown from Jer 23:29. ‖ Midrash Psalm 92 § 3 (202A): R. Joshua (b. Levi [ca. 250] see Yalquṭ Ps. § 795) said, "As when the anvil is struck and the sparks fly here and there"; R. Yose b. Hanina (ca. 280) said, "As when a rock is struck with a hammer and the pieces fly out here and there—just so was it with the 'proclamations in a great host' (Ps 68:12); for God let the word go from his mouth (at the giving of the law) and then it divided into innumerable words (read מאמרות 'words' instead of מאורות 'lights.'" ‖ Babylonian Talmud Šabbat 88B: R. Yohanan († 279) said, "What does 'The Lord gives the word which contains a great host for proclamations' (so Midr. Ps. 68:12) mean?[29] Every single word that went from the mouth of the Almighty divided into 70 languages." ‖ Exodus Rabbah 5 (71A): "Every people saw the voices" (Exod 20:18). It does not say "the voice," but rather "the voices." R. Yohanan († 279) said, "The voice went out and divided into 70 voices, into 70 languages, so that all nations could hear them; and every single people heard the voice in its language and their souls fled; but Israel heard the voices without being damaged." ‖ Exodus Rabbah 28 (88E): "Yahweh spoke these words to your whole assembly with a great voice that did not stop" (so Midr. Deut. 5:19). R. Yohanan († 279) said, "The one voice divided into seven voices and these divided into 70 voices." — The same is given anonymously in Midr. Ps. 92 § 3 (202A).

e. The Torah was made known to the nations on Ebal.[30] The base passage is m. Soṭah 7.5: Then they brought the stones and built the altar and whitewashed it with lime and

---

29. S-B: According to a manuscript reading in Buber, Midr. Ps. 92 § 3 n. 25, Rab Huna († 297) similarly says, "The word of the Torah in which there is a great host of individual regulations." — Rashi on b. Šabb. 88B: "The Lord gives the word of the proclamations that applies to a great host (= all the nations)."

30. S-B: The pseudepigrapha presuppose that it is self-evident that the nations know the Torah; however, the writings do not reflect on whence this knowledge derives; see, e.g., 4 Ezra 3:33ff.: "I (Ezra) have gone here and there among the nations and have seen them in fortune, although they had forgotten your commandments ...; or what generation would have fulfilled your commandments

wrote on it all the words of the Torah in 70 languages; for it says, "Completely understandable" (Deut 27:8; i.e., understandable for everyone, even the gentiles). Then they took the stones and came and spent the night in their place (cf. Deut 27:1–8; Josh 4:1ff; 8:30–32). — The further tradition on this issue is conflicted: whereas in the Tosefta and the Babylonian Talmud the controversy is about whether, according to Deut 27:1–8, the Torah was written on the altar before or after the stones were whitewashed, in the Jerusalem Talmud the issue is the different question of whether the altar stones in Josh 8:30ff. or the stones of the camp (night quarters) in Josh 4:3 were used to write down the Torah. α. Tosefta Soṭah 8.6 (310): R. Judah (ca. 150) said, "The Torah was written on the altar." The scholars answered him, "How then would the nations of the world have been able to learn the Torah (since the altar was immediately whitewashed, whereby the inscription must have been made unreadable)!" He said to them, "God put it into the hearts of the nations to send writers who made a transcript from the stones in 70 languages. In that hour the judgment over the nations of the world was sealed sentencing them to the pit of abyss (= gehenna) (because they knew the Torah but did not keep it)." R. Simeon (ca. 150) said, "The Torah was written on the lime. In what way? The altar was coated and whitewashed with lime and all the words of the Torah were written on this, and beneath them Deut 20:18 was written, 'So that they may not teach you to do all the abhorrent things ....' If you turn, we will accept you." ‖ A baraita in b. Soṭah 35B: How did the Israelites write down the Torah? R. Judah said, "It was written on the stones, as it says, 'Write on the stones all the words of the law' (Deut 27:8), and then they were whitewashed with lime." R. Simeon answered him, "According to your words, how were the nations of the world able to learn the Torah?" He said to him, "God gave them great insight so that they sent writers who flaked off the lime and then transcribed the Torah. And their sentence confining them to the pit of the abyss was sealed, because they could have learned (the Torah) but did not." R. Simeon said, "It was written on the lime and these words were written for them at the bottom, 'So that they may not teach you to do all the abhorrent things ...' (Deut 20:18). From that we learn that the Torah would have been accepted if they penitently turned." Rabbah b. Shela (ca. 325) said, "What was the scriptural basis for R. Simeon? Because it says, 'The nations of the world are to be burned to lime' (Isa 33:12), that is, because of the lime (on which the Torah was written)." By contrast R. Judah interpreted these words in the sense of: "as lime"; just as there is no other destiny for the lime than to be burned, so also are the nations of the world destined for burning (in gehenna). — β. A baraita in y. Soṭah 7.21D.33: "The words of the Torah were written on the stones of the camp (Josh 4:3)." These are the words of R. Judah (ca. 150). R. Yose (ca. 150) said, "They were written on the stones of the altar (Deut 27:1ff.; Josh 8:30ff.)." According to the one who says, "They were written on the stones of the camp (which remained permanently in their place), the nations of the world sent scribes on that day who made a transcript of the Torah that was written in 70 languages." According to the one who says, "They were written on the stones of the altar—were these not there for a short time only then to be hidden?"

(as Israel)? Individuals (among the gentiles) perhaps, who can be named, you will find who have kept your commandments, but nations you will not find." — See also 4 Ezra 7:37; 2 Bar. 48:38ff. in n. g.

(How then could a transcript of the Torah be made in so short a time?) Here too a miracle happened: God gave understanding into the heart of every single nation so that they made a transcript of the Torah which was written in 70 languages. For those who say, "They were written on the stones of the camp," the words in Deut 27:2 speak in their favor: "You are to coat them with lime." (The coat of lime shows that the stones had an eternal destiny.) How does the one who says, "They were written on the stones of the altar," maintain these words: "You are to coat them with lime"? (Since the altar was broken down again after the sacrifice, it did not need a coat at all!) He interprets this as follows: The coat with lime is made as mortar between the individual stones. R. Samuel b. Nahmani (ca. 260) said in the name of R. Jonathan (ca. 220, so read!): "'And the nations of the world are to be burned to lime' (Isa 33:12), that is, from lime (from the stones whitewashed with lime and inscribed with the Torah) they received their judgment, namely death." R. Abba b. Kahana (ca. 310) said in the name of R. Yohanan († 279), "'And the nations are to be completely destroyed חרוב יחרבו' (Isa 60:12), that is, from Horeb (חורב wordplay with 'ח' י) they received their judgment, namely death." (According to R. Yohanan the liability of the pagan world dates already from Sinai; according to R. Jonathan only from Ebal; see the saying of R. Yohanan in TanḥB במדבר § 7 in n. *g* below.)

f. The pagan world did not keep the Adamic and Noachic commandments. Genesis Rabbah 24 (16A): R. Judah b. Simeon (ca. 320) said, "It was determined that the Torah was to be given through the first man, see, 'This book of the histories (= Torah) belongs to Adam' (so Midr. Gen. 5:1). God said, 'This one is the object of my hand, and I should not give it (the Torah) to him?' But then God changed his mind and said, 'If he already could not abide in the six commandments I gave him, how am I to give him the 613 prescriptions, the 248 commandments, and 365 prohibitions! (On this counting of the commandments, see § Matt 22:36, #1.) Therefore, I will not give them to Adam but rather to his descendants,' as it says, 'This book belongs to the descendants of Adam' (so now Midr. Gen. 5:1)." A parallel passage can be found in Midr. Eccl. 3:11 (19A) with the scriptural proof taken from Job 28:27f.: "Then he beheld her (Wisdom = Torah) ... and said, 'She is not for Adam (לא אדם = לאדם)!'" ‖ Sifre Deuteronomy 32:28 § 322 (138A): "They are a people of lost counsel" (Deut 32:28).... R. Nehemiah (ca. 150) interpreted this in relation to the nations: "the nations (God says) have lost the seven commandments which I gave them." ‖ Leviticus Rabbah 13 (114B): Ulla of Beri (= Ulla b. Ishmael, ca. 280?) said in the name of R. Simeon b. Yohai (ca. 150), "It is like a man who went out to the threshing floor and his dog and his donkey were with him. On his donkey he loaded 5 *seahs* and on his dog 2 *seahs*. The donkey left with it, but the dog squatted. Then he removed 1 *seah* from the dog and laid it on the donkey; nevertheless, he squatted. He said to the dog, 'When you are loaded, you squat; when you are not loaded, you squat.' Just so since the children of Noah could not remain in the 7 commandments that they had accepted, he (God) came and loaded them on the Israelites." — The same is given anonymously in SDeut 33:2 § 343 (142B). ‖ A baraiata in b. Yebam. 48B: R. Hananiah b. Gamaliel (ca. 120) said, "Why are the proselytes hard-pressed in this time and why do sufferings visit them? Because they (before their conversion) did not keep the 7 commandments of the children of Noah." ‖ Mekilta Exodus (74A): R. Simeon b. Eleazar (ca. 190) said,

"If the children of Noah could not abide in the 7 commandments that were entrusted to them and which they had taken on themselves, how much less could they have done so with the commandments in the Torah. It is like a king who hired two overseers; the one he set over the supply of straw, and the other over the treasury of silver and gold. The one appointed over the straw brought himself under suspicion (because of a lack of loyalty) and mumbled that he had not been put in charge of the treasury of silver and gold. Then the one in charge of the silver and gold said to him, 'You fool, you have failed to accept responsibility (made misappropriations) with straw, so how much more would you have done so with silver and gold!' Is not the inference from the lesser to the greater warranted here? Since the children of Noah already were not able to abide in the 7 commandments, how much less would they have been able to abide in the 613 commandments." ‖ Babylonian Talmud ʿAbodah Zarah 2A.14; 2B.43: R. Hanina b. Papa (ca. 300) (according to others, R. Simlai [ca. 250]) said in a presentation, "… Immediately God will say to them (the gentiles who justify themselves in the last judgment because of their nonobservance of the Torah), 'Let the former things be taught to us,' as it says, 'Let them declare the former things to us' (Isa 43:9)." When have you kept the 7 commandments which you adopted? How do we know that they did not keep these? Rab Joseph († 333) taught as a tannaitic tradition, "'He arose and shook the earth; he saw and absolved the gentiles' (so Midr. Hab. 3:6). What did he see? He saw the 7 commandments that the children of Noah took on themselves but did not keep. Since they did not keep them, he arose and absolved them of them. Yet in that case they would have benefited (from their disobedience)! If this were so, we would find that the sinner is still rewarded." Mar bar Rabina (ca. 400) responded, "It means that they, even if they keep them (after they are freed from them), will receive no reward for them." — See the whole passage in the excursus "Depictions of the Judgment in Ancient Jewish Literature." See also b. B. Qam. 38A.5, 14.

g. The gentile world did not observe the Torah. 2 Baruch 48:38ff.: "At that (end-)time the change of the times will be made clearly visible for everyone, because they defiled themselves in all those times and they practiced deception and each one walked in his (own) ways and did not remember the law of the Most High. Therefore, fire will consume their plans and the considerations of their innards will be tested by the flame—for the judge will come and will not tarry—because each of the inhabitants of the earth could have known when he acted sinfully but they did not know my law because of their pride." ‖ 4 Ezra 7:37: "Then (in the last judgment) the Most High will speak to the nations who have awakened, 'Now look and know the one you have denied (= God), whom you have not served, whose commandments you have scorned.'" ‖ Mekilta Exodus (70A): R. Eliezer b. Yose the Galilean (ca. 150) said, "See, it says, 'He makes his word known to Jacob, his statutes and laws to Israel; he did not do so with any gentile nation' (Ps 147:19f). What have these unfortunate gentiles done that he was not willing to give the Torah to them? Answer: Laws, which they do not know, because they were not willing to accept them (see Hab 3:3–6)." ‖ Babylonian Talmud ʿAbodah Zarah 2B: (R. Hanina b. Papa, ca. 300 [according to others, R. Simlai, ca. 250] said in a presentation that the nations will say to God at the last judgment:) "Lord of the world, did you give us the Torah at all so that we did not accept it?

But how can something like this be said! It is written in Deut 33:2: 'Yahweh came from Sinai and shone upon them from Seir.' Further, it says, 'God came from Teman and the Holy One from Mount Paran' (so the Midr. on Hab 3:3)." What did he want in Seir and what did he want in Paran? R. Yohanan († 279) said, "This teaches that God circulated the Torah in every nation and language but they did not accept it until he came to Israel and they accepted it. Rather they will say (in the last judgment), 'Did we then accept it in any way so that we did not keep it?' But this is just their misfortune, because they did not accept it!" ‖ Pesiqta 200A: R. Abbahu (ca. 300) said, "It was manifest and well-known to the one who spoke and the world was made that the nations of the world would not accept the Torah. Why did he do his duty to them (by offering them the Torah)? Because this is the kind of God he is: he does not punish before he has done his duty to his creatures. Only then does he strike them out of the world, for God does not come with tyranny over his creatures." — The same is found in Tanḥ. וזאת הברכה 31B. ‖ Midrash Lamentations 3:1 (69A): R. Joshua of Sikhnin (ca. 330) said in the name of R. Levi (ca. 300), "'I am the man' (Lam 3:1); I am the one who is accustomed to chastisements (sufferings); why do you bother me? It is like a king who became angry with his matron and cast her out and removed her from the palace. She went and pressed her face behind a pillar. It happened that the king passed by and saw her. He said to her, 'Do you want to defiantly disguise your behavior?' She answered him, 'My lord king, is this (the way I was treated) at all lovely for me and pleasant and worthy of me? For no other woman took you but me!' He answered her, 'It was I who despised all women because of you!' She said to him, 'In that case, why did you then go into this and that entrance, into this and that court, into this and that place?' Not because of this and that woman? She did not take you, though! In the same way God said to the Israelites, 'You want (in your misfortune) to defiantly disguise your behavior?' They said before him, 'Lord of the world, is this lovely for us and pleasant and worthy of us? For no other nation accepted your Torah but I.' He answered them 'I am the one who despised all nations because of you!' They said to him, 'In that case, why did you have your Torah circulated among all nations?' They did not accept it, though." ‖ TanḥumaB במדבר § 7 (4A): Six names were given for it (Sinai): Mountain of God, Mount Basan, Many-peaked Mountain הַר גַּבְנֻנִּים (Ps 68:16), Mountain of Delight (Ps 68:17), Mount Horeb and Mount Sinai. ... Mount Sinai, because on it the nations of the world became loathsome to God נשתנאו (wordplay on סיני), and he spoke his judgment on them, as it says, "The gentiles are to be completely destroyed" (Isa 60:12) (because they despised the Torah). R. Abba b. Kahana (ca. 310) said in the name of R. Yohanan († 279), "The gentiles (*goyim*) will be destroyed because of Horeb, because there they received judgment (because of their rejection of the Torah)." — The same is found in Tanḥ. במדבר 187A; Num. Rab. 1 (135D); the saying of R. Yohanan is also found in y. Soṭah 7.21D.33 (see above in n. *e*) and Tanḥ. תצוה 107 A. ‖ Exodus Rabbah 5 (71A): How did the voice (of God at the giving of the law) go out? R. Tanḥuma (ca. 380) said, "With a double face: it killed the nations who did not accept the Torah, and it gave life to the Israelites who accepted it. This is what Moses said to them at the end of the forty years, 'Who is there of all flesh who would have heard the voice of the living God out of the fire, as we have, and remained alive?' (Deut 5:26). You (Israel) heard his voice and remained alive, but the nations of the world heard it and died." – The same is found in Tanḥ. שמות 65B. ‖ Exodus Rabbah 17 (79D): "Take a bunch of hyssop" (Exod 12:22). This is meant in Song 2:3 as well, "As an apple tree under the trees of the woods." Why is God compared (by Solomon in the Song of Songs) with an apple? In order to tell you: As an apple appears just like that to the eye and in it is flavor and aroma, so it acts like God. "His gums are sweets and he himself is nothing but charms" (Song 5:16). And he appeared to the nations of the world, but they did not wish to accept the Torah, because in their eyes the Torah was like something in which there is nothing. And yet therein is flavor and aroma. On flavor, see Ps 34:9: "Taste and see that Yahweh is good." And therein is enjoyment; see Prov 8:19: "Better is my fruit than exquisite and fine gold." And therein is aroma; see Song 4:11: "The scent of your clothes is like the scent of Lebanon." But the Israelites said, "We know the power of the Torah, so we do not diverge from God and his Torah;" for it says in Song 2:3: "It delighted me to sit in his shade, and his fruit is sweet to my palate." ‖ See also the citations in notes *d* and *e*.

1:21 A: They did not praise him as God or give thanks.

The pride of gentiles, which withholds honor from God, and the ungratefulness of the gentiles, which forgets God, are castigated in the following examples:

Babylonian Talmud Ḥullin 89A: R. Yohanan († 279) said in the name of R. Eleazar b. Simeon (ca. 180), "Everywhere where you find the words of R. Eliezer b. Yose the Galilean (ca. 150) in the Haggadah, make your ears like a funnel (so you do not miss the smallest word)." "Not because you were more numerous than all the nations did Yahweh become devoted to you" (Deut 7:7). God said to Israel, "I became devoted to you because you yourselves made yourselves small before me when I richly bestowed greatness upon you. I bestowed greatness on Abraham, and he said to me, 'Although I am dust and ash' (Gen 18:27); I bestowed greatness upon Moses and Aaron, and they said, 'We, who are we?' (Exod 16:17.) The same with David, and he said, 'I am a worm and not a man' (Ps 22:7). But it was not so with the nations of the world. I bestowed greatness upon Nimrod, and he said, 'Now then, we will build ourselves a city' (Gen 11:4); I bestowed greatness upon pharaoh, and he said, 'Who is Yahweh, that I should listen to his voice?' (Exod 5:2). The same with Sennacherib, who said, 'Who among all the gods of the countries would have freed your land from my hand?' (2 Kgs 18:35)! The same with Nebuchadnezzar, who said, 'I will rise to the heights of the clouds, I will make myself like the Most High' (Isa 14:14). The same with Hiram, the king of Tyre, who said, 'I am a god, I inhabit a seat of the gods in the heart of the seas' (Ezek 28:2)." ‖ See b. Ḥag. 13A (= b. Pesaḥ. 94A) at § Matt 11:23 A. ‖ Exodus Rabbah 5 (71C): "After this Moses and Aaron went and said to pharaoh, 'Yahweh, the God of Israel, has spoken thus, "Let my people go so that they may celebrate a festival for me in the wilderness" (Exod 5:1).'" R. Hiyya bar Abba (ca. 280) said, "That day was the day of the reception of the delegation in the house of pharaoh. All kings came to honor him and they brought crowns to him as gifts and they crowned him; for it was the day on which he was elevated to be the ruler of the world; they had also brought their gods along with them. When they had crowned him, Moses and Aaron stepped into the door of pharaoh's palace.

The servants went in and announced, 'Two old men stand at the door.' He answered, 'They may enter.' When they had entered, he looked at them, to see whether they wanted perhaps to crown him or present him a letter. But they did not even greet him. Then he said to them, 'Who are you?' They answered, 'We are ambassadors of the Holy One—blessed be he!' 'What do you want?' asked the king. They said 'Yahweh has spoken thus, "Let my people go!"' Then the king became angry and said, 'Who is Yahweh, that I should listen to his voice, to let Israel go? He did not think to send me a crown. He comes to me with words alone. I do not know Yahweh, and I will not let Israel go either.' Then he said, 'Wait until I have searched in my book.' At once he went into a room in his palace and looked at every nation and its gods. He began to read, 'The gods of Moab, the gods of Ammon, the gods of Sidon ....' 'I have looked for his name in my secret archive, he said to them, but I have not found it.'" R. Levi (ca. 300) told a parable which makes a comparison of a priest who had a silly slave. The priest went out to the city, and the slave went to look for his master on a burial ground. He began to call to the people who were there, "Have you not seen my master here?" They responded to him, "Is your master not a priest?" He answered, "Yes!" Then they said to him, "You fool, who has seen a priest on a burial ground!" So too Moses and Aaron said to pharaoh, "You fool, it is indeed customary to seek the dead among the living, but also the living among the dead! Our God is a living God. However, those you are talking about are dead. But our God is a living God and an eternal king!" pharaoh answered, "Is he young or old? How many years old? How many cities has he defeated? How many countries has he conquered? How many years ago did he come to power?" They answered, "The power and strength of our God fill the world. He existed before the world was created, and he will exist at the end of the whole world. He formed you and put the spirit of life in you." He responded, "What does he do then?" They said, "He stretches out the heavens and established the earth. His voice cleaves flames of fire, he topples mountains, and dashes rocks. His bow is fire, his arrows are flames, his spear is a firebrand, his shield is the clouds and his sword is lightning. He is the one who fashions mountains and hills, he covers the mountains with herbage, he causes the rain and dew to come down, he makes the grass grow and hears the animals. He forms a child in its mother's womb and leads it out into the air of the world. He topples kings and appoints kings (cf. Dan 2:21)." He answered them, "From the beginning you have spoken a lie, for I am the Lord of the world. I created myself and the Nile (see: "Mine is the Nile, and I made it" [Ezek 29:9])." In that hour he assembled all the wise men of Egypt and said to them, "Have you heard of the name of the God of this people?" They answered, "We have heard that he is a son of wise men and a son of kings of the past!" Then God said, "You call yourselves wise men and me a son of wise men (see: 'The wisest of pharaoh's counselors, their counsel is stultifying' [Isa 19:11]); how can you then say to pharaoh, 'I am a son of the wise, a son of previous kings?' See what is written of them, 'Fools, the princes of Zoan, the wisest of pharaoh's counselors, are fools' (Isa 19:11), and 'The wisdom of his wise men will be lost and the sense of his sensible ones will be hidden' (Isa 29:14)." – Then pharaoh answered them, "I do not know about your God, who he is, as it says, 'Who is Yahweh, that I should listen to his voice!' (Exod 5:2)." – In Midr. Prov. 27:17 (51A), R. Zeira (ca. 300) is named as the author; the beginning (the saying of R. Hiyya bar Abba) is also found in TanḥB וארא §2 (10A); the parable of R. Levi is likewise found in TanḥB וארא §2 (10A); the parable is found in altered form in Lev. Rab. 6 (109C). ‖ Exodus Rabbah 30 (89A): "The strength of the king lies in his love of justice" (so Midr. Ps. 99:4). When will power be attributed to God? In the hour when he makes his judgment among the nations. So you find it to be thus in the case of Nebuchadnezzar, the blasphemer; since he proudly exalted himself and said, "Is this not the great Babylon" (Dan 4:27)? God said to him, "You blasphemer, foul dankness, you proudly exalt yourself and say, 'By the strength of my power and to the honor of my glory' (Dan 4:27)? Do you not know that everything is mine? Greatness is mine, power is mine, majesty is mine and glory is mine. And so David said, 'Yours, O Yahweh, is the greatness and the power and the glory' (1 Chr 29:11); and further he said, 'Yahweh, my God, you are very great' (Ps 104:1)." God said to Nebuchadnezzar, "The bit of dominion that has been given to you stems from me." Daniel also spoke thus to him, "You, O king, to whom the God of heaven has granted dominion, power, strength and honor" (Dan 2:37). And you say: "By the strength of my power and to the honor of my glory"? Then you can see: The strength of the king lies in his love of justice. ‖ TanḥumaB ויקרא §17 (5B): When God judges all people in the future age, he will judge them with the sorcerers and adulterers (see Mal 3:5: "I will draw near to you for judgment, and will be a swift witness concerning the sorcerers and adulterers and those who swear false oaths.") Then he will declare them guilty and throw them into gehenna. God says, "With what I have given you so that you might praise and worship my name, you have cursed and slandered me and sworn falsely by my name. All creatures have been created to praise me, as it says, 'Yahweh created everything for his own sake' (Prov 16:4). And it is not enough that you do not praise me, but you also curse me!" Scripture says, "The godless are like the tossing sea" (Isa 57:20). Like the waves in the sea they proudly raise themselves high, and when each one of them has reached the shore, it is broken and retreats, and the other wave sees this, and although it too will be broken, it nevertheless raises itself proudly without turning back. So too the godless see each the other and proudly exalt themselves. Therefore they are compared with the sea (see Isa 57:20). All generations, the generation of Enosh, that of the flood, that of the destruction, have not learned from one another, but rather have proudly exalted themselves. Therefore, the godless are like the tossing sea. The godless have no rest in the world, but the righteous have rest (see Jer 30:10: "Jacob will return and have rest light-heartedly and undisturbed." ‖ See Midr. Ps. 2 § 4 (13A) along with parallels at § Heb 1:5 A, #3. ‖ Midrash Song of Songs 8:14 (134A): R. Levi (ca. 300) said, "It is like a king, who hosted a meal and invited the guests. Some of them ate and drank and praised the king, and some of them ate and drank and cursed the king. The king noticed this and wanted to bring dismay among them at his meal and disrupt this. Then the matron came up and interceded for them. She said, 'My lord king, instead of looking at those who eat and drink and curse you, look at those who eat and drink and praise you and extol your name.' Likewise, when the Israelites eat and drink and praise and extol and worship God, he hears their voice and is appeased. But when the nations of the world eat and drink and blaspheme God and revile him with their fornication which they discuss, in that hour God thinks of even destroying his world. Then the Torah approaches and intercedes and says, 'Lord of the world, instead of looking at those who blaspheme and enrage you, look on your people Israel who praise and extol and worship your great name with thanksgiving and songs and hymns.' And the holy spirit (who speaks in Scripture) calls, 'Flee, my companion' (Song 8:14), flee from the nations of the world and bind yourself to Israel." ‖ Among the pseudepigrapha, reference may be made to 1 Enoch 46:5: "He (the Messiah) will cast the kings from their thrones and from their kingdoms, because they do not exalt or praise him or gratefully recognize whence the kingdom has been conferred upon them." ‖ 4 Ezra 8:60: "For the Most High did not want men to perish. Rather the creatures themselves have dishonored the name of the one who made them and shown ungratefulness to the one who prepared life for them." ‖ 2 Baruch 82:3–9: "Now we see the fullness of the prosperity of the nations, while they act godlessly, and yet they are like a breath. And we behold the extent of their dominion, while they commit iniquity, and yet they will be made like a drop. And we see the strength of their power, while they oppose the Almighty year after year, and yet they will be counted as spittle. And we consider the glory of their greatness, while they do not observe the commandments of the Most High, and yet they will pass away like smoke. And we contemplate the beauty of their splendor, while they live in impurities, and yet they will wither like the grass that dries up. And we consider the strength of their cruel severity, while they do not think about the end, and yet they will be dispersed like a wave that flows by. And we observe their ostentatious power, while they deny the goodness of God who gave them (it), and yet they will pass away like a wave which goes by." ‖ See 2 Bar. 48:38ff. at § Rom 1:20 E, n. g.

1:21 B: They became futile (ἐματαιώθησαν) in their thoughts.

Μάταια, ματαιοῦσθαι *saepe dicitur de idolis eorumque cultu et cultoribus* (2 Kgs 17:15; Jer 2:5); *nam objecto suo conformator mens*, Bengel.

Wisdom 13:1: "All people were futile μάταιοι by nature, for whom ignorance of God was suited (see the whole passage at § Rom 1:20 D, n. *a.* ‖ Deuteronomy Rabbah 1 (196A): R. Levi b. Lahma (ca. 250, so read instead of b. Hama) said, "If the idolater becomes like the idol itself, as it is written, 'Their makers will be like them' (Ps 115:8), should not then the one who serves God all the more become like him? How do we know this? It is written, 'Blessed is the man who trusts in Yahweh. He will be (like) Yahweh as a result of his trust' (so Midr. Jer. 17:7)." ‖ Jerusalem Talmud ʿAbodah Zarah 4.44A.44: R. Zeira (ca. 300) said, "If it said in Ps 115:8, 'Their "worshipers" will be like them (the idols),' the difficulty would be that the worshipers of the sun will be like the sun, the worshipers of the moon like the moon. But it says in Ps 115:8, 'Their "makers" will be like them.'" R. Mani (II, ca. 370) said, "(Even) if it were written, 'Their "worshipers" will be like them,' there would be no difficulty; for it says in Isa 24:23, 'The moon will blush and the sun will go pale' (thus also the end of their worshipers will be shame)."

1:22: Boasting that they were wise, they became fools.

1. A similar thought may underlie the exposition in b. Sanh. 109A: R. Jeremiah b. Eleazar (ca. 270) said, "(The generation of the tower in

Gen 11) divided into three parties. The one said, 'We want to go up and live there (on the tower).' The other said, 'We want to go up and practice idolatry.' The third said, 'We want to go up and wage war (with God).' The one that said, 'We want to go up and live there,' Yahweh scattered; the one that said, 'We want to go up and wage war,' became apes, spirits, demons, and night ghosts; and concerning the one that said, 'We want to go up and commit idolatry, in their case Yahweh confused the language of all the people of the earth.'" ‖ See similar entries at § Rom 1:21 A above.

2. Pride destroys the wisdom of the wise.

Babylonian Talmud Pesaḥim 66B: Rab Judah († 299) said that Rab († 247) said, "If a man is wise, wisdom vanishes from him if he proudly boasts המתיהר. If he is a prophet, his prophecy (prophetic gift) vanishes from him."

1:23 A: They exchanged the glory of the immortal God.

1. καὶ ἤλλαξαν τὴν δόξαν τοῦ ἀφθάρτου θεοῦ. — This follows Ps 106:20 and Jer 2:11. Septuagint Psalm 106:20: καὶ ἠλλάξαντο τὴν δοξαν αὐτῶν ἐν ὁμοιώματι μόσχου ἔσθοντος χόρτον. — Septuagint Jeremiah 2:11: ὁ δὲ λαός μου ἠλλάξατο τὴν δόξαν αὐτοῦ, ἐξ ἧς οὐκ ὠφεληθήσονται.

Mekilta Exodus (40A): R. Pappos (ca. 110) said in a presentation, "'They exchanged their glory (the one who was their glory, i.e., God) for the image of a bull that eats grass' (Ps 106:20). I could understand this about the bull of the world above (see Ezek 1:10). There Scripture teaches, 'that eats grass.'" R. Aqiba († ca. 135) said to him, "Enough, Pappos!" He answered him, "How do you understand, 'They exchanged their glory for the image of a bull that eats grass'?" "I understand it to refer to an (earthly) bull below. Perhaps a bull at all possible times of the year?[31] Scripture teaches, 'that eats grass'; there is nothing uglier and more detestable than a bull at the time when it eats grass." — Parallel passages can be found in Midr. Song. 1:9 (90B); Midr. Ps. 106 § 6 (228A). ‖ In Mek. Exod. (46B) R. Judah (ca. 150) lists Jer 2:11 and Ps 106:20 among the passages in which Scripture removed offensive statements about God by means of veiled circumlocution. R. Judah said, "'... My people has exchanged its glory' (Jer 2:11); Scripture used a circumlocution (it should say 'my glory'). Likewise: 'They exchanged their glory for the image of a bull' (Ps 106:20); Scripture used a circumlocution (it should say my glory)." — The same is found anonymously in SNum 10:35 § 84 (22B) and Tanḥ. בשלח 82B; here there is the addition that the change is an improvement תִיקוּן by the Sopherim, the men of the great synagogue (at Ezra's time). ‖ Midrash Song of Songs 1:6 (88B): R. Isaac (ca. 300) said, "A woman who dwelled in the city once had an Ethiopian slave who went down with her companion to get water from a well. She said to her companion, 'My companion, tomorrow my master will dismiss his wife and take me as his wife.' The other one responded, 'Why then?' She said, 'Because he has seen her hands with soot on them (blackened).' The other one answered, 'You biggest fool in the world, let your ears hear what your mouth says! If you say about his wife who

31. S-B: This is what בשור של ימות השנה appears to mean. Midrash Song of Songs 1:9: בשיר של שאר ימות השנה. Midrash Psalm 106 § 6: בימי ניסן שהוא מזוהם.

is dear to him above all else that he wishes to dismiss her because he saw her hands with soot on them for a moment, how much more does that go for you who were completely sooted and black your whole life from your mother's womb!' So also Israel says, 'When the nations of the world slander and say, "This nation has exchanged its glory, as it says, 'They exchanged their glory ...' (Ps 106:20)": If we incurred so much guilt in a short moment (because of the golden calf), how much more does that go for you!' Israel further says to the nations of the world, 'We will tell you whom we are like. Like a king's son who went out to the commons of a city. The sun fell on his head (he got sunstroke) and his face became yellow. He went back into the city, and with a little water and with a few baths from the bathhouses his body became white again, and he returned to his beauty, as he was before. So are we, when the sun of idolatry tanned us (cf. Song 1:6B). But you are tanned from your mother's womb. While you were still in your mother's womb, you served idols. How so? If a woman became pregnant, went into the house of her idol, bowed and worshiped the idol, she herself did so along with her child (in her womb).'" ‖ The reference to Ps 106:20 in b. Tem. 28B is irrelevant for our passage.

2. How did the ancient synagogue think of the gods of the gentiles?

A. The gods of the gentiles are angels to whom God subjected the 70 nations of the world. In 1 Enoch 89:59ff., they are called "shepherds," and in rabbinic literature שָׂרֵי אוּמּוֹת הָעוֹלָם "(angel) rulers of the nations of the world" (cf. Dan 10:13, 20f.).

Septuagint Deuteronomy 32:8f.: "When the Most High distributed the nations, as he dispersed the sons of Adam (at the time of the confusion of the languages), he established the boundaries of the nations according to the number of the angels of God (variant reading: according to the number of the children of Israel). And the Lord's portion became his people Jacob, Israel his possession apportioned to him." ‖ Sirach 17:14: "For each people he (God) appointed an (angel-)ruler ἡγούμενον; but the Lord's portion is Israel." ‖ 1 Enoch 89:59f.: "He (God) called 70 shepherds and cast those sheep (Israel), in order to pasture them, and said to the shepherds and their companions, 'Each one of you is to pasture the sheep from now on and do everything that I will command you. And I will deliver them to you precisely numbered and will tell you who of them is to be killed and kill these!' Then he ceded those sheep to them." (As long as the nations of the world rule over the Israelites, the latter are handed over into the hand of the angel-rulers of the nations; but God watches that no hardships happen to them unduly.) See Jub. 15:30ff.: "But he (God) chose Israel, that they would be his people. And he sanctified them and gathered them from all the children of men; for many are the nations and numerous are the people, and they all (belong) to him, and he gave the spirits power over everyone, so that they made them stray from (behind) him. But over Israel he gave no angel or spirits power. Rather he alone is their sovereign, and he protects them and claims them for himself out of the hand of his angels and out of the hand of his spirits and out of the hand of all his powers, so that he may protect them and bless them, and they may belong to him, and he may belong to them from now until eternity." ‖ Testament of Naphtali (Hebrew) 8ff.: "I (Naphtali) warn you ... not to forget Yahweh your God, the God of your fathers, whom our father Abraham chose when the races (of men) were separated from one another in the days of Peleg. For then the Holy One came down from his high heaven and made the 70 angels of service come down (with him) and Michael was at their head. He spoke and commanded each one of them to teach 70 languages to the 70 generations of those who descended from the loins of Noah. The angels immediately came down and did as their creator had commanded. And the holy language, the Hebrew language, remained only in the house of Shem and Eber and in the house of our father Abraham, who belongs to their descendants. On that day, however, Michael delivered a message from the Holy One, the One who is highly to be praised, and said to the 70 nations, to each one in particular, 'You know the waste that burdens you, and the plot which you have developed against the Lord of heavens and earth. And now, choose for yourselves today whom you will serve, and who your intercessor in the heavenly world will be!' Then the godless Nimrod answered and said, 'For me there is no one greater than the one who taught me and my people the language of Cush in one hour!' And Phut and Mizraim and Tubal and Javan and Meshek and Tiras answered, and likewise each nation chose their (guardian) angel, and not a single one of them mentioned the name of the Holy one, the One who is highly to be praised. But as soon as Michael said to our father Abraham, 'Abram, whom will you choose and whom will you serve?' Then Abraham answered, 'I select and choose none other than the One who spoke and the world came into being, who formed me in my mother's womb, one body in the middle of another body, and put spirit and soul in it. I choose him and I will devote myself to him, I and my descendants for all eternity!' Hereupon the Most High divided the nations and gave them over and delimited for each nation their portion and lot. And from that time all nations of the earth were divided by the Most High; only the house of Abraham still remained with its creator to serve him, and after him Isaac and Jacob." ‖ Targum Yerušalmi I Genesis 11:7f.: "Yahweh said to the 70 angels who stand before him, 'Come now, let us go down and confuse their languages there so that no one will any longer understand the language the other.' Then the Memra of Yahweh appeared over the place and with it 70 angels, corresponding to the 70 nations and the individual languages of its nations. From then on, he bound his hands (those of the individual angel) and 'scattered them (humanity) from there over the surface of the whole earth' in 70 languages so that each one did not understand what the other said." ‖ Targum Yerušalmi I Deuteronomy 32:8f.: "When the Most High gave the world as a possession to the nations who had gone forth from the sons of Noah, when he separated writing systems and languages for the children of men at the time of the scattering, at the same time he cast their lot with the 70 angels, the rulers of the nations, with whom he had appeared to look at the city (Gen 11:7f.); at the same time he established the boundaries of the nations according to the sum of the number of the 70 souls of Israel who went down to Egypt. And when the holy people fell to the lot of the Lord of the world, Michael opened his mouth and said, 'This is a good portion, for the name of the Memra of Yahweh (namely אֵל) is in it (namely in יִשְׂרָאֵל).' Then Gabriel opened his mouth to worship and said, 'The house of Jacob is the lot of his possession.'" ‖ Midrash Song of Songs 2:1 (95A): R. Eleazar of Modiim († ca. 135) said, "One day in the future (at the last judgment) the ruling angels of the nations will come to indict the Israelites before God. They will say, 'Lord of the world, these (the nations) have committed idolatry, and those (the Israelites) have committed idolatry; these have committed fornication, and those have committed fornication; these have shed blood and those have shed blood ....'" – See the whole passage with parallels in the excursus "Depictions of the Judgment in Ancient Jewish Literature." ‖ Pesiqta Rabbati 21 (103B): R. Yose b. Halapta (ca. 150) said, "These (the myriads of angels who according to the haggadic interpretation of Ps 68:18 accompanied God at the giving of the law) were the ruling angels of the nations of the world." And why did they come down? R. Hiyya b. Abba (ca. 280, so read instead of Rabba) said, "For the honor of the Torah." R. Hiyya b. Yose (ca. 260) said, "For the honor of Israel." ‖ Pesiqta 151A: R. Berekhiah (ca. 340) and R. Helbo (ca. 300) said in the name of R. Simeon b. Yosena in the name of R. Meir (ca. 150), "(Jacob's dream about the heavenly ladder [Gen 28:12]) teaches that God showed our father Jacob the ruling angel of Babylon שרה של בבל, how he ascended and then descended again, and did the same with the ruling angel of Media and that of Greece and that of Edom (= Rome), how each one of them ascended and then descended again. Then God said, 'Jacob, you too, ascend!' In the moment our father Jacob was afraid and said (in himself), 'Maybe there is also for me a descent, just as there was a descent for those.' God said, '"Do not fear, Israel" (Jer 30:10). If you ascend, there will never be a descent for you.' But he did not believe and did not ascend." – The same is found in Lev. Rab. 29 (127A), but here instead of R. Simeon b. Yosena the saying is erroneously attributed to R. Simeon b. Yohai; in Tanḥ. ויצא 35B, R. Meir's name has dropped out; in Midr. Ps. 78 § 6 (174A), there are amplifications that derive from the next citation. ‖ Pesiqta 150B: R. Samuel b. Nahman (ca. 260) said, "(The angels on Jacob's heavenly ladder) were the ruling angels of the nations of the world." For R. Samuel b. Nahman said, "This teaches that God showed our father Jacob the ruling angel of Babylon, how he ascended 70 rungs, the ruling angel of Media, how he ascended 52 rungs, the ruling angel of Greece, how he ascended 180 rungs, and the ruling angel of Edom (Rome), how he ascended and kept ascending on and on without knowing how far. In the moment our father Jacob was afraid and said, 'Perhaps there is no descent for this one!'[32] But God said to him, '"Fear not, Israel" (Jer 30:10)! Even if you saw him sitting virtually כִּבְיָכוֹל at my side, I will cast him down from there, as it says, "If you (Edom; Obad 1:1) soar high like the eagle, and if you make your nest among the stars, I will cast you down from there, says Yahweh" (Obad 1:4).'" – Parallel passages can be found in Lev. Rab. 29 (127A); Tanḥ. ויצא 35A. ‖ Mekilta Exodus (43B): When the Israelites saw the ruling angel of the kingdom (Egypt) falling down, they began to strike up a song of praise.... Likewise, you will find that God in the future will not punish the kingdoms before he has first punished their ruling angels. For it says, "On that day Yahweh will visit affliction on the rulers on high (i.e., the ruling angels)" (Isa 24:21), and only then does it say, "And the kings of the earth on the earth." Additionally: "How you have fallen from heaven, you brilliant star, son of the dawn (= ruling angel)" (Isa 14:12), and after that it says, "You have been felled to the earth, who shone down on the nations." Additionally:

32. S-B: The numbers 70, 52, and 180 provide the years of the duration of the dominion of the individual kingdoms in agreement with the chronology of S. 'Olam Rab., which was received by the synagogue. Rome's dominion had still not come to an end at the time of R. Samuel b. Nahman, so its angel ascends higher and higher.

"When my sword has finished in heaven (= with the ruling angels)" (Isa 34:5), and then follows, "Behold, it will travel over Edom." – The notion that ruling angels were punished before their nations was later generally acknowledged; see b. Sukkah 29A and the next citations. ‖ Midrash Samuel 18 § 1 (49B): R. Hanina (ca. 225) said, "God never punishes a nation before he has first punished their ruling angel in heaven (see Isa 24:21; Gen 6:2, 5, 7; Exod 17:8 compared with Deut 25:17)." ‖ Exodus Rabbah 21 (83C): R. Eleazar b. Pedat (ca. 270) said, "When the Israelites went out of Egypt, they raised their eyes, and the Egyptians had pursued them, as it says, 'pharaoh drew near ... and behold, Mizraim came up behind them' (Exod 14:10). It does not say 'they came,' but rather 'he came.' When pharaoh and Egypt came out to pursue them, the Israelites raised their eyes to heaven and saw the ruling angel of Egypt flying in the air. When they saw him, they became very afraid (see Exod 14:10). What does 'And behold, Mizraim came up behind them' mean then? The name of the ruling angel of Egypt was Mizraim (Egypt); for God does not overthrow a people before he has first overthrown their ruling angel. So you find also in the case of Nebuchadnezzar that God first overthrew his ruling angel, as it says, 'The word was still in the king's mouth when the *qol* ("voice") fell from heaven.'" R. Joshua b. Abin (in the 4th cent.) said, "The ruling angel of Nebuchadnezzar had the name 'Qol,' and God cast him down. Likewise, the ruling angel of pharaoh had the name Mizraim, who had flown by to pursue Israel. When God drowned the Egyptians in the sea, he first drowned their ruling angel (see Exod 14:27: 'Yahweh threw Mizraim into the heart of the sea'; this was the ruling angel of the Egyptians; and after that he threw pharaoh and his army into it). Likewise, Exod 15:1 does not say that he cast 'their steeds and riders' into the sea but rather 'steed and its rider'; thereby their ruling angel is meant. In accordance with this Exod 14:9 should also be interpreted: 'Mizraim chased them.'" – See Exod. Rab. 15 (77B); Deut. Rab. 1 (196D). ‖ Midrash Song of Songs 8:14 (134B): עַל הָרֵי בְשָׂמִים "on the mountains of balsam" (Song 8:14). R. Simeon (ca. 280) said, "God said, 'Wait for me until I sit in judgment over their (the nations') "mountains,"' that is, over their ruling angels which are located with me in heaven." (הרי בשמים therefore = הרי בַּשָּׁמַיִם = mountains or rulers in heaven.) ... With reference to the word of R. Isaac (ca. 300), "God does not punish a people below before he has abased its ruling angel above," R. Huna (ca. 350) said, "And in favor of this, there are five passages of Scripture. The first passage of Scripture: 'On that day God will visit affliction on the host on high (= ruling angels).' After that it is written, 'And the kings of the earth on the earth' (Isa 24:21). The second passage of Scripture: 'How you have fallen from heaven, you brilliant star, son of the dawn (= ruling angel).' Then it is written, 'You have been felled to the earth ...' (Isa 14:12). The third passage of Scripture: 'When my sword has finished in heaven (with the ruling angels),' and then, 'Behold, it will come down over Edom' (Isa 34:5). The fourth passage of Scripture: 'To bind their kings with chains,' and after that, 'And their nobles with chains of iron' (Ps 149:8)." R. Tanḥuma (ca. 380) said, "'To bind their kings with chains,' pertains to the ruling angels above, 'and their nobles with chains of iron,' pertains to the rulers below." (According to Deut. Rab. 1 [196D] R. Tanḥuma is supposed to have interpreted conversely "kings" in relation to the earthly rulers and "nobles" in relation to the ruling angels.) "The fifth passage of Scripture, 'The judgment that is written is to be carried out on them (the ruling angels),' and then,

'This is a glorification for all his pious ones (below). Hallelujah!' (Ps 149:9)."[33] ‖ Genesis Rabbah 78 (50A): R. Hama b. Hanina (ca. 260) said, "(The angel with whom Jacob wrestled in Gen 32:29) was the ruling angel of Esau (= Rome). This is what 'Therefore I see your face which is like the appearance of the face of the angel' (Gen 33:10) means (so the Midr.: As his guardian angel the ruling angel of Esau also bears Esau's features)." — In Midr. Song. 3:6 (105B) the following interpretation is added to Gen 33:10: "Your face is like that of your ruling angel." Then this parable follows: It is like a king who had a tame lion and a wild dog. What did the king do? He had the lion chase after his son, after he had instilled courage in him (so read with Gen. Rab. 77), and thought to himself, "If the dog comes to set itself on my son, my son will say, 'I took on the lion, how can I not take on the dog?'" So God says to the nations of the world, when they come to set themselves on Israel, "Your ruling angel could not stand against the progenitor of these people, and you want to take them on?" — The parable is given by itself in Gen. Rab. 77 (49D); the saying of R. Hanina b. H. is further given in Gen. Rab. 77 (49D); it is anonymous in Tanḥ. וישלח 40B; here the ruling angel of Esau bears the name Sammael, who otherwise = Satan (see § Matt 4:1, #1, *c* and #2). ‖ Babylonian Talmud Makkot 12A: R. Simeon b. Laqish (ca. 250) said, "The ruling angel of Rome will one day commit three errors; for it says in Isa 63:1: 'Who is this who comes from Edom, in crimson clothes from Bozrah?' (This passage is interpreted in relation to the ruling angel of Rome who, laden with blood guilt, will escape into a city of asylum.) He errs; for the city of asylum is called only Bezer (Deut 4:43), and he goes to Bozrah. He errs; for the city of asylum is only for one who inadvertently commits homicide, and he is a deliberate murderer. He errs; for the city of asylum is only for a human being, and he is an angel." ‖ Angels of the nations are also mentioned in Pesiq. 108B; 180B; Gen. Rab. 56 (35D); Exod. Rab. 15 (77B).

B. The gods of the gentiles are demons; worshiping them is the devil's work.

Septuagint Deuteronomy 32:17: ἔθυσαν δαιμονίοις καὶ οὐ θεῷ. — The word in the text is שֵׁדִים. ‖ Septuagint Psalm 96:5: ὅτι πάντες οἱ θεοὶ τῶν ἐθνῶν δαιμόνια, ὁ δὲ κύριος τοὺς οὐρανοὺς ἐποίησεν. — The word in the text is אֱלִילִים. ‖ Septuagint Psalm 106:37: καὶ ἔθυσαν τοὺς υἱοὺς αὐτῶν καὶ τὰς θυγατέρας αὐτῶν τοῖς δαιμονίοις. — The word in the text is שֵׁדִים; targum: מַזִּיקַיָּא = "wreckers, evil spirits." ‖ Septuagint Isaiah 65:11: ἑτοιμάζοντες τῷ δαιμονίῳ τράπεζαν. — The word in the text is גַּד = divinity of fortune; targum: טַעֲוָן, generally = idol. ‖ Baruch 4:7: "You goad the one who made you by sacrificing to demons and not to God." ‖ 1 Enoch 19:1: "Then Uriel said to me, 'Here (in the place of punishment for the fallen angels) will be the angels who mixed with women (Gen 6:1ff.), and their spirits, taking various forms, make humans impure and mislead them to sacrifice to the demons as to gods.'" ‖ 1 Enoch 99:7: "Others will worship unclean spirits, demons, and all kinds of idols because of ignorance." ‖ Jubilees 22:17: "They (the nations) slaughter their sacrifices for the dead and worship demons and they eat on graves." ‖ Sibylline Oracles Preface 19ff.: "You (gentiles) will receive the reward due for your foolishness, because you gave up on

33. See, however, Wilhelm Bacher, *Die Agada der palästinensischen Amoräer* (Straßburg: Karl Trübner, 1899), 3:281.3.

praising the true and eternal God and bringing holy sacrifices to him and instead have prepared your sacrifices for demons in the underworld." ‖ Targum Onkelos Deuteronomy 32:17: "They sacrificed to demons שֵׁדִין from whom there is no benefit, divinities הַחְלָן that they did not know." – Targum Yerušalmi I: "They will sacrifice to idols which are like demons שֵׁידִין, from whom there is no benefit at all, idols that they did not know." ‖ Targum Psalms 106:37: "They sacrificed their sons and their daughters to the *mazziqin* (wreckers, demons)." ‖ Sifre Deuteronomy 32:17 § 318 (136B): "They will sacrifice to demons" (Deut 32:17). If they served the sun and the moon, the stars and the images of the zodiac or things that are of use for the world and from which the world derives enjoyment, the jealousy (of God) would not be twofold. But they serve things that are not good for them but rather that bring evil, the demons שדים. What is the manner of the *šed*? He enters the human and compels him (so that he lets him have his way with him).

C. The gods of the gentiles are people who have died who during their lives made an outstanding contribution as rulers of nations or as benefactors of their generation, and to whom therefore grateful posterity paid divine honor. This euhemeristic[34] explanation of idolatry appears to be found only in Hellenistic Jewish literature.

Letter of Aristeas 135ff.: "For they (non-Jewish humanity) make images from stone and wood and say that these are the images of those who invented something useful for their life. They then worship them, although they could grasp their own irrationality with their own hands. For if one is made into a god for this reason, namely because of his invention, they act very irrationally. For they (those made into gods) only composed something from what was created and made it useable without having created it themselves. Therefore, it is vain and foolish to divinize the likes of him; for even now there are still many people who are more inventive and more learned than the earlier ones and yet one does not at all think of worshiping them. And those who formed and invented these (figures) think that they are the wisest among the Greeks." ‖ Wisdom 14:7ff.: "Blessed is the wood by which righteousness happens; but that which is made by hands (into an idol) is accursed, both it itself and the one who made it; for he prepared it, but the perishable was called God. For in the same way both the godless and his godlessness (his godless work) are detestable to God; for that which is produced will be punished together with the producer. Therefore, affliction will be visited also on the idols (ἐν εἰδώλοις) of the gentiles, because they as creatures of God became an abomination and a vexation (offence) for the souls of human beings and a snare for the feet of the ignorant. For the beginning of whoredom is concocting idols but manufacturing them is the destruction of life; for they neither existed from the beginning, nor will they exist into eternity. For through the empty delusion of human beings they came into the world, and therefore their quick end was decided. For a father aggrieved by premature suffering made for himself an image of his child who had been suddenly taken away from him and venerated now as a god the person who had died and left behind to those subordinate to him secret rites and orders, but later the godless custom which had

---

34. S-B: Euhemerus lived ca. 340–260 BCE; see Geyza Némethy, *Euhemeri reliquiae: Collegit, Prolegomenis et Adnotationibus Instruxit* (Budapest: Kiadja a Magyar Tud. Akadémia, 1889), 5.

become solidified with time was observed as a law, and according to the commands of rulers the carved images (of the dead) were deified. Now those people who could not honor them up close because they lived far away reproduced their appearance at a distance and made a visible image of the king they venerated so that they might flatter the one absent with their zeal as though he were present. The artist's ambition drove even those who did not think about these things to intensify (amplify) their veneration; for since this one wanted to immediately please his sovereign, he compelled the appearance of his art to be as beautiful as possible. But the multitude, carried away by the charm of the work of art, considered the one who just a short time ago had been venerated as a man to be an object of worship. And this became a snare for life because they attributed to stones and pieces of wood the name that is to be attributed to no other."[35] — Appeals to euhemerism can also be found in Sib. Or. 3:545ff.; 586ff.; 721ff.; 8:45ff.; 392f.

D. The gods of the gentiles are "nothings"[a] אֱלִילִים,[36] "vanities"[b] הֲבָלִים,[37] "dead things"[c] מֵתִים,[38] in which nothing actually or really exists[d] שֶׁאֵין בָּהֶן מַמָּשׁ, which became lords only because people made them lords.[e] Their powerlessness and vanity is shown in their being produced by human hands from perishable materials,[f] in their inability to help themselves and others,[g] in the treatment that they experience from their own worshipers.[h] And even if serving the stars is loftier than the common veneration of idols, it is also true of the stars that they are only works created by God.[i] The cult of images began in the generation of Enosh. When humanity became accessible to demons at that time, they were also misled by these to serve them.[k] To the humiliation of the idolaters, at the last judgment God will grant being to the vain idols so that they themselves might punitively reproach those who venerate them with the vanity of their worshiping. Idolaters must have already experienced something similar earlier at the giving of the law on Sinai.[l] From some older religious disputations it can be gathered that idolaters tried to establish the reality of their divinities by means of the following questions: If there is no being in the idols, why does Scripture call them "gods" אלהים? Why does God inveigh against them and those who venerate them? Why does God not destroy them? How can miracles happen by means of them? The most respected scholars of Scripture entered in to deprive these questions of their probative force.[m]

a. אֱלִילִים. — Sifra Leviticus 19:4 (344A): "Do not turn to nothings אלילים" (Lev 19:4). This is one of the ten names of contempt by which the idolater is made contemptible because of what he does: (The idols are called) אלילים, because they are hollow חלולים; פֶּסֶל (image of

35. S-B: τὸ ἀκοινώνητον ὄνομα = שֵׁם הַמְיוּחָד = the name appropriate only to God; the Tetragramm is meant; here, generally, any designation for God.

36. S-B: Lev 19:4; 26:1; Isa 2:8, 20; 19:1; Hab 2:18; Ps 96:5; sing. אֱלִיל (Isa 10:10).

37. S-B: Deut 32:21; Jer 8:19; 10:8; 14:22; sing. הֶבֶל (2 Kgs 17:15; Jer 2:5; 10:15; 16:19); strengthened as הַבְלֵי שָׁוְא (Jonah 2:9; Ps 31:7).

38. S-B: Psalm 106:28.

an idol), because they have been cut out נפסלים (from stone and the like); מַסֵּכָה (a cast image), because they are poured נסוכים; מַצֵּבָה (standing image), because they stand עומדים; עֲצַבִּים (images of idols), because they are made purely from individual pieces (עצב = to form, shape); תְּרָפִים (house idols), because they putrefy מרקיבים (= תָּרַף to spoil by putrefaction); גִּלּוּלִים (chunks, images of idols), because they are dirty מגועלים (גלולים thus = גְּלָלִים "excrement"); שִׁקּוּצִים (abomination) because they are loathsome משוקצים; חַמָּנִים (pillars of the sun), because they stand in the sun בחמה (specifically at the top of the roof);[39] אֲשֵׁרִים (stakes or trees of the cult of Astarte), because they are erected by others מתאשרים (in this case אֲשֵׁרָה would be = the "erected one." If it is interpreted as the "happy one," the explanatory sentence should be rendered: "because they are made happy by others"; one would then perhaps be led to think about the fact that the moon [Astarte = moon goddess] receives its light from the sun). The parallels present only the 10 names; in Mek. Exod. (107A) חֶרֶס "sun" and תּוֹעֵבָה "revulsion" are given instead of מצבה and אשרים, and ʾAbot R. Nat. 34 (8D) lists אָוֶן instead of מצבה. — In the partial parallel SLev 26:1 (447A), מַצֵּבָה (standing image) is explained as follows: "This is Mercury on the roads" אלו הַמֶּרְקֻלִיס שע״ג הדרכים. — To honor Hermes Enodios piles of stones were heaped up on the roads and passersby would add a stone to these.[40] Therefore we read in m. Sanh. 7.6: If someone drops a stone for Mercury, this is his cult. — Tosefta ʿAbodah Zarah 6.15 (470f.): Just as the one who drops a stone for Mercury honors him, although he knows nothing of honor, likewise everyone who honors a godless man honors him although he knows nothing of honor. — Midrash Proverbs 26 § 8 (49B): R. Alexandrai (ca. 270) said, "Whoever shows a fool honor is like the one who drops a stone for Mercury." Vulgate Prov 26:8: *Sicut qui mittit lapidem in acervum Mercurii, ita qui tribuit insipienti honorem.* ‖ Midrash Psalm 96 § 2 (211A): "All the gods of the nations are nothings" (Ps 96:5). Why are they called אֱלִילִים? R. Yose (ca. 150) said, "(They mean) woe אַלְלַי for their worshipers."

b. הֲבָלִים. —Babylonian Talmud Taʿanit 5A: Rab Nahman († 320) said to R. Isaac (ca. 300), "What does 'All at once באחת they will become fools יבערו and asses' (Jer 10:8) mean? "The instruction (teaching) of the idols is wood," he answered him. R. Yohanan († 279) said, "There is one thing אחת that will burn the godless in gehenna מבערת; what is that? The idol. It is written here, 'The teaching of the vanities (הבלים = idols, idolatry) is wood (which will burn the godless in gehenna),' and it is written there, 'These (the idols) are a vanity הבל" (Jer 10:15).'" ‖ Pesiqta 119A: "What wrong did your fathers find in me that … they went after the vanity הַהֶבֶל (idol) and became a vanity?" (Jer 2:5). R. Isaac (ca. 300) said, "It is like the son of a goldsmith for whom a debtor's note was posted. He feared that someone might say that the debtor's note was for 100 pieces of gold or 200 pieces of gold. Then his creditor said to him, 'Do not fear, it is for a *homer* of bran and a *homer* of barley. Whatever it was, it will be paid for!' Likewise, God has said to the Israelites, 'My children, idolatry, for which you were so eager, is nothing in reality but rather these (the idols) are a vanity הבל, a work for mockeries.'"

---

39. S-B: Sifre Leviticus 26:1 (447A).

40. TN: Hermes Enodios was considered to be the guardian of roads.

c. מֵתִים. — Wisdom 13:18: "He (the idolater) asks the dead thing (the idol) for life, περὶ δὲ ζωῆς τὸ νεκρὸν ἀξιοῖ." — Wisdom 15:17: "As a mortal man he (the maker of idols) makes a dead thing with his godless hands." See also 13:10. ‖ Jubilees 22:17: "They (the gentiles) slaughter their sacrifices for the dead and worship demons and eat on graves." ‖ Leviticus Rabbah 6 (109C): "The dead for the living?" (Isa 8:19). R. Levi (ca. 300) said, "It is like someone who lost his son (read איבד instead of עיבד) and went to look for him among the graves. A clever man who saw him said to him, 'Is your son whom you have lost living or dead?' He answered him, 'Living.' He said to him, 'You biggest fool in the world, the dead are indeed usually sought among the living (so read with the majority of editions), perhaps the living among the dead? Everywhere the living make preparations for the needs of the dead, perhaps the dead also make preparations for the needs of the living?' Thus, our God lives and remains forever; for it says, 'But Yahweh is truly God' (Jer 10:10). What does 'truly' mean?" R. Abin (ca. 325) said, "He is a living God and an eternal king. But the gods of the nations of the world are dead מתים; for it says in Ps 115:5, 'They have a mouth and do not speak, they have eyes and do not see, they have ears and do not hear,' they are dead מתים, and we are supposed to leave the eternally Living One and worship the dead?!" — See further the similar exposition of R. Levi in Exod. Rab. 5 (71C) under § Rom 1:21 A toward the beginning. ‖ Mishnah ʿAbodah Zarah 2.3: "Meat that is supposed to be taken to idolatry (to some cultic site) is permitted (to the Israelites for usufruct because it still has not become sacrificial meat); that which comes out of such a place, though, is forbidden because it is a sacrifice to the dead זִבְחֵי מֵתִים"; these are the words of R. Aqiba († ca. 135. The halakah rejects his opinion). ‖ Mishnah ʾAbot 3.3: R. Simeon (ca. 150) said, "If three have eaten at a table without speaking words of the Torah while doing so, it is as if they had eaten from sacrifices to the dead מזבחי מתים (i.e., from sacrifices to idols); for it says in Isa 28:8, 'All tables are full of foul meat without God.'" ‖ A baraita in b. Ḥul. 13B: R. Judah b. Batera (ca. 110) said, "How do we know that a sacrifice to idols תַּקְרוֹבֶת ע"א (= תּ'עֲבוֹדַת אֱלִילִים) makes one impure by being under the same roof (i.e., as a corpse makes impure anyone who is located with it in the same enclosed space)? Because it says, 'They bound themselves to Baal Peor and ate sacrifices to the dead' (Ps 106:28). Just as a corpse makes one impure by being under the same roof, so too does a sacrifice to idols make one impure by being under the same roof." — Similarly, R. Yohanan († 279) in y. Šabb. 9.11D.10. ‖ A baraita in b. ʿAbod. Zar. 8A: R. Ishmael († ca. 135) said, "The Israelites abroad are idolaters in purity (without wanting or knowing it). How so? If a non-Israelite (*goy*) celebrates a wedding for his son and invites all the Jews in his city, Scripture counts it just as if they ate from sacrifices to the dead מזבחי מתים (= from sacrifices to idols), even if they eat from their own supply and drink from their own supply and their own servant serves them; for it says, 'He will invite you and you will eat from his sacrifice' (Exod 34:15)." ‖ See b. ʿAbod. Zar. 54B in n. *m* below.

d. Mekilta Exodus (49A): Who is like you among those whom others (= the gentiles) call "gods," and nothing actual exists in them! Concerning this it says, "They have a mouth and do not speak" (Ps 115:5). But God says two words with one utterance (all at once), something that is not possible for a human to do. For it says, "One word God has spoken and we have heard them as two" (so Midr. Ps. 62:12). ‖ Babylonian Talmud Sanhedrin 63B: Rab Judah

(† 299) said that Rab († 247) said, "The Israelites knew that nothing actually exists in an idol, and they only served the idol to allow themselves to commit fornication openly." ‖ In Midr. Lam. Introduction #24 at the end (39A), R. Samuel b. Nahman (ca. 260) has Rachel speak thus as an intercessor to God: "If I, who am flesh and blood, dust and ash, have not been jealous toward my rival (Leah), nor have I caused her to go away in dishonor and shame, why are you, the living and eternal and merciful king, jealous toward the idols in which nothing actually exists?!" ‖ Exodus Rabbah 43 (99C): R. Nehemiah (ca. 150) said, "When the Israelites had committed that act (worshiping the golden calf), Moses stepped in to mollify God. He said, 'Lord of the world, they have made a help for you, and you are angry with them? This calf which they have made should support you: you make the sun rise and this one the moon, you the stars and this one the signs of the zodiac; you make dew fall, and this one makes the winds blow; you make the rain fall, and this one makes the plants grow!' Then God said, 'Do you also go astray, Moses, like those ones do? In that thing (the idol calf) nothing actually exists!' Moses answered, 'In that case, why are you angry with your children?' This is what the words mean: 'Why, O Yahweh, should your anger burn against your people' (Exod 32:11)?" — In Deut. Rab. 1 (195B), R. Isaac (ca. 300) is named as the author. ‖ Deuteronomy Rabbah 1 (195C): If another (than Jethro) had said, "Now I know that Yahweh is greater than all gods" (Exod 18:11), then it would have been said, "Does he mean, 'Now I know'? But since Jethro knew that he had been around to all the houses of idols in the world without finding anything actually existing in them ולא מצא בהם ממש, and then came and became a proselyte, it was fitting for him to say, 'Now I know.'" ‖ Tanḥuma ויצא 36A: God said to the Israelites, "Do not go astray after idols in which nothing actually exists; 'they have eyes and do not see …; their makers will be like them' (Ps 115:5–8)." But God hears immediately when a person whispers a prayer in his heart. ‖ See Pesiq. 119A above in n. *b* toward the end; see Deut. Rab. 2 (198B) in n. *m*; see b. ʿAbod. Zar. 54B in n. *m*.

e. Mekilta Exodus (74B): "Other gods" אֱלֹהִים אֲחֵרִים (Exod 20:3). Are they then gods? Was it not said long ago: "They threw their gods into the fire, for they were not gods"? (Isa 37:19). And what does Scripture intend to teach with "other gods"? That others (the gentiles) call them gods (and thereby make them into gods). (Thus אֱלֹהֵי אֲחֵרִים = אלהים אחרים ‖ Mekilta Exodus (75A): R. Hanina b. Antigonos (ca. 150) said, "Come and see the expression which the Torah has used. (It says,) 'To Molekh' מֹלֶךְ (Lev 18:21) (and means thereby) everything that you will make into a king (lord) over yourself, even a splinter or shard (מוֹלְךָ = מוֹלֵךְ 'ruler')." Rabbi († 217?) said, "'Other gods' (is what idols are called in Exod 20:3), because they are later אַחֲרוֹנִים (the last) than the one who is the last אַחְרוֹן among the works of creation. Who is the last among the works of creation? The one who calls those things 'gods.'" (Idols are thus a creation of humans.) — Parallels to the saying of R. Hanina b. Antigonos can be found in SDeut 11:16 § 43 (81B); y. Sanh. 7.25C.4; b. Sanh. 64A.

f. On the derision of gentile idols in general, see Deut 4:28; 27:15; 28:36, 64; 29:16; 1 Kgs 18:26f.; Isa 2:8, 20; 40:19f.; 41:29; 42:17; 44:9–20; 46:1f, 5–7; Jer 2:27f.; 10:3–9, 14f.; Hos 13:2; Hab 2:18f.; Ps 115:4–8; 135:15–18; Ep Jer 4–73; Wis 13:10–19; 14:1f, 8–14; 15:4–17. — In particular see Jdt 8:19: "gods made with hands." — Jubilees 21:5: "carved images … cast images." — First Enoch 46:7: "gods which they made with their hands." — First Enoch 99:7: "They will worship stones; others will make images of gold, silver, wood and clay." — Sibylline Oracles Preface 67f.: "You venerate images of stone and effigies made by hands and heaps of stones on the streets" (see n. α toward the end). — Sibylline Oracles 3:586ff.: "Works of men, made of gold and bronze and silver and ivory, ... earthenware; paintings coated with red chalk." — Sibylline Oracles 3:605f.: (God will prepare perdition for humans because they) "honored idols, venerating works of human hands that humans themselves will throw away." — Sibylline Oracles 4:7: "Like mute idols carved from stone." — Sibylline Oracles 5:356: "gods of stone."

g. Jubilees 12:1ff.: "Abram said to Terah his father: ... 'What kind of help and advantage (comes) to us from these idols that you venerate ...? For there is no spirit in them, rather they are mute.... Why do you venerate those in whom there is no spirit? For they are the work of hands, and you carry them on your shoulders, and no help comes to you from them.'" ‖ See Maʿaśe Abraham at § Rom 1:20 D, n. *d.* ‖ Jubilees 20:8: "Do not make for yourself gods from a cast work, nor carved works, for they are a nullity and have no spirit; for they are the work of hands and everyone who trusts in them. They all trust in a nothing." ‖ 2 Enoch (B) 2:2: "Do not worship vain gods; gods who made neither heaven nor earth pass away." — 2 Enoch 66:1: "Worship the true God, not mute idols." ‖ Wisdom 13:15ff.: "He (the wood carver) also prepared for it (the idol) a box worthy of it, then he placed it on the wall, securing it with iron; lest it fall now, he cares for it, knowing that it is powerless to help itself; for it is just an image and needs help. But when he prays to it for his possessions and marriage and children, he is not ashamed to address the lifeless thing. And he calls to the weak thing for health, and he asks the dead thing for life, and he flees to the most inexperienced thing for support and for a (happy) journey he pleads with that which cannot take a step, and for earnings and business and fortune of his hands he requests power from the most powerless work of his hands." ‖ Sibylline Oracles 5:81ff.: "From their own work and wicked thoughts humans received gods of wood and stone and bronze and gold and silver; things vain, soulless, deaf and cast in the fire they have made for themselves, futilely trusting in such things." ‖ TanḥumaB נצבים § 8 (25B): R. Eleazar (ca. 270) said, "May a curse come upon Laban, who said to Jacob, 'Why have you stolen my gods?' (Gen 31:30). It (the idol) was not able to protect itself from being stolen, how could it protect others! But it is not so with Israel; for it says, 'He is your praise and he is your God' (Deut 10:21), and he protects Israel as a father protects a son; for it says, 'Behold, the protector of Israel neither sleeps nor slumbers' (Ps 121:4)." — The same is found in Tanḥ. נצבים 26A. ‖ See also y. Ber. 9.13A.15; 9.13B.22; Deut. Rab. 2 (197D) at § Matt 7:7 A, #2, n. *a.*

h. Mekilta Exodus (74B): R. Eliezer (ca. 90) said, "'Other gods' (Exod 20:3) (are what idols are called), because they (idolaters) daily make for themselves new (other) gods. How do they do that? If he has one of gold and he needs this, he makes for himself one from silver; if he needs this, he makes one for himself from copper; if he has one of copper and he needs this, he makes for himself one from iron or lead. And, likewise, it says, 'New ones come from nearby' (Deut 32:17)." R. Isaac (ca. 150?) said, "If the name of every idol were individually enumerated, all the hides (parchments) in the world would not be enough to contain them." — A parallel passage can be found in SDeut 11:17 § 43 (81B). ‖ Mekilta

Exodus (79B): "You are not to make (gods) alongside me אִתִּי" (Exod 20:23). R. Aqiba († ca. 135) said, "'You are not to make it with me אִתִּי,' as the others (non-Israelites) are accustomed to do so in their countries: if something good comes to them, they honor their gods; for it says, 'Therefore he sacrifices to his net' (Hab 1:16). If punishments come upon them, they curse their gods; for it says, 'He curses his king and his god' (Isa 8:21). But if I bring good to the Israelites, they give thanks, and if I bring chastisements (sufferings), they give thanks."

i. See Wisdom 13:1ff. at § Rom 1:20 D, n. *a.* — On serving the stars, see y. ʿAbod. Zar. 4.44A.44 at § Rom 1:21 B. ‖ Midrash Lamentations 3:24 (71B): "My portion is Yahweh, says my soul" (Lam 3:24). R. Abbahu (ca. 300) said in the name of R. Yohanan († 279), "It is like a king who came to a city and with him were generals and prefects and supreme commanders. The important people of the city sat in the heart of the city. The one said, 'I will house the generals'; and another said, 'I will house the prefects'; and another said, 'I will house the supreme commanders.' But there was a clever one there who said, 'I will house the king; for all those change (are discharged), but the king does not change.' It is the same with the nations of the world: some of them serve the sun, others serve the moon, others serve a piece of wood or a stone. But the Israelites serve only the Holy One—blessed be He! This is what 'My portion is Yahweh, says my soul' (Lam 3:24) means." — The parallel Deut. Rab. 2 (199C) with R. Isaac (ca. 300) as the author is essentially different. ‖ Leviticus Rabbah 31 (129B): R. Levi said, "Every day God sits in judgment over the sun wheel and the moon because they do not want to arise to illuminate the world. What do they say? 'Humans present incense to us,[41] humans cast themselves down before us!'" Justa b. Shunam (ca. 400) said, "What does God do with them? He sits in judgment over them, and (then) they arise and illuminate the world contrary to their will (by compulsion). This is what 'Every morning he causes his judgment to fall inevitably on the light' (so Midr. Zeph. 3:5) means. What does 'inevitably' mean? 'Unceasingly.' 'But the wicked knows no shame' (Zeph 3:5). They (the worshipers of the stars) are not ashamed (read בהתין instead of כהתין), but rather cast themselves down before them. They see how those are darkened (beaten), but they are not ashamed (to worship them)." — The same is found with variations in Midr. Ps. 19 § 11 (85A). ‖ Babylonian Talmud Roš Haššanah 31A: On the fourth (day of the week = Wednesday) they (the Levites during the temple service) sang: "God of vengeance, Yahweh" (Ps 94), because he created the sun and the moon (on the fourth day of creation) and one day he will take vengeance on those who venerate them. — The author is R. Aqiba, († ca. 13)5.

k. Jubilees 11:3ff.: "And Ur, the son of Kesed, built the city of Ara of the Chaldeans and named it according to his name and the name of his father. And they made cast images for themselves and worshiped them, each one the idol that he had made for himself as a cast image. And they began to make carved images and impure sculptures, and the evil spirits helped and misled them so that they committed sin and impurity. And the prince Mastema (= Satan) exerted himself to do all this, and he sent other spirits that had been given into his hand to execute every sort of evil deed and sin and every offense." ‖ Testament of Naphtali 3: "The gentiles, who are misled and have left the Lord, have changed their order and followed

41. This is if we read with Bacher in accordance with d. Luria מקטירין instead of מקטרגין (*Die Agada der Tannaïten*, 2:324).

stones and pieces of wood, because they followed the spirits of seduction." ‖ Genesis Rabbah 23 (15D): Much became different in the days of Enosh, the son of Seth: the mountains became rocks, and the dead began to produce worms, and their (human's) faces became ape-like, and they (humans) became accessible to demons. R. Isaac (ca. 300) said, "They were the ones who caused themselves to become accessible to demons. (They said namely,) 'What sort of a difference is there between one who bows before an image and one who bows before a human being?' 'Then they became profane' (accessible to demons; so the midrash interprets הוּחַל in Gen 4:26)." ‖ Targum Yerušalmi I Genesis 4:26: "A son was born also to Seth, and he named him Enosh. This was the generation from whose days people began to go astray (from God). And they made idols for themselves and named their idols with the name of the Memra of Yahweh (i.e., with the name Yahweh." "Memra of Adonai" is a substitute for "Yahweh"; see the excursus "Memra of Yahweh," #3, B, n. *b*–#4).

l. Midrash Psalm 31 § 4 (119B): "All those who venerate images will be put to shame" (Ps 97:7). R. Judan (ca. 350) said in the name of R. Nahman (ca. 400),[42] "One day (namely at the last judgment) God will put some actual existence מְעַט מַמָּשׁ into the idols, and they will come and cast themselves down before God; for it says, 'All the gods will cast themselves down before him' (Ps 97:7), and then they will put those who venerate them to shame." R. Phineas (ca. 360) said, "One day God will give the idols the possibility of speaking before those who venerate them, and they will say to them, 'Woe to you, for you have forsaken the One who lives forever, who is the creator of heaven and earth, and you have cast yourselves down before the one of whom it says, "They have a mouth and cannot speak" (Ps 115:5).'" R. Yohanan († 279) said, "When God revealed himself on Sinai, he gave idols the power to cast themselves down before him." Rab Tahalifa (it is uncertain which Tahalifa is intended) said, "And Scripture supports R. Yohanan, for Ps 97:7 says, 'And all the gods cast themselves down before him.' It is not written that 'they will cast themselves down,' but rather that 'they did cast themselves down.'" — See also y. ʿAbod. Zar. 4.44A.47 and Midr. Ps. 118 § 10 (242B) in the excursus "Depictions of the Last Judgment in Ancient Jewish Literature."

m. Sifre Deuteronomy 11:16 § 43 (81B): "And you venerate other gods" (Deut 11:16).... R. Yose (ca. 150) said. "Why is their name (that of the idols) given as 'other gods' אלהים אחרים? In order to give no opportunity for those who come into the world to say, 'If these were named after his (God's) name, there would be value (worth) in them.' Behold, they were named after his name, and there was (nevertheless) no value in them. And when were they named after his name? In the days of the generation of Enosh; for it says, 'A son was born also to Seth, and he named him Enosh. Then people began to name (the idols) with the name of Yahweh' (Gen 4:26; cf. Tg. Yer. I on Gen 4:26 in n. *k* toward the end). In that hour the ocean rose up and flooded a third of the world. God said to them, 'You have accomplished a new work and named after my name. I too will accomplish a new work and name according to my name; for it says in Amos 5:8, "The one who called to the waters of the sea and poured them out over the face of the earth—Yahweh Sabaoth is his name!"' (so the midr. cites the name of God in Amos 5:8)." — The parallel passage in Mek. Exod. (74B) has taken

42. S-B: The two names should be switched, unless R. Nahman refers to R. Nahman b. Samuel b. Nahman, ca. 300.

on a directly opposed sense because of the variant בשמם accepted by Weiß: if (the idols) were named after their names, there would long since be worth in them, and behold, they were named after his name (namely in Gen 4:26) and (therefore) there is no worth in them. – On the flooding of the earth in the days of Enosh, see also Gen. Rab. 23 (15D); Midr. Ps. 88 § 2 (190B). ‖ Deuteronomy Rabbah 2 (198B): The rabbis said, "Since nothing actually exists in idols, why does it (Scripture) call them gods (e.g., in Gen 20:3)?" R. Phineas b. Hama (ca. 360) said, "In order to give a recompense to everyone who separates himself from them. God said, 'Although nothing actually exists in them, I still count it for a person, when he separates himself from them, as if he served the one in whom something actually exists and came to me.'" ‖ Mishnah ʿAbodah Zarah 4.7: Someone in Rome asked the elders (namely Gamaliel II, Eleazar b. Azariah, Joshua and Aqiba, who were in Rome around 95 CE), "If he (God) takes no pleasure in idolatry, why does he not destroy it?" They said to them, "If they venerated something that the world has no need of, he would destroy it. See, they venerate the sun and the moon and the stars. Should he destroy his world because of fools?" They said to them, "In this case he should destroy what the world has no need of and allow to continue to exist what the world needs!" They said to them, "Then we would strengthen the hands of those who venerate them; for they would say, 'Recognize that these (sun, moon, and stars) are divinities; for look, these have not been destroyed!'" – The same is found expanded in several ways in t. ʿAbod. Zar. 6.7 (469); b. ʿAbod. Zar. 54B. ‖ Babylonian Talmud ʿAbodah Zarah 54B: A philosopher asked Rabban Gamaliel (ca. 90), "In your Torah it is written: 'Yahweh your God is a consuming fire, a jealous God' (Deut 4:24). Why is he jealous concerning those who venerate it (the idol) and why is he not jealous concerning the idol itself?" He said to him, "I will tell you a parable. What can this be compared with? With a king of flesh and blood who had a son, and this son had raised for himself a dog to which he gave a name after the name of his father (i.e., he named him "Abba" = my father). Now whenever he swore, he said, 'On the life of the dog Abba!' When the king heard this, with whom would he have been angry? Would he have been angry with the son or would he have been angry with the dog? Indeed, he would have been angry with the son." He said to him, "You call it (the idol) a dog, is then there not something that actually exists in it?" He said to him, "What have you perceived (i.e., what sort of reason do you have for saying that)?" He answered him, "Once a fire broke out in our city and the whole city was incinerated, but that temple of the idol was not incinerated." He said to him, "I will tell you a parable. What can this be compared with? With a king of flesh and blood against whom a city (or a province) rose up. Now when he wages war, does he wage it with the living or does he wage it with the dead? Indeed, he wages it with the living. That one answered, "You name it a dog, you name it dead; in this case, he (your God) should annihilate it from the world!" He said to him, "If they honored something that the world does not need, look, he would annihilate it. See, they venerate the sun and the moon and the stars and the zodiac and streams and valleys, should he destroy his world because of fools? And, likewise, it says, '"Should I decimate, indeed decimate everything on the face of the earth?" says Yahweh. Decimate humans and cattle, decimate the birds of the sky and the fish of the sea and everything that causes the godless to stumble?' (Zeph 1:2f; the midr. understands the words as a question.) Should he annihilate them from the world because the godless stumble because of them? Do they not then venerate humans? 'And should I eradicate humans from the face of the earth?' (Zeph 1:3)." — A parallel passage can be found with variations in Mek. Exod. (75B). ‖ Babylonian Talmud 'Abodah Zarah 55A: Agrippa's field captain asked Rabban Gamaliel (ca. 90), "In your Torah it is written, 'Yahweh your God is a consuming, a jealous God' (Deut 4:24). Is not then a wise man jealous of a wise man and a hero of a hero and a rich man of a rich man?" He said to him, "I will tell you a parable. What can this be compared with? With a man who took a wife in addition to his first wife. If the new wife is more reputable then she herself is, she is not jealous of her. If she is lower than she herself, she is jealous of her." ‖ Babylonian Talmud 'Abodah Zarah 55A: זונן said to R. Aqiba († ca. 135),[43] "My heart and your heart know that nothing actually exists מְשָּׁשָׁא (originally: there is nothing tangible) in an idol; and yet we saw people who would go (to them) broken and would come back healed (literally: as bound together). What is the reason?" He said to him, "I will tell you a parable. What can this be compared with? With a trustworthy (reliable) man who was in a city and all the inhabitants of his city used to make their deposits with him without witnesses. Then a man came and made a deposit with him in the presence of witnesses. One day he forgot it and made a deposit with him without witnesses. His (the trustworthy man's) wife said to him (her husband), 'Come, we will deny it!' He said to her, 'Because this fool acted improperly, should (or: will) we destroy our trustworthiness?' It is also so with sufferings. If one (= God) sends them over a man, he adjures them to come (over to him) only on this or that day and to do so only on this or that day and in this or that hour and to go away (from him) by the hand of this or that (doctor) and by this or that medicine. When now the time has come that they should go away, this one (the suffering person) goes into the temple of the idol. The sufferings say, 'It would be right that we not go away!' But then they say, 'Because this fool has acted improperly (with his prayer to the idol), should we nullify our oath?'" This is what R. Yohanan († 279) said, "What does 'Evil and faithful sicknesses' (Deut 28:59; so the midr.) mean? 'Evil' in their sending and 'loyal' in their oath." ‖ Babylonian Talmud 'Abodah Zarah 55A: Rabbah b. Isaac said to Rab Judah († 299), "There is a temple of an idol in our location that, when the world needs rain, appears to them (the priests of the idol) in a dream and says to them, 'Slaughter a man for me, and I will bring rain.' When they slaughtered a man for him, rain came. He said to him, 'If I were resting (dead) now, I could not tell you this word that Rab († 247) said, "What does 'Yahweh has allotted them (namely the stars) to all the nations' (Deut 4:19) mean? This teaches that he (God) has flattered them (the gentiles) with words (with smooth words has encouraged them in their serving the stars) in order to kick them out of the world (into gehenna)."'" This is what Resh Laqish (ca. 250) said, "What does 'When it comes to the mockers, he mocks; but he gives grace to the humble' (Prov 3:34) mean? If he (someone) wants to make himself impure, it is open to him (he is given the opportunity to do so); if someone wants to purify himself, he is supported in that." ‖ On God's jealousy concerning idols, see also Midr. Lam. Introduction #24 and Exod. Rab. 43 (99C) above in n. *d*.

---

43. Bacher reads Zenon and identifies this with an administrator of Gamaliel II who went by the same name (*Die Agada der Tannaïten*, 1:294). The Munich manuscript has זונין = Zonin.

E. In particular the teraphim are household gods who served as oracles for the owner. — For a haggadic interpretation of the name, see SLev 19:4 (344A) above at § D, n. *a*.

Tanḥuma ויצא 37B: "Rachel had taken the teraphim" Gen 31:34. Why did she steal them? So that it (now singular) would not tell Laban that Jacob would flee with his wives and children and his small livestock. But do the Teraphim speak then? It is as it is written, "For the teraphim speak vanity" (Zech 10:2). You can further say, "They have eyes and do not see," and that whole passage (i.e., Ps 115:5ff.). But why are the teraphim called "teraphim"? Because they are a work of shame תּוֹרֵף, a work of impurity. How were they made? They brought a man who was a firstborn, and slaughtered him and sprinkled him with salt and spices, then they wrote on a sheet of gold the name of an impure spirit and laid the sheet under his tongue with spells and put him on a wall and lit lamps before him and cast themselves before him, and he spoke with them in a whisper. This is what "For the teraphim speak vanity" (Zech 10:2) means. Therefore, Rachel stole them (to deprive her father's house of the oracle). — The preparation of the teraphim is depicted almost exactly verbatim in Pirqe R. El. 36 (19D) and Tg. Yer. I Gen. 31:19, except here not the whole corpse but only his severed head is placed on the wall to be used for oracular purposes. — In Tg. Hos. 3:4 as well, the teraphim are classified as "speaking" by the rendering מְחַוֵּי.

1:23 B: For the likeness of an image ... of birds and four-footed and crawling animals.

On the animal cult, see Let. Aris. 138f.: "What should one think of the foolishness of the others, the Egyptians and those who are like them? These have placed their trust in animals, specifically mostly in creeping καὶ τῶν ἑρπετῶν τὰ πλεῖστα and wild ones. They worship these and sacrifice to them when they are living and when they are dead." ‖ Wisdom 11:15: "For the ignorant thoughts of their (the Egyptians') godlessness, which they were wrapped up in and thus venerated senseless vermin and miserable pests, you (God) sent to them a multitude of senseless animals as punishment so that they might recognize that someone is punished by the thing he sinned with." — Wisdom 12:23f.: "Therefore, you tormented the godless who lived in foolishness in life with their own abominable works; for they had strayed far on the paths of delusion by considering even animals, despised among their enemies, as gods." — Wisdom 13:10: "But they are wretched, and their hope (depensd) on what is dead, who call the work of human hands gods: gold and silver, products of craft, and likenesses of animals ἀπεικάσματα ζῴων." — Wisdom 13:13f.: "(The wood carver) shaped (a piece of wood) like an image of a human or modeled it after a lowly animal." — Wisdom 15:18f.: "But the most hideous animals (like snakes and crocodiles) are worshiped, for compared with others they are not beautiful, to find pleasure in them as when otherwise looking at animals." ‖ Sibylline Oracles Preface 59ff.: "You human beings, why do you uproot yourselves by vainly exalting yourselves? Be ashamed that you deify cats and beasts (like crocodiles)!... Snakes, dogs and cats you worship, you fools, and venerate birds and creeping animals ἑρπετὰ θηρία of the earth." — Sibylline Oracles 3:29f.: "You stray in vain, since you venerate snakes and offer sacrifices to cats." — Sibylline Oracles 5:278ff.:

"(Until mortal humans) no longer honor what is mortal, neither dogs nor vultures, which Egypt taught you to praise with an ignorant mouth and foolish lips." ‖ Josephus, *Against Apion* 1.25: "Furthermore the contrariness of the religions caused them (the Egyptians) to greatly hate (the Jews), in that our veneration of God differs so much from that adopted by them, as the being of God differs from that of senseless animals. For it is common for them as an ancestral custom to consider these to be gods; but in particular they differ from one another in their veneration." — *Against Apion* 1.28: "'The king (Amenophis of Ethiopia),' so Manetho recounts, 'wanted to see the gods.' Which then? If those introduced among them, the steer and the goat and the crocodile and the dog-headed ones, then he indeed saw them. But the heavenly gods, how would he have been able to do that!?" — *Against Apion* 2.6: "Since you (Egyptians) venerate animals who conflict with our nature, feeding them with great care." — *Against Apion* 2.7: "(In response to the accusation that the Jews venerated the head of an ass in their sanctuary,) first I answer that, if the same had been the case among us, an Egyptian could certainly not have been berated for this, since an ass is no worse than the weasels and goats and other animals that are considered by them to be gods.... Therefore, Apion would have had to consider this, if he himself had not possessed rather the heart (the mind) of an ass and the shamelessness of a dog which is customarily venerated by them.... We therefore ascribe to asses neither honor nor any power as the Egyptians do to crocodiles and snakes by considering as fortunate and valued by the gods those who are bitten by snakes or robbed by crocodiles." — *Against Apion* 2.13: "If everyone followed the customs of the Egyptians, the world would be empty of human beings; but it would be filled with the wildest animals, since they consider them to be gods and rear them with care." ‖ Philo, *Contempl.* 1 (Mangey's ed., 2:472): "It is not even pleasant to think about what is common among the Egyptians: from everything that is under the moon, they have elevated to divine honor senseless animals, and not just tame ones, but even the wildest of animals, among the land animals the lion, among the aquatic animals the native crocodile and among the birds of the air the vulture and the Egyptian ibis." — See further Philo, *Decal.* 16 (Mangey's ed., 2:193f.) and *Legat.* 25 (Mangey's ed., 2:570). ‖ Tanḥuma שופטים 15B: God says to them (idolaters at the last judgment), "Every day you were put to shame before me: some of you venerated pigeons—many pigeons have been slaughtered! Other of you venerated stones—many stones have been dashed on the street! Others of you venerated fish—many fish have been sold in the market!" Immediately God will put them to shame; for it says, "The gentiles will see and be ashamed because of all their might, they will put their hands over their mouths and their ears will become deaf" (Mic 7:16). — A parallel can be found in TanḥB שופטים § 8 (16A). ‖ Exodus Rabbah 16 (79C): Likewise, you will find it to be so with the Israelites. When they were in Egypt, they committed idolatry without ceasing; for it says, "Everyone—the abominations of his eyes (so the midr. cites the text) they did not cast away (and they did not leave the rubbish idols of Egypt)" (Ezek 20:8). God said to Moses, "As long as the Israelites served the gods of Egypt, they will not be redeemed. Go and tell them to leave their evil works and renounce idolatry." This is what is meant by the words, "Withdraw and take for yourselves small livestock" (so Midr. Exod. 12:21), that is, withdraw your hands from idolatry[44] and take for yourselves small livestock and slaughter the gods of the Egyptians (the sheep is meant) and make ready the Passover.... A different explanation: "Delay and get for yourselves small livestock" (Exod 12:21). This is what is written: "All those who serve images will be put to shame" (Ps 97:7). In the hour when God said to Moses, that the Passover lamb should be slaughtered, Moses said to him, "Lord of the world, how can I carry out this word! Do you not know that the small livestock (specifically the sheep) are gods of the Egyptians, as it says, 'Behold, we will sacrifice the abomination of the Egyptians before their eyes; will they not then stone us?' (Exod 8:22)." God said to him, "On your life, the Israelites will not go out from here before they will have slaughtered the gods of the Egyptians before their eyes, for I want them to know that the gods of the gentiles are nothing at all." ‖ Pesiqta 55A: R. Hiyya b. Adda of Joppa (ca. 350) said, "'Withdraw and take for yourselves small livestock' (Exod 12:21), so that every single person draws out the divinity of the Egyptians (namely a sheep) and slaughters it before him." — The same is found in Pesiq. Rab. 15 (78B) with this addition at the end: "And whoever notices it, let him speak against it!" — Here the author named is R. Hiyya b. Aha of Joppa.

Comment: The Egyptian Jew Artapanus, who lived before Alexander Polyhistor (the latter ca. 80–40 BCE), allows that not only polytheism in general but also the cult of Ibis and Apis in particular were introduced among the Egyptians by Moses; see Eusebius, *Praep. ev.* 27.

1:24: Therefore, God gave them over to the desires of their hearts for impurity.

1. On the connection between idolatry and the dissolute living of the gentiles.

Epistle of Jeremiah 43: "The women with bands wound (around their chests) sit in the streets and make smoked bran. But if one of them is drawn away by some passerby and goes to bed, she ridicules another that she was not found as worthy as she and her band was not torn." ‖ Wisdom 12:3ff.: "You hated the old inhabitants of the holy land, because they committed the most hideous works of sorcery and wicked rites, and as merciless murderers of children and as celebrants of sacrificial feasts of human flesh and blood and as initiates in abominable societies and as parents who by their own hand killed souls of the helpless (children), you wanted to exterminate them by the hands of our fathers, so that the land that is dear to you above all lands might receive a worthy inhabitation by the children of God." — Wisdom 14:8–12: "That which is made with hands (= an image of an idol) is accursed, both it itself and the one who made it. For he prepared it, but the perishable thing

---

44. S-B: This interpretation of מְשְׁכוּ in Exod 12:21 is old. It is represented by R. Yose the Galilean (ca. 110) in Mek. Exod. 12:21 (14B): "Draw back from idolatry and cling to the commandment"; by R. Judah b. Batera (ca. 110) in Mek. Exod. 12:6 (6B): "Command them to separate themselves from idolatry," and by R. Eleazar Haqqapar (ca. 220) in Mek. Exod. 12:6 (6A): Draw your hands back from idolatry and cling to the commandment. This interpretation is adopted also by Tg. Yer. I on Exod 12:21: "Draw your hands back from the idols of the Egyptians." — Septuagint Exodus 12:21 with ἀπελθόντες and Tg. Onk. Exod. 12:21 with אִתְנְגִידוּ follow the ordinary interpretation of משכו = "take" or "remove."

was called 'god.' For in the same way both the godless and his godlessness are detestable to God; the work will be punished together with its author. Therefore, affliction will be visited also on the images of the idols of the gentiles, because in the creation of God they became an abomination and a vexation (offence) for the souls of human beings and a snare for the feet of the ignorant. For the beginning of whoredom is concocting idols but manufacturing them is the destruction of life." — Wisdom 14:22–30: "Then it was not sufficient for them to stray concerning the knowledge of God, but also, living in the great battle of ignorance, they call so great an evil (nevertheless) salvation! For whether celebrating sacrificial murders of children or secret mysteries or frantic debaucheries according to strange custom, they no longer keep lives or marriages pure: one kills another in a dastardly way or spites him by means of adultery; but all without exception are ruled by thirst for blood and murder, thievery and deceit, destruction, faithlessness, rioting, perjury, harassment of those who are good, forgetting good deeds, defiling of souls, exchanging genders (= unnatural sex), breakdown of marriages, adultery, and fornication. For serving inglorious (nameless) idols is the beginning and cause and end of every evil; for either they rage in (wild) lust or prophesy lies or live godlessly or swear straight out falsely. For since they trust in lifeless idols, they swear falsely without fear of punishment. But for two reasons the just punishment will come: because they wickedly thought of God by devoting themselves to idols, and because they deceitfully swore falsely by having no regard for piety." ‖ 2 Enoch 10:4–6: "And I (Enoch) said, 'Woe, woe! What an exceedingly awful place this is!' And those men (= angels) said to me, 'This place, O Enoch, is prepared for those who do not honor God, who on earth commit (do) fornication contrary to nature, which is pederasty, sodomy in the hind passage; sorceries, oaths, demonic soothsayings, and who boast of their evil deeds: stealing, lying, calumnies, jealousy, thinking of unrighteousness, fornication, manslaughter; and who steal the souls of unfortunate human beings, seeing the poor and taking their possessions—but they themselves become rich—and acting unjustly toward the possession of another; who though being able to satisfy the hungry killed the starving (hungry), who though being able to clothe undressed the naked; and who did not recognize their creator and worshiped lifeless gods, which can neither see nor hear, forming vain gods, carved images, and worship impure work of the hands. For all of these is this place prepared as an eternal inheritance. ‖ Concerning the people Israel Rab († 247) made reference to the close connection between idolatry and fornication in b. Sanh. 63B; see the passage at § Rom 1:23 A, #2, D, n. *d.*

2. The handing over of the gentile world as an imposition, a divine punishment.

TanḥumaB שמיני § 10 (14B): (What does "He makes the gentiles jump up וַיַּתֵּר גּוֹיִם" [Hab 3:6] mean?) R. Tanḥum b. Hanilai (ca. 280) said, "God released (הִתִּיר = allowed) to them what is forbidden, abominations (Lev 11:10f.) and creeping animals. With what can this be compared? With a doctor who went out to visit two sick people. He saw one was close to death, and he said to his household companions, 'Give him anything he wants to eat.' He saw that the other would return to life and said to his household companions, 'He may eat this and that food, but he may not eat this and that food.' They said to the doctor, 'Why are you differentiating between this man and that one? For to that one who is in great danger you have said that he may eat anything he wants, and to this one who will return to life you have said that he may eat this and that, but he may not eat this and that.' The doctor answered, 'Concerning that one who I saw lay near death I said, "Give to him," because he is near death. But this one for whom there is hope of life, he must take care of himself.' Likewise God released to the *goyim*, who worship the stars, abominations and creeping animals and every transgression because they are destined for gehenna; but to the Israelites, who are destined for the life of the garden of Eden, he said, '"Do not make yourselves an abomination by means of anything that swarms ... and be holy, for I am holy" (Lev 11:43f.). You may eat this, but you should not eat this because they will remain alive; for it says, "You who have clung to Yahweh your God, all of you are still alive" (Deut 4:4).'" — A parallel passage can be found in Lev. Rab. 13 (114B). ‖ Numbers Rabbah 20 (188A): "The rock, what he does is perfect; for all his ways are justice" (Deut 32:4). God did not leave the nations of the world any excuse to say in the future: "You kept us far (from yourself)!" What did God do? As he allowed kings, wise men, and prophets to arise for the Israelites, so he allowed (such ones) to arise also for the nations of the world. He appointed Solomon king over Israel and over the whole earth, and he did likewise with Nebuchadnezzar. That one built the sanctuary and said innumerable praises and petitionary prayers; and this one destroyed it and put it to shame and slandered it and said, "I will ascend to the heights of the clouds" (Isa 14:14). On David he bestowed a kingdom, and this one acquired the house (the temple) for his (God's) name; on Haman too he bestowed a kingdom, and he acquired a whole nation to butcher it. So, you find that all the great things that the Israelites received, the nations received too. In the same way he made Moses arise for the Israelites and Balaam for the nations of the world. See what a difference there is between the prophets of Israel and the prophets of the nations of the world. The prophets of Israel warned Israel about transgressions; for it says, "And you, son of man, I have appointed you as a watchman" (Ezek 3:17). But the prophet who arose from the gentiles (namely Balaam) brought about debauchery to blot the creatures out from the world (cf. Num 31:16). And not only this, but also all the prophets were merciful to Israel and the nations of the world; for Jeremiah said this, "My heart mourns over Moab like a flute" (Jer 48:36), and likewise Ezekiel, "But you, O son of man, raise a lament for Tyre" (Ezek 27:2). But that cruel one (= Balaam) appeared in order to uproot an entire nation for no reason and for nothing. Therefore, the section about Balaam was written down (in Scripture), in order to make known why God removed the holy spirit from the nations of the world. — The same is found in Tanḥ. בלק 231A. ‖ See further § Rom 3:9.

1:25: Who is blessed forever, Amen!

Doxologies are occasionally found in ancient Jewish literature, particularly at the close of a remark.

1 Esdras 4:40: "And it (truth) is the strength and the kingdom and the power and the glory of all ages. Blessed be the God of truth εὐλογητὸς ὁ θεὸς τῆς ἀληθείας." ‖ Midrash Ecclesiastes 9:10 (42B): R. Aha (ca. 320) was eager to see the face of the (dead) R. Alexandrai

(ca. 270). He appeared to him in his dream; he showed him two things: "There is nothing inside of the *mechitza* (partition) of the slain of Lydda. Blessed be he בָּרוּךְ, for he took away the disgrace of Lulianos and Pappos!" — See the whole passage at § Matt 5:10, #3; see also § Matt 10:28, #2. ‖ Mishnah ʾAbot 6 Heading: The wise taught in the language of the Mishnah. Blessed be the one who has chosen it and its teaching! ‖ The best-known example is the extraordinarily common designation of God as "the Holy One—blessed be He" הַקָּדוֹשׁ בָּרוּךְ הוּא! (see the excursus "Memra of Yahweh," #3, A, n. *k*).

1:26 A: Therefore, God gave them over to passions of shame.

1. Gentile fornication in general.

See Ep Jer 43; Wis 14:22–30 at § Rom 1:24, #1. ‖ Sibylline Oracles 3:171: "Then the arrogant and unchaste ἄναγνοι Hellenes will rule." ‖ Testament of Judah 12: "It is a custom of the Arameans that the woman who has married sits at the gate seven days for whoredom." ‖ Mekilta Exodus (17B): For they said, "We are all doomed to die" (Exod 12:33). So they said, but not according to the norm of Moses. Moses said, "Every firstborn in the land of Egypt will die" (Exod 11:5); and they thought that, if someone had four or five sons, only the firstborn among them would die. But they did not know that their wives were suspects of fornication and those were all firstborn children of other single men." ‖ Midrash Song of Songs 6:8 (123B): "There are sixty of the queens and eighty of the concubines" (Song 6:8). R. Levi (ca. 300) said, "60 and 80, that is 140;[45] 70 of them know their fathers, but not their mothers, and 70 of them know their mothers, but not their fathers. 'And virgins without number' (Song 6:8), who know neither their fathers nor their mothers (because they were abandoned and raised by others). Is this the case perhaps also with the Israelites? Scripture teaches, 'And they registered their birth relations according to their clans, by the houses of their fathers' (Num 1:18)."[46] ‖ Pesiqta Rabbati 23/24 (122A): "Honor your father and your mother" (Exod 20:12). There (see Lev 19:3) reverence lets the mother precede the father, and here in honor the father precedes the mother. R. Joshua of Sikhnin (ca. 330) said in the name of R. Levi (ca. 300), "In the tent of meeting (i.e., in the case of the commandments given in the tent of meeting), because the nations of the world do not listen (as on Sinai), the mother precedes the father with the exclusion of the non-Israelite (*goy*), because he has no father שאין לו אב." ‖ Babylonian Talmud Yebamot 98A: Raba († 352) said, "If our teachers said, 'The non-Israelite (נכרי) has no father,' you may not think (that they said this), because they are addicted to fornication and he (the father) is not known, but that we, if he is known, take this into account; rather even if he is known, we still do not take this into account. For look, concerning two (gentile) twin brothers (who converted to Judaism), in whose case the drop of sperm was one and divided into two, the conclusion (of m. Yebam. 11.2) teaches, 'They fulfill neither the ceremony of the withdrawing of the shoe

45. S-B: On the basis of Song 6:8, R. Eliezer b. Yose the Galilean (ca. 150) also assumes that the number of nations on earth is 140. See SDeut 32:8 § 311 (134B).

46. S-B: In the anonymous parallel passage Num. Rab. 9 (151B), similar ideas are expressed about Israel. Here too there are children who do not know their father, or who know neither their father nor their mother.

nor levirate marriage.' Conclude from this that the All-merciful One has released his sperm (declared it to be without owner; i.e., unfit to produce a lineage considered legitimate by the Jewish law); for it is written, 'Their flesh is the flesh of a donkey and their ejaculation (of semen) that of a horse.'" — See b. B. Qam. 88A: A proselyte has no legitimate kin above him (insofar as the Jewish law is concerned), though he does in fact have legitimate kin beneath him (for after his conversion to Judaism his descendants count as legitimate according to the Jewish law). — A further consequence of this for proselytes is found, for example, also in a baraita in b. Sanh. 57B: A proselyte whose conception did not occur in holiness (i.e., before his mother converted to Judaism) and whose birth did happen in holiness (after the mother converted) has kin on his mother's side but not on his father's side. How then? If he married a sister on his mother's side, he must (at his conversion to Judaism) dismiss her; if a sister on the father's side, he may keep her; if a sister of his father on his mother's side, he must dismiss her; if a sister on his father's side, he may keep her .... — A parallel passage can be found in b. Yebam. 98A. ‖ Babylonian Talmud Qiddušin 49B: Nine measures (*qab*) of whoredom came down to the world; Arabia got nine of them and the whole rest of the world got one. ‖ The beginning of ʾAbot R. Nat. 28: There is no fornication like that of the Arabs. ‖ Babylonian Talmud Pesaḥim 113B: Canaan commanded his sons five things: Have sex with each other, love robbery, love fornication, hate your masters and do not speak the truth. (By "the sons of Canaan" should be understood, in the first place, slaves of non-Israelite origin.) ‖ Babylonian Talmud ʿAbodah Zarah 65B: Raba († 352) delivered a gift to Bar Shishak (a great Persian figure) on one of their holidays. He said, "I know about him, that he does not serve idols." He went and met him; how he sat up to his neck in a bath of roses while prostitutes stood before him! He said to Raba, "Will you have the same in the future world?" He answered him, "Ours is far more exquisite than this." He said to him, "Is there something more exquisite than this?" He answered him, "You fear the government; we will not fear the government." He said to him, "That concerns me least of all; why should I be afraid of the government?" While they were still sitting, a servant of the king came, who said, "Get up! For the king has made a decree concerning you." As he went forth, he said to Raba, "May the eye that wishes to see your misfortune pop!" Raba answered him, "Amen!" Then the eye of Bar Shishak popped. ‖ The end of Sopherim 21: It was a custom of the Arameans for them (the fathers) to sleep with their virgin daughters and then they would marry them. ‖ Babylonian Talmud Šabbat 33B: R. Judah (ca. 150) said, "How glorious arc the works of this (Roman) nation! They have made streets, bridges, and baths." R. Yose was silent in response to that; but R. Simeon answered and said, "Everything they have made, they have made only for their own good. They have made streets to put prostitutes in them; baths to take pleasure in them; and bridges to raise taxes on them." — The works of Rome are evaluated in the exact same way in b. ʿAbod. Zar. 2B. — On brothels, see Midr. Lam. 1:15 (56A): Vespasian filled three ships with the great ones of Jerusalem (men and women) in order to put them into the brothels קָלוֹן of Rome. — A baraiata in b. Giṭ. 57B: Once 400 boys and girls were taken prisoner for shame קלון (brothels). — Babylonian Talmud ʿAbodah Zarah 17B: They (the Roman rulers) decided to bring the daughter (of R. Hanina b. Teradion, † ca. 135) into a brothel קוּבָּה שֶׁל זוֹנוֹת (literally: tent of prostitution). — The same expression is found also in b. ʿAbod. Zar. 18A; in b. ʿAbod. Zar. 18B we find instead בֵּי זוֹנוֹת = house of prostitution. See further Sib. Or. 5.387ff. at § Rom 1:27 A, A, #1. ‖ Babylonian Talmud Baba Qamma 58A.22: A man heard that his wife said to his daughter, "Why do you not commit fornication secretly?" That woman (i.e., I) has ten sons, and of those only one of those is from your father." (According to the broader context, this is a non-Jewish woman.)

2. In the face of gentile fornication, Israel repeatedly boasted about the purity of its marriages;[a] but this self-boast must be seriously qualified.[b]

a. Letter of Aristeas 152: "The majority of the rest (i.e., non-Israelites) defiled themselves in (sexual) intercourse, by committing a grievous wrong, and whole countries and cities (still) boast about this. For they not only go around with men, but they also defile mothers and daughters. But we (Israelites) abstain from these things." ‖ Sibylline Oracles 3:584ff.: "To them (the Israelites) alone the great God has given rational counsel and faith and the best sense in the breast; who do not with vain delusions honor works of human beings, made of gold and iron and silver and ivory, and images of deceased gods made of wood and stone, clay, painted with crimson, formed (?) paintings, as mortals (do) according to their vain thoughts, but rather they lift up pure arms to heaven, early in the morning (when they get up) from bed always purifying their hands with water, and they alone honor the immortal one who always rules and then the parents. Then exceptionally more than all people they think of the purity of the bed and do not mix themselves unchastely with male youth, as the Phoenicians, the Egyptians, Latins, larger Hellas, the many nations of the others, the Persians and Galatians and of all Asia, transgressing the holy law of the great God which they have transgressed." ‖ See b. Qidd. 82A at § Rom 1:27 A, B.

b. Psalms of Solomon 4:1ff., 9ff. (from before 63 BCE; the psalm is directed against a great Sadducee and his followers): "Why do you, unholy one, sit in the counsel of the pious ...? Excelling all (others) in words and behaviors, (he is ready) with harsh words to condemn the guilty in judgment. He is the first to place his hand on him as in (pious) zeal, while he himself though is involved in many sins and impurity. His eyes are directed at each woman without distinction, his tongue lies (even) in an agreement made under oath. He sins at night and in secret because he believes he remains unseen; with his eyes he holds a sinful tryst with every woman. He swiftly invades every house—harmlessly, as if he acted with no malice .... Their eyes are directed at the houses of people who (morally still) stand firm in order to destroy snakelike the wisdom of the pious by means of godless speech. His words are deceptions in order to carry out wicked desires; he does not stop until he has carried through on driving away (the people) as orphans. Thus, he has desolated houses for the sake of his godless desire, conducted deceitful talks, as if no one sees and hears (it). When his godlessness is done in one place, his eyes are directed to another house to destroy (it) with misleading talk. In all this his greed is insatiable like hell." — Psalms of Solomon 8:9f. (from soon after 63 BCE): "In chasms under the earth (they) wickedly (practiced) their abominations, a son fornicated with his mother and a father with his daughter. They committed adultery, each one with his neighbor's wife, negotiated deals with each other under oath about these things." — Psalms of Solomon 2:11ff. (from soon after 48 BCE): "They made a mockery of the sons of Jerusalem because of the harlotry in it; everyone who went on the road could go inside in broad daylight.... The daughters of Jerusalem were disgraced according to your (God's) judgment because they had defiled themselves in abominable fornication." ‖ See T. Levi 17 at § Rom 1:27 A, B, #1 below. ‖ Babylonian Talmud ʿErubin 21B: Raba († 352) publicly said in a presentation, "What does 'Arise, my beloved, let us go out to the country ...' (Song 7:12f.) mean? The community of Israel says before God, 'Lord of the world, do not judge me according to the inhabitants of the great cities among which there is thievery, fornication, vain and deceitful swearing ...' (see the whole passage at § Luke 18:11 B)." ‖ Babylonian Talmud Pesaḥim 113A: R. Yohanan († 279) said, "God daily proclaims three people (announcing their merit): a single person who lives in a big city and does not sin (protects his chastity); a poor person who returns what is found to its owner; and a rich person who tithes his crops in secret (and so goes without thanks)." Rab Safra was a single man who lived in a big city; someone learned in the tradition taught (that word of R. Yohanan) before Raba († 352) and Rab Safra; (in the process) Rab Safra's face shone. Raba said to him, "Not (one) like the lord (= like you, is what is meant here), but rather like Rab Hanina and (his brother) Rab Hoshaiah (ca. 300), who were shoe-makers in the land of Israel (namely in Tiberias). They lived in the alley of prostitutes and made shoes for the prostitutes and brought them to them. Those women looked at them, but they would not raise their eyes to look at them." – Elsewhere as well particular alleys for prostitutes would not have been lacking in Jewish cities. This can be concluded from the proverb-like saying in the mouth of Samuel († 254) in b. Ketub. 64B: "Go out and learn from the alley of prostitutes: who hires whom?" ‖ Mishnah Soṭah 9.9: Since the time adulterers increased, the drinking of bitter water (the water of jealousy) has ceased, and specifically Rabban Yohanan b. Zakkai († ca. 80) put an end to it, because it says, "I will not visit affliction on your daughters when they act as prostitutes, and your brides when they commit adultery" (Hos 4:14). – For the sense Rabban Yohanan b. Zakkai gave to this meaning of Scripture, see § Matt 12:39 A, #2. ‖ Babylonian Talmud Sanhedrin 21A: Rab Judah († 299) said that Rab († 247) said, "At that time (after the episode in 2 Sam 13:11ff.) it was forbidden (for a man) to be alone (with a married woman) and for a woman to be single. Being alone (with a married woman) is indeed a biblical prohibition! For R. Yohanan († 279) said in the name of Simeon b. Yehozadaq (ca. 225), 'Where can one draw from the Torah a hint about the issue of being alone? Because it says, "If your brother, your mother's sin, leads you astray" (Deut 13:7); if then (only) the son of the mother leads you astray, does not (also) the son of the father lead you astray? It means just this: A son may be alone with his mother, but no other man may be alone with any of the women the Torah proscribes to him to marry. Therefore, it can be said: It has been forbidden to be alone with a single woman.'" – Babylonian Talmud Qiddušin 81A: Rab († 247) said, "(A woman) can be whipped for being alone (with a man), but the rule about being alone does not prohibit her from being alone (with her husband to carry on the marriage)." Rab Ashi († 427) said, "This was said only concerning being alone with a single woman, but not about the being alone of a married woman so that her children might not be slandered (that they are bastards)." The saying of Rab is also found in b. Ketub. 13A. – Mishnah Qiddušin 4.12: A man may not be alone with two women, but a woman may indeed be alone with two men. R. Simeon (ca. 150) said, "A man may also be alone with two women if his wife is with him, and he may sleep with them in a lodging house because his wife will keep an eye on him." ‖ Mishnah Qiddušin 4.13: A single man may not give instruction as a children's teacher and a woman may not give instruction as a children's teacher. R Eliezer (ca. 90) said, "Also, whoever does not have his wife with him (so according to the Tosefta) may not serve as a children's teacher." — See b. Qidd. 82A: The single man because of the mothers of the children, the woman because of the fathers of the children. — Jerusalem Talmud Qiddušin 4.66B.24: Because his mother comes with him (the child to the teacher), because his sister comes with him. — The saying of R. Eliezer is also found in t. Qidd. 5.10 (342) and y. Qidd. 4.66B.20. — From these regulations we can infer that the leading circles of the people had very little confidence in the chastity of Jewish men and women. ‖ See further § Rom 2:22 A.

1:26 B: For their women exchanged the natural custom for the unnatural one.

1. The φυσικὴ χρῆσις and the παρὰ φύσιν χρῆσις correspond to the rabbinic כְּדַרְכָּהּ וְשֶׁלֹּא כְּדַרְכָּהּ "according to their ordinary (natural) way and according to their not ordinary (unnatural or perverse) way." παρὰ φύσιν χρῆσις refers to using a woman in a pederastic fashion. According to a word of Resh Laqish (ca. 250), this type of fornication must have been exceptionally widespread in the gentile world.[a] But the ancient synagogue was also exceedingly lax in its judgment on this point. Such use of a woman was categorically rejected by R. Ishmael († 135);[b] but the usual opinion was that the husband was allowed to do what he wanted with his own wife, and that he was therefore not forbidden from having intercourse with her in a pederastic fashion.[c] This opinion is still represented even in Schulchan ʿArukh, even if with a certain reservation.

a. Genesis Rabbah 60 (37D): Resh Laqish (ca. 250) said, "The daughters of the *goyim* (non-Israelites) take care in the place of their shame; but they expose themselves in another location." — See also Sib. Or. 5:166f.: "Adultery is in you (Rome) and nefarious mingling with boys and sacrilegious mingling with women, evil city, more unholy than any other!"

b. Sifra Leviticus 20:13 (369A): "And if a man sleeps with a male in the ways one would sleep with a woman מִשְׁכְּבֵי אִשָּׁה, they have both committed an abomination" (Lev 20:13). "A man" אִישׁ: this excludes a minor (who is younger than 9 years and 1 day old, and thus he goes unpunished); "who sleeps with a male זָכָר": a minor is also included in the wording; "in the ways one would sleep with a woman": Scripture thereby shows that there are two ways of sleeping with a woman (namely כדרכה and שלא כדרכה). R. Ishmael said, "See, this (namely משכבי אשה) was supposed to teach (that pederasty is punishable) and is devised as something that learns (namely that pederastic intercourse with a woman or her having intercourse שלא כדרכה is forbidden)." This is the same as a baraita in b. Sanh. 54A; here Rashi puts into words what משכבי אשה "learns": that whoever has intercourse with a woman, whether it be כדרכה or שלא כדרכה, is liable to punishment. — Reference can also be made to Sib. Or. 5:166f.: "Adultery is in you (Rome) and nefarious mingling with boys and sacrilegious mingling with women, evil city, more unholy than any other!"

c. Babylonian Talmud Nedarim 20A: R. Yohanan b. Dahabai (ca. 180) said, "The angels of service recounted many things to me: Why do children become lame? Because they (the parents during intercourse) invert their table.[47] Why do they become mute? Because they kiss on that place. Why do they become deaf and mute? Because they talk to each other at the time of intercourse. Why blind? Because they look at that place...." (20B:) R. Yohanan († 279) said, "These are the words of Yohanan b. Dahabai; but the scholars said, 'The halakah does not follow Yohanan b. Dahabai; rather a man is permitted to do whatever he wants to do with his wife. As with a piece of meat that comes from the butcher: if he wants to eat it with salt, he may do so; roasted, he may do so; cooked, he may do so; boiled, he may do so. It is likewise with a fish that comes from the fish shop...." A woman came before Rabbi († 217?). She said to him, "Rabbi, I had prepared the table for him (my husband), and he inverted it (see above)." He answered her, "My daughter, the Torah has allowed you (to your husband, in whatever way he wants), what can I do for you about that?!" A woman came before Rab († 247). She said to him, "I had prepared the table for him, and he inverted it." He answered, "How is it any different with a carp?" ‖ Babylonian Talmud 58B: R. Eleazar (ca. 270) said that R. Hanina (ca. 225) said, "If a Noachide (= a non-Israelite) has intercourse with his wife in an unnatural way שלא כדרכה, he has committed an offense. For it says, 'And he will cling to his wife' (Gen 2:24), and so not in an unnatural way שלא כדרכה." Raba († 352) said, "Is there then something for which an Israelite would not become liable to punishment but for which a non-Israelite (*goy*) would?[48] Rather, said Raba, if a Noachide (non-Israelite) has intercourse with the wife of another man in an unnatural way שלא כדרכה, he is exempt from punishment. What is the scriptural basis for this? Gen 2:24: ('And he will cling) to his wife,' and not to the wife of another; 'and he will cling,' and not in an unnatural way שלא כדרכה."

d. Schulchan 'Arukh אבן העזר § 25 Comment: He (the Israelite) may do whatever he wants with his wife ...; and he may have intercourse with her both in the natural way כדרכה and in the unnatural way שלא כדרכה, as long as he does not needlessly spill semen. Some ease this by saying that he may sleep with his wife in an unnatural way, even if he spills semen, as long as he does this only occasionally and not usually. — The Tosafists in b. Sanh. 58B מי are among those who speak in the latter sense.

2. Most find in Rom 1:26 B a reference to the lesbian debauchment of women designated as *frictrices* or *triabdes* (τριβάδες).

Lucian, Ἑταιρικοὶ διάλογοι 5: Τοιαύτας γὰρ ἐν Λέσβῳ λέγουσι γυναῖκας, ὑπὸ ἀνδρῶν μὲν οὐκ ἐθελούσας αὐτὸ πάσχειν, γυναιξὶ δὲ αὐτὰς πλησιαζούσας, ὥσπερ ἄνδρας....

47. S-B: Rashi gives to the phrase "Because they reverse their table" a double explanation: α. they turn their face to the neck (of the woman) when they have intercourse with their wives שלא כדרכן; β. she is on top, he is on the bottom. — The second explanation is rejected by the Tosafists in b. Sanh. 58B מי; R. Asher b. Jehiel († 1327) follows the first explanation in b. Ned. 20A.

48. S-B: Raba thereby expresses that an Israelite does not become liable to punishment by unnatural intercourse with his wife, or, as the Tosafists in b. Sanh. 58 B מי say, that an Israelite is permitted to have such intercourse with his own wife.

Ἐγεννήθην μὲν ὁμοία ταῖς ἄλλαις ὑμῖν· ἡ γνώμη δὲ καὶ ἡ ἐπιθυμία καὶ τἄλλα πάντα ἀνδρός ἐστί μοι. ‖ Martial, *Epigrams* 90.5: *Mentiturque virum prodigiosa Venus.* ‖ The halakah has something similar in view in the following passages. Jerusalem Talmud Giṭṭin 8.49C.58: As for two women who have moved to and fro מסלדות on each other (in fornication), the school of Shammai has declared them to be ineligible (to marry priests; thus, their act was viewed as harlotry), but the school of Hillel declared them to be eligible. – The parallels in b. Šabb. 65A and b. Yebam. 76A do not read מסלדות, but rather מסוללות with the same meaning. In b. Yebam. 76A Rashi gives the explanation: "they rub each other's genitals." ‖ Tosefta Soṭah 5.7 (310): As for a woman who has moved to and fro מסלסלת on top of her son who is a minor so that genital touching has occurred, the school of Shammai has declared her to be ineligible (to marry a priest), but the school of Hillel has declared her to be eligible. – Parallels can be found in y. Giṭ. 8.49C.58 with the verb מסלדת, and in b. Sanh. 69B as a baraita with the verb מסוללת. ‖ Another kind of female fornication is mentioned in b. ʿAbod. Zar. 44A: What does מִפְלֶצֶת ("idol," 1 Kgs 15:13) mean? Rab Judah († 299) said, "There was occasion for too much mockery מפליא ליצנותא" (a notarikon interpretation of מפלצת), as Rab Joseph († 333) taught as a tannaitic tradition: "She (Maacah, the mother of King Asa) had a certain kind of penis made with which she had intercourse every day." ‖ It is worded quite dully in SLev 18:3 (337A): "You are not to act as they do in the land of Egypt and as they do in the land of Canaan" (Lev 18:3). Are we then not to construct buildings or set up any planting as they do? Scripture teaches: "And you are not to walk in their statutes" (Lev 18:3). I have spoken only of statutes that were established for them and for their fathers and for their fathers' fathers. And what did they do? A man married a man and a woman a woman. A man married a woman along with her daughter, and a woman married two men. Therefore, it is said: "And you are not to walk in their statutes."

1:27 A: But in the same way the men too abandoned the natural use of woman ....

A. Fornication contrary to nature in the gentile world:

1. With men.

Sibylline Oracles 3:184ff.: "But the compulsion of godlessness among these (the Romans) will straightaway be: A man will copulate with a man, and they will place their boys in shameful houses." – See Sib. Or. 3:584ff at § Rom 1:26 A, #2, n. *a*. – See Sib. Or. 5:166f. at § Rom 1:26 B, #1, n. *b*. – Sibylline Oracles 5:387ff.: "You (Romans) who in ancient times unchastely had intercourse with boys and placed the (girls) in houses as prostitutes, who were previously pure, with abusive lust and torment and painstaking shame. For in you (Rome) a mother mingles wickedly with her son and the daughter is bound as a bride to the one who begat her." – Sibylline Oracles 5:429f.: "(In the blessed end time) there will no longer be among wretched mortals what they would have to fear, neither adultery nor wicked boy-love." ‖ See Let. Aris. 152 at § Rom 1:26 A, #2, n. *a*. ‖ Genesis Rabbah 26 (16D): "They took wives for themselves" (Gen 6:2): thereby married women are meant; "from all who were pleasing to them": thereby males (for pederasty) and livestock (for sodomy) are meant. R. Huna (ca. 350) said in the name of Rab (so read instead of "Rabbi") Joseph († 333),

"The generation of the flood was not wiped off the earth until they wrote marriage contracts for males and livestock (as for women)." – Parallel passages can be found in Lev. Rab. 23 (122B); TanḥB בראשית § 33 (12B), though here R. Idi (ca. 310) is named as the author who then as elsewhere[49] should be thought of as the tradent of Rab Joseph. – On marriage contracts for males, see also b. Ḥul. 92A at Rom 1:20 C. ‖ Babylonian Talmud Sanhedrin 108A: "All flesh had corrupted its way on earth" (Gen 6:12). R. Yohanan († 279) said, "This teaches that they (the people of the generation of the flood) made the livestock couple (copulate) with wild animals and wild animals with the livestock and everything with people and people with everything." ‖ Genesis Rabbah 50 (32A): R. Menahemah (ca. 350) said in the name of R. Bibi (ca. 320), "The people of Sodom had agreed among themselves: 'We will sleep with every foreigner who comes here and takes his money.'" —See Gen. Rab. 26 (16D): R. Joshua b. Levi (ca. 250) said in the name of Pedaiah, "That whole night Lot had prayed for mercy for the Sodomites, and they (the angels) had accepted it from him; but when they said to him, 'Bring them out to us so we may know them' (Gen 19:5), namely compel them to sleep with us, then they said to him, 'Whom do you still have here?' (Gen 19:12)." – On the sodomitic vice, see further 2 En. 10:4–6 at § Rom 1:24, #1; 2 En. 34:2: "They (the people of the generation of the flood) made the whole earth recoil by its unrighteous acts and deeds of injustice and wicked fornication, which is a man acting sodomitically (literally: "in the hind passage") with another"; see T. Naph. 4 and T. Benj. 9 further below at B, #11. ‖ Concerning the Egyptians and Canaanites, see SLev 18:3 (337A) at § Rom 1:26 B, #2. ‖ Babylonian Talmud Šabbat 149B: "As you fell from heaven, ... you who cast the lot for nations" (the midr. interprets חולש in Isa 14:21 as הֲלָשׁ "lot"). Rabbah bar Rab Hunna (in 309 became head of the school in Sura, † 322) said, "He (Nebuchadnezzar) cast the lot for the great ones of the kingdom in order to know who on the given day would be his next partner for pederastic intercourse מִשְׁכַּב זָכוּר (literally: lying with a man). Further it says, 'All the kings of the nations, they all (call: You too have become weak like us)' (Isa 14:9f.)." R. Yohanan († 279) said, "They rested from pederastic intercourse." ‖ Hiram and pharaoh and king Joash had sex like women; see TanḥB וארא § 7ff. (11B) at § John 5:18, #1. ‖ Genesis Rabbah 63 (40A): ("Esau ... became a man of the steppe" [Gen 25:27]). R. Hiyya (ca. 280) said, "He exposed himself like the steppe (which is accessible to everyone as an ownerless good). The Israelites said before God, 'Lord of all worlds, is it not enough for us that we have been made subservient to the 70 nations; must we also become subservient to this one (Esau = Rome), who had intercourse in a womanly fashion?' God said to them, 'I too will take revenge on him with the same word (namely "woman")!' This is what is written: 'The heart of the heroes of Moab on that day will be like the heart of a woman in her distress' (Jer 48:41)." (This citation is not appropriate because of the mention of Moab; apparently there is a confusion with Jer 49:22.) – The first four citations from the Sib. Or. used at the beginning of #1 are also related to Rome. ‖ See further below at B, #1 "Halakic Material."

49. See Buber on TanḥB לך לך comment 3.

2. With animals.

Here belong the passages from #1 above: Gen. Rab. 26 (16D) and b. Sanh. 108A. – See further Sib. Or. 5:393: "In you (Rome) wicked men have invented even intercourse with animals." ‖ Babylonian Talmud Yebamot 63A: R. Eleazar (ca. 270) said, "What does 'This one is at last bone from my bone and flesh from my flesh' (Gen 2:23) mean? This teaches that Adam had intercourse with all livestock and wild animals; but his mind was stilled (was satisfied) only when he had intercourse with Eve." ‖ Babylonian Talmud ʿAbodah Zarah 22B: R. Yohanan († 279) said, "When the snake had intercourse with Eve, it cast filth into her. In that case, it is also valid for the Israelites! In the case of the Israelites, because they stood at Mount Sinai, their filth came to an end; in the case of the *goyim* (non-Israelites), because they did not stand at Mount Sinai, their filth did not cease." (The filth זוּהֲמָא that the snake inflicted on Eve refers not to original sin but rather to the inclination to fornication that is contrary to nature; this came to an end for the Israelites at the giving of the law.) Parallel passages can be found in b. Šabb. 146A; b. Yebam. 103B. ‖ Babylonian Talmud Sanhedrin 105A: Balaam (is called) son of Beor (see Num 22:5) because he had intercourse with livestock בְּעִיר. – Babylonian Talmud Sanhedrin 105A: Mar bar Rabina (ca. 400) said, "Balaam had intercourse with his jenny." – A similar claim can be found in b. Sanh. 105B. ‖ All the animals of the field had intercourse with Nebuchadnezzar; see TanḥB וארא § 7ff. (11B) at § John 5:18, #1. ‖ Babylonian Talmud ʿAbodah Zarah 22B: They (the teachers) asked, "What is the case with poultry? Come and hear!" Rab Judah († 299) said that Samuel († 254) said in the name of R. Hanina (ca. 225), "I have seen a *goy* (non-Israelite) who bought a goose from the market, had sex with it, choked, fried and ate it." And Rab Jeremiah of Difti said, "I have seen an Arab who bought a haunch (leg) from the market, made a hole in it to have sex with it, had sex with it, fried it and ate it." ‖ See further at B, #2 "Halakic Material."

B. Fornication contrary to nature in Israel.

The ancient synagogue boasted that fornication contrary to nature had no place in its midst.

Sibylline Oracles 3:594f.: "Then exceptionally more than all people they (the children of Israel) remember the purity of the bed and do not mingle unchastely with a young male." – Sibylline Oracles 4:33f.: "(The pious look to God), not tending shameful longing for a strange bed, nor for the odious and appalling rape of boys." ‖ See Let. Aris. 152 at § Rom 1:26 A, #2, n. *a*. ‖ A baraita in b. Qidd. 82A: Someone said to R. Judah (ca. 150), "The Israelites are not suspected of lying with a man משכב זכור or (having sex with) livestock."

In reality the matter was probably considerably different. This is attested not merely by occasional remarks but rather above all by the preventive regulations of the halakah.

1. Fornication contrary to nature with men.

Testament of Levi 17: "In the seventh week (on which the messianic time follows) the priests will come, as will idolaters, the contentious, the greedy, the cocky, the godless, the lustful, those who rape boys, those who rape livestock." (Thereby the author of the Testaments depicts his own time as if it were before the destruction of Jerusalem.) – Testament of Naphtali 4: "I say this, my children, because I read in a holy writing of Enoch that you too will fall away from the Lord by walking in accordance with the wickedness of the gentiles, and that you will act in accordance with every sin of Sodom." (On the sin of Sodom, see § Rom 1:27 A, A, #1.) – Testament of Benjamin 9: "I (Benjamin) suppose, however, on the basis of the words of Enoch, the righteous one, that good deeds will not happen among you either. You will namely commit whoredom as Sodom did...." ‖ See the beginning of b. Sanh. 82A at § Matt 5:27 B, #4. ‖ Jerusalem Talmud Sanhedrin 6.23C.4: R. Judah b. Pazzi (ca. 320) went up to the balcony of the house of learning and saw two men (literally: two children of men, people) who were having sex with each other. They said to him, "Rabbi, remember that you are one man and we are two!" (Your testimony as one person does not count as valid before the court, but our testimony as two people against you would be valid.)

Halakic Material. Mishnah Sanhedrin 7.4: The following are stoned: He who has sex ... with a male.... ‖ Mishnah Keritot 1.1: There are 36 cases in which the Torah prescribes the punishment of eradication (namely when the act in question occurred on purpose but without warning): He who has sex ... with a male.... ‖ The scriptural basis is given in SLev 20:13 (369A): "If a man sleeps with a male in the ways one would sleep with a woman, they have both committed an abomination; they are to be killed; their bloodguilt clings to them" (Lev 20:13). "A man" אִישׁ: this excludes a minor (who is younger than 9 years and 1 day old, and thus he is not punished as a perpetrator); "who sleeps with a male": a minor is also included in the wording (therefore a man who sleeps with a minor would also be punished); "in the ways one would sleep with a woman": Scripture shows (with the plural "ways one would sleep with") that there are two ways of sleeping with a woman (כְּדַרְכָּהּ and שֶׁלֹּא כְדַרְכָּהּ). R. Ishmael († ca. 135) said, "See, this was supposed to teach (that pederasty is punishable) and is devised as something that learns (namely that intercourse with a woman שלא כדרכה is forbidden); 'they are to be killed': by stoning. You say 'by stoning,' but should the punishment be carried out instead by one of all (the other) death penalties in the Torah? Scripture teaches: 'Their bloodguilt clings to them,' and it says there (namely in Lev 20:27): 'Their bloodguilt clings to them'; as the sentence 'Their bloodguilt clings to them' there (is punished) by stoning, so too should the act be punished by stoning here. We have heard the punishment but not the warning (in Scripture). Scripture teaches: 'And you are not to lie with a male in the ways one would sleep with a woman' (Lev 18:22). There I have only a warning concerning the one who sleeps with someone; whence comes the proof concerning the one who is slept with? Scripture teaches, 'Let there be no consecrated prostitute from the sons of Israel' (Deut 23:18); and further it says, 'There were also consecrated prostitutes in the land' (1 Kgs 14:24)." R. Aqiba († ca. 135) said, "'And you are not to lie לֹא תִשְׁכַּב with a male in the ways one would sleep with a woman' (Lev 18:22); for (לֹא) תִשָּׁכֵב read 'you are not to let yourself be slept with.'" – The same is found in a baraita in b. Sanh. 54A; a further parallel, but in a different version, can be found in y. Sanh. 7.24D.65. ‖ Different from this Sifra passage is t. Sanh. 10.2 (430): He who sleeps with a male who is 9 years and 1 day old ..., they all are due to be stoned. – Here the rape of a boy under 9 years old goes unpunished; this corresponds to the opinion of Rab († 247); see b. Sanh. 54B, though here the beginning of the baraita is to be corrected according to the Tosefta. ‖ Mishnah Qiddušin 4:14: R. Judah (ca. 150) said, "Two single men are not to sleep under one coat (one blanket)"; but the scholars allowed this. – Tosefta Qiddušin 5.10 (343) adds: They said, "The Israelites are not suspected of this (that is, of משכב זכור)." See the baraita in b. Qidd. 82A above at the beginning of § Rom 1:27 A, B. ‖ Babylonian Talmud Šabbat 17B: Rab Nahman b. Isaac († 356) said, "(On the day when a decision was made about the 18 questions in accordance with the opinion of the school of Shammai,) they established (as a preventive regulation) concerning the non-Israelite child תינוק גוי that it makes one unclean as a discharge does, so that an Israelite child with him (near him) would not become accustomed to pederasty משכב זכור." – The same is found in b. ʿAbod. Zar. 36B.

Haggadic Material. A baraita in b. Sukkah 29A: The sun is beaten (a solar eclipse occurs) for many reasons: because of a presiding judge who died and was not properly mourned; because of a betrothed girl who screamed in the city, and there was no one to save her (cf. Deut 22:23ff.); because of pederasty משכב זכור and because of two brothers whose blood was spilled simultaneously (at once). ‖ Jerusalem Talmud Berakot 9.13C.42: (Why do earthquakes come into the world?) R. Aha (ca. 320) said, "Because of the sin of pederasty משכב זכור. God says, 'You have aroused your penis because of something that is not yours; on your life, I will arouse (shake) my world because of this man.'"

2. Fornication contrary to nature with animals.

See T. Levi 17 above at #1. ‖ Jerusalem Talmud Sanhedrin 6.23B.58: There was a pious man who was out and about and saw two men having sex with a female dog. They said, "We know that this pious man will go and give testimony against us, and our lord (king) David will kill us. But we will go ahead of him and give testimony against him (that he committed that act)." They gave testimony against him, and his judgment was given, that he would be killed. This is what David said in Ps 22:21: "Save my soul from the sword, my only soul from the violence of the dog." "From the sword": namely from the sword of Uriah (whom I killed by the sword of the Ammonites [see 2 Sam 11]); from "the dog": because of the dog of the pious man (who was killed though innocent). ‖ Babylonian Talmud Qiddušin 81B.22, 28: Samuel said, "It is forbidden to be alone with any women whom the Torah forbids a man to marry, and also with livestock...." (When he went into the field) Abbayye († 338/39) kept the animals away at the distance of the entire field (in order not to be suspected of sexual offense). Rab Sheshet (ca. 260) had the livestock go on a rope bridge (across the river, also so as not to come under suspicion). Rab Hanan of Nehardea came to Rab Kahana (ca. 250) in Pum Nahara (in Babylon); he saw him, how he sat there and studied, and livestock stood before him. He said to him, "Is my lord not of the opinion: 'Also with livestock' (one should not be alone)?" He answered him, "I did not think about that."

Halakic Material. Mishnah Sanhedrin 7.4: The following are stoned: He who has sex ... with livestock; additionally, a woman who lets livestock have sex with her.... ‖ Mishnah Keritot 1.1: There are 36 cases in which the Torah prescribes the punishment of eradication (namely when the act in question occurred on purpose but without warning): He who has sex ... with livestock; additionally, a woman who lets livestock have sex with her. ‖ Tosefta Sanhedrin 10.2 (430): He who has sex with livestock in the usual way and in the unusual way, a woman who lets livestock have sex with her, whether in the usual or in the unusual way בין כדרכה ... ובין שלא כדרכה, they all make themselves due for the penalty of stoning.

‖ The scriptural basis is given in SLev 20:15 (370A): "If a man ejaculates into livestock, he is to be killed, and you are to kill the livestock" (Lev 20:15). "A man": this excludes a minor (who is younger than 9 years and 1 day old, and thus he is not punished as a perpetrator); "who ejaculates into livestock": whether he is big (an adult) or small; "he is to be killed": by stoning. You say "by stoning," but should the punishment happen (instead) by one of all (the other) death penalties in the Torah? Scripture teaches: "And you are to kill the livestock"; here it talks of killing, and there (specifically Deut 13:10) it talks of killing; as the killing spoken of there means stoning, so also here it means stoning. We have learned the penalty concerning the one who has sex with the livestock; where does the proof come from concerning the penalty for those who let livestock have sex with them? Scripture teaches: "Everyone who lies with livestock is to be killed" (Exod 22:18). If the passage (because of the general expression "lie") references not (only) the one who has sex, then it should be related (also) to those who let livestock have sex with them. We have learned the penalty both for the one who has sex and for those who let livestock have sex with them; whence comes the proof about the warning? Scripture teaches: "And you are not to ejaculate into any livestock, to thereby make yourself impure" (Lev 18:23). We have learned the warning for the one who has sex; where does the proof come from for the warning for those who let livestock have sex with them? Scripture teaches: "Let there be no consecrated prostitute from the sons of Israel" (Deut 23:18); and further it says, "There were also consecrated prostitutes in the land" (1 Kgs 14:24). These are the words of R. Ishmael († ca. 135). R. Aqiba said, "This is not needed. See, it says, 'You are not to ejaculate שְׁכָבְתְּךָ' (Lev 18:23, which can be interpreted as:) 'You are not to allow your being laid with שְׁכִיבְתְּךָ' (i.e., that someone lie with you)." – The same can be found in a baraita in b. Sanh. 54B; further parallels can be found in Mek. Exod. 22:18 (100B); y. Sanh. 7.25A.10; see also b. Sanh. 15A. ‖ Mishnah Qiddušin 4.14: R. Judah (ca. 150) said, "A single man should not pasture livestock...." The scholars allowed it. – According to b. Qidd. 82A.6, 12, someone answered R. Judah, "The Israelites are not under suspicion because of livestock." – A parallel can be found in t. Qidd. 5.10 (343). ‖ Babylonian Talmud Baba Meṣiʿa 71A: Rab Joseph († 333) taught as a tannaitic tradition, "A widow should not raise a dog and should not let a young man at school live in her dwelling (literally: lodging house). The rule is given concerning the young man at school, since he can hide it (if he regularly has contact with his landlady); but in the case of the dog she must fear since it may cling to her (run after her if she has committed fornication with it, so that people can conclude from the behavior of the dog toward her about her behavior toward the dog; why is this forbidden!?)." Someone said, "Since, if she drops him a piece of meat for it, it (likewise) may cling to her (run after her), people may think that it clings to her because of the piece of flesh that she threw to him." (Since fornication can remain hidden, that prohibition was issued.) – The same can be found in b. ʿAbod. Zar. 22B. ‖ Caution about non-Israelites. Mishnah ʿAbodah Zarah 2.1: Livestock may not stay in the inns of the *goyim* (non-Jews) because they are suspected of copulating. ‖ Tosefta ʿAbodah Zarah 3.2 (463): Livestock may not stay in the inns of the *goyim*, neither male animals with men nor female animals with women, because the man causes someone to lie with the male livestock and because the woman causes someone to lie with the female livestock (see the following two citations), and it is not necessary to say in the first place that male animals may not stay with women and female animals with men. Further, livestock may not be handed over to one of their (the *goyim*'s) shepherds; also, a child may not be handed over to him (a *goy*) for school instruction or to teach him a trade if he is alone with him. – The same may be found in a baraita in b. ʿAbod. Zar. 15B. ‖ A baraita in y. ʿAbod. Zar. 2.40C.33: Livestock may not stay in the inns (of the *goyim*), neither male animals with men nor female animals with women, and it is not necessary to say in the first place that male animals may not stay with women and female animals with men. "Male animals may not stay with men": what do you have against this? His (the innkeeper's) lover stays with him, and if she does not find him, she lets the livestock have sex with her (so the man causes male cattle to be used for sex, as it says above in t. ʿAbod. Zar. 3.2); "female animals may not stay with women": what do you have against that? Her lover stays with her, and if he does not find her, he has sex with them. ‖ Babylonian Talmud ʿAbodah Zarah 22B: "Female animals may not stay with women" (see t. ʿAbod. Zar. 3.2 above). Why are they not allowed to be together? Mar Uqba b. Hama (ca. 375) said, "Since the *goyim* are often with the wives of their associates, and if he once does not find her, he finds (female) livestock and has sex with it. And if you want, I will say: Even if he finds her (the woman), he still has sex with the livestock; for the author said, 'They (the *goyim*) prefer the livestock of the Israelites to their own women.'" – The last sentence is also in b. Giṭ. 38B.

Haggadic Material. Sifra Leviticus 20:16 (371A): "And if a woman approaches any livestock so that it may have sex with her, you are to strike dead the woman and the livestock" (Lev 20:16). "You are to strike dead the woman and the livestock." If a person has sinned, how has the animal sinned? Yet because the offense (being enticed to sin) came to the person by the animal, Scripture said: "It is to be stoned." Then the inference is justified by moving from the lesser to the greater: if, because an offense came to a person by livestock, Scripture says concerning livestock, who do not know how to differentiate between good and evil, "It is to be stoned," how much more does it go for a person, who caused someone else to deviate from the way of life onto the way of death, that God will make him disappear from the face of the earth! – Babylonian Talmud Sanhedrin 55B: (Why are the person and the animal stoned?) So that the animal might not go across the street and then someone could say, "This is the animal on whose account this or that person was stoned." – Both explanations are found alongside each other in m. Sanh. 7.4; they are referred to by R. Joshua b. Levi (ca. 250) in Pesiq. 142B; Gen. Rab. 15 (11B); R. Abbahu (ca. 300) in Pesiq. 75B; TanḥB אמור § 11 (45B) and R. Jacob b. Zabdai (ca. 330) in Lev. Rab. 27 (125B); the second explanation is cited in Pesiq. 142B.

1:27 B: Receiving in themselves the retribution ... for their aberrance.

Babylonian Talmud Šabbat 33A: R. Hoshaiah (ca. 225) said, "Whoever gives himself fully to fornication, on him wounds and welts will appear; for Prov 20:30 says, 'Running wild in vice brings about welts of wounds' (so the midr.); and not only this, he is also punished with dropsy, for Prov 20:30 says, 'And blows which hit the chambers of the belly.'" Rab Nahman bar Isaac († 356) said, "Dropsy is a sign of fornication."

1:29–31: Unrighteousness, wickedness, worthlessness, greed ....

Similar vice catalogues appear rather frequently in the pseudepigrapha.

See Wis 14:22ff.; 2 En. 10:4ff. at § Rom 1:24, #1; T. Levi 17 at § Rom 1:27 A, B, #1. ‖ 3 Baruch 4: "Everything (bad) comes rather from drinking wine, such as homicide, adultery, fornication, perjury, stealing, and the like." — 3 Baruch 8: "And I, Baruch, said, 'O Lord, and why are its (the sun's) rays speckled on earth?' And the angel said to me, 'Because it has to look at the transgressions of the law and the sins of men together, such as fornication, adultery, stealing, robbery, idolatry, drunkenness, homicide, quarrels, jealousy, suspicions, grumbling, gossip, fortune telling, and the like.'" — Almost the same list is found in 3 Bar. 13.

1:30 A: Haughty.

On pride, see § Matt 23:12 and § Luke 1:51.

1:30 B: Disobeying parents.

The following story is recounted many times as an example of childish piety in the gentile world. Jerusalem Talmud Pe'ah 1.15C.14: R. Abbahu (ca. 300) said in the name of R. Yohanan († 279), "R. Eliezer (ca. 90) was asked to what extent one was supposed to honor one's father and mother. He answered them, 'You are asking me? Go and ask Damah b. Netinah.' Damah b. Netinah was the chairman of the councilmen. Once his mother hit him in the face in the presence of the whole council and her shoe fell out of her hand. He gave it to her so that she would not have to make an effort. R. Hezekiah (ca. 350) said, 'There was a *goy* (non-Israelite) from Ashkelon and a chairman of the councilmen, and his whole life he never sat on the stone that his father used to sit on, and when his father died, he made that (stone) into an idol.' Once the jasper of Benjamin (from the breastplate of the high priest) had gotten lost; someone asks, 'Who is it who owns a stone similarly precious?' Someone said, 'Damah b. Netinah owns one.' They went to him and agreed with him on a price of 100 *denars*. When he went up to get it for them, he came upon his father sleeping—some say, 'The key to the box (with the jasper) lay between the father's fingers'; others say, 'His father's feet were resting stretched out on the box'—then he went down to them and told them, 'I cannot bring it to you.' They thought, 'Maybe he wants a higher price.' They raised it to 200, raised it to 1000 (*denars*). When his father awoke from sleep, he went up and got it for them. They wanted to give him the last price they had offered (see the reading in y. Qidd. 1); but he did not take it. He said, 'Should I sell honoring my father to you for money? I do not want to gain from honoring my father.' What did God pay him as a recompense? R. Yose b. Abun (ca. 350) said, 'On that night his cow gave birth to a red cow (as she was used for the atoning water in the temple), and all Israel weighed out for him its weight in gold and took it.' R. Shabbetai (ca. 260) said, 'It is written, "Justice and the fullness of righteousness he does not decline" (Job 37:23). God does not delay the payment of wages to those who fulfill the commandments among the *goyim*.'" — Parallel passages can be found in y. Qidd. 1.61A.67; Pesiq. Rab. 23/24 (123B); Deut. Rab. (196B); in b. Qidd. 31A and b. ʿAbod. Zar. 23B, excluding other variations, Samuel († 254) is named as the author and Rab Judah († 299) as the tradent.

1:32: Since they knew God's righteous demands.

On the gentiles' knowledge of God's will, see § Rom 1:20 C. – As the one who knows and does God's will earns praise,[a] so the one who knows God's will but does not do it earns special punishment.[b]

a. Mekilta Exodus 12:28 (16B): "Then the children of Israel did as Yahweh had commanded" (Exod 12:23): this is meant to make known to you their praise; for they did as Moses and Aaron told them to. ‖ Sifra Leviticus 10:7 (192A): "They acted according to the word of Moses" (Lev 10:7); they fulfilled the commandments of our teacher Moses. Scripture has praised the Israelites in the same way in the section about sending away the impure: "And the children of Israel acted thus and sent them out in front of the camp" (Num 5:4). Scripture likewise praises Joshua: As Yahweh commanded Moses, Moses commanded Joshua, and Joshua did so (cf. Num 27:22 and Exod 17:10). ‖ Sifre Numbers 8:3 § 60 (16A): "And Aaron did so" (Num 8:3): this is meant to make known to you Aaron's praise, for he did as Moses told him.

b. Deuteronomy Rabbah 7 (204A): "To observe and to do all my commandments" (so the midr. cites Deut 28:1). R. Simeon b. Halapta (ca. 190) said, "Whoever studies the words of the Torah but does not fulfill (do) them, his punishment is heavier than the one who does not study at all. What can this be compared with? With a king who had an arboretum. He put two coloni in it: one planted trees and cut them down (again), and the other did not plant at all and did not cut down. Whom will the king be angrier at? Will he not be angrier at the one who had planted and cut them down (again)? In the same way whoever studies the words of the Torah but does not fulfill them, his punishment is heavier than the one who does not study at all. How do we know this? Because it says, 'The godless, who does not study how to be righteous, will receive pardon' (Isa 26:10, so the midr.); but if he did study and did not fulfill, he will not receive pardon." ‖ Pesiqta 13B: "There arose great anger at Israel" (2 Kgs 3:27). God said to the Israelites, "My children, the nations of the world do not know my power (Tanḥ. כי תשא: my glory) and they rise up against me; but you know my power and you rise up against me" (hence the great anger in 2 Kgs 3:27; see b. Sanh. 39B on this passage of Scripture). – A parallel passage can be found in Tanḥ. כי תשא 111B. – See further § Luke 12:47f.

2:2: But we know that God's judgment is according to truth.

2 Baruch 85:9: "Before the judgment demands his own and the truth (of the judgment) demands what is due to it, we will prepare ourselves...." – Judgment and truth likewise stand alongside each other in 4 Ezra 7:34. ‖ Mishnah ʾAbot 3.16: (R. Aqiba, † ca. 135, said,) "The judgment is a judgment of truth וְהַדִּין דִּין אֱמֶת." ‖ Mekilta Exodus 14:28 (40A): R. Pappos (ca. 110) said in a presentation, "'He is one, who will answer him? His soul demands, he carries it out' (Job 23:13). Alone he judges all who come into the world, and there is no one who could respond to his words." R. Aqiba († ca. 135) said to him, "Enough, Pappos!"

R. Pappos said, "How do you explain the words then: 'He is one, who will answer him?'" R. Aqiba answered, "One cannot respond to the words of the one who spoke and the world came into existence; rather he judges everything according to truth באמת and everything according to justice בדין." — The same is found in Midr. Song. 1:9 (90A); in TanḥB וירא § 21 (49A) the words "according to truth" are lacking; R. Aqiba's answer is completely different in TanḥB שמות § 14 (4B). ‖ A common dictum is: God's seal is truth (see the end of § John 1:14 and § John 3:33.) See 4 Ezra 7:104: "The day of decision is like the court courier and shows to all the seal of truth."

2:3: Do you think ... that you will escape God's judgment?

1 Enoch 52:7: "In those days (of the decision) no one will save himself, neither with gold nor with silver, nor will one be able to escape." — 1 Enoch 102:1: "Whither will you flee in those days, when he brings painful fire upon you, and how will you save yourselves? Will you not be terrified and afraid when he hurls his voice at you?" ‖ Psalms of Solomon 15:8f.: "Those who do injustice will not avoid the judgment of the Lord; they will be seized as by enemies skilled in war, for the sign of doom is on their forehead."

2:4 A: Or do you despise the richness ... of his forbearance?

1. μακροθυμία = α. אֶרֶךְ אַף (Jer 15:15); LXX: μακροθυμία. The targum changed the thought: "do not give an extension אַרְכָא of my disgrace." β. אֹרֶךְ אַפַּיִם (Prov 25:15); LXX: μακροθυμία. Targum: נְגִירוּתָא דְרוּחָא (a different reading: נגידותא) = length of spirit or forbearance.

2. On God's forbearance in general.

Jerusalem Talmud Taʿanit 2.65B.38: "For he is gracious and merciful, longsuffering אֶרֶךְ אַפַּיִם and rich in grace and relents from evil" (Joel 2:13). R. Samuel b. Nahman (ca. 260) said in the name of R. Jonathan (ca. 220),"אֶרֶךְ אַף (sg.) is not written here, but rather ארך אפים 'slow to manifestations of anger' (pl.); he is longsuffering with the righteous and longsuffering with the godless." R. Aha (ca. 320) and R. Tanḥum b. Hiyya (ca. 300) said in the name of R. Yohanan († 279), "ארך אף is not written here, but rather ארך אפים; he is longsuffering, before he exacts (punishment); and when he has begun to exact punishment, he is (again) longsuffering and exacts it (i.e., longsuffering in the process of exacting itself)." R. Hanina (ca. 225) said, "Whoever says that the All Merciful One is lenient וַתְּרָן (lets sins go unpunished), may his bowels disappear יִתְוַותְּרוּן (through diarrhea); he is rather longsuffering, but he exacts from his own." R. Levi (ca. 300) said, "What does ארך אפים mean? Far from anger (then follows the passage from y. Taʿan. 2.65B.43 cited in Rom 1:18 A, n. *b*). — In Pesiq. 161B the names of the authors are switched; further, a remark is attached to the dictum of R. Jonathan cited above, and the remark belongs to R. Aqiba († ca. 135) according to Pesiq. 73A; Gen. Rab. 33 (19D); Lev. Rab. 27 (128A) and Tanḥ. אמור 173A. The passage elaborated in this way states: R. Aha and R. Tanḥum b. Hiyya (so read!) said in the name of R. Yohanan, "ארך אף is not written here, but rather ארך אפים; he is longsuffering with the righteous and exacts punishment on them for the few evil works that they did in this world, in order to give them their full recompense in the future (in the future world). And he richly gives wellbeing (fortune) to the godless in this world and repays them (thereby) for the few good works that they did in this world, in order to demand their full debt from them in the future (in the future world). For it is written, 'He will repay (each) of his haters to his face, to destroy him; he will not delay ...' (Deut 7:10)." R. Samuel said in the name of R. Yohanan (read: R. Jonathan) ... as above in the name of R. Yohanan. — Parallels can be found in Midr. Ps. 86 § 7 (187B), which links itself to y. Taʿan. 2.65B.38; Midr. Ps. 103 § 11 (218B) is connected to Pesiq. 161B. The dictum of R. Hanina is also in Gen. Rab. 67 (42D); y. Beṣah 3.62D.19; y. Šeqal. 5.48D.31; b. B. Qam. 50A, but here too R. Jonathan's dictum appears briefly under the name of R. Samuel b. Nahman as the author. ‖ Seder Eliyahu Rabbah 24 (135): Just as it is God's way to be longsuffering, he is forbearing with the godless and accepts them in repentance, so you too should be forbearing with one another for the good.

3. God's forbearance is a product of his omnipotence.

Babylonian Talmud Yoma 69B: R. Joshua b. Levi (ca. 250) said, "Why are the men of the 'Great Synagogue' (the administrative body of 120 members who supposedly led the Jewish community since the days of Ezra) called by this name? Because they brought the wreath (of divine attributes) to its earlier state. Moses came and said, 'The great, strong, and dreadful God' (Deut 10:17). Jeremiah came and said, 'gentiles have torn down his temple, where is his dreadfulness?' So he did not say 'dreadful' (but rather only 'great, strong God' [Jer 32:18]). Daniel came and said, 'His children have served gentiles, where are the manifestations of his strength?' He did not say 'strong' (but rather only 'great and dreadful God' [Dan 9:4]). Then those (the men of the Great Synagogue) came and said, 'On the contrary, his strength is shown in that he suppresses his impulse (to punish and destroy) and bestows forbearance ארך אפים on the godless and these are the manifestations of his dreadfulness; for if the dreadfulness of God did not exist, how could one nation (namely the Jewish one) continue to exist among the (other) nations? And our teachers (Jeremiah and Daniel), how did they act thus and tear down the definition that Moses had established?'" R. Eleazar (ca. 270) said, "Because they knew about God that he is truthful and therefore they did not lie to him." — See Wis 11:23: "You have mercy on all because you can do everything." — Wisdom 12:16: "For your strength is the cause (principle) of your righteousness, and so that you may rule over everything, you spare everything." — See other motifs about the divine forbearance in the following section on Rom 2:4 B.

2:4 B: Misunderstanding that God's goodness leads you to repentance?

Wisdom of Solomon 11:23: "You overlook people's sins so (they) can repent." — Wisdom of Solomon 12:10: "But you punished them (only) bit by bit and gave them time to repent." ‖ Midrash Ecclesiastes 7:15 (36A): Samuel the Small (ca. 100) was asked, "What does 'Many righteous men perish in their righteousness' (Eccl 7:15) mean?" He said, "It is evident and known before the one who spoke and the world came into existence that a righteous man will one day unravel (fall). Then God says, 'As long as he is still in his righteousness, I will take him away'; for it says, 'Many righteous men perish in their righteousness.' 'And many unrighteous men live a long time in their wrongdoing' (Eccl 7:15). As long as a person is alive, God hopes that he will repent. When he has died, his hope is lost; for it says, 'His hope is lost in the death of a godless person' (Prov 11:7). It is like a band of robbers that lay locked up in prison. One of them dug an opening and all escaped. Only one of them stayed back and did not escape. When the guard came, he began to beat that man with a stick and said to him, 'Your destiny is bad and your star has sunk (read טמיע with Midr. Eccl. 11:9)! The opening lay before you, but you did not escape!' So God will one day say to the godless, 'Repentance lay before you, but you did not convert; rather "the eyes of the wicked languish and all refuge vanishes for them, and their hope—a wisping away of the soul"' (Job 11:20)." R. Josiah (I, ca. 140; II, ca. 280) said, "Because of three things God has patience מאריך פנים with the godless in this world: they might perhaps repent or they might fulfill the commandments so that God may pay them their wage in this world, or perhaps righteous sons might issue from them. For so we find: he had patience with Ahaz, and Hezekiah issued from him; with Amon, and Josiah issued from him; with Shimei (see Esth 2:5), and Mordecai issued from him." ‖ We hear a completely different motif about the divine forbearance in 4 Ezra 7:74: "The Most High has had patience long enough with the inhabitants of the world—not however for their sake, but rather because of the times that he had established (from the beginning)." ‖ On repentance, see § Matt 4:17 A.

2:6: Who will repay each one according to his works.

See Ps 62:13; Prov 24:12; Job 34:11. ‖ Mishnah ʾAbot 3.15: (Aqiba [† ca. 135] said,) "Everything is foreseen, but permission (free will) is given; the world is judged with goodness, but everything is according to the amount of the act לְפִי רוֹב הַמַּעֲשֶׂה" (i.e., according to the majority of the works). ‖ Jerusalem Talmud Pe'ah 1.16B.37: If a person's merits constitute the majority, he will inherit the garden of Eden; if transgressions constitute the majority, he will inherit gehenna. If however he has a balance (of merits and transgressions), then, as R. Yose b. Hanina (ca. 270) has said, "It is not written here (Exod 34:7; Mic 7:18): 'He who takes away sins עוונות (so read!),' but rather, 'he who takes away one sin עון.' God quickly tears off a debt note from the transgressions so that the merits cause the scale to sink (so that they gain the greater weight)." R. Eleazar (ca. 270) said, "'Grace is yours, Yahweh; for you repay everyone according to what he does' (Ps 62:13). And if he does not have (what gives the merits the greater weight over the debt), you give to him from what is yours (from your grace)." This is the opinion of R. Eleazar. For R. Eleazar said, "'He who is rich in grace' (= God in Exod 34:6) tips the scale according to grace." — Both R. Yose b. Hanina and R. Eleazar follow the opinion of the Hillelites; see the baraita in b. Roš Haš. 16B at § Matt 1:19, #1, n. *a*. — Parallels can be found in y. Sanh. 10.27C.30; somewhat differently in y. Qidd. 1.61D.47; in a different form in Pesiq. 167A; Midr. Ps. 30 § 4 (118A); 86 § 2 (187A); in the last passage the opinion of R. Yose b. Hanina is attributed to R. Phineas the priest (ca. 360) and that of R. Eleazar, at least according to the manuscript reading in Buber n. 10 on Rabbanan. See further b. Roš Haš. 17A and b. ʿArak. 8B. ‖ Babylonian Talmud Roš Haššanah 17B: R. Eleazar (ca. 280) raised the objection, "It says, 'Grace is yours, Yahweh' (Ps 62:13), and then it says (again), 'For you repay everyone according to what he does'

(Ps 62:3). First, 'You repay everyone according to what he does,' and in the end (God acts according to the words), 'Grace is yours, Yahweh.'"

2:10: Glory and honor and peace to everyone who does good, to the Jew first and also to the Greek.

On the last words, see b. B. Qam. 38A: Mar b. Rabina (ca. 400) said, "... Even if they (non-Jews) keep them (the commandments), they receive no recompense for this." Really they do not? But in a baraita it says that R. Meir (ca. 150) said, "Where does the notion come from that even a *goy* (non-Jew) who devotes himself to the Torah is like the high priest? Scripture teaches, 'The person who does them will live by them' (Lev 18:5); it does not say priests or Levites or Israelites but rather 'person.' This teaches that even a *goy* who devotes himself to the Torah is like the high priest. I mean: They do not receive a recompense for this like one who is commanded (to do something) and does it, but rather like one who it not commanded (to do something) and (nevertheless) does it. For R. Hanina (ca. 225) said, 'Greater is the one who is commanded (to do something) and does it than the one who is not commanded (to do something) and does it.'" — The same is found in b. ʿAbod. Zar. 3A. — The saying of R. Meir is also found in b. Sanh. 59A; in SLev 18:5 (338B), R. Jeremiah (ca. 110) is named as the author (perhaps Jeremiah was a slip of the pen when writing Meir?). — The saying of R. Hanina is found also in b. Qidd. 31A and b. B. Qam. 87A.

2:11: With God there is no esteem of the person.

1. οὐ γάρ ἐστιν προσωπολημψία παρὰ τῷ θεῷ = אֵין עִם יהוה מַשֹּׂא פָנִים (2 Chr 19:7).

Septuagint 2 Chronicles 19:7 οὐκ ἔστι μετὰ κυρίου ... θαυμάσαι πρόσωπον.[50] — Targum: לֵית קֳדָם יי׳ מִסַּב אַפִּין "before Yahweh there is no accepting (no preference) of a person." ‖ (Hebrew) Sirach 35:15: "For he is a God of justice and with him there is no esteem of the person אין עמו משוא פנום." — (Greek) Sirach 32:12 (according to the chapter count in Fritzsche[51]): "For the Lord is judge and with him there is no esteem of a person οὐκ ἔστι παρ' αὐτῷ δόξα προσώπου." ‖ Jubilees 5:16: "He is not one who looks at the person, and he is not one who takes a gift when he says he will execute judgment on every single person. If (one) gives everything that is on earth, he does not take a gift and does not (look at the person) and he accepts nothing from his hand, for he is a righteous judge." ‖ Psalms of Solomon 2:18: ὁ θεὸς κριτὴς δίκαιος καὶ οὐ θαυμάσει πρόσωπον. — On θαμάζειν πρόσωπον see LXX 2 Chr 19:7 above. ‖ Mishnah ʾAbot 4.22: (R. Eleazar Haqqappar [ca. 180] said,) "... He is God, he the one who forms, he the creator, he the one who pays heed, he the judge, he the witness, he the accuser, and one day he will judge, the one before whom no wrong is valid and with whom there is no forgetting and no esteeming of the person מַשּׂוֹא פָנִים

50. S-B: The LXX uses θαυμάζειν πρόσωπον instead of the otherwise usual λαμβάνειν πρόσωπον to render נָשָׂא פָנִים also in Gen 19:21; Deut 10:17; Isa 9:15, while in Lev 19:5 it translates לא תֶהְדַּר פני גדול ("You shall not honor the person of the great in a biased manner") with θαυμάζειν πρόσωπον. θαυμάζειν πρόσωπον is used for λαμβάνειν πρόσωπον also in Jude 16.

51. Otto F. Fritzsche, *Kurzgefasstes Exegetisches Handbuch zu den Apokryphen des Alten Testamentes: Die Weisheit Jesus-Sirach's*, vol. 5 (Leipzig: S. Hirzel, 1859).

and no taking of bribes; for everything belongs to him." ‖ See 1 En. 63:8 and 2 Bar. 13:8 and § Eph 6:9.

2. Balancing Num 6:26 with Deut 10:17; here the rabbinic scholars proceed from the assumption that נשא פנים has the same meaning in both passages, namely "to lift the face to someone" = to look at someone, to take account of someone.[52]

A baraita in b. Nid. 69B: The people of Alexandria asked R. Joshua b. Hananiah (ca. 90) about 12 things; three concerned words of wisdom (i.e., the halakic knowledge of the law), three concerned words of the Haggadah, three concerned foolish (trivial) things and three concerned things about ordinary life דִּבְרֵי דֶרֶךְ אֶרֶץ.... (70B): Three concerned words of the Haggadah.... A passage of Scripture says, "He does not take account (of the person) and accepts no gift" (Deut 10:17) and another passage of Scripture says, "Yahweh takes account of you" (Num 6:26). Here (Num 6), before he (God) has laid down his judicial decision (since God can change his judgment and make allowances for someone); there (Deut 10), after he has laid down his judicial decision. See R. Aqiba in the next citation. ‖ Babylonian Talmud Roš Haššanah 17B: Come and hear! The proselyte Beluriah (Veluria) asked Rabban Gamaliel (ca. 90), "In your Torah it is written, 'He takes no account (of the person)' (Deut 10:17), and then again it is written, 'Yahweh takes account of you' (Num 6:26)." Then R. Yose, the priest, attended to her; he said to her, "I will tell you a parable. What can this be compared with? With a person who borrowed a *mina* from someone else; he appointed a time (for repayment) before the king and swore to him on the life of the king. The time came, and he did not pay him. Then he came to placate the king. This one said to him, 'May the insult you have done to me be forgiven you; go and placate the other person!' So too this passage (Num 6) deals with transgressions between a person and God (since God makes allowances) and that passage (Deut 10) deals with transgressions between one person and another (since God does not make allowances in changing a decision)." (So it was said) until R. Aqiba († ca. 135) came and taught, "Here (Num 6 deals with the time) before he (God) has made his judicial decision; there (Deut 10 deals with the time) after he has laid down his judicial decision." See the interpretation of R. Joshua in the previous citation. ‖ Babylonian Talmud Berakot 20B: Rab Avira (4th cent.) said in a presentation, sometimes in the name of R. Ammi (ca. 300) and sometimes in the name of R. Asi (ca. 300), "The angels of service said before God, 'Lord of the world, in your Torah it is written: "He does not take account and takes no gift" (Deut 10:17); but do you not take account of Israel? For it is written: "Yahweh takes account of you" (Num 6:26).' He answered them, 'Should I take no account of Israel, to whom I have written in the Torah: "If you have eaten your fill, praise Yahweh your God" (Deut 8:10)—and they are so meticulous with themselves down to the size of an olive and down to the size of an egg?!'" — Here the solution is: God takes account of Israel, but not of others. ‖ Sifre Numbers 6:26 § 42 (12B): "Yahweh takes account of you" (Num 6:26), namely when you stand and pray; for it says, "He said to him: Look, I have taken account of you

52. TN: The German "*auf jemand Rücksicht nehmen*" is polyvalent in meaning and could mean "show consideration for," "take account of," "make allowances for," all of which come into play in the discussion below.

(Lot)" (Gen 19:21). Then the inference is justified by moving from the lesser to the greater: "If I have taken account of Lot אם ללוט נשאתי פנים because of my friend Abraham, should I not take account of you (the one who prays) for your sake and the sake of your fathers?" And this is what Scripture said: "Yahweh takes account of you" (Num 6:26). A passage of Scripture says, "Yahweh takes account of you" (Num 6:26), and another passage of Scripture says, "He takes no account" (Deut 10:17). How will these two passages of Scripture be maintained alongside each other? If the Israelites do the will of God, then the following is valid: "Yahweh takes account of you." And if they do not do the will of God, then the following is valid: "He takes no account." A different explanation: Before the judicial decision is sealed, the following is valid: "Yahweh takes account of you"; but after the judicial decision is sealed, the following is valid: "He does not take account (thus as R. Joshua and R. Aqiba said in a presentation in the first two citations). ‖ Numbers Rabbah 11 (164A): "May Yahweh take account of you" (Num 6:26) pertains to this world; "he takes no account" (Deut 10:17) pertains to the future world. — Parallels: the explanation of R. Yose the priest reappears as a saying of one R. Yose b. Dosai (when?) in Num. Rab. 11 (164A); excluding SNum 6:26 § 42 (12B) the explanation of R. Joshua and R. Aqiba is anonymous both in Num. Rab. 11 (164A) and in TanḥB נשא § 18 (17B); the explanation of R. Ammi and R. Asi is anonymous in Num. Rab. 11 (164A) and in TanḥB נשא § 18 (17B). ‖ See Pesiq. 156A at the end of #3 below.

3. In spite of the divine impartiality, God has a different relationship to Israel than to the nations of the world. This idea recurs in all kinds of contexts and expressions.

α. Only Israel is God's possession (see § John 1:11). — β. Only the Israelites are called friends of God (see § John 15:14). — γ. Israel is more beloved by God than all other nations; therefore, God's hatred and wrath apply only to the latter, but grace applies to Israel; therefore, Israel is also judged differently than the nations. Sifre Deuteronomy 33:3 § 344 (143B): "He loved nations" (Deut 33:3) (the rabbinic scholars took this to mean the tribes of Israel; see Tg. Onk. and Rashi on the passage): this teaches that God loves Israel as he loves no other nation and no other kingdom. — The same sentence is found again a few lines later below. ‖ Sifre Deuteronomy 33:3 § 344 (143B): "He loved nations" (Deut 33:3): this teaches that God did not show love to the nations of the world as he showed it to the Israelites. ‖ Pesiqta 15B: R. Judan (ca. 350) said in the name of R. Samuel b. Nahmani (ca. 260), "It is like a king who had an undergarment and he commanded his servant and said to him, 'Shake it out, fold it together and take care of it!' His servant said to him, 'My lord king, of all the undergarments you have, you have issued me a command concerning only this one.' He answered him, 'Because it clings closely to my flesh.' Likewise Moses said before God, 'Lord of the world, of the 70 nations that you have, you have issued me a command concerning only Israel: "Thus you are to speak to the children of Israel" (Exod 3:15); "And to the children of Israel you are to speak thus" (Exod 30:31); "Say to the children of Israel" (Exod 33:5); "Speak to the children of Israel" (Exod 31:13); "Command the children of Israel" (Lev 24:2); "And you are to command the children of Israel" (Exod 27:20); "When you take the total of the children of Israel" (Exod 30:12).' He answered him, 'Because they cling closely to me; for it says, "As a belt clings closely to a man's hips, so I have made myself cling closely to Israel" (Jer 13:11).'" — The same is found in Lev. Rab. 2 (106B); only the beginning is found in Lev. Rab. 24 (123A). ‖ Deuteronomy Rabbah 5 (202A): "You are to appoint judges and officials for yourself in all your gates" (Deut 16:18). R. Levi (ca. 300) said, "What can this be compared with? With a king who had many sons, and he loved the youngest one most of all. He also had a garden that he loved more than anything else he owned. The king said, 'I will give this garden, which I love more than anything else I own, to my youngest son, whom I love more than all my other sons.' Likewise, God said, 'Of all the nations I have created, I love only the Israelites; for it says, "When Israel was a boy, I developed a love for him" (Hos 11:1); and of everything I have created, I love only justice; for it says, "I, Yahweh, love justice" (Isa 61:8).' So, God said, 'I will give what I love to the nation I love.' This is the point of: 'You shall appoint judges and officials …' (Deut 16:18)." ‖ Midrash Song of Songs 1:2 (84B): "Your caresses are tastier than wine" (Song 1:2). "Your caresses are tastier": here the Israelites are meant; "than wine": here the nations of the world are meant. (The numerical value of יין = "wine" is) י 10, י 10, נ 50, these are the 70 nations; this teaches that the Israelites are more beloved before God than all the nations. ‖ See Pesiq. 193B in the excursus "The Feast of Tabernacles," VI, #2, n. *b.* ‖ Tanḥuma תרומה 100A: The tyrant Rufus (Tineius Rufus, who became governor of Judea around 132 CE) once asked R. Aqiba († ca. 135) and said to him, "Why does God hate us? For it is written: 'Esau I hate' (Mal 1:3)." He answered, "Tomorrow I will give you the answer." On the next day he (Rufus) said to him, "R. Aqiba, what did you dream this night and what did you see (in your dream)?" He answered him, "In the dream during the night there were two dogs, one whose name was Rufus and the other whose name was Rufina." Immediately he (Rufus) got angry and said to him, "You named your dogs only after me and my wife, so you have subjected yourself to death by the government." R. Aqiba answered him, "What difference is there then between you and them (the dogs)? You eat and drink, and they eat and drink; you think about procreation, and they think about procreation; you die, and they die. Since I named them after you, you have gotten angry; and God spreads out heaven and establishes the earth, kills and makes alive, then you take a piece of wood and call it God, naming it after him; must he not hate you all the more? This is the point of: 'And Esau I hate.'" ‖ Babylonian Talmud ʿAbodah Zarah 4A: R. Hama b. Hanina (ca. 260) interjected, "It is written, 'I have no wrath' (Isa 27:4); and it is written, 'Yahweh takes revenge and is full of wrath' (Nah 1:2). There is no contradiction: here (Isa 27:4) it pertains to Israel, there (Nah 1:2) to the nations of the world." ‖ Midrash Psalm 36 § 7 (126A): "Keep your grace for those who know you" (Ps 36:11). R. Isaac (ca. 300) said, "Do not keep your grace for the nations of the world, who do not know you." ‖ Genesis Rabbah 82 (52C): (A Roman military officer spoke to two students of R. Joshua [ca. 90],) "One passage of Scripture says, 'Yahweh has arisen for a lawsuit and stands to judge the nations' (Isa 3:13), and again it is written, 'I will sit there to judge the nations on every side' (Joel 4:12)." They said to him, "In that hour when God judges the Israelites, he will judge them while standing in that he will briefly make judgment and mitigate the same; but when he judges the nations of the world, he will judge them while sitting, while being meticulous in judgment and drawing it out for a long time." He said to them, "Your teacher R. Joshua did not explain the passages in this way, rather he said that in both passages Scripture speaks about the nations of the world: 'When God judges the nations of the world, he will judge them while sitting, while being meticulous in judgment and drawing it out for a long time; and then (he will arise and) become their accuser.'" ‖ Jerusalem Talmud Roš Haššannah 1.57A.40: R. Levi (ca. 300) said, "'He judges the earth with righteousness and speaks justice to the nations with equity' (Ps 9:9). God judges the Israelites by day, when they devote themselves to fulfilling the commandments, and the nations at night, when they celebrate about their transgressions (read with the parallels עברות instead of מצות)." Parallels can be found in Pesiq. Rab. 40 (167B), which is extensively elaborated, and Midr. Ps. 9 § 11 (44A). ‖ Mekilta Exodus 21:30 (93B): For the nations there is no redemption (atonement); Scripture teaches, "A man will surely not redeem a brother, and he will not give God his ransom. The ransom of their souls is too costly" (Ps 49:8f.). The Israelites are beloved, for God gives the nations of the world in their stead as atonement for their souls; for it says, "I will give Egypt for you as atonement" (Isa 43:3). Why? "Because you are precious in my eyes, valued, and I love you. I give people for you and nations for your life" (Isa 43:3). — The author is R. Ishmael († ca. 135). — See similar ideas in SDeut 32:43 § 333 (140A) at § Luke 24:26, I, #2, n. *m* and Tg. Isa. 53:8 at § Matt 8:17, A. ‖ Jerusalem Talmud Pe'ah 1.16B.5: God counts a good intention as an action (so that it can be recompensed as one); God does not count an evil intention as an action. God counts a good intention as a deed; for it is written: "Then the pious conferred with each other (and a commemorative book was written before him for the pious)" (Mal 3:16). God does not count an evil intention as a deed: "If I intended wrong in my heart, Yahweh would not hear it" (Ps 66:18). What you say here is relevant for Israel, but with the *goyim* (non-Israelites) it is reversed: God does not count the good intention, but he does count the evil intention. God does not count the evil intention, for it is written: "And till the sun went down he was anxious to save him" (Dan 6:15), and it is not written: "and he saved him" (read ושיזביה instead of לשיזביה. Although the king in fact kept Daniel alive until the evening, this is not viewed as saving him but only as intending to save him; see Tosafot b. Qidd. 39B מהשבה). God counts the evil intention: Because of killing, because of wickedness toward your brother Jacob (shame must cover you ...; so the midr., which relates מקטל in Obad 9 to verse 10). How so? Did Esau kill Jacob? Rather, it teaches that he intended to kill him, and Scripture reckons it to him as if he had killed him. — See a partial parallel in b. Qidd. 40A. ‖ Leviticus Rabbah 27 (125D): R. Samuel b. Nahman (ca. 260) said, "In three passages (of Scripture) God comes to go to court with Israel, and the nations of the world rejoiced and said, 'They cannot go to court with their creator; now he will exterminate them from the world.' (First) in the hour when he said to them, 'Come now, let us go to court, says Yahweh!' (Isa 1:18). When God saw that the nations of the world rejoiced, he turned it for their good; for it says, 'If your sins should be as scarlet, they are to become white as snow' (Isa 1:18). In that hour the nations were astonished and said, 'Is this a conviction and is this a rebuke? He wanted to delight למתפרגגה (Pesiq.: למתפגגה) only in his children.' Then in the hour when he said to them, 'Hear, you mountains, the lawsuit of Yahweh!' (Mic 6:2). The nations of the world rejoiced and said, 'How can these ones go to court with their creator; now he will exterminate them from the world!' When God saw that the nations of the world rejoiced, he turned it for their good;

for it says, 'My people, what have I done to you?' (Mic 6:3); 'My people, think what Balak the king of Moab planned!' (Mic 6:4). Then they were astonished and said, 'Is this a conviction and is this a rebuke, this after he said that? He wanted to delight only in his children.' And then in that hour when he said, 'Yahweh has a lawsuit against Judah and wants to settle up with Jacob' (Hos 12:3). Then (the nations) rejoiced and said, 'How can they go to court with their creator; now he will exterminate them from the world!' Immediately he turned it to their good; this is what is written, 'In your mother's womb he grabbed his brother's heel' (Hos 12:4).... Immediately the nations of the world were astonished and said, 'Is this a conviction ...' as above." — Parallels can be found in Pesiq. 76B; Num. Rab. 10 (157A); Midr. Song. 5:16 (121B); TanḥB אמור § 13 (46B). ‖ Jerusalem Talmud Pe'ah 1.16B.49: R. Huna (ca. 350) said in the name of R. Abbahu (ca. 300), "Before God there is no forgetting; see, because of Israel he becomes forgetful שׁוֹכְחָן. What is the scriptural basis? 'The one who נושא guilt' is written in Micah 7:18 (i.e., it need not be read as נוֹשֵׂא 'who takes away' or 'forgives'; it can also be read as נוֹשֵׁא = 'who forgets'). And, likewise, David says, 'You took away נָשָׂאתָ (= נָשָׁאתָ "you forgot") the guilt of your people' (Ps 85:3)." The same can be found in y. Sanh. 10.27C.45; y. Šebu. 1.33C.15; Pesiq. 167A; in another form in Midr. Ps. 32 § 2 (121B); very briefly in y. Qidd. 1.61D.48. See Pesiq. Rab. 45 (186A): "Blessed is the one who נְשׂוּי פֶּשַׁע" (Ps 32:1); do not read samekh (ס = שׂ), but rather שׁ: נְשׁוּי פֶּשַׁע = "whose transgression was forgotten." R. Berekhiah the priest (ca. 340) said, "For he (God) forgets אַנְשֵׁי our sins before him (against him)." ‖ Pesiqta 156A: It is written: "May Yahweh take account of you" (so Midr. Num. 6:26); and it is also written: "He takes no account" (Deut 10:17). Whoever repents, he takes account of him; perhaps of everyone? Scripture teaches: "of you" (thus of Israel; Num 6:26), but not of another nation. ‖ It also says of the Messiah that he will be aggressive with the nations of the world but mild with Israel (see SDeut § 1 [65A] at § Matt 1:21 B, #2, n. *b*). ‖ For further remarks that belong in this context, see § Matt 5:43, #1, n. g.

2:12 A: For as many as have sinned without the law will perish also without the law.

The gentiles protest against this conclusion in, for example:

See Lev. Rab. 2 (134B) at § Luke 16:28. ‖ Pesiqta Rabbati 21 (99A): (The emperor) Hadrian—may his bones be crushed—asked R. Joshua b. Hananiah (ca. 90) and said to him, "God has bestowed great honor on the nations of the world; for his name is connected with those first five words[53] (commandments), which God gave to the Israelites, in order to say that, when the Israelites sin, he will proclaim a dispute against them. His name is not connected with the last five commandments, which he gave to the nations of the world, in order to say that, when the nations of the world sin, he will not proclaim a dispute against them." (See the continuation of the passage at § Luke 19:22).

53. S-B: The first five commandments in the Jewish enumeration correspond to the first four commandments in our enumeration.

2:12 B: As many as have sinned with the law will be judged by the law.

The Torah as the measure of God's judgment.

2 Baruch 48:47: "On account of all this their end will incriminate them (the godless), and your law, which they have transgressed, will punish them on that day." — 2 Baruch 48:27: "My judgment exacts my own and my law exacts its justice." — See also Jub. 5:13 and 4 Ezra 7:72f. ‖ See Pesiq. Rab. 21 (107A) at § Matt 19:18 A, #2, end of n. *a.* ‖ Tanḥuma שופטים 15B: R. Hanina b. Hama (ca. 225) said, "When God judges the world, he will gather (read תופשן) them (the nations) and their gods for judgment, and he will put down posts (?) for them and have the two tablets fetched on which the 10 commandments are written and say to them, 'Have they (the nations) tended to you at all?' Then they will say before him, 'Since the day you created us, only your people Israel have tended to us.' (Then the nations will be put to shame.)" — The same is found in TanḥB שופטים § 8 (16A). ‖ Babylonian Talmud ʿAbodah Zarah 2A: R. Hanina b. Papa (ca. 300) (according to others, R. Simlai [ca. 250]) said in a presentation, "In the future (at the last judgment) God will put the book of the Torah in his lap and say, 'Whoever has devoted himself to her (Torah), let him come and receive his recompense!'" — The same is found in Pesiq. 185B; in Tanḥ. שופטים 15B, Rab († 247) is named as the author and R. Hama b. Hanina (ca. 260) as the tradent; in TanḥB שופטים § 9 (16A), R. Hama b. Hanina is the author. ‖ TanḥumaB שמיני § 14 (16B): In the future God will have a herald go out and say: "Whoever has devoted himself to the Torah, let him come and receive his recompense!" Then the nations will say, "Give us our recompense, for we too have fulfilled this and that commandment." Then God will say, "Whoever has not eaten abominable and creeping animals, let him come and receive his recompense!" In that hour they will accept their judgment, as it said, "Those who eat the flesh of pigs and abominable animals and mice, all of them will come to an end, says Yahweh" (Isa 66:17). — In the parallel Tanḥ. שמיני 150A, B, God's answer is: "Whoever has fulfilled קיים the Torah, let him come and receive their recompense (i.e., the recompense for them)!" ‖ Exodus Rabbah 29 (89A): R. Jeremiah (ca. 320) said, "If the earth quaked at the hour when God gave life to the world (i.e., at the giving of the law), how much more will this happen when he comes to punish the godless because they have transgressed the word of the Torah (see Nah 1:6; Mal 3:2)." ‖ The idea of being judged by the law can be compared with the idea that the poor are to be judged by the poor, the rich by the rich, craftsmen by their peers, the gentiles by the proselytes who have come from them, that is, they will be measured by them and be assessed according to them; see the passages at § Matt 12:41 B.

2:13: For it is not the hearers of the law who are righteous before God, but rather the doers of the law will be declared righteous.

1. Similar ideas are heard more or less in the following passages.

Sifra Leviticus 18:3 (337A): "You are to do my laws and you are to keep my statutes (so the midr.), to walk in them" (Lev 18:4). "My laws": these are the (individual) stipulations (halakoth); "statutes": these are the studies in Scripture (for the biblical basis of the halakoth); "you are to keep": this pertains to learning (study); "to walk in them": this pertains to doing (the practical carrying out of religion); "you are to keep them, to walk in them": learning (study) is not what leads (to eternal life nor is it the decisive thing), but rather doing (the practice of the religious life) is what leads. ‖ See SLev 26:3 (448A); Lev. Rab. 35 (132C); b. Ber. 17A; t. Yebam. 8.4 (250) at § Matt 23:3 B. — See Deut. Rab. 7 (204A) at § Rom 1:32, n. *b*. ‖ Babylonian Talmud Yoma 72B: R. Samuel b. Nahman (ca. 260) said that R. Jonathan (ca. 220) said, "What does 'Why then is a purchasing price in a fool's hand to acquire wisdom, since he has no understanding!' (Prov 17:16) mean? Woe to those who hate pupils of the learned (= godless pupils of the learned), who devote themselves to the Torah, without having the fear of God in them (who engage in religious practice)!" R. Yannai (ca. 225) publicly proclaimed, "Woe to the one who has no dwelling place and makes a door his dwelling! (Study is the door to the dwelling of the fear of God; meaning: Woe to the one who studies the Torah without living according to what he has learned!)" Raba († 352) said to the scholars, "I beg you, do not make yourselves heirs of a twofold hell (once by tormenting yourselves with the study of the Torah without combining true piety with study, and second by thereby cutting yourselves off from blessedness)." The saying of R. Yannai is found also in b. Šabb. 31B. ‖ Babylonian Talmud Šabbat 31A: Rabbah bar Rab Huna († 322) said, "If someone possesses knowledge of the Torah but does not have the fear of God, he is like a treasurer who has been given the inner key but not the outer key; how will he get in?" ‖ Leviticus Rabbah 25 (123B): R. Huna (ca. 350) said, "If a man has fallen into sin and made himself liable to death by God's hand (being eradicated), what is he to do to remain alive? If he used to read a page (in Scripture), let him read two; if he used to read a chapter (from the Mishnah), let him read two. If, however, he was not accustomed to read or study, what is he to do to remain alive? Let him go and become a community leader or one who raises alms (i.e., let him devote himself to religious practice), and he will remain alive. For if it said, 'Cursed is the one who does not "study" the words of this law,' there would be no way for him to stay alive; but it says, 'Cursed is the one who does not "fulfill"' (Deut 27:26); if it said, 'She (Torah = Wisdom) is a tree of life for those who toil with (the study of) her,' there would be no way for him to stay alive; but it says, 'She is a tree of life for those who cling to her (do what she asks in practice)' (Prov 3:18)." — The same is found with many variations in TanḥB וישלח § 9 (84A). ‖ Mishnah ʾAbot 5.14: There are four kinds among those go into the house of learning: the one who goes but does not act (according to what he has heard), in his hand is the recompense for going there; the one who does what he should but does not go there, in his hand is the recompense for his action; the one who goes there and does what he should is a pious man חָסִיד; the one who neither goes nor does what he should is a godless man.

2. What is more important: the study of the Torah or carrying it out in practice? In older times, greater value was clearly awarded to religious practice;[a] it was rare to grant precedence to the study of the Torah.[b] A complete reversal came about with the Hadrianic edicts, which forbade on threat of death not only the practice of the religious law but also occupying oneself with the Torah.[54] At that time an assembly of Jewish scholars in

54. S-B: See e.g., Mek. Exod. 20:6 (75B): R. Nathan (ca. 160) said, "'Those who love me and observe my commandments' (Exod 20:6): these are the Israelites, who dwell in the land of Israel and give their

Lydda decided that an Israelite may transgress any commandment in the Torah under duress from enemies, and thus may desist from performing religious commandments, if in doing so he might save his life; only the commandments concerning idolatry, fornication, and shedding blood (murder) should be observed in all circumstances; for the sake of these commandments every Israelite must accept martyrdom. It is probable that another decision, this one concerning the study of the Torah, stands in close connection to this decision. After it had been decided to abandon the performance of the religious law in situations of duress, a settlement was demanded because of another question, namely how, in view of the imperial edicts, should one hold to the teaching of the rabbis and the studies of their students? Should these too be sacrificed or be continued despite the threat of death? R. Tarfon declared in another assembly that practicing the Torah was more important than studying it. Therefore, if the more important thing, religious practice, had been abandoned by the earlier decision, so, R. Tarfon thought, it would be unjustified to demand that someone put their life at risk for the sake of the Torah of the study, which was less important. However, R. Aqiba said, "Study is more important!" And all answered, "Study is more important, for study leads to practice."[c] Hereby it was avowed that devotion to the Torah was not to be surrendered despite any persecutorial edict (see this in more detail at § Matt 5:10, #2). As was to be expected, since that time the view remained dominant that studying the Torah was more important than actually doing it in practice;[d] the opposite opinion is only rarely expressed.[e]

a. Wisdom of Solomon 6:18f.: "Concern for education is love (for Wisdom = Torah); but love is observation of her commandments; but devotion to the commandments is a guarantee of life." ‖ Mishnah ʾAbot 1.15: Shammai (ca. 30 BCE) used to say, "Make your study of the Torah into something firm; speak little but do much." ‖ Mishnah ʾAbot 1.17: Simeon († ca. 70, if the son of Gamaliel I is meant) said, "The main thing is not study, but action." ‖ Mishnah ʾAbot 3.9: The same one (R. Hanina b. Dosa, ca. 70) said, "The one whose deeds are more than his wisdom, his wisdom endures; but the one whose wisdom is more than his deeds, his wisdom does not last." ‖ Mishnah ʾAbot 3.17: The same one (R. Eleazar b. Azariah, ca. 100) said, "Everyone whose wisdom is greater than his deeds, what is he like? Like a tree that has many branches but few roots. The wind comes and uproots it and turns it over.

---

lives for the commandments. Why (it is asked) are you led out to be killed? Because I circumcised my son. Why are you led out to be burned? Because I read the Torah. Why are you led out to be crucified? Because I ate *maṣṣa*. Why are you getting beaten with a whip? Because I took a festive bouquet in my hand (on the Feast of Tabernacles)." — A similar passage is found in Lev. Rab. 32 (129C). ‖ A baraita in b. B. Bat. 60B: R. Ishmael b. Elisha († ca. 135) said, "Since the day the wicked government (Rome) took over Israel and enacts harsh edicts against us and abolishes the Torah and the obligatory commandments and prevents us from meeting to circumcise our one-week old sons ..., then we should determine concerning ourselves that we may no longer marry or beget children; as a result the seed of Abraham would automatically be destroyed. But just leave Israel alone; it is better to sin inadvertently than deliberately."

Yet anyone whose deeds are more than his wisdom, what is he like? Like a tree that has few branches but many roots; even if all the winds in the world come and blow against it, they do not move it from its place." — A parallel passage with elaborations can be found in ʾAbot R. Nat. 22 (6D). ‖ See ʾAbot R. Nat. 24 at § Matt 7:24 B. — From the NT, Jas 1:22ff. belongs here.

b. Sifre Deuteronomy 11:13 § 41 (79B): R. Yose the Galilean (ca. 110) said, "Study is greater (than action); for study preceded the dough offering by 40 years; the levying of the tithe by 54 years; the observation of the fallow years by 61 years; and the observation of the jubilee years by 103 years." (Study began immediately on Sinai, but the implementation of the prescriptions of the law that are named began only after the possession of Canaan; specifically, the dough offering began immediately after the 40 years of wandering in the wilderness, the levy of tithes began 14 years after the complete subjugation of Canaan; after another 7 years [40 + 14 + 7 = 61 years since the giving of the law] the first fallow year occurred and 42 years later [61 + 42 = 103 years] came the first jubilee year.) — The same is found in b. Qidd. 40B; here "the Galilean" must be added after R. Yose. ‖ Mekilta Exodus 15:26 (54A): "If hearing you listen (= listen closely) to the voice of Yahweh your God" (Exod 15:26). R. Eleazar of Modiim († ca. 135) said, "'Hearing': maybe then optionally? Scripture teaches: 'you listen.' It (hearing or studying the Torah) is a duty and not an option. 'If you listen': this is the most general rule (the basic principle) in which the (whole) Torah is contained." (Hearing and studying the Torah constitutes the presupposition of practicing it; therefore, the former is more important than the latter.)

c. Babylonian Talmud Qiddušin 40B: Once R. Tarfon and the elders sat with each other in the upper room of Nitzah in Lydda. The following question was raised before them, "Is study or action (practicing the Torah) greater?" R. Tarfon answered and said, "Action is greater." R. Aqiba answered and said, "Study is greater." Then all answered and said, "Study is greater; for study leads to action שהתלמוד מביא לידי מעשה." — Parallels can be found in Midr. Song. 2:14 (101B); SDeut 11:13 § 41 (79B); reference to this decision is made briefly in, for example, y. Pesaḥ. 3.30B.41; y. Ḥag. 1.76C.41:44; b. B. Qam. 17A. — On the words: "Study leads to action," see Mek. Exod. 15:26 above at the end of n. *b* and SDeut 11:13 § 41 (79A): "And learn them (the statues and the laws) and keep them, in order to do them" (Deut 5:1). The passage of Scripture shows that action depends on study, and not that study depends on action.

d. Mishnah Peʾah 1.1: There are three things for which people enjoy interest (preliminary recompense) in this world, while the capital (the main recompense) remains due for the future world: honoring father and mother, the works of love, bringing peace between one person and another, and studying the Torah, which compensates for all of them. ‖ Midrash Psalm 17 § 8 (66B): R. Yohanan († 279) said, "Studying the Torah is greater than practicing its commandments; for practicing a commandment is before (in the face of) studying the Torah as a lamp before the sun. For it says, 'The commandment is a lamp and the Torah is a light' (Prov 6:23), and Scripture further says, 'The sun to be light by day' (Isa 60:19; so Torah = light = sun)."[55] ‖ ʾAbot de Rabbi Nathan 41 (10C): Once R. Simeon b. Yohai (ca. 150) visited

---

55. See also Wilhelm Bacher, *Die Agada der palästinensischen Amoräer* (Straßburg: Karl Trübner, 1892), 1:237–8.

the sick; there he found a person who was swollen and lay there because of abdominal pains and spoke blasphemies before (= against) God. He said to him, "Stupid, you should have asked for mercy for yourself, and you speak blasphemies?!" He answered him, "May God remove them (the sufferings) from me and lay them on you!" He said, "God has acted justly toward me; for I have left the words of the Torah (and devoting myself to them) and attended to trivial things." (Fulfilling the commandments like visiting the sick therefore are trivialities in comparison to studying the Torah.) ‖ Jerusalem Talmud Ḥagigah 1.76C.42: R. Abbahu (ca. 300) was (lived) in Caesarea; he sent his son away to R. Hanina in order to improve (specifically in the study of the Torah) in Tiberias. Word was sent to him (the father): "He practices works of love (visits the sick, buries the dead, and the like)." He sent him a letter: "Did I send you to Tiberias because there are no graves (Exod 14:11) in Caesarea? Long ago it was determined on the balcony of Beth-Arim (Arum) in Lydda, 'Study takes precedence over action התלמוד קודם למעשה.'" The rabbis of Caesarea said, "What you say there is valid if there is someone (else) there who can do these things (then one should not interrupt studying the Torah for the purpose of practicing its imperatives; for someone else can do it); but if there is no one else there who can do these things, then action takes precedence over study." — The same can be found in y. Pesaḥ. 3.30B.42. — The saying of the rabbis of Caesarea is found as a baraita and in another form in b. Meg. 29A. ‖ Jerusalem Talmud Pe'ah 1.15D.40: R. Berekhiah (ca. 340) and R. Hiyya of Kefar Tehumin (3rd cent.; R. Berekhiah should be seen as the tradent of R. Hiyya, whose saying he contrasts with his own). The one said, "The value of the whole world is not equal to a single word that one studies from the Torah." The other said, "The value of doing even all the commandments of the Torah is not equal to a single word that one studies from the Torah (therefore the study of the Torah is so much more important than doing it)." R. Tanḥuma (ca. 380) and R. Yose b. Zimra (ca. 220; R. Tanḥuma is to be considered the tradent). The one (R. Tanḥuma) spoke as that one (namely as R. Berekhiah above), and the other (R. Yose b. Zimra) spoke as this one (namely as R. Hiyya from Kefar Tehumin above). ‖ Sifre Deuteronomy 11:13 § 41 (79A): (As action depends on study and not vice versa,) so we find that he (God) punishes more because of study than because of action.... And as he punishes more because of study than because of action, so he gives more recompense because of study than because of action. ‖ Babylonian Talmud Qiddušin 40B: As study takes precedence over action (in relation to value and importance), so the punitive sentence given for (neglecting) study takes precedence over the punitive sentence given for action. This corresponds to the opinion of Rab Hamnuna (ca. 290). For Rab Hamnuna said, "The beginning of judgment happens over a person only concerning the Torah (begins with the question of whether the person devotes himself to the Torah); for it says, 'If a man ceases from water (i.e., from the Torah), this is the beginning of judgment' (so Prov 17:14 is formulated). And as the punitive sentence given for (neglecting) study takes precedence over the punitive sentence given for action, so its recompense takes precedence over that given for action; for it says in Ps 105:44f., 'He gave to them the lands of the *goyim* and they took the purchase of the nations for their possession, so that they might keep (= "study" in the meaning of the midr.)

his statues and observe (= keep) his laws.'" — The proof lies in the fact that "study" is spoken of first and then "keeping."

Comment: Explanations about the recompense for studying the Torah are found, for example, in b. Ber. 14A.28; b. ʿErub. 18B.40; b. Sanh. 92A.32; b. ʿErub. 63B.11; b. Roš Haš. 18A.20; b. Meg. 16B.36; b. Ḥag. 12B.31 (= ʿAbod. Zar. 3B.35); b. Menaḥ. 110A.18; b. ʿAbod. Zar. 19A.21; b. Meg. 28B.40 (= S. Eli. Zut. 2).

e. Mishnah ʾAbot 6.4: Act more than your studying is (= than you study). ‖ Jerusalem Talmud Ḥagigah 1.76C.40: When R. Judah (ca. 150) saw how a dead man (in a funerary procession) and a bride (in a wedding procession) were praised, he would set his eyes on his students and say, "Action takes precedence over study." (He thereby would interrupt his lectures to associate with the funerary or wedding procession along with his students.) — The same is found in y. Pesaḥ 3.30B.41, but here at the beginning the name "Judah" has fallen out. The passage is found in another form in b. Meg. 29A.

2:14: When the gentiles who do not have the law by nature do what the law requires....

It was very common in rabbinic Judaism to think that God's will had been made known to the gentiles, specifically in the seven Noahic commandments, and then through the Torah itself, in that God had offered the gentiles the opportunity to accept the Torah supposedly at Sinai and then later he had made it knowable to them on Ebal (see § Rom 1:20 C). In addition to that, the Jewish law had long ceased to be an unknown entity as a consequence of the diaspora of the Jews through the whole Roman Empire and thanks to the many full- and half-proselytes who had connected themselves to Judaism. It therefore comes as no surprise if ancient Jewish literature sometimes speaks of gentiles who fulfilled God's law or specific commandments therein.[a] However it was completely foreign to the rabbinic scholars to think, as Paul claims above, that the gentiles, who do not have the law, fulfill the law by nature (i.e., by the power of the natural impulse of their conscience). Indeed, this thought is nowhere encountered in the actual rabbinic literature, though it is once clearly discernible in a pseudepigraphal writing.[b]

a. 4 Ezra 3:33ff.: "(Ezra said to God,) 'I have wandered here and there among the nations and seen them in their fortune, although they have forgotten your commandments. Now, however, weigh our sins and those of the inhabitants of the world on the scale, so that it may be shown which way the bar tips. Or when would the inhabitants of the world not have sinned before you? Or which generation would have thus fulfilled your commandments? Individuals you can name you will indeed find who kept your commandments, but nations you will not find.'" ‖ Tanḥuma שמיני § 14 (16B): In the future (at the last judgment) God will have a herald sent out: "Whoever devotes himself to the Torah, let him come and receive his recompense!" Then the *goyim* (non-Israelites) too will say, "Give us our recompense, for we too have fulfilled this and that commandment ..." (see § Rom 2:12 B). ‖

Tanḥuma עקב 6A: "Not because you were more numerous than all the nations did Yahweh become devoted to you ..." (Deut 7:7). Not because you are more numerous than all (other) nations, not because you do what is commanded more than those nations—for more than you the nations do what is commanded, without having been commanded, and they glorify my name more than you; as it says, "From the rising of the sun to its setting, my name is great among the gentiles" (Mal 1:1). You however desecrate it by your chatter: "The table of Yahweh is defiled along with its harvest, its food is contemptible!" (Mal 1:12); "for you are the least among the nations" (Deut 7:7). But because you have humbled yourselves before me, therefore I love you; as it says, "I have loved you, says Yahweh" (Mal 1:2). — In TanḥB עקב § 4 (9A) the words on which the passage depends are lacking, namely "For the nations do, moreso than you." ‖ TanḥumaB קדושים § 1 (36B): What does "The hair of his head was pure as wool" (Dan 7:9) mean? That God keeps himself pure (from debt and indebtedness) in relation to the nations. He pays them the recompense for the light commandments which they have done in this world in order to be able to judge them in the future world and declare them to be indebted, so that they cannot protest and no credit may be found for them. — Similar explanations are found in TanḥB § 4 (42A), where the author is R. Levi (ca. 300); Tanḥ. משפטים 92B, where the author is R. Simeon b. Laqish (ca. 250); Midr. Esth. 1:1 (84A), where the author is R. Samuel b. Nahman (ca. 260). ‖ See further b. B. Qam. 38A at § Rom 2:10; y. Pe'ah 1.15C.14 at § Rom 1:30 B.

b. 2 Baruch 48:38: "At that time (of the tribulations at the end of days) the change of times will become clearly visible to everyone, because they (inhabitants of the earth) defiled themselves in all those times and practiced deceit and each one passed away in his (own) deeds and did not remember the law of the Almighty. Therefore fire will consume their plans, and the deliberations of their kidneys will be tested by the flame. For the judge will come and not delay, because each one of the inhabitants of the world could have known when he sinned (namely on the basis of the knowledge of the law) and yet they did not know my law because of their pride."

2:15 A: For they show that the work (= the demand) of the law is inscribed on their hearts.

After what has been remarked on in § Rom 2:14, one cannot expect to find among the rabbis the notion that the law was inscribed on the hearts of the gentiles. Insofar as we can see, this idea is in fact encountered nowhere in the rabbinic writings. However, on the basis of Jer 31:32, in many places one does find the notion that the law of God was written on the hearts of the Israelites.[a] Once it is even said that the law of God is embedded in the evil inclination יֵצֶר הָרַע in order to restrain it.[b] See also the tablets of the heart in Jer 17:1; Prov 3:3; and 2 Cor 3:3.[c]

a. Jeremiah 31:32: נָתַתִּי אֶת־תּוֹרָתִי בְּקִרְבָּם וְעַל לִבָּם אֶכְתֲּבֶנָּה. — Septuagint: διδοὺς δώσω νόμους μου εἰς τὴν διάνοιαν αὐτῶν καὶ ἐπὶ καρδίας αὐτῶν γράψω αὐτούς. — Targum: "I will give my law into their interior and write it on their heart וְעַל לִבְּהוֹן אֶכְתְּבִנָּהּ." ‖ Midrash Ecclesiastes 2:1 (12B): R. Hezekiah (ca. 350) said in the name of R. Simon b. Zabdai (ca. 300),

"The whole Torah, which you study in this world, is vanity (nullity) compared to the Torah in the future world; for in this world a person studies the Torah and forgets (it); but concerning the future, what is written there? 'I will put my Torah in them and write it on their heart' (Jer 31:32)." – See also the following embryological poetry. Babylonian Talmud Niddah 30B: R. Simlai (ca. 250) said in a presentation, "What is a child in its mother's womb like? Like a book that lies folded together: its hands on both temples, its armpits on both knees, both heels on both butt cheeks and its head on both knees. Its mouth is closed and its navel is open; it eats from what its mother eats, and drinks from what its mother drinks; but it does not discharge any refuse; otherwise it might kill its mother. When it comes up to the air of the world, it opens up what was closed, and it closes what was open; for if it were not so, it could not live an hour. But a lamp burns (in its mother's womb) over its head in which it looks peering from one end of the world to the other, as it says, 'When his lamp shone over my head, I walked through darkness by his light' (Job 29:3). Do not marvel at this; for look, a person sleeps here and sees a vision in Spain (Apamea?). And there are no days when the person spent his time in greater happiness than in those days; for it says, 'O, if only I were as I was in the months of the time beforehand, as in the days when God protected me!' (Job 29:2) And when are the days, in which there are months but no years? Say: 'These are the months of the birth (pregnancy).' (In those months) one learns the whole Torah; for it says, 'He taught me and said to me, "Let your heart hold fast to my words, observe my commandments, and you will live"' (Prov 4:4). It also says, 'Since God's secret was over my tent' (Job 29:4). Why 'it also says'? (The first citation was already enough!) If you were to suggest that the one who said (the first word from Scripture) was a prophet (for whom the time in the womb is different from all other children of men), then come and hear (the second passage): 'Since God's secret was over my tent.' When, however, the child comes up to the air of the world, an angel comes and hits it on its mouth and makes it forget the whole Torah; for it says, 'Sin camps at the door' (Gen 4:7). And it does not go out from there before it has been forced to swear, as it says, 'For to me (read לי instead of לך) every knee will bow, and to me every tongue will swear' (Isa 45:23). 'To me every knee will bow': this pertains to the day of death, for it says, 'Before him all who sank into the dust of the grave will bow' (so Midr. Ps. 22:30);[56] 'to me every tongue will swear': this pertains to the day of birth, for it says, 'He who has guiltless hands and is of a pure heart, who does not set his soul on deceit and does not swear to what is false' (Ps 24:4). And what is the oath to which one is sworn? That one be a righteous person and not a godless person, and even if the whole world should say to you, 'You are a righteous person!,' in your own eyes you would be as a godless person and know that God is pure and his servants are pure and the soul that he has placed in you is pure; if you keep the soul in purity, it is good; but if not, look, I will take it from you." – Similar thoughts can be found in Tanḥ. פקודי 127A, though in this case they are based on the teaching about the preexistence of the souls of humanity (see § John 1:1 A, C, #3).

56. S-B: The interpretation of these words in relation to the soul's appearance before God at the hour of death derives from R. Dosa (ca. 180) according to SLev 1:1 (7B), and from R. Eleazar b. Yose (ca. 180) according to SNum 12:8 § 103 (27B). See § Matt 18:10 C.

b. Leviticus Rabbah 35 (132C): R. Levi (ca. 300) said in the name of R. Hama b. Hanina (ca. 260): "חֻקִּים 'statutes' (are what the laws of the Torah are called) because they are embedded חקוקים in the evil inclination; this is what is written, 'Woe to those for whom the statutes are embedded, who prepare distress (perdition) for them' (so the midr. appears to interpret Isa 10:1)." R. Levi said, "It is like a barren (read with Dalman אֶירֵימוֹן = ἔρημος instead of אדרימון) region that was brought into disarray by bands of robbers. What did the king do? He set up guards (read קוּסְטוֹדְיָנוֹס) there to protect it (the region). Likewise, God said, 'The Torah is called "stone" and the evil inclination is called "stone"'; the Torah is called stone: see 'So I may give you the tablets of stone and the Torah (instruction) and the commandment' (Exod 24:12). The evil inclination is called stone: see 'I will remove the heart of stone from your flesh' (Ezek 36:26). The Torah is a stone and the evil inclination is a stone: let the stone watch the stone." — A parallel passage is found in Midr. Song. 6:11 (125A).

c. Tablet of the heart. Targum Yerušalmi I Deuteronomy 6:6: "Those words that I assign to you today are to be written on the tablet of your heart כתיבין על לוח לבכון." ‖ Targum Proverbs 3:3: "Write them (goodness and truth or faithfulness) on the tablet of your heart." ‖ Targum Jeremiah 17:1: "The debts of the house of Judah ... are embedded on the tablet of their heart." ‖ Targum Song of Songs 8:9: "The merits of the Torah, to which the youths devote themselves, which are written on the tablet of the heart, will be remembered for her (the community of Israel)." — See the "inscription on the chest of man" in T. Jud. 20 at § Rom 2:15 B, #3, n. *h*.

2:15 B: With their conscience bearing witness and their thoughts indicting or excusing.

1. The OT has no particular word to designate the conscience; it attributes the activity of the conscience to the לֵב or לֵבָב, that is, the heart. Thus 1 Sam 24:6 (5); 25:31; 2 Sam 24:10; Jer 17:1; Job 27:6; Eccl 7:22. The LXX leaves לב in 1 Sam 25:31 untranslated; in Jer 17:1 it is missing altogether; in Job 27:6 it is re-expressed as οὐ γὰρ σύνοιδα ἐμαυτῷ ἄτοπα πράξας "I am not aware ..."; in the other passages לב, לבב are rendered with καρδία = "heart." — In all these passages the targumim keep לב, לבב in the Aramaic forms לִבָּא, לִבְבָא. — In the pseudepigrapha "heart" is found for "conscience" in T. Gad 5: "The righteous and humble man is unwilling to do wrong, not because he will be incriminated (condemned) by someone else, but rather by his own heart (= conscience) οὐκ ὑπὸ ἄλλου καταγινωσκόμενος, ἀλλὰ ὑπὸ τῆς ἰδίας καρδίας." — The NT maintained the OT mode of expression only sporadically; see in particular 1 John 3:19–21, where καρδία is synonymous with "conscience.

2. Though still not according to the later usual meaning "conscience," the word συνείδησις is used in LXX Eccl 10:20: καί γε ἐν συνειδήσει σου βασιλέα μὴ καταράσῃ. For συνείδησις the underlying Hebrew text has מַדָּע, which is "insight, knowledge" in 2 Chr 1:10, 11:12; Dan 1:4, 17, and "insight, understanding" in Sir 3:13; 13:8. The targum has replaced מדע with מַנְדְּעָא

= "insight, knowledge," and elucidates this word with the addition בְּחַדְרֵי לְבָבְךָ = "in the recesses of your heart." Accordingly, the Septuagint passage should be translated: "Even in your consciousness (which you alone know) do not curse the king." — Also, in Sir 42:18 many manuscripts have the word συνείδησις: ἔγνω γὰρ ὁ ὕψιστος πᾶσαν συνείδησιν. Fritzsche has accepted εἴδησιν: here both words mean "knowledge."

In biblical Greek, συνείδησις is first found with the meaning "conscience" in Wis 17:11: "Wickedness is cowardly, condemned by its own witness; but it (itself) has always (first) added what is evil, tormented by the conscience συνεχομένη συνειδήσει." In the pseudepigrapha συνείδησις = "conscience" appears in T. Reu. 4: "Until our father's end, I (Reuben) had no joy looking in the face of Jacob or speaking with one of my brothers because of the shame (with Bilhah in Gen 35:22). And up till now my conscience torments me συνείδησίς μου συνέχει με." — The word συνείδησις first appears in the NT as a generally known and conventional way of designating the conscience, though it is not present in the synoptic Gospels[57] and John. — Philo and Josephus use the synonymous τὸ συνειδός instead of ἡ συνείδησις. For Philo, see the citations in Hermann Cremer[58] on σύνοιδα; for Josephus, *Against Apion* 2.30: "For those who act according to the laws in everything, the recompense is not silver or gold, nor a coronal wreath made from the wild olive tree or from ivy or the like that proclaims him as the victor, but rather each one is completely confident in having his conscience as a witness τὸ συνειδὸς ἔχων μαρτυροῦν."

3. Like the OT, the rabbinic writings have no particular expression for the conscience. They made do with either the more general term לֵבָב ,לֵב[a] as in the OT, or attributed the functions of the conscience to the "good inclination" יֵצֶר טוֹב. The *yeṣer ṭob* is the good spirit, the spirit of truth, the inclination in the human that is oriented to the divine and eternal. It is formed by the Torah and draws its power from the Torah;[b] for this inclination, the Torah alone serves as the norm for its judgment and desire.[c] Its opponent[d] is the "evil inclination" יֵצֶר הָרַע. This term denoted the inborn sinful desire in people, the inclination of the human set on the earthly and perishable. Its power lay in making itself subservient to the natural impulses of the human body before the *yeṣer ṭob*, strengthened only later on, could exercise its countereffects. In this way the evil inclination gets a head start on the good inclination which it exploits to get its way everywhere and to accustom the human person to the unholy and ungodly from youth on. Both inclinations have their seat in the heart of the human

57. S-B: Jesus has in view the ability of the human spirit to have insight and discern in moral matters before the bar of conscience when he speaks of the φῶς τὸ ἐν σοί in Matt 6:23; Luke 11:35.

58. Hermann Cremer, *Biblisch-theologisches Wörterbuch des neutestamentlichen Gräcität*, 11th ed. (Stuttgart: Perthes, 1923).

being. As a scriptural proof, the rabbis employ particularly the word לֵבָב "heart," whose double ב refers to the two inclinations, one good and one evil.[e] According to another opinion, the good inclination lives on the right side of the person and the evil inclination on the left side. A third view assigned both kidneys as the dwelling place of each inclination. In any case the struggle between the two inclinations takes place in the heart. It was accepted that this struggle begins when the Israelite boy has completed his 13th year of life.[g] Then through instruction in the Torah the boy was supposed to ground himself so firmly in the fear of God that he could set himself on the side of the good inclination in the conflict between the two inclinations and thus aid this inclination in overpowering the evil inclination. The conflict itself is depicted in the following way. If a person wishes to perform a commandment or a good work, the evil inclination immediately interlopes to mislead the person and raises its tempting voice in the heart against doing the good. It presents to the person the idea that he will gain more from not completing the commandment or good work in question. But the good inclination also does not stay silent: admonishing and warning it refers to the Torah and demands the completion of the intended good deed.[h] The decision lies in the person's hand: he alone has to bear responsibility, and on him alone the potential guilt also falls. But even when the person decides in favor of sin, the inclination does not stop being his loyal adviser. It refers him to the ordained means of atonement, repentance, and good works.[i] If, however, the person continually follows the evil inclination, God takes the good inclination away from him completely, so that the evil inclination attains sole domination. If he continually follows the good inclination, God removes the evil inclination from him, so that only the good inclination prevails in him.[k] In this line of thought the *yeṣer ṭob* is nothing other than the conscience of the Israelite that is bound to God's Torah: as the conscience has its norm in the divine will, so the *yeṣer ṭob* has its norm in God's Torah; as the conscience warns and admonishes the person before the evil deed has been committed and pushes the person toward repentance and reversing course after sin has been committed, so also the *yeṣer ṭob*; and as the conscience fades out when it is continually ignored, so the *yeṣer ṭob* disappears fully from the heart of the Israelite who knowingly withdraws himself continually from its voice. The rabbinic scholars spoke about the *yeṣer ṭob* in this way and thereby meant in substance the conscience, not always to be sure, although this identification can be made where the context encourages it. Here we will have to see the reason why a particular word for the conscience is lacking in rabbinic literature: for the Jewish scholars, the *yeṣer ṭob* that dwells and prevails in the heart of the person was sufficient to represent all the functions of the human conscience in their lectures. — See more about the good and evil inclination in the excursus by the same name; here only a few supporting passages are given which are important for the present context.

a. Babylonian Talmud Berakot 7B: R. Yohanan († 279) said in the name of R. Simeon b. Yohai (ca. 150), "One may be indignant at the godless in this world, for it says, 'Those who forsake the Torah praise the godless; but those who keep the Torah are indignant at them' (Prov 28:4)." The baraita contains the same: R. Dosetai b. Judah (ca. 150, so read with Dèrek Ereṣ 2) said, "One may be indignant at the godless in this world (see Prov 28:4, as above); and if someone whispers to you and says, 'Look, it is written, "Do not get angry about wrongdoers and do not be envious of evildoers" (Ps 37:1),' (know) he who is struck by his heart[59] speaks in this way. Rather: 'Do not get angry about wrongdoers' in order to be like the wrongdoers; and 'do not be envious of evildoers' in order to be like evildoers (to imitate them)." The same is found in b. Meg. 6B; only the saying of R. Dosetai is found in Dèrek Ereṣ 2 (19A), though differently.

b. Babylonian Talmud Nedarim 32B: Rammi (= Rab Ammi) b. Abba said, "What does 'A small city and only a few men in it ...' (Eccl 9:14f.) mean? 'A small city': that is the (human) body; 'and only a few men in it': these are the limbs; 'and a great king came against them and surrounded them': this is the evil inclination; 'and built siege towers against them': these are the sins; 'and he met in it a poor wise man': this is the good inclination. (In the rabbinic view Wisdom = Torah; therefore, since the good inclination is called 'a wise man,' it is implied that his wisdom comes from the Torah.) 'He saved the city by his wisdom': this pertains to repentance and good works (in favor of which the good impulse counsels so that the sins may be forgiven); 'and no one thought any more about the poor man': for in the hour of the evil inclination (i.e., at the time when the evil inclination has fortune) there is no one who remembers the good inclination." — A parallel passage that is anonymous and has some differences is found in Midr. Eccl. 9:15 (45A): Why is the evil inclination called a great king? Because he is 13 years older (than the good inclination); "siege towers": these are ambush and pitfall; why is the good inclination called a poor man? Because it is not found in all people and the majority of people do not listen to it. — Additionally, Midr. Ps. 41 § 1 (130A). ‖ See Midr. Eccl. 4:13 (24A) in the following n. *c.* ‖ See T. Jud. 20 in n. *h.*

c. See ʾAbot R. Nat. 16 (5D); Exod. Rab. 36 (95D) in n. *h.* ‖ Midrash Ecclesiastes 4:13 (24A): "Better a boy poor and wise and a king old and foolish" (Eccl 4:13). "Better a boy poor and wise": this is the good inclination; and why is it called a "boy"? Because it is first joined (bound) to a person from the time he is 13 years old. And why is it called "poor"? Because not everyone listens to it. And why is it called "wise"? Because it teaches people the straight (right) way (i.e., the way prescribed by the Torah). "Than a king old and foolish": this is the evil inclination. Why does he call it a "king"? Because everyone listens to it. And why does he call it "old"? Because it is joined to him (a person) from his youth to his old age. And why does he call it "foolish"? Because it teaches a person the

59. S-B: מי שלבו נוקפו "who is struck by his heart" = who does not have a good conscience. Likewise, ויך לב דוד "and David was struck by his heart" (1 Sam 24:6 [5]; 2 Sam 24:10).

wrong (evil) way. "He who no longer knows how to be warned" (Eccl 4:13); since he does not know how much distress and chastisement will come upon him, he cannot be warned. "For he went forth from the place of thorns to rule" (so Midr. Eccl. 4:14); for it caresses people (to mislead them), hidden כָּמֵן among thorns. "For also the poor man is born under his dominion" (Eccl 4:14): under the dominion of the good inclination the poverty of the evil inclination is born.

d. The evil inclination is expressly labeled as the "opponent" of the good inclination in ʾAg. Ber. 23 (20A): "You will see and your heart לבכם will rejoice" (Isa 66:14). Should it not rather have said, "You will see and לבבכם (with two ב's) will rejoice? R. Aha (ca. 320) said, "Because only one heart (i.e., one inclination of the heart, namely the good one) will survive and God will tear out the heart of the evil inclination (at the eschaton), as it says, 'I will remove the heart of stone' (Ezek 36:26); but he will leave the good inclination, for it says, 'I will give you a heart of flesh' (Ezek 36:26), and the good inclination will rejoice that it no longer has an opponent אַנְטִידִיקוֹס (see § Matt 5:25); therefore it is said, 'You will see and your לבכם (with one ב) will rejoice.'"

e. Tosefta Berakot 7.7 (15): R. Meir (ca. 150) said, "See, Scripture says, 'You shall love Yahweh your God with your whole heart לבבך (with two ב)' (Deut 6:5), with both of your inclinations, with the good inclination and the evil inclination." — The same is found anonymously in m. Ber. 9.5; SDeut 6:5 § 32 (73A). See also ʾAg. Ber. 23 in n. *d.*

f. Numbers Rabbah 22 (193B): "The heart of the wise man goes to his right and the heart of the fool to his left" (Eccl 10:2). "The heart of the wise man does to his right": this is the good inclination, which is located on his (the person's) right side. "And the heart of the fool to his left": this is the evil inclination, which is located on the left side. ‖ A baraita in b. Ber. 61A: There are two kidneys in a person: one (with the good inclination) counsels him for the good, and the other (with the evil inclination) to evil. It is clear that the good one is located on his right side and the evil one is located on his left side; see Eccl 10:2 (as in the previous citation).

g. See Midr. Eccl. 4:13 in n. *c*; Midr. Eccl. 9:15 in n. *b*; ʾAbot R. Nat. 16 in n. *h.*

h. ʾAbot de Rabbi Nathan 16 (5D): It has been said, "The evil inclination (which is born with the child) is 13 years older than the good inclination (which is joined to the person only when the 13th year of life is completed). It gradually grew up with him from his mother's womb, then he began to profane the Sabbaths without struggling against it. After 13 years the good inclination is born (begins its opposition). (Now) when he profanes the Sabbaths, the good inclination says to him, 'You fool ריקא (= ῥαχά in Matt 5:22). Look, it says, "Whoever profanes it is to be killed" (Exod 31:14).' If he wants to kill a person, it says to him, 'You fool. Look, it says, "Whoever sheds man's blood, by man his blood is to be shed" (Gen 9:6).' If he sets out to commit a sin of fornication, it says to him, 'You fool. Look, it says, "The adulterer and the adulteress are to be killed" (Lev 20:10).'" ‖ Exodus Rabbah 36 (95D): What does "And the Torah is a light" (Prov 6:23) mean? Often it appeals to a person in his heart to fulfill a commandment (= to give alms); but the evil inclination says to him inwardly: "Why are you thinking about giving alms and (thus) depleting your wealth! Instead of giving to others, give to your children!" And the good inclination says to him: "Give alms.

See what is written, 'For the commandment (מִצְוָה in the later usage it also = alms) is a lamp' (Prov 6:23)." Just as a million wax and tallow candles can be lit by one burning lamp, and its light continues to exist, no one who gives alms למצוה depletes his wealth. Therefore, it is said, "For the commandment is a lamp and the Torah a light." ‖ Among the pseudepigrapha, see T. Jud. 20: "Know now, my children, that two spirits bother with the person, the spirit of truth (= *yeṣer ṭob*), and the spirit of deceit τὸ τῆς πλάνης (= *yeṣer ha-ra'*), and the mediator is the spirit of discretion of understanding τὸ τῆς συνέσεως τοῦ νοός, where he wants to incline. (The person makes his decision on the basis of σύνεσις, which rationally considers obligation and inclination, advantage and disadvantage.) And both that which relates to truth and that which relates to deceit (in favor of which the person decides) is written on the chest of man, and the Lord knows each one of them. And there is no time when a person's works can be hidden, because they are written on the chest of bones (bony chest) before the Lord. And the Spirit of truth witnesses everything and indicts everyone μαρτυρεῖ πάντα καὶ κατηγορεῖ πάντων, and the sinner is set aflame by his own heart and cannot lift his face to the judge."

i. See b. Ned. 32B in n. *b.*

k. 'Abot de Rabbi Nathan 32 (8C): The same man (namely R. Yose the Galilean [ca. 110]) used to say, "He (God) removes the evil inclination from the righteous and gives them the good inclination; for it says, 'My heart לבי (with one ב, i.e., the heart of the evil inclination) is pierced within me' (Ps 109:22). He removes the good inclination from the godless and gives them the evil inclination; for it says, 'The wicked man says to the godless (= to the evil inclination), "Within my heart there is no fear of God before his eyes"[60] (the complete eradication of the fear of God is a proof that the *yeṣer ṭob* has vanished from the heart).' To the middling man he gives both the latter and the former inclination. The evil inclination judges שופטו (= rules) the one who follows the evil inclination (literally: who comes to the evil inclination); the good inclination judges the one who follows the good inclination; for it says, 'He (God) himself stands at the right hand of the poor to help him to be free of those who judge his soul' (Ps 109:31)." — The same exposition is found in another form in a baraita in b. Bar. 61B: R. Yose the Galilean said, "The good inclination judges שופטו (= rules) the righteous; see Ps 109:22 (as above); the evil inclination judges the godless; see Ps 36:2 (as above); both inclinations judge the middling man; see Ps 109:31 (as above)."

2:16: Since God will judge ... through Jesus Christ.

On the involvement of the Messiah in the judgment of the world, see the excursus "Sheol, Gehenna, and the Garden of Eden," II, #10; see also § John 5:22.

2:17 A: If you call yourself a "Jew."

According to the rabbinic scholars, יְהִידִי, Aram. יְהוּדָאָה, יְהוּדַאי "Jew" denotes the individual Israelite as monotheists, as venerators of the one

60. S-B: Or: The wicked says to the godless within my heart (= to the evil inclination in my heart): There is no fear of God before his eyes.

and true God, over against the polytheistically oriented confessors of paganism. Thus, "Jew" is an honorific name in the view of the ancient synagogue.[a] Conversely non-Israelites associated something contemptible with the name "Jew,"[b] and even used it as invective.[c]

a. Midrash Esther 2:5 (93A): Why is Mordecai (Esth 2:5) called a Jew יהודי? Was he not a Yeminite (= Benjaminite)? Because he, as opposed to everyone else who comes into the world, confessed the oneness (uniqueness) of the divine name. This is what is written: "Mordecai did not bow and did not prostrate" (Esth 3:2).... "When Haman saw that Mordecai did not prostrate, he became full of anger" (cf. Esth. 3:5). But Mordecai said to him, "There is one Lord who is exalted over every exalted person; how should I abandon him and prostrate before an idol!" And (just) because he confessed the oneness (uniqueness) of the divine name, he was called a "Jew" יהודי; this means: A Jew is tantamount to a confessor of the only God (monotheist) יְהוּדִי יְחִידִי. ‖ Babylonian Talmud Megillah 13A: R. Yohanan († 279) said, "(Mordecai) stems from Benjamin and why does Scripture (Esth 2:5) call him a Jew? Because he repudiated idolatry; for everyone who repudiates idolatry is called a 'Jew' יהודי. As it is written, 'There are Jewish men here ...' (Dan 3:12)." When R. Simeon b. Pazzi (ca. 280) would begin interpreting the books of Chronicles, he would say, "All your words are one (however many different names you may give to a person, they still designate only one person), and we understand how to interpret them. 'And his wife, the Jewish woman, gave birth to Jered the father of Gedor, and Heber the father of Soco, and Jekuthiel, the father of Zanoah. And these are the sons of Bithiah the daughter of pharaoh, who Mered (according to the midr. = Moses) married' (1 Chr 4:18). Why is she (Bithiah, who was an Egyptian) called a Jew יְהוּדִית? Because she repudiated idolatry; for it is written, 'Then the daughter of pharaoh went down to the Nile to bathe' (Exod 2:5)." And R. Yohanan said that she went down to bathe herself (clean) from the idols (= idolatry) of her father's house. — In this passage יהודי or יהודית appears to be brought into etymological connection with הוֹרָה. ‖ Differently, though in content little is different, Rab Nahman († 320) explains the designation of Mordecai as a "Jew." He says in b. Meg. 12B: "'Mordecai was crowned with his law,' that is, since he held fast to the Torah as to the most beautiful crown, he was called a Jew. Jew is therefore an honorific name for all who are faithfully devoted to the law." ‖ Exodus Rabbah 42 (98D): "Yahweh said to Moses, 'I have seen this people, and behold, it is a stiff-necked people עם קשה ערף'" (Exod 32:9). What does "Behold, it is a stiff-necked people" mean? R. Judah b. פולויה (if = פְּלָיָא, then in the 4th cent.) said in the name of R. Meir (ca. 150), "They would have earned that their neck be broken להערף." R. Yaqim[61] (ca. 350) said, "There are three hard-necked[62] types: The hard-necked חָצוּף among the wild animals is the dog,[63] among the birds the rooster, and among the nations Israel." R. Isaac b. Redipah (ca. 330) said in the name of R. Ammi (ca. 300), "You think (or: do you think perhaps) that this

---

61. S-B: רב יקים, according to Bacher, is "definitely a corruption of ר״ש לקיש (= R. Simeon b. Laqish, ca. 250)" (*Die Agada der palästinensischen Amoräer*, 1:371.4).

62. S-B: חֲצוּפִים α. = firm, strict, stubborn, persistent; β, = brazen. — The last meaning does not fit the context. The parallel in b. Beṣah 23B עַזִּים α = strong, hard; β = brazen.

63. S-B: The dog is considered to be among the חַיָּה elsewhere as well; see § Matt 15:26.

amounts to shame? Rather it amounts to praise for them: either a Jew יהודי or crucified!" (A Jew prefers to be crucified before giving up his faith.) R. Abin (I, ca. 325; II, ca. 370) said, "Still now Israel is called abroad the people with a hard neck האומה של קשה עודף." – The parallel passage b. Beṣah 25B: In the name of R. Meir (ca. 150) it was taught (as a baraita): "Why was the Torah given to the Israelites? Because they are (stubborn) עַזִּים (hard, firm)." In the school of R. Ishmael († ca. 135) it was taught: "'At his right hand the fire of the law for them' (so Midr. Deut. 33:2). God said, 'These are worthy to be given the law of fire.'" Some say: "Their law is fire; for if the Torah had not been given to the Israelites, no nation and tongue would be able to exist before them." (The fire of the law is therefore supposed to tame their spirit, as R. Meir claimed at the beginning.) And this is what R. Simeon b. Laqish (ca. 250) said, "There are three stubborn עַזִּין (hard, firm) types: Israel among the nations, the dog among the wild animals, the rooster among the birds." Some say, "Also the goat (עֵז, evidently because of the same consonants in עז) among the small livestock"; and some say, "Also the caper shrub צָלָף among the trees."[64] ‖ See y. Šeb. 4.35A.62 at § Matt 5:10, #2, at the end.

b. See Meg. Ta'an. 9 = the baraita in b. Yoma 69A at § Matt 10:5 B, #4, two-thirds down; see y. Ber. 5.9A.30 at § Acts 6:15. ‖ Jerusalem Talmud Berakot 5.9A.32: R. Jonah and R. Yose (both ca. 350) came before Ursicinus in Antioch. He saw them and stood up before them. Someone told him, "You stand up before these Jews יהודאי?" He answered them, "I saw their face in combat and prevailed." ‖ See further Gen. Rab. 11 at § Matt 12:1, next to last paragraph of #2, and Midr. Lam. Introduction #17 at § Matt 12:1, last paragraph of #2.

c. Midrash Lamentations 1:11 (55A): R. Phineas (ca. 360) said, "It once happened that two whores fought with each other in Ashkelon. One said to the other while they fought, 'Are you still not leaving this place? Your face looks like a Jew יהודאיתא!' After a few days the one reconciled with the other. She said to her, "You are to be forgiven and let off for everything שרי ושביק ליך, but that thing you said to me, 'Your face looks like a Jew'—that I will not forgive you for or let you off the hook for." There it is said. 'O look, Lord, and see that I am despised!' (Lam 1:11)."

2:17 B: And you rest on the law.

The LXX uses ἐπαναπαύεσθαι many times to render נִשְׁעַן = to support oneself α. in the proper sense in 2 Kgs 5:18; 7:2, 17; β. in the metaphorical sense in Mic 3:11: ἐπὶ τὸν κύριον ἐπανεπαύοντο "to depend on the Lord" = to (unjustifiably) rely on the Lord. Targum: "To depend (rely) on the Memrah of Yahweh מִסְתַּמְכִין." – So also ἐπαναπαύεσθαι νόμῳ = to stand erect on or to rely on the law, to rest (complacently) on the law. People took some pride in the law, as if possessing it and exerting oneself in studious devotion to it were a guarantee for participation in the future salvation. – Rabban Yohanan b. Zakkai († ca. 80) already opposed this unjustifiable

---

64. S-B: The caper shrub is considered to be among the עזין because it is "unshakable" and "indestructible" due to its powerful ability to take life from other plants. Differently, in Tanḥ. בראשית 4B, the צלף = "caper bud," "caper berry" is counted among the "hard" = tangy things דברים קָשִׁים which need to be sweetened.

trust in the Torah. He used to say: If you have studied a lot of the Torah (another reading: עָשִׂיתָ "done"), do not be proud of it; for you were created for this purpose (m.ʾAbot 2.8).

See § Rom 2:23 A and 3:2[65] for passages supporting the claims that possessing the Torah is Israel's boast, that the Torah is the only good that remained for Israel, that the Torah is the source of all salvation and the pledge of divine love.

2:17 C: And you boast in God.

The Israelites boasted that God was their father (see § Matt 6:4; 6:9 B; § Mark 14:36). They also boasted that they were God's children (see § Matt 5:9 #2; 5:45 A; § John 1:12). They further boasted that they were God's possession (see § John 1:11). They moreover boasted that they were God's friends (see § John 15:14).

2:18: You know his will.

Israel's boast includes that it alone knows God's will.

(Hebrew) Sirach 45:5: "God let Moses hear his voice and let him draw near to the darkness (cf. Exod 20:21) and put the commandment in his hand, the Torah of life and insight, in order to teach his statutes in Jacob and his testimonies and laws to Israel." – (Greek) Sirach 17:10: "He established the eternal covenant with them and made his laws known to them." ‖ Baruch 3:36, 37; 4:2–4: "This is our God, there is no other beside him. He investigated every way to wisdom and gave her (wisdom = Torah) to Jacob, his servant, and to Israel, his favorite.… Turn, Jacob, and seize her, walk in the splendor of the light that comes from her! Do not surrender your honor to another, nor salvation to a foreign nation. Salvation is ours, Israel, because we know what pleases God." ‖ 4 Ezra 8:12: "You have given him (human beings) instruction by your law and teaching in your wisdom." ‖ See passages from rabbinic literature at § Luke 12:47f.; § Rom 1:32; 2:23; and 3:2.

2:19–20: You also presume to be a guide for the blind, a light for those in darkness, a tutor for the ignorant, a teacher for the uninstructed.

With these words the apostle may be thinking less of Palestinian Judaism and more of Hellenistic Judaism. The rabbinic scholars of the motherland only very rarely and very quietly espouse the idea that Israel is called to be the teacher of the gentile world. The Judaism of the Diaspora was all the more pervaded by this idea.

1. The whole of Hellenistic Jewish literature is ultimately propaganda literature: on one occasion the law of Moses is glorified in order to make the depicted Hellenism more sympathetic to the Jews, and then above all in order to win over people who believed differently to the veneration of the Jewish God. The Torah of Israel is the best and most excellent law[a] that

65. TN: No note exists at § Rom 3:2.

has ever been given. The philosopher and poets of Greece drew knowledge and wisdom from her.[b] The Torah will one day be the law of the world which will bind all humanity to the service of the one and true God.[c] It is therefore no wonder if this law already now reveals its allure in the world: scarcely ever has a Jew who has known his ancestral law fallen away from it,[d] but among the multitude of Greeks and barbarians, there has long been a great enthusiasm to imitate the customs of the Mosaic law.[e] How could the people that was the bearer of the Torah not have felt that it was a light for the gentiles,[f] a guide for the human race![g] Even Philo has no qualms about calling the Jews the priests of prophets of humanity.[h]

a. Letter of Aristeas 31: "This (Jewish) law is as a divine law, full of wisdom and flawless." ‖ Philo, *De vita Mosis* 3.23 (Mangey's ed., 2:163): "Moses is the best king and lawgiver and high priest; in conclusion I will demonstrate that he too was the most reliable of the prophets. I certainly know that everything written in the holy books are God's χρησμοί that were proclaimed by him (Moses)." ‖ Josephus, *Against Apion* 2.38: "If because of the exquisiteness of the laws we are so biased toward them (that we dread them more than men), one should concede that we have the best laws."

b. Aristobulus in Eusebius, *Praeparatio evangelica* 13.12: "It is evident that Plato followed the giving of our (Jewish) law (i.e., borrowed from it) and concerned himself with its details. (And since a Greek translation of the Mosaic laws existed long before the LXX,) it is clear that the forenamed philosopher borrowed much …, as also Pythagoras adopted much from our law and set it in the right place in his teaching.… It seems to me that Pythagoras and Socrates and Plato, who thoroughly occupied themselves with everything (in our law), came after this opinion (of Moses, namely that God's 'speaking' means an action).… Clearly also Homer and Hesiod, who borrowed from our books, teach that it (the seventh day) is holy." ‖ Philo, *Legum allegoriae* 1.33 (Mangey's ed., 1.65): "Heraclitus also in this part followed the teaching of Moses beautifully; for he says: Ζῶμεν τὸν ἐκείνων θάνατον, τεθνήκαμεν δὲ τὸν ἐκείνων βίον." — Philo, *Quod omnis probus liber sit* 8 (Mangey's ed., 2:454): "Zeno seems so to speak to have drawn the word ('Will the inept man not complain when he disagrees with the capable man?') from the source of the Jewish law" (here Philo means the narrative about Jacob and Esau in Gen 28:1ff.). ‖ Josephus, *Against Apion* 2.36: "Plato imitated our lawgiver most of all in commanding the citizens above all to learn all the laws precisely by heart." — *Against Apion* 2.39: "What first concerns the philosophers among the Greeks, they ostensibly kept the ancestral constitutions (customs). In their actions and their philosophizing, however, they followed that one (Moses) by thinking the same thing about God and teaching among themselves simplicity of life and community." — *Against Apion* 2.41: "I might boldly say that we (Jews) have been the guides εἰςηγητάς for everyone else (non-Jews) concerning most matters and also what is best. For what is more beautiful and imperishable than piety and what is more righteous than obedience to the laws? Or what is more useful than mutual concord so that people are neither split in misfortune nor proudly at each other's throats in fortune, but rather scorn death in war and devote themselves to their craft or agriculture in peace, being persuaded in everything and everywhere that God protectively looks down and prevails? If this had either been written down first or more firmly observed among the other nations, we would owe them a debt of gratitude, since we would have been (their) students; but if we see that we have implemented this most of all, and if we have shown that this was first discovered among us, then men like Apion and Molon and all who delight in lies and abuse are refuted."

c. Sibylline Oracles 3:757f.: "The immortal one in the starry heavens will bring about for humanity a common law on the whole earth (in the messianic time)." — Sibylline Oracles 3:719f.: "Let us all remember the law of the most high God, which is the most just of all laws on earth." — Sibylline Oracles 5:357: "May the law of wisdom and the glory of the righteous (?) take the lead."

d. Josephus, *Against Apion* 2.38: "No Jew would go so far from the fatherland or fear a harsh master so much that he would not dread the law more than the latter."

e. Philo, *De vita Mosis* 2.4 (Mangey's ed., 2:137): "(Our law) wins all people for itself and brings them to repentance, barbarians, Greeks, those who dwell on the mainland and on islands, nations east and west, Europe, Asia, the whole inhabited world from one end of the earth to the other. For who would not honor the seventh day ..., and who would not admire and pay homage to the so-called fast ...?" — See also *Mos.* 2.7 (Mangey's ed., 2:141): "So the celebrated and controversial (Jewish) laws are brought to the knowledge of all private persons and official persons (during the annual celebration on the island of Pharos), and this although the (Jewish) people has not enjoyed fortune for a long time.... But if their conditions should become brighter, how great would the increase presumably be!? I think that one would abandon his own laws, and everyone would part with his ancestral constitutions to turn exclusively to the veneration of these (Jewish laws). For the laws that shine bright simultaneously with the fortune of the people will darken other laws as the rising sun does the stars." ‖ Josephus, *Against Apion* 2.10: "Many of them (the Greeks) have come over to our laws. Some have stuck with them, while others, who have not maintained abstinence (self-control), have fallen away again." — *Against Apion* 2.39: "Great enthusiasm arose long ago among the masses for our veneration of God; and there is no city, neither anywhere among the Greeks nor among the barbarians, and there is no single people, where the custom of the seventh day, on which we rest from work, has not reached, and where the fasting ceremonies and the lighting of lights and many of our dietary restrictions are not observed. But they also try to imitate our concord among themselves, as well as the drive to acquire property (others: largesse with our possessions), and the love for devotion to trades and the steadfast loyalty to the laws in distress. For the thing most worthy of admiration is that the law is strengthened by itself, without the charm of sensual pleasures and bait. And as God goes forward throughout the whole world, so the law has reached all people."

f. Wisdom 18:4: "Those (Egyptians) deserved to be robbed of light and bound in darkness because they held your sons prisoner, through whom the imperishable light of the law was to be given to the world." — See further § Rom 2:19 B below.

g. Sibylline Oracles 3:194f.: "Then the people of the great God will become strong again and they will be guides of life βίου καθοδηγοί for all mortals." ‖ See Josephus, *Against Apion* 2.36 in n. *b.* ‖ See further at § Rom 2:19 A.

h. Philo, *De Abrahamo* 19 (Mangey's ed., 2:15): "He (Abraham) who was to beget not a certain number of sons and daughters, but rather a whole people, the most beloved of God among the people, who, as it seems to me, have acquired the office of priests and prophets for the whole human race." — *De vita Mosis* 1.27 (Mangey's ed., 2:104): "(The people Israel,) which out of all the other peoples was to be priests, always offering prayers for the whole human race." — See also Sib. Or. 3:582f. at § Rom 2:19 A.

2. Matters were different in Palestinian Judaism. The paucity of sources makes it impossible to determine to what extent the synagogue of the motherland in Jesus' day actually carried out its missionary vocation to the nations of the world. That people did in fact try to fulfill this task is shown by Jesus' words in Matt 23:15; an additional proof is given in the conversion to Judaism by the royal house of Adiabene (ca. 50 CE; see § Matt 23:15 A). In any case, the practical missionary task of Palestinian Judaism ceased with the destruction of Jerusalem by Titus. To be sure, in rabbinic literature many references are made to the responsibility of Israel to make God's name known to the nations of the world; but most of the time this responsibility is so strictly limited that it was hardly felt as such.[a] Furthermore, there is no lack of voices that downright forbid instructing non-Israelites in the Torah.[b] Most likely the rabbinic scholars still liked to feel as if they were teachers of the ignorant and immature in the so-called religious conversations,[c] in which they defended to individual non-Jews the Jewish teaching about faith and morals. Here they could assert the superiority of the Jewish belief in God over gentile error and make palpable their pride in the ancestral law[d] and in Israel's exaltedness over all other nations,[e] a pride for which the non-Jewish world so liked to reproach the Jews.[f] On the preceding remarks, see § Matt 23:15 A.

a. Mekilta Exodus 15:2 (44A): "This is my God, whom I will exalt ואנוהו" (Exod 15:2). R. Yose the Galilean (ca. 110) said, "Glorify נייגו and praise God before all nations of the world!..." R. Aqiba († ca. 135) said, "I will speak of beautifying the praise בנאות שבחו (i.e., of the correct praise) of the one who spoke and the world came into existence. For behold, the nations of the world ask Israel: 'What then is your companion before any (other) companion that you adjure us in this way' (Song 5:9), that you continually die in this way for his sake and are killed thus for his sake? For it says, 'Therefore you are loved by virgins' עלמות, (Song 1:3), that is, you are loved unto death עד מות. And it is also written, 'For your sake we are killed all day long' (Ps 44:23). 'Behold, you are beautiful, behold you are heroic, come and commingle with us!' And Israel answers them, 'Do you know him then? We will tell you a part of his praise (glory): "My companion is bright white and red" (Song 5:10).' When they hear that he is praised in this way, they will say to Israel, 'We want to go with you; as it says, "Where has your companion gone, you most beautiful among women? Where has your companion turned that we may seek him with you?" (Song 6:1).' Then Israel will answer them, 'You have no share in him, but rather "my companion is mine and I am his ..." (Song 2:16); "I am my companion's and my companion is mine, who pastures his sheep among the lilies"

(Song 6:3).'" – The duty to glorify God before the nations is acknowledged; but the correct worship of God consists in referring the advantage Israel has over the nations. – Parallels can be found in the anonymous saying in SDeut 33:2 § 343 (143A); the passage is split up and anonymous in Midr. Song. 1:3 (85B); 5:9 (119A); 6:1 (122A). ‖ Leviticus Rabbah 6 (109D): "For Torah and for testimony!" (Isa 8:20). The Torah adjures us with admonitions. "If they do not speak according to this word (= in this way), they will be like one who has no dawn" (Isa 8:20). R. Yohanan († 279) and R. Simeon b. Laqish (ca. 250). R. Yohanan said, "God said to the Israelites, 'My children, tell the nations of the world, "Whatever has no dawn, as this thing (namely the idol) does not, cannot make light shine on you."'" R. Simeon b. Laqish said, "God said to the Israelites, 'Tell the nations of the world, "Whoever has no dawn (such as necromancers and fortune tellers), that is, if he cannot cause light to rise for himself, how can he cause light to rise for others!"'" – Since both interpretations are only slightly different from each other, the different tradition in Tanḥ. אמור 171A should perhaps be preferred: R. Yohanan said, "God said, 'If they (the Israelites) do not speak according to this word (= in this way) to the nations of the world, they (Israel) will have no dawn, he (God) will not cause the dawn (of salvation) to rise for them.'" R. Simeon b. Laqish said, "'Whoever has no dawn': necromancers and fortunetellers cannot make the dawn rise for themselves because they are devoted to darkness, so how much less can they do so for others." – The same can be found in TanḥB אמור §3 (41A). – Here it is unambiguously laid on Israel's shoulders as a matter of conscience to call the nations of the world to the Torah and to point out to them the futility of their idolatry and magical arts. ‖ Leviticus Rabbah 6 (109C): "If anyone does not speak up and (therefore) incurs guilt" (Lev 5:1). (God said to the Israelites:) "If you do not proclaim my divinity to the nations of the world, behold, I will punish you." When (does this apply)? When they say to you: "Ask the spirits of the dead ..." (Isa 8:19). – That is, when the gentiles try to mislead Israel to sin, they should be the bulwark for those who proclaim the divine name. The author is R. Phineas (ca. 360).

b. Babylonian Talmud Sanhedrin 59A: R. Yohanan († 279) said, "A *goy* (non-Israelite) who is devoted to the Torah is guilty of death; for it says, 'Moses commanded us with the Torah as an inheritance' (Deut 33:4). It is an inheritance for us, but not for them (the non-Israelites)." – This passage is cited by the Tosafists in b. Ḥag. 13A אין with the addition: And whoever instructs him (the non-Israelite), transgresses (the prohibition): "You are not to lay a stumbling block in front of a blind man" (Lev 19:4). ‖ Sifre Deuteronomy 33:4 § 345 (143B): "As an inheritance of the community of Jacob" (Deut 33:4); do not read מוֹרָשָׁה "inheritance," but rather מְאוֹרָסָה "one who is betrothed"; for the Torah is betrothed to Israel and (therefore) is like a married woman for the nations of the world (i.e., as a wife is prohibited to every other man, so a *goy* is forbidden to occupy himself with the Torah); see Prov 6:27ff. – The same is found in Exod. Rab. 33 (94C). The interpretation מאורסה = מורשה is found also in b. Ber. 57A; b. Pesaḥ. 49B; b. Sanh. 59A. ‖ Babylonian Talmud Ḥagigah 13A: R. Ammi (ca. 300) said, "The words of the Torah are not handed on to a *goy*; for it says, 'He has not acted in this way with any (other) nation, and they do not know his laws' (Ps 147:20)." ‖ See also § Matt 7:6 A, #2.

c. Among the great number of religious disputations mentioned earlier, reference should be made to Gen. Rab. 1 (2D) at § Matt 1:18 C, #2, n. *a*; b. Sanh. 39A at § Matt 3:11 B; Gen. Rab. 81 (52A) and Gen. Rab. 32 (19D) at § Matt 10:5 B, #2, n. *g*, α; Midr. Eccl. 5:10 (27B) at § Matt 10:5 B, #2, n. *g*, β; b. Sanh. 90B at § Matt 10:5 B, #2, n. *g*, β; Gen. Rab. 4 (4A); 4 (4B); 4 (4A); 94 (59C) at § Matt 10:5 B, #5; Pesiq. 98A at § Matt 10:5 B, #5; Gen. Rab. 11 (8B) at § Matt 12:1, #2; b. Sanh. 39A at § Matt 18:20; Pesiq. 11B at § Matt 19:6; Pesiq. 40A, b. Taʿan. 7A, b. Sanh. 65B and TanḥB מקץ § 9 (97A) at § Matt 21:24; TanḥB בראשית § 2 (1B) and Gen. Rab. 27 (17C) at § Matt 21:24; b. Sanh. 90B at § Matt 22:32, #2, A; b. Sanh. 91A, b. Sanh. 90B and Gen. Rab. 14 (10C) at § Matt 22:32, #2, C; b. Sanh. 91A at § Matt 22:32, #2, C; b. Šabb. 31A at § Matt 23:15 A, n. *w*; Gen. Rab. 78 (49D) at § Matt 25:31 B, #2, n. *a*; TanḥB מקץ § 11 (98B) at § Matt 27:29; Lev. Rab. 2 (134B) at § Luke 16:28; Pesiq. Rab. 21 (99A) at § Luke 19:22; b. Sanh. 39A at § Luke 24:26, I, #2, n. *i*; Exod. Rab. 30 (89D) at § John 5:17; Midr. Eccl. 8:17 (41A) at § John 7:19; ʿAbod. Zar. 10B at § John 8:39; b. Sanh. 91B at § John 9:2, n. *a*; y. Meg. 1.72B.46 at § John 12:20, #3; Exod. Rab. 2 (68C) at § Acts 7:30 C; b. Sanh. 65B at § Acts 7:43 B; b. Ḥul. 59B at § Rom 1:20 A, n. *a*; m. ʿAbod. Zar. 4.7 and b. ʿAbod. Zar. 54B at § Rom 1:23 A, #2, D, n. *m*; b. ʿAbod. Zar. 55A at § Rom 1:23 A, #2, D, n. *m*; b. Roš Haš. 17B at § Rom 2:11, #2; Tanḥ. תרומה 100A at § Rom 2:11, #3, α. — Here a few additional conversations may be found in the following, which fog cus on Israel's special and privileged position. ‖ Midrash ha-Gadol on Lev 26:9:[66] This is what a philosopher asked Rabban Gamaliel (ca. 90). He said to him, "You (Jews) say, 'Our God will turn to us and gather us from our places of exile.'" He answered him, "Yes!" That one said to him, "Were the prophets who prophesied to you prophets of truth or prophets of a lie?" He answered him, "They were prophets of truth." That one said to him, "It is written, 'With their sheep and with their cattle they will go to seek Yahweh; but they will not find him. He has set himself loose from them חלץ מהם' (Hos 5:6). If your God has dismissed you חלץ לכם, how is he supposed to come back to you?" (חלץ is the verb that is used especially when one dismisses the sister-in-law one is obliged to marry in levirate marriage.) Rabban Gamaliel said to him, "You fool, pay attention to the words of the Torah: 'And his sister-in-law is to approach … and remove his shoe' (Deut 25:9). If it said in Hos 5:6, 'They have set themselves loose from him,' they would be like a sister-in-law who dismissed her brother-in-law and was thereby forbidden to him. Now, though, where it is written, 'He has set himself loose' (Hos 5:6), it is he (God) who has become like the brother-in-law who dismissed his sister-in-law and may turn again to her." Immediately the philosopher accepted this and agreed with Rabban Gamaliel. — The passage can be found in another form in Yebam. 102B and Midr. Ps. 10 § 8 (49A). ‖ Babylonian Talmud Ḥagigah 5B: R. Joshua b. Hananiah (ca. 90) was with the emperor (Hadrian). A sectarian מִינָא showed him (by a corresponding hand gesture), "(You Jews are) a people from whom its Lord has turned his face away." He showed him (in the same way): "His hand is stretched out over us." The emperor said to R. Joshua, "What did he show you? A people from whom its Lord has turned his face away." And I showed him: "His hand is stretched out over us." It was said to him (the sectarian): "What did you show him? A people from whom its Lord has turned his face

66. Hebrew text in Bacher, *Die Agada der Tannaïten*, 1:83.

away." And what did he show you? "I do not know." It was said, "Should a man who does not understand what has been shown to him by a gesture show something (in the same way) before the king?" He was led away and killed. ‖ Babylonian Talmud Baba Batra 10A: The tyrant Rufus, the blasphemer (i.e., Tineius Rufus, the governor of Judea), asked R. Aqiba this question, "If your God loves the poor, why does he not take care of them?" He answered him, "So that by them (i.e., by the charity practiced toward them) we may escape the judgment of gehenna." He said to him, "That would indeed (all the more) make one guilty of gehenna!" "I will tell you a parable. What can this be compared with? With a king of flesh and blood who became angry at his servant and cast him into prison and commanded that no one give him either food or drink. Then a person came to him and gave him food and drink. When the king hears of this, will he not get angry with this person? And you are called servants; as it says, 'For the children of Israel are my servants' (Lev 25:55; thus, as long as God's wrath rests on the Israelites, having compassion on them entails God's punishment)." R. Aqiba answered him, "I will tell you a parable. What can this be compared with? With a king of flesh and blood who became angry at his son and cast him into prison and commanded that no one give him either food or drink. Then a person came and gave him a drink. When the king hears of this, will he not send the person a gift? And we are called sons, for it is written, 'You are sons of Yahweh your God' (Deut 14:1; thus, as long as God's wrath lasts, having compassion on Israel entails a recompense from God)." That one said, "You are called sons and you are called servants. If you do God's will, you are called sons, and if you do not do God's will, you are called servants. And now you do not do God's will (this is proven by God's judgments on you)." He answered him, "Look, it says, 'Is it not that you break your bread with the hungry and bring the wretched, homeless into your house' (Isa 58:7). When does this apply: 'to bring the wretched, homeless into your house'? Now of course! And then it says, 'Is it not that you break your bread with the hungry'!" (The fact that God has set down the law of charity to be fulfilled precisely at Israel's times of distress and oppression is a proof that he does not leave his people even when he judges them.) ‖ See Midr. Abba Gurion 41A at § Matt 4:17 A, #1, near the end. ‖ Babylonian Talmud Yoma 56B: A sectarian said to R. Hanina (ca. 225), "Now you (Jews) are certainly impure; for it is written, 'Her filth is in her train' (Lam 1:9)." He answered him, "Come and see what is written about them: 'He dwells with them in the midst of their impurities' (Lev 16:16)." (הַשֹּׁכֵן is referred to God.) ‖ See b. 'Abod. Zar. 4A at § Luke 7:41. ‖ Babylonian Talmud Sanhedrin 39A: A sectarian said to R. Abina (I, ca. 325), "It is written, 'Is there any people on earth like your people' (2 Sam 7:23)? What does the people's greatness consist in? You too will be pooled with us; for it is written, 'All peoples are like nothing before him (God)' (Isa 40:17)." He answered him, "One of you has testified about us; for it is written, 'It (Israel) is not counted among the peoples' (Balaam says this in Num 23:9)." ‖ TanḥumaB בראשית § 20 (8A): A matron asked R. Yose (ca. 150), "It is written, 'So that your days and the days of your children may be many ... like the days of heaven above the earth' (Deut 11:21). You will (thus) remain only as long as heaven and earth remain; but heaven and earth will disappear. For Isaiah said, 'Lift your eyes to the heights and see ...' (Isa 40:26); and it is also written, 'Lift your eyes to heaven and see ..., for the heavens will disperse like smoke' (Isa 51:6)."

He said to her, "I will answer you from the same prophet, from whom you have brought forth proof; for it says, 'As the new heaven and the new earth that I will make will last before me, says Yahweh, so your seed and your name will last' (Isa 66:22)." ‖ Babylonian Talmud Pesaḥim 87B: R. Hoshaiah (ca. 225) said, "What does 'The saving acts toward Israel that his leading accomplished' (Judg 5:11) mean? God has given Israel a blessing by dispersing them among the nations." And this is what that sectarian said to R. Hanina (ca. 225), "We are better than you; it is written about you, 'Joab and all Israel stayed there six months, until they wiped out every male in Edom' (1 Kgs 11:16); and look, you have now been among us for so many years and we have not done anything to you." He said to him, "If you are willing, a student will deal with you." R. Hoshaiah dealt with him; he said to him, "(You spare us) because you do not know how to eliminate us. If you wanted to destroy us (all), they are not all among you, (and if you wanted to destroy) those who are among you, you would be called a mutilated kingdom." He answered him, "By the Roman god of fortune, we show consideration for this (בהא נחתינן ובהא סלקינן is the positive Aramaic formulation of the negative Hebrew expression לא מעלין ולא מורידין = 'one does not pull up [someone from a pit] and one does knock down' = one leaves him to his fate, does not attend to him, does not show consideration for him)." — The parallel in S. Eli. Rab. 11 (54) is very different. ‖ Midrash Psalm 9 § 9 (43B): Philip (another reading: a philosopher) asked R. Eleasa (an Amora of uncertain time):[67] "Did the prophet not say, 'If Edom (= Rome) says, "We have been wrecked"' (Mal 1:4); and further, 'They may build, but I will tear down' (Mal 1:4)? And look, everything that we (Romans) have built still stands!" He answered him, "Scripture does not speak of actual buildings but rather of plans: for as often as you sit and think and take counsel against us in order to build yourselves and destroy us, just as often God tears down your plan." He said to him, "On your life, it is so! For we want to destroy you every year, and then some elder (senator) comes and thwarts it." ‖ Leviticus Rabbah 4 (107D): R. Eleasa (see the previous citation) said, "A *goy* (non-Israelite) asked R. Joshua b. Qarha (ca. 150), 'It is written in your Torah: "Judgment is to be made in accordance with the majority" (so the midr. formulates Exod 23:2).[68] Now since we are more numerous than you, why will you not become like us in idolatry?' He answered him, 'Perhaps you have children?' He said to him, 'Now you remind me of my distress.' He said to him, 'Why?' He said to him, 'I have many children. When they sit at my table, one thanks this god and another thanks that god, and they do not get up from there until they crack each other's brains.' He said to him, 'Do you become like them?' He answered him, 'No!' He said to him, 'Instead of wanting to make us like you, make your children like yourself!' Then he rushed away from there." ‖ See b. Sanh. 39A at § John 10:16, n. *a*. ‖ Babylonian Talmud Sanhedrin 98B: R. Simlai (ca. 250) said in a presentation, "What does 'Woe to those who long for the day of Yahweh! What will this day of Yahweh be for you? It will be darkness

67. S-B: Seder Ha-doroth (in Buber, Midr. Ps. Introduction, 14A n. 54) identifies this Eleasa with Bar Eleasa, the son-in-law of R. Judah I; against this, see Bacher, *Die Agada der palästinensischen Amoräer*, 3:761–5.

68. S-B: In b. Ḥul. 11A, the principle that in judicial decisions the majority of votes is decisive is also derived from Exod 23:2.

and not light' (Amos 5:18) mean? Like a rooster and a bat that waited for the (day) light. Then the rooster said to the bat, 'I wait for the light, for the light is mine; but you, what is the light for you?'" This is what that sectarian said to R. Abbahu (ca. 300), "When will the Messiah come?" He answered him, "When darkness will cover those people (i.e., you)." He said to him, "Truly, you have cursed me!" He answered him, "In a passage of Scripture it is written, 'Behold, darkness covers the earth and darkness the nations; but Yahweh will rise over you and his glory will appear over you' (Isa 60:2)." — Pagans are like the bat for which there is darkness.

d. Josephus, *Against Apion* 2.39, toward the end: "Even if we ourselves did not recognize the excellence of all (our) laws, we would still feel compelled to be proud of them μέγα φρονεῖν ἐπ' αὐτοῖς because of the multitude of those who emulate them."

e. See Mek. Exod. 15:2 (44A) above in n. *a* and the religious disputations translated in n. *c*.

f. In the anti-Semitic circular letter that, according to R. Levi (ca. 300), Haman dispatched, there is ample reference to Jewish pride. According to Midr. Esth. 3:9 (96A), the beginning of the letter reads: "Peace to you without end! Let it be known to you that there is a person in our midst who does not in fact stem from our region but is of royal blood and descends from the seed of Amalek and belongs among the great ones of our times, and Haman is his name. He made a small and simple plea to us (the great ones of the kingdom) concerning a people that lives in our midst and is despised by all nations. But their mind is proud in them. They take pleasure in our misfortune and they commonly curse the king with their mouth. And what is the curse with which they curse us? 'Yahweh is king forever and ever, the gentiles will perish from his land' (Ps 10:16); and furthermore they say, 'To carry out revenge on the gentiles, chastisements on the nations' (Ps 149:7). And they repudiate the one who has bestowed good on them." (This is then proven in more detail by appealing to the history in the Old Testament.) — On these and similar accusations, see especially Emil Schürer.[69]

2:19 A: A guide for the blind.

1 Enoch 105:1: "'In those days (of the end time),' says the Lord, 'they (the righteous and wise Israelites) will call the children of earth (= humanity) and testify concerning the wisdom of the same (namely the apocalyptic cryptographs). Show them to them, for you are their guides.'" ‖ Sibylline Oracles 3:194f.: "Then the people of the great God will be strong again, who will be the guides of life βίου καθοδηγοί for all mortals." ‖ Sibylline Oracles 3:582f.: "They (the Israelites) will themselves be prophets, raised up by the immortal one, bringing great joy to all people." — The Israelites are presented as prophets and priests of humanity also in Philo; see § Rom 2:19f., #1, n. *h.* ‖ Josephus, *Against Apion* 2.41: The Jews are the εἰσηγηταί of the non-Jews; see § Rom 2:19f., #1, n. *b*.

69. Schürer, *Geschichte des jüdischen Volkes*, 3:150–155, 546–553.

2:19 B: A light for those in darkness.

1. φῶς. — α. Israel as the light of the world; see § Matt 5:14 A, n. *c*. — See Wis 18:4 at § Rom 2:19f., #1, n. *f*. — β. Jerusalem as the light of the world; see § Matt 5:14 A, n. *e*. — Sibylline Oracles 5:260ff.: "Let your heart no longer be tormented in your chest by the sword, you divinely born one, you rich one, the flower longed for by the Only One, noble light and worthy scion, beloved offspring, lovely, beautiful Jewish city, divinely inspired for songs."

2. τῶν ἐν σκότει. — The gentile world is like the bat, for which there is darkness; see b. Sanh. 98B at § Rom 2:19f., #2, n. *c*, toward the end. — For the equation "darkness" = "a lack of knowledge of the Torah," see Exod. Rab. 36 (95C) at § John 8:12 B; parallels here include Midr. Ps. 27 § 2 (111B); Pesiq. Rab. 8 (30A).

2:21–23: You who teach another, do you not teach yourself? You who declare that one should not steal, do you steal? You who say that one should not commit adultery, do you commit adultery? You who abhor idols, do you rob temples? You who boast in the law, do you dishonor God by transgressing the law?

These words of the apostle are confirmed and filled out by the picture suggested by R. Yohanan b. Zakkai († ca. 80) concerning the internal circumstances of the Jewish people in the last decades before the destruction of the temple. The same is found in:

Tosefta Soṭah 14:1ff. (320): R. Yohanan b. Zakkai said, "Since murderers have multiplied, the process with the calf whose neck was to be broken has ceased (Deut 21:4), because the calf whose neck was to be broken is used only in a case of doubt; but now murder is openly committed. Since adulterers have multiplied, the water of bitterness has ceased, because it had to be drunk only in a case of doubt.[70] Since salacious people have multiplied, honoring the Torah has ceased and the court proceedings have become corrupt. Since whisperers of blandishments have multiplied in court (for the purpose of influencing the judges), a blaze of wrath has come into the world, and the Shekinah (divine presence) has been removed from Israel. Since respecters (of the person)[71] have multiplied, so too the commandment has disappeared: "You are not to respect" (Deut 1:17), as has the commandment, 'You are not to be intimidated' (Deut 1:17), and people have cast off the yoke of heaven (= the law of God) and made their master a king of flesh and blood. Since those have multiplied who imposed wares on owners (dealers; for the purpose of profit, as also the judges did, according to Rashi in b. Soṭah 47B), bribery increased, and justice was perverted, and things got worse instead of better; and likewise it says, 'His sons did not walk in his ways and went after gain and took bribes and perverted justice' (1 Sam 8:3).... Since those have multiplied (especially among the judges) who say, 'I accept your

70. S-B: The Mishnah, which also accepted both these claims, adds to the second m. Soṭa 9.9: Rabban Yohanan b. Zakkai made the bitter waters cease, since it says: "I will not afflict your daughters when they play the harlot, nor your daughter-in-laws when they commit adultery; for they themselves (the husbands) go aside with harlots" (Hos 4:14).

71. TN: That is, those who unduly consider a person's prestige.

graciousness and will thank you for it,' those have multiplied of whom it is said, 'Everyone did what was right in his own eyes' (Judg 17:6), and all the authorities became foul and ever more despicable. Since those have multiplied of whom it is said, 'Everyone did what was right in his own eyes,' the base have been exalted and the exalted have been abased. Since the envious have multiplied and those who commit robbery (that is, shedders of blood), the hard-hearted have multiplied and every single one closed his hand before the other. Since those have multiplied of whom it says, 'Their heart runs after gain' (Ezek 33:31), 'those who call the bad good and the good bad' (Isa 5:20) have multiplied. Since those who have multiplied call the bad good and the good bad, the whole world has been filled with woe! Since the saliva drawers (people of a proud, malicious sort) have multiplied, students have decreased and the honor of the Torah has dwindled. Since the proud (cocky) have multiplied, the daughters of Israel have begun to marry the proud, for our generation looks only at the appearance (or: looks only at the person). Since those 'with an outstretched neck and eyes that look around lustfully' (Isa 3:16) have multiplied, the bitter waters have multiplied, but they (ultimately completely) ceased. Since those who are proud of heart have multiplied, factions have increased in Israel, and two Torahs have arisen (insofar as each party followed its own understanding and interpretation of the laws in practice). Since the students of Shammai and Hillel multiplied, who had not served (their teacher in personal dealings with him) satisfactorily, factions have increased in Israel and two Torahs have arisen. Since those who accepted gifts multiplied, lifespan has decreased and years have been shortened, and goodness has ceased. Since those who accepted alms from the *goyim* (non-Israelites) have multiplied, the *goyim* began to multiply and Israel to decrease, and there is no rest for Israel in the world." – This lament of Rabban Yohanan b. Zakkai nowhere presupposes the destruction of the temple. The yoke of the Roman emperor is indeed a burden on the people and the number of the *goyim* is growing in the land; but the Jewish authorities, even if they were despised, still occupy their office. This fits only the decades before the year 70. Many times Rabban Yohanan b. Zakkai takes the initiative to complain about factions and bribery accepted by Jewish judges. But these things emerged in large part from the number of scholars of the Scriptures (*soferim*); so Rabban Yohanan's complaint also becomes an accusation against them. Our lament is as a corroborative analogue to the woes of Jesus in Matt 23. – The Tosefta passage is found also in b. Soṭah 47B, partly elaborated by additions and with a different order of the individual sentences.

2:21 A: You who teach another, do you not teach yourself?

ʾAbot de Rabbi Nathan 29 (8A): Abba Saul b. Nannos (a Tannaim) said, "There are some people who teach themselves and not others שלמד לעצמו ואינו מלמד לאחרים; one who teaches others and does not teach himself; one who teaches himself and others, and one who teaches neither himself nor others.... The one who teaches others and does not teach himself. How might this happen, for example? A person studies a lesson two or three times, and then he teaches others, then he does not occupy himself with it any further and forgets it. This is one who teaches others and does not teach himself...." ‖ See Midr. Eccl. 8:4 (39B) at § Matt 5:45 A, n. *c.* ‖ Deuteronomy Rabbah 2 (198B): R. Simlai (ca. 250) said, "It is written, 'Their mother has prostituted herself, the one who bore them has acted shamefully' (Hos 2:7), for they desecrate my words before ordinary people (here the Torah is thought of as the mother of the learned). How so? A learned man sits there and openly states in front of the community, 'You should not charge interest on loans!' and he himself charges interest on loans. He says, 'You should not rob!' and he himself robs. He says, 'You should not steal!' and he himself steals." R. Berekhiah (ca. 340) said, "There once was a man whose coat was stolen; he went to file a suit with the judge; there he found his coat spread out on the judge's bed." R. Berekhiah also said, "There once was a man whose kettle was stolen. He went to file a suit with the judge; then he found it on his stove." ‖ Midrash Ruth 1:2 (124B): R. Berekhiah (ca. 340, so read!) asked R. Bezalel (ca. 310), "What does 'Your mother has prostituted herself' (Hos 2:7) mean? Is it possible that our mother Sarah was a whore?" He said to him, "Far from it חס ושלום! But when do the words of the Torah (= our mother) become contemptible to ordinary people מתבזין? When those who know them (those learned in Scripture) make them contemptible מבזין (by their deeds not corresponding to their words)." Then R. Jacob b. Abdima (in the 4th cent.) came and stated as a traditional teaching: "When are the words of the Torah like prostitutes to ordinary people? When those who know them make them contemptible." R. Yohanan († 279) offered (the scriptural proof) from here: "'The wisdom of the poor is despised בזויה' (Eccl 9:16). But was the wisdom of R. Aqiba († ca. 135) despised because he was poor? Rather, what should we understand by 'poor'? The one who is despised because of his words. For example, an elder זָקֵן (= teacher, scholar) sits and states, 'You should not pervert justice!' and he himself perverts justice. 'You should not respect the person!' and he himself respects the person. 'You should not take bribes!' and he himself takes bribes. 'You should not oppress the widow and orphan!' and he himself oppresses them. Samson went after his eyes; for it says, 'Get her for me, because she pleases me!' (Judg 14:2). Gideon committed idolatry; for it says, 'Gideon made an ephod out of it' (Judg 8:27). Here you see that there is no greater poor man than this one! Woe to the judge who respects the person in judgment!" — R. Yohanan's statement is also found in Midr. Eccl. 9:16 (45B). ‖ Exodus Rabbah 30 (89D): The way of God is not the way of men. The way of men is to teach others מורה to do something, while not doing it oneself; but it is not so with God. Instead, what he himself does or decides to do, he commands Israel to do and observe it. — Then the narrative is laid out about how Rabban Gamaliel (ca. 90) and his companions represented this statement once in Rome; see Exod. Rab. 30 (89D) at § John 5:17. ‖ See ʾAbot R. Nat. 1 at § Matt 6:9 C, n. *p*.

2:21 B: You who proclaim that one should not steal, do you steal?

On the whole sentence, see Deut. Rab. 2 (198B) at § Rom 2:21 A. — On the interpretation of the 7th commandment, see § Matt 19:18 A. — Here we present some passages on the 7th commandment which demonstrate the strictness of the scholars of Scripture in theory and their occasional laxity in practice.

A. Strictness in theory.

Mishnah Baba Qamma 7.7: Small livestock are not reared in Israel, though they are in Syria (because this place had not originally been a part of the land of Israel) and in the deserts in the land of Israel. (Reason: The livestock could pasture on a stranger's land and thus make its owner a thief.) ‖ Tosefta Baba Qamma 8.11 (362): Although it has been said, "Small livestock are not reared in Israel," they may be reared (kept) 30 days before a festival and 30 days before the celebration of a son's wedding, but the livestock cannot be driven outside to pasture on the road; rather, the livestock must be bound to the legs of the bed.... Tosefta Baba Qamma 8.13: It was said of R. Judah b. Baba († ca. 135) that he did everything for God's sake, except that he reared a bit of small livestock. Once he got sick, and a doctor came to him and said to him, "The only cure for you is warm milk (as it comes from the animal)." He bought himself a goat and tied it to the legs of the bed and sucked warm milk from it, for he had a cough. One time the scholars wanted to give to him (in order to visit him in his sickness). They said, "How can we go to him, since there is a robber in his house (namely the goat)!" When he had died, the scholars carefully examined all his works, and they found no fault in him, except this alone. Even he himself said in the hour of his death, "I know that there is no fault in me except this alone, namely that I transgressed the words of my colleagues." R. Ishmael († ca. 135) said, "My father's house (paternal family) was among the householders in Galilee; why was it destroyed? Because in their case only one person made decisions about procedures concerning money (instead of three persons, as prescribed), and because they reared small livestock, although we owned a small wood close to the city (this counted as wilderness, where small livestock could be kept; see the Mishnah passage above); but a field lay between it and the city, and they crossed it when they were driven out and back." – The same is found as a baraita in b. B. Qam. 79B; the account about R. Judah b. Baba is found also in y. Soṭah 9.24A.24; b. Tem 115B. ‖ Genesis Rabbah 41 (25B): "A dispute arose between the herders of Abram's livestock and the herders of Lot's livestock" (Gen 13:7). R. Berekhiah (ca. 340) said in the name of R. Judah b. Simon (ca. 320), "The livestock of our father Abraham was driven out wearing a muzzle, and the livestock of Lot was driven out without a muzzle. Then Abraham's herders said to them, 'Is robbery allowed?' ..." See Gen. Rab. 59 (37B): The camels of our father Abraham were recognizable in that place by the fact that when they were driven out, they were driven out wearing a muzzle. – Moses and David also kept their herds from robbery; see Exod. Rab. 2 (68B) at § Matt 25:21 A. – Concerning herders, tax collectors, toll keepers, and other people who are under suspicion in matters of money, see also t. Sanh. 5.5 (423) and b. Sanh. 25B at § Luke 2:8 A. ‖ Mishnah Qiddušin 4.14: Abba Gurion of Sidon (ca. 180?) said in the name of Abba Saul (ca. 150, so read with the Jerusalem Talmud), "A man should not have his son trained to be a donkey driver, a camel guide, a barber, a sailor, a herder, and a peddler; for their craft is a craft of robbers." ‖ Mishnah Baba Qamma 10.1: One should not exchange money from the coffer of toll keepers, or the bag of tax collectors. Alms are also not taken from them (for the poor box); but these are taken in one's house or on the street. – The money in the coffer of toll keepers and tax collectors is counted as robbery, because it is often raised arbitrarily, and it is forbidden to make use of what has been robbed.

B. Laxity in practice.

Babylonian Talmud Baba Qamma 113B: Rab Bibi b. Giddel said that R. Simeon the Pious (ca. 210) said, "What has been robbed from a *goy* (non-Israelite) is forbidden, what he has lost is allowed (if an Israelite finds it, he does not have to give it back to him)." What has been robbed is forbidden; for Rab Huna († 297) said, "Where do we find the proof that what has been robbed from a *goy* is forbidden? Because it was said, 'You will consume all the nations that Yahweh your God gives to you' (Deut 7:16). If they are given into your hand, but not if they are not given into your hand." What he has lost is allowed; for Rab Hama bar Guria (ca. 270) said that Rab († 247) said, "Where do we find the proof that what a *goy* has lost is allowed? Because it was said, 'Do this with everything your brother has lost (give it back to him)' (Deut 22:3). You should give it back to your brother, but you should not give it back to a *goy* (because he is not a brother)…." In a baraita: R. Phineas b. Yair (ca. 200) said, "When it is a matter of whether the divine name is (thereby) desecrated, even what he has lost is forbidden." (If, e.g., the *goyim* would see the Jew's keeping of what has been found as reason to slander the God of the Jews, what has been lost must be given back even to the *goy*.) Samuel († 254) said, "When it is a matter in which he (a *goy*) has made an error (he demands too little, gives too much, and the like), it is allowed." According to this opinion of his, Samuel bought a golden basin from a *goy* as if it were copper (bronze, read פליזא instead of פרזילא "iron") for four *zuzim* and let him lose another *zuz* (while he was counting the money). Rab Kahana (probably the elder, ca. 250) bought 120 vats from a *goy* as if 100 and let him lose another *zuz*. He said to him, "Look, I rely on (trust) you." Rabina (I, † ca. 420; II, † 499), he himself and a *goy* (i.e., jointly with a *goy*), purchased a palm to split. He said to his servant, "Get to it first and take the stem part (thus the thickest and best parts), for the *goy* knows only the number (of pieces)." Rab Ashi († 427) was out and about and saw a vine tendril in a garden on which wine grapes hung. He said to his servant, "Go and see. If they belong to a *goy*, bring them. If they belong to an Israelite, do not bring them to me." They belonged to a *goy* who sat in the garden. He said to him, "What belongs to a *goy* is allowed?" He answered him, "A *goy* takes money (as compensation), an Israelite does not take money." – Note that the victim in every case is a *goy*.

2:22 A: You who say that one should not commit adultery, do you commit adultery?

On the interpretation of the 6th commandment, see § Matt 5:27. – The passages at § Matt 5:28 show just how strict the teaching about keeping the 6th commandment was in theory, yet the following passages permit us to conclude that even the lives of respected leaders and teachers of the people in many ways did not align with this strictness.

See Pss. Sol. 4:1ff., 9ff.; 8:9f.; 2:11ff. at § Rom 1:26 A, #2; see T. Levi 17 at § Rom 1:27 A, B, #1. ‖ Babylonian Talmud Qiddušin 81A: R. Aqiba († ca. 135) had scoffed at those who commit a sin (against the 6th commandment, namely that they are not able to resist temptation). One day Satan appeared to him in the form of a woman on top of a date tree. He grabbed the tree and climbed higher and higher. When he had gotten halfway up the tree, he (Satan) left him. He said, "If it had not been proclaimed in heaven, 'Be careful (be warned) about R. Aqiba and his knowledge of the Torah,' I would have treated your life as equal to two *maahs*" (the smallest silver coins; see § Matt 5:26 B, #14). ‖ Babylonian Talmud Qiddušin 81A: R. Meir (ca. 150) had scoffed at those at those who commit a sin (against the 6th commandment). One day Satan appeared to him in the form of a woman on the (other) side of a river. Since there was no ferry, he used a rope bridge and went across. When he had gotten to the middle of the rope bridge, he left him. He said, "If it had not been proclaimed in heaven, 'Be careful about R. Meir and his knowledge of the Torah,' I would have treated your life as equal to two *maahs*." ‖ A baraiata in b. Sanh. 11A: Once a woman came into the house of learning of R. Meir (ca. 150) and said, "Rabbi, one of you has become betrothed to me by lying with me" (even if frowned upon, this was a way to legally implement an engagement; see § John 2:1 A, #5, notes *i* and *k*). Then R. Meir stood up and wrote her the bill of divorce and gave it to her (as if he were the fiancé). Then everyone stood up and wrote (the bill of divorce) and gave it to her (so that the one who had actually committed the deed would remain undiscovered). ‖ A baraita in b. Qidd. 81B: R. Meir (ca. 150) said, "Keep watch over me because of my daughter!" R. Tarfon (ca. 100) said, "Keep watch over me because of my daughter-in-law!" A student mocked him. R. Abbahu (ca. 300) said in the name of R. Hanina b. Gamaliel (ca. 120), "Only a few days passed before that student fell because of his mother-in-law." ‖ Babylonian Talmud Yebamot 37B: When Rab († 247) came to Dardeshir, he said (he announced), "Who (= which woman) wants to be married for the day?" When Rab Nahman († 320) came to Shekanzib, he said, "Who wants to be married for the day?" (The woman was then given a bill of divorce so that everything was done as legally as possible.) – The same is found in b. Yoma 18B. ‖ Babylonian Talmud Niddah 47A: Samuel († 254) inquired with his female slave (about her sexual maturity) and gave her 4 *zuzim* for sex. ‖ Babylonian Talmud Qiddušin 81A: Some women who had been taken captive had come to Nehardea (to be redeemed here) had been taken up to the house (thus onto the balcony of the house) of Rab Amram the pious (ca. 260?). He had the stairs (to the balcony) removed before them. When one of them passed by, a ray of light fell in the window (so that she became visible). Then Rab Amram took the stairs, which took more than ten men to lift, and lifted them by himself. He climbed higher and higher up. When he had gotten to the middle of the stairs, he spread his feet apart (to stand firm) and called with a loud voice: "Fire at Amram's!" The rabbis came and said to him, "You have disgraced us!" He answered them, "It is better that you have been disgraced by me in this world than to have been disgraced by me in the future world." He adjured it (the evil inclination) to depart from him. Then it departed from him like a pillar of fire. He said to it, "Behold, you are fire and I am flesh, and yet I am stronger than you!" ‖ Babylonian Talmud Berakot 20A: Rab Giddel (ca. 270) used to go and sit at the doors of the immersion baths (for women). He said to them, "The submersion is like this and that." The rabbis said to him, "Does our lord not fear the evil inclination?" He answered them, "In my eyes they are like white geese." R. Yohanan († 279) used to go and sit at the doors of the immersion baths (for women). He said, "When the daughters of Israel get out and come out from the bath, they look at me, and they will have descendants who are just as beautiful as I am." The rabbis said to him, "Does our lord not fear the evil eye?" He answered them, "I came from seed the seed of Joseph, to whom the evil eye did no violence; for it is written, 'Joseph is a young fruit tree, a young fruit tree at the spring עֲלֵי עָיִן.'" R. Abbahu (ca. 300) said, "Do not read עֲלֵי עָיִן, but עוֹלֵי עַיִן 'those who are above the eye.'" ‖ Babylonian Talmud Qiddušin 81B: R. Hiyya b. Ashi (ca. 270) used to say, as soon as he fell on his face (in prayer): "May the All Merciful One save me from the evil inclination!" One day his wife heard this, and she said, "Since he has kept clear of me for who knows how many years, why does he speak this way?" One day he was studying in his garden. She put on make-up and passed by him several times." He said to her, "Who are you?" She answered. "I am a prostitute[72] who just got back today." He requested her (to sleep with him). She said to him, "Get me that pomegranate at the top of the branch!" He jumped up, went, and brought it to her. When he came into the house, his wife had heated the oven. He went up and put himself in it (in order to take his life, Rashi). She said to him, "What are you doing?" He said to her, "This and that happened." She answered him, "It was I." He did not consider that until she gave him his sign (the pomegranate). He said to her, "In any case, I intended to do what is forbidden." ‖ Babylonian Talmud Qiddušin 81A: Rab Bibi (ca. 320) came into the house of Rab Joseph († 333). After he had eaten כְּרַךְ רִיפְתָּא (literally: the bread had been wrapped), he said to them, "Remove the stairs from under Bibi!" But Rabbah († 331) said, "In the case of a woman whose husband is in the city (= at home), one is not under suspicion because of being alone (with another man)!" In the case of Rab Bibi it was different because she was his maid of honor and (therefore) bold toward him (familiar with him; see § Matt 9:15 A). ‖ In SNum 15:41 § 115 (35B) and b. Menaḥ. 44A, it is recounted how a student of R. Hiyya (ca. 200) in the house of a prostitute came to his senses at the last moment by looking at his show fringes; see the excursus "Show Fringes," #5. ‖ On fornication in Israel, see also § Rom 1:26 and § 1:27, as well as t. Soṭah 14:1ff. at § Rom 2:21ff.

2:22 B: You who abhor idols.

1. βδελύσσω, βδελύσσομαι, is used in the LXX for תִּעֵב, שִׁקֵּץ, as well as for גָּעַל (Lev 26:11) = "abhor"; specifically, for abhorring idolatry and everything connected with it (LXX Lev 18:30; Deut 7:26; 1 Kgs 21:26); therefore, the substantive βδέλυγμα "abomination" really = idol, idolatry. Thus, it is used for שִׁקּוּץ in LXX Deut 29:17; Jer 7:30; 13:27; Ezek 11:18, 21; 20:7, 8, 30; 2 Chr 15:8; for תּוֹעֵבָה in LXX Deut 7:26; 13:14 (15); 2 Kgs 16:3; 21:2; 23:13; Ezek 7:20; for גִּלּוּלִים in LXX 1 Kgs 21:26. — Testament of Judah 23: "You will mingle with the abominations of the gentiles ἐπιμιγήσεσθε ἐν βδελύγμασι ἐθνῶν." — See also § Matt 24:15.

2. The rabbinic scholars considered it to be a foregone conclusion that by their time idolatry no longer had any place in Israel.[a] It was assumed that the evil inclination toward idolatry had been fully eradicated among the people either during the Babylonian exile or soon thereafter.[b] Since then the pagan cult had become an abhorrence תּוֹעֵבָה or abomination

72. Read הֲדָוְתָא instead of חריתא according to J. Levy, *Neuhebräisches und Chaldäisches Wörterbuch über die Talmudim und Midraschim* (Leipzig: F. A. Brockhaus, 1876), 2:16B.

שִׁקּוּץ for Israel, as it always should have been according to the OT. This abhorrence manifested itself particularly in that α. idolatry was counted among the cardinal sins alongside fornication, bloodshed, and the desecration of the divine name;[c] β. the names of idols and their locations were cacophemetiscally called deformed,[d] and that γ. any use, for the most part any usufruct of things connected to the pagan cult, was forbidden.[e]

a. Judith 8:18ff.: "Among our generation today there is neither tribe nor family, neither district nor city among us that has worshiped gods made with hands, as in earlier days; because of their devotion to such gods our fathers were given up to the sword and plunder and fell in large numbers before our enemies. But we know no other God beside him." ‖ Babylonian Talmud ʿAbodah Zarah 17A: R. Hanina (ca. 225) and R. Jonathan (ca. 220) were on a journey. They came to two paths, one of which led to the entrance of the temple of an idol and the other to the entrance of a whore house. One of them said, "We will go to the entrance of the temple of the idol, for the inclination to idolatry is slaughtered (killed in us)." The other said, "We will go to the entrance of the whore house and overcome the evil inclination, so that we may receive our recompense." When they arrived there, the prostitutes saw them and bowed (politely) before them. Then that one said to him, "How did you know this (that we would be protected from sin here)?" He answered, "Discretion will keep watch over you, understanding will protect you" (Prov 2:11).

b. Midrash Song of Songs 7:8 (128A): R. Huna (ca. 350) said in the name of R. Dosa b. Tebeth, "God created two (evil) inclinations in his world: the inclination to idolatry and the inclination to fornication. The inclination to idolatry has long been uprooted, but the inclination to fornication (still) exists. God said, 'Whoever can resist fornication, for him I count it as if he resisted both.'" R. Judah (b. Simon?, ca. 320) said, "It is like a snake charmer who had (two) snakes (adders). He held the big one at bay and left the small one (unhindered). He said, 'Whoever can resist this one, for him I count it as if he resisted both.' Thus, God uprooted the inclination to idolatry but left the one that inclines to fornication. He says, 'Whoever stands sideways toward (resists) fornication, for him I count it as if he resisted both.'" When was the inclination to idolatry eradicated? R. Bannaiah (= Benaiah, ca. 220) said, "These (the ones who eradicated it) were Mordecai and Esther"; the rabbis said, "Hananiah, Mishael, and Azariah (the contemporaries of Daniel)." ‖ Babylonian Talmud Yoma 69B: "They cried out with a loud voice to Yahweh their God" (Neh 9:4). What did they say? Rab († 247) or, as it has also been said that R. Yohanan († 279) said, "Woe, woe! (they cried). This (namely the inclination to idolatry) is what destroyed the sanctuary and burned the temple and killed all the righteous and led the Israelites out of their land into exile, and still now dances in our midst. You (O God) gave it to us so that we might receive our recompense by it (i.e., by overcoming it). We do not want it or the recompense for it!" Then a note fell to them from heaven on which it was written: אמת "truth." R. Hanina (ca. 225) said, "Conclude from this: The seal of God is 'truth' (God seals each of his decisions with the three letters אמת; cf. Dan 8:26; 10:1)." They sat fasting for three days and three nights, since it (the inclination to idolatry) had been given to them (by God). It burst forth and came like a fiery lion from the Most Holy Place. The prophet (here Zechariah is meant) said to the Israelites,

"This is the inclination to idolatry יצרא דע"ז, for it says, 'And he said, "This is godlessness"' (Zech 5:8)." While they seized it, a strand of hair was pulled from its head. Then it raised its voice, and its voice traveled 400 *parasangs*. They said, "What should we do to it? Maybe, if God wants to stop us, mercy will be shown to it from heaven!" The prophet said to them, "Throw it into a leaden kettle and cover the opening with lead, for lead strongly pulls the voice into itself (muffles it); for it says, 'He said, "This is godlessness," and he cast it into the bushel and put a stone of iron on its opening' (Zech 5:8)." Then they said, "Since it (now) is a time of delight (to raise a prayer), we will ask for mercy (also) concerning the inclination to the sin of fornication (perhaps it will also be given into our power)." They asked for mercy, and it was given into their hand. He (probably the prophet) said to them, "Watch out! For if you kill it, the world will stop (for if it dies, so does the drive for sex)." They bound it for three days. Then from the same day an egg was sought in Israel and it was not found. They said, "What should we do to it? If we kill it, the world will stop; if we ask for mercy concerning one half of it, half will not be granted in heaven." Then they blinded its eyes and let it go. As a result, people are no longer aroused to blood relations by it (the inclination to incest has stopped since then in Israel). — The same is found in b. Sanh. 64A.

c. See supporting passages at § Matt 5:21 B, #1, n. *a*; see also b. Sanh. 74A at § Matt 6:9 C, n. *h*; the passages at § Matt 6:9 C, n. *q*; b. ʿArak. 15B at § Matt 5:11 B, #2; Lev. Rab. 37 (133C) at § Matt 5:33, #3.

d. Examples can be found at § Matt 12:24, #2, n. *c*.

e. See a more detailed treatment along with supporting passages in the excursus "The Stance of Judaism toward the Non-Jewish World." See also m. ʿAbod. Zar. 2.7 at § Matt 3:4 C, n. *f*; m. ʿAbod. Zar. 2.6 at § Matt 5:13 A, #1, n. *c*; m. ʿAbod. Zar. 3.6 at § Matt 12:24, #2, n. *c*; m. ʿAbod. Zar. 5.12 at § Matt 23:25, #2; m. ʿAbod. Zar. 3.7 at § Acts 17:23; m. ʿAbod. Zar. 2.3 at § Rom 1:23 A, #2, D, n. *c*.

2:22 C: Do you rob temples?

1. In line with the complex sentence and the context, only εἴδωλα can be supplied as the object to complement ἱεροσυλεῖς. In other words, in using ἱεροσυλεῖν, the apostle was not thinking of robberies of the Jewish temple, but rather of robberies of pagan divinities and pagan shrines. In the ancient Jewish literature explicit testimonies for these instances of sacrilege against pagan holy places are rarely found. Gentiles first appear here as perpetrators.[a] A Jew was forbidden by Deut 7:25f. from any desire for gold and silver in the banned idols of the gentiles (Deut 7:25f.). If, as is to be assumed, Josephus, *Ant.* 4.8.10 had this passage of Scripture in view in connection with Exod 22:27, it would be a testimony to the fact that at Josephus' time, the prohibition of robbing pagan sanctuaries was established with Deut 7:25f.[b] Despite this prohibition, there was no lack of Jews who participated in stealing idols, whether indirectly or directly. There is one case where a Jew is said to have taken an idol in order to sell it.[c] Another time a tradition is given in which an Israelite takes stones from

one of the heaps of stones that were cast to honor Mercury and uses them to pave roads and streets.[d] The Mishnah declares that gold, garments, and equipment that a Jew finds on the head of an idol are allowed for usufruct.[e] Here one has to keep in mind that a Jew who found what had been lost by a non-Jew was not obligated to return what was found (see b. B. Qam. 113B at § Rom 2:21 B, B). Lastly, one can find the stipulation that the objects that idol priests stole from their idols and then sold were allowed to an Israelite for usufruct.[f] The Israelite was thus permitted to buy the goods in question as a fencer and exploit them to his advantage. One cannot assume that all these cases and stipulations were simply theoretical. They will have occurred and been acted on often enough in practice as well. But in that case the apostle was justified in asking the accusatory question: ὁ βδελυσσόμενος τὰ εἴδωλα ἱεροσυλεῖς;

a. Epistle of Jeremiah 10f.: "But it also happens that the priests take the gold and silver from their idols and use them for themselves, and also give these to the prostitutes in the whorehouse." Epistle of Jeremiah 15: "He also holds a combat blade in his right hand and an ax, and yet he cannot free himself from war or robbers." — Epistle of Jeremiah 18: "And as the yards (of the prison) are closed for anyone who has offended the king, as for one lead away to death, the priests keep their dwellings safe with gates and locks and bars so that they may not be plundered by robbers." — Epistle of Jeremiah 33: "The priests pilfer their clothing and use it to clothe their wives and children." Epistle of Jeremiah 37f.: "(These) gods of wood and silver and gold cannot stay safe from thieves and robbers. Those who have power over them will take their silver and gold and garments to clothe themselves." ‖ Genesis Rabbah 26 (16D): R. Simeon b. Yohai (ca. 150) taught, "A degeneracy (moral breakdown) that does not emanate from the great ones (the upper class) is not degeneracy: if the idol priests steal the idol, who swears by the idol, who brings it sacrifices?" ‖ See t. ʿAbod. Zar. 6.12 (470) in n. *f*; see also n. *d*.

b. Josephus, *Jewish Antiquities* 4.8.10: "No one should slander gods recognized (venerated) by other cities (see Exod 22:27), nor should anyone steal from foreign temples, nor steal a gift that has been dedicated to a god (see Deut 7:25f.)."

c. A baraita in b. ʿAbod. Zar. 53A: If he (the owner) has hidden (money) on it (his idol), or if something (a ruin) has collapsed on it, or if robbers have stolen it, or if the owners have left it behind and moved to a distant country, then, if they intend to return, it has not thereby become void, as in the wars of Joshua (against the pagan inhabitants of the land of Israel; that is, it has not lost its idol character and remains forbidden to the Israelite for usufruct). And it was necessary (to say all this for clarification; or as a question: was it necessary to say all this?). If he (only) taught: "If he hid something on it," I would say, "Since he did not sell it, he did not make it void"; but (he also teaches) "if something has collapsed on it"; since he did not uncover it (from the rubble), I would say, "He certainly did not make it void." This is problematic (in need of clarification). If he (only) taught: "If something has collapsed on it," I would say, "Since he might have meant that 'it may remain lying there until I want to have it, and then I will take it'" (therefore he did not uncover it, but also did not make it void); but (he also teaches) "if robbers have stolen it"; since he did not inquire about it, I would say, "He certainly did not make it void." This is problematic (in need of clarification). If he (only) taught: "If robbers have stolen it," I would say, "Since he might have meant if a gentile has taken (stolen) it, he will worship it; if an Israelite took it, he will sell it to a gentile since it is worth a lot of money, and the gentile will worship it" (therefore he did not inquire about it, but he also did not make it void); but (he also teaches) "if the owners have left it behind and moved to a distant country"; since they did not take it with them, I would say, "They did not make it void." This is problematic (in need of clarification). (Therefore, he teaches at the end:) "If they intend to return, it has not become void, as in the wars of Joshua." (This concluding remark clarifies everything that precedes it: the idol is not made void in any of the cases considered; any usufruct of the idol is therefore forbidden to the Israelite.)

d. Babylonian Talmud ʿAbodah Zarah 50A: Rab Joseph b. Abba (ca. 310?) said, "Rabbah b. Jeremiah came to our place. He came and brought with him the following tannaitic tradition: "If a *goy* (non-Israelite) has taken stones from one of the heaps to Mercury and covered (paved) roads and streets with them, these are allowed (to the Israelite for usufruct; that is, he may walk on these roads and streets; for by taking the stones from the stone heaps devoted to Mercury, the *goy* has not made these into idol shrines or desecrated them). If an Israelite has taken stones from one of the heaps to Mercury and paved roads and streets with them, they are forbidden (Israelites may not use them since an Israelite cannot desecrate a pagan shrine …)."

e. Mishnah ʿAbodah Zarah 4.2: If he (an Israelite) has found gold, garments, or equipment on his (Mercury's) head, see, these are allowed (to the Israelite for usufruct). — In the parallel passage t. ʿAbod. Zar. 6.13 (470); b. ʿAbod. Zar. 51B, we find the qualification that the things in question are allowed only if they were not used to beautify the idol.

f. Tosefta ʿAbodah Zarah 6.12 (470): If idol priests steal and sell (the idolatrous items, such as garments, equipment, etc.), lo, they are allowed (to the Israelite for usufruct).

2. If one prefers to understand ἱεροσυλεῖν as referring to the robbing of the Jewish temple, the following passages can be invoked:

Psalms of Solomon 8:11ff (from the time shortly after 63 BCE): "They (the Jewish rulers) looted διήρπαζον the sanctuary of God, as if there were no inheritance and avenger. They approached the altar of the Lord with every impurity and in a flow of blood they defiled the offerings as common meat. They spared no sin that they did not commit worse than the gentiles." ‖ Testament of Levi 14: "You (Levi's sons) are the lights of heaven like the sun and the moon. What will all the gentiles do, if you, blinded in godlessness and teaching commandments opposed to the ordinances of God, who rob the Lord's offerings and steal from his portions and, before you make an offering to him, take for yourselves the best part, consuming it scornfully with prostitutes?" ‖ Josephus, *Jewish Antiquities* 18.3.5: "There was a Jewish man who was charged with transgressing the laws and had fled the fatherland out of fear of punishment, wicked in every respect. He then stayed in Rome (at the time of the Emperor Tiberius), where he masqueraded as an interpreter of the wisdom of the Mosaic law, after he had gained three other men who were just like him in every way. A certain

Fulvia came to these men quite often. She was among the most respectable women and had bound herself to the Jewish customs (as a proselyte). They persuaded her to send purple and gold to the sanctuary in Jerusalem. When they had received it, they used it for their own expenditures, and this was why they had asked her in the first place. Then Emperor Tiberius commanded—who was a friend of Saturninus, the husband of Fulvia, who had made known what had been done to his wife—that all the Jews be expelled from Rome." ‖ TanḥumaB תרומה § 7 (46B): Our teachers said, "He (God) punished the generation of Malachi," and they answered him, "He said to them, 'Will a man cheat היקבע God?' (Mal 3:8)." R. Levi (ca. 300) said, "This (namely קבע) is an Arabic word. If an Arab wants to speak with another and says to him, 'Did you rob us גוזלינו?' he says, 'Did you קובעינו = rob us? Will then a man cheat (= rob) God?' And he said, '"And do you say, 'How are we cheating (robbing) you?' Your tithes and offerings!" (Mal 3:8), which you do not set apart as is fitting.'" — A parallel can be found in Midr. Ps. 57 § 2 (149A); see Roš Haš. 26A, B. See also Gen. Rab. 80 (51B): Yose of Maon stated as an interpreter in the synagogue of Maon, "'Hear this, you priests, and pay heed, house of Israel, and those of you from the house of the king, pay attention!' (Hos 5:1)." He said, "One day God will take the priests to judge them and will say to them, 'Why did you not make an effort with the Torah? Did you not make use of 24 priestly gifts?' Then they will say to him, 'Nothing was given to us!' 'Pay heed, house of Israel, why did you not give the 24 priestly gifts to the priests, which I wrote down for you in the Torah?' And they will say to him, 'Because of those from the patriarchal house, who took everything.' 'House of the king, pay attention, the preservation of the law lay with all of you, "And this should be the right of the priests" (Deut 18:3). Therefore the divine punitive justice will come to you and against you' (read נהפכת instead of נהפכתי)." — A parallel is found in y. Sanh. 2.20D.2. ‖ Mishnah Sanhedrin 9.6: If someone steals an offering cup ..., zealots (for the divine law) may have at him (and kill him).

2:23 A: You who boast in the law.

1. The Torah is Israel's honor and glory and jewel.

(Greek) Sirach 24:8, 10f.: "Then the creator of everything, and the one who made me (Wisdom = Torah), commanded me, gave me a resting place for my tent, and said, 'Pitch your tent in Jacob and have your property in Israel....' In the holy tent I served before him, and so a firm home arose for me in Zion; in the beloved city he likewise gave me a resting place, and in Jerusalem is my dominion." ‖ Baruch 3:35f.; 4:2ff.: "This is our God, there is no other beside him. He investigated every way to knowledge and gave her (knowledge, wisdom = Torah) to Jacob, his servant, and to his beloved Israel .... Turn, Jacob, and seize her; continue toward the splendor of the light that comes from her! Do not give your honor (glory, τὴν δόξαν σου) to another, nor your fortune (best, τὰ συμφέροντά σοι) to a foreign nation. Blessed are we, Israel; for we know what pleases God (= God's will)!" ‖ 2 Baruch 48:22ff.: "We trust in you, because your law is with us; and we know that we will not fall, as long as we hold fast to the prescriptions of your covenant. At all times salvation has been ours, also only as long as we have not commingled with the nations. For we are all one people that bears an illustrious name, we who received one law from One. And that law, which resides with us, helps us, and the sublime wisdom that is in us will support us." — 2 Baruch 77:3: "The Lord gave the law to you and your fathers before all nations." ‖ 4 Ezra 5:27: "Out of all the nations, of which there are so many, you acquired for yourself one people, and that law, which you have chosen amidst all (laws), you have bestowed on the people that you desire." ‖ Sifre Deuteronomy 32:8 § 311 (134A): When God gave Israel the Torah, he arose and looked around and mused; as it says, "He arose and measured the earth, he saw it and gave up the gentiles" (so Midr. Hab. 3:6). There was no nation among the nations that would have been worthy to receive the Torah, except for Israel. — Leviticus Rabbah 13 (114A) goes into more detail and names R. Simeon b. Yohai (ca. 150), as the author. ‖ TanḥumaB תצוה § 7 (50A): "The wise receive honor as a possession" (Prov 3:35): these are the Israelites; "but fools walk away with shame": these are the nations of the world. When did the Israelites obtain honor? When they received the Torah from Sinai. ‖ Exodus Rabbah 51 (103D): When (the Israelites) received the Torah, God clothed them with the with the splendor of his glory. ‖ Pesiqta 37A: R. Haggai (ca. 340) said in the name of R. Samuel b. Nahman (ca. 260), "You find, when the Israelites stood at Mount Sinai and said, 'Everything that Yahweh has said, we will do and obey' (Exod 24:7), then he gave to them from the splendor of the Shekinah (divinity); for it says, 'Your renown went out among the gentiles because of your beauty, because it was perfect due to my adornment, which I had laid on you, says the Lord' (Ezek 16:14)." — The same is found in Pesiq. Rab. 14 (62B); the text is anonymous in Midr. Eccl. 8:1 (38B). ‖ Pesiqta 124B: "What should I adorn you with?" (So Midr. Lam. 2:13, by connecting אעידך with the biblical עֲדָה.) How much jewelry I have adorned you with (says God)! For R. Yohanan († 279) said, "On the day when God descended onto Mount Sinai to give Israel the Torah, 60 myriads of angels of service descended, and each one of them had a crown in his hand to adorn Israel with." R. Abba b. Kahana (ca. 310) said in the name of R. Yohanan (so read instead of ר' אחא בשם ר' אחא), "There were 120 myriads (2 angels for each of the 600,000 fighting men who went out of Egypt), one to set the crown on his head, and the other to gird him with weapons." R. Huna the elder of Sepphoris (ca. 300) said, "There was a belt, as it says, 'He dismantled the dominion of the (Egyptian) kinds (for the benefit of Israel), and then he girded their (the Israelites') loins with a belt' (so Midr. Job 12:18)." — Parallel passages with variations are found in Midr. Lam. 2:13 (67B); TanḥB תצוה §7 (50A); שלח has additions in § 1 (38B); Pesiq. Rab. 33 (154A); Exod. Rab. 51 (103D); Num. Rab. 16 (181D); Midr. Ps. 103 § 8 (218A). ‖ Sifre Numbers 18:20 § 119 (40A): There are three crowns: the crown of the Torah, the crown of the priesthood, and the crown of the kingdom. Aaron received the crown of the priesthood, and he accepted it; David received the crown of the kingdom, and he accepted it. Behold, the crown of the Torah lies there so that no one of those who come into the world will be able to say, "If the crown of the kingdom and the crown of the priesthood were lying there, I would not have myself worthy to take them." Behold, the crown of the Torah lies there for everyone who comes into the world; for whoever has made himself worthy of it, I (God) will count it for him as if the three crowns were lying there and he had received all of them; and whoever does not make himself worthy of it, I will count it for him as if the three crowns were lying there and he had received none of them. And if you should say, "Is it somehow greater than those two?," R. Simeon b. Eleazar (ca. 190) has said, "Is the one who installs the king or the king greater?" Answer: "The one who installs the king." "Is the one who appoints the sovereign or the one who exercises sovereignty greater?" Answer: "The one who appoints the sovereign." All the strength of those two crowns comes only from the power of the Torah; and, likewise, it says, "By me (Wisdom = Torah) kings reign ..., by me princes rule." — The same is found more briefly in Midr. Eccl. 7:1 (31A). ‖ Mishnah ʾAbot 4.13: R. Simeon (ca. 150) said, "There are three crowns: the crown of the Torah, the crown of the priesthood, and the crown of the kingdom; but the crown of a good name stands higher than them (all)."— See ʾAbot R. Nat. 41 toward the beginning: What is the situation with the crown of the priesthood? If someone gave all the silver and gold in the world, the crown of the priesthood would not be given to him (Num 25:13). If someone gave all the silver and gold in the world for the crown of the kingdom, the crown of the kingdom would not be given to him (Ezek 37:25). But the situation is different with the crown of the Torah. Whoever is willing to labor with the Torah, let him come and take it; for it says, "O, all you who are thirsty, come to the water" (Isa 55:1); labor with the words of the Torah and do not labor with the words of vanities. ‖ Babylonian Talmud Yoma 72B: R. Yohanan († 279) said, "There were three wreaths (bindings): in the case of the altar of incense (Exod 30:3f.), in the case of the ark of the covenant (Exod 25:11) and in the case of the table for the showbread (Exod 25:24f.). Aaron received the wreath of the altar (a symbol of the priesthood) and accepted it; David received the wreath of the table (a symbol of kinghood); and the wreath of the ark of the covenant (a symbol of the Torah and of the standing of scholars) still lies there. Whoever wants to take it, let him come and take it. But if you should say, 'It is small!,' there is this against that, 'By me kings reign ...' (Prov 8:15f.)." R. Yohanan interjected, "זר is written (in the case of the ark of the covenant [Exod 25:11], which could be read as זָר), but we read it as זֵיר: if a person is worthy, (the Torah) will become his wreath זֵיר; but if he is not worthy, it will vanish זָרָה from him." — See a similar passage in Exod. Rab. 34 (94D); Tanḥ. ויקהל 125A and Num. Rab. 4 (142B). ‖ See Josephus, *Against Apion* 2.39 toward the end at § Rom 2:19f., #2, n. *d.* ‖ See additional supporting passages also at § Rom 3:1f., C.

2. The Torah is the only good that remains for Israel,[a] but also at the same time its eternally inalienable possession.[b]

a. 2 Baruch 85:3: "Now the righteous have been gathered (to their fathers), and we too have left our land, and Zion has been torn away from us; and now we have nothing outside of the Almighty and his law." ‖ Sifra Leviticus 26:44 (459A): "I will not reject them (Israel) and I will not detest them so as to wipe them out" (Lev 26:44). But what is left for them, if they have not been detested and they have not been rejected? Have not all the good gifts that have been given to them been taken away from them? And if the book of the Torah had not remained for them, they would not be any different from the nations of the world.

b. 2 Baruch 77:12ff.: "(The people said to Baruch,) 'Write a letter of admonition and a letter of promise to our brothers in Babylon, in order to strengthen them before you leave us. For the shepherds of Israel have gone missing for them, and the lamps that once shone have gone out, and the wells of the streams we once drank from have dried up. But we have been left in darkness and in a thick wood and in the driest desert.' Baruch answered,

'The shepherds and the lamps and the wells stemmed from the law. And if we too go (away), the law still remains. If you look to the law and carefully pay heed to wisdom, you will not lack a lamp and the shepherd will not go away and the well will not dry out.'" ‖ Josephus, *Against Apion* 2.38: "Even if we have been robbed of the kingdom and cities and our other goods, the law remains for us without dying." ‖ A baraita in b. Šabb. 138B: When our teachers assembled in the vineyard at Javneh (the seat of the highest Jewish authority immediately after the destruction of the temple), they said, "One day the Torah will be forgotten by Israel; for it says, 'Behold, days are coming, says Yahweh the Lord of all, when I will send a hunger over the land, not a hunger for bread, nor a thirst for water, but rather to hear the word of Yahweh. And they will stagger from sea to sea from midnight until the rising of the sun, wandering to search for the word of Yahweh, and they will not find it' (Amos 8:11f.)...." R. Simeon b. Yohai (ca. 150) said, "Far from it חָס וְשָׁלוֹם (God forbid!) that the Torah should be forgotten by Israel; for it says, 'It will not be forgotten from the mouth of its seed' (Deut 31:21). But how will I maintain then: 'They will wander to seek the word of Yahweh, and they will not find it'? They will nowhere find clear (plain) halakic assessment or clear traditional teaching." — The first part is also in t. 'Ed. 1.1 (454); for the second part, see SDeut 11:22 § 48 (84B). ‖ Exodus Rabbah 33 (94C): "Moses laid the Torah on us, an inheritance מוֹרָשָׁה for the community of Jacob" (Deut 33:4). Do not read מורשה "inheritance," but rather יְרוּשָׁה "possession": it is a possession for Israel forever. ‖ Exodus Rabbah 33 (94C): "An inheritance for the community of Jacob" (Deut 33:4). Do not read מוֹרָשָׁה "inheritance," but rather מְאוֹרָסָה "betrothed one." This teaches that the Torah is betrothed to Israel; for it says, "I will betroth you to myself forever" (Hos 2:21). — The same is in b. Ber. 57A. — The interpretation that מורשה = מאורסה is also found in b. Pesaḥ. 49B; b. Sanh. 59A.

3. The Torah is the source of salvation for Israel and the basis and pledge of divine love; see § Rom 3:2.[73]

2:23 B: Do you dishonor God by transgressing the law?

See § Matt 6:9 C, especially notes *e–r*.

2:24: For the name of God is slandered among the gentiles because of you, as it is written.

1. With the words "as it is written," one should think of Isa 52:5 and Ezek 36:20ff. — Isaiah 52:5 is cited in b. Sukkah 52B.16 and b. Meg. 24A, but without any further reference to the slander of the divine name; however, Ezek 36:20ff. is adduced rather often as a supporting passage the thought expressed in Rom 2:24 as well; for examples, see Mek. Exod. 15:2 (44B) at § Matt 6:9 C, n. *e*; b. Yoma 86A at § Matt 6:9 C, n. *l*; Midr. Lam. Introduction 15 (33A) at § Matt 6:9 C, n. *p*.

2. The converse of Rom 2:24 would be: God's name is praised among the gentiles because of Israel's virtue.

---

73. TN: No note exists at § Rom 3:2.

Jerusalem Talmud Baba Meṣiʿa 2.8C.27: R. Hanina (ca. 225) recounted this incident: The old rabbis bought a bunch of wheat from some soldiers and found in it a bag with *denars* and gave it back to them. Then they said, "Blessed be the God of the Jews!" Abba Hoshaiah of Teriyya (Turiyya?) [was a laundryman; a queen came to bathe there; she lost her jewel and a golden item; he had compassion and gave it back to her].[74] She said, "That, what is it to me? Why should I bother noticing it? I have more beautiful things than this, I have more than this (therefore you can keep what you have found)." He answered her, "The Torah commands us to give it back." She said, "Blessed be the God of the Jews!" R. Samuel b. Soseretai (= Σώστρατος) went up to Rome; the queen lost her jewel (דילניה, read with Dalman כְּלִידוֹנָה), and he found it. She sent out a herald who cried out in the city, "Whoever brings it back within 30 days will get this and that; but whoever brings it back after 30 days will be beheaded!" R. Samuel b. Soseretai did not give it back within 30 days; after 30 days he gave it back. She said to him, "Were you not in the city?" He answered, "Yes!" She said, "Did you not hear the voice of the herald?" He answered, "Yes!" She said, "And what did he say?" He answered, "Whoever brings it back within 30 days will get this and that; but whoever brings it back after 30 days will be beheaded!" She said to him, "And why did you not give it back within 30 days?" He answered her, "So that you might not say I did it out of fear of you; rather this happened out of fear of the All Merciful One." She said to him, "Blessed be the God of the Jews!" ‖ See y. B. Meṣ. 2.8C.18 at § Rom 1:14, #2, n. *c*.

2:25 A: Circumcision avails if you do the law.

The rabbinic scholars would have denied this claim: for them circumcision מִילָה as such had the power to save every Israelite[75] from the fire of gehenna and to make him a son of the future world; see the last three citations at § Matt 3:9, #3 and in the excursus "Sheol, Gehenna, and the Garden of Eden," II, #5 and #7; see also the excursus "Circumcision," #5.

2:25 B: But if you are a transgressor of the law, your circumcision has become uncircumcision.

1. Just as circumcision מִילָה literally became uncircumcision עָרְלָה for a Jew who performed an epispasm on himself (see 1 Cor 7:18), the apostle claims that περιτομή has become ἀκροβυστία in a metaphorical sense for the Jew who is a transgressor of the law; and just as the ancient synagogue declared that the former, the so-called מָשׁוּךְ, had no portion in the future world (see excursus "Circumcision," #4), the apostle also deprives the latter of any advantage attached to circumcision (see verse 25 A). — On the benefit of circumcision, see excursus "Circumcision," #5.

---

74. S-B: The words in square brackets have fallen out of the text of the Jerusalem Talmud and are supplied from the commentary פני משה on a "midrash."

75. S-B: Only a few categories were excluded, particularly those Israelites who had disavowed their people.

Wettstein (2:25B) has adduced the following citation from Exod. Rab. 19 as a proof of the idea that even the rabbis called proselytes "circumcised" מהולים and Jews "uncircumcised" עֲרֵלִים in the very way the apostle does: "*Illi proselyti sunt circumcisi: vos autem praeputiati.*" — The passage has been misunderstood because אתם "you" has been confused with אותם "they"; the correct translation reads, "Do not let the son of a foreigner who has bound himself to Yahweh say, 'Yahweh will certainly exclude me from his people'" (Isa 56:3). God said to the proselytes, "You are afraid because I have declared you unfit and have said, 'The son of a foreigner may not eat of it' (the Passover lamb)" (Exod 12:43).... The former (of whom Isa 56:3 speaks) are the circumcised proselytes הגרים מהולים (= complete proselytes), but the latter אותם (in Exod 12:43) are uncircumcised ערלים. For God declares the uncircumcised unfit and casts them down into gehenna (Exod. Rab. 19 [81B, C]). — The passage simply does not belong here at all.

2. As the corresponding λογισθήσεται in verse 26 shows, γέγονεν is used here in the sense of the rabbinic נַעֲשָׂה כְּ and means: "is counted as" or "is considered to be"; see § Rom 2:26, #2, n. *d*.

2:26: If, then, the uncircumcised one keeps the statues (just requirements) of the law, will his uncircumcision not be counted as circumcision?

1. This sentence is the converse of verse 25. The first ἡ ἀκροβυστία stands metonymically for ἀκρόβυστος; on this see § Acts 10:45, #2. — Of course, rabbinic Judaism would have denied the apostle's conclusion: οὐχ ἡ ἀκροβυστία αὐτοῦ εἰς περιτομὴν λογισθήσεται. It was generally believed that the non-Israelite who kept the Torah did not become the equal of the Israelite; rather, precisely because he was uncircumcised, he remained distant and a stranger to God, indeed even brought punishment on himself, because he concerned himself with things that he had not been given a commandment about. The opposing view of R. Meir (ca. 150)—see b. B. Qam. 38A at § Rom 2:10 and b. Sanh. 58B at § Matt 5:43, #1, n. *g*, paragraph 4—was hardly recognized in broader circles.

Yelamedenu in Jellinek, *Beth ha-Midrash* 5.162.1: There once was an *ʿakum* (worshiper of the stars = pagan, *goy*; see § Matt 5:43, #1, n. g, S-B fn. 1), who gave alms to the poor. He came before R. Aqiba († ca. 135) and said to him, "I am greater (more esteemed) than you, because I love alms (doing good); therefore God loves and exalts me." R. Aqiba answered him, "God delights only in Israel; for it says, 'Who is like your people Israel?' (2 Sam 7:23). But what the *ʿakum* do results only in offense (sin) for them; for it says, 'Mercy leads to sin for the nations' (so the midr. formulates Prov 14:34; see the next citation)." Then he went away. After some time the army came out to play on the play area. R. Aqiba was sitting and studying. He saw how each one jumped and how each one who jumped farther than the other received a larger ration. R. Aqiba saw that *ʿakum* sitting there. R. Aqiba said to him, "Why are they doing this?" He answered him, "Because whoever is able to jump farther gets a larger ration." Then R. Aqiba said, "And I will jump farther than them all, so give me the ration!" That *'akum* answered him, "As a great one among the Israelites do you not know that whoever does not have the belt of the king (the sign of belonging to him) does not get a ration?" He said to him, "And do your ears not hear what your mouth speaks? God loves only the circumcised הַמִּילָה, because it is the deal of God, and it is his belt (the sign of belonging to him), and he loves this. But the *'akum* are deemed to be nothing, because they do not have the belt of God, for they all exist for gehenna, as it says, 'Therefore Sheol has opened wide its mouth' (Isa 5:14). God said, 'The *'akum* are deemed to be nothing, do not fear them. Even if you see that they are numerous, before me they are not numerous. Do not fear them; for Yahweh your God is with you!'" ‖ A baraita in b. Bat. 10B: Rabban Yohanan b. Zakkai († ca. 80) said to his students, "My children, what does the passage of Scripture mean, 'Beneficence exalts the people, but for the nations mercy is sin' (so Midr. Prov. 14:34)." R. Eliezer (ca. 90) answered and said, "'beneficence exalts the people': this pertains to Israel, for it is written: 'Is there another people on earth like your people' (2 Sam 7:23); 'and mercy is sin for the nations': all beneficence and mercy that the nations of the world do is sin for them; for they do it only in order to thereby get older, as it says: 'So that they may offer some beneficence to the God of heaven and pray for the life of the king and of his sons' (Ezra 6:10; this is why Darius supported the building of the temple and the sacrificial cult in Jerusalem). But whoever acts this way, his beneficence is not perfect." But in a baraita it says: Whoever says, "This *sela* is for alms so that my children may stay alive and so that I may become worthy of the future world!," this is a perfectly righteous man! There is no contradiction here: in the latter case it deals with an Israelite, but in the former case it pertains to an idolater. Then R. Joshua (ca. 90) answered and said, "'Beneficence exalts the people': this pertains to Israel; see 2 Sam 7:23 (as above); 'and mercy is sin for the nations': all beneficence and mercy that idolaters do is sin for them; for they do it only so that thereby their dominion may be protracted; for it says, 'Therefore may my counsel please you, O king: Remove your sin by beneficence and your misdeeds by mercy to the poor, so that perhaps (thereby) your welfare (or your rule?) may last' (Dan 4:24)." Rabban Gamaliel (ca. 90) answered and said, "'Beneficence exalts the people': this pertains to Israel; see 2 Sam 7:23 (as above); 'and mercy is sin for the nations': all beneficence and mercy that idolaters do is sin for them; for they do it only so that they may proudly gloat, and those who proudly gloat fall into gehenna; for it says, 'A conceited impudent man is called a mocker, he effects wrath over the proud' (so Midr. Prov. 21:24), and 'wrath' means nothing other than gehenna; for it says, 'That day will be a day of wrath' (Zeph 1:15)." Rabban Gamaliel said, "We still need to hear from Modiim. R. Eleazar of Modiim († ca. 135) said, "'Beneficence exalts the people": this pertains to Israel; see 2 Sam 7:23 (as above); "and mercy is sin for the nations': all beneficence and mercy that idolaters do is sin for them; for they do it only so that they may ridicule us, for it says, 'Yahweh has summoned and brought it about, as he said, because you sinned against Yahweh and did not listen to his voice, and so this word has come over you' (Jer 40:3)." R. Nehuniah b. Haqqanneh (ca. 70) answered and said, "'Beneficence exalts the people and mercy': this pertains to Israel, and 'sin is for the nations.'" Rabban Yohanan b. Zakkai said to his students, "The words of R. Nehuniah b. Haqqanneh seem to me to be better than your words, because he ascribed beneficence and mercy to the Israelites and sin to idolaters; for he (Rabban Yohanan) too had said what Prov 14:34 means. For in a baraita it says that Rabban Yohanan b. Zakkai said to them, 'As the sin offering makes atonement for Israel, beneficence makes atonement for the nations of the world.'" (He had earlier interpreted Prov 14:34 in this way: 'Beneficence exalts the people and mercy is a sin offering for the nations'; later he gave up this explanation in favor of the interpretation of R. Nehuniah b. Haqqanneh.) — Parallels with significant differences can be found in Pesiq. 12B (see § Matt 5:43, #1, n. *g*, paragraph 4) and Tanḥ. כי תשא 111A. ‖ See b. Sanh. 58B at § Matt 5:43, #1, n. *g*, paragraph 4. ‖ Deuteronomy Rabbah 1 (196D): R. Yose b. Hanina (ca. 270) said, "A *goy* (non-Israelite) who observes the Sabbath before he has accepted circumcision is guilty of death. Why? Because it has not been commanded him." And what reason do you have to say, "A *goy* who observes the Sabbath is guilty of death"? R. Hiyya b. Abba (ca. 280) said that R. Yohanan († 279) said, "Is it not customary in the world that someone who thrusts himself between the king and his wife while they sit and chat is guilty of death? So too the Sabbath is (something) between Israel and God; for it says, 'Let it be a sign between me and the children of Israel forever!' (Exod 31:17). Therefore, any *goy* who thrusts himself between them before he has accepted circumcision is guilty of death." The rabbis said, "Moses said before God, 'Lord of the world, even if the *goyim* have not received a commandment concerning the Sabbath, will you by chance turn your face (graciously) to them, if they observe it?' God answered him, 'Are you afraid of that? On your life, even if they do all the commandments in the Torah, I will make them fall before you.' From where (is this to be concluded)? From what we read in Deut 2:31: 'Behold, I have begun to give them up before you.'"

2. In the LXX, λογίζεσθαι = "view as," "count as," most of the time serves to render חָשַׁב; see Gen 15:6; Lev 7:18; 17:4; 2 Sam 19:20; Ps 32:2; 106:31. In rabbinic usage, the following expressions are found for the idiom "to count something for someone as."

a. חָשַׁב עָלָין כְּ,[α] Aram. חֲשַׁב לֵיהּ לְ;[β] yet this expression is encountered only rarely in rabbinic literature.

α. Jerusalem Talmud Pe'ah 1.16B.17: R. Yohanan († 279) said, "Not only this (that God accepts a godless person who repents), but also all the (earlier) transgressions that he committed are counted for him as merits נחשבין עליו כּזָכִיּוֹת. What is the scriptural basis for this? 'All your garments בִּגְדֹתֶיךָ are myrrh, aloe, and cassia' (Ps 45:9); every breach of faith בְּגִידוֹת (interpretation of בִּגְדֹתֶיךָ) that you have committed against me, behold, they are (so pleasant and lovely before me) as myrrh, aloe, and cassia." — The parallels (see notes *b–d*) use other verbs, which prove how uncommon it was for the rabbinic scholars to use חשב with this meaning.

β. Active. Targum Onkelos and Yerušalmi I Genesis 15:6: "He counted it to him as righteousness (merit) וְחַשְׁבַהּ לֵהּ לְזָכוּ." — Septuagint passively: ἐλογίσθη αὐτῷ εἰς δικαιοσύνην. ‖ Passive. Targum Psalms 106:31: "It was counted for him as merit וְאִתְחֲשְׁבַת לֵיהּ לְזָכוּ." — Septuagint: καὶ ἐλογίσθη αὐτῷ εἰς δικαιοσύνην. The passive is also found, though without the second לְ, in Tg. Onk. Lev. 17:4: "It will be counted for that man as bloodguilt" הִמָא יִתְחֲשֵׁב לגברא ההוא. — Septuagint: λογισθήσεται τῷ ἀνθρώπῳ ἐκείνῳ αἷμα.

b. מָנָה לוֹ followed by a simple accusative.

Midrash Song of Songs 5:16 (121A): R. Yohanan († 279) said, "And not only this (see y. Pe'ah 1 above at n. a, α), but also all transgressions that he has committed God will count for him as merit מוֹנֶה לוֹ זָכוּת."

c. עָשָׂה לוֹ followed by a simple accusative; literally: "one makes something into something for him."

TanḥumaB ויצא § 22 (80B): Resh Laqish (ca. 250) said, "Have you heard anything greater than this? What is written? 'If the godless person turns from his godlessness and does justice and righteousness, he will live because of them' (Ezek 33:19). It is not written, 'he will live,' but rather he will live 'because of them' (because of the transgressions); for God counts them for him as merit, so that he lives because of them עושה אותם לו זכות והוא חי בהם."

d. נַעֲשָׂה לוֹ כְ (the passive or middle of the expression in n. c) "it will be made this or that for him"; see γέγονεν used by the apostle in Rom 2:25.

Babylonian Talmud Yoma 86B: Resh Laqish (ca. 250) said, "Great is repentance; for purposeful sins will be counted for him (because of it) as unintentional sins שזדונות נעשות לו כשגגות, as it says, 'Turn (in repentance), Israel, to Yahweh your God, for you stumbled (= accidentally failed) in your sin' (Hos 14:2)." See, it was an intentional sin, and he calls it an (accidental) stumbling. (Is this) really אִינִי (so)? Resh Laqish said, "Great is repentance; for (because of it) purposeful sins will be counted for him as merits זדונות נעשות לו כְזָכִיּוֹת, for it says, 'If the godless person turns from his godlessness and does justice and righteousness, he will live because of them (the transgressions he regrets)!' There is no contradiction: here (it deals with people who repent) out of love (for God), and there (with such people who repent) out of fear (of God)."

e. הֶעֱלָה עָלָיו כְּאִלּוּ or הֶעֱלָה לוֹ כְּאִלּוּ "to count something for someone as if"; what the given thing was counted as is then stated in an independent clause. The reckoning subject is usually the indeterminate "one"[α] = God or explicitly God[β] or Scripture;[γ] the allocation of recompense or punishment is seen as the purpose of the reckoning, depending on whether it results in good or bad; it can therefore also simply be said: הֶעֱלָה עָלָיו שָׂכָר כְּאִלּוּ[δ] "one counts it to him as a recompense, as if he." — The expressions named at n. e are in use almost exclusively in rabbinic usage.

α. Subject: One. — מַעֲלִין עַל כאלו, specifically for good. Sifre Numbers 15:39 § 115 (35A): "When you look at it (the *tzitzith*), you should think of all of Yahweh's commandments, to do them" (Num 15:39). This indicates (teaches) that for anyone who fulfills the commandment of the *tzitzith* one counts it as if he had fulfilled all the commandments מעלין עליו כאלו קיים כל המצוות. Here the inference is justified by moving from the lesser to the greater: if for the one who fulfills the commandment of the *tzitzith* one counts it as if he had fulfilled all the commandments, how much more is this the case (that it will be counted to him as recompense) concerning all the commandments in the Torah (or: how much more is this the case, that it would be as if he had fulfilled all the commandments, concerning all the other commandments in the Torah. The latter formulation is most probable). ‖ See m. Sanh. 4.5 at § Matt 16:26 B; Midr. Song. 1:3 (85A) at § Mark 16:15; Tanḥ. משפטים 95A at § Luke 6:35 and

SNum 15:39 § 115 (34B) in the excursus “Memra of Yahweh,” #3, B, n. *c*, δ. ‖ For bad. Leviticus Rabbah 22 (121B): R. Yohanan († 279) said, “Whoever robs someone else in the amount of a *prutah* (the smallest coin), one will count it for him as if he had killed him.” ‖ ʾAbot de Rabbi Nathan 31 at § Matt 16:26 B; m. ʾAbot 3.7 at § Luke 24:17. ‖ מַעֲלִין לְ כאלו. Midrash Song of Songs 7:8 (128A): R. Judah (b. Simon? ca. 320) said, “God eradicated the inclination to idolatry (in the case of the Israelites), but left the inclination to fornication; he said, ‘Whoever resists fornication, one will count it for him מעלין לו, as if כאלו he had resisted both.’” ‖ See Midr. Song. 2:5 (97B) at § Matt 10:14 A.

β. Subject: God; most of the time in the phrase מַעֲלֶה אֲנִי עַל כְּאִלּוּ “I (God) will count it as if.” — For good. Babylonian Talmud Menaḥot 110A: “From the rising of the sun until its setting, my name is great among the gentiles, and everywhere incense and pure sacrifice will be offered to my name” (Mal 1:11).... R. Samuel b. Nahman (ca. 260) said that R. Jonathan (ca. 220) said, “These are the students who devote themselves to the Torah everywhere. (God says,) ‘I will count it for them עֲלֵיהֶן as if they lit incense and offered pure sacrifice to my name.’” ‖ Babylonian Talmud Megillah 31B: God said to Abraham, “I have already decreed for them (your children) to read the sections about sacrifices: as often as they read them, I will count it for them as if they offered sacrifice before me, and I will forgive all their sins.” (After the destruction of the temple, reading the sections of Scripture concerning sacrifices has atoning power in the way sacrifices themselves did before the destruction.) ‖ See SDeut 11:22 § 49 (85A) at § Matt 10:14 A; b. Qidd. 30B at § Matt 15:4 A, first third; b. Ber. 8A at § Matt 18:19; Yal. Lev. 2:1 § 447 at § Mark 12:43, n. *c*; y. Roš Haš. 7.59C.51 at § John 3:3, #2, n. *c*; Midr. Song. 7:8 (128A) at § Rom 2:22 B, #2, n. *b*. ‖ For bad. See SNum 18:20 § 119 (40A) at § Rom 2:23 A, #1; SLev 19:2 (342A) at § Matt 6:9 C, n. *d*; Pesiq. Rab. 21 (107B) at § Matt 19:18 B (in the last two passages, there is also a reckoning for good).

γ. Subject: Scripture; most of the time in the phrase מַעֲלֶה עַל הַכָּתוּב כְּאִלּוּ. — For good. Mishnah ʾAbot 3.2: If someone sits and studies, Scripture counts it for him מעלה עָלָיו הכתוב as if כאלו he had fulfilled the entire Torah; for it says, “Let him sit alone and quietly, for he (God) has bestowed (recompense) on him” (so Midr. Lam. 3:28). ‖ See also b. Soṭah 5B at § Matt 5:3, #3; b. Sanh. 43B at § Matt 7:7 A, #2, n. *n*; b. Ketub. 111B and Lev. Rab. 34 (131D) at § Matt 10:40 A, #2; b. Ber. 10B at § Matt 10:40 A, #2; b. Ber. 14B at § Matt 15:2 B, #2, n. *i*; ʾAbot R. Nat. 31 at § Matt 16:26 B; b. Qidd. 70A at § Luke 1:5 B, #1; b. Menaḥ. 110A at § John 3:2; b. Sukkah 45A in the excursus “Feast of Tabernacles,” II, D. ‖ For bad. Numbers Rabbah 8 (149A): “Since he (Saul) killed the Gibeonites” (2 Sam 21:1). Where do we find that he killed the Gideonites? But since he had massacred Nob, the city of the priests, who had given them water and nourishment (see 1 Sam 22), Scripture counts it for him as if he had massacred them. ‖ See further ʾAbot R. Nat. 13 at § Matt 7:11, #3 (here there is also a reckoning for good); y. Peʾah 1.16B.5 at § Rom 2:11, #3. ‖ The form הֶעֱלָה הַכָּתוּב is found instead of the participle מעלה הכ׳ in Midr. Song. 2:5 (97B); see § Matt 10:14 A.

δ. Mishnah ʾAbot 2.2: Rabban Gamaliel b. R. Judah the prince (ca. 220) said, “... All those who labor with the community (for the community) should labor with it for God’s sake; for the merit of their fathers helps them and their righteousness lasts forever. ‘What concerns you, though, I (God) will count for you as recompense, as if you had done it מַעֲלֶה אֲנִי עֲלֵיכֶם שָׂכָר כְּאִלּוּ עֲשִׂיתֶם' (what constitutes the father's merit and righteousness)."

2:27: The natural uncircumcision (the one uncircumcised by nature) ... will judge you who, though you have the letter and circumcision, are a transgressor of the law.

The idea that one person will be measured by the standard of another person in the divine judgment, so that the latter appears as his judge (cf. Matt 12:27), is encountered quite often in rabbinic literature. See the passages at § Matt 12:41 B. Here a few others may be added.

Wisdom 4:16: The deceased righteous will judge the (still) living godless and the youth that has reached maturity the unrighteous in his old age. ‖ Pesiqta Rabbati 40 (167B): "He will judge the earth with righteousness, he will pass sentence on the nations by the righteous" (so Midr. Ps. 9:9). What does "by the righteous" mean? R. Alexandrai (ca. 270) said, "He will judge the nations by their righteous ones, by Rahab, Jethro, Ruth? How? He will say to the nations of the world (i.e., to each person among them), 'Why did you not come to me?' And if he answers, 'Because I was a wicked man forfeited to sin and I was ashamed,' God will say to him, 'Were you more than Rahab whose house was against the city wall and took in thieves and was a whore? And when she approached me, did I not accept her and cause prophets and righteous ones to arise from her? And Jethro was a priest for idols; but when he came to me, did I not accept him and cause prophets and righteous ones to arise from her? And when Ruth the Moabite came to me, did I not accept her and cause kings to arise from her?'" ‖ Jerusalem Talmud Roš Haššanah 1.57A.43: How did Samuel († 254) maintain, "'He will pass sentence on the nations by the righteous' (Ps 9:9)? He will judge them after (according to) the righteous among them; he remembers the action (behavior) of Jethro, he remembers the action of the prostitute Rahab."

2:29 A: The Jew who is in secret (in his heart, is a real Jew).

1. Since Schöttgen,[76] commentators have often adduced as a parallel to the words ὁ ἐν τῷ κρυπτῷ Ἰουδαῖος the following saying from b. Nid. 20B: *Judaei in penetralibus cordis sedent.* The complete passage reads: Ifra Hormiz, the mother of king Shabor, sent blood to Raba († 352, so that he would examine it); Rab Obadiah sat before him. He smelled it and sent word to her, "This is blood of (sexual) desire." She said to her son, "Come and see how wise the Jews are!" He answered her, "Perhaps as a blind man through a hatch (i.e., they got it right by coincidence)!" She then sent him 60 kinds of blood. He told (determined) them all; the last blood came from pests, and he did not recognize it. Then he got help: he sent her (coincidentally) a comb that kills pests. Then she said (assuming that this comb was supposed to refer to the origin of the last blood test), "The Jews sit in the chambers

---

76. Christian Schöttgen, *Horae Hebraicae et Talmudicae in universum Novum Testamentum* (Leipzig: Christoph. Hekelii B. Filium, 1733), 1:500.

of the heart (they know even the most hidden things)!" — In any case, this exclamation has nothing to do with ἐν τῷ κρυπτῷ Ἰουδαῖος. Rather it should be compared to the saying of Raba († 352): "Every student whose inside is not like his outside (who thinks differently than he acts) is no student" (b. Yoma 72B). Without altering its meaning, this sentence could be patterned after Rom 2:29 as follows: The student who is a student in secret (in his heart) and not simply outwardly, he is a real student.

2. The ancient synagogue itself had various ways of answering the question of who a real Israelite was. The merciful spirit is extolled as an especially salient trait in the essence of the true Jew.[a] Another passage adds modesty and beneficence alongside mercy.[b] According to a third passage, which states the difference between the disciples of Abraham and the disciples of Balaam (Jesus), the sure marks of the former are a benevolent eye, a lowly mind and a humble spirit.[c] Finally, in a passage where a comparison is made with the secular person, who is like the Sadducees, the distinguishing marks of the real Israelite are that he confesses two worlds,[d] that is, life after death, the resurrection, and the last judgment.

a. Babylonian Talmud Beṣah 32B: Rab Nathan b. Abba (ca. 270) said that Rab († 247) said, "The rich in Babylon will go down to gehenna." This matches the opinion of Shabbetai b. Marinos. He came to Babylon and asked them for employment, but they gave him none; for nourishment, but they did not feed him either. Then he said, "These people derive from the 'great mixture' (Exod 12:38; thus they are not real Jews); for it is written, 'He will give you mercy (toward others, so the midr.) and have mercy on you' (Deut 13:18). Whoever has mercy on people certainly derives from the seed of our father Abraham; but whoever does not have mercy on people certainly does not derive from the seed of our father Abraham."

b. Deuteronomy Rabbah 3 (200B): R. Hiyya (b. Abba, ca. 280) said, "The Israelites possess three good characteristics; they are modest, merciful, and beneficent גומלי חסדים (= doing good). Where does 'modest' come from? Because it says, 'So that fear of him may be on your faces (in the form of blushing)' (Exod 20:20). Where does 'merciful' come from? Because it says, 'He will give you mercy (toward others; see above in n. *a*) and have mercy on you' (Deut 13:18). Where does 'beneficent' come from? Because it says, 'Yahweh your God will keep his covenant for you and the love חסד (that you have shown to others; specifically, as a compensatory treasure in heaven; so Midr. Deut. 7:12).'" ‖ Jerusalem Talmud Qiddušin 4.65B.44: (When the Gibeonites made the demand of 2 Sam 21:5f., David said,) "God has given the Israelites three good gifts: they are merciful, modest, and beneficent? Where does 'merciful' come from? '(Yahweh) will give you mercy (toward others)' (Deut 13:18). Where does 'modest' come from? 'So that fear of him may be on your faces' (Exod 20:20). This is a sign for the modest man so that he does not sin; but if anyone has a shameless face, then it is certain that his ancestors did not stand at Mount Sinai (thus he does not stem from Jewish blood). Where does 'beneficent' come from? 'Yahweh your God will keep his covenant for you and love' (Deut 7:12; see above)." — Parallels can be found in y. Sanh. 6.23D.19; Num. Rab. 8 (149B); Midr. Ps. 1 § 10 (5B); Midr. Sam. 28 (67B); in b. Yebam. 79A, the beginning reads: There are three distinguishing marks for this nation (Israel): they are merciful, modest, and beneficent. The scriptural proof for beneficence is grounded in Gen 18:19, where צְדָקָה is interpreted as beneficence. The conclusion says: Anyone in whom these three characteristics are found is determined (fit, worthy) to be connected to this nation (as a proselyte).

c. Mishnah ʾAbot 5.19: Anyone in whom three things are found is a disciple of Abraham; three (different) things mark out a disciple of Balaam (= Jesus). A benevolent (a nonenvious) eye, a lowly mind and a humble spirit (are the characteristics of) a disciple of Abraham. An envious eye, a greedy mind and a proud spirit (are the characteristics of) a disciple of Balaam. And what is the difference between the disciples of Abraham and the disciples of Balaam? The disciples of Balaam will be cast down into gehenna; as it says, "You God will cast them into a deep pit" (Ps 55:24). But the disciples of our father Abraham will receive the garden of Eden as a possession; as it says, "supplying a true good for those who love me and filling their treasuries" (Prov 8:21).

d. Genesis Rabbah 53 (34A): "In (through) Isaac your seed will be named" (Gen 21:12). R. Judan (ca. 350) said, "'Isaac' is not written here, but rather 'in Isaac' ביצחק." R. Azariah (ca. 360) said in the name of Bar Hittaia (in the 4th century), "ב (Beth) means two: (your seed will be named) in the one who confesses two worlds." R. Judan b. Shalom (ca. 370) said, "It is written, 'Remember the miracles of him who made a sign for him (the seed of Abraham), specifically the judgments of his mouth' (so Midr. Ps. 105:5). I have given what proceeds from his mouth as a sign for him: whoever confesses two worlds will be named your seed; whoever does not confess two worlds will not be named your seed."

2:29 B: Circumcision of the heart.

The trope of the circumcised heart is very common in Philo. See *Migr.* 16 (Mangey's ed., 1:450); *De circumcisione* § 1f. (Mangey's ed., 2:211); *De vict. offer.* § 9 (Mangey's ed., 2:258). In rabbinic literature, it is found only rarely, except when OT passages such as Lev 26:41; Deut 10:16; 30:6; Jer 4:4; 9:25; Ezek 44:7, 9 provided reason to mention it. The image of the heart of flesh, which had the same meaning, was preferred. — The uncircumcised heart is the heart ruled by the evil inclination; circumcision happens by repentance.

Babylonian Talmud Sukkah 52A: R. Avira (in the 4th century) or, as others claim, R. Joshua b. Levi (ca. 250) said in a presentation, "The evil inclination has seven names. God names it 'evil' (see Gen 8:21), Moses names it 'uncircumcised' (see Deut 10:16, 'Circumcise the foreskin of your heart ...'), Ezekiel names it 'stone' (see Ezek 36:26, 'I will take away your heart of stone from your body and I will give you a heart of flesh ...')." (See the whole passage in the excursus "The Good and Evil Inclination.") ‖ Sifra Leviticus 26:41 (458A): "Then their uncircumcised heart will be bent" (Lev 26:41). These words pertain to repentance; for as soon as their heart bends to repent, I will have mercy on them again. For it says, "Then their uncircumcised heart will be bent, and then I will forgive their guilt" (Lev 26:41). ‖ Additionally, on the basis of Jer 9:25 and Ezek 44:9 the uncircumcised heart is discussed in Mek. Exod. 18:3 (65B); t. Ned. 2.4 (277); b. Yoma 71A; b. Taʿan. 17B; b. Moʿed Qaṭ. 5A; b. Sanh.

22B; b. Zebaḥ. 19A; however, the content of these passages is irrelevant. See a few other citations at § Acts 7:51 B.

3:1f.: What then is the advantage of the Jew? ... First (above all), they were entrusted with the revelations of God.

τὰ λόγια "the revelations" hardly differ in content from the Torah in the broader meaning of the word = Holy Scripture. – Being the people of the Torah was Israel's highest honor; this honor grew the more the Torah was glorified. Therefore, glorifying the Torah is the inexhaustible theme of the Haggadah. Here only a small portion of the relevant passages are highlighted.

A. The Torah was given only to Israel.

See a string of supporting texts at § Rom 2:23 A, #1. ‖ Exodus Rabbah 30 (89D): "He makes his words דבריו known to Jacob, his statutes and laws to Israel; he has done this with no (other) people" (Ps 147:19f.); but to whom (did he do this)? Jacob, whom he has selected from all the nations. To them (the other nations) he gave only a part (of his commandments): To Adam he gave six commandments (see § Rom 1:20 E, n. *b*), to Noah he added one more (the prohibition to eat any part of an animal that was still alive; see § Rom 1:20 E, n. *c*); to Abraham (he gave) eight (circumcision in addition to the seven Noachic commandments), to Jacob nine (the prohibition to eat the thigh muscle at the hip in addition to Abraham's eight commandments); but to the Israelites he gave everything. R. Simon (ca. 280) said in the name of R. Hanina (ca. 225, perhaps more correctly in the name of R. Yose b. Hanina [ca. 270]), "It is like a king who had a table before him decked out with all kinds of food. His servant came in, and he gave him a piece; a second servant, and he gave him an egg; a third servant, and he gave him vegetables, and so on to each one. Then his son came in, and he gave him the entire table that he had before him. He said to him, 'To them I only ever gave a part (a portion), but I set before you the whole for your enjoyment.' So also God gave to the nations only a part of his commandments; but when Israel arose, he said to them: 'Behold, the whole Torah is entirely for you!' For it says, 'He has done this with no (other) people' (Ps 147:20)." R. Eleazar (ca. 270) said, "It is like a king who went to war, and his legions were with him. He had some livestock slaughtered and allocated a portion to each man, so that he would be able to labor (at preparing them). His son saw and said to him, 'What will you give me?' He answered him, 'From what I have prepared (determined) for myself.' Therefore God gave the nations of the world the raw commandments (those not worked through in detail), so that they might labor at them. But he did not differentiate for them between impure and pure. Then the Israelites came; then he elucidated every single law for them, the punishment and the recompense for each one; for it says, 'He kissed me with the kisses of his mouth' (Song 1:1). Therefore it was said. 'He made known his statutes and laws to Israel' (Ps 147:19)."

B. The Torah separates and differentiates Israel from all other nations.

Letter of Aristeas 139: "While the lawgiver (Moses), whom God had made capable to have insight into all things, considered all this in his wisdom (namely how people become godless by keeping bad company; see § 130), he surrounded us (Israelites) with an impenetrable enclosure and with iron walls περιέφραξεν ἡμᾶς ἀδιακόποις χάραξι καὶ σιδηροῖς τείχεσιν (cf. Eph 2:14), so that we would not cultivate any fellowship with any of the other nations, pure in body and soul, free of foolish beliefs, venerating the one and powerful God above every creature." — Letter of Aristeas 142: "Lest we defile ourselves by fellowship with others and become corrupted by association with bad men, he surrounded us ἡμᾶς περιέφραξεν on all sides with purity laws for food, drink, contact, as well as what we listen to and see." ‖ 3 Maccabees 3:4, 7: "Since they (the pious Egyptian Jews) feared God and walked according to his laws, they separated themselves in what they ate. For this reason, they seemed detestable to some. In many ways they (the enemies of Israel) criticized the different (Jewish and pagan) ways of venerating God and the manners of eating, while claiming that these people are loyal neither to the king nor to the (official) authorities, but rather are hostile and act very contrary to the government." — See also from the apocrypha Tob 1:10ff.; additionally, see Esth 9:28 and Wis 2:15f. ‖ Sifra Leviticus 20:24, 26 (374A): "'I am Yahweh, your God, who has set you apart from the other nations' (Lev 20:24). See how different you are from them: among idolaters a man adorns his wife and gives her to another man; another adorns himself and gives himself to another man (for fornication contrary to nature).... 'I have set you apart from the other nations' (Lev 20:26). Look, you belong to me; but if not, you belong to Nebuchadnezzar, the king of Babylon, and his companions." ‖ Babylonian Talmud Moʿed Qaṭan 16B: "Are you not like the sons of the Cushites to me, house of Israel?" (Amos 9:7). How is this so? Was their name "Cushites"? Was it not "Israel"? As a Cushite is different only because of the color of his skin are also the Israelites different from all (other) nations by their behavior. ‖ Pesiqta 46A: R. Levi (ca. 300) opened his presentation with Lev 20:26: "'You are to be holy to me ..., and I set you apart from the other nations, so that you would belong to me ....'" R. Levi (so read instead of ר״י) said, "In all their behavior the Israelites are different from the nations of the world: in their plowing, sowing, harvesting, sheaving, threshing, in their threshing floors and winepresses, in their counting and calculating. In their plowing, see Deut 22:10: 'Do not plow with a bull and a donkey at the same time.' In their sowing, see Deut 22:9: 'Do not sow your vineyard with two different kinds (with mixed seed).' In their harvesting, see Lev 19:9: 'You are not to keep the gleanings of your harvest.' In their sheaving, see Deut 24:19: 'If you have forgotten a sheaf in your field, do not turn back to get it.' In their threshing, see Deut 25:4: 'You are not to bind the ox's mouth while it threshes.' In their threshing floors and their winepresses, see Deut 15:14: 'You are to give him provisions ... from your threshing floor and your winepress.' In their counting and calculating, for the nations of the world calculate according to the sun and Israel according to the moon, see Exod 12:2: 'This month is the first month for you.'" — The same is partly found with some differences and additions in Pesiq. Rab. 15 (69B); Num. Rab. 10 (157A); Midr. Song 5:16 (122A). ‖ Numbers Rabbah 2 (136C): "The children of Israel will camp, each one at his banner, at the signs of the houses of their fathers" (Num 2:2). This is what is written: "Who is this who shines like that dawn?" (Song 6:10). The Israelites were holy and great at their banners, and all nations looked at them and were astonished and said, "Who is this who shines ...?" The nations of the world said to them, "'Turn back, turn back, O Shulamite' (Song 7:1), join us, come to us, and we will make you princes, commanders, dukes, eparchs, and generals. 'Turn back, turn back, that we may choose you' (so Midr. Song. 7:1B, interpreting נחזה = 'to see' as 'to choose')...." And Israel answers, "'What sort of Shulamite do you want to see?' (so Midr. Song. 7:1C.) What greatness (what great thing) will you give us? Perhaps something 'like the perimeter of the camp'? (So Midr. Song. 7:1D, interpreting מְחוֹלָה 'circle dance' as מָהוֹל 'perimeter.') Are you able to give us anything that corresponds to the greatness that God has given us in the wilderness: 'The banner of the camp of Judah ...' (Num 2:3)? Are you also to give us such a thing? 'What sort of Shulamite do you want to see?' What greatness will you give us? Perhaps something 'like the remission of sin for the camp'? (So Midr. Song. 7:1D, but now interpreting מְחוֹלָה as מְחִילָה 'forgiveness.') Are you able to give us anything that corresponds to the greatness that God has given us in the wilderness? For we had sinned, and he forgave us and said to us, 'Let your camp be holy' (Deut 23:15)! Even Balaam looked at it, and his eyesight faded opposite them, because he could not harm them: 'Balaam raised his eyes and saw Israel, how it camped according to its tribes' (Num 24:2): these were the banners; then he began to say, 'Who can harm these people, who know their fathers and their families?' For it says, 'Camping according to tribes' (Num 24:2)." From this passage we learn that the banners were a greatness and a fence for Israel. Therefore, it says, "Each one at his banner" (Num 2:2). — See the significantly divergent parallel in Midr. Song 7:1 (125B); see also R. Aqiba's explanation of Song 5:9f. in Mek. Exod. 15:2 at § Rom 2:19f., #2, n. *a.* ‖ See Lev. Rab. 4 (107D) at § Rom 2:19f., #2, n. *c*, near the end; b. Sanh. 39A at § Rom 2:19f., #2, n. *c*, near the middle; b. Sanh. 39A at § John 10:16, n. *a*; see also Gen. Rab. 13 (9D = Deut. Rab. 7 [204B]; Midr. Ps. 117 § 1), where R. Joshua b. Qarha (ca. 150) has a conversation with a pagan; Num. Rab. 20 (189D) on Num 22:9.

C. The Torah as Israel's wisdom and honor and jewel.

See the citations at § Rom 2:23 A, #1. — On "wisdom" in particular, reference may be made to SLev 18:2ff. (338A): R. Judah b. Baba († ca. 135) said (with reference to Lev 18:2ff.), "... If you should think that those ones (non-Israelites) have statutes while we do not, it says against this: 'You are to keep my laws and you are to observe my statutes, to walk in them. I am Yahweh, your God' (Lev 18:4). The evil inclination could still think and say, 'Theirs are more beautiful than ours.' Then it says, 'Keep and do it; for this is your wisdom and your understanding in the sight of the nations' (Deut 4:6)." ‖ Babylonian Talmud Šabbat 75A: R. Samuel b. Nahman (ca. 260) said that R. Jonathan (ca. 220, so read instead of R. Yohanan) said, "Where does the idea come from that people are commanded to calculate the solstices and the course of the planets? Because it says, 'Keep and do it; for this is your wisdom and your understanding in the sight of the nations' (Deut 4:6). What is wisdom and understanding in the sight of the nations? Say, 'It is the calculation of the solstices and the course of the planets.'" ‖ Babylonian Talmud Qiddušin 49B: Ten *qabs* of wisdom have come into the world: the land of Israel has received nine of them (in the Torah) and the rest of the world one. ‖ On "honor." Sifre Deuteronomy 11:22 § 48 (84B): "To love Yahweh your God" (Deut 11:22). If you should say, "See, I will study Torah so that I may be called a scholar, so that I may sit in the academy, so that I may live long in the future world," Scripture teaches, "To love Yahweh your God." Study in all circumstances, then honor will also come eventually.

‖ Sifre Deuteronomy 11:21 § 47 (83B): R. Simeon b. Yohai (ca. 150, so read with Midr. Eccl. 1:4) said, "… If the Torah, which was created for Israel's honor, remains for all eternity, how much more does this go for the righteous, for whose sake the world was created!" — Parallels can be found in Midr. Eccl. 1:4 (6A); Gen. Rab. 12 (9A).

D. The Torah as the source of all salvation and life.

Sirach 17:11: "God set insight before them, and he gave them the law, which works life νόμον ζωῆς, as a lasting possession." — Sirach 32:24 (Hebrew): "He who heeds the Torah protects his soul." — Sirach 45:5 (Hebrew): "God put the commandment in his (Moses') hand, the Torah of life and insight." ‖ Baruch 4:1: "She (Wisdom = Torah) is the book of God's commandments, the law that lasts forever. Those who cling to her attain life; those who leave her fall prey to death." ‖ Wisdom 6:18: "Keeping the commandments is security of immortality." — Wisdom 7:14: "It (Wisdom = Torah) is a never-failing treasure for humans by which those who availed themselves of her attained friendship with God." ‖ Psalms of Solomon 14:2: "The law, which God offered us for our life." ‖ 2 Baruch 32:1: "If you prepare your hearts by sowing the fruits of the law in them, it will shield you in that time when the Almighty will shake the whole creation." — 2 Baruch 38:2: "Your law is life and your wisdom is fidelity." — 2 Baruch 46:5f.: "Prepare your hearts solely to obey the law …. For if you do this, the promises will come to you …, and you will not fall prey to torment." — 2 Baruch 48:24: "That law, which abides among us, helps us, and the sublime wisdom that is in us will support us." ‖ 4 Ezra 7:45: "Blessed are they who come into the world and keep your commandments." — 4 Ezra 9:29ff.: "Then (at the giving of the law) you (God) said, 'You, Israel, hear me, seed of Jacob, pay heed to my words. Today I will sow my law in your heart, which will bring fruit in you, and you will thereby attain eternal glory.'" — 4 Ezra 14:30: "Our ancestors received the law of life, but they did not keep it." — See also 4 Ezra 7:21, 127ff. ‖ While there is a vast number of supporting passages in rabbinic literature, here we limit ourselves to presenting a number from the Tannaitic period (until around 200 CE). — Genesis Rabbah 1 (3A): (R. Aqiba, † ca. 135) said (to R. Ishmael, † ca. 135), "'It is not an empty word מכם (from you = from which you can turn away)' (Deut 32:47), and if it is an empty one, that arises from you מכם (it is your own fault). Why? Because you do not understand how to interpret it, since you do not make an effort. 'But rather it is your life' (Deut 32:47). When is your life? If you make an effort with this." — This word of R. Aqiba is found in the mouth of R. Mani (ca. 370) in y. Pe'ah 1.15B.39; y. Šebiʿit 1.33B.54; y. Šabb. 1.3D.43. ‖ Mekilta Exodus 15:26 (54A): R. Eleazar of Modiim († ca. 135) said, "… What do the words, 'I, Yahweh, am your doctor' (Exod 15:26) mean? God said to Moses, 'Say to the Israelites, "The words of the Torah that I have given you are healing for you, are life for you." For it says, "They are life for everyone who acquires them" (Prov 4:22), and "It will be healing for your navel and refreshment for your bones" (Prov 3:8).'" ‖ Sifre Deuteronomy 11:12 § 40 (79A): R. Simeon b. Yohai (ca. 150) said, "A loaf of bread and a stick came down from heaven bound together. God said to Israel, 'If you do the Torah, behold, there will be bread for food; but if not, behold, there will be a stick for beating.' And where is the explanation for this found? Look, it says, 'If you are willing and obedient, you will eat the best of the land; but if you refuse and are wayward, you will be consumed by the sword' (Isa 1:19f.)." R. Eleazar (presumably of Modiim, who died ca. 135) said, "A book and a sword came down from heaven bound together. He (God) said to them, 'If you do the Torah which is written in this book, you will be kept safe from that thing (the sword); but if not, you will be punished with it.' And where is the explanation for this found? Look, it says, 'He expelled Adam and on the east side of the garden of Eden he placed the cherubim and the flash of the sword that turned to guard the way to the tree of life' (Gen 3:24)." — The parallel in Lev. Rab. 35 (132C), which presents both sayings but in reverse order, adds a clarification to the final words: "the way," which means the (generally human) good custom דֶּרֶךְ אֶרֶץ. Then it says, "to the tree of life," which means the Torah. According to Lev. Rab. 9 (110D) this interpretation of דרך עץ החיים is associated with R. Samuel (so read) b. Nahman (ca. 260). — See a further parallel in Deut. Rab. 4 (201C). ‖ Sifre Deuteronomy 32:2 § 306 (131B): R. Benaah (ca. 220) used to say, "If you do the words of the Torah for their own sake, the words of the Torah are life for you; for it says, 'They are life for those who attain them, and healing for your whole body' (Prov 4:22). But if you do not do the words of the Torah for their own sake, the words of the Torah will kill you; for it says, 'Let my teaching drip יערף like the rain' (Deut 32:2). This 'dripping" means nothing other than killing, as it says, 'They are to break the cow's neck in the valley וערפו' (Deut 21:4)." — The same is found as a baraita with variations in b. Taʿan. 7A. ‖ Sifre Deuteronomy 11:18 § 45 (82B): "Make these words of mine a remedy for your heart and soul" (so Midr. Deut. 11:18, interpreting שַׂמְתֶּם: make them a שָׂם = סַם "remedy"); Scripture shows (indicates) that the words of the Torah are like a remedy for life סם החיים. It is like a king who hit his son and gave him a big wound and put a patch on his wound. He said to him, "My son, as long as this bandage is on your wound, eat and drink what you like, and bathe in warm and in cold water, and you will suffer no harm. But if you remove it, behold, you will cause a malignant boil." God also spoke thus to the Israelites, "My children, I have created the evil inclination for you, (but) I have (also) made the Torah as a spice (remedy) for you. As long as you devote yourself to the latter, the former will not rule over you; for it says, 'When you do what is right, do you not rise above it?' (So the midr. interprets שאת in Gen 4:7: see Rashi on b. Qidd. 30B). But if you do not devote yourself to the Torah, behold, you will be surrendered into its power; for it says, 'But if you do not do what is right, sin camps before the door' (Gen 4:7). Not only this, but all its action and impulse (literally: its taking and giving משאו ומתנו, two ways to express action) is against you; for it says, 'And its desire is for you' (Gen 4:7). But if you wish, you can rule over it; for it says, 'You should be lord over it' (Gen 4:7)." — The same is found as a baraita in b. Qidd. 30B. ‖ Mekilta Exodus 13:3 (24A): R. Ishmael († ca. 135) said, "... If it is obligatory before and after the meal to say a word of praise for food that means life for a (fleeting) hour, how much more is it obligatory to say a word of praise for the Torah, in which the future world lies, before and after using it!" ‖ Sifre Deuteronomy 11:22 § 48 (83B): R. Simeon (ca. 150) used to say, "'Only guard yourself and watch out for your soul' (Deut 4:9). It is like a king who caught a bird and handed it to his servant. He said to him, 'Go about carefully with this bird for my son! If you lose it, do not think you had lost a bird worth an *issar* (see 5:26 D), but rather it will be as if you had lost your soul (life).' And likewise, it says, 'For it is not an empty word for you, but rather it is your life' (Deut 32:47); a word that you call empty is in fact your life." — At the end of Abot R. Nat. 24,

Elisha b. Abbuyah (ca. 120) is the author; in b. Menaḥ. 99B it is found as a baraita from the school of R. Ishmael († ca. 135). ‖ Deuteronomy Rabbah 4 (201D): R. Simeon (ca. 150) said, "… God says to human beings, 'My Torah is in your hand, and your soul is in my hand. If you preserve what is mine, I will preserve what is yours; if you corrupt what is mine (if you let it perish), I will corrupt what is yours.'" ‖ Deuteronomy Rabbah 4 (201D): Bar Qappara (ca. 220) said, "The soul and the Torah are compared with a lamp. The soul, for it is written: 'A person's soul is a lamp from Yahweh' (Prov 20:27). The Torah, for it is written: 'The commandment is a lamp and the Torah is a light' (Prov 6:23). God says to the person, 'My lamp is in your hand and your lamp is in my hand.' My lamp is in your hand: this is the Torah. And your lamp in my hand: this is the soul. If you preserve my lamp, I will preserve your lamp; but if you put out my lamp, I will put out your lamp. Where does support come from for this conclusion? Because it is written: 'Only guard yourself and watch out for your soul' (Deut 4:9)." — The same is found in Midr. Ps. 17 § 8 (66A); the emphasis is different in Lev. Rab. 31 (128D). ‖ Sifre Deuteronomy 32:2 § 306 (131B): As the rain is life for the world, so the words of the Torah are also life for the world. ‖ Sifre Numbers 18:20 § 119 (39B): "The Torah of your mouth is better to me than a thousand pieces of gold and silver" (Ps 119:72); for gold and silver bring a person out of this world and the future world, but the Torah brings a person into the life of the future world. ‖ Mishnah ʾAbot 6.7: Great is the Torah, for it bestows life on those who do it in this world and in the future world (see Prov 4:22; 3:8, 18; 1:9; 4:9; 9:11; 3:16, 2). ‖ Here belong the sayings of later authors. See b. Ber. 5A with R. Simeon b. Laqish (ca. 250) and R. Yohanan († 279); b. Ber. 14A with R. Yohanan († 279); b. Ber. 32B with R. Yohanan († 279); b. Ber. 8A with R. Nathan = R. Jonathan (ca. 220); b. Šabb. 63A with Rab Sheshet (ca. 260); b. Šabb. 88B with R. Hanina b. Papa (ca. 300); b. ʿErub. 54A with R. Joshua b. Levi (ca. 250), and R. Judah b. Hiyya (ca. 240); b. Yoma 72B with R. Joshua b. Levi (ca. 250) and Raba († 352): Torah as a remedy for life or poison for death; see b. Taʿan. 7A at § John 6:35 A, n. *a*; b. Ketub. 77 with R. Joshua b. Levi (ca. 250); see b. Ned. 62A at § John 6:35 A, n. *a*; y. Soṭah 7.21D.12 = Lev. Rab. 25 (123B), Midr. Eccl. 7:12 (35A) with R. Hiyya (ca. 280); b. ʿAbod. Zar. 19B with R. Joshua b. Levi (ca. 250); b. B. Bat. 16A with Raba († 352): the Torah as a remedy against the evil inclination; b. Menaḥ. 99B with R. Yohanan († 279) and R. Eleazar (ca. 270); b. ʿArak. 15B with R. Hama b. Hanina (ca. 260): the Torah as tree of life; Lev. Rab. 12 (113D) = Midr. Ps. 19 § 15 (86A), Deut. Rab. 8 (205B) with Hezekiah b. Hiyya (ca. 240) or R. Hiyya (ca. 200); Lev. Rab. 25 (123A) with R. Benjamin b. Levi (ca. 325); Lev. Rab. 25 (123B) = TanḥB וישלח § 9 (84A) with R. Huna (ca. 350); Lev. Rab. 29 (127B) with R. Jeremiah (ca. 320): the Torah as tree of life; Lev. Rab. 35 (132C) with R. Aha b. Eliashib (4th cent.): the Torah as tree of life; Deut. Rab. 4 (201D) is anonymous: Torah protects from evil spirits; Midr. Ps. 1 § 19 (9B) with R. Judan (ca. 350): Torah as tree of life; Midr. Ps. 1 § 19 (9B) with R. Isaac b. Hiyya (ca. 380): Torah as tree of life; TanḥB נח §2 (15A) with R. Judah b. Shalom (ca. 370): Torah as tree of life.

E. The Torah as the life-principle of Israel.

A baraita in b. Ber. 61B: Once the blasphemous (Roman) government ordered that the Israelites should no longer devote themselves to the Torah. Pappos b. Judah (ca. 110) came and met R. Aqiba († ca. 135), as he publicly held assemblies and devoted himself to the Torah.

He said to him, "Aqiba, are you not afraid of the blasphemous government?" He answered him, "I will tell you a parable. What can this matter be compared with? With a fox that went along the bank of a river and saw how the fish clustered in one place and then another. He said to them, 'Why do you flee?' They answered him, 'Because of the nets that men bring over us.' He said to them, 'If it should please you to come onto dry land, then we, I and you, will live (together), as my ancestors lived (together) with your ancestors!' They answered him, 'You are the one people call the cleverest among the animals? You are not clever but dumb!' If we must be afraid in the place of our life, how much more would that be the case in the place of our death! If this is also now the case with us, when we sit and devote ourselves to the Torah in which it is written, 'For it is your life and the length of your days' (Deut 30:20), how much more would this be the case (that we would have to be afraid), if we went and abandoned it (the Torah)!" ‖ See b. ʿAbod. Zar. 3B at § Matt 13:47. ‖ Mekilta Exodus 17:8 (61A): "Then Amalek came" (Exod 17:8). R. Joshua (ca. 90) and R. Eleazar ben (so!) חִסְמָא (? הֲסָמָא? [ca. 110]) said, "This passage of Scripture contains an (allegorical) interpretation and is elucidated by Job. For it says, 'Does papyrus grow tall without a marsh, does a reed shoot up high without water?' (Job 8:11). How can this be so? Is it possible for papyrus to grow without a marsh? Does a reed shoot up high without water? How can this be so? Can a reed exist without water? So too it is impossible for Israel to exist without the Torah, and the enemy came over them because they separated themselves from the words of the Torah; for the enemy comes only because of sin and because of transgression. Therefore it is said, 'Then Amalek came.'"

F. The Torah as the only good that remains for Israel. See § Rom 2:23 A, #2.

G. The Torah as the basis and guarantee of the divine love for Israel.

Mishnah ʾAbot 3.14: (R. Aqiba [† ca. 135] said,) "The Israelites are beloved; for a precious instrument has been given to them by which the world was created (the Torah is meant). It was made known to them as a particular love that an instrument had been given to them by which the world was created; for it says, 'I have given you a good teaching. Do not abandon my Torah' (Prov 4:2)." — On the Torah as God's tool in creation, see § John 1:1–4, #4. ‖ Deuteronomy Rabbah 8 (205C): "The word is very near to you" (Deut 30:14). R. Samuel b. Nahman (ca. 260) said, "What can this be compared with? With the daughter of a king whom no one had gotten to know. But the king had a friend who was permitted to come to the king at any time when the king's daughter stood before him. Then the king said to him, 'See how I love you. For no one knows my daughter, but she stands there before you.' Thus God spoke to the Israelites, 'See how beloved you are to me. For no creature in my palace knows my Torah, but I have given her to you; for it says, "It (Wisdom = Torah) is hidden from the eyes of every living thing" (Job 28:21). But in your case, "It (Torah) is not too wonderful before you, but rather the word is very near to you" (Deut 30:11, 14).' God said to them, 'My children, if the words of the Torah remain near to you, then I will also call you "near"; for it is written, "For the children of Israel, the people that is near to him. Hallelujah!" (Ps 148:14).'" ‖ Numbers Rabbah 2 (138B): "And it will happen that instead of it having been said to them: 'You are not my people,' they will be called 'sons of the living God'" (Hos 2:1).

This is what is written: "Great waters cannot extinguish love and streams do not swamp it. If one gave all the wealth of his house for love, it would only be despised" (Song 8:7). R. Samuel b. Nahman (ca. 260) said, "This passage of Scripture speaks of two kinds of love; at the beginning it speaks of (God's) love for Israel; for if all the nations of the world came together, to take away the love between him and Israel, they would not be able to. For it says, 'Great waters cannot extinguish love.' And 'great waters' means nothing other than the nations of the world; for it says, 'Woe, a roar of many nations, they roar like the roar of the sea' (Isa 17:12). 'And streams do not swamp it': these are the kings and princes; for it says, 'Therefore, behold, Yahweh will cause the powerful and mighty waters of the tide, the king of Assyria, to rise over them ...' (Isa 8:7). And at the end it speaks of (Israel's) love for the Torah. For if all the nations of the world came together and said, 'We want to sell all our possessions to do the Torah and the commandments,' God would answer them, 'Even if you sell all your possessions to acquire the Torah—it is only contemptible with you!' 'If one gave all the wealth of his house for love, it would only be despised'; for what kind of love? For love of the Torah; for it says, 'How I love your Torah' (Ps 119:97). They (the nations) said to him (God), 'Why will you not accept us?' He answered them, 'Because you sin.' They said to him, 'Do the Israelites not sin?'" R. Berekhiah (ca. 340) said, "What is written after that (after Song 8:7)? 'We have a little sister ...' (Song 8:8). God said to them, 'Just as in the case of a child, as long as it is small, its parents will not get upset with it when it sins against them, precisely because it is small.' So it is the same with the Israelites: because they are small, God does not count it against them אֵין מַעֲלֶה עֲלֵיהֶם. Recognize that this is so; for they enraged God in the days of Hosea, and then God began to make them afraid: 'They are children of whores' (Hos 2:6), 'for she is not my wife' (Hos 2:4). 'Call it, "Not my people," for you are not my people' (Hos 1:9). But if he let that out of his mouth for a moment, he did it only to bring them back to the good. He could not even bear it for one hour, but rather while he was still in his (previous) place, he regretted it: 'and it happened in the same place where he had said to them, "You are not my people," that he said to them, "Children of the living God"' (so Midr. Hos. 2:1)." — The same is found more briefly and anonymously, and with some other supporting passages, in Midr. Song. 8:7 (131B). ‖ TanḥumaB תצוה § 7 (50A): R. Abba b. Kahana (ca. 310) said, "When the Israelites stood at Mount Sinai and said, 'We will do and listen' (Exod 24:7), God loved them immediately and adjoined two angels to each one of them, one of which girded him with a weapon, while the other put a crown on his head." See the parallels to this in § Rom 2:23 A, #1. ‖ Exodus Rabbah 33 (94C): "They shall take for me לִי an offering" (Exod 25:2). This is what is written: "I have given you a good buy (= Torah, so the midr.)" (Prov 4:2). R. Berekhiah, the priest, the son of rabbis (ca. 340), said, "... According to the custom of the world, a man buys something valuable from the market; can he acquire its owner? But God gave the Torah to Israel and said to them, 'You are virtually כִּבְיָכוֹל taking (receiving) me!' Therefore, 'They are to take me לִי as an offering (so now the midr.).' Meaning: As long as Israel has the Torah, it has God." ‖ Midrash Psalm 78 § 1 (172B): God made the covenant with Israel only because of the Torah, so that it would not be forgotten from their mouth. — Meaning: As long as Israel has the Torah, God's covenant with it endures. — According to Yal. Ps. § 819, R. Samuel b. Nahman (ca. 260) is the author.

3:4 A: Absolutely not!

μὴ γένοιτο = חָלִילָה or חָס or חָס וְשָׁלוֹם. See § Matt 16:22 B. In rabbinic usage, the last phrase predominates the others by far. Therefore a few examples may be given here.

Babylonian Talmud Ḥagigah 15A: (The apostate Elisha b. Abbuyah [ca. 120]) saw that authority was given to Metatron (the highest throne angel of God) to sit down and write down the merits of Israel. He said, "It is a traditional teaching that above, there is no sitting and no fighting and no backside and no fatigue."[77] Are there two powers? Absolutely not חס ושלום!" ‖ See b. Sanh. 90A at Matt 7:15 A; S. Eli. Rab. 16 (82) at Matt 13:14f.; b. Ḥag. 4B at Matt 19:20 A; y. Ḥag. 2.77B.32 at § Acts 2:3, #2; Midr. Ruth 1:2 (124B) at Rom 2:21 A; b. Šabb. 138B at § Rom 2:23 A, #2, n. *b*.

3:4 B: Every man as a liar.

Psalm 116:11: כָּל־הָאָדָם כֹּזֵב. — Targum has the plural: כָּל בְּנֵי נָשָׁא מְכַדְּבִין. — Septuagint: πᾶς ἄνθρωπος ψεύστης.

3:4 C: So that you are justified in your words and prevail in your justice.

Psalm 51:6: לְמַעַן־תִּצְדַּק בְּדָבְרֶךָ תִּזְכֶּה בְשָׁפְטֶךָ "so that you are right in your word (speech), pure in your justice." — The targum forms the verbs transitively and makes the one praying their object: "Before you alone I have made myself guilty and done what is evil before you, so that you may declare me innocent when you speak, declare me pure when you judge מִן בִּגְלַל דִּתְזַכֵּי יָתִי בְּמַלָּלוּתָךְ תִּבְרוֹר יָתִי כַד תְּדִין. — Septuagint: ὅπως ἂν δικαιωθῇς ἐν τοῖς λόγοις σου καὶ νικήσῃς ἐν τῷ κρίνεσθαί σε. Here ἐν τῷ κρίνεσθαί σε is meant in the middle sense according to Job 9:3; 13:19; Jer 2:9 (cf. also Matt 5:40; 1 Cor 6:1) = in your judging or justice. — The apostle follows the LXX verbatim except for the fact that, according א AD he has νικήσεις instead of νικήσῃς.

1. δικαιοῦσθαι = to be justified or recognized as just, to stand as just.

For example, Psalms of Solomon 8:27 (Fritzsche): "God was justified ἐδικαιώθη ὁ θεός in his judgments among the nations of the earth." — More common is the active δικαιοῦν. Sirach 10:28: "Someone who sins against himself, who will justify him? τίς δικαιώσει;" — Sirach 13:21: "If a rich man fails, there are many defenders: he said what is forbidden and they justify him ἐδικαίωσαν αὐτόν." — Psalms of Solomon 2:16: "I acknowledge you, O God, as just ἐγὼ δικαιώσω σε with an upright heart, for in your judgments is your righteousness, O God." — Psalms of Solomon 3:5: "The righteous man falters and acknowledges the Lord as just καὶ ἐδικαίωσε τὸν κύριον (in his punishment)." — Psalms of Solomon 4:9: "The pious would acknowledge the judgment of their God to be just δικαιώσαιεν when sinners are

77. S-B: This is the ordinary interpretation according to Rashi. — However, Maimonides reads יסוד השלישי in m. Sanh 10.1 instead of תחרות "fighting," עמידה "standing," and interprets עורף "backside" = פירוד "separation" and עפוי "fatigue" = חבור "connection."

removed from the sight of the righteous." — Psalms of Solomon 8:7: "I contemplated the judgments of God since the creation of heaven and earth: I declared God to be righteous ἐδικαίωσα τὸν θεόν (= acknowledged that God is right) in his judgments from eternity."

δικαιόω corresponds to the Hebrew הִצְדִּיק, צִדֵּק, and זִכָּה = to declare someone to be (innocent), declare righteous.

Sirach 10:29 (Hebrew): "Whoever declares himself guilty מרשיע נפשו, who will declare him righteous יצדיקנו?" (The Greek translator interprets מרשיע differently; see Sir 10:28 above.) ‖ Babylonian Talmud Berakot 19A: He (the mourner) stands and acknowledges the judgment (that fell upon him by the death of an associate) as just מצדיק. ‖ Jerusalem Talmud Soṭah 8.22C.41: Zedekiah (was named the king of Judah), because he acknowledged it (the divine judgment) to be just צִידֵּק. ‖ See SDeut 32:4 § 307 (133A) at #3. ‖ Pesiqta Rabbati 40 (169A): R. Isaac (ca. 300) said, "... God said to the Israelites, 'Repent in the ten days between the new year and the Day of Atonement, and I will declare you to be righteous ואני מְזַכֶּה אתכם on the Day of Atonement and make you into a new creature.'" (By God declaring the Israelites to be righteous, all sins are forgiven; this condition of purity from sin is viewed as בְּרִיָּה חֲדָשָׁה, as new creation, new creature, because the Israelite stands before God as pure as a newborn child.) ‖ In b. ʿErub. 19A, R. Joshua b. Levi (ca. 250) speaks of those condemned to gehenna, "They will acknowledge the (divine) judgment to be just מצדיקין and say before God, 'Lord of the world, beautifully you have judged, beautifully you have declared righteous זִיכִּיתָ, beautifully you have declared guilty הִיַּבְתָּ, beautifully you have prepared gehenna for the godless and the garden of Eden for the righteous.'" ‖ Midrash Psalm 143 § 1 (266B): No one can declare himself righteous (pure) in the (divine) judgment אין אדם יכול לְזַכּוֹת את עצמו בדין. Why? "When they sin against you—for there is no one who has not sinned"(1 Kgs 8:46). — See also Tg. Ps. 51:6 above and at § Matt 11:19 B[78] and Tg. Yer. I Deut. 5:11.

2. νικήσεις, word in the text: תִּזְכֶּה. — זָכָה "to be pure," in later usage it also = to be proved right, to prevail, win.[a] The LXX and the apostle understood תזכה in the latter sense; this meaning is also present in b. Sanh. 107A (see #3).

a. Babylonian Talmud Berakot 7B: R. Isaac (ca. 300) said, "If you see the hour smiling upon a godless man, do not get worked up about him (do not get into a fight with him); for it says, 'His ways are permanent at all times' (Ps 10:5). And not only this, but he also prevails in judgment זוֹכֶה בדין; for it says, 'Your judgments are on high (in heaven), far from him' (Ps 10:5). And not only this but he also looks down on his opponents (is permitted to rejoice at their defeat); for it says, 'He breathes on all his opponents' (Ps 10:5)." — The same is found in b. Meg. 6B. — זוכה בדין "he prevails in judgment" = he wins in the trial also in b. B. Meṣ. 107B in a baraita; see § Luke 14:12 B, #1. — Aramaic זְכָא = prevail, defeat, overcome in, for example, b. Sanh. 39A: Let anyone who beats the king דזכי למלכא (in an argument) be thrown into the animal cage; see § John 10:16, n. *a.* ‖ Babylonian Talmud ʿAbodah Zarah 10B: Whoever defeats זכי the king will be thrown from the Gemonian Stairs; see § Matt 20:12. ‖ In b. Bek. 8B an emperor (Hadrian?) summons R. Joshua b. Hananiah (ca. 90): "Go, defeat

78. TN: This reference is not actually contained within § Matt 11:19 B and must represent one of the errors the authors note in their prefaces.

them זכינהו (the wise ones of Athens or of the athenaeum?) and bring them to me!" Then further below R. Joshua addresses the wise with the words: "If you prevail זכיתו, you can do what you want with me; but if I prevail זכינא over you, you are to become worn out (rotten, decrepit) on a ship."

3. Psalm 51:6 is not cited in rabbinic literature especially frequently, and when it is, the meaning is so distorted that one could think that the passage was written as a supporting passage for Rom 3:8: Let us do evil so that good may result!

Sifre Deuteronomy 32:4 § 307 (133A): When a man departs from the world, all his works accompany him and are enumerated one by one. He (God) says to him, "You did this on this and that day; or do you not believe these words?" If he says, "Yes, yes!," then God says to him, "Seal (sign) it!" For it says, "He seals by the hand of every human being" (Job 37:7). "Just and trustworthy is he" (Deut 32:4). And he (the person) acknowledges the judgment as just מצדיק and says, "Beautifully have you judged me!" And (Scripture or God) also says, "So that you are just in your words" (בדבריך, so the midr. reads), you are pure in your judgment. – See the whole passage in the excursus "Sheol, Gehenna, and the Garden of Eden," II, #3, n. *f*. – See the parallel in b. Taʿan. 11A at § Matt 12:36, #1. ‖ Yalquṭ Reubeni on Gen 8:21 from the Ten Commandments Midrash: "The inclination of the human heart is evil from youth" (Gen 8:21). This was the reason why King David said, "So that you are right in your word" (Ps 51:6). This means, "I have sinned to verify your words which you have said, 'The inclination of the human heart is evil from youth.'" (Had David not sinned, this word of God would have been belied. To spare God this dishonor, David sinned.) ‖ Babylonian Talmud Sanhedrin 107A: Raba († 352) said in a presentation, "What does 'For you alone (= exclusively in your interest) I have sinned and done evil in your eyes, so that you are right in your words (בדבריך, so!) and prevail in your judgments' (so Midr. Ps. 51:6) mean? David said before God, 'It is evident and known before you that, if I had wanted to overpower my (evil) inclination, I would have overpowered it הוה כייפינא. But I thought, lest one say, "The servant has overpowered כפייה his master!"' (People would have talked if David had overcome his passion for Bathsheba, which he could have done, and thus had nullified God's word in Gen 8:21; David sinned with Bathsheba so that God could prevail in his judgment about the human heart in Gen 8:21.)" ‖ Midrash Psalm 51 § 3 (141A): "For you alone (= only in your interest) I have sinned, so that you are right in your words" (Ps 51:6). What can David be compared with? With someone who sustained a wound (fracture) and went to a doctor. The doctor was astonished and said to him, "How great is your wound! I am very sorry for you." Then the one with the wound answered him, "You are sorry for me? Have I not sustained the wound for your sake? If not, would you get any recompense?" Likewise, David said to God, "For you alone (only in your interest) I have sinned in case you say to wrongdoers, 'Why did you not repent?' If you will accept even me (after I sinned), all wrongdoers will give in to you, and all will look to me, and I will testify to them that you accept the penitent." And likewise, God says, "Behold, I have appointed him (David, because of חסדי דוד in verse 3) as a witness for the nations" (Isa 55:4). "And not only I" (David says, will be a witness), "but also all Israel"; as it says, "You are my witnesses, says Yahweh, and my servant (= David) whom I have chosen" (Isa 43:10). – Here David sins in God's interest in order that, by his subsequent repentance, he might embolden all wrongdoers to repent. – The last three passages make clear at any rate how close Jewish thought was to the notion rejected by the apostle in verses 5–8 that punishment is undeserved when a person brings God's righteousness to light by his unrighteousness (verse 5) or when he repents so that good may result (verse 8).

3:5: I speak in a human way.

κατὰ ἄνθρωπον λέγω. Similarly, Gal 3:15; in 1 Cor 9:8, it features as a question: κατὰ ἄνθρωπον λαλῶ; in Rom 6:19: ἀνθρώπινον λέγω. But the meaning is different in each case. Romans 3:5: in the only way that can be expected of humans, that is, I speak in a foolish way; Gal 3:15: in order to make myself better understood by drawing an example from ordinary life, as people are accustomed to do; 1 Cor 9:8 as a question: am I speaking in a human way that is possibly wrong and therefore nonbinding? Romans 6:19: in the way of humans who also sometimes choose an apparently inappropriate expression in order to make their words poignant or to prevent misunderstanding. From the diverse senses in which the expression is used by the apostle, it can be seen that the phrase was not a fixed term taken from the language of the synagogue. In fact, in rabbinic literature, one does not find an idiom that fully corresponds to κατὰ ἄνθρωπον λέγω. – The following formulas certainly do not supply a proper analogue: כדאמרי אינשי "as people say";[79] היינו דאמרי אינשי "this is what people usually say";[80] הדא הוא דברייתי אמרי "this is what men usually say."[81] These formulas serve only to introduce proverbs. However, the following expressions may be drawn on for comparison.

a. דִּבְּרָה תורה כלשון בני אדם "The Torah speaks in the way humans express themselves," an exegetical principle first asserted by R. Ishmael († ca. 135) in opposition to the attempt of R. Aqiba († ca. 135) to attribute a special meaning to every pleonastic expression in Scripture (e.g., to an infinitive before a finite verb).

Sifre Numbers 15:31 § 112 (33A): "'This soul should be eradicated, yes eradicated (הִכָּרֵת תִּכָּרֵת = completely eradicated)' (Num 15:31). 'Eradicated' הכרת in this world; 'yes let it be eradicated' תכרת for the future world." These are the words of R. Aqiba. R. Ishmael responded

79. S-B: Babylonian Talmud Sukkah 56B: Abbayye († 338/39) said, "Yes, as people usually say, 'The word of a child on the street arises either from its father or from its mother.'" ‖ Babylonian Talmud Ḥagigah 2B at § Matt 9:32; see also b. B. Qam. 92A (twice); 92B.

80. S-B: Babylonian Talmud Berakot 48A: This is what people usually say, "Every cucumber is recognized by its juice." ‖ Babylonian Talmud Sanhedrin 52A at § Matt 3:17 A, n. *l*; b. Nid. 31A at § Matt 5:13 A, #4; b. Sanh. 95B at § Matt 5:25 B; b. Sanh 48B at § Matt 5:44 A, n. *g*; b. B. Meṣ. 59B at § Matt 7:3ff., #1; see also b. Sanh 98B; 106A; b. B. Meṣ. 85B.

81. S-B: Genesis Rabbah 60 (37D): This is what men usually say, "Between the midwife and the one giving birth (i.e., before the former comes to the latter) the child of the misfortunate has passed away (dead)."

to him, "Since (Scripture) says, 'eradicated' הכרת, is this soul to be eradicated (also for the future world)? The Torah speaks in the way humans express themselves" (there is no special meaning behind the pleonastic infinitive; it simply strengthens the finite verb, just as it is used in everyday speech to emphasize the verb). — R. Ishmael's rule was later applied to other pleonasms in Scripture as well; here our editions often read בלשון "in the manner of expression" instead of כלשון. For examples of the way this rule was applied, see SLev 20:1f. (363A); b. Ber. 31B; b. Yebam. 71A; b. Qidd. 17B; b. Giṭ. 41B; b. Ned. 3A; b. B. Meṣ. 31B; 94B; b. Sanh. 56B; 64B; 85B; 90B; b. Mak. 12A; b. ʿAbod. Zar. 27A; b. Zebaḥ. 108B; b. ʿArak. 3A; b. Ker. 11A; b. Nid. 32B; 44A. — The sentence from R. Ishmael cited above appears in a different form in the following expressions in notes *b, c, d.*

b. התורה דברה כדרכה "the Torah speaks in its customary way." This is how the Jerusalem Talmud conveys the rule of R. Ishmael cited above.

Jerusalem Talmud Šabbat 19.17A.27: "Should be circumcised, yes circumcised הִמּוֹל יִמּוֹל" (Gen 17:13; the infinitive המול is pleonastic). From here we have a proof for the two parts of circumcision: one (namely המול) refers to the (actual) circumcision and the other (namely ימול) refers to the exposure of the glans, (or) one refers to (actual) circumcision and the other to the fiber of flesh (that remains behind and has to be removed). Up to this point following R. Aqiba († ca. 135), who said, "The expressions are inclusive (the pleonastic infinitive adds something in addition to actual circumcision)." According to R. Ishmael, who said, "These are double expressions (implying nothing more); the Torah speaks[82] in its customary way: הלוך הלכת 'you went' (Gen 31:30), נכסף נכספתה 'you had (strong) desire' (Gen 31:30), גנב גנבתי "I am stolen, indeed stolen" (Gen 40:15)." (These three passages show that the addition of the pleonastic infinitive to the finite verb is a customary manner of expression in the Torah; correspondingly, the infinitive המול in Gen 17:13 has no special significance.) — See further examples in y. Yebam. 8.8D.58; y. Ned. 1.36C.23.

c. דרך ארץ דברה תורה "The Torah speaks in the usual way."

Sifre Deuteronomy 11:14 § 42 (80B): "'You are to gather your grain' (Deut 11:14). Why was this said? Because it says, 'This book of the Torah is not to depart from your mouth' (Josh 1:8). Should I understand this according to its wording? (Then the Torah would have to constitute the sole occupation of a human being.) Scripture teaches: 'And you are to gather' (Deut 11:14). The Torah speaks in the usual way." These are the words of R. Ishmael. (When Scripture says, "This book of the Torah is not to depart from your mouth," it means this not in an absolute sense, but rather in the ordinary way that people would have spoken this word; specifically, the Torah is to be the main occupation of a human being but not the sole occupation. Scripture itself teaches this by imposing other necessary works, e.g., collecting grain.) — This is different in the parallel in a baraita in b. Ber. 35B: "'And you are to gather your grain' (Deut 11:14). What does Scripture teach? When it says, 'This book of the Torah is not to depart from your mouth' (Josh 1:8), should the words be understood according to their written wording? Scripture teaches, 'And you are to gather your grain:

82. S-B: The ריבתה after דברה should be removed.

observe הַנְהֵג alongside them the custom of worldly occupation מִנְהַג דֶּרֶךְ אֶרֶץ.'" These are the words of R. Ishmael.

d. דרך ארץ דברה תורה כלשון בני אדם "The Torah speaks in the customary way that people express themselves."

Sifre Deuteronomy 6:7 § 34 (74B): "(Talk about the words of the Torah,) when you lie down" (Deut 6:7). Perhaps also when one lies down at midday? Scripture teaches: "And when you get up" (Deut 6:7). Perhaps also when one gets up at midnight? Scripture teaches: "When you sit in your house and when you walk on the road" (Deut 6:7). The Torah speaks in the customary way that people express themselves. (Scripture means the same thing people mean when they speak of getting up and lying down, namely getting up in the morning and lying down to sleep in the evening; one talks about the words of the Torah at this time by reciting the Shema.) ‖ The expressions in notes *a–d* do not match the Pauline κατὰ ἄνθρωπον λέγω in content.

e. לְשַׁכֵּךְ האוזן "to satisfy the ear" (Scripture says this and that).

Mekilta Exodus 19:18 (72B = Tanḥ. יתרו 89B): "Its smoke went up like the smoke of a furnace" (Exod 19:18); perhaps only like smoke? Scripture teaches: "of a furnace." If like that of a furnace, perhaps only like that of a furnace? Scripture teaches: "The mountain burned in fire" (Deut 4:11). And why does Scripture teach: "of a furnace"? To please the ear, giving it only what it always likes to hear. (To shield the majesty of God, which cannot be described with words, Scripture resorts to inadequate images so that from them the weak human ear may hear something of God's greatness and be satisfied.) Likewise (it says of God): "The lion roars, who should not fear?" (Amos 3:8). Who gave the lion power and strength? Was it not he (God)? But see, we speak periphrastically about him (in metaphorical expressions as humans do) to please the ear. Similarly (it says of God): "And see, the glory of the God of Israel came from the east (and its sound was like the sound of mighty waters"; Ezek 43:2). Who gave water power and strength? Was it not he? But see, we speak periphrastically about him from his creatures to please the ear. — In a limited way this passage can be used as a parallel to Rom 6:18f., insofar as here the use of inadequate expressions is justified on the basis of human weakness. Just as the OT Scripture uses inadequate images to shield the divine majesty in order to make the glory of God as perceptible and comprehensible to the weakness of the human ear as possible, so too in Rom 6:18f. the apostle speaks in a similarly inadequate way about the condition of Christian freedom as well as the condition of bondage in order to "please the ear" in a human way by this paradox, that is, to poignantly bring to the awareness of his weak readers that from now on their life must be wrapped up in the service of righteousness.

f. כִּבְיָכוֹל "as it were," "in a way," used most of the time to soften anthropomorphisms,[α] but also to attenuate an inauspicious statement about Israel,[β] or to excuse an expression that otherwise appears to be inappropriate.[γ] כביכול always implies *sit venia verbo*!, so that its sense could correctly be translated by: "if one may say so."

α. Mekilta Exodus 12:41 (20A): When they (the Israelites) return from exile, the Shekinah will be with them as it were כביכול (so to speak). — Mekilta Exodus 16:14 (57B): In a way כביכול God stretched out his hand and accepted the prayers of our fathers. – Mekilta Exodus 20:11 (77A): What does Scripture intend to teach when it says, "He rested" (on the seventh day; Exod 20:11)? In a way כביכול (if one may say so) he (God) had it written about himself that he created his world in six days and rested on the seventh day. See, here the inference is justified by moving from the greater to the lesser: If the one before whom there is no labor had it written about himself that he created the world in six days and rested on the seventh, how much more is this the case for humans, about whom it says: "A human being is born for travail" (Job 5:7; so that he must rest on the seventh day)! ‖ Sifre Deuteronomy 11:12 § 40 (78B): What does Scripture mean to teach when it says, "A land that Yahweh your God looks after" (Deut 11:12)? In a way כביכול God looks after only this land; but because of the looking after (literally: as a recompense for the looking after) by which he looks after it, he looks after all (other) lands in fellowship with it.... What does Scripture mean to teach when it says, "protector of Israel" (Ps 121:4)? In a way כביכול it is the case that he protects only Israel; but because of the protection by which he protects them, he protects all at the same time along with them.... What does Scripture mean to teach when it says, "My eyes and my heart are to be there for all days" (1 Kgs 9:3)? In a way כביכול it is the case that they are only there; but as a recompense for being there, they are everywhere. ‖ Sifre Deuteronomy 32:36 § 326 (139A): When God judges the nations, there is joy in his presence ...; but when he judges Israel, there is in a way כביכול sorrow in his presence.

β. Tosefta Soṭah 14.10 (321): Since those who took alms from the *goyim* (non-Jews) increased (among the Israelites), the *goyim* began in a way כביכול to increase and the Israelites to decrease. – The Erfurt manuscript does not read כביכול; it is supplied by the Vienna manuscript. To conceal the unfavorable judgment over Israel even more, the latter manuscript even reverses the statements: "the *goyim* began in a way to decrease and the Israelites to rise." The correct reading is then however suggested by the addition: אִיפְּכָא "the opposite" (should be read).

γ. Sifre Numbers 6:26 § 42 (13A): In a way כביכול the family above (= the angel world) was diminished. ‖ Midrash Psalm 97 § 2 (211B): (R. Samuel b. Nahman, ca. 260, said,) "In that hour (of the last judgment) he (God) will in a way כביכול (if one may say so) give existence to the idols, and the idols will come and prostrate before God. Then the nations of the world will be ashamed and be put to shame (see Ps 97:7)." ‖ This כִּבְיָכוֹל could be put in place of κατὰ ἄνθρωπον λέγω in Rom 3:5 without changing the meaning of the passage: כביכול if one may say so, is God not unjust to impose wrath? (Answer in verse 6:) Absolutely not!

3:6: How would God judge the world?

κρίνειν τὸν κόσμον, also in 1 Cor 6:2; John 3:17; 12:47. The corresponding דִּין אֶת־הָעוֹלָם,[a] Aram. (לְ)מְדָן יַת עָלְמָא,[b] appears only rarely in rabbinic usage. The rabbis preferred to say דין את אומות העולם "to judge the nations of the world."[c]

a. See Tanḥ. שופטים 15B at § Rom 2:12 B. – Passively: הָעוֹלָם נִידּוֹן the world is judged (e.g., m. Roš Haš. 1.2; b. Roš Haš. 16A).

b. Targum 2 Samuel 23:7: "When the great tribunal is revealed to sit on thrones of judgment to judge the world."

c. For example, TanḥB שופטים § 8 (16A); Midr. Ps. 31 § 5 (119B); Pesiq. Rab. 35 (161A).

3:8: Let us do evil so that good may result.

See § Rom 3:4 C, #3.

3:9 A: Do we have any advantage? Not at all.

Without a second thought, rabbinic Judaism would have answered the question of whether the Jews had any advantage over gentiles (= non-Jews): Certainly, quite a lot; for the gentiles are hopelessly forfeited to gehenna, but all Israel has a share in the future world. The ancient synagogue formed its judgment about the *goyim* (non-Israelites) or the nations of the world more precisely in the following way.

1. Since the covenant with Abraham[a] or, as was said most often, since the rejection of the Torah by the nations of the world God had cast off the gentiles.[b] Since then they have been regarded as nothing before him: like chaff blown away by the wind,[c] like debris that lies around worthlessly,[a] like trash burned by fire,[d] hated,[e] abhorred.[f] For this reason he lets them go their own ways without worrying about them.[g] Each one of the gentiles serve sin, wallow in vice,[h] and God does not punish them or does so only a little. They do good here and there and may have other merits to point to, and God repays them immediately: they are not to have anything good or meritorious to point to that God did not repay them for in this world, so that they bear only guilt and await only punishment for it in the next world.[i] In this way God maintains his righteousness toward each gentile.[k] Only when the measure of sin is complete will the judgment begin,[l] which happens immediately after death before God's seat of judgment. The judgment will be damnation to gehenna.[n] A few pious gentiles may constitute an exception and gain a share in the future world;[m] the mass is a *massa perditionis* that is destined for gehenna.[n]

a. Tanḥuma וישב 42A, B: Why does Scripture bother to write down their (Esau's and his descendants') genealogy? Did God have nothing else that he could have written than: "the chief Teman" (Gen 36:15), "the chief Lotan" (Gen 36:29)? This is meant to teach only that from the creation of the world God devoted himself to establishing the genealogy of the nations of the world so that there would be no opportunity for objection, in order to make known to men their shameful origin .... Since they were all children of incest, Scripture explicated them to make known their shame. But Israel is an offering of God, and he calls them "lot" and "inheritance" and "his portion"; as it says, "For Yahweh's portion is his people and Jacob the lot of his inheritance" (Deut 32:9). It is also written: "You are to be my possession from all the nations" (Exod 19:5). Further: "I have planted you as a noble vine from a completely pure seed" (Jer 2:21). And why did God devote himself from the beginning to the lineage of the nations of the world? It is like a king who had a pearl that had fallen into dust and rubble. The king had to look through the dust and rubble to pull the pearl out of it. When the king obtained the pearl, he left the dust and rubble lying and devoted himself to the pearl. Likewise, God devoted himself to the generations in the past.... But when he came upon the pearl of Abraham, Isaac and Jacob, he began to devote himself to these.

b. See supporting passages at § Rom 1:20 E, n. *e* and § Rom 1:20 E, n. *g*.

c. Midrash Song of Songs 7:3 (127A): R. Menahemah (ca. 370; so read instead of R. Nehemiah) said in the name of R. Abin (I, ca. 325), "... A parable. What can this be compared with? The straw, the chaff, and the gleanings fought with each other. One said, 'The soil is sown because of me'; and the other said, 'The field is sowed because of me.' Then the wheat said to them, 'Wait until the threshing floor comes, then we will know for whose sake the field was sown.' The threshing floor came, and when they had been brought to the threshing floor, the master of the house came out to winnow them: the chaff went away from there into the wind; he took the straw and tossed it to the ground; he took the gleanings and burned them; he took the wheat and made a pile of grain from it. The people passed by, and everyone who saw it kissed it; as it says, 'Kiss the grain' (so Midr. Ps. 2:12)! In the same way, of the nations of the world, some say, 'We are (the true) Israel, and for our sake the world was made; and others say, 'We are (the true) Israel (an allusion to the intra-church fights at the beginning of the 4th cent.), and for our sake the world was made (= we are the main thing and thus the heirs of the future world).' But Israel says to them, 'Wait until the day of God comes, then we will know for whose sake the world was created. This is what is written, 'Behold, the day is coming, burning like a furnace' (Mal 3:18). It is also written, 'You will winnow them, and the wind will carry them away' (Isa 41:16). But of Israel it says, 'But you will rejoice in Yahweh, you will glory in the Holy One of Israel' (Isa 41:16)." — The same is anonymously said in Gen. Rab. 83 (53A); sharp divergences are found in Pesiq. Rab. 10 (36A); Midr. Ps. 2 § 14 (16A). ‖ See Pesiq. Rab. 10 (35B) at § Matt 5:43, #1, n. *g*.

d. Tanḥuma במדבר 191B: God said, "The *ʿakum* (= *goyim*, see S-B footnote at § Matt 5:43, #1, n. *g*) are trash (filth). See: "The nations will be fires of lime, thorns cut away, which burn in the fire" (Isa 33:12). — The same is found in Num. Rab. 4 (141B).

e. See TanḥB במדבר § 7 at § Rom 1:20 E, n. *g*; see b. ʿAbod. Zar. 54B and Tanḥ. תדומה 100A at § Matt 15:26, n. *f*.

f. TanḥumaB נשא § 13 (16A): God said, "I have detested תיעבתי all nations in this world because they stem from unclean (incestuous) seed (see above n. *a*); but I have chosen you (Israel) because you stem from pure seed; as it says, "I have planted you as a noble vine from nothing but pure seed" (Jer 2:21). It is also written: "Yahweh your God chose you" (Deut 7:6). And also in the future (= the days of the Messiah) I will choose only you, for you are a holy seed; as it says, "They will not toil in vain, nor give birth for a sudden demise; for they are the seed of those blessed by Yahweh" (Isa 65:23). — The same is found in Tanḥ. נשא 196A.

g. See Pesiq. Rab. 10 (36B) at § Matt 5:43, #1, n. *g*.

h. See supporting passages at § Rom 1:26, 27. ‖ The following are more general in content. Sifre Deuteronomy 32:32 § 323 (138B): R. Nehemiah (ca. 150) interpreted the passage

(Deut 32:32) in relation to the nations: "In truth, you come from Sodom's vine and you stem from Gomorrah's field, you are students of the ancient snake that led Adam and Eve astray." ‖ Pesiqta 190A: "You have given increase to the people" (Isa 26:15). When you give a male child to the nations of the world, he (the gentile father) prefers the foreskin and let a curl grow (on his head, as a sign of idolatry). When he has raised him, he takes him to the temple of his idol and angers you. But when you give a male child to one of the Israelites, he counts eight days and circumcises it, and if it is his firstborn, he redeems it after thirty days. When he has raised him, he takes him to the synagogues and houses of learning and praises you every day and says, "Praise Yahweh who is worthy of praise!" A different explanation. "You have given increase to the people. To the nations of the world you give many holidays, then they eat and live wantonly, they go to the theaters and circuses and anger you with their words and their works. But the Israelites are not so: you give them holidays, and they eat and drink and rejoice; they go to the synagogues and the houses of learning and make their prayers numerous, and their additional offerings (or additional prayers) numerous and their offerings numerous." — A similar explanation is found in Pesiq. 194B.

i. Payment to the gentiles in general. Sifra Leviticus 26:9 (450A): "And I will turn to you" (Lev 26:9). A parable has been told. What can this be compared with? With a king who hired many workers and there was one worker there who worked for him many days. The workers came to receive their pay, and that worker also came with them. The king said to that worker, "My son, I will turn to you (in particular, will concern myself especially with you): to the many who have worked for me for a little while, I give a little pay; but you have a big check, and I will reckon together with you." So the Israelites ask for the payment from God in this world, and the nations of the world ask for their payment from God. God says to the Israelites, "My children, I will turn to you (in particular): those nations of the world have worked for me a little, and I will give them a little pay (immediately in this world); but you have a big bill, and I will reckon together with you accordingly (only in the future world, in order to give you a big payment). Therefore it is said, 'I will turn to you.'" ‖ Payment in this world so that only guilt and punishment remain pending for the future world. TanḥumaB קדושים § 1 (36B): What does "The hair of his head was pure like wool" mean (Dan 7:9)? That God keeps himself pure (from obligation and debt) to the nations of the world: he gives them their payment (immediately) for the light commandments that they have done in this world, in order to be able to judge them in the future world and declare them guilty, so that they may not be able to raise an objection nor any merit be found for them. — The same is found in Tanḥ. קדושים 167A.

k. See the beginning of the citation in n. *i.*

l. Babylonian Talmud Soṭah 9A: Rab Hamnuna (ca. 300) said, "God does not punish a person before his measure is full עד שתתמלא סאתו; as it says, 'When the fullness of what his evil inclination has desired is full, every force of adversity (of the divine punishment) comes upon him' (so Midr. Job 20:22)." — The same is found in b. 'Arak. 15A. ‖ Midrash Psalm 10 § 5 (47B): R. Hanina b. Papa (ca. 300) said, "The wicked man does not fall until his measure is full; as it says, 'Among the wicked lies the fullness of their wishes' (so Midr. Job 34:26) and 'When it is full ...' (Job 20:22, as in the previous quotation)."

m. See t. Sanh. 13.2 (434) with parallels at § Matt 5:43, #1, n. *g.* ‖ Babylonian Talmud Sanhedrin 105A: It is Balaam who (according to m. Sanh. 10.2) does not come into the future world. See (this implies) that other *goyim* come into it (namely the pious among them). ‖ Maimonides on m. Sanh. 10.2: The pious of the nations of the world have a share in the future world. — See also New Pesiqta in Jellinek, *Beth ha-Midrash* 6.63 lines 19ff. = *Beth ha-Midrash* 3.28 lines 2ff., translated in the excursus "Sheol, Gehenna, and the Garden of Eden," II, #10, n. *ee.*

n. See TanḥB שמיני § 10 (14B) at § Rom 1:24, #2; also see the quotations in the excursus "Sheol, Gehenna, and the Garden of Eden," II, #7, n. *d.*

2. God handles each of the gentile nations similarly to the way he deals with individual gentiles. They are not planted, they are not sown, they do not put down roots. Before God blows on them, they are dried up. They lack the character of eternity.[a] God glorifies his righteousness with them: he repays their merits[b] and lets them sit in fortune, although they are nothing before him;[c] but he delays their punishment until the measure of their sins is full.[d] Only when they have no more merit that demands payment does God's judgment break out over the nations;[e] then it will be shown that they were not made for eternity. "Never, God says, have I struck a nation and needed to do it a second time." The first strike is enough to destroy a depleted gentile nation forever; they lack the moral power for renewal.[f] So it will be until the end.

a. Midrash Song of Songs 7:3 (127A): R. Menahemah (ca. 370; so read instead of R. Nehemiah) said in the name of R. Abin (I, ca. 325), "For the nations of the world there is no being planted or sown or taking root; and all three are in one verse: 'Even before they are rightly planted, even before they are rightly sown, even before their trunk has taken root in the soil, he has already blown on them so that they wither' (Isa 40:24). But for Israel there is being planted (see Jer 32:41: 'I will plant them in this land'; Amos 9:15: 'I will plant them on their soil'). For them there is being sown (see Hos 2:23: 'I will sow them for myself in the land'). For them there is taking root (see Isa 27:6: "In the future Jacob will take root)."

b. Tanḥuma משפטים 92B: God said, "I am called the Lord (owner, bearer) of justice, and I am supposed to try to stretch out my hand against Esau (= Rome)? I cannot do that until he is repaid for the light commandment that he has performed before me in this world." (This refers to the veneration that the ancestor Esau showed to his father Isaac; Rome continually wears out this merit.) — See also the citations in n. *e.*

c. 2 Baruch 82:2ff.: "But you should know that our creator avenges us (Israel) on all our enemies.... Now we see the fullness of the welfare of the nations, as they act godlessly, and yet they are like a breath. And we look on the extent of their dominion, as they commit wickedness, and yet they will be like a drop. And we see the strength of their power, as they oppose the Almighty year after year, and yet they will be treated as spittle. And we contemplate the glory of their greatness, as they do not observe the commandments of the Most High, and yet they will pass away like smoke. And we ponder the beauty of their splendor, as they live in filthiness, and yet they will wither like grass that dries up. And we contemplate the strength of their cruel harshness, as they do not think about the end, and yet they will disperse like a wave that flows by. And we observe their swaggering power, as they repudiate the goodness of God who has given (it) to them, and yet they will pass away like a cloud that passes by."

d. 2 Maccabees 6:12–16: "I admonish all those who come into possession of this book that they not be discouraged by such cases of misfortune (as befell those who are loyal to the law), but rather to consider that the punishments happen not to destroy our people (Israel) but rather to discipline them. For God's great grace is shown in not leaving the godless (in Israel) alone for a long time but rather having them suffer punishments. While the Lord waits long-sufferingly with all other peoples and punishes them only when the measure of their sins is full, he wanted to proceed with us in a different way, so that his vengeance would not befall us at the end, after we had already reached the further extent of our sins. Therefore, he never withdraws his mercy from us, and although he chastises his people with misfortune, he does not reject them." ‖ Babylonian Talmud Soṭah 9A: R. Hanina b. Papa (ca. 300) said, "God takes vengeance on a nation only when they are eliminated; for it says, 'When the measure was full (when the measure became the measure) in the expulsion, you punished' (Isa 27:8; so the midr.)."

e. Tanḥuma משפטים 92B: R. Levi (ca. 300) said in the name of R. Simeon b. Laqish (ca. 250), "See what is written, 'And the hair of his head was pure as wool' (Dan 7:9). God said, 'When I have made myself pure vis-à-vis the nations because of the light commandments that they have fulfilled before me (i.e., when they get their full payment), in that hour it will happen that thrones (namely of the world powers) will fall.'" – In TanḥB משפטים § 4 (42A) R. Levi is the author. ‖ Midrash Esther 1:1 (84A): R. Levi (ca. 300) said in the name of R. Samuel b. Nahman (ca. 260), "It is written, 'And the hair of his head was pure as wool' (Dan 7:9); (this means:) that no creature has the slightest thing on him שאין לכל בריה אצלו כלום (cf. John 14:30: καὶ ἐν ἐμοὶ οὐκ ἔχει οὐδέν)." R. Judan (ca. 350) said in the name of R. Aybo (Aibbu, ca. 320), "It is written, 'I, I alone, have trodden the winepress, and no one from the nations assists me' (Isa 63:3). How is this so? Does God need the support of the nations so that he says, 'no one from the nations assists me'? Rather, God meant, 'When I look over the tablets of the nations (the books managed in heaven about their deeds; see § Luke 10:20, #2) and no merit is found for them any longer before me (all their merits have been fully repaid), in that hour, "I will trample them in my anger and stomp on them in my wrath" (Isa 63:3).'" R. Phineas (ca. 360) and R. Hilqiah (ca. 320) said in the name of R. Simon (ca. 280), "It says, 'It will happen on that day that I will seek to destroy all the *goyim*' (Zech 12:9). 'I will seek': how can this be? Who hinders him? Rather God means, 'When I look closely at the tablets of the nations of the world and no merit is found for them any longer before me, in that hour I will seek to destroy all the *goyim*.'" – The saying of R. Simon is found also in Tanḥ. משפטים 92B; TanḥB משפטים § 4 (42A). ‖ Babylonian Talmud 'Abodah Zarah 4A: R. Alexandrai (ca. 270) said, "What does 'It will happen on that day that I will seek to destroy all the *goyim*' (Zech 12:9) mean? What is God talking about? 'I will search their registers: if some merit is found for them, I will release them, but if not, I will destroy them.'"

f. Babylonian Talmud Soṭah 9A: Amemar (ca. 400) taught as a tannaitic tradition, "... What does 'I, Yahweh, have not done it a second time, and you, sons of Jacob, have not ceased' (Mal 3:6) mean? 'I, Yahweh, have not done it a second time': I have not struck a nation and had to do it a second time (they were destroyed already by the first blow); but you, sons of Jacob, are not destroyed (whenever my blows have hit you). This is what is written: 'I will use up my arrows against them' (Deut 32:23); my arrows come to an end, but they (the Israelites) do not come to an end."

3. The great turning point in Israel's history, the dawn of the messianic time, also signifies a turning point for the fates of the nations. Every nation that Israel has served, with the Roman world empire leading the way,[a] will be subject to destruction by the Messiah: pestilence, fire, and sword will consume them[b] and gehenna will devour them.[c] Only the nations with which Israel has had no contact up until that time or by which they have at least not been trodden upon will remain alive.[d] All the nations left over will pay homage to the Messiah. His kingdom will be a universal monarchy in the fullest sense of the word;[e] he will keep all nations under his yoke,[f] mildly with Israel, strictly with the nations,[g] quelling revolt without the sword but only by the commanding word of his mouth.[h] He will manifest his sternness in not tolerating any resident alien or foreigner on Israel's soil; only the "called" (invited) will be allowed to come to Jerusalem.[i] This is contradicted, though, by another opinion, namely that the sons of foreigners will be Israel's field workers and gardeners; this of course presupposes that foreigners remain in Israel's dwelling places.[k] Overall the agreed upon view of the ancient synagogue was probably that the gentiles would be tributaries to the Messiah and Israel in a political respect.[l] There was less unity in the judgment about the religious position that the nations of the world would occupy within the messianic world kingdom. Here there were two opposing orientations: the universalistic and the particularistic.

A. The universalistic direction was the older of the two; it was guided by the thought of Old Testament prophecy and granted the gentiles access to Israel's religious holy places. The Messiah was viewed as the redeemer of the whole world[m] and was praised as the light of the nations,[n] as the banner that the gentiles will rally around.[o] He leads all who come into the world to repentance so that all the gentiles will turn to the truth;[p] he judges and he saves all the gentiles who call upon the Lord,[q] so that great multitudes of them will attach themselves to the Israelites as full proselytes[r] and will serve God shoulder to shoulder with them, albeit from fear.[s]

B. The particularistic orientation arose especially after the year 70 CE: the destruction of the temple, the persecutions under Hadrian had generated such hatred of the pagan world empire that no one liked to be reconciled to the idea of the universality of the messianic kingdom of God. It was explained: As Israel had lived alone in this world, so in the future the gentiles should have no benefit from Israel;[t] strongly universalistic sayings in the OT were reinterpreted and explained away.[u] Gradually the belief was that in the days of the Messiah no proselytes at all,[v] or at least none from the seed of Amalek,[w] that is, from the members of the Roman Empire, would be accepted. Only those who had attached themselves to the people of God in Israel's times of suffering would be actual proselytes; but those who tried to connect themselves in times of fortune, they would not be acknowledged as proselytes.[x] R. Eliezer (ca. 90) said that in the days of the Messiah many gentiles would convert to Judaism as proselytes, but he calls them "intruding proselytes"; these were the ones who were never viewed as true proselytes.[y] The word of R. Yose (ca. 150) was interpreted in the same sense: in the future the gentiles of the world would come to become proselytes.[z] The particularistically minded circles of rabbinic Judaism did not at any rate think of a true proselytism of the gentiles in the messianic time. But in order to offer the gentiles something in a religious respect, the claim was marshaled that the Messiah would impose observance of 30 commandments on the gentiles.[aa] These 30 commandments, of which only some were enumerated,[bb] doubtlessly corresponded to the earlier Noachic commandments and were meant to eliminate the coarsest excesses of paganism and to compel the nations to bring their customs in some way into alignment with those of Israel. At the same time it can be discerned from the imposition of these 30 commandments that particularlistically oriented Judaism intended approximately the same place in a religious respect for the gentiles in the messianic time that had previously been occupied by resident strangers (גֵּר תּוֹשָׁב): just as these had to avoid what was especially offensive to the strictly law-abiding Jew without thereby ever acquiring the character of proselytes—so too will it be for the gentile world in the days of the Messiah.[cc] Their religious incorporation into Israel will consist solely in their accepting certain morals and customs; otherwise they will remain, as they were before, a pagan world inwardly estranged from God. They will be proven to be this way as soon as the nations under Gog and Magog charge against Israel at the end of the messianic period. Then those nations will cast off all the commandments laid upon them and will make common cause with the hordes of Gog.[dd] Then however God's patience will also come to an end. The great world judgment will begin: all nations will fall into gehenna[ee] or will otherwise be done away with.[ff] Israel alone will remain,[gg] its dead will arise,[hh] and the claim will then become true: All Israel has a share in the future world.[ii]

a. Supporting passages can be found in the excursus "This World, Days of the Messiah, and the Future World"; see further in n. *b.*

b. In the pseudepigrapha, fire and sword appear as the main means of destruction (e.g., Jub. 9:15; 1 En. 62:12; 63:11; 91:12; Sib. Or. 4.172ff.; 1 En. 56:7; 90:19; 94:7; 99:16; 100:1–3; 2 Bar.

70:8; 72:6). Yet it must be kept in mind that, apart from the last two passages, all the others belong to writings that do not differentiate the messianic period from the absolute end of time; in these writings the messianic judgment of the nations and the eschatological judgment of the world coincide. — In rabbinic literature, reference may be made to Tg. Yer. I Gen. 49:11: "How beautiful is the king, the Messiah, who will arise from the house of Judah. He girds his loins and comes down and marshals the battle lines against his enemies and kills kings along with their generals." ‖ TanḥumaB צו § 4 (8A): "It, the burnt offering, will remain on its fire" (Lev 6:2). By this (by עולה "burnt offering") the wicked empire (= Rome) is (allegorically) meant, which has exalted עילתה itself (interpretation of עולה); as it says, "If you soar high like the eagle, and if you make your nest among the stars" (Obad 4). And they will be judged (punished) by fire; as it says, "I looked until the animal was killed, and its head was destroyed and given to be burned with fire" (Dan 7:11). God said, "And the house of Jacob will become a fire and the house of Joseph a flame (and the house of Esau [= Rome] stubble, and they will scorch them ...)" (Obad 18). And what did he say through Moses? "It, the burnt offering, will remain on its fire" And after that (it says), "Deliverers will go up to Mount Zion to judge the mountain of Esau (= Rome), and the kingship (kingdom) will fall to Yahweh" (Obad 21). ‖ Pesiqta 67B: R. Levi (ca. 300) said in the name of R. Hama b. Hanina (ca. 260), "The one who repaid the earlier ones will also repay the later ones; as Egypt (was punished) with blood, so too Edom (Rome), as it says, 'I will give wonders in heaven and on earth: blood, fire, and pillars of smoke' (Joel 3:3).... As Egypt with pestilence, so too Edom, as it says, 'I will argue with him with pestilence and blood' (Ezek 38:22)." ‖ Tosefta Taʿanit 3.1 (218): R. Yose (ca. 150) said, "He will not bring a flood of water, but he will bring a flood of pestilence over the nations of the world in the days of the Messiah." ‖ Midrash Psalm 97 § 1 (211B): "Yahweh has acceded to his kingship (with the dawn of the messianic time) ..., the islands rejoice in great numbers" (Ps 97:1). Then he will come to fight with the nations of the world.... "Fire goes before him and consumes his enemies around him" (Ps 97:3): these are the nations of the world. ‖ In Pesiq. 51A, R. Azariah (ca. 380) interprets Song 2:10ff. in the following way, "'The winter is gone': this refers to the wicked (Roman) empire, which misleads people.... 'The rain is over, is gone': this refers to servitude.... 'The time of song זמיר has arrived': the time of the foreskin has come, to be cut off תזמר (= time of the uncircumcised, so that they may be destroyed), the time of the godless has come, to be shattered: 'Yahweh has shattered the sticks of the godless, the rod of rulers' (Isa 14:5). The time of the wicked (Roman) empire has come, to be destroyed; the time of the kingdom of heaven (the reign of God מלכות שמים) has come, to be revealed. As it says, 'Yahweh will be king over all the earth' (Zech 14:9). 'The voice of the turtledove is heard in our land': this refers to the king, the Messiah; for it says, 'How beautiful on the mountains are the feet of those who bring news of joy' (Isa 52:7). 'The fig tree reddens its fruit.'" R. Hiyya b. Abba (ca. 280) said, "Right before the days of the Messiah a great pestilence will come, and the godless will be wiped out by it." — Parallels are found in Midr. Song. 2:13 (100B); Pesiq. Rab. 15 (74B).

c. 1 Enoch 63:10; 90:18, 26f.; 91:9: All the images of the pagans will be given up; the temples will be consumed with fire, and they will be removed from the whole earth, and they (the gentiles) will be cast into the damnation of fire and will perish in anger and in the massive eternal judgment." — 1 Enoch 56:8: "In those days, Sheol will unlock its jaws. They (the nations) will sink down and their demise will be over. Sheol will devour sinners in the sight of the elect." — It should be observed here that these passages do not differentiate the messianic judgment from the last judgment. ‖ Genesis Rabbah 20 (13B): R. Levi (ca. 300) said, "In the future (= days of the Messiah) God will take the nations and cast them into gehenna. He will say to them, 'Why did you torment my children?' Then they will answer him, 'From their midst and in their midst were some who came and vilified (denounced) them, one did this to the other.' Then God will take these and those and cast them into gehenna." ‖ TanḥumaB שמיני § 10 (14B): "He (God) looked and made the nations jump up" (Hab 3:6). What does "He made jump up" mean?… R. Aha (ca. 320) said, "He made them leap to gehenna." — The same is anonymous in TanḥB ברכה § 3 (27B). ‖ See Tg. Isa. 53:8, 9 see § Matt 8:17, A. ‖ Midrash Psalm 104 § 18 (223A): "When the sun rises, they draw back" (Ps 104:22); when the sun of the king, the Messiah, rises, the nations of the world draw back; "and they will lie down in their dwellings"; where will they go? Into gehenna.

d. 2 Baruch 72:2ff.: "When the time of my Messiah comes, he will call all the nations, and he will keep some alive and kill others. The following will come from him over the nations who will live: every people that does not know Israel and has not trampled the family of Jacob, this people is to remain alive, specifically because they will submit themselves among all peoples to your people. But all who took dominion over you or (otherwise) knew you, all these are to be handed over to the sword." ‖ Pesiqta Rabbati 1 (2A): "All flesh will come (to worship before my face)" (Isa 66:23). "All flesh": the *ʿakum* (non-Israelites; see S-B footnote 1 at § Matt 5:43, #1, n. *g*); but not all the *ʿakum*; rather the Messiah will accept (only) those who did not oppress Israel. ‖ 2 Baruch 13:1–12: "Then I, Baruch, stood on Mount Zion; and behold, a voice came from the heights (of heaven) and said to me, 'Stand on your feet, Baruch, and hear the word of the Almighty God! Since you have marveled at what has befallen Zion, you are certainly to be kept (namely alive in the future world) until the end of the times, so that you may live to bear witness.' If the (now) thriving cities (of the gentiles) ever say, 'Why has the Almighty God brought punishment on us (at the dawn of the messianic time)?,' you are to say to them, you along with those who are like you, all of you who have experienced this calamity (brought on Jerusalem): 'This is the calamity and the punishments that now come upon you and upon your people, because you castigated our people at its time, so that the nations may be completely castigated and then they are to remain (in this situation).' And if they say at that time, 'How long (will this last)?,' you are to say to them, 'You who have drunk clear wine, now drink from its yeast too!' The judgment of the exalted one is impartial. Therefore, he has not preserved his own children from the beginning, but rather has tormented them as well as those who hate them, because they sinned. Then they were castigated so that they could be cleansed of sin. But now, you peoples and nations, you are to be punished, because you have trampled the earth this whole time and have taken advantage of creation, as you should not have. For I have always shown good to you, but you have always denied the goodness!'"

e. Numbers Rabbah 13 (170B): "And his (Nahshon's) offering was a silver bowl …; a silver basin, 70 *shekels* according to the *shekel* of the sanctuary" (Num 7:13). He offered this corresponding to the kings of the house of David who would arise from him, who would rule over the sea and dry land under the firmament, as for example, Solomon and the king, the Messiah. Where do we read about Solomon? (A scriptural proof follows). Where do we read about the king, the Messiah? Because it is written: "Let him reign from sea to sea and from the (Euphrates) river to the ends of the earth" (Ps 72:8). Where do we hear about his rule over the land? Because it is written: "Every king will pay homage to him, all peoples will serve him" (Ps 72:11). It also says, "And behold, one like a son of man came with the clouds of heaven; ... and power was given to him ..." (Dan 7:13, 14). "And the stone that hit the image became a great rock and filled the whole earth" (Dan 2:35). So he (Nahshon) offered a bowl corresponding to the sea that surrounds the whole world and is like a bowl.... (He also offered) a silver basin מזרק, corresponding to the world which has been made like a ball that is tossed נזרק from hand to hand. Why its weight of 70 *shekels*? Because they both (Solomon and the Messiah) would rule over the 70 nations from one end of the world to the other. ‖ Deuteronomy Rabbah 1 (196A): "Yahweh your God has multiplied you (and see, now you are like the stars of the sky in number)" (Deut 1:10). Why did he bless them (with the expression) "like the stars"?... As the stars rule from one end of the world to the other, so too Israel. ‖ Pirqe Rabbi Eliezer 11 (6C): Ten kings have ruled from one end of the world to the other. The 1st king was God, for he rules as king in heaven and on earth. (2nd–8th king: Nimrod, Joseph, Solomon, Ahab, Nebuchadnezzar, Cyrus, Alexander of Macedonia.) The 9th king, this is the king, the Messiah, for he will rule as king from one end of the world to the other; as it is written, "The stone that hit the image became a great rock and filled the whole earth" (Dan 2:35). The 10th king: he returns the kingship to its Lord (God; see the sequence in 1 Cor 15:24).

f. Psalms of Solomon 17:30f.: "He (the Messiah) will keep the gentiles under his yoke so that they will serve him, and he will manifestly glorify the Lord before the whole world and will make Jerusalem pure and holy, as it was in the beginning, so that the nations will come from the ends of the earth to see its glory, bringing as a gift their (the Israelites') exhausted sons (who lived in the diaspora until that point), and to see the glory of the Lord with which God has glorified them." ‖ Jerusalem is the metropolis for all lands in Midr. Song. 1:5 (87B); Exod. Rab. 23 (85A); TanḥB דברים 2B below.

g. See SDeut § 1 (65A) at § Matt 1:21, #2, n. *b.*

h. Tanḥuma שופטים 19A: "If you approach a city to fight against it, call out to them for peace" (Deut 20:10). (Scripture) speaks of the king, the Messiah, who will begin peacefully with them; as it says, "He will offer peace to the *goyim*, and his dominion will go from sea to sea" (Zech 9:10). "And if they answer you peacefully" (Deut 20:11), so that they bind (obligate) themselves; as it says, "They will reforge their swords into plowshares and their spears into pruning hooks. No longer will a nation raise the sword against another nation, and they will no longer wage war." (Isa 2:4). "And every people that is in it will pay tribute to you and serve you" (Deut 20:11); they are to offer gifts to him (the Messiah). As it says, "The nobles will come from Egypt" (Ps 68:32), for they will come in a hurry with their gift, "Cush, its hands will at once make an offering to God" (Ps 68:32), for they will at one come with their gift. "But if they will not make peace with you" (Deut 20:12); if a spirit of unrest (confusion) enters into them so that they rise up against the king, the Messiah, then he will immediately kill them. As it says, "He strikes the earth with the rod of his mouth and by the breath of his lips he kills the godless" (Isa 11:4). ‖ Midrash Psalm 21 § 3 (90A): What does "the אֲרֶשֶׁת (the demand) of his lips" mean? The רְשׁוּת (force) that lies in his lips. If he (the Messiah) is told, "This and that land has risen up against you." He will answer them, "The grasshopper is to go and destroy it; for it says, "He strikes the earth with the rod of his mouth" (Isa 11:4). "This and that eparchy has risen up against you." (He will answer,) "The angel of death is to go and destroy them; for it says, 'And the villain (Satan = the angel of death) kills at the behest of the breath of his lips'" (so Midr. Isa. 11:4). – A parallel passage is found in Midr. Ps. 2 § 3 (13A), where at the conclusion it is added: When they see their great distress, they will come and prostrate before the king, the Messiah, as it says, "They will prostrate before you with their face to the earth" (Isa 49:23).

i. Psalms of Solomon 17:22, 28: "Gird him (the Messiah) with power, so that he may shatter unjust rulers, purify Jerusalem of gentiles who tread upon it despicably!... Neither resident alien nor foreigner may dwell among them in the future." ‖ Babylonian Talmud Baba Batra 75B: What does "over its assemblies" מִקְרָאֶהָ (Isa 4:5) mean? Rabbah († 330) said that R. Yohanan († 279) said, "The Jerusalem of the future world (here = days of the Messiah) will not be like the Jerusalem of this world. Whoever wanted to go up to the Jerusalem of this world went up to it; but only those who are invited הַמְזוּמָּנִין there will be allowed to go up to the Jerusalem of the future world" (מִקְרָאֶהָ in Isa 4:5 is thus interpreted as "those invited to it.")

k. Babylonian Talmud Sanhedrin 91B: Ulla (ca. 280) objected, "It is written, 'He will devour death forever, and Yahweh (so the Talmud cites) will wipe the tears away from every face' (Isa 25:8). It is also written, 'The young man will die at 100. No longer will there be in that place a child who lives (a few) days' (so the Talmud cites Isa 65:20. The 1st passage denies that death exists in the messianic time; the 2nd passage presupposes it). There is no contradiction: there it deals with Israelites, here with the nations of the world. But what do the nations of the world want? (They should not be destroyed in the messianic time!) Those are meant (who are left) of whom it is written, 'Aliens זרים will be there and pasture your flocks and sons of foreigners will be your field workers and your gardeners' (Isa 61:5)." ‖ Babylonian Talmud Šabbat 32B: Resh Laqish (ca. 250) said, "Whoever meticulously observes the commandment about the show fringes will attain (will be honored), so that 2,800 servants (slaves) serve him (specifically in the days of the Messiah); for it says, 'So says Yahweh of hosts: "In those days, it will happen that ten men from every tongue of the gentiles will fasten onto the tips of a Judean's tunic with the words, 'We wish to go with you' ..."' (Zech 8:23). (10 men from the 70 nations = 700 on 1 coat string, so 2,800 for four coat strings.)" – According to SNum 15:38 § 115 (34B), this interpretation of Zech 8:23 seems to have been known already by R. Hanina b. Antigonos (ca. 150). ‖ Midrash Ecclesiastes 2:8 (13B): R. Nathan (ca. 160) said, "... The nations of the world will be the Israelites' servants (slaves) in the future (= days of the Messiah); as it is written in Isaiah,[83] 'Aliens will be there

83. S-B: כמה שכתוב בישעיה corresponds to the formula καθὼς γέγραπται ἐν τῷ Ἡσαΐᾳ (Mark 1:2). The remark at § Mark 1:2f. can be supplemented by the material here.

and pasture your flocks and sons of foreigners will be your field workers and your gardeners' (Isa 61:5)." ‖ Pesiqta Rabbati 36 (162B): In that hour (when the Messiah is revealed to his people), God will make the light of the king, the Messiah, and of Israel shine forth, and all the nations of the world will be in darkness and gloom. And they will all go to the light of the Messiah and of Israel; as it is said, "And nations (*goyim*) will go to your light and kings to the rising of your radiance" (Isa 60:3). And they will come and lick the dust under the feet of the king, the Messiah; as it says, "And they will lick the dust of your feet" (Isa 49:23). And they will all come and fall on their face before the Messiah and before Israel and will say to them, "We wish to be servants (slaves) to you and to Israel." And everyone among the Israelites will have 2,800 servants (slaves); for it says, "And it will happen on that day (so the midr.) that ten men ..." (Zech 8:23; see above).

l. See Tanḥ. שופטים 19A above in n. *h.* ‖ Babylonian Talmud Pesaḥim 118B: Rab Kahana (ca. 250) said, "When R. Ishmael b. Yose (ca. 180) became sick, Rabbi († 217?) sent word to him, 'Tell us two or three things that you have said in the name of your father.' He sent word to him, 'My father said (the first saying follows, then the second), "One day Egypt will send a gift to the Messiah. He will think it should not be accepted from them."' Then God will say to the Messiah, 'Accept it from them; a shelter has been prepared for my children in Egypt!' Immediately 'the nobles will come from Egypt' (Ps 68:32). Cush will then draw a conclusion about itself by moving from the lesser to the greater: 'If this is the case with those who have enslaved them (the Israelites), should it not all the more be the case with me, the one who has not enslaved them?' God will say to the Messiah, 'Accept it from them!' Immediately 'Cush, its hands will hurriedly offer (gifts) to God' (Ps 68:32). The wicked empire (= Rome) will draw a conclusion about itself by moving from the lesser to the greater: 'If this is the case with those who are not their (Israel's) brothers, should it not all the more be the case with us who are their brothers?' Then God will say to Gabriel, 'Hit the animal of the reed חית קנה" (Ps 68:31)! Hit the animal and prepare חיה וקנה a community for yourself!'" — A parallel can be found in Exod. Rab. 35 (95B). ‖ Targum Isaiah 16:1: "They will bring tribute מִסִּין to the mountain טור of the community of Zion to the Messiah of Israel, who will have power over all the inhabitants of the desert."[84] ‖ The gifts that the nations will offer to the Messiah are discussed further in Gen. Rab. 78 (50C); Midr. Esth. 1:1 (83B); Midr. Ps. 68 § 15 (160B); see also Midr. Ps. 87 § 6 (189B); Midr. Song. 4:8 (114A); see some passages on this point at § Matt 2:11.

m. 4 Ezra 13:25f.: "When you have seen a man arising from the heart of the sea, this is the one the Most High keeps ages long, by whom he will redeem the creation (Messiah = world redeemer); he himself will fashion a new order among those who remain."

n. See 1 En. 48:4 at § Acts 13:47; see also the admittedly mostly different passages at § Luke 2:32. ‖ See Pesiq. Rab. 36 (162B) above in n. *k.* ‖ Midrash Psalm 72 § 5 (163B): As the sun and the moon shine in this world, so will the righteous shine in the future world

---

84. S-B: The passage has been misunderstood quite often since Christian Schöttgen, *Horae Hebraicae et Talmudicae in universum Novum Testamentum* (Leipzig: Christoph. Hekelii B. Filium, 1742), 2:165, 454; Leonhard Bertholdt, *Christologia Judaeorum Jesu apostolorumque aetate* (Erlangae: J.-J. Palm, 1811), 145. See § 1 Cor 10:4.

(in the days of the Messiah); as it says, "Nations (*goyim*) will go to your light and kings to the rising of your radiance" (Isa 60:3). ‖ TanḥumaB בהעלתך § 3 toward the end.

o. Tanḥuma ויחי 57B: "The obedience of the nations will be bestowed on him" (Gen 49:10). He (the Messiah) is the one to whom the gentiles will gather; as it says, "The shoot of Isaiah, who will be the banner of the nations, the gentiles will seek him out" (Isa 11:10). – The same is found in Gen. Rab. 99 (63C). ‖ Tanḥuma ויחי 57B: "The obedience of the nations יקהת עמים will be bestowed on him" (Gen 49:10). He will blunt יקהה (read this instead of יקהת) the teeth of the nations, as it says, "They (the gentiles) will put their hand over their mouth, their ears will be deaf" (Mic 7:16). A different explanation is as follows: "The obedience of the nations will be bestowed on him." יקהת (now interpreted = יִקָּהַת = יתקהת "will be gathered") refers to the one to whom they (the nations) will one day be gathered מתקהלין; as it says, "The shoot of Isaiah ..." (Isa 11:10, as before). – The same is found in Gen. Rab. 99 (63C).

p. Midrash Song of Songs 7:5 (127B): "The word of Yahweh concerning the land of Hadrach" (so the midr. here on Zech 9:1). Hadrach: this is the king, the Messiah, who will lead (הדריך wordplay on הדרך) all who come into the world to repentance before God. ‖ Tobit 14:6f.: "All gentiles will convert to the truth and fear of God, the Lord, and will bury their idols, and all the gentiles will praise the Lord, and his people will give thanks to God, and the Lord will exalt his people."

q. Testament of Judah 24: "Then the scepter of my kingdom will shine forth, and a sapling (the Messiah) will arise on your root (that is, the root of the tribe of Judah). And by him a scepter of righteousness will arise for the gentiles, to judge and to save all who call upon the Lord." – Armenian translation: "Then the shoot will proceed from me (Judah) and the scepter (the royal rod) of the kingship will sprout and the base will be laid from your rootstock. From the same the staff (scepter) of righteousness will arise for the gentiles, to judge and to save (deliver) all who call on him."

r. Babylonian Talmud ʿAbodah Zarah 3B: R. Yose (ca. 150) said, "In the future (= days of the Messiah) the nations of the world will come to become proselytes." ‖ Tosefta Berakot 6.2 (14): Whoever sees an idol (image of an idol, temple of an idol, etc.) says (as a word of praise), "Blessed the long-suffering one! Whoever sees a place from which an idol has been destroyed says, 'Blessed be the one who has destroyed idols from our land! May it be your will, Yahweh our God, that idolatry be eradicated from our land and all places in Israel; and turn the heart of those who venerate them to serve you!' (This is followed in other editions by:) This does not need to be said abroad, because the majority consists of *goyim*." R. Simeon (ca. 150) said, "This should also be said abroad, because they will one day become proselytes; as it says, 'Then I will give purified lips to the nations, so that they all may call on the name of Yahweh, to serve him with one shoulder (Zeph 3:9).'" – The complete text is found as a baraita in b. Ber. 57B, except it reads R. Simeon b. Eleazar (ca. 180) instead of R. Simeon. ‖ Numbers Rabbah 1 (135C): (R. Joshua b. Levi [ca. 250] said,) "In the future world (= days of the Messiah) when the nations see how God is with the Israelites, they will come to attach themselves to them (see Zech 8:23 at n. *k*)." The same is found in TanḥB במדבר §3 (3A). ‖ Midrash Song of Songs 1:3 (85B): R. Berekhiah (ca. 340) said, "The Israelites said to God, 'By bringing light to the world, your name will become great in the world.' And what is this light?" Redemption. For when you bring it to us, many aliens will come and become proselytes and will be added to us, as Jethro and Rahab. ‖ TanḥumaB ויּרא § 38 (54B): God said, "In this world individuals have become proselytes by the mediation of the righteous (in Israel); but in the future world (= days of the Messiah) I will bring the righteous (among the *goyim*) under the wings of the Shekinah, as it says, 'Then I will give purified lips to the nations ...' (Zeph 3:9)."

s. Tobit 13:11: "Many nations will come from afar to the name of the Lord our God with gifts in their hands, gifts for the king of heaven. From generation to generation they will praise you and sing praise to your name." ‖ Sibylline Oracles 3:710ff.: "Then (in the messianic time) all islands and cities will say how much the immortal God loves those men (the Israelites).... They will make sweet speech resound from their mouth in songs: 'Come, bowing down to the earth, let us all beseech the immortal king, the great and eternal God. Let us send gifts to the temple, for he alone is the ruler, and let us all remember the law of the Most High God, the law that is most just among all those on earth.... Come, falling on our face in the house of God, let us regale God our creator with songs....'" Sibylline Oracles 3:772ff.: "From the whole earth they will bring incense and gifts to the house of the great God, and there will be no other house among people to be known to posterity other than this one that God has given to believing men to honor." ‖ ʾAbot de Rabbi Nathan 35 at the end: R. Simeon b. Gamaliel (ca. 140) said, "In Jerusalem one day all the nations and kings will gather; as it says, 'All the gentiles will gather at Jerusalem in the name of Yahweh' (Jer 3:17)." ‖ Genesis Rabbah 88 (56B): Who would have expected that God would raise the fallen shack of David; as it says, "On that day I will raise the shack of David" (Amos 9:11). (Who would have expected) that the whole world would be one federation; as it says, "Then I will give purified lips to the nations, so that they all may call on the name of Yahweh, to serve him with one shoulder" (Zeph 3:9)! ‖ Midrash Psalm 66 § 1 (157B): "For the leader of music, a psalm. Rejoice in God, all lands, sing the honor of his name!" (Ps 66:1f.). This is what Scripture says, "Then I will give purified lips to the nations, so that they all may call on the name of Yahweh, to serve him with one shoulder" (Zeph 3:9). R. Yohanan († 279) said, "What is the service of God? Prayer תפלה; see Deut 11:13; Ps 100:2; 95:1; Dan 6:17 compared with Dan 6:11. Say to God, '"How formidable are your works!" (Ps 66:3). As it was said to him at the sea, "Who is like you among the gods, Yahweh" (Exod 15:11)?' So too I will not say to him, 'How formidable are your works!' And likewise Isaiah said, 'It will happen, as often as there is a new moon, on that new moon, and as often as the Sabbath comes, on that Sabbath, all flesh will come to worship before my face' (Isa 66:23). And it also says, 'All the nations you have made will come and worship' (Ps 86:9), and not only just all the *goyim*, but also 'the whole earth must worship you' (Ps 66:4)! Why? Because there will no longer be any kingship or ruler for flesh and blood. Likewise, the sons of Korah said, 'All you nations, clap your hands, rejoice in God with the sound of jubilation!' (Ps 47:2). Why? "For Yahweh, the Most High, is fearsome, a great king over the whole earth' (Ps 47:3). In that hour 'Yahweh will become king over all the earth; on that day Yahweh will be one and his name will be one' (Zech 14:9)." ‖ Midrash Psalm 96 § 2 (211A): "Give to Yahweh, you families of the nations, give to Yahweh honor and power" (Ps 96:7)! This pertains to the future (days of the Messiah). "Bring a gift" (Mincha) (Ps 96:8), for it is written: "Kings will bring you gifs" (Ps 68:30). "Worship Yahweh" (Ps 96:9), for it is written: "All flesh will come to worship before my face, says Yahweh" (Isa 66:23). On that day (it will happen): "Say among the *goyim*, 'Yahweh has become king' (Ps 96:10)." For it is written, "Yahweh will be king over all the earth" (Zech 14:9). "He also established the world" (Ps 96:10), through righteousness; "so that it does not falter" (Ps 96:10), for there will no longer be any godless people in the world. "He will judge the nations equitably" (Ps 96:10); for the nations will be judged before him only equitably (justly and fairly); and there is nothing in them for them to rely on (no merit in their favor), they will be destroyed. Then "the heavens will rejoice and the earth will exult" (Ps 96:11) over the redemption of Israel. "The field will rejoice" (Ps 96:12): this is the garden of Eden that will rejoice over the joy of the righteous. – It should be noted how here the days of the Messiah in the sense of a later time are so idealized that they seem to overlap with the eschatological *ʿolam ha-ba*. ‖ Targum Zephaniah 3:9: "Then I will change the language of the nations into the one chosen one, so that they may all worship in the name of Yahweh, so that they may all serve before him with one shoulder." ‖ Targum Zechariah 14:9: "The kingship of Yahweh will be revealed over all the inhabitants of the earth. In that time they will serve before Yahweh with one shoulder; for his name will be firmly established in the world, and there will be none beside him." ‖ Tanḥuma נח 15A: God said, "In this world my creatures have been split in two because of the evil inclination and have been divided into 70 languages; but in the future world (= days of the Messiah) they will all be like one shoulder, to call upon my name, and to serve me." As it says, "Then I will give the nations pure lips ..." (Zeph 3:9). And Israel's subjugation among the nations will cease so that they may serve God with joy; as it says, "Serve Yahweh with joy" (Ps 100:2). But the nations, the idolaters, will serve him with trembling. When, for example, someone's son serves him, he serves with joy. He says, "If I ruin something before my father, he will not become angry with me, for he loves me." Therefore, he serves with joy. But a foreign slave serves with fear. He says, "If I ruin something before him, he will become angry with me." Therefore, he serves him with fear. It is the same with the nations, the idolaters. What is written about them? "Why do the gentiles rage and the nations think vain things" (Ps 2:1)? The whole psalm speaks of the nations, the idolaters. What is written at the end of the psalm? "Serve Yahweh with fear and rejoice with trembling. Kiss the Son" (Ps 2:11f.). David says to them, "Watch yourselves and do not twist the way 'lest he become angry with you and you perish in the way' (Ps 2:12)." This means: he gets angry with you because of a small matter. But what is written about Israel? "Serve Yahweh with joy, come before his face with rejoicing" (Ps 100:2). – The same is found in a briefer form in TanḥB נח § 28 (28B). ‖ Midrash Psalm 86 § 4 (187A): "All the gentiles that you have made will come and worship before you, Yahweh" (Ps 86:9), whether they want to or not, with a broken neck.

t. Sifre Deuteronomy 32:12 § 315 (135A): "Yahweh alone led it (Israel)" (Deut 32:12) (the midr. reads: Yahweh settled it for himself alone). God said to the Israelites, "Just as you alone have lived in this world without having even the smallest pleasure from the nations of the world (Text: *ʿakum*), so in the future (= days of the Messiah) I will make you live so that none of the *ʿakum* (non-Israelites) will have even the smallest pleasure from you."

– See TanḥB נשא § 13 (16A) at § Rom 3:9 A, #1, n. *f.* "In the future too I will choose only you (Israelites)."

u. Babylonian Talmud Menaḥot 110A: Rab Shimi b. Hiyya (ca. 250) held against Rab († 247), "'From the rising of the sun until its setting my name is great among the gentiles, and everywhere incense and pure offerings are offered to my name; for my name is great among the gentiles' (Mal 1:11)." He answered him, "You are Shimi (and you raise such an objection)?... Since God is everywhere, (he can say,) 'Incense is offered to my name everywhere.'" (Where God accepts incense, it is, as it were, offered to him, even if in fact the only place it can be offered is in Jerusalem; drawing any implication about the gentiles presenting offerings is thus unjustified.) "What do you mean?" R. Samuel b. Nahman (ca. 260) said that R. Jonathan (ca. 220) said, "These are the students everywhere who devote themselves to the Torah. 'I count it for them' (God says) 'as if they lit incense and offered it to my name.' 'And pure offerings': this is the study of the Torah in purity: first one takes a wife and then studies the Torah (undisturbed by impure thoughts)." ‖ TanḥumaB אחרי § 14 (34B): R. Ammi (ca. 300) asked R. Samuel b. Nahman (ca. 260), "What does 'Everywhere incense is offered to my name' (Mal 1:11) mean? The Torah warns, 'Be careful not to offer your burnt offerings at any random place that you see, but rather in the place Yahweh will choose' (Deut 12:13f.). And likewise it says, 'Anyone from the house of Israel who ... slaughters ... a bull or a lamb and does not bring it to the entrance of the tent of revelation ..., it is to be counted for such a man as bloodguilt' (Lev 17:3f.). And the prophet says, 'Everywhere incense is offered to my name?!' R. Samuel b. Nahman answered him, "What is the pure offering that is lit everywhere and offered to God's name? This is the Mincha prayer (the eighteenth prayer to be prayed toward evening); for incense is nothing other than the Mincha prayer. As it says, 'May my prayer be as incense before you' (Ps 141:2). It also says, 'Elijah came near at the time when the Mincha goes up' (1 Kgs 18:36)." – A similar anonymous explanation is found in Num. Rab. 13 (169B). ‖ Pesiqta 60B: Rab Huna (ca. 350) said, "'From the rising of the sun ... incense and pure offering (Mincha) is offered to my name' (Mal 1:11). How is this so? Is there a pure Mincha in Babylon? God only meant, 'Since you (in your studies etc.) devote yourselves to them (to the portions of Scripture that deal with offerings, it is as if you presented (the said) offerings.'" ‖ Midrash Psalm 87 § 6 (190A): When they (those who have brought the Israelites from the places of exile to Jerusalem as a votive offering for Yahweh [Isa 66:20]) depart, to separate from the king, the Messiah, the nations before the Messiah will tell of the glory of the Israelites and say, "This one is a priest and this one a Levite and this one an (ordinary) Israelite." And why? Because they had been sold as slaves and their bloodlines had gone into oblivion because of their servitude in exile, and they (themselves) were forgotten and became *goyim* by compulsion. R. Eleazar (ca. 270) said, "'And I will also take some from them as Levitical priests, says Yahweh' (Isa 66:21); from the *goyim* who bring the Israelites to the king, the Messiah; from them he designates each one who is a priest or a Levite or a (plain) Israelite. 'And I will also take from them': from those who bring and from those who are brought,[85] (for it says,) 'and also' from them I will take,

85. S-B: This is according to the reading מן המביאים ומן המובאים; see Buber n. 36.

says Yahweh (the 'and also' implies: apart from those who bring, still others, namely the ones brought)." And where did Yahweh say this? R. Phineas, the priest, b. Hama (ca. 360) said, "'What is hidden belongs to Yahweh, our God' (Deut 29:28)." — Thus, those *goyim* from whose number God will one day take priests are originally Israelites who had gradually become *goyim* while abroad under the compulsion of distress.

v. See the baraita in b. Yebam. 24B at § Matt 23:15 A, n. *r*; the same is found in a baraita in b. ʿAbod. Zar. 3B.

w. Mekilta Exodus 17:16 (64A): "Truly the hand at the throne of Yahweh, Yahweh has war against Amalek from generation to generation" (Exod 17:16). R. Eliezer (ca. 90) said, "Yahweh swore by the throne of his glory that he would accept anyone (as a proselyte), irrespective of the people he may come from, but he will not accept from Amalek (= Esau = Rome) and his house." — The same is found in Pesiq. 28B; in Tanḥ. כי תצא 23A as a baraita in the name of R. Ilai (ca. 110); in Pesiq. Rab. 12 (51A) the author is R. Eliezer b. Jacob (ca. 150).

x. Babylonian Talmud Yebamot 24B in a baraita at § Matt 23:15 A, n. *r*.

y. Babylonian Talmud ʿAbodah Zarah 24A at § Matt 23:15 A, n. *b*.

z. Babylonian Talmud ʿAbodah Zarah 3B in a baraita at § Matt 23:15 A, n. *r*.

aa. Jerusalem Talmud ʿAbodah Zarah 2.40C.13: Rab Huna († 297) said in the name of Rab († 247), "'Then they weighed my payment: thirty pieces of silver' (Zech 11:12): these are the 30 commandments that one day (in the days of the Messiah) the Noachides (= non-Israelites) will take on themselves." The rabbis said, "These are the 30 righteous people whom the world will (never) lack." ‖ Genesis Rabbah 98 (62A): R. Hanin (ca. 300) said, "The Israelites will not need the teaching of the king, the Messiah, in the future; for it says, 'The *goyim* will seek him out' (Isa 11:10), but not the Israelites. If this is the case, why does the king, the Messiah, come and what will he do? (He will come) to collect the exiles of Israel and to give them (the *goyim*) 30 commandments. This is what is written, 'Then I said to them, "If it is pleasing in your sight (give me my payment...." Then they weighed my payment: thirty pieces of silver)' (Zech 11:12)." Rab († 247) said, "These are the 30 heroes (= righteous people, without whom the world could not continue to exist)." R. Yohanan († 279) said, "These are the 30 commandments (for the Noachides in the messianic time)." ‖ Midrash Psalm 21 § 1 (89A): "For the leader of music. A psalm of David. Yahweh, the king rejoices in your strength" (Ps 21:1f.). This is what Scripture says: "It will happen on that day that the shoot of Isaiah, who will be the banner of the nations—the gentiles will seek him out" (Isa 11:10). This is the Messiah, the son of David, who will be hidden until the time of the appointed date. R. Tanḥuma (ca. 380) said, "The king, the Messiah, will come only to give the 6 (read: 30) commandments to the nations of the world, pertaining to, for example, the sukkah, the festal bouquet, and phylacteries. But all the Israelites will study the Torah from God; as it says, 'All your sons will be disciples of Yahweh' (Isa 54:13). Why (will the Messiah come only to give the *goyim* 30 commandments)? Because of the passage of Scripture: 'The *goyim* will seek him out' (Isa 11:10)." ‖ In b. Ḥul. 92A the 30 commandments already belong to the past: "Then they weighed my payment: thirty pieces of silver" (Zech 11:12). R. (read: Rab) Judah († 299) said, "These are the 30 righteous ones among the nations of the world, for whose sake the nations of the world continue to exist." Ulla (ca. 280) said, "These are the

30 commandments, that the Noachides took on themselves, but they kept only three: the one that prohibits prescribing marriage for males (pederasty); and the other that prohibits them from weighing the flesh of a dead person in a meat store (for sale); and the third, which commands them to honor the Torah."

bb. See the baraita in b. ʿAbod. Zar. 3B at § Matt 23:15 A, n. *r*; Midr. Ps. 21 § 1 (89A) above in n. *aa.*

cc. See the saying of Abbayye († 338/39) in b. ʿAbod. Zar. 24A: Rab Joseph († 333) said, "What passage of Scripture (proves the opinion of R. Eliezer [ca. 90] that in the future all will impose themselves as proselytes)? 'Then I will give the nations pure lips ...' (Zeph 3:9)." Abbayye answered him, "But it might mean (only) that they will turn away from idolatry (but otherwise remain gentiles)!" Rab Joseph said to him, "It is written, 'So that they may serve him with one shoulder' (shoulder to shoulder with Israel; Zeph 3:9)."

dd. See the baraita in b. ʿAbod. Zar. 3B at § Matt 23:15 A, n. *r.* ‖ Jerusalem Talmud ʿAbodah Zarah 2.40C.19: R. Hiyya b. Lulianai (ca. 360) said in the name of R. Hoshaiah (I, ca. 225; II, ca. 300), "One day (in the days of the Messiah) the Noachides will take all the commandments on themselves. What is the scriptural basis? 'Then I will give the nations pure lips' (Zeph 3:9). But at the end they will fall away again. What is the scriptural basis? 'Let us tear apart their bonds and cast their chains off of us' (Ps 2:3). The one refers to the commandments concerning phylacteries, and the other the commandments concerning show threads." – See further at § Rev 20:8f.;[86] here there are also various opinions about the time of the appearance of Gog and Magog.

ee. See supporting passages in the excursus "Sheol, Gehenna, and the Garden of Eden," II, #10, n. *o.* ‖ TanḥumaB צו § 4 (8A): In the future world (after the days of the Messiah) when God takes vengeance on Esau (= Rome), what will Esau do? He will drape himself in his prayer shawl like a lion (another reading: like an elder) and come and sit down next to Jacob; for it says, "If you make your nest among the stars" (Obad 4), and by the "stars" only the Israelites are meant, as it says: "Look to heaven and count the stars.... So will your seed be" (Gen 15:5). Then Jacob will say to him, "My brother, you should not be like me! For it says, 'Woe, your word is death; woe, descend into Sheol!' (Hos 13:14 is interpreted in this way by taking אֱהִי where? as = אהי = הִי woe!) Pure woe were the edicts that you issued against me! You determined that I should serve idols: if I had done it, I would have incurred death by God's hand (the punishment of eradication), and if I had not done it, you would have killed me. Therefore, 'Woe, your word is death! Woe, descend קטבך into Sheol!'" This is a Greek word (i.e., קטבך is = κατάβα "descend"!). When Esau descends into Sheol, Jacob will remain all alone; as it says, "It will happen on all the earth, says Yahweh, that two parts will be eradicated, perish, and the third part will be left" (Zech 13:8). And the third part is nothing other than Israel; as it says, "On that day Israel will be the third" (Isa 19:24).... When Esau is removed from the world, God and Israel will remain; as it says, "My dove, my uninjured one, is one" (so Midr. Song. 6:9). It also says, "Yahweh settled it (Israel) alone, and there is no foreign god alongside him" (so Midr. Deut. 32:12; see SDeut 32:12 § 315 above

86. TN: There is no entry for § Rev 20:8f.

in n. *t*). – A parallel is found in Tanḥ. צי 139B. ‖ TanḥumaB שופטים § 10 (16B): "All the gods will worship him" (Ps 97:7). The nations of the world will say to their idols (on the day of the last judgment), "Come, we will worship before God, for you have led us astray." Immediately the idols will go right along (see Isa 2:18), and then God will cast the nations of the world into gehenna. This is why it says: "All who serve idols will be put to shame" (Ps 97:7). ‖ Midrash Psalm 49 § 2 (139B): ("The children of men and the sons of man" [Ps 49:3]:) these are the 70 nations who will one day go down to gehenna.

ff. Judith 16:18: "Woe to the nations that have risen up against my people. The Lord, the Almighty, will punish them on the day of judgment by putting fire and worms in their flesh (Isa 66:24) so that they will howl from pain forever." ‖ See further the excursus "Sheol, Gehenna, and the Garden of Eden," II, #10, n. *k*.

gg. Midrash Psalm 2 § 14 (16A): The nations of the world say, "This world has been made for us." In the future, when the day of the (last) judgment comes, they will be dragged into gehenna; as it says, "And the nations will be fires of lime" (Isa 33:12). It also says, "Strike with the sickle, for the harvest is ripe ..." (Joel 4:13). But the Israelites in the future will be the only ones left; as it says, "Yahweh will leave only him (Jacob = Israel)" (Deut 32:12; so the midr.). ‖ Deuteronomy Rabbah 2 (199C): R. Judah b. Simon (ca. 320) said, "'"It will happen on all the earth," says Yahweh, "that two parts will be eradicated, perish, and the third part will be left"' (Zech 13:8). The mouths that say, 'There are two divinities' (interpretation of פי שנים; those who profess the Christian faith are meant), will be eradicated and perish. And who will still be around that day? 'The third will be left:' the Israelites are meant, who are called threefold because they consist of three classes: the priests, the Levites, and the (plain) Israelites, (or) because they stem from three fathers, Abraham, Isaac and Jacob." ‖ See further at TanḥB צו § 4 above in n. *ee*.

hh. See supporting passages in the excursus "General or Partial Resurrection of the Dead?"

ii. Mishnah Sanhedrin 10.1: All Israel has a share in the future world; for it says, "And your people, they are all righteous ones; they will possess the land (in the sense of the midr. probably more correctly: the earth) forever." See the excursus "Sheol, Gehenna, and the Garden of Eden," II, #5.

3:9 B: For we have already charged Jews and gentiles, that they all stand under sin.

The fact of general sinfulness is a firm fact of experience for the ancient synagogue. Even the best could not survive if God entered into judgment with them; for they have all sinned.[a] There is no death without sin;[b] so, since all die, all must be sinners. Alongside this affirmation there are however other statements that offset the claims just made. A whole line of men are named who went through life without any sin: above all the three patriarchs Abraham, Isaac, and Jacob; also Elijah, Hezekiah, Benjamin, the son of Jacob, Amram, the father of Moses, Isai, the father of David, Chileab, the son of David, as well as Moses and Aaron.[c] People are mentioned who never tasted sin in their life,[d] or who kept the whole Torah from the first to the last letter.[e] Finally, some rabbis could boldly ask whether they had departed even a bit from the Torah. In all seriousness they think that they completely kept the whole law of God.[f] As far as we can see, no one ever tried to balance these two lines of thought with each other.[g]

a. 4 Ezra 3:21: "Because of his evil heart the first Adam (person) strayed into sin and guilt, and likewise all who were born from him." — 4 Ezra 7:46: "Who is there among the living who has not sinned? Who among those born of a woman has not broken your covenant?" — 4 Ezra 7:68: "For all who have been born are marred by godlessness, full of sins, laden with guilt." — 4 Ezra 8:35: "For in truth there is no one of those born of woman who has not sinned, no one of the living who has not done wrong." ‖ 2 Enoch 39:8: "As fearful and dangerous as it is to stand before the face of an earthly king, how much more terrible and dangerous it is to stand before the face of the heavenly king, the ruler over the living and the dead, and of the heavenly hosts! Who will survive in that endless pain?" ‖ TanḥumaB שופטים § 7 (15B): Rabban Yohanan b. Zakkai († ca. 80) had said, "'I will draw near to you in judgment and will be a swift witness about the sorcerers and adulterers and perjurers and those who slight the day laborer in his payment, who oppress the widow and orphan and alien' (Mal 3:5). Woe to us because of the day of judgment, woe to us because of the day of rebuke!" — See the similar remark of R. Eleazar b. Azariah (ca. 100) in Gen. Rab. 93 (59B) in the excursus "Sheol, Gehenna, and the Garden of Eden," II, #10, n. *l.* ‖ Leviticus Rabbah 14 (115B): "See, I was born in sin" (Ps 51:7). R. Aha (ca. 320) said, "Even if someone were the most pious among the pious, it is still not possible that he would not in some way be in sin." ‖ A baraita in b. ʿArak. 17A: R. Eliezer the elder (ca. 90) said, "If God entered into judgment with Abraham, Isaac, and Jacob, they would not survive because of the rebuke (i.e., because of the accusation that could be made against them); for it says, 'And now come here so that I may argue with you before Yahweh because of all the blessings of Yahweh that he has done to you and to your ancestors' (1 Sam 12:7)." — Light is shed on what the three patriarchs could be accused of in Midr. Eccl. 4:3 (22B); see § Matt 5:23, D. See also the following quotation. ‖ Midrash Psalm 143 § 1 (266B): "A psalm of David. Yahweh, hear my prayer, heed my plea .... Do not enter into judgment with your servant, for before you no one living is righteous" (Ps 143:1f.). Solomon said, "A king, who sits in the seat of judgment, separates all evil, looking with his eyes. Who can say, 'I have kept my heart pure, I have become pure of sin?'" (Prov 20:8). Who can say on the day of judgment, "I am pure of my sin? No person can stand." Likewise, he says, "Who can abide the day of his arrival and who can stand when he appears?" (Mal 3:2). Who can stand on the day of judgment? And, likewise, Jeremiah says, "Ask and see if a man can give birth! Why then do I see every man with his hands on his hips like a woman giving birth and all their faces have become pale?" (Jer 30:6). There is no person on that day whose face would be light-hearted, but rather "all faces have become pale," even Abraham because of Ishmael even Isaac because of Esau and even those above (the angelic realm) because of Israel (cf. the saying of R. Yohanan on Jer 30:6 in b. Sanh. 98B). For it says, "All faces will become pale." David said to him (God), "I ask you, lo, I plea before you that you answer me and show mercy to me because of that day." This is why it says, "Yahweh, hear my prayer ..." (Ps 143:1); if you do not show me mercy, who can stand? And, likewise, Job said, "O, if you would hide me in the kingdom of the dead" (Job 14:13)! God said to him, "Forever?" He answered. "Until the judgment is over, until the anger is gone, until the wrath is gone, 'until your wrath turns.'" Likewise, David said, "Do not enter into judgment with your servant ..." (Ps 143:2). David said before God, "Will you bring me into judgment? Is there a servant (slave) who enters into judgment with his lord?" And likewise Scripture says, "If I sinned, woe to me!" (Job 10:15). Why? Everything is your servant, and everything that is his belongs to his lord (see excursus "The Nature of Ancient Jewish Slavery"). And, likewise, it says, "Just do not do two things to me (then I will not hide from your face): remove your hand from me (and do not let terror of you numb me)" (Job 13:20f). "Remember that you formed me like clay.... Did you not clothe me with skin and flesh?... You have shown me life and grace" (Job 10:9, 11f.). With all that, will you place me in judgment? Why? "A human, born of woman, ... springs up like a flower ...; do you set your eyes on him, will you bring me to judgment!" (Job 14:1–3). This is why it says, "Who can say, 'I have kept my heart pure'" (Prov 20:9)? No one can declare himself זכות righteous in the judgment. Why? If they sinned against you. But there is no one who has not sinned!" (1 Kgs 8:46). Likewise, it says, "There is no one righteous on earth, who would do good and not sin" (Eccl 7:20). Even the heavens are not pure in his eyes, even the stars are not pure in his eyes. This is why it says, "For before you no one living כל חי is righteous" (Ps 143:2). What does "no one living" mean? No one living is righteous before you, look, are the dead righteous? Rather even the holy beings החיות of the upper world cannot justify themselves היצדק before you on that day. This is why it says, "For before you no one living is righteous." ‖ See b. Ḥag. 4B at § Matt 19:20 A, near the end; see b. Sanh. 101A in n. *f.*

b. See b. Šabb. 55A at § Matt 19:20 A, near beginning.

c. See m. Qidd. 4.14; b. B. Bat. 17A; Lev. Rab. 27 (125C); y. Ber. 4.8B.38; b. Šabb. 55A at § Matt 19:20 A.

d. For example, Midr. Eccl. 1:8 (9B) at § Matt 4:17 A, #2; b. Pesaḥ. 87A; b. ʿErub. 21B; Midr. Song. 7:14 (130A).

e. Babylonian Talmud Šabbat 55A at § Matt 19:20 A. —The expression: "to keep the Torah from א to ת" is found also in b. ʿAbod. Zar. 4A; Midr. Lam. 2:1 (62A); Tanḥ. משפטים 94A; see also § Luke 15:7 B.

f. Babylonian Talmud Sanhedrin 101A: (R. Eliezer [ca. 90]) said to him, "Aqiba († ca. 135), have I left behind anything from the whole Torah (omitted anything that I would not have fulfilled)?" They (his students) said to him, "Our teacher, you have taught us, 'There is no one righteous on earth who would do good and not sin!' (Eccl 7:20)." ‖ See b. Ketub. 77B; y. Taʿan. 3.66D.35 at § Matt 19:20 A, at the end.

g. For example, b. Šabb. 55A at § Matt 19:20 A: here after the opinion of R. Ammi that there is no death without sin, opposing sayings are juxtaposed, and it says in conclusion simply: "The objection of R. Ammi remains." Thereby it is confessed that there is no known way to balance these views.

On Ἰουδαῖοι καὶ Ἕλληνες, see § Rom 1:14, #3.

3:10–12, base passage Ps 14:1–3.

1. Septuagint Psalm 14:1–3: Εἶπεν ἄφρων ἐν καρδίᾳ αὐτοῦ· οὐκ ἔστι θεός, διέφθειραν καὶ ἐβδελύχθησαν ἐν ἐπιτηδεύμασιν, οὐκ ἔστι ποιῶν χρηστότητα, οὐκ ἔστιν ἕως ἑνός. Κύριος ἐκ τοῦ οὐρανοῦ διέκυψεν ἐπὶ τοὺς υἱοὺς τῶν ἀνθρώπων, τοῦ ἰδεῖν εἰ ἔστι συνιῶν ἢ ἐκζητῶν τὸν θεόν. Πάντες ἐξέκλιναν, ἅμα ἠχρεώθησαν, οὐκ ἔστι ποιῶν χρηστότητα, οὐκ ἔστιν ἕως ἑνός. ‖ Targum Psalm 14:1–3: "The fool said in his heart, 'There is no sovereignty of God on earth.' They corrupted their actions, kept away from good and found perdition. There was no one who did good. From heaven Yahweh looked closely on the children of men to see if there was someone with understanding, who sought instruction from before Yahweh. They all went astray, they had all become indolent. There was no one who did good, not even one."

2. By the fool נָבָל who speaks in Ps 14:1, the rabbinic scholars usually understand Esau and then, by his name, Rome; see examples at Midr. Ps. 14 § 2 and 3, and also the following:

> Midrash Psalm 14 § 3 (57A): "The fool said in his heart" (Ps 14:1): this is Esau the blasphemer. Why is he called a "fool" נָבָל? R. Judah (ca. 350) said in the name of R. Samuel (b. Nahman, ca. 260), "Because he has filled the whole world with shameful things נְבָלוֹת: he has established whorehouses, filthy houses (derogatory name for the idol temples), theaters and circuses [places of idolatry, probably should be removed as an intruding gloss]." R. Huna (ca. 350) said, "Because he has filled the whole land with the corpses נְבֵילוֹת of the Israelites; as it says, 'They have given the corpses of your servants as food to the birds of the sky' (Ps 79:2)." R. Abba (ca. 290) said, "Since he has done מְנַוֵּול shameful things (or since he has defiled himself מְנוּוָּל): he set up his statues at the entrance of a house of fornication, at the entrance of the toilets and the bathhouses. This is what is written, 'Disgust at you! The pride of your heart has misled you' (Jer 49:16)." R. Jacob (probably a contemporary of the previous one) said, "Because God will one day remove it as an unripe fruit נוֹבֶלֶת that falls from a tree; as it says, 'Sons foreigners withered יִבֹּלוּ' (as an explanation of נוֹבֶלֶת; Ps 18:46)."

3:13 A: Their throat is an open grave; they deceive with their tongues.

Verbatim in agreement with LXX Ps 5:9 (= Heb. 5:10). — Targum: "Their throat is opened like Sheol, they speak smooth-tongued words with their tongue."

3:13 B: Viper poison is under their lips.

Verbatim in agreement with LXX Ps 140:3. — Targum: "The poison of vipers is under their lips."

3:14: Their mouth is full of cursing and bitterness.

The underlying text is Ps 10:7: "His mouth is full of cursing and deception and oppression." — Septuagint: οὗ ἀρᾶς τὸ στόμα αὐτοῦ γέμει καὶ πικρίας καὶ δόλου. — Targum: "His mouth is full of curses, deceit, and deception."

3:15–17: Their feet rush to shed blood. Ruin and misery are on their paths and the way of peace they have not known.

Septuagint Isaiah 59:7f.: Οἱ δὲ πόδες αὐτῶν ἐπὶ πονηρίαν τρέχουσι, ταχινοὶ ἐκχέαι αἷμα, καὶ οἱ διαλογισμοὶ αὐτῶν διαλογισμοὶ ἀπὸ φόνων. σύντριμμα καὶ ταλαιπορία ἐν ταῖς ὁδοῖς αὐτῶν, καὶ ὁδὸν εἰρήνης οὐκ οἴδασι. — Targum: "(Their feet) rush to shed innocent blood; their thoughts are thoughts of violence; robbery and corruption are on their paths; the way of peace they do not know."

3:18: There is no fear of God before their eyes.

Septuagint Psalm 36:2: οὐκ ἔστι φόβος θεοῦ ἀπέναντι τῶν ὀφθαλμῶν αὐτοῦ. — Targum: "Recalcitrance (disobedience) said to the sinner in the inner place (literally: in the middle) of my heart. There is no fear of Yahweh before his eyes." (Rashi: "Recalcitrance פֶּשַׁע, which is the evil inclination, tells the godless that there should be no fear of God before his eyes.") — In the midrash, Ps 36:2 is used to characterize the completely wicked person.

See b. Ber. 61B at § Rom 2:15 B, #3, n. *k*. ‖ Midrash Psalm 36 § 2 (125A): When David looked at the Philistine Goliath and saw that he was armed as a hero like all kinds of weaponry, he said, "Who could overpower him?" But when he saw how he jeered and blasphemed, he said, "Now I will overpower him, for he does not fear מפחד God"; for it says, "The wicked man says to the godless, 'There is no fear of God before his eyes'" (Ps 36:2). Here you learn that God judges the godless only in the hour when there is no fear of him פחדו upon them. Likewise, you find that God has said to Israel, "Your wickedness will chastise you … and realize that your falling away from Yahweh is evil and bitter and that there is no fear of me in you" (Jer 2:19).

3:19 A: But we know that what the law says, it says to those who are under the law.

1. ὅσα ὁ νόμος λέγει. Since reference is obviously being made to the scriptural citations in verses 10–18, νόμος is meant in the broader sense = Holy Scripture; for altogether the citations are taken from the Nevi'im and Ketuvim. In rabbinic usage, תּוֹרָה is used in the same way in the broader sense = Holy Scripture. On this point, see § John 10:34. Here a few other supporting passages are given.

Babylonian Talmud Sukkah 51B: Rab († 247) said, "A passage of Scripture was found (to establish the separation of the genders in the forecourt of the women; see m. Sukkah 5.1–4 in the excursus "The Feast of Tabernacles," V), which was interpreted, 'The land shall mourn separately according to their tribes: the tribe of the house of David in particular and their wives separately ...' (Zech 12:12). Then it was said, 'Is a conclusion not to be drawn by moving from the lesser to the greater? If the Torah speaks of the future (= messianic) time, when people will be occupied with mourning and when the evil inclination will have no more power over them, saying, "The men separately and the women separately, how much more does that have to be the case now, when people are occupied with something celebratory and the evil inclination (to fornication) rules in them!"'" (Here Zech 12:12 is invoked as a citation from the Torah.) ‖ In a baraita in b. Sanh. 101A—see § Matt 9:15 A, n. *aa*—the Torah bemoans the fact that she is profaned when a verse from the Song of Songs is made into a king of profane song. The Song of Songs is thus a component of the Torah. ‖ Pesiqta Rabbati 3 (9A): R. Berekhiah the priest (ca. 340) said, "We read (speak the word מַשְׂמְרוֹת in Eccl 12:11) as מַסְמְרוֹת with samekh, and yet only משמרות is written (so that מִשְׁמָרוֹת can be spoken): as the divisions מִשְׁמָרוֹת of the priesthood are 24 in number, so the books of the Torah are 24 in number (thus all the books of the OT belong to the Torah)." Parallels are found in Tanḥ. בהעלותך 209B; Num. Rab. 14 (174A). ‖ Tanḥuma יתרי 88B: R. Joshua b. Nehemiah (ca. 350) said, "... The Torah is threefold (consists of 3 parts): Torah, Nevi'im, and Ketuvim. — Here the first occurrence of "Torah" is general = OT, and the last is particular = Pentateuch, just like the νόμος that occurs twice in Rom 3:19. A parallel is found in Pesiq. 105A; see also b. Šabb. 88A. ‖ Tanḥuma ראה 8B: The Israelites said to Asaph, "Is there another Torah so that you say, 'Here, my people, my Torah' (Ps 78:1)? We received it long ago from Mount Sinai!" He answered them, "The wicked in Israel will say that the Prophets and hagiographa are not Torah and will not believe in them; as it says, 'We (read this instead of "they") have not listened to the voice of Yahweh our God as to walk in his Torahs, which he set before us by his servants, the prophets' (Dan 9:10)." See, (here it is shown) that the prophets and hagiographa belong to the Torah. This is why it says, "Hear, my people, my Torah" (Ps 78:1). — A similar exposition is found in Midr. Ps. 78 § 1 (172B): Lest anyone say, "The psalms are not Torah: in fact, they are Torah." And so too the Prophets are Torah. This is why it says, "Hear, my people, my Torah" (Ps 78:1). — See further examples at § 1 Cor 14:21.

2. τοῖς ἐν τῷ νόμῳ, to those who are in the law as their sphere of life; in substance = those who stand under the law and therefore have to expect both the punishment threatened in the law as well as the promised recompense.

Pesiqta Rabbati 21 (107A): The community of Israel said before God, "Lord of the world, you persuaded me before you gave me the Torah. Then you laid the yoke of the commandments on my neck and I incurred punishment by them. If I had not accepted the Torah, I would be like one of the (other) nations, without recompense and without punishment." — This correctly designates the position of those under the law.

3:19 B: The whole world.

πᾶς ὁ κόσμος = כֹּל הָעוֹלָם = everyone; see § John 12:19.

Babylonian Talmud ʿAbodah Zarah 3B: Rab Judah († 299) said that Rab († 247) said, "The day has twelve hours. The first three God sits and occupies himself with the Torah;

the second he sits and judges the whole world כל העולם כולה. When he sees that the world deserves to be destroyed נתהייב (cf. ὑπόδικος γένηται in Rom 3:19), he gets up from the throne of (strict) justice and sits on the throne of mercy. The third he sits and nurtures (feeds) the whole world (now in the broader sense: all creation) from the horns of the wild oxen to the eggs (nits) of vermin. In the fourth, he sits and frolics (plays) with the Leviathan; as it says, 'You formed the Leviathan, to play with it' (so Midr. Ps. 104:26)."

3:20 A: For by the works of the law no flesh will be declared righteous before him.

1. ἐξ ἔργων νόμου. — Ancient rabbinic literature has no expression that formally overlaps with ἔργα νόμου; ἔργα νόμου would have to be rendered in Hebrew with מַעֲשֵׂי תוֹרָה, and in Aramaic with עוּבְדֵי אוֹרָיתָא. These expressions are not found among the rabbinic scholars.[87] However, in 2 Bar. 57:2 we read: "At that time (namely in the days of Abraham, Isaac, and Jacob) the law was unwritten but generally known among them, and the works of the commandments *opera praeceptorum* were fulfilled at that time, and faith in the future judgment was born at that time, and hope that the world will be renewed was built up at that time, and the promise of life to come was planted at that time." Here the "works of the commandments" עוּבְדֵי מִצְוָותָא (Hebrew מַעֲשֵׂי מִצְוֹת) are exactly what the apostle calls ἔργα νόμου, except that there the singular νόμος is replaced by the multiplicity of the individual commandments. It further says in 2 Bar. 48:38: "At that (end)time the change of the times will become visibly clear to everyone, because in all those times they defiled themselves and practiced deception and each one walked in his (own) works *in operibus suis* and did not remember the law of the Almighty." The "own works" are works that each one did according to his own discretion without considering the Torah. If the individual had let himself be guided by the regulations of the Torah, as was his duty, his works would have been *opera praeceptorum*, that is, works about which the Torah provides instruction, that are done on the basis of the Torah, that proceed from observing the Torah. The apostle would have given the same meaning to his ἔργα νόμου: these are works that result from keeping the law or fulfilling the commandments.

Since, among all other works, these works of fulfilling the commandments occupied pride of place for every Israelite loyal to the law, it comes as no surprise if now and then they are called "works" as such מַעֲשִׂים in rabbinic literature, particularly when studying the Torah is mentioned alongside them. For every Jew knew that when מַעֲשֶׂה was mentioned in connection with studying the Torah, what was meant was the practical doing of the

87. S-B: The name of the midrash work מַעֲשֵׂה תוֹרָה does not belong here. It would probably best to translate it: "Effects of the Torah"; see the text in Jellinek, *Beth ha-Midrash* 2.92–101.

Torah and the result of this doing correspondingly to the מעשים, namely the works of fulfilling the commandments.

In m. ʾAbot 3.17, R. Eleazar b. Azariah (ca. 110) says, "Everyone whose wisdom (= knowledge of the Torah) is greater than his works מִמַּעֲשָׂיו, what is he like? A tree that has many branches but few roots: the wind comes and uproots it and turns it over. But everyone whose works are greater than his wisdom, what is he like? A tree that has few branches but many roots; even if all the winds in the world come and blow on it, they will not move it from its place." ‖ ʾAbot de Rabbi Nathan 24: (Elisha b. Abbuyah [ca. 120]) further said, "A person who has works מעשים and has studied the Torah a lot is like a goblet that contains a stone (controlling its balance) …"; see § Matt 7:24 B. — In both passages, מעשים is used absolutely and designates the works of the law; see also 4 Ezra 8:33.

The adjective טוֹבִים is added to this מעשים several times, but not in order to designate them as so-called "good" works (i.e., as works of mercy), but rather as beautiful, right works in contrast to the evil works of godlessness.

See this phrase several times at the beginning of ʾAbot R. Nat. 24 at § Matt 7:24 B. ‖ Mishnah ʾAbot 3.11: R. Eleazar of Modiim († ca. 135) said, "Whoever desecrates the holy gifts, whoever scorns the feast days, whoever publicly shames his companion (= another person), whoever annuls the covenant of our father Abraham, whoever uncovers his face (brazenly) against the Torah, he has no share in the future world, even if good works מַעֲשִׂים טוֹבִים are in his hand." — The parallel SNum 15:31 § 112 (33A) (see in n. *b*) proves that works that fulfill the commandments are meant by "good" works.

The expressions מעשים or מעשים טיבים never became widely used designations for works of the law. The actual technical term for this is מִצְוֹת. — מִצְוָה means (α) commandment[a] = ἐντολή, (β) the work resulting from fulfilling the commandments[b] = ἔργον νόμου. It has been common to render מצוה in the latter meaning with "fulfilling a commandment." We have also regularly followed this usage in this work. One should keep in mind, though, that "fulfilling a commandment" is not meant in the abstract = "fulfilling a commandment," but rather in the concrete sense = "fruit, result of fulfilling a commandment" = work of the law.

a. Mishnah Qiddušin 1.7: (Only) men are bound to every commandment concerning the son מִצְוַת הַבֵּן that applies to the father, but women (e.g., mothers) are free from them. Both men and women (e.g., daughters) are bound to every commandment concerning the father מִצְוַת הָאָב that applies to the son. ‖ The commandments are more precisely designated as מִצְוֹת עֲשֵׂה = Do-Commandments and the prohibitions such as מִצְוֹת לֹא תַעֲשֶׂה = Do-Not-Commandments. Mishnah Qiddušin 1.7: (Only) men are bound to all the commandments מצות עשה that are actuated at a specific time, but women are free from them; both men and women are bound to all the commandments מצות עשה that are not actuated at a specific time. Both men and women are bound to all prohibitions מצות לא תעשה, irrespective of whether they are actuated at a specific time or not, except for the prohibitions: "you are not to mar (the edge of your beard)" (Lev 19:27), "you are not to round off (the outermost parts of your head; see Lev 19:27), and "you are not to defile yourself with the dead." ‖ Mishnah Qiddušin

1.9: Every commandment מצוה that is connected to the land (Israel) is valid only (has to be observed only) in the land (Israel), but those that are not bound to the land are valid both in the land and abroad, except for the prohibition concerning the *orlah* (Lev 19:23ff.) and concerning mixed seeds (in the vineyard; Deut 22:9).

b. Sifre Numbers 15:31 § 112 (33A): R. Eleazar of Modiim († ca. 135) said, "Whoever desecrates the holy gifts (e.g., offerings), whoever scorns the feasts and whoever annuls the covenant of our father Abraham, he deserves to be cast out of the world, even if he has many מִצְוֹת 'fulfillments of the commandments' (= works of the law) in his hand." — The parallel passage in m. ʾAbot 3.11 (see above) reads מעשים טובים instead of מצוות, a proof that both expressions could be used as synonyms when appropriate. ‖ Babylonian Talmud ʿAbodah Zarah 2A: R. Joshua b. Levi (ca. 250) said, "All fulfillments of the commandments מִצְוֹת which the Israelites do in this world will come and testify in their favor in the future world." ‖ Babylonian Talmud Taʿanit 11A: "A God of faithfulness without injustice" (Deut 32:4). Just as the godless will be punished in the future world even for a light transgression (sin עֲבֵירָה) that they commit, so the righteous are punished in this world because of a light transgression that they commit—"without injustice." Just as the righteous will be repaid in the future world even for a light fulfillment of the commandments מצוה that they do, so the godless are repaid in this world even for a fulfillment of the commandments מצוה that they do. — עֲבֵירָה = work that results from transgressing the law; similarly, מִצְוָה = work that results from fulfilling the law. ‖ מצות "Fulfillments of the commandments" = "works of the law," stand alongside "good works" מעשים טובים = "works of mercy" in the saying of R. Jonathan and R. Zeira in Gen. Rab. 9 (7A); see § Matt 6:19f., #1; see the same section for further examples of the way the two expressions are set alongside each other. ‖ Sifre Deuteronomy 32:47 § 336 (141A): If kings and rulers desired to bind themselves (to relate themselves by marriage) to Esau, who had in his hand only one *mitzvah* (fulfillment of a commandment), namely that he honored his father, how much more will they have rushed to bind themselves to Jacob, who kept the whole Torah (thus had innumerable *mitzvoth* or works of the law to boast about)!

2. οὐ δικαιωθήδεται. — On δικαιόω see § Rom 3:4 C, #1.

3. οὐ δικαιωθήσεται πᾶσα σὰρξ ἐνώπιον αὐτοῦ. — Underlying passage is Ps 143:2.

Psalm 143:2: כִּי לֹא־יִצְדַּק לְפָנֶיךָ כָל־חָי "for before you no one living is righteous." — Septuagint: ὅτι οὐ δικαιωθήσεται ἐνώπιόν σου πᾶς ζῶν. — Targum: "For before you nothing that lives is righteous יִזְכֵּי" (say this instead of יְזַכֵּי). — Psalm 143:2 may be cited in 1 En. 81:5: "Proclaim everything to the son of Methuselah and show to all your children that no flesh is righteous before the Lord, for he is their creator." Yet because of the closing word one should probably think of Job 4:17 as the underlying passage. — There may be a longer exposition on Ps 143:2 in Midr. Ps. 143 § 1 (266B) at § Rom 3:9 B, n. *a*.

3:20 B: By the law comes knowledge of sin.

See 2 Baruch 48:40: "Each one of the inhabitants of earth could have known when he acted sinfully (namely by the law), and yet they did not know my law because of their pride."

3:21 A: But now a righteousness of God has been revealed without the law.

δικαιοσύνη θεοῦ. — By this term the apostle Paul understands a righteousness that God attributes to the person. It comes about by God's judicial judgment deciding in favor of the person and thereby declaring him righteous, that is, it views him as one who satisfies God requirements. It is thus actually a δικαιοσύνη ἐκ θεοῦ (Phil 3:9), a righteousness that comes only from God, is produced by God, is bestowed by God. What is decisive for the judicial judgment of God is not the efforts of the person, the works that he can boast in on the basis of fulfilling the law so that his being declared righteous by God could be viewed as the compulsory, indebted payment μισθὸς κατὰ ὀφείλημα (Rom 4:4) for those efforts—for the works of the law will never be enough for a person to be declared righteous, since the law brings only knowledge of sin (Rom 3:20)—rather being declared righteous happens χωρὶς νόμου, without the mediation of the law (Rom 3:21), as a gift, free δωρεάν, solely by grace χάριτι (Rom 3:24). But being declared righteous is, on the part of humans, mediated by the believing response to God's loving purposes in Jesus Christ διὰ πίστεως Ἰησοῦ Χριστοῦ (Rom 3:22).

According to rabbinic theology as well, the Israelite becomes righteous צַדִּיק, Aram. זַכַּאי, by gaining God's judicial judgment in his favor, by God declaring him righteous צִדֵּק, זִכָּה. To this extent it could be said that strictly speaking the righteousness of an Israelite was also a δικαιοσύνη θεοῦ, a righteousness coming from God.[88] But now the difference immediately comes in here. Specifically, even if the Israelite becomes a righteous man by God recognizing him as such, this in no way implies that his righteousness in the actual sense of the word is produced initially by God; rather, the Israelite already possesses righteousness, specifically his own righteousness, before he is judged by God. He brings it with him before God's seat of judgment, and God either recognizes it or rejects it.

---

88. S-B: The term "righteousness of God" in the sense of Rom 3:21 was foreign to the ancient synagogue. See, for example, the interpretations that have been given to the expression צִדְקַת יהוה (Deut 33:21). Generally, Moses has been taken as the subject of Deut 33:21; then צדקת יהוה has been interpreted as: (a) = צדקה of Yahweh. Sifre Deuteronomy 33:21 § 355 (147B): "He (Moses) carried out the צדקה of Yahweh" (Deut 33:21)? How? What sort of צדקות (of Yahweh) did he show the Israelites? For the whole 40 years the Israelites spent in the wilderness, did the spring not arise and the manna fall for them, did they not have enough quail and did the clouds of glory not surround them? Rather (when it is said that he showed the beneficences of Yahweh, this happens) because it says: "If a poor person is among you" (Deut 15:7; in caring for the poor he showed his people beneficences according to Yahweh's example). A different explanation is as follows: "he carried out the צדקה of Yahweh and his laws." This teaches that righteousness (in judgment) is bound with the throne of glory. (As righteousness is a pillar of the divine throne, so too Moses carried out the righteousness in accordance with Yahweh's kind of righteousness.) — (b) = what is right or meritorious before Yahweh. Targum Onkelos Deuteronomy 33:21: "He carried out meritorious things זָכְוָן before Yahweh and his laws with Israel." — Targum Yerušalmi I Deuteronomy 33:21 is similar. — See δικαιοσύνη θεοῦ = "what is right before God" (James 1:20).

Thus, it is not a matter of God's judgment producing righteousness but rather assessing it. In this way in its origin the Israelite's righteousness is in reality not a δικαιοσύνη θεοῦ, but rather one's own righteousness ἰδία δικαιοσύνη (Rom 10:3). This righteousness of one's own that is only recognized by God comes about by observing the law. Therefore, it is not a δικαιοσύνη χωρὶς νόμου (Rom 3:21), but rather thoroughly a δικαιοσύνη ἐκ νόμου (Phil 3:9; Gal 3:21; Rom 10:5; 2 Bar. 67:6 [*justitia ex lege*; cf. 51:3]) or ἐν νόμῳ (Phil 3:6) or διὰ νόμου (Gal 2:21) or in brief δικαιοσύνη νόμου (T. Dan 6; see the citations from the pseudepigrapha at § Matt 5:20 A). Every observance of the law has as its fruit a מִצְוָה "fulfillment of the law" (= work of the law) or, if formulated with a view to the thought of repayment, a merit זָכוּת, just as conversely a transgression of the law has a עֲבֵירָה "sin" and thereby a debt חוֹבָה as its consequence. The relationship that exists in number and value between fulfillments of the commands or merits, on the one hand, and transgressions and the debt of sin, on the other hand, constitutes the Israelite's particular degree of righteousness before God. But this degree is known only to God; the individual Israelite does not know his account before God. The result is considered only at the hour of death: if the works of the law or the merits outweigh the transgressions or debts, the Israelite will be declared righteous by God and he attains a share in the life of the future world. This declaration of righteousness thus does not signify a gift of divine grace that would be given freely δωρεάν, without effort in return; rather, it is the well-deserved recompense for the works of the law that the Israelite did during his life on earth, a μισθὸς κατὰ ὀφείλημα. Yet if the transgressions or debts weigh more, the person in question is considered to be completely godless and falls into gehenna. God's grace comes forth only in the case of the mediocre, that is, in the case of those whose merit and guilt are equal in the scales: according to the school of Hillel. The divine grace accepts such people, although they would have earned the punishment of gehenna; according to the school of Shammai they must repent. More precisely it was said later in the spirit of the Hillelites: God takes away one note of debt or adds something from his own, from grace, until the scale bends in the direction of the merits. — On this point, see briefly at § Matt 5:20 A; see in more detail in the excursus "Preliminary Remarks on the Sermon on the Mount."

3:21 B: Attested to by the law and the prophets.

On the twofold division of the Old Testament canon, see § Matt 5:17 A. — Here reference may also be made to:

Midrash Psalm 90 § 4 (194B): R. Levi (ca. 300) said in the name of R. Hanina (ca. 225), "The eleven psalms that Moses said (authored; according to tradition, Ps 90–100), he spoke in the order (division) of the prophets. And why were they not recorded in the Torah (by Moses)? Because the one contains the words of Torah and the other (the 11 psalms) contains words of prophecy." — Here the psalms are numbered among the prophetic books in accordance with the division of the canon into law and prophets.

3:23: For all have sinned.

On general sinfulness, see § Rom 3:9 B.

3:24: By the redemption in Christ Jesus.

On redemption by the Messiah, see § Matt 1:21 C through D.

3:25 A: Whom God presented as an atonement cover (instrument of atonement).

1. In the LXX, ἱλαστήριον renders כַּפֹּרֶת (see LXX Exod 25:17–22; 31:7; 35:12; 37:7–9; Lev 16:2, 13–15; Num 7:89). — כַּפֹּרֶת originally was probably simply = "top cover, lid," from כָּפַר "to cover" (Lev 25:17); then because of the meaning that this top cover had in the sacrificial ritual of the Day of Atonement (see Lev 16:14ff.), it was reconceived as "atonement cover" or "instrument of atonement" from כִּפֶּר "to atone." Accordingly, ἱλαστήριον = *kapporeth* = atonement cover. Similarly, Philo calls the top cover of the ark of the covenant ἱλαστήριον. *De profugis* 19 (Mangey's ed., 1:561): … "the lid of the ark of the covenant τὸ ἐπίθεμα τῆς κιβωτοῦ, but he calls it ἱλαστήριον" = atonement cover. — *De vita Mosis* 3.8 (Mangey's ed., 2:149f.): "Its (the ark of the covenant's) cover is like a lid πῶμα, τὸ λεγόμενον ἐν ἱεραῖς βίβλοις ἱλαστήριον.... Τὸ δὲ ἐπίθεμα τὸ προσαγορευόμενον ἱλαστήριον. — *De cherubim* 8 (Mangey's ed., 1.143): (Τὰ Χερουβίμ) bowed to the atonement cover ἱλαστήριον.

2. Description of the *kapporeth*.

The ark of the covenant (אָרוֹן,[89] אֲרוֹן הַבְּרִית, א׳ הָעֵדוּת) along with the *kapporeth* were lost in the destruction of the first temple; the second temple had no replacement for them; see #8 further below. What the rabbis report later about them rests solely on assumptions and combinations of different Scripture passages that seemed to provide a basis for the proposals. — According to Exod 25:11; 37:1f., the ark of the covenant was made of acacia wood and was coated inside and outside with pure gold; the *kapporeth* was made of pure gold (Exod 25:17; 37:6).[90] At least according to Scripture its

89. S-B: See a haggadic interpretation of the word אָרוֹן in y. Ber. 4.8C.20: (Why is the ark called) אָרוֹן? R. Hiyya the elder (ca. 200) and R. Yannai (ca. 225). The one said, "Because light אוֹרָה goes out into the world from there (from the tablets of the law located in the ark)." The other said, "Because a curse אֲרִירָה (because of transgression of the law) goes out into the world from there." — The closing statement in Midr. Song. 4:4 (112B) reads as follows: Because from there the curse goes out over the nations of the world (because of their nonacceptance of the Torah). Genesis Rabbah 55 (35B): It is the place from where fear יִרְאָה (because of transgression of the commands) goes out into the world.

90. S-B: In its color the gold was like purple (see Midr. Song. 3:10 [107B]; Num. Rab. 12 [165D]).

size was fixed: both the ark and its cover panel were 2.5 cubits long and 1.5 cubits wide (Exod 25:10, 17; 37:1, 6); the ark was 1.5 cubits high (Exod 25:10; 37:1), though there is no statement in Scripture about the height of the *kapporeth.* On the basis of a very dubious scriptural proof it was assumed that the *kapporeth* was 1 handbreadth high (thick).[a] Opinions diverged about the length of the cubit in view here: R. Meir (ca. 150) set the cubit at 6 handbreadths; R. Judah (ca. 150) at 5 handbreadths.[b] Since ark and cover had precisely the same length and width, the latter, if it was laid on the former, must have covered it so that it did not protrude beyond its side panels; the *kapporeth* was therefore like a cap or cover lid. Accordingly, it was assumed that it was fastened to the ark by pegs that were located on its underside and were vertically embedded in the side panels of the ark.[c] Others conceive of the *kapporeth* as an insert cover or top inlay that itself was inset onto the ark from above, specifically either so deep that the upper (external) side panel of the *kapporeth* formed precisely one face with the upper rim of the enclosing side panels of the ark, or even deeper, so that the side panels of the ark protruded a bit above its top surface. The part of the ark's side panels that stood above the *kapporeth* were then considered to be the crown frame זֵר, which according to Exod 25:11 was supposed to be made on the ark.[d] Once, it is explicitly emphasized that there was nothing separating the *kapporeth* as the cover and the tablets of the law placed in the ark,[e] that is, the ark of the covenant had no additional cover besides the *kapporeth.*[91] On the *kapporeth,* more precisely on the ends of its narrow sides, there were two cherubim with wings outspread (Exod 25:18ff.), whose faces were, according to one assumption, turned toward each other, while according to another assumption they were directed to the sanctuary of the temple.[f]

a. Babylonian Talmud Šabbat 92A: The ark was 9 handbreadths high and the *kapporeth* was 1 handbreadth high. ‖ Targum Yerušalmi I Exodus 25:17: "Its (the *kapporeth*'s) thickness should be one handbreadth פֻּשְׁכָּא." — Targum Yerušalmi I Exodus 37:6: "Its (the *kapporeth*'s) thickness was one handbreadth." Scriptural proof. Babylonian Talmud Sukkah 4B; 5A: Rab († 247) and R. Hanina (ca. 225) and R. Yohanan († 279, according to others R. Jonathan, ca. 220) said, "The ark was 9 handbreadths high and the *kapporeth* was 1 handbreadth high.... It is right that the ark was 9 handbreadths high; for it says, 'Let its height be 1.5 cubits' (Exod 25:10; see n. *b*; in R. Meir's opinion, 1 cubit = 6 handbreadths, 1.5 cubit = 9 handbreadths), but where does the notion come from that the *kapporeth* was 1 handbreadth high?" R. Hanina taught as a tannaitic tradition: "Of all the implements that Moses crafted, the Torah specified the measure of their length and width and height. In the case of the *kapporeth,* the measure of its length and width was specified, but the measure of its height

91. S-B: Christian theologians have wanted to conclude from the expression ἱλαστήριον ἐπίθεμα (LXX Exod 25:17) that the ark of the covenant had a special cover aside from the *kapporeth.*

was not specified.[92] Go and learn it from the smallest of the implements: 'Make around it (the table) a frame of one handbreadth' (Exod 25:25). Just as it is 1 handbreadth here, so also there (in the case of the *kapporeth*) it is 1 handbreadth...." Rab Huna († 297) said, "From this passage (the proof should be brought forth): 'Let him sprinkle on the front (literally: on the face) of the *kapporeth*' (Lev 16:14); and no face (of any person) is smaller than 1 handbreadth."

b. Jerusalem Talmud Šeqalim 6.49D.10: R. Yohanan († 279) said, "The ark was fashioned in accordance with a cubit that was 6 handbreadths. Which teacher in the Mishnah taught 'in accordance with a cubit of 6 handbreadths'? It was R. Meir (ca. 150). For we learned that R. Meir said, 'All cubits (that are given for the construction of the sanctuary) are cubits of medium size (= 6 handbreadths).' R. Judah (ca. 150) said, 'The cubits according to which the buildings were executed measured 6, and the cubits according to which the implements (such as the ark, *kapporeth*, etc.) were fashioned measured 5 handbreadths.'" (Then follows a detailed calculation of the volume of the ark according to both the cubit of R. Meir and that of R. Judah). Parallels are found in y. Soṭah 8.22C.44; b. B. Bat. 14A.

c. Jerusalem Talmud Šeqalim 6.49D.39: How did Bezalel make the ark? R. Hanina (ca. 225) said, "He made it from three boxes תֵּיבוֹת; two were of gold and one of wood. One of the gold ones he placed in the wooden one and then the wooden one in the golden one, and (in this way) he covered (coated) it (with gold); for it is written, 'Coat it with pure gold, inside and outside you are to coat it' (Exod 25:11). What does Scripture intend to teach with (the repeated): 'You are to coat'? It intends to include its (the wooden box's) upper rim (it should thus likewise be covered with gold)." R. Simeon b. Laqish (ca. 250) said, "He made it as one box and (then) he coated it; for it is written, 'Coat it with pure gold, inside and outside' (Exod 25:11). What does Scripture intend to teach with (the repeated): 'You are to coat'?" R. Phineas (ca. 360) said, "It intends to include the spaces between the individual sides (they too should be coated with pure gold)." — The same is found in y. Soṭah 8.22D.5; Midr. Song. 1:11 (92A). — Both of the opinions mentioned here presuppose that the three slices or layers of which the side panels of the ark consisted were level with each other at the upper rim, so that the *kapporeth*, having the same length and width, could be laid as a cover panel only on the upper rim of the ark. — Fully appropriately, Josephus then adds that the *kapporeth* was fastened by putting in pegs. *Jewish Antiquities* 3.6.5: "The cover panel τὸ ἐπίθεμα was put together with it (the ark) with golden pegs στρόφιγξι in a marvelous way, for everywhere it (the cover panel) was even with it, so that it in no way spoiled the look of the beautiful structure with protruding unevenness."

d. Babylonian Talmud Yoma 72B: Rahba (ca. 300) said that Rab Judah († 299) said, "Bezalel fashioned three arks: the middle one of wood was 9 handbreadths high (1 cubit = 6 handbreadths in the view of R. Meir); the inner one of gold was 8 handbreadths high; the outer one (of gold) was 10 handbreadths high plus some more. But in a baraita it says, 'It was 11 handbreadths high plus some more.' This does not entail a contradiction: the latter opinion is in agreement with the one who says that the thickness (of the bottom of the outer

92. S-B: See Philo, *Mos.* 3 § 8: "The length of this (cover) and the width have been specified, but not its height."

golden ark) amounts to 1 handbreadth; and the first opinion is in agreement with the one who said that the thickness does not amount to 1 handbreadth. And what does the 'plus some more' mean (in the baraita)? This is the crown (Exod 25:11)." — (α) The opinion of Rab Judah, "The wooden box, whose measurements are given in Exod 25:10, was 9 handbreadths high including its bottom. If one calculates with the thickness of the bottom being 1 handbreadth, its hollow still has a height of 8 handbreadths. The inner box of gold is 8 handbreadths high including the thickness of its bottom. Placed in the wooden box, its upper rim cuts off precisely with the upper rim of the wooden box. The outer box of gold has a height of 10 handbreadths + "some" including the thickness of its bottom, but the bottom does not measure 1 handbreadth. This + "some" is reserved for the thickness of the bottom of the outer golden box; about 10 handbreadths are left for the height. So if the wooden box with a height of 9 handbreadths together with the inner box of gold in it were placed in the outer box of gold, the side panels of the latter surpass the side panels of the latter by about 1 handbreadth. If, finally, the *kapporeth*, whose length and width are the same as the length and width of the wooden box (cf. Exod 25:10 with 25:17) is placed on top as a cover panel, it sinks down into the shell of the outer golden box surrounding the wooden box, up to the point that it comes to rest on the upper rims of the wooden and inner golden box which lie 1 handbreadth deeper. Since the thickness of the *kapporeth* itself is 1 handbreadth, now its upper side forms a surface with the upper rim of the surrounding outer golden box. — (β) The baraita: The outer box of gold has a height of 11 handbreadths + "some"; of this 1 handbreadth is reserved for the thickness of the bottom, and about 10 handbreadths + "some" are left as the height; of this 9 handbreadths are further used by the wooden box along with the inner golden box inside it which were placed inside; and 1 handbreadth + "some" are left, around which the outer golden box surpasses its insert. The *kapporeth* when laid on top sinks in until it in turn comes to rest on the upper rim of the wooden box and its insert; since the *kapporeth* itself is only 1 handbreadth thick, it is now surpassed by the side panels of the outer golden box by the + "some." This + "some" is the crown זֵיר in Exod 25:11.

e. Sifra Leviticus 16:2 (307A): "Before the *kapporeth*, which is on top of the ark" (Lev 16:2). What does Scripture intend to teach by saying this? If it said, "(Before) the *kapporeth*," there could be another (additional) cover כִּיסּוּי for the ark. Then Scripture teaches, "*Kapporeth*, which is on top of the ark"; there is one *kapporeth* for the ark, but there is not an (additional) cover for the ark. Even if there is no (additional) cover for the ark, there could still be something separating the *kapporeth* and the testimony (= the tablets of the law in the ark; e.g., a cover that was fashioned over the tablets of the law). Scripture teaches: "When the cloud of incense covers the *kapporeth*, which is over the testimony" (Lev 16:13). See, nothing separates the *kapporeth* and the testimony.

f. Cherub כְּרוּב, Aram. כְּרוּבָא, plural כְּרוּבִין.

α. Name. Babylonian Talmud Ḥagigah 13B: What does כְּרוּב mean? R. Abbahu (ca. 300) said, "'like a boy' כְּרָבְיָא, for רָבְיָא is what a child is called in Babylon." (כְּרוּב is thus composed from כְּ = "like" and רוֹבֶה, Aram. רָבְיָא, = "boy, lad.") There is a parallel in b. Sukkah 5B. ‖ Philo, *De vita Mosis* 3.8 (Mangey's ed., 2:150): Χερουβίμ, as the Greeks would say: ἐπίγνωσις καὶ ἐπιστήμη πολλή "knowledge and much insight." — כְּרוּבִין is interpreted as a notarikon[93] = כר = הֶכֵּר or הַכָּרָה "knowledge," רוֹב "plenty, a lot," בִּינָה "insight."[94] — β. Shape and size. According to R. Abbahu the cherubs were shaped like boys or lads (see b. Ḥag. 13B at α). This was probably the common opinion. Babylonian Talmud Sukkah 5B: Rab Aha b. Jacob (ca. 325) said, "It is traditional teaching that the face of a cherub is no smaller than one handbreadth...." Abbayye († 338/39) said, "Rather from here (we learn), 'The first face was the face of a cherub, the second face was the face of a human' (Ezek 10:14); but the cherub is the same thing as a human (why then are two expressions used to denote one and the same thing?)! The one (namely the face of a human) denotes a large face and the other a small face (the face of a boy)." ‖ Babylonian Talmud Baba Batra 99A: In a baraita it has been taught that Onkelos the proselyte (ca. 120) said, "The cherubs were shaped like boys." — So according to Rashi; then מַעֲשֵׂה צַעֲצֻעִים "sculpture" (2 Chr 3:10) is interpreted = מ׳ צָאֱצָאִים "shape of a child." ‖ Babylonian Talmud Yoma 54A: Rab Qattina (ca. 270) said, "When the Israelites went up (to Jerusalem) for the feast, the curtain was rolled away for them and they were shown the cherubs which hung on each other, and it was said to them, 'See, your love before God is like the love of man and wife!'" ‖ Josephus, *Jewish Antiquities* 3.6.5: "The cover (ἐπίθεμα) of the ark of the covenant had two figures; the Hebrews call them 'cherubs'; but they are winged figures ζῶα πετεινά that look like no other being that has been seen by humans." — It is incorrect to suppose that Josephus describes the cherubs here as bird-shaped; he calls them "winged figures," and he still could have thought of human figures. The situation is the same with the words of Philo in *Mos.* 3.8 (Mangey's ed., 2.150): "The cover τὸ ἐπίθεμα (of the ark of the covenant), which is called ἱλαστήριον 'instrument of atonement,' is the support for both of the winged ones τῶν πτηνῶν δυεῖν, which are called Χερουβίμ in the ancestral language." — There is in any case no need to think of bird figures, particularly since in Philo this is followed very soon by the words: πτηνὸν γὰρ ὁ σύμπας οὐρανός. ‖ Babylonian Talmud Sukkah 5B: "The house that king Solomon built for Yahweh had a length of 60 and a width of 20 (cubits) and a height of 30 cubits" (1 Kgs 6:2). It also says, "The height of the first cherub was 10 cubits and the second was just as high" (1 Kgs 6:26). And in a baraita it says, "As we find in the house of eternity (= temple) that the cherubs stood in the third part of the house (i.e., with their height reaching a 3rd part of the total height), so the cherubs also stood in the 3rd part of the house in the tent of meeting. How high was the tent of meeting? 10 cubits, for it is written, 'Let its plank be ten cubits in length' (Exod 26:16). How long were they (then)? 60 handbreadths (1 cubit = 6 handbreadths). What does the 3rd part measure? 20 handbreadths. Subtract from this the 10 handbreadths of the ark and the *kapporeth* (ark = 9 handbreadths, *kapporeth* = 1 handbreadth high), and there remain for them (the cherubs) 10 handbreadths." — According to these words the size of the cherubs corresponded precisely to the height of the ark and *kapporeth.* ‖ γ. Position. Babylonian Talmud Baba Batra 99A: How did (the cherubs) stand?

---

93. Hermann L. Strack, *Einleitung in den Talmud und Midraš*, 5th ed. (Munich: C. H. Beck, 1921), #30.

94. See Carl Siegfried, *Philo von Alexandria als Ausleger des alten Testaments: An sich selbst und nach seinem geschichtlichen Einfluss betracht* (Jena: Dufft, 1875), 215.

R. Yohanan († 279) and R. Eleazar (ca. 270). The one said, "Their faces are turned toward each other" (Exod 25:20); and the other said, "Their faces are turned toward the house (the holy place of the temple)" (2 Chr 3:13). Against the one who said "Their faces are turned toward each other," it is written: "Their faces are turned toward the house." This is not a contradiction: there (turned toward one another), it pertains to when the Israelites do God's will; here, it pertains to when the Israelites do not do God's will. Against the one who said, "Their faces are turned toward the house," see, it is written, "Their faces are turned toward each other." (This is not a contradiction:) they were turned sideways (turned partly toward the house, partly toward each other). Onkelos the proselyte (ca. 120) said, "The cherubs were shaped like boys (cf. above) and their faces were turned sideways, as when a student bids goodbye to his teacher." ‖ Babylonian Talmud Baba Batra 99A: Rabbanai said that Samuel († 254) said, "The cherubs (of the first temple) stood there by a miracle; for it says, 'The one wing of the cherub measured five cubits and the second wing of the cherub measured five cubits, ten cubits from the one end of his wings to the other end of his wings' (1 Kgs 6:24). Where then did their bodies stand (since the whole width of the holy of holies was only 20 cubits and was already taken up by the four wings)? Conclude from this the following: they stood there by a miracle." Abbayye († 338/39) objected: "Perhaps they stood such that they (the wings) stood out like those of chickens (till the middle of the back, so that the measure of their bodies was included in that of the wings)!" Raba († 352) objected: "Perhaps they (the cherubs) did not stand precisely opposite each other (so that the wing of one protruded beyond that of the other)!" Rab Aha bar Jacob (ca. 325) objected: "Perhaps they stood in a diagonal (forming an angle with their wings)!" Rab Huna b. Joshua (ca. 350) objected: "Perhaps the space (of the holy of holies) went further upward!" Rab Papa († 376) objected: "Perhaps their wings were bent (curved)!" Rab Ashi († 427) objected: "Perhaps they (the wings) were not set in a straight line (so that the wing of one cherub could be shoved under the wing of the other cherub)." See also b. Yoma 21A.

3. The location and orientation of the ark of the covenant in the holy of holies.

The ark of the covenant along with the *kapporeth* stood right in the middle of the holy of holies,[a] specifically on a stone that was called שְׁתִיָּה "foundation stone," because the world had been created starting from it.[b] From the proportions of the holy of holies it was concluded in agreement with a baraita that there was actually no room for the ark there, so that it, like the bodies of the cherubs (see #2, the end of n. *f*) stood there only by a miracle.[c] According to common assumption, the ark was to be positioned in such a way that it stood with its long sides parallel to the curtain of the holy of holies, that is, its long axis stood perpendicular to the long axis of the temple, thus in a north-south orientation. Yet this is contradicted by a passage in the Mishnah according to which the long axis of the ark was parallel to the long axis of the temple, and thus must have lain in an east-west orientation; but this passage can also be understood differently, as in fact it was in a baraita.[d] Specifically, the south-north orientation of the long axis of the ark of the covenant follows from the sayings about the sprinkling of blood toward the *kapporeth* on the Day of Atonement. All the passages agree that the blood was sprinkled onto the east front of the *kapporeth*; but the east front could not be one of the narrow sides of the *kapporeth*, since the cherubs were positioned there (Exod 25:18f.), so only a long side of the *kapporeth* was left as the east front, that is, the long axis of the ark lay in the north-south orientation.[e] There appears to have been less unity among the opinions about the affixing and orientation of the carrying rods of the ark of the covenant. Josephus assumes that the rings for the carrying rods were affixed on the long sides of the ark.[f] Then the carrying rods of the ark lay parallel to the long axis of the ark and must have been oriented north to south in the sanctuary—if the ark stood with its long sides parallel to the "holy place." However the opinion of the rabbis is that the carrying rods lay in an east-west orientation in the sanctuary, so that their front end touched the curtain of the holy of holies.[g] From this it followed, if the long sides of the ark lay parallel to the curtain, that the rings of the carrying rods were fixed on the narrow sides of the ark. This is also explicitly claimed by R. Judah (ca. 150) and is established in more detail.[h]

a. A baraita in b. B. Bat. 99A: The ark that Moses made had 10 cubits of free space on each side (in each direction; that is, it stood right in the middle of the holy of holies)"; see also b. Meg. 10B in n. *c* and Tanḥ. קדושים 169B in #8, n. *g*.

b. Tosefta Yoma 3.6 (186): A stone was there (in the holy of holies) since the days of the earlier prophets, and it was called foundation stone שתייה, and its height was 3 fingerbreadths from the earth, for from the beginning the ark was on it (hence the name "foundation stone"). But when the ark on it was taken away, incense was lit (on it) on the holy of holies. R. Yose (ca. 150) said, "Starting from it the world was established (hence the name "foundation stone"); for it says, 'God made the perfection of beauty shine forth from Zion' (so Midr. Ps. 50:2)." — See further in #8, n. *g*.

c. Babylonian Talmud Megillah 10B: R. Levi (ca. 300) said, "We have in our hands this word as a tradition from our fathers (i.e., as an ancient tradition): 'The position of the ark does not belong to the measure (of the holy of holies).' In a baraita it has similarly been taught: 'The ark that Moses made had 10 cubits (of free space) in each direction' (see in n. *a*). It is also written: 'Inside the *debir* (= holy of holies) the length was 20 cubits (and the width 20 cubits and the height 20 cubits)' (1 Kgs 6:20). It also says, 'The wing of one cherub was 10 cubits and the wing of the other cherub was 10 cubits' (cf. 1 Kgs 6:24f.; 2 Chr 3:11ff.). Where then did the ark itself stand (if it had 10 cubits of free space on its sides)? From this I conclude only that it stood there by a miracle." — A parallel is found in b. B. Bat. 99A, where R. Yohanan († 279) is named as the author alongside R. Levi; see further in b. Yoma 21A.

d. Mishnah Menaḥot 11.6: All the implements that were in the sanctuary stood with their longitudinal direction in the longitudinal direction of the temple (so from east to west). — Since the ark was among the "implements," it too must have stood in this direction. But this is contradicted by a baraita in b. Menaḥ. 98A in the most specific way: All implements in the sanctuary stood with their longitudinal direction in the longitudinal direction of the temple with the exception of the ark, whose longitudinal direction lay in the width orientation of the temple (so from north to south). — It has to be concluded that the general rule in the Mishnah was not intended so strictly that it permitted no exceptions. Perhaps it had in view only the implements that had been in the temple only until recent times; but the ark was not among them.

e. For sprinkling blood on the eastern side of the *kapporeth*, see SLev 16:14 (314A); b. Yoma 55A; Tg. Yer. I Lev. 16:14 in #6, n. *c*.

f. Josephus, *Jewish Antiquities* 3.6.5: "Into each of the two longer side panels (of the ark) two golden rings were inset, and they went through the entire piece of wood, and through them two gilded rods were laid on each side of the ark, so that it (the ark) could be moved with their help whenever it was necessary; for it was transported not by draft cattle, but rather it was carried by the priests (on their shoulders)."

g. Tosefta Yoma 3.7 (186): The two carrying rods of the ark stood out so far from the ark that they reached to the curtain (of the holy of holies); for it says, "(Both) the rods were long" (1 Kgs 8:8). Then were they perhaps not visible from inside (i.e., from the holy place)? Scripture teaches: "The tips of the rods were seen" (1 Kgs 8:8). Then perhaps they tore apart the curtain? Scripture teaches: "They were not visible outside" (1 Kgs 8:8). Say therefore, "The rods were so long that they reached the curtain, and they pushed back the curtain (outwardly), and so they were seen from inside, and concerning them one finds the following explanation (clarification) in the kabbalah (= non-Pentateuchal Scripture): 'My beloved is to me a bundle of myrrh that rests between my breasts' (Song 1:13)." — The meaning of this citation is made clear by the parallel in b. Menaḥ. 98A, B: "Both the rods pressed the curtain back and protruded so that they looked like the breasts of a woman." — Yahweh is thus the bundle of myrrh because he is enthroned on the ark of the covenant between the carrying rods which in the curtain looked like a woman's breasts. — See a partial parallel also in b. Yoma 54A, though here the anonymous interpretation of 1 Kgs 8:8 is attributed to the Babylonian Rab Judah († 299). — Babylonian Talmud Yoma 72A: R. Yose b. Hanina (ca. 270) juxtaposed the following passages: "'The rods should be in the rings of the ark. They are not to be removed from it' (Exod 25:15); and 'Bring the rods into the rings' Exod 25:14 (as if it were talking about a repeated action). How should this be understood? They sat loosely (in the rings) without slipping from these. In the baraita it likewise says: 'The rods should be in the rings of the ark.' Perhaps they are not to move from their place? It says, 'Bring the rods into the rings!' Perhaps they are to be brought in and taken out again? It says, 'The rods should be in the rings of the ark.' How is this? They sat loosely (in the rings) without slipping from these." (Rashi: "The rods were thick at the ends and thin in the middle.")

h. Babylonian Talmud Menaḥot 98B: How do we know that the rods of the ark were on its width side (that is, on its narrow sides)? Perhaps they were not on the long side of the ark. R. Judah (ca. 150) said, "Two men cannot walk (next to each other) at a distance of one and a half cubits (and carry the load on their shoulders)." (In order for there to be space for them, the carrying rods were affixed to the narrow sides.)

Only if the ark was constructed in such a way that its long axis lay in a north-south orientation, and only if the carrying rods were affixed on the narrow sides so that they pointed east to west, only then can this account for the manner the Mishnah has the high priest go on the Day of Atonement to the *kapporeth.* Mishnah Yoma 5.1ff.: He (the high priest on the Day of Atonement) took the brazier in his right hand and the spoon (with the incense) in his left hand and walked through the temple until he came between the two curtains that separated the holy place from the holy of holies. But between them there was one cubit of space.... The outer (curtain) was attached (only) on the south side and the inner one on the north side. He went between the two until he came to the north side. When he had reached the north side, he would then turn his face to the south, go further with the curtain at his left side until he came to the ark. Once he had reached the ark, he would set the pan between the two carrying rods and would shake the incense onto the coals so that the house was filled with smoke. Then he went out as he had come in.... He took the blood from the one who had stirred it up, went himself to the same place he had gone (before), stepped onto the same spot where he had stood (before), and sprinkled some of the blood.... He went out.... The ram was brought to him, he slaughtered it and collected its blood in a bowl, went into the same place he had gone (before), stepped into the same place where he had stood (before), and sprinkled some of the blood.... He went out.... — According to these words the high priest went behind the inner curtain at the north side and thereby into the holy of holies; then he would turn left and went while the curtain was at his left, southward until he came to the ark. If the carrying rods had lain on the two long sides of the ark positioned in the middle of the holy of holies, its orientation would have been the same as those of the long axis of the ark from north to south, but the high priest would not have bumped into the ark at all by going southward along the curtain. On his path he came into contact with the ark only if its carrying rods were affixed to its narrow sides and reached the curtain in a west-east orientation. Then he could, as soon as he had reached the carrying rods, put the brazier down between these and light the incense. It further says that the high priest sprinkled the blood from the same place where he had stood before and prepared the incense, that is, he stood between the carrying rods while he sprinkled the blood. But the blood was sprinkled against the long side of the *kapporeth* that was directed toward the east, and yet he stood between the rods while doing this, so it follows from this that the carrying rods lay perpendicular to the long axis of the ark. In other words, they were affixed to the narrow sides of the ark and had an east-west orientation in the holy of holies.

4. The *kapporeth* is the site of God's presence.

Here belong all the passages that speak of God's dwelling in the tent of meeting or in the first temple;[a] for here the ark of the covenant or the *kapporeth* is always thought of as the actual site of the divine presence. But there are also passages that explicitly designate the latter places themselves as the site where God stays and dwells among his people.[b]

a. Only two supporting passages follow here, one from the pseudepigrapha and one from the midrash. 2 Baruch 64:6: "The nefariousness of Manasseh became so bad that the glory of the Most High departed from the sanctuary." ‖ Pesiqta Rabbati 5 (18B): "It happened ויהי at the time when Moses had finished erecting the dwelling" (Num 7:1). Rab († 247) said, "(Wherever ויהי is written in Scripture, it indicates that what is spoken of in the passage in question) is something that was made (came into being) only now. Since the world had been created, the Shekinah (divine presence, divinity) did not dwell with those below; only after the dwelling (tent of meeting) was constructed did the Shekinah dwell with those below." R. Simeon b. Yohai (ca. 150) said, "What does ויהי 'and it happened' mean? Something that had existed, then had ceased and finally was (came into being) again as before. For you find that in the beginning of the creation of the world the Shekinah dwelt with those below; see, 'They heard the voice of Yahweh-Elohim when he went for a walk in the garden' (Gen 3:8). When the first man had sinned, the Shekinah went up into the 1st heaven (of 7). Cain arose and killed his brother; then it went up into the 2nd heaven. The generation of Enosh arose and they sinned; see, 'Then they began to name idols with the name of Yahweh'[95] (Gen 4:26); then it went up into the 3rd heaven. The generation of the flood arose, and they sinned; see, 'Yahweh saw that the wickedness of humanity upon the earth was great' (Gen 6:5); then it went up into the 4th heaven. The generation of the dispersal arose and the Shekinah went up into the 5th heaven. The Sodomites arose, and it went up into the 6th heaven, because they were sinners; see, 'The people of Sodom were wicked and sinful' (Gen 13:13). The Philistines came and sinned; see, 'King Abimelech of Gerar sent and took Sarah' (Gen 20:2); then it went up into the 7th heaven. Abraham came and secured for himself good works, and the Shekinah descended from the 7th heaven to the 6th. Isaac came and stretched his neck out on the altar, and it descended from the 6th to the 5th. Jacob came and put up tents for the Torah; see, 'Jacob was a pious man, sitting in tents (to occupy himself with the Torah)' (Gen 25:27); then the Shekinah descended from the 5th to the 4th. Levi came and made it descend from the 4th to the 3rd. Kohath came and made it descend from the 3rd to the 2nd. Amram came and made it descend to the 1st.... Moses came and made it descend to below (onto the earth); see: 'The cloud covered the tent and the glory of Yahweh filled the dwelling.'" — Parallels are found in Tanḥ. פקודי 129B; very briefly in Num. Rab. 12 (166A); TanḥB נשא § 24 (19A.18), though here the beginning has "Rabbi" instead of Rab. — This explanation apparently enjoyed a certain popularity; it is therefore later connected with various authors. R. Isaac (ca. 300), connects it to Ps 37:29 in, for example, Pesiq. 1B; Midr. Song. 5:1 (117B); Gen. Rab. 19 (13A); it is anonymous in Pesiq. Rab. 5 (18B); R. Abba b. Kahana (ca. 310), connects it to Gen 3:8 in, for example, Pesiq. 1B; Midr. Song. 5:1 (117B), though here "bar Kahana" should be added to R. Abba; Gen. Rab. 19 (13A); R. Simeon b. Yosena (ca. 270?) connects it to Song 5:1 in, for example, Pesiq. 1A; Midr. Song. 5:1 (117B); Pesiq. Rab. 5 (17B).

b. Babylonian Talmud Sanhedrin 7A: Someone had once said (to his wife), "When our love was strong, we lay on the sword's width (edge); now, since our love is no longer strong, a bed of 60 cubits is no longer wide enough for us." Rab Huna († 297) said, "Verses of Scripture are written for this. First it says, 'I will position myself there for you and will speak

95. S-B: This is how R. Yose (ca. 150), interpreted the passage in Mek. Exod. 20:3 (74B); SDeut 11:16 § 43 (81B); the same is propounded by R. Aha (ca. 320), in Gen. Rab. 23 (15D); however, R. Simon (ca. 280): Then there was a rebellion against the name of Yahweh; see Gen. Rab. 23 (15D). See § Rom 1:23 A, #2, D, n. *m*.

with you from above the *kapporeth* between the two cherubs' (Exod 25:22); and in a baraita it says, 'The ark was nine and the *kapporeth* one handbreadth high. See, there are here ten handbreadths' (thus in the beginning God managed with such a narrow space to dwell among Israel). Then it says, 'The house that king Solomon built for Yahweh had a length of 60 cubits ...' (1 Kgs 6:2). And, finally, it says, 'Thus Yahweh speaks, "Heaven is my throne" ...' (Isa 66:1)." ‖ Pesiqta 171A: R. Judan of Gallaia (ca. 275) opened his presentation with the passage: "'Does the eagle rise at your behest and build his nest on high?' (Job 39:27). God said to Aaron, 'Have I made my Shekinah dwell on the ark at the word of your mouth, or have I made my Shekinah go up from the ark at the word of your mouth?'" ‖ Pesiqta Rabbati 47 (190A): (God said to a grumbling Job), "Are you greater than Aaron? For I have shown such an honor to none of the creatures of the world as I have to him. When he went into the holy of holies (on the Day of Atonement) clothed with eight vestments, the angels of service fled before him: 'No person should be in the tent of revelation when he goes in' (Lev 16:17). The angels of service are meant: 'And their faces were like the countenance of a person' (Ezek 1:10). They showed him honor and fled before him. And my glory had filled the house, 'and the priests could not remain standing to serve before the cloud; for the glory of Yahweh filled the house' (1 Kgs 8:11). But when he went in, I showed him honor and made my glory ascend between the two cherubs. This is what 'Does the eagle rise at your behest?' (Job 39:27) means." R. Tanḥuma (ca. 380) said, "'At your behest': namely at the entrance of Aaron (= at your behest) God made his glory ascend between the two cherubs. 'Does the eagle rise': this is God; see, 'Like an eagle he stirs up his nest' (Deut 32:11). And if he stirs up his nest, 'he dwells on the rock and abides on jagged rocks and mountain peaks' (Job 39:28): although I made my glory ascend at his entrance, it dwells on the rock (= ark of the covenant). When he had gone out, it would return and fill the house." ‖ Targum Onkelos Leviticus 16:2: "I will appear in the cloud over the site of the *kapporeth*." ‖ Targum 1 Samuel 4:4: "The people sent to Shiloh and fetched the ark of the covenant of Yahweh Sabaoth whose Shekinah dwells above the cherubs." — Targum 1 Samuel 4:21, 22: "The glory (of Yahweh) is removed from Israel, because the ark of Yahweh has been led away captive." ‖ Targum 2 Samuel 6:2: "David and all the people ... headed off ... to retrieve ... the ark of Yahweh, which was named after the name of Yahweh Sabaoth, whose Shekinah dwelt on it over the cherubs." ‖ Targum Psalms 80:2: "You leader of Israel, listen, ... whose Shekinah dwells between the cherubs, shine forth!" ‖ Targum Ezek. 9:3: "The glory of the God of Israel ascended on the cherub, above which it had dwelt in the holy of holies, and it took up residence on the threshold of the house." — Almost verbatim the same in Tg. Ezek. 10:4.

5. The *kapporeth* is the site of divine revelation.

Sifra Leviticus 1:1 (7B): "'Yahweh ... spoke to him (Moses) from the tent of revelation' (Lev 1:1). Perhaps from the whole house? Scripture teaches: 'From above the *kapporeth*' (Exod 25:22). If from above the *kapporeth*, then perhaps from the whole *kapporeth*? Scripture teaches: "Between the two cherubs" (Exod 25:22)." These are the words of R. Aqiba († ca. 135). R. Simeon b. Azzai (ca. 110) said, "It is not as if I wished to give a reply to the words of my teacher, but I would like to add something to his words. It says about the glory (of God): 'Do I not fill heaven and earth?' (Jer 23:24)—see the love (of God) toward Israel, what it has made this glory do. It compresses itself, if one may say so כביכול (see § Rom 3:5, n. *f*), in order to speak from above the *kapporeth* between the two cherubs." – Parallels are found in Num. Rab. 14 (178B); Leqach Tob Exod. 25:22 (in the edition of Buber, 1:90A). ‖ See Gen. Rab. 4 (4A) at § Matt 10:5 B, #5. ‖ Sifre Numbers 7:89 § 58 (15B). "When Moses went into the tent of revelation" (Num 7:89). Why is this said? When it says, "Yahweh spoke to him from the tent of revelation" (Lev 1:1), I conclude from this the following: (he spoke) from the actual tent of revelation. Then Scripture teaches: "I will position myself in that very place for you and speak with you from above the *kapporeth*" (Exod 25:22). Now it cannot be said, "from the tent of revelation," because it has already been said, "from above the *kapporeth*." Likewise it cannot be said, "from above the *kapporeth*," because it has already been said, "from the tent of revelation." How can both passages of Scripture stand (alongside each other)? This is the rule in the Torah: when two passages of Scripture contradict each other so that they cancel each other out, they are left in their place until a (further) passage of Scripture comes and produces a balance between them. Scripture teaches: "When Moses went into the tent of revelation ..." (Num 7:89); Scripture shows that Moses went in and stood in the tent of revelation, then the voice came down between the two cherubs from the highest heaven, and he heard the voice speaking to him from inside. – The same is found in Num. Rab. 14 (177C); here at the conclusion: Moses stood in the tent and the voice came down from heaven like a fiery beam (or: like a fiery tube; read סֵילוֹן = σωλήν instead of טילין) between the two cherubs, and he heard the voice speaking to him from inside. ‖ Numbers Rabbah 14 (178B): "He spoke to him (Moses)" (Num 7:89), and not to the angels of service who were there. Scripture thus indicates that the voice went out from the mouth of God like a beam (or: like a tube) into Moses' ear, so that the angels, who were in the middle (between God and Moses), did not hear it. So it also says, "God thunders miracles with his voice" (Job 37:5). ‖ Targum Onkelos Exodus 25:22: "I will keep my word ready for you there and from above the *kapporeth* between the two cherubs that are on the ark of the testimony I will tell you everything that I will assign to the children of Israel." – Similarly, Tg. Yer. I Exod. 25:22. ‖ Targum Yerušalmi I (Num 7:89): "When Moses went into the tent of meeting to speak with him, he heard the voice of the spirit that spoke with him when it had come down from the highest heaven onto the *kapporeth*, that was over the ark of the testimony, between the two cherubs. From there the word דִּבּוּר (= God) used to speak with him."

6. The *kapporeth* is a place of atonement.

Just how close together the *kapporeth* had coalesced with the idea of atonement for the Jewish conception is shown by the rendering of the word "*kapporeth*" in the targumim with "place of atonement" בֵּית כַּפּוֹרֵי[a] (כַּפּוֹרֵי inf. *paʿel*). This designation was then transferred metonymically over to the whole space of the holy of holies.[b] – There are precise regulations concerning the way atonement was carried out before the *kapporeth* on the Day of Atonement itself. During the presentation of the atoning sacrificial blood, the high priest took his place in the same spot where he had lit the incense after his first entrance into the holy of holies, that is, he stood between the two carrying rods of the ark of the covenant, his face turned toward the west (see m. Yoma 5.1ff. in #3, n. *h* and the remark there). He was not to let the sacrificial blood drip or splatter, but rather was to sprinkle it with the index finger of his right hand, eight times in total, once against the east side of the *kapporeth* (not on the top or surface of the *kapporeth*) and then seven times lower down against the ark of the covenant (cf. Lev 16:14). But the high priest did not have to pay attention to the precise place where the sprinklings fell; rather all his attention was supposed to be directed to counting the sprinklings. What is more, a particular way of counting was prescribed in order to protect against any error in the process. It was said that while sprinkling the high priest was to be "like a lasher." Just as a lasher paid attention only to counting the strikes lest he administer more than 40 blows minus 1, though he remained unconcerned with where the individual strokes fell, so too the high priest was supposed to proceed in the process of sprinkling the atoning blood. (There is, though, a different explanation of the expression "like a lasher"; see n. *c*.) The high priest had to pause in this procedure both while offering the blood of the sin offering of the young bull (Lev 16:11ff.) as well as while offering the blood of the sin offering of the goat (Lev 16:15).[c] — As for the effects of the atonement, a distinction has to be made between the atoning power of the Day of Atonement itself and the atoning power of the individual actions performed on the day. While the former was an all-encompassing power,[d] the latter remained more or less limited. So according to rabbinic opinion the kinds of blood sprinkled on the *kapporeth* on the Day of Atonement achieve only atonement for purity violations against the temple and the holy offerings.[e]

a. Leviticus 16:2: "I will appear in the cloud over the cover panel עַל־הַכַּפֹּרֶת"; Tg. Onk.: "Over the site (place) of the *kapporeth*" עַל בֵּית כַּפּוֹרְתָא; Tg. Yer. I: "In the clouds of my glory my Shekinah will appear above the place of atonement עַל בית כַּפּוֹרֵי." ‖ In 1 Chr 28:11 the holy of holies is called "house, place of the *kapporeth*" בֵּית הַכַּפֹּרֶת; the targum: "place of atonement בית כפורי."

b. For example, Tg. 1 Kgs. 6:5, 19, 20; 2 Chr. 3:16, where בית כפורי "place of atonement" serves as a replacement for the word in the underlying text דְּבִיר "the holy of holies."

c. Mishnah Yoma 5.3f. (cf. m. Yoma 5.1ff. in #3, n. *h*): (The high priest) took the blood (of the sin offering of the young bull) from the one who had stirred it up, went in (into the holy of holies) to the same place he had gone (before), stepped onto the same spot where he had stood (before between the carrying rods of the ark), and sprinkled הִזָּה some of it (the blood) once above and seven times below, but he did not pay attention to precisely where to sprinkle (= did not sprinkle precisely) either above or below, but rather (he proceeded) like a lasher. And he used to count like this: One (this counted for the sprinkling toward the top, then he moved downward for the sprinkling), one and one, one and two, one and three, one and four, one and five, one and six, one and seven. He went out and put it (the blood) on the golden rack that was in the holy place. The goat (for the sin offering) was brought to him, he slaughtered it and collected its blood in a bowl, went in (into the holy of holies) to the same place he had gone (before), stepped onto the same spot he had stood (before), and sprinkled some of it once above and seven times below, but he did not pay attention to precisely where to sprinkle either above or below, but rather (he proceeded) like a lasher. And he used to count like this: one, one and one, one and two etc. Then he went out and put it on a second rack that was in the holy place. ‖ Sifra Leviticus 16:14 (314A): "He shall take some of the blood of the young bull and sprinkle it with his finger at the front of the cover panel and he shall sprinkle it seven times before the cover panel" (Lev 16:14). "He shall sprinkle" וְהִזָּה, but he is not to be one who lets it drip הַמַּטִּיף; "he shall sprinkle," but he is not to be one who splashes (tilts it out) הַזּוֹרֵק. "With his finger"; it is said here "his finger" and it is said there (Lev 14:16) "his finger": as his right finger, which is mentioned there, is the most skillful finger on his right hand (i.e., his index finger) is, so too is his finger, which is mentioned here, the most skillful one on his right hand. "Against the eastern side of the *kapporeth*" (so the midrash interprets Lev 16:14: על פני הכפורת קדמה); this is a main passage (literally: "builds a family"[96]): everywhere where it says "the front side of the *kapporeth*," this refers to the side facing east. A different explanation is as follows: "Against the eastern side of the *kapporeth*": while sprinkling above or below he does not need to pay precise attention, but rather (he proceeds) as a lasher. "Let him sprinkle before the cover panel (*kapporeth*) seven times," and not seven drops. — See b. Yoma 55A in a baraita from the school of R. Eliezer b. Jacob (ca. 150): "'Against the eastern side of the *kapporeth*'; this is a main passage: everywhere where it says פני, this refers to the front (eastern) side." — Targum Yerušalmi I Leviticus 16:14: "Let him take some of the blood of the young bull and sprinkle it with his right (index) finger against the front side of the *kapporeth* facing east and let him sprinkle before the *kapporeth* לִקְדָם כפורתא seven times from the blood with his right (index) finger." ‖ A baraita in b. Yoma 55A: When he sprinkled, he did not sprinkle onto the *kapporeth*, but rather against the thick side (= front side) of the *kapporeth*. When he sprinkled above, his hand faced downward, and when he sprinkled below, his hand faced upward. — Jerusalem Talmud Yoma 5.42C.36: It is written: "Let him sprinkle onto על the *kapporeth*" (Lev 16:14); perhaps onto its top (the upper surface of the cover panel)?! Scripture teaches: "And let him sprinkle before לפני the cover panel" (Lev 16:14); perhaps onto its end face (front side)?! Scripture teaches: "onto" על and "before" לפני (thus denotes a place that lets both passages hold true, and this place is the upper edge of the front side). R. Zeira (ca. 300) said, "It (the blood) had to touch (the *kapporeth*)." R. Samuel b. Isaac (ca. 300) said, "It did not need to touch it." ‖ Babylonian Talmud Yoma 54B: What does "like a lasher" mean? Rab Judah († 299) showed (with a hand gesture): like the beater (who carries out the lashing punishment). — On this point Rashi remarks, "The one who beats with the strap begins (above) from the shoulders and beats further and further down." — This is the other explanation of the phrase "like a lasher" mentioned above. In that case it should be said that the high priest began with the sprinkling of blood above and then went further and further down the ark of the covenant. — In y. Yoma 5.42C.32 the question: What does

96. See Strack, *Einleitung in den Talmud und Midraš*, 97 #3.

"like a lasher" mean? is answered by R. Samuel b. Hananiah (?)[97] in the name of R. Eleazar (ca. 270): "Like the blow of a whip." (Perhaps the opinion here is the following: as the blows of the whip were laid on top of each other, so also the sprinklings of blood. But in that case the following have the other explanation in view: as the lasher pays attention only to counting, so also the high priest; they read:) R. Yohanan († 279) said, "Lest he errs." R. Zeira (ca. 300) said, "So that he finishes his sprinklings at seven."

d. See supporting passages at § Matt 12:32, #1.

e. Mishnah Šebiʿit 1.2ff.: "In every case where beforehand (before the action) it was known (that one was unclean) and where afterward it was known (that despite his impurity one went into the sanctuary or otherwise came into contact with something holy [e.g., sacrifices]), but in the meantime (while doing the action) it was hidden (was forgotten), see, such a one is due for a rising and falling sacrifice (one appropriate to his financial situation). If it was known beforehand but not afterward, the goat prepared in the inner place (in the holy of holies) and the Day of Atonement (guilt and punishment) are held in abeyance, until it comes to his consciousness; then he has to offer a rising and falling sacrifice. If it was not known beforehand, but it was afterward, the goat prepared outside (see Num 29:11) and the Day of Atonement make atonement for him; as it says, 'Outside of the sin offering of atonement' (Num 29:11). Whatever the latter makes atonement for, the former also makes atonement for: as the (goat prepared) in the inner place makes atonement only for what was known, so also the (goat prepared) outside makes atonement only for what was known. For what was known neither beforehand nor afterward, the goats of the festivals and the goats of the new moons make atonement." These are the words of R. Judah (ca. 150). R. Simeon (ca. 150) said, "The goats of the festivals make atonement, but not the goats of the new moons. And what do the goats of the new moons make atonement for? For the clean who ate something unclean." R. Meir (ca. 150) said, "The atonement of all goats is uniform for the defilement of the sanctuary and its holy offerings." R. Simeon said, "The goats of the new moons make atonement for the clean who ate something unclean, and the goats of the festivals make atonement for something that was not known beforehand or afterward, and the goat of the Day of Atonement makes atonement for something that was not known beforehand but was afterward." It was said to him (by the scholars), "How is that? Is one permitted to offer the one and not the other?" He answered them, "One is permitted to offer." They said to him, "Since their atonement is not uniform, how is one permitted to offer one instead of the other?" He answered them, "All are offered to make atonement for the defilement of the sanctuary and its holy offerings." R. Simeon b. Judah (from Kefar Ikos? [ca. 180]) said in his name, "The goats of the new moons make atonement for the clean who ate something unclean; the goats of the festivals go beyond these, for they make atonement for the clean who ate something unclean and for something that was known neither beforehand nor afterward. The goats of the Day of Atonement go beyond these, for they make atonement for the clean who ate something unclean, and for what was known neither beforehand nor afterward, and for what was not known beforehand but

97. S-B: Perhaps R. Samuel b. Inya (ca. 360) is intended.

was afterward." It was said to him, "How is that? Is one permitted to offer the one and not the other?" He answered, "Yes!" They said to him, "In that case they could offer the goats of the Day of Atonement on the new moons, but how could they offer the goats of the new moons on the Day of Atonement in order to make an atonement that does not inhere in them?" He answered them, "They are all offered to make atonement for the sanctuary and its holy offerings. For intentional defilement of the sanctuary and its holy offerings the goat prepared in the inner place and the goat of the Day of Atonement (in association with the former one) make atonement. For all other transgressions in the Torah, the light and the heavy, the intentional and the unintentional, the known and the unknown, commandments and prohibitions, to be punished by eradication (by God) or by death by a (worldly) court, the goat sent away into the wilderness makes atonement. This is the case for the (ordinary) Israelites as well as the priests and the anointed priest (= high priest). What is the difference between the Israelites and the priests and the anointed priest? Only that the young bull (Lev 16:11ff.) makes atonement for the sanctuary and its holy offerings (while this is effected for the Israelites by the goat in Lev 16:15ff.)." R. Simeon (ca. 150) said, "Just as the blood of the goat that is prepared in the inner place makes atonement for the Israelites, so the blood of the young bull makes atonement for the priests; as the confession of sin makes atonement for the Israelites in the case of the goat sent away into the wilderness, so the confession of sin with the young bull makes atonement for the priests." – Related content is found in t. Šebu. 1.1 (445) and SLev 16:16 (315A).

7. The *kapporeth* is the holiest thing in the holy of holies.

Babylonian Talmud Menaḥot 27B: In a baraita it has been taught: If any for whom (after the expiration of the time of impurity) there is still no atonement (by the closing sacrifice) inadvertently have stepped into the forecourt, they are due for a sin offering. If it happened intentionally, they are guilty of the punishment of eradication (by God's hand). It is not necessary to say that this goes all the more for the one who needs an immersion bath in the evening (to be fully clean) and for all other unclean people. Those who are clean who have gone into the temple further inward from their area (the area accessible to them), they are together guilty of the forty (lashes); those who (have gone) within the curtain before the cover panel (are guilty) of death. R. Judah (ca. 150) said, "The whole holy place (so הֵיכָל here) and within the curtain (i.e., the foremost part of the holy of holies) makes one guilty of the 40 lashes and (the place) before the *kapporeth* makes one guilty of death. What is this difference of opinion based on? On this passage of Scripture: 'And Yahweh said to Moses, "Say to Aaron, your brother, that he is not at any time to go into the sanctuary הַקֹּדֶשׁ within the curtain before the cover panel (*kapporeth*), which is over the ark, lest he die"' (Lev 16:2)." The rabbis held, "'Into the sanctuary' (= holy place): this is meant by 'he is not to go in.' 'Within the curtain' and 'before the *kapporeth*': this is meant by 'lest he die.'" R. Judah held, "'Into the sanctuary' (= holy place) and 'within the curtain': this is meant by 'he is not to go in.' And 'before the *kapporeth*': this is meant by 'lest he die.'" – The rabbis make a distinction between: (α) holy place, (β) within the curtain and before the *kapporeth* = the holy of holies. Whoever enters into β is guilty of death; for the place within the curtain and before the *kapporeth* have the same degree of holiness. However, R. Judah makes a distinction between (α) holy place and within the curtain; whoever enters here receives the 40 lashes; (β) the place before the *kapporeth*; it is the holy thing in the holy of holies; only by coming to it is one punished with death. — In SLev 16:2 (306A.46) the controversy is as follows: "Within the curtain": this is meant to warn about the whole house. Is one guilty of death because of the whole house? Scripture teaches: "before the *kapporeth*, which is over the ark, lest he die." How is this? "Before the *kapporeth*": the threat of the death penalty pertains to this, and the warning (with the 40 lashes) pertains to the whole rest of the house. It should be noted that here the opinion of R. Judah appears to be the generally recognized one, without being explicitly mentioned. — Tosefta Kelim Baba Qamma 1.10 (570): Those who enter into the sanctuary (= the holy of holies), behold, they are guilty of death. R. Judah said, "'Before the *kapporeth*' (read הכפרת instead of הַקֹּדֶשׁ): the threat of the death penalty pertains to this, and the warning pertains to the whole rest of the house."

8. The sprinkling of blood in the holy of holies at the time of the second temple.

At the destruction of Solomon's temple, the ark of the covenant was lost along with the *kapporeth*. R. Eliezer (ca. 90) assumed that it had been taken to Babylon;[a] others thought that it had been hidden by king Josiah[b] or otherwise somewhere in the temple area;[c] according to still others, the prophet Jeremiah had hidden it away on Mount Nebo.[d] At any rate, the second temple lacked the ark of the covenant and the *kapporeth*.[e] Nevertheless, the blood of the sin offering of the young bull and of the sin offering of the goat was also offered regularly on the Day of Atonement in the holy of holies while the second temple stood, and Lev 16:3 and Lev 16:33 were invoked here.[f] According to the tradition, a stone that was three finger-breaths high, which was called אֶבֶן שְׁתִיָּה "foundation stone," was found in the place where the ark of the covenant had earlier stood:[g] the high priest carried out the atoning activity before the stone at the time of the second temple.[h] The Tosefta contains a different tradition: according to it, the high priest would have sprinkled the blood in the holy of holies onto the curtain.[i] Yet one has to assume that the passage strayed into a context foreign to its original one.

a. Tosefta Šeqalim 2.18 (177): R. Eliezer (ca. 90) said, "The ark of the covenant went into exile in Babylon; for it says, "Behold, days are coming when everything that is in your house … will be taken to Babylon; no word (so the midr.) will be left, Yahweh has said" (2 Kgs 20:17). 'Word' is nothing other than the commandments in it (i.e., nothing other than the two tablets of the law that were kept in the ark)." R. Simeon (ca. 150) said, "See, it says, 'After the course of the year king Nebuchadnezzar sent and had him brought to Babylon with the precious implements of the house of Yahweh' (2 Chr 36:10). The ark is meant here." — The same is found in t. Soṭah 13.1 (318); in y. Šeqal. 6.49C.12 as a baraita; the name of R. Simeon has fallen out, so that 2 Chr 36:10 appears as the 2nd supporting passage in the mouth of R. Eliezer. ‖ Babylonian Talmud Yoma 53B.34: It has not been taught, then it (the ark) had been "hidden." Instead it has been taught, when it had been "taken away" (see m. Yoma 5.2 in n. *h*). Here we have learned as the one who said, "The ark went into exile in Babylon." For in a baraita it says that R. Eliezer said, "The ark went into exile in Babylon"; see 2 Chr 36:10 (as previously). R. Simeon b. Yohai said, "The ark went into exile in Babylon"; see 2 Kgs 20:17 (as previously). — A completely different opinion is represented by R. Simeon in b. Yoma 53B (see in n. *c*).

b. Jerusalem Talmud Soṭah 8.22C.6: When the ark was hidden, there was hidden with it the basket with manna (cf. Exod 16:32ff.), the bowl with the anointing oil (with which the sanctuary and later some kings had been anointed), Aaron's staff with its flowers and almonds (cf. Num 17:13ff.), and the chest that the Philistines had sent as an atoning gift to the God of Israel (cf. 1 Sam 6:8). Who hid it? (King) Josiah, specifically when he saw what was written: "Yahweh will lead you and your king, whom you will appoint for yourself, to a people that neither you nor your ancestors know" (Deut 28:36). This is what is written: "He (Josiah) said to the Levites, who instructed all Israel, the ones who were holy to Yahweh, 'Put the holy ark in the house that Solomon, the son of David, the king of Israel, built; for no longer will you carry it on your shoulder'" (2 Chr 35:3). He said, "If that (ark) goes with you into exile in Babylon, you will not bring it back again to its place, but 'now serve Yahweh your God and his people Israel' (2 Chr 35:3)." — Parallels are found in b. Yoma 52B; b. Hor. 12A; b. Ker. 77B = 5B in other editions; in another version in t. Soṭah 13.1 (318).

c. 2 Baruch 6:4ff.: "Then I (Baruch) saw and, behold, four angels stood on the four corners of the city, with each one of them holding a flaming torch in his hands. And another angel descended from heaven and said to them, 'Take your torches and do not light them before I tell you! For I have been sent to communicate to the earth beforehand and to bring down upon her what the exalted Lord has commanded me. And I saw him, how he descended to the holy of holies and from there took away the curtain and the holy ephod and the atoning cover (*kapporeth*) and the two tablets and the holy vestments of the priests and the altar of incense and the 48 jewels that the high priest wore, and all holy vessels of the tent.' And he said to the earth with a loud voice, 'Earth, earth, earth! Hear the words of the Almighty God (cf. Jer 22:29) and receive these things that I entrust to you, and keep them in yourself until the last times, so that you part with them when you are commanded, so that foreigners will not be able to take possession of them. For the time has come that even Jerusalem will be temporarily surrendered until it is said that it should be constructed again, (specifically) forever. And the earth opened its mouth and devoured them.'" See also 2 Bar. 80:2. ‖ Tosefta Yoma 3.7 (186): The basket with manna, the bowl with anointing oil, Aaron's staff with its almonds and flowers (see Num 17:2ff.) and the chest in which the Philistines had sent gifts to Yahweh, the God of Israel, all of this was laid down in the holy of holies. When the ark was hidden, they were hidden with it. ‖ ʾAbot de Rabbi Nathan 41 toward the end: Things that were made and hidden are: the tent of meeting and the implements in it and the ark and the broken pieces of the tablets of the law and the basket with manna and the staff (of Moses) and Aaron's staff with its almonds and flowers and the vestments of the priesthood and the vestments of the anointed priest; but the mortar of Abtina (maker of the holy incense), the table (for the showbread) and the lampstand and the curtain still lie in Rome. ‖ Tosefta Šeqalim 2.18 (177): R. Judah b. Laqish (ca. 150) said, "The ark was hidden in its place (thus in the holy of holies); for it says, 'The rods were long and the tips of the rods were visible from the holy place at the entrance to the holy of holies; but outside they were not visible, and they are still there until today (namely hidden in the earth)' (1 Kgs 8:8)." – The same is found in t. Soṭah 13.1 (318) with R. Judah (ca. 150) as the author; in y. Šeqal. 6.49C.16, instead of R. Simeon b. Laqish, R. Judah b. Laqish should be read. ‖ Babylonian Talmud Yoma 53B: Ulla (ca. 280) said, "R. Matthew b. Heresh (ca. 130) asked R. Simeon b. Yohai (ca. 150) in Rome, 'After R. Eliezer (ca. 90) taught us once or twice that the ark went into exile in Babylon ..., what do you say?' He answered him, 'I say that the ark was hidden in its place (= in the holy of holies); for it says, "The rods were long ... and are still there until today (namely hidden in the earth)" (1 Kgs 8:8).'" Rabbah († 331) said to Ulla, "What can be concluded from the fact that it is written: 'They are still there until today'?! In every case where it is written 'Until today,' does it mean forever? Yet it is written: 'The Jebusites have lived in Jerusalem ... until today' (Josh 15:63)! Does this likewise imply that they were not led away into exile? ..." He answered him, "Here (1 Kgs 8:8) שָׁם (= there) is written, while there (Josh 15:63) שָׁם is not written; and everywhere where שָׁם is written, it means that it is forever." It was rejoined, "'From the sons of Simeon, 500 men went to Mount Seir ... and have dwelt "there" שָׁם until today' (1 Chr 4:42f.); and Sennacherib, the king of Assyria, came up long ago and mixed all countries with one another (see Isa 10:13)!" ‖ Mishnah Šeqalim 6.1f.: There were thirteen bows in the sanctuary. Those of the house of R. Gamaliel (I, ca. 40) and those of the house of R. Hananiah, the principal priest (ca. 70), bowed fourteen times. How did this excess happen? Toward the wooden booth; for from their ancestors they received the tradition that the ark was hidden there. In the case of a priest it happened that he was busy (there). He saw that the floor finish (in one place) was different from the rest. He came and told his colleague, but he had not yet finished his words when his life (his soul) went out of him. Then it was known with certainty that the ark had been hidden there. – A parallel is found in y. Šeqal. 6.49C.19; here at the conclusion: R. Hoshaiah (ca. 225) taught as a tannaitic tradition: "(That priest) hit it (that place of plaster) with a hammer, then fire went forth and burned him." See further b. Yoma 54A. ‖ Tanḥuma בהעלותך 205A: When the sanctuary was destroyed, the lampstand was hidden. This was one of the five things that were hidden: the ark, the lampstand, the fire (see y. Taʿan. 2.65A.52 in n. *e*), the holy spirit (of prophecy), and the cherubs. But when God in mercy will set out to build his house and his sanctuary, then he will have them brought back to their place, so that Jerusalem may enjoy them; as it says, "Its wilderness and wasteland will be jovial and the steppe will rejoice and bloom like the narcissus ..." (Isa 35:1f.). – This passage has mixed two traditions together, the tradition about the things hidden with the ark and about the five things that were missing in the second temple (see n. *e*). A parallel is found in Num. Rab. 15 (178D).

d. 2 Maccabees 2:1, 4–8: "It is found in the writings (in the purported memoirs of Nehemiah [2 Macc 2:13]) that the prophet Jeremiah commanded those who were led away to take something from the fire, as has been told above (2 Macc 1:19ff.).... It was also written in the writing that the prophet, as a consequence of a divine message, had the tent and the ark carried behind him, that he went to the mountain where Moses had gone up and had seen God's land of inheritance. (According to Deut 34:1, Nebo is meant.) When Jeremiah came, he found a spacious cave and he brought the tent[98] and the ark and the incense altar there and blocked the entrance. Some of his companions then came to remember the way, and they could not find it. When Jeremiah learned of this, he rebuked them and said, 'The place is to remain unknown until God brings his people back again and proves to be gracious. Then the Lord will make these things become visible, and the glory of the Lord will appear in the cloud, as it showed itself at the time of Moses.'" — The same is found in Yosippon 3.[99]

e. Josephus, *Jewish War* 5.5.5: (In the holy of holies) lay nothing at all ἔκειτο δ' οὐδὲν ὅλως ἐν αὐτῷ. ‖ Jerusalem Talmud Taʿanit 2.65A, 52: R. Samuel b. Inya (ca. 360) said in the name of R. Aha (ca. 320), "The last sanctuary lacked five things compared to the first; these are: the fire (from heaven that consumed the first offerings;[100] cf. Ezra 3:3 with Lev 9:24; 1 Chr 21:26; 2 Chr 7:1), the ark, the Urim and Thummim, the anointing oil (with which the tent of meeting and later some kings and the high priest were anointed), and the holy spirit (of prophecy). This is why it says, 'Build the house so that I may delight in it and honor (it)' (Hag 1:8). It is written. אכבד 'that I may honor' without ה (= 'it'). By this the 5 things are meant (ה according to its numerical worth = 5), that the 2nd sanctuary lacked in comparison to the 1st." — Parallels are found in y. Mak. 2.32A.5; y. Hor. 3.47C.56, though here the holy spirit is missing as a result of Urim and Thummim being counted as 2 entities. Babylonian Talmud Yoma 21B: R. Samuel b. Inya said, "What does 'So that I may delight in it and honor' (Hag 1:8) mean? We read: 'and honor "it"'! What is this other than that the ה (= it) is missing? By this the 5 things are meant which constituted the difference between the 1st and the 2nd sanctuary, namely the ark along with the *kapporeth* and the cherubs, the fire, the Shekinah, the holy spirit, and the Urim and Ṭhummim." — The Shekinah is inserted for the anointing oil; this relies on the view that God did not dwell in the 2nd sanctuary. ‖ Babylonian Talmud Menaḥot 27B: The ark and the *kapporeth* were not in the 2nd sanctuary.

f. Sifra Leviticus 16:3 (307A): "Aaron is to come into the sanctuary with this" (Lev 16:3). What does Scripture intend to teach? Since it says, "Into the sanctuary before the *kapporeth*, which is on top of the ark" (Lev 16:2), I could think: only into a sanctuary, in which the ark and the *kapporeth* are found. Whence comes the idea of going also into a sanctuary, in which the ark and the *kapporeth* are not found? Scripture says, "Aaron is to come into the sanctuary (without further additions) with this," in order to make the sanctuary, in which the ark and *kapporeth* are not found, like the sanctuary, in which they are found. ‖ Babylonian Talmud Menaḥot 27B: Since the ark and the *kapporeth* are not present in the 2nd sanctuary, should the sprinkling (of blood) not be carried out there? Rabbah b. Ulla (ca. 400?) said, "Scripture says, 'Let him (by the sprinkling of blood) cleanse of sin the holy

98. S-B: See a different tradition about the continuance of the tent in t. Soṭah 13.1: After the 1st house was built, the tent of meeting along with its boards, rings, pillars, and pedestals were hidden. But the table and the lamp that Moses had made were kept in use. — In b. Soṭah 9A, the last sentence is missing, which is the question: Where (were they hidden)? Rab Hisda († 309) said that Abimi (ca. 270) said: "Among the hollows of the Holy One."

99. Sefer Yosippon (ed. Amsterdam 1723), folio 13A.34.

100. S-B: See a variant tradition about the fire in 2 Macc 1:19–22, 31–36; Yosippon 3 (ed. Amsterdam 1723), folio 13A.14.

place of the sanctuary' (Lev 16:33, so the midr.), that is, the place that is made holy for the sanctuary (= ark)" (If the ark is not present, the place where it stood is to be cleansed of sin by the sprinkling of blood.)

g. See t. Yoma 3.6 (186) at #3, n. *b*; see m. Yoma 5.2 in the following n. *h*. ‖ A baraita in b. Yoma 5.42C.28: Before the ark was taken away, he (the high priest) would go in and out in the light of the ark. When the ark was taken away, he would grope his way in and grope his way out. R. Yose (ca. 150, read this instead of R. Yohanan) said, "Why was it (the stone that lay in the holy of holies) called "*shethiyyah* stone"? Because the world was established starting from it." R. Hiyya (ca. 200) taught: "Why is it called '*shethiyyah* stone'? Because the world was established starting from it." (Thus, *shethiyyah* stone = foundation stone). The interpretation of R. Yose appears frequently (e.g., Pesiq. 171A; Lev. Rab. 20 (119C); Num. Rab. 12 (165B); Tanḥ. אחרי 163A; קדושים 169B; TanḥB אחרי §4 (30A); קדושים §10 (39B); Midr. Ps. 11 § 2 (49B). ‖ A baraita in b. Yoma 54B: (The stone in the holy of holies was called אֶבֶן שְׁתִיָּה) because the world was established הושתת by it. We learned this according to the opinion of the one who said, "The world was created from Zion." For in a baraita it has been taught that R. Eliezer (ca. 90) said, "The world was created from its middle point; for it says, 'With the dust having run into a mass and the bits of soil having set there (in one firm point in the middle of the world)' (Job 38:38)." R. Joshua (ca. 90) said, "The world was created starting from the sides; for it says, 'He said to the snow, "Become earth!" and also to the rain and its mighty downpours' (Job 37:6)." (The masses of snow and rain becoming earth in a wide perimeter extended until they collided in the middle.) R. Isaac the smith (ca. 300) said, "God cast a stone into the sea from which the world was established; as it says, 'What have its columns sunk onto, or who laid its corṇerstone?' (Job 38:6)." (This foundation stone and cornerstone is the *shethiyyah* stone.) The scholars said, "The world was created from Zion; for it says, 'A psalm of Asaph. God … called the earth' (Ps 50:1). Furthermore it says, 'God made the completion of beauty break forth from Zion' (so Midr. Ps. 50:2), that is, the beauty of the world was completed from there." — The opinion of the scholars is also found anonymously in y. Yoma 5.42C.31; see also t. Yoma 3.6 (186) in #3, n. *b*. ‖ Tanḥuma קדושים 169B: "I made for myself gardens and parks and planted in them all kinds of fruit trees" (Eccl 2:5). What does "all kinds of fruit trees" mean? R. Yannai (ca. 225) said, "Solomon also planted pepper in the land. And how was he able to plant it? Solomon was wise and had knowledge about the actual foundation stone of the world. Why? 'God made the completion of beauty shine forth from Zion' (Ps 50:2): from Zion the whole world was completed, as we learned: Why was its (the stone's in the holy of holies) name '*shethiyyah* stone'? Because the world was established from it הושתת. And Solomon knew which strand (of earth) it was that was taken to Cush, and he planted pepper on it and immediately it bore fruits; for he said, 'I planted in them all kinds of fruit trees.' Another explanation is as follows. 'I planted in them all kinds of fruit trees.' As the navel is located in the middle of a man, the land of Israel lies in the middle of the world; as it says, 'Those who dwell there on the navel of the earth' (Ezek 38:12), and the foundation stone of the world goes out from there (see Ps 50:2, as above). The land of Israel lies in the middle of the world and Jerusalem in the middle of the land of Israel and the sanctuary in the middle of Jerusalem and the holy of holies (here called הֵיכָל) in the middle of the sanctuary and the ark in the middle of the holy of holies and the *shethiyyah* stone before the ark, for starting from it the world was established." — A parallel is found in TanḥB קדושים §10 (39A). ‖ Targum Yerušalmi I Exodus 28:30: "The great and holy name (of Yahweh) was clearly engraved (into the breastplate of the high priest), the name by which 310[101] worlds have been created. And it was (further) clearly engraved into the *shethiyyah* stone, with which the Lord of the world sealed (closed) the opening of the great deep in the beginning. Everyone who mentions (speaks) this holy name in the hour of tribulation is saved, and secrets are revealed (by this name)." ‖ Targum Ecclesiastes 3:11: "He (God) also hid before them the great name (of Yahweh) which was clearly written on the *shethiyyah* stone; for the evil inclination in their hearts was known before him, for if it (the name of Yahweh) had been given into the hand of man, he would use it to serve himself and find out what will be at the end of days into all eternity." ‖ Jerusalem Talmud Pesaḥim 4.30D.3: R. Zeira (ca. 300) said, "If women observe the custom not to weave from the beginning of the month of Ab (until the 10th of Ab), this is a (good) custom; for the foundation stone אבן שתיה (= temple) has ceased. What is the scriptural basis for this? 'When the pillars (to which the service of the temple belongs) are torn down, what work should a pious one do!' (so Midr. Ps. 11:3)." — A parallel is found in y. Taʿan. 1.64C.25.

h. Babylonian Talmud Yoma 52B: What does "When he had reached the ark" (m. Yoma 5.1) mean? (The ark was no longer present in the second temple!) The place of the ark (where it had previously stood). But it says, "He placed the pan between the two carrying rods" (m. Yoma 5.1; so these must have been present)! Say: As it were between the two carrying rods (as if it were present). — Accordingly, the atoning action was performed in the second temple in the exact same place it had been carried out in the first temple. See the Mishnah passage drawn upon (m. Yoma 5.1) at #3, n. *h.* ‖ See b. Menaḥ. 27B above in n. *f.* ‖ Mishnah Yoma 5.2: When the ark was taken away, there lay there (in the holy of holies) a stone since the days of the earlier prophets, which was called *shethiyyah*, and its height was three fingerbreadths from the earth; he placed (the pan with the incense) on this. — Tosefta Yoma 3.6 (186) is similar; see #3, n. *b.*

i. Tosefta Yoma 3.8 (186): He took the blood from the one who had stirred it up, went in to the same place he had gone (before), stepped onto the same spot where he had stood (before), and sprinkled some of it (the blood) onto the curtain עַל הַפָּרֹכֶת opposite the two carrying rods of the ark, once above and seven times below, without sprinkling precisely above or below, but rather as a lasher. And he counted in this way: one (above, then while sprinkling below:) one and one, one and two, one and three, one and four, one and five, one and six, one and seven. He went (outside) the curtain on his right and without touching the curtain; but if he touched the curtain, he touched it (it did not matter). R. Yose (ca. 150) said, "I saw it (the curtain) in Rome and there were who knows how many drops of blood

101. S-B: Haggadic interpretation of the word יֵשׁ in Prov 8:21, whose numerical value is 310. According to m. ʿUq. 3.12, the interpretation comes from R. Joshua b. Levi, ca. 250; we should understand the following as his tradents: R. Abdima of Haifa (ca. 280) in Midr. Ps. 31 § 6 (120A); R. Hanin b. Adda (ca. 300, if identical with R. Hanina b. Idi) in Midr. Ps. 5 § 2 (26A) and Rabbah bar Mari (ca. 320) in b. Sanh 100A.

on it. It was said to me, 'These are from the blood of the Day of Atonement.'" – As far as the Tosefta. The description of the first entrance of the high priest into the holy of holies for lighting the incense comes first; after a few intermediary remarks, then follows the above passage, which corresponds exactly to the Mishnah Yoma 5.3 (see #6, n. *c*) and depicts the second entrance into the holy of holies, the purpose of which was the sprinkling of the blood of the sin offering of the young bull. The penultimate sentence of our passage then discusses the exit of the high priest from the holy of holies in more detail than the Mishnah does, and in turn states for its part that the whole passage intends to actually depict an atoning action that was carried out in the holy of holies, namely the offering of the blood of the sin offering of the young bull. The great difference, though, between our passage and m. Yoma 5.3 lies in the fact that the latter has the blood sprinkled on the כַּפֹּרֶת "atoning cover" and the first on the פָּרֹכֶת "curtain." One might at first be inclined to see in פָּרֹכֶת a scribal error for כַּפֹּרֶת and correspondingly to improve the reading. In this case, the Mishnah and Tosefta would be in the greatest agreement. Yet this procedure is thoroughly contradicted by the concluding sentence of our passage which only makes sense if sprinkling the curtain with blood was discussed in what precedes. So, the Tosefta appears to follow a tradition that departs from the Mishnah. According to this tradition, at the time of the second temple, in the holy of holies on the Day of Atonement the blood would be sprinkled not on the place where the ark of the covenant had stood before, but rather on the curtain. Yet this assumption quickly becomes uncertain once again because of the statement of R. Yose at the end of our passage. This saying is also found elsewhere quite often, except that it, as can only be right, is presented in all other passages as a word of the son of R. Yose, namely of R. Eleazar b. Yose (ca. 180). Among these passages there are only two (y. Yoma 5.42D.3 and b. Yoma 57A), in which the word is cited in relation to the ceremonies of the sprinkling of blood that on the basis of Lev 16:16ff. were carried out on the Day of Atonement also in the "holy place" of the temple. Mishnah Yoma 5.4 specifies concerning this among other things also the following: (The high priest) took the blood of the young bull ... and sprinkled some of it against (onto) the curtain עַל הַפָּרֹכֶת, which is opposite the ark, from outside (i.e., not from the "holy of holies," but rather from the "holy place") once above and seven times below, without paying attention precisely to where, so that he would sprinkle precisely above or precisely below, but rather was as a lasher. And he counted thus: One, one and one, one and two .... He took the blood of the goat ... and sprinkled some of it against (onto) the curtain, which was opposite the ark, from outside once above and seven times below .... – From the two passages named above we learn then in more detail that it was a controversial question as to whether the blood had to touch the curtain or not during the process of sprinkling. The passage in y. Yoma 5.42D.3 remarks on this point: A teacher of the Mishnah taught, "It is necessary that it (the blood) touches (the curtain)." Another teacher of the Mishnah taught, "It is not necessary that it touches." R. Eleazar b. Yose said, "I saw it (the curtain) in Rome, how it was full of drops of blood. I said, 'These come from the kinds of blood that were sprinkled against it on the Day of Atonement.'" This implies: It is necessary that it touch. But you can also say, (so it will be objected against this conclusion): "It is not necessary that it touch; but if it touched, it touched (it does not matter)." – The second passage (b. Yoma 57A) reads: The following had been taught. When he sprinkles, he does not sprinkle it against (onto) the curtain עַל הַפָּרֹכֶת, but rather in the direction of the curtain כְּנֶגֶד הַפָּרֹכֶת. R. Eleazar b. Yose said, "I saw it in Rome, and there were on it who knows how many drops of blood from the young bull and from the goat of the Day of Atonement (thus the blood touched the curtain)." — Both of these passages with the word of R. Eleazar b. Yose make it very likely that our Tosefta passage also stood in a context that dealt with the cleansing of the "holy place" from sin. Only in this way do the words become understandable which come immediately before the saying of R. Yose and read: "Without touching the curtain, but if he touched the curtain, he touched it." Now these words speak of the exit of the high priest from the holy of holies and specify that if possible he should not touch the curtain in the process. But this is a condition that is not found anywhere else; it also does not fit well with the remark in t. Yoma 3.5 (186) that, in order to get between the carrying rods, the high priest pressed back the curtain with his hips when he put the incense down between the carrying rods of the ark. However, the words about touching the curtain made good sense in their original context. They related precisely to the question of whether the blood had to touch the curtain or not, and decided, as happens also in the Palestinian Gemarah above, that it does not matter. To refute this decision, reference was then made in the original content to the saying of R. Yose (read: R. Eleazar b. Yose) about the evidence of the curtain in Rome. But if, as one will be permitted to assume, our Tosefta passage is wedged into a context foreign to its original one, then it does not lend itself to establishing the assumption that at the time of the second temple, the blood was sprinkled on the Day of Atonement against curtain from outside the holy of holies.

3:25 B: In his blood.

The atoning power lies in the blood.

Sifra Leviticus 1:4 (22A): "It will pleasingly be accepted for him to make atonement for him" (Lev 1:4), by that which atones. What makes atonement? It is the blood; for it says, "The blood, by the soul it makes atonement" (Lev 17:11). See b. Yoma 5A.

3:28: For we consider that a person is justified by faith without works of the law.

1. On δικαιόω see § Rom 3:4 C. — See briefly about the rabbinic teaching on justification at § Matt 5:20 A and § Rom 3:21 A; in detail in the excursus "Preliminary Remarks on the Sermon on the Mount."
2. By faith. See § Rom 4:2f.
3. ἔργα νόμου. See § Rom 3:20 A, #1.

3:29: Or is God only (God) of the Jews? Not also of the gentiles? Yes, also of the gentiles.

The position of the ancient synagogue on the question that the apostle raises in the words above was brought to briefest expression by R. Simeon b. Yohai (ca. 150) in Exod. Rab. 29 (88D): "I am Yahweh your God" (Exod 20:2).

R. Simeon b. Yohai said, "God said to the Israelites, 'I am God over all those who come into the world, but I have united my name only to you. I am not called the God of the nations of the world, but rather the God of Israel.'" — This means: God is the God of all people, insofar as he has created them and insofar as they will stand before his judgment seat; but God is Israel's God, insofar as only this people is the people that is loved by God and destined for blessedness. See in more detail at § Rom 3:9 A; further, see also the material in the passages at § Rom 2:11, #3. — Parallels to R. Simeon's saying can be found in Midr. Ruth 1:1 (122B); Mek. Exod. 23:17 (107B); SDeut 6:4 § 31 (73A); Mek. Exod. 15:13 (50A). — On Ἰουδαῖοι and ἔθνη see § Rom 1:14, #3.

3:30: Circumcision … foreskin (see m. Ned. 3.11 at § Matt 15:5, #3 and #4).

4:2f.: If Abraham was justified by works, he has a boast, but not before God. For what does Scripture say? "Abraham believed God, and it was reckoned to him as righteousness" (Gen 15:6).

1. The thesis of the apostle is: If Abraham was found to be righteous on the basis of his works, he has a boast before men, but not therefore with God; for before God's judgment no human merit by works suffices. But Abraham did not acquire his righteousness before God by his works at all, but rather by his faith; for Scripture says, "Abraham believed God, and it was reckoned to him as righteousness." — The counterthesis of rabbinic Judaism would have been: Abraham was recognized as righteous exclusively on the basis of his works,[a] and therefore he has a great boast not simply with men,[b] but also with God.[c] But if Scripture says "Abraham believed God, and he reckoned it to him as righteousness," the faith is viewed exactly as a meritorious work as any other fulfillment of the commandments. The principle that man achieves his righteousness before God by his works is therefore not at all affected by the passage of Scripture in Gen 15:6, let alone voided. See in more detail in n. *d.*

a. Jubilees 23:10: "Abraham was complete (perfect) in all his action toward God and pleasing in righteousness all the days of his life." ‖ 2 Baruch 57:2: "At that (Abraham's) time, the law was unwritten but generally known among them, and the works of the commandments were then completed (by Abraham)." ‖ Mishnah Qiddušin 4.14 at the end: Likewise, it says in the case of our father Abraham, peace be with him: "And Abraham was old, and Yahweh blessed Abraham with everything" (Gen 24:1). We find that our father Abraham kept the whole Torah before it had been given; for it says, "As recompense for Abraham having listened to my voice and having observed what is to be observed before me, my statutes and my Torahs" (Gen 26:5). — The same is found more briefly in y. Qidd. 4.66B.51. ‖ Babylonian Talmud Yoma 28B: Rab († 247) said, "Our father Abraham kept the whole Torah; for it says, 'As a recompense for …' (Gen 26:5) (as before)." Rab Shimi b. Hiyya (ca. 250) responded to Rab, "Were they perhaps the seven (Noachic) commandments?!" (Answer:) "He also had circumcision." "Perhaps they were the seven commandments and circumcision?!" He answered him, "If this were the case, why would it say my commandments and my Torahs?" (These two expressions show that Abraham kept all the commandments of the whole Torah.) ‖ TanḥumaB לך לך § 14 (36A): "He stores up wisdom (= Torah) for the righteous" (Prov 2:7). What does "He stores up wisdom for the righteous" mean? Before the world was created, God stored up the Torah for Abraham; for it says, "As recompense for ..." (Gen 26:5 as before). This shows that Abraham observed all the commandments and all Torahs. — The same is found in ʾAg. Ber. 13 (12B). — Thus, Abraham is counted among the "righteous." Prayer of Manasseh 8: Now you, O Lord, you God of the righteous, have not imposed repentance on the righteous, Abraham, Isaac, and Jacob, who did not sin against you. ‖ 2 Baruch 58:1: "The third black water that you saw, this is the confluence of all the sins that the nations committed later after the death of those righteous ones (Abraham, Isaac, and Jacob)." ‖ Midrash Psalm 116 § 10 (239A): God said, "It is hard in my eyes to say to the righteous that they should die. It is hard in my eyes to say to Abraham that he should die, who long ago made me the creator of heaven and earth (cf. Gen 14:22), and who for the sake of my name descended into (Nimrod's) furnace (cf. Gen 15:7, where according to rabbinic interpretation אור כשדים means: fire(oven) of the Chaldeans), and who sanctified my name in my world."

b. Mishnah ʾAbot 5.3: Our father Abraham was tempted with 10 temptations, and he passed in everything, to make known how great the love of our father Abraham was (for God). ‖ Sirach 44:19ff. (Hebrew): "Abraham, the father of a multitude of nations, did not allow any blemish to fall upon his boast (his glory), who observed the commandments of the Most High and entered into the covenant with him. He made a stipulation with him in his flesh and in his temptations he was found faithful. Therefore, he determined for him in an oath that in his seed he would bless nations, that they would acquire a possession from sea to sea and from the river (Euphrates) to the ends of the earth (see Ps 72:8)." ‖ A baraita in b. B. Bat. 16B, 17A: ... The evil inclination had no power over three people, and these were: Abraham, Isaac, and Jacob, for about them it is written בכל, מכל, and כל. (In the case of Abraham: "Yahweh had blessed Abraham with everything בכל" [Gen 24:1]; in the case of Isaac: "I ate from everything מכל" [Gen 27:33]; in the case of Jacob: "I have everything כל" [Gen 33:11]. This כל, understood in an absolute sense, excludes any lack or blemish, thus also the evil inclination, from the three who are named.) ‖ Babylonian Talmud ʿAbodah Zarah 18B: R. Samuel b. Nahman (ca. 260) said that R. Jonathan (ca. 220) said, "'Blessed is the man who does not talk in the counsel of the godless' (Ps 1:1): this is our father Abraham, who did not walk in the counsel of the people of the generation of the dispersion, who were godless (see Gen 11:4). 'And who does not stand in the way of sinners' (Ps 1:1); for Abraham did not stand where the people of Sodom stood, who were sinful (see Gen 13:13). 'And who does not sit in the seat of mockers' (Ps 1:1); for Abraham did not sit in the seat of the Philistines, because they were mockers (see Judg 16:25)." — The same is found anonymously with elaborations in Midr. Ps. 1 § 13 (6B). ‖ Babylonian Talmud Makkot 24A: "Who walks irreproachably" (Isa 33:15): this is Abraham (see Gen 17:1: "Walk before my face; thus, you will be irreproachable.")

c. Jubilees 24:11: "In your (Isaac's) seed all nations of the earth will be blessed (see Gen 26:4) because your father listened to my word and observed my instruction and my commandments and my laws and my ordinances and my covenant." ‖ Genesis Rabbah 49 (31A): "The secret of Yahweh belongs to those who fear him" (so Midr. Ps. 25:14). At first the secret of Yahweh was with those who feared him (Ps 25:14); later with the righteous. See, "His secret is with the righteous" (Prov 3:32); and later with the prophets, see, "For Yahweh Elohim does nothing, unless he has revealed his secret to his servants, the prophets" (Amos 3:7). God said, "This Abraham is god-fearing." See, "No I know that you fear God" (Gen 22:12). This Abraham is the most righteous among the righteous. See, "Those who are among the righteous love you" (so Midr. Song. 1:4). This Abraham is a prophet. See, "Give the man's wife back, for he is a prophet" (Gen 20:7), and "Should I not reveal it to him (namely the destruction of Sodom; see Gen 18:17)?"

d. The central significance of faith for the religious-moral life was by no means unknown to the ancient synagogue in earlier times, as is shown especially by the pseudepigrapha. A clear proof of this lies in the fact that the righteous and pious are called in short "believers."[α] More specifically, in the understanding of the ancient synagogue faith meant first of all the confession of monotheism[β] and the teaching about future recompense:[γ] whoever confessed the one God who made heaven and earth and who will one day place humanity before his judgment, this one was among those who believe. But the concept of faith in the ancient synagogue is not thereby exhaustively accounted for. Faith was not to be simply an act of the intellect; it should also entail a decision of the will that involves the whole person and embraces the whole person. Faith therefore meant, secondly, that orientation and conduct of life that accorded with the confession of the Almighty God, the creator and leader and judge of the world. Correspondingly, faith should above all be proven and preserved in obedience to God's word and will,[δ] in trust in God's guidance and promise,[ε] in striving for fellowship with God,[ζ] in patient endurance amidst all tribulation,[η] in the secure hope of the ultimate victory of the righteous.[θ] It can be seen that faith is here valued as the fundamental driving power of the religious-moral life. — The life of Abraham was viewed as the paragon of such a life in the power of faith. Abraham, the representative of monotheistic thought[ι] and at the same time the representative of belief in the future recompense,[κ] sees his life task as winning his contemporaries to faith in the one God.[μ] Thus he, who was the first proselyte,[λ] assembled a great host of proselytes around himself[μ] and then sets an example of faith for them in his rather eventful life.[ν] And it was this life of faith, Philo explains,[ξ] that God, according to Gen 15:6, reckoned to Abraham as righteousness. Just how close Philo's view is to that of the apostle Paul is self-evident. —

The above claims, in particular the principally important ones, find their main support in passages that are taken from the nonrabbinic writings. The actual rabbinic literature, although it too can boast about faith,[ο] never rose to such a height of judgment about faith and the life of faith as we find in the pseudepigrapha and in Philo. The nomism of rabbinic Judaism kept even faith fully in its chains. We may perhaps hear a distant echo of the struggle between faith and works still in 4 Ezra (from the time shortly after 70).[π] Here the attempt is made to protect the place of faith in soteriology alongside works; but long before the struggle had been decided in favor of works. Nomism no longer valued faith as a unified orientation of life, but rather it broke up the life of faith into many individual actions of faith. Thereby each independent act of faith was pressed down to the level of an individual performance, to which a person was obligated in the particular situation of his life, just as he would have been obligated in a different situation to fulfill this or that commandment. Faith in this case no longer stood as a contrast to works but rather had now itself become a work that could be credited to a person where necessary by God as a merit just as any other fulfillment of a commandment.[ρ] Of course, the rabbinic understanding of Gen 15:6 was shaped accordingly. The moment depicted there demanded from Abraham faith in God's word and promise; he achieved this faith; thereby he had fulfilled the commandment of that hour, and therefore God could reckon that act of faith to him as righteousness, that is, a meritorious achievement.[σ] Naturally, this deprived of any validity the apostle's scriptural proof that Abraham was not declared righteous by works but rather by faith, for Abraham's faith in that hour was itself nothing other than a work.

α. Wisdom 3:9: "Those who trust in him (God) will know the truth, and those who believe οἱ πιστοί will remain in his love." (This can, however, also be translated: "Those who are faithful in love will remain with him.") ‖ Sibylline Oracles 5:158ff.: "But a great star will come down from heaven and burn … the land of Italy, because of whom many holy ones, believers πιστοί of the Hebrews, died." — Sibylline Oracles 5:426: "So that all who believe πάντας πιστούς and all the righteous may see the glory of the eternal God." See also Sib. Or. 3:69, 774. ‖ 4 Ezra 7:131: "Therefore, there will be no mourning over their (the unbelievers') doom, and joy will reign over the salvation of those who believe." ‖ 1 Enoch 46:8: "(The godless) will be driven out of the houses of his assemblies (synagogues) and of the believers, who are protected in the name of the Lord of Spirits." ‖ 2 Baruch 54:21: "At the end of the world those who have done evil will be repaid according to their misdeed, and you will glorify believers according to their faith." See also 2 Bar. 54:16. ‖ 2 Enoch 51:2: "Help the one who believes in tribulation, and no tribulation will find you in the time of your work." — In rabbinic usage, "believers" is rarely used to designate righteous or pious people. Mishnah Soṭah 9.12: Since the sanctuary was destroyed …, men of faith אַנְשֵׁי אֲמָנָה have ceased. — According to b. Soṭah 48B, this means people who believe in God without worrying about their daily bread. ‖ Babylonian Talmud Taʿanit 8A: R. Ammi (ca. 300) said, "Come and see how great those are who are full of trust (believers) בַּעֲלֵי אֲמָנָה! From where? (Learn it) from weasels and wells (which were called upon to be witnesses to a marriage promise and then avenged a broken promise). And if such was the case with the one who trusted המאמין in weasels and wells, how much more is this the case for the one who trusts in God!" — However, in the immediately preceding sentence בַּעֲלֵי אמנה means "trustworthy, reliable," as it does elsewhere most of the time. — In b. Šabb. 97A (see the passage further below in n. σ), "those who believe" and the "sons of those who believe" are people who showed faith once in a particular situation in their life. — The נֶאֱמָן in m. Demai 2.2 has been thought to refer to someone who is a "believer" up until the last time,[102] but it is in fact someone who is "certified" as a member of the *ḥaber* covenant; on this, see § John 7:49, #5.

β. Letter of Aristeas 139f.: "(The lawgiver Moses) surrounded us (Israelites) with an impenetrable enclosure and with iron walls (cf. Eph 2:14), so that we would not foster any fellowship with any of the other nations, pure in body and soul, free from foolish belief ματαίων δοξῶν, venerating the one and mighty God above all creatures. Therefore the leaders of the Egyptians, their priests, who have penetrated into many things and comprehended them, call us 'men of God,' a name that is not attributed to the others, but rather only to the one who venerates the true God: they (the others) are rather men of food and drink and clothing." — Letter of Aristeas 234: "(The king) then asked the tenth one, 'What is the highest glory?' And he said, 'To honor God! This does not mean with gifts and sacrifices, but rather by purity of soul and of the pious belief διαλήψεως ὁσίας that everything is created by God and guided according to his will. And you have this belief γνώμην continuously, as we all can conclude from your earlier and present deeds.'" ‖ Judith 14:10: "Achior, though, when he saw everything that the God of Israel had done, he believed strongly in God ἐπίστευσε τῷ θεῷ σφόδρα and had the flesh of his foreskin circumcised and was added to the house of Israel until this day." ‖ Wisdom 12:17: "You show strength when someone does not believe in your complete power ἀπιστούμενος ἐπὶ δυνάμεως τελειότητι, and you punish the defiance of those who know it." ‖ Sibylline Oracles 3:584ff.: "For the great God has given wise counsel and faith πίστιν and the best sense in the breast to them (the Israelites) alone, who ... alone honor the always ruling immortal one." — Sibylline Oracles 3:724ff.: "This is what the souls of believing people πιστῶν ἀνθρώπων will cry, 'Come, falling on our face in the house of God let us delight God our creator with songs!'" ‖ 1 Enoch 43:4: "These ('stars') are the names of the holy ones who dwell on firm land and always believe in the name of the Lord of Spirits." — Thus, those who confess the monotheistic faith are the holy ones, who are like the stars. — 1 Enoch 58:5: "After that (after the dawn of the messianic time of completion) it will be said to the holy ones that they should seek in heaven the secrets of righteousness, the lot of faith (i.e., what is intended and stored up for those who confess the one God)." — Conversely, the godless are designated in 1 Enoch as people who "deny the name of the Lord

---

102. Wilhelm Bousset, *Die Religion des Judentums im neutestamentlichen Zeitalter*, 3rd ed. (Berlin: Reuther & Reichard, 1903), 178; Paul Volz, *Jüdische Eschatologie von Daniel bis Akiba* (Tübingen: Mohr, 1903), 318.

of Spirits" (1 En. 45:1, 2) or renounce it (38:2; 41:2; 48:10; 67:8), or who "do not believe in God's name" (67:8), whose faith is directed toward idols that they have fashioned with their hands, while they have repudiated the name of the Lord of spirits (46:7). — In every case it is a matter here of denying the monotheistic faith. Likewise, in 1 En. 63:5, 7f., where the godless rulers say on the day of judgment: "Who will grant us rest that we may boast in, thank and praise and confess our faith before his glory? For we have not confessed our faith before him, nor boasted in the name of the Lord of Spirits, nor praised the Lord for all he has done. Our trust rested in the scepter of our kingdom and in our glory. On the day of our distress and tribulation he will not save us, and we will find no respite that we may confess our faith that our Lord is true in all his action, judgment, and justice and his judgments show no respect for the person." ‖ 4 Ezra 5:1: "Behold, days are coming when the inhabitants of the earth will be seized by immense dread, the area (the way?) of truth will be hidden and the land of faith (= Palestine, where those who confess the one God live) will have no fruit." See 2 Baruch 59:10: "(God let Moses see) the land of faith (= Palestine)." ‖ 2 Baruch 51:7: "But those who were saved (from eternal destruction) by their deeds, and those for whom now the law was their hope and insight their desire and the (monotheistic) faith their wisdom, for them wonderful things will appear ...." — In 2 Bar. 78:6, the 9.5 tribes that were led away are admonished: "Therefore, if you remember that you suffer now for your salvation, lest you be judged at the end and suffer torment, you will then obtain hope forever, if above all you cast out the vain erroneous belief from your heart, because of which you had to leave this place." — Then it says further in 2 Bar. 83:8: "So now direct your hearts rightly to what you believed earlier, so that you are not taken from both worlds, in that here you were led away captive and there you will suffer torment." — By "erroneous belief" the author means the idolatrous inclination of the earlier Northern Kingdom. This belief should be replaced once again by the original correct belief in the one God.

γ. 1 Enoch 60:6: "The day ... of judgment, which the Lord of Spirits has prepared for those who ... deny the righteous judgment and abuse his name." ‖ 4 Ezra 9:9ff.: "Then (at the end) those who now flout my ways will learn reverence; then they will abide in the agonies that they have scorned and mocked. For all who have not recognized me in life, when they still received beneficence from me, who spurned my law, when they still had freedom ..., they will come to realize the truth after death." ‖ 2 Baruch 42:2: "Those who believed (who lived in faith in the future recompense) will be granted the aforementioned good (the messianic salvation), and the opposite of this will be bestowed on those who scorn (because they do not believe in it)." — 2 Baruch 59:2: "At that (Moses') time the lamp of the law, which is valid forever, shone for all those who sat in darkness; to make known to those who believed the promise of their recompense and to those who did not believe the torment of fire that is stored up for them."

δ. Sirach 35:24: "The one who believes the law ὁ πιστεύων νόμῳ heeds the commandments,[103] and the one who trust in the Lord will not be put to shame." (The Hebrew text of

---

103. S-B: The phrase "to believe in the law" comes from Ps 119:66: במצותיך האמנתי.

Sir 32:24: "Whoever observes the Torah preserves his soul, and whoever trusts in Yahweh will not be put to shame.") See Sir 36:3: "The wise person will trust in the law ἐμπιστεύσει νόμῳ, and the law will be proven to him to be reliable πιστός as a question put to the Urim." ‖ Sibylline Oracles 3:283ff.: "But you (Israel), wait, believing in the holy laws πιστεύων ... ἁγνοῖσι νόμοισιν of the great God, when he lifts up to the light your weary knee." ‖ Wisdom 12:2: "You gently punish the fallen and, reminding them about where they have gone wrong, you rebuke them, so that, having been freed from evil, they may believe in you, Lord (for new obedience)." — Wisdom 15:2ff.: "Even if we sin, we still remain yours, since we know your power. But we will not, since we know that we are reckoned as your own. For to know you τὸ γὰρ ἐπίσταθαί σε is perfect righteousness, and to know of your power is the root of immortality." — The knowledge of the one God makes those who believe God's possession, but it also obligates them to avoid sin. Conversely, it is said of the godless in 4 Ezra 7:23f.: "They conceived vain thoughts and concocted nefarious lies. They also claimed that the Most High did not exist, and they did not concern themselves with his ways. They spurned his law, denied his covenant, they did not believe his commandments, they did not complete his works." ‖ 4 Ezra 7:83: "The third (torment of the godless after death) is that they see the recompense that is stored up for those who have believed the testimonies of the Most High." ‖ 2 Baruch 54:5: "You reveal what is hidden to those who are without blemish, who have submitted themselves in belief in you and your law." ‖ Mishnah Berakot 2.2: R. Joshua b. Qarha (ca. 150) said, "(In the Shema,) why does 'Hear, Israel' (Deut 6:4–9) proceed the (section) 'And if you hear' (Deut 11:13–21)? Only so that one may first take the yoke of God's lordship (the confession of the one God) on himself and then the yoke of the commandments (the obligation to live according to God's commandments)." ‖ Mekilta Exodus 15:1 (40B): "Then Moses and the children of Israel sang this song to Yahweh" (Exod 15:1). R. Nehemiah (ca. 150) said, "Whoever takes a commandment on himself in faith is worthy of the holy spirit (= spirit of inspiration) dwelling upon him; for thus we find it in the case of our ancestors, for as a recompense for our fathers believing in Yahweh, they obtained the holy spirit dwelling upon them and they sang a song. For it says, 'They believed in Yahweh and in Moses, his servant' (Exod 14:31); and (immediately after that) it says, 'Then Moses and the children of Israel sang this song to Yahweh' (Exod 15:1)." ‖ Exodus Rabbah 21 (83C): (The Israelites) obeyed God in everything that he stipulated concerning them; for it says, "And the people believed" (Exod 4:31). — Thus, to believe in God = to obey God, and conversely not to believe in God = not to obey God; so Tg. Onk. Deut. 9:23: "When Yahweh sent you out of Rekam Geah (= Kadesh-barnea) saying 'Go up and take the land that I have given you into possession,' you were recalcitrant against the stipulation of the Memra of Yahweh your God and you did not believe him and did not take his word on yourselves." — Similarly, Tg. Yer. I.

ε. See Let. Aris. 234 in n. β. ‖ 3 Maccabees 2:7: "Those who trusted you as the commander of all creation you led safely through." ‖ 2 Maccabees 7:40: "In this way, this one parted from life in purity by placing all his trust in the Lord." — 2 Maccabees 8:18: "Those ones trust in weapons, ... but we have placed our trust in the almighty God." — 2 Maccabees 15:7: "Maccabeus was unremittingly full of trust with all hope that he would receive help from the Lord." ‖ Prayer of Azariah 17: "Those who trust in you will not be put to shame." ‖ Wisdom 3:9: "Those who trust in you will know the truth." — Wisdom 16:24: "The creation calms down again to do good to those who trust in you." — Wisdom 18:6: "That (Passover) night it was proclaimed to our ancestors beforehand so that they could be securely comforted by the oaths in which they trusted." ‖ 4 Ezra 3:32: "Which tribes have believed your covenants like those of Jacob?" — 4 Ezra 5:29: "Why have those who have contradicted your promises been permitted to trample down those who have believed your covenants?" — Wisdom 8:30: "Show your love to those who have always trusted in your glory." ‖ 2 Baruch 48:22: "We trust in you, since your law is among us; and we know that we will not fall as long as we hold fast to the prescriptions of your covenant." ‖ Mekilta Exodus 17:11 (62A): "Whenever Moses lifted his hand, Israel was strong" (Exod 17:11). How? Did Moses' hands make the Israelites strong, or did his hands break Amalek? Rather, whenever he lifted up his hand, the Israelites looked to him and believed in the one who had assigned it to Moses to do this, and God performed miracles and great deeds for them. Likewise: "And God said to Moses, 'Make for yourself a serpent of fire'" (Num 21:8). How? Did he kill the serpent and make it live? Rather, as long as he did this, the Israelites looked and believed in the one who had assigned it to Moses to do this, and God made cures for them. — A parallel passage is found in m. Roš Haš. 3.7, 8. It is notable that the Mishnah of the Babylonian Talmud has both times replaced the words: "They believed in the one who had assigned it to Moses to do this" with "They submitted their heart to their Father in heaven." The Mishnah of the Jerusalem Talmud reads the same in the 2nd passage, which deals with the serpent, while in the 1st passage it has the replacement words: "They directed their heart to their Father in heaven." One recognizes from this that for the rabbinic scholars "faith in God" in this context was generally speaking synonymous with believing obedience to God's word and assurance. — On the expression: "to keep the thoughts or the heart directed to God" = "in obedience to God's word" or "to do something for God's sake," see also m. Menaḥ. 13.11 and b. Ber. 17A.

ζ. Sirach 25:11: "The fear of the Lord is the basis ἀρχή for loving him, but faith is the basis for union with him." ‖ See Wis 3:9 above in n. α. ‖ Philo, *De migratione Abrahami* 24 (Mangey's ed., 1:456): "You are to fear Yahweh your God, to worship him and to be bound to him κολληθήσῃ" (Deut 10:20). What is the glue κόλλα? Piety and faith; for the virtues bind and unite the soul with imperishable existence. For it says also of Abraham because he believed: "He drew near to God" (Gen 18:23).

η. Psalms of Solomon 2:36: "The Lord is gracious to those who patiently call on him." — Psalms of Solomon 3:3: "The righteous remember the Lord at all times; they recognize his judgments as just." See 2 Bar. 78:5. — Psalms of Solomon 14:1: "The Lord is faithful to those ..., who accept his chastisement." ‖ 2 Enoch 50:3: "Endure every blow and every wound and every evil word and affliction for the Lord's sake." — 2 Enoch 51:3: "Endure every yoke of tribulation and hardship when it comes upon you for the Lord's sake, and thus you will find your recompense on the day of judgment." ‖ 4 Ezra 8:27: "Look ... to those who have kept your covenants in sufferings." ‖ 2 Baruch 52:5f.: "The righteous, what should they do now? Take pleasure in the suffering you now suffer." ‖ 4 Maccabees 15:24: "Although this (mother) watched the demise of seven children and the manifold fullness of torments: the noble mother rendered them all void by the power of her faith in God." — 4 Maccabees 16:17ff.: "It would be a shame if you as the more youthful ones would recoil from the torments, when this aged man (the priest Eleazar) bears pains for the sake of piety. Remember that it is God by whom you share in the world and enjoy life. Therefore, you are due to endure every hardship for God's sake." (Then the ancestors etc. are pointed to; then verse 22:) "Therefore you too who have the same faith in God: do not be distressed! It would be irrational to be skilled in piety and yet unable to withstand sufferings." — 4 Maccabees 17:2: "O mother, you who with your seven boys voided the tyrant's violence, you thwarted his evil attacks and showed the nobility of faith!" — 4 Maccabees 17:9f.: "Here are buried an aged priest, an aged woman, and seven boys by the violence of a tyrant who intended to destroy the condition of the Hebrews. They saved the people, looking to God and withstanding the torments of torture."

θ. 1 Maccabees 2:59, 61: "Hananiah, Azariah, and Mishael, because they showed faith, were rescued from the fire.... And so, consider from generation to generation, that all who hope in him will gain strength." ‖ 2 Maccabees 7:20: "Greatly admirable and worthy of thoughts of praise is the mother who saw her seven sons die on one day and bore it bravely because of her hopes in the Lord." ‖ Judith 8:20: "We know no God other than him; therefore, we hope that he will not overlook us, nor one from our generation." ‖ 1 Enoch 96:1: "Hope, you righteous, for suddenly sinners will perish before you, and you will rule over them as you please." ‖ 2 Enoch 9: "This place (paradise), O Enoch, is prepared for the righteous who endure all tribulations from those who trouble their souls." — 2 Enoch 66:6: "Walk, my children, in ... faith ..., until you leave this age of pain so that you may become heirs of the endless age." ‖ 4 Ezra 6:27f.: "Then (in the messianic time) evil will be exterminated and deceit destroyed, faith in bloom, corruption will be overcome." — 4 Ezra 7:18: "The righteous can (now) bear the straits well, since they hope for capacious circumstances; but the godless endure the straits and will not see capacious circumstances." — 4 Ezra 7:33f.: "Then the end will come.... My judgment alone will remain, the truth still abide, faith will triumph." ‖ 2 Baruch 42:2: "Those who believed will be granted the aforementioned good (the messianic salvation), and the opposite of this will be bestowed on those who scorn." — 2 Baruch 54:15f., 21: "For if Adam sinned first and brought premature death upon everyone, every individual among those who stem from him have brought the future torment on himself, and likewise each individual among them has chosen the future glory for himself. For truly the one who believes receives his due from it.... For at the end of the world recompense will be made to those who have done evil, according to their misdeed, and you will glorify those who believe, according to their faith." — 2 Baruch 83:4f.: "We will quietly hope, because what has been promised to us is coming. And we will not now look at the pleasures of the nations but rather we should think of what is promised to us for the end time." ‖ Philo, *De Abrahamo* 46 (Mangey's ed., 2:39): "The only true and secure good is faith in God ἡ πρὸς τὸν θεὸν πίστις: comfort of life, fullness of good hopes, being far from sufferings, but a rich gain in good, eschewing an evil disposition, knowledge of piety, lot of blessedness, comprehensive betterment of the soul that relies on the author of all things who can do all things and wills what is best."

ι. Jubilees 11:16ff.: "The boy (Abram) began to realize the error of the earth, as everything strayed after carvings and impurities, and his father taught him writing when he was two weeks of years old, and he separated from his father so as not to worship idols with him. And he began to pray before the creator of all that he would save him from the error of the children of men, and that his lot would not fall to straying after impurity and abomination." — Jubilees 12:1ff.: "And it happened in the 6th week in its 7th year, Abram said to Terah his father, 'Father!' And he said, 'Here I am, my son!' And he said, 'What kind of help or benefit comes to us from these idols that you worship and before whom you prostrate? For there is no spirit in them; rather they are mute, and they are a straying of the heart. Do not worship them; worship the God of heaven, who brings rain and dew down upon the earth and makes everything on earth and created everything by his word, and from whose face all life emanates....' And in the 60th year of Abram's life ... Abram arose at night and burned the house of the idols.... In the 6th week, in its 5th year, Abram sat at night, on the new moon of the 7th month, to observe the stars from evening until morning, to see how it would be in the year with the rain (showers), and he was alone when he sat and observed. And a word came into his heart and said, 'All signs of the stars and the signs of the sun and the moon, all are in the hand of God. Why do I study them? When he wants, he makes it rain, morning and evening; and when he wants, he makes it not come down, and everything is in his hand.' And he prayed on this night and said, 'My God, Most High God, you alone are my God, and you have made everything, and everything that exists is the work of your hands, and I have chosen you and your kingdom. Save me from the hand of the evil spirits who rule over the thoughts of man's heart, and do not let them lead me astray away from you, my God, and ensure that I and my seed never err from now on till forever!'"(Then the calling of Abraham follows.) ‖ Testament of Naphtali (Hebrew) 8f.: "I (Naphtali) warn you ... not to forget Yahweh your God, the God of your ancestors, whom our father Abraham chose, when the races (of humanity) were separated from each other in the days of Peleg (see Gen 10:25). For then the Holy One came from his high heaven and made 70 serving angels descend (with him) and Michael was at their head.... On that day Michael delivered a message on behalf of the Holy One, the one who is highly to be praised, and said to the 70 nations: ... 'And now choose for yourselves whom you will serve, and who will be your intercessor in the height of heaven!'... But as soon as Michael said to our father Abraham, 'Abram, whom will you choose and whom will you serve?' Abraham answered, 'I select and choose none other than the one who spoke and the world came to be, who formed me in the womb of my mother, a body in the middle of another body, and who put spirit and soul in it. Him I choose and him I will cling to, I and my descendants forever.'" ‖ Genesis Rabbah 38 (23C): R. Hiyya b. Ad(d)a of Joppa (ca. 350) said, "Terah (Abraham's father) was an idolater. Once when he went on a journey, he appointed Abraham as a seller in his place. Then a man came to buy something (an idol). Abraham said to him, 'How old are you?' He answered, '50 to 60.' Abraham said, 'Woe to this man (= you), who is 60 years old and wants to worship something that is one day old!' That one was ashamed and went away. Once a woman came who had a bowl of flour in her hand. She said to him, 'Take it and offer it before them (Terah's idols).' Then he stood up, took a stick in his hand and smashed all the idols; then he put the stick in the hand of the largest among them. When his father returned, this one said to him, 'Who did such a thing to them?' He answered, 'How could I deny it before you? A woman came carrying a bowl of flour and said to me, "Take it, offer it before them!" I offered it before them. Then the one said, "I want to eat it first!" And the other said, "I want to eat it first!" Then this biggest one arose among them, took the stick and smashed them.' Terah said, 'You wish to mock (read מפלה instead of מכלה) me! Do those things have understanding?' Then Abraham said, 'Will your ears not hear what your mouth says?' Terah took Abraham and handed him over to Nimrod. This one said to him, 'We will worship the fire!' Abraham responded, 'We will worship the water, which puts out the fire!' Nimrod said, 'Let us worship the water!' Abraham said, 'In this case (i.e., if this is to be worshiped) let us instead worship the cloud that carries water!' Nimrod said, 'Let us worship the cloud!' Abraham replied, 'In this case let us instead worship the wind that disperses the cloud!' Nimrod said, 'Let us worship the wind!' Abraham replied, 'Then we will worship human beings, who endure the wind!' Nimrod said, 'Do you just want to make words? I will worship only the fire! Look, I will have you cast into it; then may the God, whom you worship, come and save you from it!' — See further § Rom 1:20 D, n. *d.*

κ. 2 Baruch 57:2: "Faith in the future world was born at that time (in the days of Abraham), and the hope that the world will be renewed was erected at that time, and the promise of the life to come was planted at that time." ‖ On the revelations granted to Abraham about the future world and particularly about the place of retributive punishment, gehenna, see § John 8:56.

λ. Mekilta Exodus 22:20 (101A): Abraham called himself a proselyte גֵּר; for it says, "I am a proselyte (so גר in the later sense; see § Acts 13:16) and resident alien among you" (Gen 23:4). ‖ Babylonian Talmud Sukkah 49B: Raba († 352) said in a presentation, "What does 'How beautiful are your steps in the shoes, you daughter of a noble man' (Song 7:2) mean? How beautiful are the steps of the Israelites, when they go up to the festival (to Jerusalem). 'You daughter of a noble man': daughter of our father Abraham, who is called a noble man; as it says, 'The nobles of the nations are gathered to the God of Abraham' (Ps 47:10). 'God of Abraham' and not 'God of Isaac' or 'of Jacob'; rather, God of Abraham, because this one was the beginning for the proselytes (the first proselyte). (Since Abraham was a proselyte, he belongs among the 'nobles' who are gathered to God)." — The same is found in b. Ḥag. 3A: ‖ TanḥumaB לך לך § 6 (32A): God said, "I so love the proselytes, and Abraham is the father of the proselytes, and then those wicked ones come (Gen 14:12ff.) and they want to set themselves on him? Woe to them! For their end is to fall before him."

μ. Genesis Rabbah 30 (18B): Abraham was determined to lead the whole world to repentance. ‖ Genesis Rabbah 39 (24B): "You are to be a blessing בְּרָכָה" (Gen 12:2). Read: בְּרֵיכָה "pool of water": just as a pool of water cleans the unclean, so you (Abraham) are to bring near those who are far away and cleanse them for their father in heaven. ‖ Genesis Rabbah 44 (27B): The word of Yahweh came to Abram in a face thus, "Fear not, Abram!" (Gen 15:1). Whom did he fear? R. Berekhiah (ca. 340) said, "He feared Shem. This is what is written, 'The islands have seen and fear, the ends of the earth quaked ...' (Isa 41:5). As the islands are marked out in the sea (by their sharp contours), Abraham and Shem were marked out in the world (by their reputation and renown). 'And they feared': this one feared that one and that one feared this one, saying, 'Perhaps he (Shem) might have something against me in his heart because I killed his descendants' (Gen 14:14ff.); and this one (Shem) feared that one (Abraham), saying, 'Perhaps he (Abraham) might have something against me in his heart because I let the godless arise.' 'The ends of the earth': this one dwelt at the end of the world, and that one dwelt at the end of the world. 'They drew near and came running' (Isa 41:5): this one drew near to that one and that one drew near to this one. 'Each helped the other' (Isa 41:6): this one helped that one with blessings, and that one helped this one with gifts. This one (Shem) helped that one with blessings: 'He (Melchizedek, according to the common rabbinic assumption = Shem) blessed him (Abraham) and said, "Blessed be Abram of El Elyon ..." (Gen 14:19)'; and that one (Abraham) helped this one (Shem) with gifts: 'And he (Abraham) gave him a tenth of everything' (Gen 14:20). 'The blacksmith stabilized it' (Isa 41:7): this is Noah, who made the ark; 'the blacksmith' צורף (Isa 41:7): this is Abraham, whom God refined צרפו in the furnace (of Nimrod); 'the one who smooths the hammer the one who strikes the anvil' הולם (Isa 41:7), for he (Abraham) smoothed his hammer and united הלם all who come into the world on a path with God; 'saying, "He (God) is good to cling to"' (so Midr. Isa. 41:7): the nations of the world are meant, who say: 'It is better to cling to the God of Abraham than to cling to the idols of Nimrod.' 'Then he stabilized it with nails' (Isa 41:7): Abraham stabilized Shem with fulfillments of the commandments and good works; and 'did not waver' (Isa 41:7): this pertains to Abraham." ‖ Midrash Song of Songs 8:8 (132A): R. Berekhiah (ca. 340) interpreted the passage in relation to our father Abraham, "'We have a little sister אחות' (Song 8:8): this is Abraham; for it says, 'Abraham was one אחד and received the earth as his own' (Ezek 33:24), and united איחה all who came into the world (in one faith) before God. — The same is found in Gen. Rab. 39 (23D). ‖ Genesis Rabbah 39 (24C): "Abram took his wife Sarai ... and all souls they had acquired עשו in Haran" (Gen 12:5). R. Eleazar (ca. 270) said in the name of R. Yose b. Zimra (ca. 220, so read instead of R. Eleazar bar Zimra), "If all who come into the world were to come meet to create even only a gnat, they would not be able to strew the soul into it, and you say, 'The souls that they had made'? Only the proselytes are meant whom they had made proselytes. But if they had thus made them proselytes, why does it say, 'that they had made עשו?' To teach you that everyone who brings a foreigner and makes him a proselyte is as if he had created him.[104] But then it should have said, 'that he had made.' Why is it said, 'that they had made'?" R. Huna (ca. 350) said, "Abraham made the men and Sarah made the women proselytes." — The same is found with the correct authorial attribution in Gen. Rab. 84 (53B); Pesiq. Rab. 43 (181A); anonymously in SDeut 6:5 § 32 (73A); Midr. Song. 1:3 (85A), among many others. ‖ Targum Onkelos Genesis 12:5: "Abram took Sarai, his wife, and Lot, the son of his brother, and all their possessions that they had acquired, and the souls that they had made subservient to

104. S-B: See the principle in b. Sanh 99B: Whoever teaches the son of another the Torah, it is as if he had created him עשאו.

the Torah in Haran, and went forth to go into the land of Canaan." — Targum Yerušalmi I is clearer: "The souls that they had made proselytes."

v. Genesis Rabbah 39 (24C): "(Abraham) solemnly called upon Yahweh" (Gen 12:8). This shows that he had the name of God called upon שהקרא by the mouth of each person. Or "He called upon": he began to make proselytes and to bring them under the wings of the Shekinah. ‖ Babylonian Talmud Soṭah 10A: "(Abraham) solemnly called upon Yahweh there, the eternal God" (Gen 21:33). Resh Laqish (ca. 250) said, "Do not read 'He called upon' ויקרא, but rather 'he made it called upon' ויקריא. This teaches that our father Abraham had the name of God called upon by the mouth of every migrant (that came with him). How so? When they had eaten and drunk and got up to thank him, he said to them, 'Have you eaten from what is mine? You have eaten from that which belongs to the God of the world! Thank and glorify and praise the one who spoke and the world came to be!'" — The same is found anonymously in Gen. Rab. 54 (34D). ‖ Genesis Rabbah 43 (26D): R. Isaac (ca. 300) said, "(Abraham) took the migrants with him, and when they had eaten and drunk, he said to them, 'Say the word of praise!' If they said to him, 'What should we say?,' he would answer them, 'Say, "Blessed be the eternal God who has fed us from what belongs to him!"' God said to him, 'My name was not known to my creatures, but you have made me known among my creatures. I reckon this to you as if you had been my companion in creating the world.' It says, 'Blessed be of El Elyon Abram, the creator of heaven and earth' (this is the reading of Midr. Gen. 14:19, which takes קינה in apposition to Abram)." ‖ Genesis Rabbah 49 (31A): R. Azariah (ca. 380) said in the name of R. Judah b. Simon (ca. 320), "(Abraham) began with mercy and ended with justice (cf. Gen 18:19, where 'righteousness' = mercy comes first and then 'justice'). How so? Abraham used to accept migrants. When they had eaten and drunk, he would say to them, 'Say the word of praise!' If they said to him, 'What should we say?,' he would answer them, 'Say, "Blessed be the eternal God who has fed us from what belongs to him!"' When he (the one in question) accepted this and said the word of praise, he had eaten and drunk and could go further (without paying anything). But if he did not accept to speak the word of praise, then Abraham would say to him, 'Pay what you owe!' If he then said, 'What do I owe you?,' he would then say to him, 'An amount of wine for 10 *pullarin* (see § Matt 5:26 C, #22), a pound of meat for 10 *pullarin*, and a loaf of bread for 10 *pullarin*. Who gives you wine in the wilderness, who gives you meat in the wilderness, who gives you bread in the wilderness!' When he then saw the hardship that beset him, he would then say, 'Blessed be the eternal God who has fed us from what belongs to him!' This is why first 'mercy' צדקה and then at the end 'justice' משפט is written (Gen 18:19)." — See also Midr. Song. 1:3 (85A). ‖ Genesis Rabbah 59 (37B): "With this I make you swear by Yahweh, the God of heaven and the God of earth" (Gen 24:3). R. Phineas (ca. 360) said, "(Abraham said,) 'Before I had made him (God) known to his creatures, he was (only) God of heaven. After I had made him known to his creatures, he was (also) God of earth.'" — The same thought is found anonymously in SDeut 32:10 § 313 (134B). ‖ Sirach 44:20 (Hebrew): In temptation he (Abraham) was found faithful. — The Greek is the same. ‖ Jubilees 17:15ff.: "And it happened in the 7th week in the 1st year in the 1st month in this (41st) jubilee, on the 12th say of this month (i.e., on the 12th of Nisan), there were voices in heaven about Abraham, that he was faithful in everything that he (God) said to him, and that he loved God and was faithful in all hardship. And Prince Mastema (= Satan) came and said before God, 'See, Abraham loves his son Isaac and delights in him above all. Tell him to bring him as a burnt offering on the altar, and you will see whether he carries out this command, and you will know whether he is faithful in everything that you try him in!' And God knew that Abraham was faithful in all his hardship; for he had tried him by his country and by the famine, and he had tried him also by the wealth of kings, and he had further tried him by his wife, when she was stolen from him, and by circumcision, and he had tried him by Ishmael and by Hagar, his maid, when he sent her away. And in everything that he had tried him in, he was found faithful, and his soul had not been impatient, and he had not hesitated to do it; for he was faithful and loved God." — Jubilees 18:15f.: "(God) said, 'By myself I have sworn,' says God, 'because you did this and you have not refused me your firstborn son whom you love, I will richly bless you and will make your seed exceedingly numerous as the stars of heaven and as the sand on the coast of the sea, and your seed will inherit the cities of its enemies. And in your name all nations of the earth will be blessed because you have listened to my word. And I have made known to all that you are loyal (faithful) to me in everything that I have said to you. Go in peace!'" — Jubilees 19:8f.: "This (the purchase of the double cave as a burial site) is the tenth temptation with which Abraham was tried, and he was found faithful and patient in spirit. And he did not say a word about the promise concerning the land that God had said, that he would give it to him and to his seed after him, but rather he requested a site here to bury his dead. For he was found faithful and was written as a friend of God on the heavenly tablets." ‖ 4 Maccabees 16:20: "It happened for his sake (for God's sake) that also our father Abraham hastened to slaughter his son, the father of nations." ‖ ʾAbot 5.3 above in n. *b*. ‖ Mekilta Exodus 22:20 (101A): Beloved are the proselytes, for our father Abraham was circumcised for the first time as a ninety-nine-year-old; for if he had been circumcised as a twenty- or thirty-year-old, a proselyte would have been able to convert only when he was younger than 20 or 30 years old. Therefore God waited with him (Abraham) until he had let him become 99 years old, in order not to shut the door for future proselytes and to give a recompense for the days and years, in order to increase the recompense of the one who does his will; as it says, "It pleased Yahweh, for the sake of his righteousness, to make the Torah great and glorious" (Isa 42:21).

ξ. On the comprehensive meaning of faith according to Philo, see *Abr.* 46 (Mangey's ed., 2:39) above in n. θ at the end. — Philo, *Quis rerum divinarum heres sit* 6 (Mangey's ed., 1:476 f.) knows how to beautifully portray the feel of Abraham's faith, as he is now seized in the consciousness of his nothingness by trembling and quaking at the thought that he should approach the infinite God, and now filled again with unspeakable joy at being able to confidently come before this God with all his concerns. "I know well, Abraham says to God, your surpassing power; I know the awesomeness of your sovereignty; with fear and trembling I come, and yet again I am comforted; for you have told me not to fear (Gen 15:1).... But when I say that I am comforted, I admit also that I am afraid and pressed down. But I have no disharmonious conflict in me, fear and confidence, as one might think, but rather the purest harmony. I satisfy myself endlessly with the mix that has determined me, not speaking candidly without fear, but also not fearing without candor. For I have learned to gauge my own nothingness and to survey the effusive height of your beneficences, and if I feel that I am earth and ash and even less, just then I have courage to approach you with entreaty...." ‖ Philo, *De migratione Abrahami* 9 (Mangey's ed., 1:442): "God deliberately determined (for Abraham) not the present, but rather the future time in the promise, by not saying, 'The land that I am showing you,' but rather 'that I will show you' (Gen 12:1), as a testimony of the faith that the soul met God with, by it proving to be thankful not based on completed facts, but rather based on the expectation of future things. For holding fast to and hanging on a good hope and being persuaded without vacillating that what was not yet present was present, it (Abraham's soul) found a perfect good as a recompense for the steadfast faith in the one who gave the promise." ‖ Philo, *Quis rerum divinarum heres sit* 18 (Mangey's ed., 1:485): "'Abraham believed God' (Gen 15:6). Someone might say, 'You deem this worthy of praise? Who would not give credence to God when he says and promises something, even if he were otherwise the most unrighteous and godless person?' To this we say, 'No, no, my dear, do not without inspection take away from the wise the praise given to him, nor attribute to the unworthy the most perfect of the virtues, faith, nor rebuke our opinion in this matter. For if you would examine more deeply and not cling so much to the superficial level, you would certainly realize that it is not easy to trust God alone without aid from something else, specifically because of our relationship to perishable being with which we are so closely bound, and this coaxes us to trust in money and honor and power and friends, in health and bodily strength and much else. To free oneself from every single one of these things and not to trust in the creature that is unreliable in itself in every respect, but instead to trust in God who in truth alone is reliable, this is the work of a great and olympic (heavenly) rationality that is captivated by nothing of what we have.'" ‖ Philo, *Legum allegoriae* 3.81 (Mangey's ed., 1:132): "The best thing is therefore to believe God and not foolish thoughts and insecure assumptions. Abraham at least believed God, and he was deemed righteous καὶ δίκαιος ἐνομίσθη (Gen 15:6)."

ο. See the citations at n. ρ.

π. 4 Ezra 9:7: "But all who are saved then (before the dawn of the messianic time) and who have then been able to escape because of their works or because of their faith that they have preserved, these are those who are left over from all the dangers that I have made known to you: they will see my salvation...." — In these words faith still appears as an equal factor in redemption alongside works. The formula is: "works or faith." However, 4 Ezra 13:23: "The same (God) who brings the tribulation in that time (before the coming of the Messiah) will also preserve those who have fallen in the tribulation, if they have works and faith in the Most High and Almighty." — Here the formula is already "works and faith," with the latter coming into consideration only temporarily alongside works; actual salvation lies with the works, but where these fall short, faith can be taken into account if necessary.

ρ. Mekilta Exodus 12:39 (19A): "And they had also not prepared provisions for themselves" (Exod 12:39). With this God wants to proclaim Israel's praise: "Before they said to Moses, 'How can we go out into the wilderness, since we have no provisions for the way,' they instead believed האמינו and followed Moses." Concerning them the explanation is given in the kabbalah (= non-Pentateuchal Scripture): "Go and proclaim in the ears of Jerusalem, ('I was mindful of the grace of your youth ..., since you walked after me in the wilderness, in an unsown land')" (Jer 2:2). What recompense did they receive for this? "Israel is consecrated to the Lord ..." (Jer 2:3). — A parallel is found in Mek. Exod. 14:15 (36A). ‖ Mekilta Exodus 14:15 (35B): Rabbi († 217?) said, "(God said,) 'The faith אֱמוּנָה, with which they have believed in me, is worthy of (merits) my splitting the sea for them; as it says, "That they should turn back and make camp" (Exod 14:2).'" — The obedience to this command (see Exod 14:4) is viewed as an act of faith, and the splitting of the sea is counted as their recompense. ‖ Mekilta Exodus 14:15 (35B): Abtalion (ca. 50 BCE) said, "The faith אֱמִינָה, with which they have believed in me, is worth (merits) that I split the sea for them; as it says, 'And the people believed. They listened ...' (Exod 4:31)." — See Mek. Exod. 14:15 (36A). ‖ Mekilta Exodus 14:31 (40B): Great is the faith אמונה, with which they Israelites believed in the one who spoke and the world came to be; for as a recompense for the Israelites having believed in Yahweh, the holy spirit (spirit of inspiration) rested on them, so that they sang a song; for it says, "They believed in Yahweh and in Moses, his servant" (Exod 14:31), and it says (immediately after that), "Then Moses and the children of Israel sang Yahweh this song" (Exod 15:1). ‖ Mekilta Exodus 15:1 (40B): "Then Moses and the children of Israel sang" (Exod 15:1). R. Nehemiah (ca. 150) said, "Everyone who takes a commandment upon himself in faith אמנה is worthy of the holy spirit resting on him; for so we find it in the case of our ancestors. For as a recompense for our ancestors having believed in Yahweh, they earned (they became worthy of) זכו the holy spirit resting on them and their singing a song; as it says, 'And they believed in Yahweh and in Moses, his servant' (Exod 14:31), and it says (immediately after that), 'Then Moses and the children of Israel sang ...' (Exod 15:1).... Likewise, you find that the Israelites were redeemed from Egypt only as a recompense for faith אמנה; as it says, 'And the people believed' (Exod 4:31)." ‖ Mekilta Exodus 15:1 (41A): "It is exquisite to praise Yahweh and to sing praise to your name, O Most High, to proclaim your grace in the morning and your faithfulness in the nights, to the ten-stringed lute and the harp, to the gentle playing (?) with the zither. For you, Yahweh, have made me rejoice because of your deeds; I will rejoice over the work of your hands" (Ps 92:2–5). Who brought about coming to this joy? This is the recompense for the faith אמנה, with which our ancestors believed in this world, which is the whole night; for so it says, "to proclaim your grace in the morning (of the future world) and your faithfulness in the nights (of this world)." And also Jehoshaphat said, "And they set off in the early morning and went to the wilderness of Tekoa. But while they went out, Jehoshaphat stood and said, 'Listen to me, Judah and you inhabitants of Jerusalem! Believe in Yahweh your God, and you will remain firm, and believe in his prophets, and you will have fortune!'" (2 Chr 20:20). It is also written, "Your eyes, are they not looking out for faithfulness (faith אמונה)?" (Jer 5:3); "And the righteous will live by his faithfulness באמונתו!" (Hab 2:4). It is also written, "They are renewed every morning; great is your faithfulness!" (Lam 3:23). And, likewise, you find that the exiled (dispersed) will be gathered only as a recompense for faith אמנה; as it says, "With me from Lebanon, O bride, with me from Lebanon, come, sing[105] because of faith מראש אמנה" (so Midr. Song. 4:8); furthermore it says, "I will betroth you to myself forever ..., and I will betroth you to myself in faithfulness אמונה" (Hos 2:21, 22). See, great is faith (faithfulness) אמונה before God.... ‖ Midrash Psalm 94 § 5 (210A): R. Levi (ca. 300) said, "Everywhere where the word לוּלֵי 'unless' is said refers to the merit of the Torah; as it says, 'Unless your Torah had been my delight' (Ps 119:92), and the merit of faith זכות האמנה; as it says, 'Unless I believed I would see the goodness of Yahweh in the land of the living' (Ps 27:13)." — Parallels are found in Midr. Ps. 27 § 7 (114B); Gen. Rab. 74 (47D). ‖ Babylonian Talmud Beṣah 15B.30: R. Yohanan († 279) said in the name of R. Eleazar b. Simeon (ca. 180), "God said to the Israelites, 'My children, lend for my sake and sanctify (by eating and drinking well) the holiness of the (Sabbath or feast) day and believe in me (trust in me האמינו בי), and I will repay (compensate you)!'" — In all these passages faith appears as a single meritorious performance that receives its recompense as such. It has become a work that, in reference to its soteriological worth, differs in no way from the works of the law (fulfilling the commandments).

σ. Genesis 15:6 in ancient Jewish literature. The following passages are worded very generally. Septuagint Gen 15:6: καὶ ἐπίστευσεν Ἀβρὰμ τῷ θεῷ καὶ ἐλογίσθη αὐτῷ εἰς δικαιοσύνην. ‖ Jubilees 14:6: "He (Abraham) believed God, and it was reckoned to him as righteousness." ‖ Babylonian Talmud Šabbat 97A: Resh Laqish (ca. 250) said, "Whoever places the pious (innocent) under suspicion will be punished in his body; for it is written: 'But look, they will not believe me (Moses)!' (Exod 4:1). And before God it was evident that the Israelites would believe דמהימני. He said to him, 'They are believers and children of believers מאמינים ובני מאמינים, but you will ultimately not believe להאמין.' They are believers, for it is written, 'And the people believed' (Exod 4:31); children of believers, 'And he believed in Yahweh ...' (Gen 15:6). But you will ultimately not believe; for it says, 'Since you have not believed in me ...' (Num 20:12). How do we know that he was punished (in his body with leprosy)? Because it is written, 'And Yahweh further said to him, "Bring your hand to your chest ..."' (Exod 4:6)." — The same is found anonymously and more briefly in Exod. Rab. 3 (69D). — In all these passages it remains uncertain exactly in what sense Abraham's faith was evaluated. The transformation of the comprehensive posture of Abraham's faith in Gen 15:6 into an isolated meritorious act of faith begins already in pre-Christian time. A first step in this direction was made by 1 Macc 2:52: "Was Abraham not found faithful πιστός (believing?) in temptation and (it) was reckoned to him as righteousness καὶ ἐλογίσθη αὐτῷ εἰς δικαιοσύνην?" — The reference to the law and works in verses 50 and 51 makes it clear that Abraham's faithfulness or faith is here conceived simply as one meritorious performance. — A second step is then made by Shemaiah (ca. 50 BCE). Mekilta Exodus 14:15 (35B): Shemaiah said, "(God said,) 'The faith האמנה with which your father Abraham believed in me merits my splitting the sea for you'; as it says, 'And he believed in Yahweh and it was reckoned to him as righteousness (= as a merit).'" — In subsequent time this interpretation of Gen 15:6 became generally common. Mekilta Exodus 14:31 (40B): Likewise you find that our father Abraham took possession of this world and the future one only by the

105. S-B: Most of the time, the rabbinic scholars interpret תשורי as "sing"; see in n. σ Exod. Rab. 23 (85A), twice.

merit of the faith בזכות אמנה with which he believed in Yahweh; as it says, "He believed in Yahweh and it was reckoned to him as righteousness" (Gen 15:6). ‖ Exodus Rabbah 23 (85A): R. Eleazar b. Yose (ca. 180) said, "When the exiles (dispersed) come there (to Mount Amana in Lebanon), they will sing a song. This is why it says, 'Sing from the peak of Amana' (so Midr. Song. 4:8). A different interpretation: 'Sing from the peak of Amana.' One day in the future (= days of the Messiah) the Israelites will sing a song; as it says, 'Sing to Yahweh a new song, for he has done miracles' (Ps 98:1). And by what merit (i.e., on the basis of what meritorious work) will the Israelites sing a song? By the merit of Abraham בזכות אברהם, who believed in God; as it says, 'And he believed in Yahweh ...' (Gen 15:6). This faith is that by which (because of which) the Israelites will take possession of (the land), and concerning it Scripture says, 'The righteous will live by his faith' (Hab 2:4). This is what 'Sing from the peak of Amana' means. 'From the peak of Senir' (Song 4:8): by the merit of Isaac; 'and of Hermon' (Song 4:8): by the merit of Jacob; 'from the dwellings of lions' (Song 4:8): this pertains to the captivity in Babylon and Media; 'from the mountains of panthers' (Song 4:8): this pertains to Edom (= Rome)." – A parallel is found in Midr. Song. 4:8 (114B). ‖ Exodus Rabbah 23 (85A): R. Simeon b. Abba (ca. 280) said, "(The Israelites became worthy of singing a song at the sea [Exod 15:1ff.] only) because of the faith בשביל האמנה with which Abraham believed God; as it says, 'He believed in Yahweh ...' (Gen 15:6). Accordingly, the Israelites became worthy of singing a song at the sea; as it says, 'Then Moses sang ...' (Exod 15:1). This is what the words mean: 'Since because of the one (by the merit of the one) who is the beginning of faith"'(i.e., by the merit of Abraham; מראש אמנה in Song 4:8 is now interpreted in this way)." – The similar saying of R. Nahman (ca. 400) in Midr. Song. 4:8 (114B) appears to be related to the song at Amana. ‖ Targum Onkelos Genesis 15:6: "And he believed in the Memra of Yahweh, and it was reckoned to him as זְכוּ." – Yerušalmi I: And he had faith in the Memra of Yahweh, and it was reckoned to him as זְכוּ that he had not uttered reproaches (words) before him. – In targumic usage, זְכוּ, determ. זְכוּתָא, most of the time means "the state of being righteous" and thus corresponds to the Old Testament צדקה; but it can also be like the Hebrew זְכוּת = "merit, meritorious action." If one considers how, in all of the citations above, Abraham's faith is glorified as a meritorious work that involves recompense, one will probably do most justice to the Jewish view if one translates זְכוּ in both targum passages not with "righteousness" = "the state of being righteous," but rather simply with "merit." Abraham's faith is recognized by God as a meritorious performance on the basis of which Abraham not only receives this world and the future one as a possession (see above Mek. Exod. 14:31 folio 40B), but also which benefits his distant descendants in multiple ways. Thus, for the rabbinic scholars, Abraham's faith constitutes a fully valid witness for the idea that man gains the favor of God's judgment and is counted as something before God only by virtue of his own meritorious works.

2. ἐλογίσθη αὐτῷ εἰς δικαιοσύνην. – Formally, the expression in y. Pe'ah 1.16B.17 comes closest: All transgressions that he (one who was earlier a penitent man) has committed will be counted to him (if he repents) as merits (righteous, meritorious actions) נחשבין עליו כזָכִיּוֹת. This is offered by the 1609 Krakau edition. Other editions such as, for example,

the 1710 Amsterdam ed. (5A.44) read: נחשבין לו בזכיות. – In Aramaic it is said: אַחֲזֵיק לֵיהּ טֵיבוּתָא "to reckon to one as a good, as merit" (e.g., b. Ber. 18B; see the whole passage at § Luke 16:24 A, near beginning). – See more about λογίζεσθαι at § Rom 2:26, #2. – When it is a matter of reckoning or imputing the merit or guilt of another, the verb תָּלָה "hang, attach" can also be used. Mishnah ʾAbot 5.18: Moses acted rightly זָכָה and he instructed the multitude to do what is right זִכָּה, and the merit זְכוּת of the multitude was imputed to him תְּלוּיָה בוֹ (literally: was attached to him); as it says, "He practiced the righteousness of Yahweh (= what is right before Yahweh) and his laws with Israel" (Deut 33:21). (It is concluded from the עִם "with" that the people's action is viewed simultaneously as the action of Moses.) Jeroboam sinned and misled the multitude to sin, and the sin of the multitude was imputed to him תָּלוּי בוֹ; as it says, "Because of Jeroboam's sins, which he committed and to which he misled Israel" (1 Kgs 15:30; the latter also belong to "Jeroboam's sins").

4:4: But to the one who deals with works, the recompense is not imputed according to grace, but rather according to obligation.

Two principles that are pertinent here are as follows: אין נוטלין שכר אלא על ידי מעשה "recompense is received only for a deed (work)" (Mek. Exod. 12:6 [6A]), and "What you (God) have done toward us (Israel) is grace, because there were no works in our hands" (Mek. Exod. 15:13 [50A]). Thus grace applies only where works are absent. – On the latter idea, see 4 Ezra 8:31–33, 36: "But you are called the Merciful One precisely because we are sinners. For precisely because we do not have works of righteousness, you will be called the Gracious One when you consent to show us grace. For the righteous, for whom many works are stored up with you, will receive a recompense from their own works.... For your righteousness and goodness, O Lord, become evident by your having mercy on those who have no treasure of good works."

4:5: His faith is reckoned as righteousness.

See y. Peʾah 1.16B.17 at § Rom 4:2f., #2 above: Transgressions will be counted as merits.

4:7 f.: Blessed are those whose transgressions have been forgiven and whose sins have been covered; blessed is a man whose sin the Lord will not impute.

The citation agrees verbatim with LXX Ps 32:1f., except the LXX (as also some manuscripts of Rom 4:8) reads ᾧ instead of οὗ in the last sentence. – The psalm passage was used many times in rabbinic literature as well.

Babylonian Talmud Yoma 86B: "(In the confession of sin on the Day of Atonement) one must specify the sins one by one; for it says, 'O, please! This people has committed a great sin, and they have made for themselves a god out of gold.'" These are the words of R. Judah b. Baba († ca. 135). R. Aqiba († ca. 135) said, "Blessed is the one whose transgression is removed, whose sin is covered" (Ps 32:1). – A vestige of this controversy is present also in t. Yoma 5.14 (191). In y. Yoma 8.45C.38 the psalm passage is not drawn on and R. Judah b. Batera appears as the one who disagrees with R. Aqiba. ‖ Midrash Psalm 32 § 2 (121B): "Blessed is the person to whom Yahweh does not impute wrongdoing, and in whose spirit is no deceit" (Ps 32:2). R. Yose b. Judah (ca. 180) said, "For when a person completely repents so that his heart is uprooted in him, God forgives him." ‖ Babylonian Talmud Yoma 86B: Rab Judah († 299) said that Rab († 247) juxtaposed the following passages: "'Blessed is the one whose transgression is removed, whose sin is covered' (Ps 32:1) and 'Whoever covers his misdeeds will not prosper' (Prov 28:13). There is no contradiction: in the one case (Prov 28) it deals with a sin that has become known; in the other case it deals with a sin that has not become known." Rab Zutra b. Tobiah (ca. 270) said that Rab Nahman († 320) said, "In the one case (Prov 28) it deals with the sins of one person against another; in the other case it deals with a person's sins against God." ‖ Pesiqta Rabbati 45 (186A): "Blessed is the person to whom Yahweh does not impute wrongdoing" (Ps 32:2). R. Simeon b. Laqish (ca. 250) said, "What can this be compared with? With a woman who has drunk the bitter water (water of jealousy) and been found pure. Then it began to be said: 'Blessed is my mother, for she did not need to drink that at all.' David said as much: 'Blessed is the one whose transgression is removed, whose sin is covered!' God answered him, 'Blessed is the person to whom Yahweh does not reckon wrongdoing.' And who are these whose transgressions God takes away? These are the Israelites, who are righteous on the Day of Atonement and who specify their sins and transgressions one by one, and God takes away their sins." ‖ See Pesiq. Rab. 45 (186A) at § Rom 2:11. ‖ Babylonian Talmud Berakot 34B: Rab Kahana (ca. 250; according to Diqduqe Soph, Rab Sheshet [ca. 260], should be read) said, "It seems to me that the one who names his sins is presumptuous; for it says, 'Blessed is the one whose transgression is removed, whose sin is covered!' (Ps 32:1)." ‖ Genesis Rabbah 22 (14D): R. Samuel b. Ammi (ca. 325, so read instead of R. Simeon b. Ammi) said, "'Of David, a song. Blessed is the one who is raised above his sin' (Ps 32:1 is now interpreted thus). Blessed is the person who is higher than his sins and whose sin is not higher than him; as it says, 'Sin is a camper before the door' (Gen 4:7). Here it is not written, 'Sin is one who encamps (feminine),' but rather, 'Sin is one who encamps (masc.)': at the beginning it is weak like a woman, but later it becomes strong like a man." ‖ Pesiqta Rabbati 45 (185B): On the Day of Atonement God cleanses Israel and atones for their guilt; as it says, 'For on this day atonement will be made for you, to cleanse you' (Lev 16:30). And if you should say, '(He cleanses) another nation as well,' (know) this: No, only Israel; for so the prophet Micah said, "Who is a God like you, who forgives guilt and passes over sin for the remnant of his inheritance" (Mic 7:18). He forgives only Israel. When David saw how God forgives the sins of the Israelites and has mercy on them, he began to declare them blessed and to boast: "Blessed is the one whose transgression is removed ..." (Ps 32:1). ‖ Pesiqta Rabbati 45 (185B): "Of David, a song ..." (Ps 32:1). This is what is said: "You have removed the guilt of your people, covered all their sins; Selah" (so Midr. Ps. 85:3). You find that on the Day of Atonement Satan comes to indict

Israel. He enumerates Israel's sins one by one and says, "Lord of the world, among the nations of the world there are adulterers, just as in Israel; among the nations of the world there are thieves, just as in Israel." God enumerates the merits זְכֻיּוֹת of Israel one by one. What does he do? He takes the scale and weighs the debts against the merits, and debts and merits balance out, and the two weighing dishes are found to hang down to the same level. Satan goes to fetch debts and lay them on the dish of the debts and thus to give this one the greater weight. What does God do? While Satan goes around and looks for debts, God takes debts away from the dish and hides them under his purple. Satan comes, without having found one debt there; as it says, "One will look for the debt of Israel, and there will be not be one" (Jer 50:20). When Satan sees this, he says to God, "Lord of the world, you have taken away one debt of your people!" When David saw this, he said, "How he removes debt and covers their sins!" Then he began to praise them: "Blessed is the one for whom one transgression is removed, one sin is covered! (Ps 32:1). ‖ Midrash Psalm 32 § 3 (122A): "Blessed is the person to whom Yahweh does not impute wrongdoing" (Ps 32:2), namely because he has performed a fulfillment of the commandments מִצְוָה (= work of the law) corresponding to it (canceling it out).

4:9: Now, this blessedness, does it pertain to the circumcision (the circumcised) or also to the foreskin (the uncircumcised)?

See Pesiq. Rab. 45 (185B) above at § Rom 4:7f., which answers as follows: "It pertains only to Israel, thus the circumcised." By contrast, in verse 10, the apostle can refer to the fact that the righteousness of faith was already attributed to Abraham, when he was still in the foreskin; but according to the official chronology of the ancient synagogue, the circumcision of Abraham happened a full 29 years later than the making of the covenant which is dealt with in Gen 15.

Seder ʿOlam Rabbah 1: Our father Abraham was 70 years old in the hour when it was spoken to him and he was between the pieces (Gen 15:10). — Since according to Gen 17:1 Abraham was 99 years old at the time he was circumcised, 29 years lay between Gen 15:1ff. an 17:10ff. See also the chronological statements at § Acts 7:6.

4:11 A: He received the sign of circumcision as a seal of the righteousness of faith.

Concerning circumcision as a sign and seal of the Abrahamic covenant, see the excursus "Circumcision."

4:11 B: Father of all who believe while in circumcision.

The synagogue similarly called Abraham the father of proselytes. See TanḥB לך לך § 6 (32A) at § Rom 4:2f., #1, n. λ.

4:12 A: Father of the circumcision (circumcised).

Abraham, the father of Israel. See § Matt 3:9 A.

4:12 B: Who walk in the footsteps of our father Abraham's faith which was present while he was in the foreskin.

See § John 8:39 and § Rom 2:29 B. ‖ Mishnah Niddah 4.2: The daughters of the Sadducees, if they are wont to walk in the ways of their ancestors ללכת בדרכי אבותיהן, behold, they are as Samaritan women; but if they depart from those to walk in the ways of the Israelites ללכת בדרכי ישראל, behold, they are like an Israelite woman.

4:13 A: For the promise to Abraham or to his seed did not come into being through the law ..., but rather through the righteousness of faith.

1. The ancient synagogue made the precisely opposite judgment: all the promises were bestowed on Abraham on the basis of his righteousness by the law, and if Gen 15:6 says that faith was reckoned to Abraham as righteousness, this faith too is viewed only as a meritorious performance that stands in one line with the works of the law. On this point, see in detail at § Rom 4:2f., #1, n. *d.* Even the objection that Abraham could not be righteous by the law because there was not yet any law at his time did not change the position of the rabbinic scholars; for in their circles it was a foregone conclusion that Abraham observed the whole Torah, although it had not yet been given.[a]

a. See 2 Bar. 57:2; m. Qidd. 4.14; b. Yoma 28B; TanḥB לך לך § 14 (36A) at § Rom 4:2f., #1, n. *a*; see Jub. 24:11 at § Rom 4:2f., #1, n. *c.* ‖ A baraita in b. Ned. 32A: Rabbi († 217?) said, "Great is circumcision; for you have no one who devoted himself to fulfilling the commandments (works of the law) מִצְוֹת as much as our father Abraham, and he was called 'perfect' תמים first because of circumcision; as it says, 'Walk before me, so you will be perfect' (Gen 17:1) and it is also written, 'And I will institute my covenant between myself and you' (Gen 17:2)." – Of the specific commandments of the Torah that Abraham observed, the following in particular are named. Jubilees 6:19: "Abraham alone observed it (the festival of weeks or Pentecost), and Isaac and Jacob and his children have observed them up until your (Moses') days. And in your days the children of Israel forgot this, until I renewed it for them on this mountain (Sinai)." – Jubilees 15:1f.: "In the 5th year of the 4th week of years of this Jubilee, in the 3rd month in the middle of the month, Abram celebrated the feast of the first fruits of the grain harvest. And he offered as a new offering to God on the altar the first fruits: a steer and a ram and a sheep on the altar as a whole offering for God; the offering of fruit and drink that go with them he offered on the altar with incense." – Jubilees 16:21: "He (Abraham) built tabernacles for himself and for his servants on this feast and was the first person to celebrate the feast on earth." – Jubilees 21:7ff. reports how Abraham introduces his son Isaac to the offerings of the Torah. ‖ Babylonian Talmud Baba Meṣiʿa 87A: Ephraim, the quarrelsome (ca. 170), the student of R. Meir, said in the name of R. Meir (ca. 150), "Our father Abraham ate the profane foods in purity (according to the stipulations of the purity laws)." ‖ Genesis Rabbah 49 (31A): R. Berekhiah (ca. 340) and R. Hiyya (ca. 280) and the rabbis there said in the name of R. Judah (ca. 150), "Not a day goes by without God stipulating a new halakah in the heavenly court; as it says, 'Listen, O listen to the din of his voice and the meditation that proceeds from his mouth' (Job 37:2). This 'meditation' pertains to nothing other than the Torah; as it says, 'Meditate over it (the book of the Torah) day and night' (Josh 1:8). Abraham knew even these halakoth." — The same is found garbled in Gen. Rab. 64 (40C). ‖ Genesis Rabbah 42 (26B): "One who had escaped came" (Gen 14:13). Resh Laqish (ca. 250) said in the name of Bar Qappara (ca. 220), "It was Og who had escaped; and why was he called Og? Because he met Abram at his arrival, as he sat there and concerned himself with the commandments about the bread cakes עוּגוֹת." — Deuteronomy Rabbah 1 (197A) is clearer: About the Passover-bread cakes. — Targum Yerušalmi I Genesis 14:13: "Og came on the day of preparation for the Passover feast. He met him (Abraham), as he prepared unleavened cakes." ‖ Babylonian Talmud Yoma 28B: Rab († 247), it has also been said, "Rab Ashi († 427) said that our father Abraham observed even the 'mixing of the foods' (see the excursus 'The Day of Jesus' Death,' C, #3); for it says, 'My Torahs' (Gen 26:5), that is, both the written and the oral (traditional) Torah (and the stipulation about the mixing of foods belonged to the latter)." ‖ Genesis Rabbah 49 (31A): R. Aha (ca. 320) said in the name of R. Samuel b. Nahman (ca. 260) in the name of R. Nathan (= Jonathan, ca. 220), "Abraham knew even the halakoth about the 'mixing of courts.'"[106] — Parallels are found in Gen. Rab. 64 (40C.15); 95 (60B.30); TanḥB לך לך § 1 (29B); § 14 (36A); Midr. Ps. 1 § 13 (7A). ‖ Targum Yerušalmi I Genesis 21:14: "Abraham headed off early in the morning, took bread and a wineskin with water and gave it to Hagar, put it on her shoulder (כספה probably a misspelling of כתפה), and bound it around her hips to make it known that she was a slave, and also the boy; then he dismissed her by a letter of divorce." ‖ Genesis Rabbah 43 (26C): "He emptied out the number of his proven men" (so Midr. Gen. 14:14). R. Levi (ca. 300) said, "As a consequence (of the reading) of the section about the officers (= Deut 20:5ff.) he reduced their number; as it says, 'Whichever man is afraid or despondent of heart, let him go and return to his house' (Deut 20:8)." — Rab's († 247) interpretation הוריקן בתורה in Ned. 32A may mean the same thing. ‖ Pesiqta 98A: R. Huna (ca. 350) said, "The earlier ancestors set apart the offerings and the tithes. Abraham set apart the great offering (the so-called offering of the priests in Num 18:8ff., cf. Deut 18:4); for it says, 'I raise my hand to Yahweh' (Gen 14:22). This 'raising' means nothing but the offering (see Num 18:26: 'Raise from this an offering for Yahweh')." — In the parallel Pesiq. Rab. 25 (127B): Abraham set apart the first tithe (Num 18:21ff.); as it says, "He gave him a tithe of everything" (Gen 14:20); in Num. Rab. 12 (167A): "First Abraham set apart the tithe" (see Gen 14:20). ‖ Concerning the institution of the morning prayer through Abraham, see § Acts 10:9 B, #4, n. *e*. ‖ Babylonian Talmud ʿAbodah Zarah 14B: Rab Hisda († 309) said to Abimi (ca. 270), "We have learned by tradition that the tractate of our father Abraham on idolatry comprised 400 chapters, and we have studied only 5 and we do not know what we say and what contradicts us." ‖ In b. Soṭah 14A, in an interpretation of Isa 53:12 referring to Moses, R. Simlai (ca. 250) says that Abraham, Isaac, and Jacob were heroes in the Torah and in the commandments.

---

106. S-B: On the Sabbath, nothing may be carried from one private area to another. Therefore, those who share the same courtyard unite their areas by putting food made from common contributions in one of the dwellings on Friday. See Strack, *Einleitung in den Talmud und Midraš*, 38f.

The question of whence Abraham acquired his knowledge of the Torah is answered in various ways.

α. From himself. — Genesis Rabbah 61 (38B): R. Simeon (ca. 150) said, "A father did not teach him (Abraham) and he did not have a teacher. From where did he learn the Torah? God appointed זימן for him his two kidneys as two teachers, and they bubbled and taught him Torah and wisdom. This is what is written: 'I will praise Yahweh, who has counseled me, even at night my kidneys admonished me' (Ps 16:7)." — Parallels are found in Gen. Rab. 95 (60B); TanḥB ויגש § 12 (106A); Midr. Ps. 1 § 13 (7A); 16 § 7 (61B). ‖ Genesis Rabbah 95 (60B): R. Levi (ca. 300) said, "From himself he (Abraham) learned Torah; as it says, 'Whoever is of devious heart will be full from his ways; but the good man from himself' (Prov 14:14)." See Num. Rab. 14 (173A) at § Rom 1:20 D, n. *e*.

β. From written traditions. — In Jub. 21:10, after Abraham has introduced his son to the Torah of offerings, he says, "So I found written in the book of my forefathers and in the words of Enoch and in the words of Noah." — The view is probably that Enoch brought down to earth transcriptions of the heavenly tablets and books and left them behind for his descendants.

γ. By divine revelation. — Mekilta Exodus 20:18 (78B): (In the vision in Gen 15) God let Abraham see the sanctuary and the order of offerings; as it says, "Take for me a three-year-old heifer …" (Gen 15:9). ‖ Genesis Rabbah 44 (27D): He said to him, "'Take for me a three-year-old heifer …" (Gen 15:9). He showed him three kinds of young bulls and three kinds of goats and three kinds of rams. Three kinds of young bulls: the young bull of the Day of Atonement, the young bull that is offered for all the other commandments, and the calf whose neck is broken. Three kinds of goats: the goat for the feast days, the goats for the new moons, and the goat for the individual Israelite. Three kinds of rams: the guilt offering in clear cases, the guilt offering in unclear cases, and the lamb for the individual Israelite. 'And a turtledove and a young dove' (Gen 15:9), that is, a turtledove and a baby dove. 'And he took all this for him' (Gen 15:10)." R. Simeon b. Yohai (ca. 150) and the rabbis. R. Simeon b. Yohai said, "He showed him all the atoning offerings, but the tenth of an *ephah* (of fine flour in Lev 4:11) he did not show him." But the rabbis said, "He showed him the tenth of an *ephah* too. It says here, 'And he took all this אֵלֶּה for him' (Gen 15:10); and it says there, 'Let him bring a food offering that is prepared from this אֵלֶּה (מ) for Yahweh' (Lev 2:8). (As in Lev 2:8, אלה pertains to the food offering, the same applies in Gen 15:10.) 'But he did not cut the birds in pieces' (Gen 15:10): God showed him that in the case of burnt offerings involving birds, one separates (the head; Lev 1:14ff.), but in the case of sin offerings involving birds, one does not separate (it; Lev 5:8)." — See also § Rom 1:20 D, notes *d* and *e*.

2. ἐπαγγελία = pledge, promise. The word is rare in the LXX. Psalm 56:9: "Lay my tears before yourself, as it is also in your pledge ὡς καὶ ἐν τῇ ἐπαγγελίᾳ σου." The underlying text has: הֲלֹא בְּסִפְרָתֶךָ = not in your book? (May be a gloss.) — In Ezek 7:26 it is uncertain whether ἀγγελία or ἐπαγγελία should be read; the word in the text is: שְׁמוּעָה "news." — The base text of Amos 9:6 has: "The one who builds his balcony in heaven and his vault אֲגֻדָּתוֹ, he has established it above the earth." Septuagint: "The one

who builds his staircase into heaven and establishes (makes firm) his pledge (promise) on earth καὶ τὴν ἐπαγγελίαν αὐτοῦ ἐπὶ τῆς γῆς θεμελιῶν." Here אֲגֻדָּה is interpreted as = אַגָּדָה "announcement" (*nomen actionis* from הִגִּיד to announce, proclaim). — Esther 4:7: "Mordecai communicated to him what had happened and the promise that Haman had given the king concerning the 10,000 talents for the treasury." The words: τὴν ἐπαγγελίαν, ἣν ἐπηγγείλατο are an addition that do not correspond to anything in the underlying text. — ἐπαγγελία is found in the general sense "pledge, promise" also in 1 Esdras 1:7: ταῦτα ἐκ τῶν βασιλικῶν ἐδόθη κατ' ἐπαγγελίαν τῷ λαῷ καὶ τοῖς ἱερεῦσι καὶ Λευίταις. — 1 Maccabees 1:15: καὶ ἤκουσεν Ἀλέξανδρος ὁ βασιλεὺς τὰς ἐπαγγελίας ὅσας ἀπέστειλε Δημήτριος τῷ Ἰωνάθαν. — Josephus, *Jewish Antiquities* 3.5.1: "The Hebrews ... occupied the foot of the mountain, with the exalted thought that Moses would return from God with the promise of the goods (with the promised goods) μετὰ τῆς ἐπαγγελείας τῶν ἀγαθῶν which he had made for them. — Josephus, *Jewish Antiquities* 5.8.11: "The heads of the Philistine community came to her (Delilah) and by promises ἐπαγγελίαις persuaded her to find out the source of Samson's strength." — ἐπαγγελία stands specifically for divine promises in, for example, Pr. Man. 6: "Immeasurable and unfathomable is the mercy of your promise (= your promised mercy)" τὸ ἔλεος τῆς ἐπαγγελίας σου. — Psalms of Solomon 12:6: "καὶ ὅσιοι κυρίου κληρονομήσαιεν ἐπαγγελίας κυρίου the Lord's pious ones may inherit (obtain) the Lord's promises." — Testament of Joseph 20: "God ... will lead you into the promise of your fathers εἰς τὴν ἐπαγγελίαν τῶν πατέρων ὑμῶν, that is, into the land promised to your fathers." — Wisdom 12:21 says ὑπόσχεσις "promise" instead of ἐπαγγελία: "With what great attentiveness you ruled your children to whose fathers you gave oaths and covenants of good promises συνθήκας ἀγαθῶν ὑποσχέσεων!?" (The ὑπισχνέομαι is likewise used in Sib. Or. 3:768f.: He, who once gave the holy law to the pious, to whom he promised ὑπέσχετο he would make the whole earth open.)

The rabbinic equivalent of ἐπαγγελία is הַבְטָחָה[a] "assurance, promise," a *nomen actionis* from הִבְטִיחַ[b] = to assure, promise. The choice of precisely the expression הבטחה to designate the divine promise indicates that absolute security or reliability was seen as the characteristic feature of the divine promise.

a. Mekilta Exodus 14:15 (35A): (God said to Moses,) "Because of the promise that I gave to your father Jacob בשביל הבטחה שהבטחתי יעקב, I split the sea for you"; for it says, "And your seed will be like the dust of the earth, and you will spread out ופרצת to the west and the east ..." (Gen 28:14). Here he intimated to him the separating (splitting) פרוץ of the sea. R. Judah b. Batera (ca. 110) said, "God said to him, 'Long ago I carried out the promise that I gave to your father Abraham הבטחה שהבטחתי אברהם'; for it says, 'And he made the sea a dry place' (Exod 14:21)." (The last sentence is certainly garbled.)[107] ‖ Genesis Rabbah 41 (25A): That whole night (in the house of pharaoh, Gen 12:17), Sarah lay stretched out on her face and said, "Lord of worlds, Abraham went out (from his fatherland) with a promise בהבטחה, and I went out (without any such promise) in faith באמנה. Abraham went out from a prison (the idolatrous house of his father), and I am in a prison!" Then God said to her, "Everything that I do, I do for your sake, and all will say, 'Because of Sarai, Abram's wife' (Gen 12:17)." — The same is found in Gen. Rab. 52 (33C). ‖ In Midr. Esth. 4:15 (98A) Mordecai says in a prayer, "This provoker of wrath (Haman) will know that you have not forgotten the promise that you gave us ההבטחה שהבטחתנו: 'But even then, while they are in the land of their enemies, I will not cast them away and I will not abhor them, so as to wear them out, or to break my covenant with them; for I am Yahweh their God' (Lev 26:44)." ‖ Numbers Rabbah 2 (137C): "The number of the children of Israel will be as the sand of the sea" (Hos 2:1). This is what is written: "Forever, Yahweh, your word stands firm in heaven" (Ps 119:89); for God had given Abraham a promise (pledge) הבטיח את אברהם and that promise הבטחה came (= was fulfilled) in the hour when the Israelites went out of Egypt. And when had God given him the promise הבטיחו? When he told him that he should go from the house of his father; as it says, "Go from your land ..." "And I will make you into a great people ..." (Gen 12:1, 2). ‖ Exodus Rabbah 19 (81B): Aquila the proselyte (ca. 110) asked our teachers (R. Eliezer and R. Joshua [ca. 90]) and said to them, "What does 'Who loves the stranger (in the later meaning = proselyte), to give him bread and clothing' (Deut 10:18) mean? Are these all the promises that he has given to the proselyte כל הַבְטָחוֹת שהבטיח את הגר, that he would give him bread and clothing?" — Concerning the proselyte Aquila, see § 1 Cor 16:19; there n. *d* has the parallels to our passage.

Besides the meaning "promise" הַבְטָחָה also has the more general meaning "trust, confidence," in, for example, m. Ber. 5.4: Whoever comes before the ark (as the prayer leader) should not answer "Amen" after the priests (after the blessing of the priests; Num 6:24ff.) due to distractibility (and because one must fear making an error during prayer), and if there is no (other) priest there except himself (the priest who speaks the blessing), he should not raise his hands (to say the blessing). But if he has confidence in himself הַבְטָחָתוֹ that he can raise his hands and then can return to his prayer (without making an error), he may do so. ‖ Genesis Rabbah 76 (49A): R. Judan (ca. 350) said, "God said to him (Jacob), 'Return to the land of your ancestors ...' (Gen 31:3), and yet Jacob was very afraid (see Gen 32:8). From this one knows that for the righteous there is no confidence הבטחה (no absolutely certain rest in the promises of God) in this world." R. Huna (ca. 350) said in the name of R. Aha (ca. 320), "(God said to Jacob,) 'Behold, I am with you' (cf. Gen 31:3) (and Jacob himself had said,) 'If God will be with me' (Gen 28:20) (and yet Jacob was afraid; Gen 32:8); from this it follows that for the righteous there is no confidence הבטחה in this world." R. Huna said in the name of R. Aha, "'I will be with you (Moses)' (Exod 3:12), and nothing bad will harm you; and further it is written, 'And it happened on the way in the night quarters that Yahweh attacked him (Moses) and intended to kill him' (Exod 4:24); but for the righteous

107. See Bacher, *Die Agada der Tannaïten*, 1:377.

there is no confidence הבטחה in this world." A parallel is found in b. Sanh. 98B. – See Hillel's (ca. 20 BCE) word in m. ʾAbot 2.4: "Do not trust in yourself before the day you die," which in b. Ber. 29A is justified by the idea that the righteous could become a godless person in the end. See further b. Ber. 4A below in n. *b.* ‖ Babylonian Talmud Berakot 17A: Greater is the confidence הבטחה, with which God has women trust הבטיחן than the men. (Proof: in Isa 32:9 women are called "light-hearted" שאננות and "trusting" בוטחות).

b. הִבְטִיחַ "to promise." – See Mek. Exod. 14:15 (35A); Midr. Esth. 4:15 (98A); Num. Rab. 2 (137C); Exod. Rab. 19 (81B) above in n. *a.* ‖ Mishnah Maʿaśer Šeni 5.13: We have done what you stipulated concerning us; so you (God) too, do what you have promised us שֶׁהִבְטַחְתָּנוּ. ‖ Babylonian Talmud Šebiʿit 35B: "All the names of God that are named at Gibeah-Benjamin (i.e., in Judg 20) are profane (not real names of God)" according to R. Eliezer (ca. 90); R. Joshua (ca. 90) said, "Holy (real names of God)." R. Eliezer said to him, "How can this be? Should he have promised מבטיח and not have kept it?" R. Joshua answered him, "What he promised הבטיח, he kept; but they have not tested whether (the oracle) related to prevailing or being defeated (see Judg 20:18ff.)." ‖ Pesiqta Rabbati 42 (178A): (Sarah said,) "'I will rejoice in Yahweh' (Hab 3:18) concerning what he promised me הבטיחני through the angels: 'Truly, your wife Sarah will give birth' (Gen 17:19). And what he promised me הבטיחני, he immediately did: 'And Yahweh visited Sarah' (Gen 21:1)."

One also commonly encounters the passive participle מֻבְטָח = one who has received a pledge may consider himself assured. Babylonian Talmud Berakot 4A: "If I did not לוּלֵא believe that I would see the goodness of Yahweh in the land of the living" (Ps 27:13). In the name of R. Yose (ca. 150) it has been taught: "Why are there two points over לולא? David said before God, 'Lord of the world, I may consider myself assured by you מובטח אני בך that you will pay out a good recompense to the righteous in the future; but I do not know whether my portion will be among them or not.'" (David's certainty of salvation is indicated by the two points over לולא.) ‖ Babylonian Talmud Berakot 4B: R. Eleazar b. Abina (ca. 340; this is to be read) said, "Whoever says the 'praise song of David' (i.e., Ps 145) three times a day may consider himself assured מובטח לו that he is a son of the future world." ‖ Babylonian Talmud ʿErubin 43B: Long ago the Israelites were assured מובטח להן that Elijah will come neither on the preparation days of the Sabbaths nor on the preparation days of the feast days nor because of the labor (for one would neglect the errands necessary for the Sabbath in order to welcome Elijah, Rashi). ‖ A barainta in b. Talmud Pesaḥ. 49A: Let a person always sell what he has in order to be able to marry the daughter of a scholar for what he sells; for if he dies or goes into exile, he may be assured מובטח לו that his sons will be scholars.... ‖ Babylonian Talmud Megillah 28B: In the school of Elijah it has been taught: Whoever studies halakoth may consider himself assured מובטח לו that he will be a son of the future world; for it says, "He has הליכות of eternity" (Hab 3:6). Do not read הֲלִיכוֹת = courses, ways, but rather הֲלָכוֹת = dictates of justice (these are what he has forever). – The same is found in b. Nid. 73A; see also S. Eli. Zut. 2 (173). ‖ Babylonian Talmud Ketubbot 111A: R. Abbahu (ca. 300) said, "Even a servant girl who lives in the land of Israel may consider herself assured מובטח לה that she will be a daughter of the future world. Here it is written, 'Who gives the breath of life to the people on it' (Isa 42:5); there it is written, 'Remain here, donkey people' (so Midr. Gen. 22:5), the people that is like a donkey (thus even male and female slaves who live in the land of Israel belong to 'the people' that Isa 42:5 speaks of). 'And spirit to those who walk on it' (Isa 42:5)." R. Jeremiah b. Abba (ca. 250) said that R. Yohanan († 279) said, "Whoever walks 4 cubits in the land of Israel may consider himself assured מובטח לו that he will be a son of the future world." — Further examples may be found in b. Giṭ. 58A.24; b. Naz. 29B.28; b. B. Meṣ. 83B.38; SDeut 31:14 § 305 (129B); Lev. Rab. 16 (116D).

4:13 B: That he would be an heir of the world.

The ancient synagogue is also familiar with Abraham as the heir of the whole world.

See Sir 44:19ff. (Hebrew) at § Rom 4:2f., #1, n. *b*; see Mek. Exod. 14:31 (40B) at § Rom 4:2f., #1, n. *d*, σ. ‖ Numbers Rabbah 12 (167A): First Abraham set apart the tithe; as it says, "He gave him a tithe of everything" (Gen 14:20), and (for this) God let him acquire heaven and earth (see on this the next two citations). ‖ Numbers Rabbah 14 (173A): God said to Abraham, "The things above and the things below are mine; as it says, 'What is under the whole of heaven belongs to me' (Job 41:3); and further it says, 'Yahweh's is the earth and its fullness' (Ps 24:1). And you have made my name known in the world. On your life, I will let you acquire the things above and the things below; as it says, 'Blessed be Abram, the acquisitor of heaven and earth, by the most high God' (so Gen 14:19 according to the midr.)." ‖ Midrash Proverbs 19 § 1 (43A): Abraham won the acquisition of heaven and earth; for it says, "Blessed be Abram, the acquisitor of heaven and earth, by the most high God!" (Gen 14:19). — The targumim did not adopt this interpretation of Gen 14:19. ‖ A different view is represented by Gen. Rab. 11 (8C): R. Yohanan († 279) said in the name of R. Yose b. Halapta (ca. 150), "Since it is not written that he observed the Sabbath, Abraham came to possess the world את העולם in a measure (in a limited way); as it says, 'Get up, go around in the land in its length and width' (Gen 13:17). However, it is written that Jacob observed the Sabbath; for it says, 'He camped before the city' (Gen 33:18.) While (the Sabbath) came with the dusk, Jacob had determined the boundary of the Sabbath when it was still day.[108] (Therefore) he took possession of the world not in measure; for it says, 'Your seed will be like the dust of the earth, and you will spread out the west and east and north and south (so, without boundary)' (Gen 28:14)." — Leqach Tob (1.72A) remarks about Gen 28:14: "You will spread out the west and east and north and south." He added the four directions of the world to him as good news בְּשׂוֹרָה; what he did not say to Abraham and Isaac, he said to Jacob. And this will come to fulfillment in the future in the days of the Messiah; as it says, "I will make you ride along on the heights of the land, and I will make you enjoy the inheritance of Jacob, your father" (Isa 58:14).

108. S-B: Jacob stops before the city; from this it was inferred that the arrival of the Sabbath prevents one from entering into a city and caused Jacob's further actions, as stated above. This provided a basis for the assumption that Scripture reported that Jacob observed the Sabbath. — On the time when the Sabbath began, see § Acts 1:12 B.

4:15 A: The law works wrath.

This thought, but limited to human parties in court, is remotely discernible in the following sentences as well: Before judgment only strict justice is valid; justice as such knows nothing of mercy or compassion; only in one case are justice and mercy united in the process of judgment, and this comes at the conclusion of a settlement; yet the views concerning the reliability of a companion diverged starkly from each other.

Mishnah Ketubbot 9.2: R. Aqiba († ca. 135) said, "In justice one does not exercise compassion אין מרהמין בַּהִין." ‖ Tosefta Sanhedrin 1.2ff. (415): A settlement פְּשׁרָה is concluded by three judges. If the procedure of judgment was concluded, a settlement may not (any longer) be achieved אין רשאי לבצוע. R. Eliezer b. Yose the Galilean (ca. 150) said, "Whoever achieves a settlement המבצע is a sinner, and whoever praises one who achieves a settlement, behold, he blasphemes (before) God. On this it has been said, 'He praises the one who concludes a settlement בוצע, he despises Yahweh' (so Ps 10:3 according to the midr.); rather let justice bore through the mountain (*pereat mundus, fiat justitia*). For Moses said thus, 'Let justice bore through the mountain!' But Aaron made peace between a person and his neighbor; as it says, 'He walked in peace and uprightness …' (Mal 2:6)." R. Eliezer b. Jacob (ca. 150) said, "What does Scripture intend to teach by saying: 'If the thieving man says a word of praise, he despises (reviles) Yahweh' (so now Ps 10:3)? A parable was told; what can this be compared with? With someone who stole a *seah* of wheat. He ground it and baked it and set some of it apart for the dough offering and gave some of it to his children to eat. What should he say as a word of praise (over the bread)? He says no word of praise. Concerning him it was said, 'If the thieving man says a word of praise, he despises (reviles) Yahweh'…." R. Joshua b. Qarha (ca. 150) said, "It is a commandment to negotiate a settlement; for it says, 'Administer judgments of truth and justice and peace in your gates' (Zech 8:16). Is it not so that wherever there is real justice there is no peace (no peaceful resolution to the complaint), and wherever there is peace, there is no real justice; but what is a case of real justice in which (where) there is peace? Say: 'This is the settlement בִּיצּוּעַ.' Likewise, it says about David, 'And David practiced justice and blessing צְדָקָה to his entire people' (2 Sam 8:15). Is it not so that where there is justice מִשְׁפָּט, there is no blessing צדקה, wherever there is blessing, there is no justice; but what is a case of justice, in which (where) there is blessing? Say: 'This is mediation בִּיצּוּעַ.' He spoke the verdict: 'He found in favor of the one who was right, and he condemned the guilty. When he would condemn a poor man, he would fetch some (from his own money) and would give to him from his own. So he was found to be one who performed a blessing צדקה toward this one, while he spoke the verdict for the other one (according to justice).'" Rabbi († 217?) said, "He spoke the verdict: 'He found in favor of the one who was right, and he condemned the guilty. So he was found to be one who performed a blessing צדקה toward the guilty; for he fetched what had been stolen underhandedly, and (simultaneously) did justice to the one who was right; for he gave him back what was his.'" R. Simeon b. Manasseh (ca. 180) said, "Sometimes a settlement should be achieved, and sometimes a settlement should not be achieved. How then? If two agree that he should administer justice, this one may say to them, if he still has not heard their speeches, or if he has heard their speeches, but does not (yet) know where justice will incline: 'Go and make a settlement ביצעו!' But if he has heard their speeches and knows where justice will incline, he may not say to them 'Go and make a settlement!'; as it is written, 'The beginning of strife is as when someone lets floods of water loose. Therefore before it comes to burs, לפני התגלע, cease from strife' (Prov 17:14); before the dispute is made clear נתגלה (wordplay), you may cease from it (in order to make a settlement), but after the dispute it made clear, you may not cease from it." — Parallels are found in y. Sanh. 1.18B.9; Sanh. 6A, B; the saying of R. Joshua b. Qarha is found also in Tanḥ. משפטים 94A.

4:15 B: Where there is no law, there is also no transgression.

Schöttgen cites Yalquṭ Reubeni 17D.10: "*Adamus non mortuus esset, nisi legem Dei cognitam habuisset*"; correctly translated, the Yalquṭ passage reads: If the first man had studied the Torah, he would not have died. — Thus, the passage does not belong here. — Yalquṭ Reubeni drew from Yalquṭ Simeoni Lev 26:3 (§ 771) and this passage in turn drew from Tanḥ. בחקותי 182A: If the first man had observed the Torah and the commandments that had been given to him, he would not have died; this is why it says, "If you walk in my statutes" (Lev 26:3).

4:16f.: Who is a father to all of us, as it is written: "I have appointed you the father of many nations" (Gen 17:5).

The interpretation of the name "Abraham" = "father of a multitude of nations" (Gen 17:4f.) caused the ancient synagogue as well to call Abraham the father of proselytes and all people.

For Abraham as the father of proselytes, see TanḥB לך לך § 6 (32A) at § Rom 4:2f., #1, n. *d*, λ. ‖ Mishnah Bik. 1.4: The following offer the first fruits without reciting (from Deut 26:5ff.): The proselyte offers and does not recite, because he cannot say: "You have sworn this to our ancestors, to give it to them" (Deut 26:3). But if his mother stemmed from Israel, he offers and recites. When he (a proselyte) prays only for himself, he says, "The God of Israel's ancestors"; when he is in a synagogue, he says, "The God of your ancestors." But if his mother stemmed from Israel, he says, "The God of our ancestors." — The baraita in y. Bik. 1.64A.15 is different: It has been taught as a tannaitic tradition in the name of R. Judah (ca. 150): "The proselyte himself offers and recites. Why? Because it says, 'I have appointed you the father of a multitude of nations' (Gen 17:5). Heretofore you were a father for Aram (thus אברם = אַב אֲרָם); but from now on and beyond you are a father for all nations." R. Joshua b. Levi (ca. 250) said, "The halakah is in accordance with R. Judah." The matter came before R. Abbahu (ca. 300) and he taught as R. Judah did. — According to t. Bik. 1.2 (100) R. Judah claimed the right of recitation for the Kenites, the descendants of Hobab, the brother-in-law of Moses, on the basis of Num 10:32. ‖ Tosefta Berakot 1.13 (2): "Your name will no longer be Abram, but rather Abraham will be your name" (Gen 17:5). Behold, at the beginning you were a father in relation to Aram, but now, look, you are a father for all who come into the world; as it says, "For I have appointed you the father of the multitude of nations" (Gen 17:5). — In b. Ber. 13A: Ultimately, he became a father for the whole world. ‖ Babylonian Talmud Šabbat 105A: R. Yohanan († 279) said in the name of R. Yose b. Zimra (ca. 220), "Where is (the proof) for the notarikon-interpretation (according to which the letters of a word are understood as an abbreviation of words) from the Torah? Because it says, 'I have appointed you the "father of a multitude" אַב הֲמוֹן of nations' (Gen 17:5). I have made you the 'father' אָב for the nations; I have made you the 'chosen one' בָּחוּר among the nations; הָמוֹן: I have made you the 'beloved one' חָבִיב (ח and ה can be interchanged with each other in the same interpretation) among the nations; I have made you the 'king' מֶלֶךְ for the nations; I have made you the 'righteous' (pious) וָתִיק among the nations; I have made you the 'faithful' (reliable) נֶאֱמָן for the nations."

4:17 A: Before God, whom he believed.

κατέναντι is not = בִּפְנֵי "before" in the sense of "opposite of" or "in comparison with,"[a] but rather = לִפְנֵי "before" in the sense of "in the eyes of,"[b] which in the targumim is קֳדָם.[c]

a. Babylonian Talmud Pesaḥim 8A: What are the righteous like (in their future glorious splendor) before the Shekinah בפני ש'? Like the light before בפני (in comparison with) a torch.

b. Mekilta Exodus 15:1 (41A): Great is faith before God לפנו הקב"ה (= in God's eyes); for as a recompense for faith (Exod 14:31) the holy spirit (spirit of inspiration) rested on them so that they sang a song.

c. Targum Onkelos Genesis 6:8: "Noah found mercy before Yahweh קֳדָם יי." ‖ Targum Onkelos Genesis 8:11: "The earth was corrupt before Yahweh קדם יי."

4:17 B: Who makes the dead alive.

See from the OT: Deut 32:39; 1 Sam 2:6; 2 Kgs 5:7; from the NT: 2 Cor 1:9; 1 Tim 6:13. ‖ Wisdom 16:13: "You have power over life and death and you lead down to the gates of the underworld and back up again." ‖ Tobit 13:2: "He chastises and has mercy; he casts into the underworld and leads up from there." ‖ The 2nd benediction of the Prayer of Eighteen Benedictions closes with the words: "Who makes the dead alive" מְחַיֵּה הַמֵּתִים!

4:17 C: Who calls the things that do not exist as existing (as though they were).

2 Maccabees 7:28: "I ask you, beloved child, look to heaven and to earth and see everything that is in them, and remember that these things were made by God from things that did not exist ἐξ οὐκ ὄντων, and the human race arose in the same way." ‖ Wisdom 11:25: "How could anything have remained if you had not willed it, or how could that not called by you τὸ μὴ κληθὲν ὑπὸ σοῦ have been preserved?" ‖ Philo, *De creat. princ.* 7 (Mangey's ed., 2:367): "For he called the nonexistent to existence τὰ γὰρ μὴ ὄντα ἐκάλεσεν εἰς τὸ εἶναι, order from disorder ...; bringing light out of darkness." ‖ Philo, *De migratione Abrahami* 9 (Mangey's ed., 1:442): "Holding fast to and hanging onto a good hope (the promise in Gen 12:1) and without swaying being convinced that what was not yet present was already pres-

ent ἤδη παρεῖναι τὰ μὴ παρόντα, it (Abraham's soul) found a perfect good as a recompense for his unshakeable faith in the one who gave the promise." ‖ Philo, *De Josepho* 22 (Mangey's ed., 2:59): "Vain are the dreams by which the soul paints and forms τὰ μὴ ὄντα ὡς ὄντα." ‖ From the rabbinic texts, see the designation of God as "the one who spoke and the world came to be." See the excursus "Memra of Yahweh," #3, A, n. *l*.

4:18: Thus (like the stars) will your seed be (Gen 15:5).

Gen 15:5 in rabbinic literature.

1. The invitation: "Look to heaven."

Babylonian Talmud Šabbat 156A: Rab Judah († 299) said that Rab († 247) said, "How do we know that Israel has no star (its fate does not depend on the stars)? Because it says, 'He brought him out' (Gen 15:5). Abraham said before God, 'Lord of the world, "the bondsman of my house will be my heir" (Gen 15:3).' He answered him, 'No, but rather the one who will issue from your body' (Gen 15:4). He said before him, 'Lord of the world, I have seen in my astrology (horoscope) that I am not destined to bear a son.' He answered him, 'Go out from your astrology, for Israel has no star.'" — The same is found more briefly in b. Ned. 32A. — Abraham was made into an astrologer by Eupolemos in Eusebius, *Praep. ev.* 9.17; by Artapanus in Eusebius, *Praep. ev.* 9.18; and by Philo, *Abr.* 15 (Mangey's ed., 2:11f.); *Abr.* 17 (Mangey's ed., 2:13). Among the rabbinic scholars, R. Eleazar of Modiim († ca. 135) appears to have been the first to attribute astrological knowledge to Abraham. See t. Qidd. 5.17 (343); b. B. Bat. 16B. — On astrology among the Jews see § John 2:4 C, γ, Comment. ‖ Genesis Rabbah 44 (27C.24): R. Samuel b. Isaac (ca. 300) said, "(Abraham said,) 'The star urges me and tells me: "Abram, you will not father a child!"' God answered him, 'It will be according to your words. Abram will not father a child, but Abraham will father a child....' 'He made him go out' (Gen 15:5)." R. Joshua of Sikhnin (ca. 330) said in the name of R. Levi (ca. 300), "Did he make him go out of the world, since it says, 'He made him go out'? Rather, he made him look at the roads of the sky; as it says, 'When he had not yet made earth and the roads' (of the sky; so Midr. Prov. 8:26)." R. Judah (b. Simon, ca. 320) said in the name of R. Yohanan († 279), "He lifted him above the vault of heaven; for it says, 'Look down at the sky' (Gen 15:5); for הַבָּטָה (the looking) is nothing other than (a looking) from above toward below." The rabbis said, "(God said to Abraham,) 'You are a prophet and not an astrologer; as it says, "Give the man back his wife, for he is a prophet" (Gen 20:7).' In the days of Jeremiah, the Israelites sought to attain this way (astrology), but God did not permit it; as it says, 'Thus says Yahweh: "Do not take to the way of the pagans and you are not to fear the signs of heaven"' (Jer 10:2). Once your father Abraham sought to attain this way, but I did not let him." R. Levi (ca. 300) said, "(God said to Abraham,) 'As long as the sandal is on your foot, it tramples down the thorn. The one who is beneath them (the stars) fears them; but the one who is above them (see the saying of R. Yohanan above) tramples them down.'" — Parallels are found to R. Samuel b. Isaac in Pesiq. Rab. 43 (179A) anonymously, and to R. Yohanan in Gen. Rab. 48 (30A); Exod. Rab. 38 (96C); Num. Rab. 12 (137C).

2. The promise: "Thus כֹּה will your seed be."

a. Interpretations that take the stars as the point of comparison.

1 Enoch 43: "Once again I saw lightning and the stars of heaven, and I saw how he called them all by name, and how they listened to him. I saw how they were weighed with a just scale according to the strength of their light, according to the breadth of their spaces and the day of their appearance, and how their orbit produces lightning. I saw their orbit according to the number of the angels, and how they keep themselves faithful among them. Then I asked the angel who went with me and he showed me the hidden things: "What are these?" He said to me, "The Lord of Spirits has shown you their symbolic meaning (a parable). These (the stars) are the names of the holy ones (i.e., the Israelites), who dwell on the firm land and who believe forever in the name of the Lord of spirits." ‖ Exodus Rabbah 38 (96C): When God said to Abraham, "Go from your land …; I will make you into a great people" (Gen 12:1f.), he said before God, "Lord of the world, what gain will I have from all these blessings? Look, I am parting from the world without children." God said to Abraham, "Do you already know that you will not father a child?" He said before him, "Lord of the world, I have seen in my star that I will not father a child." God answered, "You fear your star? On your life, as no one can count the stars, so it is impossible to count your children.… As you see these without being able to count them, so will your seed be so that no one can count them." – The same is found partially in Num. Rab. 2 (137C). ‖ Numbers Rabbah 2 (137D): God compares the Israelites with the dust, as it says, "Your seed will be like the dust of the earth" (Gen 28:14); and he compares them with the stars, as it says, "So will your seed be" (Gen 15:5). In this world they are compared with the dust.… (138A:) But in the future he compares them with the stars. As the stars shine in all of heaven, so also will these (Israel) shine in the future; for it says, "The understanding will shine like the splendor of heaven, and those who have brought many to righteousness, like the stars forever and ever" (Dan 12:3). Why are they compared with the stars and not with the sun and not with the moon? Rather Abraham is compared with the sun and Isaac with the moon and Jacob with the stars in the future. In the future the sun and the moon will be ashamed; as it says, "The moon blushes and the sun blanches, Yahweh of hosts has become king on Mount Zion and in Jerusalem and is glory before his elders" (Isa 24:23); but the stars will not be ashamed. Likewise, Abraham's and Isaac's face will turn pale in the future because of their descendants.… Abraham because of Ishmael and the descendants of Keturah, Isaac because of Esau and his princes; but there will be no shame for the stars, just as there will not be for Jacob, for he does not need to be ashamed; as it says, "Do not be ashamed, Jacob, do not let your face turn pale" (Isa 29:22)! Why? Because it says, "For when he sees his children, the work of my hands, in his midst, they will sanctify my name" (so Midr. Isa. 29:23), for they will all be righteous, "you are completely beautiful, my love" (Song 4:7). A different explanation. As the stars show honor to each other and peace dwells among them; as it says, "He makes peace in his heights" (Job 25:2), so the righteous love each other. As the stars do not fight with one another, it is just so with the righteous. Or as the stars activate only at night, so too the Israelites activate only at night because of the yoke of (worldly, hostile) sovereignty. Or as one of the stars can set the whole world on fire, it is just so with the righteous, as, for example, with Elijah, at whose word fire came down (see 2 Kgs 1:10). ‖ Leqach Tob on Gen 15:5 (1.34B): "Count the stars …" (Gen 15:5). Just as no nation can rule over the stars, so also

can no nation destroy the Israelites. Or as the stars are in the height of the world, so too will your children be, if they rise, they will rise up to heaven, but if they sink, they will sink into the dust. ‖ Genesis Rabbah 100 (64B): "Joseph spoke to their heart" (Gen 50:21). How? Can a man speak to the heart? Rather, this refers to words that calm the heart. He said to them, "You are compared with the dust of the earth; can anyone destroy the dust of the earth? You are compared with the animals of the field; can anyone destroy the animals of the field? You are compared with the stars; can anyone destroy the stars? Ten stars (= 10 sons of Jacob) tried to destroy one star (= Joseph), and they did not overcome it; how should I overcome twelve tribes! Could I change the natural order, since those (twelve tribes) correspond to the twelve hours of the day and the twelve signs of the zodiac in the firmament? ‖ Genesis Rabbah 43 (26D): When will I glorify (make great) your children like the stars? R. Eleazar (ca. 270) and R. Yose b. Hanina (ca. 270). R. Eleazar said, "When I reveal myself to them with 'thus' כֹּה: 'Thus should you speak to the house of Jacob' (Exod 19:3)." And R. Yose b. Hanina said, "When I reveal myself to their leader with thus כֹּה: 'You should tell pharaoh, "Yahweh has said, 'Israel is my firstborn son'" (Exod 4:22).'" — The כֹּה in Gen 15:5 refers to the כֹּה in Exod 19:3 and in Exod 4:22. — In a similar way R. Judah (ca. 150) connected the כֹּה of Gen 15:5 with the כֹּה in Num 6:23. See Gen. Rab. 43 (26D).

b. Interpretations that do not take the stars as the point of comparison.

Numbers Rabbah 2 (137C): What does "Thus will your seed be" (Gen 15:5) mean? R. Levi (ca. 300) said in the name of R. Yohanan († 279), "What can this be compared with? With someone who went on a journey. He wandered one, two, three, up until ten days, without encountering a city, a lodging house, a tree, water, a person. When he had wandered for ten days, he spotted a tree from afar. He said, 'Maybe there is water under it.' When he had reached it, he found it standing at a source. Since he saw that the tree was beautiful, its fruits sweet, and its branches beautiful, he sat down to cool himself in its shade. He ate from its fruits and drank from the source; this did him good and refreshed his soul. When he got up to go on, he said to the tree, 'What should I bless you with, and what should I say to you? That your trunk may become beautiful? It is already. That your shade may become beautiful? It has been beautiful for a long time. That your branches may become beautiful? They are beautiful. That your fruits may become sweet? They are sweet. That a source may break forth under your roots? A source broke forth under your roots long ago. That you may stand in a beloved spot? You stand in a beloved spot. What should I bless you with? May all the tiny plants that arise from you become like you!' Just so, when God had created the world, twenty generations arose, but there was nothing beneficial in them and no righteous person arose from them. After twenty generations God spotted Abraham, who was in the land of Babylon, which is called a faraway place; as it says, 'They came from a distant land, from Babylon' (2 Kgs 20:14). Then God said, 'Will he have the power to stand firm?' When he had been cast in the furnace and he had sanctified God's name and had succeeded in his trial, God brought him immediately to the land of Israel. He built himself a shelter and fed the migrants and led the people under the wings of the Shekinah (he made them proselytes of his faith) and made God's honor (glory) known in the world and bound his name with God's name like the angels. Then God said to him, 'What should

I say to you and what should I bless you with? That you may be a perfect righteous man before me, or that your wife Sarah may be righteous before me? You are righteous; Sarah your wife is righteous before me. Or that all the members of your house may be righteous before me? They are righteous before me. What should I bless you with? But may all the children (descendants) who will one day arise from you be like you!' Where do we get this from? For it is written, 'And he said to him, "Thus, כֹּה may your seed be (namely like you yourself)"' (Gen 15:5)." ‖ Tanḥuma וירא 26A: God said, "Long ago I said to Abraham, 'Thus will your seed be' (Gen 15:5)." What does "thus will it be" כה יהיה mean? R. Tanḥum (ca. 380) said in the name of R. Aha (ca. 320),[109] "The world will never lack 30 righteous people (like Abraham), for יהיה is 30 according to its numerical value." — In other passages the proposition of the 30 righteous people like Abraham is proven from יהיה in Gen 18:18; so by R. Alexandrai (ca. 270) in Gen. Rab. 49 (31A); by R. Mana (ca. 350) in y. ʿAbod. Zar. 2.40C.15. — The mention of the 30 righteous like Abraham, without whom the world could not endure, could be a later addition in the saying of R. Simeon b. Yohai (ca. 150) in Gen. Rab. 35 (21C).[110]

4:19 A: He looked at his own body as a dead one, being about one hundred years old.

1. νενεκρωμένον = מֵת "sexually impotent"; literally: "dead, died away."

Babylonian Talmud Šebiʿit 18A: Raba († 352) said, "This means that whoever has sexual intercourse that is forbidden as incest with a dead (flaccid) member המשמש מת goes unpunished...." Abbayye († 338/39) responded to him, "I will always tell you, 'Whoever has sexual intercourse that is forbidden as incest with a dead member is guilty.'" — Reference is made to these sentences in b. Yebam. 55B; b. Sanh. 55A.

2. ἑκατονταέτης, see Gen 21:5.

Genesis Rabbah 53 (34A): R. Phineas (ca. 360) said in the name of R. Hilqiah (ca. 320), "Who has 'said' אמר, who has 'spoken' דבר is not written here (Gen 21:7); but rather, who has 'talked' מלל. With this (Scripture), it was indicated to him that he would father a child at the age of 100. This is the numerical value of מלל (= 100)."

3. Statements about Abraham's physical condition at that time.

Genesis Rabbah 48 (30D): "My lord is old" (Gen 18:12). R. Judah (= R. Judan? [ca.350] or = R. Judah b. Shalom? [ca. 370]) said, "He grinds but brings nothing out" (euphemism; cf. Job 31:10; Judg 16:21 is also interpreted by R. Yohanan († 279) in this sense; see b. Soṭah 10A). ‖ TanḥumaB וירא § 37 (54A): She said, "Who has said מלל about Abraham?" (Gen 21:7), namely that there is youthfulness in him; and the word מלל means nothing other than "fresh" לח, as it says, "Pick ears מלילות (fresh ears still on the stalk) with your hand" (Deut 23:26). ‖ Pesiqta Rabbati 43 (180A): R. Phineas the priest b. Hama (ca. 360) said in the name of R. Hilqiah (ca. 320), "Abraham's seed קמתו של אבר' had dried up, and it became ears מלילות: 'Who has made Abraham into ears מי מלל לאבר'?'" (Gen 21:7 is now thus interpreted.) — In Gen. Rab. 53 (34A) from קמתו של אבר' came קומתו של אבר' "Abraham's form had dried up ...," probably

109. S-B: Bacher wants to read this in reverse order: R. Aha said in the name of R. Tanḥum (b. Hiyya, ca. 300). See Bacher, *Die Agada der palästinensischen Amoräer*, 3:131.

110. See Bacher, *Die Agada der Tannaïten*, 2:74.

a misunderstanding by the copyist. ‖ Genesis Rabbah 48 (30C): R. Yohanan († 279) said, "It says already, 'Abraham and Sarah were old' (Gen 18:11). What does Scripture mean to teach by saying: 'Abraham was old' (Gen 24:1)? Only because God set him back (in Gen 18:11 for the purpose of siring Isaac) into the days of his youth. Therefore, it (Gen 24:1) had to write it a second time: 'Abraham was old.'" R. Ammi (ca. 300) said, "Here (Gen 18:11) it deals with an age that had freshness (power), and there (Gen 24:1) with an age in which there was no freshness." ‖ – There is a different explanation in Gen. Rab. 47 (29C): R. Judan (ca. 350) and R. Azariah (ca. 380). R. Judan said, "'Can a child be born to a hundred-year-old?' (Gen 17:17). Why? 'Is Sarah, a ninety-year-old, to give birth?' (Gen 17:17). The man does not age, but the woman ages." (Thus, Abraham is capable of siring a child both before and after; if a child is not born to the hundred-year-old, the cause lies exclusively with Sarah.) – See the opinion of Azariah further below at the end of § Rom 4:19 B.

4:19 B: The deadness of Sarah's womb.

Babylonian Talmud Yebamot 64A: R. Ammi (ca. 300) said, "Abraham and Sarah were a טוּמְטוּם (a 'blocked up one,' whose sex organs have been overgrown with skin, so that his gender is not evident); for it says, 'Look to the rock from which you were hewn and to the well from which you were dug' (Isa 51:1), and further it is written, 'Look to Abraham, your father, and to Sarah, the one who bore you' (Isa 51:2)." ‖ Genesis Rabbah 47 (29C): R. Judan (ca. 350) said in the name of Resh Laqish (ca. 250), "(Sarah) had no womb, and God hollowed out a womb for her." – The same is found in Gen. Rab. 53 (33D); Pesiq. Rab. 42 (177A). ‖ Babylonian Talmud Yebamot 64B: Rab Nahman († 320) said that Rabbah b. Abuha (ca. 270) said, "Our mother Sarah was a barren one (אַיְלוֹנִית); for it says, 'Sarai was barren עקרה; she had no child' (Gen 11:30); she did not have a womb even." ‖ Genesis Rabbah 47 (29C): R. Judah and R. Nehemiah (both ca. 150). R. Judah said, "'I will bless you' (Gen 17:16A), to give her a son, 'and I will bless you' (Gen 17:16B) concerning the blessing of milk." R. Nehemiah answered him, "How would the good news about milk have come to her, when she was still not even pregnant? Rather Scripture teaches that God set her back into the days of her youth." ‖ Babylonian Talmud Baba Meṣiʿa 87A: "Should sweetness be mine after my fading away?" (Gen 18:12 according to the midr.). Rab Hisda († 309) said, "After the flesh had become flaccid and had gotten lots of wrinkles, the flesh again became sleek נִתְעַדֵּן (interpretation of עֶדְנָה in Gen 18:12) and the wrinkles were smoothed out and beauty returned to its place." ‖ – The view of LXX Gen 18:12 is different: "Sarah laughed within herself, saying: 'Nothing has happened to me till now (which has made my getting pregnant impossible); but my lord has gotten old.'" – This is how the LXX reads Gen 18:12: אחרי בִּלְתִּי היתה לי עֲדֶנָה. – This rendering is counted among the changes that the LXX made to the text of the Torah in Gen. Rab. 48 (30C); b. Meg. 9A; Mek. Exod. 12:40 (19B). ‖ Genesis Rabbah 47 (29C): (Continuation to the concluding citation at § Rom 4:19 A, #3:) R. Azariah (ca. 380) said, "There is also no need of this; for look, Sarah was a ninety-year-old, but she had not gotten old. Which is one who has gotten old? Every woman who is called mother so-and-so without getting angry (resenting it).

4:20 A: Considering the promise of God he did not doubt in unbelief.

1. Acceptance of the promise by Abraham.

Genesis 17:17: "Abraham fell down on his face and laughed." — Targum Onkelos Genesis 17:17: "Abraham fell on his face and rejoiced." — Targum Yerušalmi I: "Abraham fell on his face and marveled." — The same is found in the Samaritan targum. "Abraham's 'laughing' had to be mitigated." ‖ Genesis Rabbah 47 (29C): "May Ishmael live before you!" (Gen 17:18). R. Judan (ca. 350) said in the name of R. Judah b. Simon (ca. 320), "Like the friend of a king for whom the king raised the natural supply (official income). The king said to him, 'I would like to double your natural supply.' He answered him, 'May my mind not be filled with cold (disappointment?)! Oh, if only what I had earlier would not be taken away from me!' Likewise: 'May Ishmael live before you!' (Gen 17:18)." — Abraham cannot understand the greatness of the promise at first.

2. Acceptance of the promise by Sarah.

Genesis Rabbah 48 (30C.56): Sarah laughed inwardly, saying: "Am I to have sexual pleasure after my fading away, since my lord is old?" (Gen 18:12). She said, "As long as a woman gives birth, she has beautiful jewelry; and am I to have deliciousness עדנה after my fading away?" This refer to jewelry; as it says, "I put jewelry on you" ואעדך עדי (Ezek 16:11). "As long as a woman gives birth, she has her menstrual cycle; and am I to have עדנה, that is, periods עִידָנִיו after my fading away? As long as a woman gives birth, there is conception for her; and am I to have sexual pleasure after my fading away? My time would still be there, but 'And my lord is old!'"... R. Judah b. Simon (ca. 320) said, "God said, 'You declare yourself young and your lord (read אדניכם with Yalquṭ 1 § 82 instead of הבריכם) old. Have I become too old to do miracles?' (The midr. relates both instances of "My lord is old" [Gen 18:12] to God)...." R. Judan b. Simon (ca. 320) said, "Like one who had two chains in his hand; he brought them to a smith and said to him, 'Can you restore them for me?' He answered him, 'To make them in the first place, that I could have done; to recreate them for you, should I not be able to do that?' Likewise, the answer to be given them here was, 'To make them in the first place I could have done; to restore them to the days of their youth, should I not be able to do that?'" ‖ Yalquṭ Simeoni 1 § 82 from Yelamedenu: "Then Sarah denied it: 'I did not laugh'" (Gen 18:15). From this passage it has been taught that women are unfit to give testimony. And if God had not promised to Abraham that he would give him a son from Sarah, she would not have given birth, because she had not believed.

4:20 B: Giving God honor (see § Luke 17:18 and § John 9:24).

4:25: Who was given up for our transgressions.

On vicarious suffering, see § Luke 24:26, I, #2.

5:1: Now justified by faith, we have (reading ἔχομεν) peace in relation to God.

1. δικαίωσις and εἰρήνη are materially connected with each other in y. Roš Haš. 7.59C.51: R. Eleazar b. Yose (ca. 400) said in the name of R. Yose b. Qeṣarta (3rd cent.), "With every offering it is written, 'You should present,' and here in Num 29:2 'You should make' עשיתם. God said to them, 'If you come into court before me on the Day of the New Year and go forth from there in peace בשלום, I will count it for you as if you had been made a new creature.'" — If the Israelite has God's verdict in his favor, that is, is justified, in court on the Day of the New Year, then God views him as a new creature, that is, as a newborn child without sin and guilt, and the Israelite may go from there in peace. — Parallels with R. Tahlifa of Caesarea (ca. 270) as author are found in Lev. Rab. 29 toward the end (without בשלום) and Pesiq. 155B, here with בְּדִימוֹס "with acquittal" instead of בשלום. ‖ In t. Šabb. 13.5 (129) the *minim* (Jewish Christians) are accused of causing (instead of peace) enmity, jealousy, and fighting between Israel and God with their writings. See the passage at § Luke 6:22 A. — On "peace" see also 1 En. 105:2 at § Rom 1:3 A, A, #1, n. γ.

2. Romans 5:1 is among the prooftexts for assurance of salvation for the Christian; opposed to this, the lack of any certainty of salvation appears as the notable feature of the ancient Jewish religion. It is regarded as a dogma that for the righteous there is in this world no הַבְטָחָה, no confidence, no security concerning his status of salvation before God.[a] Man has no glimpse into his account before God; he does not know whether his merits or his debts form the majority. Moreover, any sin can quickly change the momentary propitious state into its opposite.[b] To be sure, a foothold is sought in the idea that the man who has once become righteous continually remains preserved from sins that could put his state of salvation into question;[c] but one cannot blindly secure oneself from the fact that some righteous people ultimately became godless. Hence the admonition: Let no one trust in himself before his death![d] Even God does not trust the righteous as long as he lives. Only after his death does he bind his name to him.[e] Reference is made to Jacob and Moses who were afraid despite divine promises. Why would they be afraid if there were an assurance of salvation?[f] Samuel is frightened when the woman of Endor summons his spirit; he fears the hour may have come for him to appear before God's seat of judgment.[g] David is completely uncertain about his future salvation, as the points above לולא in Ps 27:13 indicate.[h] Rabban Yohanan b. Zakkai († ca. 80) grounds his fear of death in his not knowing whether the garden of Eden will be opened to him or whether he will be expelled into gehenna.[i] And R. Eleazar b. Azariah (ca. 100) erupts at the thought of the coming judgment by referring to Gen 45:3 with the words: "Woe to us because of

the day of judgment! Who will stand!"[k] – With this certainty of salvation in life it is not surprising if one sought to attain certainty of salvation at least for the hour of death. Already in early times the claim was marshaled that God shows the pious briefly before his end the complete fullness of his future recompense;[l] later it was added as a complement that the hunt will be shown also to the godless, how he was captured, that is, so that the sins, that have filled his cup to the brim, come before him.[m] Thereby ample opportunity was given to casuistry to guess the otherworldly fate of the dying person from his attitude, appearance, utterances, etc.[n]

Comment: In the framework of the above remarks a whole series of statements cannot be integrated which determine in the briefest form who is a son of the future world, that is, who will have a share in eternal life. Almost universally they are more or less indifferent externals for the observation of which the surest prospect of eternal salvation is held out.[o] This immediately suggests the assumption that similar statements were calculated only to admonish the broad masses to observe certain religious duties or to warn about certain prevailing trends. Such statements can, at any rate, not be understood as a protest against the view that there is no certainty of salvation on earth for the righteous.

a. Genesis Rabbah 76 (49A): אין הבטחה לצדיק בעולם הזה there is no confidence (no certain rest in God's promises, no certainty of salvation) for the righteous in this world; see the whole passage at § Rom 4:13 A, #2, n. *a.* ‖ Apocalypse of Moses 31: "(Adam said to Eve,) 'We do not know how it will be when we appear before our creator, whether he will be angry with us or, having mercy on us, turn to us once again.'"

b. See b. Qidd. 40A in a baraita at § John 3:18.

c. See b. Yoma 38B at § Matt 19:20 A. ‖ Jerusalem Talmud Pe'ah 1.16B/45: R. Jeremiah (ca. 320) said in the name of R. Samuel b. Isaac (ca. 300), "If someone keeps himself from a transgression once, twice, three times, then God protects him from then on and beyond. What is the scriptural basis? 'Behold, God does everything twice, three times to the man' (Job 33:29)." R. Zeira (ca. 300) said, "Except that he would not turn to her again! What is the scriptural basis? 'A threefold cord is never ripped' is not written here (Eccl 4:12), but rather: 'does not rip soon.' If you overload it, it rips." – The same is found in y. Qidd. 1.61D.56; y. Sanh. 10.27C.40. ‖ See b. Ber. 29A in n. *d.*

d. So already Hillel [ca. 20 BCE] in m. 'Abot 2.4: Hillel said, "Do not trust אַל תַּאֲמִין in yourself until the day of your death." ‖ Babylonian Talmud Berakot 29A: Abbayye († 338/39) said, "It is a traditional teaching: 'A good man will not become a bad man.' No? But it is written, 'If the righteous man turns away from his righteousness and does wickedness' (Ezek 18:26)! This is someone who by nature was a godless person; but this does not apply to someone who was inherently righteous. No? But we have learned: 'Do not trust in yourself until the day of your death! For, look, Yohanan the high priest (= John Hyrcanus 135–104 BCE) served in the office of high priest for 80 years, and in the end he became a heretic (Sadducee).'" ‖ TanḥumaB מקץ § 15 (100B): No one may trust in himself until the day of his death, and likewise our teachers have taught us: "Do not trust in yourself until the day of your death!" ‖ Tosefta Qiddušin 1.14 (337): R. Simeon (ca. 150) said, "If someone was a perfectly righteous man his whole life and finally rebelled (became an apostate), he has lost everything (all his earlier merit); for it says, 'The righteousness of the righteous man will not save him on the day of his wickedness' (Ezek 33:12)."

e. See Tanḥ. תולדות 33A at § Luke 18:9.

f. See Gen. Rab. 76 (49A) at § Rom 4:13 A, #2, n. *a.* ‖ Mekilta Exodus 17:14 (64A): (R. Eleazar of Modiim [† ca. 135] said,) "He (God) gave Jacob a sign, but he did not heed it; for it says, 'Behold, I am with you and will protect you' (Gen 28:15). And he was startled and afraid; for it says, 'Jacob was very afraid and distressed' (Gen 32:8). A man to whom God gave a promise (pledge) הבטיחו was afraid and startled? But our father Jacob said, 'Woe to me, perhaps sin has caused it!'"

g. Jerusalem Talmud Ḥagigah 2.77A.24: ("Rabbi [† 217?] said,) "Samuel said to Saul, 'Why have you disturbed me ...?' (1 Sam 28:15).... I even believed that this was the day of judgment and was afraid. See, here the inference is justified by moving from the greater to the lesser: if Samuel, the teacher (master) of the prophets, of whom it is written 'All Israel became aware from Dan to Beersheba that Samuel had been commissioned as a prophet for Yahweh' (1 Sam 3:20) was afraid of the day of judgment, how much more does that go for me!" — Parallels are found in Lev. Rab. 26 (124C); Tanḥ. אמור 171B; Midr. Sam. 24 § 5 (60B).

h. See b. Ber. 4A at § Rom 4:13 A, #2, n. *b.*

i. See b. Ber. 28B at § Matt 10:28, #1, n. *c.*

k. Genesis Rabbah 93 (59B): R. Eleazar b. Azariah (ca. 100) said, "Woe to us because of the day of judgment, woe to us because of the day of rebuke (reckoning)! If (in that hour) when Joseph, the righteous, who was flesh and blood rebuked his brothers, they could not stand at his rebuke (Gen 45:3), how much more will it be the case when God, who is judge and indicter, sits on his throne of (strict) justice and judges every single one, that flesh and blood cannot stand before him!" — A few lines earlier a very similar exposition is given by Abba Kohen of Bardela (a Tannaim of uncertain time).

l. Genesis Rabbah 62 (39A): Every recompense of the righteous is prepared (determined מתוקן) for them for the future, and God shows them, as long as they are still in this world, their recompense, which he will give them in the future (= in the hereafter), and their soul will be satisfied with it and (then) they will fall asleep. R. Eleazar (ca. 270) said, "Like a meal held by the king; and he invited the guests and showed them what they would eat and drink, and their soul was satisfied, and then they fell asleep. So God shows the righteous, as long as they are still in this world, their recompense, which he will give them in the future, and then they will fall asleep, as it says, 'If I lay now, I would have rest' (security, certainty; thus the midr. appears to understand Job 3:13). From this it follows: in the hour when the righteous depart, God shows them their recompense." When R. Abbahu (ca. 300) passed away, one (God) showed him 13 rivers of balsam. He said about them, "Whose are these?" He was answered, "Yours!" He said, "These are Abbahu's?' And I said, 'In vain have I labored, for nothingness and ephemerality have I used up my strength; yet my due is with Yahweh and my recompense with my God' (Isa 49:4)." Zabdai b. Levi (ca. 240) and R. Joshua b. Levi (ca. 250) and R. Yose b. Parta (Peter, ca. 220), the three of them said (when they passed away) these three words of Scripture. When the first of them passed away, he said, "'Therefore let every pious man pray to you at the time of finding' (Ps 32:6). 'Yes, in him our heart rejoices' (Ps 33:21)." And the second said, "'You prepare a table before me in the face of my oppressors' (Ps 23:5). 'And all will rejoice who hide themselves in you' (Ps 5:12)." And the last said, "'For one day in your forecourts is better than a thousand (elsewhere)' (Ps 84:11)." And as the rabbis said, "How great is your goodness, which you hide (store) for those who fear you" (Ps 31:20). From this it follows: in the hour when the righteous depart from the world God shows them their recompense. Ben Azzai (ca. 110) said, "'Precious in the eyes of Yahweh is the death of his pious ones' (Ps 116:15), and when does God show them their recompense, which is prepared (determined) for them? Just before their death." – Ben Azzai was, as far as we can tell, the first one to express this idea.

m. Midrash Esther 1:12 (90A): R. Samuel b. Nahman (ca. 260) said in the name of R. Jonathan (ca. 220), "The godless does not depart from this world before God has shown him his hunt, how he was captured." – See further SDeut 34:5 § 357 (149B) in the excursus "Sheol, Gehenna, and the Garden of Eden," II, #3 n. *l*, at the end.

n. ʾAbot de Rabbi Nathan 25, at the beginning: Ben Azzai (ca. 110) said, "… If the spirit of wisdom (of the wise) delights in someone at the hour of his death, that is a good sign for him; but if the spirit of wisdom does not delight in him, that is a bad sign for him. If his face is directed upward, that is a good sign for him; but if his face is weighed down, that is a bad sign for him. If his eyes are set on his children (standing around him), that is a good sign for him; if his eyes are not set on his children, that is a bad sign for him. If his face is shining (serene), that is a good sign for him; if his face is dark (black), that is a bad sign for him…." The same one (Ben Azzai) said, "If he dies with a calm (clear) consciousness, that is a good sign for him; (if he dies) in confusion, that is a bad sign for him. (If he dies) while speaking, that is a good sign for him; while silent, that is a bad sign for him; with words of the Torah, that is a good sign for him; with a word of commerce (business), that is a bad sign for him; with a word of a fulfillment of a commandment, that is a good sign for him, with a word of vanity, that is a bad sign for him; in cheerfulness, that is a good sign for him, in grief, that is a bad sign for him; while laughing, that is a good sign for him; while crying, that is a bad sign for him; if he dies on the day of preparation for the Sabbath (on a Friday), that is a good sign for him; after the conclusion of the Sabbath (= on a Sunday), that is a bad sign for him; if he dies on a day of preparation for the Day of Atonement, that is a bad sign for him." – See a parallel anonymous baraita from b. Ketub. 103B in the excursus "Sheol, Gehenna, and the Garden of Eden," II, #3, n. *l*, at the beginning. ‖ Pesiqta 174B.15: R. Samuel b. Nahman (ca. 260) said, "The godless person does not go out of this world before he has expressed his judgment with his own mouth (in a certain ominous expression)." – The same is found in Lev. Rab. 21 (120A); Midr. Ps. 27 § 3 (112B).

o. Whoever says the 145th psalm three times daily, or whoever studies halakoth, may be assured that he is a son of the future world. See b. Ber. 4B and b. Meg. 28B at § Rom 4:13 A, #2, n. *b*. ‖ Whoever speaks the holy language and enjoys his fruits in purity and recites the Shema morning and evening, to him may the good news be brought that he is a son of the future world. See y. Šeqal. 3.47C.62 at § Rom 1:1 D, #2, n. *f*. ‖ Babylonian Talmud Pesaḥim 113A: R. Yohanan († 279) said, "Three types are among the heirs of the future world: (*a*) ...; (*b*) whoever raises his sons to study the Torah; (*c*) whoever speaks the parting blessing over the wine at the conclusion of the Sabbath." — The passages are easily understandable if one assumes that they intend to promote the named religious duties in a solemn form. The passage in y. Ketub. 12.35A.26 (= y. Kil. 9.32B.18) is instructive: A voice from heaven came which called to them, "Whoever has not been nonchalant in mourning Rabbi († 217?), to him let the good news be brought concerning the life of the future world (namely that he will have a share in it)." — Here, by announcing the highest recompense, the obligation is made known to the people to participate without exception in the future in the dirges for its great men. ‖ Whoever walks four cubits in the land of Israel (see b. Ketub. 111A at § Rom 4:13 A, #2, n. *b*), whoever lives in the land of Israel (see y. Šeqal. 3.47C.62 at § Rom 1:1 A, n. *f*), he may be assured that he is a son of the future world. — Likewise, b. Pesaḥ. 113A: R. Yohanan († 279) said, "Three types are among the heirs of the future world: (*a*) whoever lives in the land of Israel" (see notes *b* and *c* above). — The words are meant as a warning against emigrating from Palestine.

5:3 A: We boast even in tribulation.

In Bousset we read, "The proud word of Paul, that the pious boasts in sufferings, was not expressed and could not be expressed by a pious Jew."[111] This judgment is not correct. On the contrary, the value of sufferings was quite high in the ancient synagogue. In sufferings one saw an impetus to repentance, a means of atoning for sins, the surest way to increase merit and thereby to obtain eternal life. How could the pious Jew not have boasted in suffering! See the supporting passages for this point at § Luke 24:26, I, #2. Here only some additional citations may be added.

Psalms of Solomon 3:4: "A righteous man does not take it lightly when he is chastised by the Lord." — Psalms of Solomon 8:34: "Blessed be the Lord for his judgments by the mouth of the pious." — Psalms of Solomon 10:1: "Blessed is the man whom the Lord remembers to rebuke and whom he turns away from the evil ways with the rod, so that he may be pure of sin, so that he may not do it." ‖ 2 Baruch 52:5: "Delight in the suffering that you now suffer." ‖ A baraita in b. Šabb. 88B: Concerning those who are afflicted without afflicting in turn, who hear their slander without responding, who act out of love and rejoice in sufferings, Scripture says: "Those who love him are like the rising of the sun in its power" (Judg 5:31). — The same is found in b. Yoma 23A; b. Giṭ. 36B. ‖ Babylonian Talmud Taʿanit 8A: R. Joshua b. Levi (ca. 250) said, "Whoever rejoices in the sufferings that come over him brings salvation into the world." ‖ Dèrek Ereṣ Zuṭa 5 at the beginning (= 9 in other editions): R. Eleazar Haqqappar (ca. 180) said, "... Rejoice in the sufferings that come over you because they protect you from anguish of the belly." ‖ See further b. ʿArak. 16B; b. Sanh. 101A; Pesiq. 73A at § Matt 6:2, #4. ‖ There is also, though, no lack of examples of respected teachers like

111. Bousset, *Religion des Judentums*, 353f.

R. Yohanan († 279) and R. Hiyya b. Abba (ca. 280), who, when they themselves were sick, answered the question of whether the sufferings that had come over them were dear and valuable to them. They said, "Neither them nor their reward!" See b. Ber. 5B at § Mark 1:31 A.

5:3 B: Knowing that tribulation produces patience (... up until verse 5A).

Examples of chain inference (*sorites*) in the OT include Hos 2:23–25 and Amos 3:3–8; in the NT, aside from Rom 5:3–5, also 2 Pet 1:5–7. In the apocrypha, Wis 6:18–21; in rabbinic literature:

Seder Eliyahu Rabbah 8 (43): "The house of Israel is the vineyard of Yahweh of hosts" (Isa 5:7). R. Eliezer the elder (ca. 90) said, "'The house of Israel is the vineyard of God': do not look at it; and if you have looked at it, do not go into it; and if you have gone into it, do not make use of it; and if you have made use of it, do not eat of its fruits; and if you have looked at it and gone into it and made use of it and eaten of its fruits, that man (= you) will ultimately be eradicated from the world." — The whole is meant as a warning for Israel's enemies. — A parallel, but without allegorical meaning, is found in Bacher as a saying of Ben Zoma (ca. 110): "'Do not look at your neighbor's vineyard' (cf. Deut 23:25); if you have looked, do not enter; if you have entered, do not look upon (the fruits); if you have looked upon them, do not touch; if you have touched, do not eat; but if you have eaten, then you will rip yourself out of the life of this world and out of the life of the world to come."[112] — The saying intends to ascetically limit the permission given in Deut 23:25. ‖ See m. Soṭah 9.15 at § Matt 5:3, #3; y. Sanh. 10.28B.51 at § Luke 2:25 C, #3, n. *b*.

5:6f.: Christ died for the godless. One will hardly die for a righteous man; Someone will perhaps undertake even to die for a benevolent man

ἀσεβής, = רָשָׁע, Aram. רַשִׁיעָא, בִּישָׁא, the godless, who flouts divine and human justice. — δίκαιος, = צַדִּיק, כָּשֵׁר, Aram. צַדִּיקָא, כָּשְׁרָא, כַּשִׁירָא, the righteous, who wants to be just toward everyone, but also sacrifices nothing of his own due. — ἀγαθός = טוֹב, Aram. טָבָא, the good man = benevolent man, who goes beyond the letter of justice for the sake of others.

Mishnah ʾAbot 5.10: There are four kinds of dispositions people have: (α) If someone says, "What is mine is mine and what is yours is yours," this is a mediocre (lying on the middle line) disposition[113] מִדָּה בֵינוֹנִית. (β) Whoever says, "What is mine is yours and what is yours is mine," this is an *ʿam ha'areṣ* (who stretches the meaning of mine and yours; on the *ʿam ha'areṣ*, see § John 7:49). (γ) "What is mine is yours and what is yours is yours," this is a pious person חָסִיד (loving, gracious, benevolent). (δ) "What is mine is mine and what is yours is mine," this is a godless person רָשָׁע. — Here the רשע in (δ) corresponds to

112. Bacher, *Die Agada der Tannaïten*, 1:430.

113. S-B: Here follows: "Some say, 'This is the disposition of Sodom.'" — This is a marginal gloss which is inserted into the text in an incorrect passage that belongs after β or δ. On the conceptions of ownership of the people of Sodom, see § Matt 10:15.

the ἀσεβής; the מדה בינונית in (α) to the δίκαιος; the חסיד in (γ) to the ἀγαθός. ‖ Jerusalem Talmud Taʿanit 2.65B.32: R. Simeon b. Halapta (ca. 190) said, "The shameless (brazen) bowl over the righteous בשירא (by his importunate pleading), how much more the good of the world לְטוֹבָתוֹ שֶׁל עוֹלָם (= the good one of the world = God)." — See the parallel expressed differently in Pesiq. 161A at § Matt 19:17 B. — On טוב, טבא "good" = benevolent, see also § Mark 10:17. — Naturally טוֹב can also designate the morally good person. The passage in b. Qidd. 40A is instructive. The passage negotiates the question of why releasing the mother bird in Deut 22:7 just like honoring one's parents etc. (m. Qidd. 1.1) is not counted among the things that people enjoy the fruits of in this world, while the principal (main recompense) remains due for the future world, especially since the promise "So that it may go well for you (according to the midr.: in this life) and you may live long (= in the future world)" (Deut 22:7) corresponds precisely to the promise for honoring one's parents (Deut 5:16). Then it says that Raba († 352) said, "R. Idi (ca. 310) made it clear to me (according to Isa 3:10), 'Say: "The righteous man צדיק, if he is good טוֹב, that they (the righteous) will enjoy the fruit of their deeds (in this life)" (so the midr.). How is this so? Is there a good righteous person צדיק טוב and is there a righteous person who is not good? Only the one who is good טוב toward God and toward creatures is a good righteous person; the one who is good toward God but bad (evil) רַע toward creatures is a righteous person who is not good. (The "good" טוֹב person comprises here both the morally "good" person who fulfills his duties toward God, and the "benevolent," who is gracious, merciful toward creatures.) Similarly, you must say: "Woe to the bad godless person רשע רע! For what his hands perpetrate will be done to him" (so the midr. on Isa 3:11). How is this so? Is there a bad godless person and one who is not bad? Only the one who is bad toward God (by not fulfilling the duties toward God), and bad (unmerciful) toward creatures is a bad godless person; the one who is bad toward God but not bad (but rather merciful) toward creatures is a godless person who is not bad.'" (Irreligiosity can be connected with mercy.) — From this it follows for the question to be negotiated: since the one who lets the mother bird fly away but kills her young is not good toward creatures, observing the commandment in Deut 22:7 is, in accordance with Isa 3:10, not counted among the things that people enjoy the fruit of in this world, while the principal remains due for the future world.

5:9f.: How much more πολλῷ μᾶλλον.

1. The inference *a minori ad majus* is called in rabbinic literature קַל וָחוֹמֶר (plural: קַלִּים וַחֲמוּרִין) = "light and heavy."[a] R. Ishmael († ca. 135) enumerates ten passages in the OT in which this reasoning is found.[b] The earliest examples of *qal wahomer* in rabbinic literature may be in m. ʾAbot 1.5; see Gen. Rab. 65 (42A) at #2, A, and y. Pesaḥ. 6.33A.14 at #2, D.

a. Babylonian Talmud Roš Haššanah 25B: Rabban Gamaliel (ca. 90) said to R. Joshua (ca. 90), "From the fact that the great (respected) listen to the small, the small refer the *qal wahomer* inference to themselves נושאין קל וחומר בעצמן.

b. Genesis Rabbah 92 (58C): "Behold, money ..." (Gen 44:8). R. Ishmael taught: "This is one of the ten *qal wahomer* inferences written in the Torah (= OT). These are: 'Behold money ... we have ... brought back ... to you' (Gen 44:8); *qal wahomer*: 'How should we steal?' 'Behold, the children of Israel have not listened to me' (Exod 6:12); *qal wahomer*: 'How will pharaoh listen to me!' 'Yahweh said to Moses, "But if her father had spat in her face, would she not have been ashamed for seven days?"' (Num 12:14); *qal wahomer*: when it is a matter of the Shekinah (divinity), fourteen days! 'Behold, while I still live among you, you have been recalcitrant' (Deut 31:27); *qal wahomer*: 'let alone after my death.' 'If you have raced with those who walk and they have made you tired' (Jer 12:5); *qal wahomer*: 'how will you compete with horses?' 'And you are safe in a peaceful land'; *qal wahomer*: 'how will you manage when the Jordan is high?' (Jer 12:5 is to be counted as two passages.) 'Behold, we are already afraid here in Judah, let alone when we go beyond Keilah!' (The words '*qal wahomer*' are missing here and need to be supplied.) 'Behold, the righteous man receives his recompense on earth' (Prov 11:31); *qal wahomer*: 'how much more the godless and the sinner!' 'Then the king (Ahasuerus) said to queen Esther, "In the fortress of Susa the Jews have ... killed ... 500 men"' (Esth 9:12); *qal wahomer*: 'what have they done in the king's other territories?' 'Behold, when it was still whole, it could not be used for anything'; (*qal wahomer*:) 'let alone when it has been eaten by fire so that it has been charred!'" (The commentaries observe that 40 *qal wahomer* can easily be found in the OT. Strack.)

2. The forms of the *qal wahomer* inference.

A. The reasoning is indicated by the words קל וחומר, which should be rendered with: "all the more," "how much more," "how much less."

Examples: See Gen. Rab. 92 (58C) in #1, n. *b.* ‖ In Mek. Exod. 18:21 (68A), R. Eleazar of Modiim († ca. 135) understands by men "who are hostile to acquisitiveness" (Exod 18:21) men "who hate (= do not love) their own money"; to this he then adds the remark: "If they hate their own money, how much more קל וחומר the money of others!" ‖ Mishnah Nega'im 12.5: R. Meir (ca. 150) said, "... If the Torah thus spares his little esteemed possession מָמוֹן, how much more ק״ו his valued possession; if thus his possession, how much more ק״ו the life of his sons and his daughters; if thus that of the godless, how much more ק״ו that of the righteous." ‖ Babylonian Talmud Pesaḥim 99A: Silence is beautiful for the learned, and all the more ק״ו for the simple. ‖ Mishnah 'Abot 1.5: Yose b. Yohanan (ca. 150 BCE) said, "'Do not converse much with a woman.' It has been said that this goes for one's own wife; how much more ק״ו the wife of another." ‖ Genesis Rabbah 65 (42A): Yaqim of Zerodoth (Zereda) was the son of the sister of R. Yose b. Yoezer of Zeredag (ca. 150 BCE) and rode horses on the Sabbath (a sign of apostasy from Judaism). He (R. Yose b. Yoezer) accompanied him before the cross on which he was to be hanged. Then he (his nephew) said to him, "See my horse on which my lord (the pagan ruler) lets me ride, and see your horse (the cross) on which your Lord (God) lets you ride!" He answered him, "If this comes to those who anger him (God), how much more ק״ו those who do his will!" That one said to him, "Has anyone done his will more than you?" He answered him, "If this comes to those who do his will, how much more ק״ו those who anger him!" (See the continuation of the passage in the excursus "Sheol, Gehenna, and the Garden of Eden," III, #3, δ.) ‖ Mishnah Baba Batra 9.7: The scholars said, "His words (by which a person orally allocates his possessions) are valid on the Sabbath, because he is not permitted to write (on the Sabbath); but not on a weekday. R. Joshua (ca. 90) said, "'On the Sabbath,' they said; (thus) all the more ק"ו on a weekday!" "Likewise: For someone who is underage (who is not yet 13 years old) something may be purchased, but not for someone who is of age" (so R. Eliezer, ca. 90). R. Joshua (ca. 90) said, "'For someone who is underage,' it has been said; all the more ק"ו for one who is of age!" — "How much less," in, for example, Mek. Exod. 20:2 (74A). See § Rom 1:20 E, n. *f*.

B. The conclusion is drawn with the words: כׇּל שֶׁכֵּן = "all the more," "even more"; negatively: לֹא כׇּל שֶׁכֵּן = "all the less," "even less."

Mekilta Exodus 13:3 (24A): How do we know that a word of praise has to be said beforehand (before a meal)? R. Ishmael († ca. 135) said, "Here the *qal wahomer* inference applies. If it is obligatory to say a word of praise after one has eaten his fill (cf. Deut 8:10), does this not apply all the more לא כל שכן when one longs (for food)?" (Here the לא does not belong to the concluding formula but rather occurs because of the question form.) A parallel is found in b. Ber. 48B. ‖ Babylonian Talmud Šabbat 63A: Rabbah b. Shela (ca. 325) said, while according to others Rab Joseph b. Hama (ca. 300) said that Rab Sheshet (ca. 260) said, "What does 'Length of days is in her right hand, riches and honor in her left' (Prov 3:16) mean? Perhaps that length of days is in her right hand but riches and honor are not? Rather, that on those who devote themselves to her למיימינין בה in the right way, length of days will be bestowed, not to mention וכל שכן riches and honor; but on those who do not devote themselves to her in the right way, riches and honor, yes, but not length of days will be bestowed." ‖ Babylonian Talmud Ḥullin 5B (= 7A): If God does not let any offense come by the cattle of the righteous, how much more not לא כל שכן by the righteous themselves. ‖ See further y. Taʿan. 2.65B.32 at § Rom 5:6f.; Pesiq. Rab. 34 (159A) at § Jude 6 A, n. *g*.

C. A very common formula is: מָה אִם ... עַל אַחַת כַּמָּה וְכַמָּה שֶׁ׳ = if (this and that applies in this and that case), much and much (i.e., all the more or how much more) (it applies) toward one, that (such and such happens).

Mishnah ʿArakin 8.4: R. Eleazar b. Azariah (ca. 100) said, "If a person is not authorized to dedicate to God all his possessions (all his goods), a person all the more (in other cases) has to save his possessions מה אם ... על אחת כמה וכמה שיהא אדם הס." ‖ Mishnah Makkot 3.15: R. Hananiah b. Gamaliel (ca. 120) said, "If life is taken from someone who commits a transgression (sin), how much more על אחת כמה וכמה will life be given to someone who carries out a commandment!" ‖ Babylonian Talmud Sanhedrin 9A: R. Aqiba († ca. 135) said, "... If Scripture punishes the one who joins transgressors as the transgressors, how much more will recompense be given (by God) to someone who joins one who does a commandment as the one who does the commandment (himself)." ‖ Babylonian Talmud Qiddušin 31A: R. Hanina (ca. 225) said, "If the one who is not given a commandment but does it (is repaid), how much more does this apply to the one who is given a commandment and does it." ‖ Mishnah ʾAbot 6.3: Does the inference from lesser to greater not apply וַהֲלֹא דְּבָרִים קַל וָחוֹמֶר? How, if David, the king of Israel, who had learned only two words from Ahithophel, declared him to be his teacher, his friend, and his confidant, how much more על אחת כמה וכמה must the one who learned from someone else a chapter or a halakah or a verse or even only one letter show him honor! ‖ See further y. Qidd. 4.65B.61 at § Matt 6:9 C, n. *k*; Lev. Rab.

34 (132A) at § Matt 7:11, #1; t. Šabb. 13.5 (129) at § Luke 6:22 A; Num. Rab. 2 (138B) at § Rom 9:26, #1.

D. מָה אִם ... אֵינוֹ דִין שֶׁ׳ = if (this and that happens), is it not (entirely) right that (this and that happens)?

Jerusalem Talmud Pesaḥim 6.33A.14: (Hillel the elder [ca. 20 BC] expounded his opinion) on the basis of a *qal wahomer*: "If the Tamid offering, the preparation of which does not make one guilty of the punishment of eradication, supersedes the Sabbath, is it not right אינו דין that the Passover offering, the preparation of which does make one guilty of the punishment of eradication (Num 9:13), supersede the Sabbath?" ‖ Mishnah Yebamot 8.3: R. Simeon (ca. 150) drew a *qal wahomer* inference from the words, "He said, 'If when it is forbidden to the men by an eternal commandment (to enter the community of Israel, as, for example, the Ammonites and Moabites), it is allowed to the women (to enter) immediately, is it not right that we allow the women immediately when it is forbidden to the men for only three generations (as the Egyptians and Edomites)?'" ‖ Mekilta Exodus 19:10 (71B): "They should wash their garments" (Exod 19:10). How do we know that they were obligated to take an immersion bath? Look, I draw an inference: if one is obligated to take an immersion bath when one is not obligated to wash clothes (Lev 15:16; see Rashi at b. Yebam. 46B.4), is it not right here, where one is obligated to wash clothes, that one is obligated to take an immersion bath? There is no washing of clothes in Scripture that did not oblige one to take an immersion bath. — The same is found in b. Yebam. 46B.

5:12 A: Just as through one person sin came into the world.

See the citations at § Rom 5:15 A. ‖ Apocalypse of Moses 32: "Then Eve got up and went out, fell to the earth, and said, 'I have sinned, God, sinned, Father of all, sinned against you, sinned against your chosen angels, sinned against the cherubs and seraphs, sinned against your unshakeable throne, sinned, Lord, sinned much, and all sin has come into the creation through me.'"

5:12 B: And through sin death.

See the citations at § Rom 5:15 A.

5:12 C: And thus death permeated to all people.

The Jewish tradition names nine people who did not die. See Der. Er. Zut. 1 in the excursus "Elijah," I, #1, n. *d*; additionally, there are six over whom the angel of death has no power, that is, whose souls were taken away by God himself. See § Matt 17:3, #1, n. *f*., and finally seven whose bodies did not fall prey to decay. See § Matt 17:3, #1, n. *g*.

5:12 D: Because all sinned (see § Rom 3:9 B).

5:14 A: Death reigned.

ἐβασίλευσεν = שָׁלַט, Aram. שְׁלַט. — Over six the angel of death did not rule (had no power) שלט; see b. B. Bat. 17A at § Matt 17:3, #1, n. *f*. ‖ Over seven the worm and decay had no power שלט; see b. B. Bat. 17A at § Matt 17:3, #1, n. g. ‖ Over three the evil inclination had no power שלט; see b. B. Bat. 17A at § Matt 19:20 A, near the middle. ‖ See additionally the citations at § Rom 6:9.

5:14 B: Who is an image of the future one.

τύπος = סִימָן "presage," "type." See examples at § Luke 2:34 B; among these there is even one that designates Adam as a type for his children. — Here Gen. Rab. 54 (34D) may also be added: The rabbis (ca. 250) said, "The shepherds of Abraham got into a dispute with those of Abimelech. They said, 'The well belongs to us'; and the latter said, 'The well belongs to us!' Then the shepherds of Abraham said, 'To whomever the water rises up (by itself) to water his small livestock, the well belongs to him.' When the water saw Abraham's small livestock, it immediately rose up. Then God said to him, 'You are a sign סימן for your children: as the waters immediately rose up at the sight of your small livestock, so too will the well (in the wilderness) immediately rise up at the sight of your children'; see Num 21:17ff."

5:15 A: If by the fall of one the many died.

1. Death as a fate that came over people because of Adam's sin.

4 Ezra 3:7: "You laid one single commandment from yourself on him (Adam); but he transgressed it. Immediately you ordained death for him as well as for his descendants." — 4 Ezra 3:21f.: "For the first Adam erred into sin and guilt because of his evil heart, and likewise all who have been born from him. In this way the sickness became permanent." — 4 Ezra 7:118: "O Adam, what have you done! When you sinned, your fall came not only upon you, but also upon us, your descendants." ‖ 2 Baruch 17:3: "He (Adam) brought death (into the world) and shortened the years of those who stem from him." — 2 Baruch 23:4: "For when Adam had sinned and death had been fated for those who would stem from him...." — 2 Baruch 48:42f.: "O, what have you, Adam, done to all those who stem from you! And what should be said about the first Eve, for she obeyed the snake so that the whole multitude became prey to corruption, and innumerable are those whom the fire consumes!?" — 2 Baruch 54:15, 19: "For if Adam sinned first and brought premature death upon all, each one of those who stem from him has drawn the future torment to himself, and again each one of them has chosen the future glory.... Adam is thus the cause solely for himself; but we, each one of us, has become Adam for himself." — The last passage does not deny that death was fated for all humanity because of Adam's sin and guilt, but it adds that the responsibility for what comes after death, for torment and blessedness, rests on the individual, so that in relation to his final fate each one is in a certain way his own Adam. ‖ In an interpretation of Deut 32:32 concerning Israel (SDeut 32:32 § 323), R. Judah (ca. 150) elucidates the words "Their grapes are grapes of poison" in the following way: "You are children of the first man, who brought death as a punishment upon you and upon all his descendants who come after him until the end of all generations." ‖ Tanḥuma בראשית 5B: Our teachers

said, "Dire is slander, for it brought death upon the first man. Namely, the snake came and said to Adam and Eve, 'God knows that on the day you eat of it, your eyes will be open' (Gen 3:5); for from this tree he ate when he created his world, and every craftsman hates his craft companions; 'and you will be like God.' They listened to it and caused death for themselves and their descendants until the end of all generations. How (can this be proven from Scripture)? Because he says in the passage about him, 'Behold הֵן, man (has become like us)' (Gen 3:22). הֵן (behold) means nothing other than death; as it says, 'Behold הֵן, the time has approached that you must die' (Deut 31:14)." (The identity of the expression הן in Gen 3:22 and Deut 31:14 justifies explaining the content of each passage by appealing to the other one.) ‖ Deuteronomy Rabbah 9 (206A): R. Levi (ca. 300) said, "What can this be compared with? With a pregnant woman who was thrown into prison. There she gave birth to a son and raised him. When the king passed by the prison, that child began to cry, 'My lord king, why have I been cast into prison?' The king said to him, 'You are here because of the sin of your mother.' So also Moses said, 'Lord of the world, there are 36 commandments with the penalty of eradication (in Scripture). If a person transgresses one of these, he is guilty of death. Have I transgressed one of these? Why have you fated death for me?' He answered him, 'You are dying because of the sin of the first man; for he brought death into the world.' 'Behold הֵן! (the time has approached' [Deut 31:14]). What does הן (behold) mean? Because of the guilt of the one of whom הן (behold)! is written: 'Behold, man has become like one of us' (Gen 3:22)." — See the comment on the previous citation. ‖ Midrash Ecclesiastes 7:13 (36A): In the hour that God created the first man, he took him and led him around the trees of the garden of Eden and said to him, "See my works, how beautiful and praiseworthy they are! And everything that I have made, I have made for your sake. Direct your mind to not corrupting and destroying my world; for if you corrupt it, there is no one who can bring it into order after you; and not only this, you will also cause death for that righteous one (namely Moses)." — Then follows anonymously the parable of R. Levi from the previous citation about the child born in prison. ‖ On the words: "You will crawl on your belly" (Gen 3:14), R. Judan (ca. 350) says in Gen. Rab. 20 (13C), "God said to the snake, 'You have caused my creation (humanity) to walk about bent גְּחוּנִים because of their dead; you too will go about on your belly גְּחֹנְךָ.'" ‖ See two further supporting texts in the citation in b. Šabb. 55A in the following #2. ‖ Genesis Rabbah 16 at the end: "You will certainly die" מוֹת תָּמוּת (Gen 2:17). One death pertains to Adam and the other to Eve; one death pertains to him (Adam) and the other to his descendants. ‖ Targum Ecclesiastes 7:29: "I found that Yahweh created the first man upright (good) and just; and the snake and Eve, who misled (him) to eat from the fruits of the tree, by whose fruits those who eat of it become wise to discern between good and evil. And they caused the day of death to come upon him and upon all generations of the world." — See further the two last citations in the following #2.

2. Death as the punishment for the sin of each individual person.

Exodus Rabbah 3 (70A): Why did (Moses) flee (from the snake in Exod 4:3)? Because he had sinned with his words (in Exod 4:1 against Israel). Had he not sinned, he would not have had to flee; for the snake does not kill, but rather sin kills, as is written about the deed of R. Hanina b. Dosa (ca. 70) (see b. Ber. 33A at § Luke 10:19 A). Of course, the saying is formed with a view to the snake in Gen 3 and means that the person is himself the cause of his death by his sin. ‖ Pesiqta 76A: R. Judah (ca. 150) said, "If someone should say to you, 'If Adam had not sinned and not eaten from that tree, would he have remained alive forever and continued to live?,' answer him, 'This happened long ago with Elijah. Since he did not sin, he lives and remains alive forever.'" — Parallels are found in Lev. Rab. 27 (125C); Midr. Eccl. 3:15 (20B); Tanḥ. אמור 174B; TanḥB אמור § 12 (45B). This is found in another form in Pesiq. Rab. Additions 1 (192B.6). ‖ Babylonian Talmud Šabbat 55A: R. Ammi (ca. 300) said, "There is no death without sin and no sufferings (chastisements) without guilt. There is no death without sin; for it says, 'The soul that sins will die. A son will not bear the guilt of the father, nor the father bear the guilt of the son. The righteousness of the righteous will be upon him and the wickedness of the wicked will be upon him' (Ezek 18:20). There are no sufferings without guilt; for it says, 'I will visit their wickedness with sticks and their wrongdoing with plagues' (Ps 89:33)." It was objected, "The angels of service said before God, 'Lord of the world, why have you fated death for the first man?' He answered them, 'I commanded him an easy commandment, and he transgressed it!' They said to him, 'But did not Moses and Aaron keep the whole Torah, and they died?' He answered them, '"A gift meets the righteous as well as the godless" (Eccl 9:2).'" (Thus, there is a death even without the person's own guilt and the thesis of R. Ammi is incorrect.) Whoever speaks (like R. Ammi) views the matter as this Tannaim does. For in a baraita it has been taught that R. Simeon b. Eleazar (ca. 190) said, "Even Moses and Aaron died because of sin; for it says, 'Because you have not believed in me' (Num 20:12). Behold, if you had believed in me, your time to depart from the world would not yet have come!" (Thus R. Ammi is right: No death without sin.) It was objected: "Four died as a result of the snake's counsel (i.e., without having caused death by their own sin, thus in content = as a consequence of Adam's sin), and these are: Benjamin, the son of Jacob; Amram, the father of Moses; Jesse, the father of David; and Chileab, the son of David. Concerning all of them it is traditional teaching with the exception of Jesse, the father of David, about whom Scripture explicitly states it is the case; for it is written 'And Absalom appointed Amasa in place of Joab over the army, and Amasa was the son of a man whose name was Jether the Israelite, who had gone into Abigail, the daughter of Nahash, the sister of Zeruiah, the mother of Joab' (2 Sam 17:25). But was she the daughter of Nahash? Was she not the daughter of Jesse; as it says, 'And their (the sons of Jesse) sisters were Zeruiah and Abigail' (1 Chr 2:16)? It only means 'She was the daughter of the one who died as a consequence of the counsel of the snake נָחָשׁ' (this is why Jesse was also called Nahash)." Who (is this author to whom the tradition about those who died from the snake's counsel belongs)? If it should be said, "The author concerning the serving angels" (see above) — are, then, (as would have to be expected) Moses and Aaron there (among the four persons named)? But R. Simeon b. Eleazar is not the author (see above), for it can be concluded from this that there is a death without sin and sufferings without guilt. The objection of R. Ammi remains, though (it has not been refuted). — The last sentence shows that the whole question remained an open one for the ancient synagogue. — Parallels are found in Lev. Rab. 37 (133D); Midr. Eccl. 5:4 (25A); b. B. Bat. 17A concerning the four who died from the snake's counsel; in SNum 27:14 § 137 (51B) the saying belongs to R. Simeon

b. Eleazar. — On Jesse see also Tg. Ruth 4:22: "Obed fathered Jesse, who is called Nahash דמתקרי בחש. Since no unrighteousness or wickedness was found in him, so that he would have been given into the hands of the angel of death in order to take his soul from him, he lived many days, until the counsel was remembered before Yahweh, the counsel the snake gave to Eve, Adam's wife, to eat from the tree, by whose fruits those who eat of it become wise to discern between good and evil. And because of this counsel all the inhabitants of the earth became guilty of death, and because of this calamity Jesse, the righteous, passed away." ‖ Yalquṭ Simeoni Numbers 20:24 (§ 764) from "midrash": "Since you have been rebellious against my commandment" (Num 20:24). This is what is written, "Yahweh does not let the desire of the righteous go unappeased" (Prov 10:3). This pertains to the first man, for death was determined for all the righteous who stem from him, and they do not part from the world until they have seen the face of the Shekinah and rebuked the first man. They say to him, "You have caused death for us!" And he answers them, "In my hand was only one sin; but among you there is not one in whose hand there would not be many debts (thus you have caused death for yourselves)!" How do we know that they see the face of the Shekinah and rebuke the first man? Because it says, "I thought, 'I will no longer see Yah, Yah in the land of the living, no longer see Adam among the inhabitants of decay'" (so Isa 38:11 according to the midr.). And the righteous are punished with death for light transgressions lest the first man be made responsible (literally: touched) for them; this is why it is said, "Since you have been rebellious against my commandment."

3. οἱ πολλοί = הָרַבִּים (Dan 12:3), "the many," "the multitude."

Mishnah ʾAbot 5.18: Whoever leads the multitude to righteousness הַמְזַכֶּה אֶת־הָרַבִּים (cf. Isa 53:11; Dan 12:3), no sin comes over him. But whoever misleads the multitude to sin הַמַּחֲטִיא את הרבים, to him the possibility is not given (by God) to repent. Moses was righteous and led the multitude to righteousness זָכָה וְזִכָּה את הרבים, and the merit of the multitude וְזָכוּת הָרַבִּים was attached to him (reckoned to him); as it says, "He did the righteousness of Yahweh and his laws with Israel" (Deut 33:21; whatever in the laws Israel did, it was viewed as if Moses had done it together with them; so the merit of the multitude could be posted to him as his own merit). Jeroboam sinned and misled the multitude to sin, and the sin of the multitude was attached to him; as it says, "Because of the sins of Jeroboam, which he committed and to which he misled Israel" (1 Kgs 15:30; the sins to which he misled Israel are reckoned among the sins of Jeroboam). ‖ Tosefta Sanhedrin 13.5 (434): But the heretics and the apostates and the informers (traitors) and the libertines and the repudiators of the Torah and those who separate themselves from the ways of the community and those who deny the resurrection of the dead, and everyone who sins and misleads the multitude הרבים …, gehenna is bolted behind them, and they will be judged (punished) in it for all generations (forever).

5:15 B: How much more abundant has the grace of God and the gift in the grace of the one man Jesus Christ for the many become.

1. πολλῷ μᾶλλον. See § Rom 5:9f.

2. In Wettstein we find the following sentence about Rom 5:15 (2, 48B): Sifre ... *Dixit R. Joses: exi et disce meritum Messiae ac praemium iustorum ab antiquo Adamo* (from the first man)*; cui non fuit datum nisi unum praeceptum de negativis* (only a commandment)*, et transgressus est illud: vide quot mortes decretae sunt ei et generationibus eius et generationibus generationum usque ad finem omnium generationum. Porro quaenam mensura multiplicatur* (what measure or what property of God is greater)*? mensurane boni an mensura vindictae? Mensura boni multiplicatur, mensura vero vindictae minuitur* (is smaller)*. Rex igitur Messiah afflictus meritum* (the merit of suffering) *omnibus retribuet. S. D. Esai 53.* — We have not been able to locate this citation; we also do not believe that it is anywhere in the ancient literature. Presumably it has been confused with the following passage. Sifra Leviticus 5:17 (120A): R. Yose (ca. 150) said, "If you want to learn the recompense of the righteous in the future, go and learn from the first man מאדם הַקַּדְמוֹנִי: only one commandment was commanded him as a prohibition, and he transgressed it. Behold, how many deaths have been fated as a punishment for him and his generations and the generations of his generations until the end of his generations! And how? What measure is greater? Is the measure of the (divine) goodness greater or the measure of punishments? Say: 'The measure of goodness.' If in the case of the measure of punishments, which is lesser, who knows how many deaths have been fated for him and his generations and the generations of his generations until the end of all generations as a punishment. How much more על אחת כמה וכמה does it go for the one who abstains from *piggul* (making use of an offering beyond the allowed time) and (from the forbidden use) of the remains of the offerings, and who fasts on the Day of Atonement, that he obtains merit שֶׁמְּזַכֶּה for himself and his generations and the generations of his generations until the end of all generations." — This passage knows nothing, however, about the merit of the sufferings of the Messiah that benefit everyone. See, though, § Luke 24:26, I, #3.

5:18: To the justification of life.

δικαίωσις ζωῆς = juridical adjudication of life. The following may be compared:

Jerusalem Talmud Roš Haššanah 1.57A.49: R. Qeruspai (ca. 300) said in the name of R. Yohanan († 279), "There are three tablets (books) (which are opened on New Year's Day): one is that of the fully righteous, the other that of the fully godless, and the third that of the people in the middle. That which the one of the fully righteous concerns, they have received the judgment (the verdict) of life אֱיפּוֹפָסִי שֶׁל חַיִּים (= ἀπόφασις) already from New Year's Day. That which the one of the fully godless concerns, they have received their verdict איפופסי שלהן (of death) already from New Year's Day. That which the one of the people in the middle concerns, they have already been given ten days of repentance between New Year's Day and the Day of Atonement. If they repent, they will be written down with the righteous (for life); but if not, they will be written down with the godless (for death)." — In the parallel b. Roš Haš. 16B the words that touch on our subject read: The fully righteous will immediately be written down and sealed for life לְחַיִּים; the fully godless will immediately be written down and sealed for death לְמִיתָה. Those in the middle remain in the balance from New Year's Day until the Day of Atonement: if they earn it (if they become worthy of it by attaining merits), they will be written down for life; if they do not earn it, they will be written down for death. — The "verdict of death" איפופסין מיתה is mentioned rather frequently; see y. Soṭah 7.21D.33 at § Rom 1:20 E, n. *e.* ‖ Leviticus Rabbah 20 (120A): "Nadab and Abihu died ... when they brought strange fire before Yahweh in the wilderness of Sinai" (Num 3:4). R. Meir (ca. 150) said, "How so? Did they die in the wilderness of Sinai? Yet it is written that they received their judgment of death איפופסין שלחם למיתה from Mount Sinai." — The same is found in TanḥB אחרי § 8 (32B); see also Pesiq. 173B.3. ‖ Midrash Song of Songs 4:4 (110A): R. Abba b. Kahana (ca. 310) offered proof from this passage in the name of R. Yohanan († 279), "'And the *goyim* will be completely destroyed חָרֹב יֶחֱרָבוּ' (Isa 60:12): they have received their judgment of death איפופסין שלחם למיחת (namely from Horeb חֹרֵב, wordplay on חָרֹב)." See Num. Rab. 1 (136A); TanḥB במדבר § 7 (4B). ‖ Midrash Psalm 52 § 5 (143A): When Saul had let the judgment of death איפרפסין של מות fall upon him (Ahimelech), it says immediately: "And the king said to the runners who were around him, 'Get closer and kill the priests of Yahweh!'" (1 Sam 22:17).

5:20: The law entered in so that transgression might be abundant.

The following may be seen as a parallel in a certain sense:

Babylonian Talmud Nedarim 22B: Rab Ad(d)a b. Hanina (= Hunia, in the 4th cent.) said, "If the Israelites had not sinned, the five fifths of the Torah and the book of Joshua would have been given to them, because this contains the order (allocation) of the land of Israel. What is the scriptural basis for this? 'For in the multitude of wisdom (the nonpentateuchal writings) there is much vexation' (concerning the effort that they require; so Midr. Eccl. 1:18; cf. Rashi)." — From the same viewpoint, R. Yohanan († 279) says in y. Meg. 1.70D.51: "The Nevi'im and the Ketuvim will cease (lose their validity) one day (in the messianic time, when there will no longer be any sin); but the five books of the Torah will never cease. What is the scriptural basis? 'Yahweh spoke ... on the mountain ... with a loud voice, and it will not cease' (so Midr. Deut. 5:19)."

6:3: As many of us were baptized into Jesus Christ.

βαπτίζειν εἰς; see § Matt 28:19.

6:4: We were thus buried with him by baptism into death, so that ... we too should walk in newness of life.

The oxymoron in b. Tamid 66A (see § Matt 10:39) adduced by Schöttgen[114] is less appropriate here.

6:6: So that the body of sin might be rendered ineffective.

Babylonian Talmud Berakot 17A: When Rab Sheshet (ca. 260) would sit in fasting, he used to say after the Prayer (of Eighteen Benedictions), "Lord of the worlds, it is evident

114. Schöttgen, *Horae Hebraicae et Talmudicae*, 1:515.

before you that if a person sinned at the time when the temple stood, he would bring an offering, and from this only its fat and its blood were offered, and atonement was made for him. And now I sit fasting and my fat and my blood are diminished נתמעט (disappear). May it be the will (pleasing) before you that my fat and my blood, which disappear שנתמעט, be viewed as if I had offered them before you on the altar, and that you graciously accept me." — See the similar saying of R. Simon (ca. 280) concerning Hos 14:3 in Tanḥ. קרח 221A; Num. Rab. 18 (185A); Pesiq. 165B. ‖ Babylonian Talmud Tamid 66A: What should a person do so that he may live? Let him kill himself (= live abstemiously); see § Matt 10:39. ‖ On "body of sin" see the excursus "The Good and the Evil Inclination."

6:7: Whoever has died has been acquitted of sin.

A baraita in b. Šabb. 151B: R. Simeon b. Gamaliel (ca. 140) said, "Because of a one-day-old child, who lives, one profanes the Sabbath (by doing all the things that are necessary for mother and child); because of the dead David, the king of Israel, one does not profane the Sabbath. Because of a one-day-old child, who lives, one profanes the Sabbath. The Torah means (literally: says), 'Profane a Sabbath because of it so that it may (later) keep the Sabbath.' Because of the dead David, the king of Israel, one does not profane it: when a person has died, he is free בָּטֵל from the fulfillments of the commandments." This is what R. Yohanan († 279) said, "'Free among the dead!' (Ps 88:6); when a person has died, he has been freed נַעֲשָׂה הָפְשִׁי (= δεδικαίωται [Rom 6:7]) from the fulfillments of the commandments." — R. Yohanan's saying is also in b. Nid. 61B; Pesiq. 200B. ‖ Babylonian Talmud Šabbat 30A: The following question was asked above (i.e., before) R. Tanḥum of Naveh (Dalman: נְוֵי), "What about extinguishing a burning light before a sick person on the Sabbath?" He arose and said, "You, Solomon, where is your wisdom, where is your insight? Is it not enough for you that your words nullify the words of your father David? Must your words also cancel each other out? Your father David said, 'The dead will not praise Yah' (Ps 115:17); and you say, 'I will praise the dead who died long ago' (Eccl 4:2). And further you said, 'For a living dog is better than a dead lion' (Eccl 9:4)." — There is no contradiction. When David said, "The dead will not praise Yah," he meant it in this way: Let a man always occupy himself with the Torah and with fulfilling the commandments before he dies; for when he has died, he is free בָּטֵל from the Torah and fulfilling the commandments, and God accrues no praise by him. And this is what R. Yohanan († 279) said, "What does "Free among the dead" (Ps 88:6) mean? When a person has died, he has become free נעשה הפשי from the Torah and from fulfilling the commandments. And when Solomon said, 'I will praise the dead who died long ago' (this also applies): for when the Israelites has sinned in the wilderness, Moses stood before God and said who knows how many prayers and pleading petitions before him, and he was not heard. But when he said, 'Remember Abraham, Isaac, and Israel (Jacob), your servants' (Exod 32:13), he was immediately heard. Did Solomon not beautifully say, 'I will praise the dead who died long ago'?" ‖ See additional the citations at § Rom 7:3.

6:9: Death no longer rules over him.

κυριεύει = שָׁלַט.

Mekilta Exodus 20:19 (79A): R. Yose (ca. 150) said, "The Israelites stood at Mount Sinai (and accepted the Torah) on the condition that the angel of death should not rule over them שלא ישלט בהם מלאך המות." – See the whole passage in the version of the parallel in b. ʿAbod. Zar. 5A at § Matt 4:1 B, #4, n. *a* at the end. ‖ Exodus Rabbah 41 (97D): (God said to the angel of death at the giving of the law,) "Over every nation in the world I permit you to rule השלטתי אותך, except for this nation (Israel), to which I have given freedom (from death)." ‖ Exodus Rabbah 51 (103D): When God gave Israel the Torah, they were not destined to have the angel of death rule over them שישלוט בהם. ‖ TanḥumaB וארא § 9 (13A): R. Simeon (ca. 150) said, "Arms were given to them (on Mount Sinai as adornment), on which the great name (= 'Yahweh') was engraved, and as long as it was in their hand, the angel of death could not rule שלוט over them." ‖ See further § Rom 5:14 A. – On the freedom of the Israelites from sickness and death at the time of the giving of the law see § Matt 4:1 B, #4 and § Matt 11:5, #1, n. *c*.

6:16: Do you not know that to whomever you devote yourselves to as servants for obedience, you are (that one's) servants?

See § John 8:34.

6:19 A: I speak in a human way.

See § Rom 3:5, n. *e*.

6:19 B: To unrighteousness unto unrighteousness, … to righteousness unto sanctification.

Mishnah ʾAbot 4.2: Ben Azzai (ca. 110) said, "Hurry to carry out an easy commandment and flee from a transgression. Fulfilling a commandment brings (another) fulfillment of a commandment and a transgression brings (another) transgression; for the recompense for fulfilling a commandment שְׂכַר מִצְוָה is fulfilling a commandment and the recompense for a transgression שְׂכַר עֲבֵירָה is a transgression."

6:20: Free in relation to righteousness.

Midrash Lamentations Introduction #7 (31A): R. Abbahu (ca. 300) opened his presentation in the name of R. Yose b. Hanina (ca. 270) with: "'Her (Zion's) gates will groan and wail' (Isa 3:26). Groaning inside and wailing outside. Her gates (plural) pertains to the first and the second destruction. 'Vacated נקתה she will sit down on the earth' (Isa 3:26). 'Vacated,' that is, free נְקִיָּה (pure) of words of the Torah, free of words of prophecy, free of righteous people, free of fulfillments of commandments and good works. Therefore 'she will sit down on the earth': 'The elders of the daughter of Zion sit down on the earth in silence' (Lam 2:10)."

6:21: What fruit did you have at that time?

καρπός = פְּרִי. See § Matt 7:16 A and § Matt 12:33, #1.

6:23: The payment of sin.

1. ὀψώνια = אֲפְסַנְיָא, אָפְסוֹנִין provisions, wages, payment.

Sifre Deuteronomy 17:17 § 159 (105B): "Let him (the king) not keep lots of silver and gold for himself" (Deut 17:17); maybe also not in order to give out pay אפסניא? Scripture teaches: "Let him not keep lots for himself"; for "himself" he should not keep a lot, but he may keep much to pay out wages אָפְסְנָיוֹת. — The same is found in a briefer form in b. Sanh. 21B; in y. Sanh. 2.20C.21 with the addition: R. Joshua b. Levi (ca. 250) said, "Only the pay for the current year." ‖ Babylonian Talmud Sanhedrin 18B: The king and the high priest are (not permitted to sit in the Sanhedrin) to set an intercalary year: the king is not allowed because of the pay אפסניא (because the pay is set as a yearly allowance, so that the king has an interest in lengthening the year by inserting an intercalary month); the high priest is not allowed because of the cold (for, since he has to take a bath several times on the Day of Atonement, he has an interest in preventing the insertion of an intercalary month, lest the Day of Atonement fall in the cold time of the year). ‖ Midrash Song of Songs 1:2 (83A): R. Yose b. Hanina (ca. 270) and the rabbis said, "Like a king who allocated the wages אפסניות to his legions by generals, eparchs, and colonels; but when his son came, he gave it to him hand to hand (personally without mediation)." ‖ Also in Mek. Exod. 15:3 (45B) אפסניות should be read instead of אכסניות "quarters."

2. Literally, in Hebrew, "payment of sin" would be rendered with שְׂכַר עֲבֵירָה. See, for example, m. ʾAbot 4.2 above at § Rom 6:19 B.

7:1: The law rules over a person as long as he lives.

See the citations at § Rom 6:7.

7:2 A: A woman subjected to a man (= a married woman).

ὕπανδρος γυνή occurs only here in the NT.

Tanḥuma בלק 237B: (Zimri) seized her (the Midianite Cozbi in Num 25:6ff.) by the hair and led her to Moses. He said to this one, "Son of Amram, is this woman allowed or forbidden?" And if you should say, "This Midianite is forbidden, who allowed you that woman, who is under you אוֹתָהּ שֶׁתַּחְתֶּיךָ (= who is married to you)?" (See Exod 2:15, 21.) — In b. Sanh. 82A, אותה שתחתיך is replaced by the name בת יתרו and in Num. Rab. 20 (190C) אותה שלקחת = the one whom you married.

7:2 B: But if the man has died, she has become free from the law of the man.

Mishnah Qiddušin 1.1: The woman acquires (obtains her independence or freedom again) in a twofold way.... She acquires it by a letter of divorce or by the death of her husband.

7:3: Free from the law.

See the citations at § Rom 6:7. — See additionally, Pesiq. 200B: R. Yohanan († 279) said, "'There small and great are the same and the servant is free from his master' (Job 3:19). Scripture is talking about the hour of death; for if one is a scholar or a powerful man or a rich man, he cannot deliver himself from the hour of death; as it says, 'No one has power over the wind ... and no one is commanding over the day of death' (Eccl 8:8). 'Small': This refers to King David—peace be upon him!—who was called small; as it says, 'But David was the youngest הקטן (the small one)' (1 Sam 17:14). 'Great': Moses is meant; for it says, 'The man Moses was also very great' (Exod 11:3). 'And the servant free from his master': this pertains to the Israelites; for when a man has died, he has become free הָפְשִׁי from fulfilling the commandments." ‖ Targum Psalm 88:6: "How the godless, who died and did not turn (in repentance), became free בְּנֵי הוֹרִין from fulfilling the commandments (read מִצְוָתָא instead of מַצוּתָא 'quarrel, conflict')."

7:6 A: But now we have become free from the law ....

On Rom 7:6, see Kittel at § Acts 21:21.

7:6 B: In newness of spirit and not in the old being of the letter.

See Pesiq. 102A: R. Eleazar said, "The words of the Torah should in your eyes not be like an old ordinance כְּפְרוֹסְדַּגְמָא ישמה (= πρόσταγμα), but rather like a new ordinance כפ׳ חדשה which all like to read; this is what is written, 'Today Yahweh your God commands you to do his statutes' (Deut 26:16)." — The same thought is found in Pesiq. 107A.

7:7: You shall not desire.

Exodus 20:17: לֹא תַחְמֹד. — Targum Onkelos: לָא תַחְמֵד "you shall not desire"; Tg. Yer. I: ולא יַחֲמֵיד חד מנכון "and none of you shall desire." ‖ Deuteronomy 5:18: וְלֹא תַחְמֹד ... וְלֹא תִתְאַוֶּה "you shall not desire ... and you shall not wish." — Targum Onkelos: וְלָא תַחְמֵד ... וְלָא תֵרוֹג "you shall not desire ... and you shall not let yourself yearn." — Targum Yerušalmi I twice: וְלָא יֵירוֹג חד מנכון "let none of you yearn." — The two synonyms הִתְאַוָּה and חָמַד were differentiated from each other in the following way: α. תַּאֲוָה is a wishing in the heart; if it remains simply a wish to possess something, this wishing does not fall under the prohibition לא תתאוה (Deut 5:18). But if one devises plans in the heart to bring the wish to fruition, one has transgressed the prohibition לא תתאוה.[a] — β. חִמּוּד is likewise a desiring of the heart (to this extent, as the broader concept, it entails תאוה, as, for example, also in Exod 20:17), but חמוד aspires to realize itself immediately in actions that bring the one desiring into possession of the wished-for object. Therefore, חמוד signifies a transgression of Exod 20:17 and Deut 5:18. As a result, the objects of חמוד are limited to something that one can acquire or that one can bring into the possession of someone else. Further, it belongs to the essence of the concept חִמּוּד in Exod 20:17 and Deut 5:18 that the one who possesses the desired object consents to the transfer of the item ultimately to the one who desires it, even if under the pressure of compulsion.[b] If the one who desires the object should gain the object in question without consent, he would not fall under the prohibition לא תחמד at all, but rather under the prohibition לֹא תִגְזֹל "you shall not steal" (Lev 19:13). As a punishment for the one who with a sinful desire sets his eyes on something that is not his, it holds that he is not permitted what he wishes and that what was his in his house is taken from him.[c] Thus תאוה is counted among the things that bring a person out of the world.[d]

a. Schulchan ʿArukh חשן המשפט § 359: Anyone who wishes for the house or the wife or the objects of another or the like כל המתאוה, if he thinks in his heart about how he might acquire this item, and lets himself be misled in his heart by the item, he transgresses the prohibition: "You shall not wish" לא תתאיה (Deut 5:18); and wishing תאוה happens only in the heart. — From the words: "If he thinks in his heart about ...," it follows that he does not make himself guilty of transgressing the prohibition in Deut 5:18 as long as he does not have such thoughts. Therefore, it correctly explicitly says in ארח מישרים (p. 92): "Anyone who does not ruminate and think about how he might acquire that desired item does not transgress: 'You shall not wish' (Deut 5:18)."

b. Schulchan ʿArukh חשן המשפט § 359: If someone desires החומד the servant or the maidservant or the house or the objects of another or anything that he can acquire from him, and he inflicts serious harm on him or pressures him until he receives the desired object from him, behold, this one violates the commandment: "You shall not desire" ... Wishing התאוה leads to desiring חִמּוּד and desiring leads to robbing גָּזֵל; for if the owners (of the desired objects) do not want to sell, although they are offered much money and pressured with all kinds of harm, it results in robbery; as it says, "If they desire houses, they rob" (Mic 2:2 is cited thus). And if the owners insist before him (the one who desires) on keeping their possessions from him, if they prevent him from robbing, then it comes to bloodshed. Go and learn from the story of Ahab and Naboth! See, there you learned that the one who wishes for something המתאוה transgresses a commandment, and he who acquires an item that he wished for by the coercion by which he coerced the owners, he transgresses two commandments; this is why it says, "You shall not desire and you shall not wish" (Deut 5:18). And if he robs, he transgresses three commandments. ‖ Mekilta Exodus 20:17 (78A): "You shall not desire" (Exod 20:17); and there it says, "You shall not wish" (Deut 5:18), in order to declare someone guilty specifically for wishing and specifically for desiring. Rabbi († 217?) said, "A passage of Scripture says, 'You shall not desire' (Exod 20:17), and a passage of Scripture says, 'You shall not wish' (Deut 5:18). How will these two passages of Scripture be maintained (alongside each other)? They mean to tell you: If someone wishes for (something), he will ultimately desire it; for it says, 'You shall not wish and you shall not desire' (Deut 5:18). How do we know that if one desires, he will ultimately act violently and rob? Scripture teaches, 'When they desire fields, they rob' (Mic 2:2). 'You shall not desire your neighbor's house' (Exod 20:17): this is general (i.e., 'house' comprises all the property with everything that belongs to it, as in Gen 15:2), 'nor his servant nor his maidservant nor his cattle nor his donkey': this is particular (individual). General and particular (alongside each other), then in general only what is in particular. And if Scripture then also says, 'Nor anything that belongs to your neighbor' (Exod 20:17), it brings up again a general statement. If it summarized the general (only) in the first general statement, you could say: 'General and particular (alongside each other), then in general only what is in particular.' But it brings up again a general statement, so you may only infer according to the particular: as the particular clearly and obviously pertains to something that one acquires or that one brings into the possession of another, so too the general pertains to something that one acquires or brings into the possession of another. Or as the particular clearly and obviously pertains to personal goods that have no mortgage security, it deals (in general) only with personal goods that have no mortgage security. And if Scripture says in Deuteronomy במשנה תורה 'You shall not desire his field' (Deut 5:18), this holds: as the particular clearly and obviously pertains to something that one acquires or gives into the possession of another, it deals (in general) only with something that one acquires or gives into the possession of another. And as the particular clearly and obviously pertains to something that can come into your possession only by the consent of the owners, it deals (in general) only with something that can come into your possession only by the consent of the owners. Thus, there is an exception (it is not a transgression of Exod 20:17), if you desire חומד his (another's) daughter for your son or his son for your daughter (because the consent of the other is not necessary in all circumstances for them to be married). Or (is it a transgression of Exod 20:17) even if one desires (only) with words? Scripture says, 'You shall not desire תחמוד the silver and gold in them (idols), so that you take them for yourself' (Deut 7:25). As there (in Deut 7:25 there is no transgression of the prohibition) until one carries out the act (takes the silver and gold), so too here (in the question about desiring with words), until one carries out the act (for it belongs to the essence of חָמוּד to bring the desire to fruition in deeds)." ‖ From b. B. Meṣ. 5B, it can be concluded that different opinions ruled over the question of whether someone transgresses the commandment "You shall not desire" (Exod 20:17) when he is ready to compensate for the value of the desired object. Here namely Rab Aha of Difti says to Rabina (I † ca. 420; II † 499), "But such a person (who renounces a deposit, even if he is ready to compensate for it) transgresses the commandment 'You shall not desire' (Exod 20:17)!" (Answer:) "'You shall not desire' לא תחמוד means according to the people (a desiring) without compensating." — The Tosafists mention this explanation in b. Sanh. 25B מעיקרא. They remark on this sentence that initially the scholars had permitted perpetrators to act as witnesses, because they would compensate for the value of wrongly acquired goods (b. Sanh. 25B); so the following: "If you should say that he (a perpetrator) should have been declared ineligible (to appear as a witness) on the basis of the Torah, since he transgresses the prohibition 'You shall not desire' (Exod 20:17), it can be rejoined that the prohibition 'You shall not desire' should be understood in the case when he does not pay the value. But when he pays the value, the prohibition 'You shall not desire' does not apply at all." And if you should say "But we have said in the 1st chapter of Baba Meṣiʿa (see b. B. Meṣ. 5B above) 'You shall not desire' means (a desiring) without compensating, and from this it is to be concluded that it was understood thus only by the people, but in reality they err, because 'You shall not desire' applies even in the case of the one who pays the value," then it should be rejoined .... — At any rate, these expositions reveal that the prohibition "You shall not desire" (Exod 20:17) was very broadly conceived.

c. See Gen. Rab. 20 (13C); t. Soṭah 4.16 (301); b. Soṭah 9A at § Matt 13:12 B. — Further punishments: Pesiqta Rabbati 24 (125B): "You shall not desire" (Exod 20:17). R. Huna (ca. 350) said, "We find that the Israelites did not migrate from their own land until they transgressed the verse: 'When they desire fields, they rob ...' (Mic 2:2)." — See the narrative in b. Giṭ. 58A.34. ‖ Seder Eliyahu Rabbah 24 (131): "You shall not desire" (Exod 20:17). If you keep it, (it will come true): "No one will desire יחמוד your land" (Exod 34:24). If you transgress it, (it will come true): "When they desire, they rob ..." (Mic 2:2).

d. Mishnah ʾAbot 4.21: R. Eleazar Haqqappar (ca. 180) said, "Envy, desire הַתַּאֲוָה, and ambition bring a person out of the world."

7:8: But since sin took the opportunity through the commandment, it worked in me every kind of desire.

The two inclinations in people and the Torah: the good inclination יֵצֶר טוֹב (the arthrous form יֵצֶר הַטּוֹב is encountered very infrequently, as in, e.g., ʾAbot R. Nat. 32) takes the opportunity and ability from the Torah for every good, while the evil inclination יֵצֶר הָרַע rebels against the Torah. This is why the Torah is the best God-given means to constrain the evil inclination. See in more detail the discussion in the excursus "The Good and the Evil Inclination." See also the explanation at § Rom 2:15 B, #3.

7:10 A: The commandment that is for life.

For the Torah as Israel's life, see § Rom 3:1f., D. ‖ Further, Pss. Sol. 14:1: "The Lord is faithful to those ... who walk in righteousness with respect to his commandments, in the law that he has commanded us for our life." ‖ Tosefta Šabbat 15.17 (134): R. Aha (a Tannaim [ca. 180?]) said in the name of R. Aqiba († ca. 135), "... The commandments were given only so that one might live by means of them; as it says, 'If anyone does them, he will live by means of them' (Lev 18:5). But (they were) not (given) so that one might die by means of them. And there is nothing that excludes saving human life except for these three things: idolatry, fornication, and bloodshed (i.e., all the commandments can be transgressed if one can save life by means of them, except for the three named). In which case do these words apply? For the case when it is not a time of religious persecution; but in a time of religious persecution, one should lose his life even for the lightest commandment." See Lev 22:32; Prov 16:4. (See b. Yoma 85A in § Matt 5:10, #2 and § Matt 12:10, #2, n. *a.*) ‖ Pesiqta 102B: "A two-edged sword in their hand" (Ps 149:6). R. Judah (ca. 150) said, "פִּיפִיּוֹת (= 2 edges) means the written and oral Torah." R. Nehemiah (ca. 150) said, "פיפיות means a blade that has two edges; (the Torah is) a sword that devours on two sides, and it gives life in this world and in the future world." ‖ Midrash Song of Songs 1:2 (83A): R. Hana (read Hanina) b. Aha (ca. 330) supplied evidence for the notion (that the Torah is like a weapon) from this passage: "'Lifting praises to God with their (the pious') mouth and a two-edged sword in their hand' (Ps 149:6); as a sword devours on two sides, so the Torah gives life in this world and for the future world." — See further § 2 Cor 2:16.

7:10 B: For death.

Exodus Rabbah 5 (71A): How did the voice (of God at the giving of the law) go out? R. Tanḥuma (ca. 380) said, "It went out in a double form, and it killed the nations because they did not accept it, and gave life to the Israelites because they accepted the Torah." — See also the passages at § 2 Cor 2:16.

7:12: The commandment is ... good.

On the Torah as the good per se, see § Matt 19:17 A. — Further, SDeut 11:17 § 43 (82B): "You will quickly perish from the good land" (Deut 11:17); you will quickly go into exile and not come into a land as good as this one is. R. Judah (ca. 150) said, "'Good': this is the Torah. Likewise (Scripture) says, 'For I am giving you a good teaching; do not abandon my Torah' (Prov 4:2)."

7:14 A: The law is spiritual.

πνευματικός = stemming from the spirit of God or from the holy spirit and therefore bearing its nature in itself. The rabbis have no single equivalent word, so a circumlocution must be used to express the content.

Mishnah Sanhedrin 10.1: These are the ones who have no share in the future world: Whoever says, "... The Torah is (stems) not from God אין תורה מן השמים." ‖ Tosefta Yadayim 2.14 (683.12): R. Simeon ben Manasseh (ca. 180) said, "The Song of Songs makes the hands unclean (= is canonical), because it was spoken in the holy spirit שנאמרה ברוח הקדש (= originated by the power of divine inspiration); the book of Ecclesiastes does not make the hands unclean (is not canonical), because it stems from Solomon's wisdom (and not from the holy spirit of inspiration)." ‖ Babylonian Talmud Megillah 7A.25: Samuel († 254) thought that the book of Esther was not spoken in the holy spirit לאו ברוח הקודש נאמרה.

7:14 B: But I am fleshly, sold under sin.

1. σαρκινός. See § 1 Cor 3:1, #2.

2. πεπραμένος "sold" = "given up" already in the OT.

Deuteronomy 32:30: "If not because their rock sold them מְכָרָם and Yahweh delivered them up הִסְגִּירָם?" — Targum Onkelos: "Only because their strong one gave them up מסרנון and Yahweh delivered them up." — The same is found in Tg. Yer. I. — Septuagint: εἰ μὴ ὁ θεὸς ἀπέδοτο αὐτοὺς καὶ κύριος παρέδωκεν αὐτούς. ‖ 1 Kings 21:20: "Because you sold yourself יַעַן הִתְמַכֶּרְךָ to do what is evil in the eyes of Yahweh." — The targum mitigates this: "Because you intended to do what is evil before Yahweh." Septuagint: διότι μάτην πέπρασαι ποιῆσαι τὸ πονηρὸν ἐνώπιον κυρίου. — Similarly, 1 Kgs 21:25. ‖ 1 Maccabees 1:15: "They made foreskins for themselves and fell away from the holy covenant and tied themselves tight to the yoke of the pagans and sold themselves ἐπράθησαν to do evil."

3. The apostle's confession in Rom 7:14 stands in a curious contrast with the admonition in Sir 7:16 (Hebrew): "Do not count yourself among the people of unrighteousness" אל תחשיבך במתי עול (Strack: במתי עם = "among the people of the nation"). — The Greek version: μὴ προσλογίζου σεαυτὸν

ἐν πλήθει ἁμαρτωλῶν = do not count yourself among the mass of sinners. — See m. ʾAbot 2.13: R. Simeon (b. Nathaniel [ca. 100]) used to say, "… Do not be godless before yourself (in your own eyes)."

7:15 A: For I do not know what I do.

γινώσκω is not used here in the sense of theoretical knowledge (though the idea that the human intellect has been damaged by sin is not completely foreign to the ancient synagogue),[a] but rather in the ethical sense = to have inner communion with something. See John 17:3, 25; 1 John 4:6; 5:20; Matt 7:23; 1 Cor 8:3; 2 Cor 5:21; Gal 4:9; Phil 3:10; 2 Tim 2:19.

a. ʾAbot de Rabbi Nathan 39 (10A): (R. Aqiba? [† ca. 135] said,) "Because of his sin, humanity is not capable of knowing לידע the image of the upper world (the true essence of God), otherwise the keys would have been given to him (by God) to know how heaven and earth were created." (Absolute knowledge of God makes one capable of divine acts.) — On the division of the sentence (construing בעונו in relation to what follows rather than what precedes) and the supposed authorship of R. Aqiba, see Bacher.[115]

7:15 B: I do not do what I want, but rather that which I hate, I do.

On the struggle between the good and evil inclination in the person, see the excursus "The Good and Evil Inclination." See also § Rom 2:15 B, #3.

7:17: Sin dwelling in me.

On ἐνοικοῦσα, see Gen. Rab. 22 (15A): R. Isaac (ca. 300) said, "Initially it (sin) is a guest (temporary, staying only for a short while), and then it becomes the (permanently present and commanding) master of the house בעל הבית. This is what is written, 'Then he refused to take one of his sheep and from his cattle to prepare it for the migrant (guest) who had come to him' (2 Sam 12:4). See, here it is a guest. 'And he took the lamb of the poor man and prepared it for the man who had come to him' (2 Sam 12:4). Behold, here it is the master of the house." — In b. Sukkah 52B, Raba († 352) is named as the author of this saying, though it is expanded in one part: Initially it (the evil inclination) is called a transient man הֵלֶךְ, then it is called a guest אֹרֵחַ, and finally it is called a man (master) אִישׁ. See 2 Sam 12:4.

7:19: The evil I do not want, I do.

Jerusalem Talmud Yoma 6.43D.18: The evil inclination desires only what is forbidden it. — The same is found in y. Ned. 9.41B.62. ‖ 4 Ezra 3:21ff.: "Because of his evil heart the first Adam strayed into sin and guilt and so have all who have been born from him. Thus, the sickness became permanent: the law was in the heart of the people but together with the bad seed. So, what is good disappeared, but the evil remained."

---

115. Bacher, *Die Agada der Tannaïten*, 1:280.

7:24: Wretched man that I am, who will deliver me from this body of death!?

Similar plaintive cries. 4 Ezra 7:65ff.: “So let the human race mourn, but let the animals of the field rejoice! May all those born of woman wail, but the livestock and wild animals rejoice! Matters are much better for them than for us; for they have no judgment to expect, they do not know about a torment, nor of a blessedness that is promised to them after death. But we, what use is it to us to be able to know that we could come to blessedness one day, but (in fact) we fall in agonies? For all who have been born are disfigured by godlessness, full of sins, laden with guilt. And it would be much better for us if we did not have to face judgment after death!” — 4 Ezra 7:116ff.: “This remains my first and my last word: It would be better if the earth had never brought forth Adam[116] or at least if she had kept him from sin. For how does it help us all that we must live now in distress and have punishment to wait for after death? O, Adam, what have you done! When you sinned, your fall did not come upon you only, but rather upon us, your descendants! For how does it help us that eternity has been promised to us, if we have done works of death? That an imperishable hope has been promised to us, if we have fallen so miserably into vanity? That dwellings full of enjoyment and peace have been prepared, if we have passed away in wretchedness? That one day the glory of the Most High will shelter those who have kept themselves pure, if we have walked in shameful ways? That paradise, whose fruits remain forever, will appear, bestowing satiety and healing, if we will never come into it, because we have tarried in awful places? That the face of the pure ones will shine brighter than sunlight, if our own face will be darker than the night? For, O, in life, in as much as we committed sin, we did not remember the sufferings that await us after death!” ‖ Babylonian Talmud ʿErubin 18A: R. Simeon b. Pazzi (ca. 280) said (interpreting the double yod in וייצר in Gen 2:7), “Woe to me because of my (evil) inclination יִצְרִי! Wo to me because of my creator יוֹצְרִי! (If I resist the evil inclination, it torments me; if I give into it, God punishes me.)” — The same is found in reverse sequence in b. Ber. 61A.

8:2: The Spirit of life.

πνεῦμα ζωῆς, the divine spirit of the new life. — In the OT רוּחַ חַיִּים = “breath of life” (Gen 6:17; 7:15); Targum Onkelos and Yerušalmi I: רוּחָא דְחַיֵּי; LXX: πνεῦμα ζωῆς. — For the rabbis, the divine spirit only rarely appears as the life-working creative power of God. See § Matt 1:18 C, #2. Yet generally the assumption is widespread that the spirit is to be imparted anew in the messianic time. Here the new spirit is conceived of (α) as a spirit of prophetic endowment (see the supporting passages at § Acts 2:17–21); (β) as a spirit of a new life pleasing to God.[a]

---

116. S-B: Babylonian Talmud ʿErubin 13B: For two and a half years the school of Shammai and the school of Hillel fought. The former said, “It would be far better for a person if he had not been created than to have been created.” The latter said, “It is far better for a person that he was created than if he had not been created.” They voted and decided: “It would be far better for a person if he had not been created than to have been created; now, since he has been created, let him examine יפשפש his works!” Others said, “Let him test ימשמש his works.”

a. See T. Jud. 24; Jub. 1:23 at § Matt 1:21 D, A, n. *e*. — Also, T. Levi 18: "The glory of the Most High will be spoken over him (the high priest of the messianic end-time), and the spirit of understanding and of sanctification πνεῦμα ἁγιασμοῦ (spirit who effects sanctification) will rest on him." ‖ 4 Ezra 6:26: "Then (at the dawn of the messianic time) the heart of those who inhabit the earth will be changed and converted into a new spirit." ‖ Pesiqta 165A: "For you fell by your wrongdoing" (Hos 14:2). R. Simai (ca. 210) said, "Like a high rock that was at a crossroads, and people fell because of it. Then the king said to them, 'Chip away at it little by little until the hour comes when I remove it (once and for all) from the world.' So too God said to the Israelites, 'My children, the evil inclination is a great stumbling block, but chip away at it little by little, and ultimately I will remove it from the world;' this is what is written, 'I will remove the heart of stone from your flesh ... and put my spirit in you ...' (Ezek 36:26f)." ‖ Tanḥuma קדושים 170B: God said, "In this world the children of men are punished because of the evil inclination, but in the future I will destroy it from you." See Ezek 36:26f (as before). ‖ Tanḥuma שלח לך 216A: God said to the Israelites, "In this world you have separated yourselves from the commandments because of the evil inclination, but in the future I will destroy it from you." See Ezek 36:26f.

8:7: Enmity toward God.

ἔχθρα εἰς θεόν. — Leviticus Rabbah 7 (109D): "Enmity arouses disputes" (Prov 10:12). The enmity that the Israelites set up between themselves and their father in heaven שִׂנְאָה שנתנו ישראל ביניהם לבין אביהן שבשמים (namely by their idolatry before and after the exodus from Egypt) aroused judgments (punishments) upon judgments for them. For R. Samuel b. Nahman (ca. 260) said, "The enmity between Israel and their father in heaven was suppressed for almost 900 years, from the day when the Israelites went out of Egypt, until the year when it was aroused against them in the days of Ezekiel. This is what is written, 'Let each one of you cast away the horrid things, and they did not do this but rather were rebellious against me.... But I acted for the sake of my name, so that it would not be desecrated' (Ezek 20:7ff.)." ‖ See t. Šabb. 13.5 (129) at § Luke 6:22 A.

8:9 A: If indeed God's Spirit lives in you.

οἰκεῖ = שָׁרָה, Aram. שְׁרָא, "rest, dwell." See examples at § Luke 2:25 C, #3, notes *a* and *b*: Pirqe R. El. 39 (22A); Pesiq. 9A; Lev. Rab. 1 (105A); n. *g*: Lev. Rab. 15 (115C); n. *q*: b. Sanh. 65B; SDeut 18:11 § 173 (107B); § Luke 2:25 C, 4, n. *a*.

8:9 B: The Spirit of Christ.

For other passages that speak of the spirit of the Messiah רוחו של מלך המשיח, even if in a different sense than Rom 8:9, see § John 1:1 D.

8:11: He will make your mortal bodies alive because of (διὰ τό) his Spirit dwelling in you.

1. The holy spirit is connected with the resurrection of the dead in the inference chain of R. Phineas b. Yair (ca. 200) in m. Sotah 9.15. See the passage at § Matt 5:3. — The spirit of God appears in:

Exodus Rabbah 48 (102D): God said to Israel, "In this world my spirit has put wisdom in you, but in the future my spirit will make you live again (resurrect you)"; as it says, "I will put my spirit in you so that you will live" (Ezek 37:14). — Differently in Tanḥ. ויקהל 123A and TanḥB ויקהל § 6 (62A).

2. The light of the Torah features as the principle of the resurrection of the dead in b. Ketub. 111B. See the passage at § John 7:49, #8, n. *c*.

8:13: If you kill the aspirations of the body by (the) Spirit.

1. θανατοῦτε.

Babylonian Talmud Berakot 63B: "Be silent הַסְכֵּת and listen, Israel" (Deut 27:9); wear yourselves out כתתו (literally: pound, batter) for the words of the Torah (to learn them), as Resh Laqish (ca. 250) said. For Resh Laqish said, "How do we know that the words of the Torah endure only in the case of the one who kills himself because of them שממית עצמו? Because it says, 'This is the (right) study of the Torah, if one dies in the tent (= house of learning)' (so Midr. Num. 19:14)." ‖ Babylonian Talmud Tamid 66A: "What should a person do in order to live ויחיה?" It was answered, "Let him kill himself ימית עצמו." See the whole passage at § Matt 10:39. ‖ Babylonian Talmud Sanhedrin 43A: R. Joshua b. Levi (ca. 250) said, "Whoever slaughters (sacrifices) הזובח his (evil) inclination and confesses (his sin) because of it, Scripture reckons it to him as if he honored God in two worlds, in this one and in the future world; for it is written, 'Whoever offers confession honors me'" (so Midr. Ps. 50:23; here the double nun in יכבדנני is presumably interpreted in relation to the two worlds; on this see Lev. Rab. 9 [110D]).

2. Most of the time, the verb כָּבַשׁ, Aram. כְּבַשׁ, כְּבֵישׁ is used for trampling down, defeating, subduing the evil inclination.

Mishnah ʾAbot 4.1: Ben Zoma (ca. 110) said, "... Who is a champion? He who defeats his (evil) inclination הַכּוֹבֵשׁ אֶת־יִצְרוֹ; as it says, 'Better is a long-suffering man than a champion, and he who masters himself than one who conquers a city' (Prov 16:32)." ‖ Babylonian Talmud Tamid 66A.17: (Alexander of Macedonia asked the wise men of the South,) "Who is called a champion?" They answered him, "Who is a champion? He who defeats his inclination." ‖ Leviticus Rabbah 7 (109D): "The sacrifices of God are a broken spirit ..." (Ps 51:19). Zabdai b. Levi (ca. 240) said, "David said before God, 'I have trampled down my (evil) inclination כבשתי את יצרי and repented before you. If you accept me because of my repentance, I know that my son Solomon will begin and build the sanctuary and the altar and sacrifices that are written in the Torah will be offered on it.'" ‖ Jerusalem Talmud Taʿanit 2.65D.2: R. Yohanan († 279) said, "Abraham said before God, 'Lord of the worlds, it is patent and known before you that in the hour when you commanded me to offer my son Isaac, I could have responded and said, "Yesterday you told me, 'In Isaac your seed will be named' (Gen 21:12), and now you say, 'Offer him there as a burnt offering' (Gen 22:2)!" But far from it! I did not do this, but rather I defeated my (evil) inclination כבשתי את יצרי and did your will. So, may it now also be pleasing before you, Yahweh my God, that when the descendants of my son Isaac have fallen into distress and have no one to advocate for them, may you be the one who advocates for them. "May Yahweh see" (Gen 22:14). May you remember for them the binding of their father Isaac and be full of mercy for them.'" — The same is found in Lev. Rab. 29 (127C); Pesiq. 154A; TanḥB וירם § 46 (58A); in Gen. Rab. 56 (36A): I have suppressed my empathy כבשתי רחמי; completely different are Pesiq. Rab. 40 (171B) and Midr. Ps. 29 § 1 (116A). ‖ TanḥumaB ויקרא § 1 at the beginning: "Praise Yahweh, you angels of his, you strong champions ..." (Ps 103:20).... R. Isaac the smith (ca. 300) said, "Those who observe the fallow year are meant. And why are they called 'strong champions'? When such a one sees how his field and his trees are released (as a piece of property without an owner) and the enclosures are broken through; when he sees how his fruits are consumed, then he suppresses his inclination and says nothing. And our teachers have said, 'Who is a champion? He who suppresses his inclination.'" — The same is found in Tanḥ. ויקרא 132A.

3. To suppress the evil inclination, divine help is needed.

Babylonian Talmud Sukkah 52B: R. Simeon b. Laqish (ca. 250) said, "A person's (evil) inclination rises up powerfully against him every day and seeks to kill him; as it says, 'The godless (= evil inclination) lies in wait for the righteous and seeks to kill him' (Ps 37:32). And if God were not the one helping him שעוזר לו, he would not overpower it אינו יכול לו; as it says, 'But Yahweh does not give him over into his hand' (Ps 37:33). — In b. Qidd. 30B, R. Simeon b. Laqish is corrupted into R. Simeon b. Levi. — See further the excursus "The Good and the Evil Inclination."

8:14: Those who are led by the Spirit of God are children of God.

1. πνεύματι θεοῦ ἄγονται.

In Exod 35:21 we find alongside each other "everyone whose heart stirred him" and "everyone whose spirit impelled (made willing) him" כָּל־אִישׁ אֲשֶׁר נְשָׂאוֹ לִבּוֹ וְכֹל אֲשֶׁר נָדְבָה רוּחוֹ. — Targum Onkelos: "Everyone whose heart found delight in it כָּל גְּבַר דְּאִתְרְעִי לִבֵּהּ," and everyone whom his spirit filled אַשְׁלֵמַת. — Targum Yerušalmi I at the close: "And everyone whom his spirit filled by the power of prophecy which was with it." — Septuagint: ἕκαστος, ὧν ἔφερεν ἡ καρδία αὐτῶν, καὶ ὅσοις ἔδοξε τῇ ψυχῇ αὐτῶν. ‖ Concerning Samson, Judg 13:25 says: "The spirit of Yahweh began to drive (urge) him לְפַעֲמוֹ." — Targum: "The spirit of the power from before Yahweh began to make him strong לתקפותיה." — Septuagint: καὶ ἤρξατο πνεῦμα κυρίου συνεκπορεύεσθαι αὐτῷ. — Correctly, Lev. Rab. 8 (110C): R. Samuel b. Nahman (ca. 260) said, "After the holy spirit had begun to drive לגשגש Samson, he began it (in addition) in three passages" (Judg 14:6, 19; 15:14 are then named). — None of these verbs fully does justice to ἄγονται in Rom 8:14.

2. υἱοὶ θεοῦ. See § Matt 5:9, #2.

8:15 A: Spirit of bondage ... to fear ..., spirit of childship.

Tanḥuma נח 15A: (In the future world, i.e., in the days of the Messiah) the Israelites will serve him (God) with joy; as it says, "Serve Yahweh with joy" (Ps 100:2). But the (idolatrous; this word should certainly be deleted) nations will serve him with trembling. It is as with a person: if his son serves before him, he serves him with joy. He says, "If I spoil anything (make anything bad) before my father, he will not get angry with me, because he loves me." Therefore, he serves him with joy. But a foreign servant (opposite: servant of Israelite background) serves with trembling. He says, "If I spoil anything before him, he will get angry with me." Therefore, he serves with trembling. Just so with the (idolatrous) nations. What is written about them? "Why do the nations (*goyim*) rage and the nations contemplate idle things?" (Ps 2:1). The entire (psalm-)song speaks about the (idolatrous) nations; what is written at the end of the song? "Serve Yahweh with fear and rejoice with trembling!" (Ps 2:11).

8:15 B: In which we cry: Abba, my father!

1. ἐν ᾧ (πνεύματι). — In rabbinic literature, we find no passage in which the holy spirit is connected with the prayer of an Israelite. The passage adduced by Schöttgen,[117] Exod. Rab. 22 (= Mek. Exod. 14:31 folio 40B; see § Rom 4:2f., #1, n. *d*, ρ), is of a different kind. Here, when it is said that the holy spirit rested on Israel as a recompense for faith (Exod 14:31), so that they sang the song of the sea in Exodus 15, only the song is designated as inspired. Israel's faith was valued so highly by God that the whole people were endowed with the spirit of prophecy as a recompense for it.

2. On ἀββᾶ ὁ πατήρ, see § Mark 14:36; also see § Matt 23:9; § Matt 6:4; and § Matt 6:9 B.

8:16: He himself, the Spirit, simultaneously testifies....

The rabbinic scholars thought of the holy spirit as the spirit of witness, often when it is said to attest, confirm, or establish something by the word of God inspired by it. The most important examples are collected at § Luke 2:25 C, #4. See in particular the remarks in notes *b–d.*

8:17: If indeed we suffer with him so that we may also be glorified with him.

συνπάσχομεν — συνδοξασθῶμεν. Similarly, יִסּוּרִין "suffering" and כָּבוֹד "glory" are found alongside each other in SDeut 6:5 § 32 (73B): R. Yose b. Judah (ca. 180) said, "Sufferings are valuable before God, for the glory of God falls on the one upon whom sufferings come; as it says, 'Yahweh your God is the one who chastises you' (Deut 8:5)." (The full name of God "Yahweh Elohim" and thereby the entire glory of the godhead is connected with the one who is chastised.)

8:18: The sufferings of the present time are not worth anything in comparison with the glory that is to be revealed in relation to us.

1. οὐκ ἄξια ... πρός = not to be equal in worth with this or that. The rabbis say: דָּבָר כְּנֶגֶד פ׳ "a thing corresponds to this or that, reaches this or that, offsets this or that." More fully: דָּבָר שָׁקוּל כְּנֶגֶד פ׳ "something is of equal

117. Schöttgen, *Horae Hebraicae et Talmudicae*, 1:530.

value with this or that, offsets it." Negatively: דָּבָר אֵינוֹ שָׁוֶה לְ׳ "a thing is not equal to this or that."

Mishnah Pe'ah 1.1: These are the things of which a person enjoys the fruits (interest) in this world, while the principal (main payment) remains outstanding for him for the future world: honoring parents, bestowing works of love, establishing peace between a person and his neighbor, and the study of the Torah, which equals the rest (taken together) in value ותלמוד תורה כנגד כלם. ‖ Jerusalem Talmud Pe'ah 1.15D.53: To them (to the four things named in the previous citations) correspond four things that a person is punished for in this world, while the principal (the main punishment) remains outstanding for the future world. These are: idolatry, fornication, bloodshed (murder), and slander, which is equal to all the rest כנגד כולן. ‖ Jerusalem Talmud Pe'ah 1.15B.62: Alms and bestowing works of love equal in value (counterbalances) all the commandments of the Torah (taken together) צדקה וגמילות חסדים שקולת כנגד כל מצותיה של תורה[118]. ‖ Numbers Rabbah 18 (183C): Samuel, who was equal to Moses and Aaron ששקול כמשה ואהרן. ‖ Jerusalem Talmud Pe'ah 1.15D.40: R. Berekhiah (as a tradent of the following, ca. 340) and R. Hiyya of Kefar Tehumin (in the 3rd cent.). The one said, "Even the whole world is not equal in value אינו שוה to even just one single word of the Torah." The other said, "Even all the fulfillments of the commandments of the Torah are not equal in value אינן שוות to even just one single word of the Torah."

2. The sufferings of the present time are not worthy of the future world;[a] here it must be recalled that the ancient synagogue understood the concept "suffering" very broadly.[b]

a. 2 Baruch 15:7f.: "Inasmuch as you have said concerning the righteous that this world came to be for their sake, so too will the future world will come to be for their sake. For this world is toil and work for them with much struggle, and so that future world is a (victory) crown in great glory." ‖ 4 Ezra 5:40: "As little as you are able to do even one of all the things that I have named, just so little are you able to understand my judgment or the goal of the love (that is, the glory) that I have promised my people." — 4 Ezra 8:51ff. depicts the future glory in the following way: "But you (Ezra) ... search for the glory that your brothers (the righteous) are to inherit. For paradise has been opened for you, the tree of life planted for you; the future age prepared, blessedness determined beforehand; the city (the heavenly Jerusalem) built, the homeland elected; good works created, wisdom prepared; the germ (for sin) sealed up from you, the sickness removed from you; death hidden, Hades escaped; perishability forgotten, pain gone; but treasures of life will be revealed to you at the end." ‖ Mishnah 'Abot 4.17: (R. Jacob [ca. 170]) said, "Better is one hour in repentance and good works in this world than all the life of the future world; and better is one hour of refreshment in the future world than all the life of this world." — This passage is cited in Lev. Rab. 3 (106D); in Midr. Eccl. 4:6 (23A) the saying has been incorporated into a similar one of R. Jacob b. Qorshai (ca. 150). ‖ See also at § Luke 24:26: SDeut 6:5 § 32 (73B); b. Qidd. 40B; Pesiq. 151B; 179B; Tg. Eccl. 8:14. ‖ Sifre Deuteronomy 11:26 § 53 (86A): (Moses said to the Israelites,) "You see the righteous, how they struggle in this world. They struggle for two or three days

118. S-B: The text reads שוקלת.

(so a short time), but ultimately they will rejoice at last; for it says, 'So that he may at last do good to you' (Deut 8:16)." See further Eccl 7:8; Jer 29:11; Ps 97:11; and Prov 4:18. — Concerning sufferings (and their recompense), see also at § Luke 13:2; § Luke 24:26 I, #2; and § Rom 5:3 A.

b. Babylonian Talmud ʿArakin 16B: How far goes the end of sufferings (i.e., what should be viewed as a suffering)? R. Eleazar (ca. 270) said, "If someone has woven somebody a gown to wear and it does not fit (it is too tight)." Against this Rabbah (read: Rab or Rabbi) Zeira (ca. 300), according to others R. Samuel b. Nahmani (ca. 260) objected, "Greater than this it has been said, 'Also if one intended to mix (wine) with warm water and mixed it with cold; or with cold and one mixed it with warm. And do you think that that is everything?'" Mar b. Rabina (ca. 400) said, "Also, if one has reversed his shirt (so that he has to reverse it again to be able to wear it)." Raba († 352), according to others Rab Hisda († 309), according to others R. Isaac (ca. 300) said, according to others it was taught in a baraita: "Also if one has put his hand in the bag to take out three pieces of gold, and two came into his hand, but (this applies) only with three and two came into his hand; however, it does not apply with two and three came into his hand, because there is no toil in throwing it (the surplus piece of gold) back in again." And why all this? Because in the school of R. Ishmael († ca. 135) it was taught: "Anyone who has had forty days without suffering has his world there" (does not have any recompense to count on in the hereafter. Therefore it was believed that the concept "suffering" should be conceived as broadly as it possibly could be). In the west (= Palestine) it was said, "Punishments are set for him" (namely for the one who has gone forty days without suffering).

8:19: The longing expectation of creation awaits the revelation of the children of God.

1. ἀποκαραδοκία = tense awaiting, longing expectation.

In b. Sanh. 97B the longing expectation is expressed in connection with Hab 2:3 by the verb חִכָּה. R. Samuel b. Nahmani (ca. 260) said that R. Jonathan (ca. 220) said, "May the bone disappear of those who calculate the end, who say, 'Since he has made the fixed date (of the promise Messiah) come, and yet he (the Messiah) has not come, he will not come (at all)!' Rather 'be expectant' חַכֵּה־לוֹ; as it says, 'If he delays, be expectant!' (Hab 2:3). If you should say, 'We are expectant מחכין, but he (God) is not expectant אינו מחכה,' Scripture teaches, 'Therefore Yahweh will be expectant יחכה until he is gracious to you, and he will arise to have mercy on you' (Isa 30:18). But if we are expectant מחכים and he is expectant מחכה, who prevents it (holds up the coming of the Messiah)? The (divine) righteousness of punishments prevents it. But if the (divine) righteousness of punishments prevents it, why are we expectant מחכין? To receive a recompense (for this); as it says, 'Blessed are all who expect him חוכי לו!' (Isa 30:18)." — See the similar exposition in Midr. Ps. 14 § 6 (57B).

2. κτίσις "creation" finds its equivalent in rabbinic usage in בְּרִיָּה, בְּרִיאָה (בִּרְיָה?), plural בְּרִיּוֹת; Aram. בִּרְיְתָא, plural בִּרְיָתָא: α. creation = creating,[a] β. creation = creature, specifically comprising both the rational [b] and the irrational[c] creature.

a. Jerusalem Talmud Ḥagigah 2.77D.5: R. Yohanan († 279) said in the name of the scholars, "During the creation ביריה heaven came first (was created earlier than the earth); at the completion (the actual finalization) the earth came first. During the creation heaven came first: 'In the beginning God created heaven and earth' (Gen 1:1); at the completion earth came first, 'On the day when Yahweh Elohim made (completed) earth and heaven (Gen 2:4).'" ‖ See b. ʿAbod. Zar. 9B at § Rom 1:20 B, n. *a.* ‖ Mishnah Makkot 3.2: (The following will be scourged:) whoever has eaten swine or something defective or vermin or creeping things; if he ... has eaten ... *ṭebel* (a crop that has not yet been tithed etc.). How much *ṭebel* may one eat before he becomes guilty? R. Simeon (ca. 150) said, "However much there may be." The scholars said, "As much as an olive." Then R. Simeon said to them, "Will you concede to me that the one who eats an ant (thus vermin), however much there may be, is guilty (cf. Lev 11:42)?" Then they said to him, "Because it is (thus) in accordance with creation כבריתה (was not created bigger)." Then he said to them, "So too a grain of wheat is in accordance with creation."

b. בריה, rational being, human, spirits, angels. — On humanity, see § Mark 16:15. ‖ On spirits and angels, see Abot R. Nat. 37 in n. *c.*

c. בריה, irrational creation, whether living or lifeless. — ʾAbot de Rabbi Nathan 37: There are seven creations בריות that one is always over and above the other (of which one always has an advantage over the other): over all things he (God) created the firmament; over and above the firmament God created the stars that illuminate the world; over and above the stars he created the trees, for the trees bear fruits and the stars bear no fruits; over and above the trees he created the evil spirits, for the evil spirits go here and there and the trees do not move from their place; over and above the evil spirits he created the cattle, for the cattle work and eat and the evil spirits do not work and eat; over and above the cattle he created humanity, for humanity has reason דֵּיעָה and the cattle has no reason; over and above humanity he created the angels of service, for the angels of service go from one end of the world to the other and the children of men do not. ‖ Jerusalem Talmud Soṭah 9.24B.36: R. Judah (ca. 150) taught, "What is the explanation for this shamir (a worm that fissured rocks)? It was a creation בריה from the six days of creation...." ‖ Babylonian Talmud Sanhedrin 67B: R. Eleazar (ca. 270) said, "... A *šed* (demon) cannot make a creature בריה that is smaller than a barleycorn." ‖ Babylonian Talmud Giṭṭin 56B: A voice came from heaven and said (to the blaspheming Titus): "Godless man, son of a godless man, grandchild of the godless Esau, a small creature בריה I have in my world, 'mosquito' is its name, ... climb ashore and fight with it! When he had gone ashore, a mosquito came, invaded his nose and gored his brain for seven years." ‖ Targum Yerušalmi I Genesis 1:24: "Yahweh said, 'May the earthen clod (a soft mass of earth) allow living creatures בִּרְיָתָא to issue forth according to their kind, clean kinds and unclean kinds, cattle and creeping animals and creatures of the earth בִּרְיַת אַרְעָא, each according to their kind.'"

Comment: We know of no rabbinic passages attesting to the singular בריה with the meaning "creation" = universe, κτίσις, κόσμος. In and of itself the singular could certainly have this meaning, which is shown by 4 Ezra 7:75: "Until those times come when you will renew the 'creation'" (Syriac: עתיד אנת דתהדת בריתך) and 2 Bar. 32:6: "When the Almighty will renew his 'creation'" (Syriac: נחדת בריתה).[119] It is therefore possible that the singular could be found with this meaning even in rabbinic literature. Customarily, "creation" in the sense of "universe" was expressed by עוֹלָם, Aram. עָלְמָא = "world"; but the plural בְּרִיּוֹת and the term מַעֲשֵׂה בְרֵאשִׁית = "work of creation" also appears in this sense. Sirach 16:16: "His mercy was revealed to all his creatures לכל בריותיו." — The Greek glossator: πάσῃ τῇ κτίσει τὸ ἔλεος αὐτοῦ φανερόν. ‖ See b. Šabb. 88A at § Rom 1:20 C. ‖ ʾAbot de Rabbi Nathan 31 (8B): A single human outweighs the whole work of creation (entirety of creation) מעשה בראשית.

3. τὴν ἀποκάλυψιν τῶν υἱῶν τοῦ θεοῦ ἀπεκδέχεται.

4 Ezra 4:41: "The habitations of the souls in Hades are like a mother's womb; for as a woman who gives birth strives to rid herself of the pains of birth as soon as possible, they too strive to give back as soon as possible what was entrusted to them in the beginning."

8:20f.: The creation was subjected to futility, not according to its will…; for it itself, the creation, will also be liberated from servitude to decay into the freedom of the glory of the children of God.

The ancient synagogue admitted similar thoughts: the world was created for the sake of humanity,[a] that is, for him or to serve him.[b] Therefore, when humanity, the lord of creation,[c] sinned, this too was pulled into his corruption. All things, God said, I have called into being for the sake of humanity; humanity is lost, so what are the former to me now?[d] Or since the earth was the mother of humanity, the curse was imposed also upon her after humanity sinned, as it used to be said: "Cursed be the breasts that suckled this human!"[e] Yet most of the time the imposition of the curse on creation is simply postulated without reflecting further on its connection with Adam's sin.[f] Among the goods that were taken from the first human as a result of his sin, six in particular are named: the splendor of his face, the length of his life, the magnitude of his form, the fertility of the earth, the fertility of the trees and the brilliance of the heavenly lights. The first three affected the man himself, while the latter three affected the rest of creation.[g] In other passages the curse that affected creation because of Adam's sin also includes the slowing of the planetary cycles,[h] the lengthening of the time it takes for fruits to ripen,[i] the emergence of every kind of vermin[k] and the unruliness of the animal world.[l] Once it is said quite broadly: All things that had been created in their perfection were corrupted by Adam's sin.[m] Here the opinion is everywhere that creation fell into corruption purely as a result of human sin, apart from its own fault and therefore contrary to its own will. Alongside this view, though, there is also the different notion that creation incurred the curse of God because of its own disobedience. So the earth made inedible wood grow instead of edible wood, as God wanted.[n] The animals ate of the forbidden fruit just

119. Dalman, *Die Worte Jesu*, 1:146.

as humanity did; only the phoenix remained obedient to God. Therefore, it is permitted continually to make itself young again from time to time.[o] The moon intruded into the sun's arena,[p] and the earth defied the order to always keep God informed about Adam's actions.[q] Here other conceptions of the enmity of creation toward God probably linger.[120] There is complete agreement about the assumption that only the Messiah will remove the curse from creation: he will restore the six goods lost because of Adam, including the fertility of the earth and the trees according to Zech 8:12 and the brilliance of the heavenly lights according to Isa 30:26.[r] More elaborately, the things are mentioned that will be renewed in the future: the luminosity of the stars will be increased; living water that heals all sicknesses will flow; the trees will produce fruits every month; the destroyed cities will be rebuilt; Jerusalem will be built with sapphires; peace will reign among the Israelites; Israel will also have peace with the animals; weeping and wailing will cease; death will be no more, and groaning and cries of anguish and moans will no longer be heard.[s] — Authors like to linger with the thought that at that time even the animals will be healed of all ferocity;[t] healing is denied to only two categories: the Gibeonites and the snake.[u] — R. Abbahu (ca. 300) denied life after death as well as resurrection to animals.[v] Yet around the same time the different view appears that even the animals would have to justify themselves before God's seat of judgment.[w] How the two opinions are to be united with each other is difficult to see.

a. 4 Ezra 8:44: "The child of man that is formed by your hands is called your image because it has been created like you, and for its sake you have created everything, have you also made him like the seed of the farmer?" — See further Gen. Rab. 28 (17D) and b. Sanh. 108A in n. *d.* — Most of the time it is said that the world was created for Israel's sake. 4 Ezra 6:55, 59: "I have spoken all this before you, Lord, because you said that you created this first world for our sake (because of Israel). But if the world has been created for our sake, why do we not possess this world that is ours?" — 4 Ezra 7:11: "On their account (because of Israel) I created the (present) age." — 4 Ezra 8:1: "The Most High created this world for many but the future world only for a few." ‖ TanḥumaB בראשית § 3 (1B): R. Judah b. Shalom (ca. 370) said, "The world was created because of Israel. 'Formerly מקדם God created' is not written

120. S-B: Differently, Midr. Eccl, 1:4 (6A): "A generation goes and a generation comes, but the earth remains forever" (Eccl 1:4). R. Joshua b. Qarha (ca. 150) said, "Scripture should only have said, 'An earth goes and an earth comes, but the race (of men) remains forever.' Who was created for whose sake? Was the earth created for the race or was the race created for the earth? Was the earth not created for the race? Yet since the race did not remain in God's commands, it fades away; and since the earth remained in God's commands, it does not disappear." — The parallel SDeut 11:21 § 47 (83B) reads: R. Joshua b. Qarha said, "'A generation goes and a generation comes, but the earth remains forever.' Read here only: 'An earth goes and an earth comes, but the race (of men) remains forever.' But since they changed their words, God changed creation because of them." — Only humanity has been subjected to perishability because of his sin; conversely, the earth acquired an eternal character because it remained in God's commands. This view does not overlap with Rom 8:19ff.; cf. Gerhard Kittel, *Sifre zu Deuteronomium: Übersetzt und erläutert* (Stuttgart: Kohlhammer, 1922), 120 n.1.

here (Gen 1:1), and 'at the beginning' מתחילה is (also) not written here, but rather בראשית. What does בראשית mean? The Israelites are meant; they are called ראשית. As it says, 'Holy is Israel to Yahweh, the firstling ראשית of his harvest' (Jer 2:3). How do we know (that the world was created because of Israel)? Because we read in the passage: 'Because of ראשית (= Israel) God created heaven and earth' (Gen 1:1)." ‖ Gerim 1: When the proselyte has taken the immersion bath and gotten out of it, good (affectionate) and comforting words are spoken to him, "Hail! On whom have you hung yourself? On the one who spoke and the world came to be— blessed be he! For the world was created for Israel's sake and only the Israelites are called children of God!" – "The world was created for the sake of the righteous" is said in, for example, 2 Bar. 15:7. See § Rom 8:18, #2, *a*.

b. Genesis Rabbah 8 (6B): R. Huna (ca. 350) said in the name of R. Aybo (ca. 320): He (God) created him (the first human) with consideration, for he created (first) that which was needed for his sustenance, and then he created him (himself). The angels of service said before God, 'Lord of the world, "what is man that you are mindful of him and the child of man that you care for him?" (Ps 8:5). This wretched thing, why לָהֶן should it be created?!' He answered them, 'In that case, "the sheep and the cattle together, as well as the animals of the field" (Ps 8:8), why would they have been created? "The birds of heaven and the fish of the sea" (Ps 8:9), why would they have been created? Like a king who had a closet[121] full of every good; if he has no guests, what benefit does the king get from having filled it?' Then they said before him, 'Lord of the world, "Yahweh, our Lord, how glorious is your name in all the earth!" (Ps 8:10). Do what is of use to you (what you delight in) מה דהני לך!'" ‖ Pesiqta 36B: R. Levi (ca. 300) said in the name of R. Simeon b. Manasseh (ca. 180), "The heel of the first human (with its brilliance) darkened the sun wheel. Do not marvel at that! For according to the custom of the world a man prepares two sleeping chambers, one for himself and one for his house slave (a type of upper-slave, a manager of the house and affairs); for whom does he prepare the beautiful one? Is it not for himself? So God created the first man for his service and the sun wheel for the service of humanity בְּרִיּוֹת; it is right that this one darkened the sun wheel. If his heel was thus, then were not the features of his face much more so?" ‖ 4 Ezra 6:45f.: "On the fourth day you commanded that the brilliance of the sun come into being, the light of the moon and the order of the stars, and you commanded them to serve humanity, whom you wanted to form."

c. 4 Ezra 6:53f.: "On the sixth day you commanded the earth to bring forth before you cattle, wild beasts, and vermin; then also Adam, whom you made lord over all the creatures that you had created before him." ‖ Genesis Rabbah 19 (12D): R. Judah b. Simon (ca. 320) said, "Everything that was created after something else rules over the other thing (the earlier is dependent on the later or serves it). Heaven was created on the first and the firmament on the second day. Does the latter not support the former? The firmament on the second and the fresh verdure on the third: must the former not supply its waters (to the latter)? The fresh greenery on the third and the lights on the fourth: did the latter not call forth its fruits? The lights on the fourth and the birds on the fifth." R. Judah b. Simon (ca. 320) said,

121. S-B: Like a tower, equipped with a gallery and dome, and so called מִגְדָּל "tower."

"The *ziz* is a clean bird; when it flies, it covers (darkens) the wheel of the sun (does he not therefore rule over the lights of heaven?) And you (humanity) were created after everything to rule over everything." ‖-See Gen. Rab. 25 (16B) in n. *l*.

d. Babylonian Talmud Sanhedrin 108A: "And he wiped away everything that survived ..." (Gen 7:23). When humanity sinned, how did the cattle sin (so that it had to suffer too)? In the name of R. Joshua b. Qarha (ca. 150) it has been taught, "Like a man who prepared a nuptial chamber for his son and readied every possible kind (of food) for the meal. After a few days his son died. Then he arose and brought his nuptial chamber into disorder (destroyed it). He said, 'Did I not prepare this only because of my son? Now, since he is dead, what is this nuptial chamber to me?' God too said, 'Did I not create the cattle and the wild beasts only for the sake of humanity? Now, since humanity has sinned, what are the cattle and the wild beasts to me?'" – In Gen. Rab. 28 (17D) the parable goes as follows: R. Phineas (ca. 360) said, "Like a king who married his son and prepared the nuptial chamber; he whitewashed it and paneled it and painted it. The king got angry at his son and killed him. What did he do? He went into the nuptial chamber and began to shatter the jars, and he split the walls and tore apart the curtains (read בֵּילְוֹת instead of כיליות). The king said, 'Did I not prepare this solely for my son? My son has perished, and should this still remain?'" – Both parables are related, though, to the time of the sinful generation of the flood; but they pertain also to Adam's sin and its consequences for creation.

e. Genesis Rabbah 65 (41C): His mother said to him, "May the curse that applies to you come upon me, my son" (Gen 27:13). R. Abba b. Kahana (ca. 310) said, "When Adam sinned, was not his mother then cursed, as it says, 'May the earth be cursed because of you'? (Gen 3:17). (Rebekah meant it in the same way:) Also what affects you, let the curse that applies to you come upon me, my son!" ‖ Genesis Rabbah 5 (5A): Why was it (the earth) cursed (Gen 3:17)? It is as when someone says, "Cursed be the breasts that suckled this one (or that one)!"

f. 4 Ezra 7:11: "When Adam transgressed my commandments, the creation was judged." ‖ Genesis Rabbah 2 (3B): "The earth was תֹּהוּ וָבֹהוּ" (Gen 1:2). R. Tanḥuma (ca. 380) said, "Like the child of a king that slept in its cradle, and its nurse was worried and fretting תוהא ובוהא,[122] because she knew that one day she would accept what was hers (distress and suffering) from its hands. So too the earth saw beforehand that one day she would accept what was hers from Adam's hands; as it says, 'Cursed be the earth because of you' (Gen 3:17). Therefore, the earth was *tohu wabohu* (in the sense of the midrash = worried and fretting)." ‖ Genesis Rabbah 5 (4D): In the name of R. Nathan (ca. 160) it has been taught, "Three came into judgment, and four came out from there as guilty (condemned). Adam, Eve, and the snake came into judgment, and the earth fell into corruption נתקלקלה along with them; as it says, 'Cursed be the earth because of you' (Gen 3:17)." ‖ Numbers Rabbah 10 (158A): "Finally it (wine) bites like a snake" (Prov 23:32). Just as the snake misled Eve to drink wine[123] and the earth was cursed, as it says, "Cursed be the earth because of you"

122. S-B: תוהא and בוהא are participles of תְּהָא = to be paralyzed, unsettled, and of בְּהָא = to be afraid. – Levy thinks of θύω "to bluster" and βοάω "to scream" (*Chaldäisches Wörterbuch*, 1:195B).

123. S-B: According to the opinion of R. Meir (ca.150), who thought that the tree of knowledge was a grapevine (b. Ber. 40A; 70A); in Gen. Rab. 15 (11A) and Pesiq. Rab. 42 (175A) this opinion is represented by R. Judah (ca. 150).

(Gen 3:17), so also the third part of the world was cursed because of the wine, as it says, "Noah woke up from his wine-induced intoxication ... and said, 'Cursed be Canaan'" (Gen 9:24f.): this pertains to Ham, who was his third son. — The same is found in Num. Rab. 10 (160A.46).

g. See Gen. Rab. 12 (9A) at § Matt 1:3 D. — In particular, on the brilliance of Adam's face, see Pesiq. 36B above in n. *b.* ‖ Distress and death. 4 Ezra 7:11ff.: "When Adam transgressed my commandments, the creation was judged. Then the ways in this age became narrow and sorrowful and arduous, wretched and bad, full of dangers and close to great distress. The ways of the (future) age, however, are broad and safe and bear the fruits of life. If the living have not entered into these narrow and vain (cf. ματαιότης, Rom 8:20) ones, they cannot obtain what has been stored up for them." — 4 Ezra 3:7: "You laid on him (Adam) one single commandment; but he transgressed it. Immediately you ordained death for him, as for his descendants." — See further § Rom 5:15 A, #1. ‖ The judgment on Adam, Eve, and the snake. Pirqe Rabbi Eliezer 14 (7D.7): God called Adam and said to him, "Why did you flee before me" (cf. Gen 3:9)? He answered before him, "I heard your sound and my bones quaked; as it says, 'I heard your voice in the garden; then I was afraid because I am naked and I hid' (Gen 3:10). I hid because of my deed and was afraid because of my action; for I am naked of my commandment, as it says, 'Because I am naked.'" What clothing did the first man have? A coat of onyx (cf. Gen. Rab. 20 at the end) and a cloud of glory were made for him. When he had eaten from the fruits of the tree, the coat of onyx was taken off of him, and he saw he was naked and the cloud of glory was removed from him; as it says, "Who informed you that you are naked? Did you eat from the tree? ..." (Gen 3:11). Adam said before God, "Lord of the worlds, when I was alone, did I sin against you? But the woman that you brought to me misled me away from your words"; as it says, "The woman that you joined to me has given me from the tree, and so I ate" (Gen 3:12). Then God said to Eve, "It was not enough that you sinned, you also misled Adam to sin." She said before him, "Lord of the world, the snake misled my mind to sin before you"; as it says, "The snake misled me, and so I ate" (Gen 3:13). Then he took all three of them and imposed on them a decree of nine curses and death. (The decree concerning the snake:) He toppled Sammael (= Satan) and his horde from the place of their holiness from heaven; he cut off the snake's feet (see Gen. Rab. 20 folio 13C.33); he cursed it among all the animals and among all brutes; he ordained for it that it shed its skin once every seven years with great pain; it became one that pushes (moves itself forward by creeping) with its belly on the earth; its food is turned into dust in its body; snake venom and death are in its mouth; he appointed enmity between it and the woman, so that its head would be shattered, and in addition to all this, death. — To the woman he gave nine curses and death: the hardship of the blood of menstruation and the blood of virginity; the hardship of pregnancy; the hardship of giving birth; the hardship of raising children; her head is covered as one who mourns; she may not cut off her hair except because of whoredom; she pierces her ear as a perpetual slave or as a maidservant who serves her master; she is not certified for testimony (cannot appear in court as a witness); and in addition to all this, death. — He dismissed Adam and established over him nine curses and death: he diminished his strength by the impurity of pollution; he diminished his size by the impurity of copulation; he sows wheat and harvests thorns; his food is the vegetation of the earth like a brute; his bread is troubles; his nourishment is in sweat (read זיעה instead of זיע); and after all this, death. (The curses are obviously not fully enumerated; but see the text in Yal. 1 § 27.) — Ten curses are imposed on Eve in b. ʿErub. 100B, but with several variations from the exposition above; seven curses are named in Num. Rab. 10 (157C), though they are not individually listed.

h. Genesis Rabbah 10 (7B): "Heaven and earth and all their host were completed וַיְכֻלּוּ" (Gen 2:1). R. Hoshaiah (ca. 225) said R. Aphes (ca. 210) propounded in Antioch, "The word ויכלו in Gen 2:1 has the meaning to hit or wear down. A parable. Like a king who came into a city (a province) whose inhabitants praised him, and their praise pleased him. He arranged many pleasures (dances) and many chariot races for them. After some time they angered him. Then he reduced the pleasures and the chariot races for them. Just so, the planets, before the first human had sinned, traveled a short track and swiftly; but after he had sinned, God had them make their orbit on a long track and slowly."

i. Genesis Rabbah 10 (7C): R. Phineas (ca. 360) taught in the name of R. Hanan of Sepphoris (ca. 300) as a tannaitic tradition: "The *benoth shuaḥ* (a type of fig) ... bring forth their fruits (in ripeness) after three years. On that day (before Adam sinned) they brought forth their fruits. But in the future (in the days of the Messiah) God will heal this blow; as it says, 'He will heal the wounds of his blow' (Isa 30:26), that is, the wounds with which he struck the world (creation) he will heal."

k. Genesis Rabbah 5 (5A): "Cursed be the earth because of you" (Gen 3:17), that is, let it bring forth cursed things for you, such as mosquitoes, flies, and fleas. — The same is found in Gen. Rab. 20 (13D).

l. Genesis Rabbah 25 (16B): R. Yohanan († 279) said, "... When God created the first human, he made him lord over everything: the cow demonstrated its obedience to the plowman and the furrow demonstrated its obedience to the plowman. But when Adam had sinned, they rebelled against him: the cow did not show its obedience to the plowman and the furrow did not show its obedience to the plowman...."

m. See Gen. Rab. 12 at § Matt 1:3 D.

n. Genesis Rabbah 5 (5A): Why was it (the earth) cursed (Gen 3:17)?... R. Judah b. Shalom (ca. 370) said, "Because it transgressed a commandment; for God said to it, 'Let the earth shoot forth fresh vegetation, ... wood of fruit עֵץ פְּרִי' (Gen 3:11;) as the fruit was edible, so too was the wood to be edible. And it did not do this, but rather the earth brought forth vegetation whose fruit was edible but whose wood was not edible." — The parallel in y. Kil. 1.27B.10 is different.

o. Genesis Rabbah 19 (12D): "She also gave some to her husband who was with her" (Gen 3:6); "also" גַּם has an inclusive meaning: she made (also) livestock (domestic animals) and the wild beasts and the birds eat, and all obeyed her with the exception of one bird, whose name was חול[124] = phoenix. This is what is written: "Like the phoenix I will have long life"

124. S-B: The Babylonians said חול; see Buber, Midr. Sam. 12 (41A n. ו).

(Job 29:18). Those from the school of R. Yannai (ca. 225) said, "It (the phoenix) lives 1,000 years, and at the end of the 1,000 years a fire issues from its nest and burns it and leaves as much of it as the size of an egg. Then it has its members grow again and it (continues to) live." R. Judan b. Simeon (= Simon, ca. 320) said, "It lives 1,000 years. At the end of the 1,000 years its body is consumed and its wings lose their feathers and only as much of it remains as one egg. Then it has its members grow again." — A parallel is found in Midr. Sam. 12 § 2 (41A). — The saying about the phoenix appears in another form in b. Sanh. 108B: Hana b. Bizna (ca. 260) said, "Eliezer (the steward of Abraham's house) said to Shem, the eldest:[125] 'It is written, "According to their species they went out of the ark" (Gen 8:19) (thus the animals in the ark do not get confused, but rather lived separately from each other according to their kinds).' How did you manage this (in the ark during the flood)? He answered him, 'We had to work really hard in the ark: an animal that is usually fed during the day, we fed during the day; one that is normally fed in the night, we fed at night.... My father found the phoenix אֲוַרְשִׁינָא, as it lay in a hidden place in the ark. He said to it, "Do you not want any food?" It answered him, "I saw you, how you were driven about; then I thought I did not want to bother you." He said to it, "May it be the will (namely of God) that you not die!"'"

p. Genesis Rabbah 6 (5A): "And God made the two great lights (of heaven)" (Gen 1:16). R. Judan (ca. 350) said in the name of R. Tanḥum b. Hiyya (ca. 300) and R. Phineas (ca. 360) said in the name of R. Simon (ca. 280), "After he calls them 'great,' did he then shrink them (since it says in Gen 1:16): 'The great light to rule the day and the small light to rule the night'? (It was shrunk) only because it (the moon) interloped into the arena of the other one." — The moon's intrusion into the sun's arena is based on the fact that it is sometimes visible even by day. — R. Simeon b. Laqish (ca. 250) also says in b. Ḥul. 60B: "What is different about the goat of the new moon so that it is said that it is 'for Yahweh' (Num 28:15; whereas these words are not said about any other of the goat offerings)? God said, 'Let this goat be a reminder that I shrank the moon.'" — Other explanations try to exculpate the moon by tracing its intrusion into the sun's domain back to God. So a parallel to the above statement of R. Simon is found already in b. Ḥul. 60B: R. Simeon b. Pazzi (= R. Simon, ca. 280) opposed this: "It is written, 'God made the two great lights (of heaven)' (Gen 1:16); and it is written, 'The great light ... and the small light ...' (Gen 1:16). The moon said before God, 'Lord of the world, is it possible for two kings to make use of one throne?' He answered it, 'Go and shrink!' It said before him, 'Lord of the world, because I have said a modest word before you, should I shrink?' He answered it, 'Go and rule by day and at night (so intrude into the domain of the day)!' It said to him, 'What, then, is the glory of the light at midday, what use is it?' He answered it, 'In this way the Israelites will permanently number their days and years according to you.' It said to him, 'They must also necessarily number the solstices according to the sun; for it is written, "They are to serve for signs and seasons and days and years" (Gen 1:14).' (He answered it,) 'They are to lastingly name the righteous after you: Jacob the small (cf. Gen 27:15, 42), Samuel the small, David the small (see 1 Sam 16:11).' But since God saw that its mind was not quieted, he said, 'Present an offering because

125. S-B: According to the official chronology of the ancient synagogue, Shem survived Abraham by about 35 years. See S. 'Olam Rab. 1.

I shrank the moon.'" (Then follows the saying of S. Simeon b. Laqish above.) — Genesis Rabbah 6 (5A): R. Phineas (ca. 360) said, "For all offerings it is written, 'A shaggy goat as a sin offering'; but concerning the new moon it is written, 'A shaggy goat as a sin offering for Yahweh' (Num 28:15). God said, 'Bring an atoning offering for me, because I shrank the moon, for I am the one who caused it to intrude into the arena of its companion.'"

q. Pirqe R. El. 14 (7D): When Adam sinned, how did the earth sin, so that it was cursed? Only because it did not report his action was it cursed. For when humans commit serious sins, God sends humans plagues (that affect them themselves). But if they commit light sins, God strikes the fruits of the earth because of the sins of humans; as it says, "Cursed be the earth because of you" (Gen 3:17). — Yalquṭ Simeoni 1 § 27 presents the passage in a shortened form; the Yalquṭ edition available to us (Wilna 1898) cites from מדרש הנעלם also the following words: God announced to heaven and earth that they should be witnesses if the man sinned. When Adam sinned, though, heaven darkened its light but the earth did not know what it should do until God appeared over her and cursed her.

r. See Gen. Rab. 12 at § Matt 1:3 D.

s. Exodus Rabbah 15 (77D): "Behold, the former things, they have arrived, and I am proclaiming new things" (Isa 42:9). Is there something new in the future (in the messianic time)? But it is written, "What has been is what will be" (Eccl 1:9)! However, we find that God will one day renew עתיד לחדש ten things in the future. First: He will illuminate the world; as it says, "No longer will the sun serve as your light by day ... (but rather Yahweh will be your eternal light)" (Isa 60:19). But can a human look at God? However, what will God do about the sun? He will make it shine with 49-fold light; as it says, "The light of the moon will be like the light of the sun and the light of the sun will be seven times as the light of seven days" (sevenfold light of seven days = 49-fold light; so Midr. Isa. 30:26). And even if someone gets sick, God will command the sun to heal him; as it says, "The sun of righteousness will arise for you who fear my name, and healing is in its wings" (Mal 3:20). — Second: He will make living water issue forth from Jerusalem and heal everyone who has a sickness; as it says, "And it will happen, every living being that swarms will live wherever the stream comes ..., and they will be healthy and live" (Ezek 47:9). — Third: He will make the trees produce their fruits every month, and humanity will eat from them and be healed; as it says, "On river's banks on both sides every kind of tree with edible fruit will grow ...; every month they will bear fresh fruits; for their waters issue forth from the sanctuary, and their fruits will serve as food and their leaves as remedies" (Ezek 47:12). — Fourth: All the destroyed cities will be built up (again), and there will never again be any desolate place. Even Sodom and Gomorrah will be built up (again) in the future; as it says, "You sisters, Sodom and her daughters will return to their former state" (Ezek 16:55). — Fifth: He will build Jerusalem with sapphires; as it says, "Behold, I will mount your stones in a glimmering pattern and I will lay your foundation with sapphires" (Isa 54:11). It is also written, "I am making your battlements out of rubies" (Isa 54:12). And those stones will shine like the sun, and the nations of the world will come and behold Israel's glory; as it says, "Nations (*goyim*) will surge to your light" (Isa 60:3). — Sixth: "Cow and bear will pasture; their young will lie down together" (Isa 11:7). — Seventh: He will bring all the wild beasts and all birds and all swarms and make a covenant with them and with all Israel; as it says, "And I will make a covenant for them on that day with the wild beasts of the field and the birds of heaven ..." (Hos 2:20). — Eighth: There will be no more weeping or wailing in the world; as it says, "The sound of weeping and the sound of wailing will no longer be heard in it" (Isa 65:19). — Ninth: There will be no more death in the world; as it says, "He will devour death forever and the Almighty Yahweh will wipe away the tears from every face and remove the shame of his people" (Isa 25:8). — Tenth: There will be no more groaning or cries of anguish or sorrow, but rather all will rejoice; as it says, "The redeemed of Yahweh will return and come to Zion with rejoicing, and eternal joy will be upon their head ..." (Isa 35:10). — For other passages that belong here, see the excursus "This World, the Days of the Messiah, and the Future World"; see also Gen. Rab. 10 above in n. *i.*

t. Genesis Rabbah 95 (60A): "Come and see! All that God has dealt a blow to in this world he will heal in the future (= days of the Messiah).... And he will heal even the wild animals; as it says, 'Wolf and lamb will pasture together' (Isa 65:25) (thus the healing of the animal world = the elimination of their ferocity)." — A parallel is found in Tanḥ. ויגש 53A. ‖ Sifra Leviticus 26:6 (449A): "I will remove the wild (evil) animals from the land" (Lev 26:6). R. Judah (ca. 150) said, "I will remove them from the world." R. Simeon (ca. 150) said, "He will make them cease inflicting harm (calm them so that they no longer injure)." R. Simeon said, "When is the glory of God displayed? Is it when there are no (longer) harmful things? Or when there are harmful things, but they do not cause harm? (In the latter case of course!) Likewise, it says, 'A psalm, a song for the Sabbath' (Ps 92:1), for the day that makes the harmful things (also the *mazziqin* = demons) cease from the world, makes them cease to inflict harm. Further, it says, 'The wolf will dwell with the lamb and the panther will lie down with the young ram and the calf and the lion and the fattened ox with each other, and a small boy will lead them. The cow and bear will pasture, their young will lie down together, and the lion will eat straw like the cattle, and the infant will play at the adder's hole, and the weaned child will stretch out its hand toward the viper's den' (Isa 11:6ff). This teaches that an Israelite child will one day put its hand into the viper's eye and will take its poison from its mouth. Likewise, it says, 'The weaned child will stretch out its hand ...' (Isa 11:8): this (namely צפעוני in Isa 11:8) is a wild animal that kills people (or generally: creatures)."

u. Genesis Rabbah 95 (60A): Everything will be healed (in the future); however, that which has brought the blow upon all (i.e., the snake) will not be healed. Instead, "And the snake—dust will be its bread" (Isa 65:25), because it has brought people (creatures) to dust (killed them). — The same is found in Tanḥ. ויגש 53A.13. ‖ Genesis Rabbah 20 (13C): R. Levi (ca. 300) said, "In the future everything will be healed, except for the snake and the Gibeonites (concerning them, see Josh 9:3ff.). The snake, for it says, 'And the snake—dust will be its bread" (Isa 65:25); the Gibeonites, 'The worker who is in the city (i.e., in the sense of the midr., the Gibeonites) will work on it, from all the tribes of Israel' (Ezek 48:19)" (see the next citation). ‖ Midrash Samuel 28 § 7 (67B): (When the Gibeonites made the demand of 2 Sam 21:5f.,) David arose and removed them (excluded them from Israel): "The Gibeonites do not belong to the children of Israel" (2 Sam 21:2). Ezra also removed them; as it says, "The temple servants (= Gibeonites) dwelt on the Ophel" (read בעפל instead of בעפר) (Neh 11:21).

God will also remove them in the future: "The worker who is in the city, whom they will destroy יאבדוהו from all the tribes of Israel" (Ezek 48:19 is cited in this way by interpreting יעבדוהו as = יאבדוהו). The same interpretation is found in the parallels in Num. Rab. 8 (149B) and y. Qidd. 4.65B.49).

v. See Midr. Ps. 19 § 1 (81B) at § Matt 22:32, #2, C, at the end.

w. See Gen. Rab. 26 (17A) at § Matt 25:32, n. *b*.

8:22: So that the whole creation groans together and feels labor pains.

We hear about the earth's lament over her lost human children once in 4 Ezra.[a] Conversely, the same writing has humanity praise the irrational creation in another passage as being better than the human race because it does not have to await a future judgment.[b] — On συνωδίνει, see the image of the woes of the Messiah חֶבְלוֹ שֶׁל מָשִׁיחַ at § Matt 24:8.

a. 4 Ezra 10:9ff.: "Ask the earth, she will tell you (a visionary woman who wails about the death of her only son) that it is she who must grieve over so many who have sprung up on her. From her we have all taken our beginning, and others will come from her: but almost all pass into corruption, their multitude is destroyed. So, who should grieve more: is it not she who has lost such a multitude? Or you who suffers because of only one? Or will you rejoin: 'My wailing is not like that of the earth; I have lost the fruit of my womb that I labored for in travails and gave birth to with pain! But the earth proceeds only according to its nature the multitude that has lived on her has passed away as it came.' But I oppose you: 'As you labored with pain, just so did the earth in the beginning bring forth its fruit, the human person, for her creator.'"

b. 4 Ezra 7: 62ff.: "O earth, what have you conceived, if reason arose from the dust as every other creature! It would have been better if the dust itself had never arisen, so that reason would not have come from it. But now reason grows up with us, and thereby we suffer torment, because we knowingly pass into corruption. So, mourn the race of men, but may the animals of the field rejoice! May all those born of woman wail, but the livestock and the wild beasts should rejoice! It turns out much better for them than for us; for they do not have to await judgment, they know nothing of a torment, nor of a blessedness that was promised to them after death. But we, what does it benefit us that we can come to blessedness one day, but (in reality) we fall into torment?"

8:26: He himself, the Spirit, advocates for us.

On the Holy Spirit as intercessor and advocate, see § John 14:16, *h*.

8:27: Who searches hearts.

See § John 2:25; see the passage cited there, b. Sanh. 37B, at § Acts 28:4.

8:28: Everything serves for the good for those who love God.

Genesis Rabbah 42 (25C): An incident with R. Eliezer b. Hyrcanus (ca. 90). His brothers plowed in the plain, while he himself plowed on the mountain. His cow fell and suffered a (leg) break. He said, "For my good (best) לטובתי my cow has suffered a break!" He ran and went to Rabban Yohanan b. Zakkai († ca. 80). — The accident became the occasion for Eliezer to study the Torah and achieve high honors. ‖ See b. Taʿan. 21A at § Matt 18:8f. The passage continues (21A): Some people once wanted to send a gift to Caesar's palace. They said, "Who should go (and deliver it)?" Nahum of Gimzo should go, for he is accustomed to miracles. By him, they delivered a box that was full of gems and pearls. He went and spent the night in a lodging house. At night the inhabitants (of the lodging house) arose and took the box and filled it with dust. When he noticed this on the following morning, he said, "Even this is to the good גם זו לטובה!" When he had arrived there, the king wanted to have them all (Nahum and his companions) killed. The king said, "Do you Jews want to mock me (with a box full of earth)?" Then (the prophet) Elijah came in the form of one of them (from Caesar's circle) and said, "Maybe this dust is from the dust of their father Abraham! For when he threw dust, swords came into existence from it, stubble became arrows; for it is written, 'He made dust into his sword and fleeting chaff into his bow' (so Midr. Isa. 41:2)."[126] There was a province that was not able to be subjected (by Caesar). The attempt was made with it (with the dust) and it was subjected. Then Nahum was led into the treasury and his box was filled for him with gems and pearls and he was dismissed with great honor. When he went, he spent the night in the same lodging house. They said to him, "What did you bring with you that you were shown all this honor?" He answered them, "What I took with me from here. They tore down their dwellings and brought (their remains) to the king's palace." They said to him, "The dust that he brought here was from our things. The dust was examined and nothing was found in it, and the people of the lodging house were killed." ‖ Babylonian Talmud Berakot 60B: Rab Huna († 297) said that Rab († 247) said in the name of R. Meir (ca. 150), and it has also been taught in the name of R. Aqiba († ca. 135) as a baraita: "Let a person always be used to saying, 'Everything that the All-merciful One does, he does for the good לטב עביד,' as that experience of R. Aqiba (shows). When he was traveling once (on a trip), he came to a village. He asked for lodging, but no one granted it to him. He said, 'Everything that the All-merciful One does is for the good לטב.' He went and spent the night in the field. He had with him a chicken and a donkey and a lamp. A gust of wind came and blew out the lamp; a cat שֻׁנָּרָא came and ate the chicken; a lion came and ate the donkey. Then he said, 'Everything that the All-merciful One does is for the good.' On that night a fighting army came and led the village into captivity. Then he said to them, 'Did I not tell you, "Everything that the holy one does—blessed be He!—is all for the good הכל לטובה!?"'"

126. S-B: According to Gen. Rab. 43 (26C), the author of this interpretation is R. Judah b. Ilai (ca. 150). His opponent R. Nehemiah objected against him that, since in Isa 41:2 it does not say עפר, but כעפר, it should be interpreted: "They (the enemy kings in Gen 14) cast swords against Abraham, and these became like dust, and arrows, but these became like stubble (chaff)."

8:29 A: He determined beforehand.

προορίζειν. See rabbinic synonyms at § Matt 25:34 B and at § Acts 13:48.

8:29 B: Firstborn among many brothers.

Sifre Deuteronomy 11:10 § 37 (76A): Also, with the ways of God you will find that everything that is beloved חָבִיב (valuable, dear) precedes something else. Since the Torah is beloved above all, it was created before everything; as it says, "Yahweh created me as the firstling of his way, as the earliest of his works, long ago" (Prov 8:22); (Scripture) says further, "In primordial time I was appointed, at the beginning, since the very beginnings of the earth" (Prov 8:23). Since the sanctuary was beloved above all, it was created before everything; as it says, "A throne of glory from the beginning, the site of our sanctuary" (Jer 17:12). Since the land Israel was beloved above all, it was created before everything; as it says, "When he had not yet made earth and fields חוּצוֹת and the best clods of the earth" (so Prov 8:26 according to the midr.). "Earth": these are the other lands; חוצות: these are the fields מדברות; and "the best clods of earth": this is the land of Israel. — According to this canon, "firstborn" is tantamount to the most beloved, most valuable, most respected, the thing of highest quality. Also, *in malam partem*, someone can be designated as "firstborn"; then he features as the most dangerous or most dreaded of his kind.

1. The following are called firstborn in the good sense:

a. The Torah. Assumption of Moses 1:12f.: "He created (already) the world for the sake of his law (*propter legem suam*, so read with Clemen in Kautzsch instead of *propter plebem suam*),[127] but the same thing, the firstling of creation (*inceptionem creaturae*) has not been revealed even from the beginning of the world." ‖ Genesis Rabbah 1 (2A): The Torah said: בראשית ברא אלהים = by ראשית "firstling" God created (Gen 1:1), and the "firstling" is nothing other than the Torah; as it says, "Yahweh created me as the firstling of his way" (Prov 8:22). — It appears that the author of this interpretation was R. Hoshaiah (ca. 225); see a parallel in TanḥB בראשית § 5 (2B), though here R. Judah b. Ilai (ca. 150) is the author. ‖ Tanḥuma בראשית at the beginning: "By ראשית 'the firstling' God created" (so Gen 1:1 according to the midr.); this is what "Yahweh established the world by his wisdom (= Torah)" (Prov 3:19) means. — So "firstling" = Torah. See also the passages at § John 1:1–4.

b. Adam. See Num. Rab. 4 at § Col 1:15 B, #1.

c. Jacob. In the προσευχὴ Ἰωσήφ Jacob says about himself, "I am the firstborn among all beings brought to life by God" ἐγὼ πρωτόγονος παντὸς ζώου ζωουμένου ὑπὸ θεοῦ. — See the whole passage at § John 1:1 A, C, #1. ‖ Genesis Rabbah 63 (40B): Bar Qappara (ca. 220) taught, "Since they (Jacob and Esau in the argument about primogeniture) were like jokers, God joined in and joked along with them and confirmed primogeniture for Jacob, because it is written: 'Thus Yahweh has spoken, "Israel (i.e., Jacob) is my firstborn son."'" ‖ Genesis

127. E. Kautzsch, ed., *Die Apokryphen und Pseudepigraphen des Alten Testaments*, vol. 1 (Freiburg im Breisgau and Leipzig: J. C. B. Mohr [Paul Siebeck], 1900).

Rabbah 63 (39D): ("They named him Esau" [Gen 25:25].) R. Isaac (ca. 300) said, "(God said,) 'You have given your hog חזירתכון[128] a name, I too will give my firstborn son a name. 'Yahweh has spoken, "Israel (= Jacob) is my firstborn son" (Exod 4:22).'" See also Exod. Rab. 19 in n. *e*.

d. Israel. 4 Ezra 6:58: "But we, your people, which you have called your firstborn, your only son, your devotee and friend, we are given into their hand (the nations that are considered as nothing)!" In a comparison, Pss. Sol. 18:4: "Your chastisement (comes) over us, as over a firstborn, only son" ἡ παιδεία σου ἐφ' ἡμᾶς ὡς υἱὸν πρωτότοκον μονογενῆ. ‖ ʾAggadat Berešit 31 at the end: Because of his love for the Israelites he (God) calls them sons; as it says, "Israel is my firstborn son" (Exod 4:22). — In the parallel Midr. Eccl. 4:7f. (23B) Deut 14:1 is cited as a supporting passage. ‖ Exodus Rabbah 15 (78D): What does "Israel is my firstborn son" (Exod 4:22) mean? R. Hiyya (b. Abba, ca. 280) said, "These are the sons whose fathers were blessed for their deeds. So it was with Abraham; as it says, 'Blessed be Abraham by the Most High God!' (Gen 14:19). A different explanation is as follows. 'Israel is my firstborn son,' that is, sons of the one who received the right of primogeniture (thus as sons of Jacob). A different explanation. 'Israel is my firstborn son.' God said to pharaoh, the wicked one: 'Do you not know how very much I love the firstborn? For I have written in my Torah, "Do not work with your firstborn bull" (Deut 15:19), and whoever works with it will be punished.'" ‖ Exodus Rabbah 15 (79A): Why are the Israelites called "my firstborn son" (Exod 4:22)? Because it is written in the Torah, "He must recognize the firstborn, the son of the hated, to give him a double portion" (Deut 21:17). So too the Israelites take possession of two worlds, this world and the future world.

e. The Messiah. Exodus Rabbah 19 (81D): "Sanctify every firstborn thing to me" (Exod 13:1). R. Nathan (ca. 160) said, "God said to Moses, 'As I made Jacob the firstborn, as it says, "Israel (= Jacob) is my firstborn son" (Exod 4:22), so also I will make the king, the Messiah, the firstborn; as it says, "I will also make him the firstborn" (Ps 89:28).'" ‖ See further § Heb 1:6 A and Col 1:15 B.

2. Firstborn in the bad sense.

In Job 18:13 leprosy (?) is named as the most dangerous sickness the "firstborn of death." ‖ Jerusalem Talmud Yebamot 1.3A.50: R. Jacob b. Idi (ca. 280) said in the name of R. Joshua b. Levi (ca. 250), "It happened that the elders came to R. Dosa b. Harkinas (ca. 90) to ask him about the secondary wife of the daughter (whether the father of the widow is permitted to marry her as a levirate). They said to him, 'Are you the one who allowed secondary wives (for levirate marriage)?' He said to them, 'Have you heard "Dosa b. Harkinas (said it)?"' They answered him, '(We have heard) "ben Harkinas."' He said to them, 'Jonathan, my brother (who could thus also be designated as "ben Harkinas"), was the one (who allowed secondary wives). He is a firstborn (an exceedingly dangerous) adversary בכור שטן (not = firstborn of Satan) and belongs to the students of the school of Shammai. Watch out for him.'" — The same is found in b. Yebam. 16A.

---

128. S-B: This is what Esau (= Rome) is called, because Rome's standard animal was the boar. On "pig" as a designation for Rome, see § Matt 7:6 C, #2.

8:32 A: Who did not spare his own son.

Exodus Rabbah 29 (88D): "I am Yahweh your God" (Exod 20:2). This is what is written, "When a lion roars, who should not be afraid?" (Amos 3:8). And this is what is written, "Who should not fear you, king of the nations; for it is your due!" (Jer 10:7). The prophets said to Jeremiah, "What reason do you have to say, 'king of the nations'? All the prophets call him 'king of Israel,' and you call him 'king of the nations!'" He answered them, "I heard him say, 'I have appointed you the prophet for the nations' (Jer 1:5), and (for this reason) I said 'king of the nations,' in order to say, 'If he has not spared his children and the companions of his house אם על בניו ועל בני ביתו לא חס, should he spare others?' As it says, 'You are awesome, O God, from your sanctuary' (Ps 68:36); who should not fear you, king of the nations, who should not be afraid of you?" ‖ See b. Taʿan. 24A at § Mark 11:13.

8:32 B: How will he not grant us all things along with him?

Midrash Song of Songs 1:1 (80A): R. Simon (ca. 280) said in the name of R. Simeon ben Halapta (ca. 190), "Like a councilman, who was esteemed in the house of the king. The king said to him, 'Ask for whatever and I will give it to you!' The councilman said (to himself), 'If I ask for silver and gold, he will give them to me; if for gems and pearls, he will give them to me.' He said, 'Behold, I will ask for the king's daughter, and everything is included along with her.' So too Yahweh appeared to Solomon in Gibeon in a dream during the night (1 Kgs 3:5), and God said, 'Ask for whatever and I will give it to you.' Solomon said, 'If I ask for silver and gold and for gems and pearls, he will give them to me; instead, behold, I will ask for wisdom, and everything is included along with her.'" — The same is found in Midr. Eccl. 1:1 (4A).

8:34: At the right hand of God.

See § Matt 25:33 and the S-B footnote at § Matt 5:8B, #2, n. *b* containing a reference to Midr Ps 16 § 12 (62B).

8:36: For your sake we are killed all day long, we are counted as sheep for slaughter.

If the apostle saw a fulfillment of Ps 44:23 not only in the suffering of the "sword," but also in the suffering of every one of the situations of distress named in verse 35, which would not be impossible in itself, he would have understood the psalm passage in a broad sense, similarly to the way the rabbinic scholars commonly understood it.

a. Interpretations of Ps 44:23 that are not related to martyrdom.

Babylonian Talmud Giṭṭin 57B toward the end: R. Joshua b. Levi (ca. 250) said, "This (the word 'For your sake we are killed all day long' [Ps 44:23]) relates to circumcision which is given (ordained) for the 8th day (read לשמיני instead of בשמיני)." R. Simeon b. Laqish (ca. 250) said, "This relates to the scholars who demonstrate the rules about slaughtering in themselves." For Raba († 352) said, "A person may demonstrate everything in himself, except for slaughtering and something else" (= the appearance of leprosy, Rashi). Rab Nahman b. Isaac

(† 356) said, “This pertains to the scholars who sacrifice (literally: kill ממיתין) themselves for the words of the Torah.” This corresponds with a view of R. Simeon b. Laqish; for R. Simeon b. Laqish said, “The words of the Torah endure only in the case of the one who sacrifices ממית himself for them; as it says, ‘This is the (correct) study of the Torah, that a man dies in the tent (= house of study)’ (so Num 19:14 according to the midr.).” ‖ Sifre Deuteronomy 6:5 § 32 (73A): “Love Yahweh your God … with all your soul” (Deut 6:5), even if he takes your life (your soul). And likewise, it says, “For your sake we are killed all day long, we are counted as sheep for slaughter” (Ps 44:23). R. Simeon b. Manasseh (ca. 180) said, “Can a person be killed every day? Rather for the righteous God counts (their life and suffering) as if they were killed every day (as martyrs).”

b. Interpretations of Ps 44:23 that relate to martyrdom.

Babylonian Talmud Giṭṭin 57B: Rab Judah († 299) said, “This (the word ‘For your sake we are killed all day long …’ [Ps 44:23]) relates to the woman and her seven sons” (whose martyrdom is then recounted in detail; see specifics on this at § Matt 3:17 A, #29, n. *i* and § Luke 16:22 B, #1). Parallel reports are found in 2 Maccabees 7; 4 Maccabees 13; and also probably in Midr. Lam. 1:15 (57B), where the mother is called Miriam bath Nachtom. Here the report concludes with the words: “Then all the nations of the world cried out and said, ‘What does the God of this woman do (or: what will he do) for them who are killed for his sake every hour (all the time)?’ And concerning them it is written, ‘For your sake we are killed all day long’ (Ps 44:23)….” ‖ See b. Giṭ. 57B.25; Midr. Lam. 1:15 (56A) at § Rom 1:26 A, #1, toward the end. Those destined for disgrace fall into the sea. Ps 44:23 is thus applied to them. ‖ Mekilta Exodus 15:2 (44A): R. Aqiba († ca. 135) said, “… Behold, the nations of the world ask the Israelites, ‘What is your companion (i.e., God) more than a (different) companion, that you adjure us thus?’ (Song 5:9)? That you constantly die in this way for his sake and so are killed for his sake; as it says, ‘Therefore virgins עלמות love you’ (Song 1:3)? (Do not read עלמות ‘virgins,’ but rather עד מות:) They love you unto death. And it is also written, ‘For your sake we are killed all day long’ (Ps 44:23).” — The same is found anonymously in SDeut 33:2 § 343 (143A). ‖ Midrash Song of Songs 1:3 (85B): “Therefore virgins love you” (Song 1:3) (= therefore they love you unto death; see the previous citation); the generation of the (Hadrianic) religious persecution is meant. As it says, “For it is for your sake that we are killed all day long, we are counted as sheep for slaughter.” ‖ Midrash Song of Songs 2:7 (99A): The rabbis said, “God adjured them (see Song 2:7) in the generation of the (Hadrianic) religious persecution, ‘“by the gazelles” צבאות (Song 2:7; a designation for the generation of religious persecution), who have carried out my will צביוני in the world and in whom I have carried out my will; “or by the hinds of the field” (Song 2:7) (again a designation for the generation of religious persecution), who have spilled their blood for the sanctification of my name as the blood of a gazelle and the blood of a hart.’ This is what is written, ‘For your sake we are killed all day long’ (Ps 44:23).” ‖ Midrash Song of Songs 8:6 (131B): “Love is strong as death” (Song 8:6): the love with which the generation of the (Hadrianic) religious persecution loved God; as it says, “For your sake we are killed all day long” (Ps 44:23). ‖ Midrash Song of Songs 7:1 (125B): “Turn around, turn around, O Shulamite …, so that we may look at you” (Song 7:1).

The nations of the world say to the Israelites, "How long will you die for your God and give yourselves up for him" (read משלימין, interpretation of שולמית)? This is what is written, 'Therefore they love you unto death' (Song 1:3) (עלמות = מות [עד] על, see above). And how long will you let yourselves be killed for him; as it is written, 'For it is for your sake that we are killed all day long' (Ps 44:23)? How long will you render good to him, specifically in his interest, while he rewards you with bad things? Come to us, and we will appoint you generals and eparchs and colonels, 'and we want to see you' (= select, choose, interpretation of ונחזה בך in Song 7:1). Are you not then the elect[129] of the world? This is what is written, 'But you, see תחזה capable men from the whole people' (Exod 18:21)." And the Israelites answer them, "'Why do you look at the Shulamite? As the dance of Mahanaim?' (Song 7:1). Have you ever heard in your life, 'Abraham, Isaac, and Jacob served idols so that their sons after them should serve them?' Neither our fathers served idols, now will we serve idols after them! What could you prepare for us? A dance, as was prepared for our father Jacob when he went out from the house of Laban? (see Gen 32:2f.) ... Or could you prepare a dance for us like the one that was prepared for our ancestors at the sea; as it says, 'Then the angel of God burst forth' (Exod 14:19)? Or could you prepare a dance for us like the one that was prepared for Elisha? (see 2 Kgs 6:15–17). Or could you prepare a dance for us like the one that God will one day prepare for the righteous in the future?" (See the excursus "Sheol, Gehenna, and the Garden of Eden," III, #4, n. *n.*) — See the partial parallel in Num. Rab. 2 (136C) at § Rom 3:1f., B.

9:3: I could wish that I myself were an offering of destruction, separate from Christ, for my brothers, my relatives according to the flesh.

1. ἀνάθεμα in the usage of the LXX is "something dedicated by God or by those who belong to God for ruin, destruction."[130] The rabbinic חֵרֶם "banned" is a broader concept, insofar that it includes everything dedicated to God, not simply that dedicated for destruction. So הֶחֱרִים is synonymous with הִקְדִּישׁ in, for example, t. ʿArak. 4.24 (548): R. Eliezer (ca. 90) said, "It says in Lev 27:28: 'From people' and not 'all people,' 'from livestock' and not 'all livestock,' 'from his inherited field' and not 'his whole inherited field.' Therefore, if one dedicates (sanctifies הקדיש) all this, they are not all banned (sanctified מוחרמין)." — In this broader sense, three types of bans are discussed in t. ʿArak. 4.34 (549): There are three types of banned (devoted חֲרָמִים) things: "Everything banned that someone devotes to Yahweh by *herem*" יַחֲרִים (Lev 27:28): this is what is dedicated to the priests חרמי כהנים. "Everything banned is most holy to Yahweh" (Lev 27:28): this is what is devoted to the Most High חרמי גָבוֹהַּ. "Everything banned, which is banned

129. S-B: In accordance with the context and the passage Exod 18:21, the word in the text, מְהְזִיתָא = "mirror" must be intended in the sense of "seen" = select.

130. See Cremer, *Wörterbuch*.

in human beings, is not to be redeemed" (Lev 27:29): these are those who have been forfeited to the court's death penalty.

2. At any rate, corresponding to the usage of the LXX, ἀνάθεμα in Rom 9:3 has the narrower meaning = "devoted to ruin, an offering of destruction": the apostle declares that he is ready to fall under the curse of destruction if he could save his people by doing so. — The notion that a person could be an atoning offering for someone else by accepting the sufferings that this other had to expect as a punishment for his sins was very common in the ancient synagogue (see § Luke 24:26, I, #2 and n. *g*). Hence the not uncommon exclamation that, in content, comes near to the word of the apostle in Rom 9:3: "May I be an atonement for this and that one!" or: "I want to be an atonement for this and that one!"[a] Reference was gladly made to the great ones of the distant past, such as Moses, David, and the prophets, but also to esteemed men of the recent past, such as Rabbi († 217?) and R. Eleazar b. Simeon (ca. 180), who had supposedly suffered vicariously for the whole people and so had become an atoning offering for Israel (see § Luke 24:26 I, #2, and notes *i, k, l*). — Yet these ideas have just as little to do with the synagogue ban designated by חֵרֶם as does ἀνάθεμα in Rom 9:3 in the mouth of the apostle.

a. Mishnah Sanhedrin 2.1: When the high priest is comforted by someone else (when there is a death in his family), the whole people says to him, "Let us be your atonement אָנוּ כַּפָּרָתְךָ!" And he answers them, "May you be blessed by heaven!" ‖ Mishnah Negaʿim 2.1: R. Ishmael († ca. 135) said, "The children of Israel—I wish to be an atonement for them אֲנִי כַּפָּרָתָן!—have the color of boxwood. They are not black and not white, but rather are of a medium color." — The same is found in SLev 13:2 (235A). ‖ A baraita in b. Qidd. 31B: The son has to honor his father during his life and he was to honor him in his death.... In his death, how? If he used to say a word of teaching handed down from his mouth (i.e., in the name of his father), he should not say, "So my father said," but rather, "So my father, my lord, said. Behold, I wish to be an atonement for his burial place כפרת משכבו!" Yet he says these words only during the (first) twelve months (after the father's death). From then on he says, "May his remembrance be a blessing for the life of the future world!" — Since the dead man is assigned to the purifying fire of gehenna for 12 months, it is only during this time that the son has to declare himself ready to lighten or shorten the purgatorial fire for his father by accepting sufferings. ‖ Babylonian Talmud Sukkah 20A: Resh Laqish (ca. 250) said, "Behold, I wish to be an atonement כַּפָּרָה for R. Hiyya (ca. 200) and his sons! For when the Torah was first forgotten by Israel, Ezra came up from Babylon and established it (anew). When it was forgotten again, Hillel the Babylonian (ca. 20 BCE) came up and established it. When it was forgotten once more, R. Hiyya and his sons came up and established it." ‖ See the baraita in b. Yebam. 70A at § Luke 8:3 A, #2; see SNum 35:34 § 161 (62B) at § Luke 24:26, I, #2, n. *h*. — See also Josephus, *J. W.* 5.9 toward the end: "Accept as a recompense for our salvation my (Josephus') blood; and I myself am ready to die if you are willing to be wise after me (after my death)."

9:4: Theirs is the sonship and the glory and the covenants and the giving of the law and the temple service and the promises.

1. ἡ υἱοθεσία "sonship, childship." The rabbis lack a corresponding abstract formation. The Hebrew translation of the NT available to us (London 1852) makes do with מַעֲלַת הַבָּנִים = the position of a child, the worth of a son. — On Israel being the children of God, see § Rom 1:3 A, A, #1, α; #2, α; and #3, α.

2. ἡ δόξα = הַכָּבוֹד, Aram. יְקָרָא, "the glory," namely God's; yet, in rabbinic literature, we do not know of an example of this absolute use of כבוד and יקרא without the addition of a description of God.

3. αἱ διαθῆκαι, the covenants or the making of covenants = הַבְּרִיתוֹת. It was not uncommon to speak of multiple covenants being made.

Mekilta Exodus 23:19 (108A): "You are not to boil a kid in its mother's milk" (Exod 23:19). R. Simeon ([ca. 150], though Yalquṭ is more probably correct with R. Ishmael [† ca. 135]) said, "Why is this said in three places (outside of Exod 23:19 also in 34:26 and Deut 14:21)? Corresponding to the three covenants בריתות that God made with Israel: the one on Horeb and the other on the steppes of Moab and the third on Mount Gerizim and on Mount Ebal." — The same is found anonymously in SDeut 14:21 § 104 (95B). ‖ A baraita in Soṭah 37B: There were 48 covenants בריתות with every single commandment. See t. Soṭah 8:10 (311). — According to y. Soṭah 7.21C.54, R. Simeon (ca. 150) even claimed that 576 covenant makings happened because of each word in the Torah. This expressed the desire to illustrate the importance of the individual commandments. On the calculation of the numbers 48 and 576, see Bacher.[131]

4. ἡ νομοθεσία, the giving of the law = מַתַּן תּוֹרָה.

Babylonian Talmud Berakot 58A: In a baraita it was taught in the name of R. Aqiba († ca. 135), "'Yours, O Yahweh, is the greatness' (1 Chr 29:11) relates to the splitting of the Sea of Reeds; 'and the power' (1 Chr 29:11) to the striking of the firstborn; 'and the glory' to the giving of the law מתן תורה; 'and the honor' to Jerusalem; 'and the majesty' the sanctuary." ‖ See b. Pesaḥ. 118A at § Matt 21:9 A, #1, n. *a*. ‖ See b. Ḥul. 62B = b. Sukkah 13A at § John 19:29 B, #1. ‖ Babylonian Talmud Zebaḥim 116A.30: But it is written, "Jethro took a burnt offering and animal sacrifices for Yahweh" (Exod 18:12). This was after the giving of the law לאחר מתן תורה. This would be right according to the view of the one who said, "It was after the giving of the law." But according to the view of the one who said, "It was before the giving of the law קודם מתן תורה," what is there to be said? For it has been said: The sons of R. Hiyya (Judah and Hezekiah, ca. 240) and R. Joshua b. Levi (ca. 250). The one said, "Jethro was there (with Moses) before the giving of the law"; and the other said, "Jethro was there after the giving of the law." According to the one who said "Jethro was there before the giving of the law," it is thought that the Noachides presented peace meal offerings. Here the difference of opinion among the Tannaites underlies: "And Jethro, the priest of Midian, heard what God had done" (Exod 18:1). What information did he hear, so that he came and became

131. Bacher, *Die Agada der Tannaïten*, 2:93.

a proselyte? R. Joshua (ca. 90) said, "He heard about the war of Amalek…." R. Eleazar of Modiim said, "He heard about the giving of the law…." ‖ Mishnah Taʿanit 4.8: Likewise, it says, "Come out and look, you daughters of Zion, the king Solomon with the crown that his mother crowned him with on the day of his wedding and on the day of his heart's joy!" "On the day of his wedding": this pertains to the giving of the law מתן תורה; "and on the day of his heart's joy": this pertains to the building of the sanctuary—may it be built as soon as possible in our days, Amen! In Num. Rab. 12 (166C) "the day of his heart's joy" is interpreted in relation to the giving of the law. — Differently, Midr. Song 3:11 (108B); Exod. Rab. 52 (104D) and Pesiq. 5A. ‖ Babylonian Talmud ʿAbodah Zarah 9A: ממתן תורה עד השתא "from the giving of the law until now."

5. ἡ λατρεία, the temple service, sacrificial cult, service of God = הָעֲבוֹדָה.

Mishnah ʾAbot 1.2: Simeon the Righteous (I, ca. 300; II, ca. 200 BCE) was among the remnant of the great synagogue (in hands of which lay the leadership of the body politic in the period after Ezra). He used to say, "The world stands on three things: on the Torah, on the temple service העבודה, and on the demonstration of deeds of love." ‖ Only after the destruction of the temple was prayer designated as עֲבוֹדָה. A baraita in b. Taʿan. 2A: "To love Yahweh your God and to serve him with your whole heart" (Deut 11:13). What service עבודה is it that occurs in the heart? Say: "This is prayer תפילה." — The same is found in more detail in SDeut 11:13 § 41 (80A); see § Rom 1:9 B. ‖ הָעֲבוֹדָה = "By the temple service!" commonly serves as a formula of assurance; see examples at § Matt 5:36 F, n. *f*.

6. αἱ ἐπαγγελίαι, the promises = הַהַבְטָחוֹת (sing. הַבְטָחָה). See § Rom 4:13 A, #2.

9:5 A: Theirs are the fathers and from them is the Christ (Messiah).

οἱ πατέρες, the fathers = אָבוֹת. — The apostle mentions the fathers because it was their ancestry whom Israel had to thank for God's gift of the Messiah. At the mention of the fathers, a Jew thought above all of their merit זְכוּת, which assists their descendants (see further under § Rom 9:6). — Later midrashim report encounters between the Messiah and the fathers, some of which happen before the dawn of the messianic time in the garden of Eden, and some of which happen after the start of the messianic time on earth; see Midrash Conên (Jellinek, *Beth ha-Midrash* 2.29) at § Luke 24:26, I, #2, n. *p* and Pesiq. Rab. 37 at § Luke 24:26, I, #2, n. *m*.

9:5 B: Who is over all, God be praised forever, Amen!

On doxologies, see § Rom 1:25.

9:6: Not all who are (stem) from Israel are Israel.

The idea that simply stemming from Israel does not make a person a true Israelite and a true child of God, but rather that an Israelite is a child of God only when he does the will of God, is also expressed by some rabbinic scholars.[a] Yet this idea did not gain acceptance in broader circles.

It was repressed by another chain of thought that can be ordered like this: whoever stems from the fathers of Israel has a share in their advantages and virtues[b] and therefore also in their merit.[c] As the Israelites also relate to God, they are and remain, by the power of their stemming from the fathers, God's children[d] and will therefore one day all have a share in the future world;[e] the only one excluded from the future world will be the one who has separated himself from Israel, whether outwardly by removing the mark of the covenant on his body,[f] or inwardly by denying the future life.[g]

a. A baraita in b. Qidd. 36A: "You are children to Yahweh your God" (Deut 14:1). "When you are led like children, you are called children; but when you are not led like children, you are not called children." These are the words of R. Judah (ca. 150). — The opposing view that follows is represented by R. Meir (ca. 150); see the continuation of the citation in n. *d.* ‖ Additional passages that belong here are found at § Matt 5:9, #2 and § Gal 3:7; see also y. Ned. 3.38A.55 and Gen. Rab. 53 (34A) § Rom 9:7, #2.

b. Mekilta Exodus 15:2 (44B): "The God of my father, whom I will exalt" (Exod 15:2). (The community of Israel says,) "I am a queen, the daughter of kings; a beloved one (of God), the daughter of beloved ones (the fathers); a holy one, the daughter of holy ones; a pure one, the daughter of pure ones. Like a person who went to be engaged to a woman; soon he was ashamed of her, soon he was ashamed of her family, soon he was ashamed of her relatives. But I am not so (God is not ashamed of me when I address him with '"my" God,' and also not when I address him with 'God of my "fathers"'); rather, I am a queen, the daughter of kings etc.," as above. — Meaning: If the ancestor is holy, so too are the descendants holy.

c. On the merit of the fathers see § Luke 24:26, I, #2, n. *f* and § Matt 3:9 A, #3. — That participation in the merit of the fathers is conditioned solely by bodily descent from them follows from the fact that proselytes have to do without them, since they lack this descent (see § Matt 3:9 A, #4).

d. Babylonian Talmud Qiddušin 36A (continuation of b. Qidd. 36A in n. *a*): R. Meir said, "Whether in this case or that case (whether you are led as children or not), you are (always) called children; as it is said, 'They are witless children (but still children!)' (Jer 4:22). Further, 'children, who cannot be relied on' (Deut 32:20); further, 'Seed of wrongdoers, unholy sons' (Isa 1:4); further, 'It will happen, instead of it being said to them, "You are not my people," it will be said, "sons of the living God"' (Hos 2:1). What is meant by 'further' (for the three last supporting passages)? If you should say, 'witless (Jer 4:22), yes, they are called children then; but if they cannot be relied on, then they are not called children,' then come and hear: it says further, 'children, who cannot be relied on' (Deut 32:20). And if you should say, 'If they cannot be relied on, yes, in that case they are called children. But if they are idolaters, then they are not called children,' then come and hear: it says further, 'Seed of wrongdoers, unholy sons' (Isa 1:4). And if you should say, 'Unholy sons, yes, in that case they are called children, but they are not called proper (excellent מעליי״א) children,' then come and hear: it says further, 'It will happen, instead of it being said to them, "You are not my people," it will be said, "sons of the living God" (Hos 2:1)' (Rashi: 'because of repentance')." — Here belong also the numerous passages in which the Jewish scholars fight back against the objections of dissenters who hold that the Israelites are no longer God's people or God's children; see Midr. Ha-gadol on Lev 26:9; b. Ḥag. 5B; b. B. Bat. 10A; b. Yoma 56B at § Rom 2:19f., #2, n. *c*; Midr. Abba Gurion 41A at § Matt 4:17 A, #1, near the end; b. ʿAbod. Zar. 4A at § Luke 7:41; there are also those passages in which the claim of Christians to be the true Israel is rejected: see Midr. Song 7: 3 (127A) at § Rom 3:9 A, #1, n. *c*; Pesiq. Rab. 5 (14B) at § Matt 5:9, #2. — Reference can also be made to SDeut 1:27 § 24 (70A): "Because of Yahweh's hatred toward us" (Deut 1:27). Is it possible that God hates Israel? (The question is to be categorically answered in the negative. The Israelites as sons of "beloved ones" are in all circumstances also themselves "beloved ones" of God; see Mek. Exod. 15:2 in n. *b*.) Behold, it was said long ago: "I have loved you, says Yahweh" (Mal 1:2). Rather, they hate God! A common proverb is: Whatever is in your heart against your friend is that which is in his heart against you. (Israel imputes hatred to God, because it itself hates God.)

e. Mishnah Sanhedrin 10.1: All Israel has a share in the future world. — See Justin Martyr, *Dial.* 140: "Your (the Jews') teachers think that to those who are from Abraham's seed according to the flesh, even if they are sinners and unbelievers and disobedient to God, will be given the eternal kingdom."

f. Babylonian Talmud ʿErubin 19A: What is written, "Those who go through the valleys of tears (of gehenna)" (so Ps 84:7 according to the midr.): this pertains to those who were found guilty of gehenna in that hour, and our father Abraham comes and makes them rise up (after expiation of their guilt) and accepts them, except for the Israelite, who lay with a non-Jewish woman, whose foreskin is pulled forward, so that he (Abraham) does not recognize him (as an Israelite). — This is the passage that draws the broadest circle of those who are saved from gehenna for eternal life; see the excursus "Sheol, Gehenna, and the Garden of Eden," II, #5. — See passages that are interested in other categories of those who are excluded from blessedness at § Matt 23:13 B; see also SNum 15:31 at § Acts 21:21.

g. Mishnah Sanhedrin 10.1: These are those who have no share in the future world: whoever says, "There is no resurrection of the dead (and thereby also no future world) ..." (see the whole passage at § Matt 23:13 B). ‖ See y. Ned. 3.38A.55 and Gen. Rab. 53 (34A) at § Rom 9:7, #2.

9:7: In Isaac your seed will be named (Gen 21:12).

1. Septuagint Genesis 21:12: ἐν Ἰσαὰκ κληθήσεταί σοι σπέρμα = Rom 9:7. — Targum Onkelos: "Through (in) Isaac sons will be named for you." — Targum Yerušalmi I: "Through (in) Isaac sons will be named for you, but this son of the servant girl (Ishmael) will not be listed in your genealogy לָא מִתְיַחֵס בַּתְרָךְ (= will not be counted as your offspring)."

2. As the apostle infers from Gen 21:12 that only the children of the promise are reckoned as Abraham's seed, so the midrash infers that only those who confess two worlds, that is, those who confess the resurrection and the judgment, belong to Abraham's descendants.

Jerusalem Talmud Nedarim 3.38A.55: (If someone says,) "I pledge that I will have no benefit from the Noachides," such is allowed him from Israelites (for these do not belong to the Noachides), but it is forbidden him from the nations (the non-Israelites); "that I will have no benefit from Abraham's seed זרע אברהם," such is forbidden to him from Israelites, but allowed from the nations.[132] The Ishmaelites are not included in the general expression "Abraham's seed"; for "in Isaac your seed will be named" (Gen 21:12; and the Ishmaelites do not stem from Isaac). Further, Esau is not included in the general expression "Isaac's seed." R. Judan b. Shalom (ca. 370) said, "'In Isaac' (it says in Gen 21:12): in one part of Isaac (not Isaac in his entirety)." R. Huna (ca. 350) said, "The ב (before יצחק in Gen 21:12) means 'two': the son (of Isaac is meant in Gen 21:12) who will obtain two worlds one day, this world and the future world (so only Jacob's progeny belong to the seed of Isaac, because only they confess two worlds)." ‖ Genesis Rabbah 53 (34A): ("In Isaac your seed will be named" [Gen 21:12].) R. Judan (ca. 350) said, "'Isaac' is not written here, but rather 'in Isaac' (i.e., in one part of him)." R. Azariah (ca. 380) said in the name of Bar Hittaia (ca. 350?), "The ב (before יצחק in Gen 21:12) means 'two': in the one who confesses two worlds (your seed will be named)." R. Judan b. Shalom (ca. 370) said, "'Remember his wonders that he has done, his signs, and the judgments of his mouth, seed of Abraham, his servants, sons of Jacob, his chosen one' (Ps 105:5f). As a sign (of belonging to the seed of Abraham, says God) I have given the one who expresses (confesses) with his mouth:[133] 'Whoever confesses two worlds will be named your seed; but whoever does not confess two worlds will not be named your seed.'" — The same is found in briefer form in Midr. Ps. 105 § 1 (225A).

9:8: Children of the flesh.

On the expression, see Tg. Yer. I Num 23:19 at § John 3:6.

9:10: Who received seed from one man, our father Isaac.

1. ἐξ ἑνός. Genesis Rabbah 63 (39C): "Isaac prayed to Yahweh concerning לְנֹכַח (literally: with opposite) his wife" (Gen 25:21). This teaches that Isaac lay stretched out here and she there (opposite him). And he said, "Lord of the world, all the children that you will give me, may they be from that righteous woman!" She too spoke thus, "All the children that you will give to me, may they be from that righteous man!"

2. κοίτη = bed, sexual intercourse. In the LXX also = ejaculation of semen; so Num 5:20: καὶ ἔδωκέ τις τὴν κοίτην αὐτοῦ ἐν σοί "if anyone put his ejaculation of semen into you"; the word in the text is: שְׁכֹבֶת = ejaculation of semen; Tg. Onk.: שְׁכֻבְתָּא. — More fully: κοίτη σπέρματος = ejaculation of semen; LXX Lev 15:16: ἄνθρωπος, ᾧ ἂν ἐξέλθῃ ἐξ αὐτοῦ κοίτη σπέρματος, the word in the text is: שִׁכְבַת זֶרַע. Further examples are found in LXX Lev 15:17. 32; 18:20; 22:4. — If one understands κοίτη metonymically in the sense of "progeny," reference can be made to the fact that, for the rabbis, מִטָּה "bed, marriage bed" also has the meaning "progeny."

---

132. S-B: These sentences come from m. Ned 3.11.

133. S-B: One would expect the following: "I have given you as a sign what one expresses with his mouth."

Babylonian Talmud Pesaḥim 56A: R. Simeon b. Laqish (ca. 250) said, "'Jacob called his sons and said, "Gather together so I may proclaim to you"' (Gen 49:1). Jacob wanted to reveal to his sons the end of days; then the Shekinah went out of him (and with it the prophetic gift). He said, 'Should there be—God forbid חָס וְשָׁלוֹם!—in my progeny במיטתי (literally: in my marriage bed) anything useless (reprehensible), as in the case of Abraham, from whom Ishmael issued forth, or as in the case of my father Isaac, from whom Esau issued forth?'" ‖ Leviticus Rabbah 36 (133C): Why in the case of Abraham and Isaac is the word אף (= "also" and "anger") said, while the word אף is not said in the case of Jacob? Because his (Jacob's) progeny מטתן (literally: his marriage bed) was immaculate before him. From Abraham issued Ishmael and all the sons of Keturah; from Isaac issued Esau and all the chiefs of Edom. But as concerns Jacob, his progeny מיטתו was immaculate: all his sons were righteous men.

9:11 A: When they had not yet been born or done anything good or bad.

The Haggadah, however, tells of all kinds of bad things that Esau carried out already in his mother's womb; see Gen. Rab. 63 (39C) with parallels at § John 9:2, n. *a*.

9:11 B: So that the electing purpose of God might exist not on the basis of works but rather on the basis of (the will of) the one who calls.

A κατ' ἐκλογὴν πρόθεσις τοῦ θεοῦ οὐκ ἐξ ἔργων ἀλλ' ἐκ τοῦ καλοῦντος is depicted in the following:

Babylonian Talmud Niddah 16B: R. Hanina b. Papa (ca. 300) said in a presentation, "The angel that is appointed over conception is called Layela.[134] He takes the drop of semen, sets it before God and says before him, 'Lord of the world, what is to come into being from this drop? A strong man or a weak one? A wise one or a simple one? A rich one or a poor one? But whether a godless or righteous one is to come into being, he does not ask.'" This corresponds to the words of R. Hanina (ca. 225); for R. Hanina said, "Everything lies in the hand of heaven with the exception of (a person's) fear of God. As it says, 'And now, Israel, what does Yahweh your God demand of you, except that you fear Yahweh your God!' (Deut 10:12)." (Thus, a person's fear of God is a divine demand, the fulfillment of which depends on the will of the person.) The saying of R. Hanina is also in b. Ber. 33B and b. Meg. 25A. ‖ Babylonian Talmud Soṭah 2A: Rab Judah († 299) said that Rab († 247) said, "40 days before the formation of the embryo (i.e., in the hour of conception) a voice goes out from heaven that says, 'The daughter of this or that one is to be granted to this or that one, the house of this or that one to this or that one, the field of this or that one to this or that one!'" A parallel is found in b. Sanh. 22A. ‖ See Tanḥ. פקודי 127A at § John 1:1 A, C, #3.

---

134. S-B: Layela = angel of the night, an interpretation from Job 3:3: "Layela said, 'A boy is conceived.'"

9:12: The greater will serve the smaller.

Septuagint Genesis 25:23: καὶ ὁ μείζων δουλεύσει τῷ ἐλάσσονι = Rom 9:12. – Targum Onkelos formulates this passively: "And the great one will be subjected יִשְׁתַּעְבֵּיד to the small one." – Targum Yerušalmi I: "And the great one will be subjected to the small one, if the sons of the small one observe the commandments of the Torah." ‖ Leqach Tob Gen 25:23 (1.60B): R. Huna (ca. 350) said, "If Jacob merits it (or has merits זָכָה), the great one will serve the small one; but if not, the small one will serve the great one. And likewise, it says, 'If you (Esau) strive, though, you will shatter his (Jacob's) yoke on his neck' (Gen 27:40)." – Genesis Rabbah 63 (39D) should be understood accordingly: "The great one will serve the small one" (Gen 25:23). R. Huna said, "If he (Jacob) merits it, (Esau) will serve; but if not, he (Esau) will be served ייעבד (by Jacob)." – See a further parallel in Midr. Ps. 9 § 7 (43A).

9:13: Jacob I loved, but Esau I hated.

Septuagint Malachi 1:2f.: καὶ ἠγάπησα τὸν Ἰακὼβ, τὸν δὲ Ἡσαῦ ἐμίσησα. – The targum mitigates the expression: "I loved Jacob and removed (= cast away) רַחֵיקִית Esau." ‖ See Tanḥ. תרומה 100A at § Matt 15:26, n. *f.* ‖ TanḥumaB תרומה § 7 (46B): "You are to make carpets of goat hair" (Exod 26:7). This is what is written, "I have loved you, says Yahweh" (Mal 1:2). Who said this verse? Malachi said it. When? In the hour when he punished the Israelites, Malachi said to them, "Will a human being fleece (rob, קָבַע) God?" (Mal 3:8). They answered him, "How do we fleece you?" (Mal 3:8). Our teachers said, "He (God) punished the generation of Malachi, and they answered him. He said to them, 'Will a human fleece God?'" R. Levi (ca. 300) said, "This (namely קָבַע) is an Arabic word. (For the rabbis, קָבַע, Aram. קְבַע means 'to determine, decide'). An Arab comes to speak with someone else; then the latter says to him, 'Do you want to rob us האת גוזלינו, do you want to fleece us קובעינו? (גזל and קבע are thus synonyms.) Will a human fleece God?' Then he said, 'And you say, "How do we fleece you?" "The tithe and the offering" (Mal 3:8); for they did not set them apart, as they should have.' Then he said to them again, '"Is Esau not Jacob's brother"? (Mal 1:2).' And you say, '"Wherein did you love us?" (Mal 1:2). According to the custom of the world, when a man has sons, a firstborn and a younger one, who receives the most? The firstborn: Esau came out first, as it says, "The first came out, red" (Gen 25:25). He would have been designated to receive two portions, but I did not proceed thus. Instead, Jacob received two portions, this world and the future world.' Esau spoke thus to Jacob, '"We will decamp and move on ..." (Gen 33:12), we will both indulge in the world!' But Jacob answered him, 'Take your world there and move on; as it is said, "May my lord go before his servant ..., until I come to my lord at Seir" (Gen 33:14).'" R. Jacob (which one?) said, "I have gone through all of Scripture (to see) whether Jacob came to Seir or not, but I have not found it. And when will he get there? In the future, as it is said, 'And liberators will go up onto Mount Zion, to judge the mountain of Esau' (Obad 1:21). Therefore, 'And I loved Jacob' (Mal 1:2). Jacob is united with Esau in this world, but Esau is not united with Jacob in the future world. Solomon said, 'It (so the midr. cites the verse) will belong entirely to you alone and to no other alongside you' (Prov 5:17)." – The same is found in Tanḥ. תרומה 101B. ‖ Numbers Rabbah 23 (193C): You find that the desert will one day be inhabited land and that the inhabited land will one day be a desert." How do we know that the inhabited land will one day be a desert? "And Esau I hated, and I will make his mountain a wasteland" (so Midr. Mal. 1:3). And whence comes the idea that the desert will one day be inhabited land? "I will make the desert a pool of water and the dry land into springs" (Isa 41:18). ‖ Pesiqta Rabbati Supplement 1 (193B): "God seeks the persecuted" (i.e., he looks after him; so Eccl 3:15 according to the midr.).... Likewise, Esau persecuted Jacob: "Since he persecuted his brother with the sword and killed his compassion" (Amos 1:11). Then God said, "I love the persecuted and hate the persecutor, 'and Esau I hated' (Mal 1:3). But as concerns Jacob: 'and I loved Jacob' (Mal 1:2)." — See the parallel Lev. Rab. 27 (123C) at § Matt 5:10, #1. ‖ See Tanḥ. תרומה 100A at § Rom 2:11, #3, n. α.

9:15: I will be gracious to whom I will be gracious, and I will have mercy on whom I will have mercy.

Septuagint Exodus 33:19 = Rom 9:15. — Targum Onkelos: "I will be gracious to whom I want to be gracious, and I will have mercy on whom I want to have mercy." — Targum Yerušalmi I: "I will spare who deserves to be spared, and I will have mercy on the one who deserves mercy." ‖ Exodus Rabbah 45 (101A): Moses said, "Let me see your glory" (Exod 33:18). He wished to have firm ground under his feet concerning the recompense of the righteous and the rest of the godless.... "And I will remove my hand" (Exod 33:23); God said to him, "I will let you see the recompense of the righteous that I will give them then at the end of days...." What is written before that? "He said, 'I will make all my beauty pass by your face'" (Exod 33:19), the measure (the property) of goodness and the measure of punishment, "and I will be gracious to whom I will be gracious" (Exod 33:19): in that hour God showed him all the treasures of the recompense that have been prepared מתוקנין for the righteous. And he (Moses) said, "This treasure, to whom does it belong?" And he answered him, "To the one who gives alms" (עושה מצות = ποιεῖν ἐλεημοσύνην in Matt 6:2). "And this treasure, to whom does it belong?" "To those who raises orphans." And so it was with treasure after treasure. Later he saw a great treasure. He said, "This treasure, to whom does it belong?" He answered him, "To the one who can (point to the merit of works), I will give to him from his recompense (entitled to him); but whoever has nothing, with him I act at no cost חִנָּם (without him having a claim, thus = from grace) and I will give to him from this (treasure); as it says, 'I will be gracious to whom I will be gracious' (Exod 33:19). I will be gracious to whom I will be gracious, to whom I wish to be gracious שאני מבקש לחון; and likewise, 'And I will have mercy on whom I will have mercy' (Exod 33:19)."

9:16: Of the merciful (gracious) God.

ὁ ἐλεῶν θεός. — In rabbinic usage, simply רַחוּם, רַחֲמָן, Aram. רַחֲמָנָא = the "Merciful One" was used quite frequently as a designation for God.

a. רחום. See § Matt 5:34, #3 and the citation from m. Šebu. 4.13 at § Matt 5:34, #3, n. *b.* — The earliest example is Sir 50:19: "And all the people of the land gave praise in prayer before the Merciful One לִפְנֵי רַחוּם." — The Greek: κατέναντι ἐλεήμονος.

b. רחמן. Tosefta Baba Qamma 9.30 (366): R. Judah (ca. 150) said in the name of Rabban Gamaliel (ca. 90), "Look, it says, 'He will grant you mercy and have mercy on you and increase you' (Deut 13:18). Let this be a sign (of truth) in your hand: as long as you are merciful, the Merciful One רחמן will have mercy on you."

c. רחמנא. See the excursus "Memra of Yahweh," #3, A, n. *b* and at § 1 Cor 6:16, #2, n. *i.*

9:17: I have raised you (caused you to arise) precisely so that I might show my power in you, and so that my name might be proclaimed in all the earth.

Exodus 9:16 according to the base text: "But I have allowed you to remain הֶעֱמַדְתִּיךָ so that I might make you see my power, and so that my name might be proclaimed in all the earth." — Septuagint: "And you have been kept διετηρήθης so that I might show my strength in you, and so that my name might be proclaimed in all the earth." — The apostle follows the LXX, except for the fact that he has taken the verb הֶעֱמִיד not in the sense "allow to remain," but rather in the meaning commonly used in his time "to cause to arise." — Targum Onkelos: "But I have allowed you to remain, in order to make you see my strength, and so that the power of my name might be recounted in all the earth." — Targum Yerušalmi I: "But indeed, not for your good have I allowed you to remain, but rather in order to make you see my strength, and so that my holy name might be recounted (proclaimed) in all the earth." ‖ Exodus Rabbah 12 (75A): "For otherwise I would have stretched out my hand" (Exod 9:15). God said to him (pharaoh), "Do you think, blasphemer, that I could not destroy you from the world? Learn from the plague of pestilence at the time when I sent that pestilence: if I had send it against you and against your people (and not simply against the livestock [Exod 9:3]), you would have been destroyed from the earth. But I did not send it against you, only so that I might show you the power of my strength and so that my power might be proclaimed in all the earth. This is what is written; 'But I have allowed you to remain for this reason …' (Exod 9:16)." ‖ Mekilta Exodus 14:28 (39B): "'And the water turned back and covered the chariots …; not one among them remained' (Exod 14:28); (the water covered) pharaoh too." These are the words of R. Judah (ca. 150); for it says, "The chariots of pharaoh and his army he cast into the sea" (Exod 15:4). (R. Judah interprets עד אחד in Exod 14:28 as = "not even one.") R. Nehemiah (ca. 150) said, "(The water covered everyone) with the exception of pharaoh. Concerning him Scripture says, 'For this reason I have let you remain …' (Exod 9:16)." (R. Nehemiah interprets עד אחד: "up to one" = "with the exception of one," namely pharaoh.) ‖ (Greek) Sirach 16:14: "The Lord hardened pharaoh not to recognize him, so that his deeds (in him = LXX and Rom 9:17) might be known to everything under heaven. To all creation his mercy is evident, and he assigned his light and darkness to the diamond τῷ ἀδάμαντι." —These verses, transmitted by only two Greek manuscripts (106 and 248), but also by the Syriac and Arabic, were considered ungenuine up until now. This judgment must now be given up because the verses are found also in Hebrew Sirach 16:15, though with a different *Tendenz*: "Yahweh hardened the heart of pharaoh, who (= because he, not a final clause like the Greek) did not recognize him; for his works are evident under heaven (thus he would have been able to recognize him). His mercy was shown (was revealed) to all his creatures, and he assigned his light and his praise שבחו to the children of men בני אדם."

– Instead of שבחו, Solomon Schechter reads with the Greek and Syriac חשכו "his darkness"; the Greek turned בני אדם into ἀδάμας.

9:18: He is gracious to whom he wishes, but he hardens whom he wishes.

Exodus Rabbah 13 (75C): "I have hardened his (pharaoh's) heart" (Exod 10:1). R. Yohanan († 279) said, "On the basis of this passage the heretics (*minim*) have taken the opportunity (literally: an opening of the mouth) to say, 'It was not up to him to repent; for it says, "I have hardened his heart"' (Exod 10:1)." R. Simeon b. Laqish (ca. 250) responded to him, "May the mouth of heretics be plugged! Rather it says, 'He mocks mockers' (Prov 3:34). God warns a person once, twice, three times, and if he (then) does not go into himself (does not turn in repentance), he shuts his heart to repentance, in order to punish him with that by which he has sinned. So too it was with pharaoh, the blasphemer: after God had sent word to him five times and he did not bother with his words. God said to him, 'You have made your neck hard and hardened your heart. Behold, I will add impurity to your impurity.' This is what the words 'I have hardened his heart' mean. What does 'I have hardened' יתדבכה mean? That God made his heart like liver דְּבֵכָה; for if this is cooked a second time, it gets hardened (read instead of סיסטרא with Dalman, *Wörterbuch*: סִיסְרַטְסָא = στερέωσις solidifying). In this way, the heart of pharaoh became like liver so that he did not accept God's words. This is what the words 'I have hardened his heart' mean."

9:19: Who can resist his will?

Targum Job 9:12: "See, he destroys a person in the world, and who will raise an objection against him? Who will say to him, 'What are you doing?'" ‖ Daniel 4:32: "All those who dwell on the earth are considered as nothing. He acts according to his will with the host of heaven and with the inhabitants of the earth, and there is no one who could oppose his hand and say to him, 'What are you doing?'" ‖ Wisdom 11:21: "For your great power is always there for you to command, and who will resist the strength of your arm ἀντιστήσεται?" – Wisdom 12:12: "Who will say, 'What have you done?' Or who will resist ἀντιστήσεται your judgment?"

9:20 A: Who are you to talk back to God?

See Tg. Job 9:12 above at § Rom 9:19. ‖ Midrash Ecclesiastes 7:16 (36B): "Do not be entirely righteous and do not act overly wise" (Eccl 7:16). "Do not be entirely righteous," more than your creator. The passage speaks of Saul; as it is written, "And Saul came to the city of Amalek …" (1 Sam 15:5). R. Huna (ca. 350) and (= in the name of) R. Bannaiah (ca. 220) said, "Saul began to fight against his creator. He said, 'God said, "Go and strike Amalek" (1 Sam 15:3). If the men sinned, how did the women sin and how did the children sin and how did the cattle and oxen and donkeys sin (so that they were all exterminated)?' Then a voice went out from heaven and said, 'Do not be entirely righteous more than your creator!'" The rabbis said, "He began to fight about the calf whose neck it to be broken," and they said, "Scripture says, 'They should break the cow's neck there in the valley' (Deut 21:4); that one killed and this one has its neck broken! If a person sinned, how did the cattle sin?" Then a voice went out from heaven and said, "Do not be entirely righteous!" — Parallels are found in Midr. Sam. 18 § 2 (50A); b. Yoma 22B, though here R. Mani (II, ca. 370) is the author.

9:20 B: The figure does not say to its maker: Why have you made me thus?

Isaiah 45:9: "Will the clay טִינָא say to its maker, 'What are you making there?' Or your work, 'He has no hands'?" — Septuagint: μὴ ἐρεῖ ὁ πηλὸς τῷ κεραμεῖ, τί ποιεῖς ὅτι οὐκ ἐργάζῃ, οὐδὲ ἔχεις χεῖρας; μὴ ἀποκριθήσεται τὸ πλάσμα πρὸς τὸν πλάσαντα αὐτό; — targum: "Is it possible for the clay to say to טִינָא the one working on it, 'You have not worked on me'? Or (for) your work (to say), 'He has no hands'?" (It could also be translated: "You have not worked on me"? or "Your work has no handles"? ‖ Isaiah 29:16: "O your perversity! Or should the potter be regarded as clay, so that the handiwork should say of its maker, 'He has not made me'? And the figure say of its maker, 'He understands nothing'?" — Septuagint: οὐχ ὡς πηλὸς τοῦ κεραμέως λογισθήσεσθε; μὴ ἐρεῖ τὸ πλάσμα τῷ πλάσαντι αὐτό, οὐ σύ με ἔπλασας; ἢ τὸ ποίημα τῷ ποιήσαντι, οὐ συνετῶς με ἐποίησας; — targum: "Do you wish to reverse your actions? Behold, like clay in the hand of the potter, so you are regarded before me! Is it possible for the clay to say to the one working on it, 'You have not worked on me'? or for the creature to say to its creator, 'You do not know (understand) me'?" — Genesis Rabbah 24 (15D): R. Hoshaiah the elder (ca. 225) opened his talk with, "'Woe to those who bury themselves deep before Yahweh to cultivate secret counsel and whose works happen in darkness, so that they say, "Who sees us and who sees through us?"' Like an architect אַרְכִּיטֶקְטוֹס (so read instead of ארביטוקטוס), who built a city: Inner chambers and canals and caverns. After some time, he became the tax collector, and the citizens of the city hid themselves before him in the inner chambers and in the caverns. He said to them, 'I am the one who built the caverns; why do you hide from me like this?' Likewise, woe to those who hide themselves deep before Yahweh to cultivate secret counsel and whose works happen in darkness. 'O your perversity! Or should the potter be regarded as clay?' (Isa 29:16). They make the figure equal to the maker, the plant to the planter. 'So that the handiwork says of its maker, "He has not made me?" And the figure say of its maker, "He understands nothing?"'" ‖ See the narrative in b. Taʿan. 20A at § Matt 5:24 B, #1.

9:21: Or does the potter not have power over the clay to make from the same lump one vessel for honor but the other for ignominy?

1. On the whole sentence, see:

Isaiah 29:16; 45:9 at § Rom 9:20 B; also see Isa 64:7; Job 10:9; 33:6; but especially Jer 18:3–10. ‖ (Greek) Sirach 33:13 (= 36:13 in Fritzsche): "As the potter's clay is in his hand and all his action (with it happens) according to his pleasure: so are humans in the hand of the one who made them, to repay them according to his decision." ‖ Wisdom 15:7: "For even the potter, kneading weak earth laboriously, forms each single (vessel) for our use. But from the same clay he is accustomed to form both vessels that serve for pure dealings and those that serve for the opposite, but all in the same way. But what the usage is for each one of both kinds, of that the pot-maker is the judge." ‖ Babylonian Talmud Berakot 32A: R. Hama b. Hanina (ca. 260) said, "If these three passages of Scripture did not exist (in which Israel's religious-moral behavior is traced back to God), the feet of those who hate Israel (i.e., the feet of godless Israelites, see § Matt 3:17 A, #29, n. *i*, S-B footnote) falter. The one where it is written, 'On that day I will … gather together what has been scattered and what I have harmed הדעותי' (Mic 4:6) (i.e., in the sense of the midr.: which I have done fiercely). The other where it is written, 'Behold, like the clay in the potter's hand, so you are in my hand, house of Israel!' (Jer 18:6). And the third, where it is written, 'I will remove the heart of stone from your body and give you a heart of flesh' (Ezek 36:26)." — In b. Sukkah 52B, R. Yohanan († 279) is the author. ‖ Genesis Rabbah 72 (46C): We have learned, "(If someone calls [to God] about something past, it is an invalid prayer.) How so? If his wife is pregnant and he said, 'May it be (God's) will that my wife give birth to a male,' it is not an invalid prayer (m. Ber. 9.3)." Those from the school of R. Yannai (ca. 225) said, "The Mishnah deals with a woman who (already) sits on the birthing chair." R. Judah b. Pazzi (ca. 320) said, "Even in the case of a woman who (already) sits on the birthing chair, a change can (still) be brought about; this is what is written, 'Do I not have power just like this potter to deal with you, house of Israel? Behold, like the clay in the potter's hand, so you are in my hand, house of Israel!' (Jer 18:6). Like this potter, after he has formed a jug, smashes it and makes another one, so I too will do: even on the birthing chair I will make a change." — A parallel in briefer form is found in y. Ber. 9.14A.62.

2. σκεῦος = כְּלִי, Aram. מָנָא or מָאנָא, implement, garment, vessel. — כלי is used in an especially broad way by the rabbis, even of abstract things and people. So the Mishnah concludes with the sentence: R. Simeon b. Halapta (ca. 190) said, "Great is peace; for God has found no other vessel כלי that holds blessing for Israel than peace שָׁלוֹם (only); as it says, 'Yahweh will give strength to his people. Yahweh will bless his people with peace' (Ps 29:11)." — This word was cited rather often, for example, in SNum 6:26 § 42 (12B); see the passage at § Matt 5:9, #1. — It is used about people in the following, for example:

Babylonian Talmud Ta'anit 20A, B, where it is recounted that R. Simeon b. Eleazar (so read [ca. 190]), responds to someone's greeting with the words, "Fool, how stupid you are!" Then this one said, "Go and tell the master workman who created me: What an ugly vessel כלי you have made!" See the whole passage at § Matt 5:24, B, #1. — Also see § 1 Thess 4:4.

3. εἰς τιμὴν σκεῦος. See b. Ber. 27B and 28A: Some people came (after Rabban Gamaliel II [ca. 90] was removed from office) and said to R. Eleazar b. Azariah, "Is it pleasing to the lord to be the one who presides over the house of learning (in Gamaliel's place)?" He answered them, "I will go and confer with the people of my house (my family)." He went and conferred with the members of his family. She (his wife) said to him, "Perhaps they will remove you (soon from office)!" He answered her, "One day in possession of a vessel of honor (מָן יְקָר, so the Munich manuscript; ed. Amsterdam 1644ff.: cup of honor כָּסָא דְמוֹקְרָא) (then I am satisfied). Tomorrow it may be shattered!"

9:22: Vessels of wrath, prepared for destruction.

1. σκεύη ὀργῆς. — כְּלֵי זַעְמוֹ "vessels = weapons of his wrath" (Isa 13:5; Jer 50:25) is formally the same but different in content. — Septuagint Jeremiah 27:25: σκεύη ὀργῆς αὐτοῦ. Targum: ית מני כס דלוט קדמוהי = "the vessels of the cup of the curse before him." — Likewise, Tg. Isa. 13:5; however, LXX: οἱ ὁπλομάχοι αὐτοῦ = "his weapon fighters."

2. κατηρτισμένα εἰς ἀπώλειαν. — See the Hebrew synonyms for καταρτίζειν or ἑτοιμάζειν at § Matt 25:34 B. — Concerning זִמֵּן mentioned there, reference may here be made to b. Ber. 8B: "I have commanded my devoted ones" (Isa 13:3). Rab Joseph († 333) taught as a tannaitic tradition, "Here the priests are meant, who are devoted and prepared (or destined) המקודשין וּמְזוּמָּנִין for gehenna (= εἰς ἀπώλειαν)." — Likewise, concerning the verb כון presented there, here the following passages may be added: Midrash Psalm 3 § 3 (18B): David said before God, "Lord of the world, it is evident and known before you that Bathsheba has been determined for me שנכונה היתה לי since the six days of creation." — The parallel in b. Sanh. 107A reads: ראויה היתה = she was seen or determined. ‖ Mekilta Exodus 14:15 (36B toward the bottom): R. Eleazar of Modiim († ca. 135) said, "'Why are you crying out to me?' (Exod 14:15). Because of the children of Israel I do not need any command: 'My sons and the work of my hands command me!' (Isa 45:11). Have they not long been overseen (מוּכָנִים, taken into view, prepared) before me since the six days of creation; as it is written, 'If these orders (of creation) depart from my face, says Yahweh (so read instead of אני י״י), the seed of Israel will not (לא, as the verse is cited by the midrash) cease to be a people before me forever' (Jer 31:35)." (From the eternal existence of Israel *a parte post* is inferred its eternal existence before God *a parte ante.*)

9:23: Which he prepared beforehand for glory.

On ἑτοιμάζειν see § Matt 25:34 B. — In relation to Rom 9:23, Wettstein cites from a parable in Mek. Exod. 14:22 (37B): (The king said to his two sons:) "*Vos ambo non praeparati estis nisi ad gloriam meam*" לא כוונתם אלא לכבודי. These words should be translated: "You are concerned only about my honor." This passage thus has nothing in common with Rom 9:23.

9:25: As he says also in Hosea, "I will call what was not my people 'my people,' and those who were not beloved 'beloved.'"

1. ὡς ἐν τῷ Ὡσηὲ λέγει = כמו שאמר בהושע; God or Scripture is to be understood as the subject. — So Midr. Eccl. 2:8 (13B): כמ״ש בישעי׳, that is,: כמו שאמר בישעיה, as he (God, Scripture) said in Isaiah; or: כמו שנאמר בישעיה = as was said etc.; or: כמו שכתב בי׳ = as he has written etc.; or: כמו שכתוב בי׳ = as is written in Isaiah. — See § Mark 1:2f., #1 and § Rom 3:9 A, #3, n. *k*, S-B footnote.

2. Hosea 2:25: "I will give reprieve to those who have not been given reprieve and say to the not-my-people, 'You are my people,' and it will say (to me), 'My God!'" — Targum: "I will have mercy on those (or I will love

those) who are not beloved because of their works (or: by their works), and I will say to those to whom I said, 'Not my people,' in truth, you are my people!' And they will say (answer), 'My God!'" — Septuagint Hosea 2:23 (= 2:25 in the original text): καὶ ἀγαπήσω τὴν οὐκ ἠγαπημένην, καὶ ἐρῶ τῷ οὐ λαῷ μου, λαός μου εἶ σύ· καὶ αὐτὸς ἐρεῖ, κύριος ὁ θεός μου εἶ σύ.

Babylonian Talmud Pesaḥim 87B: R. Eleazar (ca. 270) said, "Even in the hour of his wrath God is mindful of mercy; for it says, 'For I will no longer have mercy on the house of Israel' (Hos 1:6)." (Even in this word of condemnation, the expression "to have mercy" appears.) ... R. Yohanan († 279) said, "From here (the scriptural proof can be adduced): 'I will have mercy on the those who have not been granted reprieve' (Hos 2:25)." ‖ Numbers Rabbah 2 (138C): R. Isaac (ca. 300) said, "God said to Israel, 'I am the first for good and the last for evil.' The first for good: 'And I will say to the not-my-people, "You are my people"' (Hos 2:25). And after this it says, 'And it will say (to me), "My God!"' (Hos 2:25; read אלהי instead of אל חי, which is found in Hos 2:1). But with evil he speaks as the last one, 'For you are not my people' (Hos 1:9); and after this it says, 'And I will not be yours' (Hos 1:9)."

9:26: And it will be in the place where it was said to them, "You are not my people," there they will be called sons of the living God.

1. Hosea 2:1: "And it will happen in the place where it is said to them (according to others: and it will happen, instead of it being said to them), 'You are not my people,' it will be said to them 'sons of the living God.'" — Targum: "And it will happen in the place where they were exiled among the nations, when they transgressed the Torah, and where it was said to them, 'You are not my people,' they will be made great again, so that it will be said to them, 'People of the eternally abiding God.'" — Septuagint Hosea 2:1 (= 2:1 in the original text): καὶ ἔσται, ἐν τῷ τόπῳ, οὗ ἐῤῥέθη αὐτοῖς, οὐ λαός μου ὑμεῖς, κληθήσονται καὶ αὐτοὶ υἱοὶ θεοῦ ζῶντος.

See b. Qidd. 36A at § Rom 9:6, n. *d*; see the parallel in SDeut 14:1 § 96 (94A) at § Rom 1:3 A, #3, α. ‖ Numbers Rabbah 2 (138A): "And it will happen in the place where it was said to them: 'You are not my people ...'" (Hos 2:1). Where was this said to them? When they committed that act (worshiping the golden calf), God called them "Moses' people," as it says, "Go, go down, for your people is acting perversely" (Exod 32:7). Immediately Moses girded his loins in prayer; as it says, "Moses sought to mollify Yahweh his God" (Exod 32:11). Like a king who saw his wife, how she kissed a eunuch. He said to her bridegroom (see § Matt 9:15 A), "I will dismiss her, I will cast her out, let her go to the house of her father!" He said to him, "Why?" "Because I met her as she kissed a eunuch." He said to him, "Now she will give you handsome and strong sons (from the eunuch), who will go with you to war!" He answered, "Nothing is to be expected from the one who cannot beget at all. And because of such a thing, (said the bridegroom,) from which there is no gain, you get angry?" Likewise, it says, "Why, O Yahweh, should your wrath burn against your people? ..." (Exod 32:11). Moses said to God, "The calf that the Israelites have made will now support you: it makes the torrents of rain fall down, and you make the dew break forth." God said to him, "Is anything to be expected from this thing?" Moses answered him, "And if nothing actually exists in this thing, why are you angry? 'Why, O Yahweh, should your wrath burn against your people? ... Why should the Egyptians say? ..." (Exod 32:12). "Remember Abraham ..." (Exod 32:13)." What is written after this? "And Yahweh relented concerning the disaster that he had said he would inflict on his people" (Exod 32:14). "His people" (it says here, not: "Moses' people"). Here you see, "And it will happen in the place where it was said to them, 'You are not my people ...'" (Hos 2:1). ‖ Numbers Rabbah 2 (138C): In the days of (the prophet) Hosea the Israelites provoked God. God began to put them in fear: "For they are children of whores ..." (Hos 2:6), "for she is not my wife ..." (Hos 2:4); "name it, 'Not my people,' for you are not my people" (Hos 1:9). But if he has let this slip out of his mouth for an hour, he did it only to bring them back to what is good. And he was not even able to bear it for one hour; but rather while he was still in that place, he backtracked, as it says, "And it will happen in the place where it was said to them, 'You are not my people,' they will be called 'sons of the living God'" (Hos 2:1). ‖ Numbers Rabbah 2 (138B): "And it will happen in the place where it was said to them, 'You are not my people,' they will be called 'sons of the living God'" (Hos 2:1). R. Yohanan († 279) said, "What is written before the passage? 'Go, take for yourself a wife of whoredom ...' (Hos 1:2); 'and he went and took Gomer ...' (Hos 1:3); and the whole verse, 'Name it, "Not my people ..."' (Hos 1:9). And after this it says, 'And it will happen in the place where it was said to them ...' (Hos 2:1). If he loved her where he became angry with her, how much more will this be the case if he loves her! What can this be compared with? With a king who got angry with his wife. He said, 'I will cast her out and will not spare even her children, she is not my wife, and I am not her husband.' Then he went down to the market, went to a goldsmith and said to him, 'Make golden jewelry for my wife!' His friend went and met him at the goldsmith's, who made the jewelry for his wife. He went and said to their women neighbors, 'Have you not heard that the king had a fight with his wife and said about her, "I will cast her out?" Now I have seen him at the goldsmith's, as he said to him, "Make jewelry for my wife!"' Likewise, when God got angry with Israel, he said to Hosea, '"Go, take for yourself a wife of whoredom" (Hos 1:2). I do not want her (according to the reading איני instead of אני), "for the land commits whoredom" (Hos 1:2). I will not have mercy on her, call her the "unpardoned one" (Hos 2:25). She is not mine and I am not hers, "for you are not my people, and I will not be yours" (Hos 1:9).' Then Hosea said to the nations of the world, 'Do you suppose because he said those words to them, "For you are not my people," that he is angry with them? See (read ראו instead of ראוי) what follows on this as he says to them, "And it will happen in the place where it was said to them, 'You are not my people,' it will be said to them, 'sons of the living God'"' (Hos 2:1)." ‖ Midrash Psalm 22 §7 (92B): Our teachers taught, "From anger (issues) delight, from darkness light, from wrath mercy, from affliction amplitude (well-being), from being distanced being brought near, from falling rising up. From anger delight (see Deut 9:14 and Exod 32:14); from darkness light (see Mic 7:8); from wrath mercy (see Hab 3:2 at the end); from affliction amplitude (see Jer 30:7); from being distanced being brought near ('And it will happen in the place where it was said to them, "You are not my people," it will be said to them, "sons of the living God"' [Hos 2:1]); from falling rising up (see Mic 7:8)."

2. The apostle has connected the verses Hos 2:25 and Hos 2:1 in Rom 9:25f. as if they formed one passage in the underlying text. The same is found also in rabbinic literature. See, for example, Num. Rab. 2 (138C) above under #1, where Hos 2:6, 2:4, and 1:9 are bound together without any separation, as if they were one citation.

9:27 A: Isaiah calls (loudly).

κράζει = צָוַח; the latter appears in rabbinic literature extraordinarily frequently in compounds such as: "this or that prophet calls"[a] or "the holy spirit calls."[b]

a. ʾAggadat Berešit 69 § 1 (47B): "Isaiah calls ישעיה צווח: You deaf, listen ..." (Isa 42:18); see the whole passage at § Matt 11:5, #2. ‖ TanḥumaB, addition to the parashah דברים § 1 (2B): The prophet calls and says צווח ואומר: "Then the lame will leap like a deer ..." (Isa 35:6). — TanḥumaB, addition to the parashah דברים § 2 (2B): Therefore, Solomon calls צווח and says, "Faithfully meant are the wounds (rebukes) that come from one who loves" (Prov 27:6). ‖ Exodus Rabbah 41 (98A): And the prophet calls צווח: "Indeed from early on they committed all their misdeeds all the more zealously" (Zeph 3:7). ‖ Tanḥuma כי תשא 117A: The prophet calls צווח: "Who is a God who forgives guilt?" (Mic 7:18). ‖ Tanḥuma ויקרא 134A: Solomon calls צווח: "I saw the place of justice, there was godlessness" (Eccl 3:16).

b. See examples at § Luke 2:25 C, #4, notes *b* and *c*.

9:27 B and 28: If the number of the children of Israel is as the sand of the sea, (still only) the remnant will be saved; for the Lord will carry out a verdict completely and definitively on the earth.

Isaiah 10:22f.: "For if your people Israel were as the sand of the sea, (still only) a remnant of them will return. A wearing down is decided, overflowing with righteousness; for the Lord Yahweh Sabaoth will bring about an end and what has been decided in the midst of all the earth." — Targum: "For if your people Israel were as numerous as the sand of the sea, (still) great deeds that will prove mighty and lead to righteousness will be done (only) for the remnant that did not sin or who have turned from sin; for Yahweh Elohim Sabaoth will carry out destruction and extermination against all the godless on earth." — Septuagint: καὶ ἐὰν γένηται ὁ λαὸς Ἰσραὴλ ὡς ἡ ἄμμος τῆς θαλάσσης, τὸ κατάλειμμα αὐτῶν σωθήσεται, λόγον συντελῶν καὶ συντέμνων ἐν δικαιοσύνῃ, ὅτι λόγον συντετμημένον κύριος ποιήσει ἐν τῇ οἰκουμένῃ ὅλῃ.

9:29: If the Lord Sabaoth had not left seed for us, we would have become like Sodom and been made like Gomorrah.

Isaiah 1:9: "If Yahweh Sabaoth had not left a remnant for us, we would have become like a trifle, like Sodom, we would have been like Gomorrah." — Targum: "If the goodness of Yahweh Sabaoth had not left over, had not allowed a remnant to escape according to his mercy, there would be sins with us, so that we would perish as the people of Sodom and would be exterminated like the inhabitants of Gomorrah." — Septuagint: καὶ εἰ μὴ κύριος σαβαὼθ ἐγκατέλιπεν ἡμῖν σπέρμα, ὡς Σόδομα ἂν ἐγενήθημεν, καὶ ὡς Γόμοῤῥα ἂν ὡμοιώθημεν.

In b. Ber. 19A, Isa 1:9f. is used as the biblical basis for a superstitious principle: R. Simeon b. Laqish (ca. 250) said, and it has also been taught in the name of R. Yose (ca. 150) as a baraita, "Let a person never open his mouth in favor of Satan (give him no opportunity to accuse or harm)." Rab Joseph († 333) said, "What Scripture passage (is there for this idea)? Because it says, 'We would soon have become like Sodom, we would have been like Gomorrah'[135] (Isa 1:9). What does the prophet say to them after this? 'Hear the word of Yahweh, you regents of Sodom ...' (Isa 1:10)." — Meaning: In Isa 1:9, the prophet places Israel on the same level as Sodom and Gomorrah; Satan is thereby given the opportunity to try to bring Sodom's fate over Israel. To avert this calamity, the prophet in verse 10 no longer explicitly addresses Israel, but rather the regents of Sodom and the people of Gomorrah, in order to divert Satan's eyes from Israel.

9:33: Behold, I am laying in Zion a stone of offense and a rock of vexation, and whoever trusts in it will never be put to shame.

The citation is a combination of Isa 8:14[a] and Isa 28:16.[b] — In rabbinic literature the two passages are cited only rarely.[c]

a. Isaiah 8:14: "He (Yahweh) will become a sanctuary and a stone of offense and a rock of stumbling for both houses of Israel." — Targum: "And if you do not accept (it), his Memra (i.e., God himself) will become a punisher among you and a pummeling (quaking) stone and a rock of offense for both houses of the rulers of Israel." — Septuagint: κἂν ἐπ' αὐτῷ πεποιθὼς ᾖς, ἔσται σοι εἰς ἁγίασμα, καὶ οὐχ ὡς λίθου προσκόμματι συναντήσεσθε, οὐδὲ ὡς πέτρας πτώματι.

b. Isaiah 28:16: "Behold, I have established on Zion a stone, a stone of testing, a precious cornerstone of well-founded grounding: whoever believes (trusts) here will not (have to) depart." — Targum: "Behold, I am installing in Zion a king, a mighty king, a heroic and fearsome one; I will strengthen him and I will keep him. The prophet said, 'And the righteous in whom there is trust will not be shaken when tribulation comes.'" — Septuagint: Ἰδοὺ, ἐγὼ ἐμβάλλω εἰς τὰ θεμέλια Σιῶν λίθον πολυτελῆ, ἐκλεκτὸν, ἀκρογωνιαῖον, ἔντιμον, εἰς τὰ θεμέλια αὐτῆς, καὶ ὁ πιστεύων οὐ μὴ καταισχυνθῇ.

c. (α) Isaiah 8:14, see b. Sanh. 38A at § Luke 2:34 A. — (β) Isaiah 28:16. — Midrash Ecclesiastes 3:8 (17B): R. Joshua of Sikhnin (ca. 330) interpreted the Scripture passage (Eccl 3:1–8) in relation to Israel. "'There is a time to be born and a time to die' (Eccl 3:2). God said, 'For a brief time I was a midwife for my children' (see Ezek 16:4); 'and there is a time to die' (see Num 14:35; 26:65). 'There is a time to plant' (Eccl 3:2; see Amos 9:15); 'and there is a time to uproot what is planted' (Eccl 3:2; see Deut 29:27). 'There is a time to kill' (Eccl 3:3;

135. S-B: Against the accents, Rab Joseph relates כמעט to what follows.

see Lam 2:4); 'and there is a time to heal' (Eccl 3:3; see Jer 33:6). 'There is a time to tear down' (Eccl 3:3; see Amos 4:3); 'and there is a time to build' (Eccl 3:3; see Amos 9:11). 'There is a time to cry' (Eccl 3:4; see Lam 1:2); 'and there is a time to laugh' (Eccl 3:4; see Ps 126:2). 'There is a time to wail' (Eccl 3:4; see Isa 22:12); 'and there is a time to dance' (Eccl 3:4; see Zech 8:5). 'There is a time to cast stones' (Eccl 3:5; see Lam 4:1); 'and there is a time to gather stones' (Eccl 3:5), for it is written, 'Behold, I have established a stone on Zion, a stone of testing …' (Isa 28:16)." ‖ Deuteronomy Rabbah 3 (201A): R. Tanḥuma (ca. 380) said, "What does 'There is a time to cast stones' (Eccl 3:5) mean? This means the time when Hadrian—may his bones be crushed!—wished to go up to scatter the stones of the sanctuary (on the occasion of the founding of Aelia Capitolina). 'And there is a time to gather stones': this concerns the time when God will build that (the sanctuary). Where does this idea come from? Because it says, 'Therefore the Lord Yahweh has spoken thus, "Behold, I have established a stone on Zion, a stone of testing …"' (Isa 28:16f.)."

10:2: They have zeal for God, but not according to correct knowledge.

Every page of rabbinic literature is reminiscent of this word of the apostle. One is zealous for God and wants to serve him till the last breath, and yet one does not know God's ways and goes astray. This is the truly tragic element in the religious life of the Jewish people. And the reason? The veil of Moses hangs in front of their hearts (2 Cor 3:15). Nomism has taken the passions captive, and nomism kills. Let us single out prayer, for example. The people that sang the Old Testament psalms also created prayers in a later time, the beauty of which cannot be denied. But what is the most beautiful prayer if it is prayed to satisfy one's duty to pray! The prayer character of prayer needs to be preserved absolutely: it should be the child-like expression of a pious heart before the Father in heaven. But what does the loudest protest against everything statutory in prayer accomplish, when the halakah (the legal norm) can make the blessing of prayer depend on time and place, on posture and gesture. In devotional preparation, one seeks to acquire the right attitude for prayer, and despite this the legalistic spirit that standardizes everything determines the words of the prayer, which one can use to pray without devotion, and yet this somehow does not harm the activity of prayer. And the same applies to all areas of the religious-moral life. One zealously wishes to acquire one's own righteousness by the most painstaking observation of the law and yet forfeits true righteousness, which comes from God and therefore is valid before God. "They are zealous for God," as Luther translated Rom 10:2, "but foolishly."

10:4: Christ is the end of the law.

Babylonian Talmud Baba Meṣiʿa 85B–86A is only formally similar: In the book of the first human being (in which all Adam's progeny are supposedly recorded) it is written, "Rabbi († 217?) and R. Nathan (ca. 160) are the end of the Mishnah סוֹף מִשְׁנָה, Rab Ashi († 427) and Rabina (II, † 499) are the end of teaching סוֹף הוֹרָאָה (materially = end of the Gemarah). — These words do not mean, though—and herein lies the difference from Rom 10:4—that the Mishnah and Gemarah are abrogated with the named authors, but rather that they came to a conclusion with them, so that additional material may no longer be added.

10:5: Moses writes that the person who has done the righteousness from the law will live in it.

1. On δικαιοσύνη ἐκ νόμου and δικαιοσύνη τοῦ νόμου, see 2 Bar. 6:6 and T. Dan 6 at § Matt 5:20 A.

2. ὁ ποιήσας ἄνθρωπος ζήσεται ἐν αὐτῇ. — The basis for the citation is Lev 18:5: "Keep my statues and my laws, which a person should do and through which he will live," that is, which a person should do in order to live by means of them. The rabbinic authors related the words: "through which he will live" partly to eternal,[a] and partly to temporal[b] life.

a. Sifra Leviticus 18:5 (337A): "Keep my statues and my laws, which a person should do" (Lev 18:5): (this was said) to bind keeping and doing with the statutes and keeping and doing with the laws; "so that he may live by means of them" (Lev 18:5), namely in the future world. And if you should say, "In this world"—is his end not that he will die? How do I maintain, "so that he may live by means of them"? (By the interpretation:) In the future world. ‖ Targum Onkelos Leviticus 18:5: "You are to keep my statutes and my laws, which a person should do so that he may live by means of them in eternal life. I am Yahweh." ‖ Targum Yerušalmi I Leviticus 18:5: "You are to keep my statutes and my legal ordinances; for if a person does them, he will live by means of them in eternal life and his portion will be with the righteous. I am Yahweh." ‖ See b. Sanh. 58B at § Matt 5:43, #1.

b. Sifra Leviticus 18:5 (338B): "So that he may live by means of them" (Lev 18:5), not, "so that he may die by means of them (or: because of them)." R. Ishmael († ca. 135) said, "How can one say that if it is said to a person, 'Serve idols in private, lest you be killed,' he is permitted to commit the transgression in order not to be killed? Scripture teaches, 'So that he may live by means of them,' and not, 'so that he may die by means of them (because of them).' Or is he even permitted to obey them (and serve idols) openly? Scripture teaches, '"Do not profane my holy name (which would happen by open idolatry), so that I may be sanctified" (Lev 22:32). If you sanctify my name, I will also sanctify my name because of you.'" — Parallels are found in b. Sanh. 74A; b. ʿAbod. Zar. 27B. ‖ See b. Yoma 85A at § Matt 12:10, #2, n. *a.* ‖ Jerusalem Talmud Taʿanit 4.68D.4: R. Levi (ca. 300) said, "It is written, 'Which a person should do so that he may live by means of them' (Lev 18:15), and the light of a person's eye (full vision) returns (after a whole day of fasting) only after

40 days (so two whole days of fasting should not be scheduled within a 40-day period)." ‖ Babylonian Talmud ʿAbodah Zarah 54A: Raba († 352) said, "All (of the cases of idolatrous worship mentioned in the preceding section) are included in the general rule: 'You are not to let yourselves be brought to worship them (idols)' (Exod 20:5; 23:24; Deut 5:9). But if Scripture tells you specifically, 'So that he may live by means of them' (Lev 18:5), and not 'so that he may die by means of them (because of them),' duress (the case of compulsion) is excepted (from the general rule). Then the All Merciful One writes, 'You are not to desecrate my holy name' (Lev 22:32), which applies even in duress. How should this be understood? The one (Lev 18:5) applies when it (worship) happens secretly, the other (Lev 22:32) when it happens openly."

10:6–8: Do not say in your heart, "Who will ascend into heaven?" This means (would mean) to bring Christ down. Or "Who will descend into the abyss?" This means to bring Christ up from the dead. Rather, what does it (the righteousness of faith) say? "The word is near to you in your mouth and in your heart." This is the word of faith, which we proclaim.

1. The base passage is Deut 30:11–14: "For this commandment that I am commanding you today is not too wonderful for you and it is not far away. It is not in heaven so that one would have to say, 'Who will ascend to heaven and get it for us and let us hear it so that we may do it?' And it is not on the far side of the sea so that one would have to say, 'Who will travel across the sea for us and get it for us and let us hear it so that we may do it?' Rather, the word is very near to you, in your mouth and in your heart, so you may do it." — Targum Onkelos and Yerušalmi I translate the passage verbatim; only verse 14 paraphrases the last sentence: "For the word is near to you in your houses of learning; open your mouths to study them, purify your heart to do them." — Septuagint: ὅτι ἡ ἐντολὴ αὕτη, ἣν ἐγὼ ἐντέλλομαί σοι σήμερον, οὐχ ὑπέρογκός ἐστιν, οὐδὲ μακρὰν ἀπὸ σοῦ ἐστιν· οὐκ ἐν τῷ οὐρανῷ ἄνω ἐστὶ, λέγων, τίς ἀναβήσεται ἡμῖν εἰς τὸν οὐρανὸν καὶ λήψεται ἡμῖν αὐτὴν, καὶ ἀκούσαντες αὐτὴν ποιήσομεν; οὐδὲ πέραν τῆς θαλάσσης ἐστὶ, λέγων, τίς διαπεράσει ἡμῖν εἰς τὸ πέραν τῆς θαλάσσης, καὶ λάβῃ ἡμῖν αὐτὴν καὶ ἀκουστὴν ἡμῖν ποιήσῃ αὐτὴν, καὶ ποιήσομεν; ἐγγύς σου ἐστὶ τὸ ῥῆμα σφόδρα ἐν τῷ στόματί σου, καὶ ἐν τῇ καρδίᾳ σου, καὶ ἐν ταῖς χερσί σου ποιεῖν αὐτό.

2. Deut 30:11–14 in rabbinic literature.

Babylonian Talmud ʿErubin 55A: Abdima b. Hama b. Dosa (Hasa I, an Amoraic rabbi of an uncertain time) said, "What does 'It (the Torah) is not in heaven and it is not on the far side of the sea' (Deut 30:12–13) mean? 'It is not in heaven' because if it were in heaven, you would have to ascend to it (to get it). And if it were on the other side of the sea, you would have to cross over to it (to get it)." Raba († 352) said, "'It is not in heaven': it is not with the one who raises his mind (= himself) as high as heaven because of it. And it is not with the one who makes his mind wide as the sea because of it." R. Yohanan († 279) said, "'It is not in heaven': it is not with the proud. 'And it is not on the far side of the sea': it is not with the merchants and traders." ‖ Babylonian Talmud Temurah 116A (= 16A in other editions): Rab Judah († 299) said that Samuel († 254) said, "3,000 halakoth were forgotten in the days of mourning for Moses. Then they said to Joshua, 'Inquire (with God)!' He answered them, 'It is not in heaven' (but rather on earth; therefore, there is no disclosure from heaven about it). It was (later) said to Samuel, 'Inquire!' He answered them, 'These are the commandments which Yahweh … commanded … Moses for the children of Israel' (Lev 27:34), that is, that from now on no prophet is authorized to say something new (which is not contained in the Torah)." ‖ Deuteronomy Rabbah 8 (205B): "It is not in heaven" (Deut 30:12). Moses said to the Israelites, "Lest you say, 'Another Moses will arise and will bring another Torah to us from heaven,' I have already made known to you. 'It is not in heaven,' that is, that nothing of it remained in heaven." R. Hanina (ca. 225) said, "It and all its tools (i.e., the characteristics that are necessary for successful devotion to it) have been given: its humility (the humility necessary to study it), its righteousness, its integrity and its reward." What does "It is not in heaven" mean? Samuel († 254) said, "The Torah is not found among the astrologers whose occupation is bound to heaven." It was said to Samuel, "Look, you are an astrologer (though) and (also) a great one in the Torah!" He answered them, "I busied myself with astrological observation only at the time I was free from the Torah." "When was that?" "When I went to the place of urination." — "It is not in heaven." They said to him, "Our teacher Moses, look, you told us, 'It is not in heaven and it is not on the far side of the sea'; where is it then?" He answered them, "It is somewhere close: 'in your mouth and in your heart, so you may do it' (Deut 30:14). It is not far from you, it is near to you! 'In your mouth and in your heart, so you may do it.'" The scholars said, "Solomon said seven words about the sluggish man, but what Moses said was greater than them all. How so? It was said to the sluggish man, 'Your teacher is in the land,[136] go and learn Torah from him!' And he answered them and said to them, 'I fear the lion on the way.' Where does this come from? For it says, 'The sluggish man said, "There is a lion on the way"' (Prov 26:13). It was said to him, 'Look, your teacher is in the city,[137] get up and go to him!' He said to them, 'I fear there could be a lion in the streets'; as it says, 'A lion in the streets' (Prov 26:14). (The citation is imprecise.) It was said to him, 'Look, he lives near your house!' He answered them, 'But the lion is outside!'; as it says, 'The sluggish man said, "A lion is outside!"' (Prov 22:13). It was said to him, 'He (your teacher) is in the house!' He answered them, 'But if I go and find the door closed, I will have to go away again!' It was said to him, 'It is open.' Where does this come from? Because it says, 'The door turns on its hinge, but the lazy man lies on his bed' (Prov 26:14). When he at last no longer knew what he should answer, he said to them, 'Whether the door is open or closed, I want to sleep a little more.' Where does this come from? Because it says, 'How long, you sluggard, will you lie down …?' (Prov 6:9) When he got up in the morning from his sleep, his food was set before him.

136. S-B: עיר and the following מדינה should be transposed, as the progression requires moving from the more distant to the more proximate

137. S-B: See the previous footnote.

He was too lazy to put it in his mouth. Where does this come from? Because it says, 'If the sluggard has put his hand in the bowl, he is too lazy to bring it back to his mouth' (Prov 19:24). (The citation is imprecise.) And what is the seventh (word of Solomon)? 'With the start of fall, the sluggard does not plow, and so there is nothing there when he longs (for the harvest) at harvest time' (Prov 20:4)." What does "With the start of fall, the sluggard does not plow" mean? R. Simeon b. Yohai (ca. 150) said, "It means the one who did not study Torah in his youth and would like to learn in his old age but is not able to do so; such a man longs for the harvest and there is nothing there. But what Moses said was greater than them all. Where does this come from? 'For the word is very near to you, in your mouth and in your heart to do it' (Deut 30:14)." "It is near to you." R. Samuel b. Nahman (ca. 260) said, "What can this be compared with? With a king's daughter whom no one knew. But the king had a friend who was permitted to approach the king at any time, and then the king's daughter stood before him. The king said to him, 'See how I love you; for no one knows my daughter, and she stands before you!' So too God said to Israel, 'See how beloved you are to me; for no one in my palace knows the Torah, but I have given it to you; as it says, "She (Wisdom = Torah) is hidden from the eyes of every living thing" (Job 28:21). But as for you it holds, "It is not too wonderful for you" (Deut 30:11), but rather, "The word is very near to you" (Deut 30:14).' God said to them, 'My children, when the words of the Torah are near to you, I will call you too "near ones" (= relatives); for it is written, "For the children of Israel, the people that is near to him. Hallelujah!"' (Ps 148:14)." ‖ Babylonian Talmud ʿErubin 54A: R. Isaac (ca. 300) said, "From here (Prov 22:18 can be established): 'The word is very near to you, in your mouth and in your heart, to do it' (Deut 30:14). When is it near to you? When it is in your mouth and in your heart to do it." ‖ Tanḥuma וילך 27B: Elijah, of blessed memory, said, "Once I was on the way and met someone who ridiculed me and mocked me. I said to him, 'What will you answer on the day of judgment, after you have not studied the Torah?' He answered, 'I can respond, "Because no insight and no knowledge and no understanding were given to me from heaven."' I said to him, 'What is your occupation?' He answered, 'I am a bird- and fish-catcher.' I said to him, 'Who gave you knowledge and understanding to take flax and spin it and plait it and to make nets from it in order to catch fish and birds in them and to sell them?' He answered me, 'Because insight and knowledge has been granted me from heaven.' I said to him, 'To take flax, in order to plait and spin it, so you could catch fish and birds, insight and knowledge have been given to you, but to acquire the Torah you were given no insight, although it says, "For the word is very near to you, in your mouth and in your heart, to do it" (Deut 30:14)?' Immediately he thought about it in himself and raised his voice in tears. I said to him, 'My son, do not be dismayed; for against all who come into the world, if they wish to evade the Torah, punitive testimony is given by what is written, "They will be put to shame who work on heckled flax and weave linen!" (Isa 19:9).'" — There is a parallel passage in S. Eli. Zut. 14 (195). ‖ Babylonian Talmud Baba Meṣiʿa 59A deals with the imposition of the ban on R. Eliezer (ca. 90). In the report (see the whole passage in the excursus "Excommunication from the Synagogue") it says: R. Eliezer said to them, "If the halakah is in line with my opinion, one (= God) may prove it from heaven." Then a voice from heaven went out that called, "What is your problem with R. Eliezer? For in every case the halakah is in line with his view." Then R. Joshua arose to his feet and said, "'It is not in heaven (Torah)' (Deut 30:12)." What does "It is not in heaven" mean? R. Jeremiah (ca. 320) said, "The Torah was given long ago from Mount Sinai, we will not consider a voice from heaven. For long ago on Mount Sinai it was written in the Torah, 'One should incline to the majority' (so Exod 23:2C was interpreted)." — A parallel is found in briefer form in y. Moʿed Qaṭ. 3.81C.58: A voice from heaven went out that called, "The halakah is according to my son Eliezer!" R. Joshua said, "It is not in heaven" (the Torah, but rather in Israel's hand; therefore, heavenly things are not to meddle in the halakic decisions made by the scholars of Israel).

Allusions to Deut 30:11ff. may be present in the following passages. Babylonian Talmud Soṭah 35A: "But Caleb conciliated to Moses" (Num 13:30). Rabbah († 331) said, "He misled them by words. (He thought to himself:) When Joshua began to speak, they said to him, 'The head that has been cut off (allusion to Joshua's childlessness) wants to speak?!' So Caleb thought, 'If I speak now, they will say something against me and shut my mouth.' He (therefore) said to them (to bewilder them), 'How is it that the son of Amram did just this to us?' They thought that he was speaking to curse him and they stayed silent (let him keep talking). He said to them, 'He led us out of Egypt and split the sea for us and gave us manna to eat. If he said, "Make leaders and ascend to heaven," would we not obey him? "We will surely go up and take it (the land of Israel) into possession" (Num 13:30).'" ‖ A baraita in b. Giṭ. 84A: (If someone says to his wife,) "Look, this is your letter of divorce on the condition that you ascend to heaven שתעלי לרקיע, on the condition that you descend to the abyss שתרדי לתהום, on the condition that you swallow reeds 4 cubits long, on the condition that you bring me a reed 100 cubits long, on the condition that you go across the world sea with your feet (by foot)," then it is not a letter of divorce (because the conditions are unfulfillable). The same is found in a different form in b. B. Meṣ. 94A. ‖ Baruch 3:29ff.: "Who ascended to heaven and got it (φρόνησις = cleverness) and brought it down out of the clouds? Who went across the sea and found it to bring it here for precious gold? There is no one who would know the way to it or perceive the path to it."

3. τίς ἀναβήσεται εἰς τὸν οὐρανόν; A question that denotes the impossible.

Sifre Deuteronomy 11:22 § 49 (85A): "And hold fast to him" (Deut 11:22). How so? Is it possible for a person to ascend to the heights לעלות במרום and hold fast to him? — See also b. Giṭ. 84A in #2 toward the end.

4. τίς καταβήσεται εἰς τὴν ἄβυσσον; The apostle substitutes this question for the line in the base text, "Who will go across to the other side of the sea for us?", because the latter does not relate to the story of Jesus. This change would have appeared all the more harmless to the apostle, since he does not use Deut 30:11–14 as an actual citation and as a proof text for his view, but rather simply as a rhetorical form in which he clothes his own thoughts. Thus, as shown by the words τοῦτ᾽ ἔστιν Χριστὸν ἐκ νεκρῶν

ἀναγαγεῖν, the apostle uses ἄβυσσος as a synonym for שְׁאוֹל = ᾅδης,[a] while otherwise most of the time it corresponds to תְּהוֹם = the deep.[b]

a. Septuagint Psalm 71:20: καὶ ἐπιστρέψας ἐζωοποίησάς με καὶ ἐκ τῶν ἀβύσσων τῆς γῆς (depths of the earth = Sheol, base text: מתהומות הארץ) πάλιν ἀνήγαγές με.

b. Septuagint Psalm 106:26: ἀναβαίνουσιν ἕως τῶν οὐρανῶν καὶ καταβαίνουσιν ἕως τῶν ἀβύσσων = תְּהוֹמוֹת. ‖ (Greek) Sirach 24:5: "I (Wisdom) alone encompassed the circle of heaven, and I walked in the depth of the abysses ἐν βάθει ἀβύσσων." ‖ (Hebrew) Sirach 16:18: "Behold, heaven and the heaven of heavens and the deep תהום and the earth tremble, when he steps on them." — The Greek is 16:16: ἰδοὺ ὁ οὐρανὸς καὶ ὁ οὐρανὸς τοῦ οὐρανοῦ, ἄβυσσος καὶ γῆ ἐν τῇ ἐπισκοπῇ αὐτοῦ (= at his sight) σαλευθήσονται. — See also above at #2 toward the end the contrast רקיע and תהום = heaven and the deep (ἄβυσσος) in b. Giṭ. 84A.

5. ἐν τῷ στόματί σου καὶ ἐν τῇ καρδίᾳ σου, verbatim according to Deut 30:14: בְּפִיךָ וּבִלְבָבְךָ. The LXX adds a third term: ἐν τῷ στόματί σου καὶ ἐν τῇ καρδίᾳ σου καὶ ἐν ταῖς χερσί σου "and in your hands." Philo adopted this addition in *De poenit.* § 2 (Mangey's ed., 2:406) without anything further and interprets στόμα in relation to the words, καρδία in relation to the expressions of the will, and χεῖρες in relation to a person's works.

10:11: "Everyone who trusts in him will not be put to shame" (Isa 28:16).

On Isa 28:16, see § Rom 9:33, n. *b.* — οὐ καταισχυνθήσεται. In y. Ber. 4.7D.28 R. Nehuniah b. Haqqanneh (ca. 70) closes a prayer with the words, "(May it be pleasing before you) that we do not forbid what is allowed and do not allow what is forbidden, and I would thus be found as one who will be ashamed (put to shame) מתבייש in this and in the future world." — See the whole prayer at § Matt 11:26.

10:13: Everyone who calls on the name of the Lord will be saved (obtain salvation).

The base passage is Joel 3:5: "And it will happen that everyone who calls on the name of Yahweh will be saved (escape) יִמָּלֵט." — Targum: "And it will happen that everyone who prays with (in) the name of Yahweh will be saved (escape)." — The apostle's citation corresponds precisely to the LXX. — Some rabbinic scholars interpreted Joel 3:5 as follows: Whoever is called by Yahweh's name (יִקְרָא is read as יִקָּרֵא) will be saved. See supporting passages at § Acts 2:17–21, section: Joel 3:5.

10:15: How beautiful are the feet of those who proclaim what is good as good news.

The base passage is Isa 52:7: "How beautiful on the mountains are the feet of the messenger of joy, who proclaims peace, who announces good news, who proclaims salvation, who says to Zion, 'Your God has become kind!'" — See the targum translation at § Rom 1:1 D, #3, n. *a*. — Septuagint: ὡς ὥρα ἐπὶ τῶν ὀρέων, ὡς πόδες εὐαγγελιζομένου ἀκοὴν εἰρήνης, ὡς εὐαγγελιζόμενος ἀγαθά, ὅτι ἀκουστὴν ποιήσω τὴν σωτηρίαν σου, λέγων, Σιὼν βασιλεύσει σου ὁ θεός. — In rabbinic literature, Isa 52:7 was almost without exception interpreted in relation to the messianic time. See Pesiq. Rab. 35 (161A); Leqach Tob on Num 24:17 at § Rom 1:1 D, #3, n. *b*; Der. Er. Zut., last chapter; Pesiq. 51A.20; and Pirqe Mashiaḥ at § Rom 1:1 D, #3, n. *c*.

Isaiah 52:7 is drawn into the service of superstition in b. Ber. 56B: R. Joshua b. Levi (ca. 250) said, "... Whoever has seen a mountain in a dream, let him say as soon as it is morning (after waking up), 'How beautiful on the mountain are the feet of the messenger of peace ...' before the other verse comes to his mind, 'I will raise weeping and wailing over the mountains' (Jer 9:9)." (The Scripture verse that first comes to someone's mind after waking up makes the content of the dream be fulfilled for good or evil.) See the whole passage at § Matt 1:20, n. *m*.

10:16: "Who has believed our message" (Isa 53:1)?

Isaiah 53:1: Who has believed our message לִשְׁמֻעָתֵנוּ (= the news that has come to us)? — Targum: "Who has believed our message לִבְסוֹרְתָנָא (= the proclamation that has come to us)?" — Septuagint: κύριε τίς ἐπίστευσε τῇ ἀκοῇ ἡμῶν; = "who has believed our message (what has been heard by us)?"

10:17 A: So faith comes from the message.

1. ἀκοή, 1. Hearing, 2. What has been heard and passed on as something heard = news, message, information, proclamation; synonyms: ἀγγελία and κήρυγμα. See supporting passages in Cremer, *Wörterbuch*, under ἀκοή. — The rabbinic equivalent is שְׁמוּעָה, Aram. שְׁמוּעֲתָא, a. = news, message; b. specifically, and most of the time = traditional teaching, tradition.

a. Mishnah Berakot 9.2: In the case of good news בְּשׂוֹרוֹת טוֹבוֹת one says this word of praise, "Blessed be the One who is good and who shows good!" and in the case of bad news שְׁמוּעוֹת הָרָעוֹת the one who says, "Blessed be the true judge!" ‖ Targum 1 Samuel 2:24: "The message שמועתא which I am hearing is not right (seemly)."

b. Mishnah 'Eduyyot 5.7: (Aqabia b. Mahalalel [ca. 70] said to his son,) "I have heard from the mouth of a majority, and they (my opponents) have heard from the mouth of a majority. I insisted on my tradition בשמועתי (on the traditional teaching that had come to me), and they insisted on their tradition." ‖ Babylonian Talmud Sanhedrin 88A: Rab Kahana (ca. 250) said, "If he (the dissenting scholar) says (his opinion) on the basis of tradition (traditional teaching מפי השמועה) and they (the opponents) say (their opinion likewise) on the basis of tradition, he will not be killed. If he says, 'It is thus according to my view (which has been acquired by one's own judgment)' and they say, 'It is thus according to our view,' he will not be killed. And even less if he speaks on the basis of tradition, while they say, 'It is thus according to our view.' He will be killed only when he says, 'It is thus according to my view,' while they speak on the basis of tradition." You can recognize from this that

Aqabia b. Mahalalel (see the previous citation) was not killed. R. Eleazar (ca. 270, so read instead of R. Eliezer) said, “Even if he speaks on the basis of tradition, while they say, ‘It is thus according to our view,’ he will be killed, so that disputes (factions) may not multiply in Israel. And if you should say, ‘Why was Aqabia b. Mahalalel not killed?,’ it did not happen because he did not teach the halakah for praxis.” (The dissenting scholar is killed only if he does not retreat from his opinion and if he acts and teaches others to act according to it, although it is rejected by the majority.) ‖ In b. Ḥag. 14A גיבור “hero” in Isa 3:2 is interpreted as = בַּעַל שְׁמוּעוֹת “bearer of many traditional teachings.” ‖ Jerusalem Talmud Pe’ah 3.17D.10: R. Yose b. Abun (ca. 350) said in the name of R. Yohanan († 279), “The traditional teaching שְׁמוּעֲתָא is as follows, ‘Whoever has no ground and soil is freed from the confession (prescribed in Deut 26:5ff.), because it is written: “From the soil that you have given me” (Deut 26:10; and he cannot say this since he does not possess any land).” ‖ In y. Roš Haš. 2.58B.7, מרה דשמועתא (= בעל שמועה above in b. Ḥag. 14A) designates the one who knows or bears many traditional teachings.

2. Just as שמועה, שמועתא is a technical term for the rabbis for “traditional teaching” according to the passages above, so too ἀκοή in specific NT passages perhaps should be understood simply as a technical term for “the gospel’s teaching of salvation.” Outside of Rom 10:17, see also Gal 3:2, 5; 1 Thess 2:13; and Heb 4:2.

3. ἄρα ἡ πίστις ἐξ ἀκοῆς. — The preaching of the salvific teaching is always the fundamental thing. Similarly, Mek. Exod. 15:26 (54A): R. Eleazar of Modiim († ca. 135) said, (“‘If listening you listen אִם שָׁמוֹעַ תִּשְׁמַע, that is, if you listen carefully to the voice of Yahweh your God’ [Exod 15:26]:) ‘If listening you’: perhaps optionally? Scripture teaches: ‘You listen’: it is a duty, not an option. ‘You listen’: this is the general ground rule כְּלָל (principle) with which the Torah (teaching of religion) is concerned.” — Listening to the Torah is the fundamental thing and therefore in principle the most important thing; for from hearing follow later studying and doing. See b. Qidd. 40B: Is studying (the Torah) more important or carrying it out? R. Aqiba († ca. 135) said, “Studying is more important.” All answered, “Studying is more important; for studying leads to carrying out.” On this point, see § Rom 2:13, #2.

10:17 B: But the message comes by the word of Christ.

The tidings that is the message of salvation comes by the word of Christ, in that the latter underlies the former. This can be compared with Num 24:4: “The saying of one who listens to (hears) God’s words” נְאֻם שֹׁמֵעַ אִמְרֵי אֵל. — The saying comes about by the one concerned hearing God’s words. — Targum Onkelos and Yerušalmi I: “A word of one who hears a word from before God.” — Septuagint: φησὶν ἀκούων λόγια ἰσχυροῦ.

10:19: "I will make you jealous of those who are not a people, with a foolish people I will provoke you to anger."

1. Deuteronomy 32:21: "And I will make you jealous by those who are not a people, by a foolish people I will slight you." — Targum Onkelos translates verbatim. — Targum Yerušalmi I: "And I will make you jealous by a nation that is not a nation, by the Babylonians; a foolish people will provoke you to anger." — Septuagint: κἀγὼ παραζηλώσω αὐτοὺς ἐπ' οὐκ ἔθνει, ἐπὶ ἔθνει ἀσυνέτῳ παροργιῶ αὐτούς.

2. Interpretations: (Hebrew) Sirach 50:25f.: "Against two peoples my soul feels disgust and the third is not a people: against the inhabitants of Seir and Philistia and 'the foolish people' גוי נבל (Deut 32:21) that dwells in Shechem (= Samaritans)." — The Greek is the same verbatim. ‖ Sifre Deuteronomy 32:21 § 320 (137A): "I will make them jealous by those who are not a people בְלֹא־עָם" (Deut 32:21). Do not read בלא עם, but rather בְלוֹי עַם "a reprobate people";[138] these are those who come from peoples and governments and take them (the Israelites) out of their houses (allusion to confiscations?). A different explanation is as follows: "By those who are not a people": these are those who come (stem) from Barbary and from Tunisia and from Mauretania who go about naked on the street; there is no one who is more despicable and reprehensible in the world than one who goes about naked on the street. "By a foolish people I will slight them" (Deut 32:21): these are the heretics המינים. Likewise, it says, "The fool says in his heart, 'There is no God'" (Ps 14:1). ‖ Babylonian Talmud Yebamot 63B: "By a foolish people I will slight them" (Deut 32:21). Rab Hanan bar Rabbah (ca. 250) said that Rab († 247) said, "It is a wicked wife whose prescribed marital sum is so big (that the husband, if he does not have the means to pay for the wedding, cannot dismiss the wife by divorce papers)." R. Eleazar (ca. 270) said, "The heretics are meant, and likewise it says, 'The fool says in his heart, "There is no god"' (Ps 14:1)." In a baraita (the Sifre passage above is meant) it has been taught: "These are the people of Barbary and the people of Mauretania who go about naked on the street, for there is no one who is more of an abomination and an abhorrence before God than someone who goes about naked on the street." R. Yohanan († 279) said, "These are the donors (Persians)." When it was said to R. Yohanan, "The donors have come to Babylon," he was horrified and collapsed. It was said to him, "They accept gifts (bribery)!" Then he stood up and calmed down.

10:20: I was found by those who did not seek me, I was revealed to those who did not ask about me.

1. Isaiah 65:1: "I was inquired about by those who did not ask (about me); I was found by those who did not seek me." — Targum: "I myself was inquired about מֵימְרִי by those who did not ask from before me (= about me); I looked for the teachers of my Torah among those who did not seek reverence before me." — Septuagint Codex B: ἐμφανὴς ἐγενήθην τοῖς ἐμὲ

138. S-B: In Yalquṭ Simeoni on Deut 32:21 § 945, a gloss inserted into the text explains: "The most despicable who are between the nations" הבזוין שבין האומות.

μὴ ἐπερωτῶσιν, εὑρέθην τοῖς ἐμὲ μὴ ζητοῦσιν. – Codex A reverses the two clauses of the statement, just like the apostle Paul.

2. Interpretation. As the opposing πρὸς δὲ τὸν Ἰσραὴλ λέγει in verse 21 shows, Isa 65:1 is related to the gentile world. That this is entirely permissible from the wording and context of Isa 65:1–2 should not be denied. The LXX also appears to have followed this interpretation, whereas the targum Isa 65:1 doubtlessly thought of Israel. In ancient rabbinic literature, we have found only two passages that refer to Isa 65:1; one interprets the word of the prophet in relation to Israel[a] and the other to non-Israelites.[b]

a. Midrash Psalm 10 § 2 (46B): R. Jonathan (ca. 220) said, "For three and a half years the Shekinah (divinity) had spoken and proclaimed, 'Seek Yahweh, as long as he may be found!' (Isa 55:6); but no one was there who bothered with this. And likewise, it says, 'I was inquired about by those who did not ask (about me); I was found by those who did not seek me' (Isa 65:1) …." (See the whole passage at § Luke 11:7.) The saying of R. Jonathan, though without citing Isa 65:1, is found also in Midr. Lam. Intro. #25 (39A) and Pesiq. Rab. 31 (143B).

b. Yalquṭ Simeoni on Ruth 1:1 (2 § 596 at the end) from Midr. Ruth (zuṭa): R. Tanḥuma (ca. 380) opened his talk with, "'I was inquired about by those who did not ask (about me)' (Isa 65:1): this is Rahab, the prostitute. 'I was found by those who did not seek me' (Isa 65:1): this is Ruth, the Moabite, who did not go out of the world before she had seen Solomon."

11:1 A: Has God not abandoned his people? Far from it.

1. On the expression, see, for example, Ps 94:14: "For Yahweh will not abandon his people לֹא יִטּוֹשׁ י״י עַמּוֹ." – Targum: לָא יִנְטוֹשׁ י״י עַמֵּיהּ. – Septuagint: οὐκ ἀπώσεται κύριος τὸν λαὸν αὐτοῦ.

2. It is impossible for God to abandon his people.

Babylonian Talmud Pesaḥim 87A: God said to Hosea, "Your children have sinned." He should have answered him, "They are your children, the children of Abraham, of Isaac, and of Jacob, heave your mercy upon them!" It is not enough that he did not so speak; he also said more before him, "Lord of the world, the whole world is yours, replace them with another nation!" God said, "What should I do with this old man? I will say to him, 'Go and take (for yourself) a wife of whoredom and beget children of whoredom.' And then I will say to him, 'Send them away from your face!' If he can send them away, I too will send Israel away." For it says, "Yahweh said to Hosea, 'Take for yourself a wife of whoredom and children of whoredom'" (Hos 1:2). And further it is written, "He went and took Gomer, the daughter of Diblaim.… And she became pregnant and bore a son. And Yahweh said to him, 'Name him "Jezreel"'" (Hos 1:3f.).… "Then she became pregnant again and bore a daughter, and Yahweh said to him, 'Name her "Unpardoned"; for I will no longer have mercy on the house of Israel, so that I should always forgive them'" (Hos 1:6). "And she became pregnant and bore a son, and Yahweh said to him, 'Name him, "Not my people,"' for you are not my people, and I will not be yours" (Hos 1:8f.). After two sons and a daughter had been born to him, God said to Hosea, "Should you not have learned from your teacher Moses? For after I had spoken with him, he separated himself from his wife. You also, separate yourself from her!" He answered him, "Lord of the world, I have children from her, and I cannot send her away and abandon her לגרשה (dismiss her by a bill of divorce)." God said to him, "If you, whose wife is a whore and whose children are children of whoredom, do not know which of these are yours or someone else's, (you declare yourself) you say concerning the Israelites who are the children's children of my approved ones, Abraham, Isaac, and Jacob, one of the four possessions[139] that I have acquired in my world …, 'Replace them with another nation?'…" ‖ Midrash Psalm 94 § 3 (209B): "Yahweh will not abandon his people and will not leave his inheritance" (Ps 94:14). And a (different) Scripture passage says, "For Yahweh will not abandon לא יטוש his people, for the sake of his great name" (1 Sam 12:22). R. Aybo (ca. 320) and R. Samuel b. Nahmani (ca. 260) said, "When the Israelites do God's will, he acts because of his people and his inheritance. And when they have no good works, he acts for the sake of his great name. Our teachers said, 'For the people abroad he acts because of his great name and for the people in the land of Israel he acts because of his people and his inheritance.' Therefore, 'For Yahweh will not abandon his people.'" — A parallel is found in Midr. Ruth 1:6 (127A). ‖ Also see Midr. Abba Gurion 41A at § Matt 4:17 A, #1, middle of paragraph 2; Midr. Ha-gadol on Lev 26:9 at § Rom 2:19f., #2, n. *c*.

11:1 B: From the tribe of Benjamin.

The tribe of Benjamin is exalted for its glorious deed of going down into the sea before all the other tribes when the children of Israel passed through the Red Sea. As a repayment for this, the temple was built in its territory.

Mekilta Exodus 14:22 (37B): R. Meir (ca. 150) said, "When the tribes stood at the sea, one said, 'I will go down into the sea first,' and the other said, 'I will go down into the sea first!' While they stood there and called out, the tribe of Benjamin sprang down into the sea first; as it says, 'There Benjamin, the small, רוֹדֵם, the princes of Judah רִגְמָתָם, the princes of Zebulun, the princes of Naphtali. Your God has summoned your strength; strength, O God, what you have worked for us' (Ps 68:28f.). Do not read רוֹדֵם (there ruler?), but rather: רֵד יָם = climb down into the sea (or רָד יָם = he climbed down into the sea). Then the princes of Judah began to pelt them with stones; as it says, 'The princes of Judah, their stone-throwing' (so רִגְמָתָם is understood). A parable. What can this be compared with? With a king of flesh and blood who had two sons; the one was big (grown-up) and the other was small (young). He entered his chamber during the night, and he said to the small one, 'Get me up (= wake me up) with the shining forth of the sun,' and to the big one he said, 'Get me up at the third hour (= 9 o'clock according to our counting).' The small one came to get him up with the shining forth of the sun; but the big one did not let him. He said to him, 'He said to me only, "At the third hour of the day."' And the small one said to him, 'He said to me only, "With the shining forth of the sun."' While they stood and spoke loudly, their father became alert. He said to them, 'My sons, you both have only my honor in view. I too will not detract from your recompense.' God spoke just in this way. What repayment did the

---

139. S-B: Aside from Israel, the following are mentioned as such: the Torah, heaven and earth, and the sanctuary.

sons of Benjamin receive for going down into the sea first? The Shekinah (divinity dwelt in their portion [tribal territory]); for it says, 'Benjamin is a wolf that tears apart' (Gen 49:27).[140] Furthermore, it says, 'And concerning Benjamin he said, "The darling of Yahweh dwells securely with him (God) ..."' (Deut 33:12; on this cf. b. Menaḥ. 53A at § Rom 1:7 B)." — Parallels are found in b. Soṭah 36B.42; Pirqe R. El. 42 (24A); Midr. Ps. 68 § 14 (160B); Tg. Ps. 68:28. — A different motive is given for the construction of the temple in Benjamin's territory in SDeut 33:12 § 352 (146A): Why was Benjamin worthy of having the Shekinah dwell in his portion? Like a king who came to his sons at certain times; each one said, "He will dwell with me." The smallest (youngest) among them all said, "Is it possible that my father would leave behind my adult brother and dwell with me?" He went and stood there with a downcast face and his soul was saddened. His father saw him, how he stood there with a downcast face, while his soul in him was saddened. He said, "Have you seen my youngest son, how he stands there with a downcast face, while his soul in him is saddened? Now (my) food and drink are to come from what belongs to you, but my dwelling (night quarters) are to be with him." God spoke in just this say, "The house of choosing בֵּית הַבְּחִירָה (= temple) is to be in the portion of Benjamin and the offerings from all tribes." A different explanation. Why was Benjamin worthy of having the Shekinah dwell in his portion? Because all the patriarchs were born abroad, but Benjamin was born in the land of Israel. A different explanation. Why was Benjamin worthy of having the Shekinah dwell in his portion? Because all the patriarchs were there when they sold Joseph, but Benjamin was not there when they sold Joseph. God said, "If I tell those ones to build the house of choosing, I will not be filled with mercy for them when they pray before me, and I will not make my Shekinah dwell in their portion, because they did were not merciful toward their brother." A different explanation. Why was Benjamin worthy of having the Shekinah dwell in his portion? Like a king who had many sons. When they had grown up, each one of them came and took his place (or: took possession of his place). The father loved the smallest (youngest) of them all. He ate with him and drank with him, he leaned on him when he went out, he leaned on him when he returned home. So was Benjamin, the righteous, the youngest among the patriarchs, and our father Jacob ate with him and drank with him, leaned on him when he went out, leaned on him when he returned home. God said, "In the place where this righteous one (Jacob) rested his hands (Benjamin's shoulders) I will make my Shekinah dwell." This is why it says, "And he dwells between his shoulders" (Deut 33:12).

11:2: What does Scripture say in the case of Elijah?

ἐν Ἠλείᾳ is not (as in ἐν τῷ Ἡσαΐᾳ in Mark 1:2 or ἐν τῷ Ὡσηέ in Rom 9:25) "in" Elijah, but rather "in the case of" Elijah. In citing passages,

---

140. S-B: For a proof, see Gen. Rab. 99 (63A): R. Phineas (ca. 360) interpreted the passage (Gen 49:27) in relation to the altar (in the temple): "As the wolf by itself tears apart, so too the altar tore apart the offerings by itself; 'in the morning he consumes robbery' (Gen 49:27), (correspondingly:) 'You shall prepare the first lamb in the morning' (Num 24:4); "and in the evening he apportions the spoil,' (correspondingly:) 'And you shall prepare a second lamb between the two evenings' (Num 24:4)." — Benjamin is thus compared with a wolf that tears apart because the temple with an altar that consumed the sacrifices was in Benjamin's tribal territory. On the comparison altar = wolf, see also the baraita in b. Sukkah 56B at § Luke 1:5 A, #1, n. *b*.

the rabbis likewise use the preposition בְּ = "in the case of"[a] (or: "about"), more rarely גַּבֵּי = "in the case of."[b]

a. Midrash Song of Songs 1:6 (88A): In the same way it is written in the case of Elijah כתיב באליהו; as it says, "I have been very zealous for Yahweh, God of Israel. For they have forsaken your covenant, the children of Israel" (so 1 Kgs 19:10 is cited). God said to him, "My covenant (they have forsaken), or perhaps your covenant? 'And your altars they have destroyed' (1 Kgs 19:10)." He answered him, "My altars, or perhaps your altars? 'And your prophets they have killed with the sword' (1 Kgs 19:10)." He answered him, "My prophets, (thus) what concern is that to you? 'And I alone am left over and they seek to take my soul' (1 Kgs 19:10). Come and see, what is written there? 'And he looked and behold, at his head was a roasted cake' עוגת רצפים (1 Kgs 19:6)." What does רצפים mean? Rab Samuel b. Nahman (ca. 260) said, "It means רוץ פה 'to dent the mouth': dent the yaps of all who (like Elijah) bring forth boasts against my children!" ‖ Mishnah ʾAbot 3.7: R. Eleazar b. Judah of Bartota (in Upper Galilee, ca. 110) said, "Give him (God) from what is his; for you and what is yours belongs to him. And likewise (Scripture) says in the case of David בְּדָוִד, 'For from you is everything, and from your hand we have given to you' (1 Chr 29:14)." ‖ Mishnah Taʿanit 2.1: In the case of the people of Nineveh it does not say לא נאמר באנשי נינוה: "God saw their sackcloth and their fasting," but rather, "God saw their works, that they turned from their evil ways." ‖ Additional examples are found in SDeut 11:13 § 41 (80A); Pesiq. 126B; see also § Mark 12:26.

b. Babylonian Talmud Berakot 7B: In the case of the war of Gog and Magog it is written גבי מלחמת גוג ומגוג כתיב: "Why do the gentiles rage? ..." (Ps 2:1). — See the whole passage at § Matt 1:1 B, #2.

11:4: "Who have not bowed their knee before Baal" (1 Kgs 19:18).

τῇ Βάαλ. — The LXX has the masculine τῷ Βάαλ in 1 Kgs 19:18, but it also uses the feminine in, for example, Hos 2:8 (= 2:10 in the original text); Zeph 1:4; plural αἱ Βααλίμ in 1 Sam 7:4 = images of Baal. — In Tob 1:5, ἡ Βάαλ is elucidated by the word that stands alongside it: δάμαλις = cow- or calf-shaped idol of Baal. — Since עֲבוֹדָה זָרָה, the most general designation for "idol" in rabbinic literature, was feminine, it immediately suggested itself to treat every image of an idol linguistically as feminine. So בַּעַל פְּעוֹר (Baal Peor) and מַרְקוּלִיס (stone heap of Mercury) were masculine; nevertheless, it says in the Mishnah text in b. Sanh. 60B (ed. Frankfurt am Main 1720ff.): When someone empties himself before Baal Peor, this is "her" cult עֲבוֹדָתָהּ; and when someone throws a stone on the stone heap of Mercury, this is "her" cult עבודתה. — Thus, בעל פעור and מרקוליס are here viewed as feminine without further explanation; however, the Amsterdam edition (1644ff.) and Strack in *Sanhedrin-Makkoth* (7.6)[141] read the masculine suffix.

141. Hermann Strack, *Sanhedrin-Makkoth. "Gerichtshof, Geißelstrafe"* (Munich: Hinrich, 1910).

11:9: “May their table become a snare and a trap, an offense and a retribution.”

1. The base passage is Ps 69:23: “May their table become a noose before them and a snare for the secure שְׁלוֹמִים.” — Targum: “May their table, which they dress before me with food, become a trap before them and their (sacrificial) slaughtering (שְׁלוֹמִים is interpreted as = שְׁלָמִים “peace meal offering”) an offense.” — Septuagint: “May their table become a trap before them and a retribution εἰς ἀνταπόδοσιν (שְׁלוֹמִים is interpreted as = שִׁלּוּמִים “retributions”) and an offense.”

2. The table is to serve to atone for the Israelite.

Babylonian Talmud Berakot 55A: “The altar of wood, three cubits high” (Ezek 41:22); and it is also written, “He said to me, ‘This is the table that stands before Yahweh’” (Ezek 41:22). He began with “altar” and closed with “table.” R. Yohanan († 279) and R. Eleazar (ca. 270), they both said, “As long as the sanctuary endured, the altar made atonement for Israel; but now a person’s table makes atonement for him.” — Targum Yerušalmi I Exodus 40:6 shows how this should be understood: “Place the altar of burnt offering before the entrance of the tabernacle: (this is said) because of the rich who prepare the table before their doors and care for the poor, and it will remit their guilt for them (forgive their sin), as if they offered a burnt offering on the altar.”

11:11: By their falling salvation has been bestowed on the gentiles.

See b. Pesaḥ. 87B at § Matt 23:15 A, n. *c*, as well as the citations at § Matt 21:43. ‖ Babylonian Talmud Sanhedrin 98B: “Ask and see if a man gives birth! Why do I see every man with his hands on his hips like a woman who gives birth and all their faces have turned deathly pale?” (Jer 30:6). What does “I see every man” mean? Rabbah b. Isaac said that Rab († 247) said, “This means the one to whom all power belongs (i.e., God, who takes an inner interest in the final fate of the nations of the world).” And what does ‘all their faces have turned deathly pale’ mean? R. Yohanan († 279) said, “This means the family above (the angelic world) and the family below (Israel) in the hour when God will say, ‘These ones (the Israelites) are the work of my hands and those ones (the non-Israelites) are the work of my hands. How should I destroy these ones (the non-Israelites) for the sake of those ones!’” (This word will frighten the angelic world and Israel.) Rab Papa († 376) said, “This is what the people say, ‘If the ox runs and falls, then one goes and puts a horse at its manger.’” (By Israel’s fall, the nations stepped into its place. Rashi says in more detail, “God feels pain in himself like a woman giving birth and says in the hour when he will eliminate the nations because of Israel, ‘How can I destroy those ones because of these ones!…’ If the ox runs and falls, one puts a horse in its place at its manger, which one would not have intended to do before the ox fell, because his ox is dearer to him. But if the ox is healed from its fall today or tomorrow, it is hard for one to remove his horse because of the ox after one had set it there. So too God, when he saw Israel’s fall, he gave her greatness to the nations of the world, and when the Israelites turn in repentance, God finds it hard to destroy the nations of the world because of the Israelites.”)

11:15: If their rejection has meant reconciliation of the world, what is their acceptance except life from the dead?

ἡ ἀποβολή ... ἡ πρόσλημψις.

Sirach 10:20 gloss: προσλήψεως ἀρχὴ φόβος κυρίου, ἐκβολῆς δὲ ἀρχὴ σκληρυσμός καὶ ὑπερηφανία = "the fear of the Lord is the beginning of acceptance, but hardness and pride are the beginning of rejection."

11:16 A: If the leaven is holy, so too is the dough.

1. ἀπαρχή = תְּרוּמָה "offering," for example, in LXX Exod 25:2f.; here specifically the dough offering = חַלָּה (Num 15:18ff.), see the section about the dough offering in the excursus "Taxes on Produce from the Soil." — φύραμα = עִסָּה "dough."

2. By ἀπαρχή or חַלָּה, Abraham is meant; by φύραμα, the people of Israel that stems from him is meant. The designation of a person as *ḥallah* is found also in rabbinic literature, where Adam is called the dough offering of the world. See the end of the section "dough offering" in the above-mentioned excursus.

11:16 B: If the root is holy, so too are the branches.

In the pseudepigrapha Israel is sometimes called the "plant of righteousness,"[a] the "root" of which is Abraham[b] and which will one day be in the fullest sense what this name signifies, at the time of the eschatological consummation.[c] — The designation of Abraham as עִקָּרוֹ שֶׁל עוֹלָם, which in itself could mean "root of the world," actually means the "principal thing of the world."[d] — See the parallel to Rom 11:16 (B) in Mek. Exod. 15:2 (44B) at § Rom 9:6, n. *b*.

a. 1 Enoch 10:16: "Every evil work will come to an end (by the flood) and the plant of righteousness and truth (i.e., Israel) will appear." — 1 Enoch 84:6: "Raise up the flesh of righteousness and uprightness (= Israel) as an eternal seed plant and do not hide your face from the pleading of your servant (Enoch), O Lord!" — See also the citations in notes *b* and *c*.

b. 1 Enoch 93:2, 5, 8, 10: "Enoch said, 'Concerning the children of righteousness, concerning the elect of the world, and concerning the plant of righteousness and uprightness—of this I will speak to you....' After this at the end of the third week (= world period) a man will be chosen as a plant of righteous judgment (Abraham is meant), and after him the eternal plant of righteousness (= Israel) will come.... At the end of this (the sixth week) the house of dominion (= temple in Jerusalem) will be burned with fire, and the whole generation of the elect root (= of Abraham) will be dispersed... At the end of this (the seventh week) the elect righteous ones of the eternal will be chosen to receive the sevenfold teaching about his entire creation (above all the apocalyptic wisdom of those days)."

c. Jubilees 1:16: "I (God) will change them (the Israelites, at the end of time) into a plant of righteousness with my whole heart and with my whole soul, and they will become a blessing and not a curse, and they will be the head and not the tail" (cf. Deut 28:13, 44).

d. ʾAggadat Berešit 57 (41A): "For we are aliens before you and sojourners like all our fathers" (1 Chr 29:15). So, the righteous are the principal thing עיקר in the world, but they make themselves a secondary matter טְפֵילָה (appendage). Just so you find it with Abraham: he was the principal thing of the world, but he made himself a secondary matter; as it says, "I am an alien and sojourner among you" (Gen 23:4).

11:17: But if some of the branches were broken off, you, though, who are a wild olive tree, have been grafted in among them ....

1. ἀγριέλαιος, wild olive tree, = עֵץ שֶׁמֶן (1 Kgs 6:23; Neh 8:15).

Mishnah Tamid 2.3: How so? Were all the types of wood for the pile of wood (on the altar of burnt offering) suitable? Yes, all the kinds of wood were suitable for the pile of wood with the exception of the olive wood זַיִת (noble olive tree) and the grape vine wood. The following, however, were standard: the branches of the fig tree and the walnut tree, and the wild olive tree עֵץ שֶׁמֶן.

2. ἐγκεντρίζειν, to graft, = הִרְכִּיב (Aram. אַרְכֵּיב), passive מוּרְכָּב = grafted. – The ennobling of trees by grafting הַרְכָּבָה was a very common thing for Jews in the days of the apostle. However, very tight boundaries were drawn around the practice by the *kilʾayim* law (mixing of two kinds): the graft could be inserted only in a tree of the same type (species).[a] Here, though, the apostle speaks of the opposite case that is contrary to nature (παρὰ φύσιν in verse 24), namely that the sprig from a wild olive tree is grafted into the noble olive tree. Concerning this, Eduard Riehm[142] refers to the statement of Columella, *Rust.* 5.9: "It may happen that strong olive trees bear no fruit. Then let a hole be bored into them and a fresh piece of branch from a wild olive tree be slapped into it." In Georg Benedikt Winer's *Biblisches Reallexikon*,[143] there is a complement found in the following quotation of the traveler Stephan Schulz (middle of the 18th century): "In Jerusalem I have heard from many that when a tame olive tree loses its branches, they get wild olive branches from the Jordan, graft these into the tame trunk and then it bears good fruits." Yet these quotations do not affect the sense of Rom 11:17ff., insofar as according to them the grafting aims merely to revitalize the unfruitful or aging noble trunk. Philo, *Exsecr.* § 6, converges more fully with the apostle's exposition.[b] The rabbinic literature knows nothing of engrafting wild olive shoots into a noble olive trunk, but it is familiar with the image, also borrowed from gardening techniques, of sinking a sprig of a person into the rootstock of a people.[c]

a. Mishnah Kilʾayim 1.7: One does not bring (graft) one tree on a tree (of a different kind). ‖ Tosefta Kilʾayim 1.10 (74): One does not graft אין מרכיבין olive trees onto the trunk

142. E. Riehm, *Handwörterbuch des Biblischen Altertums für gebildete Bibelleser* (Leipzig: Velhagen and Klasing, 1884), 1106A.

143. Georg Benedict Winer, *Biblisches Reallexikon*, 3rd ed. (Leipzig: Carl Heinrich Reclam, 1847), 2:171.6.

of a date palm, because this would be tree onto a tree (of a different kind). ‖ Midrash Psalm 128 § 4 (257B): R. Joshua b. Levi (ca. 250) said, "'Your wife like a fruitful grapevine within your house, your sons like in the saplings of an olive tree' (Ps 128:3): just as with olive trees זֵיתִים there is no grafting הרכבה (onto trees of a different kind, so that they cannot bring forth fruits of different kinds), so too among your sons there will be nothing objectionable." — The parallel in y. Kil. 1.27B.22 has R. Levi (ca. 300) as the author.

b. Philo, *Exsecr.* § 6 (Mangey's ed., 2:433), depicts the great hardships that will come over Palestine and its inhabitants before the dawning of the messianic time as a consequence of the Israelites' falling away from God's commandments. "In that time, though, the foreigner who converts to Judaism will be highly honored in fortunateness, marveled at, and blessed for two reasons: first because he passed over to God, and furthermore because he received as a fitting recompense a sure position in heaven τὴν ἐν οὐρανῷ τάξιν βεβαίαν, which it is not right to speak about. However, the Israelite who has sprung ὁ εὐπατρίδης from the noble stock will be cast deep down into Tartarus and thick darkness because he has tampered with the honorable tokens of his lineage παρακόψας τὸ νόμισμα τῆς εὐγενείας, so that all people who see this admonitory example may understand and learn that God loves the virtue (of the proselyte) that grows in the place of earlier enmity, whereas he lets go of ἐῶν χαίρειν the roots τὰς ῥίζας (of the old trunk), but accepts the sapling on the root stump, because he passed over, being grafted into the good fruit-bearing one τὸ δὲ στελεχόθεν ἔρνος, ὅτι μετέβαλεν ἡμερωθὲν πρὸς εὐκαρπίαν, ἀποδεχόμενος."

c. Babylonian Talmud Yebamot 63A: R. Eleazar (ca. 270) said, "What does 'In you all generations of the earth will feel blessed נברכו בך' (Gen 12:3) mean? God said to him (Abraham), 'Two beautiful saplings בְּרִיכוֹת I have sunk into you להבריך בך, Ruth the Moabite and Naamah the Ammonite." — Sinking in comes about by the proselyte adhering to Judaism.

11:22: God's goodness and severity (sternness).

1. χρηστότης = טוֹבָה, Aram. טוּבָא, goodness,[a] רַחֲמִים mercy,[b] עַנְוְתָנוּת, Aram. עַנְוְתָנוּתָא, gentleness, condescension, kindness to humanity.[c]

a. Babylonian Talmud Taʿanit 24B: Good salvation to the good teacher from the good Lord who does good to his people out of his goodness מְטוּבֵיהּ. — See the whole passage at § Mark 10:17.

b. Exodus Rabbah 12 (75A): "And now send and bring your livestock to a safe place" (Exod 9:19). Come and see the mercy of God רחמיו של הק"בה: even in the hour of his wrath he has mercy on the godless and on their livestock. Since he did not want to send the plague of hail on them, but rather on the produce of the land, he warned them that they should bring themselves and their cattle to a safe place, so that they would not be struck by the hail.

c. Deuteronomy Rabbah 7 (204D): "I led you for forty years through the wilderness" (Deut 29:4). R. Judah (ca. 150) said, "Come and see the kindness of God ענותנותו של הק"בה! It is customary in the world for someone who has a son whom he carries to set him down as soon as he makes him uncomfortable. But God, if one may say so כִּבְיָכוֹל, is not so: the Israelites were in the wilderness forty years and angered him, and he carried them; as it says, 'In the wilderness, where you have seen that Yahweh your God carried you as someone carries his son' (Deut 1:31)." ‖ Babylonian Talmud Berakot 16B: When R. Yohanan († 279) would end his prayer (of Eighteen Benedictions), he would speak thus, "Let it be the will (pleasing) before you, Yahweh our God, to look on our shame and see our misfortune, to clothe yourself in mercy ברחמיך and dress yourself with strength and drape yourself in your favor בחסידותך and to gird yourself with your grace בחנינותך and for the measure (the property) of your goodness טובך and your kindness ענותנותך to come before you."

2. χρηστότης καὶ ἀποτομία, closely related in rabbinic literature is the connection: מִדַּת הָרַחֲמִים [144] and מִדַּת הַדִּין = the measure (the divine property) of mercy and the measure of strict justice;[a] similarly, מִדַּת טוֹבָה and מִדַּת פּוּרְעָנוּת = the measure (the property) of the (divine) goodness and the measure of the (divine) punishment.[b] — The adjectives χρηστός and ἀπότομος (Wis 5:20; 12:9; 18:15) perhaps = רַךְ and חַד = "mild, gentle" and "severe, stern."[c]

a. Genesis Rabbah 12 (9C): God said, "If I create the world with the measure of mercy במדת רחמים, sins (read: הֲטָיוֹת) will increase very greatly; if with the measure of strict justice במדת הדין, how can the world continue to exist? But behold, I will create it with the measure of strict justice and with the measure of mercy; may she continue to exist!" — This connection is extraordinarily common.

b. Tosefta Soṭah 4.1 (298): Is the measure of goodness greater or is the measure of punishment greater? The measure of goodness is greater than the measure of punishment מידת הטובה מרובה או מידת פורענות מרובה מידת טובה מרובה ממידת פורענות. — Parallels are found in SLev 5:17 (120A); b. Sanh. 100A (see § Matt 7:2 B, #1); see also the passages named in the footnote.

c. See SDeut § 1 (65A) § Matt 1:21 B, #2, n. *b.*

11:26: And so, all Israel will be saved.

πᾶς Ἰσραὴλ σωθήσεται. This statement corresponds to another: כֹּל יִשְׂרָאֵל יֵשׁ לָהֶם חֵלֶק לָעוֹלָם הַבָּא "All Israel has a share in the future world" (m. Sanh. 10.1). — In substance, though, the statements do not overlap in any way. The saying of the apostle means that after the entrance of the fullness of the gentiles into the kingdom of God, Israel too as a whole people will convert and acquire a share in salvation. The saying in the Mishnah is related to the time after the resurrection and accepts that all Israel, that is, every member of the Jewish people, will share in the age of the blessed eschatological consummation that dawns with the resurrection. It is presupposed that the purifying fire of gehenna in the time between death and resurrection makes the individual Israelites who need it to participate in the life of the future world. The few Israelites who remain excluded from the future world were specified carefully by the Jewish scholars; with their small number, they do not nullify the statement: "All Israel has a share

---

144. S-B: The texts commonly, but less well, מִדָּה טוֹבָה = the good measure. See Mek. Exod. 14:4 (31A); b. Soṭah 11A; b. Yoma 76A.

in the future world." See the matter in more detail in the excursus "Sheol, Gehenna, and the Garden of Eden," II, #5.

11:28: According to election, beloved.

ἐκλογή = בְּחִירָה, verb בָּחַר, Aram. בְּחַר = to choose; synonym: בָּרַר, Aram. בְּרַר = to select.

Jubilees 15:30: "He (God) chose Israel to be his people, sanctified it, and collected it from all the children of men; for many are the nations and numerous are the people, and they all belong to him." — Jubilees 22:9: "(Abraham said,) 'My God, your goodness and your peace be upon your servant and upon the seed of his sons, so it may become your chosen people and your inheritance from all peoples of the earth.'" — 1 Enoch 93:2: "Enoch said, 'Concerning the children of righteousness, concerning the elect of the world and concerning the plant of righteousness and uprightness (three ways of designating for the Israelites)—of this I will speak to you.'" — 4 Ezra 3:13, "When they lived wickedly before you, you chose for yourself one of them, who was called Abraham." — 4 Ezra 5:27: "From all the nations, of which there are so many, you have acquired for yourself the one people." — 2 Baruch 48:19f. (in a prayer of Baruch): "Do not take his hope away from our people ...; for this is the people that you have chosen." ‖ Shema benediction Ahaba rabba: "You chose בָּחַרְתָּ us from all nations and tongues and brought us near to your great name, Sela (according to tradition = forever), in truth, so that we confess you and proclaim you in love as one. Blessed be you, Yahweh, who chose הַבּוֹחֵר his people Israel in love!" (See the whole benediction at § Matt 6:5 A, n. *b*.) ‖ Midrash Song of Songs 5:16 (121B): R. Judan (ca. 350) said in the name of R. Hama b. Hanina (ca. 260), and R. Berekhiah (ca. 340) said in the name of R. Abbahu (ca. 300), "It is written, 'I set you apart ואבדיל from the other nations' (Lev 20:26). If it were said, 'I set the nations apart from you,' there would be no way the enemies of Israel (= the nations of the world) could abide; but 'I set you apart from the nations.' If someone selects מברר what is bad from what is good, he cannot select again; but whoever selects המברר what is good from what is bad can select again. Likewise, if it were said, 'I set the nations apart from you,' the enemies of the Israelites could not abide; but it was said, 'I set you apart from the nations to belong to me,' to my name forever." R. Aha (ca. 320) said, "From this one can conclude that God told the nations of the world that they should repent and that they would (then) be brought near under his wings." (The election of Israel does not exclude, but rather includes, the possibility of the gentiles becoming proselytes.) Parallels are found in Pesiq. 46A; Pesiq. Rab. 15 (69B).

11:29: God's demonstrations of grace are irrevocable.

ἀμεταμέλητα, of God, see: וְלֹא יִנָּחֵם (1 Sam 15:29; Ps 110:4).

Babylonian Talmud Taʿanit 25A: His wife said (to R. Hanina b. Dosa (ca. 70) who lived in great poverty), "How long will we have to keep struggling with everything?" He said to her, "What should we do?" (She answered,) "Pray for mercy that something would be given to you (by God)!" He prayed for mercy: it came forth like a hand and a golden table leg was given to him. She saw in a dream: One day the righteous will eat at a golden table with three legs, and you will eat at a table with two legs. She said to her husband, "Do you like it that all the world will eat at a complete table and we at a table where something is missing?" He said to her (so read), "What should we do? Pray for mercy that it be taken from you." He prayed for mercy, and it was taken. It has been taught: "Greater was the last miracle (the taking back) than the first; for it is traditional teaching that one (= God) gives but does not take away again" דמיהב יהבי מישקל לא שקלי (see b. Ḥul. 60A at § Rom 15:19 toward the end). — Very similarly in Midr. Ruth 1:17 (129A)—see the passage in the excursus "Sheol, Gehenna, and the Garden of Eden," III, #3, n. *q*—it is relayed that a pearl from heaven was first handed to R. Simeon b. Halapta (ca. 190) and then taken away again. Here the conclusion reads: It is the manner of those above to give, but it is not their manner to take. The last miracle was weightier than the first: when he took the pearl, his hand was below (the giving hand), but when he gave it back, his hand was above like that of a man who pays another (in his hand). ‖ Babylonian Talmud ʿArakin 15A: God said to the (angel-)ruler of the sea, "Spit them (the Egyptians who sank in the Sea of Reeds) out onto the dry land." He said to him, "Lord of the world, is there a servant to whom his master has given a gift, and from whom he then takes it away again?"

11:33: O the depth of the riches and wisdom and knowledge of God! How unsearchable are his judgments and how inscrutable his ways!

2 Baruch 14:8f.: "But who, O Lord my God, understands your judgment, or who searches the depths of your way, or who contemplates the onerous load of your path, or who can contemplate your unfathomable decision, or who among those who have been born has ever found the beginning and end of your wisdom?" ‖ Babylonian Talmud Berakot 7A: R. Yohanan († 279) said in the name of R. Yose (b. Halapta [ca. 150]), "Moses requested three things from God, and he granted them to him. He asked that the Shekinah dwell with Israel, and he granted it to him (see Exod 33:16). He asked that the Shekinah not dwell with the nations of the world, and he granted it to him (see Exod 33:16). He asked God to let him know his ways, and he granted them to him; as it says, 'Let me know your ways!' (Exod 33:13). He said before him, 'Lord of the world, why is there a righteous person for whom things go well, and another righteous person for whom things go badly? Why is there a godless person for whom things go well, and another godless person for whom things go badly?' He answered him, 'Moses, a righteous man for whom things go well is a righteous man, the son of a righteous man; a righteous man for whom things go badly is a righteous man, the son of a godless man; a godless man for whom things go well is a godless man, the son of a righteous man; a godless man for whom things go badly is a godless man, the son of a godless man.'" ‖ Mishnah ʾAbot 4.15: R. Yannai (ca. 225) said, "We can explain neither the peaceful happiness of the godless nor the sufferings of the righteous." ‖ Midrash Psalm 139 § 1 (264A): "For the leader of music, a psalm of David. Yahweh, may you search and know me" (Ps 139:1). "Zophar of Naamah said, 'Can you reach the ultimate source?... They are as high as heaven, what will you do?... Its measure is longer than the earth' ..." (Job 11:7–9). No human fathoms it עוֹמֵד עליה (= comes to stand on it, and thus has firm ground under his feet). "It (Wisdom) is hidden from the eyes of all the living" (Job 28:21). Who knows it?

God, as it says, "God understands the way to her ...; for he looks to the ends of the earth" (Job 28:23f.). No human can come to the end of God's actions. And by the same token David said, "Who will utter the mighty deeds of Yahweh" (Ps 106:2). A person is not able to get to the mighty deeds of Yahweh. And by the same token Moses said (there is no further exposition). But God exists forever and he searches היקר everything. Therefore, David gave him eternity and a psalm; as it says, "To the eternal one, a psalm of David." (The superscription of Ps 139 is understood in this way here by למנצח being interpreted according to נֶצַח "perpetuity.") ‖ 4 Ezra 4:10f.: "He (the angel) further said to me (Ezra): You cannot know what is yours, what has grown up together with you, so how will you be able to understand the vessel that understands the workings of the Most High? For the ways of the Most High were created as eternal ways; but you, a mortal human, who lives in the perishable age, how can you grasp the eternal?" — 4 Ezra 5:40: "He (angel, God) said to me, 'As little as you are able to do even just one of all the things I have mentioned, just so little are you able to understand my judgment or the goal of love that I have pledged to my people.'"

11:35: Who has given to him first that he would be repaid?

Septuagint Job 41:11 (= Hebrew 41:3): ἢ τίς ἀντιστήσεταί μοι καὶ ὑπομενεῖ; ("Who will resist me and bear up?" See Job 9:4) εἰ πᾶσα ἡ ὑπ' οὐρανὸν ἐμή ἐστιν, οὐ σιωπήσομαι δι' αὐτόν. — Targum Job 41:3: "Who preempted me in the works of creation that I would have to repay? Is not everything under heaven mine?" ‖ Pesiqta 75A: R. Tanḥuma (ca. 380) opened his talk with the following, "'Who has given something to me first that I would have to repay? Whatever is under heaven belongs to me'" (Job 41:3). A single (unmarried) man is meant, who lives in a city and contributes to the salary for teachers of children and of the Mishnah (which he was not obligated to do). God says, 'It lies with me to repay him for his action and to give him a male child as a recompense.'" (This is thus a case to which the question in Job 41:3 does not apply.) R. Jeremiah b. Eleazar (ca. 270) said, "One day (at the time of the consummation) a voice from heaven will blaringly proclaim on the mountaintops, 'Everyone who has worked with God, let him come and receive his recompense!' This is what is meant by: 'At this time Jacob and Israel will be told what it is to work for God'[145] (Num 23:23): whoever has worked with God, let him come and receive his recompense![146] And the holy spirit (speaking in Scripture) says, 'Who has given something to me first that I would have to repay?' (Job 41:3). Whoever strikes up a song of praise before me, did I not first put a soul in him? Whoever circumcises before me, did I not first grant him a son? Whoever makes show tassels, did I not first give him a prayer shawl? Whoever makes an inscription on a doorpost, did I not first give him a house? Whoever makes a parapet for me (cf. Deut 22:8), did I not first give him a roof? Whoever makes a festival hut for me, did I not first give him a yard (on which to erect it)? Whoever separates a field quarter before me, did I not first give him a field? Whoever separates before me offerings and tithes, did I not first give him a threshing floor? Whoever sets apart a

145. S-B: פָּעַל אֵל interpreted as פֹּעַל אֵל "work, working for God."

146. S-B: Here the saying of R. Jeremiah b. Eleazar ends, which, apart from the parallel passages mentioned above, is also found in y. Šabb. 6.8D.20.

sacrifice before me, did I not first give him livestock? This is what is meant by: 'When a bull or a sheep or a goat is born, let it remain seven days with its mother; but from the eighth day on it will be accepted pleasingly as an offering by fire for Yahweh' (Lev 22:27)." (God first gives the animal, then he accepts it as an offering.) — Parallels are found in LevR 27 (125B); Tanḥ. אמור 174A; TanḥB אמור § 10 (45A); Pesiq. Rab. 25 (126B); Num. Rab. 14 (173A), though significantly changed.

12:1: Rational worship.

λογικὴ λατρεία "intellectual worship," comparable to עבודה שהיא בלב "worship with the heart." See SDeut 11:13 § 41 and b. Taʿan. 2A at § Rom 1:9 B.

12:3: Not to think of oneself more highly.

Concerning pride and proud people, see § Luke 1:51. See further § Eph 4:7.

12:8 A: Whoever shares, (do it) in simplicity.

ἐν ἁπλότητι "in simplicity," tantamount to: for God's sake, without selfish secondary motives.

Mishnah Menaḥot 13.11: It is said concerning the burnt offering of livestock, "An offering by fire of pleasing smell" (Lev 1:9); and concerning the burnt offering of birds, "An offering by fire of pleasing smell" (Lev 1:18); and concerning the food offering, "An offering by fire of pleasing smell" (Lev 2:2). This teaches: it is irrelevant whether one gives much or little, as long as his mind is directed to God. ‖ See also the citations at § Matt 6:3f.

12:8 B: Whoever shows mercy, (do it) with a cheerful spirit.

Leviticus Rabbah 34 (131B): R. Isaac (ca. 300) said, "The Torah means to teach you good morals, that a person, if he gives alms עושה מצוה (= ὁ ἐλεῶν), should give them with a joyful heart בלב שמח. For if Reuben had known that God would have it written about him, 'Reuben heard and saved him from their hand' (Gen 37:21), he would have carried him and brought him to his father; and if Boaz had known that God would have it written about him, 'He handed her roasted ears' (Ruth 2:14), he would have fed her with fattened calves."

12:10: Outdoing one another in honor (with showing honor).

See m. ʾAbot 4.15; b. Ber. 17A; b. Ber. 6B (dealing with offering greetings) at § Matt 5:47, n. *e*. — Concerning attending to the honor of others and the sensitivity of the rabbinic scholars to their honor being wounded, see § John 12:43, #2 and #3.

12:11 A: Not lagging in zeal.

See m. ʾAbot 2.15f. at § John 9:4 A. ‖ Mishnah ʾAbot 2.8: Rabban Yohanan b. Zakkai († ca. 80) said, "When you have done much Torah, do not be proud of yourself; for you were create for this."

12:11 B: Serving the Lord.

Mishnah ʾAbot 2.12: R. Yose (the priest, ca. 100) said, "… All your deeds should occur for God's sake." ‖ Babylonian Talmud Berakot 17A: A customary saying of the scholars of Javneh, "I am a creature and the other (the nonscholar) is a creature; I have my work in the city and he has his work in the field; I get started on my work early and he gets started on his work early; as he does not proudly place himself above me because of my work, I too will not proudly place myself above him because of his work (to read more simply with ʿArukh: As he does not proudly exalt himself because of his work, so … too I will not because of my work). And if you should say, 'I accomplish a lot and he accomplishes little!,' we have learned (see m. Menaḥ. 13.11 at § Rom 12:8 A): "It is irrelevant whether one accomplishes a lot or a little, as long as his mind is directed to God (to serve God with his work)!"'"

12:12: Persisting in prayer.

Praying without ceasing did not correspond to the Jewish outlook and custom. See § Luke 18:1.

12:13 A: Taking an (active) interest in the needs of the saints.

On the public care for the poor, see § Acts 6:3, #3 and #4. — On private benefaction see the excursus "Ancient Jewish Private Charity." Here reference may be made to a few other passages that concern supporting the scholars.

See b. B. Bat. 8A at § John 7:49, #8, n. *f*; b. Ketub. 111B at § John 7:49, #8, n. *f*. ‖ Babylonian Talmud Berakot 34B: R. Hiyya b. Abba (ca. 280) said that R. Yohanan († 279) said, "All the prophets prophesied only concerning the one who marries his daughter to a scholar and who conducts his business affairs for the benefit of a scholar and who allows a scholar use of his possessions; but concerning the scholars themselves (and their recompense) it says, 'No eye has seen, O God, except you, what is prepared for the one who awaits' (so Isa 64:3 according to the midr.)." ‖ See Pesaḥ. 53B at § Luke 23:43, #3, C, Comment. ‖ Midrash Ecclesiastes 11:1 (49B): "Cast your bread on the water's surface" (Eccl 11:1). R. Bibi (ca. 320) said, "If you want to show good (give alms), give it to those who labor over the Torah; for the water that is spoken about here is nothing other than the Torah; as it says, 'Oh, all you who are thirsty, come to the water!' (Isa 55:1)." ‖ Babylonian Talmud Taʿanit 21B: A greeting from the academy of heaven came to (was bestowed on) the bloodletter Abba every day, to Abbayye († 338/39) on every day of preparation for the Sabbath and to Raba († 352) on every day of preparation for the Day of Atonement. (Rashi: "A voice from heaven called to him, 'Peace be upon you!'" — On the heavenly academy, cf. § Luke 23:43, #3, C, Comment.) The mind of Abbayye was dejected because of (the greater honor bestowed on) the bloodletter Abba. It was said to him, "You are not able to act in accordance with his works!" What were the works of the bloodletter Abba? When he carried out the bloodletting, he had the men sit separately and the women sit separately. Further, he had a coat that had several slits in it before the lancet (so according to the reading in Arukh); if a woman came to him, he put the coat on her so that he would not be able to look at her. Further, he had a hidden place where the small coins brought (as payment) could be thrown: whoever had something threw something in there, and whoever had nothing was (in this way) not ashamed. When a diligent scholar would turn up at his place, he would not take payment from him, and after he had stood up, he gave him small coins and said to him, "Go, strengthen yourself!" — See also § Rom 15:26.

12:13 B: Pursuing hospitality.

φιλοξενία = הַכְנָסַת אוֹרְחִים. — See the praise of and recompense for hospitality in the excursus "Works of Love," II, A. — See further § Matt 10:40 A, #1 and #2.

12:14 A: Bless those who persecute you.

The opposite maxim is found in TanḥB פנחס § 4 (76A): "Yahweh spoke thus to Moses, 'Fight with the Midianites and slay them; for they fought with you by their scheming.'" (Num 25:16f.). From this, the scholars said, "If someone wants to kill you, kill him first." — What appears here as the word of the scholars is cited as a word of the Torah in b. Ber. 58A.35; 62B.21 (by R. Eleazar [ca. 270]) and b. Sanh. 72A.6 (by Raba [† 352]); it is inferred from Exod 22:1. ‖ God always sides with the persecuted, not the persecutors. See § Matt 5:10, #1. ‖ See further Midr. Ps. 56 § 1 at § Matt 5:39, final paragraph.

12:14 B: Bless and do not curse.

See § Matt 5:44 A and B. ‖ Babylonian Talmud Sanhedrin 48B: Rab Judah († 299) said that Rab († 247) said, "This is what the people say, 'Be the cursed, but not the curser!'"

12:15: Be joyous with the joyful, weep with the weeping.

Dèrek Ereṣ 6 at the end: Let a person not be gleeful among the weeping nor weep among the gleeful; let him not be awake among the sleeping nor sleep among the waking; let him not stand among the sitting nor sit among the standing. The general rule of the matter is: let a person make his spirit appear to be different from that of his companions and the rest of the children of men. ‖ Pesiqta 191B: "On a good day be of good cheer" (Eccl 7:14). R. Tanḥuma b. Hiyya (ca. 300) said, "On the day of your neighbor's joy, be of good cheer with him; 'and on the evil day see' (so the midr.)! If an evil day befalls your neighbor, see how you may show him love, to save him from it."— A parallel is found in Pesiq. Rab. 201A; Lev. Rab. 34 (131A); in Midr. Eccl. 7:14 (36A): On the day of your neighbor's joy, rejoice with him .... ‖ Babylonian Talmud Berakot 6B: R. Helbo (ca. 300) said that Rab Huna († 297) said, "Whoever eats at a groom's wedding meal and does not gladden him (does not contribute to his rejoicing) commits a transgression against the five 'voices' in Jer 33:11: The voice of rejoicing and the voice of joy, the voice of the groom and the voice of the bride, the voice of the one who cries 'Praise Yahweh Sabaoth!' Yet what is his recompense if he gladdens him?" R. Joshua b. Levi (ca. 250) said, "He is worthy of the Torah, which was given among the five voices; as it says, 'On the third day, when morning came, there were voices (plural = two voices) and bolts of lightning and a heavy thunderstorm on the mountain and a very strong voice (third voice) of the trumpet ..., and the voice (fourth voice) of the trumpet became stronger ..., and God answered him with a voice (fifth voice)' (Exod 19:16, 19)." ‖ Babylonian Talmud Taʿanit 11A: Let a person feel pain with the community. For so we find it with our teacher Moses that he inflicted pain on himself with the community; as it says, "When the hands of Moses became heavy, though, they took a stone and put it beneath him, and he sat on it" (Exod 17:12). What? Did Moses have no cushion or pillow to sit on? However, Moses spoke thus, "Since Israel remains in pain, I too will be in pain with them. And everyone who inflicts pain on himself with the community is worthy to see the comfort of the community." And if someone should say, "Who bears witness against me?, the stones of the person's house and the beams of the person's house bear witness against him; as it says, "For the stone will cry out from the wall and the beam will answer it from the woodwork" (Hab 2:11). – The following baraita precedes this saying: If the Israelites remain in pain and someone separates himself from them (in order not to suffer with them), the two angels of service who guide the person will come and lay their hands on his head and say, "So-and-so, who has separated himself from the community, will not see the comfort of the community!"

12:16 A: Not aspiring for lofty things.

See warnings against pride at § Luke 1:51. ‖ Mishnah ʾAbot 1.10: Shemaiah (ca. 50 BCE) said, "Love work, hate being the master הָרַבָּנוּת (sovereignty, dominion)." – See b. Pesaḥ. 87B: R. Yohanan († 279) said, "Woe because of dominion, for it buries the one who possesses it! You have no prophet who would not have outlived four kings. See Isa 1:1." ‖ TanḥumaB ויקרא § 4 (2B): "A person's pride will bring him low, but humility will obtain honor" (Prov 29:23). Whoever flees from dominion (from being master שְׂרָרָה), it will pursue him (this is then proven by the case of Saul on the basis of 1 Sam 10:22, 24). Abimelech, the son of Jerubbaal, pursued dominion, and it fled from him. See Judg 9:1f, 23. – Similar explanations are found in Num. Rab. 13 (168D) and Pesiq. Rab. 7 (26B). ‖ Mishnah ʾAbot 6.4: Do not seek great things for yourself and do not desire honor. ‖ See m. ʾAbot 1.13; SDeut 11:22 § 48 (84B); b. Ned. 62A; SDeut 11:13 § 41 (79B) at § Matt 23:8 A. – Mishnah ʾAbot 4.5 at § Matt 23:5 A.

12:16 B: Instead, proceed with lowly things (for lowliness and humility).

See the praise of humility at § Matt 5:3, #3; § Matt 5:5, #1; § Matt 18:4; § Matt 23:12. ‖ Babylonian Talmud Soṭah 5A at § Matt 5:45 A, n. *b*; b. Ber. 17A at § Rom 12:11 B.

12:16 C: Do not be clever in yourselves.

Proverbs 3:7: "Do not be wise חָכָם in your eyes." – Targum likewise: לָא תְהֵוִ חַכִּים "Do not be wise before yourself." – Septuagint: μὴ ἴσθι φρόνιμος παρὰ σεαυτῷ. ‖ Genesis Rabbah 44 (27A): It is written: "The wise man fears and avoids evil; but the fool is full of passion and self-confidence" (Prov 14:16). "The wise man fears": "Do not fear, Abram!" (Gen 15:1). "Do not be wise in your eyes, fear Yahweh and avoid evil" (Prov 3:7): "do not be wise in your eyes," in what you see with your eyes: Will I beget? Will I not beget? "Fear Yahweh": "Do not fear, Abram!" (Fear God so you do not have to fear anything.)

12:17 A: Repaying no one evil for evil.

See Gen. Rab. 38 (23A); Midr. Ps. 41 § 8 (131A) at § Matt 5:44 A, n. g; Exod. Rab. 26 (87B) at § Matt 5:45 A, n. *b*.

12:17 B: Mindful of what is good in the sight of all people.

Proverbs 3:4: "Thus you will acquire grace and accurate understanding in the eyes of God and of people." — Targum: "Thus, you will find grace and understanding and good (goodness) before God and before the children of men." — Septuagint: καὶ εὑρήσεις χάριν· καὶ προνοοῦ καλὰ ἐνώπιον κυρίου καὶ ἀνθρώπων.

See m. Šeqal. 3.2f.; t. Šeqal. 2.1 (175) at § Matt 17:24, #5, n. *e*. — See y. Šeqal. 3.47C.33: R. Samuel b. Nahman (ca. 260) said in the name of R. Jonathan (ca. 220), "In the Torah and in the prophets and in the hagiographa we find that a person must emerge from the hands of people (just as pure and righteous) as he must emerge from the hands of God. In the Torah, because it is written, 'So you will be pure before Yahweh and before Israel' (Num 32:22). In the Prophets, because it is written, 'The Lord God Yahweh, the Lord God Yahweh, who knows, and let Israel know' (Josh 22:22). In the hagiographa, because it is written, 'So you will acquire grace and accurate understanding in the eyes of God and of people' (Prov 3:4)." ‖ See further the citations at § Luke 2:52 and m. ʾAbot 2.1: Rabbi († 217?) said, "What is the right way of acting that a person should choose? Every way that is an honor for the one who does it and will be interpreted by people as an honor (because it meets with their approval and acclaim)." ‖ Babylonian Talmud Berakot 17A at § Matt 5.5; b. Yoma 38A at § Luke 1:9, #4.

12:18: If possible, as much as it lies with you, keeping peace with all people.

1. On peace and peaceableness, see § Matt 5:9; see b. Ber. 17A at § Matt 5:5, #1; see also § Heb 12:14 and § 1 Pet 3:10–12.

2. μετὰ πάντων ἀνθρώπων. — Sifre Numbers 6:26 § 42 (12B): "May he give you peace" (Num 6:26); peace in your coming, peace in your going, peace with all people עם כל אדם. — The same is found in Num. Rab. 11 (164B).

12:19 A: Not avenging yourselves.

On revenge and pursuing vengeance, see SLev 19:17 (352A) at § Matt 5:43, #2, n. *a*. — The scholar is permitted to avenge himself when he is personally slighted. See b. Yoma 22B at § Matt 5:43, #2, n. *b*. — The prohibition of vengeance applies to Israelites, but not to non-Israelites. See SLev 19:18 (352A) at § Matt 5:43, #1, final paragraph.

12:19 B: Make room for the wrath (of God).

τόπον διδόναι = נָתַן מָקוֹם. The latter means α. = give occasion or opportunity;[a] β. = make room;[b] γ. = to clear the field before someone so that he can operate;[c] opposite: to offer resistance עָמַד כְּנֶגֶד. — More rarely, τόπον διδόναι corresponds to: פִּנָּה מָקוֹם or עָשָׂה מָקוֹם = "make room."[d]

a. See m. Parah 3.3; b. Yoma 40B and Sir 4:4f. (Hebrew) at § Luke 14:9, #1.

b. See Midr. Ps. 55 § 3 (146B) at § Acts 12:15, #2.

c. Deuteronomy Rabbah 1 (196C): R. Joshua b. Levi (ca. 250) said, "When the enemies came to destroy Jerusalem, there were 60 myriads of demons there who stood at the door of the temple to set to work on it (to attack it). Yet when they saw how the Shekinah (divinity) silently watched (see Lam 2:3), even they cleared the field נתני מקום (without offering resistance)." ‖ Yalquṭ Simeoni Exodus 2:15 (I § 168 from Tanḥuma): "Moses fled from pharaoh" (Exod 2:15). It is written, "Come, my people, go into your chambers" (Isa 26:20). When you see a hard hour (come over you), offer it no resistance לא תעמד כנגדה, but rather make room for it תן לה מקום (so that it can operate). "Look to me!" (says God.) "When I in a certain way כִּבְיָכוֹל saw a hard hour because of your sins, I made space for it נהתי לה מקום (gave it leeway to run riot)"; as it says, "He turned back his right hand" (Lam 2:3). Everyone who resists the hour falls into its hand, and everyone who makes space for it has the hour fall into his hand. Naboth resisted the hour and he fell into its hand. Abraham made space for the hour and fled from Nimrod, and it fell into his hand (when God said to him: "I will make you into a great people"). Isaac made space for the hour, and it fell into his hand; as it says, "Abimelech came to him from Gerar" (Gen 26:26). Moses made space for the hour; as it says, "Moses fled from pharaoh" (Exod 2:15). Then the hour fell into his hand; as it says, "Also, the man Moses was very great in the land of Egypt in the eyes of pharaoh's officials" (Exod 11:3). David made space for the hour; as it says, "David escape from Naioth" (1 Sam 20:1). Then the hour fell into his hand, and Saul said to him, "See, I know that you will become king" (1 Sam 24:21). And likewise, Jacob made space for the hour; as it says, "Jacob fled to the range of Aram" (Hos 12:13). Then the hour fell into his hand; as it says, "Esau took his wives and went ... away from his brother Jacob" (Gen 36:6).

d. See b. ʿErub. 85B and Pirqe R. El. 2 at § Luke 14:9, #1.

12:19 C: "Vengeance is mine, I will repay," says the Lord.

1. The base text is Deut 32:35: "Vengeance and repayment is mine." — Targum Onkelos: "Before me is punishment and I, yes, I will repay." — Likewise, Tg. Yer. I. However, Yer. II: "Vengeance is mine, and I am the one who repays" דידי היא נִקְמְתָא ואנ הוא דמשלם. — Septuagint: ἐν ἡμέρᾳ ἐκδικήσεως ἀνταποδώσω. — One can see that the ἅπαξ λεγ. שִׁלֵּם in the base text is in every one of these cases, as in Rom 12:19, rendered by a verb.

See b. Giṭ. 7A at § Matt 5:44 A, n. g. ‖ Babylonian Talmud Giṭṭin 7A: Rab Huna b. Nathan (ca. 350) said to Rab Ashi († 427), "What does, 'And Kinah and Dimonah and Adadah' קינה ודימונה ועדעדה (Josh 15:22) mean?" He said to him, "He is enumerating the cities of the land of Israel." He answered him, "Do I know not that he is enumerating the land of Israel?" But Rab Gebiha (?) of Argiza (in Babylonia) specified its meaning as follows, "If someone harbors hatred קנאה toward someone else and keeps silent ידומם, then the one who is eternally עדי עד enthroned deals with his matter." He (Rab Ashi) said to him, "But in this case,

'Ziklag and Madmannah and Sansannah' צקלג ומדמנה יסנסנה (Josh 15:31) would have to be interpreted in the same way!" He answered him, "If Rab Gebiha (?) of Argiza were here, he would state its meaning." Rab Aha of Be-Hozai gave it the following meaning, "If someone has a complaint against someone else because he has damaged his livelihood צעקת לגימא and keeps silent ודומם, then the one enthroned in the thorn bush סנה deals with his matter." ‖ Midrash Esther 1:1 (84A): R. Simon (ca. 280) said in the name of R. Yohanan († 279), It is written, 'Vengeance and repayment is mine, for the time when their foot רגלם will falter' (Deut 32:35). How is that? Is it strength when one says, 'When the haters of the Israelites (= the godless Israelites) begin to totter, then I will exact punishment from them?' Rather, God said, 'When the commandment-fulfillments current רגילות among them come to an end, so that no merit is found for them before me any longer, in that hour vengeance and repayment is mine.'" — רגלם is thus interpreted: "what is common for them."

2. There was great concern to leave vengeance to God's discretion and to appeal to God's decision.

Babylonian Talmud Berakot 55A: R. Isaac (ca. 300) said, "Three things bring a person's sins into remembrance (before God), and these are: a wall leaning (to collapse, which nevertheless a person passes by), hoping in (the fulfillment of) prayer, and committing to God a dispute against someone else." (In these cases, God becomes attentive to the person in question so that he feels compelled to examine his book of debts, and who knows how this examination turns out. Thus, it is much better to avoid those three things, in order not to attract God's eye to oneself.) — In the parallel passage in b. Roš Haš. 16B the following words are appended: R. Abin (ca. 325) said, "Whoever commits (to divine decision) a dispute against another will be punished first; as it says, 'Then Sarai said to Abram, "The injustice that has happened to me is your fault.... Let Yahweh judge between me and you!"' (Gen 16:5). And further it is written, 'Abraham came to mourn and weep for Sarah' (Gen 23:2)." (According to the Haggadah, that Sarah died before Abraham was Sarah's punishment for the appeal she made to the divine decision.) ‖ Genesis Rabbah 45 (28C): R. Tanḥuma (which one?) said in the name of R. Hiyya the elder (ca. 200) and R. Berekhiah (ca. 340) said in the name of R. Hiyya (b. Abba [ca. 280]), "Whoever knocks on (appeals to) הַרְתִּיק strict divine justice will not go smoothly from his hand from there. Sarah was destined to attain Abraham's years of life, but since she said, 'Let Yahweh judge between me and you!' (Gen 16:5), 38 years were taken off her life (i.e., she died 38 years earlier than she was originally destined to)." ‖ Babylonian Talmud Baba Qamma 93A: R. Hanan (Hanin [ca. 310]) said, "Whoever entrusts (to divine decision) a matter against another will be punished first; for it says, 'And Sarai said to Abram ...' (Gen 16:5). Furthermore, it is written, 'Abraham came to mourn and weep for Sarah' (Gen 23:2). But these words apply only when one has an earthly court (so that there was no need to commit the matter to God's court)." R. Isaac (ca. 300, see b. Ber. 55A above) said, "Woe to the one who cries (to God) more than to the one who is cried against." The baraita likewise reads: "Both the one who cries out and the one who is cried against are included in the wording (of Exod 22:22f., according to which both are affected by the punishment), except that one (God) will act more swiftly against the ones who cries than against the one cried against."

12:20: "If your enemy is hungry, feed him; if he is thirsty, give him a drink; doing this, you will gather fiery coals on his head."

1. The base text is Prov 25:21f.: "If the one who hates you is hungry, feed him with bread, and if he is thirsty, give him a drink of water; for you will scrape burning coals on his head, and Yahweh will repay you." ‖ Targum: "If the one who hates you is hungry, feed him with bread, and if he is thirsty, give him a drink of water; for you will scrape burning coals גוּמְרֵי דְנוּרָא (literally: coals of fire) on his head and God נְשַׁלְמֵיהּ לָךְ (read instead of the *pael* the *haphel* נַשְׁלְמֵיהּ and translate either:) will deliver him to you, or: will make him your friend" (cf. in #2 ᾿Abot R. Nat. 16 (6A); Midr. Prov. 25 § 21; b. Sukkah 52A.28). — Septuagint: ἐὰν πεινᾷ ὁ ἐχθρός σου, ψώμιζε αὐτὸν, ἐὰν διψᾷ, πότιζε αὐτὸν· τοῦτο γὰρ ποιῶν ἄνθρακας πυρὸς σωρεύσεις ἐπὶ τὴν κεφαλὴν αὐτοῦ, ὁ δὲ κύριος ἀνταποδώσει σοι ἀγαθά.

2. Homiletic application of Prov 25:21f.

A baraita in b. Meg. 15B: What reason did Esther have to invite Haman? (See Esth 5:8). R. Eliezer (ca. 90) said, "She secretly laid a snare for him; as it says, 'Let their table become a snare before them' (Ps 69:23)." R. Joshua (ca. 90) said, "She had learned from the house of her father what is said, 'If the one who hates you is hungry, feed him with bread ...' (Prov 25:21f.)." ‖ Midrash Proverbs 25 § 21 (49B): "If the one who hates you is hungry ..." (Prov 25:21f.). R. Hama b. Hanina (ca. 260) said, "Even if he gets going early to kill you and he comes into your house hungry and thirsty, feed him and give him a drink. Why? 'For you will scrape burning coals on his head and Yahweh ישלם לך; do not read יְשַׁלֵּם לָךְ = he will repay you, but rather יַשְׁלְמֶנּוּ לָךְ = he will deliver him to you,' or = 'he will make him your friend.'" — It should be observed that the text here, as the targum above, reads the *piel* form יְשַׁלְּמֶנּוּ; yet should the meaning "deliver," which is not listed by the lexicographers, be assigned to the *piel*? ‖ Most of the time, the evil inclination was understood by the "hater" in (Prov 25:21). ᾿Abot de Rabbi Nathan 16 (6A): R. Simeon b. Eleazar (ca. 190) said, "I will tell you a parable: What can the matter be compared with? The evil inclination is like an iron that one has put into the fire. As long as it is in the fire, one can make from it all the implements one wants. So too for the evil inclination, it is set right תַּקָּנָה solely by the words of the Torah; as it says, 'If the one who hates you is hungry, feed him with bread (the Torah), and if he is thirsty, give him a drink of water (the Torah); for you will scrape fiery coals on his head and Yahweh ישלם לך' (Prov 25:21f.); do not read יְשַׁלֵּם לָךְ = 'he will repay you,' but rather יַשְׁלִים לָךְ = 'he will give you peace.'" ‖ Sifre Deuteronomy 11:18 § 45 (82B): If you are willing, you can become master over it (the evil inclination); for it says, "But you are to be master over it (sin = the evil inclination)" (Gen 4:7). Furthermore, it says, "If the one who hates you is hungry, feed him with bread," feed him with the bread of the Torah; "and if he is thirsty, give him a drink of water; for you will scrape fiery coals on his head" (Prov 25:21f.). ‖ Babylonian Talmud Sukkah 52A: R. Avira (in the 4th cent.), and it has been said R. Joshua b. Levi (ca. 250) said in a presentation, "The evil inclination has seven names: ... Solomon called it 'hater'; as it says, 'If the one who hates you is hungry, feed him with bread, and if he is thirsty, give him a drink of water; for you will scrape fiery coals on his head and Yahweh ישלם לך' (Prov 25:21f.); do not read יְשַׁלֶּם לָךְ = 'will repay you,' but rather יַשְׁלִימֶנּוּ לָךְ = 'he will deliver him to you,' or 'he will make him your friend.'" ‖ Pesiqta 80B: R. Berekhiah (ca. 340) related the Scripture passage Prov 25:21f. to it (the evil inclination): "'If the one who hates you is hungry, feed him with bread,' that is, with the bread of the Torah; 'and if he is thirsty, give him a drink of water,' the water of the Torah. Why? 'For you will scrape burning coals on his head and Yahweh ישלם לך'; do not read יְשַׁלֶּם = 'he will repay you,' but rather יַשְׁלִימֶנּוּ = 'he will deliver him to you,' or 'he will make him your friend.'" Parallels are found in TanḥB בשלח § 3 (28A); anonymously in Gen. Rab. 54 (34C).

3. ἄνθρακες πυρός. The base text has only גֶּחָלִים, since גַּחֶלֶת, in contrast to פֶּחָם = "black coal" designates precisely the burning or glowing coal. The targum (see above in #1) translates this more fully with: גּוּמְרֵי דְנוּרָא = fiery coals; but rabbinic literature makes use more specifically of גַּחֲלֵי אֵשׁ = "coals of fire" or "burning coals."

Mishnah ᾿Abot 2.10: R. Eliezer (ca. 90) said, "… Warm yourself at the fire of the scholars. But be careful of their (burning) coal מִגַּחַלְתָּן because you could burn yourself. Their bite is the bite of the fox, their sting is the sting of the scorpion, and their hiss is the hiss of a poisonous snake, and all their words are like burning coals כְּגַחֲלֵי אֵשׁ."

4. ἄνθρακες ἐπὶ τὴν κεφαλήν.

TanḥumaB בשלח § 20 (33B): What can this be compared with? With a baker who was at his baking oven: his enemy came then he took burning coals גחלים out and put them on his head. His friend came, and he took warm bread out and gave it to him. (It should be punctuated in this way, contrary to Buber's claim.) The glowing coals and the bread, both came out of the (same) oven; likewise God made fire fall (from heaven) on the Sodomites, and on the Israelites he made manna fall from heaven; see Exod 16:4. — According to TanḥB וירא § 19 (48B) this parable is associated with R. Berekhiah (ca. 340). — See a similar parable by R. Abun (I, ca. 325; II, ca. 370) in Gen. Rab. 51 (32C).

12:21: Overcome evil with good.

See TanḥB משפטים § 1 (40B) and ᾿Abot R. Nat. 23 at § Matt 5:44 A, notes *c* and *d*.

13:1 A: Let every soul be subject to the ruling authorities.

1. πᾶσα ψυχή = every person; similarly, in the OT, נֶפֶשׁ in the statutes in, for example, Lev 4:2; 5:1, 2, 4, 15, 17; in these instances, Tg. Onk. replaces נפש with אֱנָשׁ "person," while Tg. Yer. I replaces it with בַּר נַשׁ = person, someone.

2. ἡ ἐξουσία = רָשׁוּת, שְׂרָרָה, מַלְכוּת, Aram. מַלְכוּתָא.

רָשׁוּת in, for example, m. ᾿Abot 1.10: Shemaiah (ca. 50 BCE) said, "Love work, hate being the master רַבָּנוּת; do not make yourself known to the authorities רָשׁוּת." ‖ Mishnah ᾿Abot 2.3: (R. Gamaliel b. Judah the prince [ca. 220] said,) "Be careful about the authorities רשות; for they accept a person only for their own advantage. They seem like friends in the hour of their convenience, but they do not stand by someone in the hour of his affliction." ‖ שְׂרָרָה, see y. Pe᾿ah 8.21A.25 in the next section, § Rom 13:1 B. ‖ מַלְכוּת, see b. ʿAbod. Zar. 3B, 4A at § Rom 13:3 A; מַלְכוּתָא, s. b. Ber. 58A.32 at § Rom 13:1 B.

13:1 B: For there is no authority except from God.

In the ancient synagogue, there was little disagreement about this statement; see Dan 2:21, 37f.; John 19:11.

Wisdom 6:1ff.: "Listen now, you kings, and hear.... For sovereignty ἡ κράτησις has been granted to you by the Lord and power ἡ δυναστεία by the Most High." ‖ 1 Enoch 46:5: "He (the son of man—Messiah) will cast kings from their thrones and out of their kingdoms, because they do not exalt him nor praise him nor gratefully acknowledge whence the kingdom has been granted to them (namely by God)." ‖ 2 Baruch 82:9: "We observe their (the gentile kings') vainglorious power, while they deny the goodness of God who gave (it) to them, and yet they will pass away like a cloud that passes by." ‖ A baraiata in b. Ber. 58A.20: Whoever sees the kings of Israel says (as a word of praise), "Blessed be the one who has imparted from his majesty to those who fear him!" Whoever sees the kings of the nations of the world says, "Blessed be the one who has given from his majesty to flesh and blood!" ‖ A baraita in b. ʿAbod. Zar. 18A: When R. Yose b. Qisma (Qosma? [ca. 110]) was sick, R. Hananiah b. Teradion went to visit him. He said to him, "Hananiah, my brother, do you not know that this (Roman) nation has been made ruler by heaven? For it has destroyed his house and burned his temple and killed his pious ones and destroyed his noble ones, and yet it still exists!" ‖ Babylonian Talmud Berakot 58A.32: (When Rab Shela had gotten into a dispute with the pagan authorities in Babylonia [ca. 220] because of the exercise of criminal jurisdiction, he said in the course of the argument,) "'Yours, O Yahweh, is the greatness and the power ...' (1 Chr 29:11)." They said to him, "What did you say?" He answered them, "I said this, 'Blessed be the All-merciful one, who has bestowed dominion מלכותא on earth after the manner of heavenly dominion כעין מלכיתא דרקיעא and who has given you power שׁוּלְטָנָא and mercy in judgment!'" They said, "The honor of authority יקרא דמלכותא is dear to him." Then they gave him another staff and said to him, "Speak justice!" ‖ Babylonian Talmud Berakot 58A.40: Rab Hanan b. Rabbah (ca. 250) said that R. Yohanan († 279) said, "Even a well-overseer is appointed from heaven." (Even the smallest authoritative office is granted by God.) ‖ Jerusalem Talmud Pe'ah 8.21A.25: When R. Haggai (ca. 330) would appoint a community leader, he would give them a Torah to carry in order to say thereby that all leadership שְׂרָרָה, which is granted, is granted by the Torah: "By me (Wisdom = Torah) kings reign ...; by me princes rule ..." (Prov 8:15f.). ‖ Exodus Rabbah 30 (89A): God said to Nebuchadnezzar, "The little bit of dominion מלכית that is given to you stems from me." Daniel said to him, "You, O king, to whom the God of heaven has granted dominion, power, strength, and honor" (Dan 2:37). — See the whole passage at § Rom 1:21 A.

13:2: Whoever opposes authority opposes God's arrangement.

Genesis Rabbah 94 (60A): R. Judan (ca. 350) said, "Whoever behaves insolently toward the king is like someone who behaves insolently toward the Shekinah (divinity)." ‖ Midrash Psalm 2 § 3 (13A): "Against Yahweh and against his anointed one" (Ps 2:2). This relates to Korah, who grumbled against Aaron, Yahweh's anointed one, because of the priesthood. Moses said to him, "If my brother Aaron had taken the priesthood for himself, you would be right to grumble about him. But now God, to whom belongs greatness and dominion and strength, has granted it to him, and everyone who stands against Aaron שעומד כנגד אהרן stands only against God." This is what is written, "Against Yahweh and against his anointed one" (Ps 2:2).

13:3 A: Those who rule are not a dread to good work but rather to evil.

Babylonian Talmud ʿAbodah Zarah 3B and 4A: Rab Judah († 299) said that Samuel († 254) said, "What does 'You make people like the fish of the sea, like vermin, which has no ruler over itself' (Hab 1:14) mean? ... Just as with the fish in the sea the one that is bigger than the other devours the other, so too among the children of men, if there were no fear of the authorities מוראה של מלכות, everyone that is greater than the other would devour the other. And this is what we have learned (namely m. ʾAbot 3.2): 'R. Hananiah the head of the priests (ca. 70) said, "Pray for the wellbeing of the government מלכות; for if there were no fear of it, we would (already) have devoured each other alive, each one everyone else."'"

13:3 B: Do you wish not to fear authority? Do good.

Leviticus Rabbah 9 (111B): R. Aha (ca. 320) said, "Like a ruler who moved into a city, and with him (as prisoners) there were whole droves of bandits. Then the one (city dweller) said to another, 'How dreadful is this ruler!' But the one responded to him, 'If your acceptance is good, you do not need to fear him.' Likewise, when the Israelites heard the section about offerings, they were afraid. But Moses said to them, 'Do not fear. If you devote yourselves to the Torah, you will not be afraid of all this.'"

13:4: For it is God's servant.

θεοῦ διάκονος. — Wisdom 6:5: "Although you (kings and princes) are servants of his kingdom ὑπηρέται τῆς αὐτοῦ βασιλείας, you have not judged rightly, nor kept the law."

13:5: Therefore, it is necessary to be subject.

Here belongs the oft-cited word of Samuel († 254): דִּינָא דְמַלְכוּתָא דִּינָא "the law or ordinance of the (gentile) authorities is law" and therefore should be respected even by the Jews; see b. B. Qam. 113A at § Matt 5:46, #4, final paragraph.

13:7: Render to everyone what is owed: taxes to the one who demands taxes, tolls to the one who demands tolls, fear to the one who demands fear, honor to the one who demands honor.

1. φόρος and τέλος. — Concerning taxes and tolls, see § Matt 5:46, #1 and #2 and § Matt 17:25. — On evasion of tolls, see § Matt 5:46, #4.

2. φόβος and τιμή.

Babylonian Talmud Zebaḥim 102A: R. Yannai (ca. 225) said, "Let the fear of the authorities אימת מלכות always be upon you; for it is written, 'All these servants of yours will come down to me' (Exod 11:8). But look, Moses did not say it about him himself (pharaoh; namely, out of reverence for the king)." R. Yohanan († 279) said, "From here (the proof should be taken): 'The hand of Yahweh came over Elijah and he girded his loins and ran in front of Ahab' (1 Kgs 18:46)." — The same is found in b. Menaḥ. 98A. ‖ See b. ʿAbod. Zar. 3B and 4A at § Rom 13:3 A. ‖ See b. Menaḥ. 98A at § Acts 3:2, #1, n. *b*, third S-B footnote in this note. ‖ See b. ʿAbod. Zar. 65B at § Rom 1:26 A, #1, middle. ‖ Mekilta Exodus 12:31 (17A): "(pharaoh) summoned Moses and Aaron at night" (Exod 12:31). Why is this said? Because pharaoh had said to him, "Go away from me ..." (Exod 10:28). And Moses said, "You have spoken rightly," you have spoken beautifully and you had spoken at his time; "I will not see your face again" (Exod 10:29); but "all these servants of yours will come down to me" (Exod 11:8), for Scripture only intends to teach with this (eliminate אלה with Yalquṭ) that you (pharaoh) will ultimately be at their head and descend first (but Moses does not say this to extend him honor). This teaches that Moses honored authority חלק כבוד למלכות. And in the same way God said to him, "Honor authority"; as it says, "Yahweh spoke to Moses and to Aaron and commanded them concerning pharaoh" (so the midr. cites Exod 6:13). He commanded them to honor authority. And likewise, we find with Joseph that he honored authority; as it says, "God will answer what will turn out for the wellbeing of pharaoh" (Gen 41:16). Jacob likewise honored authority; as it says, "Then Israel made himself strong and sat up on his bed (to honor Joseph)" (Gen 48:2). Elijah likewise honored authority; as it says, "He girded his loins and ran in front of Ahab" (1 Kgs 18:46). Hananiah, Mishael, and Azariah likewise honored authority (see Dan 3:26). Daniel likewise honored authority (see Dan 6:21f.). — A parallel passage is found in Tanḥ. בא 75B. ‖ Tanḥuma וישלח 39A: "You are to say this to my lord, to Esau" (Gen 32:4). Jacob calls Esau "lord"; the Torah teaches human customs, that one may honor authority לחלוק כבוד למלכות. R. Ishmael († ca. 135) said, "See what is written, 'Yahweh spoke to Moses and to Aaron commanded them concerning the children of Israel and concerning pharaoh' (Exod 6:13); he taught them to honor authority. Likewise, our holy teacher (Judah I [† 217?]) wrote to (Caesar) Antoninus, 'Judah, your servant, offers you greetings,' to honor authority" (cf. § Rom 1:1 A, n. *b*). ‖ Sifre Deuteronomy 1:22 § 20 (69B): "You will draw near to me, all your tribal heads and elders" (Deut 5:20): the young honored the old, the old honored the heads.

13:8: Has fulfilled the law.

πληροῦν = קִיֵּם. See § Matt 5:17 B, #2.

13:9 A: You will not commit adultery, you will not kill, you will not steal, you will not covet.

οὐ μοιχεύσεις: see § Matt 5:27 A and § Rom 2:22 A. — οὐ φονεύσεις: see § Matt 5:21 B. — οὐ κλέψεις: see § Matt 19:18 A and § Rom 2:21 B. — οὐκ ἐπιθυμήσεις: see § Rom 7:7.

13:9 B: Is summarized in this saying, namely: "You will love your neighbor as yourself."

R. Aqiba († ca. 135) and Ben Azzai (ca. 110) think the same when they designate the commandment "You will love your neighbor as yourself"

(Lev 19:18) as the great all-encompassing principle in the Torah כְּלָל גדול בתורה and thereby as the *summa* of all the commandments. In the same way, R. Eleazar of Modiim († ca. 135) names the hearing of the divine word as the fundamental principle in which the whole Torah is contained הַכְּלָל שהתורה כלולה בו; on this, see § Matt 22:40. – On the commandment of neighbor love itself, see § Matt 5:43; here in notes *e* and *f*, more detail is also given about Aqiba's and Ben Azzai's "great principle in the Torah."

13:10: So, love is the fulfillment of the law.

Sifre Deuteronomy 11:13 § 41 (79B) can be compared, even though the passage deals chiefly with love for God: "To love Yahweh your God" (Deut 11:13). Perhaps you might say, "Look, I study the Torah so that I may become rich or so I may be called 'Rabbi' or so I may receive recompense!" Then Scripture teaches, "To love Yahweh your God." Everything that you do you should do only out of love.

13:11: Salvation is nearer to us than it was when we first believed.

See 1 En. 51:2 and especially 2 Bar. 23:7 at § Luke 21:28 B. – According to Pirqe Mashiaḥ (in *Beth ha-Midrash* 3.73.17) the Messiah will bring the good news to his people: קָרְבָה יְשׁוּעָה "Salvation has drawn near"; see the whole passage at § Rom 1:1 D.[147]

13:12 A: The night has advanced, but the day has drawn near.

νύξ – ἡμέρα = יוֹם – לַיְלָה. – In the face of the "night of this world" the future world (= days of the Messiah) are gladly called "day."

Genesis Rabbah 91 (58A): "I (Judah) will be surety for him (Benjamin) .... If I do not bring him to you (Jacob) ..., I will be guilty 'all days' before you" (Gen 43:9). The future world is meant, which is entirely day זה העולם הבא שכולו יום. – See additional examples in the excursus "This World, the Days of the Messiah, and the Future World," II, D, #2.

13:12 B: The works of darkness (cf. Isa 29:15; Prov 2:13).

TanḥumaB נה § 8 (17B): "Your judgments are a great depth" (Ps 36:7). This pertains to the works of godlessness: just as the depth is darkness, so too are the works of godlessness darkness; as it says, "Their works happen in darkness" (Isa 29:15). ‖ See Gen. Rab. 1 (2C) at § John 3:19 A, #1. ‖ The passage from b. Sanh. 104B adduced by Wettstein: "*Flevit propter noctem*" (Pindar, *Thren* 1.2), that is, "*propter opera noctis*" has been understood wrongly. לילה should not be understood in a metaphorical, but rather in a literal sense: since Israel wept in a frivolous way without reason on the night which Num 14:1 speaks about, it must now weep a true weeping in the night of Lam 1:2.

13:14 A: Put on the Lord Jesus Christ.

See § Luke 24:49, #2.

---

147. S-B: Here ישוע should be improved with ישועה.

13:14 B: Make no provision for the flesh (to stir up its) desires.

Babylonian Talmud Berakot 32A: What does "Dizahab" (Deut 1:1) mean? Those from the school of R. Yannai (ca. 225) said, "Moses spoke thus before God, 'Lord of the world, the silver and gold which you gave to Israel in abundance until they said, "It is enough" (thus דִּי זָהָב = דַּי זָהָב "enough gold") caused them to make the (golden) calf.'" Those from the school of R. Yannai said, "The lion does not roar at the basket full of straw, but rather at the basket full of meat." R. Hoshaiah (ca. 225) said, "Like a person who had an emaciated cow with strong limbs; then he fed it with vetches and it kicked him. He said to it, 'Who has caused you to kick me?' Only the vetches with which I fed you." R. Hiyya b. Abba (ca. 280) said that R. Yohanan († 279) said, "Like a person who had a son; he bathed him and anointed him, fed him and gave him drink, put a bag (with gold) around his neck and put him at the door of prostitutes. What should that son do so as not to sin?!" Rab Aha b. Huna (a contemporary of Rab Hisda [† 309]) said that Rab Sheshet (ca. 260) said, "This is what the people say, 'A full stomach is of a bad sort.'"

14:1: The one who is weak in faith.

τὸν ἀσθενοῦντα τῇ πίστει. Comparable in form: מְחוּסַּר אֲמָנָה "lacking faith"; קְטַנֵּי אֲמָנָה "those who are small in faith" = doubting. See examples at § Matt 6:30 B.

14:2: One has confidence to eat everything, but the weak eats (only) vegetation (vegetables).

Verse 21 shows that the weak abstained from consuming meat and wine. These would have been Christians who in principle eschewed any consumption of meat and wine in order not to unknowingly eat meat offered to idols or drink wine used for pagan libations. We hear of such voluntary abstinence in the ancient synagogue as well, albeit due to different motives.

Tosefta Soṭah 15.11–15 (322): After the sanctuary was destroyed, the abstemious increased in Israel, who neither ate meat nor drank wine. R. Joshua (ca. 90) concerned himself with them, He said to them, "My children, why do you not eat meat?" They answered him, "Should we eat meat, when the Tamid offering was daily offered on the altar, and now it has ceased?" He said to them, "Why do you not drink wine?" They answered him, "Should we drink wine, when the libation of wine was offered on the altar, and now it has ceased?" He said to them, "We should also not eat figs or wine grapes, since from these the first fruits were offered on the Feast of Weeks; we should not eat bread, since the two first fruit loaves (Lev 23:17) and the showbread loaves were offered; we should not drink water, since a libation of water was offered on the Feast of Booths." Then they were silent. He said to them, "It is not possible not to grieve at all, since the decision (fate) is already set (enacted); but it is also not possible to grieve excessively." Rather, the scholars said, "If someone whitewashes his house with lime, he leaves a small amount (un-whitewashed) in remembrance of Jerusalem; if someone arranges everything necessary for a meal, he leaves a small amount in remembrance of Jerusalem; if a woman applies all her make-up, she leaves a small amount in remembrance of Jerusalem; for it says, 'If I forget you, Jerusalem, may my right hand forget (perhaps: its use), may my tongue cleave to my palate, if I do not remember you, if I do not exalt Jerusalem as the peak of my joy' (Ps 137:5f.). Whoever mourns for Jerusalem is worthy to see its joy; as it says, 'Rejoice with Jerusalem and exult in her, all you who love her! Rejoice with her in bliss, all you who mourned for her!' (Isa 66:10)." — Parallels are found in b. B. Bat. 60B; Midr. Ps. 137 § 6 (262B); see also the baraita in b. B. Bat. 60B at § John 8:33 A.

14:5 A: One sets one day apart more than another.

In b. Sanh. 65B, the governor Tineius Rufus asks R. Aqiba († ca. 135), "What is the difference between the one day (the Sabbath) and the other days?" See the whole passage at § Acts 7:43 B. ‖ The following passages belong in the area of superstitious selection of days.

Babylonian Talmud Pesaḥim 112B: In a baraita it has been taught: Let one not go out alone at night, not on the midweek nights[148] (i.e., on the nights up until Wednesday) and not on the Sabbath nights, because the (demon queen) Igrat bat Mahalat goes out (on them), she herself and 18 myriads of angels of destruction, and every single one has power by itself to destroy. ‖ A baraita in b. Pesaḥ. 112A: Let one not drink water, neither on the midweek nights nor on the Sabbath nights, and if he drinks, his blood is on his head (= he bears the responsibility) for the danger. What danger? That of the evil spirit (Igrat bat Mahalat, see the previous citation). But if he is thirsty, what is his remedy? Let him say the sevenfold "voice" which David said concerning water (in Ps 29:3–9), and then let him drink. ‖ Babylonian Talmud Šabbat 129B: Samuel († 254) said, "The 1st day of the week (Sunday), Wednesday, and Friday (are appropriate) for bloodletting, but not Monday and Thursday." For the author said, "Whoever has the merit of the fathers (which supports him) may have his blood let on Monday and Thursday; for the upper and lower court agree." (Monday and Thursday are the court days for the earthly courts; then the heavenly court, which meets daily, might remember the sins of the one who has his blood let, and turn the bloodletting toward the worse.) Why not on Tuesday? Because then Mars (the star of bloodshed and punishments) applies in the even (paired) hours[149] (and in all paired things and even numbers, the demons make trouble; see the excursus "Ancient Jewish Demonology"). But he also applies on Friday in the even hours (namely in the 6th hour)! Since many are accustomed (to have their blood let) on it, "May Yahweh protect the simple" (Ps 116:6). Samuel said, "Wednesday, the fourth, Wednesday, the fourteenth, Wednesday, the twenty-fourth (of the month), the Wednesday that does not have four more days after it (in the month) is a danger (for bloodletting). The day of the new moon and the following day mean (concerning bloodletting) an enfeeblement; the third day after it is a danger; the day of preparation for a feast day (means) an enfeeblement;

---

148. S-B: לֵילֵי רְבִיעִיּוֹת can mean "nights up until the 4th days of the week" = "Wednesday nights." This is how it was translated above, as is common overall. However, it can also mean "nights in the early rains" (in the month of Marcheshvan), and it clearly has this meaning in Lev. Rab. 35 (132C). Presumably it should also be understood with this meaning above.

149. S-B: Mars rules on Tuesday except in the 1st hour (6–7 o'clock in the morning) and in the 8th hour, and so in an even numbered hour; on the planet table, see § John 2:4 C.

the day of preparation for the Feast of Weeks is a danger. And the rabbis have ordained it as a preventive measure for all preparation days for feast days on account of the Feast of Weeks, for on it a wind goes out whose name is Ṭibbuach טִבּוּחַ (= slaughter); for if the Israelites had not accepted the Torah, it would have butchered them, their flesh, and their blood. ‖ Babylonian Talmud Sanhedrin 65B: R. Aqiba († ca. 135) said, "(A soothsayer מְעוֹנֵן, see Lev 19:26; Deut 18:10) is one who calculates times and hours and says, 'Today is good to go out, tomorrow is good for shopping.'" See also SLev 19:26 (358A) at § Luke 24:16, n. *a*.

14:5 B: Let each one be fully convinced in his own mind.

See Sir 5:10: היה סָמוּךְ על דעתך "be firm in your mind." The Greek: ἴσθι ἐστηριγμένος ἐν συνέσει σου. — Sirach 35:22 (according to the chapter numbering in Fritzsche): "In every work trust your soul" πίστευε τῇ ψυχῇ σου. — The Hebrew text (Sir 32:23): "In all your deeds protect your soul."

14:6: He thanks God.

On the table prayer, see § Matt 14:19 B. — It cannot be decided with any certainty whether, by εὐχαριστεῖ (= בֵּרֵךְ), the apostle thought of the blessing before the meal or the thanksgiving afterward or both. In any case, he means: If a person says a blessing over what is to be eaten or gives thanks at the close of the meal for what has been eaten, he always confesses and praises God as the giver of food; but thereby he eats to God, to serve and honor God. — Babylonian Talmud Beṣah 16A also deals with an act of eating to God's honor; see the passage at § Matt 6:11, near the end and § Matt 12:1, #2 where parallels can be found as well.

14:8 A: If we live, we live to the Lord.

Mishnah ʾAbot 2.12: R. Yose the priest (ca. 100) said, "All your deeds should happen for God's sake." — In Pesiq. Rab. 23 (115B), Hillel the elder (ca. 20 BCE) is the author. It is said about him in b. Beṣah 16A that all he did happened for God's sake; see the passages at § Matt 12:1, #2.

14:8 B: So, whether we live or die, we are the Lord's.

Tanḥuma ואתחנן 5A: In that hour (the angel of the throne) Metatron came and prostrated before him and said to him, "Lord of the world, Moses was yours in his life and is yours in his death בחייו שלך הוא ובמותו שלך הוא."

14:10: For we will all be presented before the judgment seat of God.

1. Mishnah ʾAbot 4.22: (R. Eleazar Haqqappar [ca. 180]) said, "Those who are born are destined to die and those who died to come to life again and the living to be judged, so one may know, so one may make known and know that he is God, he the former, he the creator, he the one who takes notice, he the judge, he the witness, he the accuser, and that he will one day judge, before whom no injustice holds and no forgetting and no respect of persons

and no acceptance of bribes; for everything belongs to him. Know too that everything happens according to account. And do not let your evil inclination make you sure that there is a place of refuge in Sheol; for apart from your will you were created, and apart from your will you were born, and apart from your will you live, and apart from your will you will die, and apart from your will you will have to give an account and reckoning before the king of kings of kings—blessed be He!"

2. On βῆμα = בֵּימָה, see § Matt 27:19 A.

14:11: "To me every knee will bow and every tongue will confess God" (Isa 45:23).

In rabbinic literature, "Before him all will bow who sink in the dust" (Ps 22:30) is used almost without exception as scriptural proof for the appearance of all people before God's seat of judgment. See ʾAbot R. Nat. 25 (7A); SLev 1:1 (7B); Midr. Ps. 22 § 32 (99A) and parallels at § Matt 5:8 B, #2. We have found the application of Isa 45:23 (in connection with Ps 22:30) as a supporting passage only once, specifically in b. Nid. 30B. See the passage at § Rom 2:15 A, n. *a*. — Isaiah 45:23 is in another place interpreted concerning the acceptance of the gentiles as proselytes.

Midrash Psalm 100 § 1 (212B): "A psalm for confession (of the gentiles to Yahweh). Exult in Yahweh, all the world!" (so Ps 100:1 according to the midr.). R. Jacob b. Abbayye (ca. 340; so read instead of: R. Jacob in the name of R. Abbahu)[150] said in the name of R. Aha (ca. 320), "'A psalm for confession.' God said, 'Let all nations confess me; I will accept them (as proselytes); as it says, "I have sworn by myself, what is right has gone out from my mouth ... that every knee will bow to me, every tongue will swear to me" (Isa 45:23). At the time when every knee will bow to me, every tongue will swear to me, I will accept them.'"

14:12: Each of us will give an account about himself to God.

λόγον δώσει = עָתִיד לִיתֵּן דִּין וְחֶשְׁבּוֹן; on this, as well as on the whole of verse 12, see § Matt 12:36, #1 and #2.

14:13: Not to cause a stumbling or an offense for your brother.

πρόσκομμα and σκάνδαλον = מִכְשׁוֹל, תַּקָּלָה, Aram. תַּקָּלָא, תּוּקְלָא; see § Matt 18:7 B and C and § 1 Cor 8:13. — The base passage in the Old Testament is Lev 19:14: "You will not lay a stumbling block מִכְשֹׁל in front of a blind person." — Septuagint verbatim the same: καὶ ἀπέναντι τυφλοῦ οὐ προσθήσεις σκάνδαλον. The same is found in Tg. Onk. (תַּקָּלָא) and Tg. Yer. I (תּוּקְלָא). — Deuteronomy 27:18 then gained influence over the interpretation: "Cursed is the one who leads astray a blind person on the way!" — Septuagint and Tg. Onk. are verbatim the same. However, Tg. Yer. I and II read: "Cursed is whoever leads astray a stranger אַכְסְנָיָא (= ξένος) on

150. Bacher, *Die Agada der palästinensischen Amoräer*, 3:122..

the way, for this one is like a blind man (in his lack of familiarity with the way)." — Correspondingly, Tg. Yer. II also interpreted Lev 19:14 as follows: "And (you will not lay a stumbling block) in front of a stranger אכסניא, who is like a blind man." This metaphorical reinterpretation of "blind" is old; it is present already in SLev 19:14 and b. B. Meṣ. 5:11. In the 1st passage, the phrase "to lay a stumbling block in front of a blind person" is identical in meaning to, "to wickedly counsel an unsuspecting person (out of selfish motives)";[a] and in the 2nd passage with: "to cause an innocent to sin."[b]

a. Sifra Leviticus 19:14 (350A): "You will not lay a stumbling block in front of a blind person" (Lev 19:14); in front of someone who is blind (inexperienced, clueless) in a matter. He comes and says to you, "How is it with the daughter of this or that man in respect to (her marrying into) the priesthood?" You should not say to him, "She is fitting," when she is only unfit. If he seeks counsel from you, you should not give him counsel that is not appropriate for him. You should not say to him, "Leave at the early morning hour," when thieves could beat him. "Leave at the midday hour," so that he would be parched (get sunstroke). You should not say to him, "Sell your field and buy yourself a donkey," while you are being underhanded toward him and want to buy it from him yourself. If you say, "I will give him good counsel," behold, the matter is entrusted to the heart (which is indeed invisible to people, but not to God); for it says, "And you should fear your God. I am Yahweh" (Lev 19:14).

b. Mishnah Baba Meṣiʿa 5.11: The following transgress proscriptions (in lending for interest): the lender (creditor), the borrower (debtor), the guarantor, and the witnesses. And the scholars said, "The scribe too (for the certificate of debt). They commit a transgression because of: 'You are not to give (your money at interest)' (Lev 25:37); and because of: 'You are not to take from him' (Lev 25:36); and because of: 'You are not to be as a usurer to him' (Exod 22:24); and because of: 'You are not to impose interest on him' (Exod 22:24); and because of: 'And you will not lay a stumbling block in front of a blind person and you will fear your God. I am Yahweh' (Lev 19:14)." — See b. B. Meṣ. 75B: Abbayye († 338/39) said, "The creditor transgresses all these (prohibitions). The debtor commits one transgression because of: 'You are not to let your brother impose interest' (Deut 23:20; so the midr.); and: 'You are not to let your brother impose interest' (Deut 23:21; so the midr.); and: 'You will not lay a stumbling block in front of a blind person' (Lev 19:14; here the creditor is thought of as the one who is ignorant of the law to whom the debtor gives the opportunity to sin with his offer of interest). The guarantor and the witnesses commit a transgression only because of: 'You are not to impose interest on him' (Exod 22:24)." — Leviticus 19:14 is employed in the same sense in a baraita in b. Pesaḥ. 22B: R. Nathan (ca. 160) said, "How do we know that a person may not give a cup of wine to a Nazirite or a limb of a live animal to a Noachide? Scripture teaches, 'You will not lay a stumbling block in front of a blind person' (Lev 19:14)." (The Nazirite and the Noachide could thereby be misled to sin.) — A parallel is found in b. ʿAbod. Zar. 6A. ‖ ʿAbod. Zar. 6A: ("It is forbidden to trade with gentiles for three days before their feasts" [m. ʿAbod. Zar. 1.1].) The following question was raised by them (the teachers): Because of what merit? Or perhaps because of: "You will not lay a stumbling block in front of a blind person" (Lev 19:14)? (Trading livestock, e.g., could supply the gentiles with sacrificial meat that they present to idols.) ‖ Babylonian Talmud ʿAbodah Zarah 21B, 22A: R. Simeon b. Eleazar (ca. 190) said, "A person (a Jew) should not lease his field to a Samaritan, because it is named after him (the Jewish owner) and a Samaritan does work on it on the interfeast days (and thereby sins).... This being the case (that a Samaritan does work that is not allowed), why is (the second reason) given in the context: 'Because it is named after him'? It would arise from: 'You will not lay a stumbling block in front of a blind person' (Lev 19:14)! (By leasing the field to the Samaritan, the Jew becomes for him an occasion to transgress the law of rest on interfeast days.) He says one thing and one more thing. One, because of 'In front of a blind man ...'; and another thing "Because it is named after him.'" ‖ Babylonian Talmud Moʿed Qaṭan 5A: (Where can an allusion to marking graves be found in the Torah?) Abbayye († 338/39) said, "From here: 'And you will not lay a stumbling block in front of a blind person' (Lev 19:14)." (A grave that is not recognized and avoided makes the Israelite unclean and causes him to sin by his impurity.) ‖ Babylonian Talmud Moʿed Qaṭan 17A: A maid of the house of Rabbi († 217?) saw a man, how he struck his grown son. She said, "This man should be under the ban, since he commits a transgression due to: 'You will not lay a stumbling block in front of a blind person' (Lev 19:14). For in a baraita it has been taught that Scripture says, 'You will not lay a stumbling block in front of a blind person,' about someone who strikes his grown son" (and thereby might give the son an opportunity to sin against his father). ‖ Babylonian Talmud Baba Meṣiʿa 75B: Rab Judah († 299) said that Rab († 247) said, "Whoever has money and lends without witnesses commits a transgression because of: 'And you will not lay a stumbling block in front of a blind person' (Lev 19:14)" (by leading the debtor into temptation to disavow the loan). ‖ Babylonian Talmud Baba Meṣiʿa 90A: Come and hear! Some people reached out to the father of Samuel († 254): "Those cattle, which Arameans (gentiles) steal and castrate, what is the case with them?" (Castrating animals was forbidden to Jews; in order to circumvent the law, Jews had non-Jews ostensibly steal the animals and castrate them in order then to get them back from them.) He sent word to them, "A ruse has been carried out against them, so outfox them (the Jewish owners), and they should sell them" (so that they get nothing from their cunning)! Rab Papa († 376) said, "The westerners (= Palestinians) were of the same opinion as R. Hidqa (ca. 120); for they said, 'Castration has been forbidden to Noachides' (see b. Sanh. 56B.1, 13 and b. Sanh. 56B at § Rom 1:20 E, n. *c*). Thus, they committed a transgression because of: 'And you will not lay a stumbling block in front of a blind person' (Lev 19:14)." (By the cattle owners having had the castration carried out by non-Jews, they caused the latter to transgress the Noachic commandments.)

14:17: Joy in the Holy Spirit.

A baraita in b. Pesaḥ. 117A: (The psalm superscription:) "Of David, a psalm" indicates that the Shekinah (divinity, here = holy spirit) rested on him, and then he said the song (the psalm in question is thus inspired). (The psalm superscription:) "A psalm of David" indicates that he said the song, and then the Shekinah rested on him. This teaches you that the Shekinah does not rest (on a person) as a consequence of idleness, nor as a consequence of anguish, nor as a consequence of a hoax, nor as a consequence of recklessness, nor as a consequence of useless words (idle gossip), but rather as a consequence of joy in a commandment; as it says, "And now fetch me a musician who plays strings, and it happened, when the musician played, the hand of Yahweh came upon him." ‖ See y. Sukkah 5.55A.42 in the excursus "The Feast of Tabernacles," IV, n, *p*.

14:18: Pleasing to God and approved by people.

See § Rom 12:17 B.

14:19: So, let us pursue what pertains to peace and edification.

τὰ τῆς εἰρήνης, see § Rom 12:18. — τὰ τῆς οἰκοδομῆς, see § Matt 16:18, #2 and § Matt 21:42, #2.

14:20: Everything is clean, but it is bad for a person who eats under offense (against conscience).

This can be compared with the tenet in b. Pesaḥ. 110B.3, 5 about the attitude toward the so-called זוּגוֹת (זוּגִים) = "pairs." The superstitious person considered all pairs—including even numbers, for example, eating 2, 4, 6 etc. fruits—as hazardous, because evil spirits made mischief with them (see in more detail in the excursus "Ancient Jewish Demonology"). Concerning this, it is said:

Babylonian Talmud Pesaḥim 110B: In the west (Palestine), they were not especially particular about pairs (this superstition was not revered). Rab Dimi of Nehardea (head of the school in Pom Beditha in Babylonia [385–388]) was very particular about pairs even when it came to marking (sold) vats (of wine). It happened that a vat burst (the vat had inadvertently been marked with an even number of markings). The general rule here is: Whoever is particular about it (whoever feels bound to the superstition in his conscience), with him they (the demons) are particular about it (they harm him when he occasionally disregards the זוגות); but whoever is not particular about pairs, with him they are (also) not particular about it. All the same, one should take it into consideration (since there might be some special meaning in the זוגות).

14:21: It is good (right) not to eat meat or drink wine or (do anything else) that offends your brother.

Sifre Deuteronomy 14:21 § 104 (95A): "For you are a holy people for Yahweh your God" (Deut 14:21). Sanctify yourself in what is allowed to you:[151] if things are allowed, but others treat them as forbidden, you are not entitled to treat them as allowed before their eyes. — The same is found as a baraita in b. Ned. 15A and as the citation in the mouth of Abbayye († 338, 39) in b. Pesaḥ. 50A, B. — Babylonian Talmud Pesaḥim 51A shows how the words are meant: Rab Hisda († 309) said, "(The statement 'If things are allowed, but other treat them as forbidden …') pertains to the Samaritans. Why to the Samaritans? Because these

151. S-B: This is an improvement of the translation of the passage at § Matt 10:5.

people take advantage of it (the easements that they have seen among the Jews) and they would take advantage of it in other cases (namely to obtain further easements)." The impetus of the baraita is thus an essentially different one than that of Rom 14:21: the Jew should refrain from what is allowed not because another could take offense at the Jew's permissive action because of the narrowness of his conscience, but rather because the other would consequently take further license because of the broadness of his conscience.

14:23: Everything that does not (occur) from faith is sin.

See b. B. Bat. 10B at § Matt 5:7, #5, where several times it is stated that all benefactions and works of love of the gentiles are only sin because they are done (not for God's sake, but rather) from selfish motives.

15:3: "The insults of those who insult you have fallen upon me" (Ps 69:10).

The citation is verbatim according to the LXX Ps 68:10, except the apostle has used ἐπέπεσαν instead of ἐπέπεσον. ‖ Targum Psalms 69:10: "Zeal for your sanctuary has consumed me, and the insults of the godless who insult you when they join (equate) their idols to your glory, have fallen upon me." — The verse is interpreted in relation to David in b. Zebaḥ. 54B; see the passage at § John 2:17.

15:4: Whatever was written beforehand was written for our instruction.

See the passages presented at § Rom 1:2 B, n. *b*, according to which only those prophecies were recorded that were needed for the Torah, thus for Israel's instruction, or for the following generations.

15:9: So that the gentiles ... praise God.

The baraita in b. Meg. 14A which has been adduced as a parallel does not prove what it is supposed to prove. It reads: After the Israelites had gone into the land (Canaan), other lands were no longer suitable to have a song (to God) sung in them; but after the Israelites had gone into exile, (all lands) became suitable again (namely, so that the Israelites might sing a song to God in them. The passage does not speak about the gentiles at all; see the parallel passage b. ʿArak. 10A at § Matt 21:9 A, #1, n. *e*).

15:10: And again he says.

καὶ πάλιν λέγει = וְאוֹמֵר.[a] Here the וְ represents the πάλιν, while the subject should be understood as either God or Scripture. For the fuller formula הַכָּתוּב אוֹמֵר "Scripture says," see also § Mark 1:2f. and § John 19:37 A; further, see § 1 Cor 6:16.

a. Mishnah Berakot 9.5: It was ordained that people should greet each other with God's name (Yahweh); for it says שֶׁנֶּאֱמַר: "And lo, Boaz came from Bethlehem and said to the shearers, 'Yahweh be with you!' And they answered him, 'Yahweh bless you!'" (Ruth 2:4). And again (Scripture) says וְאוֹמֵר, "Yahweh be with you, you valiant hero!" (Judg 6:12). And again (Scripture) says ואומר, "Do not despise your mother when she has grown old" (Prov 23:22) (the ancient forms of greeting still have their significance for later times). And again (Scripture) says ואומר, "It is time for Yahweh to act (also by saying his name in a greeting); they have broken your Torah" (Ps 119:126). — On the whole passage, see the comments on b. Mak. 23B at § Matt 5:47, n. *c*. — In b. Ber. 54B.31, six citations are introduced with ואומר one after another. — Further examples are found in this work wherever several supporting passages are connected to each other in a scriptural proof.

15:11: "Praise the Lord, all you gentiles, and let all the nations extol him" (Ps 117:1).

1. Midrash Psalm 117 § 1 (240A): A philosopher asked R. Joshua b. Hananiah (ca. 90), "Which is the day on which all the world will be the same (one) and the nations will worship before God?" He answered him, "On one day they will all rejoice." "When?" "When the rain showers are withheld, all are in distress, and when the rain showers fall, all rejoice and praise God; as it says, 'All the nations that you have made (will come and prostrate before you)' (Ps 86:9)." "When?" "'When you are great and do wonders' (so Ps 86:10 according to the midr.). And 'wonders' means nothing other than rain showers; as it says, 'To the one who ... does countless wonders, who gives rain on earth' (Job 5:9f.). Therefore, it says, 'Praise Yahweh, all you peoples, praise him all you nations!' (Ps 117:1)." — In the parallel passages Gen. Rab. 13 (9D) and Deut. Rab. 7 (204B), the questioner is a "gentile" and the one asked is R. Joshua b. Qarha (ca. 150) or Rabban Yohanan b. Zakkai († ca. 80). ‖ Midrash Psalm 117 § 3 (240B): (When the angel Gabriel saved the three men from the furnace [see b. Pesaḥ. 118A at § Luke 1:19 A, #4, n. *h* and § Matt 21:9 A, #1, n. *b*]) Hananiah said, "Praise Yahweh, all you peoples!" (Ps 117:1); Mishael said, "Praise him, all you nations" (Ps 117:1); Azariah said, "For great is his grace over us" (Ps 117:2); Gabriel said, "And Yahweh's faithfulness lasts forever!" (Ps 117:2).

2. τὰ ἔθνη = גּוֹיִם, οἱ λαοί = אֻמִּים.

Midrash Psalm 117 § 2 (240A): R. Simeon (ca. 220), the son of our holy teacher, asked his father (Judah I [† 217]), "(In Ps 117:1) who are 'all the peoples' גוים (ἔθνη) and who are 'all the nations' אומים (λαοί)?" He answered him, "'All the peoples': these are the peoples who have oppressed Israel. 'All the nations': these are the nations who have not oppressed them. All the nations will say, 'How is that?' If those who have oppressed the children of Israel praise God, must we who have not oppressed them praise him all the more? This is why it says, 'Praise Yahweh, all you peoples, praise him all you nations!' (Ps 117:1). Then the Israelites will say, 'Then we must praise him all the more!' They will begin to say, 'For great is your grace over us!' (Ps 117:2). And the earth will say, 'And Yahweh's faithfulness lasts forever!' (Ps 117:2). What does 'And the faithfulness' mean? This pertains to the faithfulness of the covenant that you established with the fathers; as it says, 'And I will remember my covenant with Jacob' (Lev 26:42)."

15:12: "The root of Jesse will come and the one who arises to rule over the peoples, in him the peoples will hope" (Isa 11:10).

Except for the omission of a few words at the beginning, the citation follows LXX Isa 11:10 verbatim. — The base text is: "And it will happen on that day, the root of Jesse, which will be a banner for the peoples—the gentiles will seek him, and his place of rest will be glorious." — Targum Isaiah 11:10: "And it will happen in that time, then the scion (literally: grandchild) of Jesse will be as a sign for the peoples, kingdoms will be in thrall to him, and the place of his abode will be in glory."

Midrash Psalm 21 § 1 (89A): "For the leader of music, a psalm of David. Yahweh, the king rejoices over your strength" (Ps 21:1). This is what Scripture said: "And it will happen on that day, the root of Jesse, which will be a banner for the peoples—the gentiles will seek him" (Isa 11:10). This is the Messiah, the son of David, who remains hidden until the time of the appointed day (until the time of the end). ‖ See Gen. Rab. 98 (62A) and Midr. Ps. 21 § 1 (89A) at § John 4:25 B.

15:16 A: Administering the gospel of God in a priestly way.

ʾAbot de Rabbi Nathan 4 (2D): The study of the Torah is more beloved before God than burnt offerings (so according to the text of the Frankfurt edition [1720ff.]). For when someone studies the Torah, he acquires knowledge of God; as it says, "Then you will acquire insight in the fear of Yahweh and obtain knowledge of God" (Prov 2:5). From here it follows for a scholar who sits and speaks in the community, that Scripture counts it to him as if he offered fat and blood on the altar.

15:16 B: The offering of the gentiles.

προσφορὰ τῶν ἐθνῶν = the offering that the gentiles themselves are; τῶν ἐθνῶν is thus a genitive of apposition. — Similarly, Isa 66:20: "And they will bring all your brothers from the nations as an offering מִנְחָה (Tg.: קוּרְבָּנָא, LXX: δῶρον) for Yahweh on steeds and on chariots ...." On this, see § Matt 2:11 and Midr. Ps. 87 § 6 at § Rom 3:9 A, #3, B, n. *u*.

15:19: In power of signs and wonders.

The power to do wonders was ascribed in many ways also to the rabbis. On healing diseases, see b. Ḥag. 3A at § Matt 9:32; b. Ber. 5B at § Mark 1:31 A; b. Ber. 34B at § John 4:47ff.; on raising the dead, see § Matt 10:8 A, #2 and § John 11:44 A; on the lethal glance of the rabbis, see § Acts 13:9 B, n. *b*; also see b. B. Meṣ. 59B at § Matt 3:17 A, n. *d*; on their magical arts, see § Luke 24:16, n. *c*. — Here the following may be added as well:

Babylonian Talmud Ḥullin 60A: Caesar's (Hadrian's) daughter said to R. Joshua b. Hananiah (ca. 90), "Your God is a carpenter, for it is written, 'He sets his beams in the waters' (Ps 104:3). Tell him to make me a winch." He said, "Okay then (I will do it)." He prayed about her, and she became leprous. She was put on a street in Rome and given a winch; for it was the custom to give a winch to a leprous person in Rome, so that he would sit on the street and wind up yarn, so that people would see him and pray for mercy for him. One day he (R. Joshua) passed by that place; she sat there and wound yarn on the street of Rome. He said to her, "Is the winch that my God gave you nice?" She said to him, "Tell your God to take what he has given me." He said to her, "Our God gives, but he does not take."

15:20: Seeking my honor in proclaiming the gospel not where Christ has (already) been named (preached).

See the principle of Hillel (ca. 20 BCE): "In a place where there are no men, strive to be a man" (m. ʾAbot 2.5).

15:26: To arrange a contribution (κοινωνίαν τινὰ ποιήσασθαι).

1. κοινωνία in the passive sense = what is shared, given, is safeguarded by LXX Lev 6:2 (= Hebrew 5:21). Here the phrase in the underlying text, תְּשׂוּמֶת יָד = "what is given into the hand" is translated with κοινωνία. — With their use of שׁוּתָּפוּת יְדָא, the targumim think of a jointly pursued endeavor. — In the NT, the term λογία, which is found twice in Paul (1 Cor 16:1, 2) is an actual *terminus technicus* for fund raising or collection. The other New Testament designations for "collection" are simply circumlocutions for the concept, which represent what a collection essentially should be, namely a service or demonstration of love by those who can and want to help (διακονία, Rom 15:31; 2 Cor 8:4; 9:1; cf. Acts 11:29; 12:25; λειτουργία, 2 Cor 9:12; χάρις, 1 Cor 16:3; 2 Cor 8:4, 6, 7, 19). — Alongside εὐποιΐα = "doing good" (Heb 13:16), κοινωνία should be understood as a *nomen actionis* and signifies "sharing." — Translated literally into Aramaic, κοινωνίαν ποιήσασθαι (Rom 15:26) would be לְמֶעְבַּד שׁוּתָּפוּת and would be tantamount to, "to conduct a company business." This is found in b. Pesaḥ. 112A.26, where R. Aqiba's († ca. 135) rule of savviness, "Get involved with someone on whom the hour smiles," is elucidated by Rab Papa († 376) as follows: "One should not buy from him and one should not sell to him, but rather let one conduct a joint endeavor with him אלא למעבד שותפית בהדיה."

In the apocrypha, voluntary gifts of love are sometimes called ἀποστολαί = "sendings." 1 Esdras 9:51: ἀποστείλατε ἀποστολὰς τοῖς μὴ ἔχουσιν = Neh 8:10: שלחו מנות לאין נכון לו "send gifts to the one for whom nothing is prepared." ‖ 1 Esdras 9:54: καὶ δοῦναι ἀποστολὰς τοῖς μὴ ἔχουσι = Neh 8:12: לְשַׁלַּח מָנוֹת. ‖ 1 Maccabees 2:18: "You (Mattathias) and your sons will be honored with silver and gold and many gifts ἀποστολαῖς πολλαῖς." ‖ 2 Maccabees 3:2: "It happened that even the kings … glorified (honored) the sanctuary (in Jerusalem) with the most valuable gifts ἀποστολαῖς ταῖς κρατίσταις." ‖ In the epistle of Caesar Julian to the Jewish communities,[152] the tribute to be paid to the patriarch by the Jewish communities is called "ἀποστολή." From another, different non-Jewish source, we learn that the men appointed by the patriarch for the collection or receipt of this tribute were called "*apostoli*."[153] Ancient rabbinic literature does not mention this tax for the patriarch and its collection by specially commissioned men; but for "*apostoli*," one would expect the term שְׁלוּחִים, Aram. שְׁלוּחֵי (see § Rom 1:1 B, #2) and, correspondingly, for 'ἀποστολή' שְׁלִיחוּת, Aram. שְׁלִיחוּתָא. In the NT too, "ἀπόστολοι" appear as those who deliver the collection gifts; see 2 Cor 8:23; Phil 2:25; see ἀποστείλαντες in Acts 11:30.

2. Since the destruction of Jerusalem, the impoverishment of the position of a scholar became a serious concern for Palestinian Judaism. Insofar as purely private benefaction did not helpfully intervene, recourse was made to the so-called מַגְבַּת חֲכָמִים, "raising a collection for the scholars." The most respected scholars were appointed (presumably by the patriarchate) to gather the collection in the specified districts both in Israel and abroad. It seems that there were always at least two collectors who together had to carry out the task (see § Acts 6:3, #4, A, notes *c* and *d*). The gifts were delivered to the collectors in the localities either at a specific place, or the collectors spoke about it in individual houses. The revenue was registered; often the collectors put the names of the most generous benefactors at the top of the collection lists. It was thought that in this way a particularly special repayment from God was secured for the donors for their munificence.

Jerusalem Talmud Horayot 3.48A.39: It happened that R. Eliezer (ca. 90) and R. Joshua (ca. 90) and R. Aqiba († ca. 135) went into the region of Antiochia to raise a collection for the scholars מגבת חכמים. There was a certain Abba Judah there, who practiced benefaction with a benevolent eye. Once his wealth declined, and he saw our teachers and was about to sink into despair because of them. He went into his house and he looked afflicted. His wife said to him, "Why do you look afflicted?" He said to her, "Our teachers are here and I do not know what I should do." His wife, who was even more beneficent than he was, said to him, "You still have one field left. Go and sell half of it and give it to them." He went and did so. Then he came to our teachers and gave it to them.[154] Our teachers prayed for him (read נתפללו instead of נתפללה) and said to him, "Abba Judah, may God fill out ימלא חסרנותיך your want!" When they had gone from there, he went down to plow the half of his field. While he was plowing the half of his field, his cow sank down and broke a leg. He got down to pick it up again. Then God illumined his eyes, and he found a treasure. He said, "For my good has my cow's foot been broken." When our teachers returned, they asked about him. They said, "What does Abba Judah do?" It was answered them, "Who can look at the face of

---

152. S-B: See the text in Heinrich Grätz, *Geschichte der Juden von den ältesten Zeiten bis auf die Gegenwart*, 2nd ed. (Leipzig: Leiner, 1900), 4:493 n. 34.

153. See Codex Theodos. 16, 8, 14 in Grätz, *Geschichte der Juden*, 4:477 n. 21.

154. S-B: Here the gifts are not requested in individual houses, but rather are delivered to the collectors in a specified collecting location.

Abba Judah? (He has become so rich and noble that no one can greet him anymore.) Abba Judah has cattle, Abba Judah has camels, Abba Judah has donkeys, Abba Judah is now again as he was before." He came to our teachers and inquired about their welfare. They said to him, "How is it going for Abba Judah?" He answered them, "Your prayer has brought fruits and fruits of fruits (compound interest)." They said to him, "Although others had given more than you, we wrote you down as first in the list טוֹמוֹס (τόμος)." They took him and sat him at their side and applied this verse to him: "A person's gift makes room for him and leads him close to great ones" (Prov 18:16). — Parallels are found in Lev. Rab. 5 (108B): מגבת צדקה לחכמים "Raising a benevolent offering for the scholars"; Deut. Rab. 4 (201A): R. Aqiba is not mentioned; לגבות לעסק מצות עמילי תורה "to raise contributions for benevolent purposes for the sake of those who are assiduous in the Torah." ‖ Jerusalem Talmud Pesaḥim 4.31B.61: Once the rabbis needed a free will offering נִידְבָא.[155] R. Aqiba († ca. 135) was sent out and one of the rabbis with him. They came and wanted to come into his house (a certain Ben Mebii Yayin; in Midr. Esth., the man is called בַּרְבּוּחִין).[156] Then they heard the voice of a child who said to him, "What should we buy for you today?" He answered him, "Endives, but not ones from today, but rather from yesterday; for they have wilted and are (therefore) cheap." Then the rabbis left him and went from there (they thought that they should not request a gift from such a poor man who had nothing to eat). After they had requested alms from everyone, they went to him. He said to them, "Why did you not come to me first, as you (otherwise) used to?" They answered, "We had come (here) already, but we heard the voice of a child that said to you, 'What should we buy for you today?' And you answered him, 'Endives, but not from today, but rather from yesterday, for they have wilted and are cheap.'" He said to them, "You know what was going on with me and the child, but not what goes on between me and my creator. Anyhow, go and tell her (my wife) to give you a modius of *denars*." (1 modius = 8.754 liters; 1 *denar* was about 65 pennies.) They went and told her. She said to them, "How did he say it to you: a 'lump' or a 'rounded down' (modius)?" They answered her, "He told us without more precisely specifying." She said to them, "I will give you a lump sum, and if he meant a lump sum, it happened according to his words; but if not, I will deduct the lump sum from my dowry (which the wife had to return in case of a divorce or her husband's death)." When her husband heard this, he doubled her prescribed marital sum (which had to be paid out to the wife in case the marriage was terminated). — There is a parallel in Midr. Esth. 1:4 (86A).

15:33: The God of peace.

ὁ θεὸς τῆς εἰρήνης is found also in Rom 16:20; Phil 4:9; 1 Thess 5:23; 2 Thess 3:16; Heb 13:20. — Testament of Dan 5: "If you speak the truth, each one to his neighbor, you will not stray into desire (other manuscripts: anger) and turmoil, but rather you will be in peace and have the God of peace τὸν θεὸν τῆς εἰρήνης." ‖ Great is peace, for God's name is "peace."

---

155. S-B: The parallel passage Midr. Esth. 1:4 (86A) speaks more precisely of the "raising of a collection for the scholars" מגבת חכמים.

156. S-B: Here the gifts are requested in individual houses.

As it says, "He called him 'Yahweh peace'" (Judg 6:24)! See SNum 6:26 § 42 (12B) at § Matt 5:9, #1.

16:3: My co-workers.

συνεργός can have a Hebrew equivalent in חָבֵר, insofar as the latter generally designates any "companion" or "peer," and thus if appropriate, also a work companion. But it is incorrect that συνεργός should be a Greek translation of חָבֵר, which is used as a *terminus technicus.* חָבֵר (Aram. חַבְרָא, חֲבֵרָא) as a *terminus technicus* denotes: α. the member of the *ḥaber* covenant, whose members had obligated themselves to strictly observe the laws of tithing and purity. See § John 7:49, #5; β. the scholar who had not reached ordination and thereby not the title of "rabbi." In order to offer this scholar some compensation, the rabbis called him "colleague" חָבֵר; see § Acts 6:6, at the end of #4. The συνεργοί of the apostle do not overlap in any way with these two categories of חֲבֵרִים.

16:16: With a holy kiss.

On kissing, see § Matt 26:49.

16:19: But I want you to be wise about good, but pure concerning evil.

Babylonian Talmud Sanhedrin 21A: "Jonadab was a clever man" (2 Sam 13:3). Rab Judah († 299) said that Rab († 247) said, "He was a man who was clever for evil איש חכם לרשעה." ‖ Targum Yerušalmi I Genesis 3:1: "The same was clever for evil חַכִּים לְבִישׁ."

16:20: The God of peace will crush Satan under your feet shortly.

1. On ὁ θεὸς τῆς εἰρήνης, see § Rom 15:33.

2. συντρίψει, if there is a reference to Gen 3:15, = שׁוּף, שְׁפַף, to grind, crush. — A material parallel is found in T. Levi 18: "Beliar will be bound by him (the high priest of the messianic time), and he will give his children power to tread on the evil spirits πατεῖν ἐπὶ τὰ πονηρὰ πνεύματα."

16:22: I, Tertius, who wrote this letter, greet you.

Scribes to whom a letter is dictated are also mentioned in rabbinic literature.[a] To certify the authenticity of the letter, the sender then put his own signature or at least a sign beneath it.[b]

a. See t. Sanh. 2.6 (416) at § Matt 4:12, #2; see Gen. Rab. 75 (48C) at § Rom 1:1 A, n. *b.*

b. Tosefta Baba Qamma 7.4 (358): A parable was told. What can the matter be compared with? With a king of flesh and blood who gets engaged to a woman. He brings the scribe and the ink and the quill and the document and the witnesses. If she has committed an offense, she brings everything; it is enough for her that the king gives her (in the certificate of divorce) the mark of identification from his hand. ‖ Babylonian Talmud Giṭṭin 36A:

Rab († 247) signed a fish (as a signature); R. Hanina (ca. 225) signed a palm branch; Rab Hisda († 309) signed a *samekh* ס; R. Hoshaiah (ca. 225) signed an *ʿayin* ע; Rabbah bar Huna († 322) a mast. — The same is found in b. B. Bat. 161B. ‖ See b. B. Bat. 12B at § Luke 2:25 C, #3, n. *o*.

16:23: Erastus, the city treasurer.

On οἰκονόμος τῆς πόλεως, see § Luke 16:1.

16:25: In accordance with the revelation of the secret that was kept secret since eternal times.

1. On μυστήριον, see § Matt 13:11. — According to verse 26, μυστήριον means the participation of the gentiles in the kingdom of God.

2. σεσιγμένον = kept secret. — This statement can be compared with passages which claim that the secret of the starting time of the messianic era is hidden in God's heart, so that no human can calculate the arrival of the Messiah in advance.

Pesiqta Rabbati 1 (4B): Rabbi († 217?) said, "You cannot calculate (the starting time of the days of the Messiah); for it says, 'The day of vengeance is in my (God's) heart' (Isa 63:4)." ‖ Babylonian Talmud Sanhedrin 99A: "The day of vengeance is in my heart" (Isa 63:4). R. Yohanan († 279) said, "To my heart I have revealed it, to my limbs I have not revealed it." R. Simeon b. Laqish (ca. 250) said, "To my heart I have revealed it, to the angels of service (to say nothing of human beings) I have not revealed it." ‖ Midrash Psalm 9 § 2 (40B): R. Samuel (ca. 260, according to another reading, R. Saul; see the parallel in Midr. Eccl.) taught as a tannaitic tradition in the name of R. Judah (ca. 150), "If someone should say to you when the time of redemption will come, do not believe him; for it is written, 'The day of vengeance is in my heart' (Isa 63:4). The heart has not revealed it to the mouth. To whom would the mouth have revealed it?" — The same with variations was taught by R. Saul from Nave (in the 4th cent.) as a tannaitic tradition in the name of R. Simeon (ca. 150) in Midr. Eccl. 12:9 (54B). ‖ Midrash Psalm 9 § 2 (41A): R. Berekhiah (ca. 340) and R. Simon (ca. 280) said in the name of R. Joshua b. Levi (ca. 250), "I (says God) gave you three signs about the grave of Moses; as it says, 'He buried him in the valley, in the land of Moab, across from Beth Peor' (Deut 34:6). At the end it says, 'No one knows the site of his grave' (Deut 34:6). If no human being was able to figure out a matter in which I gave you sign after sign, how much more does this go for the end time קֵץ, of which it says, 'These words are hidden and sealed until the end of time' (Dan 12:9)!" — The same is found in Midr. Eccl. 12:9 (54B), though here the tradent is R. Judah b. Simon (ca. 320); see also b. Soṭah 13B, though here there is no application to the messianic קֵץ.

3. μυστήριον χρόνοις αἰωνίοις σεσιγμένον. — 1 Enoch 9:6 mentions heavenly secrets of primordial time (eternity), which according to 1 En. 7 and 8 mean every kind of magical potion, incantation, and miscellaneous arts that the fallen angels had revealed to men: "You have seen what Azazel (one of the fallen angels) did, how he taught every kind of iniquity

on earth and revealed the heavenly secrets of primordial time τὰ μυστήρια τοῦ αἰῶνος (= עוֹלָם)[157] which humanity took an interest in knowing."

16:26: In accordance with the ordinance of the eternal God.

ὁ αἰώνιος θεός. — 1 Enoch 1:3: "The great holy one will go out from his dwelling and the God of eternity ὁ θεὸς τοῦ αἰῶνος (= אֱלֹהֵי עוֹלָם, Isa 40:28; אֵל עוֹלָם, Gen 21:33; LXX in both passages: θεὸς αἰώνιος) will step from there onto Mount Sinai...." ‖ Baruch 4:8: "You have forgotten the eternal God" τὸν ... θεὸν αἰώνιον. — ὁ αἰώνιος appears by itself in, for example, Bar 4:10, 14, 20, 22. ‖ Susanna 35: "Her heart trusted in the Lord her God ..., in that she said in herself, 'Lord, eternal God ὁ θεὸς ὁ αἰώνιος, you who know everything before it arises....'" — In Theodotion 42: "Eternal God ὁ θεὸς ὁ αἰώνιος, you who know what is hidden ...." ‖ Assumption of Moses 10:7: "The Most High God will arise, who alone is eternal" *summus deus aeternus solus.* ‖ 1 Timothy 1:17: "To the eternal king" τῷ βασιλεῖ τῶν αἰώνων.

157. See Dalman, *Die Worte Jesu*, 1:135.

The First Letter of Paul to the Corinthians

1:1: Paul, called to be an apostle.

On Paul, see § Rom 1:1 A; on "called to be an apostle," see § Rom 1:1 B.

1:2 A: To the church of God in Corinth.

1. ἐκκλησία, see § Matt 16:18, #3.

2. ἐν Κορίνθῳ. — Corinth is not mentioned in ancient rabbinic literature. However, one does find the adjective קָלְנְתְיָא (wrongly קלוניתא) = Κορίνθιος in t. Yoma 2.4 (183) and b. Yoma 38A; see the passages at § Acts 3:2, #3, n. *b*.

1:2 B: Called to be saints (see § Acts 9:13).

1:2 C: In every place, theirs and ours.

See Kaddish de-Rabbanan: "Over Israel and over our teachers and over their students and over the students of their students who occupy themselves with the holy Torah in this place and in every single place דִּיבְאַתְרָא הָדֵין וְדִיבְכָל אֲתַר וַאֲתַר, may there be for you and for them and for us favor and grace and mercy from before the Memra of heaven and earth (i.e., from the God of heaven and earth), and say, 'Amen!'"

1:9: God is faithful.

The seal of God is אֱמֶת "truth" (faithfulness); see y. Sanh. 1.18A.55 at § John 1:14, #2, toward the end. ‖ Deuteronomy Rabbah 3 (200A): The rabbis said, "From the faithfulness (reliability, uprightness) of flesh and blood you recognize the faithfulness אוּמְּנוּת of God." An incident with R. Phineas b. Yair (ca. 200), who lived in a city of the south; and people came to procure provisions there. They had two *seahs* of barley in their possession, which they put at his house as a deposit. They forgot these and continued traveling. R. Phineas b. Yair sowed them every year, brought them to the threshing floor and gathered them together. After seven years, those business companions came to reclaim those (two *seahs*), so that they would be given back to them. R. Phineas b. Yair immediately recognized them again. He said to them, "Come and take your treasures! See, from the faithfulness of flesh and blood you recognize the faithfulness of God." — The same is found more briefly in y. Demai 1.22A.4. ‖ The closing formula that occurs quite often in the Holiness Code in Lev 17–26: "I am Yahweh" is interpreted in the Sifra (e.g., on Lev 18:2, 4, 5, 6, 19; 19:37) as "I am faithful to pay what is due" אני נאמן לשלם שכר. — The same occurs twice in Midr. Song. 5:16 (121B.37, 41).

1:10 A: That there not be factions among you.

σχίσμα = מַחֲלוֹקֶת, plural מַחֲלוֹקוֹת.

Tosefta Soṭah 14.1ff.: ... Since those things that are made of wood have increased, factions מחלוקת have increased in Israel.... Since the students of Shammai and Hillel who had not served (their teacher) in a sufficient way have increased, factions מחלוקות have increased in Israel ... (see the whole passage at § Rom 2:21–23). ‖ See t. Sanh. 7.1 (425) in the excursus "The Day of Jesus' Death," B, #1, toward the beginning. ‖ Mishnah ʾAbot 5.17: Every faction (dispute מחלוקה) for God's sake is ultimately abidingly successful ...; see the whole passage at § Matt 21:25, toward the middle. ‖ See b. B. Meṣ. 59B at § Matt 8:26. ‖ See Der. Er. Zut. 5 at § Matt 12:25. ‖ Babylonian Talmud Sanhedrin 110A: Rab († 247) said, "Whoever clings to factionalism מחלוקת transgresses a prohibition; for it says, 'He should not be like Korah and his crowd' (so Num 17:5 according to the midr.)." Rab Ashi († 427) said, "He deserves to be leprous; here it is written, 'By the "hand" of Moses' (Num 17:5); and there it is written, 'Bring your "hand" to your breast' (Exod 4:6)." R. Yose (ca. 350) said, "Whoever carries on a controversy חוֹלֵק (arouses factions) against the kingdom of the house of David deserves to be bitten by a snake." (See the continuation of the passage in b. Sanh. 110B at § Luke 10:16.) ‖ Leviticus Rabbah 9 (111B): Hezekiah (ca. 240) said in the second place, "Great is peace; for in the case of all migrations (in the wilderness) it is written (in the plural), 'They set out and they made camp,' that is, in conflict (faction מחלוקת) they set out and in conflict they made camp. But when they all came before Mount Sinai, they all became one camp; as it says, 'And Israel made camp there' (Exod 19:2). "The children of Israel made camps there,' is not written here, but rather, 'Israel made camp there' (in the singular). Then God said, 'Behold now the hour when I will give the Torah to my children (because of their unity)!'" ‖ Genesis Rabbah 26 (17B): R. Aha (ca. 320) said in the name of R. Joshua b. Levi (ca. 250), "Factionalism המחלוקת is wicked as the (sin of the) generation of the flood. It says here, 'Renowned men' (Gen 6:4); there it says, 'Called for an assembly of the community, renowned men' (Num 16:2). Just as 'renowned men' there (Num 16:2) were men of factionalism מחלוקת, so too here (Gen 6:4)'"renowned men' are men of factionalism." ‖ Babylonian Talmud Sanhedrin 110A: "Moses set out and went to Dathan and Abiram" (Num 16:25). Resh Laqish (ca. 250) said, "From here it is shown that one should not cling to factionalism מחלוקת." ‖ Jerusalem Talmud Pe'ah 1.16A.23: R. Samuel ben Nahman (ca. 260) said in the name of R. Jonathan (ca. 220), "Slander is permitted against people of factionalism (factious people בַּעֲלֵי מַחֲלוֹקֶת); and what is the scriptural basis? 'I (the prophet Nathan) will come after you (Bathsheba) and confirm your words' (1 Kgs 1:14; although these words contained slander against the factious Adoniyahu)." ‖ Pesiqta 190B: R. Isaac (ca. 300) said, "There are three who are called 'wicked,' and these are: whoever stretches his hand out against his neighbor (see Exod 2:13); whoever borrows and does not repay (see Ps 37:21); and whoever is a man of factionalism בעל מחלוקת. How do we know this? From the crowd of Korah; for it says, 'Get away from the tents of these wicked men' (Num 16:26)."

1:10 B: That you be fashioned in the same mind and in the same opinion.

A baraita in b. Megi. 9A: It happened that king Ptolemy (II Philadelphus [283–247 BCE], for the purpose of producing the Greek translation of the Bible) gathered 72 elders, and he put them in 72 rooms, without making known to them why he gathered them. Then he approached every single one and said to them, "Write down for me the Torah of your teacher Moses." Then God gave counsel into the heart of every single one so that they all agreed in one mind לדעת אחת. ‖ Admonitions to unity are frequent in ancient rabbinic literature; see § Matt 5:9, #1 and § Luke 2:14 B. — Also b. Ber. 12A; R. Helbo (ca. 300) said, "(On the Sabbath when the priests on duty for the week were relieved) the departing group said to the incoming group, 'May the one who makes his name dwell in this house make love and brotherhood and peace and amity dwell among you.'" — A parallel passage is found in y. Ber. 1.3C.40. ‖ Babylonian Talmud Berakot 16B: When R. Eleazar (ca. 270) had ended his prayer (i.e., the Prayer of Eighteen Benedictions), he would say (as his private prayer), "May it be pleasing before you, Yahweh our God, to make love and brotherhood, peace and amity, to dwell in our lot (territory), and to make our borders rich in students; to give success at our end with a happy departure and with fullness of our hope and to give us our portion in the garden of Eden; to grant us a good companion and a good inclination in your world; that we may get started early and obtain the hope of our life, to fear your name, and that rest for our souls for the good may come before you (specifically as a need to be satisfied)." — In y. Ber. 4.7D.57, this prayer is attributed to R. Yohanan († 279), while (there in line 36) the following prayer of R. Eleazar is reported: "May it be pleasing before you, Yahweh my God and God of my fathers, that no hate for us arise in the heart of anyone and no hate for anyone in our hearts, that no jealousy of us arise in the heart of anyone and that no jealousy of anyone in our heart. May your Torah be our work all the days of our life, and may our words be a prayer before you!" ‖ Babylonian Talmud Berakot 16B: Rab Safra (ca. 300) would say after his prayer, "May it be pleasing before you, Yahweh our God, to grant peace in the upper family (= the angelic world) and in the lower family (= Israel) and among the students who devote themselves to your Torah, whether they devote themselves to it for its own sake (i.e., out of pure motives) or not for its own sake (for selfish secondary purposes). But concerning all who do not devote themselves to it for its own sake, may it be your will that they devote themselves to it for its own sake!" ‖ Leviticus Rabbah 21 (120B): "Wage war by bundles for your own good" (so Prov 24:6 according to the midr., as תחבולות "clever measures" is interpreted as = חֲבִילוֹת "bundles"). R. Nathan (ca. 350) and R. Aha (ca. 320) said in the name of R. Simon (ca. 280), "If you have committed bundles of transgressions, do bundles of fulfillments of commandments corresponding to them. (The sins mentioned in Prov 6:17ff. are then chosen as examples.) 'Proud eyes'; (corresponding to these, do the commandment:) 'They will be tied on your head between your eyes' (Deut 6:8). "A tongue of lies"; (corresponding to this:) 'And teach your children them' (Deut 11:19). 'Hands that shed innocent blood'; (correspondingly:) 'And bind them as a sign on your hand' (Deut 6:8). 'A heart that has fashioned unholy thoughts'; (correspondingly:) 'And these words that I offer you today will be close to your heart' (Deut 6:6). 'Feet that are quick to run to evil'; (correspondingly:) 'Be quick to circumcise,' for it is completed between the knees (of the one circumcising). 'Whoever speaks lies without hesitation as a false witness'; (correspondingly:) 'You are my witnesses, says Yahweh' (Isa 43:10). 'And whoever stirs up disputes between brothers'; (correspondingly:) 'Seek peace and pursue it' (Ps 34:15)." ‖ Midrash Song of Songs 8:13 (133B): "You who dwell in the gardens (= the community of Israel), the companions (= angels) obey your voice; let me (= God) hear it" (so Song 8:13 according to the midr.). R. Nathan (ca. 350) said in the name of R. Aha (ca. 320), "Like a king (simply למלך), who got angry with his servants and locked them in the cell house (prison). What did the king do? He took his whole entourage of armed forces and those who served him and went to hear what they said. He heard how they say, 'Our lord king, he is our glory, he is our life; may we never cause our lord to lack anything!' Then he said to them, 'My children, raise your voices so that your companions around you may hear it!' So the Israelites, when they have occupied themselves with their work for six whole days, set off early on the Sabbath day and come to the synagogue and recite the Shema and come before the ark and read out from the Torah and read the prophets-*haphṭare*. Then God says to them, 'My children, raise your voices so that your companions may hear it! The companions are none other than the angels of service. And make it your goal not to hate one another or envy one another or fight with one another or shame one another, lest the angels of service say before me, "Lord of the world, Israel does not occupy itself with the Torah you have given them; for behold, enmity and envy and hate and disputes exist between them." Therefore, be people who fulfill it (the Torah) in peace.'"

1:15: You were baptized in my name.

See § Matt 28:19, #2.

1:17: The cross.

ὁ σταυρός = צְלוּב, Aram. צְלִיבָא, pole, cross. A distinction was made here between the beam which stood upright when placed in the earth (קוֹרָה), and the cross beam going out from it, which was called simply עֵיץ "wood."

Genesis Rabbah 56 (35C): "Abraham took the wood for the burnt offering and placed it on his son Isaac" (Gen 22:6), as the (offender) who carries the cross צלוב on his shoulder. — Pesiqta Rabbati 31 (143B): Like a person who is laden with his cross. ‖ In y. Sanh. 6.23C.57, in the report about the hanging of 80 sorceresses by Simeon b. Shaṭah (90–70 BCE) it says three times: "Bring to the cross!" אייתי לצליבא. ‖ Targum Esther II on 9:13: "The cross צליבא (for Haman) had sunk three cubits into the earth." — See more at § Matt 27:26, #2.

1:19: "I will bring to naught the wisdom of the wise, and I will render void the sense of the sensible" (Isa 29:14).

1. Isaiah 29:14 in the base text: "Therefore, behold, I will act remarkably again with this people, remarkably and wondrously, and the wisdom of its wise people will perish and the sense of its sensible people (the insight of its insightful people) will be hidden." Targum: "Therefore, behold, I will again strike this people with wondrous blows, and the wisdom of their wise ones will perish, and insight will be hidden from their insightful ones." ‖ Septuagint: διατοῦτο ἰδοὺ, προθήσω τοῦ μεταθεῖναι τὸν λαὸν τοῦτον, καὶ

μεταθήσω αὐτούς, καὶ ἀπολῶ τὴν σοφίαν τῶν σοφῶν καὶ τὴν σύνεσιν τῶν συνετῶν κρύψω.

2. Isaiah 29:14 was used only rarely in ancient rabbinic literature.

Babylonian Talmud Šabbat 138B: Rab († 247) said, "One day the Torah will be forgotten by Israel (pass into oblivion in Israel); for it says, 'Yahweh will make your blows (plagues) extraordinary (wondrous) וְהִפְלָא' (Deut 28:59). What this 'make extraordinary' הַפְלָאָה means, I do not know; but since it says, 'Therefore, behold, I will act remarkably again with this people, remarkably and wondrously הפלא ופלא' (Isa 29:14), say: The 'making extraordinary' pertains to the Torah (namely to its being forgotten by Israel)." — Apparently this interpretation is taken from Isa 29:14B: "The wisdom of its wise people will perish ...." ‖ Midrash Lamentations 1:9 (54A): When R. Yose of Milhayya (ca. 250) had passed away, R. Yohanan († 279) and Resh Laqish (ca. 250) went up to show the (last) service of love to him, and R. Isaac Passaqa (of Pasqath?) went up with them. There was an old man there who wanted to come and begin a talk about him (the deceased); but he was not allowed to. R. Isaac Passaqa said to him, "You want to open your mouth before those lions of knowledge in the Torah?" Then R. Yohanan said to them, "Let him, for he is an old man; he should come in, for he is at his (dwelling) place (and will go before us, who are strangers who come from a different place)." He came and began his talk and said, "We find that the demise (death) of the righteous is far worse (harder, heavier) before God than the 98 (literally: "one hundred minus two") chastisements (threatened punishments) in the repetition of the Torah[158] and more difficult than the destruction of the sanctuary. In the case of the chastisements it is written, 'Yahweh will make your blows extraordinary (wondrous)' (Deut 28:59; here והפלא is written only once), and in the case of the destruction of the sanctuary it is written, '(Jerusalem) went to rack and ruin wondrously פְּלָאִים (plural = two wondrous deeds)' (Lam 1:9). But concerning the demise of the righteous it is written, 'Therefore Yahweh says, "Behold, I will act remarkably הפליא again with this people, remarkably and wondrously הפלא ופלא"' (Isa 29:14; thus, there is a threefold mention of the wondrous), and why all this? 'The wisdom of its wise people will perish (with the death of a righteous man) and the insight of its insightful people will be hidden' (Isa 29:14B)." Then R. Isaac Passaqa said, "Blessed be the mouth of this man!" R. Yohanan said to him, "If you had not allowed him, where would we have heard this pearl?"

1:20 A: Where is a wise man? Where is a scribe? Where is an inquirer of this age?

1. On the whole statement, see Isa 33:18: "Where is the counter? Where is the weigher? Where is the one who counted the towers?" — With this, see b. Ḥag. 15B: Samuel († 254) met Rab Judah († 299), as he clasped tightly to the bolt of the door (so Levy, *Chaldäisches Wörterbuch*, 3:616A, according to Rashi) and cried. He said to him, "Astute man,[159] why are you crying?" He answered him, "Is what is written about teachers a small thing: 'Where is

158. S-B: מִשְׁנֵה תוֹרָה = Deuteronomy.

159. S-B: Interpretation uncertain. Levy שִׁינְנָא = "astute"; Dalman שַׁנְנָא = "equipped with large teeth"; Bacher: "This may denote Judah's steadfast endurance in learning" (*Die Agada der babylo-*

the counter סופר? Where the weigher שוקל? Where the one who counts the towers סופר את המגדלים?' Where the counter? For they have counted all the letters in the Torah. Where the weigher? For they have weighed the *qal wahomer* inferences (inferences *a minori ad majus*, see § Rom 5:9) in the Torah. Where the one who counts the towers? For they have taught 300 halakoth about the "tower that hangs in the air" (see m. Ohal. 4.1ff.)." And R. Ammi (ca. 300) said, "Doeg and Ahithophel asked 300 questions about the tower that hangs in the air, and (yet) we have learned: 'Three kings and four private persons have no share in the future world' (and among them are Doeg and Ahithophel; but if there no share came to these), what will come over us?" He said to him, "Evil thoughts (like envy, jealousy) were in their heart" (m. Sanh. 10.2). — See a parallel in a different form in b. Sanh. 106B.

2. On σοφός = חָכָם and γραμματεύς = סוֹפֵר, see § Matt 2:4, #2.

3. συνζητητής perhaps = דּוֹרֵשׁ, דַּרְשָׁן "inquirer, interpreter, lecturer." Pesiqta Rabbati 23 (115A): R. Simeon b. Laqish (ca. 250) said in the name of R. Eleazar b. Azariah (ca. 100), "When God created the first man, he created him as an unfinished mass גּוֹלֶם, and he lay there (reaching) from one end of the world to the other. God made every generation and its righteous ones, every generation and its godless ones, every generation and its searchers דורשיו, every generation and its leaders מנהיגיו (cf. καθηγηταί at § Matt 23:10) pass by him (in a vision)." — The parallel Gen. Rab. 24 (16A) reads: R. Judah b. Simon (ca. 320) said, "While the first man lay there as an unfinished mass before the one who spoke and the world came into being, he showed him every generation and its inquirers דורשיו (= συνζητηταί), every generation and its wise ones חכמיו (= σοφοί), every generation and its scribes סופריו (= γραμματεῖς), every generation and its leaders מנהיגיו (= καθηγηταί)." ‖ Babylonian Talmud Soṭah 49B toward the end: When Ben Zoma (ca. 110) died, inquirers (lecturers) דַּרְשָׁנִין ceased.

1:20 B: The wisdom of the world.

On the stance of rabbinic Judaism toward "Greek wisdom," see the excursus "The Stance of Judaism toward the Non-Jewish World." — Here reference may also be made to:

Tanḥuma מעית 244B: Let our teacher teach us: How many gifts (i.e., how much of what is given as a gift or present) were created in this world? Our teachers taught, "God created three gifts in the world: wisdom and strength and prosperity. If someone obtains one of these, he receives the most precious things in the world. If he has obtained wisdom, he has obtained everything; if he has obtained strength, he has obtained everything. When (= in which case)? When they are gifts of heaven (God) and come from the power of God's strength. But the strength and prosperity of men (when they originate from a man's own power) are nothing at all; for Solomon said, 'Again I saw under the sun (that the swift cannot hold power over the course, nor heroes over war, nor the wise over bread, nor the understanding over prosperity, nor the clever over favor; for time and destiny meet them all)' (Eccl 9:11). And Jeremiah likewise said, 'Yahweh says, "Let the wise not boast (in his wisdom, nor the strong boast in his strength, nor the rich in his prosperity)"' (Jer 9:22).

---

nischen Amoräer: Ein Beitrag zur Geschichte der Agada und zur Einleitung in den babylonischen Talmud [Straßburg: Trübner, 1878], 51.27).

And when these gifts do not stem from God, they ultimately disappear from him (the person)." The wise have taught that two wise men have arisen in the world, one from Israel and the other from the nations of the world; Ahithophel from Israel and Balaam among the nations of the world, and both have been destroyed from this and from the future world. Two strong men have arisen in the world, one from Israel and the other from the nations of the world; Samson from Israel and Goliath from the nations of the world, and both were destroyed from the world. Two rich men have arisen in the world, one from Israel and the other from the nations of the world; Korah from Israel and Haman from the nations of the world, and both were destroyed from the world. Why? Because their gift was not from God, but rather they had snatched it. — The same is found in Num. Rab. 22 (193A); TanḥB מטות § 7f. (80A).

1:21: Since ... the world did not discern God by wisdom.

See on this the remark at § Rom 1:20 D.

1:22: Since Jews demand signs and Greeks look for wisdom.

On demanding signs, see § Matt 12:38 and § Matt 16:1. — On Ιουδαῖοι καὶ Ἕλληνες, see § Rom 1:14, #3.

1:23: An offense to Jews.

σκάνδαλον, see § Matt 18:7 B and C and § Rom 14:13.

1:25: The weakness of God is stronger than men.

See the unabbreviated oxymoron in Tg. 2 Chr. 10:10: "My weakness is stronger than the strength of my father." — Base text: "My little finger is thicker than the loins of my father."

1:26: Not many wise, not many powerful, not many of noble birth.

1. On the whole statement. — Babylonian Talmud Nedarim 80B: Samuel († 254) said, "Messiness of head hair leads to blindness; messiness of clothing leads to lunacy; messiness of the body leads to ulcers and rash." The message was sent from there (from Palestine to Babylonia): "Pay heed to messiness, pay heed to the companionship (of scholars), pay heed to the sons of the poor (to raise them to study the Torah); for from them the Torah proceeds; as it says, 'Water (= Torah) flows from its (Israel's) small ones' (the midr. interprets Num 24:7 מִדָּלְיָו 'from its gullies' = מִדַּלָּיו 'from its small ones'). From them the Torah proceeds. And why is it not found that scholars proceed from scholars?" Rab Joseph († 333) said, "Lest it be said that the Torah is an inheritance for them." Rab Sheshet b. Idi (ca. 350) said, "Lest they pridefully look down on the community." Mar Zutra (ca. 400) said, "Because they (presumptuously) take possession of the community." Rab Ashi († 427) said, "Because they call the people 'asses.'" Rabina (I, † ca. 420; II., † 499): "Because they do not say a blessing over the Torah at the start (of busying themselves with it)." ‖ Conversely, R. Yohanan († 279) says in b. Ned. 38A: "God makes his Shekinah rest only on a strong, prosperous, wise, and humble man; one learns all this in Moses. (He was strong; for erecting the tent of meeting

and carrying both tablets of the law [Exod 40:19; Deut 9:17] required strength. He was prosperous [Exod 34:1], namely from the chippings from the tablets of stone which were supposedly hewn from sapphire. He was wise [Ps 8:6] and humble [Num 12:3].)"

2. εὐγενής = אַבְגֵּינוֹס, אַבְגֵּינֵיס, הוּגְנַס, of noble birth, noble, highbred.

Midrash Ecclesiastes 1:1 (4B): "Ecclesiastes, son of David" (Eccl 1:1), a king, son of a king; a wise man, son of a wise man; a righteous man, son of a righteous man; a noble man, son of a noble man אבגינוס בן אבגינוס. ‖ Genesis Rabbah 48 (30B): Abraham said, "If I see the Shekinah (divinity) wait for them (the three men in Gen 18:2), then I know that they are great men; and if I see them show each other honor, then I know they are of noble birth (read with ʿArukh הוגנסין instead of מהוגנין)."

1:27: The weakness of the world.

Exodus Rabbah 17 (79D): There are things that appear small, yet God has still commanded to perform who knows how many commandments with them. Hyssop appears to people as if it were nothing שאינו כלום (cf. τὰ μὴ ὄντα, 1 Cor 1:28); but before God its power is great; for he has treated it as equal to cedar in many passages: in the purification of the leper (see Lev 14:4) and in the burning of the (red) cow (see Num 19:6). Further, he commanded to perform a commandment in Egypt with hyssop; as it says, "Take a bunch of hyssop, dip it in blood ... and touch the lintel ... with the blood" (Exod 12:22). So it says also of Solomon, "He spoke about the trees, from the cedar, which grows in Lebanon, to hyssop, which grows on the wall" (1 Kgs 5:13), to teach you that small and great are the same before God, and that he performs wonders by means of small things and by hyssop, which is the smallest of the plants, he redeemed Israel.

1:30: Who has become for us ... righteousness.

Midrash Psalm 21 § 2 (89B): The deputy סָגָן (סֵגֶן?) of a king of flesh and blood is not called by his name; but God called Moses by his name; as it says, "Behold, I have made you into a god for pharaoh" (Exod 7:1), and the same with Israel; as it says, "I myself have spoken: you are gods" (Ps 82:6). He also calls them "holy"; as it says, "They are to be holy to their God" (Lev 21:6), and further it is written, "You are a holy people to Yahweh" (Deut 7:6). He also calls the king, the Messiah by his name; for it says, "And this is the name he will be called by: 'Yahweh our righteousness'" (Jer 23:6). — The last sentence is missing in the parallel passages Tanḥ. וארא 70A; TanḥB וארא § 7 (11B); Exod. Rab. 8 (73A). ‖ See also the passages at § Matt 1:21 B, #2, n. *k*.

2:9: But rather, as it is written: "What no eye has seen or any ear has heard or has arisen in the heart of any person, what God has prepared for those who love him."

Opinions on the origin of this citation have been divided since time immemorial. For a time, Origen oscillated between whether it was a free citation of Isa 52:15 or derived from a lost writing. Later he explains that it was taken from a (Jewish) Apocalypse of Elijah. This last opinion of his is followed by the so-called Ambrosiaster and Euthalius. Clement of Alexandria may also have supposed the Apocalypse of Elijah as the source of the quotation. However, Jerome declares most definitely that it should be traced back to Isa 64:3.[160] In the so-called Second Letter of Clement to the Corinthians (from the 2nd half of the 2nd century), chapter 11 reads: Ἐὰν οὖν ποιήσωμεν τὴν δικαιοσύνην ἐναντίον τοῦ θεοῦ, εἰσήξομεν εἰς τὴν βασιλείαν αὐτοῦ καὶ λημψόμεθα τὰς ἐπαγγελίας, ἃς οὖς οὐκ ἤκουσεν οὐδὲ ὀφθαλμὸς ἴδεν οὐδὲ ἐπὶ καρδίαν ἀνθρώπου ἀνέβη. The author does not indicate in any way that the concluding words are a quotation; rather, he uses them as if they were his own words. It may be concluded from this that the citation had already become a familiar saying at that time. However, in his so-called First Letter to the Corinthians, chapter 34, toward the end, Clement of Rome introduces our quotation with a formula that he elsewhere uses to introduce Old Testament passages, namely: λέγει γάρ, that is, "for he" = God, or "for it" = Scripture "says." Then the citation itself follows in this form: ὀφθαλμὸς οὐκ εἶδεν καὶ οὖς οὐκ ἤκουσεν καὶ ἐπὶ καρδίαν ἀνθρώπου οὐκ ἀνέβη, ὅσα ἡτοίμασεν τοῖς ὑπομένουσιν αὐτόν. The divergences from the Pauline quotation are so stark in respect to the complex sentence and the wording that it seems debatable whether Clement intends to cite 1 Cor 2:9 or whether he independently means to adduce an Old Testament passage. If the latter is the case, the closing words τοῖς ὑπομένουσιν αὐτόν (in Paul: τοῖς ἀγαπῶσιν αὐτόν) = "those who wait on him" would make it doubtful that Clement had Isa 64:3 in view. The same would then have to be supposed in the case of the apostle. Yet it must be kept in mind that both Paul and Clement did not follow the wording of the base text in rendering Isa 64:3,[a] but rather the meaning that had generally been assigned to the prophetic passage by Jewish scriptural scholarship.[b]

a. The base passage is Isa 64:3: "From eternity no one has witnessed, nor heard, nor has any eye seen a God besides you, who works for the one who waits for him." — Septuagint: ἀπὸ τοῦ αἰῶνος οὐκ ἠκούσαμεν, οὐδὲ οἱ ὀφθαλμοὶ ἡμῶν εἶδον θεὸν πλήν σου, καὶ τὰ ἔργα σου, ἃ ποιήσεις τοῖς ὑπομένουσιν ἔλεον. — Targum: "Since eternity no ear has heard the news of great deeds, nor heard a word to make one tremble, nor has any eye seen what your people have seen, (namely) the presence of your glory, O Yahweh; for besides you there is no (God), who will create for your people the primordial righteous ones (the righteous, as they were at the beginning), who wait for your redemption."

b. The base passage (Isa 64:3) according to rabbinic understanding. We will start with b. Sanh. 99A: R. Hiyya b. Abba (ca. 280) said that R. Yohanan († 279) said, "All the prophets prophesied only up until the days of the Messiah (i.e., all their prophecies do not extend beyond the messianic time, but rather will find their fulfillment in this age); but for the future world (which follows on the days of the Messiah) it may be said, 'No eye has seen, O God,

160. See the passages on this in Schürer, *Geschichte des jüdischen Volkes*, 3:361ff.

except you, what he (God) is preparing[161] for the one who waits for him' (Isa 64:3)." — This understanding of Isa 64:3 is also found in the mouth of R. Yohanan in b. Sanh. 99A.27 and 30; b. Ber. 34B.24, 28. In Midr. Prov. 13 § 25 (37A) the exposition is as follows: R. Levi (ca. 300) said, "Come and see how great the goodness is that God stores up for the righteous for the future! For it says, 'How great is your goodness, which you store up for those who fear you, which in the face of the children of men you show to those who trust in you.'" R. Yohanan said, "Not so! Rather, an eye can be made to see only what it can see, and an ear can be made to hear only what it can hear, but what he (God) has prepared for the righteous for the future, no eye can see and no ear can hear; as it says, 'No eye has seen, O God, except you, what (God) is preparing for the one who waits for him' (Isa 64:3)." — Just how old this interpretation is, its distinctive characteristic being the vocative understanding of אֱלֹהִים, cannot be indicated with certainty. R. Simeon b. Halapta (ca. 190), appears as the earliest named author representing the view, who says in Midr. Eccl. 1:8 (9B): "All good things, blessings and comforts, which the prophets have seen in this world (in a vision), they have seen only for the penitent (whose recompense will be precisely those goods); but of the one who all his life has not tasted sin at all (i.e., of the perfectly righteous) it holds: 'No eye has seen, O God, except you, what (God) is preparing for the one who waits for him' (Isa 64:3)." — Yet it is in no way said that R. Simeon b. Halapta was the actual originator of this interpretation. It is found anonymously already in SNum 27:12 § 135 (51A) in the following context: "Enough from you" (Deut 3:26). God said to Moses, "Much is stored up for you, much preserved for you"; as it says, "How great is your goodness, which you store up for those who fear you" (Ps 31:20). Furthermore, it says, "From eternity no one has witnessed, nor heard, nor has any eye seen, O God, besides you, what (God) is preparing for the one who waits for him" (Isa 64:3). The fact that this explanation of the prophetic passage can be presented anonymously in the old halakic midrashic work called Sifre is a proof that it was already generally known and common in the tannaitic period (until about 200 CE), and that, furthermore, the name of its actual originator may have passed into oblivion. In any case, there is no basis for the assumption that this interpretation of Isa 64:3 was not yet common in the days of the apostle Paul. — Among the later scholars, apart from R. Yohanan already mentioned above, this interpretation is represented in particular by R. Samuel b. Nahman (ca. 260), R. Levi (ca. 300) and R. Berekhiah (ca. 320) in Midr. Eccl. 1:8 (9A); also by R. Hiyya b. Abba (ca. 280) in b. Šabb. 63A, R. Asi (ca. 300) in Exod. Rab. 45 (101A), and R. Hanina b. Agil (ca. 300) in Midrash Abba Gurion (ed. Buber 5A); Leqach Tob on Esth 1:6 (ed. Buber 45B), Midr. Esth. 1:5 (87A); it is found anonymously in, for example, Midr. Eccl. 12:9 (59B); Midr. Ps. 9 § 2 (40B); Tanḥ. בראשית 2A; כי חשא 118B; אלה דברים 1A; TanḥB דברים § 2 (1A); Pesiq. Rab. 37 (163A).

161. S-B: Perhaps also passively: "what is (being) prepared for the one who waits for him"; then יַעֲשֶׂה would have been read as יֵעָשֶׂה.

2:11: For who among men is acquainted with (knows) what belongs to man?

See b. Pesaḥ. 54B in a baraita at § Luke 2:25 B and Mek. Exod. 16:32 (59B) with parallels at § John 2:25.

2:14f.: The natural person ... the spiritual (person).

There are no corresponding expressions for ψυχικός and πνευματικός in ancient rabbinic literature. The terms רוּחָנִי = πνευματικός and נַפְשִׁי = ψυχικός belong to a later time.

2:16: Who has known the mind of the Lord (see § Rom 11:34).[162]

3:1: Not as to spiritual people, but rather as to fleshly people.

1. πνευματικός, see § 2:14f.

2. σάρκινος, = "fleshly," does not have an equivalent in rabbinic literature; therefore some circumlocution must be used for it.[a] The only adjective formed from בָּשָׂר (flesh), namely בַּשְׂרָנָא, means "fleshly"[b] in the sense of stout.

a. βραχίονες σάρκινοι "fleshly arms" (LXX 2 Chr 32:8); base text: זְרוֹעַ בָּשָׂר = "arm of flesh." The targum paraphrases as: "Strength of flesh" תְּקוֹף בִּשְׂרָא, that is, fleshly or human strength, has become his help. ‖ βασιλεὺς σάρκινος (Add Esth 4:7; in Fritzsche [p. 48, 49]); Hebrew = מֶלֶךְ בָּשָׂר וָדָם "king of flesh and blood" = human king; examples at § Matt 16:17 B. ‖ καρδία σαρκίνη "a fleshly heart" (LXX Ezek 11:19; 36:26); base text: לב בשר, "heart of flesh." — The targum paraphrases: "A heart that fears me, to do my will."

b. Babylonian Talmud Ketubbot 61A: A woman who eats coriander (during her pregnancy) will have fleshy children בְּנֵי בִישְׂרָנֵי.

3:3 A: You are still fleshly.

σαρκικός is to σάρκινος as "fleshly" is to "fleshen," that is, while σάρκινος is ethically more or less a neutral concept,[163] σαρκικός[164] in certain circumstances brings the ethical aspect sharply to expression; see, apart from 1 Cor 3:3, particularly 1 Pet 2:11; differently, Rom 15:27; 1 Cor 9:11; 2 Cor 1:12; 10:4. — In rabbinic literature, there is no corresponding adjective for either σάρκινος or σαρκικός. Since בָּשָׂר "flesh" in the OT, like σάρξ in the NT, is assessed ethically (see, e.g., Gen 6:3, 12, 13), the same could be applied to both the circumlocution σάρκινος (see § 1 Cor 3:1, #2) and to the circumlocution σαρκικός. Franz Delitzsch, therefore, explicitly claims:

162. TN: There is no entry for § Rom 11:34. Perhaps § Rom 11:33 is intended?

163. S-B: See § 1 Cor 3:1, #2, n. *a*.

164. S-B: In extra-biblical Greek, σαρκικός is foreign; see Cremer, *Wörterbuch*.

"σαρκικοί ... corresponds to the ... Hebrew בני הבשר."[165] Unfortunately, Delitzsch does not adduce any passages. However, if he thereby meant that as בני הבשר "children of the flesh" would denote those people who lived "according to the flesh" κατὰ σάρκα or "fleshly" σαρκικῶς, this would be mistaken. בְּנֵי בָשָׂר, Aram. בְּנֵי בִסְרָא, means simply "children of men" or "human beings."[a] There is no moral evaluation whatsoever of those who are so designated; at the most, their frailty and nothingness comes into consideration. The rabbinic scholars never made the attempt to emphasize or even develop the ethical aspect that occasionally is appropriate for the Old Testament בָּשָׂר.[b] Their psychological interest was not concentrated on the concepts בָּשָׂר and רוּחַ = σάρξ and πνεῦμα, as happens in the NT, but rather on the concepts יֵצֶר הָרַע "evil inclination" and יֵצֶר טוֹב (almost always without the article) "good inclination"; and since they do not assign the seat of the "the evil inclination" to the בָּשָׂר, but rather to the גּוּף "body" or to the לֵב "heart,"[c] they had no occasion to engage in special reflections about the בשר. This is also, though, the reason that the rabbis do not have any linguistic equivalent for the New Testament σάρκινος and σαρκικός. Of course, the rabbinic scholars too in fact knew of "fleshly oriented" people. They just speak of them with different expressions: these are the people in whom the evil inclination reigns; those who have fallen prey to sin; the godless who rise up against God or do not fear God and do other things like this.[d]

a. In the ʿAlenu prayer, which is attributed to the Babylonian Rab († 247), it says according to the text in Dalman: "Therefore we hope in you, Yahweh our God, that we will quickly see the glory of your might (majesty), that idols will disappear from the earth and the nothings will be fully eliminated, that the world will be stabilized (brought into order) in the kingdom of the Almighty and all children of flesh כֹּל בְּנֵי בָשָׂר (= all people) will call on your name."[166] ‖ Targum Isaiah 40:5: "The glory of Yahweh will be revealed, and all children of flesh כָּל בְּנֵי בִסְרָא (= all people"; base text: כל בשר; LXX: πᾶσα σάρξ) will see it, because he has decided it by the Memra of Yahweh (= in himself)." ‖ Targum Ezek. 21:4: "All children of flesh (= all people) will see that I, Yahweh, have kindled it (the fire), and it will not go out." ‖ Targum Psalms 78:39: "He remembered that they are children of flesh בני בסרא (= people, the word in the text is simply בשר, LXX: σάρξ), a breath that goes away and does not return." ‖ The singular בַּר בִּישְׂרָא also occurs. Targum Yerušalmi I Deuteronomy 5:23: "For where is any child of flesh הי דין כל בר בישרא (= any person; base text: מי כל בשר; LXX: τίς γὰρ σάρξ), who would have heard the voice of the Memra of the living God speaking from the midst of the fire and would have remained alive?"

b. The following targum passages appear to be an exception. Targum Isaiah 40:6: "The voice of one who says, 'Prophesy!' And I answered and said, 'What should I prophesy?'

165. Franz Delitzsch, "Horae Hebraicae et Talmudicae: Ergänzungen zu Lightfoot und Schöttgen," *Zeitschrift für die gesammte lutherische Theologie und Kirche* 38 (1877): 209.

166. Dalman, *Die Worte Jesu*, 1:307.

All the godless כָּל רַשִׁיעַיָא (base text: כל הבשר = all flesh; LXX: πᾶσα σάρξ) are like grass and all their strength like the chaff in the field." ‖ Targum Zechariah 2:17: "All the godless כל רשיעיא (base text: כל בשר; LXX 2:13: πᾶσα σάρξ) will pass away before Yahweh; for he has revealed himself from his holy dwelling." — It would seem that the ethical aspect, which is fitting for the Old Testament בשר, could not be emphasized more strongly than it is in these two passages, in which כל בשר is replaced simply by all the godless," and it seems it would be unavoidable to infer that the targumist understood by "flesh" the sinful being of man, just as in the NT. And yet this is all only apparent. In the targum to Isa 66:24, we read, "They will go out and see the corpses of guilt-laden men, who rose up against my Memra; for their souls will not die and their fire will not go out and the godless will be judged (punished) in gehenna, until the righteous צַדִּיקַיָא (base text: כל בשר; LXX: πᾶσα σάρξ) say about them, 'We have seen enough!'" — As the words "all flesh" were rendered with "the godless" in Tg. Isa. 40:6 and Tg. Zech. 2:17, the same words are here rendered by "the righteous." This is conceivable only if כל בשר was an absolutely neutral concept for the targumist. To him כל בשר = "all flesh" means nothing more than "all human beings," and precisely for this reason he can, depending on the context, replace it sometimes with "the godless" and other times with "the righteous." So these passages, rightly understood, only confirm what was said in the text above, namely that the rabbinic scholars made no attempt to emphasize and develop the ethical aspect that is every so often fitting for the Old Testament בשר.

c. Babylonian Talmud Šabbat 105B: "There should be no foreign god in you" (so Ps 81:10 according to the midr.). What sort of foreign god is found in a man's body גוף? Say: This is the evil inclination. ‖ Exodus Rabbah 15 (76C): If the Israelites have sunken into sins as a consequence of the evil inclination, which is in their body בגופן, and turn in repentance, God will forgive them their sins every year (on the Day of Atonement). — On the heart or a person's interior as the seat of the *yetzer ha-ra'*, see § Rom 2:15 B, #3, notes *d–f* and in the excursus "The Good and Evil Inclination."

d. Babylonian Talmud Berakot 61B: The evil inclination judges = rules the godless (see § Rom 2:15). ‖ Sifre Deuteronomy 11:18 § 45 (82B): God said to the Israelites, "My children, I have created the evil inclination for you, I have created the Torah for you as the cure. As long as you occupy yourselves with it, the former will not rule over you.... However, if you do not occupy yourselves with the Torah, you will be given into its power (so that you live according to its will, i.e., κατὰ σάρκα)." — See the whole passage at § Rom 3:1f., D. ‖ Genesis Rabbah 59 (37A): "Yahweh had blessed Abraham with everything" (Gen 24:1). R. Levi (ca. 300) said, "With everything (in the absolute sense): he let him rule over his (evil) inclination (so that he walked according to the will of the good inclination = κατὰ πνεῦμα)." ‖ In an allegorical interpretation of Num 21:27ff., it says in b. B. Bat. 78B: ... What does המושלים (bard of maxims, Num 21:27) mean? These are those who rule over their (evil) inclination (= who walk according to the spirit, the good inclination).... "It devoured Ar of Moab" (Num 21:28): this is the one who pursues his evil inclination (= who lives according to the flesh), as a donkey foal runs after a pretty jenny. (See the whole passage at § Luke 1:51, n. *p.*) ‖ Jerusalem Talmud 'Abodah Zarah 1.39A.13: Jeroboam's pride made him fall as prey to sin completely החליטתו (= made him a person who followed only his evil inclination). ‖ Babylonian Talmud

Yoma 86B: The repentance of those who have sunk into sin המוחלטין suspends punishment, even if the decree of punishment (by God) had been sealed over him. ‖ See Pesiq. Rab. 40 (167B) at § Rom 2:27. ‖ Sifre Deuteronomy 32:15 § 318 (136A): You find that the people of the generation of the flood rose up מרדו against God only as a result of (good) food and drink and as a result of welfare. — This judgment is then repeated about the people of Sodom, the generation of the tower and the generation of the migration in the wilderness, the members of the kingdom of the ten tribes and, lastly, the contemporaries of the Messiah; on the last words, see § Matt 1:21. ‖ Also see Tg. Isa. 66:24 above in n. *b*. — In the Targum Ezek 11:19 and 36:26, the heart of flesh is a heart that fears God, to do his will; accordingly, the heart of stone is a heart that does not inquire about God in anything and lives according to its own desire (= κατὰ σάρκα). See also § Rom 2:29 B.

3:3 B: In a human way.

κατὰ ἄνθρωπον, see § Rom 3:5.

3:5: Servants, through whom you came to believe.

διάκονος = עֶבֶד in, for example, b. Hor. 10A: Rabban Gamaliel (ca. 90) and R. Joshua were traveling together on a ship. Rabban Gamaliel had bread with him, and R. Joshua bread and flour. The bread of Rabban Gamaliel came to an end; he counted on the flour of R. Joshua. He said to him, "Did you know that this long delay would arise for us, so that you brought flour with you?" He said to him, "A star arises every 70 years and leads ships astray; then I thought it might arise and lead us astray." He answered him, "You know all that, and you go by ship (to eke out a living)?" He said to him, "Instead of you being surprised at me, I am surprised at two students you have on the mainland, R. Eleazar Hisma (?) and R. Yohanan b. Gudgeda. They know how to calculate how many drops are in the sea and have no bread to eat and no clothes to wear." Then he made it his purpose to prioritize them. When he had landed, he sent for them; but they did not come. He sent for them again, and they came. He said to them, "Did you think that I would bestow a dominion שְׂרָרָה on you? I bestow on you one service עַבְדוּת; for it says, 'And they spoke to him and said, "If you will become a servant עֶבֶד for this people today ..."' (1 Kgs 12:7)."

3:8: Each one will receive his own recompense according to his own labor.

Mishnah ʾAbot 5.23: Ben He He (a student of Hillel, thus a contemporary of Jesus) said, "The recompense is according to labor לְפוּם צַעֲרָא אַגְרָא."[167] — On the ancient Jewish teaching about recompense, see the excursus "The Parable of the Workers in the Vineyard."

3:10: As a wise builder I laid the foundation.

1. ἀρχιτέκτων = אַרְכִּיטֶקְטוֹס, אַרְכִּיטֶקְטוֹן;[a] Hebrew אוּמָּן[b] "artificer," "artisan" or בַּנַּי, Aram. בַּנָּאָה[c] "architect," "builder."

167. S-B: As vocalized by Dalman; the ordinary vocalization is לְפוּם.

a. See Gen. Rab. 24 (15D) at § Rom 9:20 B; parallels to Gen. Rab. 24 that also have the loanword ἀρχιτέκτων are found in Tanḥ. נשא 195A; TanḥB נשא § 8 (15A); Midr. Ps. 14 § 1 (56A); Num. Rab. 9 (150D), though here instead of ארכיטיקון one should read ארכיטקטון.

b. See the beginning of Gen. Rab. 1; the beginning of Tanḥ. בראשית; S. Eli. Rab. 31 (160) at § John 1:1–4, #4.

c. See examples at § Matt 21:42, #2.

2. θεμέλιος = תֵּימֶלְיוֹס, but only rarely in rabbinic literature.

See Yelamedenu in Yalquṭ 1 § 766 at § Matt 16:18, #2. ‖ Genesis Rabbah 3 (3C): R. Judah (ca. 150) said, "Light was created first. A parable. Like a king who wanted to build a palace, and that place was dark. What did he do? He lit lamps (torches) and lanterns to know how he could set down the base stones (foundations) תימליוסים." (Dalman, *Wörterbuch*, reads the form תֵּימֶלְיוֹסִים = θεμελίωσις "foundation" instead of the plural תימליוסים.)

3. On the image of building, see § Matt 16:18, #2 and § Matt 21:42, #2.

3:11: No one can lay another foundation alongside the one that lies already, which is Jesus Christ.

Abraham is sometimes viewed as the foundation or cornerstone of the world. See Yelamedenu in Yalquṭ 1 § 766 at § Matt 16:18, #2 and Pirqe R. El. 24 at § Matt 21:42, #1.

3:12: Gold, silver, precious stones, wood, hay, straw.

1. χρυσίον = זָהָב, Aram. דְּהַב, det. דַּהֲבָא "gold"; its use in buildings is attested in b. Sukkah 51B in a baraita and b. B. Bat. 4A at § Matt 24:1; m. Šeqal. 4.4 at § Matt 17:24, #6; t. Menaḥ. 13.18 (533) at § John 18:13, n. *b*; Josephus, *J. W.* 5.5.3 at § Acts 3:2, #2, n. *a*.

2. ἀργύριον = כֶּסֶף, Aram. כְּסַף, det. כַּסְפָּא "silver" is mentioned rarely as an adornment on buildings; see as an example Josephus, *J. W.* 5.5.3 at § Acts 3:2, #2, n. *a*.

3. λίθοι τίμιοι, valuable stones, α. = gems[a] אֲבָנִים טוֹבוֹת (sing.: אֶבֶן טוֹבָה), so Rev 17:4; 18:12, 16; 21:11, 19. Yet gems appear only rarely as a building material[b] and then most of the time only for the time of the eschatological consummation.[c] — β. = precious stone אֲבָנִים יְקָרוֹת,[d] singularly also אֶבֶן בָּחוּר וָטוֹב.[f] By this is meant valuable building material like marble and alabaster,[e] and in certain circumstances also a stone that is fitting because of its size and form, particularly as a cornerstone.[f] Since the list in 1 Cor 3:12 is a *climax descendens*, λίθοι τίμιοι should be understood in the sense of β.

a. Babylonian Talmud Baba Batra 16B: R. Simeon b. Yohai (ca. 150) said, "A gem אבן טובה hung on the neck of our father Abraham; for every sick person who saw him was immediately healed. When our father Abraham departed from the world, God hung the stone on the sun wheel." Abbayye († 338/39) said, "This is what the people say (in a proverb): 'When the sun rises, sickness is lifted.'" — The parallel in t. Qidd. 5.17 (343) reads מרגלית טובה "precious pearls" instead of אבן טובה. ‖ Babylonian Talmud ʿAbodah Zarah 8B: The Romans had it inquired of the Greeks: … "Pearl and gem אבן טיבה, which of them should be the underlayment (mounting) for the other?" They sent word to them: "The pearl for the gem (the latter is thus more precious than the former)." ‖ See Exod. Rab. 30 (91B) at § Matt 13:46.

b. Rev 18:16.

c. Rev 21:19. ‖ See b. B. Bat. 75A with parallels at § John 20:29; Pesiq. 137B at § Matt 5:25 B.

d. So אבנים יקרות (1 Kgs 7:9, 10).

e. See the baraita in b. Sukkah 51B at § Matt 24:1.

f. See Pirqe R. El. 24 at § Matt 21:42, #1.

4. ξύλα = עֵצִים (sing.: עֵץ) "wooden."

Genesis Rabbah 1 (2C): R. Joshua b. Levi (read: R. Joshua of Sikhnin, ca. 330) said in the name of R. Levi (ca. 300), "Whoever builds needs six things: water, earth (such as silt, sand, clay), wood עֵצִים, stones, pipe, and iron. And if you should say, 'He is wealthy and does not need pipe,' look, he still needs the measuring pipe; as it is written, 'A linen cord was in his hand and the measuring pipe' (Ezek 40:3)."

5. χόρτος "grass" = חָצִיר, עֵשֶׂב; also "dry grass" = hay חָצִיר יָבֵשׁ,[a] so 1 Cor 3:12. There is no evidence from rabbinic literature for the use of hay in building. However, the rabbis do use the expression "hay" in the metaphorical sense of humanity when it is necessary to emphasize their worthlessness and nothingness.[a]

a. Midrash Psalm 119 § 20 (248A): "The impudent mock me to no end; (nevertheless) from your Torah I have not departed." (Ps 119:51). With what did they mock me (the community of Israel)? Mocking, they said to me, "The one who has driven you into exile (= God) will not bring you back again." And so it says, "The face of Yahweh dispersed them, he will not look at them again" (Lam 4:16). It further says, "'Out of the way! Unclean!,' it was called out to them; 'Out of the way, out of the way, do not touch! ...'" (Lam 4:15). They said among the gentiles, "They may no longer abide" (Lam 4:15). Therefore, it was said, "The impudent mock me to no end; (but still I have not departed from your Torah." And again, they said to me, "Do not circumcise and do not keep the Sabbaths and do not read in the Scripture!" But I feared you and did not listen to them, for they are hay חציר יבש (dry grass): as the grass חציר does not endure, so too their words will not endure forever. And so Scripture says, "The grass חציר is dried up, the flower withered" (Isa 40:7). But as you abide forever, so too your words will abide forever; see Isa 40:8. — See also 2 Bar. 82:2ff. at § Rom 3:9 A, #2, n. *c*.

6. καλάμη = תֶּבֶן "straw." — Chopped straw was often blended as a binding material in the silt or clay that was used for building.[a] — Like "hay" (see above in #5), the expression "straw" also served metaphorically as a designation of the worthless mass of humanity.[b]

a. Tosefta Šebiʿit 5.18 (68): Straw תבן from the fallow year may not be put into a pillow or into silt (used for building). (The straw grown in other years could of course be used because it was freely at the disposal of the field owner.) ‖ After the year 70, houses were not to be entirely whitewashed with lime any longer, as a sign of mourning over the destruction of the temple. Either a piece of the house remained without whitewash or straw chaff was blended into the whitewash, whereby it became unsightly. The issue is addressed in the following baraita in b. B. Bat. 60B: One may not whitewash his house (completely) with lime.

If one has mixed in sand or straw תבן, it is permitted. R. Judah (ca. 150) said, "If sand has been mixed in, this is (buffing) mortar and prohibited. Straw is permitted." — A parallel passage is found in b. Šabb. 80B. — The baraita stems from t. Soṭah 15.9 (322).

b. See Pesiq. Rab. 10 (35B) at § Matt 5:43, #1, n. *g*; see Midr. Song. 7:3 (127A) at § Rom 3:9 A, #1, n. *c*. See the parallel that belongs here in Midr. Ps. 2 § 14 (16A) at § Heb 1:5 A, #3.

3:16: Do you not know that you are a temple of God and the Spirit of God lives in you?

Babylonian Talmud Taʿanit 11A: R. Eleazar (ca. 270) said, "Let a person always apply the standard to himself (regard himself) as if the Holy One (God) dwelt שָׁרוּי in his body בְּתוֹךְ מֵעָיו; for it says, 'The Holy One in your interior, and I will not come in a blaze of anger'" (Hos 11:9; for this reason, a person should not impose any self-selected fast on himself, if his strength cannot bear it).

3:18: If anyone thinks that he is wise among you in this age, let him become foolish, so that he may become wise.

Mishnah ʾAbot 4.1: Ben Zoma (ca. 110) said, "Who is wise חָכָם? Whoever learns from every person; as it says, 'From all who have taught me, I have become intelligent' (so Ps 119:99 according to the midr.)." ‖ Mishnah ʾAbot 5.7: Seven things apply to the ignorant גֹּלֶם and seven to the wise חכם. The wise man does not speak before someone who is greater in wisdom than he is; he does not interrupt someone else; he does not rush to answer; he asks in accordance with the proposition (under discussion) and answers in accordance with the matter (which he was asked about); he speaks about the first thing first and about the last thing last; concerning what he has not heard, he says, 'I have heard nothing,' and he concedes the truth. And the contrary is true of the ignorant." ‖ Babylonian Talmud Tamid 32A: (Alexander of Macedonia asked the elders of the south,) "Who is called a wise man חֲכָמִים?" They said to him, "Who is a wise man? The one who sees (in advance) what will be הַנּוֹלָד." ‖ Babylonian Talmud Niddah 70B: (The people of Alexandria asked R. Joshua b. Hananiah [ca. 90],) "What should a man do so that he may become wise ויחכם?" He said to them, "Let him spend a lot of time in the academy and reduce his business." They answered him, "Many have done this and it has not helped them at all, but rather let one ask for mercy from the one to whom wisdom belongs; as it says, 'For Yahweh gives wisdom, from his mouth stems knowledge and insight' (Prov 2:6)." R. Hiyya (ca. 200) taught: "Like a king of flesh and blood who prepared a meal for his servants and gave to his friends from what was before him. What does this let us hear (what can be concluded from this)? That the one without the other is insufficient (so both are necessary, to study diligently and to pray)." ‖ Mishnah ʾAbot 2.5: Hillel (ca. 20 BCE) said, "… No one who conducts a lot of business becomes wise מַחְכִּים." See ʿErub. 55A at § Rom 10:6–8, #2. ‖ Babylonian Talmud Berakot 55A: R. Yohanan († 279) said, "God gives wisdom only to the one in whom there is wisdom (already); for it says, 'He gives wisdom to the wise and knowledge to the understanding' (Dan 2:21). R. Tahalifa b. Maʿreba heard this and said it before R. Abbahu (ca. 300). The latter said to him, "You teach it from there (Dan 2:21), we teach it from here; as it is written, 'I have put wisdom in the heart of everyone who is of wise heart.'" See on this TanḥB מקץ § 9 (97A) at § Matt 21:24.

3:21: Everything is yours.

Mishnah ʾAbot 6.1: R. Meir (ca. 150) said, "Everyone who devotes himself to the Torah for its own sake obtains many things; and not only this, but also the whole world is worthy of being there for him בְּדַי הוּא לוֹ." — See also statements such as "The world was created only for Israel's sake or for the sake of the righteous"; see § Rom 8:20f.; also SDeut 11:21 § 47 (83B) at § Rom 3:1f. C, toward the end.

4:1: Stewards of God's secrets.

οἰκονόμος, see § Luke 16:1. — μυστήρια, see § Matt 13:11.

4:2: The one be found faithful.

πιστὸς εὑρέθη = נִמְצָא נֶאֱמָן, see Exod. Rab. 2 (68B) at § Matt 25:21 A.

4:3: By any human day.

ἀνθρωπίνη ἡμέρα perhaps = דִּינֵי אָדָם[a] or דִּינֵי בָשָׂר וָדָם[b] "human judgments"; here, as it seems, דִּין is always in the plural; opposite: דִּינֵי שָׁמַיִם = "divine judgments."

a. Mishnah Baba Qamma 6.4: If someone starts a fire by means of a deaf-mute person, an imbecile, or a minor (by leaving the fire to them), he is free from human judgments בדיני אדם, but guilty before divine judgment בדיני שמים. ‖ A baraita in b. B. Qam. 55B: R. Joshua (ca. 90) said, "Whoever does four things is free from human judgments מדיני אדם, but guilty before divine judgment בדיני שמים; and these are: whoever breaks through (tears into) a fence in front of someone else's cattle (so that they can run out of there); whoever weighs down someone else's standing grain before a fire (so that it catches on fire); whoever hires false witnesses to give testimony (for himself or against someone else); and whoever knows testimony that would support someone and yet does not give it." — Further examples are found in b. Qidd. 24B; b. B. Qam. 99B; also see § Matt 5:21, C, #2, section ג.

b. Mekilta Exodus 21:14 (86B): "If anyone acts wickedly toward his neighbor רעהו so that he kills him by deceit" (Exod 21:14). "His neighbor": this excludes the others (i.e., the non-Israelites; see § Matt 5:43, #1, n. *a*). Issi b. Aqabia (ca. 150, read in this way!) said, "Before the giving of the law, we (Israelites) would have been warned about bloodshed (namely in Gen 9:6), and after the giving of the law would easements have come about for them instead of making it more serious? In truth (with certainty) it has been said (according to traditional interpretation = "as immemorial tradition" it has been said), 'He is free from human judgments מדיני בשר ודם, but their matter is left to heaven (= God).'" — See the whole passage at § Matt 5:21, A, #1, n. *a*. The preceding translation, which understands the beginning of Issi's saying as a question seems more correct to us than the translation used at § Matt 5:21, A, #1, n. *a*.

4:5: Who will illumine what is hidden in darkness and reveal the counsel of hearts.

A baraita in b. Soṭah 3A: R. Meir (ca. 150) said, "A person commits a transgression in secret, but God exposes him in the open." ‖ Midrash Psalm 14 § 1 (56B): R. Jeremiah (ca. 320) said, "What does 'The heart is deceitful more than anything, and it is corrupt; who can know it' (Jer 17:9) mean? It is also written after this: 'I, Yahweh, search the heart, test the kidneys' (Jer 17:10). I am the one who looks into the heart and tests the kidneys and reveals what is hidden ומגלה את הנסתרות. And likewise, Daniel said, 'He reveals what is deep and hidden; he knows what is in darkness, and light dwells with him' (Dan 2:22)."

4:7: What do you have that you did not receive?

Mishnah ʾAbot 3.7: R. Eleazar b. Judah of Bartota (ca. 110) said, "Give him (God) from what is his; for you and what is yours belong to him. And so (Scripture) says in the case of David (see § Rom 11:2 ἐν Ἠλείᾳ): 'For everything is from you, and from your hand we have given to you' (1 Chr 29:14)." — Numerous supporting passages for the statement that God is the giver of everything are found in the so-called table discussions of the Letter of Aristeas 187–292. Some examples follow here. 195–200: "The king (Ptolemy) asked the following one (among the Jewish translators of the Torah), what the highest (good) for his life is. And he responded, 'The knowledge that God rules everything and that in our actions we do not carry out our decisions, but rather God completes and guides everything by his power.' He confirmed to this one too that he spoke rightly and asked the next one how he might keep his power intact and ultimately pass it on to his descendants in the same condition. And he answered, 'If you always ask God to give you good thoughts for your undertakings, and if you admonish your progeny not to be proud of their power and their prosperity, since it is God who gives this, and they do not have from themselves the most high power over all.' He agreed with this view and asked the following one how he could bear strokes of fate equably. And he replied, 'If you understand that all people are destined by God to experience the greatest evils as well as the greatest goods, and that it is impossible for a person not to share in these, but God, whom one must beseech (for this) bestows fortitude.' He thanked this one too and said that the thoughts that they all expressed were right. I want to ask just one more thing.... Then he asked the man, 'What is the essence of fortitude?' And he answered, 'When the right decision is executed in the hour of danger with resolution. But all will be completed for your advantage (by God), O king, since you want what is right.' All agreed and loudly showed their approval. But the king said to the philosophers, for there were not a few there, 'I think that these men are outstanding in aptitude and wisdom, since they have extemporaneously answered such questions properly, all proceeding from God in their speech.'" — Letter of Aristeas 210: "The king said to the next one, 'What is the disposition of piety?' And he answered, 'To be convinced that God works and knows everything in everything, and that a person who acts unjustly or wickedly cannot remain hidden from him. For as the God of the whole world does good, you too can be flawless, if you imitate him.'" — Letter of Aristeas 224f.: "He asked the following one how he might avoid jealousy. And after a pause he answered, 'If you bear in mind above all that God bestows on all kings esteem and high honor, and that no one is king from himself. For all wish to attain this power, but they cannot, because it is a gift of God.' He praised him with many words and asked the next one how he might scorn his enemies. And he answered, 'If you show benevolence to all people and gain their friendship, you will not have to be afraid of anyone. Yet to be congenial to all people and to have received (this) as a beautiful gift from God, this is the best thing.'" — Letter of Aristeas 229: "He asked the next one, 'What is equal to beauty in value?' And he answered, 'Piety; for it is the greatest beauty. Yet its power is love, which is a gift of God.'" — See further Letter of Aristeas 219, 223, 227, 231, 237f., 239f., 243, 248, 252, 259, 266, 269, 276, 290, 292.

4:8: Would that you reigned, so that we too might reign with you!

On the participation of the righteous in the last judgment, or on the execution of the divine verdict by them, see the excursus "Sheol, Gehenna, and the Garden of Eden," II, #10.

4:9 A: As those forfeited to death.

See § Rom 8:36.

4:9 B: A spectacle ... for the angels.

On the angels' concern for the experience of the pious, see the citations at § Luke 1:19 A, #4, n. *h*.

4:11: Up to the present hour we hunger and thirst and are naked.

Mishnah ʾAbot 6.4: This is the right way to the Torah (and also the deftness of those who acquire it): Eat bread with salt "and drink water in a measured way" (Ezek 4:11), sleep on the earth and live a life of privation, but labor with the Torah. If you act in this say, "Blessed are you, and it shall be well with you!" (Ps 128:2). "Blessed are you," in this world; "and it shall be well with you," for the future world.

4:12 A: We toil, working with our own hands.

On the esteem of manual labor and on the rabbis who fed themselves by the work of their hands, see § Mark 6:3 and § Acts 18:3, #1 and #2. — Sometimes it was precisely the most respected scholars who found themselves constrained to manual labor as a consequence of their poverty. So Hillel (ca. 20 BCE) originally earned his livelihood as a day laborer and R. Meir (ca. 150) as a scribe. See b. Yoma 35B and Midr. Eccl. 2:18 (15A) at § Matt 20:2 B. — R. Aqiba († ca. 135) daily gathered a bundle of straw (another reading: a bundle of wood), which he then sold, to eke out a living. See ʾAbot R. Nat. 6 (3B) at § Matt 12:41 B. — Here reference may be made also to the following report about R. Joshua (ca. 90).

Babylonian Talmud Berakot 28A: (When Rabban Gamaliel [ca. 90] had lost the patriarchate because of his imperious demeanor toward R. Joshua,) he said, "I will go and propitiate (conciliate with) R. Joshua." When he came into his house, he saw that the walls of his house were blackened. He said to him, "From the walls of your house it is recognized that you are a smith פֶּחָמִי (also = 'coal burner')." He answered him, "Woe to the generation whose leader (caretaker פַּרְנָס) you are [and woe to the ship whose helmsman you are]! For you do not know the needs of the students, what they survive on and how they feed themselves." He said to him, "I humble myself before you נַעֲנֵיתִי לָךְ (see § Matt 5:24 B, #1, first S-B footnote in section), pardon me!" But he did not heed him at all. "Do it (Rabban Gamaliel continued) for the honor of my father!" Then he mollified him. — The parallels in y. Ber. 4.7D.18 and y. Taʿan. 4.67D.35: (Rabban Gamaliel) went to R. Joshua. He met him as he sat there and made needles מְחַטִּין. He said to him, "What do you live on?" He answered him, "And you need to know this now for the first time? Woe to the generation whose leader you are!" He said to him, "I humble myself before you." — See also b. Hor. 10A § 1 Cor 3:5.

4:12 B: Shamed, we bless; persecuted, we endure.

See the citations at § Matt 5:11 A; also Der. Er. Zut. 1; b. Sanh. 7A; Midr. Ps. 16 § 11 (62A) at § Matt 5:11 B, #7; lastly, the passages at § Matt 5:10, #1 and § Rom 12:14 B.

4:13: We have become as the refuse of the world, the filth of all (in general).

περικάθαρμα in LXX Prov 21:18[a] = atoning sacrifice, ransom money; the word in the text is כֹּפֶר; similarly, περίψημα = ransom money (Tob 5:18).[b] However, this meaning is quite foreign to the significance of the two words in our passage, or at least it is not demanded by the context. Therefore, it would be more appropriate to understand περικάθαρμα = discharge, refuse (what is removed in sweeping out) and περίψημα = dirt, filth (what is removed in washing away). In this case, the Aramaic זְכָא, plural זְכִין, זְכִיא,[c] would correspond to the former, and the Hebrew טִנּוּפֶת[d] to the latter. κίβδηλον and ἀκαθαρσία are used in this sense in Wis 2:16.[e]

a. Septuagint Proverbs 21:18: "The godless man is the ransom περικάθαρμα for the righteous man."

b. Tobit 5:18: "Do not add money to money, but rather let it be a ransom περίψημα for our child."

c. Babylonian Talmud Moʿed Qaṭan 10B: Raba († 352) said, "If someone cleans (his courtyard on the days between feast days) of refuse זיכיא with a view to the twigs (pieces of wood, simply to collect them for himself), it is permitted; but if with a view to the soil (to clean this), it is prohibited. How should one conceive of this? If he takes big pieces and leaves the small ones lying, it happens with a view to twigs (and it is then permitted); if he takes the big and small pieces, it happens with a view to the soil (and is prohibited)." — A similar passage is found in b. B. Bat. 54A.

d. Tanḥuma במדבר 191B: God said, "Idolaters are filth טנופות. As it says, 'The nations will become scenes of fire of lime, chopped off thorns that catch fire' (Isa 33:12); ... but the Israelites are righteous ones, are pure wheat." — The same is found in Num. Rab. 4 (141B); a starkly different version is found in TanḥB במדבר § 22 (10A).

e. Wisdom 2:16: "We (the godless) are considered as dross (or chaff) κίβδηλον by him (the pious man) and he keeps his distance from our ways as from impurities ὡς ἀπὸ ἀκαθαρσιῶν."

4:14: As my beloved children.

1. The following are called "children" בָּנִים in the metaphorical sense: α. the Israelites in their relationship to God; see § Matt 5:9, #2; β. community members gathered for worship in their relationship to the presenting scholar; see Gen. Rab. 33 (20A) at § Matt 3:9 A, #3; γ. students in relation to the teacher; see § John 13:33; see also b. B. Bat. 10B at § Matt 5:7, #5; b. Sanh. 13B at § Acts 6:6, #3, n. *a*; Der. Er. 6; b. Sanh. 30B. — The reason is stated in b. Sanh. 19B: R. Samuel b. Nahman (ca. 260) said that R. Jonathan (ca. 220) said, "If someone teaches someone else's son Torah, Scripture reckons it to him as if he had begotten him; for it says, 'These are the descendants of Aaron and Moses' (Num 3:1). Furthermore, it is written, 'These are the names of the sons of Aaron' (Num 3:2; although they were sons of Aaron, they are first called descendants of Aaron and Moses). This teaches you that Aaron had begotten them and Moses had taught them, and therefore they were called by his name." — See further § 1 Cor 4:15 B and § 4:17.

2. "Beloved children," Aramaic = בְּנַיָּא חֲבִיבַיָּא, in, for example, Midr. Esth. Intro. 82A, see § Matt 5:9, #2; or בְּנִין רְחִימִין, in, for example, Tg. Amos 9:7: "'Are you not considered as beloved children before me, house of Israel?,' says Yahweh."

4:15 A: For even if you have ten thousand teachers.

παιδαγωγός became a frequent loanword in rabbinic literature in the form פְּדָגוֹג or פְּדָגוֹגָא.

Sifre Numbers 11:5 § 87 (23B): "We remember … the cucumbers and the melons and the leeks and the onions and the garlic" (Num 11:5). R. Simeon (ca. 150) said, "Why did the manna transform (in taste) into everything (food) that they wanted, except for these five kinds? A parable. Like a king of flesh and blood who gave his son over to a tutor פדגוג, and he sat and gave him instructions and said to him, 'It is (above all) to be seen to that he does not eat any harmful food or drink any harmful drink!' And that son grumbled about his father in everything, saying, '(This is happening) not because he loves me, but rather because he (himself) cannot eat it (and therefore does not allow it to me either).'"— Another parable, in which R. Simeon uses the "pedagogue," is found in Pesiq. 17A; see § Mark 4:30, #1. ‖ Sifre Deuteronomy 1:20 § 19 (69A): "'You came to the mountains of the Amorites, which Yahweh, our God, will give us' (Deut 1:20). A parable. Like a king who gave his son over to a tutor פידגוג, and this one led him around and showed him (everything) and said to him, 'All these vines are yours and all the vineyards and all these olives are yours. When he had gotten tired of showing this to him, he said to him: 'Everything that you see is yours….'" ‖ Jerusalem Talmud Sanhedrin 10.28B.51: R. Hunia (ca. 350) said in the name of R. Eleazar (ca. 270), "Why is (the king's) name Ahaz אָחָז? Because he took possession of the synagogues and houses of learning אָחַז. Why did he take possession of them? He was like a king who had a son and gave him over to his tutor לפידגוגו. But this one sought to kill him. He said,

'If I kill him, see, I am guilty of death. Instead, look, I will take his wet nurse away from him, and then he will die by himself.'" (See the continuation of the passage with the application of the parable at § Luke 2:25 B.) ‖ See Deut. Rab. 2 (198D) at § Luke 15:18 A; see Pesiq. 101B at § Acts 19:9, #2. ‖ Numbers Rabbah 1 (135A): "Did I not (said God) make three tutors פדגוגין arise for them, Moses, Aaron, and Miriam? By the merit of Moses you ate the manna; ... by the merit of Aaron I surrounded you with the clouds of glory; and the spring came into existence for them by the merit of Miriam...." ‖ Deuteronomy Rabbah 2 (197D): "May Yahweh hear you on the day of trouble" (Ps 20:2). The rabbis said, "What can this be compared with? With a king's son who took to a bad way (became degenerate), and he had three tutors פדגוגין. The first said, 'Let chains weighing 100 pounds be made for him!' The second said, 'He cannot survive with 100-pound chains, rather let chains weighing 12 pounds be made for him!' The third came and said, 'How can he survive with 12-pound chains! Let chains weighing 1 pound be made for him.' So Moses said, 'Let chains weighing 100 pounds be made (for Israel); as it says, 'Many troubles and evils will come' (Deut 31:17). David said, 'Let chains weighing 12 pounds be made for Israel'; as it says, 'May Yahweh hear you on the day of trouble' (Ps 20:2), as the day has 12 hours. When Jeremiah arose, he said before him, 'Lord of the world, they have no power to endure, as David said, 'On the day of trouble.' Instead, let chains weighing 1 pound be made for them; as it says, 'It is a time of distress for Jacob, but he will be saved out of it' (Jer 30:7)."

4:15 B: Not many fathers.

The following are viewed as "father" in a metaphorical sense: α. a guardian who raises an orphan;[a] β. Anyone who makes a non-Israelite a proselyte to Judaism;[b] γ. a teacher who teaches the Torah to someone.[c]

a. Babylonian Talmud Sanhedrin 19B: Whoever raises an orphan in his house, Scripture reckons it to him as if he had begotten it. ‖ Exodus Rabbah 46 (101C): "But now, Yahweh, you are father" (Isa 64:7). God said to the Israelites, "You leave behind your fathers Abraham, Isaac, and Jacob and call me father?" They answered him, "We acknowledge you as father." Like an orphan who was raised in the house of a guardian אַפִּיטְרוֹפּוֹס (= ἐπίτροπος). This one was a good and faithful person and raised it and protected it, as he should have. When he wanted to marry her off, the scribe came to write down the marriage contract. He said to her, "What is your name?" She answered, "So and so." He said to her, "And what is your father's name?" Then she began to be silent. Her guardian said to her, "Why are you silent?" She answered him, "Because I know only you as a father to me"; for whoever raises is called father אָב, but not the begetter. The orphan: these are the Israelites; as it says, "We became orphans, fatherless" (Lam 5:3). Their good and faithful guardian: this is God. The Israelites began to call him "our Father"; as it says, "But now, Yahweh, you are Father" (Isa 64:7). God said, "You leave behind your fathers and you call me 'our Father'? For it says, 'Look to Abraham, your father!'" (Isa 51:2). They said to him, "Lord of the world, whoever raises is father אָב and not the begetter; as it says, 'For you are our father, for Abraham knows nothing about us and Israel (= Jacob) does not know us' (Isa 63:16)."

b. Genesis Rabbah 84 (53B): R. Eleazar (ca. 270) said in the name of R. Yose b. Zimra (ca. 220), "If all those who come into the world came together to create even just one mosquito, they would not be able to do it, and you say, 'The souls that they had made in Haran' (so Gen 12:5 according to the midr.)! This means rather the proselytes, whom Abraham had converted. And why does it say, 'Which they had made' and not 'Which they had converted'? To teach you that everyone who brings the proselyte (to God) is as if he had created him."

c. Babylonian Talmud Sanhedrin 99B: Resh Laqish (ca. 250) said, "Whoever teaches the son of his neighbor Torah, Scripture reckons it to him as if he had created him; for it says, 'The souls that they had made in Haran'" (Gen 12:5; see the previous citation). See b. Sanh. 19B at § 1 Cor 4:14, #1. ‖ Babylonian Talmud Nedarim 41A: When Rabbi († 217?) had learned the halakah according to thirteen (different) kinds, he taught R. Hiyya (ca. 200) seven of them. Ultimately Rabbi became ill; then R. Hiyya repeated before him those seven kinds which he had taught him, but the (other) six were gone (had been forgotten). There was a fuller there who had listened to Rabbi, when he studied them. R. Hiyya went to him and learned them before the fuller. Then he went and repeated them before Rabbi. When Rabbi saw the fuller, he said to him, "You have made (created) me and Hiyya." Some say that he said to him, "You made Hiyya, and Hiyya made me." See also m. B. Meṣ. 2.11: If it is a matter of a lost item of his father and a lost item of his teacher, that of his teacher takes precedence; for his father brought him into this world, while his teacher, who has taught him wisdom, brings him into the life of the future world. – Babylonian Talmud Sanhedrin 101A: (When R. Tarfon, R. Joshua, R. Eleazar b. Azariah, and R. Aqiba made a sickbed visit to R. Eliezer [ca. 90]), R. Eleazar b. Azariah answered and said, "You are better for Israel than a father and a mother; for a father and a mother (have value and significance) in this world, but the master in this world and for the future world." – See further § 1 Cor 4:17.

4:15 C: For through the gospel I have fathered you.

See the previous section 4:15 B, n. *c.*

4:17 A: Who is my beloved child.

See § 1 Cor 4:14 and § 4:15 B, n. *c.* ‖ Sifre Deuteronomy 6:7 § 34 (74A): "Impress them upon your children" (Deut 6:7): these are your students. And so, you find everywhere that the students are called "sons" בָּנִים; for it says, "You are sons to Yahweh your God" (Deut 14:1). Furthermore it says, "The sons of the prophets came out" (2 Kgs 2:3). How so? Were they the sons of the prophets? Were they not students? Rather, from this it emerges concerning students that they are called "sons." And likewise, you find in the case of Hezekiah, the king of Judah, that he taught the whole Torah to Israel, and he called them "sons" בנים; as it says, "My sons, do not be careless" (2 Chr 29:11). And as the students are called "sons," so the teacher is called "father" אָב; as it says, "And Elisha saw and cried out, 'My father, my father, the chariots of Israel and its riders!' and he saw him no more" (2 Kgs 2:12). Additionally, it says, "And Elisha became ill with a sickness from which he was going to die, and the king of Israel came to him and wept and fell on his face and said, 'My father, my father'" (2 Kgs 13:14; the quotation is imprecise).

4:17 B: My ways.

ὁδός = nature and manner; see § Acts 9:2 B.

4:19: If the Lord wills (see § Jas 4:15).

4:21: Should I come to you with a stick?

ῥάβδος = stick, rod; in rabbinic usage, the most practicable word might be מַקֵּל;[a] in substance, this is synonymous with רְצוּעָה,[b] Aram. רְצוּעֲתָא, the "thong."

a. Sifre Deuteronomy 11:12 § 40 (79A): R. Simeon b. Yohai (ca. 150) said, "A bread and a stick מקל came down from heaven tied together. God said to the Israelites, 'If you do the Torah, behold, there will be bread to eat; but if not, behold, there is the stick to be beaten with.' And where is the interpretation of this matter found? Look, it says, 'If you are willing and obedient, you will eat the best of the land. But if you refuse and are recalcitrant, you will be consumed by the sword; for Yahweh has spoken' (Isa 1:19f.; the end of the quotation is imprecise)." — There is a parallel in Lev. Rab. 35 (132C). There the words, "you will be consumed by the sword חרב" are interpreted as follows: "you will eat locust pods הָרוּבִין." According to what follows and Lev. Rab. 13 (114B), this interpretation is associated with R. Aha (ca. 320); see § Luke 15:16, n. *d.* ‖ Pesiqta 120A: R. Yohanan († 279) said, "Like a king who had two sons; he got angry with the first and took the stick את המקל and beat him and burned him...." — The same is found in Midr. Lam. Intro. #2 (30A). ‖ Babylonian Talmud Sanhedrin 7B: When Rab Huna († 297) would go to a court session, he would say, "Bring me my tools: Stick מקל and thong רצועה (for chastisement) and bugle horn (which was blown when the ban was imposed) and sandals (to carry out the ceremony of the removal of the shoe in the case that levirate marriage was refused). 'I commanded your judges at that time' (Deut 1:16)." R. Yohanan († 279) said, "Be swift with the stick and thong" (apply them diligently as judges, to put fear into the community; cf. Rashi on the passage). — On מקל as a walking stick, see § Matt 10:10 D.

b. See b. Sanh. 7B toward the end of n. *a.* ‖ Genesis Rabbah 20 (13C): R. Eleazar (ca. 270) said, "In your life have you ever seen that, when a person has hit another with a stick מקל, he also hits him again with a thong רצועה? Likewise: 'You will be cursed among all brutes מכל הבהמה' (Gen 3:14), how much more (= then even more) 'among all the beasts of the field' (Gen 3:14)." — In the case of בהמה, domesticated animals, the gestation period lasts up to 12 months, whereas in the case of wild animals חית השדה it is usually a shorter time. Yet in the case of the snake, according to the rabbinic view, at least 7 years. If the snake was thus cursed with a curse that is more difficult than that of domesticated animals, then certainly more than the wild animals, whose curse is milder. In the same way, hitting with a stick is the harder punishment, so no one then smites with the thong as a milder punishment. ‖ Numbers Rabbah 16 (181C): "Amalek dwells in the land of the south" (Num 13:29). Why did (the scouts who returned) begin with Amalek? Like a child who had gotten lost and was beaten with the thong; whenever people wanted to put fear into him, they reminded him of the thong with which he had been beaten. In the same way, Amalek was a terrible thong (a scourge from God) for Israel. ‖ Tosefta Sukkah 2.6 (194): R. Meir (ca. 150) said, "When the heavenly lights are beaten (during solar and lunar eclipses), it is a bad sign for the haters of Israel (= for the godless Israelites, see § Matt 3:17 A, n. *i*, S-B footnote in this section), because they are used to beatings (punishments). He told a parable. What can the matter be compared with? With a school teacher who walks into his classroom and says, 'Bring me the thong!' Who is afraid? The one who is used to being beaten." ‖ The punishment of scourging was carried out with the רצועה, which was made particularly for this purpose (see § 2 Cor 11:24).

5:1 A: Fornication.

πορνεία = זְנוּת, Aram. זְנוּתָא. — We have not found an actual definition of זְנוּת in ancient rabbinic literature. In general it can be said that "fornication" was understood to refer to α. all extramarital sexual intercourse[a] and β. any sexual intercourse of married people whose marriage, even if sealed in a legal form, somehow was not in accordance with rabbinic stipulations.[b] Correspondingly, זוֹנָה "whore" in the broadest sense of the word was applied to any woman who had intercourse in a whorish way, that is, either extramaritally or in an illegitimate marriage.[c] Alongside this, though, there are also explanations that conceive of the זוֹנָה in a narrower sense.[d]

a. Babylonian Talmud ʿAbodah Zarah 36B: According to the Torah only marriage by second-degree of kinship (formal marriage) אִישׁוּת דֶּרֶךְ הַתְנוּת is prohibited (with non-Israelites); then someone came and forbade also whorish sexual intercourse דֶּרֶךְ זְנוּת. — Here זנות stands in contrast to אישות; thus "whorish sexual intercourse" overlaps in substance with "extramarital sexual intercourse." — The passage is found in more detail at § Matt 5:27 B, #4.

b. Babylonian Talmud Ketubbot 3A: Whoever gets engaged (to a woman) gets engaged to her in the sense of (according to the stipulations of) the rabbis. Therefore, the rabbis can annul his engagement (in case the marriage does not align with their statutes). Rabina († ca. 420) said to Rab Ashi († 427), "In case he got engaged by money, it can be left alone; but what should be said if it happened because of sexual intercourse?[168] (It cannot be undone and just as little can the engagement be made invalid!) The rabbis have equated his intercourse (by which the engagement came about) to a whorish intercourse בְּעִילַת זְנוּת (so that it remained without legal marital consequences)." — The same is found in b. Yebam. 90B; b. Giṭ. 33A; 73A; see b. Yebam. 110A; b. B. Bat. 48B. — In certain circumstances, the illegitimacy of a marriage could be discovered only later. In that case, the entire earlier marital life of the married couple was counted as whorish cohabitation.

c. Babylonian Talmud Yebamot 61B: The scholars (ca. 100) said, "A 'whore' זוֹנָה is only a female proselyte (before her conversion to Judaism) and a freedwoman (for according to Jewish law, no legitimate marriage is in any way possible for a priest with these two categories) and a woman who had whorish sexual intercourse בעילת זנות." — The same is found in SLev 21:7 (379A).

---

168. S-B: A woman was acquired in engagement either by presenting money (monetary equivalent) or by delivering a certificate or by intercourse; see § John 2:1 A, #5, notes *i* and *k*.

d. A baraita in b. Yebam. 61B: "A whore זוֹנָה is a whore, as her name proves (= in the literal sense of the word)." These are the words of R. Eliezer (ca. 90. — Rashi: "The one who goes astray from under her husband to another; for in the view of R. Eliezer a whore is only a married woman." — The last remark is not correct; see further below). R. Aqiba († ca. 135) said, "A whore זונה is a prostitute מוּפְקֶרֶת." R. Matthew b. Heresh (ca. 130) said, "Even if her husband goes to make her drink (the water of jealousy), and he has intercourse with her on the way (which was forbidden up until the outcome of the case), he makes her a whore זונה" (here the view is that whoredom = illegitimate intercourse). R. Judah (ca. 150) said, "A whore is a barren woman אַיְלוֹנִית."[169] (Then follows the explanation of the scholars, which is presented above under n. *c*; then follows:) R. Eliezer (ca. 90) said, "An unmarried man who sleeps with an unmarried woman, but not for the purpose of marriage, makes her a whore" (here the view is that whoredom = extramarital intercourse). Individual pieces of this are found also in SLev 21:7 (379A) and b. Yebam. 6.5.

5:1 B: That a man has his father's wife (as a wife).

1. γυνὴ τοῦ πατρός "the father's wife" = אֵשֶׁת אָב. — In Lev 18:7 and 8, we read אֵם "mother" and אֵשֶׁת אָב "the father's wife," and in Lev 18:9 and 11, בַּת אִמֶּךָ "your mother's daughter" and בַּת אֵשֶׁת אָבִיךָ "the daughter of your father's wife" are parallel to each other. In such cases, אֵם designates the biological mother and אֵשֶׁת אָב the stepmother. In the above passages, the LXX has used μητήρ for אם and γυνὴ πατρός for אשת אב. It thus proves that even for them γυνὴ πατρός was common in the sense of "stepmother." Undoubtably, in 1 Cor 5:1, the apostle understood the stepmother by γυνὴ τοῦ πατρός. — Likewise, in rabbinic usage, אשת אב, Aram. אִתַּת אָב, means first and above all α. the stepmother;[a] but then also in general β. "the father's wife," without the expression in any way reflecting that this wife was a blood relative of a son of the father in question. The term "the father's wife" emphasizes that it is a wife who is the legitimate bride of the father, as opposed to a woman whom the father in question had "raped" אֲנוּסָה or "misled" מְפוּתָּה, who had entered into sexual intercourse with the father, but was not thereby his legitimate wife. In this case אשת אב "the father's wife" can denote both a "biological mother" as well as a "stepmother."[b] Yet these are the exceptions, for which the context is decisive; אשת אב primarily denotes the stepmother.

a. אֵשֶׁת אָב; examples are offered by the citations further below. — אִתַּת אָב, see Tg. Onk. Lev. 18:8: "You are not to uncover the nakedness of your father's wife אתת אבוך, it is the nakedness of your father." — Targum Yerušalmi I Leviticus 18:8: "You are not to defile תבזי the nakedness of your father's wife אתת אבוך, because it is the nakedness of your father." —

169. S-B: See b. Yebam. 61B: What is the scriptural basis for R. Judah? Because it is written: "They will eat and not be satisfied, they will commit fornication and not spread out (increase in number)" (Hos 4:10). Every case of intercourse in which there is no question of spreading out (as is the case with a barren woman) is simply an intercourse of fornication זְנוּת.

Targum Onkelos Leviticus 18:11: "The nakedness of your father's wife's daughter בת אתת אבוך, who is raised by your father, she is your sister. You are not to uncover her nakedness." – Targum Yerušalmi I Leviticus 18:11: "The nakedness of your father's wife's daughter, who has been sired by your father, she is your sister. You are not to defile her nakedness."

b. Sifra Leviticus 20:11 (369A): "A man who lies with his father's wife has uncovered the nakedness of his father" (Lev 20:11). "A man": this excludes minors (under nine years, who is not a "man"); "who lies with his father's wife": this means a wife of his father אשת אביו, who is his (the son who had intercourse) (physical) mother, or a wife of his father אשת אביו, who is not his (physical) mother (thus his stepmother). (Here, as can be seen, both the actual mother and the stepmother are called אשת אביו.) His mother, who is not the (legitimate) wife of his father (but rather perhaps one who was raped by the father), whence comes the notion (that the son's intercourse with her is prohibited in the same way)? Scripture teaches: "He has uncovered the nakedness of his father" (Lev 20:11). This is open (unnecessary, superfluous) to compare on the basis of inference by analogy. – Babylonian Talmud Sanhedrin 53B: Raba († 352) said, "R. Judah (the anonymous author of the Sifra passage above [ca. 150]) thought 'the nakedness of your father' (Lev 18:7): this is your father's wife, and he shows this by an inference by analogy, and (your father's wife) means both his father's wife who is his (physical) mother, as well as his father's wife who is not his (actual) mother (but rather his stepmother). His mother, who is not the (legitimate) wife of his father (but rather perhaps one whom he raped), whence comes the notion (that intercourse with her is also prohibited to her son)? Scripture teaches: 'You are not to uncover the nakedness of your mother,' she is your mother (Lev 18:7; she too can stand in this relation to your father by marital right)!" ‖ Targum Yerušalmi I Leviticus 20:11: "A man who sleeps with his father's wife אתת אבוי, whether it be his (physical) mother or another, has defiled the nakedness of his father. They are both to be killed, yes killed."

2. In the rabbinic view, the offenses of fornication had been prohibited to the pre- and extra-Israelite world or the Noachides in the seven Noachic commandments (see § Rom 1:20 E). Ancient Jewish literature relatively rarely speaks specifically about the incestuous action and conduct of the gentiles. In this regard the gentiles are charged with the absolute worst excesses,[a] though alongside this it is also acknowledged that their natural sexual sensibility was still strong enough to reject certain marriages between relatives which were also prohibited to Jews by the Torah. So R. Meir (ca. 150) thinks that among the gentiles it is not accepted for a brother and sister to marry if both were born from a single mother,[170] nor to marry the sister of the father on the maternal side,[171] nor the sister of the mother on the maternal or paternal side.[172] However, among the gentiles, in contrast to Jewish marital law, no offense is caused by a marriage between

170. S-B: However, cf. also the Tosafists on b. Sanh 58A נשא.

171. S-B: That is, if the father and his sister had a common mother.

172. S-B: The scholars were against this opinion of R. Meir, if the mother and sister stemmed from the same father.

a brother and sister who stemmed from one and the same father, and just as little by a marriage to the sister of the father on the paternal side, to the brother's wife, to the wife of the father's brother and to the mother-in-law.[b] Marrying one's own mother was considered taboo by the gentile just as by the Jew.[c] According to (a scattered?) Jewish view, only a slave could marry his mother, just as he was also entitled to marry his daughter.[d] However, according to another Jewish view, a non-Jew did not have the right to wed his own daughter.[e] The conflicting positions of the ancient synagogue on the question of whether a gentile is permitted to marry the stepmother ("the father's wife") is striking. R. Aqiba († ca. 135) answered the question in the negative; R. Eliezer (ca. 90), the unswerving representative of older traditions, answered it affirmatively. R. Meir follows the latter, though with the assumption that such a marriage is not offensive to non-Israelites.[f] All these legal marital questions gained real significance for ancient Judaism when it had to regulate marital law about proselytes. We will therefore return to this in #4 and reserve providing and discussing the main proof text b. Sanh. 57B until then; see #4, n. *b*.

a. See Let. Aris. 152 at § Rom 1:26 A, #2, *a*. ‖ See Sib. Or. 5:387ff. at § Rom 1:27 A, A, #1. ‖ In b. Yebam. 97B there are some conundrums concerning tricky family relationships. Two of these begin with the words: A non-Israelite נָכְרִי slept with his mother אמו and sired a daughter, or two daughters, by her. — Such conundrums would hardly have been composed unless daily life had supplied examples of this; see also b. Ker. 15A.

b. See the baraita in b. Sanh. 57B in #4, n. *b*.

c. Marriage to the mother was prohibited to the proselytes, who came from paganism, lest they might say: "We are coming from a greater holiness into a smaller holiness." This implies that even the gentile saw something unseemly in marrying one's own mother. — Concerning the Jew, see #3.

d. Babylonian Talmud Sanhedrin 58B: Rab Hisda († 309) said, "A slave is permitted (to marry) his mother אמו and likewise his daughter; he is separated from the entirety of non-Judaism גוי, and he has not entered into the entirety of Israel."

e. Babylonian Talmud Sanhedrin 58B: Come and hear! Why did Adam not marry his daughter? So that Cain could marry his sister; as it says, "I said, 'The world is to be built with grace'" (with benevolence; so the midr. understands Ps 89:3). Otherwise, would she not have been forbidden? After she was permitted, she remained permitted. Rab Huna († 297) said, "A non-Israelite גוי is permitted (to marry) his daughter (cf. Schulchan ʿArukh in #4, n. *c*), and if you should say, 'Why then did Adam not marry his daughter?' (this happened) so that Cain could marry his sister, so that the world would be built by grace." Yet there are others who say that Rab Huna († 297) said, "A non-Israelite is forbidden (to marry) his daughter! Learn from this that Adam did not marry his daughter. But this (the objection) is nothing: there, the reason was that Cain might marry his sister so that the world would be built by grace."

f. A baraita in b. Sanh. 58A: (God said to the first man,) "Therefore a man will leave his father and his mother" (Gen 2:24; in the sense of the midr.: to refrain from marrying her). R. Eliezer (ca. 90) said, "'His father,' that is, his father's sister; 'his mother,' that is, his mother's sister." R. Aqiba († ca. 135) said, "'His father,' that is, his father's wife (stepmother); 'his mother,' that is, his mother in the literal sense. 'And cling' (Gen 2:24), but not to a man; 'to his wife,' but not to someone else's wife; 'so that they become one flesh': these are those who can become one flesh (body), so domestic and wild animals are excluded, who cannot become one flesh (with the man)." — See the whole passage at § Matt 19:5. There it is applied and interpreted in relation to the proselyte who converts to Judaism. Yet in its original meaning, according to the understanding of R. Eliezer and R. Aqiba, the passage pertains to the Noachides in general. Eliezer considers it forbidden for a Noachide to marry his father's sister and R. Aqiba considers it forbidden for a Noachide to marry his father's wife (= stepmother); this implies, as the Tosafists rightly emphasize נשא in b. Sanh. 58A, that R. Eliezer declared that a Noachide was permitted to marry his father's wife (stepmother), while conversely R. Aqiba had no objection against a Noachide marrying his father's sister. R. Meir (ca. 150) partly follows the older traditions of R. Eliezer and correspondingly declares that a Noachide who becomes a proselyte is permitted to marry his father's wife (stepmother), specifically because there is no reason to worry that the proselyte will say that he is coming from the greater holiness of paganism to the smaller holiness of Judaism. Thus, it is expressed that, according to R. Meir's view, it was not prohibited among the gentiles to marry the stepmother, so that the proselyte, in his converting to Judaism, could not take offense if such a marriage was permitted to him also on the part of Judaism; see b. Sanh. 57B with the explanation in #4, n. *b*.

3. The relatives an Israelite is forbidden to marry are listed in Lev 18:6ff. In order to secure the individual prohibitions from any transgression as much as possible, the Sopherim broadened the banned circle of relatives in each case to a member a generation above and below. There were the so-called שְׁנִיּוֹת, the second degrees of relation whom it was forbidden to marry; see § Matt 2:4, final paragraph; § Matt 15:2 A, #2 toward the end; and § John 2:1 A, #3, ε — Marriage to one's own mother (Lev 18:7) and marriage to the father's wife (= stepmother; Lev 18:8; 20:11; Deut 23:1; 27:20) were among the prohibited incestuous marriage of the first degree.[a] The unmarried mother (who had given birth outside of marriage) was like the married mother (who had given birth as a legitimate wife) in this regard.[b] The occasional case of sexual intercourse with the mother and the stepmother was treated exactly as the formally completed marriage.[c]

A. Son and biological mother.

If the incestuous act had been committed intentionally, specifically before witnesses and despite warning, the death penalty was in order, which had to be carried out as stoning.[d] If the act happened intentionally, but without witnesses and without warning, in theory the perpetrator became subject to eradication by God's hand.[e] If the action had occurred unintentionally, it was to be atoned for by two sin offerings: one was presented because the action had been carried out with the "mother," and the other was presented because the action had been carried out with "his father's wife." R. Judah (ca. 150) considered only one sin offering necessary, namely because the action happens with the "mother."[f] These stipulations held whether or not the father was still alive.[g]

B. Son and stepmother.

The act committed intentionally or unintentionally with the stepmother was punished exactly in the same way as the action with one's own mother. Yet the two sin offerings took on partly different meanings: one was presented because of the "father's wife" and the other because of a "married woman" (because of a wife). It made no difference whether the action had occurred during the father's life or after his death, or whether it had occurred after the engagement or after the marriage of the stepmother.[h] Yet after the father's death, only one sin offering had to be presented, because the widow was no longer legally considered a "married wife" אֵשֶׁת אִישׁ; see Rashi on m. Sanh. 53A.

C. Son and a woman raped or misled by the father.

A woman who had been raped אֲנוּסָה or misled מְפוּתָּה by the father, who remained in his house without him marrying her, could not in marital law be viewed as a legitimate wife (אֵשֶׁת אִישׁ or אֵשֶׁת אָב). If her own unmarried son slept with her, he was, as the son of his "mother," just as much an offender as in the situation where the son had done the same with a mother married by rite (see A); for whatever the marital relation of his mother to his father might be, she was and remained for him his biological mother.[i] Yet if another son of that father had intercourse with her, he remained exempt from punishment, because he had slept with neither his "mother" nor a legitimate "wife of his father";[k] indeed he could even marry her. R. Judah (ca. 150) wished to forbid the latter;[l] others considered it to be permitted only after the father's death.[m]

That incestuous intercourse with the wives of the father happened even in Israel is attested to by Gen 35:22; 49:4; 2 Sam 16:21f.[n] A later time accused King Amon and his biological mother of this transgression;[o] the same sort of case is discussed also in b. Ker. 87A (= 15A in other editions), though only hypothetically.[p] General accusations in this regard are raised by Pss. Sol. 8:9f.[q]

a. Here we will present all the targumim on the passages named. — Targum Onkelos Leviticus 18:7: "You will not uncover the nakedness of your father and the nakedness of your mother; she is your mother, you will not uncover her nakedness." —Yerušalmi I: "The nakedness of your father and the nakedness of your mother you will not defile (disparage); a woman should not have sexual intercourse with her father and a man should not have sexual intercourse with his mother; she is your mother, you will not uncover her nakedness."

‖ Onkelos Leviticus 18:8: "The nakedness of your father's wife (= your stepmother) you will not uncover, it is the nakedness of your father." — Yerušalmi I: "The nakedness of your father's wife you will not defile (disparage), because it is the nakedness of your father." ‖ Targum Onkelos Leviticus 20:11: "A man who lies with his father's wife has uncovered the nakedness of his father; they should both be killed, they are guilty of death." — Yerušalmi I: "A man who has sexual intercourse with his father's wife, whether she is his (biological) mother or a different woman, has defiled (disparaged) the nakedness of his father; they should both be killed; they are guilty of death by the casting of stones." ‖ Onkelos Deuteronomy 23:1: "A man should not marry his father's wife, and he is not to uncover the tip of his father." — Yerušalmi I: "A man should not marry the woman his father has raped or misled, and even less his father's wife (the stepmother), and he is not to uncover the tip which his father has uncovered (not touch a woman that his father has touched)." ‖ Targum Onkelos Deuteronomy 27:20: "Cursed is whoever lies with his father's wife; for he has uncovered his father's tip, and all the people will say 'Amen!'" — Yerušalmi I: "Cursed is whoever has sexual intercourse with his father's wife; for he has uncovered the tip which his father has uncovered; they will all answer together and say: Amen!"

b. See section C.

c. Leviticus 18:7, 8; 20:11; Deut 27:20 pertain to occasional intercourse, Deut 23:1 to marriage.

d. Mishnah Sanhedrin 7.4: These are the ones who were stoned: whoever sleeps with the mother. ‖ Jerusalem Talmud Sanhedrin 7.24D.18: Whoever sleeps with the mother.... Where does the prohibition (the warning) for the one who sleeps with the mother come from? "You will not uncover your mother's nakedness" (Lev 18:7). — The scriptural proof is presented differently (as well as anonymously, but according to R. Judah [ca. 150]) in SLev 20:11 (369A): "A man who lies with his father's wife" Lev 20:11; this means a wife of his father, who is his (the son who slept with the wife) (actual) mother, (and also) a wife of his father, who is not his (actual) mother (thus his stepmother. Therefore everything that is said about the former holds also for the former, who is his actual mother).... "They will both die by death; their bloodguilt clings to them" (Lev 20:11). They are to die a death by stoning. You say, "By stoning," or not rather by any of all the death penalties that appear in the Torah? Scripture teaches, "Their bloodguilt clings to them" (Lev 20:11), and there (Lev 20:27) it (similarly) says, "Their bloodguilt clings to them." Just as "their bloodguilt on them," which is spoken about there, is punished by stoning, so too "their bloodguilt on them," which is spoken of here, is punished by stoning. The punishment we have heard; the prohibition (the warning) we have not heard. Scripture teaches, "You will not uncover the nakedness of your father and the nakedness of your mother" (Lev 18:7). The "nakedness of your father": this applies to your father's wife (in the most general sense). Or is the "nakedness of your father" not meant in the literal sense (= you will not uncover the shame of your father)? See, you have to infer: It says here in Lev 20:11, "The nakedness of his father" (so read instead of "of your father"). And it says there in Lev 18:7, "The nakedness of your father you will not uncover." As with "nakedness of his father" (so read instead of "your father's"), which is spoken about there (Lev 20:11), Scripture speaks about his father's wife (so read), so too

Scripture speaks about your father's wife with "nakedness of your father," which is spoken about here (Lev 18:7), and this means both a wife of his father, who is his (the son's) mother, and a wife of his father, who is not his mother (but rather his stepmother). — Unlike in y. Sanh. 7.24D.18 above, R. Judah has not taken the scriptural proof from Lev 18:7: "You will not uncover your mother's nakedness," because he used these words as a scriptural proof for the woman that father had raped or misled; see C. — A parallel passage is found in b. Sanh. 54A. — On the death penalty by stoning, see also see also Tg. Yer. I on Lev 20:11 above in n. *a*. — The author of Jubilees 33:1ff. particularly strictly inculcated the prohibition of incest with mother and stepmother. He too already attests to stoning as the atoning punishment; see the passage in n. *n*. — On the process of stoning, see § Acts 7:58 A and B.

e. Mishnah Keritot 1.1: Thirty-six cases of the punishment of eradication (see § Matt 5:21 B, #2, א) appear in the Torah: whoever sleeps with his mother.... ‖ On the scriptural proof, see y. Sanh. 7.24D.20: Eradication כָּרֵת, whence (can it be proved from Scripture)? "For if anyone does any of all abominations (among which incest with mother and stepmother is also listed), the souls (persons) that do them will be eradicated from the midst of their people" (Lev 18:29). — Sifra Leviticus 18:29 (341A): "For if anyone does any of all abominations" (Lev 18:29), whether all of them or a part of them, "the souls will be eradicated." What does Scripture mean to teach? Since it says "every man" (Lev 18:6), I might think that only the man is punished with eradication because of the woman. Whence comes the notion that the woman is also punished with eradication because of the man? Scripture teaches, "Souls" (persons), look, here the two (both) are being discussed. ("The souls) that do them" (Lev 18:29); what does Scripture mean to teach? Since it says "No man will approach his biological relatives" (Lev 18:6), are they to make themselves guilty of eradication simply because of the approach קְרִיבָה? Scripture teaches, "That do them" (carry out the act) and not "That approach." "From the midst of their people" (Lev 18:29), but their people remains intact (in peace).

f. Mishnah Sanhedrin 7.4: Whoever sleeps with the mother is guilty (for two sin offerings) because of her: "because of the mother" and (since the mother is simultaneously the father's wife, also) "because of the father's wife." R. Judah (ca. 150) said, "He is guilty (for one sin offering) 'because of the mother.'" ‖ Tosefta Sanhedrin 10.1 (430): R. Judah (ca. 150) said, "Whoever sleeps with the mother, is guilty only 'because of the mother.'"— The controversy between R. Judah and the rabbis is dealt with in detail in b. Sanh. 53A.32–54A.37.

g. This follows from the analogous stipulation concerning the "father's wife"; see n. *h*.

h. Mishnah Sanhedrin 7.4: These are the ones who are stoned: whoever sleeps with ... the father's wife.... ‖ Jerusalem Talmud Sanhedrin 7.24D.21: From where in Scripture can the prohibition (warning) be proven for the one who sleeps with the father's wife? "You will not uncover the nakedness of your father's wife" (Lev 18:8).... The punishment, from where can that be shown? "A man who lies with his father's wife has uncovered his father's nakedness; they are both to be killed" (Lev 20:11). — On the scriptural proof about the punishment of stoning, see SLev 20:11 (369A) in n. *d*. ‖ On the punishment of eradication see m. Ker. 1.1: Thirty-six cases of the punishment of eradication (cf. above in n. *e*) appear in the Torah: whoever sleeps with ... his father's wife. — The scriptural proof for the punishment of eradication in y. Sanh. 7.24D.22 is as follows: Eradication (for the one who sleeps with his father's wife,) whence can this be shown? "For if anyone does any of these abominations, the souls that do them will be eradicated from the midst of their people" (Lev 18:29). – On the interpretation of this passage, see SLev 18:29 above in n. *e.* ‖ Mishnah Sanhedrin 7.4: Whoever sleeps with the father's wife (inadvertently) is guilty because of her (for two sin offerings): "because of the father's wife" and (since she is as such simultaneously a married woman אֵשֶׁת אִישׁ, also) "because of a married woman" (cf. Lev 18:20), both during his father's life and after his father's death,[173] both after the engagement[174] and after the marriage. – Tosefta Sanhedrin 10.1 (430): R. Judah (ca. 150) said, "Whoever sleeps with the father's wife is guilty (for one sin offering) 'because of the father's wife' (and not a second one 'because of a married woman')." – Abbayye († 338/39) referred to this baraita in b. Sanh. 54A. ‖ Babylonian Talmud Sanhedrin 54A: From where do the rabbis take the prohibition (the warning) concerning the father's wife? From: "You will not uncover the nakedness of your father's wife" (Lev 18:8; see also y. Sanh. 7.24D.21 above in n. *h*). And R. Judah (ca. 150)? He needs this for the prohibition (the warning) concerning his father's wife after the death. And the rabbis? For them this follows from the close of the passage: "It is the nakedness of your father" (Lev 18:8).... And from where do the rabbis take the punishment concerning his father's wife after the death? You can be answered, "From that passage: 'He has uncovered the nakedness of his father' (Lev 20:11) ... they take the punishment concerning his father's wife after the death (because the close of Lev 20:11 deals explicitly with the punishment)."

i. Tosefta Sanhedrin 10.2 (430): Whoever sleeps with the mother, who is a widow for the high priest, a divorced woman or a woman dismissed by the removal of the shoe for an ordinary priest, or who has been raped or misled by his father, or who falls into any category of the women whom his father is forbidden to marry: he is guilty. – Explanation: The high priest was forbidden to marry a widow, the ordinary priest was forbidden to marry a divorced woman or a woman who had been dismissed by the removal of the shoe; see § John 2:1 A, #3, A, notes γ and δ. If the marriage was nevertheless sealed, it still counted as a marriage, but it made the high priest and the ordinary priest, as well as their male progeny from such marriages, unfit for the execution of priestly functions. Women who had been raped or misled by the father, however, were as his wives. Finally, the father could not seal any valid marriage at all with women whom it was forbidden to marry and for which marriages the legal death penalty or eradication was due; in no case were the women in question legally considered as wives. If a son from these relationships of his father slept with his mother, he was an offender in each case; for however different the legal marital relationship of the mother to the father might be, she always remained the mother in relation to the son. – See related thoughts, though in connection with the different opinion of R. Judah (ca. 150), in b. Sanh. 53A. ‖ Sifra Leviticus 20:11 (369A):

---

173. S-B: After the father's death, the sin offering "because of a married wife" ceased; see Rashi on b. Sanh. 53A.

174. S-B: From the time of the engagement, the woman was considered by marital law to be a wife in every respect; see § John 2:1, #5.

"His mother, who is not his father's wife (but maybe one he had raped or misled), from where can it be shown (that the son is forbidden to sleep with her)? Scripture teaches: '(You will not uncover your mother's nakedness,) she is your mother' (Lev 18:7), in the most general sense (thus also the unmarried mother is included). Now I hear only the prohibition (the warning) treats his mother who is not his father's wife like his mother who is his father's wife. Where do the punishments come from? Look, you can make an inference: here (Lev 20:11) the nakedness of his father is talked about, and there (Lev 18:7) the nakedness of his father is talked about; as the nakedness of his father which is talked about there (Lev 18:7) treats his mother who is not his father's wife like his mother who is his father's wife, so too here (in the punishment in Lev 20:11) it treats his mother who is not his father's wife like his mother who is his father's wife." — This is the argumentation of R. Judah (ca. 150). A parallel passage is found in b. Sanh. 54A.14. By contrast, it is asked in b. Sanh. 54A.36: From where do the rabbis prove the punishment because of his mother who is not his father's wife? Rab Shisha b. Idi (ca. 350) said, "In the Scripture passage, 'She is your mother' (Lev 18:7), Scripture has treated his mother who is not his father's wife like his mother who is (at the same time) his father's wife."

k. Tosefta Sanhedrin 10.2 (430): Whoever sleeps with the father's wife, who is a widow for the high priest, a divorced woman or a woman dismissed by the removal of the shoe for an ordinary priest, is an offender (guilty). If she is a woman who has been raped or misled by his father, or who falls into any category of the women whom his father is forbidden to marry, he is not subject to punishment. — A widow who is married to a high priest and a divorced woman or a woman dismissed by the removal of the shoe who is married to an ordinary priest still count as wives, even though such marriages are prohibited. Therefore, if a son of her husband from another marriage sleeps with her, he sins against her as his father's wife and consequently becomes subject to punishment. However, a woman who has been raped or misled by the father or any woman who is forbidden to him, with whom he could not seal a valid marriage at all, is not considered as the father's wife at all. Therefore, if a son of the father from another marriage sleeps with her, he has committed an offense neither against his own mother nor against his father's wife; therefore, he goes without being punished.

l. Mishnah Yebamot 11.1: One (namely a son of the father) may marry a woman who has been raped or misled by his father.... R. Judah (ca. 150) forbade marriage with a woman who has been raped or misled by his father. ‖ Tosefta Yebamot 12.1 (254): R. Judah forbade marriage with a woman who has been raped or misled by his father; for it says, "A man should not marry his father's wife nor uncover the tip of his father" (Deut 23:1). Furthermore, "You will not uncover the nakedness of your father's wife; it is the nakedness of your father" (Lev 18:8). Additionally, "He should keep her as a wife; he cannot dismiss her in his life" (Deut 22:29). (The words that then follow: נתנו עיניין לו, probably meant as a question = "does the passage refer to this?" were originally probably a marginal comment; they are missing in the Vienna manuscript.) — The parallel in b. Yebam. 97A is as follows: Rab Giddel (ca. 270) said that Rab († 247) said, "What was the scriptural basis of R. Judah's view? Because it is written, 'A man should not marry his father's wife nor uncover the tip of his father' (Deut 23:1): the tip that his father has seen, he should uncover. And whence comes the idea that this is written about a woman who has been raped? Because it is written before the passage: 'The man who lay with her should give the girl's father fifty pieces of silver' (Deut 22:29)." — Deuteronomy 23:1 is named as the scriptural basis for R. Judah also in SDeut 23:1 § 246 (119B) and y. Yebam. 11.11D.40. In the latter passage it says, "A man should not take his father's wife" (Deut 23:1): this is his father's wife; "nor should he uncover the tip of his father": this is a woman raped by him. — The opinion of R. Judah is represented also by Tg. Yer. I Deut. 23:1; see above in n. *a*.

m. In treating the statement: "One may marry a woman raped by his father," b. Yebam. 97A says in conclusion: And if you want, say, "After the death (of the father he may marry her)." — Yet these words are understood completely differently and related to the sister-in-law who awaits the fulfillment of levirate marriage by the "father" named in Deut 23:1: "One should not uncover the tip of his father" = one should not marry the father's sister-in-law who awaits the fulfillment of levirate marriage by the father. Concerning this then: and if you want, say, "After the death (of the father he may marry his father's sister-in-law)."

n. Ancient Jewish literature comes to speak quite frequently of Reuben's sin with Bilhah in Gen 35:22. Jubilees in particular took this case as an opportunity to inculcate most emphatically the prohibition against incest with the father's wife. Therefore, the whole passage follows here. Jubilees 33:1ff.: "Jacob went out and dwelt toward the south in Magdaladraef (= מִגְדַּל עֵדֶר אֶפְרָת).[175] And he went to his father Isaac, he and his wife Leah, on the new moon of the 10th month. And Reuben saw Bilhah, Rachel's maid, his father's concubine, as she bathed in water privately, and he came to love her. And at night he came secretly into the house of Bilhah and found her sleeping in her bed alone in her house. And he slept with her, and she woke up and saw that Reuben slept with her on the bed, and she uncovered her tip and seized him and shouted and recognized that it was Reuben. And she was ashamed because of him and took her hand from him, and he fled. And she mourned very much about this, but she told no one (about it). And when Jacob came and looked for her, she said to him, 'I am not pure for you, because I am defiled for you; for Reuben has defiled me and at night he slept with me while I was sleeping and did not know, until he uncovered my tip and slept with me.' And Jacob became very angry at Reuben, because he had slept with Bilhah; for he had uncovered the cover of his father. And Jacob no longer approached her, because Reuben had defiled her. And every man who uncovers the cover of his father, his act is very evil; for it is condemned before God. Therefore, it is written and ordained on the heavenly tablets (see § Luke 10:20, #4) that a man may not sleep with his father's wife or uncover the cover of his father; for it is impure. Both the man, who sleeps with his father's wife, and the woman will die of death; for they have done an impure thing on the earth. And let there no longer be any impurity before our God within the people that he has chosen as his possession. And, furthermore, it is written, 'Cursed be everyone who sleeps with his father's wife; for he has exposed the shame of his father! And all the holy ones of God said, "May it be! May it be!"'

175. Littmann in Kautzsch, *Apokryphen und Pseudepigraphen*, vol. 1.

(cf. Deut 27:20). Yet you, Moses, command the children of Israel to keep this word. For (it is) a capital sin and it is impurity, and there is no forgiveness to atone for the man who has done this in eternity, but rather he is to be brought to death and to be killed and to be stoned and to be eliminated from the midst of the people of our God. For the man who does this in Israel will not be allowed to live one day on earth, since he is condemned and impure! And one should not say, 'Reuben received life and pardon after he had slept with his father's concubine, while she (still) had a husband, and while her husband, his father Jacob, was (still) alive.' Yet the ordinance and the judgment and the law had up until then (still) not been completely revealed to all; for (only) in your days (it is) as a law of time and days and an eternal law for eternal generations. And for this law there is no end of days and there is no pardon for this, except that they both be eliminated from the midst of the people: on the day on which they have done it they should be killed. But you, Moses, write it down for Israel so that they may keep it and act according to this word and not stray in sins of death; for the Lord, our God, is a judge who does not respect persons and does not accept any gift. And say this speech of the covenant to them, that they listen and beware and guard against this and not die nor be removed from the earth. For all who do this on the earth are before our God impurity, abomination, defilement, and desecration. And there is no greater sin than the fornication they commit on earth. For Israel is a holy people to God, its Lord, and it is a people of inheritance and it is a priestly people and it is a royal people and it is a possession, and it should not be that anything impure appears in the midst of the holy people."[176] — Elsewhere, most of the time, reference is made to Reuben's repentance or the attempt is made to euphemize his deed; yet there is also no lack of passages that punish his offense as sharply as possible; see T. Reu.1, 3, 4; SDeut 33:5f. § 347 (144A.19–144B.3); b. Šabb. 55B; b. Soṭah 7B; Pesiq. 159A; Gen. Rab. 82 (52D); 84 (53D); 98 (61C.19—61D.10); Num. Rab. 13 (169C; 171B.50–171C.17).

o. Babylonian Talmud Sanhedrin 103B: Manasseh tore down the altar, Amon burned the Torah and presented a type of lizard שְׂמָמִית on the altar (Rashi explains: spider webs קוּרֵי עַכָּבִישׁ, because he abolished all things and every temple service, until the spiders wove their threads across the altar). Ahaz permitted incest, Manasseh slept with his sister, Amon slept with his mother. "This Amon heaped up much guilt" (2 Chr 33:23). R. Yohanan († 279) and R. Eleazar (ca. 270). The one said, "He burned the Torah"; the other said, "He slept with his mother. She said to him, 'Do you have the smallest enjoyment in the place from which you came?' He answered her, 'Am I not doing it simply to offend (God)?'"

p. Babylonian Talmud Keritot 87A: Rab Ad(d)a b. Ahaba (ca. 250) said, "With the godless man, the son of a godless man, it is accurate that he sleeps with his mother and begets two daughters. Then he sleeps again with one of these and begets a son. His son sleeps with his mother's sister, who is his sister, who is his father's sister."

---

176. S-B: In the passage above, Jub. 33:1ff., W. Singer sees strong support for his assumption that Jubilees was authored by an anti-Pauline Jewish Christian (*Das Buch der Jubiläen oder die Leptogenesis* [Stuhlweissenburg, Hungary: Singer, 1898], 34ff., 245, 320). Specifically in Jub. 33:1ff, the anonymous opponent of the apostle refers to the incestuous incident in Corinth in order to make clear for him the corrupt consequences of his law-free preaching. Hence the strikingly sharp tone which the author of Jubilees adopts precisely with the mention of prohibitions of incest.

q. See Pss. Sol. 8:9f. at § Rom 1:26 A, #2, n. *b*.

4. According to the fundamental views of the rabbinic scholars, the OT's prohibitions against incest (Lev 18) did not come into consideration at all for proselytes. At his conversion to Judaism the proselyte was equivalent to a newborn child (see § John 3:3, #3): just as a newborn child had no opportunity in his past to automatically create incestuous relationships, but rather can produce such relationships only in his later life, a proselyte is pure from his past of all incestuous relationships; he does not leave behind any blood relatives in the gentile world, and he does not take any blood relatives with himself from the gentile world over into Judaism. Only after his conversion is he in the position to establish a legitimate marriage and thereby also legitimate blood relatives in accordance with Jewish marital law. According to this view, a proselyte at his conversion could of course not be encumbered by any sort of consanguineous marriage that would offend the Old Testament prohibitions of incest in Lev 18. Yet, for reasons of convenience, the ancient synagogue never brought this principled standpoint to bear in practice. Lest the proselytes say: "We are coming from a greater holiness into a smaller holiness"[a] (to the extent that marriages that had been forbidden to them in their gentile phase were now permitted to them in Judaism), Jews considered it appropriate to ban proselytes from intermarriages that the gentile world also took offense at. However, all further stipulations of Jewish marital law, in particular those concerning the second degrees of relation whom it was forbidden to marry שְׁנִיּוֹת (see above in #3 at the beginning), were not to be imposed on proselytes as a matter of obedience.[a] In practice the matter took more precise shape. The rabbinic scholars considered it a firm principle that a non-Israelite נָכְרִי had no father (see Pesiq. Rab. 23/24 and b. Yebam. 98A at § Rom 1:26, #1). Thus, for a proselyte, blood relationship could come into question only as it pertained to relations on the maternal, not paternal, side.[b] The following norm resulted from this for regulating consanguineous marriage among proselytes: the proselyte is forbidden to marry a woman who is a blood relative from his mother's side, but he is permitted to marry a woman whose relationship to him is determined by descent from a common father. An example: the proselyte is permitted to marry his paternal sister, because his mother is not the mother of his sister. However, he is forbidden to marry his maternal sister, since his mother is also the mother of his sister. Or: the proselyte is permitted to marry his father's sister who, with the father, stems only from the same father; for his father's mother is not also his sister's mother. In other words, the mother of the bride (the aunt) is not simultaneously also the grandmother of the groom (the nephew). However, the proselyte is forbidden to marry his father's sister who, with the father, stems from the same mother, since now the mother of the

bride would also the grandmother of the groom at the same time. – As a consequence of this rule, there was no objection if a proselyte married his father's wife, that is, his stepmother; for by her marriage to his father, no blood relationship arose for the stepson himself in the literal sense of the word. Only when the stepmother was already otherwise a maternal blood relative of her stepson did the marriage have to be avoided.[b] – Generally speaking this rule would have corresponded with the views of the gentile world about which intermarriages were permitted and which were not; see above in #2. In any case, though, the Jewish scholars had reason to suppose that their ruling about intermarriages for proselytes fully overlapped with the wishes of the proselytes themselves, namely in the sense that the proselytes could now no longer have the perception that they had stepped from a greater holiness into a smaller holiness. Only if the regulation was supported by the agreement of the proselytes themselves does it become understandable that it so quickly found general recognition in rabbinic circles. Yet there was no lack of divergent opinions about specifics. We will learn about some of these in n. *b*, where we will see also the view of R. Aqiba († ca. 135), who did not want to recognize the marriage of a proselyte to his stepmother; see also above in #2, n. *f*. Yet apart from such details, the rule became effectively decisive for practice. A later time came to recognize it as a valid halakah.[c]

a. Babylonian Talmud Yebamot 22A: "Have the second degrees of relation whom it is forbidden to marry שְׁנִיּוֹת been set for proselytes, or have the second degrees of relation whom it is forbidden to marry not been set for proselytes?" He (Rab Nahman, † 320) said to him (Raba, † 352), "If the actual blood relatives have already been set for them just so that they could not say that they have come from a greater holiness קדושה המורה into a smaller holiness קדושה קלה, can it then be in question that the rabbis have not set for them the second degrees of relation whom it is forbidden to marry?"

b. A baraita in b. Sanh. 57Bf.: A proselyte, whose conception (generation) did not occur in holiness (= in paganism or before the conversion to Judaism) and his birth happened in holiness (after the conversion to Judaism), he has the mother's blood relatives שאר האם, but not the father's blood relatives.[177] How is this? If he married his maternal sister, he must

177. S-B: Rashi: "Every proselyte who converts to Judaism is like a child who was just born, without father and mother and (other) relatives, and no blood relations from before rest on him. (This is the principled view of the ancient synagogue, which was discussed at the beginning of #4 above.) However, our rabbis have forbidden to marry all (women) who are forbidden to him in the gentile world, lest they be able to say that they have come from a greater holiness into a smaller holiness (the view of appropriateness)."

dismiss her[178] (separate from her); his paternal sister, he may keep her;[179] the sister of the father on the maternal side (when the father and his sister stem from the same mother), he must dismiss her; the sister of the father on the paternal side, he may keep her; the sister of the mother on the maternal side, he must dismiss her; the sister of the mother on the paternal side, he must, as R. Meir said, dismiss her;[180] but the scholars said, "He may keep her." For R. Meir said, "He must dismiss any woman who is prohibited because of blood relation with the mother; he may keep a woman who is forbidden because of blood relation with the father. Furthermore, he is permitted his brother's wife[181] and the wife of his father's brother; also all other women who are forbidden (to the Israelites) are allowed to him; this includes his father's wife (his stepmother).[182] If he has married a

---

178. S-B: Rashi: "If he has married his maternal sister who was born before their mother converted, or who converted with their mother and whom he married when he was an adult, he must dismiss her, for she is his sister, and he is different from a Noachide. And according to our rabbis (he must dismiss her), lest they be able to say that they have come from a greater holiness etc." (Here it is implied that even among the gentiles it was not accepted to marry one's maternal sister; this is then presented explicitly as R. Meir's view. Rashi continues:) "For R. Meir (ca. 150) thought that the maternal sister was forbidden to the Noachides and likewise also the sister of his father on the mother's side and the sister of his mother on the father's side...." – On the parallel b. Yebam. 98A Rashi remarks, "If he has married his maternal sister who was born when she (the mother) was a gentile, he must dismiss her. Although (in principle) she is not his sister, since he is like a newborn child, this preventive regulation has been enacted, lest he come and marry his sister who was born after him (thus after the mother converted to Judaism); for if he marries her, there is (for him) the punishment of eradication, since the birth of both (brother and sister) happened in holiness (after the mother's conversion)."

179. S-B: Rashi: "The prohibition about the sister applies for Noachides (non-Israelites) only in the case of the maternal sister; for it is written, 'She is actually my sister, my father's daughter, but not my mother's daughter and has become my wife' (Gen 20:12). Thus, the father's daughter is allowed to them, but the mother's daughter is not allowed to them." – In the parallel passage b. Yebam. 98A, Rashi says, "Everyone knows that the *goy* (non-Israelite, the text under the pressure of censorship: Samaritan) has no father. And if he too comes and marries a daughter of his father who was begotten from another woman after he converted to Judaism, we will not worry about it, for see, he is not his son."

180. S-B: Rashi: "This is a preventive regulation because of his maternal sister" (lest one infer from the hypothetical permission that it is also allowed to marry one's own maternal sister).

181. S-B: Rashi: "His brother's wife, even of his maternal brother, and after the (brother's) death, and even if his brother had married her after he had become a proselyte, or if he had married her when he was a non-Israelite (text: Samaritan), and had kept her after he had become a proselyte. For in the case of Noachides (non-Israelites) there is no prohibition concerning the brother's wife, and there is no need to be concerned that they might perhaps say (they have come from a greater holiness into a smaller holiness)." – A baraita in b. Yebam. 98B: In any case, (the proselyte) is allowed (to marry) his brother's wife. But does this not mean if his brother married her when he became a proselyte? No also, if he had married her when he was a gentile. – Tosefta Yebamot 12.2 (254) is different: If a proselyte woman and her sons converted to Judaism at the same time, and their conception and birth had not happened in holiness (= before the conversion), ... they do not become liable to punishment because of (marrying) the brother's wife. If their conception had not occurred in holiness, but their birth had occurred in holiness, ... they do become liable to punishment because of (marrying) the brother's wife.

182. S-B: The Tosafot on b. Yebam. 98B אשת comment on the words: "This includes his father's wife": This baraita aligns with the opinion of R. Eliezer (ca. 90); but R. Aqiba († ca. 135) had a different opinion and prohibited his father's wife, but he allowed his father's sister (cf. #2, n. *f*). והה״ג (= "and the Halakoth Gedoloth," 1st half of the 9th century) lay down (declare as valid halakah) in accordance with the opinion of R. Aqiba, since R. Eliezer was a follower of Shammai (?). – The Pisqe Tosafoth (14th century) § 178 on Yebamot chapter 11 accordingly declare: "The proselyte is forbidden his father's wife." – Rabbenu Asher († 1327) first mentions this stipulation of Yebam. chapter 11, but then adds, "Others stipulate in accordance with the view of R. Eliezer in the name of the rabbis of R. Meir, who shared his (R. Eliezer's) opinion" (namely in the baraita from b. Sanh. 57Bf. presented above in the text). –

woman along with her daughter, he will marry the one and dismiss the other, and actually he should not marry her (but it happens, so his action is valid).[183] If his wife dies, he is also permitted (to marry) his mother-in-law." Some say that his mother-in-law is forbidden to him.[184] — A parallel passage is found in b. Yebam. 98B. — The partial parallel in y. Yebam. 11.12A.2: If a proselyte converts to Judaism and (when he was still a gentile) had married a woman together with her daughter or a woman together with her sister (on the mother's side and they converted with him to Judaism), he will marry the one, and dismiss the other. For which case is this said? If he has not lain with either of them after his conversion; but if he has lain with one of them after his conversion, the one with whom he has lain is his wife. And if he had lain with both of them, then he has lain with them if he has lain with them (he may keep them both). "A proselyte who (before his conversion) had married his sister, whether on the paternal or maternal side, has to dismiss her (after his conversion)." These are the words of R. Meir (ca. 150). R. Judah (ca. 150) said, "He dismisses his maternal sister (lest he be able to say that he has come from a greater holiness into a smaller holiness, Commentary פני משה), but he may keep her if she is from the paternal side (since blood relation with the father also does not count among the gentiles, פני משה)." "He must dismiss his mother's sister, but he may keep his father's sister." These are the words of R. Meir. R. Judah said, "He dismisses his mother's sister on the mother's side (i.e., when the mother and her sister have a common mother), but he may keep his mother's sister on the father's side. He may marry all other women who are prohibited (to the Israelites) to marry (פני משה: this includes also his father's wife = his stepmother). 'He is not obliged to dismiss her' (if he had married her as a gentile and then converted, פני משה) it does not say, but rather 'he may marry her.' See, at the outset (actually) it is forbidden (after he has converted to Judaism, פני משה)." — The tradition about marriage to the sister is also in Gen. Rab. 18 (12C). — In tractate Gerim the transmitted text is corrupt, see Kirchheim, *Massekheth Gerim* (p. 42, note 2).

c. Schulchan ʿArukh יורה דעה #269 § 1: It is the law of the Torah that a proselyte is permitted to marry his mother or his maternal sister, if they have converted to Judaism; but the scholars have prohibited this, lest they be able to say: "We have come from a greater holiness into a smaller holiness." In the same way, if a proselyte has slept with his mother or his sister while she was still in the gentile world, behold, he is as one who has slept with

---

Yet Schulchan ʿArukh finally determined as halakah (albeit with qualification): "A proselyte may marry his father's wife" (see the passage in the following n. *c*). Thus, the divergent opinions cited above were thus not generally accepted in the long run.

183. S-B: Rashi on the parallel passage b. Yebam. 98B: "'If he has married a woman together with her daughter': this pertains to an ordinary proselyte who married a woman and her daughter when he was still a gentile (but not to a proselyte like the one dealt with in the baraita above who was born only after his mother converted to Judaism) and they (later) converted with him to Judaism. For if a proselyte were meant who was born in holiness, he could not marry a woman and her daughter (at all).... 'He will marry the one and dismiss the other,' lest one come and permit in Israel a woman together with her daughter."

184. S-B: The parallel passage in b. Yebam. 98B adds: The one aligns with the opinion of R. Ishmael († ca. 135) and the other aligns with the opinion of R. Aqiba († ca. 135). Whoever forbids it shares the opinion of R. Ishmael ...; and whoever allows it shares the opinion of R. Aqiba; cf. also b. Yebam. 94B.

a Samaritan woman (he has defiled himself because he has done what is prohibited, but he has not thereby become an incestuous man). § 2: What is the law about proselytes with respect to women who are forbidden because of blood relation? If he had gotten married when he was still a non-Israelite (*ʿakum*, see § Matt 5:43, #1, n. *g*, first S-B footnote in section) to his mother or his maternal sister, and then they converted to Judaism, he is compelled to separate from them. However, if he was married to other women who (the Israelites) are forbidden to marry and then he and his wife converted to Judaism, he is not compelled to separate from them. § 3: The *ʿakum* is forbidden (to marry) his mother's blood relatives after he has converted to Judaism on the basis of the words of the scribes (*sopherim*), but he is allowed the father's blood relatives even if he knows with certainty that the person in question is his paternal blood relative, for example, twin brothers, with whom it is clear that the father of one is also the father of the other. At any rate, no preventive regulations have been issued because of his father's blood relatives. For this reason, a proselyte may marry his paternal brother's wife and the wife of his father's brother and his father's wife (his stepmother) and the wife of his son, even if she had first married his brother or his father's brother or his son after they had converted to Judaism. Likewise, he is allowed his mother's sister on the father's side (when the mother and her sister have the same father) and his paternal sister and his daughter (cf. b. Sanh. 58B in #2, n. *e*) if they have converted to Judaism. (Here the qualification is: Yet there are those who forbid his father's wife.) However, he may not marry either his paternal sister or his mother's sister on the mother's side (when the mother and her sister have the same mother), nor his brother's wife on the mother's side if his maternal brother had married her after they[185] converted to Judaism. But if his brother had married her when he was an *ʿakum*, behold, she is permitted for him. § 4: Two twin brothers who were not conceived in holiness but who were born in holiness (after the mother converted to Judaism) make themselves guilty (subject to punishment) because of the brother's wife, but they are not allowed to carry out either the ceremony of the removal of the shoe, nor levirate marriage. § 5: Whoever has married a female proselyte together with her daughter who is also a proselyte, or two maternal sisters, may stay together with one of them and he must dismiss the other. § 6: If he married a female proselyte and she has died, he may marry her mother or her daughter, because preventive regulations have been issued only for the time she is alive. § 7: A man is permitted to marry two paternal sisters who are female proselytes, since preventive regulations have not been issued about the father's blood relatives. § 8: Preventive proscriptions about second degrees of relation whom it is forbidden to marry הַשְּׁנִיּוֹת have not been issued for proselytes. Therefore, a proselyte may marry his mother's mother; a man may also marry a female proselyte as well as her mother's mother and the granddaughter (daughter's daughter) of her daughter; and it is the same with all other second degrees of relation who are forbidden. § 9: A proselyte who converts to Judaism and his wife must keep apart from each other for three months in order to differentiate between the seed that is sowed in holiness (after the conversion), and the seed that was not sowed in

185. TN: The German is ambiguous and could mean after "she" or "they" converted.

holiness. (Addition: And if he does not wish to keep her, there is no need of any certificate of divorce, but rather she can go away from him without a certificate of divorce.)

5. A gentile was permitted to marry the stepmother. This was the older view of Judaism represented by R. Eliezer (ca. 90). The opposite opinion found is advocated in R. Aqiba († ca. 135); see above in #2, n. *f.* In agreement with the older view, the baraita in b. Sanh. 57Bf. declared that the marriage of a proselyte to his stepmother was permissible; of course, R. Aqiba maintained his negative position also in this matter. Only in the post-talmudic period was it brought up that R. Eliezer, the representative of the older view, was a follower of Shammai, and Aqiba's view, according to which a proselyte could not marry his stepmother, became halakah. The definitive decision in Schulchan ʿArukh returned to the oldest practice and declared that such a marriage was permitted, although some resisted this judgment; see #4 notes *b* and *c*. Consequently, it may be securely assumed that in the New Testament period the majority of Jewish scholars had no objection to a gentile or a proselyte marrying the stepmother. This position of the ancient synagogue concerning marriages which were questionable would not have remained unknown even in Corinth. In that case, though, it may have been precisely this view which served not only as the reason invoked by the incestuous man of 1 Cor 5 to justify his offense, but also as the means to relax the whole Christian community there in its own tepid and slack behavior toward the offender in its midst. At any rate, here we have an example of how completely meaningless the Jewish halakah had become for the apostle, who had grown up in rabbinism, in deciding big moral questions.

5:5: To hand over to Satan the man so conditioned, for the destruction of the flesh.

παραδοῦναι = מָסַר, Aram. מְסַר, "to hand over, deliver."[a] — Satan comes into view as the one who executes the penal judgments of God; see § Matt 4:1 B, #3, C and the excursus "Ancient Jewish Demonology," #6.

a. Exodus Rabbah 21 (84A): R. Hama b. Hanina (ca. 260) said, "When the Israelites went out of Egypt, the angel Sammael (= Satan) stood there to accuse them." R. Hama b. Hanina (ca. 260) explained this in the name of his father (R. Hanina b. Hama [ca. 225]): "A parable. Like a shepherd who took his small livestock across a river. A wolf came to attack the small livestock. The shepherd, who had experience, what did he do? He took a large ram and handed it over מסרו to the wolf. He said, 'He may wrestle with this one until we have crossed over the river, and then I will get it.' So, when the Israelites went out of Egypt, the angel Sammael stood there to accuse them. He said before God, 'Lord of the world, up until now they have committed idolatry, and you will split the sea for them?' What did God do? He handed Job over מסר to him, Job who was among pharaoh's counselors; for it says of him, 'He has an upright and righteous man' (Job 1:1). God said to Sammael, 'May he be in your hand!' God said (to himself), 'While he occupies himself with Job, the Israelites will have gone down into the sea and come up again (reversed in the text: go up to the sea and down), and then I will save Job.' This is what Job said, 'I was carefree שליו when he smashed me' (Job 16:12). Job said, '"I was his שָׁלֵו in the world when he smashed me and grabbed my neck and shattered me" (Job 16:12), in order to make me a target for the sake of his people; as it says, "And made me a target for his benefit" (Job 16:12). It further says, "God handed me over יַסְגִּירֵנִי (Tg.: ימסרנני) to the evildoer" (Job 16:11), gave me up מסרני into the hand of Satan, and lest the Israelites come out from the court as godless, he cast הרטה me into his hand; see, "He cast me ירטני into the hand of evildoers" (Job 16:11).' In that hour God said to Moses, 'Moses, look, I have handed Job over מסרתי to Satan; what do you have to do now? "Tell the children of Israel to go forth" (Exod 14:15).'"

5:6: A little leaven.

ζύμη "leaven" = שְׂאוֹר, סְאוֹר, see § Matt 16:6; but here, instead of y. Ḥag. 2.76C.37, one should read y. Ḥag. 1.76C.37.

5:7 A: Clean out the old leaven.

Underlying the admonition is the commandment to remove (clear away) בִּעֵר (substantive: בִּעוּר) everything leavened from the houses before the Passover feast; see Exod 12:15, 19; 13:7. The most important stipulations about this are the following:

Mishnah Pesaḥim 1.1: On the night of the 14th (of Nisan) one searches for what is leavened by the light of a lamp. There is no need to look in any space where leavened items are not brought. — Mishnah Pesaḥim 1.3: R. Judah (ca. 150) said, "One searches on the night of the 14th and on the morning of the 14th and in the hour of removal" (which happened by burning at 11 o'clock in the morning). However, the scholars said, "If one has not searched on the night of the 14th, let him search on the 14th; if one has not searched on the 14th, let him search during the feast; if one has not searched during the feast, let him search after the feast. (Even after the feast what is found must be destroyed, since its use is prohibited"; see m. Pesaḥ. 2.2. The halakah aligns with the scholars.) And whatever one wants to keep (for eating, as long as leavened food was allowed to be eaten on the 14th of Nisan; see further below), let one put it aside for safekeeping, so that one does not have to look for it." — Mishnah Pesaḥim 1.4: R. Meir (ca. 150) said, "(Leavened items) are eaten the whole 5th hour (10–11 o'clock in the morning) and burned at the beginning of the 6th hour (ca. 11 o'clock)"; R. Judah (ca. 150) said, "They are eaten the whole 4th hour and set aside for the whole 5th hour and burned at the beginning of the 6th hour." — Mishnah Pesaḥim 1.5: R. Judah also said, "Two unusable thank offering cakes lay on the roof of the portico (of the outer forecourt). As long as they lay there, all the people ate (leavened substances). When one of them was taken away, one set it apart, did not eat, but did not burn it. When both had been removed, all the people began to burn it." — Mishnah Pesaḥim 2.1: As long as it is permitted to eat (leavened substances), it is given to the livestock, to the wild animals, and to the fowl to eat and it is sold to non-Israelites, and it is (generally) allowed for consumption. Once the time for this is over, its consumption is prohibited, and one does not light (even just a) oven and stove with it. R. Judah said, "There is no way of removing leavened substances except for burning. However, the scholars said, 'It can (also) be crumbled and scattered or tossed into the sea.'" (The halakah does not align with R. Judah.) — Mishnah Pesaḥim 2.2: The leavened substance of a non-Israelite, which existed while Passover went by, is permitted for consumption, while that of an Israelite is prohibited; for it says, "It will not be seen by you" (Exod 13:7). — Mishnah Pesaḥim 2.3: ... Leavened bread on which a heap or rubble has fallen is like that which has been removed. Rabban Simeon b. Gamaliel (ca. 140) said, "Everything that a dog cannot trace." — Mishnah Pesaḥim 2.7: The bran for chickens is not soaked (lest they become leavened) but scalded. A woman should not soak the bran which she takes with her to bathe; but she may dry it to rub on her body. One may not chew grain and put it on his wound, because it will become leavened. — Mishnah Pesaḥim 2.8: Flour is not put into fruit pulp nor into mustard; but if one has put it in (mustard), it should immediately be eaten. R. Meir forbids this. (The halakah does not align with him; however, consuming flour in fruit pulp is prohibited in every case.) ... The water which is used by the baker should be poured out, because it allows for leavening. — Mishnah Pesaḥim 3.1: The following is removed on Passover: Babylonian puree (consisting of whey, salt, and moldy bread [b. Pesaḥ. 42A]), Median mead (because barley water was used for it [b. Pesaḥ. 42B]), Edomite vinegar (because it is made with barley [b. Pesaḥ. 42B]), Egyptian beer (because it was made from barley [wheat], safflower, and salt [b. Pesaḥ. 42B]), the wash used by dyers (a kind of bran water [b. Pesaḥ. 42B]), the starch used by cooks, and the paste used by scribes. R. Eliezer (ca. 90) said, "Also what women use to baste. (The halakah does not accord with him.) This is the rule: Everything that is a type of grain is removed on Passover (insofar as it has come into contact with water and thereby is susceptible to leavening). See, these are included in the warning (prohibition), but in their case there is no mention of being eradicated (by God's hand). (In m. Mak. 3.2, flagellation is appointed for the consumption of leavened substances.) — Mishnah Pesaḥim 3.2: Dough in the cracks of a baking tray—if so much as an olive is in any place, one is obligated to remove it; if less, it is negligible because of its small amount. — Mishnah Pesaḥim 3.5: "*Śe'ur* (שְׂאוֹר, here not leaven, but rather dough that just starts to leaven and gets small rifts that do not cohere) should be burned; but whoever eats it is free (from the punishment named in the next sentence). Dough with rifts should be burned, and whoever eats it is guilty of death (another reading: of eradication). What is *śe'ur*? (Its rifts) are like grasshopper horns. Dough with rifts? Its rifts have united with each other." These are the words of R. Judah. But the scholars said, "The one is like the other. Whoever eats it is guilty of death (another reading: of eradication)." (The halakah aligns with the scholars.) (They also said, "What is *śe'ur*? Any (dough) whose appearance has become mealy, like a person whose hairs have bristled." — Mishnah Pesaḥim 3.6: "If the 14th (of Nisan) falls on a Sabbath, one removes everything before the Sabbath." These are the words of R. Meir. However, the scholars said, "At its (ordinary) time" (see above m. Pesaḥ. 1.4). R. Eleazar b. Zadok (ca. 100) said, "The offering for the priests before the Sabbath, what is profane at its time (the halakah accords with his opinion)." — Mishnah Pesaḥim 3.7: Whoever is on the road to slaughter his Passover offering or to circumcise his son or to eat the engagement meal in the house of his father-in-law (i.e., to fulfill an obligatory commandment) and remembers that he has something leavened in his house (according to 3.8 at least the size of an egg), he should return if he can return and remove it and (then) return to his fulfilling the commandment; and if not, it (the leavened substance) should be destroyed in his heart. (Whoever is going) to rescue someone from an army, from the force of a torrent, from a conflagration or a collapse, let him destroy (the leavened substance) in his heart. But (whoever goes) to determine for himself a feast day residence (on the border of the Sabbath area) for the sake of arbitrarily self-appointed purposes (which do not contribute to fulfilling an obligatory commandment) should return immediately. — See parallels in t. Pesaḥ. 1.1–2.13.

5:7 B: For our Passover, Christ, has also been sacrificed.

The Passover sacrifice is counted among the sacrificial offerings in, for example:

Mishnah Zebaḥim 1.1: All sacrificial offerings that were not slaughtered in their name remain suitable, but they are not counted for the owners as fulfilling an obligation, except for the Passover and sin offerings (which become unsuitable).

5:10: To go out of the world.

ἐκ τοῦ κόσμου ἐξελθεῖν literally = אֲזַל מִן עָלְמָא.

Targum Ecclesiastes 1:4: "King Solomon said in the spirit of prophecy, '(It is) a good generation of the righteous that goes out of the world because of the sins of an evil generation of the godless who will come after them. But the earth remains for all eternity to bear the punishment that comes over the world because of the sins of the children of men.'"

5:11 A: To have no fellowship ... not even to eat together with such a person.

Analogous stipulations existed for interactions between the members of the pharisaic *ḥaber* covenant and the *'amme ha-areṣ*; see § John 7:49, #8. Concerning the interaction of Jews with gentiles, see the excursus "The Stance of Judaism toward the Non-Jewish World."

5:11 B: A drunkard.

μέθυσος "drunkard" = סֹבֵא (Prov 23:21), Tg.: רָוֵי, LXX: μέθυσος. Particularly the wine drinker οἰνοπότης (Matt 11:19) = סָבֵי חֲמַר in Tg. Onk. Deut. 21:20, where the word in the text is סֹבֵא, or = שַׁתָּאֵי בְחַמְרָא in Tg. Yer. I Deut. 21:20; in the Jerusalem Talmud, שתיי חמר is used for this, and in the Palestinian midrashim שתוי חמר[186] or שתוי דחמר (so Pesiq. Rab. 14 [62B]). In this connection, the Jerusalem Talmud also uses the participial form שָׁתוּי.

---

186. S-B: See passages in the parallels adduced further below for y. Šeqal. 3.47C.3.

Jerusalem Talmud Šeqalim 3.47C.3: A matron saw him (according to the context, R. Jonah [ca. 350] but see further below), how his face shone (bright red). She said, "My good sir, my good sir, one of these three things is true of you: either you are someone who drinks wine דשתוי חמרא, or someone who lends (money) for interest, or someone who rears pigs." He answered her, "May this woman's spirit become a breath! For none of these three things is true of me. Rather, my teaching is with me; for so it is written, 'A person's wisdom makes his face shine' (Eccl 8:1)." — As the parallels (y. Šabb. 8.11A.34; y. Pesaḥ. 10.37C.30) show, a sentence at the beginning of our passage has fallen away, according to which the one addressed by the matron is not R. Jonah, but rather R. Judah b. Ilai [ca. 150]; the same is found in the further parallels Pesiq. 37B; Pesiq. Rab. 14 (62B); Midr. Eccl. 8:1 (39A) and TanḥB חקת § 19 (58A), except that these texts replace the matron with a גוי = non-Israelite. The beginning of our passage is found also at § Matt 11:19 A with the note that the conclusion is presented with parallels at § Luke 15:15. For the obvious reason given in the foreword to volume II, this reference to Luke 15:15 is not in fact right; this lack is made up for here.

5:11 C: A robber.

ἅρπαξ α. = לִיסְטִים (ληστής), see § Luke 10:30 B; β. = גַּזְלָן, see § Luke 19:8 B. — It is worth noting the distinction between who is a robber גזלן according to the rabbis and who is one according to the Torah.

Babylonian Talmud Sanhedrin 26B: (The passage deals with the question of whether people who are unreliable as witnesses because of their disreputable activities should be made known publicly or not. Here it says:) Two robbers גזלנין were signatories (as witnesses) to a deed of donation. Rab Papa b. Samuel (ca. 340) wanted to declare them valid, because they (the two witnesses) had not been publicly made known (as robbers). Raba († 352) said to him, "If one must demand that someone who is a robber according to the rabbis גזלן דרבנן be publicly made known, should one also demand that someone who is a robber according to the Torah גזלן דאורייתא be publicly made known?" — A person who counts as a "robber according to the rabbis" is, for example, a usurer or a gambler, thus someone who by disreputable means of acquisition makes his own that which belongs to others. By contrast, a robber according to the Torah is a literal robber who by force makes his own that which belongs to someone else. The apostle would also have understood ἅρπαξ in the broadest sense and thereby would have understood someone who seeks to enrich himself at the expense of another, whether by force or by some other improper means.

5:12: Those outside.

οἱ ἔξω = הַחִיצוֹנִים, a designation for those who are devoted to a different religious community.

Mishnah Megillah 4.8: If someone binds (his tefillin) on his forehead or on his flat hand, behold, this is a way of sectarianism דֶּרֶךְ הַמִּינוּת; if he covers them with gold or binds them on his sleeve, behold, this is a way of outsiders דֶּרֶךְ הַחִיצוֹנִים. (Bertinoro: Associated with a sectarian who stands outside the teaching of the scholars.) ‖ Mishnah Sanhedrin 10.1: R. Aqiba († ca. 135) said, "Also anyone who reads books that are located outside (outside of the canon) (has no share in the future world)." — While סְפָרִים הַחִיצוֹנִם are talked about here, in b. Sanh. 100B the sentence in the Mishnah repeats the idea with the words: "R. Aqiba said, 'Also anyone who reads in a book of outsiders בספר החיצונים.'" This corresponds to the explanation that immediately follows about ספרים החיצונים: It has been taught: (Anyone who reads) in the books of the sectarians בספרי מינין (has no share in the future world). ‖ See t. Ḥag. 2.5 (234) at § Matt 3:16, n. *b.* There the words "Ben Zoma is already outside" כבר בן זומא מִבַּחוּץ are interpreted: he is no longer with himself, he is out of his mind. A different interpretation is as follows: he is already outside the bounds drawn for cosmological and theosophical studies, that is, in danger of falling prey to sectarianism.

5:13: Remove the wicked man from yourselves (from your midst).

Underlying this statement is Deut 13:6 or one of the parallels, such as Deut 17:7, 12; 19:19; 21:21; 22:21, 22, 24; 24:7. — Deuteronomy 13:6: וּבִעַרְתָּ הָרָע מִקִּרְבֶּךָ = "remove הָרָע from your midst." הָרָע is a neuter noun = "evil"; this necessarily follows from Deut 22:21, where הרע relates back to a female person, and from Deut 22:24, where it relates back to several people. — The LXX sometimes translates הרע as a neuter noun, τὸ πονηρόν (so Deut 13:6 [5]; 19:19), and sometimes as a masculine noun, τὸν πονηρόν (so Deut 17:7; 21:21; 24:7 and 17:12); in 22:21, 22, 24 the variants fluctuate between τό and τόν. — Targum Onkelos and Yerušalmi I, like Sifre Deuteronomy, have only the masculine form; it probably was the only common form in the days of the apostle.

Targum Onkelos Deuteronomy 13:6: "You shall remove from your midst the one who does what is evil" וּתְפַלֵּי עָבֵד דְּבִישׁ מִבֵּינָךְ. — Yerušalmi I: "You shall remove evildoers from your midst" ותפלון עבדי בישתא מביניכון. ‖ Sifre Deuteronomy 13:6 § 86 (92B): "Remove evil from your midst" (Deut 13:6): remove evildoers עושי רעות from Israel! See further SDeut 17:7, 12; 21:21; 22:22; 24:7.

6:1: Some of you dare ... to seek justice among the unrighteous (= non-Christians) and not among the saints?

1. A Jew was forbidden to seek justice among non-Jews.

A baraita in b. Giṭ. 88B: R. Tarfon (ca. 100) said, "Wherever you find courts of non-Israelites, even if their judgments (laws, legal procedures, legal decision) correspond to those of the Israelites, it is not justified for you to be connected with them; for it says, 'These are the legal statutes that you are to lay before them' (Exod 21:1), "them" (the Israelites) and not 'strangers' (non-Israelites)." — The parallel passage Tanḥ. משפטים 93A names R. Simeon (ca. 150) as the author. ‖ Tanḥuma משפטים 91A: How do we know that litigating Israelites who have an issue דִּין with each other are forbidden to come together before the *ʿakum* (non-Israelites), even if they know that the *ʿakum* will decide the matter according to the laws of Israel? Scripture teaches, "That you are to lay before them" (Exod 21:1), the Israelites, but not the *ʿakum*; for whoever abandons the judges of Israel and runs before the *ʿakum* repudiates God first and then repudiates the Torah; as it says, 'For their rock is not like our rock and our enemies should be judges?' (so the midr. appears to interpret Deut 32:31).... God said to the Israelites, "If you conduct a lawsuit and do not come together (argue with each other מזדקקין) before the nations of the world (as judges), then I will build the sanctuary for you, and the Sanhedrin will sit in it; as it says, 'I will bring back your judges as in the beginning ...' (Isa 1:26)." ‖ Mekilta Exodus 21:1 (81B): R. Eleazar b. Azariah (ca. 100) said, "Look, if the *goyim* (non-Israelites) decide in accordance with the laws of Israel, may I not conclude from this that they (their decisions) are valid? Scripture teaches, 'These are the legal statutes' (Exod 21:1): you may judge what is theirs (the legal matters of the non-Israelites), but they may not judge yours."

2. On ἅγιοι see § Acts 9:13.

6:2: Do you not know that the saints will judge the world?

1. The oldest passages that deal with the active participation of the righteous in the judgment of the world are the following:

Septuagint Daniel 7:22: καὶ τὸ κρίμα (judgment) ἔδωκεν ἁγίοις ὑψίστου. ‖ Wisdom 3:8: "They (the righteous) will judge gentiles and rule over nations" κρινοῦσιν ἔθνη καὶ κρατήσουσι λαῶν. ‖ Jubilees 24:29: "Whoever is saved (on the day of wrath and fury) from the enemy's sword and from the Hittites, whom the righteous people (Israel) will obliterate under heaven by a judgment." ‖ 1 Enoch 38:5: "The kings and rulers will be destroyed at the (end) time and will be delivered into the hand of the righteous and holy ones." — 1 Enoch 48:9: "I will deliver them (the kings of the earth) into the hands of my elect ones; like straw in the fire and like lead in the water, they will burn before the face of the righteous and sink down before the face of the holy ones, so that no trace of them will be found." — 1 Enoch 95:3: "Do not fear sinners, you righteous; for the Lord will once again (at the end time) deliver them into your hand, so that you may execute judgment on them as you please." — 1 Enoch 96:1: "Have hope, you righteous, for suddenly sinners will perish before you, and you will rule over them as you please." — 1 Enoch 98:12: "Woe to you who love the works of unrighteousness; why do you hope in something good for yourselves? Know that you will be given into the hand of the righteous; they will cut off your necks and mercilessly kill you."

See the supporting texts from rabbinic literature in the excursus "Sheol, Gehenna, and the Garden of Eden," II, #10, n. *m*.

2. On κρίνειν τὸν κόσμον, see § Rom 3:6.

6:3: Not rather matters of external life?

βιωτικά, in substance = legal cases that deal with money and money's worth. The rabbinic scholars differentiate between lawsuits about money דִּינֵי מָמוֹנוֹת and capital trials דִּינֵי נְפָשׁוֹת; the former—disputes about assets in the broadest sense of the word—correspond to the legal cases about βιωτικά.

Mishnah Sanhedrin 4.1: What is the difference between disputes about assets (lawsuits about money) and capital trials? Disputes about assets are judged by three (judges), capital trials by twenty-three....

6:5: Is there no wise person among you who would be able to arbitrate with his brother?

1. Disputes about assets were as a rule to be judged by three judges.[a] However, these three judges did not necessarily have to be experts, authorized legal professionals, and could also be lay judges.[b] In certain circumstances a scholar who possessed authority for the judicial office could also decide lawsuits about money entirely by himself, if he, for example, was the only authorized judge in his locale. Indeed, even a nonauthorized judge could as an individual issue a valid ruling in lawsuits about money, if the two parties had declared in advance that they would be subject to his decision.[c] In his question above in verse 5, the apostle also may have had in view such a judge who, as the man trusted by both parties, was able to make a decision.

a. Mishnah Sanhedrin 1.1: Disputes about assets (lawsuits about money דִּינֵי מָמוֹנוֹת) are judged by three (judges).

b. Babylonian Talmud Sanhedrin 3A: Disputes about assets are judged by three laypeople הֶדְיוֹטוֹת (ἰδιώτης), robberies and bodily injuries by three authorized judges מוּמְחִין (who were authorized as judges by the Patriarch or by a court). ‖ Babylonian Talmud Baba Meṣiʿa 32A: We have learned (namely in m. Ketub. 11.2): "A widow may sell (from the estate of her husband for her livelihood and the livelihood of her children) without the consultation of the court." Abbayye († 338/39) said to him (Rab Safra [ca. 300]), "But has it not been said about this that Rab Joseph b. Minyumi said that Rab Nahman († 320) said, 'A widow does not need (in this matter) a court of authorized judges, though she does need a court of (three) lay (judges)?'"

c. A baraita in b. Sanh. 4Bf.: Disputes about assets are judged by three (judges); but if there is a judge there who is authorized for the community, he may judge the case by himself. Rab Nahman († 320) said, "I, for example, judge disputes about assets by myself." And likewise R. Hiyya (the elder? [ca. 200]) said "I, for example, judge disputes about assets by myself." The following question was raised by them, "I, for example, who have studied the traditional law and who possess understanding and who has obtained authorization (to dispense justice); but if someone has not obtained authorization, is his legal decision (which he has cast as an individual judge) not really a legal decision, or is his legal decision still a (valid) legal decision, although he has not obtained any authorization?" Come and hear! Mar Zutra b. Nahman (b. Jacob [ca. 320]) had (as an individual judge) made a legal decision (in a lawsuit about money) and made a mistake in doing so (his verdict was mistaken, so that the question arose whether he was obliged to pay damages to the wronged party). He came before Rab Joseph († 333). The latter said to him, "If they (the two parties) accepted you (as judge and subjected themselves in advance to your verdict), you do not need to pay damages; but if not, go and pay!" Conclude from this: If he has not obtained authorization, his legal decision is a (valid) legal decision (in the case that both parties accepted him as a judge). — See the analogous case in y. Ned. 10.42B.4: R. Zeira (ca. 300), Rab Judah († 299), and Jeremiah b. Abba (ca. 250) said in the name of Samuel († 254), "Three who know how to make a way out (to annul vows) may annul (vows) as one (single) elder (scholar)." They meant: "Wherever no elder is present (three laypeople may annul vows)." However, the rabbis of Caesarea said, "Also in wherever an elder is present (they may do this)." The same is found in y. Ḥag. 1.76C.56.

2. σοφός "a wise man." The choice of this expression may have been influenced by the fact that a scholar who was the only one of his kind in a locale and was authorized to make legal decisions bore, alongside other titles such as דַּיָּין "judge" or זָקֵן "elder," also the title חָכָם = σοφός "wise man, learned one."

Tosefta Nedarim 5.5 (281): If anyone renounces usufruct of the city (in which he lives) by a vow, he seeks for his vow to be annulled by a "wise man" חכם who is in the city.

6:9: Will not inherit the kingdom of God.

For this expression, the rabbis say "the future world" or "to inherit the life of the future world"; see examples at § Matt 19:29 B.

6:12: Everything is permissible for me.

ἔξεστιν = מוּתָּר, see § Matt 16:19 B, #1, n. *b*, β, or = רְשׁוּת בְּיָד "permission is in the hand" = freedom is given, permission is granted.

Sifre Deuteronomy 11:24 § 51 (85A): What does Scripture mean to teach with: "Every place on which the sole of your foot treads will belong to you" (Deut 11:24)? God said to them, "Every place that you will subjugate except for these places, behold, it belongs to you." Or are they permitted רשות בידם to subjugate outside of the land only before they have subjugated the land? Scripture teaches, "And you will dispossess nations which are bigger and more powerful than you" (Deut 11:23); then it says, "Every place on which the sole of your foot treads will belong to you" ‖ A baraita in b. Pesaḥ. 110A: Whoever drinks paired (cups), his blood be upon his head (he has to bear the responsibility for this himself)! Rab Judah († 299) said, "When does this apply? When he does not see the face of the street (does not go out) (between the individual cups), but if he sees the face of the street, he is permitted הרשות בידו (to drink cups in paired numbers)."

6:13: God will annul this (stomach) and this (food).

This statement corresponds to what is said in § Matt 22:28 about the married life of the resurrected, not the views of the ancient synagogue.

6:16: For, it says, the two will become one flesh.

1. On the citation of Gen 2:24 see § Matt 19:5.

2. φησίν corresponds to the rabbinic אוֹמֵר,[a] as its subject should be understood as either "Scripture" or a designation of God. In fuller formulas, it is said הוּא אוֹמֵר[b] "he says" = it says, הֲרֵי הוּא אוֹמֵר[c] "see, it says," וְכֵן הוּא אוֹמֵר[d] "and likewise it says." If the subject is explicitly added, it is said: הַכָּתוּב אוֹמֵר[e] "Scripture says," אָמַר הַכָּתוּב[f] "Scripture said," אָמַר קְרָא[g] "a verse of Scripture has said," הַקָּדוֹשׁ בָּרוּךְ הוּא אוֹמֵר[h] "the Holy One—blessed be He!—says," or רַחֲמָנָא אֲמַר[i] "the All Merciful One said." See also § Rom 15:10.

a. Mishnah ʾAbot 6.2: And it says וְאוֹמֵר: "The tablets were a work of God, and the writing was the writing of God, engraved on the tablets" (Exod 32:16). ‖ Further examples are found in m. ʾAbot 6.7, 9, 10, 11.

b. Mekilta Exodus 12:13 (10B.5): "And when I see the blood" (Exod 12:13); I see the blood of the binding of Isaac, as it says: "And Abraham named this place 'Yahweh sees …'" (Gen 22:14); and there it says הוּא אוֹמֵר: "At the time of choking, Yahweh saw it and relented about the calamity …" (1 Chr 21:15). What did he see? The blood of the binding of Isaac. Also, m. Sanh. 10.3 (twice); t. Yoma 2.8 (185, 7); t. Taʿan. 4.8 (220.17); t. Sukkah 4.1 (298.13 twice); 4.2 (298.18, 20, 22); 4.3 (299.3); 4.4 (299.6); 4.5 (299.11); Mek. Exod. 15:7 (47B.6); 17:14 (64A.2); b. Šabb. 98B.3; 111A.7; 152B.20, 22, 23; b. Sanh. 6B.28.

c. Tosefta Ḥagigah 3.20 (237, 22): R. Judah (ca. 150) said, "See, it says הֲרֵי הוּא אוֹמֵר, 'Let it serve the community of the children of Israel to preserve the purification water; it is a sin offering' (Num 19:9); for all are certified concerning its preservation." ‖ See also t. Soṭah 6.1 (303.11); 6.7 (304.21); 6.9 (305.14); 6.10 (305.26); Mek. Exod. 12:1 (1B.18); 12:6 (6B.21); 13:3 (24A.3); 13:19 (29A.22); y. Ber. 9.13A.46; 9.14C.7.

d. Tosefta Berakot 4.18 (11.7): Why did (the tribe of) Judah receive the kingdom? Because it sanctified God's name at the (red) sea. For when all the tribes came and stood at the sea, this one said, "I will go down first!" And that one said, "I will go down first!" Then the tribe of Judah jumped and went down first and sanctified God's name at the sea, and about that hour it says, "Help me, God, for the water comes to my soul; I have sunk into the mire of the deep" (Ps 69:2f.). Likewise it says וְכֵן הוּא אוֹמֵר, "When Israel went out of Egypt, the house of Jacob from a people with a different language, Judah became his sanctuary, Israel his dominion" (Ps 114:1f.); since Judah sanctified God's name at the sea, Israel became his dominion. ‖ See also t. Ber. 7.1 (14.14); 7.2 (15.3); t. Pesaḥ. 9.2 (170.20); t. Yoma 1.12 (181.24); t. Sukkah 3.3 (196.1); 3.8 (196.10); t. Roš Haš. 4.7 (213.2); Mek. Exod. 14:10 (33B.4); 15:1 (41B.1); 15:7 (46B.21).

e. Tosefta Demai 5.17 (55.12): Concerning them (the priests and Levites who assist on the barn floors to receive offerings and tithes) Scripture says הַכָּתוּב אוֹמֵר, "Their chiefs judge for a bribe and their priests give wisdom for a price" (Mic 3:11). ‖ Further examples are found in t. Šabb. 13.5 (129.7, 10); t. Ḥag. 2.3f. (234.8, 9, 10, 11); b. Šabb. 75A.12; 88B.11; 116A.29; b. Sanh. 76B.5, 8, 12.

f. Genesis Rabbah 51 (32D.40, 44): Scripture said אָמַר הַכָּתוּב, "Do not attack Moab ..." (Deut 2:9).... Scripture said, "Do not attack them (the sons of Ammon)" (Deut 2:19). ‖ See further t. B. Qam. 7.5 at § 1 Cor 7:23 B.

g. Babylonian Talmud Sanhedrin 4B.34: A verse of Scripture said אָמַר קְרָא: "You are not to boil a kid in its mother's milk" (Exod 23:19). ‖ See further b. Sanh. 10A.15; 11B.29; Šabb. 27B.29; 96B.2; 116B.34; 120B.36; 127B.41; 131B.5.

h. Babylonian Talmud Šabbat 152B.19: Concerning the body of the righteous the Holy One—blessed be He!—says, "He enters into peace; they will rest on their beds" (Isa 57:2).

i. Babylonian Talmud Sanhedrin 29A.37: The All Merciful One said, "You shall not have mercy or conceal anything for his sake" (Deut 13:9). ‖ See further b. Sanh. 36A.10; 36B.11; 42B.32; 47A.11; 90A.2; b. Ber. 47B.32.

6:18: The fornicator sins against his own body.

εἰς τὸ ἴδιον σῶμα ἁμαρτάνει. — The Hebrew expression that corresponds in wording, חָטָא בַּגּוּף or פָּשַׁע בַּגּוּף, means (a): "on one's own" or "to sin in relation to one's own person" (opposite: to mislead others to sin) and (b): "to sin with the body."

a. Babylonian Talmud Roš Haššanah 17A: The school of Hillel (in the 1st cent.) said, "... The Israelites who have acted wickedly in relation to their own person, and those from the gentile world who have acted wickedly in relation to their own person פושעי ישראל בגופן ופושעי אומות העולם בגופן will go down into gehenna and be judged there for 12 months.... But those who have sinned and misled the multitude to sin והחטיאו את הרבים ... will go down into gehenna and be judged there from generation to generation." — See the unabbreviated passage in the excursus "Sheol, Gehenna, and the Garden of Eden," II, #2, n. *a*.

b. Babylonian Talmud Roš Haššanah 17A: "The Israelites who have acted wickedly בגופן" (see n. *a*), who are they? Rab († 247) said, "This means the head that does not don tefillin." "Those from the gentile world who have acted wickedly" (who are they?). Rab said, "(Those who have acted wickedly) by sinning sexually בעבירה." — In both his answers Rab has interpreted בגופן = "with their body." ‖ A baraita in b. Sanh. 109A: The people of Sodom have no share in the future world; for it says, "The people of Sodom were wicked and sinned very greatly against Yahweh" (Gen 13:13); "wicked" in this world, "and sinned" for the future world. Rab Judah († 299) said, "'Wicked' with their body בגופן, 'and sinned' with their wealth. Wicked with their body, for it says, 'How could I do this great wickedness' (Gen 39:9)! (Just as 'wickedness' in Gen 39:9 means fornication, so too in Gen 13:13; therefore בגופן = 'with their body.') 'Sinned' with their wealth; for it says, 'There might be a sin in you' (Deut 15:9). (Just as the sinful behavior in Deut 15:9, the failure to loan, pertains to money, so too the sinfulness of the Sodomites in Gen 13:13.) 'Against Yahweh' (Gen 13:13): this means blasphemy; 'very greatly,' because they sinned on purpose." In a baraita it has been taught: "Wicked" with their wealth, "and sinned" with their body בגופן. Wicked with their wealth, for it is written, "And your eye may be wicked (with greed, thus in matters of wealth) toward your poor brother" (Deut 15:9). Sinned with their body בגופן, for it is written: "How could I sin against God" (Gen 39:9) (by fornication, thus בגופן = with their body)! "Against Yahweh" (Gen 13:13): this means blasphemy; "very greatly": this pertains to bloodshed, for it says, "Manasseh shed a very great deal of much innocent blood" (2 Kgs 21:16). ‖ Targum Onkelos Genesis 13:13: "The people of Sodom acted wickedly with their wealth and made themselves guilty with their bodies בְּגְוִיָתְהוֹן (= by fornication) very much before Yahweh." ‖ Targum Yerušalmi I Genesis 13:13: "The people of Sodom were wicked toward each other with their wealth and made themselves guilty with their body by fornicating and shedding innocent blood and committed idolatry and rose up very much against the name of Yahweh."

6:19 A: That your body is a temple of the Holy Spirit in you.

See § 1 Cor 3:16.

6:19 B: You are not your own.

οὐκ ἐστὲ ἑαυτῶν perhaps = אֵינְכֶם לְעַצְמְכֶם "you do not belong to yourselves."

Mishnah Giṭṭin 9.3: The main thing (the essential content) of a certificate of emancipation (for a female slave) is: "Behold, you are a free woman בַּת חוֹרִין (in the case of a male slave: בֶּן חוֹרִין); behold, you belong to yourself אַתְּ לְעַצְמֵךְ."

6:20: You were bought at a price.

τιμῆς. For the rabbis = בְּטִימֵי "for a price."

Genesis Rabbah 2 (3B): R. Abbahu (ca. 300) said, "Like a king who bought two slaves, both with one bill of sale and for one and the same price בטימי אחת." — The same expression is found in this text in lines 22, 27, 29.

7:1: It is good for a man not to touch a woman (i.e., to remain unmarried).

This principle did not align with the views of the ancient synagogue. The common opinion of rabbinic scholars was rather that it was an absolutely obligatory commandment for a man to get married. At most, it was disputed whether this commandment applied also to women. See the supporting texts for this at § John 2:1 A, #1. — See further t. Qidd. 1.11 (336) at § John 2:1 A, #3, D, n. *c*.

7:2: Because of the instances of fornication, each one should have his wife.

A baraita in b. Qidd. 29B: (The father is obligated to teach his son Torah and to acquire a wife for him; see t. Qidd. 1.11 at § John 2:1 A, #3, D, n. *c*.) Let him study Torah and then take a wife; but if it is not possible for him to be without a wife, let him take a wife (to stay protected from fornication), and then let him study Torah. Rab Judah († 299) said that Samuel († 254) said, "The halakah is as follows: he takes a wife, and then let him study Torah." R. Yohanan († 279) said, "Millstones (concern for wife and children) on his neck, and then he is supposed to dedicate himself to the Torah?!" But they are not of different views: this one (the word of Samuel) applies to us (Babylonians), and that one (the word of R. Yohanan) applies to them (in Palestine). Rab Hisda († 309) extolled Rab Hamnuna (ca. 300) as a significant person before Rab Huna († 297). Then Rab Huna said to Rab Hisda, "When he comes to you, bring him to me." When he (Rab Hamnuna) came, Rab Huna noticed that he did not wear a turban (literally: had no cloth wrapped around). He said to him, "Why are you not wearing a turban?" He responded, "Because I am not married." Then that one turned his face away from him and said to him, "You are not to see my face again until you have gotten married!" Rab Huna acted this way with his face; for Rab Huna said, "If someone is twenty years old and has not taken a wife, all his days are full of sins (of fornication). Do you really mean full of sins (of fornication)? Rather say: All his days are full of thoughts of sins (of fornication)." (See the continuation of the passage at § John 2:1 A, #2, n. *a*.) ‖ Babylonian Talmud Yebamot 63A: R. Hiyya's (ca. 200) wife used to aggravate him a lot. When he would encounter something (that she might like), he would wrap it in his cloth and bring it to her. Then (his nephew) Rab († 247) said to him, "But she aggravates her lord (so why all these courtesies)!" He responded to him, "It is enough that they (wives) raise our children and keep us from the sin (of fornication)." — See further § 1 Cor 7:5 B.

7:3: The man should pay the debt (not withhold the marital obligation) to the woman, but also in the same way the woman the man.

Performing the marital obligation is among the things that every man owes his wife.[a] Whoever does not fulfill his obligation is called a sinner.[b] Yet in the same way the woman is not entitled to withhold marital intercourse from the man.[c] Refusing the marital obligation is punished on both sides with a fine[d] and entails the dissolution of the marriage.[e] Yet the man should not compel his wife to have intercourse;[f] conversely, from a woman who freely requests her husband to have intercourse men full of insight issue forth as progeny, such as did not exist even in the time of Moses.[g] The decision about the question of how often a man is obligated to have intercourse is based on his status and occupation.[h]

a. Mekilta Exodus 21:10 (85A): "('He is not to diminish her diet of meat שְׁאֵרָהּ, her covering [clothing] כְּסוּתָהּ or her intercourse עֹנָתָהּ' [Exod 21:10].) שְׁאֵרָהּ, this is her food (sustenance); likewise it says, 'Those who eat the flesh שאר of my people' (Mic 3:3). Furthermore, it is written, 'He made meat שאר rain on them like powder' (Ps 78:27). כְּסוּתָהּ should be interpreted according to its wording (so = covering or clothing). And עוֹנָתָהּ: this means intercourse דֶּרֶךְ אֶרֶץ. As it says, 'He slept with her and had intercourse with her ויענה' (Gen 34:2)." These are the words of R. Josiah (ca. 140). R. Jonathan (ca. 140) said, "שארה כסותה is covering (clothing) that is appropriate for her body: if she is young, he is not to give her that of an old woman; if she is old, he is not to give her that of a young woman. (Thus, שארה כסותה = as her body, so her covering.) And עונתה (= as the season): he should not give her (clothing) for summer in the rainy season (= winter time) nor give her what is for the rainy season in the summer, but rather he should give every single thing at its time. (That he has to provide her) sustenance, whence comes this idea? An inference is drawn from the lesser to the greater: if you are not entitled to withhold from her things that do not signify sustenance, it is right and just that you are not entitled to withhold things from her that do signify sustenance. Intercourse, where does this come from? An inference is drawn from the lesser to the greater: if he is not entitled to withhold from her things which were not the reason she was taken in the first place, it is right and just that he is not entitled to withhold from her things which were the reason she was taken in the first place." Rabbi († 217?) said, "שארה (now understood as 'her flesh'): this is intercourse; as it says, 'To any of your biological relatives' אֶל־כָּל־שְׁאֵר בְּשָׂרוֹ (Lev 18:6). Furthermore, it is written, 'She (the female blood relative) is the flesh of your father' (Lev 18:12), 'she is the flesh of your mother' (Lev 18:13). כסותה should be interpreted according to its wording (thus = covering, clothing). עונתה, this is her food; as it says, 'He oppressed you ויענך (by refusing to provide sustenance) and made you hunger' (Deut 8:3)." — This baraita is referred to in b. Ketub. 47B. Concerning the words in m. Ketub. 4.4: "The husband is obligated (with respect to his wife) to provide her sustenance מְזוֹנוֹתֶיהָ, her ransom (from hypothetical imprisonment) and her burial," Raba († 352) remarks: "This teacher of the Mishnah viewed 'sustenance' (in m. Ketub. 4.4) in the sense of the Torah (Exod 21:10)." To explain this sense, the Mekilta passage above then follows, though with a different authorial attribution. The interpretation the Mekilta gave to Exod 21:10 is found also in y. Ketub. 5.30B.4. ‖ See further b. Ned. 15B at § 1 Cor 7:5 A, near the end.

b. Babylonian Talmud Yebamot 62B: R. Joshua b. Levi (ca. 250) said, "Whoever knows about his wife that she is God-fearing and is not mindful of her (does not have intercourse with her) is called a sinner; as it is said, 'If you know that your tent (= your wife) is peace, and you are mindful of your dwelling (= wife), you will not sin'" (so the midr. on Job 5:24; in the opposite case: you are a sinner).

c. See m. Ketub. 5.7 in n. *d.*

d. Mishnah Ketubbot 5.7: If a woman rebels against her husband (denies him the marital obligation), her prescribed wedding sum is reduced (see § John 2:1 A, #4, C) by seven *denars* each week. R. Judah (ca. 150) said, "Seven *tropaics* (see § Matt 5:26 B, #19 and D). Up to how much is deducted? Up to the amount of her prescribed wedding sum. R. Yose (ca. 150) said, "You can always deduct more; an inheritance might fall to her from another side, and then it can be claimed from her. Likewise, if the man rebels against his wife (denies her the marital obligation), three *denars* are added to her prescribed wedding sum every week." R. Judah said, "Three *tropaics.*"

e. This follows from t. Ketub. 5.6 (266); see § 1 Cor 7:5 A.

f. Babylonian Talmud ʿErubin 100B: Rammi b. Hama (ca. 320) said that Rab Asi (ca. 250) said that a man is forbidden to compel his wife to fulfill the obligatory commandment (of intercourse); for it says, "Whoever forces intercourse sins" (so Midr. Prov. 19:2, by understanding רגלים "feet" in accordance with Judg 5:27 = "intercourse"). Further, R. Joshua b. Levi (ca. 250) said, "Whoever compels his wife to fulfill the obligatory commandment (of intercourse) will be given wayward children." Rab Iqa b. Hinenah (Hinnana) said, "What passage of Scripture (is there for this)? 'Also without the will (of the woman agreeing to intercourse) the soul (of the child begotten) will not be good' (so Midr. Prov. 19:2). The baraita is the same: 'Also without the (consenting) will (of the woman) the soul will not be good' (Prov 19:2): this refers to the one who compels his wife to fulfill the obligatory commandment (of intercourse), 'and whoever rushes with intercourse sins' (Prov 19:2): this refers to the one who repeats intercourse (several times consecutively)." Really? Yet Raba († 352) said, "Whoever wants to ensure that all his children are male, let him repeat intercourse (several times consecutively)!" There is no contradiction: the one is with the (consenting) will (of the woman), and the other is without the (consenting) will (of the woman).... (Line 35:) R. Hiyya (ca. 280) said, "What does 'Who teaches us by the animals of the earth and makes us wise by the birds of heaven' (Job 35:11)? 'Who teaches us by the animals': this refers to the female mule who kneels down and then urinates; 'and makes us wise by the birds of heaven': this refers to the rooster who coaxes (the hen first) and then gets on her." R. Yohanan († 279) said, "If the Torah had not been given, we could learn chastity from the cat (who buries its filth) and the prohibition of robbery from the ant (whose diligence makes robbery unnecessary) and the prohibition of fornication from the dove (who remains loyal in mating) and propriety in intercourse from the rooster who coaxes and then gets on her. How does he persuade her (the hen)?" Rab Judah († 299) said that Rab († 247) said, "This is what he says to her, 'I will buy you a dress that reaches to your feet.' But when he has gotten on her, this is what he says to her, 'This rooster will lose his crest if he has (money) and does not buy you (the dress)!'"

g. Babylonian Talmud 'Erubin 100B: R. Samuel b. Nahman (ca. 260) said that R. Yohanan († 279) said, "Every wife who invites her husband to fulfill the obligatory commandment (of intercourse) will be granted sons as did not exist even in the generation of Moses. For concerning those in the generation of Moses it is written, 'Choose wise and insightful and respected men, for each of your tribes' (Deut 1:13); and further it is written, 'Then I took the heads of your tribes, wise and respected men' (Deut 1:15), but 'insightful ones' he did not find (since they are not mentioned in verse 15). However, in the case of Leah it is written, 'She went to meet him and said, "You must come to me, for I have hired you!"' (Gen 30:16). And further it is written, 'And from the sons of Issachar (thus the son of Leah whom she conceived after she made the request of Jacob, see Gen 30:18), skilled in "insight" concerning the times, in understanding what Israel had to do—their heads were two hundred, and all their brothers under their command' (1 Chr 12:32). Yet is it the case (that the request from the wife was a praiseworthy thing)?" Rab Isaac b. Abdima (ca. 300) said, "Eve was cursed with ten curses; for it is written, 'To the woman he said, "I will make much more"' (Gen 3:16). This refers to the two kinds of blood drops, first to the blood of menstruation and then to the blood of virginity; 'your pains': raising children is meant; 'and your pregnancy': this is the pain (the troubles) of pregnancy; 'in pain you will bear children': this is to be understood according to the wording; 'and you will desire your husband': this teaches that the wife longs for her husband when he goes on a trip; 'and he will be lord over you': this teaches that the wife invites him in her heart (but not explicitly with words), but the man invites with his mouth (and therein his being lord is revealed). This is a beautiful virtue in women, as we say, that she relates obligingly toward him. Yet these are only seven (curses)." When Rab Dimi (ca. 320) came, he said (as the three other curses), "She is covered like a mourner and banned from everyone and shut up in prison (Rashi: 'The king's daughter is completely glorious within' [Ps 45:14]). What does 'banned from everyone' mean? If it meant because she is forbidden to be alone (with other men), well, he (the man) is also forbidden to be alone (with other women). Rather, it is because she is forbidden to have two men simultaneously (while the man may have many women at the same time); 'banned from everyone' thus = forbidden to any man except her husband." In a baraita it has been taught (concerning the three other curses): She has to let her hair grow long like (the demoness) Lilith, she sits while urinating, like livestock, and she serves as a cushion to the man. But that is indeed a praise for her! (Then follows b. 'Erub. 100B.35; see in n. *f* at the end.) — The beginning of the passage is found also in b. Ned. 20B; here, instead of R. Yohanan, R. Jonathan (ca. 220) is rightly named as the author.

h. In general, the rabbis warn about excessive sex; for example b. Giṭ. 70A: There are eight things for which much of them is harmful and a little of them is beneficial. These are: traveling, intercourse, prosperity, work, wine, sleep, warm water (as bath and drink), and bloodletting. — Babylonian Talmud Berakot 22A applies specifically to scholars: Scholars should not be found to be like roosters (with chickens). ‖ Specific stipulations. Mishnah Ketubbot 5.6: "Performing the martial obligation, which is discussed in the Torah (Exod 21:10), is obligatory for idlers (people without a particular job) daily, workers twice a week, donkey drivers once a week, camel drivers once every thirty days, mariners once every six months." These are the words of R. Eliezer (ca. 90). — See b. Ketub. 62A: "Workers twice a week." Yet in a baraita it has been taught: Workers once a week! R. Yose b. Hanina (probably the younger, ca. 270) said, "There is no contradiction: here (twice a week) deals with those who carry out their work in their own city; there (once a week) with those who carry out their work in another city." A baraita says as much: "Workers twice a week"; in what case do these words apply? If they carry out their work in their own city. However, if they carry out their work in another city, once a week. ‖ Babylonian Talmud Ketubbot 62B: When do scholars have intercourse? Rab Judah († 299) said that Samuel († 254) said, "From one day of preparation for the Sabbath to the other day of preparation for the Sabbath (i.e., on every Friday evening); for it says, 'Which gives its fruit at its time' (Ps 1:3)." Rab Judah († 299), or, as has been said, Rab Huna († 297), or, as has been said, Rab Nahman († 320) said, "This refers to the one who serves his bed (performs intercourse) from one day of preparation for the Sabbath to the other day of preparation for the Sabbath." ‖ Babylonian Talmud Niddah 38A: Samuel († 254) said, "A woman gets pregnant and gives birth only after 271 or 272 or 273 days." He said this in agreement with the earlier pious ones. For in a baraita it has been taught: The earlier pious ones served their bed (performed intercourse) only on the fourth day of the week (= Wednesday), so that their wives would not be in danger of desecrating the Sabbath (by giving birth on the Sabbath). On the fourth day of the week and not after that (on the fifth and sixth day of the week)? Say: From the fourth day and onward. Mar Zutra (probably the younger, † 417) said, "What was the scriptural basis for the earlier pious ones? Because it is written, '(Yahweh) granted her pregnancy הֵרָיוֹן' (Ruth 4:13). הריון equates to 271 in its numerical value."

7:5 A: Do not withhold from each other, except by agreement.

Mishnah Yebamot 6.6: No one should withdraw from procreation, unless he (already) has children. The school of Shammai said, "(He must have) two sons"; the school of Hillel said, "A son and a daughter; for it says, 'He created them male and female' (Gen 5:2). If he has taken a wife and waited with her for ten years without her giving birth, he may not delay longer (to fulfill the obligation to procreate; he therefore has to marry another woman instead of the barren woman). If he dismisses her, she may marry another man, and the second husband may wait with her ten years once again. If she has had a miscarriage, you should count (the ten years) from the hour of the miscarriage." ‖ Tosefta Yebamot 8.4 (249): The school of Shammai said, "Two sons, like the sons of Moses; as it say, 'The sons of Moses, Gershom, and Eliezer' (1 Chr 23:15)." The school of Hillel said, "A son and a daughter; as it says, 'He created them male and female' (Gen 5:2)." R. Nathan (ca. 160) said, "The school of Shammai said, 'A son and a daughter'; the school of Hillel said, 'Either a son or a daughter.' If someone has taken a wife and waited with her for ten years without her giving birth, he may not delay, but rather he sends her away and gives her the prescribed marital sum; perhaps he was not worthy to be built from her. Even though there is no proof for the present question, the following is a valid indication: 'Sarai, Abram's wife, took the Egyptian woman, Hagar, her slave woman, after the end of ten years from the time Abram settled in the land of Canaan and gave her to him as a wife' (Gen 16:3). According to our way, we learn from this that the stay outside the land (of Israel) is not included in the count (of the ten years). If he was sick, or if she was sick, or if her husband traveled to a country overseas or was thrown into prison, this time is also not included in the count (of the ten years). If he dismissed her (after the ten years of waiting), she can go and marry another; perhaps she was not worthy to be built from him. How many times may she get married? Three times; after that she may get married only to a man who has a wife and children. However, if she has married a man who is without wife and children, she leaves without her prescribed marital sum, because her marriage was a mistake." — See another parallel in b. Yebam. 61B. ‖ Mishnah Ketubbot 5.6: If someone abstains from intercourse with his wife by a vow, this is valid for two weeks according to the school of Shammai, but for one week according to the school of Hillel. Students may go away to study the Torah for thirty days without the consent (of their wives), but workers may go away for one week. ‖ Tosefta Ketubbot 5.6 (266): If someone abstains from intercourse with his wife by a vow, this has validity for two weeks according to the school of Shammai, as in the case of a woman who gives birth to a female (see Lev 12:5); for one week according to the school of Hillel, as in the case of a woman who gives birth to a male, and as the days of her separation (see Lev 12:2). If it is supposed to have validity beyond his time, he has to dismiss the woman and he gives her the prescribed marital sum. — Parallels are found in y. Ketub. 5.30A.61 with the addition: Students may go away to study the Torah without the permission of their wives for thirty days, but with the permission of their wives for however long; b. Ketub. 61B: With permission, as long as he wants. — In b. Ketub. 62B, the scholars even champion the principle: "Students may go away to study the Torah without permission for two or three years." ‖ Mishnah Ned. 2.1: If someone says to his wife, "I am making a vow not to have intercourse with you," see, he is subject to the word: "He should not desecrate his word" (Num 30:3; he thus has to keep the vow if he does not look for a way to dissolve it). — See b. Ned. 15B: Yet he is obligated (to have intercourse) with her on the basis of the Torah: "He should not diminish her food, her covering, and her intercourse" (Exod 21:10)! This deals with someone who says, "May the pleasure of intercourse with you be forbidden to me!" In this case he desires no satisfaction for himself from intercourse. For Rab Kahana (ca. 250) said, "(If a woman says to her husband,) 'May intercourse with me be forbidden to you by a vow,' he may compel her to have intercourse, for she is obligated to do so. However, if she says, 'May the pleasure of intercourse with you be forbidden to me by a vow,' it is forbidden; for no one is allowed to enjoy anything that is forbidden to him."

By law, intercourse was forbidden, for example, on the Day of Atonement. Mishnah Yoma 8.1: On the Day of Atonement, it is forbidden to eat, drink, wash, anoint, put on sandals, and to have intercourse (to serve the bed).

7:5 B: Lest Satan tempt you because of your lack of self-control.

Babylonian Talmud Qiddušin 29B: Rab Hisda († 309) said, "The fact that I am more excellent (achieve more) than my peers derives from the fact that I got married at 16. If I had married at 14, I would have been able to say to Satan (when he would tempt me to unchastity): An arrow in your eyes (= you cannot touch me)!" ‖ Yalquṭ Simeoni Deuteronomy 23:14 (1 § 934): "Among your implements you should have a spade" (Deut 23:14). The words of the Torah were said secretly (allegorically) and euphemistically: You should not sit there without a wife, make a sheath for your weapon. Whoever goes out with sword pulled out, Satan will ultimately have power over him, so that he strikes and kills another and becomes guilty in his soul. Likewise, whoever sites there without a wife with his sword pulled out, the evil inclination will have power over him. He goes out with it onto the street, Satan stands there and strives to destroy him out of the world; as it says, "If you act rightly, is there not joyful courage? But if you do not act rightly, sin camps before the door" (Gen 4:7). And Satan urges him to drink from a cup that is not his (= to fornicate with someone else's wife), and destroys himself from the world; as it says, "Whoever commits adultery with a woman is senseless; (anyone who wants to wreck his life does this)" (Prov 6:32). If, however, the sword is hidden in its sheath, no harm comes to him: when you have taken a wife, the evil inclination will have no power over you; as it says, "You will experience that your tent (= your wife) is peace" (Job 5:24). ‖ See further b. Qidd. 81A (twice) at § Rom 2:22 A.

7:6: Yet I say this as a permission, not as a command.

In the rabbinic view, it is an obligatory commandment to get married (see § 1 Cor 7:1, 2). By contrast, the apostle does not want his statement in verse 2, "Everyone should have his own wife," to be construed as such an obligatory commandment, as if every Christian had to enter into marriage. Rather, his opinion is that getting married should be viewed as a matter of free discretion. Therefore, everyone who chooses to enter into marriage may see in his statement "Everyone should have his own wife" only the apostle's declaration of consent to his decision, but not a strict commandment; for Christians are permitted to get married but are not commanded.

7:9: It is better to marry than to be in heat.

A baraita in b. Qidd. 21B: (Deut 21:11:) "If you see among those in prison," at the time of arrest; "a woman," even a wife; "of beautiful form": the Torah speaks only about the evil inclination (with a view to the sinful passion of the man, not to endorse the practice and impel one to it); for it is better מוּטָב that the Israelites eat meat from dying but ritually slaughtered animals than that they eat meat from dying but not ritually slaughtered animals. (The lesser evil is to be preferred.) — The parallel passage tractate Semaḥot 7 (16A): If she (the prisoner of war) wishes to become a proselyte, he has her take an immersion bath and then he emancipates her, and he is immediately allowed (to have intercourse with) her. R. Simeon b. Eleazar (ca. 190) said, "First, he has her take an immersion in the name of a female slave, then he emancipates her, and he is immediately allowed her. And why is all this? So that the holy seed (of Israel) not mix with the nations of the lands. It is better that the children of Israel eat ..." (but the text is corrupt here). ‖ Babylonian Talmud Yoma 29A: Thinking about the sin (of fornication) is worse than the sin (itself) הִרְהוּרֵי עֲבֵירָה קָשׁוּ מֵעֲבֵירָה. ‖ On πυροῦσθαι see b. Qidd. 81A at § Rom 2:22.

7:10: That the woman not get a divorce from the man.

On divorce see § Matt 5:31, 32; on the fact that even Jewish women had the possibility to trigger a divorce from their husband, see § Mark 10:12; on divorce in gentile marriages, see § Matt 5:31, B and § Mark 10:12, B.

7:11: Or she should be reconciled to the man.

According to Jewish law, the reconciliation of the couple was still possible without further formalities even after a certificate of divorce was drawn up, as long as the certificate of divorce had not been delivered into the hand of the wife or her representative. The husband only had to declare the certificate of divorce to be invalid (see § Matt 5:31, A, #5). — If the marriage had been legally divorced, it was absolutely forbidden for a divorced woman to return to her husband: a. if she had otherwise married after that (see Deut 24:1ff.); b. if the divorce had occurred because of defamation (because of the wife's immoral behavior). It was disputed whether it was possible for a divorced woman to return to her husband if the reason for her dismissal had lain in her vows or in her childlessness (see § Matt 5:31, A, #7).

7:14: But now they (your children) are holy.

Israel is holy seed זרע הקדש; see above tractate Semaḥot 7 at § 1 Cor 7:9. The proselyte shares in this holiness קְדֻשָּׁה as soon as he has converted to Judaism. It is therefore said that his children who were born to him while he was still in the gentile world were not begotten or born in holiness. However, it is said that the children who were conceived and born after he and his wife have converted to Judaism were begotten and born in holiness.

Mishnah Ketubbot 4.3: If the daughter of a female proselyte converted to Judaism with her mother and had intimacy (as an engaged woman), she will be strangled. The stipulations about the door of her father's house (Deut 22:21) and about the hundred pieces of silver (Deut 22:19) also do not apply to her (since these are valid only for women who were born as Israelites). If her conception did not occur not in holiness שלא בקדשה (= before the mother converted to Judaism) and her birth was in holiness בקדשה (= after her conversion), she will (in case she has intimacy as an engaged woman) be stoned (as an Israelite woman who has intimacy as an engaged woman). However, the stipulations about the door of her father's house (Deut 22:21) and about the hundred pieces of silver (Deut 22:19) also do not apply to her. If her conception and her birth happened in holiness בקדשה (= after the mother converted to Judaism), she counts as a daughter of Israel in every respect. ‖ Mishnah Yebamot 11.2: If the sons of a female proselyte converted to Judaism with her, they carry out neither the ceremony of the removal of the shoe (to avoid levirate marriage) nor levirate marriage, even if the conception of the first did not occur in holiness (before the conversion) and his birth occurred in holiness (after the conversion) and the conception and the birth of the second occurred in holiness (for the first one stems from a time when the levirate law did not apply to him). ‖ Babylonian Talmud Yebamot 42A: Raba († 352) responded, "A proselyte and his wife who have converted to Judaism must wait for three months (after their conversion in order to have intercourse). What needs to be tested in this case? Something here also needs to be tested: it is a test to differentiate between the seed that is sown in holiness (after the conversion) and the seed that is not sown in holiness (before the conversion)." — See further examples in t. Bek. 6.3 (540) at § Luke 2:22f., n. *f*; b. Sanh. 57B at § Rom 1:26 A, #1; t. Yebam. 12.2 (254) at § 1 Cor 5:1 B, #4, n. *b*, fifth S-B footnote in section.

7:16: For who knows, O woman, you may save your husband!

Genesis Rabbah 17 (12A): It once happened that a pious man was married to a pious woman; but they did not acquire any children from each other. Then they said, "We are of no use to God." They got up and separated from each other. He went and took a godless wife, and this woman made him godless. She went and took a godless husband and made him righteous. You see that everything depends on the woman. — A counterpart to this is found in t. Demai 2.17 (48): R. Simeon b. Eleazar (ca. 190) said in the name of R. Meir (ca. 150), "It once happened that a woman was married to a *ḥaber* (a member of a Pharisaic covenant with the law; see § John 7:49, #5 till the end) and tied the tefillin around his hand. Then she married a tax collector and tied the customs slip on his hand." — The same is found in b. ʿAbod. Zar. 39A; b. Bek. 30B.

7:18: Let him not pull (his foreskin) up.

See the excursus "Circumcision."

7:19: Circumcision is nothing.

See the remark at § Rom 2:25 A, B and 2:26; see also § Acts 21:21. Incidentally, there were also a few uncircumcised Jews; however this was not because they would have paid homage to the principle: ἡ περιτουὴ οὐδέν ἐστιν. When some sons in a family had died as a result of circumcision, the boys born later could remain uncircumcised; see more on this point in the excursus "Circumcision."

7:23 A: You were bought at a price (see § 1 Cor 6:20).

7:23 B: Do not become slaves of human beings.

Tosefta Baba Qamma 7.5 (358): (Rabban Yohanan b. Zakkai [† ca. 80] said,) "It says, 'Let his master (the master of the Hebrew servant who does not wish to depart as a free person but rather wishes to remain in his master's house) pierce his ear with an awl' (Exod 21:5f.). Why is the ear pierced instead of any of the other members? Because he heard from Mount Sinai: 'To me (God) the children of Israel are servants עבדים; they are my servants' (Lev 25:55); (nevertheless) it (the ear) cast away the yoke of heaven (of God) and made the yoke of flesh and blood its master המליכה. Therefore Scripture says, 'Let the ear come and be pierced, because it has not retained what it heard.'" — Parallel passages are found in y. Qidd. 1.59D.26; Mek. Exod. 21:6 (83B); b. Qidd. 22B. ‖ A baraita in b. B. Meṣ. 75B: Three cry out and are not heard. These are: whoever has money and lends without witnesses; whoever procures a master for himself הקונה אדון לעצמו; and whoever has a wife who rules over him. What does "Whoever procures a master for himself" mean? Some say: "Whoever attaches his money to a non-Jew (declares it alien in order to circumvent certain stipulations of the Jewish law; for thereby he gives the non-Jew the possibility of reclaiming the money as his money)." Others say: "Whoever signs over his wealth to his children during his lifetime." Still others say: "Someone who fares poorly in one place and (nevertheless) does not move to another place."

7:26: I think that because of the present distress it may be good for a person to be as he is (unmarried).

See the explanation of R. Ishmael b. Elisha († ca. 135) in the baraita in b. B. Bat. 60B at § John 8:33 A.

7:33: The married person is concerned about the (things) of the world.

This care is dramatically depicted in Midr. Eccl. 1:2 (4B): R. Samuel b. Isaac taught in the name of R. Simeon b. Eleazar (ca. 190), "The sevenfold 'vanities,' that Ecclesiastes (1:2) spoke, corresponds to the seven worlds (ages of life) that a person sees (lives through). As a one-year-old child he is like a king: he rests in a litter and all hug and kiss him. As a child of two or three years he is like a pig: he reaches his hands into gutters. As a ten-year-old he jumps along like a kid. As a twenty-year-old he whinnies like a steed, gets cleaned up and looks for a wife. When he has taken a wife, behold, he is like a (pack) donkey; when he has sired children, he makes his face shameless like a dog to provide bread and nourishment; and when he has gotten old, he is like a monkey. The (last) thing that was said applies to the *'amme ha'areṣ* (those ignorant of the law); but about the sons of the Torah it is written: 'King David was old' (1 Kgs 1:1): even though he was old, he was (still) a king."

7:34: The one who is unmarried is concerned about the things of the Lord.

Babylonian Talmud Soṭah 22A: R. Yohanan († 279) said, "We have learned from a virgin about the timidity to sin and from a widow about receiving recompense. 'From a virgin about timidity to sin.'" For R. Yohanan heard a virgin, as her face fell and she said, "Lord of the world, you have made the garden of Eden, and you have made gehenna; you have made the righteous, and you have made the godless. May it be pleasing before you that no children of men fall by me (because of me)." "From a widow about receiving recompense"; for a widow, in whose neighborhood there was a synagogue, came daily and prayed in R. Yohanan's house of learning. He said to her, "My daughter, is there not a synagogue in your neighborhood?" She said to him, "Rabbi, will I not be granted recompense for the steps?"[187]

7:35 A: Not to put a runner around you.

See the narrative in b. ʿAbod. Zar. 4A at § Luke 7:41.

7:35 B: Persevering abiding with the Lord.

Wetstein relates the participial form προσεδρεύων = "persevering abiding" to εὐπάρεδρον and finds this word again in פראדורן in Exod. Rab. 33 (94C). However, the last is a corruption of פַּרְאֶדְרוֹן = πάρεδρος = "table companion." The passage from Exod. Rab. 33 should be translated as follows: As along as a groom has not married his fiancée, he is a table companion in the house of his father-in-law. When he has married her, behold, her father comes to her (to the house of his son-in-law).

---

187. S-B: See Gen. Rab. 39 (24A): Why did God not reveal to Abraham the land he was to go to (Gen 12:11)? To make him precious in his eyes and to give him a recompense for every single step. ‖ Genesis Rabbah 55 (35C): "Abraham got up and went" (Gen 22:3); recompense is to be given to him for the getting up and for the going. ‖ TanḥumaB ויגש § 8 (104B): R. Levi (ca. 300) said, "Since Orpah, his (Goliath's) mother, went four miles with her mother-in-law (Ruth 1:7ff.), God repaid her and made four heroes arise from her (see 2 Sam 21:22)." R. Isaac (ca. 300) said, "She went 40 steps with him, so God gave her recompense to her and gave her Goliath, who blasphemed God for forty days (see 1 Sam 17:16)." — There is a parallel in Midr. Ruth 1:14 (127B).

7:36: The virgin ..., if she is beyond her bloom.

1. A virgin's life was divided into three parts: קְטַנּוּת (the time of her being a minor),[a] נַעֲרוּת (girlhood), and בַּגְרוּת (the time of puberty).[b]

a. Babylonian Talmud Yebamot 100B: What is a קְטַנָּה female minor? One who is between 11 years old and 1 day and 12 years old and 1 day. — This deals specifically with a *qeṭanna*, who is permitted to use smooth materials during intercourse to protect against becoming pregnant. In other cases the determination of time can therefore be different. A baraita in b. Ketub. 29A: A girl is a *qeṭanna* from the time she is 1 day old until the time she brings the two hairs (= until the 12th year of life is complete). This is what R. Meir (ca. 150) claims, whereas in the same passage the scholars declare that a girl becomes a *qeṭanna* at 3 years old and 1 day. It can be seen that the starting age can be differently determined; at any rate, the end-time of being a קְטַנּוּת is 12 years and 1 day. So also t. Nid. 2.6 (642); b. Yebam. 12B; b. Ketub. 39A; b. Nid. 45A.

b. Babylonian Talmud Ketubbot 39A: Samuel († 254) said, "Between (the onset of) נַעֲרוּת girlhood and (the onset of) בַּגְרוּת the time of puberty there are only 6 months." — According to this, a girl is a *naʿara* (girl) from 12 years old and 1 day until she is 12 years old and 6 months. From then on, she is called a בּוֹגֶרֶת pubescent; see also b. Nid. 65A and y. Yebam. 1.3A.8.

2. The time when a virgin begins "to be beyond her bloom" was doubtlessly viewed as the beginning of puberty. This follows from the admonitions to hurry to get daughters married as soon as they were pubescent; see the citations at § John 2:1 A, #2, n. *e*. Here the following may also be referred to:

Leviticus Rabbah 21 (120C): R. Aqiba († ca. 135) looked in the holy spirit and said to them (his students), "Let whoever has a pubescent daughter go (home) and get her married."

7:39 A: If the husband has passed away, she is free.

1. κοιμᾶσθαι = דְּמַךְ "pass away"; see examples at § Matt 27:45.

2. ἐλευθέρα ἐστίν. — Mishnah Qiddušin 1.1: A woman is acquired נִקְנֵית (as a wife) in three ways and she regains herself וְקוֹנָה אֶת־עַצְמָהּ (becomes free from the husband to enter into another marriage) in two ways. She is acquired by money, by a certificate, and by intercourse.... She regains herself by a certificate of divorce and by the husband's death.

7:39 B: To marry whoever she wants.

The words are reminiscent of a formula in certificates of divorce.

Mishnah Giṭṭin 9.3: The essential content of a certificate of divorce is the following: See, you are allowed to anyone! R. Judah (ca. 150) said, "(The formula is in Aramaic:) And this is to be from me for you the paper of repudiation and the letter of dismissal and the document of divorce, so that you may go to let yourself be taken as a wife by any man you want לְהִתְנַסְבָא לְכָל גְּבַר דְּתִצְבְּיָן".

8:1 A: Meat sacrificed to idols.

εἰδωλόθυτον "meat that has been sacrificed to idols" = בְּשַׂר זִבְחֵי מֵתִים "meat of sacrifices for the dead" (= for idols); see § Rom 1:23 A, #2, D, n. *c*. A Jew was forbidden both to consume or to derive benefit from meat sacrificed to idols.

Mishnah ʿAbodah Zarah 2.3: The following things from gentiles are forbidden, and their prohibition is at the same time a prohibition of usufruct: Wine, vinegar of gentiles that was originally wine (of a gentile), Hadrianic shards (according to the commentaries, unkilned shards that were imbued with wine which Roman soldiers dissolved in water on their marches in order to use this liquid as a drink after the clay components had settled), skins without hearts (i.e., skins of animals whose heart had been torn out while the body was still alive to sacrifice it to idols). R. Simeon b. Gamaliel (ca. 140) said, "If the tear (the hole) is round, the skin is prohibited; if it is oblong, it is permitted." "Meat that is supposed to first be brought to an idol is permitted (for usufruct), but after it has been brought out it is prohibited (in every respect), because it is like a sacrifice for the dead זבחי מתים." These are the words of R. Aqiba († ca. 135). ‖ Tosefta Ḥullin 2.18 (503): If (an animal) is slaughtered for לְשׁוּם (= εἰς ὄνομα, in the name of, in regard to) the sun, for the moon, for the stars, for the zodiac signs, for the archangel Michael, or for a small worm, behold, it is meat of sacrifices for the dead בשר זבחי מתים (= meat sacrificed to idols, and as such is prohibited). ‖ Tosefta Ḥullin 2.20 (503): Meat that is found in a gentile's possession is permitted for usufruct (but not for consumption); that which is found in the possession of a sectarian (including Jewish Christians) is prohibited (even) for usufruct. Meat that comes out of an idol temple, see, it is meat sacrificed to idols בשר זבחי מתים.

8:1 B: Knowledge puffs up.

1. On the high evaluation of knowledge דַּעַת, דֵּעָה in rabbinic circles see the citations at § Matt 5:3, #2. Here reference may also be made to Midr. Sam. 5 § 9 (30B): "For Yahweh is a God of knowledge" (1 Sam 2:3). Rabbi († 217?) said, "I wonder why (the 4th benediction of the Prayer of Eighteen Benedictions) is omitted on the Sabbath: 'You bestow knowledge on human beings'; for if there is no knowledge in someone, how can he pray!" R. Phineas (ca. 360) said, "Great is knowledge (knowing) הדעת, for it is set between two names of God: 'Then you will gain insight in the fear of Yahweh and acquire the knowledge of God' (Prov 2:5). Furthermore, it says, 'For Yahweh is a God of knowledge' (1 Sam 2:3)." R. Eleazar (ca. 270) said, "Great is knowledge (knowing), for it weighs at least as much as the sanctuary, 'the place you prepared for your dwelling, Yahweh, the sanctuary, Yahweh, that your hands have prepared' (Exod 15:17)." (Proof: as "knowledge" in Prov 2:5 stands between two names of God, so too does "sanctuary" in Exod 15:17, so "knowledge" is of the same worth as "sanctuary.") The rabbis said, "One may not have mercy on someone in whom there is no knowledge. And what is the scriptural basis? 'For it is not a people of insight. Therefore, its creator will not have mercy on it' (Isa 27:11)." — Individual parts of this are found also in y. Ber. 4.8B.8 and b. Ber. 33A.23.

2. On the condemnation of pride and the commendation of humility see § Luke 1:51 and § Matt 5:3, #3.

8:4 A: There is no idol in the world.

See the judgments of the ancient synagogue about idols at § Rom 1:23 A, #2.

8:4 B: And that there is no God but one.

On יהוה אֶחָד (Deut 6:4), see § Mark 12:29.

8:5: For even if there are so-called gods.

Mekilta Exodus 15:11 (49A): Who is like you among those who call themselves gods? Pharaoh called himself a god; as it says, "Since he says, 'The Nile River is mine, and I created it'" (Ezek 29:9). It was the same with Sennacherib; as it says, "Who is there among the gods of the lands (who would have delivered your land from my hand)?" (2 Kgs 18:35). It was the same with Nebuchadnezzar; as it says, "I will rise on the heights of clouds" (Isa 14:14). It was the same with the prince of Tyre; as it says, "Say to the prince of Tyre, 'Yahweh Elohim says, "Because your heart is proud (and you have said, 'I am a god ...')"'" (Ezek 28:2). Who is like you among those whom others call gods, and yet there is nothing actually in them?! Of them it says, "They have a mouth and do not speak" (Ps 115:5). Yet God says two words with one utterance (i.e., at once), which flesh and blood cannot do; as it says, "God spoke one word and I heard it as two" (so Ps 62:12 according to the midr.).

8:10 A: If someone ... sees you lying at table in an idol house.

It was forbidden for a Jew to consume or benefit from meat sacrificed to idols; see § 1 Cor 8:1 A; thereby he was also banned from participating in idol sacrifice meals. — The following gives some indication about the more general question of when and how an Israelite is guilty of idolatry:

Mishnah Sanhedrin 7.6: The idolater (will be stoned). It is the same whether he serves the idol (in the common cult style) or sacrifices or burns incense or presents a drink offering or prostrates before it or accepts it as God or says to it, "You are my God." However, whoever hugs, kisses, sweeps the dust off, sprinkles, bathes, anoints, clothes, or puts shoes on (an idol) transgresses a prohibition (namely: "You shall not honor them" [Exod 20:5; 23:24; Deut 5:9], without however thereby being guilty of actual idolatry and the punishment of stoning). Whoever makes an oath in its name and fulfills הַמְקַיֵּם it in its name[188] transgresses a prohibition (namely Exod 23:13: "You shall not mention the name of other gods; it shall not be heard on your lips"; see the baraita in b. Sanh. 63B). If anyone empties himself before Baal Peor, this is his cult, and if anyone casts a stone for Mercury, this is his cult. (See § Rom 1:23 A, #2, D, n. *a* toward the end and § Rom 2:22 C, #1, notes *d* and *e*.)

---

188. S-B: Rashi († 1105), Maimonides (1135–1204), Rabbenu Asher († 1327), and Bertinoro († 1510) interpret המקים = "whoever swears." However, קַיֵּם does not have this meaning in the Mishnah.

8:10 B: Will he not be built up?

οἰκοδομηθήσεται. – The rabbis use בָּנָה "build" in the same metaphorical sense.[a] Hence בַּנָּיָה דְאוֹרָיְתָא "builder of the Torah" is a predicate of honor for the scholars and בַּנָּיִין "master builders" a designation for the students.[b] – See also § Rom 14:19.

a. A baraita in b. Ned. 40A: R. Simeon b. Eleazar (ca. 190) said, "If the young people say to you, 'Build' בנה and the old people, 'Tear down' סתור, listen to the old and do not listen to the young; for the building בִּנְיָן of the young is a tearing down סְתִירָה and the tearing down of the old is building. Rehoboam, the son of Solomon, is a sign of this." – Parallels are found in b. Meg. 31B and t. ʿAbod. Zar. 1.19 (461); in the latter passage, the saying is related specifically to the building of the temple. ‖ See b. Ber. 63A at § Gal 2:18.

b. See examples at § Matt 21:42, #2.

8:13: Lest I set a stumbling block for my brother.

On σκανδαλίζειν and σκάνδαλον see § Matt 5:29, C; 18:6 A; 18:7 B and C; and § Rom 14:13. See also b. Ḥul. 5B (= 7A) at § Rom 5:9f., #2, B; b. Soṭah 22A: "Lest any children of men fall by me" שלא יכשלו בי בני אדם at § 1 Cor 7:34.

9:1: Are you not my work in the Lord?

See on this § 1 Cor 4:14, #1; § 4:15 B, notes *b* and *c*.

9:7 A: Who goes to the battlefield at his own expense?

On ὀψώνια see § Rom 6:23, #1.

9:7 B: Who plants a vineyard and does not eat its fruit?

The halakah precisely regulated workers' eating from the crops under their hands.

Mishnah Baba Meṣiʿa 7.2: The following (workers) may eat (from the fruits which relate to their work) on the basis of the Torah: whoever works on what clings to the ground at the time when the (field) work on it is done. (According to this, a worker may eat, e.g., fruit, wine grapes, vegetables when he picks and gathers them in ripe condition; cereals when the type of crop in question is scythed.) Whoever works on what is (already) detached from the soil, as long as the work on it is not yet (completely) done. (The work on the gathered grain, fruit, vegetables is considered done when the crops are ready for tithing; as long as this is not the case, the one working on them may eat of them. Yet this is valid only in the case of that which grows out of the earth (thus, e.g., all animal products are excluded). The following are those who may not eat: whoever works on what clings to the ground at the time when the (field) work on it is not yet done (e.g., whoever thins dense onions). Whoever works on what is (already) detached from the soil, after the work on it is (completely) done (and the crops have been tithed); and whoever works on what does not grow out of the earth. – Mishnah Baba Meṣiʿa 7.3: If the worker worked with his hands but not with his feet; with his feet but not with his hands; or only with his shoulders (as a load carrier), he may eat. R. Yose b. Judah (ca. 180) said, "Only if he works with his hands and feet." — Mishnah Baba Meṣiʿa 7.4: If he worked with figs, he may not eat wine grapes; with wine grapes, he may not eat figs. However, he may abstain (from eating) until he comes to the place of the most beautiful items and (then) eat. This has all been said only for the time of working; but in order to recover the time lost to the owners (by eating), it has been determined that the workers should eat when they go from one row (of trees or beds) to another, or when they return from the winepress. — Mishnah Baba Meṣiʿa 7.5: A worker may eat cucumbers up to the value of a *denar* (about 65 pennies) and dates up to the value of a *denar*. R. Eleazar חסמא (ca. 120) said, "The worker may no longer when he receives his wage; but the scholars allowed it. Yet a man is instructed not to be a glutton, whereby he would close the door in front of him (because no one would hire him to work anymore)." — Similar statements are found in t. B. Meṣ. 8.8 (388); b. B. Meṣ. 91B.14; 92A.3. ‖ Tosefta Baba Meṣiʿa 8.3 (387): Workers may eat their bread with fish broth in order to be able to eat a lot of wine grapes, and the owner may give them wine to drink, so that they may not be able to eat a lot of wine grapes. — The same is found in B. Meṣ. 89A.38. ‖ Tosefta Baba Meṣiʿa 8.6 (387): If someone guards four or five cucumber fields, he should not fill his stomach from one of them, but rather let him eat from each one in exact proportion. — The same is found in b. B. Meṣ. 93A.20 as a quotation in the mouth of Rab Kahana (II, ca. 375). ‖ Tosefta Baba Meṣiʿa 8.7 (387): R. Yose b. Judah (ca. 180) said, "As threshing (of which it says in Deut 25:4: 'You shall not bind the mouth of an ox when it treads') refers specifically to something where one works with his hands and feet and his whole body, the worker is excluded (from the right to eat the crops under his hands) who works with his hands but not his feet, or with his feet not but with his whole body (see against this m. B. Meṣ. 7.3 above). As threshing refers specifically to something where the work is not yet done, the worker is excluded (from the right being discussed) who kneads or bastes or bakes, where the work was finished. As threshing refers specifically to something that grows out of the earth, the worker is excluded (from the right above) who milks or prepares butter or cheese from something that does not grow out of the earth (cf. m. B. Meṣ. 7.2 above). As threshing refers specifically to something that is detached from the soil, the worker is excluded (from the right above) who pulls up garlic or onions, so something that clings to the soil (and where the field work is not yet done; cf. above m. B. Meṣ. 7.2 toward the end). As threshing refers specifically to something where the work is not yet done for tithes, the worker is excluded who separates the dates and figs (that stick together) with which the work for the tithes is done." — Parallels are found in y. B. Meṣ. 7.11B.50; b. B. Meṣ. 89A.5. ‖ Babylonian Talmud Baba Meṣiʿa 88B: ("When you come to your neighbor's vineyard, eat grapes as you please" [Deut 23:25]) in a baraita: "As you please." As you are free from punishment when you bind your own mouth (refrain from consuming wine grapes), so too you are not subject to punishment if you bind the mouth of the worker (arrange with him that he refrain from consuming them while he works with them). — The same is found in b. B. Meṣ. 92A.41. ‖ Sifre Deuteronomy 23:25 § 266 (121B): "When you come to your neighbor's vineyard" (Deut 23:25). (The passage is interpreted by the rabbis in relation to the workers in the vineyard.) Perhaps at any time? Scripture teaches: "But you will not put any in your container" (Deut 23:25), so at the time when you put them into the owner's containers (i.e., at harvest time). "Your neighbor's": the others (= non-Israelites) are excluded. "Your neighbor's": the Most High is excluded (a vineyard that has been hallowed to God). "Eat," but one should not crush; "grapes," but not figs. From this passage it has been said (see above m. B. Meṣ. 7.4): If he worked with wine grapes, he may not eat figs; with figs, he may not eat wine grapes; but he may abstain (from eating) until he comes to the place of the most beautiful items and (then) eat. R. Eleazar (ben) חסמא (ca. 120) said, "How do we know that a worker may no longer eat when he receives his wage? Scripture teaches: כנפשך, that is, corresponding to your person (= the value of your work)." Yet the scholars said, "'Until you are full' (Deut 23:25): this teaches that the worker may eat beyond his wage (cf. above m. B. Meṣ. 7.5). 'But you will not put any in your container' (Deut 23:25), also not in the hour when you put them in the owner's containers."

9:7 C: Or who pastures a flock and does not eat from the milk of the flock?

According to Pesiq. 79B (= y. Ter. 8.46A.28), milking was the business of shepherds; see the passage at § Matt 15:26, n. *c*. This was indeed natural when shepherds stayed far from home most of the year with their range animals in uncultivated mountain and wood districts (see § Luke 2:8 B). Likewise, it was also natural that the milk from their flocks served to nourish them. The halakah even permits milk to be purchased from the shepherds in the range areas.[a] This shows that the shepherds away from home could more or less do what they wanted with the revenues from the dairy business. It was different as soon as the shepherds drove their cattle onto the cultivated land at home and regularly returned with them in the evening to the villages. Here the rule was not only that milk could not be bought from the shepherds,[b] but also there was the further stipulation that we have already learned at § 1 Cor 9:7 B, namely that the shepherd was not entitled to consume his flock's milk while he tended them.[c] In his statement, the apostle had in view the more common case, where the shepherd is in a distant range area with his flock.

a. Tosefta Baba Qamma 11.9 (370): Goats and shorn wool and picked wool may not be purchased from shepherds (because they were presumably stolen by the shepherd), though stitched items can be bought from them, because the stitched items are their property. Milk and cheese may also be bought from them in the grazing area במדבר, not in the area where they live (in their home area). In any place, four or five sheep and four or five sheep wools may be purchased from them (since the owner would notice if such a large theft were committed by the shepherd), but not two sheep or two sheep wools. R. Judah (ca. 150) said, "Barn animals may be purchased from them, but not range animals. The rule about this is as follows: Nothing can be purchased from a shepherd that he could steal without the owner noticing, but anything can be purchased from him that he could not steal without the owner noticing." — There is a parallel in b. B. Qam. 118B.

b. Mishnah Baba Qamma 10.9: Wool and milk may not be purchased from shepherds. – See the more precise stipulation in t. B. Qam. 11.9 above in n. *a*.

c. See on this m. B. Meṣ. 7.2 and t. B. Meṣ. 8.7 at § 1 Cor 9:7 B. ‖ Babylonian Talmud Baba Meṣiʿa 89A: As threshing refers specifically to something that is a product of the soil and that a worker may eat from at the time when the work is completed, so too a worker may eat from anything that is a product of the soil. Excluded here is the one who milks and makes butter and cheese; for these are not products of the soil, and a worker may not eat from them.

9:8: Surely I do not say this in a human way!?

See on this § Rom 3:5.

9:9 A: You shall not bind the mouth of a threshing ox.

1. κημόω or φιμόω = חָסַם, Aram. חֲסַם, "to tie up the mouth," "to put on a muzzle חָסוֹם." Animals were accustomed to this because they regularly wore a muzzle on the way to the grazing area in order to be kept from grazing on someone else's land.

Tosefta Šabbat 4.5 (115): A cow shall not go out (on the Sabbath) with her muzzle. – There is a parallel in b. Šabb. 53A. ‖ See Gen. Rab. 41 (25B) at § Rom 2:21 B, A.

2. The wording of the law. Deuteronomy 25:4: לא תחסם שור בדישו "You shall not bind the mouth of an ox while it threshes." ‖ Targum Onkelos: "You shall not close the mouth of an ox לא תחוד פום while it threshes." ‖ Targum Yerušalmi I: "You shall not bridle לא תזממון the ox's mouth at the time when it threshes. Also a (childless widowed) sister-in-law who has fallen to a leprous man or someone who is (otherwise) not fitting for her, you shall not bind her to him." (On this addition see further below at § 9:9 B; 9:10; in Tg. Yer. II this is lacking.) ‖ Septuagint: οὐ φιμώσεις βοῦν ἀλοῶντα.

3. The prohibition against having an ox thresh with a bound mouth was reckoned among the things that distinguished the Israelites from all the other nations.[a] Therefore a Jew had to observe prohibition even when he threshed with a cow borrowed from a gentile, whereas a gentile was not obligated to do this when he carried out his threshing work with an Israelite's cow.[b] Ways of circumventing the law, which were attempted in the most diverse forms, were prohibited. Yet it was conceded that the owner could feed the threshing animal beforehand so that it would eat as little as possible during the treading process itself, or that he could strew threshed straw over the full layers of grain spread out for threshing so that the animal would eat only the latter.[c] There were special stipulations for grain that was destined to be an offering or a tithe, which therefore neither the owner nor his cattle were allowed to consume. In this case, one found a way by hanging a muzzle full of grain to eat around the neck of the threshing animals so that they would leave the feed under their

feet untouched.[d] Transgressing the prohibition was punished by scourging. Additionally, the threshing animal and, if it had been borrowed or rented, its owner were to be indemnified for the feed that had been drained by the animal while it worked.[e] On the reason for the law, see Josephus, *Ant.* 4.8.21.[f]

a. Pesiqta 46A: R. Levi (ca. 300, so read instead of "R. Judan") said, "In all their working, the Israelites are different from the nations of the world, in their plowing, their sowing, their harvesting, their sheaving, and their threshing, with their barn floor and their winepress, in their counting and their calculating.... In the case of their threshing; as it says, 'You shall not bind the mouth of an ox while it threshes' (Deut 25:4)." — The same is found in Num. Rab. 10 (157A); Pesiq. Rab. 15 (69B); with several additions, also Midr. Song. 5:16 (122A).

b. Tosefta Baba Meṣiʿa 8.11 (388): When an Israelite threshes with the cow of a non-Israelite, (if he binds its mouth,) he transgresses the commandment: "You shall not bind the mouth" (Deut 25:4). However, when a non-Israelite (*goy*) threshes with an Israelite's cow, he does not transgress the commandment: "You shall not bind the mouth."

c. Babylonian Talmud Baba Meṣiʿa 90A: Rammi b. Hama (ca. 320) asked, "How about when someone sticks a thorn in its (the threshing cow's) mouth? If someone sticks a thorn in it, this is the best kind of binding. But what about when a thorn sits in her mouth (which got in there by itself? Do you have to take it out or not?) Or what about when someone lets a lion camp outside near her (so that she cannot eat due to fear)? If one causes it to camp, that is the best way of binding. But what about when the lion camps outside by itself? Or what about when someone situates her young outside? What about when she is thirsty for water? What about when someone spreads a cover over the threshing layers? Explain at least one. For in a baraita it has been taught: The cow's owner may let his cow go hungry (if he rents it to someone else for threshing) so that it eats a lot of the threshing grain; further, the owner may untie a bundle of straw in front of the animal (and spread it out over the threshing layer) so that it does not eat a lot of the threshing grain. (Spreading out the straw is like spreading out a cover; if the former is allowed, then so too is the former!) Here (in the case of spreading out the straw), though, the matter is different, because the animal can eat in the ordinary way (which it cannot do when a cover is spread out. If you want, you can also say: The owner may untie a bundle of straw in front of the animal at the beginning (before beginning to thresh) so that (afterward) it will not eat a lot of the threshing grain." R. Jonathan (ca. 220) asked R. Simai (ca. 210), "What about binding the mouth outside (outside of the barn floor area and before beginning to thresh)? The All Merciful One said, 'An ox "while" it threshes,' and this (binding the mouth outside) does not happen 'while' it threshes! Or does the All Merciful One perhaps mean: 'You should not thresh while its mouth is bound?'" He answered him, "You can learn it from your father's house (R. Jonathan had a priestly ancestry). 'You shall not drink wine or intoxicating drink, you and your sons with you, when you enter the tent of revelation' (Lev 10:9). (It says,) 'When you enter,' which is forbidden, but drinking and (then) entering is allowed? The All Merciful One says indeed: 'To make a difference between holy and profane' (Lev 10:10). Rather, as there should be no drunkenness at the time of entering, so also here there should be no closing of the mouth at the time of threshing (whether it is put on before or after threshing begins)." ‖ Babylonian Talmud Baba Meṣiʿa 90B: It has been said, "As for closing the mouth by calling (the animal) …, the one in question (who does it) is guilty (subject to punishment)" according to R. Yohanan († 279). Resh Laqish (ca. 250) said, "He is exempt from punishment." – The same is found in b. Sanh. 65B.

d. Mishnah Terumot 9.3: Whoever beats (crops that are determined to be an offering or tithe) acts laudably. Yet how should the one who threshes with cattle act? Let him hang baskets around the neck of the (threshing) cattle and put the same kind of crop (which is already threshed) in it; thus he will be found as one who does not bind the mouth of the cattle, and as one who does not feed it an offering (which was prohibited to any nonpriest). ‖ Tosefta Baba Meṣiʿa 8.11 (388): Whoever threshes an offering and a second tithe (with cattle), (if he binds the mouth of the cattle,) transgresses the commandment: "You shall not bind the mouth" (Deut 25:4). What should he do? Let him hang baskets around the neck of the cattle and put the same kind of crop in it. ‖ We find something different in a baraita in b. B. Meṣ. 89B: When cows stomp the grain or thresh an offering and tithe, (if the animal's mouth is bound), one does not transgress the commandment: "You shall not bind the mouth" (Deut 25:4) (because this commandment pertains only to threshing and not stomping, and also only to threshing ordinary grain and not to grain for offerings and tithes). Yet because of the appearance of evil (since others do not know that it is an offering or tithe), a bunch of the same type of crop is taken and hung on its mouth in a feeding basket. R. Simeon b. Yohai (ca. 150) said, "Let one take vetches and hang them on it; for animals like this more than anything else." – The same is partly found in t. B. Meṣ. 8.10 (388).

e. A baraita in b. B. Meṣ. 91A: Whoever binds a cow's mouth and threshes with it receives lashes and refunds (the cow's owner) four *qabs* for a cow and three *qabs* for a donkey. – Tosefta Baba Meṣiʿa 8.12 (388): Whoever binds a cow's mouth must (afterward) give her no less than six *qabs* and a donkey no less than three *qabs.* ‖ A baraita in b. B. Meṣ.90B: Whoever binds a cow's mouth … is exempt from punishment and receives lashes only if he threshes (with it). – The same is found corrupted in t. B. Meṣ. 8.12 (388).

f. Josephus, *Jewish Antiquities* 4.8.21: "Also, one should not bind the mouth of an ox on the barn floor when it treads out the ears: for it is not right to withhold the fruit from the co-workers who have labored to produce it." – Josephus does not here mean to establish a general principle that applies to workers in other areas of life as well, as the apostle does with his interpretation of Deut 25:4. Josephus' principle relates only to the stipulation in Deut 25:4 being discussed: since the ox is a co-worker in extracting the grain crop by its threshing, it should not be deprived of consuming this crop. Josephus is certainly not concerned to broaden the law by an analogous interpretation of its wording. Similar rationales for the law's prescriptions, like the one Josephus has attempted here for Deut 25:4, are found elsewhere as well (see § 1 Cor 9:9 B).

4. Halakic extensions of the law in Deut 25:4 by inferences.

A. Expanding the law to different animals and different kinds of work.

Mishnah Baba Qamma 5.7: With an ox and with every other kind of cattle, the same stipulations of the law apply concerning falling into a pit (see § Matt 12:11), concerning keeping away from Mount Sinai (Exod 19:13), concerning the replacement of double value (in case of theft, see Exod 22:3 and § Matt 19:18 A), concerning delivering one that has gotten lost (Exod 23:4; Deut 22:1ff.), concerning unloading the burden (from an animal that has collapsed [Exod 23:5]), concerning binding the mouth (while threshing [Deut 25:4]), concerning binding of different kinds (Lev 19:19; Deut 22:10), and concerning rest from work on the Sabbath. Likewise, the same goes for wild beasts and fowl. If this is the case, why is it always only an ox or a donkey that is talked about in the stipulations of the law that are in question? Because Scripture expresses itself according to the (most common) kind of being. ‖ Sifre Deuteronomy 25:4 § 287 (125A): "You shall not bind the mouth of an ox ..." (Deut 25:4). Here I hear only about an ox; whence comes the idea that one has to act the same way with wild beasts and fowl as one would with an ox? It says, "You shall not bind the mouth," in the most general sense. If this is the case, why is it also said, "the ox's"? It means: You may not bind the ox's mouth, but you may a person's (namely when one arranges with a worker that he has to refrain from consuming the crops under his hands; see b. B. Meṣ. 88B at § 1 Cor 9:7 B). ‖ Sifre Deuteronomy 25:4 § 287 (125B): "When it threshes" (Deut 25:4). Here I hear only about it threshing. How do we know that all other kinds of work are included here? Scripture teaches: "You shall not bind," in the most general sense (the work can be any kind of work).

B. Extending the law to people.

Babylonian Talmud Baba Meṣiʿa 88B: It therefore follows (on the basis of Deut 23:25f.) that a person (who works in service of someone else) may eat of what clings to the ground (see above § 1 Cor 9:7 B), and (on the basis of Deut 25:4) that an ox may eat of what has been detached from the ground. How do we know that a person may eat of what has been detached from the ground? One draws a conclusion by moving from the lesser to the greater: if an ox, who is not permitted to eat of what clings to the ground, is permitted to eat of what has been detached from it, is it not right that a person, who may eat of what clings to the ground may (also) eat what has been detached from it? If this applies to an ox, about which you have received the prohibition about binding the mouth, can you then say it about people, about whom you have not received the prohibition about binding its mouth? In the case of people, one should infer from the ox the prohibition about binding the mouth by moving from the lesser to the greater: if you are prohibited from binding the mouth of an ox, the life of which you have not been commanded to preserve, is it not right that you are prohibited from binding the mouth of a person, whose life you are commanded to preserve?... But where (from Scripture) can it be shown that a person may eat from what has been detached from the ground (that his mouth may be bound just as little as that of the threshing ox?) Scripture says, "Grain ... grain" (Deut 23:24) twice: If this does not apply to a person in the case of what clings to the ground, let it be interpreted in relation to a person in the case of what has been detached. R. Ammi (ca. 300) said, "A person needs no particular Scripture verse at all for what is detached. It is written, 'When you come to your neighbor's vineyard' (Deut 23:25) (the passage is referred to workers in a vineyard). Can this not be referred to the case when he has rented it out to carry a load? (In this case he has crops detached from the ground under his hands, and he is permitted to eat of them according to Deut 23:25.) ...." Rabina (I?, † ca. 420; II?, † 499) said, "Neither a person in the case of what is detached nor cattle in the case of what clings to the ground need any particular Scripture verse; for it is written, 'You shall not bind the mouth of an ox while it threshes.' Since all animals are included in the prohibition concerning binding the mouth (cf. #4, A, above), since we understand "ox" from "ox" in the Sabbath commandment,[189] in this case the All Merciful One would have had to write only: 'You shall not thresh while the mouth is closed.' Why then 'ox,' as the All Merciful One (Deut 25:4) has written? In order to compare (to treat as equal) the one who binds the mouth with the one whose mouth is bound, and the one whose mouth is bound with the one who binds the mouth. As the one who binds the mouth may eat from what clings to the ground, so too may the one whose mouth is bound eat from what clings to the ground. And as the one whose mouth is bound may eat from what has been detached from the soil, so too may the one who binds the mouth eat from what has been detached from the soil." — The short meaning of this long exposition is: as the ox's mouth cannot be bound during threshing, so too the worker may eat from the fruits that no longer cling to the ground which he has under his hand while he works. In other words, the law in Deut 25:4 can be applied analogously to people working on the harvested crops.

9:9 B and 9:10: Yet God is not concerned about oxen, is he? Or does he speak entirely for our sake? For it has been written for our sake that it is fitting that the plower plows and the thresher threshes in hope of partaking.

1. When the apostle asks, "Yet God is not concerned about oxen, is he? Or does he speak entirely for our sake?," he is certain that his question will find a concurring answer. He himself then confirms this answer by continuing: "For it (the law in Deut 25:4) has been written for our sake that it is fitting that the plower plows and the thresher threshes in hope of partaking." The apostle distinguishes between the literal sense of the stipulation in Deut 25:4 and the idea underlying it. Paul is sure that the simple literal sense would not do justice to the actual intention of the lawgiver because of his certainty that God did not give his law for the sake of oxen, but rather for the sake of humanity. So the deeper sense, the actual meaning of the stipulation has to be searched for. He then discerns this in that every worker, thus also the spiritual worker, is entitled to expect that he will receive his sustenance from the things that benefit from his work. However, if this is the fundamental idea of the stipulation in Deut 25:4, then also the appeal to the law is proven to be justified, an appeal that in verse 8 is clothed in the words: "Does not the law also say this?"

189. S-B: This means that in a commandment about the Sabbath only the ox is named as a representative of all other domestic animals and that accordingly in Deut 25:4 too, "ox" includes all other domestic animals. However, there is no such Sabbath commandment. See Exod 20:10; 23:12, and Deut 5:14.

This spiritualizing method of interpreting the letter of the law, which the symbolic-allegorical interpretation of the law served as an effective means, had already appeared early in Hellenistic Judaism. Already the author of the Letter of Aristeas applied it in a comprehensive way.[a] Yet it reached its highpoint in Philo of Alexandria (born perhaps ca. 20–10 BCE). Without doubt the allegorical interpretation of the law was a danger to the law itself. For if the highest goal to strive for was a life in accordance with the idea of the law, why then would one need to observe the external letter of the law? So it appeared as if a law-free Judaism would have to be the necessary consequence of the allegorical interpretation of the law. In fact Philo had to inveigh against people who drew this last conclusion from his allegorizing, who dispensed with the literal observation of the commandments concerning the Sabbath and circumcision in order to live for only the idea that was embodied in these commandments.[b]

a. Letter of Aristeas 142ff.: "Lest we (Israelites) defile ourselves by fellowship with others and become corrupted by interaction with bad men, he (the lawgiver) surrounded us on all sides with purity laws, in food, drink, contact, in what we listen to, and see. For altogether all the stipulations are the same (in value) in their deeper meaning, since all are determined by one power; and individually each of the regulations about prohibited and permitted food has a deep reason. For the sake of example, though, I will briefly elucidate one or the other. For do not think only of the view refuted long ago that Moses gave these laws because of mice and weasels or such animals (cf. 1 Cor 9:9: μὴ τῶν βοῶν μέλει τῷ θεῷ;). Rather, these holy commandments were given for the purpose of righteousness, to awaken pious thoughts, and to form character. For the birds that we eat are all tame and are characterized by cleanliness, since they use wheat and pulses for food, such as doves, turtledoves, chickens, partridges, geese, and others of the sort. The forbidden birds, as you will find, however, are wild and flesh-eating, they oppress the others with their power and nourish themselves by eating the previously named tame birds in a wicked way. And not only these, but they also steal lambs and young goats and attack people, corpses, and live bodies. By calling them unclean, he (the lawgiver) indicated that those to whom the law is given should cultivate righteousness in their soul and oppress no one by relying on their power and take something from him, but rather should conduct their life in righteousness, as the previously named tame birds who consume pulses growing on the earth and do not use force to destroy weaker or related (beings). Thereby the lawgiver meant to signify to the wise, to be righteous, not to use force, and not to oppress others by relying on their power. For if it was not even fitting to touch the previously named (beings) because of their particular nature, how should one not be fully on guard against one's character becoming corrupted along these lines? Now, he gave us all the stipulations about permitted food with these (the birds) and the (other) animals in allegorical discourse. For to be cloven-hoofed and to have split claws is an allegory of the fact that all one's actions must be directed by discernment toward what is right. For the power of the whole body and its activity rest on shoulders and legs. He compels us to direct all our actions toward righteousness by discernment by inferring this teaching from this, but also teaching that we are differentiated from all people.... Yet whoever possesses the kind of discernment mentioned also has memory, as he has shown. For all (animals) that are cloven-hoofed and ruminate represent memory for the understanding. For rumination is nothing other than the memory of life and existence. For he (Moses) believes that life endures by nourishment. Therefore, he admonishes through Scripture: 'Remember the Lord your God who has done great and wonderful things for you'.... Therefore, he admonishes by a (particular) provision to remember that everything named is preserved by the divine power. For he has determined every time and every place to constantly remember God, the sovereign and preserver. He commands namely in the case of food and drink to offer a benediction first and only after that to consume. And with clothing he also gave us a marker of remembrance (the show tassels). Likewise, he commanded to mount the proverbs on gates and doors (the mezuzah) so that we might remember God. And he explicitly commands us to put the mark of remembrance on our hands (the tefillin). Thereby he clearly shows that we have to perform every deed with righteousness by remembering our stipulation but above all the fear of God.... This has shown the deep wisdom in discernment and remembrance, as we have interpreted the cloven hoof and rumination. For the law was not given without purpose or thought, but rather for the sake of truth and to instruct us in correct principles."

b. Philo, *De migratione Abrahami* § 16 (Mangey's ed., 1:450): "There are certain people who regard the wording of the laws τοὺς ῥητοὺς νόμους as symbols σύμβολα of spiritual truths and search the latter out with great care but disregard the former. In rebuke, I would like to accuse these people of recklessness. For one has to consider both of them, both a search for the hidden sense that is as precise as possible, as well as an irreproachable observance of the obvious (literal) sense. However, those people live as in a wilderness entirely for themselves, or as if they were disembodied souls and knew nothing about a city or a town or a house or of any human society at all; they look beyond the opinion of the majority and trace the naked (pure) truth as it is in itself. Holy Scripture teaches such people to take care of a good reputation and to abolish none of what is contained in the laws, which have been determined by men who were divinely inspired and greater than those who are among us. For since the seventh day teaches that the creative power belongs to the unbegotten one, but passivity (suffering) belongs to what is created, we should still not abolish what has been ordained in the law concerning it, like kindling fire or cultivating land or carrying burdens or accusing or judging or demanding back deposits or collecting debts or otherwise doing what is allowed in the days that are not sanctified. Or since the feast is a symbol σύμβολον of the soul's joy and gratitude to God, we should nevertheless not forsake the festal gatherings at the yearly recurring times. Or since circumcision indicates the cutting off of the lusts and all the passions and the removal of godless thoughts ..., we should still not do away with the law given concerning circumcision. For we would also have to disregard the holiness of the temple and myriad other things if we observed only what has become evident by symbols. Rather, one should think that the one (the literal meaning) corresponds to the body and the other (the allegorical meaning) to the soul. As one must care for the body since it is the house of the soul, so too must one carefully observe the literal sense of the laws. For if the latter is observed, the former (the allegorical meaning) will also be more clearly recognized, which finds its symbolic expression in the first; and this totally apart from the fact that (only in this way) does one avoid the reproach and accusations of the multitude."

2. Symbolic-allegorical scriptural interpretation found a place in the Palestinian houses of learning as well. There its representatives were called דּוֹרְשֵׁי רְשׁוּמוֹת "interpreters of hints" or דורשי חֲמוּרוֹת "interpreters of difficult passages of Scripture," unless one prefers to read ד׳ חוֹמְרוֹת = "interpreters of pearls." The last expression would show the high evaluation that the allegorists must have enjoyed: their sayings were regarded as precious pearls.[190] As can only be expected, symbolic-allegorical scriptural interpretation in Palestine was applied above all to the nonlegal parts of Scripture. Yet there are a great number of such interpretations in the case of legal texts as well. We will go into more detail with respect to the latter kind in the present context. Here the examples to be quoted will make clear the great difference that existed between Alexandrian and Palestinian allegory. The interpretations of the law in rabbinic writing that are of a symbolic-allegorical sort can be grouped most simply in the following manner.

A. Symbolic interpretation tends to be used when explaining the reasons for a law.

Tosefta Baba Qamma 7.1ff. (357): The thief pays a double compensation; yet if he has slaughtered and sold (the stolen animal), he pays a four- and fivefold compensation. The robber, in either event, compensates for only the actual value (cf. Exod 22:3; 21:37; and 22:2). His students asked R. Yohanan b. Zakkai († ca. 80), "For what reason did the Torah set a heavier penalty for thieves than for robbers?" He answered them, "The robber has put the honor of the servant (= the person stolen from) and the honor of his lord (= God) on the same level; the thief shows the servant honor far beyond the honor of his lord; the thief makes the eye above (= the eye of God) as it were into one that does not see and the ear into one that does not hear; as it says, 'Woe to those who bury themselves deep before Yahweh to nurture secret counsel, and whose works happen in darkness and who say, "Who sees us and who sees through us?"' (Isa 29:5). Those who say, 'Yah does not see us and the God of Jacob does not notice it' (Ps 94:7). For they said, 'Yahweh does not see us, Yahweh has forsaken the land' (so Ezek 9:9 is cited)." – Meaning: The thief hides from men. He supposes that God had not seen him. So, he thinks more highly of men than of God. The robber acts openly and thereby at least does not set men higher than God; hence the different punishments for the two. – There is a parallel in b. B. Qam. 79B. ‖ Tosefta Baba Qamma 7.3ff. (357): R. Yohanan b. Zakkai († ca. 80) said five words as a kind of pearl חוֹמֶר:[191] (The 1st and 2nd words pertain to the nonlegal matters; the 3rd word is:) "If אֲשֶׁר a leader sins ..." (Lev 4:22).

190. On the individual designations, see Bacher, *Die Agada der Tannaïten*, 1:29f., 31f.

191. Bacher, *Die Agada der Tannaïten*, 1:29f.

Blessed אַשְׁרֵי is the generation whose leader brings a sin offering because of unintentional sin![192] Further he said (the 4th word), "Let his master pierce his ear with an awl" (Exod 21:6). Why is the ear pierced instead of all the other members? Because he heard from Mount Sinai: "For to me the children of Israel are servants, they are my servants" (Lev 25:55), and (nevertheless) it cast from itself the yoke of God and made the yoke of a man its master. Therefore Scripture says, "Let the ear come, so that it may be pierced, because it has not kept what it heard." (Parallels are found in Mek. Exod. 21:6 (83B); b. Qidd. 22B; y. Qidd. 1.59D.26.) ... It further says (5th word): "(You shall build) an altar of stones; you will not brandish iron over them" (Deut 27:5). Why is iron declared unfit (objectionable) instead of all other kinds of metal? Because the sword is destined to be made from it. The sword is a sign סִימָן (σημεῖον? symbol) of punishment and the altar a sign of atonement. That which is a sign of punishment should be kept far from that which is a sign of atonement. And see, the inference from the lesser to the greater is valid: if, because they make atonement between Israel and their father in heaven, Scripture says about stones, which neither see nor hear nor speak, that "You may not brandish iron over them," how much more does it go for the sons of the Torah, who are an atonement for the world, that none of all the wreckers (evil spirits) may touch them! See, it says, "You shall build the altar of Yahweh your God out of unbroken שלימות (which can also mean = 'peaceful') stones" (Deut 27:6). Concerning the stones which make peace between Israel and their Father in heaven (by the sacrifices presented on them), God says, "They should be unbroken (perfect) before me!" How much more does it go for the sons of the Torah, who are bringers of peace (so שְׁלֵימִים might mean here) for the world, that they should be perfect שְׁלֵימִים before God! (Parallels are found in Mek. Exod. 20:25 (81A); tractate Semaḥot 8, at the end.) ‖ Tosefta Baba Qamma 7.10 (359): R. Meir (ca. 150) said, "Come and see, how beloved (expensive, worthy) is the work before the one who spoke and the world came into being: since he (the thief) let the (stolen) ox free from its work, he must refund five times as much; in the case of sheep, since it is not responsible for any work, he refunds four times as much (cf. Exod 21:37)." Rabban Yohanan b. Zakkai († ca. 80) said, "Come and see, how gently God deals with the honor of human beings: since the (stolen) ox walks away on its own feet, (the thief) pays a fivefold amount; in the case of a sheep, since he must carry it (which affects its value), he refunds a fourfold amount." — Parallels are found in Mek. Exod. 21:37 (95A); b. B. Qam. 79B. ‖ Sifre Deuteronomy 18:3 § 165 (106B): "Let the priest be given the upper part of the leg and the jawbone and the stomach" (Deut 18:3). R. Judah (ca. 150) said, "The allegorists דורשי רשומות have said, 'Let him give him the upper part of the leg instead of the hand, and so it says, "Then (Phinehas) arose from the midst of the community and took a spear in his 'hand'" (Num 25:7). "The jawbone": this refers to the law, and so it says, "Then Phinehas went and prayed" (so Ps 106:30 according to the midr.). The stomach for: "The womb, into her womb" (Num 25:8).'" — The three things that are due to the priests are thus symbols that should remind people of the deed of Phinehas the priest. — In the parallel b. Ḥul. 134B, we read דורשי חמורות. ‖ Semaḥot 8 (16D): The allegorists ד' חמודת (read: חמורות) have said, "'You shall

192. S-B: Parallels include SLev 4:22 (89B); b. Hor. 10B.

tear down their altars ...' (Deut 12:3). How did the trees and stones sin (so that they should be destroyed)? Only because a stumbling block has come to man because of them has Scripture said, 'You shall tear down.' Look, here the inference from the lesser to the greater is valid: if, because a stumbling block comes to man because of them, the Torah said about trees and stones, which have neither merit nor guilt, give neither good nor evil, 'And you shall tear down' (Deut 12:3), how much more does this go for the person who has caused another to sin and turned life on the way of death!" ‖ Sifre Numbers 5:15 § 8 (4A): "Let the husband ... bring a tenth of an *ephah* of barley flour as her (the wife suspected of not being loyal) offering for her sake" (Num 5:15). R. Simeon b. Gamaliel (ca. 140) said, "Permit me, you scholars, to say a kind of pearl כמין חומר: As her (the suspected woman's) action is an action of cattle, so her offering is the feed of cattle." — In b. Soṭah 15A.34 and Num. Rab. 9 (155A) Rabban Gamaliel (ca. 90) is the author. ‖ Jerusalem Talmud Yoma 7.44B.37: (Let him put on a sacred white undergarment, and let white leg coverings be over his flesh ..." [Lev 16:4].) Why in white garments? R. Hiyya b. Ba (ca. 280) said, "As the service above (in heaven) is, so is the service below. As above 'a man among them was clothed in linen' (Ezek 9:2), so too below he should wear a sacred white undergarment." — The same is found in Lev. Rab. 21 (120C). ‖ Jerusalem Talmud Šeqalim 2.46D.20: ("The redemption price for a firstborn was 5 *shekels*" [Num 18:15f.]. "The temple tax is half of a *shekel*" [Exod 30:13ff.].) R. Berekhiah (ca. 340) and R. Levi (ca. 300) said in the name of R. Simeon b. Laqish (ca. 250), "Since they sold the firstborn of Rachel (= Joseph) for 20 silver pieces (4 silver pieces = 1 *shekel*, 20 silver pieces = 5 *shekels*), everyone shall redeem his firstborn son for 20 silver pieces (= 5 *shekels*)." R. Phineas (ca. 360) said in the name of R. Levi (ca. 300), "Since they sold the firstborn of Rachel for 20 silver pieces, so that 1 *tibea* (= half a *shekel* = 2 silver pieces) fell to each of them (the 10 brothers, without Benjamin), everyone shall pay 1 *tibea* (= half a *shekel* = 1 double *drachma*) as his *shekel* (or temple) tax." — The same is found in Pesiq. 19B. ‖ ʾAggadat Berešit 79 (53B): R. Aha (ca. 320) said, "Why are the names of the tribes given on the stones (of the high priest's breastplate)? (See Exod 28:9ff.) Since they were all called priests at Sinai; as it says, 'And you shall be to me a kingdom of priests' (Exod 19:6), God said, 'It is not possible for all to be able to present (offerings) on the altar, so all their names shall be written on the heart of the high priest: when the high priest enters to sacrifice before me, it is as if every one of them were a high priest before me, clothed in priestly garments.'" ‖ Leviticus Rabbah 16 (116D): "Let the priest command that two living clean birds be brought for the one who is cleansed (of leprosy)" (Lev 14:4). R. Judah b. Simon (ca. 320) said, "These were noisy (loudly chirping) birds. God said, 'Let the voice come and make atonement for the tribe (of the slanderer, for leprosy is usually the punishment for slander).'" ‖ "On the first day take for yourselves magnificent tree fruits, palm branches ..." (Lev 23:40); on this, see R. Abin in Lev. Rab. 30 (128A) in the excursus "The Feast of Tabernacles," II, C, #1. ‖ Babylonian Talmud Soṭah 46A: R. Yohanan b. Saul (ca. 220) said, "Why did the Torah say, 'Let the cow be brought into the valley (where it is neither plowed nor seeded)' (Deut 21:4). God said, 'Let what has not yet borne fruits (= a young cow) come, so that its neck may be broken in a place that bears no fruits (= valley) and make atonement for the one who has not been allowed to bear fruits (= someone who has been murdered).'" ‖ See Pesiq. 189A in the excursus "The Feast of Tabernacles," I, C, last paragraph. ‖ Leviticus Rabbah 3 (106D): "Let him remove its goiter with the feathers" (Lev 1:16). R. Tanḥum b. Hanilai (ca. 280) said, "A bird flies and flutters around everywhere and eats on all sides and eats from stolen and robbed goods. Here God says, 'Since this gullet is full of stolen and robbed goods, it shall not be presented on the altar.' Therefore, it says, 'Let him remove its goiter' (Lev 1:16). Yet the large livestock at its master's manger does not eat from all sides, from stolen and robbed goods; therefore this one is brought as an offering (see Lev 1:13)."

B. Allegorical interpretation is applied where terms and expressions are reinterpreted to give a different meaning to individual stipulations within a law or a different reference to a whole law. This type of law-allegorizing was never given free range entirely, though. It would touch on the letter of the Torah, and then one would shy away from it. There are therefore only a few examples.[a] According to the 32 middot of R. Eliezer b. Yose the Galilean (ca. 150)[193] the halakah adopted only two of these interpretations.[b]

a. Mekilta Exodus 21:19 (88B): "If he gets up and walks outside with it" (Exod 21:19). I take from this: within the house. Scripture teaches: "outside." I take from this: even if he wastes away. Scripture teaches: "with his staff," that is, in his healthy strength על בוריו. (As מַשְׁעֵן and מַשְׁעֵנָה "staff" and "support" in Isa 3:1 stand allegorically for bread and water, or for protective superiors, so too in Exod 21:19 מִשְׁעַנְתּוֹ "his staff" should be interpreted allegorically = "healthy strength" בּ͏ִירִי. The reason for this reinterpretation would have been that the whole thrust of the law in Exod 21:18f. appears to allow the one who struck the blow to go unpunished only in the case when the one who was struck regains his complete health.) This is one of the three words that R. Ishmael († ca. 135) interpreted parabolically (i.e., allegorically) as he sat there (and presented). Likewise: "If the sun has risen over him (the thief, and he is slain), there is bloodguilt because of him" (Exod 22:2). Does the world rise only over him; does it not rise over the whole world? (What are these words supposed to mean?) Just that as the sun means peace in the world, so too, if it is certain concerning him (the thief) that he intended to act peacefully toward him (the one stolen from; that is, without intending to kill him), and he (the one stolen from) killed him, this one (the one stolen from) is guilty (of manslaughter). Likewise: "They are to spread out the dress (of the woman whose virginity is under suspicion) before the elders of the city" (Deut 22:17), that is, the things should be presented as clearly as a garment. Even here (Exod 21:19) you will have to say: "with his staff," that is, in his healthy strength. — Parallels are found in SDeut 22:17 § 237 (117B); y. Ketub. 4.28C.11; Mek. Exod. 22:2 (95B); y. Sanh. 8.26C.5. ‖ Sifre Deuteronomy 21:13 § 213 (113A): "'She should mourn her father and her mother' (Deut 21:13). Her actual father and her actual mother." These are the words of R. Eliezer (ca. 90). R. Aqiba († ca. 135) said, "'Her father and her mother' means nothing other than idols; as it says, 'Those who say to wood, "You are my father"' (Jer 2:27)." — The same is found in b. Yebam. 48A. — The point of the reinterpretation is that a captive woman should be married only after she converts to Judaism. ‖ Targum Yerušalmi I Deuteronomy 24:6: "A man should not

193. See Strack, *Einleitung in den Talmud und Midraš*, 100–108.

impound the lower and the upper millstone (on this explanation, see § Matt 18:6 C, #1, n. *g*); for in that way he impounds necessities that are used to prepare sustenance for every soul (for everyone). And let there not be a man who holds grooms and brides at bay (young married couples on their wedding night) by magic (hinders intercourse; cf. the German 'Nestelknüpfen'); for in doing so he destroys מְחַבֵּל (or: he wards off?) a soul that was to proceed from them." — Here two interpretations of Deut 24:6 stand alongside each other, one literal and one allegorical. The latter owes its origin to the hermeneutical principle, which was often used and which for the haggadah in particular was extraordinarily fruitful, that two passages of Scripture that follow one after the other should be related in content and explained from each other.[194] Since the preceding verse (Deut 24:5) speaks about the marital joy of a young couple, the converse prohibition not to hinder them in this joy by magic was put into verse 6. Allegory served as the means of proof: רֵחַיִם lower millstone = woman (cf. Job 31:10); רֶכֶב upper millstone = man; and חָבַל impound = חָבַר bind, hold at bay. On the whole, though, we have an example of how a completely different law could be put in place of another by means of allegory. The original law corresponding to the wording is not thereby meant to be abolished; it maintains its validity in its full scope. However, one could be proud of having found by allegorical interpretation the halakic basis for a prohibition, which the Torah does not explicitly mention otherwise. — In Tg. Yer. II, the allegorical interpretation is as follows: "And you shall not hold at bay grooms and brides; for anyone who does this is like someone who denies the life of the future world." — Underlying this is the view that the blessed time of consummation could only dawn when the number of human souls determined beforehand by God had in fact seen the light of the world. Whoever hinders a couple from procreating thereby impedes the coming of the future world and thus is regarded as one who has denied that world; on this understanding, see § John 1:1 A, C, #5. — It is difficult to say how old this allegorical interpretation of Deut 24:6 is. Yet it is already present in an interpretation on Gen 3:16 by R. Yose the Galilean (ca. 110), except R. Yose makes not someone else but rather the husband himself the "binding one" or the "one who holds at bay." Genesis Rabbah 20 (13D): "He shall be master over you" (Gen 3:16). R. Yose the Galilean said, "Is he supposed to be master over her in every respect? Scripture teaches, 'He shall not bind (= hold at bay) the lower and the upper millstone (not withhold intercourse from the woman by an oath)' (Deut 24:6)." ‖ Another example, where two sections of Scripture following each other became an opportunity for allegorically interpreting a stipulation of the law, is found in the passage Tg. Yer. I Deut. 25:4 presented above at § 1 Cor 9:9 A, #2: You shall not bridle the mouth of an ox at the time when it threshes. You shall also not bind a (childless widowed) sister-in-law who has fallen (in levirate marriage) to a leper or someone else who is (otherwise) not fitting for her (literally: you shall not put a muzzle for his sake). — Here the levirate law in verse 5 immediately follows on the prohibition against binding the mouth of a threshing ox (Deut 25:4). The inner relation of both laws with each other and to each other was established in the manner above by allegorically reinterpreting the prohibition against binding the ox's mouth into the other prohibition against binding

194. S-B: Sifre Numbers 25:1 § 131 (47A): R. Aqiba († ca. 135) said, "Every passage of Scripture that is right next to another should be interpreted from the latter."

a widowed sister-in-law unconditionally and without exception to just any brother-in-law, or thus being able as it were to put a muzzle on her. The prescription not to put a muzzle on a threshing ox was not of course thereby supposed to be abolished, but rather the allegorical interpretation aimed only at finding a biblical basis for the halakah already established long ago that exceptions to the levirate law are permissible. ‖ On Lev 19:14 see § Rom 14:13.

b. The 32 *middoth* (regulations) of R. Eliezer b. Yose the Galilean #26 (according to the wording in the Babylonian Talmud, at the beginning of tractate Berakot): "With the words of the Torah (with the literal stipulations of the law), you may not apply parabolic (allegorical) interpretations, except for the three words that R. Ishmael interpreted as parabolic speech. And the halakah complies with his words in two cases: (α) 'If he gets up and goes outside with his staff' (Exod 21:19), that is, in his healthy strength על בוריו; for if you should say, 'With his stick' he would be sick (which the law in Exod 21:18f. obviously does not mean). Rather it teaches that Scripture speaks of the staff of his (healthy) body, as when he supports himself on his stick. Likewise: (β) 'If the sun has risen over him, there is bloodguilt because of him' (Exod 22:2). How can this be? Did the sun rise over him alone? Rather, as the sun means peace in the world, so too in the case of the one manslayer: if the owner knows that he (the thief) wants only peace, behold, the owner (if he slays him) is guilty because of his blood. In these two cases, the halakah accords with R. Ishmael. And the third word (of R. Ishmael, which, however, has not been adopted by the halakah): 'And they shall spread out the dress' (Deut 22:17); they shall present the words clearly like a garment."

C. Allegorical interpretation of an entire law is also applied when reinterpretation is used to obtain a point of contact or material for haggadic expositions of any kind. Such allegorizations of the law did not at all affect the law in question. They ultimately signified a harmless homiletic playfulness. Therefore its usage never caused trouble.

Leviticus Rabbah 13 (114C): (R. Samuel b. Nahman [ca. 260] said,) "Moses beheld the empires in their proceedings עֵסוּק (effectiveness). (But you shall not eat this one of the animals that chew the cud and of those that have the cloven hoof:) 'The camel' גָּמָל (Lev 11:4). Babylon is meant, for it says, '(Daughter of Babylon, you devastator,) blessed is the one who repays you for your actions which you have done to us' את גמולך שגמלת לנו (Ps 137:8). 'The rock badger' (Lev 11:5): Media is meant." The rabbis and R. Judah b. Simon (ca. 320). The rabbis said, "As the rock badger has in itself signs of uncleanness and signs of cleanness, so the kingdom of Media suppled a righteous man (= Mordecai) and a godless man (= Haman)." R. Judah b. Simon said, "The last Darius, the son of Esther, was clean from his mother (mother's side) and unclean from his father. 'And the hare' (Lev 11:6): Greece is meant. The mother of Ptolemy had the name אַרְנֶבֶת = Λαγώς 'hare.' (Ptolemy I Lagi [323–285] is meant.) 'And the pig' (Lev 11:7): Edom (= Rome) is meant...." R. Phineas (ca. 360) and R. Hilkiah (ca. 320) said in the name of R. Simon (ca. 280), "Of all the prophets, only two have made it (the pig = Rome) known (depicted it more precisely), Asaph and Moses. Asaph said, 'The pig from the forest strips it (the vine = Israel) bear' (Ps 80:14). Moses said, 'And the pig; for it has a cloven hoof ...' (Lev 11:7). Why is it (Rome) compared with a pig? To tell you that as the pig stretches out its hooves when it sets itself down and (thereby) says, 'See that I am clean' (for my hoof is split), so the kingdom of Edom proudly rises up and commits acts of violence and robs (and in the process acts) as if it set down a judgment seat (acts only according to justice).... A different explanation. 'The camel' (Lev 11:4): this is Babylon. 'For it chews the cud': for it praises God." R. Berekhiah (ca. 340) and R. Helbo (ca. 300) said in the name of R. Samuel b. Nahman (ca. 260; so read instead of R. Ishmael b. Nahman), "Every single thing that David said was summarized by that blasphemer (Nebuchadnezzar) in one verse; as it says, 'Accordingly, I, Nebuchadnezzar, praise, exalt, and extol the king of heaven ...' (Dan 4:34).... 'And the rock badger' (Lev 11:5): this is Media; 'for it chews the cud.' It praises God, as it says, 'Thus says Cyrus, the king of Persia, ("Yahweh has given all the kingdoms of the earth to me ...")' (Ezra 1:2). 'And the hare' (Lev 11:6): this is Greece; 'for it chews the cud.' It praises God. When Alexander of Macedonia caught sight of R. Simeon the Righteous, he said, 'Blessed be the God of Simeon the Righteous!' 'The pig' (Lev 11:7): this is Edom; 'but it does not chew the cud,' for it does not praise God; and it is not enough that it does not praise God, it even reviles and slanders and says, 'Who is there for me in heaven?!' (Ps 73:25). A different explanation. 'The camel': this is Babylon; 'for it chews the cud' מעלה גרה ('brings up the cud'), for it exalted Daniel (see Dan 2:49). 'And the rock badger': this is Media; 'for it chews the cud'; for it exalted Mordecai (see Esth 2:21). 'And the hare': this is Greece; 'for it chews the cud': for it exalted the righteous. When Alexander had caught sight of Simeon the Righteous, he had set himself on his feet (had stood in front of him). The sectarians (perhaps Samaritans) said to him, 'You stand up before a Jew?' He answered them, 'When I went out to battle, I saw his form (his image) and conquered.' 'And the pig': this is Edom; 'and it does not chew the cud,' for it does not exalt the righteous. It is not enough that it does not exalt them, it even kills them. This is what is written, 'I was angry with my people; I desecrated my possession' (Isa 47:6). 'My possession': this is R. Aqiba († ca. 135) and those he trained. A different explanation. 'And the camel': this is Babylon; 'for it chews the cud' מעלה גרה, for it brought גררה a (different) kingdom (was superseded by a following kingdom). 'And the hare':[195] this is Greece; 'for it chews the cud': brought a (different) kingdom. 'And the rock badger': this is Media; 'for it chews the cud': for it brought a (different) kingdom. 'And the pig': this is Edom; 'and it does not chew the cud': for it will not bring (another) kingdom (Rome is the fourth and last empire). And why is it called 'pig' חֲזִיר? Because it will give back מְהַזֶּרֶת the crown to its Lord (= God). This is what is written, 'Liberators will go up onto Mount Zion to judge the mountain of Esau, and the kingship will fall to Yahweh' (Obad 21)." — See the parallel passages at § Matt 7:6, C, #2. Here reference may also be made to Tanḥ. שמיני 150A and TanḥB שמיני § 14 (16A). ‖ Genesis Rabbah 65 (41C): R. Isaac (ca. 300) said, "... 'And let the goat שָׂעִיר bear all their sins עֲוֹנֹתָם' (Lev 16:22). (The goat:) this is Esau, for it says, 'See, my brother Esau is a hairy man אִישׁ שָׂעִיר' (Gen 27:11). 'All their transgressions,' that is, the transgressions of the smooth one עֲוֹנוֹת תָּם (= Jacobs); as it says, 'And Jacob was a smooth תָּם man' (Gen 25:27)." ‖ Pesiqta 55B: R. Berekhiah (ca. 340) said in the name of R. Isaac (ca. 300), "'Let this month חוֹדֶשׁ be for you the beginning רֹאשׁ of the months; let it be the first for you' (Exod 12:2). Renew חדשו your works,

195. S-B: This and the next sentence should be transposed.

for the head ראשׁ and the first will come one day. The head: this is Nebuchadnezzar; as it says, 'You are the head of gold' (Dan 2:38). The first: this is Esau (= the 4th empire); as it says, 'The first one came out red' (Gen 25:25). And who will take vengeance for you on the head and the first? God, who is the first; as it says, 'I, Yahweh, am the first and with the last, I am the same' (Isa 41:4). And who will take vengeance for you on Media, on the 'tenth' of the month (Exod 12:3)?" For R. Abin (I, ca. 325; II, ca. 370) said, "(בֶּעָשׂר in Exod 12:3 means:) בָּא עָשׂוֹר 'the number ten comes,' the ten of Haman (i.e., the 10,000 talents that Haman promised for the edict of murder in Esth 3:9) and his ten sons. Who will take vengeance for you on them? The two delegates, Mordecai and Esther: Mordecai outside and Esther inside (in the palace). Who will take vengeance for you on Greece? (Here presumably there is missing an indication that Greece is meant by the lamb mentioned twice in Exod 12:3.) The Hasmoneans who daily presented the two Tamid offerings. Who will take vengeance for you on Edom? The one who waits נְטִירוּתָא (a name for the Messiah; see § Matt 1:21 B, #2, n. *m*); as it says, 'Let it be for you for safekeeping' (Exod 12:6)." — A parallel passage is found in Pesiq. Rab. 15 (79A). ‖ Pesiqta 40B: ("Tell the children of Israel to bring a red cow without flaw, with no flaw in its body, which has never had a yoke put on it" [Num 19:2].) "A cow": Egypt is meant; for it says, "Egypt is a magnificent little cow" (Jer 46:20). "Red" pertains to Babylon; for it says, "You are the head of (red) gold" (Dan 2:38). "Without flaw" pertains to Media. R. Hiyya b. Abba (ca. 280; so read instead of R. Judah b. Abba) said, "The kings of Media were flawless, and God had nothing against them other than that they served idols that had been handed down to them from their ancestors. (The relative clause aims to portray their idolatry in a milder light.) 'With no flaw in its body' pertains to Greece. When Alexander of Macedonia had caught sight of Simeon the Righteous, he had set himself on his feet (had stood up in front of him) and said, 'Blessed be the God of Simeon the Righteous!' His palace gentry said to him, 'You set yourself on your feet in front of a Jew?' He answered them, 'When I went into combat, I saw a form that was like his, and conquered.' 'Which has never had a yoke put on it': this refers to Edom (Rome) who did not accept God's commandments. And it is not enough that it did not accept them; it reviles and even slanders and says, 'Who is there for me in heaven?!' (Ps 73:25). 'And you shall hand it over to the priest Eleazar' (Num 19:3). Why was it prepared by Eleazar and not by Aaron? Because the latter was complicit in making the (golden) calf. 'And let it be led out in front of the camp' (Num 19:3), because he (God) will one day dispel its (Edom's = Rome's) archangel from his *mechiṣa* (his heavenly dwelling). 'And let it be slaughtered before him' (Num 19:3); for it says, 'Yahweh has an offering festival (sacrificial festival) in Bozrah (the Edomite capital)' (Isa 34:6). 'And the cow will be burnt before his eyes' (Num 19:5); (for it says,) 'And it (the 4th animal = Rome) was given over to be burned with fire' (Dan 7:11). 'Its hide and its flesh and its blood' (Num 19:5): it itself together with the leaders and eparchs and generals. This is what is written, 'Your prosperity and your trade goods, your wares ... (will sink into the heart of the sea)' (Ezek 27:27)." R. Samuel b. Isaac (ca. 300) said, "Also those who belong to my (Israel's) community and come and bind themselves to your (Rome's) community, they too 'will sink into the heart of the sea on the day of your foundering' (Ezek 27:27)." — A different explanation. "A cow" (Num 19:2): the Israelites are meant; for it is written,

"Like a stubborn cow, Israel has become stubborn" (Hos 4:16). "Red": this refers to Israel; "With a body redder than pearls (corals?)" (Lam 4:7). "Without flaw": this refers to Israel; "My dove, my flawless (unscathed) one" (Song 6:9). "With no flaw in its body": this refers to Israel; "And there is no flaw in you" (Song 4:7). "Which has never had a yoke put on it": this refers to the generation of Jeremiah, which did not accept God's yoke. "And you shall hand it over to the priest Eleazar": this refers to Jeremiah "from the priests at Anathoth" (Jer 1:1). "And let it be led out in front of the camp": "And he led the people to Babylon, into captivity" (Ezra 5:12). "And let it be slaughtered before him": "And they slaughtered the sons of Zedekiah before his eyes" (2 Kgs 25:7). "And the cow shall be burned": "He burned the house of Yahweh and the house of the king" (Jer 52:13). "Its hide and its flesh ...": "And all the houses of Jerusalem and the great house he burned with fire" (so 2 Kgs 25:9 is quoted). Why does he call it a "great house"? It was the school of R. Yohanan b. Zakkai († ca. 80), where the greatness and the praise of God were taught. "And let him take it" (Num 19:6): this refers to Nebuchadnezzar. "The priest": this refers to Jeremiah; for it says, "Take him and keep an eye on him" (Jer 39:12); "Cedar and hyssop and crimson": Hananiah, Mishael, and Azariah are meant. "And cast in the midst of the burning cow": "The flame of the fire killed them" (Dan 3:22). "And gather it" (Num 19:9): this is God, as it says, "He will raise a banner for the gentiles and gather the exiles of Israel" (Isa 11:12). "A man": this is God, as it says, "Yahweh is a man of war" (Exod 15:3). "A clean one": this is God, as it says, "You whose eye is too pure to look at evil" (Hab 3:13). "The ashes of the cow": these are the exiles of the Israelites. "And put them down outside the camp in a clean place": this is Jerusalem, which is clean. "And let it serve the community of the children of Israel for safekeeping," because in this world the Israelites are declared unclean and clean according to the word of the priest; but in the future world it will not be so; for it says, "I will sprinkle clean water over you so that you may be clean from all your uncleanness and I will cleanse you from all your idols" (Ezek 36:25). — Parallel passages are found in Pesiq. Rab. 14 (65A); TanḥB חקת § 27 and 28 (60A). ‖ Tanḥuma כי תצא 20A: "If there is a man among you who is not clean ..." (Deut 23:11). The Israelites are meant who had defiled themselves with idolatry; as it says, "You will scatter them like unclean things. 'Away with you!' you will call to it" (Isa 30:22). "He shall thus go out to the camp" (Deut 23:11); for they will go into exile in Babylon. "In the evening, though" (Deut 23:12), in the evening (at the end) of empires God will declare it (Israel) clean; as it says, "When Yahweh has washed away the filth of the daughters of Zion" (Isa 4:4). "And when the sun goes down" (Deut 23:12): when the king, the Messiah, comes; as it says, "And his throne will be like the sun before me" (Ps 89:37). "He may come into the camp" (Deut 23:12): these are the Israelites when they come into the sanctuary. "And you shall have a place יָד outside the camp" (Deut 23:13): this refers to the merit of Abraham (יד = handle to grab on to, to support). R. Phineas (ca. 360) said, "'And you shall go out there' (Deut 23:13): outside of Babylon. 'And you shall have a spade among your implements' (Deut 23:14); Nebuchadnezzar will demand of them that they serve the idol, and they will say, 'We will not venerate your God' (Dan 3:18). (אֲזֵנֶךָ is interpreted = אָזְנְךָ 'your ear': you shall have a peg to clog your ear against idolatrous impertinences.) 'And cover your refuse' (Deut 23:4): this refers to covering the idolatry that was in Jerusalem. 'For Yahweh your God walks in the midst of your camp' (Deut 23:15); Yahweh revealed himself immediately over them (Hananiah, Mishael, and Azariah) and saved them out of the fire. 'So let your camp be holy' (Deut 23:15); then God will sanctify them (Israel); as it says, 'They will be called "the holy people," "the redeemed of Yahweh"' (Isa 62:12)." ‖ Leviticus Rabbah 15 (116A): "If someone gets a swelling שְׂאֵת on the skin of his flesh" (Lev 13:2): this refers to Babylon because of the words "Then you will raise ונשאת this song of mockery against the king of Babylon and say, 'How the slave driver has ceased, the מַדְהֵבָה come to an end'" (Isa 14:4). R. Abba b. Kahana (ca. 310) said, "'The מדהבה has come to an end': this is a government that says, 'Do without and bring!' מדוד והבא." R. Samuel b. Nahman (ca. 260) said, "A government that makes a person's face blush מדהבת when he comes to it." The rabbis said because of the words: "Its head was of gold" (Dan 2:32) and "You are the head of gold דַּהֲבָא" (Dan 2:38; Babylon is called מדהבה in Isa 14:4). "'A rash' סַפַּחַת (Lev 13:2): this refers to Media, which let the godless Haman arise, who crushed ששף (so read instead of ששך; שף is supposed to interpret ספחת). He did it like a snake because of the words, 'You will creep on your stomach (... you will crush his heel תשופנו)' (Gen 3:14f.). 'A light spot' בַּהֶרֶת (Lev 13:2): this refers to Greece, which bulged מבהרת (so read instead of מכחדת) with its edicts over Israel and said to them, 'Write on the ox's horn that you have no share in the God of Israel' (= renounce your God; see § John 1:1 D, first S-B footnote). 'A leprous disease' (Lev 13:2): this refers to Edom (= Rome), which (by Esau) came from the power of the old man (= Isaac, who blessed him with the words, 'But if you toil, you will break his [Jacob's] yoke' [Gen 27:40], and therefore it [Rome] is the most difficult of all the exiles, like a leprous disease, *Kommentar Matthenoth Kehunna*); because of the words: 'And if it becomes a leprous disease on the skin of his flesh (he should be brought to Aaron the priest)' (Lev 13:2), because in this world the priest looks at leprous diseases. 'But in the future world,' says God, 'I will declare you clean.' This is what is written, 'I will sprinkle clean water over you so that you may be clean' (Ezek 36:25)." ‖ Leviticus Rabbah 17 (117B): "When I cause a leprous disease to arise in a house of the land of your possession" (Lev 14:34): this refers to the sanctuary; as it says, "Behold, I will desecrate my sanctuary, the pride of your strength" (Ezek 24:21). "The one whose house it is shall come" (Lev 14:35): this is God; as it says, "Because of my house, which lies desolate" (Hag 1:9). "And notify the priest" (Lev 14:35): this is Jeremiah; as it says, "From the priests at Anathoth" (Jer 1:1). "Some sort of disease appears to be in my house" (Lev 14:35): this is the filth of idolatry. Some say, "This is the idol of Manasseh. This is what is written, 'And behold, north of the altar gate there was an image of jealousy at the entrance בביאה' (Ezek 8:5). What does בביאה mean?" R. Aha (ca. 320) said, "Woe! Woe! בְּיָיה בְּיָיה (thus Woe! twice as an interpretation of ב in front of ביאה in Ezek 8:5). The resident alien dispels the lord of the house!" R. Berekhiah (ca. 340) said, "It is written, 'The bed is too short to stretch out' (Isa 28:20). The bed cannot hold a wife and her husband and her lover at the same time: 'the cover is too narrow to hide under' (Isa 28:20). You have prepared a great affliction for the one about whom it is written, 'He gathers the waters of the sea as into a pipe' (Ps 33:7) (how can such a God dwell with an idol in one house!). 'And the priest shall command that the house be cleared out' (Lev 14:36). 'And he (Shishak) took the treasures of the house of Yahweh ...' (1 Kgs 14:26). 'And the house shall be torn down' (Lev 14:45). 'And he (Nebuchadnezzar) destroyed this house' (Ezra 5:12).

'And it shall be carried out to the camp' (so the midr. cites Lev 14:45). 'And he led the people away to Babylon' (Ezra 5:12). Perhaps forever? Scripture teaches, 'And other stones shall be taken' (Lev 14:42); for it says, 'Therefore Yahweh the Lord has said, "Behold, I have established a stone on Zion, a stone of testing, a precious cornerstone with a firmly established substructure: whoever trusts will not have to give way"' (Isa 28:16)." ‖ See TanḥB תרומה § 6 (46A) at § John 1:1 A, D. — Further examples are found in Tanḥ. צו 139B; תזריע 157A; TanḥB תזריע § 16 (21B); Tanḥ. תרומה 100B; Exod. Rab. 35 (95B); Num. Rab. 7 (148B).

Among the citations in A–C, there is no passage that distinguishes between the literal meaning and the deeper significance of a law. In every case of allegorizing, the literal sense always retains its full validity, and even when a law is given a different meaning or another reference by allegorical reinterpretation (cf. the examples under B), the literal sense is not thereby abolished. At the most, a different letter of the law takes the place of the original letter of the law. This is the difference between the allegory of the Alexandrians and that of the Palestinian scholars. The Alexandrians see in the wording of the laws more or less an external form, a shadowy symbol; only the allegorical interpretation is what gives spirit and life to the letter by freeing the deeper significance, the actual spiritual substance from the shell of the literal sense. Whoever clings only to the letter of the law expends his strength on the external and therefore ephemeral. By contrast, whoever clings to the deeper sense of the commandments which makes the underlying idea the guide of life, he alone does justice to the actual intentions of the lawgiver. — The nomism of rabbinic Judaism was entirely different. How do we know, asks R. Eleazar b. Azariah (ca. 100) in SLev 20:26 (374A), that a person should not say, "I do not like to eat pork, I do not like to lie with women whom it is forbidden to marry," (but rather that he should say,) "I do like it, but what should I do, since my Father, who is in heaven, has made this decision over me?" Scripture teaches, "I have set you apart from the nations so that you might belong to me" (Lev 20:26). So he will be found as someone who sets himself apart from sin, and as one who accepts the yoke of God's lordship (the kingdom of heaven). In SLev 18:4 (338A) we read, "My statutes" (Lev 18:4). Here, what is meant are the stipulations (in the Torah) to which the evil inclination and the *ʿakum* (gentiles, non-Israelites) take exception, such as those concerning consuming pork, clothing made of mixed material, the removal of the shoe by the sister-in-law (in the case when levirate marriage is refused), the cleansing of lepers, the red cow, the goat sent into the wilderness, to which the evil inclination and the *ʿakum* take exception. Here it says, "I, Yahweh, have established them. You are not entitled to take exception to them."[196] Finally, Rab († 247) says in Tanḥ. שמיני 149B: "All the ways of God are

196. S-B: See the whole passage at § Rom 1:20 E, n. *a*.

irreproachable (cf. Ps 18:31). What does God care (why does God inquire) if an animal is ritually slaughtered and eaten or if it is killed by stabbing (a nonritual manner) and eaten? Do you do him any good or harm him at all? Or what does God care if something clean or pleasing is eaten? Solomon said, 'If you are wise, you are wise for your own sake; but if you are a mocker, you alone have to bear it' (Prov 9:12). See, the commandments were given only to purify humanity[197] by means of them; as it says, 'Every word of Yahweh is purification' (so Ps 18:31 according to the midr.)."[198] — These passages correctly render the fundamental standpoint of nomistic Judaism: God has given his law as it is, and as it is, it should be kept. A person is not entitled to take exception of any sort to it; it should be enough for him to know that it is God's will. Whoever acts accordingly acknowledges God's lordship and will be purified by the law and will receive his recompense. According to this view, allegorical interpretation of the law that looks for the idea, for the deeper sense of the individual commandments has no justification whatsoever. It could not give the law new content or new life; at the most, it could dissipate and dissolve the law as it was written. It was therefore only logical when this kind of interpretation of the law was not cultivated in the schools of the motherland. In the whole of ancient rabbinic literature we know of only two passages where one may rightly see paltry vestiges of this kind of interpretation. However, both passages raised a plaque on which they warn about this method of interpretation.[a]

a. Mishnah Megillah 4.9 (= m. Ber. 5.3): If (while presenting during a religious service) someone says "Your mercy extends to a bird's nest" ..., he shall be told to be silent. — It was supposed that in such a person, there was an allegorist, for whom the idea of the supreme divine mercifulness was the most important thing in the law in Deut 22:6f. — See b. Meg. 25A: Why (is he told to be silent)? Two Amorites in the west (Palestine) had different opinions about this. R. Yose b. Abin (ca. 350) and R. Yose b. Zebida (ca. 350). One (namely the latter) said, "Because he brings envy (jealousy) into creation (as if God had mercy on birds but not the rest of creation)." And the other said, "Because he makes the properties of God into pure mercy, while those (commandments) are only (divine) stipulations (which as such should be followed)." Someone came into the presence of Rabbah († 331) before the ark (as the prayer leader). He said, "You care about the bird's nest, care about and have mercy on us! You care for it (the bird) and its young, care about and have mercy on us!" Rabbah said to him, "How this one of the rabbis knows how to put his Lord (= God) in a gracious mood" (of course this is to be understood ironically)! Abbayye († 338/39) said to him, "But we have learned: 'He shall be commanded to be silent'!" What Rabbah intended (with his words) was to sharpen Abbayye's repartee. — The same is found in b. Ber.

197. S-B: The following words: "and the Israelites" should probably be struck as a gloss.

198. S-B: Parallels are found in TanḥB שמיני § 12 (15B); Gen. Rab. 44 (27A), though here Rab is explicitly named as the author; see also Lev. Rab. 13 (114B); Midr. Ps. 18 § 25 (76B) and Midr. Sam. 4 § 1 (27A).

33B. — In the Jerusalem Talmud, the Mishnah above is commented on in y. Meg. 4.75C.7 as follows: R. Phineas (ca. 360) said in the name of R. Simon (ca. 280), "(Whoever says 'Your mercy extends to a bird's nest') is like someone who causes a quarrel (dispute) about the properties of God: your mercy extends to a bird's nest, but your mercy does not extend to that man (= to me?)." R. Yose (ca. 350) said in the name of R. Simon (ca. 280), "He is like one who sets a specified measure (a boundary) to the properties of God: your mercy extends up to a bird's nest (and no further)." A teacher of the Mishnah said, "(The על should mean) 'up until' עד." Another teacher of the Mishnah said, "'to' על." Whoever taught "to" is a support for R. Phineas (see above); whoever taught "up until" is a support for R. Yose. R. Yose b. Bun (ca. 350) said, "Those who make God's properties into pure mercy do not act well (rightly)." — The same is found in y. Ber. 5.9C.15. ‖ The second passage that belongs here is Tg. Yer. I Lev. 22:28: "My people, children of Israel, as our father in heaven is merciful, so you should be merciful on earth: a steer or a sheep, you should not slaughter it with its young on the same day." — R. Yose b. Bun (ca. 350) comments on this paraphrase in y. Ber. 5.9C.20: "Those who translate (Lev 22:28 as) 'My people, children of Israel, as I am merciful in heaven, so you should be merciful on earth: a steer or a sheep, you should not slaughter it with its young on the same day,' do not do so rightly. They make the properties of God (the parallel in y. Meg. 4.75C.11 should perhaps be preferred as correct: the commandments of God) into pure mercy." — R. Yose b. Bun thinks the commandments of the Torah are divine regulations that should simply be followed as such. Therefore, interpreters were wrong to search for the motives and deeper significance of a law, especially when their main purpose was to find only divine mercy everywhere and divine punitiveness nowhere. — See the parallel from y. Meg. 4.75C.11 at § Luke 6:36.

The baraita in b. Sanh. 99A may be a third passage that belongs here, if its text were more certain than it is. The passage reads: R. Eleazar of Modiim († ca. 135) said, "… And whoever propounds interpretations in the Torah that do not correspond to the halakah … has no share in the future world." — It seems reasonable to suppose that the interpretations of the Torah that were contrary to the halakah at the time of Modiim were the explanations to which the law was subject among Christians or Alexandrians. In this case, the words might have contained an official condemnation of allegorical interpretation of the law. However, in the older sources that the baraita above stems from, either the following whole sentence is missing, "whoever propounds interpretations of the Torah that do not correspond to the halakah" (so SNum 15:31 § 112 folio 33A), or the following words are missing, "that do not correspond to the halakah" (so ʾAbot R. Nat. 26 folio 7C, while they are attested only weakly in m. ʾAbot 3.11 and y. Pesaḥ. 6.33B.48). When the words שלא כהלכה are missing, it should be translated: "And whoever uncovers his face against the Torah (i.e., masters the Torah in an impertinent, disrespectful way) has no share in the future world." Here the baraita originally would have had very little to do specifically with allegorical interpretation of the law. Only a later time that wanted to give a concrete reference to the expression "to uncover the face against the Torah" used the addition שלא כהלכה to bestow on the whole statement the meaning that it now has in b. Sanh. 99A, namely that, under the threat of the loss of eternal blessedness, it is forbidden to propound interpretations of the law that do not correspond to the halakah. Here the later time certainly was no longer thinking of allegorical interpretation of the law—as perhaps would have to be assumed by R. Eleazar of Modiim and his contemporaries—but rather in the most general terms of any interpretation of Scripture that inevitably led to results that were not in accord with the received halakah. — On the whole saying of R. Eleazar of Modiim see § Acts 21:21.

9:11: The spiritual ..., the fleshly.

The rabbis have no expressions to replace πνευματικός and σαρκικός; see § 1 Cor 2:14f. and § 3:1, 3. In content, the following contrasts could be drawn on for comparison.

In 1 Enoch 108:8ff., the righteous are portrayed as people "who loved God ... and did not love any item in the world ...; who did not long for earthly food ..., but whose spirits were found pure ..., who loved heaven more than their earthly life." ‖ See t. Pe'ah 4.18 (24) at § Matt 6:19f., #1, second paragraph. ‖ In b. Šabb. 33B, R. Simeon (ca. 150) says of people he sees doing field work: "They leave the life of eternity חיי עולם and occupy themselves with the life of the (fleeting) hour חיי שעה." ‖ Babylonian Talmud Ketubbot 105B: Abbayye († 338/39) said, "If the people of a certain place love a budding scholar, this does not happen because he is particularly excellent, but rather because he reprimands them in heavenly things מִילֵּי דִשְׁמַיָּא but not censoriously." — The "heavenly things" are juxtaposed in b. Ber. 7B with מִילֵּי דִידֵיהּ, the individual, personal concerns of a person. ‖ In b. Pesaḥ. 113A Rab († 247) says to his son Aibo, "Come, I will teach you worldly things מִילֵּי דְעָלְמָא: When the dust (from a purchase) is still on your feet, sell!" (Meaning: quick turnover of goods is most profitable.) ‖ See b. B. Meṣ. 59A at § Col 3:19. — See also § John 3:12.

9:12: But I have made no use of this authority.

1. ἐξουσία = רְשׁוּת = "permission, authority"; then also = "optional" in contrast to מִצְוָה "commanded" or קֶבַע "stipulated."

2. Parallel passages.

Babylonian Talmud Berakot 10B: Abbayye († 338/39), or, it has also been said, R. Isaac (ca. 300), said, "Whoever wants to make use הרוצה להנות (of someone else's goods) may make use of them like Elisha. (There is no supporting passage, though one may think of 2 Kgs 4:8ff.) And whoever does not want to make use of them does not have to make use of them, like Samuel of Ramah; as it says, 'He returned to Ramah, for his home was there' (1 Sam 7:17)." R. Yohanan († 279) said, "Wherever he went, he had his household with him (so as not to live at the expense of others)...." R. Yose b. Hanina (ca. 270) said in the name of R. Eliezer b. Jacob (II, ca. 150), "Whoever accepts (hosts) as a guest a student of the scholars in his house and grants him use of his possessions, Scripture reckons it to him as if he presented the daily offering (the Tamid offering)." ‖ Numbers Rabbah 18 (183D): "I have not taken (even) a donkey from them" (Num 16:15). What I could have taken according to common custom, (Moses said,) I have not taken from them. According to the custom of the world a person who deals with what is sacred receives his recompense from what is sacred, and when I went down from Midian to Egypt, I could have taken a donkey from them according to common custom, since I went down in their interest, but I did not take it from them. And likewise, Samuel the righteous said, "'Look, here I am, testify against me before Yahweh and before his anointed one: whose ox have I taken or whose donkey have I taken?' (1 Sam 12:3). The ox, which I presented for them as an offering, to ask for mercy for them, and likewise to anoint a king for them, whose was it? (Was it not one that belonged to me?) For it says, 'Take a calf with you' (1 Sam 16:2). And likewise, it says, 'The people have a sacrificial offering today on the Bama (high place)' (1 Sam 9:12). I have not taken from what belongs to them. And when I again managed their legal matters and concerns, I went around through all the cities of Israel; as it says, 'He went about year after year and successively visited Bethel … and administered justice in all these places' (1 Sam 7:16). According to the custom of the world the parties go to a judge, but I went around from city to city and from place to place and the donkey (used in the process) belonged to me." — The same is found in TanḥB קרח § 19 (46A).

9:13: Do you not know that those who work with what is holy eat from what comes from the sanctuary?

The same principle in Num. Rab. 18 (183D; see above at § 9:12, #2): According to the custom of the world a person who deals with what is sacred (works with what is hallowed) receives his recompense from what is sacred בנוהג שבעולם אדם שהוא עושה בַהֶקְדֵּשׁ נוטל שכרו מן הַהֶקְדֵּשׁ. — Verbatim the same in TanḥB קרח § 19 (46A).

9:14: So too the Lord ordained that the preacher of the gospel make his living from the gospel.

See § Matt 10:10 E and § 1 Cor 9:7, 9, 12, 14. ‖ Babylonian Talmud Šabbat 114A: R. Yohanan († 279) said, "For what sort of student of the scholars are the inhabitants of a city obliged to do the work he otherwise would do (from which he has sustenance)? The one who leaves his affairs and occupies himself with the affairs of God." ‖ Babylonian Talmud Yoma 72B: R. Yohanan († 279) juxtaposed the following: "'Make a wooden ark for yourself' (Deut 10:1), and 'They shall make the ark from acacia wood' (Exod 25:10). From the fact (that the assignment given to Moses was ultimately to be carried out by the whole people) it follows that the inhabitants of a city are obligated to do for a student of the scholar the work (from which he lives)." ‖ On the nonremuneration of instruction see § Matt 10:8 B.

9:16: For if I preach the gospel, (this) is nothing to boast about for me; for necessity is imposed on me.

Mishnah ʾAbot 2.8: Rabban Yohanan b. Zakkai († ca. 80) … said, "If you have done עָשִׂיתָ much Torah, do not be proud of it; for you were created for this."

9:17 A: Voluntarily ..., involuntarily.

ἑκών ... ἄκων, perhaps = בְּרָצוֹן "with consent, voluntarily" and בְּאוֹנֶס "out of compulsion, compulsorily,"[a] or = מִדַּעְתִּי "with my consent" and בְּעַל כָּרְחִי, עַל כָּרְחִי "against my will."[b]

a. Babylonian Talmud Ketubbot 9A: When it is uncertain whether a woman (has lost her virginity) by compulsion באונס or by consent ברצון....

b. In b. Giṭ. 21A it is said of divorce that it can happen both with her (the wife's) consent and against her will בין מדעתה ובין בעל כורחה, while it says of an endowment that it is valid with her consent מדעתה, but invalid if against her will בעל כורחה.

9:17 B: For if I do this voluntarily, I have a recompense.

See b. B. Qam. 38A at § Rom 2:10; see b. Qidd. 31A at § Rom 5:9f., #2, C; see y. Peʾah 1.15C.14 § Rom 1:30 B. — On the teaching about recompense, see the excursus "The Parable of the Workers in the Vineyard."

9:18: That I make the gospel gratuitous.

On the nonremuneration of instruction, see § Matt 10:8 B.

9:24: In a race.

στάδιον = אִסְטָדִין, אִצְטָדִין, אִסְטַדְיָא, אִצְטַדְיָה.

Mishnah ʿAbodah Zarah 1.7: One may not build with them (the non-Israelites) any hall of judgment, any place of execution, any stadium אִסְטַדְיָא, nor any judgment seat (because in these places perhaps an Israelite could be condemned or killed). ‖ Mishnah Baba Qamma 4.4 toward the end: An ox from the stadium אִצְטָדִין is not guilty of death (when it kills a person in the bullfights); for it says, "If a steer strikes" (Exod 21:28) (namely on its own), and not if it is provoked to strike. ‖ Tosefta ʿAbodah Zarah 2.6f. (462): If someone goes to the races (read איצטדינין instead of איצטרטיונין) and to the siege ramparts and (there) sees sorcerers, snake charmers, buffoons, jesters, equestrian show performers, secular celebrations, and festivals for images (at the close of the Saturnalia), this is considered the seat of mockers; as it says, "And does not sit in the seat of mockers, but rather has his delight in Yahweh's Torah" (Ps 1:1f.). Here you learn that this leads a man to abandon the study of the Torah.... Whoever sits at the racetrack (read איסטדין instead of איסטרטין) is like one who sheds blood. R. Nathan (ca. 160) permitted it for two reasons: because one can cry out and save life, and because one can give testimony for a woman (in case her husband is killed in the animal fights) so she can marry again. Parallel passages are found in y. ʿAbod. Zar. 1.40A.27; b. ʿAbod. Zar. 18B.

9:25 A: The one who fights exercises abstinence in all things.

1. ὁ ἀγωνιζόμενος. — Of the number of "fighters" the rabbinic writings mention specifically gladiators[a] (לוּדִי, לוּדָאָה, לוּדָר = *ludarius*) and wrestlers[b] (אַתְלֵיטִים = ἀθλητής).

a. Exodus Rabbah 30 (91B): "Maintain justice and practice righteousness, for my salvation is near to come" (Isa 56:1). Like a person who came to a city and heard that an act of clemency was to be given (on which occasion animal fights also usually took place). He went and asked a gladiator לודר (who was participating in the animal fights) and said, "When will the act of clemency be arranged?" He answered him, "It is far away." He went and asked the one who was arranging the act of clemency. He said, "It is near." Then he said, "But I asked the gladiator and he said to me, 'It is far away!'" He answered him, "How did you get the idea to ask the gladiator about this? Does he wish me to arrange the act of clemency? Does he not know that he has to go down (into the arena) and (perhaps) be killed?" So the Israelites asked Balaam, "When will salvation come?" He answered them, "I see him (the star), but not now; I catch sight of him, but not near!" (Num 24:17). God said to them, "Is this your opinion too? Do you not know that Balaam will ultimately go down into gehenna and that he (therefore) does not want my salvation to come? Rather, be like your father, who said, 'I (Jacob) hope for your salvation, Yahweh' (Gen 49:18). Hope in salvation, for it is near. Therefore, it says, 'My salvation is near to come' (Isa 56:1)." ‖ Babylonian Talmud Giṭṭin 47A: Resh Laqish (= R. Simeon b. Laqish, ca. 250) was sold (in recent years) to the gladiators לודאי (i.e., the leaders of the gladiatorial fights). He took a sack with him and a round stone (that lay in the sack). He said, "On the last day it is traditional to do for him (the gladiator) everything that he wants from them (since almost certain death awaits him, every wish should be fulfilled for him), so that he may pardon them for his blood." On the last day they said to him, "What is it that you wish?" He answered them, "I wish to seize you and put you down and inflict on each of you one whole and one half blow with the sack." He seized them and put them down; when he had inflicted on each of them a blow with the sack, the soul (of the person in question) departed. If he gnashed with his teeth, he said to him, "You want to play a joke on me? You still have a half blow with the sack from me waiting!" When he had killed them all, he went from there. — For further examples see b. Giṭ. 46B.36; y. Ter. 8.45D.8.

b. Genesis Rabbah 22 (15B): R. Simeon b. Yohai (ca. 150) said, "The word ('The voice of your brother's blood cries out to me from the earth' [Gen 4:10]) is difficult to say and impossible for the mouth to explain. Like two wrestlers אתליטין, who stood there and wrestled with each other before the king. If the king had desired, he could have separated them; but the king did not want to separate them. Then one overpowered the other and killed him, and he cried out and said (dying), 'Who will demand justice for me before the king?' Likewise: 'The voice of your brother's blood cries out to me from the earth.'" ‖ Genesis Rabbah 77 (49D): Like a wrestler אתליטים, who stood there and wrestled with the king's son. When he raised his eyes and saw the king standing there with him, he bowed down before him (so too the angel who wrestled with Jacob when he saw the Shekinah standing there with him). — In the parallel passage Midr. Song. 3:6 (105B) R. Levi (ca. 300) is the author and instead of the "athlete" we read of a "robber chief." ‖ Tanḥuma ויגש 51A: R. Simeon b. Laqish (ca. 250) said, "Like two wrestlers אתליטין, who had seized each other. When one of them realized that he would be overcome, he said (to himself): Now he will overpower me and then I will be ashamed before everyone here! What did he do? He kissed the other's hand and mollified the wrath of the stronger wrestler. (So Joseph revealed himself when the anger of his brother Judah flared up.)" ‖ See Exod. Rab. 21 (84B) at § 1 Cor 9:25 B, #1.

2. πάντα ἐγκρατεύεται = מְצַעֵר עַצְמוֹ מִכֹּל דָּבָר; see b. Taʿan. 11A in n. *c*. – If one disregards fasting,[a] the broad territory of ascesis was relatively untouched by the halakah; a certain personal freedom reigned in accordance with the old principle: "Whoever wants to make himself into an individual in everything that belongs to asceticism צַעַר (i.e., into someone particularly eminent who takes on, e.g., fasting ahead of the multitude) may do so, and if a student of the scholars does it, a blessing will come to him (for it)" (y. Ber. 2.5C.67). Therefore it comes as no surprise if judgments about asceticism diverged quite widely. While on the one hand there was never a lack of men who sought salvation in ascesis[b] and made the case for asceticism,[c] on the other hand there were others who were more or less harshly opposed to it.[d] Yet even when one was well-disposed toward asceticism, one did not neglect warning about overdoing it: one should not expect of the multitude more than they could bear.[e] Above all self-mortification was not allowed to lead to shaming others.[f]

a. On fasting see the excursus "Fasting" and § Luke 18:12 A, #2.

b. Celebrated ascetics of the older period included, for example, R. Zadok (ca. 50; see b. Giṭ. 56A at § Luke 18:12, A, #2); Nahum of Gimzo (ca. 90; see b. Taʿan. 21A.26 at § Matt 18:8f.); Hanina b. Dosa (ca. 70; see b. Taʿan. 24B at § Luke 15:16, n. *d*); R. Phineas b. Yair (ca. 200; see m. Soṭah 9.15 at § Matt 5:3, #3). R. Aqiba († ca. 135) should also be named here; see b. Sanh. 65B at § Luke 2:25 C, #3, n. *q* and ʾAbot R. Nat. 26 (7C): R. Aqiba said, "A (protective) fence for honor (respect) is not laughing (the 'not' is not in the text, but it should be supplied according to the 2nd recension of ʾAbot Nathan 33); a fence for wisdom is silence; a fence for vows is abstinence פְּרִישׁוּת (setting apart); a fence for purity is holiness; a fence for humility is timidity to sin." – More briefly, m. ʾAbot 3.13: (R. Aqiba) said, "The tradition (the traditional interpretation of the law, see § Matt 15:2 A, #2) is a fence for the Torah; vows are a fence for abstinence פרישות; a fence for wisdom is silence."

c. Babylonian Talmud Taʿanit 11A: R. Eleazar (ca. 270) said, "(Whoever abstains in all things המצער עצמו מכל דבר) is called a holy one; for it says, 'He (the Nazirite) shall be holy by letting the hair on his head grow long' (Num 6:5). If he who abstains ציער עצמו from just this one thing is called 'holy,' how much more does this go for the one who abstains in everything!"

d. Babylonian Talmud Taʿanit 11A: Samuel († 254) said, "Whoever sits fasting is called a sinner. He thought like this teacher of the Mishnah. For in a baraita it has been taught that R. Eleazar Haqqappar (ca. 180), the son of Rabbi, said, 'What does Scripture mean to teach by "And he shall make atonement for him (the Nazirite) for the way he has sinned against the soul" (so Num 6:11 according to the midr.). How is this meant? Against what soul did he sin? (It says this) only because he abstained from wine שציער עצמו מן היין. Is the inference from the lesser to the greater not justified? If he who abstained from wine is called a sinner, how much more does this go for the one who abstains in all things!'" – Parallels are found in b. Naz. 22A; b. B. Qam. 91B. ‖ Jerusalem Talmud Qiddušin 4.66B.57: R. Hezekiah (ca. 350) and R. Kohen (ca. 330?) said in the name of Rab († 247), "A person will one day have to give an account for everything his eye saw which he did not enjoy." ‖ Babylonian Talmud ʿErubin 54A: Samuel († 254) said to Rab Judah († 299), "Astute man,[199] hurry up and eat; hurry up and drink; for the world which we will leave is like a marriage feast (that quickly passes away along with its fullness)." Rab († 247) said to Rab Hamnuna (ca. 290), "My son, if you have it, enjoy it, for in Sheol there is no good living and there is no delaying death. And if you should say, 'I want to leave my children a certain amount,' who will deliver you a message in Sheol (that it has in fact come into their possession)? The children of men are like the vegetation of the field: these thrive and those wither." — See Sir 14:11 (Hebrew): "My son, if you have it, enjoy it...." 14:12: "Remember that there is no good living in Sheol, and death does not tarry; and what has been determined with Sheol is not made known to you...." 14:14: "Do not deny yourself the good of the day...." 14:18: "Like the green of the leaf on a verdant tree: one withers and the other sprouts, so the generations of flesh and blood: one dies away and another develops."

e. So R. Ishmael († ca. 135) and Rabban Simeon b. Gamaliel (ca. 140); see b. B. Bat. 60B and t. Soṭah 15.10 (322) at § John 8:33 A; see further the explanation of R. Joshua (ca. 90) in t. Soṭah 15.11–15 at § Rom 14:2.

f. Jerusalem Talmud Berakot 2.5D.10: It has been taught: "Whoever wants to make himself into an individual in everything that belongs to asceticism (see above #2 at the beginning) may do so." ... R. Zeira (who himself was a great faster, ca. 300) said, "Only, he should not despise others (by proudly looking down on those who lag behind him in self-mortification as inferiors)."

9:25 B: They, to receive a perishable crown, but we an imperishable one.

1. φθαρτὸν στέφανον. — See Josephus, *Against Apion* 2.30 at § Rom 2:15 B, #2. ‖ Exodus Rabbah 21 (84B): ("I will harden the heart of the Egyptians ..., so that I may be glorified by means of pharaoh," so Exod 14:17 according to the midr.) R. Simeon b. Laqish (ca. 250) said, "Like two wrestlers אתליטים, of which one was weak and the other was strong. The strong one overpowered the weak one and received a crown נָטַל עֲטָרָה for his head. Who caused the strong one to receive the crown? Not the weak one? Likewise, who caused God to receive glory and honor? Not the pharaoh? ... Therefore, it says, 'So I may be glorified by means of pharaoh בפרעה' (Exod 14:17)."

2. ἡμεῖς ἄφθαρτον. — See 2 Bar. 15:7f. at § Rom 8:18, #2, n. *a.* ‖ See b. Ber. 17A at § Matt 5:8 B, #2, n. *b.* ‖ Tanḥuma פקודי 127B: An angel takes the embryo and brings it from the mother's womb to the garden of Eden (the heavenly place of the blessed) and shows to it the righteous, as they sit in glory and their crowns are on their heads. ‖ In b. Šabb. 104A it says the following concerning the sequence of the letters ז, ח, ט, י, כ, and ל in the alphabet: If you do this (namely show beneficence to the poor) God will nourish זן you and be gracious חן to you and do good מטיב to you and give you an inheritance ירושה and make a crown for you in the future world כֶּתֶר לעולם הבא.

199. Strack, *Einleitung in den Talmud und Midraš*, 139.

9:27 A: I subdue my body and make it a servant.

See m. ʾAbot 4.1: Ben Zoma (ca. 110) said, "... Who is a hero? Whoever defeats הַכּוֹבֵשׁ his (evil) inclination, as it says, 'Better is a patient man than a hero, and whoever controls his anger than one who conquers a city' (Prov 16:32)."

9:27 B: Lest I preach to others and myself be disqualified.

See t. Yebam. 8.4 (250) at § Matt 19:12 C.

10:1 A: Our ancestors were all under the cloud.

Mekilta Exodus 13:21 (30A): "Yahweh went before them in a pillar of cloud by day to lead them, and at night in a pillar of fire to give them light" (Exod 13:21). One finds that there were seven clouds: "Yahweh went before them in a pillar of cloud by day" (Exod 13:21; 1st cloud); "so that your cloud stands over them and you go before them in a pillar of cloud" (Num 14:14; 2nd and 3rd cloud); "and when the cloud tarried a long time" (Num 9:19; 4th cloud); "when the cloud arose ...; but when the cloud did not arise ...; for the cloud of Yahweh was over the dwelling by day" (Exod 40:36–38; 5th–7th cloud). Seven clouds: four on their (Israel's) four sides, one above, one below, and one that went before them, lifting up every lowly thing and bringing low every high thing; as it says, "Every valley must be raised up and every mountain and hill be brought low, and the uneven become level and the mountainous ridges a plain" (Isa 40:4). And it (the cloud going before them) slay the snakes and scorpions ahead of them, swept and blew before them. R. Judah (ca. 150) said, "There were thirteen clouds: two on each side, two above, two below, and one that went before them." R. Josiah (ca. 140) said, "There were four: one before them, one behind them, one above, and one below." Rabbi (Judah I, † 217?) said, "There were two." — Parallels are found in SNum 10:34 § 83 (22A); with variations, Num. Rab. 1 (135B); Tanḥ. בשלח 78B; במדבר 185B; TanḥB במדבר § 2 (1B). ‖ Targum Yerušalmi I Exodus 13:20ff.: "They left from Sukkoth, the place where they were covered with the clouds of glory ענני יקרא, and camped in Etham beside the desert. And the glory of the Shekinah of Yahweh went before them by day in a pillar of cloud to lead them on the way, and at night again the pillar of cloud was behind them to be dark for those who set after them (pursued them), and a pillar of fire was there to give light before them, so that they could move by day and by night. And the pillar of cloud by day and the pillar of fire at night did not cease to go along before the people."

10:1 B: All went through the sea.

Mishnah ʾAbot 5.4: Ten miracles happened for our ancestors in Egypt (namely the exemption from the ten plagues) and ten at the sea. — See on this the next citation. ‖ Mekilta Exodus 14:16 (36A): "And you, lift up your staff" (Exod 14:16). Ten miracles happened for Israel at the sea. The sea was split, and it became like a vault (tunnel); as it says, "You pierced with his staff the head of his princes who approached fast to scatter me" (Hab 3:14). (How this passage was understood is not evident.) It was divided into 12 parts (according to the number of the 12 tribes; see further below Tg. Yer. I Exod. 14:21f.); as it says, "Stretch out your hand over the sea and split it" (Exod 14:16). (The passage offers no proof for the number twelve.) The sea became dry ground; as it says, "The children of Israel will go on dry ground" (Exod 14:16). It became clay; as it says, "You tread the sea, your steeds the clay of mighty waters" (so Hab 3:15 according to the midr.). It became crumbled; as it says, "You have crumbled the sea by your power" (Ps 74:13, so the midr). It became sheer boulders; as it says, "You smash the heads of the dragons on the water (so it must have been as hard as stone)" (Ps 74:13). It became sheer pieces (we should probably imagine an ice formation); as it says, "Who carved up into pieces the Sea of Reeds" (Ps 136:13). It became sheer heaps; as it says, "By the breath of your nose the waters became heaps" (so Exod 15:8 according to the midr.). They (the waters) became like a heap; as it says, "The flowing water stood like a heap" (Exod 15:8). He made freshwater issue forth for them from salty water; as it says, "He made flowing water issue forth from the stone (the frozen saltwater) and water flow down like streams (of freshwater)" (Ps 78:16). He made the sea congeal in two parts and it became like (translucent) clumps of ice; as it says, "The floodwaters congealed in the heart of the sea" (Exod 15:8). — The same is found in Tanḥ. בשלח 79B; in a different form in ʾAbot R. Nat. 33 (8D). ‖ Exodus Rabbah 21 (84B): R. Nehorai (ca. 150) said in a presentation, "The Israelite woman went through the sea, and her child was holding onto her hand. If it cried, she stretched out her hand and took an apple or a pomegranate from the midst of the sea and gave it to him; for it says, 'He led them in the floodwaters as in the wilderness' (Ps 106:9). Just as they did not go without anything in the wilderness, so too they did not go without anything in the floodwaters." ‖ ʾAbot de Rabbi Nathan 33 (8D): "The flowing water stood like a pipe" (the midr. reads נֵד in Exod 15:8 as נוֹד).... And the pipes let oil and honey flow into the mouths of the children and they sucked from them; as it says, "He suckled them with honey from the rock (the blocks of ice from the frozen sea)" (Deut 32:13). ‖ Targum Yerušalmi I Exodus 14:21f.: "The water was split into 12 divisions (sections) according to the 12 tribes of Jacob. And the children of Israel walked in the sea as on dry ground, and the water became firm (congealed) like walls in a stretch of 300 miles to their right and to their left." ‖ See Mek. Exod. 14:22 (37B) at § Rom 11:1 B.

10:2: All were baptized into Moses.

On βαπτίζειν εἰς see § Matt 28:19.

10:3, 4 A: Spiritual food ..., spiritual drink.

See πνευματικός at § 1 Cor 2:14f. and § Rom 7:14 A.

10:4 B: They drank from a spiritual rock that followed them.

Mishnah ʾAbot 5.6: Ten things were created on the eve of the Sabbath (of the week of creation) at twilight: the opening of the earth (Num 16:32), the opening of the well (which accompanied Israel on their migration in the wilderness), the mouth of the jenny (Num 22:28), the rainbow (Gen 9:13), manna (Exod 16:15), the staff (of Moses, Exod 4:17), the shamir,[200] script (the form of letters), spelling (the connection of letters into words, or = writing

200. S-B: The shamir was a worm that split stones on which it was laid. See b. Giṭ. 68A; b. Soṭah 48B. In the Mishnah the shamir is mentioned in m. Soṭah 9.12: "With the destruction of the sanctuary

tools), and the tablets of the law. Some say, "Also the demons and the grave of Moses and the ram of our father Abraham (Gen 22:13)." Still others say, "Also the tongs (the first one) for the tongs to be made (further by humanity)." — The same is found with several differences in b. Pesaḥ. 54A; Tg. Yer. I Num. 22:28. The oldest source, Mek. Exod. 16:32 (59B), does not mention the well and instead reads at the end: The cave in which Moses and Elijah stood. ‖ Tosefta Sukkah 3.11ff. (196): It was the same well that was with Israel in the wilderness; it was like a rock that was full of holes and like a sieve, and the water dripped and rose as from the opening of a flesh.[201] It (the rock well) went up with them onto the mountains and climbed down with them into the valleys; wherever Israel lingered, it lingered opposite them at the entrance to the tabernacle of meeting. The rulers of Israel went with their staffs around it and sang this song about it; as it says, "Rise, O well! Sing to it!" (Num 21:17). The water bubbled and rose up like a column, and each one went with his staff to his tribe and to his family; as it says, "The well which the princes dug, which the nobles of the people bored with the scepter, with their sticks ...; from Mattanah to Nahaliel and from Nahaliel to Bamoth and from Bamoth to the valley ..." (Num 21:18f.). It flowed around the whole camp of Yahweh and watered "the face of the desert" (Num 21:20), and it became large streams; as it says, "Streams surged" (Ps 78:20). And they (the Israelites) sat in barks and each one came to the other; as it says, "They went in the steppes on the stream" (Ps 105:41; or as the parallels Tanḥ. חקת and Num. Rab. 19 cite in accordance with Isa 33:21: "They went with ships on the stream"). The water that rose up on the right side flowed off on the right side, and that which rose up on the left side flowed off on the left side. However, what remained became a great stream and flowed into the great sea, and all the delights of the world were brought from there; as it says, "You have lacked nothing the forty years that Yahweh your God is with you" (Deut 2:7). — Parallels are found in Tanḥ. במדבר 185B; חקת 229B; TanḥB במדבר § 2 (2A); Num. Rab. 1 (135B); 19 (187C); Tg. Yer. I Num. 21:16ff. ‖ Tanḥuma קדושים 168B: When the Israelites had gone out of Egypt and wandered in the wilderness, God made manna come down for them and brought for them quails (from the sea) and made the stream arise for them. And every tribe made itself a water channel and directed the water to itself; and they planted figs and pomegranates there and they brought forth fruits even on the same day, as at the beginning of the creation of the world "fruit trees brought forth fruit according to their kind" (Gen 1:11). When Adam sinned, wheat was sown and thorns and thistles arose; when the well had vanished, what is written? "There was no place for sowing and fig trees and the grapevine and pomegranate trees" (Num 20:5). Why all this? "And there was no water to drink" (Num 20:5). ‖ See Midr. Song. 4:14 at § John 4:10, n. *a* toward the end. ‖ It was generally assumed that the well from the rock in the wilderness had been given to the Israelites by God due to the merit of Miriam. It was therefore called in short "the well of Miriam" בְּאֵרָהּ שֶׁל מִרְיָם. — Babylonian Talmud Taʿanit 9A: R. Yose b. Judah (ca. 180) said, "Three good providers arose for Israel: Moses, Aaron, and Miriam. And three good gifts were given by means of them.

---

the shamir disappeared."

201. Thus according to the readings in J. Levy, *Neuhebräisches und Chaldäisches Wörterbuch über die Talmudim und Midraschim* (Leipzig: F. A. Brockhaus, 1889), 4:4:44B פכפך.

These are the well and the (pillar of) cloud and the manna. The well because of the merit of Miriam, the pillar of cloud because of the merit of Aaron, the manna because of the merit of Moses. When Miriam died, the well disappeared; as it says, 'Miriam died there' (Num 20:1), and then it says, 'And there was no water for the community there' (Num 20:2). However, by the merit of the two (others) it returned. Aaron died, and then the clouds of glory disappeared; as it says, 'The Canaanite, the king of Arad, heard' (Num 21:1). What sort of message did he hear? He heard that Aaron had died and the clouds of glory had disappeared. Then he thought that the authorization had been given to him to fight with Israel.… Yet they both (?) returned because of the merit of Moses. Moses died, and then all (three) disappeared; as it says, 'I wiped out the three shepherds (in the sense meant by the midr. = Miriam, Aaron, and Moses) in one month' (Zech 11:8). How? Did they die in one month? Did Miriam not die in Nisan and Aaron in Ab and Moses in Adar? Rather (that passage) teaches that the three good gifts that had been given by means of them ceased and together disappeared in one month." — Parallels are found in S. ʿOlam Rab. 10; t. Soṭah 11.10 (315); see also Lev. Rab. 27 (125D); Num. Rab. 1 (135A, B); TanḥB במדבר § 2 (1B). — Another tradition just as old traced back the acquisition of the three good gifts above to the merit of Abraham. Babylonian Talmud Baba Meṣiʿa 86B: R. Hama b. Hanina (ca. 260) said, and likewise it has been taught in the school of R. Ishmael († ca. 135), "As a recompense for three things they (Israel) obtained three things. As a recompense for the sour milk and the sweet milk (Gen 18:8), they received the manna; as a recompense for Abraham standing before them (Gen 18:8), they received the pillar of cloud; as a recompense for 'Let some water be fetched' (Gen 18:4), they received the well of Miriam." ‖ Mekilta Exodus 16:35 (60A): Miriam died, and then the well disappeared; Aaron died, and then the clouds of glory disappeared; Moses died, and then the manna disappeared. R. Joshua (ca. 90) said, "When Miriam died, the well disappeared; but by the merit of Moses and Aaron they returned. When Aaron died, the pillar of cloud disappeared; but by the merit of Moses both (?) returned. When Moses died, all three disappeared, no more to return." ‖ Babylonian Talmud Šabbat 35A: R. Hiyya (ca. 200) said, "Whoever wants to see the well of Miriam should climb onto the height of Carmel and look out, then he will see a kind of sieve in the sea (from Tiberias), and this is the well of Miriam." Rab († 247) said, "(He will see) a pure well moving back and forth, and this is the well of Miriam." — See the parallels at § Matt 4:18 A, #2 under the heading "The Well of Miriam." — On a healing by the well of Miriam in the Sea of Gennesaret, see Lev. Rab. 22 (121B) at § John 5:4 B.

10:4 C: But the rock was Christ (the Messiah).

Schöttgen[202] and Leonhard Bertholdt[203] have tried to find an interpretation of the following rock applied to the Messiah in Tg. Isa. 16:1. The passage has been translated: "They will send gifts to Israel's Messiah, who will be mighty, because he was the rock in the wilderness for the community

202. Schöttgen, *Horae Hebraicae et Talmudicae*, 2:165, 454.

203. Bertholdt, *Christologia Judaeorum Jesu apostolorumque aetate*, 145.

of Zion." — The correct translation is as follows: "They shall send tribute to Israel's Messiah, who will be mighty (rule) over the inhabitants of the wilderness, to the mountain of the community of Zion (i.e., to Jerusalem)." ‖ The apostle's interpretation can be more easily compared with what Philo says about the ἀκρότομος πέτρα (in LXX, this translates צוּר הַחַלָּמִישׁ in Deut 8:15) in *Leg.* 2.21 (Mangey's ed., 1.82): "The ἀκρότομος rock is the wisdom of God, which he separated ἔτεμεν as highest and first ἄκραν καὶ πρωτίστην of his powers, from which he waters the souls that love God." See Philo, *Det.* § 31 (Mangey's ed., 1:213): "He suckled them with honey from the rock and with oil from the hard stone" (Deut 32:13). By the hard and unbreakable stone, he means the wisdom of God.... In another passage, making use of a synonymous expression, he calls this rock, "manna," the divine Logos, the oldest of everything that exists. — Thus, the watering rock = wisdom = Logos. ‖ In rabbinic literature Mek. Exod. 17:6 (60B) is noteworthy: "Behold, I will stand there before you" (Exod 17:6). God said to him, "Everywhere where you find the footsteps of a man, I am there before you." — The words seem to imply that wherever Israel may turn, God will go with them to give water to his people. The rock that goes with them is thus God. Targum Yerušalmi I Exodus 17:6 understood the words differently, though, namely as a designation of the rock that Moses was supposed to hit just then: "I will stand there before you at a place where you will see a footstep on Horeb; and you shall hit it with the stone of your staff." (It should be noted that the last words were interpreted by R. Yose b. Zimra [ca. 220] to mean that Moses' staff was made of sapphire; see Mek. Exod. 17:6 folio 60B.28.)

10:5: But God was not pleased with the majority of them; for they were struck down in the wilderness.

Mishnah Sanhedrin 10.3: "The wilderness generation has no share in the future world; they too will not stand in the (last) judgment (they have already received their judgment and their punishment and remain excluded from the resurrection); for it says, 'In this wilderness they shall be wiped out (namely in this world), and there they shall die (namely for the future world)' (Num 14:35)." These are the words of R. Aqiba († ca. 135). R. Eliezer (ca. 90) said, "Concerning them it says, 'Gather to me my devout ones, who have made a covenant with me by sacrifice' (Ps 50:5; cf. Exod 24)." ‖ Tosefta Sanhedrin 13.10f. (435): "The wilderness generation has no share in the future world, and they will not come to life again in the future world; for it says, 'In this wilderness they shall be wiped out,' in this world, 'and there they shall die,' in the future world (Num 14:35). It further says, 'I swore in my anger, "Truly they shall not enter my rest (in eternal life)!"' (Ps 95:11)." These are the words of R. Aqiba. R. Eliezer said, "'They will come into the future world'; and concerning them David said, 'Gather to me my devout ones, who have made a covenant with me by sacrifice' (Ps 50:5). What does Scripture mean to teach with: 'I swore in my anger' (by which

R. Aqiba tried to establish his view)? In my anger I have sworn, but I (later) changed my mind." R. Joshua b. Qarha (ca. 150) said, "Those words (in Ps 50:5) were spoken only about the (later) generations; as it says, 'Gather to me my devout ones' חסידיי, because they have done acts of love גמילות חסד for me; 'who have made a covenant with me' כורתי בריתי, because they were eradicated נכרתו because of me; 'by sacrifice' עלי זבח, because they exalted (glorified) עילו me and were slaughtered נזבחו because of me." (R. Joshua b. Qarha thus follows the opinion of R. Aqiba.) R. Simeon b. Manasseh (ca. 180) said, "They will come (into the future world, the opinion of R. Eliezer), and concerning them it says, 'Those redeemed (from Egypt, so the midr.) by Yahweh will return and come to Zion with rejoicing' (Isa 51:11)." — Additional parallels are found in y. Sanh. 10.29C.5; b. Sanh. 110B as a baraita. — ʾAbot de Rabbi Nathan 36 (9C) names R. Eliezer and R. Joshua (both ca. 90) as representatives of the opposing views; the stricter view of R. Aqiba is attributed to the former and the milder view of R. Eliezer is attributed to the latter. Bacher considers the authorial attribution in ʾAbot R. Nat. to be correct.[204]

10:6: Our examples.

τύπος; the rabbis use טוּפּוֹס, טְפּוֹס, and דְּפּוֹס, but, it seems, only with the meaning "figure, model, shape, formula, form." When they want the meaning "example," in place of τύπος, they use סֵימָן, סֵימָנָא (σημεῖον). See examples at § Luke 2:34 B and § Rom 5:14 B.

10:7: And do not be idolaters, as some of them were; as it is written, "The people sat down to eat and drink and got up to play" (Exod 32:6).

1. ἐκάθισεν. — The rabbis often deduced from Exod 32:6 the exegetical rule that the word "sit" or "sit down" means perdition in Scripture.

Sifre Numbers 25:1 § 131 (47A): "Israel sat in Shittim, when the people began to play the harlot with the daughters of Moab" (Num 25:1). "Sitting" means in every case only perdition קלקלה (corruption, sin); as it says, "The people sat down to eat and drink ..." (Exod 32:6). It further says, "And they sat down to eat" (Gen 37:25). ‖ Exodus Rabbah 41 (98A): Everywhere you find a case of "sitting," there you find being misled to sin תקלה. For so we find it with the generation of the tower; as it says, "They found a lowland plain in the land of Shinar and settled down there" (Gen 11:2). And how were they misled to sin there? They said, "Well, we will build ourselves a city!" (Gen 11:4). (Further:) "And they sat down to eat" (Gen 37:25); and it is written, "And they sold Joseph" (Gen 37:28). (Further:) "And Israel sat in Shittim" (Num 25:1). How were they misled to sin there? "The people began to play the harlot with the daughters of Moab" (Num 25:1). And what happened in the end? "There were 24,000 who died by the plague" (Num 25:9). And here (Exod 32:6) too it deals with sitting to commit idolatry: "The people sat down to eat and drink ..." (Exod 32:6). God said to Moses, "They rose up to play with the idol." ‖ Babylonian Talmud Sanhedrin 106A:

---

204. Bacher, *Die Agada der palästinensischen Amoräer*, 1:136.

R. Yohanan († 279) said, "Everywhere where it says, 'He sat,' it means nothing other than misery"; see Num 25:1; Gen 37:1, 2; 47:27, 29; 1 Kgs 5:5 compared with 11:14. ‖ Genesis Rabbah 38 (23B): R. Isaac (ca. 300) said, "Everywhere where you find a case of sitting in Scripture, Satan rushes to disperse." R. Helbo (ca. 300) said, "Everywhere where you find composure (comfortable living), Satan appears as the accuser." R. Levi (ca. 300) said, "Everywhere where you find a case of eating and drinking, Satan appears as the accuser."

2. παίζειν = צָחַק to laugh, joke, play. — In later times, it was a firm exegetical canon that when צחק appears in Scripture, nothing other than idolatry should be understood.[a] In earlier times, this rule is first found in the mouth of R. Aqiba and R. Ishmael[b] (both † ca. 135).

a. Exodus Rabbah 1 (65A): When Ishmael (the son of Abraham) was 15 years old, he began to fetch an idol from the market and he played with it and venerated it, as he had seen others do. "Immediately Sarah saw the son of the Egyptian Hagar, whom she had borne to Abraham, playing מצחק" (Gen 21:9), and "playing" means nothing other than idolatry. — The same is found in Tanḥ. שמות 59B. ‖ Exodus Rabbah 41 (98A): "The people sat down to eat and drink, and they rose up to play" (Exod 32:6), namely with the idol. ‖ Targum Yerušalmi I Exodus 32:6: "And the people settled down to eat and drink and they rose up to frolic with strange service (pagan worship)." — See Rashi on Gen 21:9: מצחק לשון עבודת גלולים שנאמר ויקומו לצחק.

b. Tosefta Soṭah 6.6 (304): R. Simeon b. Yohai (ca. 150) said, "R. Aqiba explained four words, but I do not explain them like he did. I prefer my words to his words." R. Aqiba explained מצחק (playing, laughing, Gen 21:9): "'Playing' (laughing) means nothing but idolatry; as it says, 'And they rose up to play' (Exod 32:6)." (R. Simeon himself explains the צחק in Gen 21:9 as Ishmael laughing about the fact that a double portion of the inheritance would fall to him as the firstborn.) — Similarly, SDeut 6:4 § 31 (72A), though without referring to Exod 32:6. — In Gen. Rab. 53 (34A), Aqiba's interpretation is attributed to R. Ishmael; the proof text is likewise Exod 32:6.

10:8: 23,000 fell on one day.

The targumim and midrashim everywhere read the number 24,000 following Num 25:9.

Targum Onkelos Numbers 25:9: "There were 24,000 who died of the plague." ‖ Targum Yerušalmi I Numbers 25:9: "The total of those who died from the plague was 24,000." ‖ Jerusalem Talmud Soṭah 7.21D.17: R. Samuel b. Nahman (ca. 260) said in the name of R. Jonathan (ca. 220), "... From the tribe of Simeon 24,000 had already fallen in Shittim." ‖ Babylonian Talmud Sanhedrin 106A: "And (also) Balaam, the son of Beor, slaughtered them with the sword" (Num 31:8). What did Balaam want there? R. Yohanan († 279) said, "He had come to receive his recompense for the 24,000 (who had fallen as a result of his counsel in Shittim)." ‖ Tanḥuma וישב 45A: R. Judah b. Shalom (ca. 370) said, "There is nothing worse than a woman. Know: When they made the calf, it is written, 'About 3,0000 men of the people fell on that day' (Exod 32:28). But because of a woman 24,000 fell in Shittim." — See further Num. Rab. 20 (190D) and Midr. Eccl. 3:16 (21A) at § Luke 2:25 C, #4, n. *c*, paragraph 3.

10:9 A: As some of them tested (him).

Mishnah ʾAbot 5.4: Our ancestors tested God ten times in the wilderness; as it says, "And they tested me ten times and did not listen to my voice" (Num 14:22). ‖ A baraita in b. ʿArak. 15A: R. Judah (ca. 150) said, "Our ancestors tested God (in the wilderness) with ten trials: two at the (Red) Sea, two with water, two with manna, two with the quails, one with the calf, and one in the wilderness of Paran. Two at the sea: once while going down and once while coming up. While going down, as it is written, 'Were there no graves in Egypt (have you led us away to die in the wilderness)?' (Exod 14:11). While coming up, as in the view of Rab Huna († 297); for Rab Huna said, 'The Israelites of that time were among those of little faith קטני אמנה.' This aligns with the opinion of Rabbah bar Mari (ca. 320); for Rabbah bar Mari said, 'What does "They were recalcitrant at the sea, at the Sea of Reeds; yet he helped them for the sake of his name" (Ps 106:7, 8) mean? This teaches that the Israelites were recalcitrant in that hour and said, "As we come up from this side, the Egyptians will come up from the other side!" Then God said to the archangel of the sea, "Vomit up those ones (the Egyptians) onto dry land (so the Israelites may see that they are dead)!" He said before him, "Lord of the world, is there a servant who is given a gift by his master who then takes it away from him again?" God answered him, "I will give you (as a replacement) one and a half times as much as they number" (cf. Exod 14:7: 600 with Judg 4:3: 900). He said before him, "Lord of the world, is there a servant who demands something from his master (if he, e.g., forgets a promise)?" He answered him, "Let the stream of Kishon be surety (cf. Judg 4:7ff.; 5:21)!" Immediately he vomited them up onto dry land, as it is written, "And Israel saw the Egyptians dead on the shore of the sea" (Exod 14:30).' Two with water, in Marah and in Rephidim. In Marah, as it is written, 'And they came to Marah but could not drink the water of Marah' (Exod 15:23). (After this,) it is written, 'There the people grumbled against Moses' (Exod 15:24). In Rephidim, as it is written, 'They camped in Rephidim, and there was no water to drink' (Exod 17:1). (After this,) it is written, 'There the people quarreled with Moses' (Exod 17:2). Two with manna, as it is written, 'You shall not go out on the seventh day' (so the midr. cites Exod 16:29), and they (nevertheless) went out (see Exod 16:27). Furthermore, 'Do not let anything remain' (so Exod 16:19 is cited), and they (nevertheless) let some remain (see Exod 16:20). Two with the first quails and with the second quails. With the first quails: 'When we sat by the fleshpot' (Exod 16:3); with the second quails, 'And the rabble that was among them developed a craving' (Num 11:4). With the calf, as it is (in the narrative of Scripture). In the wilderness of Paran (with the scouts), as it is."

10:9 B: And were killed by the snakes.

Numbers Rabbah 19 (187A): "Then Yahweh sent fiery serpents against the people" (Num 21:6). Why did he punish them with snakes? Since the snake had begun with slander and had been cursed, and they had not learned from it, God said, "Let the snake, which began with slander, come and punish the one who speaks slander; 'whoever tears down a wall is bitten by a snake'" (Eccl 10:8). A different explanation. Why did he punish them with snakes? Even if the snake eats all the tidbits that there are in the world, they will turn to dust in their mouths; for it says, "And the snake—dust is its bread" (Isa 65:25). And they

(Israelites) eat manna which turns into many flavors (see § John 6:31, #2); as it says, "And he gave them their desire" (Ps 106:15) (so that they ate in the manna every food that they desired). Furthermore, it says, "You have lacked nothing the forty years that Yahweh your God is with you" (Deut 2:7). So, let the snake come, which eats many kinds of things, while they have just a taste in their mouths, and punish those who eat one sort of thing and taste many kinds of things. "Fiery serpents" (Num 21:6), because they burn the soul (life). R. Judan (which?) said, "'Fiery serpents,' because the cloud burned them (cf. Mek. Exod. 13:21 at § 1 Cor 10:1 A) and made a fence out of them for the camp, in order to make known to you the miracles that God did for them; he set these upon on them."

10:10: As some of them grumbled and perished by the destroyer.

1. It is frequently assumed that with these words the apostle had in view the report in Num 14:2ff.; he may have been thinking of Num 17:6ff. as well. At least the Wisdom of Solomon 18:20–25 depicted a similar punishment for the grumbling people by the destroyer ὁ ὀλοθρεύων solely on the basis of the latter passage.[a]

2. ὁ ὀλοθρευτής corresponds with הַמַּשְׁחִית (Exod 12:23), which the LXX and Hebrews 11:28 rendered with ὁ ὀλοθρεύων. For the fuller expression הַמַּלְאָךְ הַמַּשְׁחִית in 2 Sam 24:16 and 1 Chr 21:15, the LXX has ὁ ἄγγελος ὁ διαφθείρων, or ὁ ἄγγελος ὁ ἐξολοθρεύων. — Targum Onkelos has in Exod 12:23: חַבָּלָא "the destroyer"; Yer. I: מַלְאֲכָא מְחַבְּלָא "the destroying angel"; Tg. 2 Sam. 24:16: מלאכא דִמְחַבֵּל "the angel who devastated"; Tg. 1 Chr. 21:15: מלאכא מְחַבְּלָא "the destroying angel."

3. While in the OT הַמַּשְׁחִית retained its appellative meaning, מַשְׁחִית in rabbinic literature has become a proper name for a specific angel who is sometimes also called הֶשְׁחֵת[b] = "destruction"; most of the time this angel Mashḥit appears in connection with angels of the same sort such as אַף "wrath," חֵימָה "fury," קֶצֶף "anger," and הֶשְׁמֵד "extermination."[c] From the names it is not difficult to recognize that their bearers were originally nothing but personifications of divine will of anger and punishment. Only gradually did independent angels develop from these; they were then designated generally "angels of destruction" מַלְאֲכֵי חַבָּלָה according to their task of bringing destruction over the godless.[d] Since a reputation of particular severity and cruelty attached to these angels, it was further written about them that God expelled them from being close to him, so that his mercy could prevail before they were able to obtain divine consent for the execution of punishment that lay with them.[e]

4. Aside from the "angels of destruction" designated with the names above, the ancient synagogue knows countless other angels of plague and punishment who are also called "angels of destruction" מַלְאֲכֵי חַבָּלָה.[f] As those who execute the divine punitive will, they are in principle among the "angels of service"[g] מַלְאֲכֵי הַשָּׁרֵת; in fact, however, most of the time they

are juxtaposed in opposition with these.[h] In this case the term "angels of service" was conceived of more narrowly and was understood to include only those angels who carried out God's good and gracious will. The term "angels of service" overlaps in content in this case approximately with the "angels of peace" or "of mercy" מַלְאֲכֵי שָׁלוֹם or מ׳ רַחֲמִים (contrary of מלאכי הַזַּעַם = angels of wrath).[i] Alongside this view about the angels of destruction, though, a different one had appeared early on. An inference was made about their being from their effect. Since their action was always only directed to destruction, they themselves were counted among the evil angels[k] and were associated with the angels of Satan.[l] In this way they formed the sharpest contrast to the good angels of service and peace.[m]

5. It cannot be decided whether with ὀλοθρευτής in 1 Cor 10:10 the apostle Paul thought specifically of the angel of judgment called Mashḥit or generally of any of the many angels of destruction. In favor of the former, there is the definite article before ὀλοθρευτής; in favor of the latter, there is the fact that the apostle speaks generally of an angel of destruction in 2 Cor 12:7 under the designation "angel of Satan."

a. Wisdom 18:20ff.: "The peril of death seized also righteous ones, and a destruction of the multitude occurred in the wilderness; but the wrath did not persist for long. For an irreproachable man (namely Aaron, see Num 17:11ff.) quickly became a champion: Maintaining the weapon of his own office, prayer, and atoning incense, he stood up against the fury and put an end to perdition by showing that he was your servant. Yet he did not conquer the wrath by strength of body nor by force of weapons, but rather by the word he overcame the punisher τὸν κολάζοντα, calling to mind the oaths and covenants with the fathers. For when the dead were already falling on each other in heaps, he interceded and checked the wrath and cut off its way to the living. For on his garment, which reached to his feet, there was (depicted) the whole world and the honors of the fathers on four rows of cut stones (see the description of the high priest's breastplate in Exod 28:15ff.) and your majesty (the words: "holy to Yahweh" [Exod 28:36]) on the diadem of his head. To these the destroyer ὁ ὀλοθρεύων yielded, this is what he heard; for the mere test of the wrath was sufficient." — See Tg. Yer. 1 Num. 17:11f. in n. *c*.

b. Exodus Rabbah 41 (98A); 44 (100B); see the passages among the parallels to Midr. Eccl. 4:2f. (22B) in n. *c*.

c. Midrash Ecclesiastes 4:2f. (22B): "I praised the dead who had died long ago" (Eccl 4:2). R. Joshua (b. Levi, ca. 250) interpreted the passage in relation to Israel. "When they stood at Mount Sinai and had strayed into that deed (worshiping the golden calf), there was no nook on the ground or floor of the mountain where Moses would not have bowed down and sought for intercession and mercy over Israel; but no answer was granted him. Then the five angels of destruction מלאכי חבלה set to work on him: Qeṣeph (anger), Mashḥit (destroyer), Heshmed (extermination), Af (wrath) and Ḥema (fury). Immediately Moses was afraid of them. What did he do? He clung to the work of the fathers. Immediately he mentioned them and said, 'Remember Abraham, Isaac, and Israel (= Jacob), your servants.' God said to him, 'Moses, what do the fathers of world have on me (what claims of justice could they raise)? If I wished to be exacting with them, I would have something against them. Against Abraham I have that he said, "How shall I know that I will possess it?" (Gen 15:18). Against Isaac I have something; as it says, "Isaac loved Esau" (Gen 25:28), while I hated him, as it says, "And Esau I hated" (Mal 1:3). Against Jacob I have that he said, "My way is hidden from Yahweh" (Isa 40:27).' But when Moses said, 'Which you have sworn by yourself' (Exod 32:13), for the sake of your name, God was filled with mercy; as it says, 'And Yahweh repented' (Exod 32:14). Immediately three angels of destruction מלאכי חבלה, Qeṣeph and Mashḥit and Heshmed, went away from him and two remained, Af and Ḥema. This is what is written, 'Af and Ḥema terrified me' (Deut 9:19). Moses said before him, 'Lord of the world, can I stand against the two of them?' 'Take one for yourself and I will take one!' This is what is written, 'Arise, Yahweh, against your Af' (so Ps 7:7 according to the midr.). And whence comes the idea that Moses stood against the one angel Ḥema? It says, 'Then he would have destroyed them, unless Moses, his chosen one, has stepped into the gap before him to dissipate his Ḥema, lest he cause destruction' (Ps 106:23). About that hour it says, 'I praise the dead (the fathers and their merit) more than the living' (Eccl 4:2), as, for example, I and my companions." — Parallel passages are found in Deut. Rab. 3 (200C), where the author is R. Hiyya b. Abba (ca. 280); the names of the angels are Af, Ḥema, Qeṣeph, Mashḥit, and מְכַלֶּה (= exterminator); Exod. Rab. 44 (100B), R. Isaac (ca. 300); Af, Ḥema, Qeṣeph, Heshmed, and Heshḥeth (= Mashḥit); Exod. Rab. 41 (98A), anonymous; Af, Ḥema, Qeṣeph, Heshmed, and Heshḥeth; Tanḥ. כי תשא 116A, anonymous; Qeṣeph, Af, Ḥema, Mashḥit, and Heshmed; TanḥB כי תשא § 13 (57A), anonymous; Af, Qeṣeph, מַשְׁבִּיר (= shatterer), Mashḥit, and Ḥema; Midr. Ps. 7 § 6 (33A), author: R. Samuel b. Nahman (ca. 260) with the interpretation: "Af: this is the angel who is set over (divine) wrath; Ḥema: this is the angel of fury; Qeṣeph: this is the angel of anger; Mashḥit: this is the destroying angel; Heshmed: this is the exterminating angel." ‖ Babylonian Talmud Šabbat 55A: Who were the six men in Ezek 9:2? Rab Hisda († 309) said, "They were Qeṣeph, Af, Ḥema, Mashḥit, Mashbir (see above TanḥB כי תשא § 13), and Mekhalle (see above Deut. Rab. 3)." ‖ Babylonian Talmud Nedarim 32A: R. Judah b. Zebina (ca. 300)[205] said in a presentation, "In the hour that our teacher Moses showed himself lax in circumcision, Af and Ḥema came and devoured him and left nothing of him except for his feet. Immediately Zipporah took a sharp stone and cut off her son's foreskin (Exod 4:25). Immediately he let him out of him (Exod 4:26). In that hour our teacher Moses wanted to kill them; as it says, 'Stand back from Af and let go of Ḥema!' (Ps 37:8. Some say, 'He killed Ḥema, because it says, "I no (longer) have Ḥema"' (Isa 27:4). Yet it says, 'I was terrified of Af and Ḥema!' (Deut 9:19). (Since this word was spoken after the giving of the law, Ḥema could not have been killed at the time of Exod 4:25f.! Answer:) There were two (angels named) Ḥema; or if you want, say: The host of Ḥema (the division of angels subject to him) is meant (in the later passage Deut 9:19)." — Targum Yerušalmi I Exodus 4:24ff. speaks only about one angel of destruction. ‖ Targum Yerušalmi I Numbers 17:11f.: "Moses said to Aaron, 'Take the incense censer and put fire from the altar on

205. So read with Bacher, *Die Agada der palästinensischen Amoräer*, 3:581, instead of R. Judah b. Bizna.

it and put incense of fragrant spices on the fire and bring it quickly to the community and make atonement for them; for the destroyer מְחַבְּלָא, who was restrained at Horeb and whose name is Qeṣeph, has gone out from Yahweh at his behest and has begun to kill.' And Aaron took it, as Moses had said, and hurried into the midst of the gathering. And behold, Qeṣeph began to arrange destruction in the people, and he (Aaron) took the incense of fragrant spices and made atonement for the people."

d. See Midr. Eccl. 4:2f. in n. *c*, where the term "angels of destruction" occurs twice; also, y. Taʿan. 2.65B.43 in n. *e*.

e. See y. Taʿan. 2.65B.43 at § Rom 1:18 A, n. *b*; see Tanḥ. תזריע 155B at § Rom 1:18 A, n. *a*.

f. In 1 Enoch, the "angels of destruction" bear the name "angels of punishment." 1 Enoch 53:3: "I have seen how the angels of plague (= angels of punishment) stayed (there) and prepared all sorts of instruments of torture for Satan (for his purposes)." — 1 Enoch 56:1: "There I saw hosts of angels of punishment going and holding whips and chains of iron and bronze." — 1 Enoch 62:11: "The angels of punishment will receive them (the godless rulers at the dawn of the messianic age) to take vengeance on them for mistreating his (God's) children and chosen ones." — 1 Enoch 63:1: "In those days (at the beginning of the messianic age) the powerful and the kings who own the land will implore the angels of punishment to grant them a little reprieve." — 1 Enoch 66:1: "Then he (Enoch) showed me (Noah) the angels of punishment who are ready to come and let loose all the powers of the subterranean waters to bring judgment and destruction on all who sojourn and dwell on land." ‖ In rabbinic literature, the fixed name for the angels of punishment and judgment is "angels of destruction" מַלְאֲכֵי חַבָּלָה. Babylonian Talmud Sanhedrin 106B: R. Yohanan († 279) said, "Three angels of destruction set to work on Doeg (who, according to m. Sanh. 10.2, is among those excluded from the future world). The first made him forget what he had learned, the other burned his soul, the third scattered his ashes in the synagogues and houses of learning." ‖ Jerusalem Talmud Šebuʿot 6.37A.57: R. Samuel b. Nahman (ca. 260) said, "The angels of destruction do not have joints to jump; for it says, 'Where do you come from?' Satan (here counted among the angels of destruction) answered, '... From wandering on the earth' (Job 1:7)." (Wandering presupposes a gliding, not a jumping movement.) — The same is found in Lev. Rab. 6 (109B). ‖ See also tractate Kallah 18A at § Matt 5:22 G; b. Ber. 51A at § Matt 15:2 B, #2, n. *h*; Tanḥ. משפטים 99A at § Matt 18:10 B; b. Šabb. 55A at § Luke 1:19 A, #4, n. *h*; b. Pesaḥ. 112B at § Rom 14:5 A (18 myriads of angels of destruction); Num. Rab. 11 (164B) and b. Ketub. 104A below in n. *h*.

g. See the principle in b. B. Meṣ. 59A: R. Eleazar (ca. 270) said, "Everything is punished by the hands of one appointed (by God), except for insult; for it says, 'Insult in his (God's) hand' (Amos 7:7)." (See the whole passage at § Matt 5:22 F, toward the end.) According to this the angels of destruction are, as punishing angels, God's appointees and as such are among the angels of service. See further b. Šabb. 119B in n. *k*, where both the good and the bad angels (= angels of destruction) are explicitly called "angels of service."

h. See Num. Rab. 11 (164B) at § Luke 16:22 A, #2; See b. Ketub. 104A at § Luke 16:22 A, #2.

i. Angels of peace. In 1 Enoch, the *angelus interpres* who answers Enoch's questions is called "angel of peace." 1 Enoch 40:8: "Then I asked the angel of peace who accompanied me and showed me every hidden thing." — 1 Enoch 52:5: "That angel of peace answered me, saying, 'Wait a little and everything hidden that the Lord of Spirits has planted will be revealed to you.'" — 1 Enoch 53:4: "Then I asked the angel of peace who accompanied me, 'For whom do they prepare those instruments of torture?'" — Almost verbatim the same in 1 En. 54:4. — 1 Enoch 56:2: "I asked the angel of peace who accompanied me, saying, 'To whom are the ones carrying the scourges going?'" — The *angelus interpres* is designated as an angel of peace because he is not one of the angels of punishment or plague; see above in n. *f.* ‖ In rabbinic literature the designation "angel of peace" is found only rarely. Babylonian Talmud Ḥagigah 5B: "And if you do not listen, my soul will weep secretly because of wantonness" (Jer 13:17).... Is there a kind of weeping before God? Rab Papa († 376) said, "There is no sadness before God; for it says, 'Splendor and glory are before him, power and joy where he is' (1 Chr 16:27). There is no contradiction: the one (Jer 13:17) goes for the inner and the other (1 Chr 16:27) for the outer chambers (of God). And in the outer chambers (there would be) no (weeping)? It is written, 'The Lord Yahweh Sabaoth called on that day to weeping and to mourning, to sheering and to girding with sackcloth!' (Isa 22:12). In the case of the destruction of the sanctuary it is somewhat different; then the angels of peace מלאכי שלום also wept; as it says, 'Behold, their heroes cry out outside, the angels of peace weep bitterly' (Isa 33:7)." ‖ See Tanḥ. תזריע 155B at § Rom 1:18 A, n. *a.* — The parallel TanḥB תזריע § 11 (20A): Only the angels of peace and the angels of mercy מלאכי רחמים stand before God; but the angels of wrath מלאכי הזעם are far from him; see Isa 13:5. ‖ See t. ʿAbod. Zar. 1.17f. (461) below at the end of n. *i.*

Angels of mercy. — Numbers Rabbah 20 (189A): "The wrath of God burned because he (Balaam) accompanied them, and the angel of Yahweh confronted him on the way as his adversary (שָׂטָן)" (Num 22:22). It was an angel of mercy (a merciful angel) מלאך של רחמין, but he became his adversary (Satan). — See also TanḥB תזריע § 11 at the end of the previous section.

Angels of wrath. — See Tanḥ. תזריע 155B at § Rom 1:18 A, n. *a.* ‖ See TanḥB תזריע § 11 at the end of the previous section.

On the equivalence of angels of service with angels of peace, see t. Šabb. 17.2f. (136) and the parallel t. ʿAbod. Zar. 1.17f. (461) at § Matt 18:10 B: here the expression "angels of service" is replaced by "angels of peace" in the 1st instance in the parallel passage.

k. A baraita in b. Šabb. 119B: R. Yose b. Judah (ca. 180) said, "Two angels of service מלאכי השרת accompany a person on the eve of the Sabbath from the synagogue into his house, a good one and an evil one אחד טוב ואחד רע. (It should be noted that the evil angel [= angel of destruction] is here counted among the angels of service, because he is regarded as God's appointee.) If he comes into his house and finds the (Sabbath) lamp burning and the table covered and his bed prepared, the good angel מלאך טוב says, 'May it be (God's) will that it is the same on the next Sabbath!' And the evil angel מלאך רע answers, 'Amen!' against his will! However, if it is not so, the evil angel says, 'May it be (God's) will that it is the same on the next Sabbath!' And the good angel and the good angel answers, 'Amen!' against his will." ‖ Sifre Deuteronomy 34:5 § 357 (149B): When God takes away the soul of the godless, he gives it over to the evil angels, the cruel angels למלאכים רעים למלאכים אַכְזָרִים (i.e., the angels of destruction), so that they tear their souls out (of the body painfully). (See the whole passage at § Luke 16:22 A, #2, last paragraph.) — According to Num. Rab. 11 and b. Ketub. 104A (see above n. *h*) it is angels of destruction who concern themselves with the souls of the godless; thus, מלאכים רעים = מלאי חבלה.

l. On the "angels of Satan" see § Matt 25:41 B. — Already in 1 Enoch the angels of punishment or plague (= angels of destruction) are called simply "Satans," because they serve Satan as their head. 1 Enoch 40:4: "I (Enoch) heard the fourth voice (i.e., the voice of the fourth angel of the presence named Phanuel), that it repelled the Satans (= angels of destruction or punishment) and did not allow them to come before the Lord of Spirits to accuse those who dwell on land." — 1 Enoch 65:6: "An order has gone out from the face of the Lord concerning those who dwell on land, that this (the flood) be their end, because they know all the secrets of the angels, every act of violence of the Satans (= angels of punishment or angels of destruction)." — 1 Enoch 53:3: "I (Enoch) saw how the angels of plague (= angels of destruction) tarried there and prepared all kinds of instruments of torture for Satan (for his use)." — Here the angels of destruction are in Satan's service.

m. In t. Šabb. 17.2f. (see the passage in detail at § Matt 18:10 B), R. Eliezer b. Yose the Galilean (ca. 150) gives the advice: "Travel together with a righteous man, because the angels of service accompany him; do not travel together with a godless man, because the angels of Satan accompany him." — The same is found in the parallel t. ʿAbod. Zar. 1.17f., except instead of "angels of service" we read "angels of peace."

10:11: Whom the ends of the ages have reached.

τέλος = קֵץ, pl. קִצִּין. — קֵץ designates a fixed point of time and is thus tantamount to an appointed time;[a] specifically, the dawn of redemption, the appointed time for the appearance of the Messiah is called הַקֵּץ,[b] which can be more fully called קֵץ הַגְּאוּלָּה[c] = time, appointed time of redemption, or קֵץ מָשִׁיחַ[d] = time of the arrival of the Messiah. And since in the post-Christian synagogue the days of the Messiah are synonymous with the end of the present age (עוֹלָם הַזֶּה) קֵץ can also be used to mean the "end" in the most general sense. In this meaning the expression קֵץ הַיָּמִים[e] = "end of days" is closest to the term τὰ τέλη τῶν αἰώνων. — See also § Matt 24:3 and § Matt 24:6 C.

a. Babylonian Talmud Nedarim 41A: R. Alexandrai (ca. 270) said that R. Hiyya b. Abba (ca. 280), or according to others R. Joshua b. Levi (ca. 250), said, "When the time set for a person קיצו של אדם (i.e., his life's end) has come, everything masters him." ‖ Pesiqta 106B: When God revealed himself to Moses in the thorn bush, he covenanted with him and said, "When you lead the people out of Egypt, you will serve God on this mountain" (Exod 3:12). And Moses looked and said, "When will this happen?" But when the fixed time הקץ came, God said to him, "The month has come בָּא חֹדֶשׁ (this is supposed to interpret בַּחֹדֶשׁ in Exod 19:1) which you have looked for." ‖ TanḥumaB מקץ § 3 (95B): Straightaway the cupbearer forgot Joseph, until his fixed time קִצּוֹ came to get out (of prison). ‖ Mekilta Exodus 12:42 (20A): (R. Eliezer [ca. 90] said,) "What does Scripture mean to teach with 'This very night is an observance (or pausing) for Yahweh' (Exod 12:42)? This very night it was when God said to our father Abraham, 'Abraham, I will redeem your children one day (from Egypt); and when the appointed time הקץ came, God did not delay for even a moment.'"

b. Dèrek Ereṣ 10 (20B = 11 in other editions): R. Yose (ca. 150) said, "Whoever specifies the קֵץ (i.e., the point of time for the messianic redemption) has no share in the future world." ‖ Babylonian Talmud Sanhedrin 98A: R. Abba (ca. 290) said, "The קֵץ (the dawn of the messianic age) has been revealed to you nowhere more clearly than in the words, 'But you, mountain of Israel, shall bear your leaves and bear your fruit for my people Israel, for their arrival is near' (Ezek 36:8)." ‖ Leviticus Rabbah 19 (118D): "Say to those who are rushing of heart" (Isa 35:4).... R. Joshua b. Levi (ca. 250) said, "As, for example, those who force דוחקין (i.e., try to hasten) the קֵץ (the dawn of the messianic age)." ‖ Midrash Song of Songs 2:7 (99A): R. Yose b. Hanina (ca. 270) said, "Two entreaties are here (Song 2:7 and 3:5): one to Israel and the other to the nations of the world. God entreats the Israelites not to revolt against the yoke of the kingdoms of the world; and he entreats the kingdoms of the world not to make the yoke on Israel heavy. If they make the yoke on Israel heavy, they would cause the קֵץ (the messianic end) to come before its (appointed) time." ‖ Midrash Psalm 78 § 18 (178B): "Then Yahweh arose as one who sleeps" (Ps 78:65). R. Berekhiah (ca. 340) said in the name of R. Eleazar (ca. 270), "Before the קֵץ (the messianic end) comes, God acts like one who sleeps, if one may say so; as it says, 'Then Yahweh arose as one who sleeps.' But when the קֵץ comes, he is 'like a hero shouting with joy from wine' (Ps 78:65)." ‖ Since the קֵץ, the appointed dawn of the messianic redemption, was calculated very differently, קֵץ can be spoken of also in the plural, that is, קִצִּין. Babylonian Talmud Sanhedrin 97B: R. Samuel b. Nahman (ca. 260) said that R. Jonathan (ca. 220) said, "May the bones of those who calculate the קיצין (the times of redemption) be blown away! For they say, 'Since he (God) has made the (alleged) time of redemption הקץ draw near and he (the Messiah) has not come, he will not come at all....'" ‖ Babylonian Talmud Sanhedrin 97B: Rab († 247) said, "All the (calculated) times of redemption קיצין have passed (and the Messiah has not come); the matter depends only on repentance and good works." ‖ In Tg. Yer. I Gen. 49:1, the plural קִיצַיָּיא גְנִיזַיָּא (= hidden times of redemption) probably means all the times of redemption that the history of Israel has to have up until the messianic redemption. — The plural קיצים is also found in Lev. Rab. 19 (118D); see also Midr. Song. 2:8 (99A).

c. Midrash Psalm 9 § 2 (40B): R. Samuel (ca. 260) taught as a tannaitic tradition in the name of R. Judah (ca. 150), "If anyone says to you when the time of the messianic redemption קץ הגאולה will come, do not believe him, because it is written, 'The day of vengeance is in my heart' (Isa 63:4). The heart has not revealed it to the mouth, so to whom would the mouth have revealed it?" — The parallel passage Midr. Eccl. 12:9 (54B) has different authorial attributions. ‖ Midrash Lamentations 3:21 (71A): R. Abba b. Kahana (ca. 310) said in the name of R. Yohanan († 279), "... Tomorrow, when the time of the messianic redemption קץ הגאולה comes, God will say to the Israelites, 'My children, I marvel at you, how you waited for me all these years! ...'" — The parallel passages Pesiq. 139B and Pesiq. Rab. 21 (106A) read only קץ instead of קץ הגאולה. ‖ Numbers Rabbah 5 (145A): Lest God's name be desecrated (among the nations) because of the Israelites, he (God) will bring the sealed time of the messianic redemption קץ גאולה החתום for them; as it says, "I will sanctify my great name that is profaned among the gentiles.... And I will take you from the gentiles and gather you from all lands ..." (Ezek 36:23f.). ‖ In other passages קץ הגאולה is used as a paraphrase. Pesiq. Rab. 41 (174A): "O that the salvation of Israel would come from Zion!" (Ps 14:7). O that the קץ (the appointed time of the messianic age of salvation) would come so that I could bring your redemption! ‖ Midrash Psalm 17 § 10 (67A): R. Joshua of Sikhnin (ca. 330) said in the name of R. Levi (ca. 300), "God said, 'I have twice sworn in one oath[206] by myself that I will bring the קץ and redeem you from servitude to the kingdoms of the world.'"

d. Babylonian Talmud Megillah 3A: He (Jonathan b. Uzziel, contemporary of Jesus) also wanted to publish the targum on the hagiographa; then a voice from heaven came forth that said to him, "Enough with you!" Why? Because it contained the time of the Messiah קץ משיח. – See also Tg. Yer. I Gen. 49:1: "(Jacob wanted to tell his sons the secret or hidden times of redemption קִיצַיָּיא.) But when the glory of the Shekinah of Yahweh appeared (at Jacob's bed), the time קִיצָא when the king, the Messiah, will one day come was hidden from him."

e. TanḥumaB ויחי § 1 (106A): Jacob wanted to reveal (to his sons) the end of days קץ הימין (cf. Dan 12:13);[207] then it was hidden from him. – The parallel passage Gen. Rab. 96 toward the beginning reads only קץ. ‖ Pesiqta 131B: R. Azariah (ca. 380) and R. Abbahu (ca. 300) said in the name of Resh Laqish (ca. 250), "You find, when sins triggered the enemies to infiltrate Jerusalem, they took Israel's heroes and tied their hands together behind their back. Then God said, 'It is written, "I am with him in distress" (Ps 91:15); my children are in distress and I should be in freedom?' 'Then he withdrew,' if one may say so, 'his right hand before the enemy' (Lam 2:3). Finally, he revealed to Daniel, 'But you, go to the end לקץ' (Dan 12:13)! He answered him, 'To give an account and a reckoning?' He said, 'And rest' (Dan 12:13). He answered, 'Do you mean eternal rest?' God said, 'And rise up' (Dan 12:13). He answered before him, 'Lord of the worlds, with whom? With the righteous or with the godless?' He said, '"In your lot" (Dan 12:13), with the righteous who are like you.' He answered, 'When?' God said to him, 'At the end of the ימין' (Dan 12:13). He answered, 'At the end of days לקץ הימים or at the end of the right hand לקץ הימין?' He said to him, 'At the end of the right hand; at the end of the right hand that is enslaved.' God said, 'I have set an appointed time קץ for my right hand; for as long as my children are enslaved, my right hand shall be enslaved. When I redeem my children, I will redeem my right hand'; see Ps 60:7." – Parallel passages are found in Midr. Lam. 2:3 (65B); Midr. Ps. 137 § 7 (263A); Pesiq. Rab. 31 (144B; 145A).

10:12 A: Whoever thinks he stands.

ἑστάναι = עָמַד, concisely: stand firm.

Babylonian Talmud Sanhedrin 89B: R. Simeon b. Abba (ca. 280) said, "... God said to Abraham, 'In how many trials have I tried you and you have stood firm in them all עמדת

206. S-B: This refers to the twofold לכן = "therefore" in Isa 30:18 which according to 1 Sam 3:14 is understood as a formula for an oath.

207. S-B: In the text there is, strikingly, הקץ הימין.

בכלן; now stand firm for me עמוד לי in this trial (the offering of Isaac) as well, lest it be said there was nothing in the earlier (trials)!'"

10:12 B: Let him take care not to fall.

Mishnah ʾAbot 2.4: Hillel (ca. 20 BCE) said, "Do not trust in yourself until the day of your death אַל תַּאֲמֵן בְּעַצְמְךָ עַד יוֹם מוֹתְךָ." – On warnings about pride see in detail § Luke 1:51; see also § Gal 6:3.

10:13: No temptation has seized you except a human one.

πειρασμός = נִסָּיוֹן, pl. נִסְיוֹנוֹת. – On being tempted by God see § Matt 4:1 A; on being tempted by Satan see § Matt 4:1 B, #3, A.

10:16: The cup of blessing.

τὸ ποτήριον τῆς εὐλογίας = כּוֹס שֶׁל בְּרָכָה, Aram. כָּסָא דְבִרְכְּתָא = "cup of blessing." In rabbinic literature, this is the term especially for the cup of wine over which the thanksgiving prayer is spoken at the close of a meal; see the excursus "An Ancient Jewish Feast." At Passover, it was presumably the "third" cup of wine over which the thanksgiving blessing was spoken as the "cup of blessing" after dinner; see the excursus "The Feast of the Passover." – On the "cup of blessing" at the meal of the righteous in the future world see the excursus "Sheol, Gehenna, and the Garden of Eden," III, #4, n. *y*.

10:19: That an idol is something?

On the judgments made by the ancient synagogue about the pagan gods and idols, see § Rom 1:23 A, #2, A. – On this question see SDeut 11:16 § 43 (81B): Are they gods?

10:20: What they sacrifice, they sacrifice to demons and not to God.

Deut 32:17 underlies these words; on the interpretation see § Rom 1:23 A, #2, B.

10:21 A: You cannot drink the cup of the Lord and the cup of demons.

The ancient synagogue regarded consuming pagan libation wine as a sign of apostasy from Judaism.

Tosefta Horayot 1.5 (474): Whoever eats what is abominable is an apostate מְשֻׁמָּד. (Such a person is:) He who eats carrion, what has been torn apart (not ritually slaughtered), abominable and creeping animals, as well as whoever eats pork and drinks (pagan) libation wine יין נֶסֶךְ and desecrates the Sabbath and pulls forward the foreskin. R. Yose b. Judah (ca. 180) said, "Also whoever wears blended fabric (clothes made of wool and linen)." R. Simeon b. Eleazar (ca. 190) said, "Also whoever does something without his evil inclination (lust, passion) desiring it." — The same is found as a baraita in b. Hor. 11A. ‖ On the question of from what point of time gentile wine should be considered libation wine, m. ʿAbod. Zar. 4.8: A winepress whose grapes have been trodden may be purchased from a non-Israelite, even if he takes (the grapes) with his hand and lays them in heaps (of grapes under the clamping bar). It does not become libation wine (is not regarded as such) before it has flowed down into the vat. When it has flowed down into the vat, what is in the vat is prohibited, but the rest permitted. — On libation wine, see also the excursus "The Stance of Judaism toward the Non-Jewish World."

10:21 B: Table of the Lord.

שֻׁלְחַן יהוה (Mal 1:7); LXX: τράπεζα κυρίου. Targum: פָּתוּרָא דיי, "Table of Yahweh" = altar of God. ‖ Testament of Judah 21: "The Lord chose it (the tribe of Levi) even before you (Judah), to bring him near and to eat his table ἐσθίειν τράπεζαν αὐτοῦ and the first fruits from the meal of the children of Israel." ‖ Mishnah ʾAbot 3.3: R. Simeon (ca. 150) said, "If three have eaten at a table without saying words of the Torah, it is as if they had eaten sacrifices to the dead (= sacrifices to idols); as it says, 'Every table is full of filthy food without God' (Isa 28:8). However, if three have eaten at a table and spoken words of the Torah, it is as if they had eaten from the table of God מִשֻּׁלְחָנוֹ שֶׁל מָקוֹם—blessed be He!—as it says, 'And he said to me, "This is the table that stands before Yahweh"' (Ezek 41:22)." ‖ Tosefta Ḥagigah 2.10 (236): Your table should not be full (of food on a feast day) and the table of your Lord שולחן רבך (= altar of God) empty (of freewill feast offerings). — Parallel passages are found in y. Yom Ṭob 2.61C.3; b. Beṣah 20B; see also b. Ḥag. 7A.

10:24: No one should seek his own interests, but rather those of others.

Mishnah ʾAbot 5.10: Whoever says, "Mine is yours and yours is yours" is a pious man. (Whoever says,) "Mine is mine and yours is mine" is a godless man. — See the whole passage at § Rom 5:6f. — A maxim of egoism is found in b. B. Meṣ. 30A: Rab Judah († 299) said that Rab († 247) said, "'So that no poor should be among you' (Deut 15:4) (i.e., according to Rashi, 'Do not impoverish yourself.' From this the following principle is then inferred): What is yours takes priority over what is any (other) person's שלך קודם לשל כל אדם." ‖ The rule in b. Sanh. 9B is different: Raba († 352) said, "אָדָם קָרוֹב אֵצֶל עַצְמוֹ and no one can proclaim himself a wicked person." — According to the lettering, the Hebrew words could be translated: "Each one is a neighbor to himself," but its meaning does not overlap with the German proverb. According to m. Sanh. 3.1, 4, people who are related to one of the legal parties are ineligible to participate in the legal proceedings as judges or witnesses. From this it is inferred that no one can proclaim himself a wicked person, accuse himself of a crime and thereby appear as a witness against himself, since everyone is the nearest relative to himself. — The same principle is also found in b. Sanh. 25A; b. Yebam. 25B; see also b. Ketub. 18B and § 1 Cor 13:5.

10:25: Everything that is sold in the meat shop, eat.

1. μάκελλον = מקולין, מקילון, read with Dalman מָקְלוֹן; the latter means α. in general = shop,[a] β. specifically = meat shop.[b]

a. Sifre Numbers 25:1 § 131 (47B): In that time (when the Israelites dwelled in Shittim), the Ammonites and Moabites rose up and built shops מקולים from Beth-Ha-yeschimoth to the mountain of snow הר השלג and put women in them who sold all kinds of roasted grains כִּסָּנִין.

b. See b. Menaḥ. 29B at § Matt 5:10, #3, near the beginning; see b. Ḥul. 92A at § Rom 1:20 E, n. *c*, toward the end.

2. A Jew was permitted to obtain meat from a pagan meat shop if the animal had not been slaughtered by a non-Israelite,[a] if the meat had not come into contact with the pagan cult,[b] and if the owner of the shop gave the assurance that he did not carry in his store inferior meat that the Jew was forbidden to eat (טְרֵיפָה).[c]

a. Mishnah Ḥullin 1.1: Whatever a non-Israelite has slaughtered is regarded as carrion and defiles by being carried. ‖ Tosefta Ḥullin 1.1 (500): Slaughtering done by a *min* (sectarian) is considered an idolatrous one and slaughtering done by a non-Israelite גוי is unsuitable. ‖ Tosefta Ḥullin 2.20 (503): Meat in the hand (in the possession) of a gentile is allowed for usufruct (but not for consumption, because presumably the slaughtering did not occur in a ritual way as kosher slaughter did); if (it is) in the hand of a sectarian, it is prohibited (even) for usufruct. Whatever is brought out of the house of an idol, see, it is meat from sacrifices for the dead (= idols), while (?) it is said, "Slaughtering done by a sectarian is (as if for) idolatry, their bread is (like) bread of a Samaritan[208] and their wine is (like) wine offered to idols and their fruits are (like) untithed (and therefore forbidden) fruits and their books (those authored by them as well as the holy writings in their possession) are (like) books of sorcery and their sons are (as) bastards." — The same is found as a baraita in b. Ḥul. 13A. ‖ Babylonian Talmud Ḥullin 13A: "Slaughtering done by a non-Jew (*nokhri*) is regarded as carrion and defiles by being carried" (m. Ḥul. 1.1). The Gemarah on this: As carrion, yes; no prohibition of usufruct attaches to it. Who is the Mishnah teacher (who taught this)? R. Hiyya b. Abba (ca. 280) said that R. Yohanan († 279) said that it does not align with the view of R. Eliezer (ca. 90); for R. Eliezer said, "The mind of the non-Jew (text: כותי = the Samaritan) is continuously directed toward idolatry (but even the usufruct of an idol sacrifice is prohibited)." R. Ammi (ca. 300) said, "The author in the Mishnah taught: 'Slaughtering done by a non-Jew is regarded as carrion.' It follows from this that slaughtering done by a sectarian is as for idolatry (and thus forbidden even for usufruct)."

b. Mishnah ʿAbodah Zarah 2.3: Meat that is to be brought into idolatry is permitted (for usufruct); but what is brought out is forbidden, because it is a sacrifice for the dead (= sacrifice to idols). These are the words of R. Aqiba († ca. 135; the halakah corresponds to his words). — See b. ʿAbod. Zar. 32B: Which teacher of the Mishnah (taught the first sentence of the Mishnah above)? R. Hiyya b. Abba (ca. 280) said that R. Yohanan († 279) said that it

208. S-B: Mishnah Šebiʿit 8.10: R. Eliezer (ca. 90) said, "Whoever eats bread from Samaritans (so according to Rashi on b. Ḥul. 13A), it is as if he ate pork."

corresponds to the opinion of R. Eliezer (ca. 90); for R. Eliezer said, "A *goy*'s (non-Israelite's) mind is always oriented toward idolatry." "However, what is brought out is forbidden, because it is like a sacrifice for the dead." Why? Because it is impossible to be anything but a sacrifice to idols. Who (is the author)? It is R. Judah b. Batera (ca. 110). For in a baraita it has been taught: R. Judah b. Batera said, "How do we know that the idol sacrifice makes one unclean (as a corpse does) by tenting (by being with it in one and the same enclosed space)? Because it says, 'They consorted with Baal Peor and ate sacrifices for the dead (idol sacrifices)' (Ps 106:28). As a dead person makes one unclean by tenting, so too an idol sacrifice makes one unclean by tenting (therefore, the meat that has been brought out of an idol temple is prohibited even for usufruct)."

c. Babylonian Talmud Ḥullin 94B: One (Jewish) butcher once said to another, "If you had apologized to me, would I not have given you some of the ox of the cattle feeder, which I slaughtered yesterday?" He responded to him, "I have eaten from the very best." He said to him, "Where did you get it from?" He answered him, "This or that non-Jew had bought it and given it to me." He said, "I slaughtered two (oxen), and this one (from which that non-Jew and you got some) was torn apart (*ṭerefah*, and therefore forbidden for consumption)." Rabbi († 217?) said, "Because of this fool, who did something inappropriate (by selling prohibited meat to a non-Jew and putting it on the market, should we forbid all meat shops מקולין?" Rabbi abided by his principle in this; for he said, "If there are meat shops מקולין and the butchers (in them) are Israelites, the meat that is in the hand (in the possession) of a non-Israelite (as the owner of a meat shop) is permitted (for the Jewish butchers there make sure that only ritually slaughtered meat is sold)."

10:27: If one of the unbelievers invites you and you want to go, eat everything that is set before you, without discriminating for the sake of conscience.

The convivial exchange of a law-observant Jew with a non-Israelite was so complicated in the motherland that one tried as much as possible to get himself out of an invitation to a gentile's house; see on this the excursus "The Stance of Judaism toward the Non-Jewish World." The issue took form in many different ways abroad. We present an exposition that deals with the participation of Jews in gentile wedding celebrations.

A baraita in b. ʿAbod. Zar. 8A: R. Ishmael († ca. 135) said, "The Israelites abroad are idolaters in purity (innocence = unwitting). How so? There is a gentile who prepares a wedding meal for his son and invites all the Jews in the city to it: even if they eat what is theirs (what they have brought with them) and drink what is theirs and their own servant stands before them (waiting on them), Scripture (still) reckons it to them as if they ate sacrifices for the dead (idol sacrifices); for it says, 'He (the idolater) will invite you and you will eat from his sacrifice' (Exod 34:15). Here I would like to say: Until he has (actually) eaten (only from that point does he unwittingly make himself an idolater)!" Raba († 352) said, "In this case Scripture should (only) say, 'And you will eat from his sacrifice'; what then does 'He will invite you' mean? From the hour of the invitation (he makes himself an idolater unwittingly).

Therefore, it is forbidden (to participate) the whole thirty days (of the wedding celebration), irrespective of whether he said to him, 'On the occasion of the wedding celebration (I invite you),' or if he did not say to him, 'On the occasion of the wedding celebration.' From then on, though, (so beyond the 30th day) it is forbidden to participate, if he says to him: 'On the occasion of the wedding celebration'; but if he does not say to him, 'On the occasion of the wedding celebration, he is permitted to participate.' However, if he says to him, 'On the occasion of the wedding celebration, for how long (is participation prohibited)?' Rab Papa († 376) said, '12 months of a year.' And from when beforehand (before the wedding celebration) is it forbidden? Rab Papa said in the name of Raba († 352), 'From the point when barley (for wedding beer) is poured into mortar (for shelling).' But it is permitted after twelve months of a year? Rab Isaac b. Mesharshia (ca. 400?) once came into the house of a gentile after twelve months of a year, and he heard him, how he gave thanks (to his idol). Then he went away without eating! With Rab Isaac b. Mesharshia it was somewhat different because he was a notable man." — In t. ʿAbod. Zar. 4.6 (466), R. Simeon b. Eleazar (ca. 190) is named as the author of the opening statement instead of R. Ishmael.

10:28: Yet if someone says to you, "This is meat sacrificed to idols," do not eat.

This can be compared with an analogous stipulation in m. ʿAbod. Zar. 1.5. After listing the things an Israelite cannot sell to a gentile under any circumstances because he would use them for pagan cultic purposes, the passage says generally: "All other things without a specific statement (about intention) are permitted (to be sold), but in the case of an explicit statement (of their being destined for pagan cultic purposes), it is prohibited."

10:31: Do everything to God's honor.

Mishnah ʾAbot 6.11: Everything that God has created in his world, he has created only for his honor לִכְבוֹדוֹ; as it says, "Everything that is called by my name and that I have created, formed, and made for my honor" (Isa 43:7); furthermore, "Yahweh is king forever and ever" (Exod 15:18). — The same is found as a generally recognized principle with Prov 16:4 as the supporting text in b. Yoma 38A. ‖ Pesiqta Rabbati 23 (115B): Hillel the elder (ca. 20 BCE) used to say, "Let all your action happen for God's sake" כל מעשיך יהיו לשם שמים! — See the whole passage at § Matt 12:1, #2, end of penultimate paragraph; Also see b. Beṣah 16A in the same paragraph at § Matt 12:1, #2. — Hillel's saying is found in the mouth of R. Yose the priest (ca. 100) in m. ʾAbot 2.12. ‖ Mishnah Ḥag. 2.1: Whoever does not preserve the honor of his creator (is not mindful of it), it would be better for him if he had not come into the world. ‖ See b. Meg. 3A at § Matt 3:17 A, n. *h*, #2. See a similar saying in the mouth of Rabban Gamaliel (ca. 90) in b. B. Meṣ. 59B in the excursus "Excommunication from the Synagogue." — See also § Luke 17:18.

10:32: Do not become a stumbling block to Jews or Greek or the church of God.

1. On ἀπρόσκοποι see the passages at § Rom 12:17 B.

2. On Ιουδαῖοι καὶ Ἕλληνες see § Rom 1:14, #3.

10:33: By not seeking my own benefit … (cf. 10:24).

11:4: Any man who has something on his head while praying or prophesying dishonors his head (i.e., Christ).

1. The question of whether the Jewish male world in the New Testament period would have ordinarily gone about with covered or uncovered head cannot be answered with a simple yes or no. In fact, in this respect, complete arbitrariness ruled. On the one hand, R. Joshua (ca. 90) thinks that a man going out with a bare-headed appearance is just as characteristic for him as going out with a covered head is for a woman.[a] Since the latter was the common practice, the former must have also been the recognized custom. However, on the other side, we can set the generally known fact of experience that men could sometimes have a covered head, sometimes an uncovered head, as they pleased, while boys typically went about with a bare head.[b] Accordingly, no more or less fixed custom would have developed at all. And this would have been the case for the motherland Palestine. Only in Babylonia might head covering have been just as much the sign of a married man as no head covering was regarded as the mark of an unmarried man.[c] In Palestine a man's uncovered head was viewed as a symbol of his freedom,[d] and precisely for this reason men who were particularly strict about the law made it their concern never to go out with a bare head, in order to demonstrate to everyone that God's lordship and the fear of him were upon him at all times.[e] As a consequence of this view, a respected man could see it as a sign of irreverence and impertinence when an inferior approached him with an uncovered head.[f] Yet with the very same justification others could consider precisely the uncovering of the head as a sign of reverence and subservience.[g] With such confusedly intersecting views, it is no wonder if no unified practice could develop. The majority would have behaved according to the rule that was later handed down as the practice of R. Yohanan († 279): "One covered one's head with a turban in winter because of the cold and let it remain uncovered in summer because of the heat."[h]

a. Genesis Rabbah 17 (12A): (R. Joshua was asked,) "Why does a man go out with his head uncovered ראשו מגולה, and a woman with her head covered ראשה מכוסה?" He answered them, "Like someone who committed a sin and is (therefore) ashamed before people. Therefore, she goes out with her head covered (because the woman brought sin into the world)."

b. Babylonian Talmud Nedarim 30B: Men sometimes cover their head מיכסו רישייהו, sometimes expose their head מגלו רישייהו; but women always cover it and boys always leave it uncovered.

c. Babylonian Talmud Qiddušin 29B: Rab Hisda († 309) extolled Rab Hamnuna (ca. 300) as a significant person before Rab Huna († 297). That man said to him, "When he comes to you, send him to me." When he came, he (Huna) saw him (Hamnuna), that he did not wear a cloth (a type of turban around his head). He said to him, "Why did you not spread a cloth?" He answered him, "Because I am not married." Then he turned his face away from him and said to him, "Behold, you are not to see my face again until you have gotten married!"

d. Targum Onkelos Exodus 14:8: "Yahweh hardened the heart of pharaoh, the king of Egypt, and he pursued the children of Israel, and the children of Israel went out with uncovered head בְּרֵישׁ גְּלֵי." — Base text: ביד רמה = "by (God's) raised hand." Targum Onkelos also rendered ביד רמה in Num 33:3 with בריש גלי, the same as in Tg. Yer. I; see § Acts 13:17 B, #1. ‖ Exodus Rabbah 18 (80D): God said to pharaoh, "You will let my children go at night? You shall not let my children go at night; rather, they should go out with head uncovered בְּרֹאשׁ גָּלוּי (i.e., as free men) and in the middle of the day." ‖ Targum Judges 5:9: "Deborah said by prophecy, 'I am sent to extol the scribes of Israel. For when this distress happened, they did not cease to search in the Torah; and now it befits them well that they sit in the houses of assembly with uncovered head בריש גלי (as free men) and teach the people the words of the Torah and worship and praise before Yahweh.'"

e. Babylonian Talmud Qiddušin 31A: Rab Huna b. Joshua (ca. 350) said, "I do not go four cubits with an uncovered head בְּגִילּוּי הָרֹאשׁ (literally: with the exposure of the head)." He said, "The Shekinah (divinity) abides over my head." — In the parallel b. Šabb. 118B: "May it prove advantageous for me that I have not gone four cubits with an uncovered head בגילוי הראש!" ‖ Babylonian Talmud Šabbat 156B: Concerning the mother of Rab Nahman b. Isaac († 356) the Chaldeans (astrologers) had said ..., see § John 2:4 C, under the comment on astrology.

f. Babylonian Talmud Qiddušin 33A: Rabina (I, † ca. 420) sat before R. Jeremiah of Difti. Then a man passed by him without covering his head ילא מיכסי רישיה. He said, "How impudent this man is!" ‖ See tractate Kallah 18B at § Matt 1:16, #7.

g. See Pesiq. 77A in #2, n. *m.*

h. Jerusalem Talmud Berakot 2.4C.11: R. Yohanan wore both (the head and the arm tefillin) in winter, since he had wrapped his head (with a turban); but in summer he would wear only the arm tefillin, since he had not wrapped his head (with a turban). See Pesiq. Rab. 22 (112A).

2. As the Jewish male world in the New Testament period was not bound by any custom to go about in ordinary life with a covered head, so too they were not obligated to appear with a covered head before God in religious and liturgical actions. The older halakah prescribes only that a man not come naked before God. Therefore, he should cover his nakedness while reciting the Shema and cover himself up to his chest while praying.[a] The older period thus knows nothing about covering the head while praying.

Yet without doubt there was an effort by circles that were particularly strict about the law to develop the religious custom in this direction. From previous times, the custom had been adopted that a mourner (see Ezek 24:17, 22; cf. also Mic 3:7) and a leper (see Lev 13:45) had to sit covered up to the moustache.[b] The halakah then extended this stipulation to those on whom the ban had been imposed for some reason.[c] Then the members of the pharisaic *ḥaber* covenant, which had been established to observe the tithing and purity laws punctiliously (see § John 7:49, #3–7), voluntarily took it upon itself in times of general distress in the land and after a fruitless period of certain fast days to sit before God covered like mourners and those placed under the ban, until mercy on the people appeared from heaven.[d] In all these cases, being covered before God was supposed to signify that one felt the punishing hand of God in pain and sorrow. Yet it did not stop there. Those who were strict about the law, above all the rabbinic scholars, began to implement self-covering before God on other occasions as well. So one covered himself in prayer,[e] in leading prayer in the synagogue,[f] in administering justice,[g] in dissolving vows,[h] in visiting the sick,[i] and in waiting for the arrival of the Sabbath.[k] The prayer shawl טַלִּית (see § Mark 12:38, #2 and #3), which was long and broad enough to cover the body with the head, served as a covering. Of course, the self-covering now had a different significance than in the previously mentioned cases. Here one wanted to express that one was aware of and certain of the presence of the divinity with the heads of the prayer, the judge, etc. and therefore covered himself before him in humility and reverence.[l] The custom may have gained currency from this if a prayer shawl was not available to cover at least the head in prayer. Our sources offer only sparse material on this point; yet, it seems that at the beginning of the 4th century praying with a covered head was already a fixed custom in broad circles.[m]

a. Tosefta Berakot 2.14 (4): If someone stands naked in a field or if someone does his work naked, he should cover himself with straw or with gleanings or with something else to recite the Shema by heart. For it has been said, "There is no praise for a man who stands there naked; for when God created man, he created him naked; as it says, 'When I made clouds his frock and dark mist his diapers' (Job 38:9). 'When I made clouds his frock': here the (embryo) head is meant; 'and dark mist his diapers': here the placenta is meant (cf. y. Nid. 3.50D.11)." See, if the covering of a frock or of a hide is tied around his hips, he may recite the Shema; but in neither case may he pray (the Prayer of Eighteen Benedictions) until he has covered his heart (his chest). — The same is found as a baraita in b. Ber. 24B. ‖ Mishnah Berakot 3.5: If someone has gotten into a bath and gotten out and can cover (clothe) himself and recite the (morning) Shema before the sun shines, he should get out and cover himself and recite; but if not, he should cover himself (in the bath) with water (up to the throat) and recite. Yet he should not cover himself with dirty water or with water where anything has been soaked before he has poured in (fresh) water. ‖ Tosefta Berakot 2.15 (4): A person should not stick his head in the bosom (lap) to recite the Shema. If he is surrounded with a cover from within (i.e., on a bare body), he may recite it. If two sleep under a cover, they may not recite the Shema, but rather one should cover himself with his cover and recite and the other should cover himself with his cover and recite. If his son or his daughter (with whom he sleeps under one cover) are still small, he may do it. See B. Ber. 24A.

b. See § 1 Cor 11:5 A, n. *g*.

c. See b. Taʿan. 14B in n. *d*; also see the excursus "Excommunication from the Synagogue."

d. A baraita in b. Taʿan. 14B: (After a fruitless period of the final fast days of a communal fast) the members (of the pharisaic) covenant of associates do not greet each other; they respond to the greeting of people ignorant of the law (*ʿamme haʾareṣ*) who greet them with a slack lip and a bowed head; they also cover themselves and sit like mourners and like those under the ban, like people who have received a reprimand from God (a mild degree of the ban), until mercy is shown to them from heaven.

e. ʾAbot de Rabbi Nathan 6 (3C): Naqedimon (Nicodemus) b. Gurion (ca 70) went into the house of learning, covered himself and stood praying. ‖ See b. Šabb. 10A and b. Meg. 16A at § Mark 12:38, #4, n. *a*. ‖ Jerusalem Talmud Berakot 7.11D.11: R. Ba b. Hiyya b. Abba (ca. 320) said, "If one has eaten while moving, one stands quietly and says the blessing (after the meal); if one has eaten while standing, one sits down and says the blessing; if one has eaten while sitting, one lies down (as one lies at table during a meal) and says the blessing; if one has eaten while lying at table, he wraps himself up and says the blessing. If one does this, he is like the angels of service; as it says, 'With two (wings) he covered his face and with two wings he covered his feet' (Isa 6:2)." ‖ A baraita in b. Ber. 51A: Ten things have been said about the cup of blessing (over which the table thanksgiving prayer is spoken): It requires … covering (of the one who takes it to speak the table thanksgiving prayer over it)…. Rab Papa († 376) covered himself and sat (to say the thanksgiving prayer); Rab Asi (ca. 300) spread a cloth over his head (and said the thanksgiving prayer).

f. See b. Roš Haš. 17B at § Mark 12:38, #4, n. *a*.

g. See b. Šabb. 10A and SDeut 1:13 § 13 (68A) at § Mark 12:38, #4, n. *b*.

h. Passages at § Mark 12:38, #4, n. *c*.

i. See the baraita in b. Šabb. 12B at § Mark 12:38, #4, n. *d*.

k. Babylonian Talmud Šabbat 25B: Rab Judah († 299) said that Rab († 247) said, "This was the custom of R. Judah b. Ilai (ca. 150): On the eve of the Sabbath a pan full of warm water was brought to him, he washed his face, his hands and his feet and covered himself and sat in linen throws that had show threads (*tzitzit*) (to await the Sabbath) and was like an angel of Yahweh Sabaoth." ‖ Babylonian Talmud Šabbat 119A: R. Hanina (ca. 225) covered himself and stood there until the evening of the day of preparation for the Sabbath. He said, "Well now, we will go to meet the Sabbath, the king!" (In the text, since שַׁבָּת is feminine: המלכה "the queen.")

l. Babylonian Talmud Sanhedrin 22A: Rab Hana b. Bizna (ca. 260) said that R. Simeon the Pious (ca. 210) said, "The one who prays must view himself as if the divinity stood in front of him." ‖ Babylonian Talmud Berakot 6A: Rabin b. Ad(d)a (ca. 350) said that R. Isaac (ca. 300) said, "How do we know that God dwells in a synagogue? Because it says, 'God is there in the community of the Almighty' (Ps 82:1). Where do we get the idea concerning ten persons who pray, that the Shekinah is with them? Because it says, 'God is there in the community of the Almighty' (Ps 82:1) (and a community עדה is formed by ten people according to Num 14:27). Where do we get the idea concerning three who sit in judgment, that the Shekinah is with them? Because it says, 'In the midst of the judges' (so Ps 82:1 according to the midr.)." ‖ God on the bed of the sick person: see b. Šabb. 12B at § Mark 12:38, #4, n. *d*.

m. Pesiqta 77A: "My people, ... how have I afflicted you" (Mic 6:3). R. Berekhiah (ca. 340) said, "Like a king who sent his command to a city. What did the people of the city do? They took it, got on their feet, exposed their heads פורעין ראשיהם (out of reverence for the king) and read it in trepidation and fear, with trembling and with shaking. Just so God said to Israel, 'It is my command to recite the Shema; but I have not burdened you and not told you to recite it standing on your feet, nor with your heads uncovered, but rather "while you sit in your house, and when you walk on a path, and when you lie down, and when you get up"' (Deut 6:7)." — Here reciting the Shema with a head that is not uncovered is taken for granted. — Parallels are found in Tanḥ. אמור 175B; TanḥB אמור § 13 (46B). In Lev. Rab. 27 (125D) R. Isaac (ca. 300) is the author.

11:5 A: Every woman who prays or prophesies with her head unveiled dishonors her head.

The halakah required Jewish women to cover their head when they appeared outside the house.[a] Going outside with a bare head was recognized as something disgraceful for a woman, so that her husband could dismiss her for doing so,[b] even without being obligated to pay the agreed upon divorce sum (German: *Hochzeitsverschreibung*).[c] Conversely, forcibly exposing a woman's head was considered to be such a serious insult that the Mishnah imposed on the perpetrator a penalty of 400 *zuz* in payment for the humiliation.[d] In their own house and probably in its yard, women seem to have observed the stipulations about covering the head only a little, as an occasional remark in the Babylonian Gemarah shows.[e] It would probably have been only the more stringently oriented circles within the Jewish women's world that would have valued appearing even in their own homes with a covered head at all times.[f]

In addition to mentioning covering the head, our sources also mention veiling or covering a woman's face. Among the ten curses that God is supposed to have spoken over Eve, there is one that she is to be veiled like a mourner. This entails that her face had to be covered to the mouth.[g] This corresponds to Rashi's remark on b. Šabb. 80A, namely that decent women (i.e., living in seclusion) go about veiled מעוטפות and would have only left one eye uncovered in order to see.[h] Just how stringently decent women would have maintained veiling their face even at home can be recognized best from the fact that it is considered possible that even the husband's nearest relatives would not know his wife's facial features.[i]

With the strong emphasis on a woman's obligation to cover her head and to veil her face, it is striking that our sources do not explicitly tell us about the way in which and the means by which the head was covered and the face was veiled. To think of a shroud, as eastern women are accustomed to wear today, is ruled out. For the Mishnah knows only the Jewish women living in Arabia as shrouded רְעוּלוֹת;[k] it follows from this that the shroud was not in use among women in Palestine. Completely in passing b. Ketub. 72A deals with whether the little knitting basket, when women placed it on their head, should be seen as a head covering in keeping with the law.[l] Yet this belongs to the area of casuistry and gives us no information about our question. Due to the silence of the sources, we are automatically driven to assume that no particular means was used to cover the head or veil the face, but rather both were taken as given when a woman appeared with the headdress that was custom at the time. This requires us to go into the latter briefly here.

A woman's hair was first tied together in braids[m] (קְלַע, קְלִיעָא, קְלִיעֲתָא). After a woolen cloth כִּפָּה (= little cover)[n] that reached down to the eyes was immediately spread over the hair, the hair braids were put together over this cover on the head.[n] Depending on the thickness and length of the braids, the set-up on the head would have to be higher or lower. Then a headband (שָׁבִיס or טוֹטֶפֶת) was tied around the forehead over the כִּפָּה that served as an underlay for this. The headband reached from one ear to the other and was held in place with bands that fell to the chin.[o] Corresponding to the כִּפָּה under the hair braids, a חִפּוּי, that is, a small cover, was then spread over the hair braids. This was called a כְּבוּל and, as the name shows (כָּבַל = to tie, bind), served to hold the braids together.[p] Then followed a net (שְׂבָכָה, סְבָכָה, סִבְכָא, סְבַכְתָּא), which clasped the braids and gave the whole hairstyle its actual stability; bands on its sides served to fasten it.[q] Net and headband (שביס, טוטפת) were trimmed with all kinds of decorations, especially with bands and ribbons,[r] which, as already said above, fell down in part forward over the face. In one passage, finally, in addition to the net (סבכתא), a type of shroud (בָּיְיבָא) is also mentioned, which according to Levy[209] and Samuel Krauß[210] served as a veil for the face. Yet the reading בייכא is not certain; ʿArukh reads בייכא, which Levy interprets as יְיכָא, "band," with the preposition בְּ.[211] Moreover, this saying is found in the mouth of the Babylonian scholar Raba († 352), so we are not entitled to assume that the designated item was in use in Palestine as well.

This hairstyle with its bands and ribbons and cloths was probably the covering that became a requirement for Jewish women. In this regard,

209. Levy, *Chaldäisches Wörterbuch*, 1:217A.

210. Samuel Krauß, *Talmudische Archäologie* (Leipzig: Fock, 1910), 1:189.

211. Levy, *Chaldäisches Wörterbuch*, 2:238B.

it is instructive to consider the proceeding against the Soṭah (woman suspected of adultery) at a holy place. The purpose of the proceeding is the dishonoring, the debasing of the accused.[s] This is accomplished by exposing פְּרִיעָה the woman's head and chest[t] in the presence of the multitude. The head is exposed by the priest pulling down or destroying סָתַר the woman's headdress by grabbing the כִּפָּה, the small cover under the hair braids and stepping on it. This satisfies the regulation in Num 5:18: "The priest פרע את ראש"; according to the rabbinic interpretation, this meant, "The priest shall expose the head": the woman now stands there publicly as one whose ראש פרוע, whose head is exposed, to whom the greatest insult that could befall her has been done. Accordingly, "exposing the head" פרע את ראש of the woman is tantamount to "destroying or dismantling the headdress";[u] conversely, "making the proper headdress" is tantamount to "covering the head," that is, in other words, according to the Jewish view, the covering of a woman's head, and also, if we think of the bands and ribbons and the כִּפָּה that fell down over the face, the veiling of a woman's face, consists in the orderly headdress.[v]

a. Sifre Numbers 5:18 § 11 (5A): (The regulation in Num 5:18: "The priest shall expose the woman's hair") teaches about the daughters of Israel, that they cover their heads שהן מכסות ראשיהם. Even if there is no proof for this, it is implied when it says, "Tamar put ashes on her head" (2 Sam 13:19). ‖ Babylonian Talmud Ketubbot 72A: In a baraita of the school of R. Ishmael († ca. 135) it has been taught: (The regulation in Num 5:18: "The priest shall expose the woman's hair") is a warning for the daughters of Israel, that they not go out with an exposed head בפרוע ראש. ‖ Babylonian Talmud Nedarim 30B: Men sometimes cover their head, sometimes leave their head bare; but women always cover it and boys always leave it uncovered (always go about with a bare head). ‖ Numbers Rabbah 9 (152D): "The priest shall expose the woman's head" (Num 5:18). Why? Because it is a custom for the daughters of Israel to have their head covered (ראשיהן מכוסות, literally: concerning their heads to be covered). And therefore he exposed her head and said to her: "You have separated yourself from the custom of the daughters of Israel, whose custom it is to be covered on their head מכוסות, and you have wandered in the ways of non-Israelite women (הגוים), who go about with an exposed head (ראשיהן פרועות, literally: as to their heads exposed); see, you get what you wanted (namely an exposed head)." ‖ See Gen. Rab. 17 (12A) at § 1 Cor 11:4, #1, n. *a*. — See also the citations in notes *b* and *c*.

b. Jerusalem Talmud Soṭah 1.16B.28: How do we know that a woman should be dismissed (with a certificate of divorce) if she goes out with an exposed head ראשה פרוע? Scripture teaches, "Because he has found something disgraceful in her" (Deut 24:1). — See the saying of Rab Sheshet (ca. 260) in b. Ber. 24A: (Exposed) hair on a woman is ערוה = licentious. — Babylonian Talmud Sanhedrin 109B narrates how all people recoiled when they saw the woman of a house sitting at the door with unraveled hair.

c. Mishnah Ketubbot 7.6: The following (wives) are dismissed without the prescribed marital sum: ... The one who goes out while her head is exposed וראשה פרוע. — Whether

יראשה פרוע is translated: "while her head is exposed (uncovered)" or "while her hair is unraveled," there is no difference in content, because the exposure of the head consists in the disbanding of the hair; see on this below. ‖ Tosefta Ketub. 7.6 (269): (R. Meir [ca. 150] said,) "If she (a wife) goes out while her head is exposed ..., she is to be dismissed without the prescribed marital sum, because she has not behaved toward him (the husband) according to the law of Moses and of Israel." ‖ Tosefta Soṭah 5.9 (302): (R. Meir said,) "It is a godless man who sees his wife going out while her head is exposed (and nevertheless does not separate from her).... It is an obligatory commandment to dismiss her (by divorce)." — Parallel passages are found in b. Giṭ. 90A; Num. Rab. 9 (152B).

d. Mishnah Baba Qamma 8.6: If someone exposes a woman's head פרע ראש האשה on the street, he pays 400 *zuz*.... It once happened that someone exposed a woman's head on the street, and she came before R. Aqiba († ca. 135), and he declared him guilty to give her 400 *zuz*. He said to him, "Rabbi, give me time (deferral of payment)." And he gave him time. He observed her, how she stood at the entry to her yard (and he went in) and he smashed before her a flask that had 1 *as* of oil. Then she exposed גִּלְּתָה her head and took up the oil with her hand and put her hand on her head. Then he called witnesses against her and came before R. Aqiba. He said to him, "Rabbi, I am to give this woman 400 *zuz* (who exposed and dishonored herself)?" He answered him, "You said nothing; for if someone injures himself although he is not justified to do so, he is still free (from the obligation to compensate); others are obligated to do so if they have injured him."

e. See b. Ketub. 72A in n. *l*.

f. Jerusalem Talmud Megillah 1.72A.52: It once happened that Simeon b. Qimhit[212] (a high priest) went forth with the king of the Arabs on the eve of the Day of Atonement at the entrance of darkness (from the sanctuary). Then a bit of spit sprayed from his (the king's) mouth onto his (the high priest's) frock and made him (Levitically) unclean[213] (so that he could not officiate). His brother Judah went in and provided the high priestly service in his stead. So their mother (Qimhit) saw two sons as high priest in one day. Qimhit had seven sons, and they all provided the high priestly service. Then the scholars had it asked of her: "What good works do you have (that such an honor has been bestowed on you in your sons)?" She answered them, "May this and that come over me if the beams of my house ever say the hair of my head or the fringe of my shirt!" (She kept her head covered even in her house.) It was said, "All flours are flour, but the flour[214] of Qimhit (קימחא דקימחית, wordplay) is fine flour." And the following was applied to her, "All honor is bestowed on the king's daughter in the innermost part of the house; her dress is made of gold weavings" (since high priests in clothes made of gold issued from her) (Ps 45:14). Parallel passages are found in y. Yoma 1.38D.7 (see § John 18:13, first S-B footnote); y. Hor.

---

212. S-B: Here Qimhit is the name of the mother of Simeon. — Josephus, *Jewish Antiquities* 18.2.2, calls a certain high priest Simon, son of Κάμιθος (ca. 17–18 CE), who is probably identical with our Simeon b. Qimhit; cf. Emil Schürer, *Geschichte des jüdischen Volkes im Zeitalter Jesu Christi*, 4th ed. (Leipzig: Hinrichs, 1907), 2:271.

213. S-B: According to this passage, the spit of a gentile makes one unclean just as the spit of one tainted by genital discharges; cf. Lev 15:8.

214. S-B: "Flour" = "progeny" corresponds to the euphemistic "to mill" = "to copulate."

3.47D.12; Pesiq. 174A; Lev. Rab. 20 (120A); Tanḥ. אחרי מות 164B; TanḥB אחרי § 9 (33A); Num. Rab. 2 (139A). Instead of Simeon b. Qimhit, we read Ishmael b. Qimhit in t. Yoma 4.20 (189); b. Yoma 47A; and ʾAbot R. Nat. 35 (9B).

g. The eighth curse of Eve is as follows in b. ʿErub. 100B: She shall be veiled like a mourner עטופה כאבל. – On this passage Rashi says, "She is ashamed to go out with an exposed head בראש פרוע." – In the parallel passage Pirqe R. El. 14 (7D): On her head she should be covered מכוסה like a mourner. – The following passages give an overview about the veiling of a mourner. Babylonian Talmud Moʿed Qaṭan 15A: A mourner is obligated to veil (עֲטִיפָה) the head, because the All Merciful One said to Ezekiel said, "You shall not cover your moustache" (Ezek 24:17), which entails that the whole (rest of the) world is obligated to do so. ‖ According to Pirqe R. El. 17 (9B) a mourner was recognized by having his moustache covered שפמו מכוסה (cf. Lev 13:45). ‖ Jerusalem Talmud Moʿed Qaṭan 3.82D.6: (A mourner) must cover his mouth; specifically, he should cover יכסינה it below מִלְּרַע. Rab Hisda († 309) said, "Lest it be said, 'He has pain in his mouth' (and that is why he covers it, but not because of mourning)." ‖ Babylonian Talmud Moʿed Qaṭan 24A: Samuel († 254) said, "… Any veiling עטיפה, that is not like the veiling of the Ishmaelites, is not a veiling." Rab Nahman († 320) showed: "Up to the beard dimples" (i.e., according to Rashi, "Up to the dimples in the cheeks below the mouth"). ‖ Rashi on b. Moʿed Qaṭ. 24A: "While the mourner is veiled מכוסה in the days of his mourning, on the Sabbath he must expose his nose and his moustache and his sideburns in order to show that mourning does not take place on the Sabbath."

h. On the words in m. Šabb. 8.3—"Whoever (on the Sabbath) carries out (from a private area into a public one) as much makeup as is needed to cover one eye (is guilty to present a sin offering)"—Rab Huna [† 297] remarks in b. Šabb. 80A: "For decent women put makeup on (only) one eye." Rashi says, "Decent women who go about veiled מעוטפות expose מגלות only one eye in order to be able to see, and they put makeup on this.… It is not necessary for the female inhabitants of a village to be secluded so much; for there one does not find banter and frivolity (exuberance), … and they do not cover their face and they put makeup on both their eyes."

i. Meg. 10B: R. Samuel b. Nahman (ca. 260) said that R. Jonathan (ca. 220) said, "Every young woman who lives decently (in seclusion) in the house of her father-in-law, merits that kings and prophets issue from her. How do we know this? Because it is written about Tamar, 'Judah saw her and took her for a prostitute, because she had covered כסתה her face' (Gen 38:15). Because she had covered כסתה her face (in that hour) he would have taken her for a prostitute? Rather, since she had (earlier) covered כסתה her face in the house of her father-in-law, so that he did not know her, she had been deemed worthy for kings and prophets to issue from her." – The beginning of this explanation is also in b. Soṭah 10B. ‖ TanḥumaB וישב § 17 (94A): R. Yohanan († 279) said, "Because (Tamar) covered כסתה her face as long as she was in the house of her father-in-law (Judah did not recognize her). On the basis of this passage (Gen 38:15) our teachers said, 'A man needs to come to know his daughter-in-law (lest he fall because of her).'" ‖ Genesis Rabbah 85 (54D): R. Hiyya b. Zabda (an Amorite of uncertain time) said, "A man must be mindful of getting to know (the appearance of) his wife's sister and his female relatives, lest he stumble because of one of them." From whom do you learn that? From Judah (namely in Gen 38:15). ‖ Exodus Rabbah 41 (97D): R. Simeon b. Laqish (ca. 250) said, "As a bride decently lives reserved all the days she resides in the house of her father so that no man gets to know her מכירה, but when she prepares to go under the wedding canopy, she exposes מגלה her face as if to say, 'Whoever knows a testimony about me, let him come and witness against me (against the moral purity)': so a student of the scholars must decently live reserved as a bride and be known by his good works as a bride who unveils herself מפרסמת (by exposing her face in the wedding chamber)." – See a parallel passage with differences in Midr. Song. 4:11 (115B) at § Matt 9:15 B, n. *g*.

k. Mishnah Šabbat 6.6: Arab Jewish women may (on the Sabbath) go out shrouded רְעוּלוֹת (because the shroud is a part of their everyday dress). (Rashi says, "Arab women usually veil their head and their face with the exception of the eyes").

l. Babylonian Talmud Ketubbot 72A: According to the Torah, the little knitting basket appears to be enough (for women to cover their head; see above at SNum 5:18 § 11 in n. *a*, where ashes appear to be sufficient to cover the head). But according to Jewish law (which here goes beyond the law of Moses), even a little knitting basket is prohibited (as a head covering). R. Asi (ca. 300) said that R. Yohanan († 279) said, "With a little knitting basket there is nothing of an exposed head פרוע ראש (i.e., it suffices as a head covering)." R. Zeira (ca. 300) demurred, "Where? If one should say, 'On the street,' we have the Jewish law (which rejects the little knitting basket as insufficient); rather, in the yard (the little basket suffices). Yet, if this were so (that women must keep their head covered even in the yard), our father Abraham would no longer have any daughter who could dwell with her spouse (they would all have to be dismissed, since the women are little concerned with covering their head in their own homestead)." Abbayye († 338/39)—or as it is also said, Rab Kahana (probably the younger, ca. 300)—said, "From one yard to another or in a passage (that is not taken by many people a woman may cover herself with the little knitting basket, but not in a public area)."

m. See y. Meg. 1.72A.52 in n. *f*. – The Patriarch Gamaliel (II, ca. 90) testifies about the wife of R. Aqiba († ca. 135) that she sold her hair braids so that her husband could occupy himself with the study of the Torah; see y. Šabb. 6.7D, 56; y. Soṭah 9.24C.8.

n. Mishnah Ketubbot 5.8: The husband has to give his wife a small covering כִּפָּה for her head, a waistband for her hips and shoes from one feast to another (i.e., on each of the three great festivals). – The כיפה was thus a necessary and quickly worn out piece of clothing for every woman. That it was made out of wool is attested to by the expression כיפה של צמר in, for example, b. Šabb. 57B.25, 26, 27. ‖ Jerusalem Talmud Šabbat 5.7B.45: As the כיפה with which she (the woman) covers her eyebrows. ‖ Tosefta Šabbat 4.7 (115): R. Simeon b. Eleazar (ca. 190) said, "With any small covering הִיפּוּי under her hair a woman may go out on the Sabbath (since there is no concern that she will pull it out to show to other women; for in doing so she would unravel her hairstyle), but with a small cover over her hair she may not go out on the Sabbath." – By a small covering under the hair, the כיפה is meant.

o. שָׁבִיס "headband," frequently called in, for example, t. Kelim B. Bat. 5.15 (595) שבים של שבכה "headband of the net," evidently because the net was fastened on it. In this Tosefta passage, it is also asked, "And how long does it (the שבים) measure? So long that it reaches from one ear to the other." ‖ טוֹטֶפֶת. – Mishnah Šabbat 6.1: A woman may not go out (on the Sabbath) ... into a public area ... with a headband טוטפת, nor with bands (סַנְבּוּטִין, other reading: סַרְבִיטִין) on it if they are not sewed on. – Mishnah Šabbat 6.5: A woman may go out (on the Sabbath) ... into the yard ... with a headband and with bands on it if they are sewed on. – More generally it says in t. Šabb. 4.6 (115): R. Eliezer (ca. 90) said, "A woman may go out (on the Sabbath) ... with a headband טוטפות and bands סרביטין they are sewed on." – Babylonian Talmud Šabbat 57B appears to refer to this baraita: "... A woman may go out (on the Sabbath) ... with a headband טוטפת and bands fastened on it סרביטין." – Then follows in b. Šabb. 57B: What is a headband טוטפת and what are bands סרביטין? R. Abbahu (ca. 300) said, "A headband goes from one ear to the other; the bands reach to the chin."

p. In m. Šabb. 6.1, כָּבוּל is listed among the things with which a woman may not go into a public area on the Sabbath. Already R. Yannai (ca. 225) declares in b. Šabb. 57B that he does not know what should be understood by כבול, whether the "slave rope" or a small woolen cover. However, R. Abbahu (ca. 300) says in b. Šabb. 57B.26, "The opinion of the one who said that it means the small cover of wool is plausible." Then it says further that a baraita reads the same: "A woman may ... go out into the yard ... (on the Sabbath) with a כבול." (On this, see m. Šabb. 6.5 in the foregoing n. *o*.) R. Simeon (ca. 150) said, "Also with a כבול into a public area." R. Simeon b. Eleazar (ca. 190) said as a general rule, "With everything that is beneath the hairnet שבכה she may go out; with everything that is above the hairnet she may not go out (on the Sabbath)" (and the כבול is among the things below the hairnet, so she may go out with it). – Accordingly, the כָּבוּל was a small woolen cover that was worn above the hair braids but under the net, as the כִּיפָּה was worn under the hair braids.

q. The net is mentioned together with its bands in, for example, m. Šabb. 15.2: In tying certain knots (on the Sabbath), one does not make oneself subject to punishment.... So, a woman may tie knots in ... the bands of the net חוּטֵי סְבָכָא. – That the net was located over the כָּבוּל is attested to by the general rule of R. Simeon b. Eleazar at the end of the previous n. *p.*

r. Concerning the bands on the headband טוטפת see n. *o*; concerning those on the net see n. *q*. – It is said generally in m. Šabb. 6.1: A woman may not go out (on the Sabbath into a public area) with bands of wool, with bands of linen, with ribbons on her head. – This would have meant bands and ribbons on the headband and net. ‖ Tosefta Kelim Baba Batra 5.16 (595): Metal plates, (metallic) platelets, and (other) jewelry on the headband שבים are clean and are liable to uncleanness when they are connected with the headband; the ribbons on it (on the headband) are clean; stitches (by which the ribbons are bound to the headband) are considered a connection (so that the ribbons become unclean with a headband).

s. Mishnah Soṭah 1.6: The measure a person uses to measure will be used (by God) to measure him: she primped herself for sin, so she dishonors (defaces) נִוְּלָהּ God. – Mishnah Soṭah 1.7: If she was clothed with white clothes, she will be clothed with black. If there were gold items on her, necklaces, nose rings and other rings, they will be removed from her to disgrace her.... Everyone who wishes to see her may come and see her, except for her male and female slaves, because her heart is proud toward them (and consequently she would all the more not confess her guilt). And all the women may see her; for it says, "All the women are warned not to act according to your fornication" (Ezek 23:48). ‖ Sifre Numbers 5:18 § 11

(5A): R. Yohanan b. Beroqah (ca. 110) said, "One does not dishonor מנוולים the daughters of Israel beyond what is written in the Torah (namely in Num 5:18): 'A linen cover (curtain) was spread out between him (the priest) and the people....' He was answered, 'As she did not look after God's honor, her honor will not be looked after, but rather she defiled it with this entire dishonor: whoever wished to see her was allowed to, with the exception of her male and female slaves, because her heart is proud toward them. Both men and women, both relatives and those distant to her may see her; for it says, "All the women are warned ..." (Ezek 23:48).'" ‖ Tosefta Soṭah 3.2 (295): She stood before him (her paramour), so the priest sets her before all (the people), so that they may see her disgrace; cf. b. Soṭah 8B.

t. Numbers 5:18: "The priest shall set the woman before Yahweh יפרע את ראש האשה." Rabbinic interpreters understood פרע here in the sense of "expose": "The priest shall expose the woman's head." This results from their making, in addition to the head, also the woman's breasts an object of פרע. A baraita in b. Soṭah 8A: "(The priest) shall expose the woman's head" (Num 5:18). Here I hear only about her head; from where do we hear about her body? Scripture teaches: האשה "the woman" (i.e., the woman herself, Num 5:18). The same is found in Num. Rab. 9 (155B). — The "commandment of exposure" מצות פריעה, which is mentioned sometimes in the case of the Soṭah, should therefore be understood to include both the exposure of the head and that of the chest. Sifre Numbers 5:18 § 11 (5A): "'(The priest) shall expose the woman's head' (Num 5:18). The priest turned behind her and exposed her in order to fulfill in her the commandment of exposure." These are the words of R. Ishmael († ca. 135). — The same is found a few lines further with R. Yohanan b. Beroqah (ca. 110). — Correspondingly, the passages that deal with the execution of the commandment of exposure regularly report also of the exposing of the woman's chest; see n. *u.*

u. Carrying out the exposure regulation. Mishnah Soṭah 1.5: The priest seized her clothes. If they were torn, they were torn, and if they were ripped, they were ripped, until he exposed מגלה her heart (i.e., her chest), and destroyed (pulled down, סותר) her hair. R. Judah (ca. 150) said, "If her heart (bosom) was beautiful, he did not expose it לא היה מגלהו, and if her hair was beautiful (sumptuous), he did not destroy it לא היה סותרו (lest the sensuality of the young priests and other onlookers be aroused)." — The opinion of R. Judah was not recognized. — The same is found in t. Soṭah 1.7 (293); Num. Rab. 9 (155B). ‖ Babylonian Talmud Soṭah 8A: What does Scripture mean to teach with "He shall expose her head" (Num 5:18)? This teaches that the priest destroyed סותר her hair. — The same is found in Num. Rab. 9 (155B). ‖ In t. Soṭah 3.3 (295) it says more precisely about destroying the hair: The priest removed the small cover כִּפָּה from her head and laid it under his feet. — The same is found in b. Soṭah 8B. When the כיפה, which lay under the hair braids, was pulled off, the braids fell from the head, and the head was thereby exposed פרוע. Conversely, the head was considered to be covered מכוסה as long as the hair was arranged properly. Thus, when it says in, for example, b. Ketub. 72A that a woman should not go out בפרוע ראש, it is one and the same thing whether בפרוע ראש is translated "with an exposed head" or "with unraveled hair"; for the exposed head of a woman is one whose hair is unraveled and thus became disarrayed. However, linguistically, it has to be maintained that for the rabbinic scholars פרע הראש first meant "to expose the head." This is shown specifically by the following passages. In Pesiq. 77A (see the passage with parallels at § 1 Cor 11:4, #2, n. *m*) it is said of men who hear a royal edict: פורעון ראשיהם = "they bared their heads," and not "they unraveled their hair," so that it became disarrayed. — Of a virgin bride, it says in m. Ketub. 2.1 that on the wedding day her head is exposed ראשה פרוע. This entails also that her hair is unraveled, that is, was not arranged in the normal hairstyle; but the translation has to maintain that ראשה פרוע means "her head was exposed." That it has to be translated in this way is shown by Exod. Rab. 41 (97D)—see the passage in n. *i*—where Resh Laqish replaces it with "she exposes מגלה her face." — In the passage b. Ketub. 72A, presented in n. *l*, R. Yohanan says, "With the little knitting basket there is nothing in the way of a פרוע ראש." This is true if פרוע ראש designates the exposed head; for the exposure of the head is eliminated by the basket being set on it; but it would not be true if פרוע ראש meant the unraveled hair that was in disarray; for unraveled hair remains unraveled hair, even if a little basket is put on top of it. — In SNum 6:5 § 25 (8B) we read about the words: "By letting his hair freely grow long" (Num 6:5). Why is this said? Because it says, "The leper in whom the defect is shall have his clothes torn and his hair shall be פרוע" (Lev 13:45). פרוע means "he shall let his hair grow long." You say: פרוע means "he shall let his hair grow long"; or should פרוע not rather be understood according to its wording (in its customary sense)? (It is then decided that it means "to let grow long," that is, פרע is taken in the meaning "to unravel" as "to let grow wild".) — What פרע means "according to its wording" is not, however, said; but in view of the meaning "to unravel" or "to let grow wild" we can understand by the "wording" only the meaning "to expose." So also Friedmann *ad loc*: שיהא ראשו מגולה = "his head shall be exposed." Here we have proof from the sources that the ordinary meaning (the wording) of פרע for the rabbinic scholars was "to expose." Only in the case of Lev 10:6; 13:45; and 21:10 was פרע interpreted as = "unravel," that is, "to let grow wild"; see Tg. Onk. and Tg. Yer. I on the passages mentioned. Yet R. Aqiba († ca. 135) also wants to understand פרע in Lev 13:45 with the meaning "expose"; see SLev 13:45 (260A); b. Moʿed Qaṭ. 15A. Likewise, R. Alexandrai (ca. 270) in Midr. Lam. Intro. 21 (34B) interpreted the words וראשו יהיה פרוע in Lev 13:45 in an allegorical interpretation as "his head shall be exposed." This is proven not only by the passage adduced "He uncovered the cover of Judah" (Isa 22:8), but rather also the added explanation "one uncovered what was concealed" גלי דכסייה; see Midr. Eccl. 10, 18 (49A). — In the passages of Leviticus mentioned, the LXX understood פרע as "expose," as in Num 5:18.

v. Pesiqta Rabbati 26 (129B): Like a high priest to whom the lot fell to make her drink the water of jealousy. The woman was brought to him, and he exposed פרע her head and undid פרסם her hair. Then he took the cup to make her drink. He looked at her (and saw) that it was his mother.... — Here one clearly recognizes that the covering and the veiling of a woman consisted in her hairstyle. As long as the headdress was arranged properly, the priest did not know who stood before him; for the headdress veiled her face. Only when he undid the hair was the head exposed and he recognized his mother.

Comment: Lightfoot's (2:907) opinion that Jewish women would have participated in the religious gatherings in the temple unveiled cannot be established from the rabbinic sources. The passage adduced by Lightfoot, b. Qidd. 81A, reads as follows: (R.) Abin (ca. 325) said, "The crowd (and the improper behavior of the multitude that happens in a crowd) occurs in the year at the festival סקבא דשתא ריגלא." — According to the context, this is about the improper interaction of the two genders at the great religious gatherings. Rashi and the Tosafists remark on R. Abin's saying that the men and women would have cast glances at each other at these gatherings. The Tosafists also add that some say, "Therefore, after Passover and the Feast of Booths they used to fast." — The promiscuous temper that was widespread between men and women in the temple at the Feast of Booths is complained about elsewhere as well; see t. Sukkah 4.1ff. in the excursus "The Feast of Tabernacles," #V, middle. However, it cannot be concluded from this that the women would have visited the temple without wearing a veil. Their veil was certainly not so firm and tight that they could not have been loosened at any moment.

11:5 B: For it is one and the same thing with a shorn woman.

A shorn woman was considered ugly and blemished.

Mishnah Nazir 4.5: If one of the types of blood (from Num 6:14) has been sprinkled for her (the Nazirite woman), her husband can no longer override her (Nazirite) vow. R. Aqiba († ca. 135) said, "Even if only one of all the animals (Num 6:14) has been slaughtered for her, he can no longer dissolve her vow. In which case are these words valid? For sheering in purity (Num 6:18), but in the case when sheering happens because of impurity (see Num 6:9) he may dissolve it; for he can say, 'I do not like a blemished woman אשה מנוולת.'" Rabbi († 217?) said, "Even in the case of sheering in purity (Num 6:18) he can dissolve it; for he can say, 'I do not like a shorn woman אשה מגילהת.'" —This is changed somewhat in t. Naz. 3.14 (287). ‖ Sifre Deuteronomy 21:12 § 212 (112B): "She shall sheer her head and prepare her nails" (Deut 21:12). R. Eliezer (ca. 90) said, "She shall cut (the nails)"; R. Aqiba († ca. 135) said, "She shall let them grow long." R. Eliezer said, "Here there is discussion of an action concerning the head and an action concerning the nails. As the action that is mentioned concerning the head deals with doing away with something, so too the action that is mentioned concerning the nails deals with a doing away (so a cutting)." R. Aqiba said, "There is discussion of an action concerning the head and an action concerning the nails. As the action that is mentioned concerning the head (i.e., the sheering) is a disfigurement נִיוּוּל, so too the action that is mentioned concerning the nails is a disfigurement (thus it means letting grow long)." However, a proof for the words of R. Eliezer is: "Mephibosheth, the son of Saul, went down to meet the king (David); he had prepared neither his feet nor his beard (by cutting his nails ...)" (2 Sam 19:25). — The same is found as a baraita in b. Yebam. 48A.

11:6: But if it is shameful for a woman to have (her hair) cut or to be shorn.

See the citations at § 1 Cor 11:5 B.

11:7 A: While he (the man) is the image and glory of God.

Numbers Rabbah 3 (140D): "You shall inspect ... every male" (Num 3:15). Why every male? And why does he not mention females? Because the glory כבוד of God arises from men.

11:7 B: Woman is the glory of man.

Rashi on Isa 44:13 "According to beauty of human beings" כתפארת אדם: this refers to the woman; for she is her husband's glory תפארת. – So too b. Ketub. 66A can say vice versa: In an insult to his wife there is an insult to him (the husband, read ליה instead of לה).

11:10 A: Therefore a woman is required to have authority over her head.

According to the halakah, an exposed head רֹאשׁ פָּרוּעַ, by which the bride revealed herself in the wedding procession on her wedding day, was a proof of her virginity.[a] If we add that an uncovered head otherwise was regarded as a symbol of freedom (see § 1 Cor 11:4, #1, n. *d*), the bride's appearing with an exposed head signified that she was a free virgin who up until then had never been under the authority רְשׁוּת of a man.[b] Only with her marriage does she pass over into a man's power נכנסה לרשות הבעל, so that from then on her husband's authority is over her רשות בעלה עליה.[c] The covering of her head serves as an outward sign of this changed status of a woman: by a married woman only going out with a covered head according to Jewish law (see § 1 Cor 11:5 A), she acknowledges that a man's authority is upon her.[d] It is from this perspective that the apostle speaks when he says in 1 Cor 11:10: "A woman is obligated to have an authority, that is, a sign acknowledging the authority of a man, namely the head covering, on her head." As can be seen, the head covering itself, the symbol of a man's authority, is thereby designated metonymically as "authority" ἐξουσία = רְשׁוּת. In his essay, "Die 'Macht' auf dem Haupte 1 Cor 11, 10," Gerhard Kittel assumes that ἐξουσία is the literal translation of the Aramaic שלטוניה, which according to y. Šabb. 6.8B.48 means something like "headband" or "veil."[215] According to Kittel, the apostle rendered this word literally with ἐξουσία, assuming that its root שלט is connected with שָׁלַט = "to have authority," so that this word in 1 Cor 11:10 should not be translated with "authority" at all, but rather simply with "shroud" or "veil." – In this case, though, the metonymic usage of ἐξουσία would be avoided; but would a Greek reader ever have understood ἐξουσία to denote a veil?

a. Mishnah Ketubbot 2.1: If a woman who is widowed or divorced says (concerning her husband): "You married me as a virgin," and yet he says, "No, rather I married you as a widow," and in case there are witnesses that she went out (on her wedding day) in a wedding procession (הִינוּמָא = הִימוּנָא = ὑμεναῖον) and with an exposed head, her prescribed marital sum (to which she was entitled as a widow or divorcée) amounts to 200 *zuz*. – 200 *zuz* was the amount that was due to a woman married as a virgin (see § John 2:1 A, #4, C). If this sum is awarded her in an adversarial proceeding against her husband, it is thereby recognized that she was a virgin when she married. Her virginity is proven not only by

215. Gerhard Kittel, "Die 'Macht' auf dem Haupte 1 Cor 11, 10," *Arbeiten für Religionsgeschichte des Urchristentums* 1.3 (1920).

the wedding procession but also by her appearing, as confirmed by witnesses, on her wedding day with an exposed head. In accordance with this, R. Simeon b. Laqish (ca. 250) says in Exod. Rab. 41 (97D)—see the passage at § 1 Cor 11:5 A, n. *i*—that a virgin bride shows herself under the wedding canopy with an exposed face, as if she intended to say, "Whoever knows of testimony against me (against my moral purity), let him come and testify against me!" — Thus, here too the bride's exposed head is a sign of her virginity.

b. The commentary פני משה on y. Ketub. 2.21B.4 offers the singular opinion that a bride's head being uncovered on her wedding day was a sign of mourning for Jerusalem; see § Matt 9:15 B, n. *g*, S-B footnote. — Babylonian Talmud Sanhedrin 58B is noteworthy: When Rab Dimi (ca. 320) came (namely from Palestine to Babylonia), he said, R. Eleazar (ca. 270) said that R. Hanina (ca. 225) said, "A Noachide (= non-Israelite) who has designated a slave girl for his slave (as a wife) and then has intercourse with her will be killed for this. From what point in time? Rab Nahman († 320) said, 'From the time she was named the girl of so and so (the slave in question).' From what point in time is she released again? Rab Huna († 297) said, 'From the time she uncovered her head on the street.'" — Thus, a woman's head being uncovered indicates her singleness.

c. See "to hand over to the authority of a man," in, for example, m. Ketub. 7.7f. at § John 2:1 A, #3, n. *u*; see m. Ned. 10.5 at § John 2:1 A, #5, n. *p*. — The expression "The authority of her husband is upon her," is found in, for example, t. Qidd. 1.11 (336): What are the obligatory commandments for the son concerning the father? He feeds him and gives him to drink, he clothes him and covers him, he leads him in and out, he washes his face and his hands and his feet, whether man or woman (regardless of whether the person in question is a son or daughter, every child has to fulfill these duties); Except that a man (son) has in his hand the possibility to do this, while a woman (the daughter as a married woman) does not have in her hand the possibility to do this because the authority of her husband is upon her (who can forbid her to fulfill these duties). ‖ Sifra Leviticus 19:3 (343A): Why is it said in Lev 19:3: "איש (a man = everyone) shall have respect for his mother and his father (and not איש ואשה = man and woman)?" Because the man has the possibility to do this, while the woman does not have the possibility to do this, because the authority of others (above all of her husband) is upon her.

d. See b. Sanh. 58B in n. *b*.

11:10 B: Because of the angels.

1. Considered by itself, the requirement that a woman have a covering on her head because of the angels could have its basis in the fact that the angels should not be aroused to sexual desire by seeing a woman uncovered. Traditions, according to which members of the spirit world burned with sensual passion for the daughters of the children of men and then had sex with them, circulated in various forms in the ancient synagogue.[a] However, these traditions always pertain only to evil spirits or fallen angels. Yet in 1 Cor 11:10 the apostle speaks of ἄγγελοι *per se*, and since in his usage elsewhere he understands this to refer only to good angels, the idea of their

theoretical sexual attraction is completely ruled out as an explanation of the words διὰ τοὺς ἀγγέλους.[b]

a. Eve used to have sexual intercourse with the devil and the demons, specifically with the latter for 130 years; see § Matt 4:1 B, #2, n. *c* and in the excursus "Ancient Jewish Demonology," #2, A, at the end. — The "sons of God" in Gen 6:2ff., which were explicitly understood by the older pseudepigrapha, Josephus, and some rabbinic passages to include angels, take for themselves as wives daughters of men and sire giants with them; see the citations at § Jude 7 and in the excursus "Ancient Jewish Demonology," #2. — Ashmedai, king of the demons, has intercourse with Solomon's wives; see b. Giṭ. 68A in the excursus "Ancient Jewish Demonology," #3, n. *e*. — The book of Tobit recounts how the evil spirit Asmodeus (= the just-named Ashmedai), aroused with sensual passion, kills seven rivals from the world of men, lest they take Sarah, Raguel's daughter, for themselves (Tob 3:8, 17; 6:14ff.; 8:1). — Babylonian Talmud Berakot 54B: Rab Judah († 299) said, "Three things need guarding (from the evil spirits). These are a sick man, a woman who has recently given birth, and newlyweds (literally: a groom and a bride)." Some have said, "Also a mourner"; some have said, "Also students of the scholars at night." — Rashi names the envy or jealousy of a demon as the reason for the bridal couple. Like Asmodeus, the demon thus begrudges the man the bride that he himself would like to possess. Therefore he looks for a way to harm them both.

b. In contrast to the evil spirits, the angels are denied sexuality; see Pesiq. Rab. 43 (179B); B. Ḥag. 16A and Gen. Rab. 8 at § Matt 22:30 B.

2. A particular class among the angels of service is constituted by the guardian angels who are attached to individual people; see § Matt 18:10 B and § Acts 12:15. There were different opinions about their number. R. Abin (I, ca. 325) and R. Aha (ca. 320) speak of one guardian angel (see Midr. Eccl. 10:20 and parallels at § Matt 18:10 B, two-thirds down). R. Eliezer b. Yose the Galilean (ca. 150) knows of two of them (see t. Šabb. 17.2f. at § Matt 18:10 B); likewise, R. Yose b. Judah (ca. 180) and Rab Hisda († 309), see b. Šabb. 119B at § Matt 18:10 B, as well as R. Zeriqa (ca. 300) in b. Ḥag. 16A at § Matt 18:10 B, toward the end and the baraita in b. Taʿan. 11A at § Matt 18:10 B, toward the end. According to R. Eliezer b. Yose the Galilean (ca. 150), both guardian angels are good angels or angels of peace; see t. Šabb. 17.2f. and t. ʿAbod. Zar. 1.17f. at § Matt 18:10 B; Rab Hisda appears to be of the same opinion in b. Šabb. 119B at § Matt 18:10 B. However, according to R. Yose b. Judah, one is a good angel and the other is a bad angel in b. Šabb. 119B at § Matt 18:10. R. Isaac (ca. 300) represents the view that the number of guardian angels increases depending on the multitude of the fulfillments of commandments that a person has to show: "If a person does all the commandments, many angels are given to him" (Tanḥ. משפטים 99A at § Matt 18:10 B). R. Joshua b. Levi (ca. 250) speaks of one thousand and ten thousand angels who protectively surround the Israelites (Tanḥ. משפטים 99A); yet he elevates from their midst one whom he calls "image" of the man and in whom he probably sees the actual guardian angel of the

person in question; see Midr. Ps. 55 § 3 at § Acts 12:15, #2 and Tanḥ. משפטים 99A at § Matt 18:10 B. R. Levi (ca. 300) seems to have thought about our question similarly to R. Joshua b. Levi; see Tanḥ. משפטים 99A at § Matt 18:10 B. Lastly, b. Ber. 60B deals with guardian angels without naming them or giving a specific number.[216] — The noblest task of the guardian angels is to keep the person from the pestering of the demons; see Tanḥ. משפטים 99A at § Matt 18:10 B and Midr. Ps. 55 § 3 at § Acts 12:15, #2. They accompany him on all his paths, particularly on journeys, in order to avert dangers from him; see t. Šabb. 17.2f. at § Matt 18:10 B; Gen. Rab. 59 (37B) at § Matt 18:10 B, near end; for this reason they are often designated as angels who accompany human beings (accompanying angels); see t. Šabb. 17.2f. and b. Šabb. 119B at § Matt 18:10 B and b. Ḥag. 16A; b. Taʿan. 11A at § Matt 18:10 B, near end. Yet the guardian angels also participate in a person's correct halakic good conduct. If, on Friday evening when he returns home from the synagogue, an Israelite finds the Sabbath lamp lit and the table covered and everything prepared properly, the good guardian angel says, "May it be just so on the next Sabbath!" And the evil angel answers contrary to his will, "Amen!" Yet if he does not find everything in the right way, the evil angel says, "May it be just so on the next Sabbath!" And the good angel answers contrary to his will, "Amen!" See b. Šabb. 119B at § Matt 18:10 B. Here the good angel clearly emerges as the protector of pious custom: it distresses him when a house unauthorizedly flouts the tried and true order for celebrating the arrival of the Sabbath, while the evil angel feels satisfaction in this case. Further, the guardian angels, whether indirectly or directly, have to give an account before God and testify about all the doings of the person he is commanded to guard; see Midr. Eccl. 10:20 and b. Ḥag. 16A at § Matt 18:10 B, toward end. Depending on the standing of the person before God, they proclaim for him salvation and peace or cursing and punishment; see b. Šabb. 119B and b. Taʿan. 11A at § Matt 18:10 B. Finally, though, the guardian angels can, when a person's measure is full, also become enforcers of the divine punitive will against him; in this case, they give him into the power of the evil spirits; so R. Levi in Tanḥ. משפטים 99A at § Matt 18:10 B. — Since the guardian angels also had their place in the faith of the early Christian communities (see Matt 18:10 and Acts 12:15), it is not difficult to draw certain lines of connection

216. S-B: Babylonian Talmud Berakot 60B: If one enters a toilet, one says (to the guardian angels), "Be honored, you honored ones, holy servants of the Most High! Give honor to the God of Israel! Stay away from me until I have gone in and satisfied my need and come to you again!" Abayye († 338/39) said, "A person shall not say they should leave him and go from there; rather, let him say, "Protect me, protect me! Help me, help me! Guard me, guard me! Wait for me, wait for me, so that I may go in and come back out, for so is the way of the children of men!" When he comes out, he says, "Blessed be the One who formed humanity in wisdom and created many holes and cavities in him! It is evident and known before the throne of your glory that, if one of them were opened or shut, a person could not exist before you."

between the Jewish conceptions about them listed above and 1 Cor 11:10: a woman should remember that, as those appointed by God to protect all natural arrangements in the world, the angels have an obvious interest in a woman recognizing and keeping the primordial order of creation which included her subordination to a man. For this reason, a woman should not grieve the angels by removing her head covering, which is the sign of her subjection to a man, and thus revealing that she disregards that ancient order of creation. She would compel the angels, certainly to their pain, to accuse her before God and appear as witnesses against her. For this reason, a woman should keep her head covered, not least "because of the angels," so that they can exercise their office joyfully and not have to turn from guardian angels into accusing angels.

3. On 1 Cor 11:10, Wetstein cites the following passage from Johann Christoph Wagenseil: *Malus est angelus, qui vocatur Usiel, si videat mulierem nudato capite. R. Simeon f. Yohai: Si mulieris capillus nudus est, veniunt mali spiritus, eique insident, et omnia, quae in domo sunt, perdunt.*[217] – Literally, the passage in its entirety reads thus in Wagenseil: "The חכמי הקבלה [those who are wise in the kabbalah, knowledgeable in the tradition] write that every woman should be strongly warned about chastity and בפרט [in particular] with the hair, how much evil sorrow comes from it, from heaven and earth, upon herself and upon her husband and upon her children, and brings poverty into the house. Writing about which ר׳ שמעון בן יוחאי, when a hair goes out from a woman [namely from the headdress so that it streams loosely on her head], the evil רוחות [spirits] come and sit on it and destroy everything in the house, and the גמרא [Gemarah] counts three things in a woman as a disgrace; when they scream high [= loudly], and when they show their body, and when her hair goes out from her." – As shown by the reference to those "wise in the kabbalah," the passage is of a later date. However, that some attention was already given in an earlier time to the fluttering hair on a woman's head is proved by b. Šabb. 57B, where a special headband (אִיסְטְמָא = στέμμα or בִּיזְיוֹנֵי) is mentioned that was designed specifically to hold together and cover the hair that fluttered loose around a woman's head פָּרוֹחֵי. Later generations then fashioned their own ideas about these hairs; according to the citation above, for example, the evil spirits rested on them to wreak the greatest calamity in the house. This assumption is grounded in the idea that according to the Gemarah the hairs that are loosed from the headdress are a disgrace. This refers to the saying of Rab Sheshet (ca. 260) in b. Ber. 24A: "A woman's hair is something unchaste עֶרְוָה." And by every measure in which a person sins, he is punished: since the woman sinned with her hair, the evil spirits

217. Johann Christoph Wagenseil, *Sota* (Altdorf: Endter, 1674), 43.

then take possession of it. — The above citation contributes in no way to explaining the words διὰ τοὺς ἀγγέλους in 1 Cor 11:10; not simply because of its late origin, but above all because it deals with evil spirits, whereas 1 Cor 11:10 refers to good angels.

11:12: For as the woman is from the man, so too does a man come by a woman, but everything comes from God.

Genesis Rabbah 22 (14D): R. Ishmael († ca. 135) asked R. Aqiba († ca. 135) and said to him, "Since you have served Nahum of Gimzo (ca. 90) 22 years (as a student), according to whom the words אַךְ (only) and רַק (only) exclude and the words אֶת־ (with) and גַּם (also) include, what does the אֶת־ mean that is written here (Gen 4:1: קניתי איש את־יהוה)?" He answered him, "If it said, קניתי איש י״י, the matter would be difficult (it would have to be translated 'I have brought forth a man of Yahweh'); but it says את י״י = 'with Yahweh('s help)....' Originally Adam was created from the earth and Eve was created from Adam מאדם; from then on (humans were formed) by our image according to our likeness, not a man without a woman and not a woman without a man and neither without the Shekinah (divinity)." — In y. Ber. 9.12D.49, 52 and Gen. Rab. 8 (6C), R. Simlai (ca. 250) is the author.

11:14: If a man wears long hair, it is a dishonor to him.

1. Ezekiel 44:20 decrees the following concerning the priests: "They will not shear יְגַלֵּחוּ their head bald and they will not let their hair grow wild. They shall cut כָּסוֹם יִכְסְמוּ their hair properly."[218] The haircut stipulated for the priesthood here, which evidently intends to keep the medium between being shorn bald and long-flowing hair, probably corresponded by and large to the hairstyle of the entire Jewish male world in Jesus' days. Thus, they wore, as we would say, half-length hair; yet it must be maintained that this half-length hair was, compared to our conceptions, long rather than half-length.[a]

a. Krauß refers to the following passages in this connection.[219] According to m. Naz. 1.2, the life-long Nazirite could have his hair shorn as soon as it became a burden to him.

---

218. S-B: In the first clause, the targum has retained the verb גַּלַּח and renders כסם with סַפַּר. Accordingly, גִּלַּח, Aram. גַּלַּח, was tantamount to "sheer bald," while סִפֵּר, Aram. סַפַּר, signified a sheering where the hair was cut less short. This aligns with the meaning of the word in SLev 19:27 (359A): "גִּלּוּחַ means a sheering where a destruction הַשְׁחָתָה (of the hair to the roots) occurs, as it happens with the sheering knife תַּעַר." (The same is found in b. Mak. 21A; b. Naz. 58A; b. Qidd. 35B.) Yet the usage was not bound to this rule: גִּלַּח often means simply "sheering" in the same way as סִפֵּר (see, e.g., m. Moʿed Qaṭ. 3.1). — Babylonian Talmud Sanhedrin 22B says: "What does כסום יכסמו (Ezek 44:20) mean? It has been taught: Like the Julian hairstyle. What is the Julian hairstyle? Rab Judah († 299) said that Samuel († 254) said, "A cutting where the hairs individually come to stand (without falling on each other)." Rab Ashi († 427) said, "The tip of one hair next to the root of another." Rabbi († 217?) was asked, "What was the hairstyle of the high priest like?" He answered them, "Go out and take a look at the hairstyle of Ben Eleasa (Rabbi's son-in-law)." In a baraita: Rabbi said, "Not for nothing did Ben Eleasa waste his money, but rather to demonstrate the hairstyle of the high priest." — Accordingly, the high priest would have worn hair that had been shorn very short.

219. Krauß, *Talmudische Archäologie*, 1:644 n. 830.

Rashi remarks on this (b. Naz. 4A) that he had it cut every 30 days. This accords with the view that R. Nehorai (ca. 150) represents in b. Naz. 5A; see § Luke 1:15 D, notes *g* and *h*. If it had been customary to wear short hair, it could not have been so long after 30 days that the Nazirite would have been able to experience it as a burden; only if the hair was already long from the start could it have reached an onerous length. – In m. Ohal. 3.4, it says: "If a dead man is found outside (a house) but his hair is inside, the house is unclean" (For the hair clinging to a corpse makes something unclean just as the corpse itself does). The casuistry would hardly have designed this case if men's hair was short-shorn everywhere. – In m. Makš. 1.5, R. Yose (ca. 150) declares: "If someone presses his hair (to dry it, perhaps after getting wet in a downpour) with his mantle, what flows down (in the sense of Lev 11:38) is apt to make unclean an object onto which it falls." This case also presupposes that longer hair is customary.

2. However, hair was not allowed to grow beyond a certain length. It was feared that one became unsightly by hair that was too long or, as it is said more often, defaced מְנוּוָּל. For this reason, it was cut as soon as it began to hang in a wild and disordered fashion around the head.

Numbers Rabbah 10 (160B): Why did God command the Nazirite not to sheer his hair (see Num 6:5)? Because sheering him makes him appear fine and handsome; as it says of Joseph, "He was shorn and changed his cloths" (Gen 41:14). Yet letting the hair grow long signifies pain and mourning (as is shown, e.g., in the case of one on whom the ban is imposed or in the case of a mourner, who had to let their hair grow long and wild). Therefore, God said, "Since this Nazirite abstained from wine to keep himself from fornication, he shall let his hair grow long in order to appear ugly and to mortify himself, so that the evil inclination might not charge against him (Literally: not jump on him)." ‖ Numbers Rabbah 10 (160C): Letting the hair grow long is a defacement (נִוּוּל = ἀτιμία in 1 Cor 11:14); for he does not scrub his head (to clean it). ‖ Mishnah Taʿanit 2.7: "It was forbidden for the division of priests who served and those who assisted with the sacrifices to be shorn or to change their clothes; but on the 5th (day of the week) they were allowed to do it to honor the Sabbath." Concerning this, it is asked in b. Taʿan. 17A: What was the reason? Rabbah bar bar Hana (ca. 280) said that R. Yohanan († 279) said, "Lest they report to their posts defaced (מנוולין, i.e., with uncut hair)." – Parallel passages are found in b. Moʿed Qaṭ. 14A; y. Moʿed Qaṭ. 3.81C.34. ‖ Mishnah Moʿed Qaṭan 3.1: "The following may be shorn on the inter-festival days (of Passover and the Feast of Tabernacles): whoever comes from abroad or out of captivity, whoever is released from prison, one on whom the ban was imposed whom the scholars have absolved; likewise, one who has had himself absolved of a vow by a scholar, a Nazirite (whose status as a Nazirite has already passed) and a leper who passes from his uncleanness to his cleanness. (Sheering is allowed for all of these because they previously had no opportunity for it.) ... However, it is forbidden for all other people." Babylonian Talmud Moʿed Qaṭan 14A says about this: Why is it forbidden to all other people? ... Lest they come to the festival defaced מנוולין (= unshorn). – In y. Moʿed Qaṭ. 3.81C.31, R. Simon (ca. 280) is the author. – Good practice thus required that everyone who attached some importance to his appearance have his hair cut before the festival. In particular, the upper-class man was obliged to get his hair cut more frequently. A baraita in b. Sanh. 22B: A king has his hair cut daily (see Isa 33:17), the high priest from one preparation day of the Sabbath to the next (i.e., every Friday, to honor the Sabbath), the ordinary priest once every 30 days (which is inferred from the word correspondence in Ezek 44:20 and Num 6:5). — The same is found in b. Ta'an. 17A; see Num. Rab. 10 (161B); Mek. Exod. 15:1 (43A).

3. Artificially curling the hair, which had been considered beautiful at an earlier time, was later viewed as something foppish and sinful.

The judgment from the earlier period. See t. Ned. 1.36D.43 at § Acts 18:18 B, #2, n. *c.* — The judgment of later generations. Genesis Rabbah 22 (15A): R. Ammi (ca. 300) said, "The evil inclination (= the devil) does not go about on the sides but rather in the middle of the street, and if he sees someone who gropes about with his eyes (moves his eyes right and left), clips around on his hair and raises himself on his heels, he says, 'He belongs to me' הדין דידי. What is the scriptural basis? 'If you have seen a man who is wise in his (own) eyes—the fool (i.e., the evil inclination) has hope because of him' (so Prov 26:12 according to the midr.)." ‖ Genesis Rabbah 87 (55C): "The wife of his master raised her eyes to Joseph" (Gen 39:7). "So, men of understanding, listen to me!" (Job 34:10). What is God's stratagem? "He repays a man for his action" (Job 34:11). R. Meir (ca. 150), R. Judah (ca. 150), and R. Simeon (ca. 150) said, "'And the wife of his master raised her eyes to Joseph'; what is written before the passage? 'And Joseph was fine in form and fine in appearance' (Gen 39:6). Like a hero who stood on the street and groped about with his eye (see the previous citation) and clipped around on his hair and raised himself on his heel. He said, 'This becomes me, this makes me look good, a handsome hero (is what I am like)!' Then it was said to him (by God), 'If you are a hero, if you are fine, behold, a she-bear (= Potiphar's wife) is before you, get up, strike her down (read קפהינה instead of קפחניה)!' ... God said to Joseph, 'You are a bachelor (and have become proud); on your life, I will arouse the she-bear against you!'" ‖ Mishnah Soṭah 1.7, 8: A man is measured by the measure with which he measures. ... Absalom swaggered with his hair, so he remained hanging by his hair. — Parallel passages are found in t. Soṭah 3.16 (297); Mek. Exod. 15:1 (43A). ‖ See Pesiq. Rab. 26 (129A) at § Luke 7:33f.

11:15 A: If a woman has long hair, it brings honor (glory) to her.

That a woman lets her hair grow long is counted among the curses that were laid upon Eve after the fall;[a] yet it cannot be concluded from this that long hair on a woman was interpreted as ἀτιμία. On the contrary, long and full hair was, according to Jewish judgment, an adornment for a woman,[b] while, conversely, shorn hair was viewed as a disfigurement for a woman.[c]

a. Babylonian Talmud 'Erubin 100B: Rab Isaac b. Abdima (ca. 300) said, "Eve was cursed with ten curses. ... In a baraita it has been taught: She must let her hair grow long like Lilith (a demoness of the night, the queens of the *shedim*; see the excursus "Ancient Jewish Demonology"). — In the parallel— see § Rom 8:20f., n. *g*—Pirqe R. El. 14 (7D): She may not cut her hair except because of whoredom.

b. Midrash Song of Songs 4:1 (109A): R. Levi (ca. 300) said, "... If a woman binds her hair together in the back (in braids), it is an adornment תַּכְשִׁיט for her."

c. See passages at § 1 Cor 11:5 B.

11:15 B: Her hair is given to her instead of a covering.

Sifre Deuteronomy 31:14 § 305 (130A): It once happened that Rabban Yohanan b. Zakkai († ca. 80) rode on a donkey, and his students walked behind him. Then he saw how a girl gathered up the barley corns under the feet of the animals of the Arabs. When she saw Rabban Yohanan b. Zakkai, she wrapped herself in her hair, stepped in front of him and said to him, "Rabbi, take care of me!" — See the whole passage at § John 3:1, #1, n. *d*.

11:16 A: Argumentative.

φιλόνεικος perhaps = מַקְשֶׁה, Aram. מַקְשָׁאָה, מַקְשְׁיָא, "one who likes to make objections," or = קַנְתְּרָן, קַנְטְרָן "quarrelsome." — The students of R. Meir (ca. 150) had made themselves unpopular by their obsession with raising objections all the time. R. Judah (ca. 150) therefore tried to exclude them from the house of learning as "quarrelsome ones."[a] One of them, Ephraim, in fact received the epithet מַקְשָׁאָה = "the objection raiser," "the dispute addict."[b] People were averse to spats and disputes because it was typical for them to spread and perpetuate themselves.[c]

a. A baraita in b. Naz. 49B: After the death of R. Meir, R. Judah said to his (own) students, "The students of R. Meir shall not come here (into the house of learning), for they are quarrelsome קנתרנין, and they come here not to study Torah, but rather they come to overcome me in the halakoth."

b. Genesis Rabbah 48 (30C): ("Abraham took sour milk and sweet milk and the young steer ..." [Gen 18:8].) And where was the bread (which is mentioned beforehand in verse 5)? Ephraim Makshaah from the students of R. Meir said in the name of R. Meir, "She (Sarah) had received menstruation and the dough had become unclean (so the promised bread had to be eliminated)."

c. Babylonian Talmud Sanhedrin 7A: "The beginning of a quarrel is like when floods are unleashed" (Prov 17:14). Rab Huna († 297) said, "A dispute תִּגְרָא is like the channel of a water breakthrough: if it expands, it keeps expanding." Abbayye, the elder († 338/39), said, "It is like a board at the edge of a body of water (read לגמלא דגודא instead of: לגודא דגמלא): if it lies there once, it keeps lying there."

11:16 B: We have no such custom.

συνήθεια presumably = סוּנֵיתָא in Gen. Rab. 50 (32A): R. Isaac (ca. 300) said, "A great dispute arose (between Lot and his wife) about the salt. He said to her, 'Give these guests a little salt.' But she answered him, 'Do you want to introduce this bad custom סוניתא בישא here too?'"

11:19: For it is necessary that there be factions among you, so that those who are approved among you may be revealed.

Factions מַחֲלוֹקוֹת (sing. מַחֲלוֹקֶת) were considered evil. See t. Soṭah 14.1ff. at § Rom 2:21–23; see t. Sanh. 7.1 = the baraita in b. Sanh. 88B in the excursus "The Day of Jesus' Death," B, #1; see also § Matt 12:25. — Only one dispute that led to factions was recognized as legitimate, namely one that was conducted for God's sake, that is, without self-serving secondary purposes. See m. ʾAbot 5.17 at § Matt 21:25, middle.

11:20: The Lord's Supper.

In rabbinic literature, holy communion may be mentioned in Midr. Eccl. 1:8 (9A). See § Matt 4:13.

11:22: And do you humiliate those who have nothing?

The ancient synagogue took care in several ways to carefully take into account the feelings of the poor.

A baraita in b. Moʿed Qaṭ. 27A: In an earlier time the rich sent (the food for a meal of mourning; see the excursus "Works of Love") to the house of mourning in silver and gold plates and the poor in baskets of peeled wicker; but since the poor were ashamed מתביישין because of this, it was ordered that everyone should bring something in baskets of peeled wicker for the sake of the honor of the poor. In a baraita: In an earlier time the rich provided in a house of mourning something to drink from white glasses (i.e., they sent drinks to the meal of mourning in vessels of white crystal glass) and the poor from (cheap) colored glasses; but since the poor were ashamed מתביישין because of this, it was ordered that everyone should provide drinks from colored glasses for the sake of the honor of the poor. — The 2nd baraita is also in t. Nid. 9.17 (651). ‖ Babylonian Talmud Moʿed Qaṭan 27A: In an earlier time, the face of the rich (who had passed away) was left uncovered (on the bier), while the face of the poor was covered, because their face was black due to famines; but since the poor were ashamed מתביישין because of this, it was ordered that everyone's face should be covered for the sake of the honor of the poor. In an earlier time, the rich were carried out on biers with straps (or thongs to the grave site) and the poor in a wicker basket; but since the poor were ashamed because of this, it was ordered that everyone be carried out in a wicker basket for the sake of the honor of the poor. — The 2nd part is also in t. Nid. 9.16 (651). ‖ At the dances of the virgins in the vineyards of Jerusalem on the 15th of Ab and on the Day of Atonement white dresses had to be borrowed so that the women who did not own them would not be ashamed. See Taʿan. 4.8 at § John 2:1 A, #3, n. *l*. In the baraita in b. Taʿan. 31A, it says about this: The king's daughter borrowed (the white dress) from the daughter of the high priest, and she borrowed from the daughter of the presiding priest, and she from the daughter of the one anointed for war, and she from the daughter of the common priest, and all (other) Israelite women from each other, lest she who did not have one be ashamed. ‖ See further b. Ḥag. 5A; y. Šeqal. 5.49B.2 at § Matt 6:3f.

11:23: I received from the Lord what I delivered to you.

παραλαμβάνειν = קִבֵּל, παραδιδόναι = מָסַר.

Mishnah ʾAbot 1.1: Moses received קִבֵּל the Torah (specifically both the written and the oral Torah) from Sinai and delivered it וּמְסָרָהּ to Joshua, Joshua to the elders, the elders to the prophets, and the prophets delivered it מְסָרוּהָ to the men of the great synagogue (according to tradition, a group of 120 men that led the Jewish community in the time after Ezra). — For further examples see m. ʾAbot 1.3; m. Peʾah 2.6 = TanḥB במדבר § 27 (11A); m. Zebaḥ. 1.3. ‖ On the institution of holy communion, see the excursus "The Feast of the Passover."

11:31: If we judged ourselves, we would not be judged.

See TanḥB משפטים § 4 (41B): R. Eleazar (ca. 270) said, "If there is justice below, justice is not administered above; but if there is no justice below, justice is administered above (this should be read). How so? If those below execute justice, justice is not administered above; for this reason God said, 'Keep justice below, lest you cause me to execute justice from above.'" — The same with variations is found in Deut. Rab. 5 (202A); Midr. Ps. 72 § 3 (163A); very briefly in Gen. Rab. 26 (17A).

11:32: If we are judged, we are chastised by the Lord, lest we be condemned with the world.

In the apocrypha and pseudepigrapha we often encounter the notion that the judgments of God that come upon the pious are intended as disciplinary punishments for their good.

2 Maccabees 6:12: "I admonish the readers of this book not to let themselves be cast down by these misfortunes, but rather to remember that the punishments are not meant to destroy but rather to chastise παιδεία our people." ‖ Judith 8:27: "For as he tested them (the fathers) to examine their hearts, so too he has not punished us, but rather for a warning εἰς νουθέτησιν the Lord chastises those who are near to him." ‖ Wisdom 12:22: "While you chastise παιδεύων us, our enemies afflict us in ten thousand ways, so that we remember your goodness when we judge κρίνοντες, but when we are judged κρινόμενοι, we hope for mercy." — Wisdom 12:2: "You punish ἐλέγχεις lightly those who have fallen, and reminding them of where they have fallen short, you reprimand νουθετεῖς them so that, when they have been freed from evil, they may believe in you, O Lord." ‖ Sirach 18:13: "He has mercy on those who accept chastisement παιδείαν." ‖ Psalms of Solomon 3:3f.: "Righteous men remember the Lord at all times; they acknowledge his judgments are just. A righteous man does not take it lightly when he is chastised παιδευόμενος by the Lord; his delight is constantly before the Lord." — Psalms of Solomon 8:25f., 29: "Yes, God, you have shown your judgment to us in your righteousness; our eyes have seen your judgments, O God. We have praised your eternally glorious name as righteous; for you are the God of righteousness, you judge Israel with chastisement ἐν παιδείᾳ.... We have indeed proven to be obstinate, but you have been our disciplinarian παιδευτής." — Psalms of Solomon 10:1ff.: "Blessed is the man whom the Lord remembers with reprimand ἐν ἐλέγχῳ and whom he averts from the evil way with the rod, so that he may be pure of sin and not do it. Whoever offers his back to the rod will be pure; for the Lord is good to those who accept chastisement παιδείαν. For he levels the ways of the righteous and does not devour them with chastisement ἐν παιδείᾳ." — Psalms of Solomon 13:7ff.: "The chastisement ἡ παιδεία of the righteous as a consequence of (their) ignorance cannot be compared with the downfall of the godless. The righteous man is chastised παιδεύεται secretly, lest the godless rejoice over the righteous. He warns

the righteous as a beloved son and chastises him as a firstborn. For the Lord preserves the righteous, and he repays their transgressions with chastisement ἐν παιδείᾳ." — Psalms of Solomon 16:11: "May grumbling and faint-heartedness in distress stay far from me when you chastise me for improvement ἐν τῷ σε παιδεύειν εἰς ἐπιστροφήν when I have sinned."

11:33: Wait for one another.

If one wishes to understand ἐκδέχεσθαι in the sense of "await," "wait for" = הַמְתִּין, the following parallel passage can be invoked:

Babylonian Talmud Berakot 5B: Abba Benjamin (a Tannaim of uncertain time) said, "When two enter (the synagogue) to pray and one of them is done earlier with his prayer and does not wait for the other ולא המתין את חברו, but rather goes away, his prayer is shattered before his face; as it says, 'You who strike yourself in the face, should the earth become desolate because of you?' (So Job 18:4 according to the midr.) And not only this, but also he causes the Shekinah (divinity) to be removed from Israel; as it says, 'And the rock moves away from its place' (Job 18:4); and 'rock' is nothing other than God; as it says, 'You neglected the rock that begat you' (Deut 32:18). Yet if he waits for him המתין לו, what is his recompense?" R. Yose b. Hanina (here the elder, at any rate a Tannaim, is intended) said, "He becomes worthy of these blessings; as it says, 'If you would have listened to my commandments, ... your seed would be as the sand and the descendants of your body as its grains ...; and your prosperity would be like a stream and your righteousness like the waves of the sea' (Isa 48:18f.)."

12:2: To dumb idols.

See Lev. Rab. 6 (109C) at § Rom 1:23 A, #2, D, n. *c*; Mek. Exod. 15:11 (49A) at § Rom 1:23 A, #2, D, n. *d*; Sib. Or. 4:7 at § Rom 1:23 A, #2, D, n. *f*, toward the end; Jub. 12:1ff. and 2 En. 66:1 at § Rom 1:23 A, #2, D, n. *g*.

12:3: May Jesus come under a curse!

ἀνάθεμα = "to fall prey to destruction, a curse," see § Rom 9:3. — In a Hebrew NT available to us (London 1852), ἀνάθεμα Ἰησοῦς is rendered with לְיֵשׁוּעַ חֵרֶם = "the ban for Jesus." There is no common corresponding expression at the time of the apostle. Then, ἀνάθεμα Ἰησοῦς would have been translated with אָרוּר יֵשׁוּ,[a] Aram. לִיט יֵשׁוּ[b] = "may Jesus be cursed!" or with מְחֳרָם יֵשׁוּ[c] = "may Jesus be under the ban!" An authority of the 3rd century teaches us that in the expression "cursed אָרוּר be so and so!," there is entailed a ban, a curse, and an oath.[d] — On the narrative in b. Sanh. 107B that Jesus was placed under the ban by his reputed teacher Joshua b. Perahiah, see § Matt 2:14.

a. Jerusalem Talmud Megillah 3.74B.66: Rab († 247) said, "(After the reading of the Esther scroll at the feast of Purim,) one must say, 'Cursed אָרוּר be Haman, cursed אֲרוּרִים his sons!'" ‖ Babylonian Talmud Soṭah 37B: Cursed ארורין be his father and mother! ‖ A baraita in b. Soṭah 49B: Cursed ארור be the man who breeds pigs, and cursed וארור the man who teaches his son Greek wisdom! — See the parallel b. B. Qam. 82B in detail at § Matt 8:30, n. *b*. ‖ Babylonian Talmud Sanhedrin 52A: One says, "Cursed ארור be the one who produced such a (disgraceful daughter)! Cursed be the one who reared such a one! Cursed be the one from whose loins such a one issued forth!" — The author is R. Meir (ca. 150).

b. Genesis Rabbah 5 (5A): Cursed לייטין be the breasts that suckled him! ‖ Targum Onkelos Genesis 27:29: "May those who curse you be cursed לִיטִין, and may those who bless you be blessed!"

c. Jerusalem Talmud Moʿed Qaṭan 3.81D.38: May this man be banned מְחָרָם! ‖ Jerusalem Talmud Moʿed Qaṭan 3.81D.40: (R. Simeon b. Laqish [ca. 250] said to robbers who had stolen figs,) "May these people be banned מחרמין!" They answered him, "May this man (= you) be banned מחרם!"

d. Babylonian Talmud Šebuʿot 36A: In a baraita it has been taught: "Cursed" אָרוּר (be so and so)! This entails a ban נִידּוּי, a curse קְלָלָה, and an oath שְׁבוּעָה. A ban, for it is written, "Curse Meroz, says the angel of Yahweh, curse, yes, curse its inhabitants!" (Judg 5:23). And Ulla (ca. 280) said, "Barak put Meroz under the ban שמתיה with 400 (blasts of the) trumpet. A curse, for it is written, 'And those men shall stand there for the curse' (Deut 27:13). Furthermore, it says, 'Cursed be the man who makes a carved or cast image' (Deut 27:15). An oath, for it is written, 'Since Joshua pronounced this oath at that time, by saying, "Cursed be the man before Yahweh who arises and builds up this city Jericho!"' (Josh 6:26)."

12:5: Different kinds of services.

On διακονία see b. Hor. 10A: Rabban Gamaliel (ca. 90) directed his mind to putting (R. Eleazar חסמא and R. Yohanan b. Gudgeda, two students, who lived in the most bitter poverty) in the top place (conferring an office upon them). When he landed (after a sea voyage), he sent for them but they did not come. He sent for them again, and they came. He said to them, "Did you suppose that I meant to give you a dominion שְׂרָרָה? I intend to give you a service עַבְדוּת; for it says, 'And they spoke to him and said, "If you become a servant עֶבֶד of this people today …"' (1 Kgs 12:7)."

12:12ff. (Metaphor of the body and its members).

The metaphor of the body and its members in rabbinic literature.

Tosefta Taʿanit 2.5 (217): As long as Rabban Gamaliel (ca. 90) was alive, the halakah was commonly in accordance with his words. After the death of Rabban Gamaliel, R. Joshua (ca. 90) sought to do away with his words. Then R. Yohanan b. Nuri (ca. 110) rose to his feet and said, "I see that the body is judged in accordance with the head בתר רישא גיפא אזיל: as long as Rabban Gamaliel was alive, the halakah was commonly in accordance with his words. Now when he is dead, you want to do away with his words!" R. Joshua answered him, "We will not listen to you. If the halakah had been determined in accordance with the opinion of Rabban Gamaliel, no one could raise an objection against it." — See a parallel in b. ʿErub. 41A, although here it mistakenly mentions R. Simeon b. Gamaliel (ca. 140). See also Pirqe R. El. 42 (24A): Everything is judged according to the head הכל הולך אחר הראש. ‖ Midrash Psalm 14 § 1 (56A): "For the leader of music. Of David. The fool says in his heart, 'There is no God'" (Ps 14:1). This is what Scripture said, "I, Yahweh, search the heart; I test the kidneys"

(Jer 17:10). Why does (Scripture) mention the heart and the kidneys of all the members? Yet the eyes are judged according to the heart; as it says, "That you not follow after your heart and your eyes" (Num 15:39). And likewise the ears and (all) 248 members are judged according to the heart, and the heart completes the thought according to the counsel of the kidneys. For this reason, Scripture mentions only heart and kidney in the verse "and God searches the heart and tests the kidneys." — It should be observed how here heart and kidneys take the place of the head. ‖ Midrash Psalm 39 § 2 (128A): "I said, 'I will guard my ways lest I sin with my tongue' (Ps 39:2). It happened with the king of Persia that he was dying and became excessively emaciated. The doctors said to him, 'There is no recovery for you until someone brings you the milk of a lioness לביאה and you drink it until you have recovered.' He sent for king Solomon, the son of David, and they took with themselves a lot of gold in their hand. Immediately Solomon sent servants and had Benaiah, the son of Jehoiada summoned. He said to him, 'How can we find the milk of a lioness?' Benaiah said to him, 'Give me ten goats.' Then he and the king's servants went to a lion's den. There, there was a lioness who suckled her young. On the first day he stayed far away and threw one to her, and she ate it. On the second day, he got a little closer and threw her another one, and so on day after day. At the end of the ten days he went and he got right next to her until he played with her, and he fingered her udder and took some of her milk and went on his way. They came to Solomon, and he dismissed them in peace, and they went their way. When they had gotten half the way behind them, that doctor saw in his dream, how his members fought with one another. The feet said, 'Not one among all the members is like us; for if we did not go, the body could not bring the milk.' The hands answered and said, 'Not one is like us; for if we had not fingered (the udder), (the body) could not bring the milk.' The eyes said, 'We are above all; for if we did not show the way to it (the body), nothing at all would have happened.' The heart answered and said, 'I am above you all; for if I had not given counsel, you would have not benefited from the matter.' The tongue answered and said, 'I am better than you; for if there were no speaking, what would you do?!' Then all the members arose and responded to the tongue, 'How is it that you do not shy away from comparing yourself with us, you who sit in a place of gloom and darkness and have no bones in yourself as all (the other) members?' The tongue answered them, 'Today you will (still say) that I am master among you!' When the man woke from his sleep, he kept the dream in his heart and went further on his way. He came to the king and said to him, 'Here you have milk from a dog כַּלְבָּא, which we have sought for your sake so that you may drink it.' Immediately the king became angry with him and commanded that he be hanged. When he went to be hanged, all the members began to tremble. Then the tongue said to them, 'Did I not tell you today that there is nothing in you? If I save you, will you confess to me that I rule over you?' They said to it, 'Yes!' Immediately the tongue said to those who should hang him, 'Lead me back to the king!' They led him back to the king. He said to him, 'Why did you command that I be hanged?' He answered him, 'Because you brought me milk from a dog כַּלְבְּתָא.' He said to him, 'What does it matter to you if it leads to your healing?!' And also, the lioness לְבִיָּא is also called "dog" כַּלְבְּתָא. He took some of it and drank and was healed, and it turned out that it was lion's milk, and he let him go in peace. Then all the members said to it (the tongue), 'Now we confess to you that you rule over all the members.' This is what is written, 'Death and life is in the hand of the tongue' (Prov 18:21). David said, 'I said, "I will guard my ways lest I sin with my tongue"' (Ps 39:2)." — Here too the heart takes the place of the head. ‖ Babylonian Talmud Šabbat 61A: Whoever intends to anoint his whole body anoints his head first, because it rules (as king) over all his members.

12:14: The body is not one member, but rather many.

It was thought that the body of a man had 248 members and the body of a women had 252 members.

Genesis Rabbah 69 (44B): ("My soul thirsts for you, my flesh yearns for you" [Ps 63:2].) The rabbis said, "As my soul thirsts for you, so the 248 members רמ״ה איברים, that are a part of me, yearn for you." ‖ Babylonian Talmud Nedarim 32B: Rammi bar Abba (ca. 270) said, "It is written 'Abram' and it is written 'Abraham.' At first God made him rule over 243 members (numerical value of אברם), and in the end (after circumcision) he made him rule over 248 members (numerical value of אברהם = 248); these (5 members that he gained dominion over in the end) were the two eyes, the two ears, and the tip of the (male) member." ‖ Babylonian Talmud Bekorot 45A: Rab Judah († 299) said that Samuel († 254) said, "It once happened with the students of R. Ishmael († ca. 135) that they dissected[220] a prostitute who had been condemned by the king (by the government) to be burned. They examined and found 252 members in her. He said to them, "You have examined a woman? (and with her it is thus;) for Scripture added to her two door pivots and two doors (beyond what is in a man)." In a baraita: R. Eliezer (ca. 90) said, "As a house has door pivots, so a woman has door pivots; as it says, 'She knelt down and gave birth, because her door pivots turned in her' (so 1 Sam 4:19 according to the midr.)." R. Joshua (ca. 90) said, "As a house has doors, so a woman has doors; for it says, 'It (the night when Job was conceived) did not close the doors of my mother's womb' (Job 3:10)." ‖ See also b. Mak. 23B; Pesiq. 101A at § Matt 22:36, #1, notes *d* and *e*; Midr. Ps. 14 § 1 at § 1 Cor 12:12ff.

12:17: If the whole body (were) an eye.

Babylonian Talmud ʿAbodah Zarah 20A: … If a person were all eyes like the angel of death מלא עינים כמלאך המות. It has been said of the angel of death that he is completely full of eyes שכילו מלא עינים.... — See the whole passage at § Matt 5:28 A, third paragraph and § Matt 4:1 B, #3, C at the beginning (b. ʿAbod. Zar. 20B).

12:26: If one member suffers, all the members suffer too.

Mekilta Exodus 19:6 (71A): Just as when one lamb suffers because of one of the others, the others feel (perceive) it, so too all the Israelites feel it when one of them is killed, and they are pained because of it. It is not so with the nations of the world. Instead, when one of them is killed, all rejoice over his fall. ‖ Leviticus Rabbah 4 (107D): Hezekiah (ca. 240) taught, "'Israel is a scattered lamb' (Jer 50:17). The Israelites are compared with a lamb: just as when a lamb is struck on its head or on one of its members מאבריו, all its members feel it,

---

220. So Levy, *Chaldäisches Wörterbuch*, 4:566B.

so too all the Israelites feel it when one of them sins." ‖ Jerusalem Talmud Soṭah 1.17A.51: The measure by which a person measured will be measured to him (by God).... She (the woman suspected of adultery) began to sin first with the hips and then with the stomach; therefore, the hips are struck first and then the stomach (cf. Num 5:27), and the whole rest of the body does not go free (m. Soṭah 1.7). R. Abba b. Pappi (ca. 350) applied this in a farewell speech: "If with the measure of punishment that is smaller (than the measure of goodness) one member suffers and all the other members feel it אבר אחד לוקה ושאר כל האיברים מרגישין, how much more does it apply with the measure of goodness (that all other members feel it when one member experiences something good)!"

13:1 A: With tongues ... of angels.

It is said of the voice of angels that they reach from one end of the world to the other [a] and that no human can endure them.[b] Rabban Yohanan b. Zakkai († ca. 80) was credited with understanding even the speech of angels;[c] yet it was presupposed about the angles themselves that only the holy language was understandable to them.[d] At the most, the angel Gabriel constitutes an exception, insofar as he alone is in control of all seventy languages of the world.[e]

a. ʾAbot de Rabbi Nathan 2 (2B): If the voice of Gabriel, who is one of a thousand times a thousand and ten thousand times ten thousand who stand before him (God), does from one end of the world to the other, how much more does this go for the king of all kings, the Holy One—blessed be He!—who created the whole world, who created those above and who created those below!

b. Exodus Rabbah 28 (88C): R. Samuel b. Nahmani (ca. 260) said that R. Jonathan (ca. 220) said, "What does 'The voice of Yahweh in power' (Ps 29:4) mean? Can this be said? Is it not true that no creature can stand before the voice of an angel; as it says, 'And his body was as Tarshish ... and the voice of his words was like the voice of the roar (of great waters)' (Dan 10:6)?! And as for God, of whom it is written, 'Do I not fill heaven and earth?' (Jer 23:24), should it be necessary for him to speak with power? Rather, 'the voice of Yahweh in power' (means:) with the power of all (other, i.e., ordinary) voices."

c. Babylonian Talmud Baba Batra 134A: It was said of Rabban Yohanan b. Zakkai († ca. 80) that he did not leave behind (and therefore understood and mastered) Scripture and the Mishnah, the Gemarah (here = tradition), the halakah and the haggadah, the subtleties of the Torah and of the scholars, the inferences from the lesser to the greater and from word correspondences, the calculation of the solstices and of the letter values (of individual words), the parables of the millers and the fox fables, the speech of demons and the speech of palm trees[221] and the speech of the angels of service. — The same is found in b. Sukkah 28A; in ʾAbot R. Nat. 14 (5B), the last sentence is missing.

---

221. S-B: There are people who on a windless day take a spot between trees that stand close to each other and pull a cloth from one tree to the other; they observe the mutual shaking of the branches and draw several properties from this; see Levy, *Chaldäisches Wörterbuch*, 4:545B from ʾArukh סח 1.

d. Babylonian Talmud Soṭah 33A: Rab Judah († 299) said, "No one should ever pray for his needs in the Aramaic language; for R. Yohanan († 279) said, 'Whoever prays for his needs in the Aramaic language, the angels of service (who bring prayer before God) do not attend to him, because the angels of service do not understand the Aramaic language (but rather only the holy = Hebrew language).' There is no contradiction (with the sentence in m. Soṭah 7.1: The following things may be said in any language: ... the Shema, the [Eighteen Benedictions] prayer, etc.). In the one case (in the case of the saying of Rab Judah and R. Yohanan) it deals with the prayer of an individual (which needs the support of an angel), and in the other case (in the Mishnah) it deals with the prayer of the community." — The saying of Rab Judah and R. Yohanan is also found in b. Šabb. 12B. — Against the idea that the angels do not understand Aramaic, other passages assert that even in the temple voices were heard in the Aramaic language. The objection is refuted with the remark that these voices are a voice from heaven (*bath-qol*), and so are not the speech of an angel, or that the speaker was the angel Gabriel, who had knowledge of all languages. See b. Soṭah 33A at § Luke 1:11 A.

e. See b. Soṭah 33A with parallels at § Luke 1:11 A; b. Soṭah 36B at § Luke 1:19 A, #4, n. g.

13:1 B: Sounding bronze.

See b. B. Meṣ. 85B: Ulla (ca. 280) said, "This is what people say (in a proverb), 'The stater (a coin) in the flask calls: "Cling! Cling!"'" (Unimportant people make the biggest fuss about themselves.) — Genesis Rabbah 16 (11B): R. Joshua of Sikhnin (ca. 330) said in the name of R. Levi (ca. 300), "People say to the Euphrates, 'Why does your voice (your rushing) not sound widely?' It answers, 'I do not need it to; my works make me known....' People say to the Hiddekel (Tigris), 'Why does your voice sound widely?' It answers, 'May at least my voice be heard and heeded!' People say to the fruit trees, 'Why does your voice not sound widely?' They answer, 'We do not need it to; our fruits testify for us.' People say to the non-fruit-bearing trees (i.e., to the trees whose fruits are inedible for humans), 'Why does your voice sound widely?' They answer, 'So that our voice may be heard and we may be seen.'" — Partial parallels are found in SDeut 1:8 § 6 (66B); Midr. Eccl. 10:11 (48B).

13:1 C: A noisy cymbal.

1. κύμβαλον in the LXX in the plural = צֶלְצְלִים (2 Sam 6:5; Ps 150:5), = מְצִלְתַּיִם (1 Chr 13:8; Ezra 3:10; cf. Neh 12:27); in rabbinic literature = צִלְצַל, Aram. צַלְצְלָא, cymbal, basin. — On κύμβαλον ἀλαλάζον see Ps 150:5: בְּצִלְצְלֵי שָׁמַע, with cymbals of sound = with resounding cymbals; LXX: ἐν κυμβάλοις εὐήχοις with beautiful-sounding cymbals; targum: בְּצַלְצְלָן דְּשָׁמְעִין בִּלְחוֹדֵיהוֹן, with cymbals that one listens to alone (because according to m. ʿArak. 2.5—see further below—they were present in the temple in only one exemplar). A different reading in Levy is: בצילצלון דמשמעין לבדוחא, with cymbals that are sounded for merriment.[222] — Also, Ps 150:5: בְּצִלְצְלֵי תְרוּעָה, with cymbals

222. Levy, *Chaldäisches Wörterbuch*, 2:329A.

of noise; LXX: ἐν κυμβάλοις ἀλαλαγμοῦ, with cymbals of noise; targum: בְּצַלְצְלָן דְּמַשְׁמְעִין בְּיַבָּבָא, that are sounded with noise (or: "in mourning," in contrast to: "for merriment," see the reading in Levy above).

2. The cymbals in the temple service.

Josephus, *Jewish Antiquities* 7.12.3: "The cymbals κύμβαλα were wide and large made of bronze χάλκεα." ‖ Mishnah ʿArakin 2.5: The cymbal was there alone הַצִּלְצָל לְבַד, that is, it existed in only one exemplar. — On this, see b. ʿArak. 13B: How do we know this? R. Asi (ca. 300) said, "Scripture says, 'And Asaph played loudly with the cymbals בַּמְצִלְתַּיִם' (1 Chr 16:5); thus, there were two (because of the dual ending); but since they performed only one task (one cymbal cannot do anything without another) and only one man used them, they were called 'one' (the cymbals were spoken of in the singular צִלְצַל)." — צלצל אחד is also found in t. ʿArak. 2.1 (544). ‖ Tosefta ʿArakin 2.3 (544): The cymbal צלצל in the sanctuary was made of copper נְחֹשֶׁת and damaged since the days of Moses. The scholars had master workmen (experts) who come from Alexandria in Egypt, who restored it; but its voice (its sound) was not as lovely as it had been. — The parallel y. Sukkah 5.55C.42 adds: Then (the repair) was eliminated and the cymbal was once again as it had been. — There is a parallel in b. ʿArak. 10B as a baraita. ‖ Mishnah Šeqalim 5.1: Ben Arza was appointed (as head) over the cymbal. ‖ Jerusalem Talmud Šeqalim 5.48D.51: When the head of the priests waved cloths, Ben Arza struck the cymbal (as a sign that the Levites should strike up the temple song). ‖ Jerusalem Talmud Sukkah 5.55B.52: The sound of the (temple) cymbal was heard from Jericho (i.e., as far as Jericho).

13:2: So that I move mountains.

On the saying "to uproot mountains" = "to make the impossible possible," see § Matt 17:20.

13:3 A: If I used all my possessions to feed (the poor).

In principle, no limits were imposed on benefaction. "The following things have no (legal) measure: the edges of a field (which are meant for the poor), the first fruits, festal pilgrimages (and the sacrifices to be brought for them), works of love and study of the Torah" (m. Pe'ah 1.1). Nevertheless, in order to avert the impoverishment of the benefactor, certain norms had been established that prevented giving all one's possessions for beneficent purposes; see a little on this at § Luke 18:12 B, #3, and in detail in the excursus "Ancient Jewish Private Charity."

13:3 B: And if I hand over my body to be burned.

παραδιδόναι = מָסַר. See examples at § John 10:11 B and § Acts 15:26. — The purpose of this handing over is to sanctify the divine name; see § Matt 6:9 C, notes *n* and *o*; b. Ber. 20A at § John 9:16 B. — On burning, see Num. Rab. 2 (137D) and b. Pesaḥ. 53B at § Matt 6:9 C, n. *o*; b. Sanh. 92B at § Matt 6:9 C, n. *a*.

13:3 C: But if I do not have love, I gain nothing.

Babylonian Talmud Sukkah 49B: R. Eleazar (ca. 270) said, "Alms צדקה will be repaid only according to the measure of love חסד that is contained in them; as it says, 'Sow for alms and harvest according to the measure of love' (Hos 10:12)."

13:5 A: It does not seek its own.

See § 1 Cor 10:24. ‖ Deuteronomy Rabbah 11 (206D): R. Isaac (ca. 300) said, "If an ignorant man הֶדְיוֹט speaks to another, it will harm him. And Moses said, 'Why, O Yahweh, should your wrath burn against your people?' (Exod 32:11). But his heart was pure within him; for he did not seek what he himself did not need, but rather what the Israelites needed." ‖ Midrash Psalm 2 § 2 (13A): R. Isaac (ca. 300) said, "If a person says to another, 'Why are you doing such and such?,' the other one gets angry. But the righteous say to God, 'Why?,' and he does not get angry and they will not be punished. And why will they not be punished? Because they seek good not for themselves שלא ביקשו טובה לעצמן, but rather for Israel's sake."

13:5 B: It does not reckon evil.

Here belongs also bearing a grudge for wrong experienced; see SLev 19:18 at § Matt 5:22, C.

13:7: It covers everything (see § 1 Pet 4:8).

13:8 A: Love never falls away (never ceases).

Mishnah ʾAbot 5.16: Any love that depends on something, if the thing ceases בָּטֵל, so too the love ceases וּבְטֵלָה אַהֲבָה. But a love that does not depend on something never ceases אֵינָהּ בְּטֵלָה לְעוֹלָם. What is a love that depends on something? This is the love of Amnon and Tamar (cf. 2 Sam 13). And one that does not depend on something? This is the love of David and Jonathan.

13:8 B: But whatever prophecies there may be, they will be done away with.

See y. Meg. 1.70D.51; Pesiq. 79A; b. Nid. 61B at § Matt 5:18 B, #1, under discussion about noneternal portions of the writings more broadly called the Torah.

13:12 A: Now we look through (= by means of) a mirror.

ἔσοπτρον = mirror. In rabbinic literature, the most common expressions for "mirror" are מַרְאָה, the Aramaic מַחְזִיתָא and the loanword אִסְפַּקְלַרְיָא, סְפֶקְלַרְיָא = σπεκλάριον.

1. מַרְאָה.

Tosefta Šabbat 13.16 (130): On the Sabbath one may not look in a mirror במראה (because one could thereby be misled to carry it); but if it is fixed on the wall, see, it is allowed.[223] ‖ Genesis Rabbah 4 (4A): A Samaritan asked R. Meir (ca. 150) and said to him, "... Is it possible that the one of whom it is written, 'Do I not fill heaven and earth?' (Jer 23:24), spoke with Moses between the two (carrying) rods of the ark of the covenant?" He answered him, "Fetch me a big mirror מראות גדולות (i.e., a magnifying mirror made of highly polished metal)!" Then he said to him, "Look at your image in it!" He saw it was big. Then R. Meir said, "Fetch me a small mirror מראות קטנות (a minification mirror)!" He fetched him a small mirror; he said to him, "Look at your image in it!" He saw it was small. Then he said to him, "If you who are flesh and blood can change into any size you choose, how much more does this go for the one who spoke and the world came into being—blessed be He! Consequently, if he wishes, 'Do I not fill heaven and earth?' and if he wishes, he speaks with Moses between the two rods of the ark of the covenant." ‖ Mishnah Kelim 14.6: If (by polishing and buffing) one has made a mirror מראה in the cover of a metal container, R. Judah (ca. 150) declares it clean. However, the scholars declare it unclean. If a mirror מראה that has been shattered no longer reflects most of the face (literally: "lets one see" מַרְאָה), it is clean. — Similar content is found in t. Kelim B. Meṣ. 4.12f. (583).

2. מִחְזִיתָא.

Targum Onkelos Exodus 38:8: "He made the iron basin and its frame out of ore (copper), from the mirrors מֶחְזְיָת (so read instead of מחזין) of the women who came to pray at the entrance of the tent of meeting." ‖ Targum Isaiah 3:23: "The mirror מחזיתא and the fine linens (read קַרְפַּסַיָּא with Dalman instead of קרטסיא) and the crowns and the covers." ‖ The Hebrew form מַחֲזוֹת is found in Mek. Exod. 18:21 (68A); see further below #3, β.

3. אִסְפַּקְלַרְיָא (סְפֶּקְלַרְיָא) means α. in general, mirror; β. specifically, the mirror of the astrologers; γ. glass (glass slabs, window glass).

α. Mishnah Kelim 30.2: A mirror אספקלריא is clean; but a basin that has been made into a mirror is unclean. If, however, it has been made as a mirror from the beginning, it is clean. — A similar claim is found in t. Kelim B. Bat. 7.7 (597). ‖ Targum Yerušalmi I Exodus 38:8: "He made the iron basin and its frame from ore from the women's copper mirrors אספקלירי נחשא."

β. Mekilta Exodus 18:21 (68A): R. Eleazar of Modiim († ca. 135) said, "'Yet you, look for תחזה capable men from the whole people' (Exod 18:21), namely by a mirror באספקלריא, by the sort of mirror מַחֲזִית kings usually look into (for their astrological calculations and determinations)." ‖ Genesis Rabbah 91 (57C): "Jacob saw that there was grain in Egypt" (Gen 42:1). Was Jacob then in Egypt, so that he saw the grain in Egypt; as it says, "He saw that there was grain in Egypt"? And did he not say to his sons, "Behold, I have heard that there is

223. S-B: According to b. Šabb. 149A, this deals with a mirror made from metal מראה של מַתֶּכֶת. Rab Nahman († 320) in the name of Rabbah b. Abuha (ca. 270) provides the following as a reason for the prohibition: "Since a person could be led thereby to remove hairs that have become loose." In y. Šabb. 6.7D.42, R. Aha (ca. 320) in the name of R. Ba (ca. 290) gives the following as a reason: "Since a woman might see a white hair (on her head) and rip it out and thereby make herself guilty of a sin offering."

grain in Egypt" (Gen 42:2)? Yet since the day Joseph was stolen, the holy spirit (of prophecy) had moved from him so that he saw and yet did not see, so that he heard and yet did not hear (his seeing and hearing were piecemeal in comparison with his earlier prophetic gifting). And why is it not said, "There is 'food' in Egypt"? For Scripture says, "There is 'grain' שֶׁבֶר in Egypt" (Gen 42:1); and was it not already said, "The whole land of Egypt hungered" (Gen 41:55)? What does Scripture mean to teach by saying: "There is grain שבר in Egypt"? Yet do not read: "There is שֶׁבֶר," but rather: "There is סֵבֶר (hope)." For he saw in the (astrological) mirror באספקלריא that there was hope in Egypt. And who was this? This was Joseph.

γ. Jerusalem Talmud Berakot 8.12B.44: If a light נר is in his breast or in a lantern or between glass ספקלריא, one sees the flame without using its light; one uses its light without seeing the flame. One never speaks praise about it until one sees the flame and uses its light. — In the parallel b. Ber. 53B, "between glass" is missing. ‖ Targum Yerušalmi I Exodus 19:17: "Moses led the people toward the Shekinah of Yahweh from the camp, and at once the Lord of the world tore the mountain free and set it in the air, and it was translucent like glass כאספקלריא, and they were under the mountain." ‖ Babylonian Talmud Soṭah 30B: "From the mouth of children and infants you have established a power" (Ps 8:3). R. Meir (ca. 150) said, "How do we know that even the children sang the song (in Exod 15) in the womb? Because it says, 'In the assemblies they praised Yahweh as God from the source of Israel' (in the womb; so Ps 68:27 according to the midr.). Yet they did not see! (How can it then say, 'This is my God' [Exod 15:2]?)" R. Tanḥum (ca. 380) said, "Their (the pregnant women's) body became for them as bright (translucent) glass כאספקלריא המאירה, so that they saw." — In the parallel passage Midr. Ps. 8 § 5 (39A), Rab († 247) is named as the author instead of R. Tanḥum. — In a similar content in another passage we find זְכוֹכִית = glass instead of אספקלריא. Specifically, as is narrated in Midr. Ps. 8 § 4 (38B), when at the making of the covenant at Sinai God demanded of Israel guarantors for the diligent observance of the Torah, and specifically guarantors who were not burdened with any debt, they said to God, "Who are those who are not indebted to you?" He said to them, "The children!" Immediately they brought the children in the womb and from the mother's breast, and their (the pregnant women's) bodies congealed as into glass כזכוכית, and they (the embryos) saw God from their bodies and spoke with him. ‖ A baraita in b. Yebam. 49B: All the prophets looked through glass that was not bright (translucent) באיספקלריא שאינה מאירה, but our teacher Moses looked through bright (translucent) glass. ‖ Leviticus Rabbah 1 (106A): What is the difference between Moses and all the other prophets of Israel? R. Judah b. Ilai (ca. 150) and the rabbis. R. Judah said, "The prophets looked from the midst of nine glass panes איספקלריות; as it says, 'The sight of the appearance that I saw was like the appearance that I saw when I came to destroy the city, and appearances as the appearance I saw at the river Chebar' (Ezek 43:3) (the nine glass panes are inferred from the nine-fold appearance of the verb ראה and its derivatives in this verse; here the plural "appearances" is counted twice). Moses, however, looked out from one glass pane; as it says, 'I let (Moses) look and not in riddles' (Num 12:8; here ראה occurs only once)." The rabbis said, "All the prophets looked out of a wet (fogged) glass pane; as it says, 'I have multiplied visions and given images (parables) by the prophets' (Hos 12:11). (The multiplicity of revelations to the prophets and the speech of these in visions and parables is a proof that they have beheld what has been revealed to them not in clear and definite outlines but rather in blurred ones—as through a fogged glass pane.) But Moses looked out from a clear glass pane; as it says, 'He saw the form of Yahweh' (Num 12:8)." R. Phineas (ca. 360) said in the name of R. Hoshaiah (I, ca. 225; II, ca. 300), "Like a king who reveals himself to a member of his court in his image; for in this world the Shekinah (divinity) has revealed itself to individuals, but in the future, 'The glory of Yahweh will be revealed, and all flesh will see it, for Yahweh's mouth has spoken it' (Isa 40:5)." ‖ Tanḥuma צו 143A: "If a prophet arises for you, I, Yahweh, will manifest myself in a vision" (Num 12:6); my Shekinah (divinity) will be revealed to him not by a bright (translucent) glass pane באספקלריא מאירה, but rather in a dream and vision. ‖ Babylonian Talmud Sanhedrin 97B: Abbayye († 338/39) said, "In every generation the world does not have less than 36 righteous people who can welcome the face of the Shekinah (as the Israelites did formerly at the Red Sea); as it says, 'Blessed are all who hope in him לו' (Isa 30:18); לו is 36 in its numerical value." Really? Yet Raba († 352) said, "The line (of the righteous) before God is 18,000 *parasangs* long; as it says, 'All around 18,000' (Ezek 48:35)!" There is no contradiction: in the one case (with Abbayye) it deals with those who look through a bright (translucent) glass pane באיספקלריא המאירה, and in the other case with those who look through a glass pane that is not bright (translucent)." — There is a parallel in b. Sukkah 45B.

13:12 B: In a riddle, but then face to face.

The underlying text is Num 12:8: "I speak to him (to Moses) mouth to mouth, and let him see and not in riddles בְּחִידוֹת." — Septuagint Numbers 12:8: "I will speak with him mouth to mouth, in (personal) appearance ἐν εἴδει (וּמַרְאֶה interpreted = בְּמַרְאֶה) and not in riddles δι' αἰνιγμάτων." — Targum Onkelos: "Word for word I speak with him, in (personal) appearance בְּחֵיזוּ (= במראה) and not in riddles בְּחִדְוָן." — Targum Yerušalmi I: "Word for word I speak with him, for he separated himself from intercourse, and as a visible appearance חֵיזוּ and not in a hidden way did I reveal myself in the thorn bush." — See also Lev. Rab. 1 (106A) at § 1 Cor 13:12 A, #3, γ. — On seeing God, see § Matt 5:8 B.

13:13: Greater than all these (= the greatest of these) is love.

The rabbinic scholars sometimes counted piety חֲסִידוּת and sometimes humility עֲנָוָה as the greatest among all the virtues גדולה מכולן; see b. ʿArak. 16B and b. ʿAbod. Zar. 20B at § Matt 18:15, n. *e* and the second S-B footnote within that section.

14:8: If a trumpet gives an unclear sound, who will prepare for war?

The call to men fit to bear arms for war occurs by means of blasting the שׁוֹפָר (trumpet). See Judg 3:27; 6:34; 1 Sam 13:3; Jer 4:5; Ezek 7:14.

14:11: A barbarian.

βάρβαρος, see § Rom 1:14, #2.

14:16 A: The one in the position of an uninformed person.

1. ἰδιώτης = הֶדְיוֹט (so ordinarily, Dalman הֶדְיוֹט). This loanword, which appears not infrequently in rabbinic literature, denotes α. the (profane) person as opposed to the divinity; β. the private citizen as opposed to the king; γ. the layperson as opposed to any expert or learned person and δ. specifically the ignorant person as opposed to one knowledgeable in the law.

α. Mishnah Qiddušin 1.6: The claim of the Most High (to an item purchased from the temple funds begins) with the payment of the purchase money; the claim of a person הדיוט (the ordinary buyer) with the actual taking possession. His (the person's) pledge before the Most High (that such and such will be devoted to God) is tantamount to its (the item's) transfer to the person הדיוט (the ordinary recipient). — A parallel passage is found in t. Qidd. 1.9 (335). ‖ The Most High גָּבוֹהַּ opposite הדיוט is also found in t. Meg. 3.2 (224); 3.5 (224); t. Ḥag. 2.10 (235); t. B. Qam. 4.3 (351); SNum 28:26 § 148 (55A); Num. Rab. 8 (149A); see Mek. Exod. 19:19 (73A). ‖ Pesiqta 158B: R. Alexandrai (ca. 270) said, "If a person הדיוט uses a broken vessel, it is a disgrace for him; but the Holy One—blessed be He!—is not so. Rather, all his objects are broken vessels: 'Yahweh is near to those who are brokenhearted' (Ps 34:19); 'the one who heals the brokenhearted' (Ps 147:3); 'a broken and shattered heart you will not despise' (Ps 51:19)."

β. Mishnah Sanhedrin 10.2: Three kings and four private citizens הֶדְיוֹטוֹת have no share in the future world (which commences with the resurrection). The three kings are: Jeroboam, Ahab, and Manasseh.... The four private citizens are Balaam, Doeg, Ahithophel, and Gehazi. ‖ Mekilta Exodus 17:14 (63A): Moses said before him, "Lord of the world, has a decision been made that I shall not enter there (Canaan)? 'Therefore you shall not bring this community into the land' (Num 20:12) (means:) with the status of kings; so I will enter as a private citizen כהדיוט!" He answered him, "A king does not enter as a private citizen!" — This juxtaposition of מלך and הדיוט appears a few more times in the subsequent negotiation. It is also found in, for example, b. Ber. 34A, B; Tanḥ. אמור 171B; see also the next citation. See further t. Šabb. 7.18 at § 1 Cor 16:19, n. *o*. — Here we may also draw in the frequent designation of the ordinary priests as כֹּהֵן הֶדְיוֹט; as such he is contrasted with the high priest. Mishnah Yoma 7.5: The high priest serves in eight garments and the ordinary one הַהֶדְיוֹט in four: in a robe, in trousers, in a turban, and in a belt. In addition, the high priest wears the breastplate (of decision) חֹשֶׁן and the ephod אֵפוֹד and the overgarment מְעִיל and the leaf on the forehead צִיץ. In these they consulted the Urim and Thummim; but they did not consult them for (in the interest of) a private citizen להדיוט, but rather only for a king and for a court and for one whom the community (the whole) needed. ‖ Babylonian Talmud Yoma 12A: This would be acceptable according to the opinion of one who says, "The high priest's belt was the same as the belt of the ordinary priest כהן הדיוט; but according to the opinion of one who says, "The high priest's belt was not the same as the belt of the ordinary priest, what can be said?" ‖ Mishnah Makkot 3.1: (In the case of punishment by scourging, the following are forbidden:) a widow of the high priest (see Lev 21:14), a divorced woman (see Lev 21:7), and one who has removed the shoe from an ordinary priest.

γ. Mishnah Sanhedrin 7.10: Whoever misleads (to idolatry will be stoned). This refers to a layperson הדיוט who misleads a layperson. — On this, b. Sanh. 67A remarks: "Whoever misleads. This refers to a layperson." The reason (he is stoned) is because he is a layperson. If he were a prophet, he would be executed by strangulation. (Layperson here = nonprophet, but prophet = an expert person.) "Who misleads a layperson." The reason (he is stoned) is because he misled an individual. If he had misled the multitude, he would be executed by strangulation. See on this y. Yebam. 16.15D.33 at δ. ‖ Babylonian Talmud Sanhedrin 3A: Disputes about assets are judged by three lay judges הֶדְיוֹטוֹת, theft and bodily injuries by three legal experts מוּמְחִין (approved, appointed judges). ‖ Mishnah Moʿed Qaṭan 1.8: A layperson הדיוט (who is not a tailor by trade) may stitch (on the interfestival days) as ordinarily. The tailor by craft אוּמָּן may make only uneven stitches (so that his stitching is not ordinary stitching).

δ. Jerusalem Talmud Yebamot 16.15D.53: "Whoever misleads (to idolatry will be stoned). This refers to a *hedioṭ* who misleads a *hedioṭ*" (m. Sanh. 7.10, see above in γ). Yet if he is a scholar חָכָם, then not? If he is misled, he is not a scholar; and if he misleads, he is also not a scholar. — In contrast to חָכָם, the הדיוט is ignorant. — So too in Deut. Rab. 11 (206D); see § 1 Cor 13:5 A; also, SNum 12:8 § 103 (28A): Do not the imprudent and ignorant קלי הדעת וההדיוטות act this way? — In this sense הדיוט is ultimately synonymous with עַם הָאָרֶץ, that is, like this term, it designates a person who knows nothing about the law and does not like to know anything (see § John 7:49). So t. Taʿan. 4.12 (221): On the 9th of Ab (the day of the destruction of Jerusalem), no greeting is offered to the חֲבֵרִים (the members of the pharisaic covenant with the law for the observation of the commandments about tithing and purity), to the ignorant הדיוטות but with limp lip (i.e., unclearly). — In the parallel b. Taʿan. 14B in a baraita (see § 1 Cor 11:4, #2, n. *d*), it says עמי הארץ instead of הדיוטות. — See further Exod. Rab. 36 (95C) at § John 7:49, #1, n. *d* and Midr. Prov. 6:20 (28B) at § John 7:49, #8, n. *g*.

2. In accordance with rabbinic usage, ἰδιώτης in 1 Cor 14:16 could very well refer to one who was a layperson compared to an orator. Yet the connection ἰδιῶται ἢ ἄπιστοι in 1 Cor 14:23f. makes it more probable that by ἰδιώτης the apostle understood someone who was ignorant, who had been removed from Christianity up until that time.

14:16 B: How should he say Amen! to your thanksgiving?

1. On the various meanings of אָמֵן see § Matt 5:18 A.

2. According to Jewish custom, at religious celebrations the whole community had to say "Amen!" in the following instances:

α. After the individual blessings that the prayer leader recited in connection with the prayers or on other occasions.[a] This applied only for religious services that took place in the synagogues. In the temple service, instead of "Amen," people said, "Blessed be the name of his glorious kingdom forever and ever!"[b]

β. After each of the three sections in which the priests issued the Aaronic blessing of Num 6:24–26.[c] This too applied only for religious services in synagogues; in the service in the temple, the priestly blessing was said in one section,[d] and if the name of Yahweh crossed the priest's lips, the people fell down and said "Blessed be the name of his glorious kingdom forever and ever!"[e]

3. Outside of the religious service, the individual Israelite had to answer with "Amen!" in the following instances:

α. Any blessing that he witnessed[f] (e.g., at a common meal). With his "Amen!" he expressed that he too made the blessing he heard his own;

β. Any adjuration that he heard from another's mouth; he thereby recognized the adjuration as binding for him. If, for example, the adjuration had been that its hearer should give testimony in a specific legal case, his "Amen!" obliged him to actually appear as a witness before the court;[g]

γ. A blessing that was spoken over him. His "Amen!" expressed the desire that the blessing be fulfilled;[h]

δ. A curse or an imprecation when he agreed with them.[i]

4. After prayers that closed without a blessing, the Amen! was not common in the mouth of the one who prayed or of the one who heard the prayer. However, there are some examples; see these at § Matt 5:18 A, #1.

5. Special issues when saying Amen. The one who said the blessing could not join in with the subsequent Amen! of those present.[k] The Amen! itself was supposed to be spoken in a prolonged way, not quickened or abbreviated. It was absolutely prohibited if the preceding blessing had not been heard. Such an Amen! was called an "orphaned" Amen when it was nevertheless spoken.[l] Moreover, the one who answered with "Amen!" was not supposed to speak louder than the one who had presented the blessing.[m]

6. The passages in n. *n*, which deal with the praise and recompense given for saying Amen, show the value that was attributed to the practice.[n]

a. A baraita in b. Sukkah 51B: R. Judah (ca. 150) said, "Whoever has not seen the double column hall (of the synagogue) in Alexandria in Egypt has not seen the glory of Israel. It was said, 'It was like a great basilica, one portico inside another. Sometimes 120 myriads of people were there, twice as many as had gone out from Egypt. Moreover, there were 71 golden armchairs there corresponding to the 71 members of the great Sanhedrin, and each one was worth not less than 21 myriads of gold talents. In the middle there was a wooden rostrum בֵּימָה (see § Matt 27:19 A), and the overseer of the synagogue stood on it with cloths in his hand, and when the moment came when the people had to answer with "Amen!," he waved with a cloth and all the people answered "Amen!"'" ‖ Babylonian Talmud Taʿanit 16B, in connection with m. Taʿan. 2.2ff., depicts the course of a fasting religious service in the land (outside of the temple district) and in the temple. With respect to the former, it says, "The elder (who was to say the prayers) said before them (the community) 24 blessings (thanksgivings): the 18 said every day (i.e., the Prayer of Eighteen Benedictions), plus six he added. These six were seven, as we have learned: In the seventh he said, 'Blessed be you who shows mercy to the land!' (m. Taʿan. 2.4)." Rab Nahman b. Isaac († 356) said, "What is the seventh? The seventh serves to extend (lengthen), as it has been taught: 'He extends with "Israel's Redeemer."'"[224] And for his conclusion he said, "May the one who heard Abraham on Mount Moriah hear you and listen to the voice of your cry on this day, 'Blessed be the Redeemer of Israel.'[225] After him, the people answered, 'Amen!' The overseer of the synagogue said to them, 'Blow the trumpet, you sons of Aaron! Blow the trumpet!' Then he (the praying elder) said, 'May the one who heard our ancestors at the Sea of Reeds hear you and listen to the voice of your cry on this day; blessed be the one who remembers the forgotten!' After him, the people answered, 'Amen!' The overseer of the synagogue said to them, 'Make noise, you sons of Aaron! Make noise!' And so happened with every single blessing: with the one he said, 'Blow the trumpet תקעו!' and with the other he said, 'Make noise הריעו!' In which case do these words apply? For the land; but in the sanctuary it was not so." (See the continuation of the passage in n. *b*.) ‖ Babylonian Talmud Soṭah 39B: R. Zerah (= Zeira, ca. 300) said that Rab Hisda († 309) said, "The caller (who calls on the co-workers during the religious service to wait on their office when the sequence arrives at them) may not call on the priests (to issue the Aaronic blessing) before the Amen! has ceased in the mouth of the community (after the penultimate benediction מוֹדִים אֲנַחְנוּ in the Prayer of Eighteen Benedictions), and the priests may not begin with the blessing until the calling has ceased in the mouth of the caller, and the community may not answer Amen! until the blessing has ceased in the mouth of the priests, and the priests may not begin with the other blessing (the blessing had to be spoken in three sections in the land) until the Amen! has ceased in the mouth of the community (after the 1st or 2nd section of the blessing)...." R. Zerah also said that Rab Hisda said, "The community may not answer Amen! until the blessing has ceased in the mouth of the reader (of Scripture), and the reader may not read from the Torah until the Amen! has ceased in the mouth of the community (in response to his blessing before the Scripture reading)."

b. Babylonian Talmud Taʿanit 16B (continuation of b. Taʿan. 16B in n. *a*): In the sanctuary the people did not answer Amen! How do we know that the people did not answer Amen! in the sanctuary? Because it says, "'Arise, bless Yahweh your God from everlasting to everlasting, and may your holy name be praised which is exalted above every blessing and every praise' (Neh 9:5). Should there, with all the blessings, be only one praise (with which the people respond to all the previous blessings)? Scripture teaches, 'Which is exalted above every blessing and every praise': with every (single) blessing, give him (in response) a praise. How then in the sanctuary (in the case of a religious service of fasting)? He (the leader of

224. S-B: The six added thanksgivings were interpolated between the 7th and the 8th benediction of the Prayer of Eighteen Benedictions; yet the 7th benediction (called "Israel's Redeemer") itself was added too; this addition was counted as an extra thanksgiving, as in the Mishnah, so there were in total not six but seven additional thanksgivings.

225. S-B: This conclusion constitutes the expansion of the 7th benediction of the Prayer of Eighteen Benedictions; as part of the 7th benediction, he ends with the same words with which this also ended, namely with "Israel's Redeemer." The Mishnah counted this expansion as the first of the seven (six) additional blessings that were added to the Prayer of Eighteen Benedictions at a fasting ceremony. See further in the excursus on fasting and fasting ceremonies.

prayer) said, 'Blessed be Yahweh Elohim, the God of Israel, from everlasting to everlasting, blessed be the redeemer of Israel!' And after him the people answered. 'Blessed be the name of his glorious kingdom forever and ever!' Then the synagogue overseer said to them, 'Blow the trumpet, O priests, you sons of Aaron! Blow the trumpet!' Then he (the leader of prayer) said, 'May the one who heard Abraham on Mount Moriah hear you and listen to the voice of your cry on this day! Blessed be the God of Israel, who remembers the forgotten!' After him the people answered, 'Blessed be the name of his glorious kingdom forever and ever!' The synagogue overseer said to them, 'Make noise, O priests, you sons of Aaron! Make noise!' And so it was with every blessing. With the one he said, 'Blow the trumpet!' and with the other he said, 'Make noise!,' until he had finished them." R. Halapta (ca. 120) observed this custom in Sepphoris and R. Hananiah b. Teradion († ca. 135) in Sikhni; but when the matter came before the scholars, they said, "This custom has been observed only at the east gate and on the temple mountain." — Parallels are found in a baraita in b. Taʿan. 16B.31; 16B.35 in a baraita; t. Taʿan. 1.9ff. (215); t. Ber. 7.22 (17); y. Ber. 9.14C.10; b. Ber. 63A.7; b. Soṭah 40B; the sentence about R. Halapta and R. Hananiah in the Babylonian Talmud is also found in m. Taʿan. 2.5.

c. See b. Soṭah 39B above in n. *a.* ‖ Mishnah Berakot 5.4: Whoever comes before the ark (as the leader of prayer) should not answer Amen! after the priests (i.e., after the three sections in which the blessing was spoken by the priests) because of confusion (lest he become confused and err in what he himself had to say after them).

d. See m. Tamid 7.2 in the excursus "The Memra of Yahweh," #3, B, n. *a*, α and the S-B footnote in that section.

e. See b. Taʿan. 16B in n. *b* and m. Yoma 6.2 at § Matt 6:13 C, #1.

f. In b. Ber. 47A it is taught as a tannaitic tradition: The one who (at a banquet) breaks the bread may not break it until the Amen! has finished in the mouth of those who respond. (Before the bread is broken a blessing is said over the bread: "Blessed be you, Yahweh our God, who makes bread proceed from the earth!" This blessing is answered with "Amen!" by those participating in the meal. Only after this Amen! has faded may the bread be broken.) ‖ Jerusalem Talmud Berakot 3.6A.12 = Jerusalem Talmud Moʿed Qaṭan 3.82B.55: If a mourner says the blessing (at table), the people do not then answer Amen! And if others say the blessing, he (the mourner) does not answer Amen! What you say applies only on workdays; but on the Sabbath (on which mourning customs are not observed; see, for example, y. Moʿed Qaṭ. 3.82B.26) ..., if he says the blessing, the people then answer Amen! and if others say the blessing, he then answers Amen! ‖ Mishnah Berakot 8.8: People answer Amen! after an Israelite says a blessing; but people do not answer Amen! after a Samaritan says a blessing until the whole blessing has been heard (he may have said something unseemly. — The same is found in t. Ber. 3.26 (8). ‖ Genesis Rabbah 66 (42C) in a baraita: If a *goy* (non-Israelite) blesses God (השם = the name), people then answer Amen! (But if he blesses him) with a name (with the name of an idol), people do not then answer Amen! — The same is found in y. Sukkah 3.54A.13. In y. Ber. 8.12C.45 we find only the first sentence. ‖ Babylonian Talmud Berakot 53B: Samuel († 254) asked Rab († 247), "What about saying Amen after school children?" He answered him, "People say Amen! after all people, except for school children, because they (their blessings) are performed for practice (and are not meant as actual blessings). Yet these words apply except when they read the Haftarah (a reading from the prophets), but when they read the Haftarah (when they say the blessings that belong with the reading from the prophets), people answer Amen!"

g. See m. Šebu. 4.3 at § Matt 5:18 A, #1, n. *a*, end; y. Soṭah 2.18B.1 and b. Šebu. 36A at § Matt 5:18 A, #1, n. *a*, beginning. — Yet it did not necessarily have to be an adjuration that one acknowledged as binding by saying Amen; by saying Amen, one could affirm someone else's proper explanation or word. Babylonian Talmud Ketubbot 66B: Rab Judah († 299) said that Rab († 247) said, "It happened with the daughter of Naqedimon b. Gurion (see § John 3:1) that the scholars determined (for the time of her widowhood) 400 gold coins daily for the spice box. Then she said to them, 'You make such determinations for your daughters?' (The sum was not enough for her.) And they answered after her, 'Amen!'" (Thereby they affirmed their determination.) — Yet it says in b. Ketub. 65A: R. Abbahu (ca. 300) said that R. Yohanan said, "It happened with the daughter-in-law בכלתו of Naqedimon b. Gurion that the scholars determined 2 *seahs* of wine (1 *seah* = 13.13 liters) for her as an ingredient for the cooking pot from one preparation day for the Sabbath to the next (so weekly). Then she said to them, 'You make such determinations for your daughters?' It has been taught that she was waiting for levirate marriage. And they did not answer after her Amen!" — On the daughter of Naqedimon b. Gurion, see § John 3:1, #1, n. *d*; there you will also find parallels to our passage. — See further b. Šebu. 36A at § Matt 5:18 A, n. *a*.

h. Jerusalem Talmud Sukkah 3.54A.14: R. Tanḥuma (ca. 380) said, "If a non-Israelite גוי blesses you answer after him Amen!; for it is written, 'You are blessed by all the nations' (so Deut 7:14 according to the midr.). A *goy* encountered R. Ishmael († ca. 135) and blessed him. He said to him, 'Your word (the answer to be given to you) has been said long ago.' Another encountered him and cursed him. He said to him, 'Your word has been said long ago.' His disciples said to him, 'Rabbi, as you spoke to the one as you spoke to the other.' He said to them, 'Is it not written, "May whoever curses you be cursed, and may whoever blesses you be blessed?"' (Gen 27:29)." — Parallels are found in y. Ber. 8.12C.46; Gen. Rab. 66 (42C). — See further b. Šabb. 119B at § Matt 18:10 B.

i. Mishnah Soṭah 2.5: ("The priest shall implore the woman with an oath of cursing. … And the woman shall say, 'Amen! Amen!'" [Num 5:21, 22].) To what is she saying Amen! Amen!? Amen! to the cursing; Amen! to the adjuration. ‖ A baraita in b. Soṭah 37B: "You shall give the blessing on Mount Gerizim and the curse on Mount Ebal" (Deut 11:29).… As the former and the latter answer and say "Amen!," so the former and the latter also answer the blessing and say, "Amen!" ‖ See b. Šebu. 36A and b. ʿAbod. Zar. 65A at § Matt 5:18 A, #1, n. *a*.

k. Tosefta Megillah 4.27 (227): Whoever presents the benedictions that go with the Shema and says the blessings over fruits and the commandments,[226] shall not answer Amen! after himself (to his own blessings), and if he answers, see, it is a type of ignorance דרך הַבּוּרוּת. ‖ A baraita in b. Ber. 5.9C.59: Whoever presents the benedictions that go with the

226. S-B: For example: "Blessed be you, Yahweh our God, king of the world, who sanctified us by his commandments and commanded us to dwell in the sukkah, or: to make a festal bouquet, or: to wear show threads, or: to put on tefillin, or: to wash our hands, etc. etc.

Shema, and whoever comes before the ark (as the leader of prayer), and whoever raises his hands (as the priest for blessing), and whoever reads from the Torah, and whoever reads the closing reading from a prophet, and whoever says the blessing over any of all the commandments that are said in the Torah: he shall not answer Amen! after himself; and if he answers, see, he is uneducated בּוֹר. One author taught, "See, he is an uneducated man"; There is (another) author who taught, "See, he is a wise man." Rab Hisda († 309) said, "Whoever said, 'See, he is a wise man,' means this about someone who answers Amen! (all the way) at the end; and whoever said, 'See, he is uneducated,' means this about someone who answers Amen! after every single blessing."

l. Tosefta Megillah 4.27 (227): One should answer neither an orphaned Amen אמן יְתוֹמָה (see further below), nor a broken off Amen א׳ קְטוּפָה (perhaps אָמֵי without ן). Ben Azzai (ca. 110) said, "Whoever answers an 'orphaned' Amen, his children will be orphaned; whoever answers a 'broken off' (interrupted), his days (life) will be broken off (shortened); whoever answers a 'protracted' אֲרוּכָה one, (God) will lengthen his days and years." ‖ A baraita in b. Ber. 47A: One should answer neither an expedited Amen א׳ חֲטוּפָה (perhaps אֲמֶן or אֱמֶן), nor a broken off Amen, nor an orphaned Amen; one should also not (hastily) throw a blessing from one's mouth. Ben Azzai said, "Whoever answers an orphaned Amen, his children will be orphaned; an expedited one, his days will be expedited; a broken off one, his days will be broken off; but whoever draws (his voice) out long when saying Amen, his days and his years will be lengthened." — See further parallels y. Ber. 8.12C.42 and y. Sukkah 3.54A.11. ‖ Jerusalem Talmud Sukkah 3.54A.12: What is an "orphaned" Amen? R. Huna (ca. 350) said, "This refers to one who is obligated to say the blessing, and he answers (Amen!) without knowing what it is about." (An orphaned Amen is thus an Amen that is given in response without the one responding having heard the preceding blessing.) — The same is found with a somewhat different text in y. Ber. 8.12C.44.

m. Babylonian Talmud Berakot 45A: Rab Hanan b. Abba (ca. 250) said, "How do we know that the one who answers Amen! may not raise his voice louder than the one who says the (preceding) blessing? Because it says, 'Glorify Yahweh with me (thus not beyond me) and let us exalt his name together (thus not more than each other)' (Ps 34:4)."

n. Deuteronomy Rabbah 7 (203D): There is nothing greater before God than the Amen that the Israelites answer. ‖ Deuteronomy Rabbah 7 (204A): R. Judan (ca. 350) said, "Whoever answers Amen! in this world will be worthy to answer Amen! in the future age." ‖ Babylonian Talmud Berakot 53B: Rab († 247) said to his son Hiyya, "My son, hurry up and say the blessing (do not be sluggish with it)!" And likewise, Rab Huna († 297) said to his son Rabbah, "Hurry up and say the blessing!" This means that he who says the blessing is more excellent than the one who answers Amen! But in a baraita it has been taught that R. Yose (ca. 150) said, "Greater is the one who answers Amen! than the one who says the blessing!" R. Nehorai (ca. 150) said to him, "By heaven! It is so; you can recognize it by the following: for look, the squires go and instigate war and the heroes go and win the victory." (Those who say the blessing began in order to win God's favor; but those who answer Amen! actually obtain it.) This applies conditionally. For in a baraita it has been taught: Both the one who says the blessing and the one who answers Amen! are included in the wording (namely of Neh 9:5: "Arise, bless Yahweh your God" pertains to those who say the blessing, "and they shall praise your glorious name ..." pertains to those who answer with Amen!; both categories are accordingly of equal worth); but those who hurry to say the blessing are greater than the one who answers Amen! — A parallel passage is found in b. Naz. 66A. ‖ Babylonian Talmud Šabbat 119B: R. Joshua b. Levi (ca. 250) said, "Whoever answers with all his strength—'Amen! May his great name be praised!'—his judicial decree is torn apart (by God; God overturns the punishments imposed on him); for it says, 'Israel's repayment was overturned because the people proved willing; praise Yahweh!' (so Judg 5:2 according to the midr.). Why was the repayment overturned? Because they praised Yahweh (with blessings and the Amen! that follows them)." R. Hiyya b. Abba (ca. 280) said that R. Yohanan († 279) said, "Even if the stain of idolatry were upon him (the one who answers Amen!), (God) forgives him. It is written here (Judg 2:5): 'For overturned repayment,' and there (Exod 32:25) it is written: 'For the people were exuberant.' (Just as פְּרֹעַ in Judg 5:2 refers to forgiveness, so too with פָּרוּעַ in Exod 32:25 there is the indication that there will be forgiveness for the people despite their idolatry.) Resh Laqish (ca. 250) said, "Whoever answers Amen! with all his strength, (God) will open the gates of the garden of Eden for him; for it says, 'Open the gates, so that a righteous people that answers Amen! may come in' (so Isa 26:2 according to the midr.); do not read שומר אמונים (= that maintains loyalty), but rather שאומרין אמן = that says Amen!" ‖ Jerusalem Talmud Šebuʿot 4.35C.31, 34: From what point in time (i.e., from what age) will the Israelites' little children be made alive again (resurrected)?... It has been taught in the name of R. Meir: "From the point when it knows to answer Amen! in the synagogue. What is the scriptural basis? 'Open the gates, so that a righteous people that answers Amen! may come in' (Isa 26:2; see the previous citation)." — There is a parallel in b. Sanh. 110B, though here it says explicitly about Isa 26:2: Do not read: שומר אמונים, but rather שאומר אמן = that says Amen! ‖ Numbers Rabbah 4 (142D): It once happened that a man stood in a synagogue, and his son stood opposite him, and all the people answered after the prayer leader (literally: after the one who had come before the ark) "Hallelujah!" But his son answered words of absurdity דְּבָרִים שֶׁל תַּפְלוּת. They said to him, "See how your son answers words of absurdity!" He answered them, "What should I do to him? He is a child and jokes around." On the following day he acted again in the same way. All the people answered after the prayer leader "Amen! Hallelujah!" and his son answered words of absurdity. They said to him, "See how your son answers words of absurdity!" He answered them, "What should I do to him? He is a child and jokes around." For the whole eight days of the festival he answered words of absurdity, and he did not say a single word to him. And that year and the next year and the third year had not passed when that man died and his wife died and his son died and his grandchildren and 15 people from his house parted from the world, and there remained only a couple of the man's sons: one was lame and blind, and the other was insane and godless.

14:19: Five words.

On the number five, see the detailed essay by Gerhard Kittel entitled "Die Fünfzahl als geläufige Zahl und als stilistisches Motiv."[227] Kittel names examples from the NT for the round number character of five: the five words in 1 Cor 14:19 = a few words; the five sparrows in Luke 12:6; the five in a house in Luke 12:52; the five yokes of oxen in Luke 14:19; the five pounds in Matt 25:15; the five virgins twice in Matt 25:2; the five days in Acts 20:6; 24:1, presumably = a few days. The same may be the case with the five months in Rev 9:5; the five Samaritan men in John 4:18; the rich man's five brothers in Luke 16:28; the live loaves at the feeding in Matt 14:17; 16:9; and Paul's fivefold flagellation in 2 Cor 11:24. — Kittle refers to the following passages from rabbinic literature:

Mishnah Baba Meṣiʿa 4.12: The merchant may take (buy grain) from five threshing floors and put them in storage, wine from five winepresses and put them in a vat. — Here five is a round number for "several." ‖ Mishnah Yebamot 15.7: "If someone has gotten engaged to five (= several) women and does not know which one he is engaged to while each one says, 'He got engaged to me,' he must give each one a certificate of divorce and put down the amount of the prescribed marital sum for them. Then he may depart (the matter is settled for him)." These are the words of R. Tarfon (ca. 100). R. Aqiba († ca. 135) said, "There is no way to let him escape his transgression until he gives a certificate of divorce and sets down the amount of the prescribed marital sum for each one." "If someone has stolen from five people (= from several people) and does not know from whom he stole, while each one says, 'He robbed me,' he may put down the plunder before them and then depart." These are the words of R. Tarfon. R. Aqiba said, "There is no way for him to escape his transgression until he compensates each one for the theft." — In the discussion about this Mishnah, b. Yebam. 118B adduces the further tradition: R. Tarfon and R. Aqiba did not have differing opinions about someone who has purchased something from five (= several) people and does not know from whom he purchased it: he may put down the purchasing price for them and depart. ‖ Tosefta Šabbat 8.31 (121): "Whoever carries out two date kernels (on the Sabbath makes himself guilty), and for livestock, if it was enough to fill a pig's mouth with; and how many fill a pig's mouth? One." Others said, "We count five." (If the kernels are meant to serve as counting markers, one makes himself guilty if he goes out with five.) — The same is found in b. Šabb. 90B as a baraita in the following form: "Whoever carries out date kernels, if it is for planting (he makes himself guilty) with two, if it is for eating, then with however many fill a pig's mouth; and how many fill a pig's mouth? One. If it is for heating, then with however many it takes to cook a small egg; if it is for counting, then with two." Others said, "With five." — In the last two passages, though, five is certainly intended as a definite, and not a round, number.

---

227. Gerhard Kittel, "Die Fünfzahl Als Geläufige Zahl Und Als Stilistisches Motiv," *Arbeiten Zur Religionsgeschichte Des Urchristentums* 1.3 (1920): 39ff.

14:20: Do not be children in understanding.

Babylonian Talmud Soṭah 46B: "Five small boys came out of the city" (2 Kgs 2:23). What does "small boys" mean? R. Eleazar (ca. 270) said, "(They are called 'boys' נערים) because they were empty מנוערים of the fulfillments of the commandments; 'small' קטנים because they were among those who are small in faith קטני אמנה." ‖ In the same way, it was conversely said זִקְנֵי תוֹרָה = elders in Torah knowledge. Mishnah Qinnim 3.6: R. Simeon b. Aqashya (a Tannaim of uncertain time) said, "The older the elders from the ordinary people (*ʿam ha'areṣ*) become, the more their insight dims; as it says, 'He removes speech from the eloquent and takes away the insight of the aged' (Job 12:20). However, it is not so with the elders in Torah knowledge, but rather the older they become, the surer their insight becomes; as it says, 'Wisdom is among the aged, and length of life is insight' (Job 12:12)." — See the similar saying of R. Ishmael b. Halapta (ca. 180) in b. Šabb. 152A (so read instead of 152B) at § John 7:49, #1, n. *a.* ‖ Here the expression "orphan boy" can also be related to the designation of someone who is not adequately instructed about a principle. Babylonian Talmud ʿAbodah Zarah 13B.24: R. Jacob (probably b. Abun, ca. 325) bought a sandal (from a gentile), R. Jeremiah (ca. 320) bought a loaf of bread (from a gentile; in fact both did so during a gentile fair, which was forbidden in certain cases). Then the one said to the other, "You orphan boy יַתְמָא, did your teacher act this way?" Then the other said to him, "You orphan boy, did your teacher act this way?" ‖ A second example is found in b. Ketub. 17B; see § Matt 6:17 A, #1, n. *b.*

14:21: It is written in the law.

Since the apostle cites a passage from the prophet Isaiah, he intended νόμος in the broader sense = Holy Scripture or OT. תורה = OT is also used in rabbinic literature; see § John 10:34 and § Rom 3:19 A. Here a few additional supporting texts follow.

Babylonian Talmud Sanhedrin 91B: "Then Joshua built אז יבנה Yahweh an altar" (Josh 8:30). It does not say "he built" בנה, but rather "he will build" יבנה. From this passage we have a proof from the Torah for the resurrection of the dead. (The book of Joshua thus belongs to the Torah; therefore Torah = OT.) ‖ Babylonian Talmud Sanhedrin 104B: "May this not happen to you, all you wanderers" (so Lam 1:12 according to the midr.). Raba († 352) said that R. Yohanan († 279) said, "From this passage we have a proof from the Torah for wishing away another's calamity (Lam = Torah)." ‖ A baraita in b. ʿErub. 58A: R. Joshua b. Hananiah (ca. 90) said, "You have nothing that would be better for measuring than iron chains; but what should we do? For, look, the Torah says, 'In his hand was a measuring line' (Zech 2:5)" (thus, Zech = Torah). ‖ Babylonian Talmud Moʿed Qaṭan 5A: R. Simeon b. Pazzi (ca. 280) said, "Where does the Torah refer to marking graves? Scripture teaches, 'If he sees a human bone, he will erect a marker next to it' (Ezek 39:15)" (Torah = Ezek). ‖ Babylonian Talmud Yebamot 4A: R. Eleazar (ca. 270) said, "Where can the סְמוּכִין (i.e., the hermeneutical method of interpreting two adjacent passages of Scripture by using the content of both for each) be proved from the Torah? Because it says, '(His ordinances) are joined together סְמוּכִין forever and ever, made with truth and rightness' (Ps 111:8)" (Torah = the book of

Psalms). — The same is found in b. Ber. 10A with R. Yohanan († 279) as the author. ‖ Babylonian Talmud Giṭṭin 36A: The witnesses sign the certificate of divorce to preserve the world (i.e., for the sake of order). To preserve the world? It happens on the basis of Torah! For it is written, "Write it on a bill (of sale) and sign it!" (Jer 32:10). (The passage is cited thus; so, Torah = Jer.) — Reference may also be made to b. Bek. 50A.24 and 28, where R. Hoshaiah (ca. 225) and Abbayye († 338/39) adduce Ezek 7:22 as a Torah citation; in b. ʿArak. 11A.25, Ps 19:9 is counted among the words of the Torah.

14:23: But if amateurs or unbelievers have come (into the church assembly).

A similar case is discussed in Deut. Rab. 8 (205A) as follows: "Wisdom is too high for fools; therefore, he does not open his mouth in the gate" (Prov 24:7).[228] What does "Wisdom is too high for fools" mean? R. Tanḥuma (ca. 380) said, "A fool comes into the synagogue and sees them, how they negotiate with each other about the teaching, and he does not understand what they say. Then he is ashamed, as it says, 'In the gate he does not open his mouth.' By 'gate,' nothing other than the Sanhedrin is meant; for it is written, 'His sister-in-law shall go to the elders at the gate' (Deut 25:7)." — A different explanation goes as follows. The rabbis said, "A fool comes into the synagogue and sees them busy with the Torah, and he says to them, 'How does a person begin to study the Torah?' They answered him, 'He first reads the (Esther) scroll,[229] then the book of the Torah, then the prophets, and then the hagiographa.' When he has finished Scripture, he studies the exposition of the Mishnah, then the Halakoth (the individual halakic laws), and then the Haggadoth (the nonhalakic interpretations of Scripture). When he hears this, he (the fool) says in his heart, 'When am I supposed to study all that?' and goes away from the gate. Hence, 'In the gate he does not open his mouth.'"

14:25 A: He will fall on his face and worship God.

See § Matt 2:2 B; § Matt 9:18; and § Luke 22:41 B, #2 and #3.

14:25 B: Truly, God is among you!

Underlying this statement are scriptural words like Isa 45:14;[a] Zech 8:23;[b] see also Deut 4:7.[c] We may also compare passages where the pagan recognition of the superiority of the Jewish belief in God leads to the glorification of God and Israel.[d]

a. Midrash Song of Songs 4:8 (114B): R. Ishmael b. Yose (ca. 180) said, "My father (so read) said, 'Even pharaoh, the king of Egypt, and Tirhakah, the king of Cush, were both in that miracle. Namely, they had come to help Hezekiah. But when Sennacherib noticed, what did Sennacherib, the blasphemer, do with them? In the evening he bound them, and in the middle of the night the angel went out and struck the armies of Sennacherib with the plague;

---

228. TN: The German *Tor* can mean either "gate" or "fool."

229. S-B: The commentary Matt. Keh. here understands a scroll with the alphabet.

as it says, "The angel of Yahweh went out and struck 185,000 in the camp of the Assyrians" (Isa 37:36). In the morning Hezekiah set off early and found them in chains. He said, "They appear to have come to help me!" Then he freed them, and they went and told of God's wonders and mighty deeds. This is what is written, "Thus says Yahweh, 'The acquisition of Egypt and the gain of Cush'" (Isa 45:14). "The acquisition of Egypt": this is pharaoh; "the gain of Cush": this is Tirhakah, the king of Cush; "and the Sabeans, those long men" (Isa 45:14): these are their masses of armies; "will come over to you": this is Hezekiah and his army; "and fall before you": they were given over to you long ago; "they will go behind you, coming in chains," in hand shackles (read בְּכִירוֹמָנִיקְיָא, from χειρομάνικον "hand shackle," instead of בקרקומניקיא); "and they will prostrate before you": this is Jerusalem; "and they will pray for you": this is the sanctuary. And what did they say? "God is only in you and there is no other God at all" (Isa 45:14).'" — This exposition, albeit more briefly, is also actually found in the short text S. 'Olam Rab. 23, which is attributed to the father of R. Ishmael.

b. Sifre Numbers 15:38 § 115(34B): R. Hanina b. Antigonos (ca. 150) said, "What does (Scripture) say about everyone who fulfills the commandment about the show threads? 'In those days,' it is said, 'ten men from every tongue of the gentiles will seize the tips of a Judean's tunic (saying, "We will to go with you; for we have heard God is with you")' (Zech 8:23)." ‖ See b. Šabb. 32B at § Rom 3:9 A, #3, B, n. *k*, middle.

c. See y. Ber. 9.13B.22 at § Matt 7:7 A, #2, n. *a*, first third.

d. For examples, see Pesiq. 11B at § Matt 19:6; y. B. Meṣ. 2.8C.27 at § Rom 2:24, #2. ‖ At § Matt 4:17 A, #1, end, there is a conversation of R. Meir with a commander, cited from Midr. Abba Gurion, 2nd version 41A. The latter ends the conversation with the words: "You have overcome me. You are truth and your Torah is truth!" ‖ Pesiqta 98A: A Samaritan came and asked R. Meir (ca. 150), "Do you not say that your father Jacob is the truth?" He answered, "Yes! For it is written; 'You will bestow truth on Jacob' (Mic 7:20)." The Samaritan said, "Jacob set apart the tribe of Levi (namely for God as a tithe), so one of ten tribes. Should he not have set apart (given as a tithe) also one of the remaining two tribes?" "You think," responded R. Meir, "that there were twelve. I think that there were fourteen; for it says, 'Ephraim and Manasseh shall belong to me like Reuben and Simeon' (Gen 48:5)." The Samaritan retorted, "Do you not thereby support my words even better? When you have added flour, you add water to it as well!" (If there were 14 tribes, then, beyond the first ten, there were four more for tithing!) R. Meir said to him, "Will you grant me that there were four mothers (the mothers of the sons of Jacob)? So, four firstborns are deducted from them (the 14 tribes). For a firstborn if not tithed, because he is already holy (devoted to God), and what is holy does not release what is holy (so there remain 10 tribes for tithing, and Jacob accomplished this fully by setting apart the tribe of Levi)." Then the Samaritan cried out, "Salvation to your nation in whose midst you reside!" — Parallels are found in Gen. Rab. 70 (45A); TanḥB ראה § 12 (12B).

14:26: Everyone has a psalm.

A baraita in b. Pesaḥ. 117A: "All songs and hymns that David said in the book of Psalms, he said concerning himself," according to the words of R. Eliezer (ca. 90). R. Joshua (ca. 90) said, “He said them concerning the community צִיבּוּר (= the whole).” However, the scholars said, “Some of them concerning the community and some of them concerning himself: those that are spoken in the singular, concerning himself; those spoken in the plural, concerning the community. Those that mention singing נִיצּוּחַ (cf. למנצח in the headings) or a melody נִיגּוּן (see נגינה in the headings) pertain to the future; those designated as משכיל (a didactic poem) were spoken by an interpreter. The heading ‘of David, a song’ teaches that the Shekinah (spirit of prophecy) rested on him, and then he said the song (in question). The heading ‘a song of David’ teaches that he said the song, and then the Shekinah rested on him. This intends to teach you that the Shekinah does not rest on someone in indolence, nor in distress, nor in jest, nor in levity, nor in pointless (idle) speech, but rather only with a word of joy in a commandment; as it says, ‘But now fetch me a string musician! And it happened that when the string musician played, the hand of Yahweh came over him’ (2 Kgs 3:15).” — Concerning the psalms designated as משכיל, the view is that they arose under the influence of the prophetic spirit in an assembly gathered for a religious service and were proclaimed directly to the community by an interpreter. Rashi on Ps 88:1 renders the tradition as follows: “In every case where it says משכיל, (the psalm in question) was spoken by an interpreter; for the prophet had set an interpreter before himself, and when the spirit of prophecy came to him, he told the prophecy to the interpreter, and the latter made it known.” This assumption is based on a later custom in religious services, in which an interpreter presented loudly and openly what the presenting scholar told him beforehand in a whisper; see the excursus “The Ancient Jewish Synagogue Service.”

14:27: If someone speaks in a tongue: two or at most three, and one after another, and someone should interpret.

In the synagogue service, the Torah reading was read by seven on the Sabbath, by six on the Day of Atonement, by five on festival days, by four on new moon days and on the interfestival days of Passover and the Feast of Booths and by three on the afternoon of the Sabbath and in the weekday services (Mondays and Thursdays); in each case, they read one after the other. The reading of the prophetic lesson (Haftarah) and the interpreter’s office each required one person; see in more detail the excursus “The Ancient Jewish Synagogue Service.” — Here we highlight only a few passages to illuminate the ἀνὰ μέρος in 1 Cor 14:27.

Mishnah Megillah 4.1: If one reads the Esther scroll (on the feast of Purim) standing or sitting, whether one has read it or two have read it, they have done their duty (in reading). — Rashi: “Or two have read it”: at the same time יַחַד. — Bertinoro († 1510): “Two”; since the Esther scroll is beloved, they (the hearers) direct their thoughts to it and listen (so that they understand what is read, even if two read from it simultaneously). Accordingly, it cannot be doubted that at least the Esther scroll was allowed to be read by two people simultaneously. ‖ Tosefta Megillah 4.20 (227): (It is always so) that one reads from the Torah and one interprets (translates into Aramaic), and one shall not read and two interpret, nor shall two read and one interpret, nor shall two read and two interpret. (It is always so) that one reads from the prophets (the Haftarah) and one interprets, and one shall not read and two interpret, nor shall two read and two interpret. From the Esther scroll one reads and one interprets, one reads and two interpret, two read and two interpret. — Parallels are found in a baraita in b. Meg. 21B: From the Torah one reads and one interprets; it shall not be that one reads and two interpret. From the prophets one reads and two interpret; it shall not be that two read and two interpret. From the Hallel (see § Matt 21:9) and from the Esther scroll even ten may read and ten interpret. What is the reason? Since it is beloved, they direct their thoughts to it and listen (= Bertinoro above). — Rashi: "It shall not be (with a Torah lesson) that one reads and two interpret," and certainly two may not read, and the reason is that two voices (simultaneously) are not heard (= understood). "From the prophets one reads and two interpret"; for the interpretation (of the targum) is only there in order to allow the women and ignorant people (*'amme ha'areṣ*) to hear it, since they do not know the holy language, and the targum is the language of the Babylonians, and we must repeat it by interpreting the Torah (lesson), so they may understand the commandments; but in interpreting the prophets (lesson) no consideration is paid to all this (so two may interpret at the same time, even if this undermines understanding). — Jerusalem Talmud Megillah 4.74D.30: In a baraita it has been taught: From the Torah one reads and one interprets, and one does not read and two interpret, nor do two interpret and one read;[230] nor do two read and two interpret. From the prophets one reads and one interprets, and one reads and two interpret; nor do two read and one interpret, nor do two read and two interpret. From the Esther scroll one reads and one interprets, one reads and two interpret, two read and one interprets, two read and two interpret. — Jerusalem Talmud Megillah 4.74D.26: In a baraita it has been taught: Two may not read from the Torah while one translates. R. Zeira (ca. 300) said, "Because of the blessing.[231] But in a baraita it has been taught: Two shall not interpret and one read! Can you also then say, 'because of the blessing'? (No, since the interpreter did not have to say any blessing at all!) Rather (the reason is) that two voices (simultaneously) cannot enter an ear." — The same is found in y. Ber. 5.9C.44. — As emerges with perfect clarity from the added explanations, the passages deal with a potential simultaneous reading and interpretation of the Scripture lesson by two or more people. With the Torah lesson, this procedure is forbidden in all the passages; with the prophetic lesson it is permitted for two people to interpret simultaneously, as long as one reads (b. Meg. 21B and y. Meg. 4.74D.30); with the Esther scroll, two may read simultaneously (m. Meg. 4.1); furthermore, two may interpret, whether one or two read (t. Meg. 4.20); even ten may read and interpret (b. Meg. 21B); similarly, y. Meg. 4.74D.30 permits all the possible cases. ‖ Falling completely outside the framework of the stipulations above is y. Meg. 4.74D.28 = y. Ber. 5.9C.47: In a baraita it has been taught:

230. S-B: The last two statements mean the same thing; perhaps the text is corrupt?

231. S-B: Before beginning the Torah lesson the reader had to say, "Blessed be Yahweh, highly to be praised!" The community answered, "Blessed be Yahweh, highly to be praised, forever and ever!" Then he said the actual blessing: "Blessed be you, Yahweh our God, king of the world, who elected us from all the nations and gave us his Torah! Blessed be you, Yahweh, giver of the Torah!" Since this blessing, so R. Zeira thinks, was not said by two people at the same time, so too, the Torah could not be read by two [simultaneously].

Two may read from the Torah, but two may not read from the prophets. R. Ulla (ca. 280) said, "There are readings (plural, so several readings) in the Torah (lesson), but there are not readings in (the) prophetic (lesson)." — Levy remarks: "The readings from the Pentateuch were originally commended, but the readings from the prophets (the Haftaroth) were not originally commended. Therefore, two people may read simultaneously from the Pentateuch, because the community directs its attention to it; this is not allowed with the Haftarah" (*Chaldäisches Wörterbuch*, 4:379A). Levy thus assumes that even the Torah lesson could be read by two people simultaneously. The same is supposed by a gloss to the parallel passage y. Ber. 5 (ed. Amsterdam 1710, folio 24A); it refers to the custom where people who were not skillful in reading were supported by the synagogue overseer. Yet the old period knows nothing about this custom. — R. Ulla, who is evidently not aware of a simultaneous reading of the Torah lesson by two people, adopts another way of interpreting the baraita above: he understands it to refer to several people reading the Torah lesson one after the other and can accordingly add that, with the prophetic lesson, there were not any such readings by several people one after another. In any case, R. Ulla was wrong about the actual meaning of the baraita: above all, as has to be concluded from the baraita, two persons were never allowed to read the Torah lesson one after the other; the smallest number was three. — Yet as may be the case with the baraita above, it is clear also according to the other passages that in fact it was permitted in the ancient synagogue for several people to recite simultaneously the prophetic lesson and the Esther lesson and their targumim and that this also occurred. By contrast, the apostle determines for his community's religious services that, when there are people who speak in tongues, only two, or at most three of them, should speak, and not at the same time, but rather ἀνὰ μέρος, singly, in a sequence, one after the other (= καθ' ἕνα in verse 31); but one interpreter suffices.

14:34 A: The women shall be silent in the assemblies.

The ancient synagogue did not in principle forbid women from speaking publicly in religious gatherings, though they did forbid this in practice.[a] They should participate in the services to listen[b] and to learn the commandments from the targum presentation.[c]

a. Tosefta Megillah 4.11 (226): Everyone is included in the number of the seven people (who are summoned to read the Torah lesson on the Sabbath), even a child, even a woman. (This implies that in principle women were also permitted to read; the following words show the actual practice:) A woman is not allowed to come (before the lectern) to read publicly. ‖ A baraiata in b. Meg. 23A: All are included in the number of the seven people, even a child and even a woman. But the scholars said, "A woman shall not read from the Torah for the sake of the honor of the community." — It appears that women were summoned to read the Torah lesson in order to be honored; however, according to custom, they had to forgo carrying out this office. ‖ Sifre Deuteronomy 22:16 § 235 (117B): "The girl's father shall speak to the elders" (Deut 22:16). From here it follows that a woman does not have the right to speak in the place of a man (or: instead of a man?). — Women were also forbidden to instruct children; see m. Qidd. 4.13; b. Qidd. 82A; y. Qidd. 4.66B.24 at § Rom 1:26 A, #2, n. *b*, end.

b. A baraita in b. Ḥag. 3A: Once R. Yohanan b. Beroqah (ca. 110) and R. Eleazar Hasama (?) went to visit R. Joshua in Peqiin. He said to them, "What was new in the house of learning today?" They answered him, "We are your students and drink from your water (and you ask us? See § John 4:14, #3)." He said, "All the same, it is impossible for there to be nothing new in a house of learning. Whose Sabbath (presentation) was it?" "It was the Sabbath of R. Eleazar b. Azariah (ca. 100)." "What was the haggadic presentation about today?" They answered him, "About the section, 'Assemble (the people, men and women and children and your foreigner in your gates' [Deut 31:12])." "And what did he present about it?" "'Assemble the people, men and women and children': if the men come to learn, and the women come to listen לשמוע, what do the children come for? To give recompense to those who bring them." He said to them, "A precious pearl was in your hand, and you wanted to keep it from me!" — Parallels are found in t. Soṭah 7.9 (307); Mek. Exod. 13:2 (23A); y. Ḥag. 1.75D.34; y. Soṭah 3.18D.59; Num. Rab. 14 (173C).

c. See Rashi on b. Meg. 21B at § 1 Cor 14:27, first third.

14:34 B: They shall be subordinate, as even the law says.

Presumably with these words the apostle had Gen 3:16 in view. However, the term νόμος cannot be pressed. Traditional custom was also regarded as Torah; see, for example, Roš Haš. 19A: Words of tradition are as words of the Torah.

14:35 A: If they want to learn something, they should ask their husbands at home.

There was no unanimity on the question of whether women should be instructed in the Torah. The general persuasion was probably that there was at least no obligation for a father to have his daughters instructed in Scripture.

Mishnah Soṭah 3.4: Hardly has she (the woman suspected of adultery) drunk the water of jealousy before her face turns yellow, her eyes come out, and her veins swell (literally: she becomes full of veins). And one calls out, "Get her out! Get her out!," lest she defile the court. If she has merit, this defers (the punishment) for her. Some merit keeps it suspended for a year, another kind of merit two years, another kind three years. On this basis Ben Azzai (ca. 110) said, "A person is obligated to teach his daughter Torah so that, if she must drink (the water of jealousy), she knows that merit suspends (defers) (the punishment)." R. Eliezer (ca. 90) said, "Whoever teaches his daughter Torah is like one who teaches her wantonness (she is only made shrewd about her punishment)." — On this, b. Soṭah 21B says: R. Abbahu (ca. 300) said, "What is the scriptural basis for R. Eliezer? Because it is written, 'I, Wisdom, make prudence dwell' (שכנתי interpreted as *piel*): when wisdom enters a person, shrewdness עַרְמוּמִית enters simultaneously." ‖ Jerusalem Talmud Soṭah 3.19A.3: A matron asked R. Eliezer (ca. 90), "If, in the deed with the (golden) calf it was a matter of one and the same sin, why did they die three kinds of death?"[232] He answered her, "A woman's wisdom is only in her distaff; as it is written, 'And every woman with a wise heart spun with her hands' (Exod 35:25)." His son Hyrcanus said to him, "Since you had no word from the Torah to answer her, you have lost me 300 *kors* of tithe per year (which that matron used to give him)." He answered him, "May the words of the Torah be burned, but they shall not be handed over to women!" — Parallels are found in Num. Rab. 9 (156C); b. Yoma 66B. ‖ Babylonian Talmud Qiddušin 29B: "A father is obligated to teach his son Torah" (b. Qidd. 29A); where do we learn this? Because it is written, "And teach it to your sons" (Deut 11:19; so the midrash); and if his father does not teach him, he himself is obligated to have himself taught, because it is written, "And study it" (Deut 5:1). And she (a mother or a wife), how do we know that she is not obligated (to make her son study Torah)? Because it is written, "And teach it" (Deut 11:19) and "Study" (Deut 5:1). Everyone who is commanded to study is commanded to teach (to have taught); and everyone who is not commanded to study is not commanded to teach. And she (a mother or a wife), how do we know that she is not obligated to have herself taught? (Because it is written,) "And teach them" (Deut 11:19) and "Study" (Deut 5:1). Everyone who is commanded concerning another, to teach him, is commanded to have himself taught; and everyone who is not commanded concerning another, to teach him, is not commanded to have himself taught. And how do we know that others are not commanded to teach her (a woman)? Because Scripture says, "And teach it to your sons" (Deut 11:19), but not your daughters.

14:35 B: It is shameful for a woman to speak in an assembly.

See the saying of Samuel († 254): The voice of a woman is a shameful (indecent) thing קול באשה ערוה; see b. Ber. at 24A § Matt 5:28 A, first third.

14:36: Has the word of God issued from you?

Jerusalem Talmud Nedarim 6.40A.30: Hananiah, the son of the brother of R. Joshua (ca. 110, see Midr. Eccl. 1:8 at § Matt 4:13), decreed a leap year abroad (which was prohibited; see t. Sanh. 2.13; y. Sanh. 1.19A.1; y. Ned. 6.40A.25; b. Sanh. 11B). Rabbi (Judah I [† 217?], though for chronological reasons here this cannot possibly be correct) sent three letters for him to R. Isaac (ca. 150) and R. Nathan (ca. 160; both scholars must have stayed in Babylonia at that time). In one he wrote, "To the holiness of Hananiah" (i.e.: "To his holiness, Hananiah"); and in one he wrote, "The little goats that you left (here in Palestine) have become goats (great scholars)"; and in one he wrote, "If you will not accept (renouncing your unauthorized procedure), then go out to the wilderness of thorns (cf. Gen 50:10) and slaughter (sacrifices) and let Nehunyon (probably a leading figure in Babylonia; in b. Ber. 63B, we find Ahiyya instead) sprinkle (the blood on the altar; in other words: establish a different religious community and break with Judaism)." He read the first letter, and showed them honor; the second, and showed them honor; the third—he tried to bring them into contempt. They said

232. S-B: By the sword (see Exod 32:27); by the plague (see Exod 32:35); and by dropsy, as the woman who drinks the water of jealousy (see Exod 32:20). So according to Num. Rab. 9 (156B); b. Yoma 66B; b. ʿAbod. Zar. 44A and y. Soṭah 3.19A.8.

to him, "You cannot do that, for you have already shown us honor." R. Isaac arose and cried out, "Is it not written in the Torah, 'These are the feasts of Hananiah, the son of the brother of R. Joshua'?" They answered him, "'The feasts of Yahweh' (is written; see Lev 23:4)." He said to them, "With us (in Palestine it is so)!" R. Nathan arose and made the decree (with the prophetic lesson), "Shall the Torah go out from Babylon and the word of God from Nehar Peqod" (= Nehar Paqor?; probably where Hananiah dwelt)? They answered him, "For the Torah will go out from Zion and the word of Yahweh from Jerusalem" (Isa 2:3). He said to them, "With us (it is so)!" Hananiah went and complained about this to R. Judah b. Batera in Nisibis. He said to him, "After them, after them (i.e., follow them)!" — The same is found in y. Sanh. 1.19A.7; differently in b. Ber. 63A.

14:40: Everything should happen respectably and orderly.

1. εὐσχημόνως perhaps = כְּהוֹגֶן[a] "in accordance with propriety" and κατὰ τάξιν = כְּסֵדֶר[b] "in the proper sequence."

a. Genesis Rabbah 93 (59B): R. Hama b. Hanina (ca. 260) said, "Joseph did not act rightly כְּשׁוּרָה (because, according to Gen 45:1, he remained alone with his brothers); for if one of them had moved a footstep toward him, he would have immediately died." R. Samuel b. Nahman (ca. 260) said, "He acted with propriety and rightly כהוגן וכשורה; he knew the integrity of his brothers. He said (to himself), 'Far be it from my brothers to be suspected of shedding blood.'"

b. Babylonian Talmud Yoma 73A, B: David did not inquire (of the Urim and Thummim) in the right order שלא כסדר; but he was answered in the right order כסדר. (David asked, "Will the inhabitants of Keilah deliver me into his hand? Will Saul come down ...?" [1 Sam 23:11]. The second question should have been asked first. God answered in the right order: "He will come down.") When he realized that he had not asked in the right order, he asked once more in the right order; for it says, "Will the inhabitants of Keilah deliver me and my people into Saul's hand?" (1 Sam 23:12). And Yahweh said, "They will."

2. The ancient synagogue was by no means lacking in stipulations about propriety and order in religious matters, especially in the life of religious services. Examples are found in the following passages:

Babylonian Talmud Soṭah 39B: Rab Hisda († 309) said, "The priests (who had to issue the blessing with raised arms and outstretched fingers) may not bend their finger joints until they turn their face away from the community (after finishing the blessing). (Then follows the section of b. Soṭah 39B presented at § 1 Cor 14:16 B, #6, n. *a*, up until the marked break; this is filled out as follows:) R. Zeira also said that Rab Hisda said, "The priests may not turn their face away from the community until the prayer leader begins with (the last benediction of the Prayer of Eighteen Benedictions): 'Give peace' שִׂים שָׁלוֹם; they may also not move their feet and go from there until the prayer leader has finished (the benediction): 'Give peace.' (Then comes the close of the citation presented at § 1 Cor 14:16 B, #6, n. *a*, which is followed by the following words:) The interpreter may not begin with the targum, until the Scripture verse (that is read) comes to an end in the mouth of the reader, and the reader may not begin with the next verse until the targum has come to an end in the mouth of the interpreter...." R. Tanḥum (b. Hanilai, ca. 280) said in the name of R. Joshua b. Levi (ca. 250), "The reader of the Haftarah (prophetic lesson) may not read from the prophets until the Torah scroll has been rolled up." R. Tanḥum also said that R. Joshua b. Levi said, "The reader may not uncover the lectern (remove the covering) in the presence of the community for the sake of the honor of the community." R. Tanḥum also said that R. Joshua b. Levi said, "The community may not leave until the book of the Torah has been taken and put in its place (where it is kept)." ‖ Mishnah Berakot 9.5: One may not act imprudently opposite the east gate (of the temple), for it is precisely opposite the house of the Most High. And one may not go to the temple mountain with his staff or his footwear (cf. Exod 3:5) or his money bag or with dust on his feet; and he may not make it into a shortcut (the same is said of a synagogue in m. Meg. 3.3), and how much less (may he) spit there. ‖ See t. Sukkah 4.1ff. (198) in the excursus "The Feast of Tabernacles," V, middle. ‖ Sifre Deuteronomy 1:22 § 20 (69B): "You all approached me" (Deut 1:22); in disorder (in a muddle) בְּעִרְבּוּבְיָא. But it goes on to say, "You approached me, all your tribe heads and elders" (Deut 5:20); the young honored the elders, the elders honored the heads. But here it says, "You all approached me and said" (Deut 1:22); in disorder: the young shoved the elders, the elders shoved the heads. — Of course, approaching God in a confused muddle is meant as a reprimand. See b. ʿAbod. Zar. 2A: R. Hanina b. Papa (ca. 300), it has also been said R. Simlai (ca. 250), presented the following: "In the future God will bring the book of the Torah in his bosom and say, 'Let everyone who devoted himself to the Torah come and receive his recompense!' Immediately the nations of the world will gather and come in disorder בערבוביא; as it says, 'All the nations will gather at once (confusedly)' (Isa 43:9). God will say to them, 'Do not come in disorder (in a mix) before me, but rather every nation and its scholars shall come for itself!' For it says, 'And (nations) shall gather for themselves לְאֻמִּים' (Isa 43:9). Yet לְאֹם means nothing but dominion מלכות; as it says, 'And one sovereign לְאוֹם will be stronger than another' (so Gen 25:23 according to the midr.; Targum Onkelos also translates ומלכו ממלכו ותקף here = 'and one dominion will be stronger than another'). Yet is there disorder (medley) before God? (Rashi: 'Will they not all be surveyed with one glance?') Rather, they shall not stand there in disorder (confusedly) so they may hear what he will say to them." (See the continuation of the passage in the excursus "Depictions of the Judgment in Ancient Jewish Literature.")

15:3: That Christ died for our sins according to the Scriptures.

1. On suffering and specifically on the vicarious suffering of the Messiah, see § Luke 24:26, I, #2–4.

2. The rabbis would have rendered αἱ γραφαί with כִּתְבֵי הַקֹּדֶשׁ "Scriptures of holiness" = Holy Scriptures. הַכְּתוּבִים by itself is a designation of the hagiographa, that is, the Scriptures contained in the 3rd part of the OT.

Mishnah Šabbat 16.1: One may save all the Holy Scriptures כתבי הקדש from a fire (on the Sabbath), whether they may be read or not.

15:6: But several have fallen asleep.

On the trope of "falling asleep" κοιμᾶσθαι, Aram. דְּמַךְ, = "die," see examples at § Matt 27:45, #1; see also § Matt 9:24.

15:8: As to an untimely birth.

ἔκτρωμα "untimely birth" (miscarriage) = נֵפֶל (Aram. נְפִילָא, נִפְלָא), also = שְׁלִילָא, which in the first place means "embryo." — Job 3:16 and Ecclesiastes 6:3 נֵפֶל; in both passages, the LXX has ἔκτρωμα; the targum has נפלא in the 1st passage, שלילא in the 2nd. — Babylonian Talmud Soṭah 22A paraphrases נֵפֶל with: קטן שלא כלו לו חדשיו = "a child whose months (in the womb) have not finished." This paraphrase is then interpreted with reference to certain students of the scholars; see the passage at § Matt 9:3 A, #2, n. *a*. However, this passage contributes nothing to the understanding of ἔκτρωμα in 1 Cor 15:8; yet it proves that the metaphorical application of the expression "untimely birth" to certain adults was not unknown.

15:9: I who am not adequate (worthy). (See § Luke 15:19, 21.)

15:15: We will be found.

εὑρίσκεσθαι = נִמְצָא, "to be found as one who." So already 1 En. 108:10: "He has determined a recompense for them (the humble), because they were found as those who loved heaven more than their earthly life and praised me, while they were oppressed by evil men, while they had to hear abuse and blasphemy from them and were cursed." — In rabbinic literature נמצא is used frequently in this sense; see, for example, SLev 10:3 (188A) at § Matt 11:19 B; t. Sanh. 1.2ff. at § Rom 4:15 A; y. Ber. 4.7D.28 at § Rom 10:11. ‖ Sifre Deuteronomy 11:21 § 47 (83A): "Which (the land of Canaan) Yahweh swore to your fathers to give them" (Deut 11:21); "to give you," is not written here, but rather "to give them." Here we will be found as those who learn (i.e., from this we can learn) the resurrection of the dead from the Torah.

15:19: If we have hope in Christ only in this life, we are more wretched than all (other) people.

See the saying of Raba († 352) in b. Yoma 72B at § Matt 23:15 B.

15:22: For as in Adam all die.

See § Rom 5:15 A.

15:23: Then those who are Christ's at his arrival.

The assumption that the dead will resurrect at the beginning of the messianic age was widespread in the ancient synagogue; see the excursus "General or Partial Resurrection of the Dead?"

15:24: Then the end, when he will hand over the kingdom to his God and Father.

Pirqe Rabbi Eliezer 11 (6C): Ten kings have ruled from one end of the world to the other. The first king was God; for he reigns as king in heaven and on earth. (2nd–8th world rulers: Nimrod, Joseph, Solomon, Ahab, Nebuchadnezzar, Cyrus, Alexander of Macedonia.) The ninth king, this is the king, the Messiah; for he will reign as king from one end of the world to the other; as it says, "The stone that struck the image, became a great rock and filled the whole earth" (Dan 2:35). The tenth king: The kingship returns to its lord. He who was the first king is the last king; as it says, "I am the first and I am the last, and aside from me there is no God" (Isa 44:6). And furthermore it is written, "Yahweh will become king over the whole earth" (Zech 14:9). The kingship returns to its owner and then "the idols will disappear completely" (Isa 2:18), "and Yahweh will be exalted on that day" (Isa 2:17), and he pasture his sheep and make them lie down. As it says, "I will pasture my sheep and I will make them lie down" (Ezek 34:15, as cited by the midr.). And we will see him face to face; as it is written, "For they will see face to face how Yahweh returns to Zion" (Isa 52:8). Amen!

15:25: Until he puts all enemies under his feet.

On Ps 110:1 see the excursus "The 110th Psalm in Ancient Jewish Literature."

15:26: Death will be done away with as the last enemy (see § 1 Cor 15:54).

15:28: So that God may be all in all.

Sifre Deuteronomy 6:4 § 31 (73A): "Yahweh, our God, Yahweh is one" (Deut 6:4); over all who come into the world. "Yahweh, our God," in this world; "Yahweh is one," in the future world. And likewise, it says, "And Yahweh will become king over all the earth; on that day Yahweh will be one and his name will be one" (Zech 14:9). ‖ Babylonian Talmud Pesaḥim 50A: "And Yahweh will become king over all the earth; on that day Yahweh will be one and his name will be one" (Zech 14:9). Is he (God) not one now? R. Aha b. Hanina (ca. 300; read: R. Asi [ca. 300] in the name of R. Yohanan [† 279])[233] said, "The future world is not like this world: in this world people say to good news, 'Blessed be the one who is good and bestows good!' And people say to bad news, 'Blessed be the judge of truth (the truthful judge)!' In the future world he is completely the one who is good and who bestows good! 'And his name will be one.' What does 'one' mean? Is his name not one now?" Rab Nahman b. Isaac († 356) said, "The future world is not like this world: in this world it (the name) is written with *yod he* (יהוה) and read with *aleph daleth* (אדני); but in the future world it is entirely one, it will be read with *yod he*, and it will be written with *yod he*." ‖ Targum Zechariah 14:9: "And the kingship of Yahweh will be revealed over all the inhabitants of the earth. At that time they will serve (before) Yahweh with one shoulder, because his name is valid in the world, and there is none beside him." ‖ See Pirqe R. El. 11 (6C) at § 1 Cor 15:24.

---

233. See Bacher, *Die Agada der palästinensischen Amoräer*, 1:337.5.

15:29: What will those who are baptized for the dead do?

The passage, for example, adduced by Lightfoot (2:923A) to explain ὑπὲρ τῶν νεκρῶν with the meaning of "over the dead" (b. Moʿed Qaṭ. 27B) does not belong here, since the prepositional modifier used there, עַל גַּבֵּי, does not mean "over," but rather "in the case of." Rightly translated, the passage reads as follows:

In an earlier period, in the case of על גבי who had died during menstruation, people used to immerse the items (that she had come into contact with while she was alive, for the purpose of Levitical cleansing), and because of this the living menstruants felt ashamed. Then it was ordered that people should immerse items in the case of all women (who had died) for the sake of the honor of the living menstruants. In an earlier period people used to immerse (the items) in the case of those who were afflicted by a flow, and because of this those who were afflicted by a flow who were alive felt ashamed. Then it was decreed that people should immerse items in the case of all, for the sake of the honor of those who were afflicted by a flow who were alive.

15:32: Let us eat and drink; for tomorrow we die.

The citation follows LXX Isa 22:13 verbatim. — The base text: "Eat and drink, for (so they say) tomorrow we die!" — Targum Isaiah 22:13: "Let us eat and drink, because we will die, we will not live!" ‖ See b. Taʿan. 11A at § Luke 12:19. ‖ Tanḥuma קדושים 168B: "When you come into the land and plant all kinds of trees for food" (Lev 19:23). God said to the Israelites, "Even if you find the land full of all kinds of good, you should not say, 'We will sit and not plant.' Rather be mindful of the plantings; as it says, 'When you plant all kinds of trees for food.' As you will find plantings at your entry that others have planted, so too you will plant for your children, lest anyone say, 'I am old; how many years will I still live. Why should I get up and labor for others? Tomorrow I will be dead!'" Solomon said, "He has made everything fitting for its time, and he has put eternity into their heart" (Eccl 3:11). הָעֹלָם (eternity) is written without *waw* (instead of העולם). Why? If God had not veiled העלים (interpretation of העלם without ו) from the heart of men the (day of) death, no one would plant, for he would say, "Tomorrow I will be dead, so why should I get up and labor for others?" Therefore God veiled the day of death from the hearts of the children of men, so that he might build. If he merits it, it will be for himself; if he does not merit it, for others.

15:33: Bad company corrupts good morals.

See the proverb in b. Sanh. 93A: If two bits of firewood are dry and one fresh (moist), the dry ones set the fresh one on fire.

15:35 A: How will the dead be resurrected?

This question also occupied the school of Shammai and of Hillel.

Genesis Rabbah 14 (10C): "And he formed" וייצר (Gen 2:7). (Why is וייצר written with two *yod's*?) This refers to two formations, one formation in this world, and one formation in the future world. The school of Shammai and the school of Hillel. The school of Shammai said, "His (humanity's) formation (at the resurrection) in the future world is not like his formation in this. In this world it begins (in the womb) with skin and flesh and ends with tendons and bones; but in the future it begins with tendons and bones and ends with skin and flesh. For so it says with Ezekiel's dead, 'I looked, and behold, tendons and flesh grew on them and skin covered them' (Ezek 37:8)." R. Jonathan ([ca. 140?] or Ben Eleazar? [ca. 220]) said, "From Ezekiel's dead we learn nothing. Who were Ezekiel's dead like? Like someone who gets in a bath: what he first takes off, he puts first (back) on." The school of Hillel said, "His formation in the future world is just like his formation in this world. In this world it begins with skin and flesh and ends with tendons and bones; the same in the future: it begins with skin and flesh and ends with tendons and bones. For so Job says, 'Will you not pour me out like milk?' (Job 10:10)? 'You have poured me out' is not written here, but rather 'you will pour me out'; and 'as whey you have made me curdle' is not written here, but rather 'you will make me curdle'; 'with skin and flesh you have clothed me' is not written here, but rather 'you will clothe me'; 'with bones and tendons you have woven me' is not written here, but rather 'you will weave me.' Like a bowl that is full of milk; as long as no one puts abomasum in it (as curdling material), the milk sways back and forth; but after the abomasum is added, it is drawn together and stands still. This is what Job said, 'Will you not pour me out like milk ..., clothe me with skin and flesh ...?' (Job 10:10f.)." — The same is found in Lev. Rab. 14 (115B).

15:35 B: With what sort of body will they come?

The Syriac Apocalypse of Baruch deals with this question in detail: first the dead rise in their former corporeality, so that they may be identified; but then they will be changed from one glory into another.

2 Baruch 50:1–51:10: "Hear, Baruch, this word, and write everything that you learn in the memory of your heart! For surely the earth will give back the dead then (at the time of the resurrection of the dead) that is now receives in order to keep them, while changing nothing in their appearance (in their form); but rather as it has received them, it will give them back in the same way, as I (God) have handed them over to her, just so will she make them rise. For then it will be necessary to show those who live that the dead have come to life (again), and that they those who had departed have come (back). And when those who know (each other) now have recognized one another, the judgment will be mighty.... And after the determined day has passed, then the appearance of those who are in debt will change (and) also the glory of the appearance of those who act rightly. For the appearance of those who behave godlessly now will become worse than it is, as they must (also) suffer torment. Also the glorious appearance of those who now have acted righteously on the basis of my law, who had insight in their life and who had planted the root of wisdom in their heart—their splendor will then shine in various forms, and the appearance of their faces will change into their luminous beauty so that they may accept and receive the immortal world that is then promised to them. For all the more will those who then draw near have to sigh because they neglected my law and stopped up their ears lest they hear wisdom and be able to accept insight. When they see that those over whom they regard themselves as

now being exalted are exalted and are glorified more than they will be, the former and the latter will be changed: the latter into the splendor of the angels, and the former will all the more waste away, into eye-popping appearances and forms too (wonderful) to be looked at. For first they look at them and then they (themselves) go to suffer torment. But those who have been saved by their behavior (from this) and those for whom now the law has been their hope and insight their desire and faith their wisdom, wonderful things will appear to them when the time for them comes; for they will see the world which is invisible to them now, and they will see the time that is hidden from them now. And time will not make them age either; for in the (heavenly) heights of that world they will dwell and be like the angels and be comparable to the stars. And they will be changed into all possible forms that they could (only) wish for themselves: from beauty into magnificence and from light into the splendor of glory."

15:36: Ignorant.

ἄφρων perhaps = שׁוֹטֶה (fool); the latter particularly in the expression שוטה שבעולם = "Fool in the world" = you biggest fool in the world! — See some examples at § Matt 5:22 E, n. *b*.

15:37: A naked grain.

See b. Sanh. 90B at § Matt 10:5 B, #2, n. g, β. ‖ Babylonian Talmud Ketubbot 111B: R. Hiyya b. Joseph (ca. 260) said, "The righteous will then rise in their clothes. An inference from the lesser to the greater from the wheat grain: If the wheat grain that comes (literally: is buried) naked עֲרוּמָּה into the earth comes out in who knows how many clothes, how much more does it go for the righteous that they will rise in their clothes!" ‖ Pirqe Rabbi Eliezer 33 (17C): R. Eliezer (ca. 90) said, "All the dead will rise at the resurrection of the dead and come up in their clothes. Where do you learn this from? From the seed of the earth by an inference from the lesser to the greater from the wheat grain ..." (as in the previous citation). ‖ Jerusalem Talmud Ketubbot 12.35A.11: Antoninus[234] asked Rabbi (Judah I [† 217?]): What does "It is changed like the clay of the seal" (Job 38:14) mean?" He answered him, "He who brings back the generation (at the resurrection) clothes it (too)." — Rabbi understood the Job passage as follows, "It will be changed, like loam, into a (new) character (into a new form), and then they will stand each in his own robe (that God gives to them)."

15:39: Not every flesh is the same flesh, but rather there is one for humans, another flesh for animals, another flesh for birds, another flesh for fish.

The diversity of flesh is expressed halakically in, for example, the following way:

---

234. S-B: The historicity of the narratives about the friendship between Judah I and the emperor Antoninus cannot be determined. Marcus Aurelius Antoninus (161–180) and Septimius Severus (193–211), who were in Palestine, could be in view. See Strack, *Einleitung in den Talmud und Midraš*, 133.

Mishnah Ḥullin 8.1: "'No flesh may be cooked in milk' (cf. Deut 14:21; Exod 23:19; 34:26), except for the flesh of fish בְּשַׂר דָּגִים and of locusts (whose flesh is not to be viewed as actual flesh). It is also prohibited to bring together on one table (flesh) with cheese, except for the flesh of fish and of locusts. Whoever swears off flesh by a vow is permitted the flesh of fish and locusts (for the same reason as before). Birds עוֹף may be brought together on a table with cheese, but not eaten together." These are the words of the school of Shammai. The school of Hillel said, "They may neither be put on it together nor eaten together." ‖ Pesiqta 35B: R. Jacob of Kefar Neburaya (ca. 350; on this reading, see Buber on the passage) had taught in Lydda as halakah that fish were subject to ritual slaughtering. When R. Haggai (ca. 340) heard this, he had him come and said to him, "On the basis of which passage do you teach this?" He answered, "On the basis of 'The waters shall teem with one swarm of living beings and flying animals shall fly over the earth' (Gen 1:20). Just as birds are subject to ritual slaughtering, so too fish are subject to it (because they are named as a swarm in the water alongside the winged animals in Gen 1:20, so that what applies to one also applies to the other)." R. Haggai commanded, "Put him down so he may be lashed (because of his false halakic teaching)." He responded, "A person who has taught the words of the Torah should be lashed?" The former said, "You have not taught beautifully (rightly)." He said, "And how is it with them (fish)?" He said to him, "That follows from this passage of Scripture, 'Can small livestock and cattle be slaughtered (ritually) for them so that it would be enough for them? Or can all the fish of the sea be gathered for them?' (Num 11:22)." (The word "slaughter" is written only in the case of the small livestock and cattle, but not in the case of fish.) He said to him, "Only strike efficiently, for this is good for the acceptance (of the right teaching; read with Buber בְּקִילְטָא = 'for the acceptance' instead of בקילתא)." Parallels are found in Gen. Rab. 7 (5D); Num. Rab. 19 (186A); Midr. Eccl. 7:23 (37B); TanḥB חקת § 15 (56A); Pesiq. Rab. 14 (61A).

15:41: For one star differs from (another) star in glory.

Sifre Deuteronomy 11:21 § 47 (83A): Likewise, it says, "A song for the ascents" (Ps 121:1). "A song of ascents" is not written here, but rather "a song for the ascents": for the one who will one day make ascents (ranks) for the righteous in the future. Rabbi († 217?) said, "'A song for an ascent' is not written here, but rather 'a song for ascents.' For there (in the hereafter) one ascent (rank) (of the blessed) is higher than another. Or since this ascent is higher than that one and this one (in turn) is higher than that (third) one, should I conclude from this that there will be enmity, envy, and fighting among them (the blessed)? Scripture teaches, 'Those who have led many to righteousness are like the stars forever and ever' (Dan 12:3). Just as there is no enmity or envy or fighting among the stars, so too there will be no enmity or envy or fighting among the righteous, and just as with the stars the light (the splendor of light) is not like the glory of another, so too with the righteous (in the hereafter)." — On ranks among the blessed and on the various kinds of splendor of their faces see § Matt 5:8 B, #2, n. *b*; § Matt 17:2 A; and in the excursus "Sheol, Gehenna, and the Garden of Eden," III, #3.

15:42 A: It is sowed in perishability.

According to the general assumption, the decomposition of the corpse takes place over the course of 12 months.[a] Completely singular is the view in b. Šabb. 152B that the bodies of the righteous would turn to dust only one hour before the resurrection.[b] In broader circles, it was believed that worm and decomposition had no power over only seven people.[c]

a. See b. Šabb. 152B at § Luke 23:43, #3, D.

b. Babylonian Talmud Šabbat 152B: Rab Mari (ca. 330?) said, "'The dust returns to the earth as what it had been' (Eccl 12:7)". Some diggers (of graves) who were digging on the land that belonged to Rab Nahman (according to Yalquṭ on Eccl 12:7, the baraita refers to Isaac [† 356]), and R. Ahai b. Josiah (ca. 180, who was buried there) snorted at them. They came and said to Rab Nahman, "A man snorted at us!" Rab Nahman came and said to him, "Who is it?" He answered, "I am Ahai b. Josiah." He said to him, "Did Rab Mari not say that the righteous turn to dust?" He answered, "Who is Mari? I do not know him!" "Yet (replied Rab Nahman) in Scripture it says, 'The dust returns to the earth as what it had been'!" He said to him, "Whoever made you read Ecclesiastes did not make you read the Proverbs (of Solomon); for it says, 'Envy (passion) is decomposition of the bones' (Prov 14:30); whoever has envy in his heart, his bones decompose; but whoever does not have envy in his heart, his bones do not decompose." Rab Nahman felt him (the dead man) and saw that there was something in him. He said to him, "Let my lord arise and come into the house!" He answered him, "You have made it clear concerning your knowledge that you have not read even the prophets; for it is written, 'You will know that I am Yahweh when I open your graves (and make you climb out of your graves)' (Ezek 37:13)." (A dead person may leave the grave only at God's bidding.) He said to him, "But it is written, 'For you are dust and you shall turn back to dust' (Gen 3:19)!" He answered him, "This happens an hour before the resurrection of the dead."

c. See b. B. Bat. 17A at § Matt 17:3, #1, n. g.

15:42 B: It is raised in imperishability

On this see § Luke 20:36 A; see also 2 Bar. 50:1–51:10 above at § 1 Cor 15:35 B.

15:43: It is raised in glory (splendor).

See 2 Bar. 50:1ff. at § 1 Cor 15:35 B.

15:45 A: So it is also written, "The first man Adam became a living soul" (Gen 2:7).

Genesis 2:7 in the base text: וַיְהִי הָאָדָם לְנֶפֶשׁ חַיָּה = "and man became a living soul (a living being)." — Septuagint: καὶ ἐγένετο ὁ ἄνθρωπος εἰς ψυχὴν ζῶσαν. — Targum Onkelos: "And it (the breath of life) became in Adam a speaking spirit לְרוּחַ מְמַלְּלָא." — Targum Yerušalmi I: "And the breath became in Adam's body a speaking spirit, for the illumination of the eyes and for the hearing of the ears." — In rabbinic literature the passage was little used.

Babylonian Talmud Taʿanit 26B: R. Yose (ca. 150) said, "The individual is not authorized to afflict (chasten) himself by fasting; he (as someone incapable of work) may need people and the people might not have mercy on him." Rab Judah († 299) said that Rab († 247) said, "What is the scriptural basis for R. Yose? Because it is written, 'Man became a living soul' (Gen 2:7); the soul (says God) that I have put in him, keep it alive!" — The saying of R. Yose is also found in t. Taʿan. 2.12 (218). ‖ Genesis Rabbah 14 (10D): "And man became a living soul" (Gen 2:7). R. Judah (= R. Judan [ca. 350]) said, "This teaches that he (God) made for him a pointy little tail like a wild animal (חַיָּה "living" is interpreted = חַיָּה "wild"); yet then he took it away from him for the sake of his honor." Rab Huna (ca. 350) said, "He (God) made him a slave, who is strained[235] (subject) in his own interest (literally: for himself); for if he does not work, he has nothing to eat." — ויהי לנפש חיה is here understood as follows: "he became servile to the soul that had to be kept alive." — Parallels are found in Midr. Lam. 1:14 (56A.20) and Midr. Eccl. 2:17 (15A).

15:45 B: The first man Adam ..., the last Adam.

The speculations made by the later kabbalistic literature about the "first" and the "last" person, אָדָם קַדְמַאי and אָדָם בָּתְרָאָה, and about the "upper" and "lower" person, אָדָם עִילָּאָה and אָדָם תַּתָּאָה, have no analogue in the older rabbinic literature. Indeed here, presumably in order to prevent a confusion of the proper name "Adam" with the appellative אָדָם = "human being," Adam is generally called the "first human being" אָדָם הָרִאשׁוֹן, א' הַקַּדְמוֹנִי (Aram. א' קַדְמַאי, א' קַדְמָאָה),[a] but nowhere is another human being juxtaposed to him as the "second" or "last" Adam (human being). When Abraham or the Messiah are at one point celebrated as the restorer of what has been ruined by Adam's guilt, Abraham is designated as the "great man"[b] opposite the "first" man according to Josh 14:15 and the Messiah as the "son of Perez" or as the "son of Nahshon" or even simply as the Messiah.[c] Yet, there is no trace of the term "second" or "last" man, though it would have been very appropriate in these passages.

a. אדם הראשון. — Babylonian Talmud ʿErubin 18B: R. Meir (ca. 150) said, "The first man was a great pious man. When he saw that death was imposed as a punishment because of him, he sat 130 years fasting." ‖ A baraita in b. Pesaḥ. 54A: R. Yose (ca. 150) said, "... At the passing of the (creation) Sabbath God bestowed on the first man insight after the manner of the upper (divine) insight, and he (Adam) took two stones and rubbed them against each other, and fire came from them." ‖ Pesiqta 76A: R. Judah (ca. 150) said, "If someone should say to you, 'Would the first man have remained alive forever if he had not sinned and eaten from that tree?,' answer him, 'Elijah lived long ago; since he did not sin, he lives and remains forever.'" ‖ Pesiqta 36B: "Who is like the wise man?" (Eccl 8:1). This refers to the first

235. S-B: Read with the parallels מְכֻבָּן "strained" instead of מְהוֹרר "freed from."

man, of whom it is written: "You were the seal of proportion, full of wisdom and perfect in beauty" (Ezek 28:12).... R. Levi (ca. 300) said in the name of R. Simeon b. Manasseh (ca. 180), "The curve of the first man's heel darkened the sun wheel (by its splendor)." ‖ Babylonian Talmud ʿErubin 18B: R. Jeremiah b. Eleazar (ca. 270) said, "All those years that the first man was in banishment, he sired spirits, demons, and ghosts." — אדם הקדמוני. — See SLev 5:17 (120A) at § Rom 5:15 B, #2. ‖ Numbers Rabbah 10 (158A): "You will be like one who lies on the tip of a mast" (Prov 23:34); this is the first man, who was the head (tip) of all the children of men; for as a consequence of wine he was punished with death. — אדם קדמאה (קדמאי). — Targum Psalms 69:32: "My prayer will be more beautiful before Yahweh than the fat and select bull that the first man א׳ קדמאי sacrificed and whose horns had come in earlier than its hooves." — In the parallel b. Ḥul. 60A.24, which names Rab Judah († 299) as the author, we read א׳ הראשון; see also ʾAbot R. Nat. 1 (1C). ‖ Targum Psalms 92:1: "A praise and a song that the first man א׳ קדמאה said on the day of the Sabbath." — Adam is viewed as the author of the 92nd psalm already in ʾAbot R. Nat. 1 (1C); Gen. Rab. 22 (15C): R. Levi (ca. 300) said, "The first man said this psalm (namely Ps 92)." ‖ Targum Ecclesiastes 6:10: "Whatever happens in the world has been given its name long ago, and it has been made known to the children of men since the day the first man א׳ קדמאה existed." ‖ Targum Job 15:7: "Were you born like the first man without father and mother?" (Read כקדמאי אדם instead of בקדמאי א׳.)

b. Genesis Rabbah 14 (10C): "Yahweh Elohim formed the man" (Gen 2:7), in the merit of Abraham. R. Levi (ca. 300) said, "'The great man among the Anakim' (Josh 14:15): this is Abraham. And why does he call him 'great'? Because he was determined (worthy) to be created before the first man א׳ הראשון. Yet God said, 'He may act corruptly and then there will be no one who could come to bring back into order (restore) in his place. Behold, I will first create Adam; for if he acts corruptly, Abraham will come and restore in his place.'" — Abraham is often identified as the "great man among the Anakim" in the midrash; see, for example, SLev 18:3 (337A); Yalquṭ on Josh 14:15; Gen. Rab. 43 (26D); y. Šabb. 16.15C.33; Midr. Ps. 22 § 19 (95A); Sop. 16 § 10; 21 § 9; Pesiq. 154A.2: Lev. Rab. 29 (127B). — Parallels to Gen. Rab. 14 include Midr. Eccl. 3:11 (19A) in two forms; Midr. Ps. 34 § 1 (123A).

c. See Gen. Rab. 12; Exod. Rab. 30 at § Matt 1:3 D; see Num. Rab. 13 (170A) at § Matt 1:4, #2, n. *b*.

15:47: The first man from the earth.

Genesis 2:7: "Then Yahweh Elohim formed the human being from the dust of the earth עָפָר מִן הָאֲדָמָה." — Septuagint: καὶ ἔπλασεν ὁ θεὸς τὸν ἄνθρωπον χοῦν ἀπὸ τῆς γῆς. — Targum Onkelos follows the base text verbatim: עַפְרָא מִן אַדְמְתָא.

Genesis Rabbah 14 (10D): "From the dust of the earth" (Gen 2:7). R. Berekhiah (ca. 340) and R. Helbo (ca. 300) said in the name of R. Samuel b. Nahman (ca. 260), "He was created from the place of his atonement; as it says, 'You shall make for me an altar of earth אדמה' (Exod 20:24). God said, 'Behold, I will create him from the place of his atonement; O, that he might endure!'" (The dust of the earth used to form Adam stemmed from the site on which the temple's altar of burnt offering later stood in Jerusalem.) ‖ Jerusalem Talmud Nazir

7.56B.50: R. Judan b. Pazzi (ca. 320) said, "God took a spoonful (of dust) from the site of the altar and created the first man from it. He said, 'O, that he would be created from the site of the altar and that he would endure!' This is what is written, 'Yahweh Elohim formed the human being from the dust of the earth' מן האדמה; furthermore it is written, 'You shall make for me an altar of earth אדמה' (Exod 20:24). Just as אדמה (earth), which is mentioned there, signifies the altar, so too here it signifies the altar." See also Pirqe R. El. 20 at the beginning. ‖ Babylonian Talmud Sanhedrin 38A: In a baraita it has been taught: R. Meir (ca. 150) said, "The dust of the earth (used to create) the first man was gathered from the whole world; as it says, 'Your eyes saw my unformed mass' (Ps 139:16), and further it says, 'The eyes of Yahweh wander over the whole earth' (Zech 4:10)." (Just as here the eyes of Yahweh survey the whole earth, "your eyes" in Ps 139:16 indicate that the unformed dust of Adam was seen from the whole world.) Rab Hoshaiah (ca. 225) said in the name of Rab († 247), "The body (torso) of the first man stemmed (from the soil) from Babylon and his head (from the soil) from the land of Israel and his limbs (from the soil) from the other lands, his buttocks, as R. Aha (ca. 320) said, (from the soil) from Fortress of Agma (which was in Babylon and lay very deep, Rashi)." ‖ Pirqe Rabbi Eliezer 11 (6B): God said to the Torah, "We will make a man in our image and according to our likeness" (Gen 1:26). And the Torah answered and said, "Lord of the worlds, the world is yours and this man, whom you will create, is yours; but he is 'transitory and full of turmoil' (Job 14:1) and will fall into the power of sin. If you do not act long-sufferingly with him, it would be better for him if he did not come into the world." God said to her, "Am I called 'long-suffering' and 'great in grace' for nothing (without reason)?" Then he began to gather the dust of the earth for the first man from the four corners of the earth: red, black, white, and yellow. Red: this is the blood; black: these are the entrails; white: these are the bones and sinews; yellow: this is the body. And why did he gather his dust from the four corners of the world? God said, "So that, if a person comes from the east to the west or from the west to the east, or to whatever other place he wants to go, and his end comes to depart from the world, the earth in that place may not say, 'The dust of your body is not from me, and I will not accept you; go back to the place from which you were created!' This means to teach you that, wherever a person may go, and his end comes to depart from the world, from there the dust of his body stems, and thither he returns, and that dust raises its voice; as it says, 'For you are dust and you will return to dust' (Gen 3:19)." ‖ Targum Yerušalmi I Genesis 2:7: "Yahweh Elohim created the man with two inclinations (the good and the evil inclination) and took (brought) dust from the place of the sanctuary (in Jerusalem) and from the four sides of the world, and he mixed it together with all the waters of the world, and he created him red, brownish, and white."

15:50: Flesh and blood cannot inherit the kingdom of God.

βασιλεία θεοῦ is eschatological here. — On the expression "inherit the future world," see § Matt 19:29 B.

15:51: We will not all sleep, but we will all be changed.

The change of the pious who are alive at the time of the resurrection is entailed by the idea of the resurrection. Ancient Jewish literature rarely refers to the change of those who are alive.[a] Fourth Ezra might be the only passage that directly excludes such a change.[b]

a. 1 Enoch 90:33ff. (Shepherd vision): "All who had been killed or scattered (the martyrs and the exiles), ... gathered in that house (the new Jerusalem), and the Lord of the sheep (God) greatly rejoiced because all were good and returned to his house ... I saw that a white young bull (= Messiah) was born with great horns. All the animals of the field and all the birds of heaven (= the non-Jewish world) feared him and implored him at all times. I looked until all their kinds were changed and all became white young bulls (according to 1 En. 85ff., a symbol of the Sethians and patriarchs). The first among them (the Messiah) became a buffalo, and that buffalo became a great animal and received great and black horns on his head." ‖ 1 Enoch 51:1ff.: "In those days the earth will give back those who have been accumulated in her, and also Sheol will give back what it has received, and hell will issue what it owes. He (the Messiah) will select the righteous and holy ones among them; for the day of their redemption has come ... All (also those who are alive then) will become angels in heaven. Their countenance will shine for joy, because in those days the Elect One (= Messiah) has arisen; the earth will rejoice, the righteous will dwell on her and the elect will go about and walk on her." ‖ 1 Enoch 62:15ff.: "The righteous and elect will arise from the earth and cease to lower their gaze, and they will be clothed with a robe of glory (with a transfigured body). And this will be your robe, a robe of life with the Lord of Spirits: your clothes will not wear out and your glory will not fade before the Lord of Spirits." ‖ 1 Enoch 108:11ff.: "I (God) will call the spirits of the good who belong to the generation of light and I will transfigure those born in darkness, who have not been repaid in their flesh with honor, as would have been fitting for their fidelity. I will lead forth into a bright light those who loved my holy name, and I will set each one on a throne of his glory. They will shine throughout endless times, for righteousness is the judgment of God. For he will repay with fidelity the faithful in the dwelling (of the people) of righteous ways. They will see how those born in darkness are cast into darkness, while the righteous shine. Yet sinners will cry out loudly when they see how they (the righteous) shine; and they too will go where days and times have been determined for them." ‖ 2 Baruch 49:1–51, 10: "Yet I (Baruch) will beseech you further, O Almighty One, and will plead for grace from the one who created everything: In what form will those who are alive on your day (continue to) live? Or how can their subsequent splendor (if they continued to live in their old body) last? Will they then put on their current form and be clothed with the limbs bound with ligaments, which are now in sins, and with which sins are carried out? Or will you change those who were in the world, just as the world (itself)?" (See the continuation in 50:1–51:10 at § 1 Cor 15:35 B.) ‖ According to Gen. Rab. 12, the Messiah will bring back six goods that were lost because of Adam's sin. Thereby, humanity in the days of the Messiah will receive back the original splendor of its face, an immortal body, and the length of its primordial body; see the passage with parallels at § Matt 1:3 D. ‖ Babylonian Talmud Sanhedrin 92A: (A baraita from the school of Elijah:) The righteous whom

God will resurrect one day (in the days of the Messiah) will not return to dust; as it says, "And it will be that whoever remains in Zion and whoever is left in Jerusalem will be called holy, everyone who is written among those living in Jerusalem" (Isa 4:3). Just as the Holy One (= God) remains forever, so too they remain forever. And if you should say, "What will happen with the righteous (those who were alive and resurrected then) in those years, in which God will renew his world; as it says, 'So that Yahweh alone may be exalted on that day' (Isa 2:11)?," (know:) God will make wings for them, so that they may fly over the water like the eagles. As it says, "Therefore, we will not fear when the earth changes, for we will be in the midst of the sea when the mountains falter" (so Ps 46:3 according to the midr.; see Rashi). And if you should say that this might cause them pain, Scripture teaches: "Those who hope in Yahweh receive new strength, so that they may rise up on wings like eagles, run and not grow faint, walk and not grow weary" (Isa 40:31).

b. 4 Ezra 7:28ff: "My son, the Christ, will be revealed with all who are with him and will give joy to those who remain for 400 years. After these years my son, the Christ, will die and all who have human breath. Then the world will change into the silence of the primordial time (i.e., into chaos) for seven days, as in the very beginning, so that no one remains. After seven days, though, the age that now sleeps (i.e., the future world) will awake and perishability will itself perish. The earth will give back those who rest in it, the dust will release those who sleep in it, the chambers (of Sheol) will restore the souls that have been entrusted to them. The Most High will appear on the throne of judgment. Then comes the end … Then the pit of torment will appear and opposite the place of refreshment; the oven of gehenna will be revealed and opposite the paradise of blessedness." (Since there are none alive at the resurrection of the dead, they do not need to be transformed.)

15:52 A: In a moment (see § Luke 4:5).

15:52 B: At the last trumpet.

On the trumpet, see § Matt 24:31, #2; see also b. Sanh. 92A at § Matt 22:32, #2, C, middle. ‖ Targum Yerušalmi I Exodus 20:15 (= 20:18 in the original text): "The whole people saw … the voice of the trumpet as if it would revive the dead." ‖ Alphabet-Midrash of R. Aqiba (in Jellinek, *Beth ha-Midrash* 3:31.28): How will God revive the dead in the future world? God will take a great trumpet in his hand, 1,000 cubits long according to the cubit of God, and he will blow into it, and its sound will go from one end of the world to the other. At the first trumpet blast the whole earth will quake; at the second trumpet blast the dust will separate (from the earth surrounding it); at the third trumpet blast their bones will be gathered; at the fourth trumpet blast their limbs will grow warm; at the fifth trumpet blast skin will be drawn over them; at the sixth trumpet blast the spirits and souls will enter into their bodies; at the seventh trumpet blast they will become living and stand on their feet in their clothes; as it says, "The Lord Yahweh will blow into the trumpet …; Yahweh Sabaoth will shield them …" (Zech 9:14ff.).

15:54: Death has been swallowed up into victory (in victory).

1. Isaiah 25:8 according to the base text: "He will swallow up death forever לָנֶצַח." – Septuagint: κατέπιεν ὁ θάνατος ἰσχύσας = "death devoured mightily (evermore)." – Targum: "Death will be forgotten forever." – The rendering of לָנֶצַח with εἰς νῖκος shows that נֶצַח is interpreted from נְצַח, Aram. נְצַח = "prevail." This interpretation stems from LXX 2 Sam 2:26; Job 36:7; Lam 5:20; Amos 1:11; 8:7.

2. Isaiah 25:8 in rabbinic literature.

See m. Moʿed Qaṭ. 3.9 at § Matt 9:23, n. *e.* ‖ Genesis Rabbah 26 (16C): R. Hanina (ca. 225) said, "Death will exist in the future (in the days of the Messiah) only among the Noachides (i.e., among the non-Israelites)." R. Joshua ben Levi (ca. 250) said, "Neither among the Israelites nor among the nations of the world; for it is written, ('He will swallow up death forever) and Yahweh Elohim will wipe away the tears from every face' (Isa 25:8)." What does R. Hanina do with "From every face'? (He interprets it as follows:) "From the face of the Israelites." Yet it is written, "For the young man will die as a hundred-year-old" (Isa 65:20). This is a buttress (literally: this supports) for R. Hanina. What does R. Joshua b. Levi do with it ? (He interprets it as follows:) "(Only as a hundred-year-old) is he determined for the measure of punishments (only at 100 years old does the age of accountability begin)."[236] Yet it is written: "They appear like sheep for the underworld; death pastures them, and they trample down the righteous" (Ps 49:15). This is a buttress for R. Hanina. What does R. Joshua b. Levi do with it? (He interprets it as follows:) "Whereas in this world pharaoh (and his armies) existed in their time, Sisera (and his armies) in their time, Sennacherib (and his armies) in their time (and were punished), in the future God will make the angel of death their guardsman; this is what is written, 'And the righteous will go down to them (in gehenna) in the morning (to feast their eye on their punishments); their form will be brought to the decay of Sheol, for he (God) had no dwelling' (so Ps 49:15 according to the midr.). This teaches that Sheol decays, but their body does not decay. And why all this? Because they had stretched out their hands to the dwelling (= temple). This is what is written, 'I have built a house as a dwelling for you' (1 Kgs 8:13)." (The last citation is supposed to show that the "dwelling" in Ps 49:15 should be understood as the temple.) ‖ See b. Sanh. 91B = b. Pesaḥ. 68A at § Rom 3:9 A, #3, B, n. *k.* ‖ Midrash Ecclesiastes 1:4 (5B): "I have made a separation and I will heal it" (so Deut 32:39 according to the midr.). R. Hanina[237] (ca. 225) said in the name of R. Simeon b. Laqish (ca. 250) and R. Joshua of Sikhnin (ca. 330) in the name of R. Levi (ca. 300) in the name of R. Yohanan († 279, so read with Bacher[238]), "It is not written here, 'I have struck' הכיתי, but rather 'I have separated' מחצתי: I have erected a separation (partition, barrier) between those above (= angels) and those below, so that those above remain alive and those below in this world die. But in the future

236. S-B: According to R. Eliezer b. Yose the Galilean (ca. 150) the age of accountability in the generations before the flood also began only in the 100th year of life; see Gen. Rab. 26 (16C).

237. S-B: R. Hanina as the tradent of Resh Laqish is striking but not impossible; or is R. Hanina b. Pap(p)a (ca. 300) in view?

238. Bacher, *Die Agada der palästinensischen Amoräer*, 1:338.

there will be no more dying at all; as it says, 'He will swallow up death forever' (Isa 25:8)." ‖ Midrash Lamentations 1:13 (55A): R. Yohanan († 279) said in the name of R. Simeon b. Yohai (ca. 150), "Wherever it says, 'And he said' (where one 'he said' is followed by a second 'he said'), it is said only so that it may be interpreted" (it entails a particular thought. Then the passage names and interprets as examples Ezek 10:2; 1 Kgs 20:13; Esth 7:5 and finally Lev 21:1f.:) "Yahweh said to Moses, 'Say to the priests, the sons of Aaron, and say to them.'" Why this twofold saying? With the first he said to him, "He shall not become unclean by a corpse among his brethren"; with the second he said to him, "If a dead man of obligation (who has no relatives and therefore his burial is the obligation of every Israelite) comes under your hands, you may become unclean because of him. For in this world you (priests) may become unclean by a dead man of obligation, but in the future you will not become unclean at all by a dead person, because in the future there will be no death; as it says, 'He will swallow up death forever ...' (Isa 25:8)." — The same is found in Tanḥ. אמור 172A; in TanḥB אמור § 5 (42B) and in Lev. Rab. 26 (124D) the sentence about the future is lacking. ‖ See Exod. Rab. 15 (77D) at § Rom 8:20f. introductory comment and n. *s.* ‖ See Pesiq. 189A at § John 3:29 B. ‖ See Pesiq. Rab. 36 (161A) at § Luke 24:26, I, #4, n. *k.* ‖ Deuteronomy Rabbah 2 (199B): God said, "Since in this world the evil inclination is found, they have killed each other so that they had to die; but in the future I will root the evil inclination out of you, and there will be no more dying in the world; as it says, 'He will swallow up death forever' (Isa 25:8)." ‖ Tanḥuma ירתי 90B: God said, "In this world the years (of life) have been shortened because of the evil inclination; but in the future 'he will swallow up death forever' (Isa 25:8)." ‖ Exodus Rabbah 30 (89C): In his (the Messiah's) days God will swallow up death; as it says, "He will swallow up ..." (Isa 25:8).

15:55: Where, O death, is your victory? Where, O death, is your sting?

1. Hosea 13:14 according to the base text: "Where are your plagues דְּבָרֶיךָ, O death? Where is your destruction קָטָבְךָ (say *qoṭobekha*, from קְטֵב), O Sheol?" — Septuagint: ποῦ ἡ δίκη (right) σου θάνατε; ποῦ τὸ κέντρον σου ᾅδη; — targum: "Now I myself מֵימְרִי (literally: 'my word') will be killing לְקָטוֹל among them and my word destruction לְחַבָּלָא; since they have transgressed my Torah, I will remove my Shekinah from them." (The last sentence renders the base text's clause: "Remorse will hide from my eyes.")

2. Hosea 13:14 in rabbinic literature.

Babylonian Talmud Pesaḥim 87B: R. Eleazar (ca. 270) said, "God exiled Israel to Babylon only because the latter is as deep as Sheol; as it says, 'From the power of Sheol I will free them; from death I will redeem them ...' (Hos 13:14)." ‖ Babylonian Talmud Yebamot 17A: What does Harpania mean? (The name of a city in Babylonia that was disreputable due to its many intermarriages.) R. Zera (= Zeira, ca. 300) said, "Mountain, to which they will all turn (from their illegitimate origin)." In a baraita it has been taught: Whoever does not know his family and his stock will turn there. Raba († 352) said, "And it (the city Harpania) is deeper than Sheol; for it says, 'From the power of Sheol I will free them ...' (Hos 13:14;

thus, there is a restoration from Sheol); but for its (Harpania's) illegitimate ones, there will be no restoration." ‖ See an interpretation of קטבך in Hos 13:14 = κατάβα "go down" into Sheol in TanḥB צו § 4 (8A) at § Rom 3:9 A, #3, B, n. *ee*.

3. In קֶטֶב in Deut 32:34 and Ps 91:6 the ancient synagogue frequently saw a dangerous demon; see the excursus "Ancient Jewish Demonology," #5.

15:58 A: Be ... abounding in the Lord's work at all times.

See the interpretations in the midrash of the saying: "It is time for Yahweh to act; they have broken your Torah" (Ps 119:126). — See Yalquṭ on Num 27:2 with parallels in t. Ber. 7.24 etc. at § Matt 12:30. ‖ Mishnah Berakot 9.5: R. Nathan (ca. 160) said, "Your Torah is broken (stipulations of the Torah may be suspended) when it is time for Yahweh to act." — Jerusalem Talmud Berakot 9.14C.27: R. Nathan (ca. 160) inverted the Scripture passage (Ps 119:126): "Your Torah is broken when it is time for Yahweh to act." R. Hilkiah (ca. 320) said in the name of R. Simon (ca. 280), "Whoever occasionally forces his study of the Torah breaks (destroys) the covenant. What is the scriptural basis? 'They have broken your Torah, acting occasionally for Yahweh' (so now Ps 119:126)." In a baraita it has been taught: R. Simeon b. Yohai (ca. 150) said, "When you see that men hopelessly withdraw their hands completely from the Torah, then go and hold fast to it, and you will receive the recompense for them all. What is the scriptural basis? 'If they have broken your Torah, it is time for Yahweh to act' (so now Ps 119:126)." Parallels are found in Midr. Sam. 1 (21A and 21B). ‖ Babylonian Talmud Berakot 63A: It says, "It is time for Yahweh to act; they have broken your Torah" (Ps 119:126). Raba († 352) said, "This passage can be interpreted from its beginning with a view to its end; it can (also) be interpreted from its conclusion with a view to its beginning. It can be interpreted from its beginning with a view to its end: 'It is time for Yahweh to act.' Why? Because your Torah has been broken. It can be interpreted from its conclusion with a view to its beginning: 'They have broken your Torah' (its stipulations have been partly suspended, see the explanation of R. Nathan above); why? 'Because it is time for Yahweh to act.'"

15:58 B: Knowing that your labor is not in vain (empty) in the Lord.

Mishnah ʾAbot 2.16: (R. Tarfon [ca. 100] said,) "The master over your work (God) is reliable, who will pay you your recompense for your work."

16:1: Concerning the collection for the saints.

On λογία = collection see § Rom 15:26, #1. — See further about the nature of collections at § Rom 15:26, #1 and #2.

16:2: Every first of the week each of you should set aside something.

1. μία σαββάτου = אֶחָד בַּשַּׁבָּת "the first of the week" = Sunday; see on this § Matt 28:1 B.

2. παρ' ἑαυτῷ τιθέτω. — In the ancient Jewish view it was also allowed to appoint alms for the poor on a Sabbath.

Babylonian Talmud Šabbat 150A: R. Eleazar (ca. 270) said, "One may appoint alms for the poor on the Sabbath." — The same is found in Tanḥ. בראשית 2B.

16:7 A: For I do not want to see you now in passing.

ἐν παρόδῳ = לְפִי דֶרֶךְ,[a] in passing, casually, incidentally, *en passant.* — The Aramaic equivalent to לפי דרך is אֲגַב אוֹרְחָא;[b] for this, one can also say אֲגַב גְּרָרָא[c] (actually: by going by).

a. Mishnah Sukkah 2.1: In passing לְפִי דַרְכֵּנוּ we learn from this that whoever sleeps under a bed (in the sukkah) does not do his duty (to dwell in the sukkah). ‖ Mishnah ʿEduyyot 2.3: In passing לְפִי דַרְכְּךָ we learn from this that a woman may write her own certificate of divorce and a man his own receipt (about the prescribed marital sum paid out); for the validity of a deed depends on those who have signed it. ‖ Babylonian Talmud Sanhedrin 76B: Rab Kahana (ca. 250) said in the name of R. Aqiba († ca. 135), "Be on guard against someone who gives you counsel casually לְפִי דַרְכּוֹ (he could have ulterior motives)." The same is found in Der. Er. Zut. 8 toward the beginning.

b. Babylonian Talmud Ber. 2A: In passing אֲגַב אוֹרְחֵיהּ he lets us conclude from this. ‖ Babylonian Talmud Ketubbot 105B: I remembered to deliver it to the Lord incidentally אֲגַב אוֹרְחֵי.

c. Babylonian Talmud Baba Meṣiʿa 4B: Here is the main passage; there he mentions it casually אֲגַב גְּרָרָא. — Similarly in the parallel passage b. Šebu. 40B; however, b. Zebaḥ. 12A has אֲגְרָרָא instead of אגב גררא.

16:7 B: If the Lord allows.

See § Jas 4:15. — The abbreviation אי״ה = אם ירצה השם, "if God (the name) wills"; or = אם יגזור השם, "if God should decide," or = אם יעזור השם, "if God helps"—belongs to a later time.

16:9: A door is open for me.

θύρα = פֶּתַח, Aram. פִּתְחָא "opening, door," or = דֶּלֶת "door."

Sifre Deuteronomy 3:24 § 27 (71A): "You began" (Deut 3:24). You have opened a door פֶּתַח for me (gave the possibility, opportunity) so that I might come and pray before you for your children when they sinned with the deed with the (golden) calf; as it says, "Let go of me, so I may destroy them" (Deut 9:14). How so? Had Moses seized God? Rather, he said before him, "Lord of the world, you have opened a door for me so that I might come and pray before you for your children; I have come and prayed for them, and you have heard my prayer and forgiven their sins. I meant that I was together with them in prayer; but they have not prayed for me." ‖ Deuteronomy Rabbah 3 (200D): When (the Israelites) were on the brink of crossing the Jordan, (Moses) reminded them of everything that he had prayed for them in their defense; for he thought that they would pray for mercy for him, that he might enter with them (into the land of Canaan). What does "You cross over today" (Deut 9:1) mean? R. Tanḥuma (ca. 380) said that Moses cast himself down (read מחבט instead of מחבש) before them and said to them, "You are going over; I am not going over!" Thereby he opened a door פתח for them, to see whether they might pray for mercy for him; but they did not understand him. ‖ Genesis Rabbah 38 (23B): "And now it will not be unattainable for them" (Gen 11:6). R. Abba b. Kahana (ca. 310) said, "This teaches that God opened for them (the generation of the tower) the door of repentance פתח של תשיבה; for it says, 'And now.' This means nothing but repentance, as it says, 'And now, Israel, what does Yahweh your God demand of you, except that you fear Yahweh?' (Deut 10:12)." ‖ See Midr. Song. 5:2 (118A) at § Acts 14:27; parallels to this are found in Pesiq. 163B and Pesiq. Rab. 15 (70A). ‖ The opposite, "to close a door," in, for example, m. B. Meṣ. 7.5: The worker may eat cucumbers (with which he performs work) himself for a *denar* and also dates for a *denar*. R. Eleazar Hasama (?, ca. 110) said, "A worker may not eat (of the fruits with which he works) beyond his wage." The scholars, however, allowed it. But, people are taught that he should not be greedy and should close the door before himself סוֹתֵם אֶת הַפֶּתַח (since no one else would hire him as a worker). ‖ Genesis Rabbah 46 (29A): Abraham could have been circumcised at 48 years old when he knew this creator! However, (he was circumcised only at 99 years old) so as not to close the door לנעול דֶּלֶת to proselytes (lest they think that one could convert to Judaism only in one's prime). ‖ Babylonian Talmud Baba Qamma 7B: In this case the door would be closed נעלת דלת to borrowers (because no one else would be willing to lend). — Similarly, b. B. Qam. 8A: Why has it been said that a creditor (at the repayment of his claim) is paid from material of mediocre quality? Lest the door be closed before borrowers. (If the creditor were paid, e.g., with bad ground and soil, no one would lend anymore.)

16:10: For he is carrying out (doing) the Lord's work.

Jeremiah 48:10: "Cursed is whoever does עֹשֶׂה Yahweh's work מְלֶאכֶת יהוה with laxity." — Septuagint: ἐπικατάρατος ὁ ποιῶν τὰ ἔργα κυρίου ἀμελῶς (negligently). — Targum: "Cursed is whoever works עביד on work before Yahweh עובדא מן קדם ײ׳ with guile (deceit)."

16:13: Stand (firm) in faith.

Tanḥuma צי׳ 142A: R. Berekhiah the priest (ca. 340) said, "Since God saw that only the tribe of Levi would stand firm עימדין in their faith (their fidelity באמונתן), he came down with them (the angels) opposite the camp of the Levites."

16:14: Let everything happen among you in love.

Sifre Deuteronomy 11:13 § 41 (79B): "Everything that you do, you should do only out of love"; see the whole passage at § Rom 13:10.

16:17: Because they filled out your lack.

It was customary to call out this word of comfort to someone affected by a loss: "May God fill out your lack" יְמַלֵּא חֶסְרוֹנְךָ.

See y. Hor. 3.48A.39 at § Rom 15:26, #2; here in the plural: חסרנותוך "your lacks"; in the parallel Lev. Rab. 5 (108C): חסרונך. — In a similar narrative in Midr. Esth. 1:4 (86A) the wish is:ברייך ימלא חסרונך "May your creator fill out your lack!" ‖ Babylonian Talmud Berakot 16B: Just as someone says to a man because of his ox or because of his donkey that died,

"May God fill out for you your lack" ימלא לך חדתונך!, so too one says to him because of his male or female slave (who died), "May God fill out for you your lack!"

16:18: For they reassured my spirit and yours.

Babylonian Talmud Šabbat 152A: Rab Judah († 299) said, "If someone who has passed away has no comforters (i.e., no relatives to mourn him), ten people (of the place in question) go and sit (as mourners) in their stead." Someone who had passed away in Rab Judah's neighborhood had no comforters. Then Rab Judah took ten people every day who sat at his place (as mourners). After the seven days (of mourning) he appeared to him in a dream of Rab Judah (so!) and said to him, "May your mind be reassured, for you have reassured my mind תניה דעתך שהנחת את דעתי!" ‖ Babylonian Talmud Berakot 28B: Abbayye († 338/39) wanted to reassure the mind of Rab Joseph († 333) לאניחי דעתיה דרב יוסף. ‖ In b. Taʿan. 21A—see the passage at § Matt 18:8f.—Nahum of Gimzo (ca. 90) says, "My mind was not reassured לא נתקררה דעתי (literally: did not cool down) until I said, 'May my whole body be full of leprosy!'" ‖ See also m. ʾAbot 3.10: (R. Hanina b. Dosa [ca. 70]) said, "In whomever the spirit of men finds soothing, in that one the spirit of God finds soothing כל שרוח הבריות נוֹחָה ממנו רוח המקום נוֹחָה ממנו; but in whomever the spirit of men does not find soothing, in that one the spirit of God (also) does not find soothing (gratification)." ‖ Mishnah Šebiʿit 10.9: Whoever pays back a debt in a fallow year (although it is remitted by this year), in him the spirit of the scholars finds soothing (gratification) רוח חכמום נוֹחָה הימנו. Whoever borrows from a proselyte whose children converted with him to Judaism need not (in case he dies) pay back his children; but if he does pay back, the spirit of the scholars finds soothing in him. All movable goods are obtained (taken into possession) by drawing them to oneself; but whoever keeps his word (even if this pulling close is omitted), in him the spirit of the scholars finds soothing."

16:19: Aquila.

The name Ἀκύλας is written עֲקִילַס in rabbinic literature; only very occasionally does one encounter עֲקִילוֹס or אֲקִילַס;[a] according to DMZ XXIX, 236f., a neo-Punic inscription knows the spelling אקילא as well. — The most famous bearer of this name in rabbinic literature is the proselyte Aquila עֲקִילַס הַגֵּר,[b] the author of the Greek translation of the Bible that followed the original text as closely as possible not only in content but also in form and was intended to supplant the LXX in the circles of Hellenistic Judaism as much as possible.[c] On the fragments of this translation still in existence, see Strack and Schürer.[239] — The time of the proselyte Aquila can be determined quite precisely. Since R. Eliezer (ca. 90), R. Joshua (ca. 90), and R. Aqiba († ca. 135) were his teachers,[d] his period of activity falls in the first third of the 2nd century. This is corroborated by statements that bring him into personal and familial relation to the emperor Hadrian

239. Hermann Strack, *Einleitung in das Alte Testament einschliesslich Apokryphen und Pseudepigrapha*, 6th ed. (Munich: Beck, 1906), 223–224; Schürer, *Geschichte des jüdischen Volkes*, 3:437.

(117–138).[e] According to SLev 25:7, the region of Pontus appears to have been his home.[f] Aside from the citations from his translation of the Bible,[g] only a few sayings of his survived.[h]

In addition to the proselyte Aquila, another proselyte by the name of Onkelos, אוֹנְקְלוֹס (אונקלס) הַגֵּר,[i] is also mentioned in rabbinic literature; he is supposed to have been the son of a certain Qaloniqos or Qalonymos.[k] Relktions of a personal kind with the emperor Hadrian are attributed to him as well.[l] A different tradition makes him the son of Titus' sister.[m] Among the Jewish scholars, Rabban Gamaliel II (ca. 90) appears to have been particularly close to him. This emerges specifically from the two Tosefta passages Kelim B. Bat. 2.4 and Miqw. 6.3.[n] However, a different Tosefta passage (t. Šabb. 7.18 along with the parallel b. ʿAbod. Zar. 11A) also brought him into a closer personal relationship with Gamaliel the Elder גמליאל הזקן (ca. 40–50).[o] Yet since his dealings with Gamaliel II (the grandson of Gamaliel the Elder) are secured against all doubt by the testimony of R. Joshua b. Qabosai (ca. 120) in t. Miqw. 6.3,[n] the הזקן after גמליאל in both of the passages named should be removed as erroneous. If the relations with the emperor Hadrian attributed to the proselyte Onkelos require his work to have occurred in the first third of the 2nd century, this would be best confirmed by his contact with Rabban Gamaliel II. Apart from this, we learn only a little more[p] about him. Among this, it deserves to be particularly mentioned that in the observance of the rabbinic stipulations for his person, he was inclined to understand the applicable regulations even more strictly than the letter required.[q]

The above statements about Aquila and Onkelos agree in that both men were proselytes, both lived and worked at the same time, and personal relations with the emperor Hadrian are attributed to both men. If one adds also the similarity of both names, we are pressed to suppose that the two men were one and the same person. This supposition becomes a certainty by the realization that one and the same episode in the rabbinic writings is sometimes tied to the name Aquila and at other times to the name Okqelos.[r] Indeed, we even find that the proselyte Onkelos is introduced precisely as the translator of a passage of Scripture into Greek as otherwise is said about the proselyte Aquila.[s] Accordingly, it can hardly be doubted that at least the older period identified both men with each other. And they would have been right to do so. The difference of the two names carries little weight against this; they were presumably two dialectically different forms of one and the same name, unless one accepts with Schürer that the name אונקלוס is simply a corruption of עקילס.[240] — Only later generations judged differently. For them, the two different names are sufficient proof

240. Schürer, *Geschichte des jüdischen Volkes*, 3:437.

that there were also two different men who bore them. One of them, the proselyte Aquila, was the author of the Greek translation of the Bible, and the other, the proselyte Onkelos, was the author of the Aramaic targum to the Pentateuch named after him. The first formulation of this hypothesis is already found in the Babylonian Talmud.[t] Yet precisely here, it also becomes clear that the whole hypothesis rests on a misunderstanding, namely on a confusion of Aquila's Greek translation of the Bible with the Aramaic targum to the Pentateuch, which was later called the Targum Onkelos. In reality, the latter was not the work of a single man at all, but rather a work that took several centuries to complete.

a. On עקילוס see Midr. Eccl. 1:11 in n. *g*; on אקילס, Gen. Rab. 1 in n. *h*.

b. עקילס הגר, see y. Meg. 1.71C in n. *c*; Tanḥ. משפטים 92A in n. *e*; Gen. Rab. 70 in n. *d*; y. Ḥag. 2.77A.32 in n. *e*; Gen. Rab. 93 in n. *g*; y. Qidd. 1.59A.9 in n. *g*.

c. Jerusalem Talmud Meg. 1.71C.9: R. Jeremiah (ca. 320) said in the name of R. Hiyya b. Ba (= Abba, ca. 280), "The proselyte Aquila עקילס הגר translated תִּרְגֵּם the Torah (in the broader sense = OT) before R. Eliezer and before R. Joshua, and they praised him and said to him, 'You are the most beautiful יפיפית among the children of men' (Ps 45:3)." — That this passage is about the translation of the Torah into Greek follows from יפיפית, which in the mouth of R. Eliezer and R. Joshua is meant as a play on Gen 9:27: "May Japheth dwell in the tents of Shem," that is, according to the interpretation of Bar Qappara (ca. 220): "The language of Japheth (Greece) shall be spoken in the tent of Shem" (y. Meg. 1.71B.46). — See the remains of Aquila's Greek translation contained in the rabbinic writings in n. *g*. Concerning his work Jerome, *Epist.* 57 *ad Pammachium* cp. 11 aptly judges: *Aquila autem proselytus et contentiosus interpres, qui non solum verba, sed etymologias quoque verborum transferre conatus est, jure projicitur a nobis. Quis enim pro frumento et vino et oleo possit vel legere vel intelligere* χεῦμα, ὀπωρισμόν, σιλπνότητα, *quod nos possumus dicere fusionem, pomationem et splendentiam. Aut quia Hebraei non solum habent* ἄρθρα, *sed et* πρόαρθρα (Jerome is referring to the article ה and the *nota accusativi* את), *ille* κακοζήλως *et syllabas interpretatur et litteras dicitque* σὺν τὸν οὐρανὸν καὶ σὺν τὴν γῆν, *quod Graeca et Latina lingua omnino non recipit.* — The translation of Gen 1:1 complained about here goes back to an interpretation of R. Aqiba († ca. 135), who was a teacher of Aquila. We learn about this in Gen. Rab. 1 (3A): R. Ishmael († ca. 135) asked R. Aqiba and said to him, "Since you served Nahum of Gimzo (ca. 90) for 22 years as a student, who said that אַךְ (only) and רַק (only) have an exclusive and אֵת (*nota accusativi*)[241] and גַּם (also) have an inclusive meaning: what is the את doing that is written here (Gen 1:1)?" He answered him, "If it said בראשית ברא אלהים שמים וארץ (in the beginning God created heaven and earth), one might think that 'heaven' and 'earth' were divinities (since שמים and ארץ without an article seem like proper names); ... yet it says את השמים, to include sun, moon, and stars, and את הארץ, to include trees, herbage, and paradise." — The את before השמים and before הארץ thus means: "whatever is associated with it,"

241. TN: The Hebrew word that signals the accusative (direct object) can also mean "with."

"whatever belongs with it." Aquila received this interpretation of R. Aqiba and expressed it by means of his σύν before τὸν οὐρανόν and τὴν γῆν.

d. Genesis Rabbah 70 (44D): The proselyte Aquila came to R. Eliezer and said to him, "Is it the whole gain of a proselyte that it says about him, 'He loves the stranger (proselyte), to give him bread and raiment' (Deut 10:18)?" He answered him, "How so? Is it something small in your eyes for whose sake an old man (namely Jacob) cast himself down in prayer; as it says, 'And if he (God) gives me bread to eat and clothes to wear'? (Gen 28:20)." He (R. Eliezer) wanted to give him the answer with a reed stick (i.e., so fleetingly, without detailed exposition); then he went to R. Joshua (to be instructed by him). A different explanation. The proselyte Aquila came and asked R. Eliezer and said to him, "See the love with which God loves the proselyte; as it says, 'He loves the stranger (proselyte) to give him bread and raiment'! (Deut 10:18). How many peacocks I have, how many pheasants I have; even with my slaves there is no question about it!" Then he shouted at him (sent him away from himself), and he went to R. Joshua. Then his (R. Eliezer's) students said to him, "Rabbi, this, for whose sake did old man (Jacob) cast himself down in prayer, you give to him with a reed stick?" (The text is evidently corrupt; the question of the students presupposes that R. Eliezer and Aquila had previously talked about Gen 28:20.) He (R. Joshua) began to mollify him with words. "'Bread' (so he said to him) means the Torah; for it is written, 'Eat of my bread' (Prov 9:5); 'raiment' means the robe of honor (of the scholars, טַלִּית). If a man obtains knowledge of the Torah, he obtains the robe of honor. And not only this, but they (the proselytes) may also marry their daughters into the priesthood, and their sons become high priests and present sacrifices on the altar ..." Some people said, "If the patience אֲרִיכוּת פָּנִים that R. Joshua showed Aquila had not been there, the latter would have returned to his old manner (i.e., remained a gentile); and the following was applied to him (R. Joshua): "Better a patient man than a hero" (Prov 16:32). — Parallel passages with variations: Exod. Rab. 19 (81B); Num. Rab. 8 at the end; Midr. Eccl. 7:8 (34B). For the additional parallel TanḥB לך לך § 6 (32A), see n. *r.* — The student relationship of Aquila to R. Eliezer and R. Joshua emerges also in y. Meg. 1—see the passage in n. *c*—in the expression: Aquila translated before R. Eliezer and before R. Joshua. — That R. Aqiba was also among his teachers is shown by y. Qidd. 1.59A.9 in n. *g*; see also Jerome, *Comm. Isa.* 8:11ff.: *Aqibas, quem magistrum Aquilae proselyti autumant.* — See also the next citation.

e. Tanḥ. משפטים 92A: Aquila,[242] the proselyte, was the son of (the emperor) Hadrian's sister and wanted to convert to Judaism, but he was afraid of his uncle Hadrian. He said to him, "I would like to conduct some business." He answered him, "If you lack silver and gold, behold, my treasure chambers are before you." He said to him, "I would like to conduct some business by going abroad in order to learn the thoughts of men, and I would like to consult with you, as should be done." He answered him, "If you see a business that is despised and underfoot, attend to it; for in the end it will rise up, and you will be rich!" He went to the land of Israel and studied the Torah. After some time R. Eliezer and R. Joshua met him. They saw his face changed and they said to each other, "Aquila

242. S-B: Behind in brackets אונקלוס = Onkelos.

studies the Torah." When he came to them, he began to lay out many questions, and they gave him answers. He went to his uncle Hadrian. He said to him, "Why has your face changed? Should I suppose that your commercial venture suffered losses? Or has somebody hassled you?" He answered him, "No!" and said to him, "You are my relative, and so should someone hassle me?" He said to him, "And why has your face changed?" He answered him, "Because I studied Torah; and not only this, but also because I have been circumcised." He said to him, "Who told you to do this?" He answered him, "I consulted with you." He said to him, "When?" He answered, "When I said to you, 'I would like to conduct business,' and you said to me, 'If you see a business that is despised and underfoot, attend to it, for in the end it will rise up.' I have now gone around to all the nations and I have seen no people so despised and underfoot as Israel, and in the end it will rise up, for so Isaiah said, 'So says Yahweh, the redeemer of Israel, its Holy One to the one whose soul is despised, who is detested by the people, a slave of rulers: kings will see and rise up, princes, and they will cast themselves down because of Yahweh, who is faithful, the Holy One of Israel, and he has chosen you' (Isa 49:7)." Then his observer (l. סִנְקָתֶדְרוֹס = συνκάθεδρος instead of סקנדרוס) said to him, "Shall they remain (can they remain alive) of whom you said that kings will rise up before them; as it says, 'Kings will see and rise up'?" Then Hadrian hit him on his jawbone and said to him, "When one puts on a bandage, then on a wound! (One takes measures against present dangers, but not ones that lie very far off.) If one sees a page (arms bearer, servant of the company), one will not rise before him now, and that is why it is said that kings will see and rise up before them!" Then the observer said to him, "If that is the case, what will you do? Get him (Aquila) out of the way (literally: hide him); since he has become a proselyte, kill him." He answered him, "Aquila, the son of my sister, was, when he was still in his mother's womb, destined to become a proselyte." What did his observer do? He climbed onto his roof, plunged down, and died; and the holy spirit (the spirit of inspiration that speaks from Scripture) says, "May all your enemies, Yahweh, perish!" (Judg 5:31). Then Hadrian said to him, "Behold, the observer is dead; will you not tell me why you did this (accepted circumcision)?" He answered him, "Because I wanted to study Torah." He said to him, "You could have studied Torah but you should not have gotten circumcised!" Aquila answered him, "You give a general provision; but only once he has seized his weapons (begins the battle)! Likewise, a person can never ever study Torah unless he has been circumcised; as it says, 'He makes his words known to Jacob' (Ps 147:19), that is, to one who is circumcised like Jacob; 'he has not done this to any non-Israelite' (so the midrash understands Ps 147:20); for all idolaters are uncircumcised." — The same is found in TanḥB משפטים § 3 (41A). ‖ Exodus Rabbah 30 (90A): Once Aquila said to King Hadrian, "I would like to convert to Judaism and become an Israelite." He answered him, "You have a longing for this people? How despised I have made them, I have slaughtered them! You wish to mingle with the shabbiest among all the nations? What have you seen in them that you wish to become a proselyte?" He answered him, "Every child among them knows how God created the world, what was created on the first day, and what he created on the second day, and how long ago it is that the world was created, and what the world stands on and its Torah is truth." He said to him, "Well then, study their Torah, but do not get circumcised!" Aquila answered him, "Even the wisest man in your kingdom and an elder (senator) of a hundred years cannot learn their Torah unless he is circumcised; for it is written, 'He makes his words known to Jacob, his statutes and laws to Israel. He has not done this with any nation' (Ps 147:19f.); and whom (did he do it with)? The children of Israel." ‖ Jerusalem Talmud Ḥagigah 2.77A.32: R. Judah b. Pazzi (ca. 320) said in the name of R. Yose b. Judah (ca. 180), "Hadrian asked the proselyte Aquila, 'Do you say the truth (with the claim) that this world rests on the wind?' He answered him, 'Yes!' He said to him, 'How can you prove this to me?' He answered him, 'Have (young) camels brought to me!' Camels were brought to him. He weighed them down with heavy burdens, had them (immediately) get up and lie down; so he took them and strangled (choked) them. He said to him, 'You have them, make them get up!' He answered him, 'After you have choked them!?' He said to him, 'Have I taken anything away from them? Is it not the air that went out from them?'" ‖ Epiphanius, *De mensuris et ponderibus* § 14 also knows about Aquila's relationship with Hadrian: καὶ λαβὼν τὸν Ἀκύλαν ... τὸν ἑρμηνευτὴν ... καὶ αὐτοῦ (the Emperor Hadrian's) πενθερίδην, ἀπὸ Σινώπης δὲ τῆς Πόντου ὁρμώμενον....

f. Sifra Leviticus 25:7 (429A): "Whatever is in your land" (one may eat of the land yield of the Sabbath year [Lev 25:6f.]). "Whatever is in your land" may be eaten, (but) not whatever עקלים had carried out for his slaves to פנדוס. – The Malbim edition does not indicate what is going on with the word עקלים; in the commentary, it is replaced simply by עקילס (Aquila); on פנדוס, it is remarked: "This was a location in Syria." This place name is not encountered elsewhere in the older rabbinic literature. – Yalquṭ (ed. Wilna, 1898 § 659) presents the Sifra passage in the following form: "Whatever is in your land," this they may eat, not what Aquila had carried out for his slaves to Pontus שהוציא עקילס לעבדיו לפונתוס. If this text is correct, we can take from it that Aquila owned an estate in Pontus, which he had worked by slaves. This would suggest the assumption that he himself came from Pontus. As is well known, ecclesial authors also make Pontus his home territory. Irenaeus in Eusebius, *Hist. eccl.* 5.8.10: Θεοδοτίων ... ὁ Ἐφέσιος καὶ Ἀκύλας ὁ Ποντικὸς, ἀμφότεροι Ἰουδαῖοι προσήλυτοι. – Epiphanius (see the citation at the end of the previous n. *e*) names Sinope in Pontus as his hometown. In the text of Yalquṭ, though, the spelling פינתוס instead of פינטוס is notable.

g. Jerusalem Talmud Šabb. 6.8B.52: Aquila translated (תִּרְגֵּם) בָּתֵּי הַנֶּפֶשׁ ("smelling bottles," Isa 3:20) with אסטו מוכריאה (= στομαχάρια, trusses? Dalman). ‖ Jerusalem Talmud Yoma 3.41A.20: Aquila translated "opposite the lampstand" (נברשתא) (Dan 5:5) as "opposite the torch" לַמְפָּדָס (= λάμπαδος). ‖ Jerusalem Talmud Sukkah 3.53D.21: R. Tanḥuma (ca. 380) said, "Aquila translated הָדָר (= 'splendor,' Lev 23:40) as הידר (= ὕδωρ, 'water') 'a tree that grows by the water.' – The same is found in Pesiq. 183B; Lev. Rab. 30 (128B); in b. Sukkah 35A, this interpretation is attributed to Ben Azzai (ca. 110). – Pesiqta 84B: "I clothed you with colorful embroidered cloth" רִקְמָה (Ezek 16:10); R. Simai (ca. 210) said, "In purple. Aquila translated: פילקטון (read פְּקְלְטוֹן = ποικιλτόν = 'colored garment')." – Parallel passages with different variants can be found in Midr. Song. 4:12 (116B) and Midr. Lam. 1:1 (42B); on the last passage, see n. *s*. ‖ Genesis Rabbah 46 (29A): שַׁדַּי ("the Almighty," Gen 17:1). Aquila translated: אַכְסִיּס ואנקוס (read אִקְנוֹס) = ἄξιος καὶ ἱκανός. (שדי has thereby been dissolved into שֶׁ and דַּי = who is

דַּי, i.e., "worthy and sufficient.") ‖ Genesis Rabbah 93 (58D): It is written, "Golden apples in silver settings" (Prov 25:11). Aquila, the proselyte, translated "Golden apples on silver דִּסְקָרִין (= δισκάριον =) plates." ‖ Leviticus Rabbah 33 beginning: "Death and life is in the hand of the tongue" (Prov 18:21). Aquila translated: (read מִיצְטְרָא מזכירין (וּמְכֵירִין (= μυστρίον καὶ μαχαίριον =) spoon and sword; death on the one side and life on the other. ‖ Leviticus Rabbah 33 (130C): What does לַבָּלָה (= "the worn-out one" in Ezek 23:43) mean? Aquila translated: פּוֹרְנֵי (read פִּלְאָה) פיליא (= παλαιὰ πόρνη =) "old whore who weakened her paramours." ‖ Midrash Esther 1:6 (87A): חוּר כַּרְפַּס (= "white cloth and linen," Esth 1:6); the Targum Aquila: אירינין קרפינון (read אִירִינוֹן קַרְפְּסִינוֹן = εἰρίνεον καρπάσινον =) woolen material, linen cloth. ‖ Midrash Song of Songs 1:3 (85B): עַלְמוּת (Ps 48:15); the Targum Aquila: אֲתָנַסְיָא (= ἀθανασία =) immortality; a world in which there is no dying. — In this interpretation, either על מות is understood as = "beyond dying," or עַל is taken as = אַל so that אל מות (cf. Prov 12:28) would have to be translated as: "where there is no dying." The explanation added speaks in favor of the latter understanding. — The same is found in Lev. Rab. 11 (113C); in the other parallel passages, the אתנסיא is more or less distorted, see y. Meg. 2.73B.36; y. Moʿed Qaṭ. 3.83B.54 and Midr. Eccl. 1:11 (10A); in the last passage the name Aquila is written עֲקִילוֹס.

Sometimes the Greek translation word is not invoked but rather its Hebrew equivalent. Jerusalem Talmud Qiddušin 1.59A.9: R. Yose (= Asi [ca. 300]) said in the name of R. Yohanan († 279), "Aquila, the proselyte, translated the words 'And she is a maidservant intended for a man' (Lev 19:20) before R. Aqiba with 'Encountered before a man' כתושה לפני איש (= slept with by a man)." ‖ Genesis Rabbah 21 (14B): "And a holy one said to someone לפלמוני, who then spoke" (Dan 8:13). R. Huna (ca. 350) said, "'To a certain one' לפלנייה (is what לפלמוני means). Aquila translated it as 'לפנימי' (= 'to the innermost one'): this is the first man whose inward part was from that of the angels of service (in the closest proximity to God). — Levy and Krauß want to recover the Greek πνεῦμα in פנימי.[243] This is hardly correct, since the clarifying words "inner part of the angels of service" make sense only if פנימי is intended with the meaning "the innermost one." — The LXX simply retained פלמוני with its τῷ φελμουνί.

h. Genesis Rabbah 1 (2D): ("In the beginning God created" [Gen 1:1].) R. Judan (ca. 350) said in the name of Aquila אקילס, "It befits this one (namely God) to be called 'God.' According to the custom that rules in the world, a king of flesh and blood is glorified in a city even before he has built public or private baths for it; first he mentions his name and at the end his work קטיזמה (= κτίσμα). Yet the Only One works for the world first and then is glorified." — The saying is occasioned by the word sequence in Gen 1:1: first comes the verb ברא, and then God's name follows אלהים. — See further the remarks of Aquila in the citations in n. *e.*

i. אונקלוס הגר; see this designation in t. Kelim B. Bat. 2.4 and t. Miqw. 6.3 in n. *n*; t. Šabb. 7.18 in n. *o*; b. B. Bat. 99A in n. *p*; t. Demai 6.13 and t. Ḥag. 3.3 in n. *q*; tractate Semaḥot 8 at § John 19:39.

k. אנקלוס בר קְלוֹנִיקוֹס; see b. Giṭ. 56B in n. *m*. — אנקלוס בר קְלוֹנִימוֹס; see b. ʿAbod. Zar. 11A in n. *l*.

---

243. Levy, *Chaldäisches Wörterbuch*, 4:64B; Samuel Krauß, *Griechische und lateinische Lehnwörter im Talmud, Midrasch und Targum* (Berlin: S. Calvary & Co., 1898), 2:460.

l. Babylonian Talmud ʿAbodah Zarah 11A: Onkelos, the son of Qalonymos, had converted to Judaism איגייר (= had become a proselyte). The emperor (Hadrian) sent out a horde of Romans to him. He drew them close by passages of Scripture, and then they became proselytes. He again sent out a horde of Romans to him and said to them, "Do not say the smallest things to him (do not let yourselves be drawn into a discussion with him)!" When they had taken him and gone away (with him), he said to them, "I want to tell you something from ordinary life: A court official carries the (offering) fire before the imperial palace commander, and he before the *dux* (commander of the provincials), and he before the proconsul (ἡγεμών, *praeses provinciae*), and he before the commander of the imperial headquarters (κόμης, *comes*); does this latter one carry the fire before ordinary people?" They answered him, "No!" He said to them, "God bore the fire before the Israelites; as it says, 'Yahweh went before them by day …' (Exod 13:21)." Then they became proselytes. Then he sent another horde out to him. He said to them, "Do not talk with him about anything!" When they had taken him and went away (with him), he caught sight of a door post capsule (mezuzah); he laid his hand on it and said to them, "What is this?" They said to him, "You tell us!" He said to them, "According to the custom of the world a king of flesh and blood sits inside and his servants guard him outside; and behold, while his servants are inside, God guards them outside; as it says, 'Yahweh will watch over your going out and your coming in now and forever' (Ps 121:8)." They became proselytes. He no longer sent anyone out to him.

m. Babylonian Talmud Giṭṭin 56B: Onkelos, the son of Qaloniqos, the son of Titus' sister, wanted to become a proselyte. He went, made Titus arise by necromancy, and said to him, "Who is esteemed in that (the hereafter) world?" He answered him, "Israel!" "How is it that a person should join with them? …" (See the whole passage in the excursus "Sheol, Gehenna, and the Garden of Eden," II, #8, n. *o*).

n. Tosefta Kelim Baba Batra 2.4 (592): If they are hollowed out so that they (in their deepened or hollowed out place) can take something, however much, the ladle with which the priests mix the dough (combine the flour with the water) and also the cover (? חפית) of a pot are unclean; but if not, they are clean. It once happened that the cook of the proselyte Onkelos set bread (on a pot cover) before Rabban Gamaliel (II), and 85 elders sat there (in the house of Onkelos as guests). Rabban Gamaliel took it (the cover) and observed it. Then he gave it to his neighbor and this one in turn to his neighbor. When he saw that they said nothing about it, Rabban Gamaliel took a thread from a towel of the student who sat before him, and he stretched it out about it, and it became clear that it had been hollowed out. Then he declared it unclean. ‖ Tosefta Miqwaʾot 6.3 (658): It once happened that Rabban Gamaliel (II) and the proselyte Onkelos came to Ashkelon, and Rabban Gamaliel took an immersion bath in a bath house while the proselyte Onkelos took one in the sea. R. Joshua b. Qabosai (ca. 120, a son-in-law of R. Aqiba) said, "I was with them, and Rabban Gamaliel took an immersion bath only in the sea."

o. Tosefta Šabbat 7.18 (118): One may organize a funeral fire in the case of kings, and this is not among the (forbidden) Amoritic (= pagan) customs; for it says, "In peace you will die, and as for your fathers … they will light funeral fires for you" (Jer 34:5): And just as funeral fires are lit in the case of kings, so too in the case of the patriarchs נְשִׂיאִים, but not in the case of private persons הדיוטות. What should one light in his case? His bed (bier) and all his personal effects. It happened when Rabban Gamaliel the Elder died that the proselyte Onkelos burned more than 70 *minas* for him. – The same is found in b. ʿAbod. Zar. 11A.

p. A report about the placement of the cherubim above the ark of the covenant is connected with his name in a baraita in b. B. Bat. 99A: The proselyte Onkelos said, "The cherubim (above the ark of the covenant) were 'a work of sculpture' (2 Chr 3:10), and their faces were turned sideways מְצוּהָדִין, as when a student says goodbye to his teacher."

q. Tosefta Demai 6.13 (57): The proselyte Onkelos received his portion (in his father's inheritance) from his brothers. He decided concerning himself difficultly and cast his portion into the Dead Sea. – According to m. Demai 6.10 a proselyte was allowed to accede to the inheritance with the things from the estate of his gentile father which did not have any connection to idolatry. Onkelos thus made no use of this right, but rather did away with his inheritance. ‖ Tosefta Ḥagigah 3.3 (236): The proselyte Onkelos ate all his life (his ordinary food) according to the measure of the purity regulations that applied to the consumption of what is holy (i.e., he ate his profane food according to the purity regulations that applied to the priests concerning the consumption of the offering).

r. The debate of Aquila with R. Eliezer and R. Joshua about the recompense of a proselyte (see the passages in n. *d*) plays out in TanḥB לך לך § 6 (32A) between the proselyte Onkelos and an elder. – While in t. Demai 6.13 (see the passage in n. *q*) the proselyte Onkelos is the one who does away with his paternal inheritance, in y. Demai 6.25D.34 the very same thing is narrated about the proselyte Aquila. – See also the variant אונקלוס in Tanḥ. משפטים in n. *e*.

s. In n. *g*, Pesiq. 84B discussed how Aquila translated רקמה in Ezek 16:10 with ποικιλτόν. The parallel passage Midr. Lam. 1:1 (42B) reads instead: "Onkelos translated ...."

t. Babylonian Talmud Megillah 3A: R. Jeremiah (ca. 320)—it has also been said R. Hiyya b. Abba (ca. 280)— said, "The proselyte Onkelos said (authored) the targum to the Torah (i.e., to the Pentateuch) on the basis of the interpretation of R. Eliezer and of R. Joshua. Jonathan b. Uzziel (a contemporary of Jesus) said the targum to the prophets on the basis of the interpretation of Haggai, Zechariah, and Malachi." – Alongside the Aramaic Prophets Targum Jonathan b. Uzziel, here the targum to the Torah of the proselyte Onkelos can refer only to the Aramaic Pentateuch targum, which subsequently was called, generally, the Targum Onkelos. Yet, the worth of the tradition relayed in b. Meg. 3A is shown by the parallel passage that is presented above in n. *c* from y. Meg. 1.71C.9. According to the latter, the saying of R. Jeremiah and R. Hiyya b. Abba is not about an Aramaic targum at all, but rather about the Greek translation of the Bible by Aquila. Due to a misunderstanding, the anonymous tradent of b. Meg. 3A reinterpreted Aquila's Greek translation as Onkelos' Aramaic targum. Thus, he became the originator of the erroneous opinion that the Aramaic targum to the Pentateuch in circulation at his time was authored by the proselyte Onkelos. In this way the name of Onkelos became tied with a writing with which the historical proselyte Aquila, alias Onkelos, in fact had not the slightest to do.

16:20: With a holy kiss.

On "kiss" see § Matt 26:49. — In addition to the passage adduced there (Gen. Rab. 70 [45B]), we may add the further parallels Exod. Rab. 5 (70C); Midr. Ruth 1:14 (128A) and Midr. Sam. 14 § 5 (45A).

16:21: With my hand.

See § Rom 16:22, n. *b*.

16:22: Maran atha.

μαρὰν ἀθά is a transcription of the Aramaic מָרַן אֲתָא = "our Lord is coming." — If one wishes to understand it as an imperative, the Aramaic would have had to presuppose either מָרַנָא תָא "our Lord, come!" (against this, though, is the Greek spelling of the two words); or מָרַן אֲתָא "our Lord, come!" — Other interpretations include the following: α. μαρὰν ἀθά (synonymous with the previous ἀνάθεμα, see § Rom 9:3 and § 1 Cor 12:3) = שֵׁם אֲתָא "the name (Yahweh, God) is coming" = שָׁמַתָּא "ban." Yet breaking up the word שַׁמַּתָּא into שֵׁם אֲתָא cannot be proven in rabbinic literature; here we find in b. Moʿed Qaṭ. 17A only the following haggadic interpretation of the word: What does שמתא (ban) mean? Rab († 247) said, "Death is there" שָׁם מִיתָה; Samuel († 254) said, "May he be a devastation" שְׁמָמָה יִהְיֶה. — β. μαρὰν ἀθά = Aram. מָרַן אָתָא "our Lord is the sign," according to Klostermann, a formula of offering during the brotherly kiss.[244]

244. August Klostermann, *Probleme im Aposteltexte neu erörtert* (Gotha: Friedrich Andreas Perthes, 1883), 220.

The Second Letter of Paul to the Corinthians

1:3 A: The Father of compassion.

R. Meir (ca. 150) once presented God's compassion (οἰκτιρμοί = רַחֲמִים) as God's cosuffering in the following way.

Mishnah Sanhedrin 6.5: "A hanged man is a curse of God קִלְלַת אֱלֹהִים" (Deut 21:23). R. Meir said, "When a person suffers pain מצטער (as the criminal during hanging), what expression does the Shekinah (divinity) use? It is light קַלַּנִי (interpretation of קִלְלַת in Deut 21:23) on my head, it is light קלני on my arm! (A euphemism for: 'It is too heavy for me on my head, it is too heavy for me on my arm!') If God thus suffers pain מצטער because of the blood of the godless that is shed, how much more because of the blood of the righteous!" — R. Meir thus interprets Deut 21:23 to mean: "A hanged man is a heavy pain for God." — See the numerous variants on the passage in Hermann L. Strack's *Sanhedrin-Makkoth*.[245] ‖ Babylonian Talmud Sanhedrin 46B: How does he (R. Meir) interpret (קללת in Deut 21:23 with his קַלַּנִי)? Abbayye († 338/39) said, "Like one who says, 'It is not light!' קַל לֵית (קללת is thus interpreted by separating the word)." Raba († 352) responded to him, "In that case he should have said, 'My head is heavy for me, my arm is heavy for me!'" Rather, Raba said, "Like one who says, 'The world is light for me קִיל לִי' (euphemistically = the world is too heavy or unbearable for me)." — A parallel without authorial attribution is found in y. Sanh. 6.23D.42.

1:3 B: And God of all comfort.

In b. Ketub. 8B.27, Resh Laqish (ca. 250) says at the funeral service for the deceased son of R. Hiyya b. Abba to his interpreter R. Judah b. Nahman, "Speak a word (of comfort) concerning the mourners!" He began and said, "Our brothers, who are wearied and bowed down by this grief, direct your heart to examine this: this exists (remains) forever; a path has existed since the six days of creation; many have drunk, many will drink; the drink of those who come later is just like the drink of those who come earlier. Our brothers, may the Lord of comforts בַּעַל נֶחָמוֹת comfort you! Blessed be the one who comforts those who mourn!"

1:7: As you are companions of suffering, so too of comfort.

See b. Taʿan. 11A at § Rom 12:15.

1:9: The condemnation of death.

ἀπόκριμα = אֱיפּוֹפָסִן (ἀπόφασις); see y. Soṭah 7.21D.33 at § Rom 1:20 E, n. *e*; see also § Rom 5:18.

---

245. Strack, *Sanhedrin-Makkoth*, 20*.

1:11: Intercede for us.

On interceding for others, see y. Šabb. 2.5B.25 at § Acts 27:9, #2; b. Ber. 34B at § John 4:47ff.; y. Hor. 3.48A.39 at § Rom 15:26, #2; see also § Jas 5:16 B.

1:12 A: The witness of our conscience.

On συνείδησις see § Rom 2:15 B, #2.

1:12 B: Not in fleshly wisdom.

On σάρκινος and σαρκικός see § 1 Cor 3:1, 3.

1:16: To Judea.

Ἰουδαία probably in the broader sense = land of Israel. — In rabbinic literature יְהוּדָה is a designation only for the province Judea (see examples at § Matt 4:12, #1), not for the whole Jewish land; see the names of the latter at § Matt 2:20.

1:17: So that with me yes should be yes and no, no?

See § Matt 5:37. — The meaning of the question emerges from verses 18f.

1:22 A: (God) who has also sealed us.

Both σφραγίζειν and חָתַם are used concerning persons.

See b. Roš Haš. 16B at § Rom 5:18 and § Matt 1:19, #1, n. *a.* ‖ Tosefta Berakot 7.13 (16): Blessed be the one who ... sealed חתם his (Isaac's) descendants with the mark of the covenant (circumcision). ‖ The seal of God is חתם. See y. Sanh. 1.18A.55 with parallels at § John 1:14, #2, final paragraph.

1:22 B: (God) who put the down-payment of the Spirit in our hearts.

ἀραβών (ἀῤῥαβών), a Semitic word that came to be commonly used among the Greeks via the Phoenicians, corresponds to the biblical עֵרָבוֹן "pledge," "down-payment." Already the LXX in Gen 38:17, 18, 20 translated ערבון with ἀῤῥαβών. Yet, in the passages named, Tg. Onk. and Tg. Yer. I render ערבון with מִשְׁכּוֹנָא "pledge," although in Aramaic עַרְבוֹנָא is also found with the meaning "pledge"; see, for example, b. Šabb. 105B. — In commercial life, it is the recipient, the buyer, who gives a pledge for the payment to be rendered to the one giving or selling. So says R. Aqiba († ca. 135) in a figurative sense in m. ʾAbot 3.16: הַכֹּל נָתוּן בָּעֵרָבוֹן "everything is given on pledge or bail." — He means that everything someone possesses is bestowed on him by God; yet, with the soul as ערבון or a pledge, humanity is liable for the correct use of the gifts and goods bestowed. — The converse case is also known, where the giver gives the recipient a pledge. In Midr. Esth. 3:10 (97A) it says, "The rabbis said, 'Ahasuerus hated the Israelites more than the wicked Haman.' According to the usual custom the buyer

לָקוֹחַ gives the seller a pledge ערבון, but here (Esth 3:10) the seller gave a pledge; this is what 'Then the king removed his signet ring from his hand and gave it to Haman' (Esth 3:10) means." – The following legend deals with a pledge that God gave.

Babylonian Talmud Pesaḥim 118B: R. Nathan (ca. 160) said, "The words 'The truth of Yahweh lasts forever' (Ps 117:2) were spoken by the fish in the sea." This aligns with the opinion of Rab Huna († 297). For Rab Huna said, "The Israelites of that generation (who went out of Egypt) were of little faith." It also aligns with what Rabbah b. Mari (ca. 320) said in a presentation, "What does 'They were recalcitrant at the sea, as the Sea of Reeds' (Ps 106:7) mean? It teaches that the Israelites were recalcitrant in that hour and said, 'As we rose up on one side (out of the sea), so too the Egyptians will rise up on the other side!' Then God said to the (angel) prince of the sea, 'Spit them (the Egyptians) out onto dry land!' He answered him, 'Lord of the world, is there any servant to whom his lord gives a gift and then takes it back from him?' God said to him, 'I will give you one and a half (times as many) as them (the Egyptians to be spit out land).' It was said to him, 'Lord of the world, is there a servant who can ask his lord (to fulfill a promise that has been given)?' He said to him, 'The stream Kishon shall be surety for me.' Immediately he spit them onto the dry land, and the Israelites came and saw them; as it says, 'And Israel saw the Egyptians dead on the shore of the sea' (Exod 14:30). What is going on with 'one and a half times as many as them'? See, with pharaoh it is written, '600 choice chariots' (Exod 14:7); and with Sisera it is written, '900 (so 1.5 times as many) cast-iron chariots' (Judg 4:3). When Sisera came, it says, 'The stars from heaven fought' (Judg 5:20). When the stars of heaven came down against them ..., they came down to refresh themselves and to bathe in the stream Kishon. Then God said to the stream Kishon, 'Go and deliver your pledge ערבונך (the armies of Sisera that were given by me as a pledge).' Immediately the stream Kishon swept them away and cast them into the sea (into the territory of the prince of the sea); as it says, 'The stream Kishon swept them away, the primordial stream' (Judg 5:21). What does 'primordial stream' mean? A stream that he made a surety from time immemorial. In that hour the fish of the sea rose up and said, 'The truth of Yahweh lasts forever!'"

2:4: Trepidation (affliction) of heart.

συνοχὴ καρδίας, see צָרוֹת לְבָבִי "the afflictions (narrows) of my heart" (Ps 25:17), from צָרַר "compress, constrain." – Septuagint: αἱ θλίψεις τῆς καρδίας μου. – Targum: עָקְתִין דִּלְבָבִי (from עוק "to be narrow, compressed") = the afflictions of my heart. – συνοχή may be even close to מְצוּקוֹתַי "my constraints" that is also found in Ps 25:17, a word that comes from צוק "to be narrow." – Septuagint: αἱ ἀνάγκαι μου. – Targum: שְׁנוּקַי "my chokings, anxieties." – צַר and מְצוּקָה are also found alongside each other in Job 15:24. – Septuagint: ἀνάγκη δὲ καὶ θλῖψις. – Targum: עָקָא וּמְעִיקָא "tribulation and affliction." – Septuagint Job 30:3 rendered שׁוֹאָה "devastation, destruction" very freely with συνοχή.

2:7: Lest I be devoured.

καταποθῆναι = נִבְלַע. — In Gen. Rab. 94 (59D) Benjamin says, "I gave my sons names with a view to what happened to him (Joseph): Bela בֶּלַע (Gen 46:21), because he (Joseph) was devoured (torn) away from me שנבלע ממני." See also § 1 Cor 15:54.

2:12: When a door was opened for me (see § 1 Cor 16:9).

2:13 A: I did not find rest for my spirit (see § 1 Cor 16:18).

2:13 B: Since I did not find my brother Titus.

1. ἀδελφός, see § Matt 5:22, B and § Acts 23:1.

2. εὑρεῖν = find, meet. The Aramaic שְׁכַח, *aphel* אַשְׁכַּח is used with the same meaning in rabbinic literature.

Babylonian Talmud Qiddušin 70A: (Rab Judah [† 299]) came and met him (Rab Nahman [† 320]) אשכחיה, as he made a rail. (See the continuation of the passage at § John 5:2, #3, n. *a*.) ‖ Babylonian Talmud Yebamot 110B: Rab Nahman († 320) said, "I met Rab Ada b. Ahaba and Rab Hanna, his son-in-law, אשכחיה, as they sat at the market of Pumbedita and raised questions (objections)." ‖ Babylonian Talmud Baba Meṣiʿa 85B: "I (Rab Habiba b. Surmaqi [4th century]) saw that scholar to whom (the prophet) Elijah was to report שְׁכִיחַ (i.e., to whom he used to report)." — See the whole passage at § Luke 23:43, #3, C, n. *c*, comment. ‖ See b. Sanh. 98A at § Luke 24:26, I, #4, n. *e*.

2:13 C: To Macedonia (see § Acts 16:9 B).

2:15 A: For we are the aroma of Christ for God.

Genesis Rabbah 34 (21A): "And Yahweh smelled the pleasing odor" וַיָּרַח יהוה אֶת־רֵיחַ הַנִּיחֹחַ (Gen 8:21).[246] He smelled the odor ריח of our father Abraham, as it will have arisen from (Nimrod's) furnace, and he smelled the odor ריח of Hananiah, Mishael, and Azariah, as they will have arisen from the furnace.... He smelled the odor ריח of the generation of the (Hadrianic) religious persecution. ‖ Targum Song of Songs 7:9: "The name of Daniel, Hananiah, Mishael, and Azariah will be heard on all the earth, and their odor ריחיהין will spread like the odor of the apples of the garden of Eden." ‖ Targum Song of Songs 7:14: "If it is the will from before Yahweh to redeem his people from exile, it will be said to the king, the Messiah, 'Already the time of exile has ended and the merit of the righteous has become sweet before me like the odor of balsam כְּרֵיחַ בַּלְסָמוֹן ...; now then, receive the kingdom (the kingship) that I have preserved for you.'" ‖ See Midr. Song. 1:3 (85A.) at § Matt 26:7 A. ‖ See further TanḥB לך לך § 3 (30A); Tanḥ. לך לך 15A, B; Midr. Song. 1:3 (84B); Tanḥ. יתרו 86B; TanḥB יתרו § 2 (35A).

---

246. S-B: Septuagint Gen 8:21: καὶ ὠσφράνθη κύριος ὁ θεὸς ὀσμὴν εὐωδίας. — Targum Onkelos and Yerušalmi I render the verse as "And Yahweh accepted his offering with pleasure בְּרַעֲוָא" in order to avoid the anthropomorphism.

2:15 B: And among those who are perishing.

We can compare the rabbinic passages where joy is attributed to God at the demise of the godless; see, for example, SNum 18:8 § 117 (37A); SDeut 32:36 § 326 at § Luke 15:7 A. ‖ Midrash Psalm 104 § 27 (224B): R. Simeon b. Abba (ca. 280) said, "From the beginning of the book (of Psalms) up till here, there are 104 psalms; but 'Hallelujah!' is not written in them until the godless are completely destroyed from them world. It says, 'May the godless be no more! Bless Yahweh, my soul! Hallelujah! ' (Ps 104:35). And what is the reason? 'When the wicked perish, rejoicing reigns' (Prov 11:10)." — See b. Ber. 9B below. — Predominantly, though, in agreement with Ezek 18:32; 33:11, the view was that God took no joy in the demise of the godless; see § 2 Pet 3:9 B.

2:16: To the one, an odor from death to death, but to the other an odor from life to life.

In a similar expression in rabbinic literature סַם, Aram. סַמָּא = powder, spice, medicine, remedy is used instead of ὀσμή "odor."

A baraita in b. Taʿan. 7A: R. Benaiah (ca. 220) said, "To everyone who occupies himself with the Torah for its sake (without self-seeking ulterior aims), it becomes a medicine of life סַם חַיִּים; for it says, She (Wisdom = Torah) is a tree of life to those who seize it' (Prov 3:18); furthermore it says, 'There will be healing for your navel' (Prov 3:8); and furthermore it says, 'Whoever finds me has found life' (Prov 8:35). However, to everyone who occupies himself with the Torah not for its own sake, it will became a medicine of death סַם הַמָּוֶת; for it says, 'Let my teaching drip like rain' (Deut 32:2); and the dripping עריפה means nothing except killing, as it says, 'They shall break וערפו the neck of the cow there in the valley' (Deut 21:4)." — The same is found without the image of medicine in SDeut 32:2 § 306 (131B); see § Rom 3:1f., D, middle ‖ In SDeut 11:18 § 45 (82B), שַׂמְתֶּם in Deut 11:18 is interpreted = "make it a שם" = סם "remedy"; see the passage at § Rom 3:1f., D, middle. — In the parallel in b. Qidd. 30B, שַׂמְתֶּם is dissolved into סם תָּם = "a perfect remedy." ‖ Babylonian Talmud Yoma 72B: R. Joshua b. Levi (ca. 250) said, "What does 'This is the Torah that Moses set before שָׂם the children of Israel' (Deut 4:44) mean? If he (a person) merits it, it will become for him a medicine of life סם חיים; if he does not merit it, it will become for him a remedy of death סַם מִיתָה." And this is what Raba († 352) said, "If it is handled rightly, it is a remedy of life סַמָּא דְחַיּוֵי; if it is not handled rightly, it is a remedy of death סַמָּא דְמוֹתָא."[247] — Raba's saying is somewhat different in b. Šabb. 88B.19. ‖ Babylonian Talmud ʿErubin 54A: R. Judah b. Hiyya (ca. 240) said, "Come and see that the manner of flesh and blood is not as God's manner. The manner of flesh and blood is that one person gives another a medicine סַם; for one it is good and for another it is bad. Yet it is not so with God: he gave the Torah to Israel as a medicine of life סם חיים for the whole body; as it says, 'And healing for his whole body'

247. S-B: Raba once also used תֶּבֶל "spice" basically synonymously with סַם, סַמָּא. Babylonian Talmud Baba Batra 16A: God created the evil inclination, but he also created the Torah against it as a spice תַּבְלִין (= remedy).

(Prov 4:22)." ‖ Leviticus Rabbah 16 (116B): "This is the law for the leper" (Lev 14:2). This is what is written, "Who is the man who desires life?" (Ps 34:13). It once happened that a spice merchant was peddling in the cities that are around Sepphoris, and he called out and said, "Who wants to buy a medicine for life סם חיים?" People paid attention to him (literally: they looked at him). R. Yannai (ca. 225) was sitting and interpreting the literal sense of Scripture in his dining room. He heard the man as he called out, "Who wants a medicine for life?" He said to him, "Come up here and sell to me!" He answered him, "You do not need it, nor does anyone like you." He pressed him. Then he came up to him, pulled out a book of Psalms and showed him the verse: "Who is the man who desires life?" What is written after that? "Keep your tongue from evil …; turn away from evil and do good!" (Ps 34:14f.). R. Yannai said to him, "Solomon too proclaims this and says, 'Whoever guards his mouth and his tongue guards his soul from dangers (Prov 21:23)." R. Yannai said (probably later to his students), "My whole life I have read this verse (Ps 34:13) without knowing what the simple literal meaning was getting at until this spice merchant came and taught me who the man is who desires life. Therefore, Moses warned the Israelites and said to them, 'This is the law for the leper,' the law for the one who brings out a bad name (bad reputation = slander) המוציא שם רע (notarikon interpretation of המצורע 'the leper.' Leprosy was generally considered to be a punishment for slander.)." — The same is found with multiple variations in TanḥB מצורע § 5 (23A). — A similar narrative where the term סם is not used is connected with the name R. Alexandrai (ca. 270) in b. ʿAbod. Zar. 19B. ‖ See the additional passages Deut. Rab. 1 (195C); Midr. Song. 2:3 (96B); Lev. Rab. 1 (106A); Gen. Rab. 61 (38D); Num. Rab. 11 (162D); Midr. Ps. 1 § 5 (3B); Tanḥ. לך לך 16A. ‖ סם המות as a medicine for death is frequently simple poison, so m. Ḥul. 3.5; Tg. Yer. I Gen. 24:33, Gen 40:1; Tg. Jer. 11:19; Tg. 1 Chr. 1:20.

2:17: Who huckster the word of God.

Anyone who hucksters ὁ καπηλεύων God's word wants to derive benefit for himself from proclaiming the word like a huckster κάπηλος from selling his wares. He achieves this purpose above all by proclaiming the word in a way that pleases the hearers' old, natural man. Rabbinic sayings are also directed against both; see the citations at § Matt 10:8 B, n. *a* and § Matt 23:8 A; see also b. Ketub. 105B at § Matt 18:15, n. *e*, toward the end.

3:1: Letters of recommendation (see § Acts 9:2 A, #1).

3:2: Written into our hearts (see verse 3).

3:3 A: Not with ink.

τὸ μέλαν "the black," "the ink" is sometimes found with the same meaning in rabbinic literature as well in the form מֵילָן, מְלַנְיָה (= μελάνη).[a] The most common term for "ink" in rabbinic literature, though, is דְּיוֹ (already Jer 36:18),[b] Aram. דְּיוֹתָא[c] (Gesenius connects this etymologically with דָּוָה "to flow slowly," while Levy thinks of דִּיהָ "to be faint, dark"[248]). The production of *deyo* occurred in a relatively simple way. Soot from the smoke of burning oil served as its main component; the soot of olive oil was considered the best. The soot was mixed with olive oil and some balsamic resin and then stored to dry.[d] When needed, the mass was dissolved in water[e] and the *deyo* was ready to use.[249] R. Meir (ca. 150), who was a לִבְלָר (*libellarius*), that is, a Torah scroll scribe by trade, introduced an innovation by adding water of copper vitriol to old usable ink קַנְקַנְתּוֹס, קַלְקַנְתּוֹס (= χάλκανθος). Thereby the ink acquired the ability to bind more closely with the writing material (paper, parchment, etc.), and the durability of the writing correspondingly increased. Yet thereby there was also the possibility that the causticity of the copper vitriol would attack the writing material and gradually eat away at it. This danger appears to have been actualized, which early on triggered a certain opposition to the improved *deyo*. The prescription in Num 5:23 in particular was referred to, according to which the imprecations against the woman suspected of adultery had to be written with fadeable ink, which could simply not be done with R. Meir's ink.[f] However, the opposition cannot have lasted long. Already in the Tosefta, a passage is found that makes the addition of קנקנתוס appear to be completely taken for granted.[g]

a. Genesis Rabbah 1 (2B): R. Huna (ca. 350) and R. Jeremiah (ca. 320) said in the name of R. Samuel b. Isaac (ca. 300), "... Like a king ..., who said, 'Take this ink and this quill מֵילָנִין וְקַלְמִין for my son!'" See the passage at § Eph 1:4, #3. ‖ ʿArukh[250] presented two citations from Yelamedenu; in one it says: מילן וקלמין "ink and quill" and in the other שהירה היא כמילניה "it is black like ink."

b. Jeremiah 36:18: "I wrote (the words) on the book with ink בַּדְּיוֹ." — The LXX left בדיו untranslated. — Targum: "I wrote on the book בִּדְיוֹתָא."

c. Mishnah ʾAbot 4.20: Elisha b. Abbuyah (the apostate, ca. 120) said, "Whoever studies as a child, what is he like? The ink לִדְיוֹ that is written on new paper נְיָר. And whoever learns as an old man, what is he like? The ink that is written on worn down paper (from which earlier writing has been wiped off)." ‖ See tractate Sopherim 16 § 8 and ʾAbot R. Nat. 25 at § John 21:25. ‖ Genesis Rabbah 58 (37A): R. Eleazar (ca. 270) said, "How many (bulks of) ink דְּיוֹת (plural) have been poured out, how many quills קולמוסין (= κάλαμος) have been broken to write 'the sons of Heth' ten times (in Gen 23)!" ‖ Babylonian Talmud Niddah 20A: (Black blood, one of the five kinds of blood that are distinguished in m. Nid. 2.6f. in the case of the woman, is) black like black dye חֲרֵת (e.g., boot blackness). Rabbah bar Rab Huna († 322) said, "Like black dye that they call (in Palestine) דְּיוֹ ink (blackness). In a baraita it has likewise been taught: Black like black dye חרת and the soot שְׁהוֹר that is called ink דיו. But then they

248. Levy, *Chaldäisches Wörterbuch*, 1:393A.

249. S-B: From the method of production we also realize that the *deyo* was less of a liquid ink than in our sense and more of a sticky type of ink.

250. See J. Levy, *Neuhebräisches und Chaldäisches Wörterbuch über die Talmudim und Midraschim* (Leipzig: F. A. Brockhaus, 1883), 3:102B.

should have said 'ink' דיו! If it said 'ink,' I might think, 'like the thinness of the ink כְּפִכְהוּתָא דְּדְיוֹתָא (like the upper, brighter mass of the ink)'; he thus makes us hear: 'like the blackness of the ink דִּדְיוֹתָא (read חֲרָתָא) כי חרותא (i.e., as deeply black as the sediment of the ink).'" – See a further example of the Aram. דיותא in n. *b*.

d. Babylonian Talmud Šabbat 23A: R. Joshua b. Levi (ca. 250) said, "All oils are good (useable) for ink לְדְיוֹ, but olive oil is among the choicest." The question has been raised by them (the scholars): To mix (knead the soot) or to make the smoke (for the purpose of making the smoke)? Come and hear! For Rab Samuel b. Zutra taught as a tannaitic tradition: "All oils are good for ink דיו, but olive oil is among the choicest both for mixing (kneading) and to make smoke." Rab Samuel b. Zutra taught as a tannaitic tradition: "All kinds of smoke כל העשנים are good for ink לדיו, but the smoke from olive oil is among the choicest." (Rashi on b. Šabb. 23A cites the following passage from the responses of the Geonim: "A glass jar would be filled with smoke from olive oil until it became black. Then the blackness (the soot) was scraped off and some olive oil was added and mixed with it and left to dry in the sun; then it was pulverized into ink לתוך הדיו.") Rab Huna († 297) said, "All resins are good for ink לדיו, but resin from a balsam tree is the best of all."

e. Mishnah Šabbat 1.5: The school of Shammai said: "(On a day of preparation for the Sabbath), ink (soot) דְּיוֹ, dye stuff, and vetches פַּרְשָׁנִין (according to Dalman, camel lentil, *ervum ervilia*) not be softened, unless they can be sufficiently softened when it is still day (so before the arrival of the Sabbath)." Yet the school of Hillel allowed this. – On softening the mass of ink with water, see also t. Šabb. 11.18 (126) in n. *g*.

f. Mishnah Soṭah 2.4: The priest may not write (the imprecations against the woman suspected of adultery in Num 5:19–22) with resin (chicle) nor with copper vitriol קנקנתום nor with anything else that leaves a trace, but rather with ink בדיו; for it says, "And he shall wipe out" (Num 5:23), so a writing that can be wiped out. Jerusalem Talmud Soṭah 2.18A.60: "And (the priest) shall write" (Num 5:23); with ink בדיו or with red dye or with resin (chicle) or with copper vitriol? Scripture teaches: "And he shall wipe out" (Num 5:23). If he is supposed to wipe out, then with drinks or fruit juices? Scripture teaches: "He shall write" (Num 5:23). How so? A writing that can be wiped out. And what kind is that? In which there is no copper vitriol. Yet in a baraita it has been taught: If he wipes out (the imprecations not from a sheet of parchment written ad hoc, but rather) from a Torah scroll, it is valid (and ink without further specification, with which the Torah scrolls are written, is the kind to which copper vitriol has been added! Why is the copper vitriol forbidden above?)! It should be interpreted according to the expert in the tradition who has taught: R. Meir (ca. 150) said, "As long as we studied under R. Ishmael († ca. 135), we did not add any copper vitriol to the ink בדיו" (i.e., the baraita about wiping out the Soṭah parashah from a Torah scroll stems from a time when the ink used to write Torah scrolls was not mixed with copper vitriol). ‖ Babylonian Talmud 'Erubin 13A: Rab Judah († 299) said that Samuel († 254) said in the name of R. Meir, "When I (R. Meir) studied under R. Aqiba († ca. 135), I put copper vitriol קנקנתום in the ink הַדְּיוֹ, and he said not a word to me. When I came to R. Ishmael († ca. 135), he said to me, 'My son, what is your occupation?' I said to him, 'I am a (Torah scroll) scribe.' He said to me, 'My son, be careful in your occupation; for your occupation is an occupation with heaven (= with heavenly or divine things); perhaps you will let one letter drop out or you will write one letter too many, and then you would be found as one who destroys the whole world.' I said to him, 'I have something, and copper vitriol is its name, which I put in the ink.' He answered me, 'Is copper vitriol put into ink? Does the Torah not say, "(The priest) shall write and wipe out" (Num 5:23), so a writing that can be wiped out?'" — The opposed tradition, according to which adding copper vitriol was forbidden by R. Aqiba but allowed by R. Ishmael, comes first. — After that there follows a mediating tradition with the following content. In a baraita it has been taught: R. Judah (ca. 150) said that R. Meir said, "For everything copper vitriol is put into ink, except the section about the woman suspected of adultery." — A parallel to the whole is found in b. Soṭah 20A.

g. Tosefta Šabbat 11.18 (126): "If (on the Sabbath) someone brings the ink הדיו (i.e., the soot powder for ink) and someone else adds the water and another person adds the copper vitriol, the last two are guilty (of transgressing the Sabbath commandment because the work is completed by them). If someone brings the copper vitriol and someone else adds the water and another person adds the ink, the last one is guilty (because he has added the main thing). If someone brings ink and another adds water ..., the latter is guilty." These are the words of Rabbi († 217?). R. Yose b. Judah (ca. 180) said, "The latter is not guilty until he mixes (for only then is the work completed)."

3:3 B: Inscribed on tablets, namely hearts of flesh.

See § Rom 2:15 A. — Here we may add Tg. Song. 4:9: "Your love, my sister, community of Israel, who is like a bride, is engraved (impressed) in the tablet of my heart."

3:6 A: Of a new covenant.

There appears to be a polemic against the idea of a new covenant in Midr. Song. 1:14 (93B); see the passage at § Luke 24:26, I, #2, n. g, second third, as well as the S-B footnote there.

3:6 B: The letter kills.

This principle is acknowledged in a certain sense in the saying of R. Yohanan († 279) in b. B. Meṣ. 30B: R. Yohanan said, "Jerusalem was destroyed only because they judged according to the justice of the Torah (i.e., according to the strict letter of the law). Should they have rendered verdicts of bowl judges (who could be bought for a bowl of food)?[251] Rather say, 'Because they rendered their verdicts on the basis of the (letter of the) law of the Torah and did not act "within the line of justice."'" — The line of justice limits whoever judges according to the letter of the law; the one who punishes more harshly than the letter of the law demands goes beyond the line of justice; whoever judges more mildly than the letter of the law proscribes, who exercises mercy instead of strict justice, remains

251. See Levy, *Chaldäisches Wörterbuch*, 3:19B.

"within the line of justice." Since the Jerusalemites failed here because they always regulated their behavior toward one another only according to the letter of the law, the destruction of their city came as a punishment upon them, so that in this case it was true: the letter of the law kills! – On the expression "within the line of justice," see also § Matt 5:41 B.

3:7 A: The ministry of death.

1. διακονία, see § 1 Cor 12:5.

2. διακονία τοῦ θανάτου. – By contrast, Tanḥ. כי תשא 114B: God engraved the tablets in order to give them words of life. – Exodus Rabbah 41 (97C): God engraved the tablets for them to give them life. – Exodus Rabbah 41 (97D): (When God wrote the tablets of the law,) he busied himself with this to give them the Torah, which is completely life. (See § 2 Cor 3:7 B, B, n. *x*.) – See also § Rom 3:1f., D.

3:7 B: In letters engraved in stones.

With these words, the apostle is thinking of the "tablets of the testimony" לֻחֹת הָעֵדוּת (Exod 31:18; LXX: πλάκες τοῦ μαρτυρίου; Tg. Onk. and Yer. I: לוּחֵי סָהֲדוּתָא) or the "tablets of the covenant" לוּחֹת הַבְּרִית (Deut 9:9; LXX: πλάκες διαθήκης; Tg. Onk. and Yer. I: לוּחֵי קְיָמָא), which, since they are made of stone, can also as a shorthand be called "tablets of stones" לוּחֹת הָאֲבָנִים (Deut 9:9; LXX: πλάκες αἱ λίθιναι; Tg. Onk.: לוּחֵי אַבְנַיָּא = "tablets of stones"; Tg. Yer. I: לוּחֵי מַרְמֵירָא = "tablets of marble"). In rabbinic literature the stone tablets of the law are most often called, depending on whether the writer is referring to the broken tablets or the tablets that remained unbroken, "the first tablets" לוחות הראשנים and the "second" or the "last tablets" לוחות השניים, or לוחות האחרונות.[a] – The legend with which the old synagogue crowned this "work of God" (Exod 32:16), "written by the finger of God" (Exod 31:18) is not as lavish or grand as would be expected. It seems all the more appropriate to compile the available material.

A. The first tablets.

They were counted among the items that had been created on the Friday of the week of creation in the dusk immediately before the arrival of the Sabbath of creation.[b] The material from which they were formed was precious sapphire;[c] according to a different opinion, they were cut out from the sun.[d] Although they were made of sapphire, they could be rolled together; this was one of the miracles by which they were continually glorified.[e] Yet the tablets were supposed to be made of stone so that the Israelites would remember that the only person who could study the Torah successfully was the one who made his jaw לְחָיַיִם (wordplay on לוחות) as hard as stone;[f] or because the death penalties that the Torah ordains were carried out by stoning most of the time; or because the tablets of the law were bestowed on the Israelites either by the merit of Jacob, who is called the "stone of Israel" in Gen 49:24, or by the merit of the temple, of which it is said, "Behold, I have established a stone on Zion ..." (Isa 28:16f.), or by the merit of the Messiah, who in Dan 2:34f., is referred to by the stone that will one day smash the image seen in the dream.[g] — The duality of the tablets of the law was also not meaningless: the two tablets were supposed to be like two witnesses between God and Israel or like two bridesmen or like two scribes for a document. Or the duality was chosen in view of (corresponding to) heaven and earth or in view of groom and bride, to the written and the oral Torah, to this and the future world.[h] — Both tablets were the same size,[i] specifically their length and width were each six handbreadths and their thickness three handbreadths;[k] according to a different opinion, they would have been six handbreadths long and only three handbreadths wide (and thick).[l] Their weight was equal to the weight of forty *seahs*; yet by a miracle their weight was carried by the writing that God's hand had engraved.[m] — On the tablets there were only the Ten Commandments[n] (the ten words עֲשֶׂרֶת הַדְּבָרִים, already Exod 34:28; LXX: οἱ δέκα λόγοι; Tg. Onk.: עַשְׂרָא פִּתְגָּמִין; Tg. Yer. I: עֲשַׂרְתֵּי דִּבּוּרַיָּא), either so that each tablet contained five commandments or each tablet contained all ten commandments.[o] Additionally, the further view sporadically appears that on each tablet the Ten Commandments would have been written twice or even four times.[p] The transcription of the commandments was "God's writing," written by the middle finger of the divine hand,[q] "engraved on the tablets" (Exod 32:16). Some supposed that the engraving completely penetrated the tablets so that the words could also be read on the back side, though with the letters in the reversed order. In the process an extraordinary thing also happened with the ס and (the final *mem*) ם, so that their center, which as a consequence of the engraving that penetrated the whole tablet lost any hold in the tablet, did not fall out but rather was held fast in it. This was a further miracle that distinguished the first tablets.[r] Everywhere here the engraving of the commandments appears as a work of God. Others, for whom this view seemed all too anthropomorphic, conceived the course of events in such a way that the ten commandments would have been engraved in the two tablets by themselves by the power of the divine voice. At the most one can assume that the finger of God somehow lent a hand to the engraving voice, perhaps as a teacher leads the hand of a writing child.[s] Always, though, the first tablets were a work of God, stemming not from earth, but rather from heaven.[t] Therefore, woe to the person who handles the Torah in a contemptible, insulting way![u] Conversely, if the Israelites had been able to dedicate themselves to these tablets, the words of the Torah would never have been forgotten by them;[v] furthermore, no nation, indeed not even death, would have ever gained authority over them; for חָרוּת עַל הַלּוּחוֹת "engraved on the tablets" read as חֵרוּת עַל הַלּוּחוֹת means: "Freedom because of (on the basis of) the tablets!"[w] Unfortunately, though, while God still sat above to engrave the tablets, the Israelites below already formed a calf for idolatry![x] – Moses had spent forty days with God to learn the Torah, but he repeatedly forgot what he learned. Finally God handed the two tablets to him as a gift.[y] In this very moment—it was on the 17th of Tammuz[z]—the people sinned with the golden calf. Then God wanted to rip the tablets out of Moses' hand; yet Moses gripped the two tablets (Deut 9:17) and tore them from God's hand. This is what the word of praise in Deut 34:10ff. refers to: "No other prophet has arisen in Israel like Moses ... with all that strong hand...." "Blessed is the hand, said God, that is stronger than I!"[aa] – According to a different opinion, the tablets themselves tried to flee from Moses' hands when they saw Israel's sin. Then Moses grabbed and seized them (Deut 9:17).[bb] A third opinion is that the writing on the tablets did in fact flee when it saw the people's idolatrous conduct and returned to the place from which it had gone out; and since this writing had carried the tablets up until that point, as the soul carries the body, now after the flight of the writing the tablets became so heavy for Moses that they fell from his hands and shattered.[cc] This is an attempt to attenuate and justify the unauthorized nature of Moses' breaking the tablets. Similar attempts are also made elsewhere.[dd] Yet, on the other hand, there is no lack of passages in which Moses is made thoroughly responsible for breaking the tablets.[ee]

B. The second tablets.

Forty days after the first tablets were broken, on the basis of Moses' intercession, God forgave the people for the sin with the golden calf and said to Moses, "Cut two stone tablets like the first!" (Exod 34:1; Deut 10:1). These second tablets had arisen in God's thoughts already in the beginning of creation.[ff] Now the day had come—it was on the 28th of Ab[gg]—when God's purpose would be realized. At the same time God revealed to Moses a sapphire quarry in his tent with the instruction to take from there the material for the second tablets.[hh] As these were like the first tablets in their material, so too in their form and their appearance.[ii] Yet their difference from each other was greater than their similarity. First, the second tablets did not come from heaven, but rather from earth; this was due to Israel's sin with the calf.[kk] – Next, the one who made the two tablets was not God but Moses. This had various reasons. Originally God had intended the second tablets only for Moses and his descendants; here it seemed proper that the maker of the tablets was also the one who received them.[ll] Additionally, Moses had been the steward with whom God had stored the first tablets as a deposit in a certain sense. But if a steward destroys a deposit, he is fully responsible for a replacement.[mm]

Finally, Moses had acted as a mediator between God and Israel; as such, he also had to be responsible for the damage that Israel's sin had caused.[nn] — Above all, though, the first and second tablets differed from each other by the content that was written on them. So (in Exod 20:12) the following words were missing on the first tablets: "So it may go well with you" יִיטַב, which are found only on the second tablets (see Deut 5:16). God did not want טוב "good" to be written on the tablets that would be smashed.[oo] The main thing, though, was this: the second tablets contained not only the Ten Commandments, but also the special regulations that went with them, halakoth, derivations from Scripture (midrash), and haggadoth[pp] (on the expressions see Strack, *Einleitung*, 4f. § 6–8). — The traditions conflict on the question of who wrote the second tablets. Sometimes the view is that they were written by Moses and signed by God.[qq] Other passages know only God as the one who did the writing.[rr] These variations are due to the interpretation of ויכתב "and he wrote" (Exod 34:28) in reference to Moses (instead of God). After Moses had spent forty days again with God (Exod 34:28), the two tablets were given to him on the 10th of Tishri, that is, on the Day of Atonement, as a sign that God forgave Israel the sin of falling away.[ss] Since then the two tablets were in Israel's possession. They were kept in the ark of the covenant; the broken tablets were also located there.[tt] That the latter were kept in a special ark of the covenant is claimed only by a tradition that appears around the end of the 2nd century.[uu] The fate of the ark of the covenant then later became the fate of the tablets of the law as well: since the destruction of the first temple, both have been lost. See the views about the whereabouts of the ark of the covenant at § Rom 3:25 A, #8. — R. Yohanan († 279) lived in the faith that the ark of the covenant exists for all eternity; he also did not doubt the endurance of the tablets of the covenant.[vv]

a. Deuteronomy Rabbah 3 (201B): Why were the first tablets לוחות הראשונות (here construed as feminine) a work of heaven and the second השניים a work of man מעשה אדם? (See the whole passage in n. *kk*). ‖ Tanḥuma עקב 8A: As the first (tablets) הראשונים were given among voices of voices (= among many thundering voices?), so were the second השניים; as the first for 60 myriads, so too the second. ‖ Additional examples can be found everywhere in the following citations.

b. See m. ʾAbot 5.6 at § 1 Cor 10:4 B; see Mek. Exod. 16:32 (59B) at § Heb 9:4, #4, n. *a*. See further b. Pesaḥ. 54A; ʾAbot R. Nat. 2 (2A.16) and Tg. Yer. 1 Num. 22:28.

c. Sifre Numbers 12:3 § 101 (27B): It says, "The tablets were a work of God" (Exod 32:16); it further says, "They saw the God of Israel and under his feet like a work of sapphire tiles" (Exod 24:10). (Scripture) compares "work" with "work": just as the work that is mentioned there (Exod 24:10) is made of sapphire, so too is the work that is mentioned here (Exod 32:16) made of sapphire. ‖ See further Tanḥ. עקב 8A in n. *o*. — See the tablets of marble above at the beginning of Tg. Yer. Deut 9:9.

d. Midrash Song of Songs 5:14 (120A): "His hands are golden rollers" גְּלִילֵי זָהָב (Song 5:14); this refers to the tablets of the covenant; as it says, "And the tablets were a work of God" (Exod 32:16).... R. Menahemah (ca. 370) said in the name of R. Abin (ca. 325), "They were cut out from the sun."

e. Midrash Song of Songs 5:14 (120A): R. Joshua b. Nehemiah (ca. 350) said, "(The tablets of the covenant) were a miracle: they could be rolled together (although they were made of sapphire)."

f. Babylonian Talmud ʿErubin 54A: R. Eleazar (ca. 270) said, "What does 'The tablets of stone' (Exod 31:18) mean? If someone himself makes his cheekbones (jaw) like a rock that is not broken, what he has learned remains with him; but if not, what he has learned does not remain with him." — Parallels without authorial attribution are found in Tanḥ. עקב 8A and Exod. Rab. 41 (97D). — See the question: Why are they called tablets of the law לוּחוֹת? Because being occupied with them happens with the cheekbones לְחִי (by loudly debating, reciting and memorizing) (Tanḥ. כי תשא 115B).

g. Tanḥuma עקב 8A: "Tablets of stone" (Exod 31:18), because most of the death penalties in the Torah happen by stoning. Or "tablets of stone" by the merit of (because of) Jacob, of whom it says, "From where the shepherd is, the stone of Israel" (Gen 49:24). Or "tablets of stone" by the merit of (because of) the sanctuary; as it says, "Behold, I have established a stone on Zion" (Isa 28:16f.). And Resh Laqish (ca. 250) said, "By the merit of (because of) the Messiah (so read instead of 'Moses'), who is called 'stone'; as it says, 'Until a stone was torn loose without (human) hands' (Dan 2:34)." — Individual elements from this can be found also in Tanḥ. כי תשא 115A; TanḥB כי תשא § 12 (56B); Exod. Rab. 41 (97D).

h. Deuteronomy Rabbah 3 (201B): Why two tablets? The rabbis said, "God said, 'They shall be witnesses between me and my children, corresponding to two witnesses, corresponding to two bridesmen, corresponding to groom and bride, corresponding to heaven and earth, corresponding to this world and the future world.'" — Parallels are found in TanḥB כי תשא § 12 (56B); Tanḥ. כי תשא 115A; Exod. Rab. 41 (97D). In Tanḥ. עקב 8A the following pairs are newly added: Corresponding to two scribes סופרים, corresponding to the two Torahs, the written and the oral Torah.

i. Exodus Rabbah 41 (97D): "Two tablets לֻחֹת of the testimony" (Exod 32:15). R. Hanina (ca. 225) said, "לחת (defective) it is written, 'the one was not bigger than the other.'" — The same is found in Tanḥ. כי תשא 115A. Tanḥuma עקב 8A adds the positive formulation: "Rather both were the same."

k. A baraita in b. Ned. 38A: "The length of the tablets was 6 and their width 6 and their thickness 3 handbreadths." — Similarly, y. Šeqal. 6.49D.17, 21, 31, 36 and b. B. Bat. 14A. — This is the opinion of R. Meir and of R. Judah (both ca. 150). — Only the length is specified as 6 handbreadths in Exod. Rab. 28 (88B).

l. Jerusalem Talmud Soṭah 8.22C.49, 63; 22D.3: Each of the tablets had a length of 6 and a width of 3 handbreadths. — Parallels are found in y. Taʿan. 4.68C.12 (see in n. *aa*); Tanḥ. כי תשא 121A and Tanḥ. עקב 8B.

m. Jerusalem Talmud Taʿanit 4.68C.19: R. Ezra (= Azariah, ca. 380) said in the name of R. Judah b. Simon (ca. 320): The tablets had a weight of 40 *seahs* (cf. § Matt 13:33, #1), and the writing (on them) carried them (gloss: as the soul carries the body). — See further Exod. Rab. 47 (102A) in n. *o*.

n. The view that the tablets contained only the 10 commandments underlies, for example, the following interpretation in b. Ber. 5A: R. Levi b. Hama (= Lahma, ca. 260) said that R. Simeon b. Laqish (ca. 250) said, "What does 'So that I may give you the tablets לוחות of stone and the Torah and the commandments, which I have written to teach them' (Exod 24:12) mean? The 'tablets': these are the Ten Commandments (for only these were on them); 'Torah': this is Scripture (= written Torah = Pentateuch); 'and the commandment': this is the Mishnah (= the traditional law); 'that I have written': these are the Prophets and hagiographa; 'to teach them': this is the Gemarah. This teaches that they were all given to Moses from Sinai."

o. Jerusalem Talmud Šeqalim 6.49D.44: How were the tablets (with the Ten Commandments) written? R. Hananiah b. Gamaliel (ca. 120) said, "Five were on one tablet and five on the other tablet. This is what is written, '(He proclaimed to you … the ten words) and wrote them on two stone tablets' (Deut 4:13), five on one tablet and five on the other tablet." The rabbis said, "Ten on one tablet and ten on the other tablet. This is what is written, 'He proclaimed to you his covenant that he commanded you to practice, the ten words (and wrote them on two stone tablets)' (Deut 4:13) ten on one tablet and ten on the other tablet." — Parallels are found in y. Soṭah 8.22D.10; Midr. Song. 5:14 (120A); Mek. Exod. 20:16 (78A), and here there is also a proof of how the five commandments on the two tablets corresponded to each other. The 1st commandment, "I am Yahweh your God," corresponds to the 6th (according to Jewish numbering), "You shall not murder." Scripture indicates that Scripture reckons it to the one who sheds blood as if he degraded the image of the king. — The 2nd commandment, "You shall have no other God aside from me," corresponds to the 7th, "You shall not commit adultery." Scripture indicates that Scripture reckons it to the one who serves idol as if he committed adultery with respect to God …." ‖ See further Exod. Rab. 47 (102A), where, though, the text is hardly in order. ‖ Tanḥuma עקב 8A: How many (read כמה instead of במה) commandments were on each tablet? Five commandments were on (each) tablet, and between each one a kind of waves גללים had been set (as a separation), as it says Song 5:14: "His hands (according to the foregoing interpretation = 'the tablets') are golden waves (so גלילי is interpreted), covered with sapphires," for they (the tablets) were made of sapphire. — On the "waves" between the individual commandments, see y. Soṭah 6 in n. *pp*. — The statement "Five commandments on each tablet" is also found in TanḥB כי תשא § 20 (60A); likewise, Josephus, *Ant.* 3.5.8.

p. Jerusalem Talmud Šeqalim 6.49D.48: R. Simeon b. Yohai (ca. 150) said, "Twenty commandments (i.e., the Ten Commandments twice) were on one tablet and twenty on the other tablet; for it is written, 'And he wrote them on two stone tablets' (Deut 4:13), twenty on one tablet and twenty on the other tablet." (The proof text is not probative; Exod 32:15 would fit better "Tablets written on both their sides; they were written on here and there," so on each side of one tablet there were two Ten Commandments). R. Simai (ca. 210) said, "Forty commandments (i.e., the Ten Commandments four times) were on one tablet and forty on the other tablet; (for it is written,) 'They were written on here and there,' four times טֶטְרָגֵינָה

(= τετράγωνον)." — The commentators understand טטרגינה to mean "square shaped" and try to present in greater detail the form of the square in which the Ten Commandments were written four times on each tablet. — Parallels are found in y. Soṭah 8.22D.14; Midr. Song. 5:14 (120A).

q. Pirqe Rabbi Eliezer 48 (28A): R. Ishmael († ca. 135, though the name might be a pseudonym) said, "The five fingers of the right hand of God are together the basis of redemptions. With the little finger he (God) showed Noah how he should make the ark (see Gen 6:15). With the finger that is the second from the little finger (i.e., with the fourth finger), he struck the Egyptians (see Exod 8:15). With the finger that is the third from the little finger (i.e., with the middle finger), he wrote the tablets; for it says, 'Stone tablets that were written by the finger of God' (Exod 31:18). With the fourth finger that is second from the thumb (= index finger), God showed Moses what the Israelites should give as a ransom for the soul; as it says, 'This זֶה (in the sense of the midrash, the coin that was showed to Moses) they shall give' (Exod 30:13). With the thumb and the whole hand God will one day destroy the sons of Esau (= Romans), because they oppress the children of Israel, and likewise the sons of Ishmael, who are its enemies; as it says, 'Your hand is exalted over your oppressors, and all your enemies will be eradicated' (Mic 5:8)."

r. Babylonian Talmud Šabbat 104A: Rab Hisda († 309) said, "The final *mem* ם and the *samekh* ס, that were on the tablets, were there by a miracle (in that their middle part did not fall out as a result of the engraving)." Furthermore, Rab Hisda said, "The writing on the tablets was read from inside (on the front of the tablets) and from outside (on the back of the tablets) (because the engraving went through the tablets); for example, נבוב (on one side had to be conversely read on the other side as) בובנ, רהב as בהר, סרן as נרס." (These words are given as examples without appearing in the ten commandments.)

s. Mekilta Exodus 20:18 (78B): "'And all the people saw the voices (and the flames)' (Exod 20:18). They saw the visible and heard the audible." These are the words of R. Ishmael († ca. 135). R. Aqiba († ca. 135) said, "They saw and heard the visible, and there was not any word that did not proceed from the mouth of the Almighty and was engraved in the tablets; as it says, 'The voice of Yahweh flashes flames of fire' (while striking the tablets, whereby the commandments were engraved in them) (Ps 29:7)." ‖ Something similar is found in a more expansive version in Midr. Song. 1:2 (82A). At the conclusion here it says: "R. Berekhiah (ca. 340) said R. Helbo (ca. 300) taught me, 'The word itself was engraved by itself, and when it was engraved, his voice went from one end of the world to the other; as it says, "The voice of Yahweh flashes sparks of fire" (Ps 29:7).' I said to R. Helbo, 'Yet it is written, "Written by God's finger" (Exod 31:18)!' He answered me, 'Choker, do you mean to choke me (with your objection)?' I said to him, 'Yet what then does "Stone tablets written by God's finger" (Exod 31:18) mean?' He said to me, 'Like a student who writes and his teacher regulates (guides) his hand.'" — A partial parallel is found in SDeut 33:2 § 343 (143A).

t. Pirqe Rabbi Eliezer 46 (26B): R. תהנא (perhaps תַּחְנָה?) said, "The tablets (the first ones) were not created from earth, but rather from heaven, a work of the hands of God; as it says, 'The tablets were a work of God' (Exod 32:16). They are the tablets that were from before (from eternity). 'And the writing was God's writing' (Exod 32:16). It was the writing that was from before."

u. See m. ʾAbot 6.2 at § John 8:32.

v. Babylonian Talmud ʿErubin 54A: R. Eleazar (ca. 270) said, "What does 'Engraved on the tablets' (Exod 32:16) mean? If the first tablets לוחות הראשונות had not been broken, the Torah would not have been forgotten by Israel."

w. Tanḥuma כי תשא 115A: "Engraved" חָרוּת (Exod 32:16). What does חרות mean? R. Judah and R. Nehemiah and the rabbis (all ca. 150). R. Judah said, "Freedom חֵרוּת from the kingdoms of the world"; and R. Nehemiah said, "Freedom from the angel of death"; and the rabbis said, "Freedom from suffering." R. Eliezer b. Yose the Galilean (ca. 150) said "If the angel of death had come and said before God, 'For nothing you have created me in this world!', God would have answered him, 'I have made you the ruler over the idolaters; yet this nation, on which I have bestowed freedom חֵרוּת on the tablets, is exempt!' And how do we know that is the case? Because it is written, 'I myself have said, "You are gods and all sons of the Most High"' (Ps 82:6). You have corrupted your works, 'Truly, you shall die like men!' (Ps 82:7)." — Parallels are found in Tanḥ. שלח 214A; TanḥB כי תשא § 12 (56B); שלח additions § 1 (38B); Lev. Rab. 18 (118A); Exod. Rab. 41 (97D); Tanḥ. עקב 7B. ‖ Babylonian Talmud ʿErubin 54A: Rab Aha b. Jacob (ca. 330) said, "(If the tablets had not been broken,) no nation or tongue would have obtained power over them (the Israelites); for it says, 'חרות (Exod 32:16); do not read חָרוּת "engraved," but rather חֵרוּת "freedom."'" — The interpretation חָרוּת = חֵרוּת, though applied in a different way, is found also in m. ʾAbot 6.2; see § John 8:32. ‖ Tanḥuma כי תשא 115B: "Written by the finger of God" (Exod 31:18); if the first tablets had reached the Israelites (come into the possession of the Israelites), no creature could have obtained power over them.

x. Tanḥ. כי תשא 114B: R. Levi (ca. 300) said, "The Israelites sat below and chiseled out the calf; as it says, 'He took it from their hand and formed it with a chisel' (Exod 32:4). And God above engraved the tablets to give them words of life; as it says, 'And he gave (the two tablets) to Moses when he had finished speaking with him' (Exod 31:18)." — The same is found in Exod. Rab. 41 (97C). ‖ Exodus Rabbah 41 (97D) is similar in an expanded version.

y. Babylonian Talmud Nedarim 38A: R. Yohanan († 279) said, "At the beginning Moses had learned the Torah, but he forgot it until it was given to him as a gift; as it says, 'He gave (= gave as a gift) to Moses the two tablets when he had finished speaking with him' (Exod 31:18)." — In the parallel y. Hor. 3.48B.41 at the end there is the addition: And why all this? In order to give an answer (by reference to Moses) to the weakly gifted (who want to withdraw from studying the Torah). — See further TanḥB כי תשא § 12 (56B); Tanḥ. כי תשא 115A; Exod. Rab. 41 (97D).

z. Seder ʿOlam Rabbah 6: On the 17th of Tammuz he went down and shattered the tablets. ‖ See m. Taʿan. 4.6 at § Matt 24:2, #2. — There is a parallel in Meg. Taʿan. toward the end; see further, b. Taʿan. 28B, b. Yoma 4B and Pirqe R. El. 46 (26B).

aa. Jerusalem Talmud Taʿanit 4.68C.12: R. Samuel b. Nahman (ca. 260) said in the name of R. Jonathan (ca. 220), "The length of the tablets was six handbreadths and their width three. And Moses grasped two handbreadths (of them) and God two handbreadths; and two handbreadths consisted of the free space in the middle (between the hands of Moses and God). When the Israelites committed that deed (with the golden calf), God tried to tear them out of Moses' hand; but Moses' hand was strong and tore them away from him. This is what Scripture at the end (of the Torah) praises and says, 'With all that strong hand' (Deut 34:12). May well-being come upon the hand that is stronger than I!" – There is a parallel in Tanḥ. עקב 8B.

bb. Jerusalem Talmud Taʿanit 4.68C.17: R. Yohanan († 279) said in the name of R. Yosa b. Abbayye (Abbai?, ca. 230), "The tablets tried to flee from there, and Moses gripped them; as it says, 'Then I gripped the two tablets' (Deut 9:17)."

cc. Jerusalem Talmud Taʿanit 4.68C.18: In the name of R. Nehemiah (ca. 150) it has been taught as a tannaitic tradition: "The writing itself fled (from the tablets)." R. Ezra (= Azariah, ca. 380) said in the name of R. Judah b. Simon (ca. 320), "The tablets had a weight of 40 *seahs* and the writing (on them) carried them (as the soul carries the body, gloss). When the writing fled, they (the tablets) became too heavy for Moses' hands, so they fell and shattered." – A similar text is found in Pirqe R. El. 45 (25D); Tanḥ. עקב 8B and b. Pesaḥ. 87B.

dd. ʾAbot de Rabbi Nathan 2 (2A):[252] When Moses saw that wicked deed which they committed by making the calf, he said, "How can I give them the tablets! I would bind them with commandments that would be too heavy for them and they would be declared guilty of death by God (= of eradication)! For it is written on them, 'You shall have no other God aside from me' (Exod 20:3)." He turned back. Then the seventy elders saw this, and they ran after him. He gripped one end of the tablet and they grabbed the other end of the tablet; yet the strength of Moses was stronger than all of them; as it says, "With all that strong hand and all the amazing great deeds that Moses did before the eyes of all Israel" (Deut 34:12). He looked at the tablets and saw that the writing had fled from them. He said, "How can I give the Israelites the tablets on where there is actually nothing!? Rather, I will seize them and shatter them; as it says, 'Then I seized both tablets and threw them out of both my hands and shattered them' (Deut 9:17)." R. Yose the Galilean (ca. 110) said, "I want to tell you a parable. What can the matter be compared with? With a king of flesh and blood who said to his appointee, 'Go and betroth for me a beautiful and graceful (pious?) virgin נַעֲרָה (a girl between 12 and 12.5 years old) whose works are beautiful.' His appointee went and betrothed one for him. After he had betrothed her, he went and found her, how she committed fornication with another man. Immediately he drew an inference from the lesser to the greater by himself (at his own impulse) and said, 'If I deliver the marriage contract to her, she will from now on be found as one who is guilty of death, and will be dismissed by my lord forever.' So too Moses the righteous drew an inference by himself from the lesser to the greater. He said, 'How can I hand over these tablets to the Israelites! I would bind them with commandments that would be too heavy for them and declare them guilty of death; for it is written on them, "Whoever sacrifices to gods other than Yahweh alone shall be under the ban" (Exod 22:19). Rather, I will seize them and smash them.' And thus he was thinking of what was good; rather, the Israelites might say, 'Where are the

252. S-B: The translation follows the more accurate text of the ed. Frankfurt a. M. 1720 ff.

first tablets that you brought down? There were only lying words!'"[253] R. Judah b. Batera (ca. 110) said, "Moses shattered the tablets only because it had been told him by the mouth of the Almighty; as it says, '"I speak with him mouth to mouth" (Num 12:8). Mouth to mouth I (also) told him (without writing it in Scripture), "Shatter the tablets!"'" Some say, "Moses shattered the tablets only because it had been told him by the mouth of the Almighty; as it says, 'And I saw, and behold, you had sinned against Yahweh your God' (Deut 9:16), and (the words) 'And I saw' he only said because he saw that the writing had fled from them (the tablets) (therein Moses found the command to shatter the tablets himself)." Others (according to the tradition, this refers to the students of Meir) said, "Moses shattered the tablets only because it had been told him by the mouth of the Almighty; as it says, '(I laid the tablets in the ark ...), and they were there, as Yahweh commanded me' (Deut 10:5). (The words) 'As commanded me,' he only said because the command had been given to him to shatter them." R. Eleazar b. Azariah (ca. 100) said, "Moses shattered the tablets only because it had been told him by the mouth of the Almighty; as it says, '(With ... amazing great deeds) that Moses did before the eyes of all Israel' (Deut 34:12). Just as he was commanded there and he did it (i.e., as he acted there on the basis of a commandment), so too here (in the case of the tablets) he was commanded and he did it (shattered them)." R. Aqiba said, "Moses shattered the tablets only because it had been told him by the mouth of the Almighty; as it says, 'And I seized the two tablets' (Deut 9:17). What does a person seize? What he can shatter (according to the reading לשברן)." R. Meir (ca. 150) said, "Moses shattered the tablets only because it had been told him by the mouth of the Almighty; as it says, 'Which אֲשֶׁר you shattered' (Deut 10:2). Blessing upon your strength (literally: may your strength strengthen יישר כוחך, interpretation of אשר) because you shattered!" (This word of thanks from God is a testimony that Moses shattered the tablets with divine approval.) — See a similar exposition at b. Šabb. 87A.7, 21; y. Taʿan. 4.68C.7; Exod. Rab. 46 (101B); b. Menaḥ. 99A; y. Taʿan. 4.68C.10; Deut. Rab. 5 (202C); Tanḥ. עקב 8B; Exod. Rab. 46 (101A).

ee. Deuteronomy Rabbah 3 (201A): "Hew for yourself two stone tablets" (Exod 34:1). This is what Scripture said, "Do not be too hasty in your spirit to anger; for anger rests in the breast of a fool"(Eccl 7:9). And who was it that got angry? It was Moses, as it says, "Then Moses' wrath burned, and he threw the tablets from his hand" (Exod 32:19). God said to him, "Behold, Moses, you quench your wrath with the tablets of the covenant; do you want me to quench my wrath? Then you will see that the world cannot endure even for one hour." Moses said to him, "And what should I do?" He answered him, "You have to accept the sentence (the penalty, read קָטָדִיקִי instead of קטריקי); you have shattered them and you have to replace them!" This is what is written, "Hew for yourself two stone tablets" (Exod 34:1). — See also the citations in notes *mm* and *nn*.

ff. Pirqe Rabbi Eliezer 3 (2C): Ten things arose in (God's) thought (before the world was created): Jerusalem and the spirits of the fathers (?) and the ways (the faring) of the righteous (materially = the garden of Eden) and gehenna and the waters of the flood and

253. S-B: The parable of R. Yose the Galilean is anonymous in Exod. Rab. 43 (99A); Tanh. עקב 8A.

the second tablets and the Sabbath and the sanctuary and the ark of the covenant and the light for the future world.

gg. Seder ʿOlam Rabbah 6: On the 18th of Tammuz (one day after the tablets were shattered), Moses arose and prayed for mercy for Israel; as it is written, "Then I threw myself down before Yahweh for 40 days and 40 nights when I cast myself down because Yahweh told me" (Deut 9:25). In that hour God pardoned the Israelites and told Moses that he should hew the second tablets and climb up; as it says, "In that time (i.e., 40 days after the 18th of Tammuz) Yahweh said to me, 'Hew for yourself two stone tablets like the first and climb up the mountain and make yourself a wooden ark'" (Deut 10:1). He descended on the 28th of Ab[254] to hew two tablets; as it says, "He hewed two stone tablets like the first and Moses started early in the morning" (Exod 34:4) and climbed up on the 29th of Ab. (See the continuation of the passage in n. *ss.*)

hh. Leviticus Rabbah 32 (129D): How did Moses become rich? R. Hanin (ca. 300) said, "God created a sapphire quarry (shaft) for him in the midst of his tent, and this is how he became rich. This is what is written, '"Hew for yourself" (Exod 34:1); the chippings belong to you!' In that hour Moses said, 'The blessing of Yahweh who makes rich' (Prov 10:22)."[255] – In the parallel in y. Šeqal. 5.49A.42, there is a shaft of gems and pearls that God created for Moses in his tent and his prosperity arose from it. – Further parallels with the sapphire shaft: Midr. Eccl. 9:11 (44A); 10:20 (49B). Further, Tanḥ. עקב 8A: "Hew for yourself" (Exod 34:1); the chippings shall be yours! R. Levi and R. Hanin (both ca. 300) said, "Where did he hew them from?" The one said, "From beneath the throne of glory he hewed them." And the other said, "In the midst of his tent God created for him a shaft, and from there he hewed the two stone tablets. He took the chippings for himself, and he became rich; for (the tablets) were made of sapphire." ‖ Additional parallels are found in SNum 12:3 § 101 (27A) and Pirqe R. El. 46 (26B). ‖ Targum Yerušalmi I Deuteronomy 10:1, 3 has the second tablets hewn like the first from marble.

ii. Exodus Rabbah 47 (102A): "He wrote on the tablets" (Exod 34:28). This teaches that the first and the last tablets were alike (read שוים instead of שונים). – Similarly, TanḥB כי תשא § 20 (60A) with the correct reading שוים.

kk. Deuteronomy Rabbah 3 (201B): "Hew for yourself two stone tablets like the first" (Deut 10:1). Rabban Yohanan b. Zakkai († ca. 80) was asked, "Why were the first tablets a work of heavens and the second a work of man מעשה אדם?" He answered them, "What can this be compared with? With a king who took a wife; and he got paper and a scribe from his own possessions (at his own expense), he bedecked her from his own possessions and he led her into his house. The king saw her frolicking with one of his slaves. He became furious with her and sent her away. Her bridesman came to him and said to him, 'My lord, do you not know where you took her from? Did she not grow up among slaves? And since she

254. S-B: 40 days after the 18th of Tammuz; these 40 days comprised the last 12 days of Tammuz and the first 28 days of Ab; hence, the descent and hewing of the tablets was on the 28th of Ab.

255. S-B: Moses' wealth is connected with the chippings from the second tablets elsewhere as well; see y. Šeqal. 5.49A.40 and b. Ned 38A.5 (R. Hama b. Hanina, ca. 260); anonymously in b. Ned 38A.24; Midr. Eccl. 10:20 (49B).

grew up among slaves, her heart (mind) is forward (trusting) toward them.' The king said to him, 'What do you want? That I reconcile with her שאתרצה לה? Get paper and a scribe from your own possessions! And behold, here is the writing from my hand (i.e.: and I give you my signature as a certification for this)!' Moses said the same to God when the Israelites blundered into that deed (with the calf). He said to him, 'Do you not know the place you led them out from, from Egypt, the seat of idolatry?' Then God said to him, 'What do you want? That I reconcile with them שאתרצה להן? Get the tablets from your own possessions! And behold, here is the writing of my hand! "And I will write on the tablets"' (Exod 34:1)." — See Exod. Rab. 47 (101D) in n. *qq*.

ll. Babylonian Talmud Nedarim 38A: R. Yose b. Hanina (ca. 270) said, "The Torah was given only to Moses and his seed; for it says, 'Write down for yourself' (Exod 34:27); 'Hew for yourself' (Exod 34:1); as their chippings belong to you, so too does their writing (what is written on them) belong to you (alone). Yet Moses acted with a benevolent eye and gave it to the Israelites, and concerning him Scripture says, 'Whoever has a benevolent eye will be blessed' (Prov 22:9)." — A similar explanation with the authorial name R. Simeon b. Halapta (ca. 190) is found in Exod. Rab. 47 (101D) at n. *rr*.

mm. Deuteronomy Rabbah 3 (201A): "Hew for yourself two stone tablets" (Deut 10:1). R. Isaac (ca. 300) said, "It is written, 'If he thus sins and is guilty, he shall return the theft that he has robbed, or what he has acquired by extortion, or the thing entrusted (deposit) which has been deposited with him, or the lost thing that he found' (Lev 5:23). God said to Moses, 'Were the tablets not an item entrusted to you? You have shattered them and you must replace them.'" — The same is found anonymously in Tanḥ. עקב 8B.

nn. Deuteronomy Rabbah 3 (201A): R. Isaac (ca. 300) said, "Our teachers taught (namely in m. B. Bat. 5.8): 'If the vat has been broken, it is broken for the negotiator סַרְסוֹר (the broker between buyer and seller had to bear the loss).' God said to Moses, 'You are the negotiator (the mediator סַרְסוֹר = μεσίτης) between me and my children; you have shattered (the tablets), you have to make compensation!' How do we know this? For it is written, 'And Yahweh said to Moses, "Hew for yourself two stone tablets like the first, and I will write on the tablets the words that were on the first tablets that you have broken"' (Exod 34:1)."

oo. Babylonian Talmud Baba Qamma 54B: R. Hanina b. Agil (ca. 300) asked R. Hiyya b. Abba (ca. 280), "Why was the word "good" טוב not said in the first words (i.e., in the commandments of the first tablets), whereas the word "good" was said in the last words (in the commandments of the last tablets)?" He answered him, "Instead of asking me, 'Why was the word "good" not said in them?,' ask me instead whether the word 'good' was said in them or not; for I do not know whether the word 'good' was said in them or not. But appeal to R. Tanḥum b. Hanilai (ca. 280), who used to associate with R. Joshua b. Levi (ca. 250) who was knowledgeable in the haggadah." He went to him (to R. Tanḥum b. Hanilai). He said to him, "I have not heard from him (R. Joshua b. Levi), but Samuel b. Nahum, the brother of the mother of R. Aha b. Hanina (the latter ca. 300)—some say, the father of the mother of R. Aha b. Hanina—said to me, 'Because they ultimately were to be broken (that is why טוב was missing on the first tablets).' Yet if it is the case that they were ultimately to be broken, so what?" Rab Ashi († 427) said, "חָס וְשָׁלוֹם = God forbid! What is good would have ceased in Israel!"

pp. Jerusalem Talmud Soṭah 8.22D.17: Hananiah, the son of the brother of R. Joshua (ca. 110) said, "Between the individual commandments (on the tablets) there were the special stipulations and sections of Scripture that pertain to them (so according to the parallel in Midr. Song.), 'filled like the sea' (so Song 5:14B according to the midr.), like the great sea." R. Simeon b. Laqish (ca. 250) used to say when he came to this passage of Scripture (Song 5:14B), "Hananiah, the son of the brother of R. Joshua taught me beautifully. Just as the sea has small waves between the individual big waves, so between the individual commandments (on the tablets) there were the special stipulations and sections of Scripture that pertain to them." — Parallels are found in y. Šeqal. 6.49D.52; Midr. Song. 5:14 (120A). ‖ Exodus Rabbah 46 (101B): Moses began to grieve over breaking the tablets. God said to him, "Do not grieve over the first tablets that contained only the Ten Commandments; I will give you the second tablets so that on them there will be the halakoth and the derivations from Scripture and the haggadoth (the nonhalakic interpretations of Scripture). This is what is written: 'He will make known to you the secrets of his wisdom, for they are two-fold in true knowledge' (Job 11:6). And not only this but also the good news may apply to you that I have forgiven you your sin; as it says, 'And know that God will forgive you your guilt' (Job 11:6)." ‖ Similarly, Exod. Rab. 47 (102B).

qq. TanḥumaB כי תשא § 17 (59A): "Write for yourself" (Exod 34:27). "I wrote the first tablets (God said); as it says, 'Written by the finger of God' (Exod 31:18); but you write the second for yourself!" What can this be compared with? With a king who took a wife and wrote her a marriage contract on his very own (on paper, which he himself delivered). It was not long before she committed an offense and he cast her out. Her bridesman came and reconciled her with the king. The king said to her, "See, I am reconciled נתרציתי; but go and make a different marriage contract!" — The same is found in a somewhat expanded form in Exod. Rab. 47 (101D) with the conclusion: Let me place my initials on it (as certification)! This is what is said: "And I will write on the tablets" (Deut 10:2). — See Deut. Rab. 3 in n. *kk*.

rr. Exodus Rabbah 47 (101D): "Write for yourself" (Exod 34:27); by your merit (because of you), God said to Moses, "I will give them (Israel) the Torah." R. Simeon b. Halapta (ca. 190) said, "This is what Moses said to the Israelites, 'And he (God) wrote on the tablets like the first writing ..., and Yahweh gave them to me' (Deut 10:4). To me he gave them; but I acted with a benevolent eye toward you and gave them to you. Therefore, it says, 'Write for yourself,' by your merit." — The same is found in TanḥB כי תשא § 17 (59A).

ss. Seder 'Olam Rabbah 6: Moses came down on the 28th of Ab (see above in n. *gg*) to hew the two tablets; as it says, "He hewed two stone tablets like the first, and Moses got going early in the morning" (Exod 34:4) and ascended on the 29th of Ab. God taught him the Torah for a second time (the text uses the passive construction to avoid using the name of God); as it says, "Yet I remained on the mountain, as the first days, 40 days and 40 nights" (Deut 10:10).... He climbed down on the 10th of Tishri,[256] and that was the Day of Atonement.

---

256. S-B: The 40 days consist of one day in Ab, 29 days in Elul, and 10 days in Tishri.

And he brought them the good news that God was reconciled; as it says, "Forgive our wrong and our sins and accept us as your possession" (Exod 34:9). This is why this day is appointed as a statute and as a remembrance for the (coming) generations; as it says, "And this shall be for you an eternal statute" (Lev 16:34). ‖ Babylonian Talmud Taʿanit 30B: The Day of Atonement ..., this is the day when the last (= second) tablets were given. ‖ See further Tanḥ. כי תשא 119B and Pirqe R. El. 46 (26C).

tt. See b. B. Bat. 14A at § Heb 9:4, #2, n. *a.* ‖ Babylonian Talmud Berakot 8B: The tablets and the broken pieces of the (first) tablets lay in the ark. ‖ Jerusalem Talmud Soṭah 8.22C.48 = y. Šeqal. 6.49D.15: There were four tablets in the ark, two broken and two whole. – The same is found in the same passage three more times.

uu. See the baraita in y. Soṭah 8.22B.57 at § Heb 9:4, #2, n. *a.*

vv. Babylonian Talmud Soṭah 35A: R. Yohanan († 279) said, "... The ark (of the covenant) endures forever."

3:7 C: So that the children of Israel could not look at the face of Moses because of the splendor (glory) of his face ....

1. Exodus 34:29f. in the base text: "And it happened, when Moses came down from Mount Sinai—and the two tablets of the testimony were in Moses' hand, when he came down from the mountain, and Moses did not know that the skin of his face shone (cast rays קָרַן) as a result of his talking with him. Aaron and all the children of Israel saw Moses, and behold, the skin of his face shone קָרַן, and they were afraid to approach him." – Septuagint: ὡς δὲ κατέβαινε Μωυσῆς ἐκ τοῦ ὄρους, καὶ αἱ δύο πλάκες ἐπὶ τῶν χειρῶν Μωυσῆ· καταβαίνοντος δὲ αὐτοῦ ἐκ τοῦ ὄρους, Μωυσῆς οὐκ ᾔδει, ὅτι δεδόξασται ἡ ὄψις τοῦ χρώματος (τοῦ χρωτὸς) τοῦ προσώπου αὐτοῦ ἐν τῷ λαλεῖν αὐτὸν αὐτῷ. καὶ εἶδεν Ἀαρῶν καὶ πάντες οἱ πρεσβύτεροι Ἰσραὴλ τὸν Μωυσῆν, καὶ ἦν δεδοξασμένη ἡ ὄψις τοῦ χρώματος τοῦ προσώπου αὐτοῦ· καὶ ἐφοβήθησαν ἐγγίσαι αὐτῷ. – Targum Onkelos Exodus 34:29f.: "And it happened, when Moses came down from Mount Sinai—and the two tablets of the testimony were in Moses' hand when he descended from the mountain, and Moses did not know that the splendor of the glory of his face was great due to his speaking with him. Aaron and all the children of Israel saw Moses, and behold, the splendor of the glory of his face was great, and they were afraid of approaching him." – Targum Yerušalmi I Exodus 34:29f.: "And it happened at the time when Moses came down from Mount Sinai—and the two tablets of the testimony were in Moses' hand when he descended from the mountain, and Moses did not know that the splendor of his facial features gleamed אִשְׁתַּבְהַר, which had been bestowed on him by the splendor of the glory of the Shekinah of Yahweh at the time he spoke with him. Aaron and all the children of Israel saw Moses, and behold, the splendor of his facial features gleamed, and they were afraid of approaching him."

2. Where did the splendor of Moses' face come from?

a. From the splendor of the glory of Yahweh, when he passed by Moses (Exod 33:21ff.) or spoke with Moses on the mountain.

Tanḥuma כי תשא 121A: From where did Moses acquire the rays (literally: the horns) of glory (splendor) קַרְנֵי הַהוֹד? Our teachers—blessed be the memory of them!—said, "From the cave, as it says, 'When my glory passes by, I will set you in the hollow of the rock' (Exod 33:22). Then God put his hand on him, and thus he acquired the rays of glory (splendor). It likewise says, 'Rays from his hand came to him there where there is concealment from his strength' (so the midrash appears to interpret Hab 3:4)." Some say, "At the time when God taught him the Torah (on the mountain) he received from the sparks (rays) that went from the mouth of the Shekinah, the rays of splendor (glory) קרני ההוד." – In the parallels TanḥB כי תשא § 20 (60A) and Exod. Rab. 47 (102A) we find only the 1st explanation. – On the 2nd explanation, see Tg. Onk. and Yer. I in #1.

b. From writing down the Torah on the mountain.

Exodus Rabbah 47 (102A): R. Judah b. Nahman (ca. 280) said in the name of R. Simeon b. Laqish (ca. 250), "While Moses wrote with a writing instrument (on the mountain), some (of the fiery ink) was left in it. He put it (the writing instrument) over his head, and the rays of splendor (glory) קרני ההוד came to him from it; as it says, 'And Moses did not know that the skin of his face shone (cast rays)' (Exod 34:29)." – The same is found in TanḥB כי תשא § 20 (60B) with R. Judah b. Nehemiah (read: Nahman) as the author; in Tanḥ. כי תשא 121A, read R. Simeon b. Laqish instead of "Rab Samuel." ‖ Tanḥuma יתרו 90A: You find that when God gave the Torah, everything was made of fire; as it says, "At his right hand there was the fire of the law for him" (Deut 33:2). Resh Laqish (ca. 250 = R. Simeon b. Laqish in the previous citation) said, "The Torah was made of fire, its parchment was made of fire, its writing was made of fire, its sewing (to bind the pieces of parchment) were made of fire; as it says, 'At his right hand there was the fire of the law for him' (Deut 33:2). Even the face of the mediator סַרְסוֹר (= Moses) was of fire; as it says, 'And they were afraid to approach him' (Exod 34:30)…." ‖ See another parallel in Deut. Rab. 3 (200D).

c. From the tablets of the law.

Deuteronomy Rabbah 3 (200D): R. Samuel b. Nahman (ca. 260) said, "Moses received the splendor of the face זיו הפנים from the tablets. When the tablets were given to him hand to hand, he received from this the splendor of the face. When the Israelites committed that deed (with the calf), he took them and shattered them. Then God said to him, 'When you ordained (them) for Israel (composed them as a presentation), I gave you the splendor of your face as your recompense; and now you have broken the tablets!'" ‖ Exodus Rabbah 47 (102A): R. Berekhiah the priest (ca. 340) said in the name of R. Samuel (b. Nahman, ca. 260), "The tablets had a length of 6 handbreadths and a width of 6 handbreadths; and Moses grasped 2 handbreadths (when they were given to him) and the Shekinah 2 handbreadths and there were 2 handbreadths in the middle, and thus Moses received the rays of splendor (glory) קרני ההוד." – Parallels are found in Tanḥ. כי תשא 121A; TanḥB כי תשא § 20 (60B).

d. From Moses' role as a mediator between God and Israel; see Deut. Rab. 3 (200D) at § John 2:1 A, #4, E, n. *w*.

e. From Moses' humility of not feasting his eye on the splendor of the Shekinah.

Babylonian Talmud Berakot 7A: R. Samuel b. Nahman (ca. 260) said that R. Jonathan (ca. 220) said, "Moses received זכה three things as a recompense for three things. As a recompense for "And Moses hid his face"(Exod 3:6), he received the appearance (the splendor) of the face קלסתר פנים. As a recompense for "For he was afraid" (Exod 3:6), he received:

"And (Aaron and the children of Israel) were afraid to approach him" (Exod 34:30). As a recompense for "To look at" (Exod 3:6), he received: "And he sees the form of Yahweh" (Num 12:8). — The same is found as a saying of "our teachers" in Tanḥ. בראשית 1B. ‖ Pesiqta 173A: ("They looked at God" [Exod 24:11].) R. Tanḥuma (ca. 380) said, "This teaches that they proudly raised their heart and stood on their feet (trod firmly) and feasted their eyes on the Shekinah." R. Joshua of Sikhnin (ca. 330) said in the name of R. Levi (ca. 300), "Moses did not feast his eyes on the Shekinah, and so he had enjoyed the splendor of the Shekinah. He did not feast his eyes; for it is written, 'Moses hid his face; for he was afraid to look at God' (Exod 3:6). And he enjoyed the Shekinah. How do we know? Because it is written, 'Moses did not know that the skin of his face shone (cast rays)' (Exod 34:29).... 'Nadab and Abihu died before Yahweh' (Num 3:4)." — Parallels are found in Lev. Rab. 20 (119D); TanḥB אחרי § 7 (32B); Tanḥ. אחרי מות 164B.

3. The rays of splendor remained upon Moses even after death.

Pesiqta Rabbati 21 (102A): R. Simeon b. Yohai (ca. 150) said, "If a hole were bored from the grave of Moses, the whole world could not endure because of his light. And if this is the case with a hole, what would it be like with the (whole) grave?! And if this is what it would be like with the grave, what would it be like with Moses (himself)?!" ‖ See Tg. Onk. Deut. 34:7: Moses was 120 years old when he died; his eye had not grown dim, and the splendor of the glory of his face had not changed.

4. "Moses did not know that the skin of his face shone" (Exod 34:29).

Babylonian Talmud Šabbat 10B: R. Hama b. Hanina (ca. 260) said, "Whoever gives a gift to someone else does not need to make him know it; for it says, 'Moses did not know that the skin of his face shone' (Exod 34:29)." — The opposing view takes precedence. — There is a parallel in b. Beṣah 16A.

5. ὥστε μὴ δύνασθαι ἀτενίσαι.

Sifre Numbers 5:3 § 1 (1B): R. Simeon b. Yohai (ca. 150) said, "Come and see, how bad the power of sin is. Before (the Israelites) had stretched out their hands toward sin (with the golden calf), what is said of them? 'The appearance of the glory of Yahweh was like a consuming fire' (Exod 24:17), and yet they were not afraid and did not tremble. Yet when they had stretched out their hands toward sin, what is said of them? 'And Aaron and all the children of Israel saw Moses, and behold, the skin of his face shone, and they were afraid to approach him' (Exod 34:30)." ‖ Pesiqta 45A: R. Abba b. Kahana (ca. 310) said, "There were seven ramparts of fire glowing in each other[257] (on Sinai), and the Israelites saw them without fearing or being afraid. Yet when they sinned (with the calf), they themselves could not look at לא היו יכולים להסתכל the face of the mediator סַרְסוֹר; as it says, 'Aaron and all the children of Israel saw Moses, and behold, the skin of his face shone, and they were afraid to approach him' (Exod 34:30)." R. Phineas (ca. 360) said in the name of R. Abin (ca. 325) in the name of R. Hanin (ca. 300), "Even the mediator סרסור (i.e., Moses) felt the force of the sin (with the calf) ...."; see the continuation at § Rom 1:18 A, n. *b*, toward end; there are also the parallels there. ‖ Leviticus Rabbah 20 (119D): As a recompense for Moses being afraid

257. S-B: So with Bacher according to the reading תוססות instead of בוססות (*Die Agada der Tannaïten*, 2:493.6).

(to look at God) in Exod 3:6, he obtained (was worthy of זכה) (Aaron and the children of Israel) being afraid to approach him (Exod 34:30). — Parallels are found in Pesiq. 173A and Tanḥ. אחרי מות 164B; see also b. Ber. 7A above at #2, *e*.

3:13: As Moses put a veil over his face.

In ancient rabbinic literature we have not encountered any passage that refers to the "veil of Moses" (Exod 34:33ff.). — Rashi (without indicating that he is following older traditions) comments on Exod 34:33 that Moses put the veil over the rays of splendor, lest all feast their eyes on them.

3:15: As soon as Moses is read out.

On the liturgical reading of Scripture, see the excursus "The Ancient Jewish Synagogue Service."

3:17: Where the Spirit of the Lord is, there is freedom (see § John 8:32).

3:18: We are being transformed from glory to glory into the same image.

See 2 Bar. 50:1–51:10 at § 1 Cor 15:35 B.

4:6: Who said, "Let light shine out of darkness."

Tanḥuma בהעלותך 204B: "The seven lamps shall cast their light on the front side of the lampstand" (Num 8:2). Flesh and blood light a lamp by a burning lamp; can a lamp be lit with darkness? Yet God ignites a light from the darkness; as it says, "Darkness was over the primordial waters" (Gen 1:2). What is written after this? And God said, "Let light come into existence!" (Gen 1:3). God said, "I had light brought forth הוצאתי from the darkness, and would I need your lamps? Yet why did I tell you this? To exalt (glorify) the perennial lamp." — The same is found in Num. Rab. 15 (178D). See also Midr. Ps. 22 § 7 at § Rom 9:26, #1, end.

4:7: In earthen vessels.

ἐν ὀστρακίνοις σκεύεσιν, Aramaic = בְּמָנֵי דְפַחָרָא see b. Ta'an. 7A at § Matt 21:24. In Hebrew "earthen vessels" are called כְּלֵי חֶרֶס ,כ חֶרֶשׂ; this term appears often in m. Kelim 2–4, where their uncleanness is discussed.

On the commonness of earthen vessels, see Gen. Rab. 14 (10C) at § Matt 22:32, #2, C, beginning. Also, SDeut 11:22 § 48 (84A): Just as it is not possible for wine to be kept in golden or silver vessels, but rather only in one that is the lowliest of vessels, (namely) in an earthen vessel בִּכְלִי חֶרֶשׂ, so too the words of the Torah can only be kept in someone who humbles himself. See also Midr. Song. 1:2 (84A) and b. Ta'an. 7A.

4:11: We who are alive are constantly being given over to death for Jesus' sake (see § Rom 8:36 ff.).

4:3: According to what is written, "I believed, therefore I have also spoken."

The obscure words of the base text in Ps 116:11 could be translated, "I believe that I will speak," or "I believe when I speak." — The targum interprets it as follows: "I trust that I will speak in the community of the righteous." — The LXX: "I believed, therefore I spoke" ἐπίστευσα, διὸ ἐλάλησα. The apostle followed this text. — In ancient rabbinic literature there does not appear to be any reference to these words in Ps 116:11.

4:16: Even if our outer person is being destroyed, our inner one is being renewed day by day.

1. ὁ ἔξω ἡμῶν ἄνθρωπος ..., ὁ ἔσω ἡμῶν. Formally similar, though different in substance is b. Yoma 72B; see § Luke 11:40.
2. ἀνακαινοῦται, see § Eph 4:23.

4:17: The momentary lightness of our tribulation is bringing about for us ... an eternal weight of glory.

See § Rom 8:18. ‖ 2 Baruch 48:50: "For truly you (the righteous), just as you have endured many toils in this short span of time in this perishable world in which you live, will receive much light in that endless world." ‖ On the significance of sufferings see § Luke 24:26, I, #2 and § Rom 5:3 A.

4:18: What is seen is temporary (transitory); but what is not seen is eternal.

See 2 Bar. 44:7ff.

5:1: Our earthly dwelling of the tent.

σκῆνος "tent" is a metaphorical expression for "body" in Biblical Greek in Wis 9:15: "A perishable body weighs down the soul, and the earthly tent τὸ γεῶδες σκῆνος burdens the thoughtful spirit." — 2 Peter 1:13, 14 has σκήνωμα instead. — The body is the dwelling of the soul already in Job 4:19, where people are called "inhabitants of clay houses" שֹׁכְנֵי בָתֵּי חֹמֶר because their body comes from the earth. Septuagint: τοὺς κατοικοῦντας οἰκίας πηλίνας. See also Isa 38:12. — In rabbinic literature בַּיִת "house" was not a common image for "body"; Levy adduces only one example from b. Ber. 44B: "Woe to the house (= body) through which a beet passes! (i.e., whose main nutrition consists of beets)."[258] — Rashi interprets בית here with כֶּרֶס = "stomach, body."

5:2: To put on our dwelling from heaven.

The clothes of glory that the righteous receive are a parallel idea; see § Matt 17:2 B.

---

258. Levy, *Chaldäisches Wörterbuch*, 1:224A.

These heavenly clothes are mentioned particularly often in the Christian Ascension of Isaiah (2nd century CE), for example, 7:22; 8:14f.; 8:26; 9:2, 17f., 24ff. (according to the chapter division in Gfrörer). They are juxtaposed with the *vestimenta carnis*; for example, 9:9: *Et ibi vidi Enochum omnesque, qui cum eo, qui caruerunt vestimento carnis, et aspexi eos in vestimento superno, et fuerunt sicut angeli.*

5:3: We will be found (see § 1 Cor 15:15).

5:4: Not to put off, but rather to put on.

On ἐκδύσασθαι see 4 Ezra 14:13f.: "You yourself (Ezra) shall renounce the perishable life, let go of mortal cares. Cast away the burden of humanity, put off the weak nature. Leave aside the agonizing questions and rush to go from this temporality!"

5:6: At home in the body, we are away from the Lord.

On these words, Wetstein 2:190 comments, "Gemarah Moed Katon f. 85 (this folio does not exist): *eum, qui terrena magis curat quam coelestia, vocat indigenam* ציבא *in terra et advenam* גייורא *in coelo*." — Presumably Wetstein had in mind the following claim from y. Ḥag. 1.76A.11; b. ʿErub. 9A; b. Yoma 47A; b. B. Qam. 42A: יציבא בארעא וגיורא בשמי שמייא = "Should the ancestral one (the Israelite) be on the earth and the proselyte in the highest heaven?" (i.e., should the proselyte have it better than the Israelites?, a proverbial mark of a proof that leads to an illogical result). The expression knows nothing about an earthly minded person being called "a native of earth" and "a stranger in heaven."

5:10 A: We must all appear before the judgment seat of Christ.

See § Rom 14:10; on the Messiah's judicial role in particular, see § Matt 25:31 B, #3, n. *a* and § John 5:22.

5:10 B: So that each one may receive.

κομίσηται perhaps = נָטַל. — Sifre Numbers 15:41 § 115 (35A): Why did God give us commandments? Was it not so that we might do them and receive a recompense וניטול שכר? ‖ Babylonian Talmud ʿAbodah Zarah 2A: Whoever has occupied himself with the Torah, let him come and receive his recompense ויטול שכרו.

5:10 C: That which has been done with the body.

In some ways, this should be grouped with the Rabbi's conversation with Antoninus in b. Sanh. 91A; see § Matt 10:28, #1, n. *c*, middle.

5:13: Even if we are beside ourselves.

ἐξέστημεν. — In t. Ḥag. 2.5 (234), R. Joshua (ca. 90) says, "Ben Zoma is already outside כבר בן זומא מבחוץ (= no longer within himself, out of his senses); only a few days passed and Ben Zoma was different." — See the whole passage with parallels at § Matt 3:16, n. *b*. — In b. Pesaḥ. 50A the verb אִיתְנְגִיד is used when someone is delirious or senseless in fevered dreams; literally= to be pulled away, carried off; see the passage at § Matt 5:10, #3, first third.

5:15: That one died for all.

On the vicarious suffering of the righteous, see § Luke 24:26 I, #2, introduction and I, #4 notes *d–q*.

5:17: A new creation.

καινὴ κτίσις = בְּרִיָּה חֲדָשָׁה, an expression that was not coined by the apostle, but rather was adopted from the language of the school; see § John 3:3, #2. Here we can add another passage in which those whose sin has been forgiven are called "new creation."

Midrash Psalm 18 § 6 (69A): R. Simon (ca. 280) said, "Not everyone who wants to say a song says it (= may say it). Rather, concerning everyone to whom a miracle happened and who said a song (for it), it is certain that his sins have been forgiven and he has become like a new creation."

5:18: Who reconciled us with himself.

In place of καταλάσσειν in rabbinic literature specifically the two verbs רִצָּה and פִּיֵּיס come into play. α. רִצָּה, Aram. רַצִּי, really "to make benevolent, agreeable" = "to pacify, reconcile"; הִתְרַצָּה = to reconcile oneself, to be conciliated, appeased; אַרְצִי (Aram.) = to act kindly, to be conciliated.[a] — β. פִּיֵּיס, Aram. פַּיֵּיס, "to pacify, reconcile"; הִתְפַּיֵּיס, Aram. אִתְפַּיֵּיס ,אִפַּיֵּיס, = "to reconcile, to allay, to be conciliated."[b] — The expression "to make peace between one person and another" עָשָׂה שָׁלוֹם בֵּין ,הֵטִיל שלום בין is related in substance, insofar as the peace presupposes reconciliation.[c] — It is the task of the offender to initiate reconciliation;[d] yet there is also the case where reconciliation proceeds from the one offended.[e]

a. Tosefta Šeqalim 1.6 (174): The communal offering achieves reconciliation and atonement מרצין ומכפרין between Israel and their Father in heaven. ‖ Mishnah Yoma 8.9: The Day of Atonement does not atone for the sins of one person against another until he has reconciled with the other עַד שֶׁיְּרַצֶּה אֶת־חֲבֵירוֹ. — The same is found in SLev 16:30 (324A). ‖ Babylonian Talmud Berakot 33B: In the presence of Rabbah († 331) someone (as the leader of prayer) went before the ark and said, "You have mercy on a bird's nest; have mercy and pity on us!" Then Rabbah said (ironically), "How this outstanding scholar knows how to pacify (conciliate לרצויי) his Lord!" ‖ On התרצה see Deut. Rab. 3 at § 2 Cor 3:7 B, n. *kk* and TanḥB כי תשא § 17 at § 2 Cor 3:7 B, n. *qq*; also, Pesiq. 163B at § Matt 5:24, B, #1, first third. ‖ ארצי. — Babylonian Talmud Taʿanit 23B: (Abba Hilkiah [ca. 50] said to his wife,) "We will climb up to the roof and plead for mercy. Perhaps God will be kind מרצי (he will show himself to be conciliated) and make rain come."

b. See y. Yoma 8.45C.19; b. Yoma 87A; b. Ber. 31B at § Matt 5:24, B, #1; Roš Haš. 17B at § Matt 5:24, B, #1, end. — Babylonian Talmud Yoma 86B: R. Isaac (ca. 300) said that in the west (= Palestine) it has been said in the name of Rabba b. Mari (ca. 320), "Come and see that God's manner is not like the manner of flesh and blood. The manner of flesh and blood is that when someone has hurt someone else with words, it is doubtful whether he can be conciliated by him מתפיים, or whether he cannot be conciliated by him. And if you say that he can be conciliated by him, it is doubtful whether he can be conciliated with words or whether he cannot be conciliated with words. Yet God, when someone has committed a transgression secretly, can be conciliated מתפיים by him with words; as it says, 'Take with you words and turn back to Yahweh your God' (Hos 14:3). Not only this but also he knows to thank him as well; as it says, 'Accept thanks (good)' (Hos 14:3). Not only this but also Scripture counts it to him as if he offered young bulls; as it says, 'So we will pay young bulls—our lips' (Hos 14:3). And if you should say, 'young bulls of obligation,' Scripture teaches, 'I will heal their falling away, I will love them as a freewill offering' (Hos 14:5)." — אפיים "to be reconciled" appears twice in b. Yoma 87A at § Matt 5:24, B, #1, beginning.

c. Pesiqta 137B: Sometimes (a judge) makes peace עוסה שלום between two people in a dispute, but sometimes he does not make peace between them. Therefore, the two people do not go from there as those who act kindly toward each other (= who are reconciled מרציין with each other). See the whole passage at § Matt 5:25 B.

d. See the citations at § Matt 5:24, B, #1.

e. See b. Yoma 87A at § Matt 5:24, B, #1, beginning.

5:19 A: God was in Christ reconciling the world to himself.

On the unity of atonement and reconciliation, see t. Šeqal. 1.6 (174) at § 2 Cor 5:18, n. *a*.

5:19 B: By not counting their sins against them.

1. On λογίζεσθαι see § Rom 2:26, #2.

2. Forgiveness for wrong is the result of reconciliation; see the parable in b. Roš Haš. 17B at § Matt 5:24, B, #1, end.

5:21 A: Him who knew no sin.

τὸν μὴ γνόντα ἁμαρτίαν. This expression is most closely approximated by: אינו יודע מהו טעם חטא "he who does not know what the taste of sin is."[a] Most of the time it was said: לא טָעַם טַעַם חטא "not to taste the taste of sin"[b] or more briefly: לא טעם חטא "to not taste sin."[c] See the similar expression: "to not taste death" at § Matt 16:28.

a. Tanḥuma צו·144B: R. Asi (אסיא, ca. 300) said, "Why do school children begin by studying the 3rd book (and not the 1st book) of Moses? Because all the offerings are written there and because up until now they are still pure and do not know what the taste of sin and guilt is. Therefore God said that they should first begin with the section about offerings: 'Let the pure come and occupy themselves with the work of the pure! Therefore, I reckon it to them as if they stood there and offered sacrifices before me.'" — The same is found much abbreviated and without the expression that concerns us here in Pesiq. 60B; Pesiq. Rab. 16 (83B); Lev. Rab. 7 (110A).

b. Babylonian Talmud ʿErubin 21B: Raba († 352) said in a presentation, "What does 'The mandrakes give off a fragrance' (Song 7:14) mean? This pertains to the youth of Israel who have not tasted the taste of sin." The same is found anonymously in Midr. Song. 7:14 (130A). – In b. Pesaḥ. 87A, Rab († 247) gives the same interpretation to the words in Ps 144:12A. ‖ Midrash Ecclesiastes 1:8 (9B): R. Simeon b. Halapta (ca. 190) said, "All the goods, blessings and comforts that the prophets saw in this world they saw for the penitent; but for the one who has not tasted the taste of sin his whole life, the following applies, 'No eye has seen, O God, except for you, what is prepared for the one who hopes' (so Midr. Isa. 64:3)."

c. Babylonian Talmud Yoma 22B: Like a one-year-old child who has not tasted sin. – See the whole passage at § Matt 5:24, B, #1, second third.

5:21 B: Righteousness of God (see § Rom 1:17 A and § Rom 3:21 A).

6:2: At the suitable time I heard you ....

1. Isaiah 49:8 in the base text: "Thus says Yahweh, 'At the time of pleasure בְּעֵת רָצוֹן I will hear you and on the day of salvation וּבְיוֹם יְשׁוּעָה I will help you.'" – Targum: "Thus says Yahweh, 'At the time when you do my will רְעוּתִי, I will accept your prayer, and on the day of trouble I will cause redemption and help to arise for you.'" – Septuagint: οὕτως λέγει κύριος· Καιρῷ δεκτῷ ἐπήκουσά σε, καὶ ἐν ἡμέρᾳ σωτηρίας ἐβοήθησά σοι.

2. καιρὸς δεκτός = עֵת רָצוֹן.

Babylonian Talmud Sanhedrin 102A: "At the time of pleasure I will hear you" (Isa 49:8). In the name of R. Yose (ca. 150) it has been taught, "This is the time that is set for salvation (for the good לטובה)." ‖ Babylonian Talmud Berakot 7B: R. Yohanan († 279) said in the name of R. Simeon b Yohai (ca. 150), "What does 'I direct my prayer to you, Yahweh, at the time of pleasure עת רצונא (Targ: בְּעִדָּן רַעֲוָא)' (Ps 69:14) mean? When is the time of pleasure? In the hour when the community prays." R. Yose b. Hanina (ca. 270) said, "From here (this opinion can be established): 'Thus says Yahweh, "At the time of pleasure I will hear you"' (Isa 49:8)." ‖ Babylonian Talmud Taʿanit 24B: "This is the time of pleasure to beg for mercy." – See the whole passage at § Mark 10:17.

6:10: As poor who yet make many rich.

See the saying of Abbayye († 338/39) in b. Ned. 40B, as well as Lev. Rab. 1 (105D) at § Matt 5:3, #2, middle. ‖ Babylonian Talmud Berakot 17B: "Listen to me, you strong-hearted, who are far from kindness" (so Isa 46:12 according to the midr.). Rab († 247) and Samuel († 254); according to others R. Yohanan († 279) and R. Eleazar (ca. 270). The one said, "The whole world is supported by (God's) kindness; yet these (the strong-hearted, who are understood in a laudatory sense by the midrash) are supported (by the strength of their virtuousness) by (their own) arm." The other said, "The whole world is supported by their (the strong-hearted's) merit, and they are also not supported by their own merit (since the righteous often lack what is necessary to live)." This is like what Rab Judah († 299) said in the name of Rab († 247); for Rab Judah said that Rab said, "Daily a voice from heaven goes out from Mount Horeb and calls, 'The whole world is supported because of Hanina (b. Dosa, ca. 70), and my son Hanina (because of his poverty) can be satisfied with one measure of carob from one preparation day for the Sabbath to the next!'" — The saying about R. Hanina b. Dosa is also found in b. Taʿan. 24B. — A similar controversy about the "strong-hearted" in Isa 46:12 occurs between R. Yohanan († 279) and R. Simeon b. Laqish (ca. 250; tradent R. Abbahu [ca. 300]) in y. Maʿaś. Š. 5.56D.7.

6:14: Do not pull at a different yoke for unbelievers (for the sake of unbelievers).

The apostle may have had in mind the Kilʾayim law, which forbids joining animals of a different kind under one yoke[a] in Deut 22:10, although the LXX in Lev 19:19 rendered the term כִּלְאַיִם directly with ἑτερόζυγον.[b] This would have to be translated: "Do not be different yoke companions (ones not appropriate for them) with unbelievers."

a. Mishnah Kilʾayim 8.2, 3: With two kinds of livestock and two kinds of wild animals, with livestock and a wild animal, with a wild animal and livestock, with two kinds of unclean and two kinds of clean animals, with one unclean and one clean, with one clean and one unclean animal, one may not plow; one may also not make them draw nor steer them fastened together. Whoever steers them receives the forty (lashes), and whoever sits on the cart also receives the forty. R. Meir (ca. 150) clears the latter.

b. Septuagint Leviticus 19:19: τὰ κτήνη σου οὐ κατοχεύσεις (mate) ἑτεροζύγῳ.

6:15 A: Beliar.

Βελίαρ (= בְּלִיַּעַל "worthlessness, malice") is a name for the devil in the pseudepigrapha.[a] — Rabbinic literature does not know Beliar as a name for Satan but does give some haggadic interpretations of the Old Testament בני בליעל.[b]

a. Jubilees 1:20: "O Lord, may your mercy over your people be great, and fashion for them a right mind, and may the spirit of Belhor (= Beliar) not rule them, to accuse them before you and to woo them away from all the ways of righteousness, so that they perish far from your face." — Jubilees 15:33: "All the sons of Beliar will leave their sons without circumcision as they were born." ‖ Martyrdom and Ascension of Isaiah 2:4: "Manasseh (the king) also changed his mind so that he served Belial (= Beliar); for the prince of injustice, who rules this world, is Belial, whose name is Matanbukus (?)." — See further Mart. Ascen. Isa. 3:11; 5:3, 4. ‖ See Sib. Or. 3:63ff. at § 2 Thess 2:3 B, n. *d.* ‖ Beliar is mentioned most often in the Testaments of the 12 Patriarchs; see, for example, T. Reu. 2. 4; T. Sim. 5; T. Levi 18, 19; T. Jud. 19; T. Iss. 7; T. Zeb. 9; T. Dan 1, 4, 5; T. Naph. 2; T. Jos. 7; T. Benj. 3, 6, 7.

b. Sifre Deuteronomy 15:7ff. § 117 (98B): "Guard yourself, lest a thought, a despicable בְּלִיַּעַל one, arise in you yourself" (Deut 15:9). Be careful not to abstain from mercy; for whoever abstains from mercy toward another, Scripture makes him equal to an idolater, and he casts the yoke of heaven (God) from himself. As it says, "a despicable one" בליעל, (i.e.,)

בְּלִי עוֹל = "without yoke." — Thus, בליעל = one who casts God's yoke from himself. — See the whole passage at § Matt 5:42, #1. — ‖ Mishnah Sanhedrin 10.4: The inhabitant of an unfaithful city has no share in the future world (which begins with the resurrection of the dead); for it says, "Men, despicable people בני בליעל, have gone out from your midst" (Deut 13:14). — The probative quality of the passage appears to lie in בליעל being interpreted = בלי עָל = "who does not rise up, resurrect." It was also taken this way at § Acts 12:2. Yet a baraita in b. Sanh. 111B on the Mishnah above interprets בני בליעל in Deut 13:14 = בניס שפרקו עול = "sons who have cast off the yoke," so בליעל as above in SDeut 15:7ff. = בלי עול = "without yoke." Then the thought would be that the people who have cast off God's yoke and fallen away from Judaism obviously forfeit the resurrection and the future world.

6:15 B: What part (is there) for a believer with an unbeliever?

μερίς = חֵלֶק, in, for example, Josh 22:25: "You have no part חלק (LXX: μερίς) in Yahweh." See § John 2:4 A and § John 1:1 A, D, the first S-B footnote in that section.

7:1 A: Promises.

On ἐπαγγελία see § Rom 4:13 A, #2.

7:1 B: Let us cleanse ourselves from every defilement…, perfecting holiness…!

Conversely, holiness appears in the service of purity in ʾAbot R. Nat. 26 at the beginning: R. Aqiba († ca. 135) said, "… Holiness is a fence for purity סייג לטהרה קדושה."

7:4: Much boldness.

παρρησία, see § John 7:4.

7:10: Godly sorrow brings about repentance unto salvation.

See the citations at § Matt 4:17 A, #3.

7:13: Because his spirit was reassured by all of you (see § 1 Cor 16:18).

8:4: The benefaction and the fellowship of service.

1. χάρις in the meaning "favor, benefaction" also = חֶסֶד, Aram. חִסְדָּא. So in the common expression גְּמִילוּת חֲסָדִים "demonstration of benefaction, bestowal of love"; see examples in the excursus "Works of Love." Also, גָּמֵיל חִסְדָּא "doer of benefaction" = benefactor; גמל חסד "to bestow benefaction."

Jerusalem Talmud ʿAbodah Zarah 3.42C.17: (At the funeral of R. Samuel b. Isaac [ca. 300]) a voice from heaven went out that cried, "Woe, for Samuel b. Isaac, the performer of benefaction גמיל חיסדא, has passed away!" ‖ Jerusalem Talmud Ḥagigah 2.77D.39: One of them (of the two pious men in Askalon) passed away, and no labor of love was bestowed him לא איתגמל ליה חסד (at his funeral). The son of the tax collector Maayan died, and the whole city took time off (from work) to bestow on him the (last) labor of love מיגמול ליה חסד. — See the whole passage at § Luke 16:24 C.

2. On κοινωνία see § Rom 15:26, #1.

8:10: From last year.

ἀπὸ πέρυσι. — In the Mishnah, the previous year is called אֶשְׁתָּקַד, put together from שתא קדמאה "earlier year" with the א added at the beginning facilitating the pronunciation. שתא דא are likewise put together in אֶשְׁתָּדָא = "this year." — Examples can be found in m. Šeqal. 6.5; y. Maʿaś. Š. 4.55B.28.

8:12: If the willingness is present, it is pleasing according to what it has.

Mishnah Menaḥot 13.11: It does not matter whether someone offers much or little if he only directs his heart to God. — This statement in the Mishnah originally deals with the different offering capacities of rich and poor, but then in b. Ber. 17A.27 as a motto in the mouth of the rabbis of Yavneh it is applied generally to any person's offering: it is not the greatness of the gift that gives it its worth before God, but rather the attitude of the giver behind it. ‖ See b. Sukkah 49B at § 1 Cor 13:3 C.

8:13 A: Not so that there may be relief for others (and in contrast) suffering for you, but rather (so that it may be) in accordance with equality.

See the principle of b. Ketub. 50A in a baraita: Whoever wishes to give his possessions (as a gift) may not give more than the fifth part; perhaps he himself will (later) draw from people.

8:13 B: For their lack.

ὑστέρημα = חֶסְרוֹן, see § 1 Cor 16:17.

8:15: The one who had much did not have more, and the one who had little did not lack.

Exodus 16:18 in the base text: "The one who collected much did not have a surplus and the one who collected little did not lack." — Septuagint: οὐκ ἐπλεόνασεν ὁ τὸ πολὺ καὶ ὁ τὸ ἔλαττον οὐκ ἠλαττόνησεν. — Targum Onkelos: "The one who had much did not have any left over; and the one who had little did not lack." — Targum Yerušalmi I: "The one who had collected much did not have any left over from the mass, and the one who had collected little did not have any lack from the mass (in measure)."

8:19: Chosen by the churches.

Nothing more specific is stated in rabbinic literature about the sponsors of the people involved in raising collections for Jewish scholars. One may assume that the collectors were delegated by the patriarchate; see § Rom 15:26, #2.

8:21: We intend what is fitting (proper) not only before the Lord but also before people (cf. § Rom 12:17 B).

8:23: Emissaries from the churches.

On ἀπόστολοι see § Rom 15:26.

9:5: Your blessing that was previously promised.

εὐλογία "blessing" = gift of blessing, that is, a gift that is accompanied by blessings. בְּרָכָה has the same meaning in, for example, Gen 33:11; 1 Sam 25:27; 30:26; 2 Kgs 5:15; Prov 11:25. The LXX most often translate ברכה in these passages with εὐλογία = gift of blessing; only in 1 Sam 30:26 is the word left untranslated, while in Prov 11:25 they understand passively the actively intended נפש ברכה = "a soul that gives gifts of blessing," and renders it with ψυχὴ εὐλογουμένη = "a soul that is blessed." — The targumim mostly replace ברכה in the passages above with תִּקְרוּבְתָּא = "gift"; Yer. I has in Gen 33:11 דורון = δῶρον, "gift" and the targum to 1 Sam 30:26 מַתְּנָא = "gift." Only Tg. Prov. 11:25 retains ברכה in the Aramaic form בִּרְכְתָא: "A soul of ברכהא will be well-nourished, and the one who teaches also learns." Levy understands נפש דברכהא passively (cf. the LXX on Prov 11:25 above) = "the blessed person";[259] but this can hardly be right because the parallelism demands an active formulation: a soul that gives blessing = gifts of blessing, will be well-nourished, that is, a soul that blesses will itself be blessed, just as one who teaches also learns at the same time. — In the actual rabbinic literature, we know of no passage where ברכה would without doubt mean "gift of blessing."

9:6 A: Whoever sows scarcely will also reap scarcely.

3 Baruch 15: "Give a hundredfold recompense to our friends and to those who painstakingly did good works; for those who sow well will also reap well." ‖ A baraita in Lev. Rab. 30 (127D): On New Year's Day, a person's subsistence (for the next year) is determined (by God). This does not include what he distributes for the Sabbaths and the feast days and days of the new moon; also what the children bring into the house of their teacher (as a gift). If (for these purposes) he adds מוסיף, one (= God) adds to him; if he reduces פוחת, one reduces for him. — בְּצִמְצוּם "in scarcity" = sparingly, meagerly (opposite: בְּרֶיוַח "in abundance") appears only later in rabbinic writings.

9:6 B: Whoever sows with blessing will also reap with blessings.

See b. B. Qam. 17A at § John 4:10, n. *c*. — There is a parallel in b. ʿAbod. Zar. 5B with R. Benaiah (ca. 220) as the author.

259. Levy, *Chaldäisches Wörterbuch*, 1:163A.

9:7: God loves a joyful giver.

Proverbs 22:9 may underlie the aphorism, where the LXX translates: ἄνδρα ἱλαρὸν καὶ δότην εὐλογεῖ ὁ θεός. In the base text the passage reads: "Whoever has a benevolent eye will be blessed." — Targum: "Whoever's eye is benevolent will be blessed."

ʾAbot de Rabbi Nathan 13 (5B.1, 25): Shammai (ca. 30 BCE) said, "Accept every person with a cheerful face.... This teaches: if someone should give all the gifts in the world to someone else, yet his face look sullenly toward the earth, Scripture reckons it to him as if he had given him nothing. Yet if he accepts another with a cheerful face, Scripture reckons it to him, even if he had given him nothing, as if he had given him all good gifts." ‖ Babylonian Talmud Soṭah 38B: R. Joshua b. Levi (ca. 250) said, "One gives the cup of blessing (of thanksgiving after the meal) to say a blessing only to the one who has a benevolent eye; as it says, 'Whoever has a benevolent eye will be blessed' (Prov 22:9). Do not read יבורך 'he will be blessed,' but rather יברך 'he shall say the blessing.'" ‖ See b. Ned. 38A at § 2 Cor 3:7 B, n. *ll*. ‖ Leviticus Rabbah 34 (131B): R. Isaac (ca. 300) said, "... If someone wants to give alms, he should give with a cheerful heart בלב שמח."

9:9f.: He scattered, gave to the poor, his righteousness remains for eternity.... Seed for the sower and bread for food, ... the products of your righteousness.

In verse 9, Ps 112:9 is cited following the LXX; in verse 10, in the words σπέρμα τῷ σπείροντι καὶ ἄρτον εἰς βρῶσιν and γενήματα τῆς δικαιοσύνης, the apostle uses expressions that are found in LXX Isa 55:10 and Hos 10:12. Neither in the scriptural citation from Ps 112:9 nor in the words γενήματα τῆς δικαιοσύνης is there any need to understand δικαιοσύνη to mean "alms" or "charity" in general. In the present context δικαιοσύνη means nothing other than a person's righteous posture that corresponds with the divine expectation, a posture that drives the person specifically to charity. — In rabbinic literature, though, Ps 112:9 was understood differently; here, צדקה in Ps 112:9 is interpreted as the charity of the God-fearing, in accordance with the later meaning of צְדָקָה.

Leviticus Rabbah 34 (132A): R. Tarfon (ca. 100) gave R. Aqiba († ca. 135) six hundred silver talents. He said to him, "Go, buy yourself the property where we busy ourselves with the Torah and from which we (simultaneously) can have our subsistence." He took the talents and distributed them to the students and teachers of the Mishnah and those who occupied themselves with the study of the Torah. After some days he met with him. He said to him, "Did you buy for yourself that property that I told you about?" He answered him, "Yes!" He said to him, "Can you show me it?" He answered him, "Yes!" He took him and showed him the students and teachers of the Mishnah and those who occupied themselves with the study of the Torah. He said to him, "Does a person give away something for free? Where is the receipt אַפּוֹכִי (ἀποχή) for it?" He answered him, "In David,[260] the king of Israel,

260. S-B: "In David" = "in the Book of Psalms."

in whom it is written, 'He scattered (and) gave to the poor, his alms צדקתו are pending (like a sure mortgage) forever' (Ps 112:9)." — Parallel passages are found in Pesiq. Rab. 25 (126B); tractate Kallah 18B. ‖ Babylonian Talmud Baba Batra 10B: R. Abbahu (ca. 300) said, "Solomon, the son of David, was asked, 'How far does the power of alms (charity) כחה של צדקה extend?' He answered them, 'Go and see what my father David clearly stated, "He scattered (and) gave to the poor, his arms are certain forever, his horn is raised in honor"' (Ps 112:9)."

10:2: According to the flesh (cf. § 1 Cor 3:1, 3).

11:2: A pure bride.

ἁγνή = טְהוֹרָה — see Midr. Song. 4:11 (115B) at § Matt 9:15 B, n. *g*. — By contrast, the confession of guilt for the woman suspected of adultery is as follows in m. Soṭah 3.3: "I am unclean טמאה אני." — On clean and unclean in a sexual sense, see also Num 5:28. Targum Onkelos and Yerušalmi I render טהורה here with דַּכְיָאָה = "clean" and the verb נטמאה with אִסְתָּאָבַת = "she has defiled herself."

11:3: As the snake in its cunning deceived Eve.

On the snake's cunning, see Gen. Rab. 19 (12D); ʾAbot R. Nat. 1 (1B) at § Matt 15:2 A, #4; also see 2 Bar. 48:42f.; Tanḥ. בראשית 5B at § Rom 5:15 A, #1, middle; Pirqe R. El. 13 at § Matt 4:1 B, #2, n. *a*; Num. Rab. 8 (149B) at § Matt 4:1 B, #2, n. *d* and the passages in n. *e* there.

11:6: An amateur in speech.

ἰδιώτης, see § 1 Cor 14:16 A, #1.

11:7: In vain I preached the gospel of God.

See § Matt 10:8 B; see also § 1 Cor 9:9 B and 9:10.

11:8: Taking pay.

ὀψώνιον, see § Rom 6:23, #1.

11:14: For Satan himself changes himself into an angel of light.

1. On the ability of Satan to change himself into any form, see § Matt 4:1 B, #3, A.

It is said about the fallen angels in general in 1 Enoch 19:1: "Then Uriel said to me (Enoch), 'Here the angels will stand who have mingled with women; and their spirits, taking many forms, defile people and mislead them to sacrifice to demons as gods.'"

2. Satan changes himself into the form of the angels.

Life of Adam and Eve 9: "18 days passed (of the 40 days of Adam's repentance); then Satan became angry and changed himself into the luminous form of the angels ...." ‖ Apocalypse of Moses 17: "At once the snake (which had been acquired for Satan's seduction tactics) hung on the wall of Paradise. At the hour when the angels of God went up to worship

God, Satan adopted an angelic form and praised God like the angels. And he bent over the wall so that I (Eve) saw him (in the form) like an angel."

11:22 A: Are they Hebrews?

עִבְרִי "Hebrew" is α. the name of the people which the Israelites bear in distinction to the other nations; see, for example, Pirqe R. El. 10 at § Matt 12:39 B, #3. — On the rabbinic interpretations of the name, see Gen. Rab. 42 (26C) at § John 5:2, #1. — β. A designation of Hebrew- (Aramaic-)speaking Jews in contrast to Greek-speaking Jewish Hellenists. So 2 Cor 11:22 and Phil 3:5; Acts 6:1; see § John 5:2, #2.

11:22 B: Are they Israelites?

יִשְׂרָאֵל, originally the honorific name for Jacob[a] (Gen 32:29), designates α. the whole Jewish people[b] and β. the individual Jew[c] as a member of the people of God.

a. Genesis Rabbah 77 (49C): R. Berekhiah (ca. 340) said in the name of R. Simon (ca. 280): "'No one is like the God of Jeshurun' (Deut 33:26). And who is like the God of Jeshurun? Israel, the old man (= Jacob). Just as it is written of God, 'Yahweh "alone" is exalted there' (Isa 2:11), so too 'Jacob remained "alone"'(Gen 32:25)."

b. Mishnah Sanhedrin 10.1: All Israel has a share in the future world. ‖ Babylonian Talmud Roš Haššanah 32B: R. Abbahu (ca. 300) said, "The angels of service said before God, 'Lord of the world, why do the Israelites ישראל not say (with the verb in the plural) a song before you on the Day of the New Year and the Day of Atonement?' He answered them, 'While the king sits on his judgment throne and the books of life and death are opened before him, should Israel say a song (verb in the singular)?'"

c. The individual Israelite ישראל is frequently mentioned alongside or in contrast to the priest; see, for example, t. Ketub. 1.2 (260) and m. Ketub. 1.5 at § John 2:1 A, #4, C, n. *m.*

11:22 C: Are they Abraham's seed? (see § John 8:33 A).

11:24: From the Jews I received five times forty (lashes) minus one.

1. τεσσεράκοντα παρὰ μίαν = forty except for one. — Josephus: πληγὰς μιᾶ̣ λιπούσας τεσσαράκοντα (*Ant.* 4.8.21) or πληγὰς τεσσαρακοντα μιᾶς λειπούσης (*Ant.* 4.8.23). — Mishnah Makkot 3.10: אַרְבָּעִים חָסֵר אַחַת = forty minus one. — Numbers formed by subtraction are also found elsewhere in rabbinic literature.

Tanḥuma ראה 9B: The curses in the Torah of the priests (= 3rd book of Moses) comprise 30 verses minus one and the blessings 11. ‖ Tanḥuma אתם נצבים 25B: The Israelites heard 100 curses minus one or two. ‖ See m. Šabb. 7.2; b. Šabb. 49B; b. B. Qam. 2A at § Matt 12:2, notes *a* and *b.*

2. τεσσεράκοντα in the absolute without πληγαί corresponds to the absolute אַרְבָּעִים without מַכּוֹת among the rabbis.

A baraita in b. Šabb. 95A: Whoever on the Sabbath milks, stirs a paste, makes cheese in the amount of a dried fig etc., is guilty of a sin offering, if it happens unintentionally; if he does it on purpose on a (inter-)festival day, he will receive forty (lashes) לוֹקֶה ארבעים. — Additional examples are given in the following citations.

3. ἔλαβον. — In rabbinic literature three verbs in particularly are used for this: לָקָה (Aram. לְקָא) = to be hit, to receive flogging;[a] קִבֵּל (Aram. קַבֵּיל) = to obtain, receive;[b] and סָפַג = to absorb, bring upon oneself.[c]

a. Mishnah Makkot 1.1: How are witnesses treated as false (what happens to them)? If they said, "We testify against (the priest) so-and-so that he is the son of a divorced woman or the son of a woman who carried out the removal of the shoe,"[261] one does not say (on the basis of Deut 19:19), "Let him instead be treated as the son of a divorced woman or as the son of a woman who carried out the removal of the shoe, but rather he is punished with the forty (lashes) לוקה ארבעים." If they said, "We testify against so-and-so that he is guilty (of manslaughter) to flee to a sanctuary city," one does not say, "Let him instead flee to a sanctuary city, but rather he is punished with the forty (lashes)."

b. See m. Mak. 3.11 in #4, n. *c*.

c. Mishnah Kil᾿ayim 8.2, 3: No one may plow … with two (heterogeneous) kinds of livestock; nor may one make them draw or steer them when they are tied together. Whoever steers them brings upon himself the forty (lashes) סוֹפֵג את הארבעים, and whoever sits on the cart (also) draws upon himself the forty. R. Meir lets the latter off.

4. The punishment of flagellation followed on the pronouncement of three judges.[a] The number of blows was set at 40 by Deut 25:3; yet this passage was interpreted so that in fact only 39 were administered.[b] Before carrying out the flagellation, the wrongdoer was evaluated to see how many strokes he could endure at once without jeopardizing his body or life. If the evaluation showed that he could not bear the 39 blows all at once, the number was lowered. Yet the number had to be divisible by three,[c] because a third of the blows were applied on the chest and two thirds on the back of the delinquent.[d] — Mishnah Makkot 3.12ff. contains more detail about the execution of flagellation;[e] the main offenses that were punished with the penalty of flagellation are enumerated in m. Mak. 3.1ff.[f]

a. Mishnah Sanhedrin 1.2: The lash strokes מַכּוֹת are determined by three (judges). In the name of R. Ishmael († ca. 135) it has been said, "By twenty-three." — On this, b. Sanh. 10A: Lash strokes by three. Where do these words come from? Rab Huna († 297) said, "Scripture says, 'And they judge them' וּשְׁפָטוּם (Deut 25:1); these are two (the plural of the verb presupposes at least 2 judges). Yet there is no court that consists of an even number of judges; so one more is added to them; see, here there are three …." In the name of R. Ishmael († ca. 135) it was said, "By twenty-three." What was R. Ishmael's scriptural basis? Abbayye († 338/39) said, "It is established by the analogy of the word רָשָׁע = the guilty person; this is said about those who are guilty of death. Here it is written, 'If the "guilty" one should receive blows'

261. S-B: These women were not allowed to be married by priests; it happened, though, so the sons of such marriages were excluded from all priestly functions

(Deut 25:2), and there it is written, 'One who is "guilty" of death' (Num 35:31). Just as there (the imposition of the death penalty) is by twenty-three, so too here (the imposition of flagellation) is by twenty-three." Raba († 352) said, "Flagellation מַלְקוּת occurs for the death penalty (so 23 judges are appropriate for imposing it)."

b. Mishnah Makkot 3.10: How many strokes of the lash is he given? Forty minus one; for it says, "With the number forty" (so the midrash, which connects the last word of Deut 25:2 with the first word of verse 3), that is, a number that comes close to forty (so 39). R. Judah (ca. 150) said, "A whole forty. And where does he receive לוֹקֶה the surplus one? Between his shoulders." ‖ Numbers Rabbah 18 (185A): "He shall give him forty blows, not more" (Deut 25:3); this corresponds to the forty curses with which the snake, Eve, Adam, and the earth were cursed (cf. Pirqe R. El. 14 [7D] at § Rom 8:20f., n. *g*), and the scholars said one less because of the words "not more." ‖ Targum Yerušalmi I Deuteronomy 25:2f.: "If the culprit is found guilty to receive blows, the judge shall have him lie down and in his presence have him scourged according to the measure of his guilt in his trial. He shall strike forty times (with the whip), but he shall strike him one time less; he shall not complete (the number of the forty blows); he might strike him beyond the thirty-nine blows and he may be brought into (mortal) danger; and your brother should not be made contemptible while you look at him."

c. Mishnah Makkot 3.11: He is evaluated (the delinquent concerning the question of how many lashes he can bear without being endangered) only for a number of blows that can be divided in three parts. If he has been evaluated to receive forty לְקַבֵּל אַרְבָּעִים, he receives one part of the strokes לָקָה מִקְצַת and, if he is not able to receive לקבל forty, he is let off (the rest are waived). If he has been assessed to receive eighteen, yet after he has received them he can receive לקבל forty, he is let off (the first assessment remains binding). If he committed a transgression, in which two prohibitions (and so two transgressions) were contained, and in an evaluation he was evaluated (so that he could bear the two merited scourgings at once, perhaps in the amount of 42 blows), he is scourged (all at once) and then is free (the remainder of the second forty blows are waived); but if not (i.e., if he could not be evaluated as strong enough to bear both scourgings at once), he is lashed (first for the one transgression) and healed and then scourged again (for the other transgression).

d. See m. Mak. 3.12ff. in n. *e*.

e. Mishnah Makkot 3.12ff.: How is he scourged מלקין? Both his hands are tied to a pillar here and there (Bertinoro: a pillar, perhaps 2–1.5 cubits high, was fixed in the ground, and he himself was bent down and stretched out on the pillar; then both his hands were tied on both sides of the pillar). The attendant of the synagogue takes hold of his clothes—if they were torn, they were torn; if they were ripped, they were ripped—until he exposed his heart (breast); and a stone lay behind him (the offender). The attendant of the synagogue stood on it with a thong of calfskin in his hand that was folded one to two and two to four (so that the thong that was originally just one-fold was now four-fold), and two (thin) thongs were threaded in it up and down[262] (through holes in the thong folded together four times

---

262. S-B: Babylonian Talmud Makkot 23A: Two (thin) straps. It has been taught: With donkey skin, as the Galilean presented before Rab Hisda († 309): "An ox knows its owner and a donkey its

in order to give it stability and cohesiveness). The handle on it (the whip) was one handbreadth long, and its (the whip's) width was one handbreadth, and it reached (around) to the navel (of the delinquent). And he beat him a third from the front and two thirds from behind. And he did not beat him while he (the one being scourged) stood or sat, but rather while he was bent down; as it says, "And the judge shall have him lie down" (Deut 25:2). And the one beating beat him with his one hand with all its strength. The reader read out,[263] "If you do not carefully carry out all the words of this law etc., Yahweh will make your blows (plagues) extraordinary …." (Deut 28:58f.). Then he returns to the beginning of the passage of Scripture (reads it again, if the scourging drags on for an extended time). Then (he reads), "Keep the words of this covenant and do them …" (Deut 29:8) and closes with, "He is merciful, expiates iniquity and does not destroy, and many times he turns away his anger and does not arouse his whole wrath" (Ps 78:38). Then (if necessary) he returns to the beginning of the Scripture passage again. If he dies under his hand, he (the beater) is exempt from punishment. Yet if he adds one stroke and he dies, he must flee because of him (to a city of asylum). If he (the one scourged) defiles himself, whether by excrement or by urine, he (the one scourged) is free (because this defilement already signifies a degradation in the sense of Deut 25:3). R. Judah (ca. 150) said, "A man by excrement, but a woman (also) by urine."

f. Mishnah Makkot 3.1ff.: These are the ones who are scourged הַלּוֹקִין: whoever sleeps with his sister (Lev 18:9, 11; 20:17) or his father's sister or his mother's sister (Lev 18:12f.; 20:19) or his wife's sister (Lev 18:18) or his brother's wife (Lev 18:16; 20:21) or his father's brother's wife (Lev 18:14; 20:20) or a menstruant (Lev 18:19). (Further, it is forbidden to scourge) a widow of the high priest (Lev 21:14); and the divorced wife of an ordinary priest (Lev 21:7) and one who has carried out the ritual of removing the shoe of an ordinary priest; a female bastard or temple bondwoman (*nethina*, cf. Josh 9) of an Israelite; an Israelite woman of a bastard or a temple bondsman. In the case of a widow who is also a divorcée, one (the high priest) is guilty of two prohibitions; in the case of a divorcée who has carried out the rite of removing the shoe, one (the ordinary priest) is guilty of only one prohibition (because the *chaluṣa* is only forbidden to the priest by the rabbis and the prohibition is based on Lev 21:7 in the same way as the prohibition against marrying a divorced woman). (The following are also scourged:) an unclean person who has eaten what is holy (Lev 7:20), and whoever has come into the sanctuary while unclean (Num 5:3); whoever has eaten tallow (forbidden fat, Lev 3:3, 4, 17) or blood (Lev 3:17) or anything holy left beyond the time (Exod 29:34) or anything objectionable (offering food more than 2 days old, Lev 7:18) or unclean (Lev 7:19); whoever has slaughtered or presented (animal sacrifices) outside the temple (Lev 17:4, 9) and whoever ate something leavened on Passover (Deut 16:3) and whoever ate or did work on the Day of Atonement (Lev 23:29, 31) and whoever copied the (holy) oil of anointing or the (holy) incense (Exod 30:32f., 37f.) and whoever anointed himself with the holy oil

---

lord's manger; but Israel does not know" (Isa 1:3). God said, "Let him come who knows his Lord's manger, and let him punish the one who does not know his Lord's manger!"

263. S-B: A baraita in b. Mak. 23A: The greatest among the judges reads, the second counts (the blows) and the third says (before each blow), "Hit him!" — According to other passages, the one who did the beating seems himself to have counted; see m. Yoma 5.3f.; b. Yoma 54B and y. Yoma 5.42C.32 at § Rom 3:25 A, #6, n. *c*.

of anointing and whoever ate carrion (not ritually slaughtered food) or anything damaged (*ṭerefah*) or bugs or worms; whoever has eaten something untithed or a first tithe, from which the heave offering had not been set apart (Num 18:26), or a second tithe (which had become unclean and was not allowed to be eaten in Jerusalem without being resolved; see m. Maʿaś. Š. 3.9) or anything holy (Lev 22:10) which had not been redeemed .... Furthermore, whoever eats first fruits before he has recited (the prescribed section of Scripture from Deut 26:5–10), whoever eats a most holy offering outside the parts that hang around (= outside the temple court) and less holy offerings or second tithes outside the walls (of Jerusalem); whoever breaks a bone of a pure Passover lamb: he receives 40 lashes. — This enumeration, though, is not by any means complete; so according to m. Mak. 3.5ff., for example, someone who observes certain pagan customs is also scourged, as is a Nazirite who drank wine or defiled himself with corpses or cut his hair, and in Palestine the punishment of scourging was imposed on scholars instead of the ban, see the excursus "Excommunication from the Synagogue."

11:31: Who is blessed forever.

On occasional doxologies see § Rom 1:25. Here a few more follow. Tanḥuma מצורע 160B: The Holy One—Blessed be He! Blessed be his name forever!—also determined all the sufferings for a person before he created him. ‖ Tanḥuma האזינו 28B: Why does David say, "Seek his face forever" (1 Chr 16:11)? To teach you that the Holy One—Blessed be He! Blessed be his name!—sometimes appears and sometimes does not appear, sometimes listens and sometimes does not wish to listen, sometimes answers and sometimes does not answer .... ‖ Targum Yerušalmi I Exodus 24:18: "Moses entered the cloud and ascended to the mountain, and on the mountain Moses learned the words of the Torah from the mouth of the Holy One—Blessed be his name!—for forty days and forty nights." ‖ ʾAbot de Rabbi Nathan 31 (8B): The Holy One—Blessed be He! Blessed be his great name forever and ever!—created the whole world by his wisdom by his insight.

11:32: Of king Aretas.

Aretas IV (ca. 9 BCE until 40 CE) in inscriptions is called חרתת מלך נבטו רחם עמה "Harithath, king of the Nabateans, who loves his people" ΣA.[264] It is uncertain whether the name means the one "diligent in profession, seed of industry," as Delitzsch supposes.[265]

11:33: I was let down through a (window) opening in the wall.

Perhaps one should think of a building like the one mentioned in m. ʿArak. 9.5: A house that is built in the (city) wall is not viewed, as R. Judah (ca. 150) said, like a house of a walled city. R. Simeon (ca. 150)

---

264. See Emil Schürer, *Geschichte des jüdischen Volkes im Zeitalter Jesu Christi*, 4th ed. (Leipzig: Hinrichs, 1901), 1:738.

265. Franz Delitzsch, "Horae Hebraicae et Talmudicae: VIII. Zweiter Brief an die Korinther," *Zeitschrift für die gesammte lutherische Theologie und Kirche* (1877): 454.

said, "The outer wall counts as its wall." — The house therefore is not an appendage to the wall, but rather the wall counts as a part (the back wall) of the house.

12:2 A: I know a man.

This way of speaking about oneself is reminiscent of the replacement of the 1st and 2nd person of the personal pronoun with: "this (that) man, this (that) woman."

Babylonian Talmud Ketubbot 49B: This man (= I) is not asking about his children; see § Luke 12:24 A. ‖ Babylonian Talmud Baba Meṣiʿa 85B: Two sparks of fire came and hit this man (= me) and blinded his eyes; see § Luke 23:43, C, n. *c*, comment. ‖ Babylonian Talmud Berakot 56A: May it be (God's) will that this man (= you) be given into the power of a government that will not have mercy! See § Matt 1:20, n. *k*. ‖ Babylonian Talmud Baba Qamma 58A: That woman (= I) has ten sons; see § Rom 1:26 A, #1 toward the end. ‖ Genesis Rabbah 38 (23C): Woe to this man (= you)! See § Rom 4:2f., #1, *d*, n. ι. ‖ Midrash Lamentations 1:1 (47A): This man (= you) ascends to greatness; see § Luke 1:63 A, #2, n. *c*, second third. ‖ Leviticus Rabbah 34 (132A) twice: Give this woman (= me) alms. ‖ Pesiqta 40A: Has the spirit of confusion (possession) never gone into this man (= into you)? See § Matt 21:24. ‖ Jerusalem Talmud Maʿaśer Šeni 4.55C.14: This woman (= I) has seen in a dream a room of the house burst apart; see § Matt 1:20, n. *i*. ‖ Babylonian Talmud Sanhedrin 98B: When darkness covers that people (= you); see § Rom 2:19–20, #2, n. *c*, end. — The possessive pronoun can also be replaced in this way. Leviticus Rabbah 32 (130A): You have cut off the life of this man (= my life).

12:2 B: Who was transported.

The pseudepigrapha often mention people being transported; see, for example, 1 En. 39:3; 52:1; 71:1; 71:5: Then the spirit transported Enoch to the heaven of heavens. — 3 Baruch 2ff.; 2 En. 3:7, 8, 11; etc. ‖ Babylonian Talmud Pesaḥim 50A: R. Joseph, the son of R. Joshua b. Levi (ca. 250), fell ill and was transported (in his fevered dreams) אִיתְנְגִיד; see § Matt 5:10, #3, first third. The parallel in b. B. Bat. 10B also uses the verb אִינְּגִיד; it is otherwise in Midr. Ruth 1:17 (128A). — The passage cited by Wetstein, b. B. Meṣ. 89 (he must mean 86A), does not deal with the transporting of, but rather with the dying of Rabbah b. Nahmani († 331).

12:2 C: To the third heaven.

ἕως τρίτου οὐρανοῦ, in the apostle's mind = to the highest heaven, to the immediate vicinity of God. The ancient period denoted the highest heaven as "heaven of heavens."[a] In this expression, it was found that, numerically, two heavens were taught. On the basis of the fuller formula: "Heaven and the heaven of heavens" (1 Kgs 8:27), others supposed that there were three heavens.[b] Around the middle of the 2nd century, rabbinic circles spoke of seven heavens.[c] This view then became the dominant one. It is doubtful whether Rabban Yohanan b. Zakkai († ca. 80) already based his exposition in b. Ḥag. 13A (= b. Pesaḥ. 94A, B) on seven heavens; see the passage at § Matt 11:23 A. In any case, though, some of the pseudepigrapha are already familiar with seven heavens.[c] Differently, 2 Enoch refers to ten heavens[d] and 3 Baruch to five heavens.[e]

a. 1 Enoch 1:3f.: "The great holy one will go out from his dwelling and the God of eternity will go from there to Mount Sinai (for the last judgment), he will be visible with his armies and he will appear in the power of his might from the heaven of heavens." — 1 Enoch 71:5: "Then the spirit transported Enoch to the heaven of heavens."

b. Midrash Psalm 114 § 2 (236A): The Rabbanan said, "There are two firmaments (= heavens); for it says, 'He who rides along in the heaven of heavens' (Ps 68:34)." Our teachers said, "(There are) three (heavens); for it says, 'Heaven and the heaven of heavens' (1 Kgs 8:27)." — Yet this fuller formula was also interpreted as referring to two heavens; so b. Ḥag. 12B: R. Judah (ca. 150) said, "There are two firmaments; for it says, 'Behold, to Yahweh your God belong heaven and the heaven of heavens' (Deut 10:14)." — Likewise, Rab († 247) in Deut. Rab. 2 (199B).

c. Babylonian Talmud Ḥagigah 12B: R. Meir (ca. 150, so read with ʾAbot R. Nat. 37 instead of "Resh Laqish," ca. 250) said, "There are seven (firmaments = heavens), and they are: וִילוֹן (= velum, curtain), רָקִיעַ (firmament), שְׁחָקִים (thinning, in the sense of the midrash = grinding), זְבוּל (dwelling), מָעוֹן (dwelling), מָכוֹן (place), and עֲרָבוֹת (according to the midr., tantamount to עֲרָפֶל = the darkness). — The וילון is nothing actual (permanently existing), but rather comes in the morning (to cover the stars, like a curtain) and disappears in the evening (so the stars appear) and so daily renews the work of creation; as it says, 'Who stretches out heaven like a towel of gauze (= curtain) and spreads it out like a tent to dwell in' (Isa 40:22). — The רקיע, to which the sun and moon, stars and the planets are affixed; as it says, 'God set them on the רקיע (the firmament) of heaven' (Gen 1:17). — שחקום, in which are the millstones, which grind the manna for the righteous; as it says, 'He commanded the *shechaqim* above (= the clouds, which the midrash interprets as "the grinders") and opened the door of heavens and made manna rain down on them for food' (Ps 78:23f.). — זבול, in which the (heavenly) Jerusalem and the (heavenly) sanctuary and an altar is built, at which Michael, the great prince, stands and on which he brings the offering; as it says, 'I have built a house as a dwelling זבול for you, a place מכון for your throne forever' (1 Kgs 8:13). And how do we know it (זבול) is called 'heaven'? Because it is written, 'See from heaven and look down from your holy and splendid dwelling (זבול)' (Isa 63:15). — מעון, in which the divisions of the angels of service are, who say a song at night, but remain silent by day for the sake of Israel's honor (because by day the latter praise God); as it says, 'By day Yahweh offers his goods (to those below, so the angels have to remain silent) and by night his song (sung to him by the angels) is with me (united with the one sung by me during the day, according to Rashi's interpretation)' (Ps 42:9) .... And how do we know it (מעון) is called heaven? Because it says, 'Look down from your holy dwelling מעון from heaven' (Deut 26:15). — מכון, in which the storage rooms of snow and the storage rooms of hail are, and the balcony of harmful dew and the balcony of the waters (that harm crops, Rashi) and the chambers of the storm wind and the cavern of fog, and their doors are fire; as it says, 'Yahweh will open his good treasure to you' (Deut 28:12; it follows from this that with God there are also treasures for punishment, and these are found precisely in the 6th heaven) .... And how do we know it (מכון) is called heaven? Because it says, 'May you hear from heaven in the place מכון of your throne' (1 Kgs 8:39). – ערבות, in which righteousness, justice and mercy are, the treasures of life and the treasures of peace and the treasures of blessing and the souls of the righteous (who have died) and the spirits and souls that shall one day be created (i.e., embodied; here souls themselves are thought of as preexistent), and the dew with which God will one day bring the dead back to life. Righteousness and justice; for it is written, 'Righteousness and justice are the foundations of your throne' (Ps 89:15). Mercy, for it is written, 'He put on mercy as armor' (Isa 59:17). The treasures of life; for it is written, 'For with you is the source of life' (Ps 36:10). The treasures of peace; for it is written, 'He called it "Yahweh is peace"' (Judg 6:24). And the treasures of blessing; for it is written, 'He will receive blessing from Yahweh' (Ps 24:5). The souls of the righteous; for it is written, 'The soul of my lord will be bound with the bundle of those who live with Yahweh your God' (1 Sam 25:29). The spirit and the souls that will one day be created; for it is written, 'The spirit would faint before me and the souls that I have created' (Isa 57:16). The dew with which God will one day bring the dead to life; for it is written, 'You showered a rain of gifts, O God, you raised up your inheritance when it was exhausted' (Ps 68:10). (Rashi: 'The passage is written about the giving of the law, since their soul went out; as it says, "My soul went out at his word."') There (in the Araboth) are the *Ofanim* (angels of the wheels) ..."; see the continuation at § Matt 25:31 B, #2, *a*. Then follows: Rab Aha b. Jacob (ca. 325) said, "There is another firmament (so an eighth) above the heads of the holy *chayyoth*; for it is written, 'And there was an appearance above the heads of the *chayyoth* like a firmament that looked like noble crystal' (Ezek 1:22)." – Parallel passages that mostly give the names of the seven heavens only briefly, though, include 'Abot R. Nat. 37 (9D); Pesiq. 154B; Lev. Rab. 29 (127C). In the last two passages, there are the introductory words: "All sevens are beloved" (before God); additionally, וילון and מכון are replaced by שמים and שמי שמים. ‖ Midrash Psalm 114 § 2 (236A): R. Eleazar (ca. 270) said, "There are seven (firmaments): וילון, רקיע, שחק, זבול, מעון, מכון, ערבות, and the glory of God is in the Araboth." R. Halapta b. Jacob (ca. 350?) said in the name of R. Judah b. Simon (ca. 320), "God saw the works of the righteous, and he took pleasure (ערב, which is supposed to interpret the name of the heaven Araboth) in their works." R. Phineas, the priest, b. Hama (ca. 360) said, "In the firmament whose name is Araboth God sows the works of the righteous, and they bring fruits; as it says, 'For they will enjoy the fruit of their deeds' (Isa 3:10)." – The saying of R. Eleazar is also found in Deut. Rab. 2 (199); the names the 7 heavens are שמים, שמי שמים, רקיע, שחקים, מעון, זבול, ערפל. ‖ See Pesiq. Rab. 5 (18B) at § Rom 3:25 A, #4, n. *a*; according to this passage, R. Simeon b. Yohai (ca. 150) would also have assumed there were seven heavens. But according to the parallel Pesiq. Rab. 17B, which is not cited there, we should instead read R. Simeon b. Yosena (ca. 270?). ‖ Seven heavens are also mentioned in b. Roš Haš. 32A; b. Menaḥ. 39A; Exod. Rab. 15 (78D); Pesiq. 7B; Pirqe R. El. 18; Midr. Ps. 92 § 2 (201B); Tanḥ. תרומה 101B. – Among the pseudepigrapha, T. Levi 2f. and Apoc. Mos. 35 are aware of seven heavens.

d. 2 Enoch 22: "In the tenth heaven Araboth, I (Enoch) saw the face of the countenance of the Lord."

e. 3 Baruch 11: "The angel took me (Baruch) from this one (the 4th heaven) and brought me to a fifth heaven." — A sixth and seventh heaven are not mentioned; yet in Kautzsch (II, p. 450, n. *a*), Ryssel remarks, "It should be assumed and is confirmed by the citation in Origen that this passage too originally ... spoke of seven heavens." — The citation in question from Origen (*Princ.* 2.3.6) reads: *Denique etiam Baruch prophetae librum in assertionis huius testimonium vocant, quod ibi de septem mundis vel caelis evidentius indicatur.*

12:4 A: Into paradise.

1. παράδεισος = גַּן עֵדֶן. — Rabbinic Judaism spoke of the garden of Eden in a threefold sense. It was understood to refer to α. Adam's paradise, which was secluded in hiddenness somewhere after the fall; β. the heavenly paradise that serves as the abode of the righteous in heaven with God in the intermediary period between death and resurrection; γ. the eschatological paradise that will appear as the site of the blessed on earth, whether in the days of the Messiah or at the dawn of the future world. Rabbinic scholars consistently identified this eschatological paradise with Adam's paradise, and its reappearance was expected at the time of the consummation. 4 Ezra has the eschatological paradise descend from heaven to earth, while 2 Baruch conversely transfers the blessed consummation from earth to heaven, specifically to the heavenly paradise. See on this in more detail in the excursus "Sheol, Gehenna, and the Garden of Eden"; individual elements are also found at § Luke 23:43, #2. — 2 Corinthians 12:4 and Luke 23:43 use παράδεισος to refer to the heavenly world of souls, that is, the paradise listed above under β.

2. Just as the third heaven and paradise appear in close connection with each other in 2 Cor 12:2 and 4, so too in Apoc. Mos. 37: "Then the Father of all stretched out his hand, sitting on his throne, lifted up (the dead) Adam and gave him to the archangel Michael with the words, 'Lift him into paradise up to the third heaven and leave him there until that great and dreadful day of my event that I will bring to the world.'"

12:4 B: Inexpressible words that no one can speak.

2 Enoch 17: "In the middle of the heavens I (Enoch) saw an armed host, which served the Lord with trumpets and instruments and uninterrupted voice and beautiful voice and with beautiful and ceaseless and different sorts of (or 'excellent') song, which is impossible to express." — See also Rev 14:3: No one could learn the song.

12:7 A: A thorn for the flesh was given to me.

σκόλοψ = sharp stake, thorn, barb, a metaphorical term for something that causes pain in any way.

1. Numbers 33:55: "If you do not drive out the inhabitants of the land before you, what you leave of them will become thorns שִׂכִּים (LXX: σκόλοπες) in your eyes and barbs צְנִינִם

(LXX: βολίδες) in your sides, and they will oppress you in the land in which you dwell." – The targumim avoided the image. Onkelos: "It will happen that those whom you leave will become hordes that will seize weapons against you, and army camps that will encircle you." – Yerušalmi I: "It will happen that what you leave will become like those who look at you with an envious eye סָכְיָין (interpretation of שִׂכִּים) and will surround you like shields at your sides." – Yet ʿArukh knows of a different reading: "They will become thorns סִכִּין in your eyes." – Pesiqta 112A: R. Samuel b. Nahman (ca. 260) opened his presentation with the following, "'If you do not drive out the inhabitants of the land before you' (Num 33:55). God said to the Israelites, 'I told you, "You shall strictly carry out the ban with them ..."' (Deut 20:17); yet you did not do so. Rather, 'Rahab, the prostitute, and her family and all her relatives Joshua left alive' (Josh 6:25). See, Jeremiah will come from the descendants of the prostitute Rahab and bestow on you words full of 'thorns in your eyes' and full of 'barbs in your sides' (Num 33:55)." ‖ R. Levi (ca. 300) applied Num 33:55 to King Saul, who spared Agag. Therefore, Haman arose from him, "who, God said, will make hard words become thorns in your sides and barbs in your sides" (Midr. Esth. Intro. 81B).

2. Ezekiel 28:24: "There shall no longer be for the house of Israel a thorn that causes bitter pain סִלּוֹן מַמְאִיר (LXX: σκόλοψ πικρίας) and a thorn that hurts קוֹץ מַכְאִב (LXX: ἄκανθα ὀδύνης) among all those that surround them. – The targum translates freely and without the image: "There shall no longer be for the house of Israel among all their neighbors a king who would do evil to them, nor a ruler who would oppress them. – The Aramaic סִלְוָא = "prick, thorn" can metaphorically be used even for "ban." Babylonian Talmud Baba Batra 151B: (Rab Nahman [† 320] sent word to Rab Dimi b. Joseph,) "If you do not come, I will strike you with a thorn סילוא that will not draw any blood (i.e., with the ban)."

3. The expression: "to throw a thorn in the eyes" הטיל קוֹצִים בעינים = to cause someone bitter grief seems to have a proverbial character; see, for example, b. Sanh. 38A at § Luke 2:34 A.

12:7 B: An angel of Satan to slap me.

1. ἄγγελος σατανᾶ, see § Matt 4:1 B, #2 and § Matt 25:41 B.

2. κολαφίζειν "to slap" may = סָטַר; see m. B. Qam. 8.6 at § Matt 5:39 B. – Nebuchadnezzar is handed over to an angel of Satan so that he might beat (scourge נגד) him; see Exod. Rab. 20 at § Matt 4:1 B, #2, n. *h*.

13:1: Every word should be supported by the mouth of two or three witnesses (see § Matt 18:16).

13:11 A: Maintain peace (see § Rom 12:18).

13:11 B: The God of peace (see § Rom 15:33).

13:12: With a holy kiss (see § 1 Cor 16:20).

The Letter of Paul to the Galatians

1:4 A: Who gave himself.

διδόναι = מָסַר or נָתַן. — Examples can be found at § John 10:11 B and § Acts 15:26. — Reference may also be made to b. Sanh. 110B.10.

1:4 B: From the present evil world.

1. ὁ αἰὼν ὁ ἐνεστώς is the time that is immediately approaching which, since every moment turns into the present, belongs to αἰὼν οὗτος = עוֹלָם הַזֶּה.

2. On αἰῶν πονηρός, see 1 En. 48:7: "The wisdom of the Lord of Spirits revealed him (the Son of Man-Messiah) to the holy ones and the righteous; for he protects the lot of the righteous, because they have hated and despised this world of unrighteousness and have hated all its deeds and ways in the name of the Lord of Spirits." ‖ In Lev. Rab. 26 (124C), the spirit of Samuel that appears from the hereafter says to Saul: "When I was with you (alive), I was in a world of falsehood בעלם דשקר, ... but now I am in a world of truth בעלם דקושטא."

1:5: To him (be) glory for all eternity!

On occasional doxologies, see § Rom 1:25 and § 2 Cor 11:31.

1:6 A: Who called you (see § Rom 1:6).

1:6 B: Gospel (see § Rom 1:1 D).

1:8 A: An angel from heaven.

The interference of heavenly beings in the halakic decisions of the rabbinic scholars is similarly objected to in B. Meṣ. 59A; see § Rom 10:6–8, #2, second third. — See also: If Moses and Samuel came, they could not permit this and that; see y. Yebam. 12.13A.33 at § Matt 23:13 A, #1. — Babylonian Talmud Yebamot 102A: Rab († 247) said, "If Elijah came and said, 'The ceremony of the removal of the shoe may be performed with a shoe,' people would listen to him. (If, however, he said,) 'It may not be performed with a sandal, people would not listen to him, since the people already observe the custom with a sandal.'"

1:8 B: May he be forfeited to the curse!

On ἀνάθεμα see § Rom 9:3 and § 1 Cor 12:3.

1:13: In Judaism.

ὁ Ἰουδαϊσμός "Judaism" = the Jewish religion.[a] — In rabbinic literature there is no exact equivalent. Levy does have יַהֲדוּת = "Judaism," since in Midr. Esth. 3:7 (95B) he wants to read ביהדותן.[266] However, in accordance with Dalman, the correct reading here is found in ed. Pesaro: יִחוּדָם.[b] An approximation of Ἰουδαϊσμός in rabbinic literature would be דָּת יְהוּדִית = Jewish law, Jewish religion.[c]

a. 2 Maccabees 2:21; 8:1; 14:38. — 4 Maccabees 4:26: "(Antiochus Epiphanes) tried by means of torture to compel each one among the people to eat unclean food and to renounce Judaism ἐξόμνυσθαι τὸν Ἰουδαϊσμόν."

b. Midrash Esther 3:7 (95B): (Hananiah, Mishael, and Azariah) did not change their God and their laws, but rather held fast to their monotheism (to their confession of the oneness of God) ביחודם.

c. דת יהודית, see m. Ketub. 7.6 at § Matt 5:32 A, #2, β. ‖ By contrast, y. Ketub. 4.28D.64: (In an Alexandrian marriage contract) it was written, "When you (the engaged woman) have come into my house, you shall be to me as a wife according to the law of Moses and the Jews." — Tosefta Ketubbot 4.9 (265) has instead: "according to the law of Moses and Israel." This formula appears twice more in t. Ketub. 7.6 (269).

1:14: A zealot for my ancestral traditions.

On the esteem and significance of the ancestral traditions, see § Matt 15:2 A.

1:16: Flesh and blood.

σὰρξ καὶ αἷμα = בָּשָׂר וָדָם = human being; see § Matt 16:17 B.

1:19: James, the brother of the Lord.

A report of Josephus about the death of James.

Antiquities 20.9.1: "Annas the younger, who as we have said obtained the high priesthood (in 62 CE, cf. § John 18:13), had a truculent manner and was immensely audacious. He affiliated with the party of the Sadducees, who, as we have already presented, are stern in their judgments before all (other) Jews. With this character of his, Annas thought, when Festus (the governor) had died and (his successor) Albinus was still on the road, that the appropriate moment had come to make a court (against his opponents). First among these he had the brother of Jesus, the so-called Messiah, named James, and some others, brought in, and he accused them of transgressing the law and handed them over to be stoned. Yet precisely the most law-abiding among the inhabitants of the city and those who were especially exacting with the laws, were outraged by this and secretly sent word to the king (Agrippa II, from 50–100 CE) and had it requested of him to make Annas cease and no longer act this way; for also in what had occurred earlier he did not act justly. Yet some of them encountered Albinus on his way from Alexandria and indicated to him that it was not

266. Levy, *Chaldäisches Wörterbuch*, 2:224A.

right for Annas to form a court without his (Albinus') consent. Albinus, persuaded by their words, wrote to Annas full of anger and threatened him that he would demand an account from him. King Agrippa therefore took from him the office of the high priest, after he had held it for three months, and appointed Jesus, the son of Damneus (perhaps 62–63 CE). — Concerning this passage and its parallels in ecclesial authors, as well as concerning the year of James' death—the year 62 is not at all certain—see Schürer.[267] — Annas the younger was murdered in Jerusalem by Idumeans during the Jewish war (*J. W.* 4.5.2).

2:1: I went up (see § Luke 18:10 A).

2:2: To those who were esteemed.

οἱ δοκοῦντες perhaps = הַחֲשׁוּבִין.

Babylonian Talmud Taʿanit 14B: R. Eleazar (ca. 270) said, "A respected person אָדָם חָשׁוּב may not (during a public fast) fall down on his face, unless he receives an answer like Joshua, the son of Nun (see Josh 7:10)." Also, R. Eleazar said, "A respected person may gird himself with sackcloth, unless he receives an answer like Jehoram, the son of Ahab (see 2 Kgs 6:30)." (For if he did not receive an answer, his reputation in the community would dwindle, according to Rashi.)

2:6: God does not look at anyone's person (see § Rom 2:11).

2:7: The gospel of the foreskin, ... of circumcision.

ἀκροβυστία = non-Israelites, περιτομή = Israelites, see § Acts 10:45, #2.

2:9: Who were considered to be pillars.

See b. Ber. 28B at § Matt 10:28, #1, n. *c*; ʾAbot R. Nat. 25 (7A) at § Matt 5:8 B, #2, n. *a*, middle. ‖ Exodus Rabbah 2 (69A): Moses said, "Here I am" (Exod 3:4). God answered him, "You stand where the pillar of the world עמודו של עולם (= Abraham) stood." Abraham said, "Here I am" (Gen 22:11), and you say, "Here I am." ‖ Targum Yerušalmi I Genesis 46:28: "He sent Judah before himself to Joseph, to show the way before him and to subject the pillars עַמּוּדַיָא of the land (the mighty)." ‖ Babylonian Talmud Ketubbot 104A.12: (When Bar Qappara [ca. 220] announced the death of Rabbi to the people of Sepphoris in an oblique way, he said,) "The lions of God (= angels) and the pillars מְצוּקִים (= the pious on earth) grasped the holy ark (= Rabbi); the lions of God overcame the pillars and the holy ark was led away captive!" — Parallels are found in Midr. Eccl. 7:11 (35B); 9:10 (43B); in y. Kil. 9.32B.9 and y. Ketub. 12.35A.18, מצוקים is replaced by יְצוּקִים "the established ones" = the powerful; see § Matt 26:25.

2:12: He ate together with the gentiles.

See the excursus "The Stance of Judaism toward the Non-Jewish World"; see also § 1 Cor 10:27.

---

267. Schürer, *Geschichte des jüdischen Volkes*, 1:581f.

2:15: Not sinners from the gentiles.

"Sinners" in short = gentiles in, for example, Pss. Sol. 1:1: "I cried out to the Lord in my utmost distress, to God, when sinners (= Syrian authorities) harassed me." — Psalms of Solomon 2:1f.: "In his arrogance the sinner (= Pompey) brought down firm walls with a ram, and you did not hinder it. Foreign gentiles mounted your altar, walked on it arrogantly with their shoes."

2:16: By the works of the law no flesh will be declared righteous (see § Rom 3:20 A).

2:18: If I build again what I tore down.

καταλύειν = סָתַר, οἰκοδομεῖν = בָּנָה.

Babylonian Talmud Berakot 63A: (Hananiah, the son of the brother of R. Joshua [ca. 110] decreed leap years in a prohibited way in Babylonia; a delegation of two scholars is sent to him to thwart his actions.) When he saw them, he said to them, "What have you come for?" They answered him, "We have come to study Torah." Then he had it announced, "These are great men of the age, and their fathers served in the sanctuary ...." Then he began to declare something unclean and they declared it clean; he prohibited something and they allowed it. Then he had it announced about them: "These are men of mendacity and desolation." They said to him, "You have already built בנית (by praising us), so you cannot tear down סתור (by slandering us; your tearing down would give the lie to your building); you have already set up a fence, so you cannot make a breach." (See the continuation according to the parallel in y. Ned. 6.40A.30 at § 1 Cor 14:36.) ‖ See b. Ned. 40A at § 1 Cor 8:10 B, n. *a*.

2:21: If righteousness comes by the law, Christ died for nothing.

Since the law was the sole source of all salvation and life for the ancient synagogue—see § Rom 3:1f., particularly section D—they consequently did not know a dying Messiah.

3:2: By the proclamation of faith (see § Rom 10:17 A).

3:5: Who supplies you.

ὁ ἐπιχορηγῶν, in rabbinic literature, one would say הַמַּסְפִּיק or הַמְסַפֵּק and, in the case of particularly abundant provision, הַמַּשְׁפִּיעַ.

Mekilta Exodus 17:7 (60B): R. Eliezer (ca. 90) said, "They pronounced (with Exod 17:7), 'If he supplies מספק our needs, we will serve him; but if not, we will not serve him.'" ‖ A baraita in b. Sanh. 108A: The generation of the flood became arrogant only because of the good that God richly provided השפיע for them.... God said, "Because of the good I have richly provided שהשפעתי for them, they have incensed me." — The same is then said further below also about the Sodomites.

3:6: Abraham believed God and it was reckoned to him as righteousness (see § Rom 4:2f.).

3:7: Those from faith are sons of Abraham.

The idea that only those who comport themselves in accordance with Abraham's moral manner are children of Abraham was also not foreign to the ancient synagogue; see § Rom 9:6. See further m. ʾAbot 5.19 at § Matt 10:1 A, #2 and b. Beṣah 32B at § John 8:33 A.

3:8 A: Since Scripture foresaw.

The same personification of Scripture is found in the rabbinic formula: מה ראתה תורה "What has the Torah seen," that is, on what basis has it prescribed this or that?

Tosefta Baba Qamma 7.2 (357): R. Yohanan b. Zakkai († ca. 80) was asked by his students, "What has the Torah seen (why has the Torah found it good) to impose a severer penalty on a thief than on a robber? (see the continuation at § 1 Cor 9:9f. B, #2, A.). — The parallel in b. B. Qam. 79B simplifies things without ראתה: Why has the Torah imposed a severer penalty on a thief than on a robber? ‖ Sifra Leviticus 23:22 (410A): Eurydemos b. Yose (ca. 180) said, "What has Scripture seen so as to ordain (the prescription in Lev 23:22 concerning the edge of the field and gleanings) between Passover and the Feast of Weeks on the one hand and the Day of the New Year and the Day of Atonement on the other? To teach that one (= God) reckons it to the one who fulfills the commandment concerning gleanings, what is forgotten, the edge of the field and tithing for the poor as if the sanctuary existed and he presented his offerings in it." ‖ The expression "what has Scripture seen?" is synonymous with another, "what has God seen?" Exodus Rabbah 9 (73C): What has God seen מה ראה הב"ה so as to (in Exod 7:9) put the (earthly) government (pharaoh) alongside a snake? Just as the snake bends, so too the government bends its ways.

3:8 B: It proclaimed beforehand to Abraham: "In you all the gentiles (nations) will be blessed" (Gen 12:3).

1. Genesis 12:3 in the base text: "All families of the earth will be blessed in you (regard themselves as blessed in you) וְנִבְרְכוּ בְךָ." — Septuagint: καὶ ἐνευλογηθήσονται ἐν σοὶ πᾶσαι αἱ φυλαὶ τῆς γῆς. — Targum Onkelos: "Because of you בדילך all families of the earth will be blessed יִתְבָּרְכוּן." — Targum Yerušalmi I: "In you all the families of the earth will be blessed." — Rashi: "There are many haggadoth on this, and this is its literal sense: A man will say to his son, 'Be like Abraham!' (i.e., a father will bless his son with Abraham's name). And all the expressions 'ונברכו בך' in Scripture should be understood in the same way. And this proves it: 'Israel will bless יְבָרֵךְ with you, saying, "May God make you like Ephraim and like Manasseh!"' (Gen 48:20)." — Just as Tg. Onk. has all the families of the earth blessed for Abraham's sake, that is, because of Abraham's merit or

righteousness, so too Jub. 18:15f. sees in all nations of the earth being blessed a recompense for Abraham's obedience to God's word: "In your name all the nations of the earth will be blessed because you listened to my word." (See the whole passage at § Rom 4:2f., #1, n. *d*, v.) — Similarly, Jub. 24:11: "In your (Isaac's) seed all the nations of the earth shall be blessed (Gen 26:4) because your father listened to my word and observed my instruction and my commandments and my laws and my ordinance and my covenant."

2. Rabbinic Judaism found the fulfillment of the promise in Gen 12:3 in a long series of blessings of a spiritual and corporal nature, which were bestowed on the nations of the earth for Abraham's sake and through him. The world was created only for Abraham's sake[a] and to him alone humanity owes its continued existence despite its sin;[b] he also became the one who introduced God's grace into the world.[c] Abraham taught a world sunken into idolatry about the one God[d] and thereby made God king over heaven and earth;[e] he exemplified for humanity the monotheistic faith in God[f] and united them in this faith.[g] He led those far away to repentance[h] and brought them under the wings of the Shekinah (i.e., made them proselytes);[i] therefore, God loves proselytes and appointed Abraham as their father.[k] No one entered into a business relationship with Abraham without taking his blessing with them. At his intercession, barren women were remembered with children, sick people recovered from their sufferings; even when those suffering just saw him they were immediately healed.[l] By his merit rain and dew came down, and even the ships on the ocean were protected for his sake.[m] All kings came from east and west to ask him for counsel,[n] and when he departed from this life, they all united in this lamentation, "Woe to the world, which has lost its ruler; woe to the ship, which has lost its helmsman!"[o]

a. Genesis Rabbah 12 (9B): R. Joshua b. Qarha (ca. 150) said, "'When they were created' בְּהִבָּרְאָם (Gen 2:4); (read:) באברהם: for Abraham's sake (heaven and earth were created)." — Parallels are found in TanḥB בראשית § 16 (6A) and לך לך § 4 (31A) with R. Tahlifa (?) and Midr. Ps. 104 § 15 (222B) with R. Judan (ca. 350) as the author. ‖ Tanḥuma B היי שיה § 6 (60A): R. Halapta b. Kahana (when?) said, "By his (Abraham's) merit this and the future world were created." ‖ See Yelamedenu in Yalquṭ 1 § 766 at § Matt 16:18, #2.

b. See Gen. Rab. 14 (10C) at § 1 Cor 15:45 B, n. *b*. ‖ See Gen. Rab. 14 (10C) at § Matt 16:18, #2.

c. Genesis Rabbah 60 (37C): "Show grace to my lord Abraham" (Gen 24:12). Since you have begun to do it, complete it as well. R. Haggai (ca. 330) said in the name of R. Isaac (ca. 300), "Everyone needs grace, even Abraham; for whose sake grace moves through the world, needed it, as it says, 'Show grace to my lord Abraham.'" ‖ Sifre Deuteronomy 32:8 § 311 (134A): Before our father Abraham had come, God had judged the world so to speak as a cruel man. The people of the generation of the flood had sinned, and he made them float likes pipes on the water (so according to the reading in Yalquṭ, see Friedmann ad loc.); the people of the tower had sinned, and he scattered them from one end of the world to the other; the Sodomites had sinned, and he judged them with fire and brimstone. Yet after our father Abraham had come into the world, he obtained to take these sufferings on himself (to atone for sin), which began to approach little by little (not all at once); as it says, "A famine arrived in the land, and Abram went to Egypt." ‖ Genesis Rabbah 49 (31C): R. Levi (ca. 300) said, "'Should the judge of the whole earth not do justice?' (Gen 18:25). (Abraham said to God,) 'If you want the world, strict justice will not happen, and if you want strict justice, there will be no world. You grasp the rope at both its ends: you want the world and you want strict justice. But if you do not ease up a bit, the world cannot endure!' Then God said to him, 'Abraham, "you love righteousness and hate godlessness" (Ps 45:8), you love to declare my creatures righteous and hate godlessness, you refuse to declare them guilty; "therefore, God, your God, anointed you with the oil of joy before your companions" (Ps 45:8)....' And Yahweh said, 'If I find 50 righteous people in Sodom, ... I will forgive the whole place for their sake.'" (Thus, grace overcame strict justice.)

d. Supporting passages can be found at § Rom 4:2f., #1, nn. *d*, ι and partly also in ν.

e. See Gen. Rab. 59 (37B) at § Rom 4:2f., #1, n. *d*, ν.

f. Supporting passages can be found at § Rom 4:2f., #1, n. *d*, ν.

g. Midrash Song of Songs 8:8 (132A) at § Rom 4:2f., #1, n. *d*, μ. – Genesis Rabbah 39 (23D): R. Berekhiah (ca. 340) opened his presentation with, "'We have a little sister' (Song 8:8). This is Abraham who united (in the monotheistic faith in God) all who come into the world." Bar Qappara (ca. 220) said, "Like one who knits together a tear." – In TanḥB לך לך § 2 (30A), the whole is attributed to R. Eleazar Haqqappar (= Bar Qappara). ‖ Genesis Rabbah 44 (27B) at § Rom 4:2f., #1, n. *d*, μ.

h. Genesis Rabbah 30 (18B); 39 (24B) at § Rom 4:2f., #1, n. *d*, μ. For a parallel to the latter passage at § Rom 4:2f., we may add as a parallel Num. Rab. 11 (162C).

i. Genesis Rabbah 39 (24C) with parallels; Tg. Onk. and Yer. I on Gen 12:5 at § Rom 4:2f., #1, n. *d*, μ; Gen. Rab. 39 (24C) and Mek. Exod. 22:20 (101A) at § Rom 4:2f., #1, n. *d*, ν. ‖ Babylonian Talmud Yebamot 63A at § Matt 1:5 B, #2, n. *a*.

k. TanḥumaB לך לך § 6 (32A) at § Rom 4:2f., #1, n. *d*, λ.

l. Genesis Rabbah 39 (24B): R. Levi (ca. 300) said, "No one bought a cow from Abraham without being blessed by him, and no one sold him a cow without being blessed by Abraham. How so? When our father Abraham prayed for barren women, they were remembered, and if for sick people, they recovered." Rab Huna (ca. 350) said, "Not only if Abraham went to a sick person, but also if a sick person only saw him, the sick person recovered." ‖ See b. B. Bat. 16B at § 1 Cor 3:12, #3, n. *a*.

m. Genesis Rabbah 39 (24B): "In you all families of the earth will be blessed" (Gen 12:3); the rain (comes) by your merit, the dew (comes) by your merit. ‖ Genesis Rabbah 39 (24B): R. Hanina (ca. 225) said, "Even the ships that traveled on the ocean were protected by Abraham's merit." – See b. Yebam. 63A.

n. Babylonian Talmud Baba Batra 16B: R. Eleazar of Modiim († ca. 135) said, "Our father Abraham had astrological skills, for all the kings of the east and west got to his door early (to get counsel from him, Rashi)." – There is a parallel in t. Qidd. 5.17 (343).

o. See b. B. Bat. 91A at § Matt 23:10, n. *b*.

3:10: "Cursed is anyone who does not remain in everything written in the book of the law, to do it!" (Deut 27:26.)

1. Deuteronomy 27:26 in the base text: "Cursed is anyone who does not fulfill יָקִים (literally: bring about) the words of this Torah, to do them (by doing them)." — Septuagint: ἐπικατάρατος πᾶς ἄνθρωπος, ὅς οὐκ ἐμμένει ἐν πᾶσι τοῖς λόγοις τοῦ νόμου τούτου ποιῆσαι αὐτούς. — Targum Onkelos: "Cursed is everyone who does not uphold יְקַיֵּם (= fulfill) the words of this Torah, to do them." — Yerušalmi I: ... "Cursed be the man who does not uphold יְקִים (?) the words of this Torah, to do them...." ‖ The addition "all" is found not only in the LXX and Gal 3:10, but also in the Samaritan targum: ארור דלא יקים ית כל מלי "cursed is everyone who does not fulfill all the words"; also in Lev. Rab. 25 and y. Soṭah 7.21D.6; see #2.

2. Rabbinic interpretations of Deut 27:26.

Leviticus Rabbah 25 (123A): "When you come into the land and plant all kinds of trees for food" (Lev 19:23). This is what is written: "She (Wisdom = Torah) is a tree of life for those who hold fast to it מַחֲזִיקִים בָּהּ" (Prov 3:18). ... R. Huna said in the name of R. Benjamin b. Levi (ca. 325), "... If it were said, '(Cursed) is everyone who does not study,' there would be no continued existence for those who hate Israel (= for the godless Israelites, see § Matt 3:17 A, n. *i*, S-B footnote). But it says, '(Cursed) is everyone who does not uphold (= establish, support, יקים now taken in this sense) all (so! see above in #1) the words of this Torah' (Deut 27:26). Therefore, it is said, 'She is a tree of life for those who establish (strengthen, so now מחזיקים) her' (Prov 3:18)." R. Huna (ca. 350) said, "If a person stumbles in sin and is guilty of death by God's hand (= by eradication), what should he do to remain alive? If he was used to reading one page in Scripture, let him read two pages; and if he was used to studying one chapter of the Mishnah, let him study two. If he was not used to reading in Scripture or studying from the Mishnah, what should he (then) do to stay alive? Let him go and become a leader of the community or a raiser of alms, and thus he will remain alive. For if it said, 'Cursed is whoever does not study,' there would be no continuing in existence (for him); but (it says), 'Cursed is everyone who does not uphold (= whoever does not help support, establish, strengthen) יקים'; if it said, 'She is a tree of life for those who toil (studying) with her,' there would be no continuance in existence (for the one who neglects this), but (it says), 'She is a tree of life for those who establish her.' (It further says,) 'Being under the protection of wisdom (occupying oneself with the Torah) is like being under the protection of silver (the right use of money)' (Eccl 7:12)." R. Aha (ca. 320) said in the name of R. Tanḥum b. Hiyya (ca. 300), "If a man has studied and taught and observed and practiced (done עשה) (Torah) and was able to oppose (evil) and he did not oppose it to establish להחזיק (good), and he did not establish, behold, he is included in the 'Cursed.' This is what is said, 'Cursed is whoever does not uphold יקים (= does not help strengthen and support)' (Deut 27:26)." — The slant of the passage pertains to weakening יָקִים, in order to take away the sharpness of the curse in Deut 27:26. — A partial parallel is found in TanḥB וישלה § 9 (84A): R. Huna (ca. 350) said, "... If a person is not a son of the Torah, let him support a teacher of the Bible or a teacher of the Mishnah, who teach the Torah, and he will be worthy (earn) to remain alive; for it says, 'She is a tree of life for those who support her (by supporting her teachers with money).'" ‖ Jerusalem Talmud Soṭah 7.21D.6: It is written, "Cursed is whoever does not uphold (so the midrash) all (so! see above in #1) the words of this Torah" (Deut 27:26). How so? Is there a falling Torah תורה נופלת (so that needs to be upheld)? Simeon b. Yaqim (ca. 270) said, "This pertains to the overseer of the synagogue who stands there (in the synagogue, upholding the reading of Scripture and the order of the religious service)." R. Simeon b. Halapta (ca. 190) said, "This refers to the lower court; for Rab Huna († 297) and Rab Judah († 299) said in the name of Samuel († 254), 'Because of this word Josiah tore his garment' (2 Kgs 22:11) and said, "It is my responsibility to uphold להקים (the Torah; to supervise its implementation).'" R. Aha (ca. 320) said in the name of R. Tanḥum b. Hiyya (ca. 300), "If someone studies and teaches and observes and does and is able to establish (to support) and does not establish, behold, he is included in the 'cursed.'" See also Midr. Eccl. 7:11 (35A).

3:11: The righteous one will live as a result of faith (Hab 2:4).

1. Habakkuk 2:4 according to the base text: "The righteous will live by his faithfulness בֶּאֱמוּנָתוֹ!" – Septuagint: ὁ δὲ δίκαιος ἐκ πίστεώς μου ζήσεται. – Targum: "The righteous will remain alive (survive) ותקימון because of their rectitude (truth קוּשְׁטְהוֹן)."

2. Habakkuk 2:4 in the midrash (cf. § Matt 22:40).

See Mek. Exod. 15:1 (41A) and Exod. Rab. 23 (85A) at § Rom 4:2f., #1, n. d, ρ and σ. ‖ Babylonian Talmud Makkot 23B: R. Simlai (ca. 250) said in a presentation, "613 commandments were told to Moses (cf. § Matt 22:36). 365 prohibitions in accordance with the number of the days in the solar year and 248 commandments, corresponding to the parts of a human being ... David came and reduced them (all the commandments) to 11; for it is written, "Who may reside in your tent and who may dwell on your holy mountain? [1.] Whoever walks irreproachably and [2.] does righteousness and [3.] speaks the truth in his heart; [4.] he does not slander with his tongue, [5.] he does not do evil to his neighbor, and [6.] he does not take up abuse against his companion; [7.] the reprehensible man is despised in his eyes; yet [8.] those who fear the Lord he honors; [9.] he swears to (his own) disadvantage and does not alter anything; [10.] he does not give his money for interest [11.] nor does he accept a bribe against the innocent ..." (Ps 15:1). Isaiah came and reduced them to 6; for it is written, "[1.] Whoever walks a righteous path and [2.] speaks in an upright way, [3.] whoever despises gain by extortion, [4.] shakes his hand from taking any bribe, [5.] whoever stops his ear so that he does not hear of bloodshed, and [6.] closes his eyes firmly so that he does not see evil: he will dwell on the heights ...." (Isa 33:15f.). Micah came and reduced them to 3; for it is written, "He has declared to you, O human being, what is good and what Yahweh desires from you: rather [1.] to do justice and [2.] to strive for love and [3.] to walk secretly (so the midrash) with your God" (Mic 6:8). "To do justice": this is dispensation of justice; "to strive for love" pertains to the works of love; "to walk secretly with your God": this refers to escorting out a dead person and bringing a bride under the wedding canopy .... Isaiah came again and reduced them to 2; for it says, "Thus says Yahweh, 'Maintain justice and practice righteousness'" (Isa 56:1). Amos came and reduced them to 1; for it says, "Thus says Yahweh to the house of Israel: Seek me and you will live!" (Amos 5:4). Rab Nahman b. Isaac († 356) objected, "I think that 'seek me' refers to the whole Torah (and all the commandments contained therein). Rather, Habakkuk came and reduced them to 1; for it says, 'The righteous will live by his faith!' (Hab 2:4)." — According to this (Babylonian) tradition, the sentence referring to the prophet Habakkuk is not associated with R. Simlai, but rather with the period of Rab Nahman b. Isaac; the tradition added him as a conclusion to the whole instead of the rejected verse from Amos. The Palestinian tradition in TanḥB שופטים § 10 (16B) is different. Here it says, "Micah came and reduced them to 3 (see Mic 6:8); Amos came and reduced them to 2, as it says, 'Seek me and live!' (Amos 5:4). Habakkuk came and reduced them to 1 (see Hab 2:4)." — Midrash Psalm 17 at the end (the passage is missing in the ed. Buber) links up with b. Mak. 23B. — As for Jewish judgments about the explanation of R. Simlai, Grätz considers them to be the first attempt to trace all the laws of Judaism to principles.[268] See § Matt 22:40. — Bacher sees here a historical proof of how the prophets and before them David draw up an ever smaller number of religious, mostly ethical fundamental commandments, the fulfillment of which was regarded as equal in value with fulfilling the numerous commandments of the Torah, and this list was seen as the quintessence of what Israel's teaching required from those who confess it.[269] — Rashi, in whom the thoughts, sentiments, and views of the ancient synagogue continue to live on powerfully, explains: "At the beginning they (the Israelites) were righteous and could accept the yoke of many commandments; but the later generations were not as righteous, and if they had wanted to observe all the commandments, there would be no person who would have merit (who would be righteous). So David came and reduced the commandments to 11, so that merit could be earned if these 11 commandments were kept; and the following generations likewise continually reduced the number of commandments even further." — Rashi might have hit upon the view of the Makkot passage most accurately. For R. Simlai, faith does not count as the great all-encompassing principle of the religious-moral life, but rather is for him synonymous with the confession of monotheism. Faith as such is the smallest accomplishment that can be required of someone. If an Israelite had no merit to point to in the area of fulfilling the law, he can still achieve this faith. And precisely because the faith as a monotheistic confession of God represents the smallest conceivable accomplishment of an Israelite before God, the prophet Habakkuk, in the opinion of R. Simlai, made it the single requirement for his degenerate contemporaries. This signifies a complete devaluation of the faith that is spoken of in Hab 2:4. Since R. Simlai many times distinguished himself as an opponent of Christianity,[270] one may ask whether this devaluation does not contain a polemical dig

---

268. Grätz, *Geschichte der Juden*, 4:265f.

269. Bacher, *Die Agada der palästinensischen Amoräer*, 1:557.

270. S-B: Jerusalem Talmud Berakot 9.12D.44: The *minim* (Jewish Christians) asked R. Simlai, "How many divinities created the world?" He answered them, "Are you asking me? Go and ask the first man, as it says, 'Ask the earlier times ...' (Deut 4:32). 'When the gods created בראו אלהים (the plural of the verb) Adam on the earth' is not written here, but rather, 'From the day when God created ברא (the singular, so the plural אלהים is not several gods, but one God) Adam on the earth.'" They said to him, "Yet it is written, 'In the beginning ברא אלהים' (Gen 1:1) (אלהים in the plural)!" He said to them, "Is בראו 'created' (plural) written? Is not rather ברא 'created' (singular) written?" R. Simlai said, "Whenever the *minim* present (read שפקרו instead of שפרקו) heretical explanations, they have their answer ...."

at the emphasis of faith on the part of Christians. If, on the Christian side, Hab 2:4 was invoked to indicate the pivotal significance of faith for a person's justification before God, R. Simlai could argue that, on the contrary, it was precisely the prophet Habakkuk who considered faith to be the smallest demand that he thought he could expect of his religiously degenerate period. The implication would then be: What does this one puny demand of faith from the church mean in the face of the 613 commandments, the fulfillment of which the law-loyal synagogue demands of its members! ‖ Midrash Ecclesiastes 3:9 (17B): R. Isaac b. Marion (ca. 280) said, "'The righteous will live by his faith' (Hab 2:4), (i.e.,) the righteous will live by the work of his hands (אֱמוּנָה is interpreted as אוּמָּנוּת 'work of his hands'). Even the righteous one who lives eternally (= God) lives by the work of his hands. God said, 'First I killed the firstborn of Egypt; as it says, "In the middle of the night, Yahweh had slain every firstborn in the land of Egypt" (Exod 12:29). Also, every firstborn that is born to you, you shall sanctify for me; as it says, "Sanctify for me every firstborn" (Exod 13:2). You shall sanctify for me the firstborn because of the work of his hands (as a recompense for my action with the firstborn in the land of Egypt).' Consequently, 'the righteous will live by the work of his hands (i.e., his fulfillments of the commandments).'"

3:12: Whoever does them (the commandments) will live by means of them.

See § Rom 10:5 and § Rom 3:1f.

3:13 A: By becoming a curse for us.

On the idea that a person could become a curse of elimination or an atoning sacrifice for another person, see § Rom 9:3, #2.

3:13 B: "Cursed (is) everyone who hangs on a tree" (Deut 21:23).

Deuteronomy 21:23 according to the base text: "For a hanged man is a curse of God" קִלְלַת אֱלֹהִים תָּלוּי. — Here אלהים is a subjective genitive, so קללת אלהים = a curse on God's part, that is, one cursed by God. So rightly the LXX: κεκατηραμένος ὑπὸ θεοῦ πᾶς κρεμάμενος ἐπὶ ξύλου. So too the apostle, although he has left אלהים untranslated. By contrast, the rabbinic

---

Again they asked him, "What does 'We will make man in our image and according to our likeness' (Gen 1:26) mean?" He said to them, "'Then the gods created man in their image' is not written, but rather, 'Then God created man in his image' (singular)...." Again they asked him, "What does 'The Lord God Yahweh אל אלהים יי״, the Lord God Yahweh, he knows' (Josh 22:22) mean?" He said to them, "'They know' is not written here, but rather 'he knows' is written...." Again they asked him, "What does 'The Lord God Yahweh אל אלהים יי״ speaks and summons the earth' (Ps 50:1) mean?" He said to them, "Is 'speak and summon' (plural) written here? There is only written, 'speaks and summons the earth'!..." Again they asked him, "What does 'A holy God' אלהים קדושים (adjective in the plural) (Josh 24:19) mean?" He said to them, "'Holy are they' is not written, but rather, 'is he, a jealous God he is' ...." Again they asked him, "What does 'What great people is there that has a God so near to it אלהים קרובים' (adjective in the plural) (Deut 4:7) mean?" He said to them, "'As Yahweh our God, whenever we call to them,' is not written, but rather, 'whenever we call to him.'" — See parallels with various differences, abbreviations, contractions in Gen. Rab. 8 (6C); Exod. Rab. 29 (88C); Deut. Rab. 2 (198A); TanḥB בראשית § 7 (3A); קדישים § 4 (37A); Midr. Ps. 50 § 1 (139B).

scholars almost universally (see an exception at § 2 Cor 1:3 A) understood אלהים as an objective genitive; קללת אלהים thus = "a curse or imprecation against God."[a]

a. See m. Sanh. 6.4; SDeut 21:22 § 221 (114B); Tg. Yer. I Deut. 21:22f. and b. Sanh. 46B at § Matt 26:65 B, #3. See a parallel to the last passage in t. Sanh. 9.7 (429). ‖ Jerusalem Talmud Qiddušin 4.65B.61 also belongs here, where R. Hoshaiah (ca. 225) understands קללת אלהים = "desecration of the divine name"; see § Matt 6:9 C, n. *k*; parallels include Num. Rab. 8 (149C) and Midr. Sam. 28 § 6 (67A). ‖ Targum Onkelos Deuteronomy 21:23: "His corpse should not remain overnight on the cross, but rather you shall bury him on the same day; since he had incurred guilt before God, he was crucified." — Here קללת אלהים is interpreted to mean "flippant behavior against God"; אלהים is also an objective genitive.

3:15 A: In a human way (see § Rom 3:5).

3:15 B: No one nullifies or adds something to a person's established testament.

1. διαθήκη in profane authors = testament; in the LXX = בְּרִית "contract"; in the NT α. = contract, β. = testament (writ of inheritance). דְּיַתֵיקָא, דְּיַתֵיקֵי, adopted in rabbinic literature, means α. generally "decree,"[a] β. specifically "last will" = testament.[b]

a. Midrash Song of Songs 5:11 (119B): R. Simeon b. Yohai (ca. 150) said, "The book of Deuteronomy ascended and prostrated before God and said before him, 'Lord of the world, you have written in your Torah': "A decree (regulation דייתיקי), that has become partly void has become completely void" (there is no supporting passage given); yet king Solomon is trying to tear out a *yod* that is written in the Torah ...." — See the parallel in y. Sanh. 2.20C.39 at § Matt 5:18 B, #1. There, though, דייתיקי was translated with "testament." ‖ Numbers Rabbah 2 (137A): (Moses feared that dissensions might arise between the tribes because of the camp regulations.) God said to him, "Moses, why does this concern you? They do not need you; by themselves they will know their places. A regulation דייתיקי is in their hand from their father Jacob, how they should encamp with their banners. I will make no innovation for their sake; they have the order (sequence) already from their father Jacob. As they carried him (as a corpse) and surrounded his bier, they shall also surround the dwelling (the tent of meeting)."

b. Examples in the following citations.

2. דְּיַתֵיקֵי "testament." — The testament to be recorded in writing[a] was supposed to give the bequeather the security that his possessions would be apportioned after his death in the way he wanted among those entitled to the inheritance. Yet last wills decided orally were also valid. "It is an obligatory commandment," as is said in a generally recognized saying of R. Meir (ca. 150), "to fulfill the words of a dead man" (see b. Ketub. 70A.1, 4; b. Giṭ. 15A.6, 16). In a formal respect, it was desirable that a testament include the words: "This shall be in place and be valid. When I die,

my goods should be given to so-and-so."[b] In a material respect, it was regarded as an absolute requirement that the stipulations of the testament not violate recognized law. Jewish inheritance law had formed especially on the basis of Num 27:8ff. Its essential regulations were approximately the following. If a father dies, the sons first of all have the right of inheritance.[c] The firstborn among them has to receive a double portion of what every other brother receives,[d] though only from the goods that were actually in the father's possession when he passed away. As for the goods that were expected to accrue only later, the claim of the firstborn to a double portion of the inheritance did not apply.[e] — After the sons, their sons had the right of inheritance in the second place,[f] so the grandsons of the bequeather. However, if one of the sons had only daughters surviving him, in this particular case these daughters took the place of their father; they were therefore equally entitled heirs alongside the sons, or the grandsons of the bequeather.[g] — The bequeather's own daughters came into consideration only in the third place;[h] thus, as heirs of the father, they were less favorably positioned than the bequeather's granddaughters in the particular case mentioned above. This anomalous relationship gave rise to disputes between Pharisees and Sadducees over a long period; the dispute ended in the Pharisees' favor such that the superior right of the granddaughters over the bequeather's own daughters was recognized in the case mentioned.[i] If the father left behind sons and unsupported daughters, the sons were the sole heirs, although the daughters had to be supported from the father's possessions until they married. If the father's estate did not amount to more than was necessary to supported the daughters, the sons in fact went away empty-handed, although they were the real heirs.[k] — In the fourth and fifth place, the bequeather's brother and the brothers of his father, or their heirs, had the right of inheritance.[l] — The case was similar with a mother's inheritance. The sons had the first claim to it,[m] but the firstborn did not receive a double portion of the inheritance.[n] The daughters were not considered alongside the sons; the unmarried among them did not even have the right to be supported from the mother's possessions, as from the father's.[o] Only if there were no sons did the daughters appear as the mother's heirs.[p] There were also differences of opinion about this in earlier times.[q] — If a testator violated these basic regulations concerning the right of inheritance, the testament was void.[r] However, it could also be declared invalid for other reasons, for example, when there was a justifiable doubt as to whether a testament found with the dead person actually corresponded to his last wishes and intentions.[s] The testator himself had the right at any time to replace one testament with a different one.[t]

a. See the conventional phrase: הכותב דייתיקי "whoever writes a testament"; examples in t. B. Bat. 8.8ff. (409); see also the beginning of n. *t*.

b. Tosefta Baba Batra 8.10 (409): How do we know something is a testament (read דייתיקי instead of דייתוקי)? (Where it is written:) "This shall be in place and be valid. When I die, my goods should be given to so-and-so." ‖ Jerusalem Talmud Pe'ah 3.17D.58: What is a testament? (Where it is written:) "It shall belong to me and remain; and when I die, my goods should be given to so-and-so." ‖ A baraita in b. B. Meṣ. 19A: What is a testament? (Where it is written:) "This shall be in place and be valid. When he dies, his goods will belong to so-and-so." — Accordingly, the quintessence of a testament (in distinction from a deed of donation, see further below in #3) consists in the testator retaining the right of disposition over his goods until death.

c. So as not to tear apart the Mishnah passage, we present it here undivided; further below we will refer to it in the relevant passages. Mishnah Baba Batra 8.2: This is the case with the order of inheritance: "If a man dies and does not have any sons, let his estate pass to his daughter" (Num 27:8). The son (thus) has priority over the daughter, and all physical descendants of the son have priority over the daughter; the daughter (of the bequeather) has priority over the brothers (of the bequeather), and the physical descendants of the daughter have priority over the brothers (of the bequeather); the brothers (of the bequeather) have priority over the brother of the father (of the bequeather), and the physical descendants of the brothers (of the bequeather) have priority over the brothers of the father (of the bequeather). This is the general rule: whoever has priority in the right of inheritance, that person's physical descendants (likewise) have priority.

d. Sifre Deuteronomy 21:17 § 217 (113B): "To give him (the firstborn) a double portion" (Deut 21:17); double the amount that one (of the other brothers receives); or two shares of all the goods (so that the firstborn receives two-thirds of the whole inheritance and the other brothers together receive one third)? Look, you can infer the following: since he inherits with one, he inherits (in the same way) with five. As we find, if he inherits with one, twice as much as one, so too, if he inherits with five, twice as much as one. Or turn to this conclusion: since he inherits with one, he inherits (in the same way) with five. As we find, if he inherits with one, he gets two portions of all the goods (the firstborn gets two-thirds of everything and the brother one-third), so too, if he inherits with five, two portions of all the goods. — In the following, the first inference is recognized as the correct one. — The same is found in b. B. Bat. 122B as a baraita.

e. Mishnah Bekorot 8.9: The firstborn does not receive a double portion … from what is expected (prospective) as from what is in the possession (of the father). — The statement is repeated rather often in, for example, b. B. Bat. 55A; 119A; 145B. ‖ For the scriptural proof, see SDeut 21:17 § 217 (114A): "To give him (the firstborn) a double portion of everything that is his" (Deut 21:17); this teaches that the firstborn does not receive (a double portion) from what is expected as from what is in the possession (of the father).

f. All physical descendants have priority over the daughter; see m. B. Bat. 8.2 in n. *c.*

g. A baraiata in b. B. Bat. 115A: "The son has priority over the daughter" (see m. B. Bat. 8.2 in n. *c*); here I hear only: "the son"; the son of the son or the daughter of the son or the son of the daughter of the son, how do we know (that they have priority over the biological daughters of the bequeather)? Scripture teaches, "He does not have אין לו a son" (Num 27:8), that is, inquire about him עיין עליו (whether he does not have other descendants of a son; they would then have priority over the bequeather's own daughters).

h. Mishnah Baba Batra 8.2 in n. *c.*

i. Babylonian Talmud Baba Batra 115B: Rab Huna († 297) said that Rab († 247) said, "If someone says, 'The daughter inherits (equally) with the daughter of the son,' even if it were the patriarch נָשִׂיא in Israel, one does not listen to him; for this is a practice of the Sadducees. For in a baraita it has been taught: On the 24th of Tebet (December/January) we returned to our law; for the Sadducees had said, 'The daughter inherits (equally) with the daughter of the son.' Rabban Yohanan b. Zakkai († ca. 80) dealt with them. He said to them, 'You fools, where do you get this from dies?' And no one was there who would have responded a word to him, apart from an old man (elder), who twaddled against him and said, 'If the daughter of his son, who comes by virtue of the right of his son, inherits from him (the grandfather), would it not all the more be right for his daughter, who comes by virtue of his right?' Then he read him this passage of Scripture, '"These are the sons of Seir the Horite, who were the (earlier) inhabitants of the land: Lotan and Shobal and Zibeon and Anah" (Gen 36:20); and further it is written, "These are the sons of Zibeon: Aiah and Anah" (Gen 36:24). This teaches that Zibeon slept with his mother and sired Anah (because Anah is designated once as a son of Seir and then as a son of Zibeon the son of Seir. It simultaneously follows from this that the grandchildren are also called "sons" because the right of the fathers passes over to the grandsons) ....' He answered him, 'Rabbi, you want to dismiss me with that (and view the matter as settled? The Sadducees also concede that the sons of a son have the right of inheritance before the daughters of the bequeather; the dispute, though, is not about the sons of a son, but rather about the daughters of a son!).' He said to him, 'You fool, should our perfect Torah not be like your vain twaddle? What goes for the daughter of the son, whose right is well-founded alongside the brothers (of her father, since she inherits instead of her father, just like the daughters of Zelophehad alongside the brothers of their father instead of their father inherited from their grandfather Hepher [Num 27:7])—you mean to say this about a daughter, whose right is unfounded alongside her brothers (since she cannot inherit together with them)?' Then they were overcome, and that day was made a feast day."

k. Mishnah Baba Batra 9.1: If someone dies and leaves behind sons and daughters, if the fortune is large, the sons inherit, and the daughters are provided for. If the fortune is small, the daughters are provided for, and let the sons beg at the doors. ‖ Babylonian Talmud Baba Batra 139B: How much is a "large" fortune? Rab Judah († 299) said that Rab († 247) said, "Whatever is enough to provide for these and those (sons and daughters) for 12 months." When I said this before Samuel († 254), he answered, "These are the words of R. Gamaliel b. Rabbi (ca. 220)." Yet the scholars said, "Whatever is enough to provide for these and those, until they become nubile." It has also been said, "When Rabin (ca. 325) came, he said that R. Yohanan († 279)—according to others Rabbah bar bar Hana (ca. 280)—said that R. Yohanan said, 'If these and those can be provided for from it until they are nubile, it is a large fortune; but if less time than this, see, it is a small fortune. And if it is not enough for these and those until they are nubile, do the daughters get everything?'" (so as a question, Rashi.) Rather, Raba († 352) said, "One takes from this the livelihood for the daughters until they are nubile, and the rest belongs to the sons." — A different regulation for the obligation to provide for unsupported daughters is found in b. Ketub. 68A: In a baraita it has been taught: Rabbi († 217?) said, "A daughter who is to be supported by the brothers receives a tenth of the fortune (left by the father)."

l. See. B. Bat. 8.2 in n. *c.*

m. Mishnah Baba Batra 8.1: A man (son) inherits his mother's estate. ‖ Babylonian Talmud Baba Batra 110B: Where do these words come from? The rabbis taught (as a baraita): "And every daughter who receives an inheritance from the tribes of the children of Israel" (Num 36:8). How can a daughter receive an inheritance from two tribes (since it says in Num 36:8: "from the tribes," and therefore several)? It is possible only when her father comes from one tribe and her mother from another tribe, and they died and she inherited their estate. (In circumstances where there are no male descendants as heirs, the daughter can inherit the estate of both the father and the mother.) Here I hear only that the daughter (inherits the mother's estate where applicable). Where does the son come from? You can draw an inference from the lesser to the greater: if a daughter, whose right to the goods of the father is small, has a good right (on the basis of Num 36:8) to the goods of the mother, is it not proper for a son, who has a good right to the goods of the father to have a good right to the goods of the mother? And learn also from the passage you are coming from (i.e., proceeding from the goods of the father): just as there (with the inheriting from the father) the son has priority over the daughter, so too here the son has priority over the daughter.

n. Mishnah Baba Batra 8.4: The son (who is a firstborn) receives a double portion of the inheritance from the goods of the father, but he does not receive a double portion of the inheritance from the goods of the mother.

o. Mishnah Baba Batra 8.4: The (unsupported) daughters are provided for from the goods of the father, but they are not provided for from the goods of the mother.

p. See b. B. Bat. 110B in n. *m.*

q. Babylonian Talmud Baba Batra 111A: R. Yose b. Judah (ca. 180) and R. Eleazar b. Yose (ca. 180) said in the name of R. Zechariah b. Haqqassab (ca. 150?): Both the son and the daughter are equal with respect to the goods of the mother (i.e., the daughters inherit together with their brothers, both parties are equally entitled to inheritance). What is the reason? It is enough if what is inferred is like that which it is inferred from. (The right of inheritance of the son with respect to the goods of the mother is inferred only from the right of inheritance of the daughter; see b. B. Bat. 110B in n. *m.* Here the right of the son cannot extend beyond the right of the daughter from which it itself was inferred!) — It is then further established that the halakah is not in accordance with R. Zechariah b. Haqqassab.

r. Mishnah Baba Batra 8.5: If someone says, "My firstborn son so-and-so should not receive a double portion of the inheritance; my son so-and-so should not inherit with his brothers" (and thus be disinherited), he has said nothing (his ordinance is invalid); for he has made a decree contrary to what is written in the Torah. ... If someone says, "Such-and-such man (who does not belong to the family) shall inherit my estate," while he has a daughter (who has a right to inherit); "my daughter shall inherit my estate," while he has a son, he has said nothing; for he has made a decree contrary to what is written in the Torah.

R. Yohanan b. Beroqah (ca. 110) said, "If he said it (namely: so-and-so shall inherit my estate) concerning someone who has a right to inherit his estate, his words are valid; but if he said it concerning someone who does not have a right to inherit his estate, his words are invalid." — Babylonian Talmud Baba Batra 130A: Rab Judah († 299) said that Samuel († 254) said, "The halakah is not in accordance with R. Yohanan b. Beroqah." Likewise, Raba († 352) said, "The halakah is in accordance with R. Yohanan b. Beroqah." — Babylonian Talmud Baba Batra 130B: R. Zeriqa (ca. 300) said that R. Ammi (ca. 300) said that R. Hanina (ca. 225) said that Rabbi († 217?) said, "The halakah is in accordance with R. Yohanan b. Beroqah."

s. Mishnah Baba Batra 8.6: If some has died and a testament דיתיקי is find bound around his hips (so that there is no doubt that it is a testament of the man who has passed away), this is nothing at all (since one does not know whether the dead person did not ultimately change his instructions; for otherwise he would have handed it over to the heirs as a certification of their claims). ‖ Mishnah Baba Meṣiʿa 7.1: If one finds a certificate of divorce, a certificate of emancipation for slaves, testaments דייתיקי, deeds of donations, or receipts, behold, one does not give them back (to the issuer or loser); for one can assume that they were indeed written, but one then considered (later) not to hand them over (but rather to annul them).

t. Tosefta Baba Batra 8.10 (409): Whoever writes a testament דויהיקי, can (later) renounce it. ‖ A baraita in y. B. Bat. 8.16B.61: R. Simeon b. Gamaliel (ca. 140) said, "One testament annuls another." — Likewise, Rab Dimi (ca. 320) in b. B. Bat. 135B; 152B.

3. מַתָּנָה "donation." — Alongside the testamentary decree, in the course of time another procedure developed for assigning an inheritance: the bequeather divided (cf. διεῖλεν in Luke 15:12) his fortune by way of a private donation מַתָּנָה, Aram. מַתְּנָא, מַתַּנְתָּא. This procedure doubtlessly secured him a rather large freedom in his decisions. For since it was now a matter, at least according to the letter, not of actually apportioning the inheritance, but rather of bestowing gifts, the gift-giver was not bound by the legal right of inheritance (see #2), but rather the division of goods could be carried out completely according to his own discretion without consideration of the applicable law of inheritance, indeed even in contradiction to it. In this way, for example, there was the possibility of simply ignoring the claim of the firstborn to a double portion of the inheritance; a son who turned out badly would be completely passed over in the division of the goods. Indeed, even a stranger could be made the sole lord of the whole fortune when all the family members who had the right to inherit were excluded. The scholars, nevertheless, did not approve of the latter, though they did not dare to dispute the validity of the donation. Yet in the case of these gifts, the recipient could not be designated as an heir and the gift itself could not be designated as an inheritance. In that case, the conditions would have taken on the character of a regulation of inheritance and thereby would have readily fallen under the legal stipulations concerning inheritance.[a]

The gift-giver could divide his fortune as a gift both in days of health[b] and in the face of death.[b] In both cases, though, particular regulations applied.

A. Dividing the goods in days of health. — This happened in the way of concluding a contract, and so, as a rule, in written form.[c] The certificate had to include the words that the donation should be valid "from today and after death." This implied that the donation was legally binding immediately for both parties, but could be implemented only after the death of the gift-giver.[d] The latter thereby lost any further right of disposal over the goods donated, though he retained the unlimited enjoyment of them until his death. Thus, if he sold a portion of the goods donated, at the moment of his death, the sale terminated automatically, and the buyer had to surrender the acquired goods to the recipient of the gift (legatee) without any compensation. Nor, though, could the recipient of the gift freely dispose of the goods bestowed as long as the gift-giver was still alive. If he sold, for example, the donation in whole or in part, the buyer could start the sale only at the death of the gift-giver; before then, the latter has the full right of enjoyment to the gift that had been sold.[e] The contract of donation became legally binding for both parties when the certificate that set up the conditions was delivered to the one who was to receive the gift;[f] withdrawing from the contract was possible for both parties only on the basis of a new agreement. In this respect, the gift-giver was less favorably positioned than the testator: whereas the latter could unilaterally annul his testament at any time, the former needed the consent of the recipient of the gift in order to annul a donation.[g]

B. Dividing the goods in the face of death. — This happened orally most of the time according to the principle: "the words of a seriously ill person are as good as if they were written down and delivered (in the form a certificate)" (b. B. Bat. 151A; b. Giṭ. 13A).[h] Donations made orally by a seriously ill person became settled at the moment of his death. If he recovered from his illness, though, he could revoke them all, provided that they were stipulated only in case of death.[i] Likewise, with his recovery, all his donations automatically became invalid whenever he had donated all his goods in the face of death; for since he had not reserved anything for the period of his own life in case of his recovery, one could infer that he had stipulated the gifts only in the case of his death.[k]

a. Mishnah Baba Batra 8.5: If someone orally divides his goods (as gifts) to his sons, and gives to one more and to another less or makes the firstborn like them (the others, and thus does not assign to him a double portion of the inheritance, his words are valid. Yet, if he says, (he gives it to them) "as an inheritance," he has said nothing (his words are not valid). If he wrote (in a document written out concerning the donation), whether at the beginning or in the middle or at the end, (he gives it to them) "as a gift," his words are valid.[271] ... If someone signs over his goods (as gifts) to others (not to people who are among his heirs) and leaves behind (passes over) his (own) children, what he has done is done (i.e., it retains its applicability, it is valid). However, the mind of the scholars finds no pleasure in him. R. Simeon b. Gamaliel (ca. 140) said, "If his children did not behave appropriately, let it be thought well of him (he has acted rightly)!"

b. One says, "as a healthy person" בָּרִיא = in days of health and "as a seriously ill person" שְׁכֵיב מְרַע = in the face of death; see, for example, b. B. Meṣ. 19A in n. *d.*

c. See the set phrase: "if someone signs over his goods (as gifts)," in, for example, m. B. Bat. 8.5 in n. *a.* This passage also shows, though, that the dividing of possessions as gifts could also happen orally.

d. Mishnah Baba Batra 8.7: "If someone signs over his goods to his sons (as a gift in days of health), he must write (in the deed of donation), 'From today and after death'" (cf. by contrast what is said about a testament in #2, n. *b*). These are the words of R. Judah (ca. 150). R. Yose (ca. 150) said, "It is not necessary (to write 'from today,' the date of the deed of donation suffices; for זמנו של שטר מיכיה 'the date of a certificate is probative '" [b. B. Bat. 136A]). — The significance of the words: "from today and after death" is briefly summarized in b. B. Bat. 136A as follows: "Receive the principle from today, the interest after death," that is, the principle belongs to the son from the day of the signing over, but the free right of disposal and the interest is his only after the death of the father. Until then the latter has the interest at his disposal; see m. B. Bat. 8.7 in n. *e.* ‖ Tosefta Baba Batra 8.10 (409): What is a (deed of) donation מתנה? (Where it is written:) "From today my goods shall be given to so-and-so." ‖ Jerusalem Talmud Pe'ah 3.17D.59: What is a deed of donation מתנה? (Where it says,) "Behold, all my goods are given to so-and-so as a gift from now on," and here it must be written: "from today." ‖ A baraita in b. B. Meṣ. 19A: What is a testament? (Where it says,) "This shall be in place and be valid. When he dies, his goods belong to so-and-so." A deed of donation מתנה is anything where it is written, "From today and after death." Thus, if it is written, "From today and after death," he acquires (the gift), and if not, does he not acquire it? Abbayye († 338/39) said, "This is what he meant. What gift from a healthy man בריא is like the gift of a seriously ill man שכיב מרע, which is acquired only after death? Anything where it is written, 'from today and after death.'" — The difference between testament and deed of donation thus consists in the testament leaving to the testator the free right of disposal over his goods, whereas the deed of donation takes it from the gift-giver, though it does not transfer it to the recipient of the gift as long as the gift-giver is still alive. This goes together with the fact that a testament, but not a donation, was revocable; see n. *g.*

---

271. S-B: Tosefta Baba Batra 7.17 (408): If he wrote "as an inheritance" below (later) and "as a gift" above (previously); "an inheritance" above and "as a gift" below; "as an inheritance" on both sides and "as a gift" in the middle, his words are valid because he mentioned the term "gift." — Babylonian Talmud Baba Batra 129A: When Rab Dimi (ca, 320) came (from Palestine to Babylonia), he said that R. Yohanan († 279) said, "(If he wrote,) 'This and that field shall be given to this or that man as a gift and he shall inherit,' this is what 'as a gift at the beginning' means. (If he wrote,) 'He shall inherit it and it shall be given to him as a gift,' this is what 'as a gift at the end' means. (If he writes,) 'He shall inherit it and it shall be given to him and he shall inherit it,' this is what 'as a gift in the middle' means. — Thus, even the word 'inherit' may appear in a deed of donation, as long as the term 'gift' is not missing.

e. Mishnah Baba Batra 8.7: If someone signs over his goods (as a gift) to his son after his death, the father cannot sell them, because they are signed over to his son, and the son cannot sell them because they are in the father's power. If the father (nevertheless) sells them, they are sold until he dies; if the son sells them, the buyer has nothing of them until the father dies.

f. See b. B. Bat. 151A and b. Giṭ. 13A above in the text, section B, at the beginning: "The words of a seriously ill man are as good as if they were ... delivered," that is, they are as legally binding as a certificate handed over. ‖ Jerusalem Talmud Ketubbot 11.34B.9: The words of a seriously ill person are valid like those which a healthy man has written and delivered. – Only at the delivery of the certificate to the one authorized does its content become binding for the issuer. ‖ Babylonian Talmud Baba Batra 77A: Documents (and what is written down in them) are acquired by delivery (handing over).

g. Tosefta Baba Batra 8.10 (409): Whoever writes a testament can renounce (it); whoever (writes) a deed of donation מתנה cannot renounce. ‖ A baraita in y. B. Bat. 8.16B.61: R. Simeon b. Gamaliel (ca. 140) said, "One testament annuls another, but one deed of donation does not annul another."

h. That the donations of a seriously ill person could also be established in writing is shown by b. B. Bat. 151B and y. Pe'ah 3.17D.56 in n. *i.* Mishnah Baba Batra 9.6 in n. *k.* – The scriptural proof for the donation of a seriously ill person is less clear in its first portion; in b. B. Bat. 147A, it reads: R. Zeira (ca. 300) said that Rab said, "From where in the Torah do we know that the donation of a seriously ill person (i.e., the stipulation that a seriously ill person can legally divide his goods orally as gifts)? Because it says, 'And you shall let his inheritance pass over to his daughter' (Num 27:8); there is another passing over that is like this one. And what is it? This is the donation of a seriously ill person." Rab Nahman († 320) said that Rabbah b. Abuha (ca. 270) said, "From here (the proof should be drawn): 'And you shall give his inheritance to his brothers' (Num 27:9). There is another giving that is like this. What is it? This is the donation of a seriously ill person. (According to Rashi, the superfluous: 'and you shall let pass over,' or 'and you shall give' in Num 27:8, 9 is supposed to refer to a different 'passing over,' or a different 'giving.') ...." Rab Manasseh b. Jeremiah (when?) said, "From here: 'In those days Hezekiah became sick unto death, and the prophet Isaiah, the son of Amoz, came to him and said to him, "Arrange צו your house, for you will die and not remain alive"' (2 Kgs 20:1); by an ordinary (oral) arrangement צַוָּאָה (arrange your house and not by an elaborate testamentary decree)." R. Rammi b. Ezekiel said, "From here: 'Ahithophel ... went to his house and arranged ויצו his house and hanged himself' (2 Sam 17:23); by an ordinary (oral) arrangement צואה (he arranged his house)."

i. Jerusalem Talmud Pe'ah 3.17D.56: A healthy man who has written a testament, and a seriously ill person who has written a deed of donation, can withdraw. ‖ Babylonian Talmud Baba Batra 151B: So Samuel († 254) said, "If a seriously ill person has signed over all his goods to others, he can, even if they (those given the gift) had taken possession of them from his hand, renounce if he remains alive, doubtlessly because he had made the arrangements only because of dying (in case of his death, and since this eventuality did come about, all the donations bound up with it are invalid)." ‖ Babylonian Talmud Baba

Batra 151B: The halakah is: The donation of a seriously ill person that pertains only to a portion of his goods needs appropriation (to be valid), even if he has died. An arrangement because of death (in case of death) does not need appropriation, namely when he has died. If he remained alive, though, he can withdraw, even if they had appropriated the property. ‖ Babylonian Talmud Baba Batra 151A: The sister of Rab Dimi b. Joseph possessed a piece of an arboretum. As soon as she became ill, she gave it to him (her brother). When she remained alive, though, she withdrew. Once she got sick, and she had word sent to him, "Come, take possession of it!" He sent word to her, "I do not like it." She sent word to him, "Come, take possession of it, however you please." He came, left some of it behind (see in n. *k*) and acquired it from her (took possession of it). When she remained alive, she withdrew. She came (with her matter) before Rab Nahman († 320). He sent word to him (her brother), "Come (to me)!" He did not come; he said (to himself), "Why should I go, I left some of it behind and acquired it from her (so it is a done deal)!" He sent word to him, "If you do not come, I will strike you with a thorn that does not make any blood flow (i.e., with the ban)." He said to the witnesses, "How did the matter transpire?" They said to him, "She said this, 'Woe, that woman is dying (= woe, I am dying)!'" Then he said to them, "If this is the case, that was an arrangement in the case of death, and one may withdraw from an arrangement in the case of death (if one remains alive)."

k. Mishnah Baba Batra 9.6: If a seriously ill person has signed over all his goods to others, but has left a small piece of land (for his own needs), however much it may be, his donation is valid. If he has not left any land, however much it may be, his donation is invalid. (Since the person in question reserved nothing for the period of his own life, it is clear that the donation was intended in case of death; after this eventuality has not materialized, the donations are invalid.) ‖ Babylonian Talmud Baba Batra 149B: If he has left land, however much it may be, his donation is valid. How much is: "however much it may be"? Rab Judah († 299) said that Rab († 247) said, "As much land as suffices for his sustenance"; and Rab Jeremiah b. Abba (ca. 250) said, "As much personal property as suffices for his sustenance."

3:16 A: And to his seed. He does not say, "And to his seeds," as concerning many, but rather as concerning one, "And to your seed."

1. The passage drawn on is Gen 13:15 or 17:8; see also 22:18.

2. λέγει; the subject is either God or Scripture; see § Rom 15:10 and § 1 Cor 6:16.

3. The interpretation of the number plays a certain role even in halakic exegesis.

Mishnah Šabb. 9.2: How do we know (on the basis of Scripture) that one may sow five rows of (different kinds of) seeds on a bed that is six handbreadths square, and specifically four on the four sides of the bed and one in the middle (without therefore needing to fear transgressing the law of mixed seeds)? Because it says, "For as the earth brings forth its sprout and as a garden lets its seeds זֵרוּעֶהָ sprout" (Isa 61:11). It does not say "its seed" זַרְעָהּ (singular), but rather זרועיה "its seeds" (plural). — Meaning: Just as a garden may be arranged with different kinds of seeds on the basis of the plural זרועיה, so too a bed that is a small garden for itself; yet one must pay heed so that the different types of plants do not get mixed up with each other, but rather stand well-ordered in separated rows. ‖ See m. Sanh. 4.5 at § Matt 5:21 B, B, #3, n. *c* and § Matt 26:60, #2. See also the parallel in Gen. Rab. 22 (15B).

3:16 B: To your seed, which is Christ.

The words "your seed" in Gen 13:15; 17:8; 22:18 are nowhere, as far as we can see, interpreted to refer to the Messiah in ancient rabbinic literature. – On the designation of the Messiah as "different seed" זרע אחר or as "seed from another place" זרע ממקים אחר, see § Matt 1:5 C, #2, n. *c*.

3:17 A: The law, which came 430 years later.

On the 430 years, see § Acts 7:6.

3:17 B: The promise (see § Rom 4:13 A, #2).

3:18: For if the inheritance (came) from the law ... (see § Rom 4:13 A).

3:19 A: It was added because of transgressions (cf. § Rom 5:20).

3:19 B: Enacted by angels.

The presence of angels at the giving of the law is ancient Jewish traditional material. This idea is already mentioned in a tradition that is supposed to have been brought from Babylon (see Pesiq. Rab. 21 in the following #6), and is alluded to in LXX Deut 33:2 as well (see in the following #2). Opinions diverge concerning the purpose of the angels at the giving of the law. It is once stated generally in Pesiq. Rab. 21 (103B): Why did (the angels) come down (at the giving of the law)? R. Hiyya b. Rabba (?) said, "To honor the Torah," and R. Hiyya b. Yose (?) said, "To honor Israel." – The following traditions come into consideration more precisely.

1. The angels who were present at the giving of the law were the ruling angels of the nations. That is probably to say that the Torah was made known to them just as to the nations represented by them; see § Rom 1:20 E.

Pesiqta Rabbati 21 (103B): R. Yose b. Halapta (ca. 150) said, "(The angels present at the giving of the law) were the ruling angels of the nations of the world."

2. The angels present at the giving of the law was comprised of only God's entourage.

Septuagint Deuteronomy 33:2: Κύριος ἐκ Σινὰ ἥκει, καὶ ἐπέφανεν ἐκ Σηεὶρ ἡμῖν, καὶ κατέσπευσεν ἐξ ὄρους Φαρὰν, σὺν μυριάσι Κάδης, ἐκ δεξιῶν αὐτοῦ ἄγγελοι μετ᾽ αὐτοῦ. ‖ Pesiqta Rabbati 21 (104A): R. Judan (II), the patriarch (ca. 250), said, "According to the custom of the world, when a king of flesh and blood goes out to a *majuma* celebration (or more generally: to a celebration of peace), he goes out with ten children of men (as his entourage). But when he goes out to war, he goes out with armies and with legions. Yet with God it is not so. Rather, when he revealed himself at the Sea of Reeds to lead the battle of his children, he appeared to them without anyone else: "Yahweh is a man of war" (Exod 15:3). And when God came down onto Mount Sinai to give Israel the Torah, Michael and his banner, Gabriel and his banner came down with him: "Yahweh Elohim will come and all his holy ones with him" (so the midrash cites Zech 14:5; the targum also translates: And all his holy ones with him). — Parallels are found in Midr. Ps. 18 § 17 (73B), where R. Judah the patriarch is the author; the tradition is anonymous in SNum 12:5 § 102 (27B) and in Exod. Rab. 29 (88D); in Num. Rab. 11 (164B), R. Simeon (ca. 150) is the author. ‖ Pesiqta 108A: "The chariots of God are ten-thousand-fold, אַלְפֵי שִׁנְאָן (thousands of repetition = innumerable thousands, probably a gloss to interpret 'ten-thousand-fold')" (Ps 68:18). R. Eleazar b. Pedat (ca. 270) said, "In a place where there are clusters of people, there is a crowd; but when God came to Sinai, thousand times a thousand and ten thousand times ten thousand, אלפי שנאן, came down with him. Despite their number, they had free space; as it says, 'Moab was unhindered שַׁאֲנַן from his youth' (Jer 48:11)." (According to this, שאנן should be interpreted by means of letter transposition as אלפי שנאן = "thousands unhindered.") — Parallels are found in Pesiq. Rab. 21 (103B); Exod. Rab. 29 (88C).

3. In case Israel did not accept the Torah, the angels were to destroy the godless Israelites or even the whole world.

Pesiqta 107B: "The chariots of God are ten-thousand-fold, אַלְפֵי שִׁנְאָן" (Ps 68:18). R. Eleazar b. Pedat (ca. 270) said, "And they all came down sharpened (well-armed שְׁנוּנִין, interpretation of שִׁנְאָן) to destroy the enemies of the Israelites (= the godless Israelites, see § Matt 3:17 A, n. *i*, S-B footnote); for if they had not accepted the Torah, they would have destroyed them." The parallel in Midr. Ps. 68 § 10 (160A) reads "to destroy the world." ‖ Pesiqta Rabbati 21 (103B): (אלפי שנאן [Ps 68:18]:) The rabbis (ca. 300) said, "They came down sharpened שנונים against the world, to destroy them (if necessary)."

4. The angels supported the Israelites so that they could bear the bodily strain that was bound up for them with the giving of the law.

Mekilta Exodus 20:18 (78B): "The people saw and quaked וינועו and stood at a distance" (Exod 20:18). The "quaking" means nothing but a "staggering" זִיעַ; as it says, "Staggering, the earth staggers" (Isa 24:20). "And they stood at a distance," outside (a radius) of 12 *mils* (12 *mils* amounted to the extent of the camp); this indicates that the Israelites staggered back 12 *mils* and then again went forward 12 *mils*, so 24 *mils* with every single word (commandment). Thus they were found as those who went 240 *mils* (1 *mils* = 1.5 kilometers) on that day. In that hour God said to the angels of service, "Go down and support your brothers; as it says, 'The kings of the hosts (= angel) move on, move on' (Ps 68:13) (or transitively: move, lead); 'move on,' at the going away (of the Israelites), 'and move on,' at the returning." — A parallel that does not mention the angels is found in SDeut 32:10 § 313 (134B). The elements of this fiction are already in R. Aqiba († ca. 135); see Mek. Exod. 19:4 (70B). ‖ See a similar exposition of R. Joshua b. Levi (ca. 250) in b. Šabb. 88B.

5. The angels adorned the Israelites as a recompense for accepting the Torah. According to another view, this honor was bestowed only on the tribe of Levi.

Babylonian Talmud Šabbat 88A: R. Simai (ca. 210) contended, "In the hour that the Israelites put the 'We will do' before 'We will hear' (see Exod 24:7), 60 myriads of angels of service (corresponding to the 600,000 valiant men who had gone out from Egypt) came to every single one of the Israelites and bound two crowns to him, one corresponding to the 'We will do,' and one corresponding to the 'We will hear.' Yet when the Israelites had sinned (with the calf), 120 myriads of angels of destruction came down and took them away from them; as it says, 'Then the adornment from Mount Horeb was torn away from the children of Israel' (so Exod 33:6 according to the midrash)." ‖ See Pesiq. 124B at § Rom 2:23 A, #1, middle; to the parallels adduced there, we can add also Pesiq. Rab. 21 (102B). ‖ Pesiqta Rabbati 21 (102B): "The chariots of God are ten-thousand-fold. Thousands of repetition" (Ps 68:18). R. Abudemi (Εὔδημος) of Hefa (Haifa, ca. 280) said, "I have learned in my collection of tradition: 22,000[272] angels of service came down with God onto Mount Sinai, and in the hand of each one was a crown to adorn each individual from the tribe of Levi." R. Levi (ca. 300) said, "Evident and known it was before the one who spoke and the world came into being that not all the tribes would endure in their oath in their innocence,[273] that, however, the tribe of Levi would endure in its innocence. Therefore, they came down with God onto Mount Sinai, and in the hand of each one was a crown to adorn each one of the sons of the tribe of Levi." — See parallels with different authors at points in Pesiq. 107A; TanḥB יתרו § 14 (38B); Midr. Ps. 68 § 10 (159B), among many others.

6. The angels explained the law and the scope of its individual regulations to the Israelites.

Josephus, *Jewish Antiquities* 15.5.3, has Herod say: "What Hellenes and barbarians unanimously consider the most impious, that is what they (the Arabs) did to our emissaries by butchering them, since the Hellenes declared heralds holy and sacrosanct and we learned the best of our teachings and the holiest in the laws by angels from God δι' ἀγγέλων παρὰ τοῦ θεοῦ." ‖ It says generally in Pesiq. Rab. 21 (103B): In a tradition that has come in their hand (with those who returned) from exile, it was found written: Two myriads of the אַלְפֵי שִׁנְאָן among the angels came down with God onto Mount Sinai to give Israel the Torah. R. Eleazar (ca. 270) said, "שנאן, that is, they were the most beautiful and the most excellent." (אלפי is interpreted as the plural of אלפא = the first, most noble; שנאן = שנאין = who were beautiful, excellent; אלפי שנאן thus = the first among the beautiful = the most beautiful.) — In the parallels in Pesiq. 107B and Midr. Ps. 68 § 10 (160A), which are quite different in other ways as well, the words "to give Israel the Torah" are missing. ‖ Midrash Song of Songs 1:2 (82A): "He kissed me with the kisses of his mouth" (so Song 1:2 according to the midrash). R. Yohanan († 279) said, "An angel brought out the word (commandment) from God with each commandment and circulated it to each one of the Israelites and said to him, 'Do you

272. S-B: This number is obtained from Ps 68:18 as follows: רבוא = 10,000; רבותים = 2 × 10,000 = 20,000; אלפי שנאן = 1,000 repeated = 2,000; so, altogether, 22,000.

273. S-B: The word in the text is corrupt; see Buber on Pesiq. 107B note קמה.

accept this commandment? This sort of and this many laws are entailed in it, and this sort of and this many punishments, this sort of and this many requirements, this sort of and this many commandments, this sort of and this many inferences from the lesser to the greater, this sort of and this much recompense.' If the Israelite said to him, 'Yes!,' he would then say to him, 'Do you accept the divinity of the Holy One—blessed be He!?' If he then said to him, 'Yes, yes!,' he kissed him immediately on his mouth. This is what is written, 'It was shown to you so that you might know' (Deut 4:35), namely by an emissary שליח (= angel)." Yet the rabbis said, "The commandment itself went around to each one of the Israelites and said to him, 'Do you accept me? ...'" ‖ Here we should also refer to the fact that, according to the book of Jubilees, it was the angel of the presence, who went before Israel, who partly himself wrote down the law for Moses on the basis of the heavenly tablets, and partly dictated to Moses out of his head; see Jub. 1:27ff.; 2:1ff.; 6:22; 30:12, 21; 50:1f.

3:19 C: By the hand of a mediator.

μεσίτης = סַרְסוֹר; the latter designates α. generally[a] any negotiator or broker, β. specifically Moses as the mediator of the law.[b]

a. See, for example, Deut. Rab. 3 (201A) at § 2 Cor 3:7 B, n. *nn*.

b. See Deut. Rab. 3 (201A) at § 2 Cor 3:7 B, n. *nn*; see Pesiq. 45A at § 2 Cor 3:7 C, #5. ‖ Jerusalem Talmud Megillah 4.74D.9: R. Haggai (ca. 330) said, "R. Samuel b. Isaac (ca. 300) came into the synagogue. He saw how Huna stood and interpreted without having arranged another for himself (as an interpreter). He said to him, 'You are forbidden to do this; as it (the Torah) was given by the hand of a mediator עַל יְדֵי סַרְסוֹר, so too must we use it by the hand of a mediator (i.e., by means of an interpreter).'" ‖ Exodus Rabbah 3 (69B): "Moses said to God, 'Behold, I אנכי will come to the children of Israel'" (Exod 3:13). R. Simeon of Lydda (ca. 320?) said in the name of R. Simon (ca. 280) in the name of Resh Laqish (ca. 250), "Moses said, 'I will one day be made a mediator סרסור between you and your children, if you give them the Torah and say to them, "I אנכי am Yahweh your God"'" (Exod 20:2). ‖ See Tanḥ. יתרו 90A at § 2 Cor 3:7 C, #2, n. *b*.

3:21 A: God forbid.

See § Matt 16:22 B and § Rom 3:4 A.

3:21 B: For if a law had been given that could make alive, righteousness would actually come from the law.

That the law could give life and should give life was the settled conviction of the ancient synagogue; see § Rom 3:1f. D. — On righteousness from the law see § Matt 5:20 A; § Rom 3:20 A and § Rom 3:21 A.

3:22: Scripture locked up everything under sin.

See § Rom 3:9 B.

3:24: So the law became our tutor unto Christ.

παιδαγωγός, for the rabbis is פְּדָגוֹג, and פֵּידָגוֹג, = tutor.[a] Yet פדגיג is also used when tutoring activity is not actually mentioned; in that case, it stands in a broad sense for אֶפִּיטְרוֹפּוֹס (ἐπίτροπος) = overseer, caretaker, guardian.[b] In rabbinic literature we have not encountered any passage in which the law is designated as פדגוג, though it is once spoken of in 4 Maccabees 5:33 (in Fritzsche's verse numbering) as παιδευτής.[c]

a. See Pesiq. 17A at § Mark 4:30, #1; see Pesiq. 101B at § Acts 19:9, #2. ‖ Genesis Rabbah 28 (17D): R. Judan (ca. 350) said, "Like a king, who handed over his son to a tutor לפדגוג; he misled him, though, to a bad way of life." ‖ Genesis Rabbah 31 (18D): Like the son of a king who had a tutor פדגוג; whenever he sinned, his tutor was thrashed.

b. Numbers Rabbah 1 (135A): God said to the Israelites, "Have I not caused three פדגוגין to arise for you: Moses, Aaron, and Miriam?" — Then it is explained that the Israelites were indebted to Moses for the manna, to Aaron for the clouds of glory, and to Miriam for the well that followed them in the wilderness. In view of these three goods, Moses, Aaron, and Miriam are elsewhere called the three good פַּרְנָסִין, that is, "caretakers"; see, for example, b. Taʿan. 9A at § Matt 23:10, n. *a*; פדגוגין is meant in this sense in Num. Rab. 1 as well; the parallels in Tanḥ. במדבר 185A and TanḥB במדבר § 2 (1B) read גואלים = "redeemer" instead of פדגוגין.

c. In 4 Maccabees 5:33 the old priest Eleazar says, "I will not lie to you, tutor law παιδευτὰ νόμε!"

3:27: All who were baptized into Christ have put on Christ.

1. On βαπτίζειν εἰς see § Matt 28:19, #2. — 2. On ἐνδύσασθαι Χριστόν see § Luke 24:49, #2.

3:28: There is no Jew or Greek, there is no slave or free, there is no male or female; for you are all one in Christ Jesus.

1. The contextual meaning is: those who believe in Christ form a spiritual unity, for which the natural differences of an ethnic, social, and gender kind have lost their significance. Transferred to the religious outlook of the ancient synagogue, the statement would be: Those faithful to the law form a spiritual unity, for which the differences of natural life have become trivial. This thought would simply have been unimplementable for the synagogue, because precisely those natural differences decisively determined the relationship of everyone to the law: the one born a Jew had a different relationship to the law than the proselyte, a man had a different relationship to the law than a woman, a free person a different relationship than a slave. Thereby, the basis of a spiritual unity for those loyal to the law was withdrawn from the outset.

A. The proselyte and the law.

A distinctive relationship to the law was least apparent in the case of the proselyte. If he had undergone circumcision and the immersion bath, he became like a Jew in every respect.[a] This entailed that he had to fulfill the law in precisely the same way as the one born a Jew. Nevertheless, some particularities remained in his relationship to the law. This was the case with the presentation of firstlings and with certain expressions in prayer.[b] This was bound up with the fact that as a former non-Jew he did not belong to Abraham's physical progeny. This natural ethnic particularity thus did not at all lose its significance by his conversion to the Jewish religion of the law, but rather continued to maintain a lasting influence on the manner of the way he fulfilled the law. The appropriation of salvation was also lastingly influenced by this ethnic element: the proselyte, as one born a non-Jew, did not share in the merit of Israel's ancestors; he therefore remained dependent exclusively on his own merit in acquiring the righteousness of the law.[c]

a. See b. Yebam. 47A at § Matt 3:6 A, #6, n. *a.*

b. See m. Bik. 1.4 at § Matt 3:9 A, #4; see also, y. Bik. 1.64A.15 and t. Bik. 1.2 (100) at § Rom 4:16f.

c. Numbers Rabbah 8 (150B) at § Matt 3:9 A, #4.

B. The woman and the law.

The unfavorable opinion that existed in rabbinic circles in many ways about the world of women partly comes to expression in the relationship to the law that the ancient synagogue assigned to women; see § Eph 5:25, n. *e.* Josephus formulated this opinion in *Against Apion* 2.24 in the words: γυνὴ δὲ χείρων ἀνδρὸς εἰς ἅπαντα "the woman is in every respect less than the man." It can accordingly be readily assumed that an equal relationship to the law would not have been granted to the inferior woman alongside the fully valued man; reality was also denied to it. We differentiate here more precisely between a woman's relationship of the prohibitions and her relationship to the commandments in the Torah.

α. In relation to the prohibitions, woman and man were fully equal, that is, she had to observe them exactly as he did; only in relation to the three prohibitions that are contained in Lev 19:27 and 21:1f. did she hold a special place because of her gender.[a] Furthermore, she stood under all the regulations of civil and criminal law; she therefore had to appear for any damage that she may have caused, and also otherwise had to anticipate the same punishments as a man, including the death penalty.[b] However, apart from a few exceptions, she did not have the important right to appear as a witness.[c] Some other differences that existed in a religious and legal respect between her and a man and that in turn were partly grounded in her gender are enumerated in m. Soṭah 3.8.[d]

β. The relationship of a woman to the commandments of the Torah was regulated in an essentially different way. It was declared that she was obligated only to those commandments whose fulfillment was not bound to a particular time.[e] Accordingly, she was, for example, free from dwelling in a sukkah on the feast of booths, as well as from bearing the festal bouquet (*lulab*, see the excursus "The Feast of Tabernacles," II, A, n. *l*.); also from blowing the shofar on the New Year, from wearing *tzitzit* (show tassels) and *tefillin* (prayer straps), from reciting the Shema,[f] etc.; for these religious obligations were all dependent on time. However, she was obligated to mount the mezuzah (a door post inscription containing Deut 6:4–9 and 11:13–21) and a railing around the roof (Deut 22:8), to hand over lost property (Deut 22:3), to release a mother bird (Deut 22:6f.), to say the Prayer of Eighteen Benedictions and the meal prayer;[g] for the fulfillment of these obligations was not bound to a specific time.[274] However, there was nothing like a consistent implementation of this principle. There was a whole series of obligatory commandments that a woman was exempt from, although these obligations were not bound to a specific time. So a woman was free from studying the Torah, from the duty to procreate (see § John 2:1 A, #1), from redeeming the firstborn son,[h] generally from all the obligations that a father had to fulfill for his son, while conversely she was obligated as a daughter to do everything for her father that a son had to do for him.[i] However, the three commandments that were obligatory for a woman and that can genuinely be described as the obligatory commandments for a woman, namely the observation of the menstruant נִדָּה, the setting apart of the dough offering for the priesthood, and the lighting of the Sabbath lamp, were unique.[k] In some passages, the woman is put on the same level as slaves and children when it comes to fulfilling certain commandments.[l] More than anything else, this proves the inferior position that a woman occupied in relation to the law in comparison to a man.

a. Mishnah Qiddušin 1.7: Both men and women are bound by all the prohibitions (in the Torah), irrespective of whether time is the reason to do it or whether time is the reason not to do it, except for: "You shall not mar the edge of your beard" (Lev 19:27); "You shall not sheer round the extremity of your head" (Lev 19:27); and "You shall not defile yourself with a corpse" (Lev 21:1). (All women are exempt from the first two of these three prohibitions because they are not relevant at all for their gender, whether due to nature or custom. The third prohibition pertains to the priesthood; the wives of priests and the daughters of priests are exempt from it because the prohibition applies only to the "sons of Aaron" according to the wording of Lev 21:1.)

b. Babylonian Talmud Qiddušin 35A: In the school of R. Eliezer (ca. 90) it has been taught, "Scripture says, '(These are the legal statutes) that you shall set before them' (Exod 21:1). Scripture sets a woman on the same level as a man concerning all the legal statutes in the Torah (whether they deal with civil or criminal proceedings)." ‖ Sifre Numbers 5:6 § 2 (2A): "If a man or woman (commits some sin)" (Num 5:6). R. Josiah (ca. 140) said, "Why is it

274. S-B: On the appearance of women in the sanctuary at the three great pilgrimage festivals, see § Luke 2:41.

said (in Num 5:6) 'A man or a woman'? When it says, 'If a man opens a cistern or if a man digs a cistern' (Exod 21:33), I hear only about a man here. How do we know that it applies also to a woman? Scripture teaches, 'A man or a woman' (Num 5:6). This means that a woman is set on the same level as a man concerning all sins and damages that are mentioned in the Torah." – The same is found more briefly in Num. Rab. 8 (149D). ‖ Babylonian Talmud Qiddušin 35A: Rab Judah († 299) said that Rab († 247) said—and it has also been taught in the school of R. Ishmael († ca. 135), "Scripture says, 'If a man or a woman commits some sin of men' (Num 5:6); Scripture put a woman on the same level as a man concerning all the punishments in the Torah." – The same is found in b. Pesaḥ. 43A. ‖ Babylonian Talmud Qiddušin 35A: In the school of R. Hezekiah (ca. 240) it has been taught, "Scripture says, 'Kill the man or the woman' (cf. Lev 20:27; Deut 17:5); Scripture puts a woman on the same level as a man concerning all the death penalties in the Torah."

c. Sifre Deuteronomy 19:17 § 190 (109B): Should even a woman be fit to give testimony? It says here (Deut 19:17): "'Two' (men)," and it says there (Deut 19:15): "'Two' (witnesses)"; as the two that are mentioned here (Deut 19:17) are men and not women, so too are the two who are mentioned there (Deut 19:15) mean neb and not women. ‖ Yalquṭ Simeoni 1 § 82 from Yelamedenu: "'Then Sarah denied, "I did not laugh"' (Gen 18:15). It has been taught from this passage that women are unfit to give testimony." ‖ See m. Šebu. 4.1. 2 at § Matt 5:33, #1, n. *c*. ‖ Babylonian Talmud Baba Qamma 88A: Ulla (ca. 280) said, "... If a woman, who is suitable to come into the community (to be accepted there), is unfit to give testimony, is it not all the more the case that a slave, who is not suitable to come into the community, is unfit to give testimony?" ‖ Mishnah Roš Haššanah 1.8: This is the rule: for any sort of testimony for which a woman is not suitable, neither are they (slaves) suitable. ("A woman may, e.g., testify that a man has died, so that his widow can marry, or that a woman suspected of adultery has become unclean for her husband by keeping herself concealed with her paramour," Rashi.)

d. Mishnah Soṭah 3.8: What are the differences (in a religious-legal respect) between a man and a woman? A man (with leprosy) unbinds his hair (lets his hair grow wild) and tears his clothes (Lev 13:45); but a woman does not unbind her hair and does not tear her clothes. A man may dedicate his son as a Nazirite by a vow, but a woman may not (see § Luke 1:15 D, #2, final discussion after n. *aa*). A man (who is a Nazirite) may sheer himself because of the sacrifices appointed for the Nazirite vow of his father, but a woman may not. A man may sell his daughter, but a woman may not. A man may give his daughter (who is a minor) in engagement, but a woman may not. A man is stoned naked, but a woman is not. A man may be sold because of what he has stolen (if he cannot replace it), but a woman may not.

e. Mishnah Qiddušin 1.7: Men are bound to all the commandments (in the Torah) for which a specific time is the occasion, and women are exempt from them; both men and women are bound to all the commandments for which a specific time is not the occasion.

f. Mishnah Sukkah 2.8: Women and slaves and children are exempt from the sukkah. ‖ A baraita in b. Qidd. 33B: What are the commandments for which a specific time is the occasion (from which women are thus exempt)? The sukkah, the festal bouquet, blowing the shofar, the show fringes and the tefillin. ‖ Mishnah Berakot 3.3: Women, slaves, and children are exempt from reciting the Shema and from the tefillin.

g. A baraita in b. Qidd. 34A: What are the commandments for which a specific time is not the occasion (to which women are thus bound)? The mezuzah, the rail (around the roof), handing over a lost item (which was then found by a woman), and setting free a mother bird. ‖ Mishnah Berakot 3.3: Women, slaves, and children ... are bound to the Prayer (of Eighteen Benedictions), the mezuzah, and the table prayer (after a meal; however, they are not counted among the persons who are called upon to sing the blessing after the meal, m. Ber. 7.2; see the excursus "An Ancient Jewish Feast").

h. Babylonian Talmud Qiddušin 34A: Yet is this (what is said in m. Qidd. 1.7 in n. *e* above) a general rule? Look, women are bound to unleavened bread (on the feast of Passover), to the joy of the feast (Deut 12:12; 16:11, 14f.) and to the assembly (Deut 31:12), although they are commandments for which a specific time is the occasion, and furthermore, see, women are exempt from studying the Torah, from the duty of procreation, and from redeeming the (firstborn) son, although these are not commandments for which a specific time is the occasion! ‖ It is notable that a woman was excluded precisely from the study of the Torah, which was so highly valued (m. Pe'ah 1.1). This implied that the Torah was really laid down for the sphere of Israelite men, but not for the sphere of Israelite women. See b. Ḥag. 3A at § 1 Cor 14:34 A, n. *b*; m. Soṭah 3.4; b. Soṭah 21B; y. Soṭah 3.19A.3 at § 1 Cor 14:35 A.

i. Mishnah Qiddušin 1.7: Men are bound by every commandment concerning a son that a father is obligated to, whereas women are exempt from these; but both men and women are bound to all the commandments concerning a father that are obligatory for a son. ‖ On the duties of a father to a son, see b. Qidd. 29A at § Acts 18:3, #1 and t. Qidd. 1.11 (336) at § John 2:1 A, #3, D, n. *c*. – On the duties of a son to a father, which also therefore had to be observed by a daughter, see t. Qidd. 1.11 (336) at § 1 Cor 11:10 A, n. *c*. – See also at § 1 Cor 11:10, n. *c*, SLev 19:3 (343A); somewhat differently, b. Qidd. 30B.

k. Mishnah Šabbat 2.6: Due to three transgressions women die in the hour of bearing children, namely if they are not diligent about menstruation and the dough offering and lighting the (Sabbath) light. – On this, y. Šabb. 2.5B.34: In the case of menstruation. The first man was the blood of the world; as it is written, "A mist arose from the earth" (Gen 2:6). (The passage, compared with what precedes and follows, is supposed to prove that the life of the plant world arose only with the creation of Adam; so Adam means the life of the world. And since according to a different view, life is in the blood, Adam can now be called the blood of the world. It is more obvious simply to interpret אָדָם = אַדְמָא = blood.) And Eve caused death for him. Therefore, the commandment about menstruation was handed (by God) to the woman. Additionally, in the case of the dough offering. The first man was the pure dough offering for the world; as it is written, "Then Yahweh-Elohim formed man from the dust of the earth" (Gen 2:7). (Adam thus is the first thing that was lifted from the dust of the earth.) This corresponds to what R. Yose b. Qeṣarta (in the 3rd century) said, "If a woman beats her dough in water, she takes away from the dough offering (for the priest). And Eve caused death for him; therefore, the commandment about the dough offering was handed to the woman. And in the case of lighting the (Sabbath) light. The first man was the lamp נֵר

(light) of the world; as it says, 'The spirit of the man is a lamp of Yahweh' (Prov 20:27). And Eve caused death for him; therefore, the woman was handed the commandment concerning the (Sabbath) light." In a baraita: R. Yose (ca. 150) said, "There are three things that hang together with death (to the extent that not observing them leads to death), and these three were handed to the woman, namely: the commandment about menstruation and the commandment about the dough offering and the commandment about lighting the (Sabbath) light. — See similar expositions in t. Šabb. 2.10 (112); b. Šabb. 31B; 32A; Gen. Rab. 17 (12A).

l. See b. B. Qam. 88A and m. Roš Haš. 1.8 in n. *c*; m. Sukkah 2.8 and m. Ber. 3.3 in n. *f*; m. Ber. 3.3 in n. *g*. ‖ Yalquṭ Simeoni on Samuel § 78 (from Yelamedenu): "Why were women connected with children and slaves concerning the fulfillment of the commandments (placed on the same level as them)? Because they have a heart only (for their husband). Likewise, the heart of the slave is directed only to his lord. Women and slaves still have a human lord over them, and serving him claims their heart in such a way that it lacks the time and strength to serve God. Therefore, lesser demands are made of women and slaves than are made of men and free people concerning fulfilling the commandments."

C. The slave and the law.

A non-Israelite slave who passed into the possession of a Jew was made a proselyte by circumcision and an immersion bath. He thereby for the most part entered into the same relation to the law in which a woman stood, that is, he was bound only by those commandments whose fulfillment was not dependent on a specific time. The time and strength of the slave belonged in the first place to his human lord; therefore, the binding nature of the commandments for the slave generally ceased when fulfilling them would have put pressure on the master's right to his working power. This stood out particularly in the case of a slave's vows: if these hindered the slave's services for his lord, they were simply invalid. Babylonian Talmud Ḥagigah 4A is also instructive: "How can it be proved," it is asked here, "that slaves are not obligated to appear in the temple at the festivals? Rab Huna († 297) said, 'Scripture says, "Three times a year every one of your males shall appear before the Lord Yahweh" (Exod 23:17). He who has only one Lord (should appear). This excludes the one who has another (second) lord.'" The principle: "Serving a lord takes priority over serving God" unmistakably underlies these words. Only when a stipulation of the law explicitly directed itself to a slave, as, for example, in the Sabbath commandment (Exod 20:10), did he have to observe the commandment in question as a free Israelite did. See more detail on this with supporting passages in the excursus "The Nature of Ancient Jewish Slavery."

2. Only if one does not pay attention to the context of Gal 3:28 and deduces from it the general idea that before God all people are equal can a few parallels from rabbinic literature be adduced.[a] Yet one must be careful not to assume that the idea of the equality of all people before God found general acceptance in the ancient synagogue.[b]

a. Exodus Rabbah 21 (83C): R. Judah b. Shalom (ca. 370) said in the name of R. Eleazar (ca. 270), "If a poor man comes to someone to say something before him, he does not listen to him; if a rich man comes to say something, he immediately listens and accepts it. Yet with God it is not so, but rather all are alike before him שוין לפניו, women and slaves and poor and rich. You can recognize it (from the following); for look, in the case of Moses, the master of all the prophets, it is written, what is written in the case of the poor man. In the case of Moses it is written, 'A prayer of Moses, the man of God' (Ps 90:1), and in the case of the poor man it is written, 'A prayer of a poor man, when he is afflicted and pours out his lament before Yahweh' (Ps 102:1). The former is called 'prayer' and the latter is called 'prayer' to let you know that all are alike before God in prayer." ‖ Seder Eliyahu Rabbah 7 (36): "I (Elijah) take for myself heaven and earth as witnesses: whether a gentile or an Israelite בין גוי ובין ישראל, whether a man or a woman בין איש ובין אשה, whether a servant or a servant-girl בין עבד ובין שפחה recites this passage of Scripture, 'To the north before Yahweh' (Lev 1:11), God remembers the binding of Isaac, the son of Abraham." — This passage is also found in the addenda to Lev. Rab. 2 (134C). — Seder Eliyahu Rabbah 10 (48): "'Deborah, a prophetess' (Judg 4:4). What reason was there for Deborah to judge the Israelites and to be a prophetess over them? Was not Phineas the son of Eleazar present? I (Elijah) take for myself heaven and earth as witnesses: whether a gentile or an Israelite, whether a man or a woman, whether a servant or a servant-girl—on each one the holy spirit (= the spirit of prophecy) rests according to the measure of works that he does." ‖ Seder Eliyahu Rabbah 14 (65): (God said to Moses,) "Is there respect of a person before me? Whether a gentile or an Israelite, whether a man or a woman, whether a servant or a servant-girl—if he fulfills a commandment, its (the commandment's) recompense is at its (the commandment's) side; as it says, 'Your righteousness is (unchangeable) like the mountains of God' (Ps 36:7)." — See further the saying of R. Joshua in t. Sanh. 13.2 (434) at § Matt 5:43, #1, n. *g*, 2nd paragraph in note, and that of R. Meir in b. Sanh. 58B at § Matt 5:43, #1, n. *g*, 4th paragraph in note.

b. See the passages at § Rom 2:11, #3 and § Matt 5:43, #1, n. *g*.

4:1 A: As long as the heir is a child.

νήπιος corresponds to the rabbinic קָטָן; the latter adjectivally = "small, underage," substantively = "child, boy, a minor"; opposite: גָּדוֹל = an adult, one who is of age, or אִישׁ = man.[a] A Jewish boy was considered a קטן until he was 13 years and 1 day old;[b] with the completed 13th year of life, he became of age גדול. Physiologically, the age of 13 years and 1 day was designated as the time of puberty.[c] A 13-year-old boy was of age, though, only in a religious-legal perspective, insofar as he was obligated to observe all the commandments in the Torah with the completed 13th year of life and was responsible all by himself to consciously fulfill them.[d] He acquired all legal rights and responsibilities only once he completed the 20th year of life.[e]

a. Babylonian Talmud Niddah 46B: We find that Scripture places a boy on the same level as an adult שהשוה הכתוב הקטן כגדול. ‖ Babylonian Talmud Niddah 46B several times uses the expression: מופלא סמוך לאיש, that is, a minor who knows clearly how to say a vow is on the brink of the (the age of being a) man. ‖ Sifre Numbers 6:2 § 22 (7A): "If a man איש" (Num 6:2), so not a boy קטן; for one could infer: if when Scripture does not put women on the same level as men,[275] it puts boys קטנים on the same level as adults גדולים, would it not be right for it here (Num 6:2), where it places women on the same level as men, to put (also) boys קטנים on the same level as adults גדולים? Scripture teaches: "If a man" איש, and not a boy קטן.

b. Mishnah Niddah 5.6: In the case of a (boy) who is 12 years and 1 day old, his vows are subject to review (to see whether the boy knows what it is about); in the case of one who is 13 years and 1 day old, his vows (automatically) are valid (for with this age he has become of age).

c. Babylonian Talmud Niddah 45B; 46A: If he has not brought forth both hairs (as a sign of puberty), he is a minor קטן.

d. See m. Nid. 6.11; m. ʾAbot 5.21; b. Ketub. 50A and Gen. Rab. 63 (40A) at § Luke 2:42.

e. Babylonian Talmud Giṭṭin 65A: There are three measures (rules) in the case of one who is not of age קָטָן: if he throws away a stone (that is given to him) while he takes a nut, he can acquire something for himself but not for others (he can, e.g., keep a gift).... In the case of older boys (according to the commentaries, those who are 7–8 years old), their purchase is a purchase and their sale is a sale in the case of movable goods (the same in m. Giṭ. 5.7).... If they have reached the age of being able to make a vow (see m. Nid. 5.6 above in n. *b*), their vows are a vow and their dedications (to the temple) are a dedication.... However, he may sell from the (immovable) goods (to be inherited from) the father only when he is 20 years old.

4:1 B: He is in no way different from a slave.

The point of comparison is the lack of the right of self-determination.

Babylonian Talmud Giṭṭin 38A: A slave over whom his lord has authority is called a slave. (Such a one was a slave of non-Jewish origin.) ‖ Babylonian Talmud Nazir 61A: This excludes a slave whose soul is not his own (who is not his own master). — The same is found in b. Naz. 62B. ‖ Mishnah Baba Meṣiʿa 1. 5: That which is found by his son and his daughter, if they are minors, is that which is found by his Canaanite (= non-Jewish) slave..., they belong to him (to the father, or the lord). ‖ Babylonian Talmud Pesaḥim 88B: That which a slave has acquired, his lord has acquired (it belongs to his lord). Similarly, y. Qidd. 1.60A.26; b. Qidd. 23B.21. 24. ‖ Tosefta Baba Qamma 11.2 (370): If a son does business with that which is his father's, and likewise if a slave does business with that which is his lord's, behold, it (what is acquired) belongs to the father, behold, it belongs to the lord. ‖ Genesis Rabbah 67 (42D): A slave, whose is he? (His) goods, whose are they? A slave and everything that is his belongs to his lord. See TanḥB תולדות § 24 (72B); Deut. Rab. 1 (196C); b. Meg. 16A. — See further in the excursus "The Nature of Ancient Jewish Slavery."

275. S-B: This refers to Lev 21:1ff.; see m. Qidd. 1.7 at § Gal 3:28, B, β, n. *a*.

4:2 A: He is under guardians and administrators.

1. On ἐπίτροπος = אֶפִּיטְרוֹפּוֹס, see § Luke 8:3 A, #3 and § Gal 3:24. – On οἰκονόμος, see § Matt 24:45; § Luke 12:42; and § Luke 16:1.

2. The nature of guardianship was regulated and developed on all sides already in the Mishnaic period (until about 200 CE). The guardian was named with the foreign appellative אֶפִּיטְרוֹפּוֹס[276] = ἐπίτροπος, the ward יָתוֹם (= orphan, Aram. יְתוֹמָא, יַתְמָא), fem. יְתוֹמָה. Most of the time, it appears to have been the father who before his death determined the guardian for his underage children.[a] In this case, the guardian may have come into his office by the responsible local court.[b] If the father had failed to name a guardian, the court appointed one.[c] Occasionally orphans are mentioned who were supported by the father of a household or by an elder.[d] It should be understood that the orphans in question who did not have an actual guardian had their affairs handled by a neighbor or other acquaintances. One may conclude from this that it was not absolutely necessary to name a particular guardian. Even several guardians for a ward are mentioned;[e] we should here think of rather large legacies which were too great to be managed by one guardian. The plural ἐπίτροποι in Gal 4:2 thus is not striking. – In selecting a guardian, a father was virtually unrestricted. Only an *ʿam ha'areṣ* (one who did not know the law, who did not concern himself with rabbinic stipulations, see § John 7:49) was not to be entrusted with a guardianship.[f] Further, a relative who might have a personal interest in the inheritance was also not to be named as a guardian.[g] Additionally, it was frowned upon to name women and slaves as guardians; however, if they were appointed by a testator, the judicial authority usually did not then raise objections against them.[h] There is also the case where a father appoints his grown son as a guardian for his underage siblings.[i] Among the tasks of a guardian were, in the first place, to care for the physical and spiritual wellbeing of those entrusted to his care. In this respect, he fully took the place of the father:[k] he looks after the livelihood[l] of the wards, he makes the earnings ready to use by setting aside what accrues to it,[m] he pays the temple tax for the wards,[n] slaughters the Passover lamb for them,[e] sees to the sukkah and the festal bouquet for the Feast of Booths for them, he buys them a Torah book, the tefillin, the *tzitzit* (tassels) for their clothes, and the inscription capsule on their doorposts.[o] In order to finance the livelihood and education in the law for the wards, the guardian was even allowed to sell properties (houses, fields, etc.) from the estate,[o] which otherwise he was not permitted to do. – In addition to this first task of a guardian to see to the livelihood and education of the wards, there was another, namely, to faithfully manage the entire inheritance of

---

276. S-B: One also finds אפיטרופא and אפיטרופיא.

the children for their benefit. The worth that was attributed precisely to this part of the guardian's activity we can already see linguistically from the fact that אפיטרופוס denoted not simply the guardian, but rather at the same time also the administrator.[p] Guardian and administrator were exactly one and the same thing in the consciousness of the people. When he came into his office, the guardian formally acquired possession of the whole fortune that belonged to the wards[r] החזיק (ירד) בנכסי היתומין, without though being permitted to derive the right of acquisition for himself from this, as is explicitly emphasized.[q] As long as the property had not yet been acquired, the guardian could still rescind his guardianship אֶפִּיטְרוֹפְּסוּת, and after the property had been acquired, withdrawing was no longer allowed.[r] The uppermost guideline for administering the goods of the wards was preserving them and, insofar as it was relevant, increasing them. Sales that could decrease the value of the goods were therefore prohibited. Real estate could not be sold if one intended to invest the proceeds from them in movable property.[s] Also, all dubious transactions with the fortune had to be avoided: the guardian was not to sell distant plots to buy ones that were closer.[t] He was to avoid lawsuits in matters pertaining to his wards, or at least conduct them with the approval of the judicial authority.[u] Even expenses for purposes that were in themselves good and commendable (e.g., alms) were not to be paid from the funds of the wards.[v] Unscrupulous guardians were removed by the judicial authority.[w]

The duration of a guardianship depended of course on the age of the wards: the younger the latter were, the longer the former had to last. Yet here we lack explicit evidence. It is once said incidentally in a parable that a king who went to a distant country appointed a guardian for his son until he came of age.[x] This would also have been the general rule elsewhere, since the guardianship came to an end when the wards came of age (see § Gal 4:1). "For a bearded man (one of age)," it says, "a guardian is not appointed" אפיטרופא לדיקנני לא מוקמינן (b. B. Meṣ. 39A). — However, a guardian is once mentioned who could continue his guardianship after the wards had come of age. At issue here, though, is the unauthorized behavior of an unfaithful and reckless guardian who thinks he can compete for a right of acquisition for himself by administering the goods beyond the time when his wards come of age.[y] Correctly understood, then, the passage shows rather that guardianships had to end when the wards reached their majority. — Sometimes there is mention of a guardian "forever" לעולם, who is juxtaposed with a guardian "for a short time" לשעה (literally: for one hour). The former would have been arranged for the whole period when the wards were minors, whereas the latter was appointed for a specific matter, and after it had been dealt with his guardianship automatically ceased.[z]

After a guardianship ended, the guardian gave an account of his administration.[aa] Also, an oath could be required of him that he had not enriched himself by the fortune of his wards. It was disputed, though, whether a guardian appointed by a father or by the court was obligated to give this oath. The halakah on this point appears to have been conflicting.[bb] Once a guardianship ended, all rights and powers of the guardian ceased; it was said, "As soon as a guardian is out of his guardianship, he is like all other men" (t. B. Bat. 2.5 [399]; t. Ketub. 9.3 [271]).

a. Mishnah Giṭṭin 5.4: If orphans (wards) are supported by the father of a household, or if their father named a guardian for them, he must tithe their fruits. ‖ See m. Giṭ. 5.4 in n. *c*; see t. B. Bat. 8.17 (410) in n. *h.* ‖ Pesiqta 123A: R. Eleazar (ca. 270) said, "Earlier when someone in Jerusalem who was near death named guardians (pl.) for the orphans and his widow claimed her prescribed marital sum from the orphans, they went to the judge and found him and the guardian suspicious (because of bribery)."

b. See t. B. Bat. 8.17 (410) in n. *h.*

c. Mishnah Giṭṭin 5.4: A guardian named by the father of the orphans has to swear, while one named by the court does not need to swear (see n. *bb*). ‖ See t. B. Bat. 8.17 (410) in n. *h.* ‖ Babylonian Talmud Ketubbot 100A: Rab Nahman († 320) said that Samuel († 254) said. "If orphans want to apportion the goods of their father (among themselves), the court appoints a guardian for them...." The same is found in b. Giṭ. 33B; b. Yebam. 67B. ‖ See m. B. Qam. 4.4 in n. *z.* ‖ See further b. B. Meṣ. 39A.

d. See m. Giṭ. 5.4 above in n. *a.* ‖ Tosefta Terumot 1.13 (26): R. Simeon b. Manasseh (ca. 180) said, "If orphans are supported by the father of a household, or if their father has given support for them, or if the court has given support for them, he tithes (their fruits) and lets them eat for the sake of order in the world." ‖ Babylonian Talmud Giṭṭin 52A: Orphans who were supported by an old man owned a cow. The old man took it and sold it for them. Then the relatives came before Rab Nahman († 320) and said to him, "How it is that he has sold it?" He answered them, "We have learned: 'If orphans are supported by the father of a household ... (i.e., the support is viewed as a guardian, so the action associated with it should be recognized as valid)'" (m. Giṭ. 5.4).

e. Mishnah Pesaḥim 8.1: A ward for whom guardians אפיטרופין (plural) have slaughtered (namely the Passover lamb) can eat from whatever part he wants. ‖ See Pesiq. 123A above in n. *a.*

f. A baraita in b. Pesaḥ. 49B: Six things have been said about the *ʿamme ha'areṣ*: ... They are not named as a guardian over orphans ...

g. Babylonian Talmud Baba Meṣiʿa 39A: Rab Huna († 297) said, "... One does not appoint a relative (as an administrator or guardian) over the goods of a minor, nor any indirect relative (related by marriage) over the goods of a minor .... This refers to a brother on the maternal side (whom the mother brought into the marriage); for since no one hinders him, he might come to take possession of them (for himself)."

h. Tosefta Baba Batra 8.17 (410): A court does not make women or slaves guardians in the first place. Yet if their (the orphans') father has appointed them for this during his life, they are made guardians (by the court). — The same is found in t. Ter. 1.11 (26). From the wording in t. B. Bat. 8.17 it can be inferred that the court had a certain right of confirmation concerning guardians that were appointed by fathers. — Babylonian Talmud Giṭṭin 52A: One (a court) does not make women, slaves, and minors guardians. However, if the father of the orphans has appointed them for this, he has the authority for his in his hand. (The appointment is therefore valid.) — A woman is found as a guardian also in b. B. Bat. 131B: Rab Judah († 299) said that Samuel († 254) said, "If someone has signed over all his goods to his wife, he has thereby only made her a guardian (for his underage children). (Rashi: 'No one who leaves behind children gives everything to his wife; when he does so, he only has the purpose of making her a guardian, so that his children bestow reverence on her.') ... If he has signed over all his goods to his wife and to a stranger (who does not belong to the family), he has given it to the stranger as a gift, but he has made his wife a guardian." (The first sentence is also found in b. B. Bat. 144A.) — Then the text also mentions a minor whom the father has set as a guardian; see b. Giṭ. 52A above. It says on this: What is the case when he has signed over all his goods to his underage son? It has been said: Rab Hanilai b. Idi (ca. 260) said that Samuel († 254) said, "Even his small son who lies in the cradle (the father has made a guardian as soon as he has signed over to him all his goods; here he has been guided by the wish that his other children honor this youngest son)"; see also the next citation in n. *i*.

i. Babylonian Talmud Baba Batra 131B: It stands to reason that if someone has signed over all his goods to his underage son, he has thereby only made him a guardian (for his underage siblings, so that they honor him and obey him). See the similar regulations in n. *h*.

k. Reference may also be made here to the haggadic interpretation of the word אפיטרופוס, which is found in Bertinoro († 1510) on m. Giṭ. 5.4: פאטור (πατήρ) means "father," פיס (παῖς) means "children" (so the whole אפיטרופוס = father of the children). — The source from which Bertinoro created this remains unknown to us. This interpretation is found later as well in Mosheh Margelit in his commentary *Pene Mošeh* on y. Giṭ. 5.4.

l. Babylonian Talmud Giṭṭin 52A: (Against the words: "The guardian must tithe their fruits" [m. Giṭ. 5.4]—see above in n. *a*) the objection has been raised: It says, "'You' (shall withdraw)" (Num 18:28) ... and not the guardians, "you" and not the one who withdraws what does not belong to him. Rab Hisda († 309) said, "There is no contradiction: here (m. Giṭ. 5.4) what is at issue is setting apart tithes to feed (the wards immediately); there, to store the fruits. In a baraita it says: 'The guardians set apart the offering and the tithes to feed (the wards), but not to store (the fruits).'" — See further t. Ter. 1.13 (26) in n. *d*; t. B. Bat. 8.14 (409) and b. Giṭ. 52A in n. *o*.

m. Tosefta Baba Batra 8.14 (409): The guardians set apart the (priestly) offering and tithes for the goods of the wards. — See further m. Giṭ. 5.4 in n. *a*; t. Ter. 1.13 in n. *d;* and b. Giṭ. 52A in n. *l*.

n. Tosefta Šeqalim 1.8 (174): Guardians who pay the temple tax for the wards are responsible for the premium (when the money is exchanged).

o. Tosefta Baba Batra 8.14 (409): Guardians set apart the (priestly) offering and tithes for the goods of the wards. They may sell houses, fields and vineyards, livestock, slaves and slave-girls to feed the wards, to make them a sukkah, a festal bouquet, and tassels for their clothes and all other commanded items that are named in the Torah; furthermore, to buy a Torah scroll and a prophets scroll, anything (at all) that is prescribed by the Torah. – The same is found in t. Ter. 1.10 (26) with the closing words: "Something that is firmly fixed by the Torah (in its scope)." (This excludes, e.g., payments for benevolent purposes since the amount is not set by Scripture.) – ‖ Babylonian Talmud Giṭṭin 52A: Guardians may sell for wards livestock, slaves and slave-girls, houses, fields and vineyards to feed them, but not to deposit (the money received); they may also sell for them fruits, wine, oil, and flour to feed them, but not to deposit (the money). They make for them a festal bouquet, a willow (for the Feast of Booths), a sukkah and tassels for their clothes, and everything that has a fixed measure; the trumpet (blowing at the New Year) should be included; they also buy them a Torah book, tefillin, and doorpost capsules (*mezuzoth*), and everything that has a fixed measure; the Esther scroll should also be included.

p. See the citations at § Luke 8:3 A, #3.

q. Mishnah B. Bat. 3.1: Guardians do not have the right of acquisition חֲזָקָה. (To acquire houses, wells, and artificially watered fields, three years had to pass without their ownership being contested, while according to R. Aqiba [† ca. 135] ordinary types of landed property could be acquired already by use that went uncontested for 14 months [m. B. Bat. 3.1].)

r. Tosefta Baba Batra 8.12 (409): Before guardians have acquired possession of the goods of the wards, they can withdraw (from the guardianship); after they have acquired possession of the goods of the wards, they can no longer withdraw.

s. Tosefta Baba Batra 8.16 (410): (Guardians) may sell slaves to buy landed property for them, but not landed property to buy slaves for them. Rabban Simeon b. Gamaliel (ca. 140) said, "Not even slaves to buy landed property for them." (Having numerous slaves raised the esteem of a family.) A parallel passage is found in b. Giṭ. 52A. ‖ A baraita in y. Giṭ. 5.47A.12: A guardian may sell slaves but not landed property. – The meaning is different in the parallel in y. Ter. 1.40A.51.

t. Tosefta Baba Batra 8.15 (410): (Guardians) may not sell far away in order in turn to buy nearby, nor sell cheap in order in turn to buy expensive. – A parallel passage is found in b. Giṭ. 52A.

u. Tosefta Baba Batra 8.15 (410): (Guardians) may not conduct lawsuits so that the wards become indebted or prevail, so that obligations may be imposed on them or removed from them—unless they have been authorized by the court. A parallel passage is found in t. Ter. 1.11 (26); differently, b. Giṭ. 52A. ‖ Jerusalem Talmud Baba Qamma 4.4B.42: R. Yohanan († 279) said, "Originally, one (the court) did not appoint a guardian so that they (the orphans) would become indebted, but rather so that they might prevail (in legal proceedings); and if they became indebted, they became indebted." R. Yose b. Hanina (ca. 270) said, "Both originally as well as recently one did not appoint a guardian for the wards, neither to win nor to lose a legal proceeding" (i.e., legal proceedings should be avoided in all circumstances). – The same is found in y. Giṭ. 5.47A.13.

v. Tosefta Terumot 1.10 (26): Guardians may not ransom any prisoners for them (the wards, i.e., at their expense), nor determine alms for the poor in the synagogue; this is a matter that has no amount determined by the Torah. Further, they are not authorized to release slaves as free people, though they may sell them to others, and they may then release them as free people. Rabbi († 217?) said, "I think that if he (the slave) pays his worth, he can free himself." — The same is found in t. B. Bat. 8.14 (409); b. Giṭ. 52A.14, 19.

w. Babylonian Talmud Giṭṭin 52B: It has been said, "A guardian who harms (his wards) is removed," as said by Rab Huna († 297) in the name of Rab († 247). The school of Shela said, "He is not removed." The halakah is as follows: he is removed.

x. Sifre Deuteronomy 1:11 § 11 (67B).

y. To the saying of Rab Huna adduced in n. *g* from b. B. Meṣ. 39A, Raba († 352) adds the remark, "From the saying of Rab Huna I take that one cannot acquire the goods of a minor even if he has come of age (and the guardian does not cede the administration)."

z. Jerusalem Talmud Terumot 1.40B.48: It says: "'You' (shall withdraw)" (Num 18:28) and not "the guardians" (so that the latter may not set apart the tithes etc. from the fruits of their wards). Yet we have learned (see m. Giṭ. 5.4 above in n. *a*): If orphans (wards) are supported by a father of a household, or if their father has appointed a guardian for them, he must tithe their fruits! (How is this contradiction to be overcome?) The companions (of the scholars) said, "Here what is at issue is a guardian forever (this one may tithe) and there what is at issue is a guardian for a short time (this one may not tithe)." — The same is found in y. Giṭ. 5.47A.9. — A guardian named in this ad hoc way is mentioned, for example, in m. B. Qam. 4.4: If the ox of a deaf-mute, feeble-minded, and minor has struck (has become apt to strike), the court appoints a guardian for them and warns them in the presence of the guardian. —Jerusalem Talmud Baba Qamma 4.4B.42—see the passage in n. *u*—also deals with a guardian who is appointed specifically for conducting a legal proceeding.

aa. Tosefta Terumot 1.11 (26): "At the end (of their guardianship) guardians must reckon with the wards (give an account in their presence)." So Rabbi († 217?). Rabban Simeon b. Gamaliel (ca. 140) said, "The wards are due no more than what their guardians have left for them" (a reckoning is therefore pointless). — The same is found in t. B. Bat. 8.15 (410). — In b. Giṭ. 52A Rabban Simeon b. Gamaliel says, "A guardian does not need to" (give an account to the wards).

bb. Mishnah Giṭṭin 5.4: A guardian who has been named by the father of the orphans must swear; if the court has named him, he does not need to swear. Abba Saul (ca. 150) said this the other way round. — In t. B. Bat. 8.13 (409), the tradition is as follows: A guardian who has been named by the father of the orphans must swear; if the court has named him, he does not need to swear. Abba Saul said, "Even the one named by a court must swear because he is as one who receives a recompense." — See discussions about this in y. B. Qam. 4.4B.49; y. Giṭ. 5.47A.19 and b. Giṭ. 52B.

4:2 B: Until the time set by his father.

That a father could determine the duration of the guardianship and the time of his children's coming of age as he pleased cannot be proved from Jewish sources; see, however, above at § 4:2, A, notes *x–z*.

4:3: The elements of the world.

στοιχεῖα τοῦ κόσμου refer to the religious regulations and customs of the pre-Christian world, which in comparison with the gospel can be evaluated only as *rudimenta disciplinae mundi*, as the rudiments of the religious education of humanity. — The expression יְסוֹדוֹת הָעוֹלָם = "elements of the world" in a physical sense belongs only to the post-Talmudic period.

4:4 A: The full measure (literally: the fullness) of time.

τὸ πλήρωμα τοῦ χρόνου is the moment that rounds off the time appointed by God. In substance, it is related to the expression συντέλεια τοῦ αἰῶνος, see § Matt 13:39 A and § Matt 24:3. — Concerning the messianic time appointed by God for redemption = קֵץ, see § Matt 24:6 C and § Acts 1:6.

Tobit 14:5: "God will have mercy on them again and make them return to the land; and they will build the house (temple), not like the first was until the times of the course of the world have been filled ἕως πληρωθῶσι καιροὶ τοῦ αἰῶνος." — In א: ἕως τοῦ χρόνου οὗ ἂν πληρωθῇ ὁ χρόνος τῶν καιρῶν "until the point in time when the point in time of the times is full." ‖ 4 Ezra 4:35ff.: "This question of yours (about the dawn of the time of salvation) the souls of the righteous in their chambers have already asked; they said, '... When will the fruit on the threshing floor of our recompense finally appear?' Yet the archangel Jeremiel answered and said, 'When the number of those like you is full. For he (God) has weighed the age on the scale, he has measured the hours with the measure and counted the times by number. He does not disturb them and he does not awaken them (before the time), until the declared measure is fulfilled *usquedum impleatur praedicta mensura*.'" ‖ 4 Ezra 11:44: "Then the Most High considered his times: behold, they were at an end, and his eons, they were full *et saecula eius completa sunt*." ‖ 2 Baruch 40:3: "His (the Messiah's) dominion will endure forever, until the world dedicated to destruction comes to an end and until the times foretold are full *donec impleantur tempora praedicta*." — We have not encountered the expression מְלוֹא עִתִּים, which would correspond verbatim to πλήρωμα τοῦ χρόνου. — See also § Eph 1:10.

4:4 B: Born of a woman.

γενόμενος ἐκ γυναικός = יְלוּד אִשָּׁה "born of a woman," α. a simple circumlocution "human being," see 4 Ezra 7:46 at § Rom 3:9 B, n. *a*; 4 Ezra 7:65ff. "all those born of women" at § Rom 8:22, n. *b*; Tanḥ. משפטים 99A at § Matt 18:10 B; Num. Rab. 4 (141B) and Lev. Rab. 35 (132B) at § Matt 11:11 A, with a disparaging connotation = "frail, sinful human," see ʾAbot R. Nat. 2 (2A) at § Eph 4:8 B, #2, n. *b* and b. Šabb. 88B at § Matt 11:11 A; Midr. Ps. 143 § 1 (266B) at § Rom 3:9 B, n. *a*. — Synonymous with "one born of women" is "one born of the earth" = "human being." 2 Enoch 50:1: "I have set down in a writing the work of each person. And no one born on the earth can hide nor can his works remain hidden."

4:4 C: Born under the law.

The Messiah subject to the Torah: Tg. Isa. 9:5: "He (the Messiah) takes the Torah upon himself to keep it." ‖ Targum Isaiah 53:11f., see § Matt 8:17, A, 2nd paragraph. ‖ Targum Psalm 45:10f., see § Heb 1:8f. ‖ Targum Song of Songs 8:1f.: "In that time the king, the Messiah, will be revealed to the community of Israel, and the children of Israel will say to him, 'Come, be our brother, and we will go up to Jerusalem to imbibe with you the bases of the Torah, as a child sucks at the breast of its mother.... I will escort you, O king, Messiah, and lead you into the sanctuary, so that you may teach me to fear Yahweh and to walk in his Torah.'" ‖ Midrash Psalm 2 § 9 (14B), see § Rom 1:3 A, A, #3, β. ‖ Midrash Psalm 110 § 4 (233B): Likewise, it says of the Messiah, "His throne was established (so the midrash) by grace, and he sits on it with faithfulness in the tent of David" (Isa 1: 5). God says, "He will still quietly and I will wage war. Therefore, it says, 'He sits on his throne with faithfulness in the tent of David.' And what does he have to do? To read and to study in the Torah, which is called 'fidelity' אמת"; see Ps 19:10 and Prov 23:23.

4:6: Crying: Abba, my father.

1. The term that corresponds to κράζειν, צְוַח, Aram צְוַח, = "to cry loudly, yell," is said extraordinarily frequently about the Holy Spirit in rabbinic literature. See examples at § Luke 2:25 C, #4, notes *b* and *c*.

2. On ἀββᾶ ὁ πατήρ see § Mark 14:36.

3. That the ancient synagogue knows of no cooperation of the Holy Spirit in the prayer of an Israelite, see § Rom 8:15 B.

4:8: You served gods, who by nature are not gods.

See the opinions of the ancient synagogue about pagan divinities at § Rom 1:23 A, #2.

4:10: You are observing days and months and times and years?!

Presumably R. Eleazar of Modiim († ca. 135) already accused the apostle of despising the holy times. Galatians 4:10 could be adduced as proof for this (see § Acts 21:21).

4:14: You received me as an angel of God, as Christ Jesus.

See the principle: The one sent (authorized) by someone is as he himself (see § Matt 10:40 B).

4:19: Whom I am anew bearing in pain.

See § 1 Cor 4:15 B.

4:23: The one who (is) from the free woman (is begotten) by virtue of the promise.

1. ἐκ τῆς ἐλευθέρας = from Sarah. — The passage adduced by Schöttgen, Tg. Job 3:19, does not belong here, since בר הורין should not be translated with "born free," but rather simply with "free." The whole passage reads: "Jacob, who is called young, and Abraham,

who is called old, is there and (likewise) Isaac, the servant of Yahweh, who went out free from the binding (on the altar in Gen 22) before his Lord."

2. By virtue of the promise; see § Rom 4:18–20.

4:24 A: This has an allegorical meaning.

ἅτινά ἐστιν ἀλληγορούμενα, which in rabbinic literature might be שנאמרו כמין משל or שנאמרו כמשל = which is said in the manner of a parable (see § 1 Cor 9:9).

4:24 B: From Mount Sinai.

Interpretation of the name Sinai.

TanḥumaB במדבר § 7 (4A): "Yahweh spoke to Moses in the wilderness of Sinai" (Num 1:1). It (Mount Sinai) was called by six names: mountain of God, mountain of Basan, mountain of summits, mountain of longing (these four names come from Ps 68:16f.), Mount Horeb, and Mount Sinai. — "Mountain of God," because God sat on it in judgment;[277] as it says, "These are the legal statutes that you are to lay before them" (Exod 21:1). — "Mountain of Basan" בָּשָׁן, that is, mountain where God came (ש)בא שם (a notarikon interpretation by changing ן to ם). — "Mountain of summits" הַר גַּבְנֻנִּים (literally: mountain of hunches or humps), that is, mountain where he declared all (other) mountains unsuitable (for the giving of the law). How do we know this? Because it says, "Or a hunchback or a sickly emaciated one (who were unsuitable for priestly service)" (Lev 21:20). — "Mountain of longing," for God longed to be enthroned on it; as it says, "Mountain which God desired for his seat" (Ps 68:17). — "Mount Horeb" חֹרֵב, for on it the sword חֶרֶב was drawn; as it says, "The adulterer and the adulteress shall be killed" (Lev 20:10), "the murderer shall be killed" (Num 35:16). — "Mount Sinai" סִינַי, for on it the nations of the world made themselves abhorrent נִשְׂתַּנְּאוּ to God, and he spoke their judgment; as it says, "And the nations shall be completely destroyed" (Isa 60:12) (because they rejected the Torah on Sinai). R. Abba b. Kahana (ca. 310) said in the name of R. Yohanan († 279), "The nations will be destroyed because of Horeb, because they received their judgment there (due to the rejection of the Torah)." — Parallels are found in Tanḥ. במדבר 187A; Num. Rab. 1 (135D), though here the text is partly corrupted; the saying of R. Yohanan is also found in y. Soṭah 7.21D.33 (see § Rom 1:20 E, n. *e*); Tanḥ. תציה 107A and Midr. Song. 4:4 (110A.11). ‖ Exodus Rabbah 2 (68C): "He came to the mountain of God, Horeb" (Exod 3:1). It has five names: mountain of God, mountain of Basan, mountain of summits, Mount Horeb, and Mount Sinai. ‖ Exodus Rabbah 51 (104A.5): This mountain (namely Horeb) is called by three names: mountain of God, Mount Horeb, and Mount Sinai. ‖ Babylonian Talmud Šabbat 89A: One of the rabbis said to Rab Kahana (II, ca. 375), "Have you heard (has it been made known to you) what Mount Sinai means?" He answered him, "Mountain on which miracles נִסִּים happened for the Israelites. Then it should be called 'Mount Nisse' הַר נִיסַּאי = 'Mountain of miracles'! Rather, (the name means:) Mountain that became a good sign (portent) סִימָן טוֹב for the Israelites. Then it should be called 'Mount

277. S-B: God will also hold the last judgment on Sinai (1 En. 1:3ff.).

Semana' הַר סִימָנָא = 'Mountain of the sign'!" He said to him, "Why have you not appeared before Rab Papa († 376) and Rab Huna b. Joshua (ca. 350), who have thought about the haggadah of Rab Hisda († 309) and of Rabba (Rabbah) b. Huna († 322)? For both said, 'What does "Mount Sinai" mean? Mountain on which hate שִׂנְאָה descended upon the nations of the world (because of their failure to accept the Torah).'" This is what R. Yose b. Hanina (ca. 270) said, "It (Sinai) has five names: Wilderness of Zin, because the Israelites נצטוו received commandments on it; wilderness of Kadesh, because the Israelites were sanctified נתקדשו on it; wilderness of Kedemoth (Deut 2:26), because on it that age-old thing (i.e., the Torah) was given; wilderness of Paran, because in it the Israelites increased פרו ורבו; wilderness of Sinai, because on it hate שִׂנְאָה descended upon the nations of the world (because of their failure to accept the Torah). And what is its (actual) name? Horeb is its name." This differs from the opinion of R. Abbahu (ca. 300). For R. Abbahu said, "'Mount Sinai' is its (actual) name. And why is it called Mount Horeb? Because on it devastation (destruction חוּרְבָּה) descended upon the nations of the world." ‖ While in the previous passages סִינַי is somehow connected with שִׂנְאָה "hate," the late Pirqe R. El. 24 (23B) tried to establish a connection with סְנֶה "thorn bush, bramble." The passage reads: R. Eleazar of Modiim († ca. 135) said, "Since the day when heaven and earth were created, the name of the mountain was 'Horeb,' but when God revealed himself to Moses in the thorn bush סְנֶה, because of the סְנֶה (because of the thorn bush) it was called Sinai סִינַי, which is Horeb."

4:24 C: Hagar.

Ἄγαρ = הָגָר means "beautiful." In the haggadah, the name was once connected with the Aramaic אַגְרָא "recompense."

Genesis Rabbah 45 (28B): R. Simeon b. Yohai (ca. 150) said, "Hagar was a daughter of pharaoh, and when pharaoh saw the (miraculous) actions that happened to Sarah in his house, he took his daughter and gave her to him (Abraham). He said, 'It is better that my daughter is a servant-girl in his house than a mistress in the house of someone else.' This is what is written, 'She had an Egyptian slave and her name was Hagar' (Gen 16:1), (i.e.,:) 'She is your recompense' הא אגריך! (or: behold, your recompense!)."

4:25: The present Jerusalem.

ἡ νῦν Ἰερουσαλήμ; in rabbinic literature: ירושלם של עולם הזה = "the Jerusalem of this world" or "of this age"; opposite: י׳ של עולם הבא = "the Jerusalem of the future world" or "of the future age." See, as an example, b. B. Bat. 75B at § Rom 1:6.

4:26 A: The Jerusalem above.

The ancient synagogue also knows of a Jerusalem above ירושלם של מַעְלָה, but not, as in Gal 4:26, as a congregation or community of people, but rather as a city that is built in heaven (cf. Heb 12:22; Rev 3:12; 21:2, 10).

2 Baruch 4:1ff.: "The Lord said to me (Baruch), 'This city (Jerusalem) will be given up for a time and the people will be temporarily chastised; but the world will not pass away.

Or do you think that this is the city about which I said, "I have engraved you on the palms of my hands" (Isa 49:16)? It is not this city whose buildings now stand before you that is the (future) one that is (already) revealed with me, which is prepared here (in heaven) beforehand, since the time when I had decided to create paradise. And I showed it to Adam, before he sinned; and when he had transgressed the commandment, it was taken away from him, just as paradise was. And then I showed it to my servant, Abraham, in the night between the halves of the sacrifices (Gen 15). And further, I showed it also to Moses on Mount Sinai, when I showed him the likeness of the tent and all its implements. And so it is already now kept with me, just as paradise is.'" ‖ See 4 Ezra 8:52 at § Eph 2:10 B. ‖ Babylonian Talmud Taʿanit 5A: Rab Nahman (b. Jacob, † 320) said to R. Isaac (ca. 300), "What does 'In your midst a holy one, and I will not come into the city' (so Hos 11:9 according to the midr.) mean? Since I am a holy one in your midst, I will not come into your city?" He answered him, "This is what R. Yohanan († 279) said, 'God said, "I will not enter the Jerusalem above י׳ של מעלה until I enter the lower Jerusalem י׳ של מִטָּה (which is to be rebuilt)." Is there then a Jerusalem above לְמַעְלָה? Yes, for it is written, "Jerusalem, which is built like the city that is its companion (like it)" (i.e., like the Jerusalem above, so Ps 122:3 according to the midr.).'" — The saying of R. Yohanan is also found in Midr. Ps. 122 § 4 (254B). ‖ Tanḥuma פקודי 125B: You find that a Jerusalem is erected above למעלה like the Jerusalem below י׳ של מטה. Out of great love for the lower one he made another one above; as it says, "Behold, I have engraved you on my hands, your walls are always before me" (cf. above 2 Bar. 4:1ff.).... Likewise, David said, "Jerusalem, which is built like the city that is its companion (like it)" (Ps 122:3). This means the following: like the city that Yahweh built (in heaven). The targum (on Ps 122:3) reads: Jerusalem, "which is built in heaven is like a city in order to join the one on earth (as a companion)." And (God) swore that his Shekinah would not enter the upper one until the one below was built (again). How beloved are the Israelites before God! ‖ See b. Ḥag. 12B at § 2 Cor 12:2 C, n. *c*. — On the Jerusalem that descends from heaven, see § Rev 3:12 C.

4:26 B: Which is our mother.

This trope is already found in Isa 50:1; Jer 50:12; Hos 4:5. In rabbinic literature, the following are designated as "mother": a. the community or the people of Israel; b. the land of Israel; c. Jerusalem (Zion); d. the Torah.

a. See b. Ber. 35A, partly = b. Sanh. 102A, at § Matt 14:19 B, #1, n. *a*. ‖ Jerusalem Talmud Berakot 9.14C.23: "Do not despise your mother when she has grown old" (Prov 23:22).... R. Zeira (ca. 300) said, "If your people has grown old, come and fence it about, as Elkanah did, who accustomed the Israelites to the festival pilgrimages (see 1 Sam 1:3)." — There is a parallel in Midr. Sam. 1 § 1 (21B).

b. Jerusalem Talmud Moʿed Qaṭan 3.81C.40: R. Hanina (ca. 225) said to a priest, "The brother of this man (= your brother) left the womb of his mother (= the land of Israel) and hugged the womb (breast) of a foreign woman (joined himself to a foreign land), and may he (God) be blessed that he struck him with plagues! And you want to do the same?"

c. 2 Baruch 3:1ff.: "Then I (Baruch) said, 'O Lord, my God! Have I come into the world to see the perdition of my mother (the destruction of Jerusalem)? No, no, Lord! If I have found mercy in your eyes, take my spirit (from me) beforehand, so that I may go to my fathers and not have to look at the destruction of my mother. For two things press me greatly: namely, that I not face you, but that my soul cannot see the perdition of my mother.'" ‖ 4 Ezra 10:6f.: "(Ezra says to a mother mourning her son,) 'You who are more foolish than all women, do you not see our mourning and misfortune? Is Zion, the mother of us all, herself in deep mourning, in heavy suffering, in bitter lamentation (about her destruction)!'" – In the passage Pesiq. Rab. 26 (132B), which in a certain sense offers a parallel to 4 Ezra 10, the corresponding passage reads: "I (the prophet Jeremiah) answered and said to her (the lamenting mother), 'You are not better than my mother Zion אמי ציון, and she has become a place of pasture for the animals of the field!' Then she answered and said to me, 'I am your mother Zion!'" ‖ Targum Song of Songs 8:5: "In that hour (at the time of the resurrection of the dead) Zion, who is Israel's mother דהיא אמן דישראל, will bear her children and Jerusalem will receive the exiles." – See also Bar 4 and 5.

d. See Deut. Rab. 2 (198B) and Midr. Ruth 1:2 (124B) at § Rom 2:21 A. ‖ Jerusalem Talmud Berakot 9.14C.23: "Do not despise your mother when she has grown old" (Prov 23:22). R. Yose b. Bun (ca. 350) said, "When the words of the Torah have grown old in your mouth (appear old to you), do not despise them! What is the scriptural basis? 'Do not despise your mother (= Torah) when she has grown old' (Prov 23:22)." – There is a parallel in Midr. Sam. 1 § 1 (21B). ‖ – See also m. Ber. 9.5 at § Matt 5:47, n. *c*, where Prov 23:22 is likewise interpreted in reference to the Torah, specifically to old morals and customs mentioned in it. ‖ Numbers Rabbah 10 (158C): "Words for king Lemuel, a saying with which his mother punished (admonished) him" (Prov 31:1); this refers to the Torah, which punished (admonished, read שמיסרתו instead of שמסרתו) Solomon, which is called the mother of those who study her; as it says, "If you call insight 'mother'" (so Prov 2:3 according to the midr..); אם is written (which should not be read as אִם = "if," but rather as אֵם = "mother"). – This interpretation of Prov 2:3 is also found in Tg. Prov. 2:3.

4:27: For it is written, "Rejoice, barren woman, who does not give birth; break forth and cry out, you who are not in labor; for the children of the lonely one are many more than of the one who has a husband."

Isaiah 54:1 in rabbinic literature.

Targum: "'Praise, Jerusalem, you who were like a barren woman who did not give birth, break out in song and rejoice, you who were like a woman who did not become pregnant; for the children of Jerusalem destroyed will be more numerous than the children of an inhabited city,' says Yahweh." ‖ Pesiqta 141A: "Rejoice, barren woman!" Isa 54:1. R. Reuben (ca. 300) said, "קרינא תעקר (on these incomprehensible words, see below and Midr. Song. 1:5)." R. Meir (ca. 150) said, "'Rejoice, barren woman עֲקָרָה!' (Say,) עֲקוּרָה 'Destroyed,' nation, that the nations of the world have destroyed (eradicated) שעקרוה. This is what is written, 'Remember, Yahweh, the children of Edom the day of Jerusalem who said, "Tear down, tear down, down to the ground with her!"' (Ps 137:7)." ‖ Babylonian Talmud Berakot 10A: A sectarian said to Beruriah (Beluriah = Veluria, the wife of R. Meir), "It is written,

'Rejoice, barren woman, who has not given birth!' Since you have not given birth, rejoice?!" She answered him, "You fool, look at the conclusion of the passage; for it is written, '"More numerous are the children of the lonely one than the children of the married one," says Yahweh.' But what does 'who has not given birth' mean? Rejoice, community of Israel, who is like a barren woman because she has not given birth to children for gehenna like you!" ‖ Midrash Song of Songs 1:5 (87B): R. Bebai (ca. 320) said in the name of R. Reuben (ca. 300), "'Rejoice, barren woman!' (Isa 54:1). Look, is barrenness a thing to rejoice about?[278] Rather: Rejoice, barren woman, who has not born children for gehenna." ‖ Pesiqta 142A: "For more numerous are the children of the lonely one than the children of the married one" (Isa 54:1).... R. Levi (ca. 300) said, "During her construction, she made the godless arise for me like Ahaz, Manasseh, and Amon; during her destruction, she made righteous ones arise for me like Daniel and his company, Mordecai and his company, Ezra and his company." R. Aha (ca. 320) said in the name of R. Yohanan († 279), "She made more righteous ones arise during her destruction than there were righteous ones whom she made arise for me during her construction." — The same is found in Midr. Song. 4:4 (112A). ‖ Pesiqta 135A: R. Levi (ca. 300) said, "Everywhere it says, 'She did not have' אין לה, it will be hers (later). 'Sarah was barren. She did not have a child' (Gen 11:30); and it will be hers, 'Sarah suckles children' (Gen 21:7). 'Peninnah had children and Hannah did not have children' (1 Sam 1:2); and it will be hers, 'Yahweh visited Hannah and she (also) became pregnant and bore three sons and two daughters' (1 Sam 2:21). 'Zion does not have any who inquire about her' (Jer 30:17); and it will be hers, 'A redeemer comes for Zion' (Isa 59:20). And likewise, 'Rejoice, barren woman, who has not given birth!' (Isa 54:1); and she will have children, 'You will say in your heart, "Who has given birth to these for me?"' (Isa 49:21)." — Parallel passages are found in Gen. Rab. 38 (23C); Pesiq. Rab. 32 (148A); Midr. Lam. 1:2 (50B); 1:17 (59B). ‖ Pesiqta 141A.3: "He settles the barren woman of the house as a happy mother of children" (Ps 113:9). There are seven barren ones (in Scripture): Sarah, Rebekah, Rachel, Leah, the wife of Manoah, Hannah, and Zion.... "He settles the barren woman of the house": this is Zion: "Rejoice, barren woman, who has not given birth" (Isa 54:1); "as a happy mother of children": "You will say in your heart: who has given birth to these for me?" (Isa 49:21).

4:29: Just as then the one begotten according to the flesh persecuted the one according to the Spirit.

Jewish tradition also knows of a persecution (hostility) of Isaac by Ishmael; it was found indicated in מְצַחֵק in Gen 21:9.

Tosefta Soṭah 6.6 (304): R. Ishmael († ca. 135) said, "מצחק means nothing but shedding blood; as it says, 'May the boys arise and joust וישחקו before us ...' (2 Sam 2:14ff.). This teaches that Sarah had seen how Ishmael took arrows and shot them with the purpose of killing Isaac; as it says, 'Like a senseless man who hurls firebrands, arrows, and death' (Prov 26:18)." — In the parallel in Gen. Rab. 53 (34A), R. Eliezer b. Yose the Galilean (ca. 150) is the author. Here the following words are then attached: R. Azariah (ca. 380) said in the name

278. S-B: הא רנה עקרותא; according to this passage, the words designated as incomprehensible in Pesiq. 141A, קרינא תעקר, should be changed. The concluding sentence has fallen out completely there.

of R. Levi (ca. 300), "Ishmael said to Isaac, 'We will go and inspect our portions on the field.' And Ishmael took bows and arrows and shot in the direction of Isaac and acted as if he were joking מצחק. This is what is written, 'Like a senseless man who hurls firebrands, arrows, and death, so is a man who has deceived his neighbor and says, "In truth, I was (only) joking"' (Prov 26:18f.)." — In both passages, as well as in SDeut 6:4 § 31 (72A), there are still other interpretations of מצחק, especially in relation to fornication and idolatry; see t. Soṭah 6.6 at § 1 Cor 10:7, #2, n. *b*.

4:30f.: "The son of the slave-girl shall not inherit with the son of the free woman." So we, beloved brothers, are not children of the slave-girl, but rather of the free woman.

See the opposite verdict in ʾAbot 5.19 at § Matt 10:1 A, #2.

5:1 A: For freedom Christ has set us free.

Of course, for the ancient synagogue, the Messiah as a liberator from the law is never in view; as redeemer גּוֹאֵל he brings his people only political freedom. It says about this briefly in Tg. Lam. 2:22: "Proclaim freedom חֵירוּתָא for your people, the house of Israel, through the Messiah, as you did through Moses and Aaron on the day of Passover." — See further at § Matt 1:21 C and D; see also m. ʾAbot 6.2 at § John 8:32.

5:1 B: Do not let yourselves be held again by a yoke of servitude.

On the yoke of the Torah or the commandments, see § Matt 11:29 A, notes *b* and *c* and § Acts 15:10.

5:6: In Christ Jesus neither circumcision nor foreskin can do anything.

See § Acts 21:21.

5:14 A: The whole law is fulfilled in one word.

See § Matt 22:40.

5:14 B: "Love your neighbor as yourself" (see § Matt 5:43).

5:15: If you bite and devour one another, watch out that you not be consumed by one another.

Babylonian Talmud Šabbat 152B: "Passionateness is erosion in the bones" (Prov 14:30). If passionateness dwells in someone's heart, his bones rot; but if passionateness does not dwell in someone's heart, his bones do not rot.

5:16: Spirit ... flesh.

These contrary ideas overlap in many ways with the rabbinic terms "good and evil inclination"; see the excursus by the same name.

5:19–21: See a similar catalog of vices at § Rom 1:29ff.

5:21: Will not inherit the kingdom of God (see § 1 Cor 15:50).

5:22: But the fruit of the Spirit is love, joy, peace, patience ….

On καρπός = פְּרִי see § Matt 7:16 A. – On the list of virtues, see m. ʾAbot 6.5f. further below at § Gal 6:2 A.

5:24: Have crucified the flesh.

See b. Tamid 66A and b. Ber. 63B at § Matt 10:39.

5:26: Let us not seek after idle praise.

See warnings against seeking praise and honor at § Matt 23:8 A and § John 12:43.

6:1: Restore such a person.

On correcting a person, see § Matt 18:15ff.

6:2 A: Bear one another's burdens.

In m. ʾAbot 6.5f., 48 requirements are listed that are to be made of those assiduous in the Torah, among which is also that he helps the other bear his yoke. – Since these requirements contain a whole series of virtues that were especially desirable in scholars of Scripture, the whole passage may be rendered here unabbreviated in view of the list of virtues in Gal 5:22: Greater is the Torah than the dignity of priests and the dignity of kings. For the dignity of kings is acquired by 30 merits, that of priests by 24, but the Torah by 48, namely: [1]study, [2]hearing of the ear, [3]preparation of the lips, [4]insight of heart, [5]understanding of heart, [6]dread and fear, [7]humility עֲנָוָה, [8]joy שִׂמְחָה,[279] [9]subservient dealings with the scholars (see § Matt 10:1 A, #1; § Matt 23:11), [10]sticking together with companions, [11]discussions with students, [12]understanding thought, [13]Bible, [14]Mishnah, [15]little business, [16]little sleep, [17]little pleasure, [18]little merriment, [19]little worldly occupation, [20]long-suffering אֶרֶךְ אַפַּיִם, [21]a good heart, [22]believing the scholars, [23]bearing sufferings. [24]Whoever knows his place, [25]whoever is happy with his portion, [26]whoever makes a fence for his words, [27]whoever does not praise himself, [28]whoever is beloved, [29]whoever loves God, [30]whoever loves people, [31]whoever loves alms, [32]whoever loves correction, [33]whoever loves uprightness, [34]whoever keeps himself from (greed for) honor, [35]whoever does not exalt himself because of his learning, [36]whoever does not rejoice at (his own) decisions in the law, [37]whoever bears a yoke with his neighbor נוֹשֵׂא בְעוֹל עִם חֲבֵרוֹ, [38]whoever judges him according to the good side, [39]whoever brings him to the truth (so that he may be established on it), [40]whoever helps him to peace, [41]whoever thinks over his learning, [42]whoever asks and answers (in the house of learning), [43]whoever hears and studies, [44]whoever studies in order to teach, [45]whoever studies in order to do, [46]whoever makes his teacher wise, [47]whoever observes exactly what is heard, [48]whoever

279. S-B: The holy spirit rests only on those of joyful heart; see y. Sukkah 5.55A.42 in the excursus "The Feast of Tabernacles," IV, n. *p*.

says a word in the name of an author. ‖ In Gen. Rab. 1 (2B), it said about the great of the land that with the king they bear his burden שנושאין עמו במשאו; see the passage at § Matt 16:17 B.

6:2 B: So you will fulfill the law of Christ.

A Torah of the Messiah was also spoken of in rabbinic circles; yet this was not understood to be a Torah that would supersede the Torah of Moses and set itself up in its place, but rather a new interpretation of the old Torah that the Messiah would bring and teach in the power of God so that his Torah would in a certain way appear as a new Torah. However, we have encountered the term תורתו של משיח = ὁ νόμος τοῦ Χριστοῦ only once.[a] See in more detail in the excursus "Preliminary Remarks on the Sermon on the Mount."

a. Midrash Ecclesiastes 11:8 (52A): The Torah that a person studies in this world is nothing in comparison to the Torah of the Messiah.

6:3: For if someone thinks that he is something, though he is nothing, he deceives himself.

Midrash Ecclesiastes 9:10 (42B): (R. Hiyya appeared to Resh Laqish [ca. 250] in a dream and said to him,) "Whoever is nothing but acts as if he were something, it would be better for him if he had not been created מאן הוא דכלום ודבר בגרמיה כלום נוח ליה אם לא נברא."

6:6: Let the one who is instructed in the word share all (possible) goods with the one instructing.

See Lev. Rab. 30 (127D) at § 2 Cor 9:6 A.

6:7: Whatever a person sows, this he will also reap.

See 4 Ezra 9:17: "As the ground, so the seed, as the flowers, so the color; as the effort, so the work, as the farmer, so the harvest."

6:8 A: Whoever sows to his flesh ...; whoever sows to the Spirit.

The same image is found in 4 Ezra 9:31: "Today I sow my law in your heart, which will bring forth fruit in you, and you shall thereby obtain eternal glory."

6:8 B: Will reap destruction from the flesh ..., will reap eternal life from the Spirit.

On the salutary workings of the good inclination and on the bad consequences of the evil inclination, see the corresponding section in the excursus "The Good and the Evil Inclination."

6:10 A: Since we have a period of time (fitting for this), let us do good.

Leviticus Rabbah 34 (131A): "A caring man does good to his own soul" (Prov 11:17); this refers to Hillel the elder (20 BCE). When he would say goodbye to his disciples (whom he escorted), he would always go further with them. His disciples said to him, "Rabbi, where are you going?" He answered them, "To show love to a guest in the house." They said to him, "Do you have a guest every day, then?" He said to them, "This pour soul—is it not a guest in the body? Today it is here, tomorrow it is not here!"

6:10 B: Especially to the companions of faith.

Mekilta Exodus 22:24 (102A): "If you lend money to my people who is poor alongside you" (Exod 22:24). "My people": if an Israelite and a *goy* (non-Israelite) stand before you to borrow something, my people takes priority; if a poor man and a rich man, the poor man takes priority; if your poor (those who are related to you) and the poor of your city, your poor take priority over the poor of your city; if the poor of your city and the poor of another city, the poor of your city take priority; for it says, "to the poor alongside you" (to the one who is nearest you). – Parallels are found in Tanḥ. משפטים 97B; TanḥB משפטים § 8 (43A); b. B. Meṣ. 71A, here as a tannaitic tradition taught by Rab Joseph († 333).

6:15: A new creation (see § 2 Cor 5:17 and § John 3:3, #2).

6:16: On whom (may) peace and mercy (come) and upon the Israel of God.

In prayer requests for individuals, it is common for all of Israel to be in mind.

The Prayer of Eighteen Benedictions 19: "Bestow peace ... and mercy on us and on your (whole) people Israel!" ‖ Kaddish de-Rabbanan at the end: "May there be great peace from heaven ... and mercy upon you and upon us and upon all communities of the house of Israel for life and for peace! and answer, Amen!" – The same concluding words are found also in the kaddish of the religious service. ‖ Babylonian Talmud Šabbat 12B: R. Judah (ca. 150) said (as a prayer when visiting the sick), "May God have mercy on you and on the sick of Israel!" R. Yose (ca. 150) said, "May God have mercy on you among the sick of Israel." ‖ In the meal prayer בִּרְכַּת הַמָּזוֹן it says, "May the one who created peace in his heights create peace upon you and upon all Israel! and answer: Amen!"

6:17: I bear the marks of Jesus on my body.

στίγμα "mark, identifier," perhaps = רוֹשֵׁם, רוּשְׁמָא, רִשּׁוּם. – A mark was imprinted by, for example, a master on his slave to identify them as his property.

Tosefta Makkot 4.15 (443): Whoever imprints a mark הָרוֹשֵׁם on his slave so he may not escape is exempt from punishment (in respect to the prohibition against tattoos in Lev 19:28). ‖ Reference may also be made to the stigmatization of Egyptian Jews with the ivy leaf in 3 Macc 2:29: "Those registered should be marked χαράσσεσθαι, specifically by fire on their body with an ivy leaf as a sign of Bacchus παρασήμῳ Διονύσου κισσοφύλλῳ."

6:18: Brothers.

On this form of address, see § Acts 23:1.

The Letter of Paul to the Ephesians

1:1 A: To the saints (see § Acts 9:13).

1:1 B: In Ephesus.

Εφεσος = אֶפְסוֹס or אוֹבֵיסוֹס.

Jerusalem Talmud Megillah 1.71B.47: "The sons of Japheth: Gomer and Magog and Madai and Javan and Tubal and Meshech and Tiras" (Gen 10:2). Gomer is Germania, Magog is Getia (Transylvania), Media is like his name (thus Media), Javan is Ephesus אווסוס (proconsular Asia Minor), Tubal is Bithynia (in Asia Minor), Meshech is Moesia, Tiras: R. Simon (ca. 280) said, "Persia," but the rabbis said, "Thrace." ‖ In the parallel in Tg. 1 Chr. 1:5, we read אוביסוס.

1:4: As he chose us in him (Christ) before the foundation of the world.

1. ἐκλέγεσθαι = בָּחַר, בָּרַר, see § Rom 11:28; on ἐκλεκτοί § Col 3:12 B, #1.

2. ἐκλέγεσθαι ἐν = בָּחַר בְּ. — Genesis Rabbah 44 (27A): "You I have chosen and not rejected" (Isa 41:9): I have chosen you in Abraham בחרתיך באברהם, and I have not rejected you in Abraham ולא מאסתיך באברהם.

3. πρὸ καταβολῆς κόσμου. — It is similarly said of Israel that God created it, that is, decided to create it before the world had been created; see the citations at § Matt 25:31 B, #1 and § John 1:1 A, B, n. *a*. — In Gen. Rab. 1 (2B), Ps 74:2 serves as the proof text for the ideal preexistence of Israel: "Remember your community that you created (so קנית in Ps 74:2 is understood by the midrash) in prehistoric times (absolutely = before the creation of the world)." — In the same text, R. Huna (ca. 350) and R. Jeremiah (ca. 320) say in the name of R. Samuel b. Isaac (ca. 300), "The thought (idea) of Israel preceded everything else. Like a king who was married to a matron but he had no son from her. Once it happened that the king was going across a street. He said, 'Take this ink and this pen for my son!' Then everyone said, 'You do not have a son and (yet) he says, "Take this ink and this pen for my son!"' They said again, 'The king is a great astrologer; if the king had not seen that he would have a son rise from her, he would not have said, "Take this ink and this pen for my son."' Likewise, if God had not seen that after 26 generations the Israelites would accept the Torah, he would not have written in the Torah (that was preexistent), 'Command the children of Israel,' 'Say to the children of Israel.'"

1:5: Predestining us.

On the verbs of determination, see § Matt 25:34 B and § Rom 9:22f.

1:9 A: The secret of his will.

μυστήριον, see § Matt 13:11 and § Rom 16:25.

1:9 B: According to his pleasure (will).

1 Enoch 49:4: "He (the Messiah) will judge the hidden things, and no one will be able to speak vacuously before him; for he has been chosen before the Lord of Spirits according to his pleasure." — On the divine εὐδοκία see also § Luke 2:14 C.

1:10: Fullness of the times.

Just as מְלוֹא הָעוֹלָם "fullness of the world" encompasses all creatures that fill the world,[a] so too τὸ πλήρωμα τῶν καιρῶν (sg.: τὸ πλήρωμα τοῦ χρόνου, Gal 4:4) "fullness of the times" denotes the moment that completes a certain time; as long as this moment has not arrived, the time in question is not yet complete or full. In substance, "fullness of time" of course always denotes the end of a fixed period of time; See the citations at § Gal 4:4 A.

a. Genesis Rabbah 1 (2C.7): R. Bannaiah (ca. 220) said, "The world and its fullness מְלוֹאוֹ was created only because of the Torah; for it says, 'Yahweh established the earth because of wisdom (= Torah)' (so Prov 3:19 according to the midr.).

1:12: We who have hoped beforehand in the Christ (Messiah).

Hoping in the Messiah was a prominent feature in the piety of broad circles of the Jewish people, see Luke 2:25, 38.

2 Baruch 30:1: "And then, when the time of the arrival of the Messiah is complete (i.e., after the course of the messianic period), he (the Messiah) will return in glory (to heaven). Then all who fell asleep in hope in him will arise." ‖ Targum 2 Samuel 23:4: "God will do good to you (the righteous) (in the days of the Messiah), because you have longed for the years of comfort (= for the messianic age) that are to come." ‖ Targum Jeremiah 31:6: "There is lengthening of life and much good that will come to the righteous who have longed for the years or comfort that will come, who have said, 'When will we arise and go up to Zion, to appear before Yahweh our God?'" ‖ Midrash Ecclesiastes 3:9 (17B): In the future the godless will be judged (punished) in gehenna; then they will grumble against God: Look, we had waited for the (messianic) salvation of God, and now this comes upon us?! (See the whole passage at § Matt 22:2–14, near end.) ‖ Pesiqta Rabbati 34 (159A): "An oath is before me" (God says), "that I myself will testify for the good for each one who waits for my kingdom (which will appear with the Messiah); as it says, 'Therefore, wait for me, for the day when I will arise as a witness'" (so Zeph 3:8 with the LXX and targum). ‖ Babylonian Talmud Šabbat 31A at § Matt 5:13 A, #4.

1:13 A: The gospel (see § Rom 1:1 D).

1:13 B: You were sealed (see § 2 Cor 1:22 A).

1:14: A down payment (see § 2 Cor 1:22 B).

1:15: Faith in the Lord Jesus.

πίστις = אֱמוּנָה in, for example, Midr. Esth. 3:9 (96B). (Here it is said against the Jews in a bill of indictment:) Although they are in exile, they mock us (non-Jews) and the faith in our gods ואת אמונת אלהינו.

1:18: That he illumine the eyes of your heart.

See the saying of Bar Qappara (ca. 220) about the soul as the light of the human being in Deut. Rab. 4 (201D) at § Rom 3:1f, D, second third.

1:20: At his right hand.

See § Matt 25:33 and § Matt 26:64.

1:21: Above every authority and power and force and dominion.

1. As some passages in the pseudepigrapha show, ἀρχή, ἐξουσία, δύναμις, and κυριότης are names for specific classes of angels,[a] which are derived from their action or task. That what is being spoken about is in fact classes of angels whose members are conceived of as personal beings follows from the fact that, for example, in place of "authority" and "dominion" one can also say "all the angels of authority, all the angels of dominion."[b] Nevertheless, it is still notable that one passage even speaks of "incorporeal powers" and "principalities" (probably = ἀρχαί).[c] — Among the New Testamenst parallels to Eph 1:21, one may mention Eph 3:10 (ἀρχαί and ἐξουσίαι), Rom 8:38 (ἄγγελοι, ἀρχαί, and δυνάμεις), Col 1:16 (θρόνοι, κυριότητες, ἀρχαί, and ἐξουσίαι), 1 Pet 3:22 (ἄγγελοι, ἐξουσίαι, and δυνάμεις). If we disregard the general ἄγγελοι, the NT knows of five relevant classes of angels here: apart from the four in Eph 1:21, there are also the θρόνοι in Col 1:16. — The pseudepigrapha raise the number to ten by naming the following in addition to the five classes of angels already mentioned in the NT: the great archangels, the cherubim, the seraphim, the many-eyed (nine legions), and the ophanim (or angels of the wheel).[d] — Rabbinic Judaism, which concerned itself far less with angelology than the pseudepigraphic literature, most of the time distinguishes between only two classes of angels: the angels of service and the angels of destruction; both classes are essentially identical with the angels of peace and the angels of Satan; see § 1 Cor 10:10 and § Matt 25:41 B. A different division names four classes of angels alongside one another: the ophanim (angels of the wheel), the seraphim, the holy beings (*hayyoth*), and the angels of service.[e] The angels of the throne appear as an additional, special class which are sometimes enumerated as four, and at other times as seven; on the latter, see § Rev 8:2.

a. Testament of Levi 3: "The second (of the seven heavens) has fire, snow, ice, prepared for the day when the Lord ordains, in the great judgment of God. In it all the spirits πνεύματα of those who serve for judgment over the godless (i.e., the spirits of plague or the angels of destruction). In the third there are the powers of the hosts αἱ δυνάμεις τῶν παρεμβολῶν, which are ordained for the day of judgment to exact revenge on the spirits of error and of Beliar (= Satan. These δυνάμεις are, as shown by the addition of τῶν παρεμβολῶν and their dwelling in the 3rd heaven, not = the δυνάμεις in Eph 1:21). Yet those in the 4th above this one (the 3rd) are holy ἅγιοι; for in the one that is above all (7), there dwells the great glory in the Most Holy Place, high above every holiness. In the following (so the 5th heaven) are the angels of the face of the Lord οἱ ἄγγελοι τοῦ προσώπου κυρίου, who serve there and plead with the Lord for all mistakes of the righteous. Yet they bring to the Lord a wise pleasing odor ὀσμὴν εὐωδίας λογικήν and a bloodless offering. In the one above that (so read instead of: 'the one under that,' thus in the 6th heaven) are the angels who bring to the angels of the face of the Lord (in the 5th heaven) the answers (to their pleas for the righteous). In the one following that (the 7th heaven) there are thrones, powers, in which praise songs are ceaselessly offered to God θρόνοι (καὶ) ἐξουσίαι, ἐν ᾧ ἀεὶ ὕμνοι τῷ θεῷ προσφέρονται." ‖ 1 Enoch 41:9: "Neither an angel nor a power can hinder it, because he will determine a judge (namely the Messiah) for them all, and he will judge them all before him."

b. 1 Enoch 61:10: "He will summon the whole host of heaven, all saints in the heights, the host of God, the cherubim, seraphim, and ophanim, all angels of authority, all angels of dominion, the elect one (= Messiah), and the other powers that are on dry land (and) over the water (the elementary spirits who preside over visible nature)."

c. 2 Enoch 20f.: "Those men (= angels) raised me (Enoch) from there (the 6th heaven) into the 7th heaven. And I myself saw a very great light and fiery hosts of great archangels, incorporeal powers and dominions, principalities and powers, cherubim and seraphim, thrones and many-eyed ones, nine legions, the luminous stands of the ophanim.[280] And I was afraid and quaked with great fear. And those men seized me and led me after them and said to me, 'Be courageous (comforted), O Enoch, do not fear!' And they showed the Lord from afar, sitting on a very high throne. [Since the Lord dwells here, what is in the 10th heaven? In the 10th heaven is God, which is called Arabat (= עֲרָבוֹת Ps 68:5) in the Hebrew language.] And all the heavenly hosted came, stood on ten levels according to the order (rank) and prayed to the Lord; and they came again to their places in joy and gladness and in immeasurable light singing songs with small ('tender') and gentle voices; but the glorious ones who serve him do not go away, standing before the face of the Lord, doing his will, the cherubim and seraphim standing around his throne, the six-winged and many-eyed, and they cover his whole throne, singing with a soft voice before the face of the Lord, 'Holy, holy, holy is the Lord, the Lord Sabaoth; heaven and earth are full of your glory.'"

d. See 1 En. 61:10 and 2 En. 20f. in notes *b* and *c*.

e. Babylonian Talmud Ḥagigah 12B: There (in the 7th heaven, which is called Araboth) are the ophanim (angels of the wheel, see Ezek 1:15ff.) and the seraphim and the holy beings

280. S-B: Recension B: "I myself saw a great light and all the fiery hosts of the incorporeal archangels and the luminous stand of the ophanim." — "Incorporeal archangels," if the text is right, is completely singular.

חַיּוֹת (see Ezek 1:5ff.) and the angels of service. ‖ Babylonian Talmud Roš Haššanah 24B: "You shall not make me" (= depict me; this is how Exod 20:23 is interpreted, by reading אִתִּי as אוֹתִי); you shall not make me according to the likeness of my servants, who serve before me on high, such as the ophanim and seraphim and the holy *chayyoth* and the angels of service. — The חֵילֵי שְׁמַיָּא (e.g., 1 Kgs 22:19; Ps 96:11) = "powers of heaven" mentioned in the targumim are synonymous with "hosts of heaven," and can thus in certain circumstances also mean the stars; see Isa 34:4; Tg. Ps. 148:1, where they are called חֵילֵי אֲנְגְלֵי = powers or hosts of angels. See § Matt 24:29 B.

2. It is explicitly said about the ranks among the angels in 2 Enoch Intro.: "The Lord took him (Enoch) up (into heaven), so that he might see ... the luminous and many-eyed stand of the servants of the Lord and the unreachable throne of the Lord and the ranks and the rallies of the incorporeal hosts." — 2 Enoch 20 (see above n. *c*) more precisely distinguishes 10 ranks that are probably supposed to correspond to the 10 classes of angels, mentioned in the same work, that stand in the 10th heaven before God. Testament of Levi 3 (see above #1, n. *a*) also presupposes rankings in the angel world; here, the rank of the individual classes of angels depends on the heaven that is assigned as their dwelling place: the higher heaven, the higher the rank of its inhabitants. The 2nd heaven is where the angels of destruction dwell, the spirits of plagues who execute judgment on godless humans; they occupy the lowest level. Then come one level higher in the 3rd heaven the powers of the hosts that shall take revenge on the evil spirits on the day of judgment. Only in the 4th heaven do the dwellings of the holy angels begin. With the adjective "holy" these angels are contrasted with the angels of punishment in the 2nd and 3rd heaven; because of their task or business with evil people and spirits, the latter are more or less themselves considered as evil (see § 1 Cor 10:10, #5, n. *k*). The angels of the face, who are appointed to serve the righteous, occupy the 5th and 6th heaven. The inhabitants of the 6th heaven are in rank one level higher than those of the 5th heaven, insofar as they have to mediate the communication of the latter with God. At the highest level are the angels of the 7th heaven. In their number we also find the "thrones" and "powers" or "authorities," as in the Testaments of the 12 Patriarchs and 2 Enoch 20 (above n. *c*). We have to assume that the ἀρχαί, ἐξουσίαι, δυνάμεις, κυριότητες, and θρόνοι of the NT are also dealing with the highest classes of angels. — In ancient rabbinic literature, we do not hear anything explicitly about ranks within the angelic world. However, we can tell from occasional remarks that this idea was not entirely unknown to the rabbinic scholars. So the archangels are called "kings of the angels" or "princes of those above."[a] This implies that they knew about angels who were subordinate to them in rank. The particular emphasis about the 4 or 7 angels of the face who stand before God belongs here as well (see § Rev 8:2). Only in posttalmudic period is

there once again talk of 10 different ranks for the classes of angels, which thereby links up with the tradition that we have already become familiar with above in 2 Enoch 20; see on this Weber (2nd ed., p. 168).

a. See Pesiq. 45A at § Rom 1:18 A, n. *b*; see Gen. Rab. 78 (49D) at § Luke 1:19 A, #3, n. *a*.

2:1: Dead because of your transgressions and sins.

Just as νεκρός here denotes the one dead spiritually, so too can מֵת be used in this sense. See two passages at § Matt 8:22.

2:2 A: According to (subject to) the ruler of the power (ruler) of the air.

The words denote the devil as the prince of the demonic powers that dwell in the air; see T. Benj. 3 at § Eph 2:2 B. — On Satan as the prince of demons and owner of a kingdom, see § Matt 12:24, #3 and § Matt 25:41 B. — On the air as the dominion of demons, see the excursus “Ancient Jewish Demonology,” #4.

2:2 B: (According to the ruler) of the spirit that is now at work.

The pseudepigrapha speak similarly of the spirit of Beliar: the spirit that is Beliar's spirit proceeds from Beliar into people to corrupt them. Here, Beliar is used everywhere as a name of Satan.

Jubilees 1:20: “May your mercy, O Lord, be high over your people, ... and may the spirit of Belhor (= Beliar) not rule them to accuse them before you and to lure them away from all the ways of righteousness, lest they perish far from your face.” ‖ Testament of Joseph 7: “I (Joseph) noticed that the spirit of Beliar τὸ πνεῦμα τοῦ Βελίαρ agitated her (Potiphar's wife).” ‖ Testament of Benjamin 3: “Whoever fears God and loves his neighbor cannot be struck by the spirit of Beliar, which dwells in the air ὑπὸ τοῦ ἀερίου πνεύματος τοῦ Βελίαρ, since he is shielded by the fear of God.” — Testament of Benjamin 6: “The counsel of a good man is not in the hand of the spirit of the seduction of Beliar.”

2:2 C: In the sons of disobedience.

For similar expressions formed with בֵּן or בַּר, see § Matt 8:12 A.

2:3: We were children of wrath by nature.

1. τέκνα ὀργῆς. — Apocalypse of Moses 3: “God says to the archangel Michael, ‘Tell Adam, “The secret that you know (which one?), do not tell to your son Cain; for he is a son of wrath”’” (cf. Gen 4:11).

2. φύσει. — Wisdom 13:1: “Foolish (futile) were all men by nature φύσει, for whom ignorance of God was inherent and who were not able to recognize from visible goods the One Who Is.” See also 4 Maccabees 5:24; 15:10; 16:3 (verse numbering according to Fritzsche).

2:4: God, though, who is rich in mercy.

πλούσιος ἐν ἐλέει, see Exod 34:6: רַב חֶסֶד "great in grace," LXX: πολυέλεος. — Targum Onkelos: "Who richly shows benevolence." — Yerušalmi I: "Who richly shows grace." — For an application of Exod 34:6 by the school of Hillel, see b. Roš Haš. 16B at § Matt 1:19, #1, n. *a*.

2:6: And gave us a seat with him in the heavenly places in Christ Jesus.

Philo says of the proselyte that, as a fitting recompense for his connection to God, he receives a secure place in heaven τὴν ἐν οὐρανῷ τάξιν βεβαίαν; see *Exsecr.* § 6 at § Rom 11:17, #2, n. *b.* ‖ See 4 Maccabees 17:5, where the mother of the seven martyr brothers is praised with the words: "The moon does not stand in heaven with the stars as nobly as you—you who led your seven boys star-like in light to piety—you stand there honored by God and together with them in heaven you have a firm dwelling" (so Deißmann renders the words: καὶ ἐστήρισαι ἐν οὐρανῷ σὺν αὐτοῖς).

2:8: It is the gift of God.

θεοῦ τὸ δῶρον. — Mekilta Exodus 16:25 (58B): Then Moses said, "Eat it today היום" (Exod 16:25).... R. Eleazar of Modiim († ca. 135) said, "If you (the wilderness generation) manage to observe the Sabbath (this day היום), God will one day give you six good gifts שש מִדּוֹת טובות: the land of Israel and the future world (the heavenly world of souls) and the new world (after the days of the Messiah) and the kingship of the house of David and the priesthood and the Levitehood. Therefore, it says, 'Eat it today'...." See a parallel in Mek. Exod. 18:9 (66B). ‖ See SDeut 6:5 § 32 (73B) at § Luke 24:26, I, #2. ‖ Tanḥuma מטות 244B: Let our teacher teach us: How many gifts מתנות (goods to be bestowed as a gift by God) have been created in the world? Our teachers taught us: God has created three gifts מתנות in the world: wisdom and power (strength) and prosperity. If a man obtains one of them, he has received the treasure of the whole world.... When? If they are God's gifts מתנות שמים.... Yet the power (strength) and prosperity of man (that originates from himself) are nothing....

2:10 A: Created for good works.

1. ἔργα ἀγαθά = מַעֲשִׂים טוֹבִים, α. generally: "beautiful, righteous works,"[a] so too Eph 2:10; β. specifically: works of mercy (the so-called "good" works).[b]

a. See examples at § Rom 3:20 A, #1.

b. See examples in the excursus "Ancient Jewish Private Charity."

2. κτισθέντες. — Mishnah ʾAbot 2.8: R. Yohanan b. Zakkai († ca. 80) used to say, "If you have done much Torah (i.e., you have done many righteous works in accordance with the Torah), do not be proud about it; for you were created for this כִּי לְכָךְ נוֹצַרְתָּ."

2:10 B: That God prepared beforehand.

4 Ezra 8:52 also says of good works that they were created for the righteous: "Since for you (the righteous) Paradise has been opened, the tree of life has been planted; the future

age is prepared, the blessedness determined beforehand; the city (the heavenly Jerusalem) built, the homeland chosen, good works created, wisdom prepared" (see Gunkel on this passage).

2:11: Foreskin … circumcision (see § Acts 10:45, #2).

2:12: Not having hope.

More or less the same is meant by those rabbinic sayings which claim that the nations of the world are destined for gehenna; see, for example, t. Sanh. 13.2 (434); Pesiq. Rab. 10 (36B); TanḥB שמיני § 10 (14B) at § Matt 5:43, #1, n. *g*; b. Ber. 10A and Midr. Song. 1:5 (87B) at § Gal 4:27.

2:13: You who were once far off were brought near in the blood of Christ.

μακράν … ἐγγύς. — "Far ones" רְחוֹקִים (sing. רָחוֹק) and "near ones" קְרוֹבִים (sing. קָרוֹב) is a frequent designation for "non-Israelites" and "Israelites." It is supposed to express the relationship in which the latter and the former stand to God.[a] Conversely, though, even God can be called the "near one" or "ally" קָרוֹב of Israel.[b] According to the designation above, the verb קֵרֵב signifies bringing a non-Israelite near to God, that is, accepting him as a proselyte, and רִחַק keeping a non-Israelite's distant = not accepting him as a proselyte.[c] However, the designation "near ones" and "far ones" did not remain completely limited to Israelites and non-Israelites. One also spoke of "near ones" and "far ones" even within Israel. In this case, the "near ones" were mostly the righteous who always held out for God, and the "far ones" were the godless who fell away from God in their sins. There are other interpretations, though.[d]

a. In Midr. Esth. 3:9 (96A), the wise men of the nations of the world who assembled before Ahasuerus explain Haman's plan of destruction as follows: "If you destroy the Israelites from the world, the world exists only for the sake of the Torah, which was given to the Israelites.… And not only this but also all the nations are called 'strangers' נָכְרִים before God, but the Israelites are called 'near ones' (or 'related ones') קרובים; this is what is written, 'And even the stranger who does not belong to your people Israel' (1 Kgs 8:41). Yet the Israelites are called 'near ones' קרובים; as it says, 'For the children of Israel, the people that is near to him עם קרובו' (Ps 148:14).… And God is called one who is 'near' to Israel; as it is written, 'Yahweh is near קרוב to all who call on him, to all you who call on him in truth' (Ps 145:18). And no nation is near to קְרוֹבָה to God except for Israel; as it says, 'For which great nation that has a God so near to it as Yahweh our God whenever we call to him?'(Deut 4:7). And if a person lays his hand on those who are near to God, how will he escape, since he rules over those above and below and the soul of every living thing is in his hand to exalt and to humble, to kill and to make alive!" ‖ Numbers Rabbah 8 (149A): God said to David, "If you keep away תרחק those who are far הרחוקים (this refers to the Gibeonites), you will also ultimately remove לרחק those who are near חקרובים." — A few lines later, the same is described as a word of God to Joshua. ‖ Numbers Rabbah 8 (149D): Why all this (that which is recounted in 2 Sam 21 about the Gibeonites)? To make known that God draws near מקרב those who are far הרחוקים and rejoices over those who are far as those who are near כקרובים; and not only this but also he offers the greeting of peace to those who are far before he does to those who are near; as it says, "Peace, peace to those far and near!" (Isa 57:19). — The same is found in Midr. Sam. 28 § 6 (67B). ‖ Numbers Rabbah 8 (149D): If God brings near קירב those who are far הרחוקים, even when they do not become proselytes for God's sake, it does not even have to be said concerning the proselytes of righteousness (full and complete proselytes). ‖ Numbers Rabbah 8 (149A): Who is a God like this who loves those who love him and draws near those who are far as those who are near מקרב רחוקים כקרובים, who come for his sake. ‖ See further y. Ber. 9.13B.35 and Lev. Rab. 14 (115A.15 and 21).

b. Midrash Psalm 118 § 10 (242B): The Israelites (when they stand before God in judgment) will be afraid of the judgment. Then the angels of service will say to them, "Do not fear the judgment.... Do you not know him (the judge)? He is one near to you קרובכם (= your ally); as it says, 'For the children of Israel, the people that he is near to'" (whose ally he is; this is how Ps 148:14 is now interpreted). — See further Midr. Esth. 3:9 (96A) above in n. *a*.

c. See Num. Rab. 8 (149A; 149D; 149D; 149A) above in n. *a*; see Gen. Rab. 39 (24B and 24C) at § Rom 4:2f. #1, n. *d*, μ. ‖ Mekilta Exodus 18:6 (66A): R. Eliezer (ca. 90) said, "It was said to Moses (by God), 'I am the one who spoke and the world came to be; I am the one who draws near המקריב, and not the one who removes המרחק; for it says, "Am I a God only of the one who is near, says Yahweh, and not a God also of the one who is far?" (Jer 23:23). I am the one who drew Jethro near and did not remove: you too, when someone comes to you to become a proselyte, and when he comes only for God's sake (without corrupt ulterior motives)—you too shall draw him near קרבהו and not remove him ולא תרחיקהו.' From here you learn that a person should always push away with the left hand while the right hand brings near, and not as Elisha did to Gehazi, whom he pushed away (with both hands) (2 Kgs 5:27)." See § Matt 23:15 A, n. *m*. — The same is found in Tanḥ. יתרו 88A. ‖ See further y. Qidd. 4.65B.21; Tanḥ. קדושים 170B and Tg. Isa. 48:16.

d. See b. Ber. 34B at § Matt 4:17, A, #2, top of 3rd paragraph. ‖ Drawing near and removing illegitimate families from the community of Israel is dealt with in m. ʿEd. 8.7: R. Joshua (ca. 90) said, "I have received from R. Yohanan b. Zakkai († ca. 80), who had heard from his teacher and the latter in turn from his teacher, as a halakah from Moses from Sinai, that Elijah will not come to declare unclean or clean, to remove or to bring near לרחק ולקרב, but rather to remove those brought near by force הַמְקוֹרָבִין and to bring near those removed by force הַמְרוּחָקִים. A family from Beth-Seriphah was on the far side of the Jordan, and a certain Ben Zion removed them by force (despite their well-known legitimacy, he declared them illegitimate); and another family was there that Ben Zion brought near by force (declared them legitimate). Elijah will similarly declare unclean or clean, remove or bring near." R. Judah (ca. 150) said, "Elijah will come to bring near, but not to remove." R. Simeon (ca. 150) said, "To settle differences of opinions." The scholars said, "Neither to remove nor to bring near, but rather to establish peace in the world (see Mal 4:6f.)." — A parallel passage is found in Midr. Song. 4:13 (117A).

2:14 A: For he is our peace.

Derek Ereṣ Zuṭa, Pereq ha-schalom (21B): R. Joshua (ca. 90) said, "Great is peace, for the name of God is 'peace' (see Judg 6:24)." R. Yose the Galilean (ca. 110) said, "Also the name of the Messiah is 'peace'; as it says, 'Eternal father, prince of peace' (Isa 9:5)...." R. Yose the Galilean said, "Great is peace; for when the king, the Messiah, is revealed to Israel, he will rise up only with peace; as it says, 'How beautiful on the mountains are the feet of the one who brings news of joy, who proclaims peace!' (Isa 52:7)." — See also § Col 1:20. ‖ See Tanḥ. שופטים 19A at § Rom 3:9 A, #3, B, n. *h*.

2:14 B: The two.

On the two-fold division of humanity into Jews and non-Jews, see § Rom 1:14, #3.

2:14f.: Who tore down the dividing wall of the fence, the hostility, by doing away by means of his flesh with the law of the commandments consisting of regulations.

The hostility that existed between Jews and non-Jews is described as a fence that separated them from each other. Yet if, according to the following words, the elimination of this hostility occurred by the abolition of the law, this implies that the actual cause of this hostility was precisely the law of Moses which separated and distinguished Jews from non-Jews.

1. The image of a fence (or of a wall) גָּדֵר, סְיָג is found quite often in ancient Jewish literature; in rabbinic writings the fence is viewed solely in accordance with its protective significance,[a] while the separating and dividing that is characteristic of a fence appears particularly in two passages of the Letter of Aristeas as a basis for comparison.[b]

a. The natural and moral world order as a fence for the world. Babylonian Talmud Baba Batra 15B: What does "And his (Job's) livestock have spread out פרץ in the land" (Job 1:10) mean? R. Yose b. Hanina (ca. 270) said, "Job's livestock broke through פרץ the fence of the world גדרו של עולם (= the natural order); according to the course of the world, wolves kill goats, but with Job's livestock, goats killed wolves." — Leviticus Rabbah 26 (124A): R. Samuel b. Nahman (ca. 260) said, "It was said to the snake, 'Why are you found between the fences (walls) גדרות?' It answered, 'Because I have broken through the fence of the world גדרו של עולם (the moral world order) (by misleading humans to sin).'" R. Simeon b. Yohai (ca. 150) taught, "The snake first broke through the fence of the world גדרו של עולם. Therefore, it became an executioner for all who break through fences (now = stipulations of the scholars, see further below)." — The saying of R. Samuel b. Nahman is also found in y. Pe'ah 1.16A.65; Num. Rab. 19 (185C); Deut. Rab. 5 (202B); Midr. Eccl. 10:11 (48A); Pesiq.32A; Tanḥ. הקת 223B; TanḥB הקת § 8 (54A). — The saying of R. Simeon b. Yohai is also in Midr. Eccl. 10:11 (48A). ‖ The Torah as a fence for Israel against sin; and hence Moses and the Sanhedrin as the law-giving entities who fence the rifts that Israel's sin tear open. Leviticus Rabbah 1 (106A): R. Eleazar (ca. 270) said, "Although the Torah was given as a fence for Israel סיוג לישראל from Sinai (to keep them from sin), they were first punished because of it after it was reviewed again in the tent." — Leviticus Rabbah 1 (105B): "Abigedor" (1 Chr 4:18; thus read as a word, it is Moses). R. Huna (ca. 350) said in the name of R. Aha (ca. 320, so read instead of: R. Huna bar Aha), "Many fencers גודרין have arisen for the Israelites, but this one (Moses) was the father of all (hence the name Abigedor = father of fencing)." — Babylonian Talmud Baba Batra 91B: "יֹשְׁבֵי ... גְדֵרָה (Inhabitants of Gederah)" (1 Chr 4:23): this refers to the Sanhedrin who fence in גדרו the rifts of the Israelites (by drawing a fence around the Torah to prevent further transgressions; see Rashi on the passage). ‖ The intensifying preventive regulations גְּזֵירוֹת of the rabbis are a fence for the Torah in order to protect it from transgressions. See passages at § Matt 15:2 A, #2, #3, and #4. — Additional examples are found in SDeut 11:22 § 48 (83B) and Pesiq. 90B. ‖ The legitimacy of marriages is a fence for Israel. Numbers Rabbah 2 (136D): "Balaam raised his eyes and saw Israel, how it camped according to its tribes" (Num 24:2); these are the banners (of the individual tribes). Then he arose to say, "Who may touch these children of men, who know their fathers and their families (by virtue of the legitimacy of marriages)? For it says, 'Which camped according to its tribes.'" From here we learn that the banners (and the legitimacy of lineage vouched by them) were something great and a fence גדר for Israel. ‖ Lastly, one may cite also m. ʾAbot 3.13: (R. Aqiba [† ca. 135] used to say:) The (oral) tradition is a fence סְיָג for the Torah; vows are a fence סְיָג for abstemiousness; a fence סְיָג for wisdom is silence.

b. See Let. Aris. 139 and 142 at § Rom 3:1f., B.

2. Hostility between Jews and non-Jews. — On hatred on the Jewish side, see the excursus "The Stance of Judaism toward the Non-Jewish World" and § Matt 5:43, #1, n. *g*. — A little known testimony for the deeply rooted mistrust of Jews toward non-Jews is found in b. B. Bat. 91B: R. Yohanan († 279) said, "I remember how it was said in the house of learning, 'Whoever agrees with them (non-Jews) falls into their hands, and whoever trusts מתרחיץ them, what is his is theirs (they take everything away from him).'" — Rashi relates the last statement to Isa 39:2. — The hostility on the part of the non-Jewish world in many ways was based on the proud separation that the Jewish people persisted in vis-à-vis the other nations. It was also common to accuse them of a hostile attitude toward pagan authority and ingratitude toward their benefactors.[a] Hostility and hate are accompanied at the same time by scorn and mockery.[b]

a. The richest repository for all the accusations and recriminations that the pagan world raised against the Jews is and remains Josephus' writing against Apion; see also Josephus' passing remark in *Ant.* 16.6.8. In the following we limit ourselves to providing a few passages from other ancient Jewish literature.

α. Citations from non-rabbinic writings. 3 Maccabees 3:4ff.: "The Jews worshiped God, and by living according to his law, they made a separation with respect to eating, for which reason they appeared hateful to some. However, since they adorned their behavior with good conduct, as is appropriate for the righteous, they were highly esteemed in the eyes of all men there. This good conduct of the people, which was spoken of much by all, was not considered at all by the foreigners; on the contrary, they talked much about the difference concerning their worship of God and eating, by saying that these men were not loyal to the king nor to the authorities, but rather were hostile and were opposed to the common good." — In 3 Macc 3:16ff., the following statements about the Jews are found in the supposed edict of king Ptolemy IV Philopator, 222–204: "We went also to Jerusalem and went up to show reverence to the sanctuary of the impious who never abandon their ignorance. The latter indeed accepted our appearance gladly with words, but in fact they wrong-mindedly refused us entrance, since we wished ... to enter their temple, as they were driven by ancient arrogance.... Manifesting their hostile attitude toward us in this way, as if they alone among the nations could raise their necks high against kings and their benefactors, they will not acquiesce to anything rightful.... We also wanted to make them (the Jews) partakers in the citizenship of the Alexandrians and to make them companions of the eternal religious services (the Dionysian mysteries). Yet they took this in a contrary sense, rebuffing good with inherent ill will, and inclined as they are constantly to evil, they not only rejected the citizenship despised (by them), but also abhor both by word and by silence the few among them who are well-inclined toward us, constantly expecting as a consequence of their shameful manner that we would again abrogate what was ordained as soon as possible. Therefore, since we are fully persuaded by proofs that they are ill-disposed toward us in every way, and since we want to prevent, in the case of unrest that might suddenly break out in the future, that these nefarious people be at our back as traitors and barbarous enemies: we have ordained that as soon as this edict is enacted, those designated as well as women and children, enclosed on all sides with iron chains, be brought to us with abuse and torment for inexorable and shameful death, as is fitting for enemies. When they have been punished, we are of the opinion that in the time to come our affairs will become stable and of the best order." — 3 Maccabees 4:1: "Everywhere this decree reached, among the heathen a public feast took place with shouts and joy, because the hostility that had long been fixed in their mind would now freely appear publicly." — See also 3 Macc 7:3f. ‖ In the Additions to Esther 3:14, it is said in Artaxerxes' edict of destruction against the Jews: "Haman indicated to us that a certain ill-disposed people is mixed in with the nations on earth, in its laws opposed to every (other) nation and the commandments constantly despising kings, so that the dominion impeccably led by us cannot achieve rest (cf. Esth 3:8). In view of the fact that solely this people constantly persists in opposition to everyone, differentiated by a strange way of life of laws and ill-disposed toward our affairs it carries out the worst evil deeds, so that the kingdom cannot be stable: so we have decreed that all those named in the writing of Haman together with women and children be absolutely destroyed by enemy swords without any mercy or sparing on the 14th day of the 12th month, Adar in the present year, so that those previously and currently hostile-minded go down to Hades by force on one day and so that in the future our public affairs may be well-established and made unshakable until the end."

β. Citations from rabbinic writings. — Hate and hostility in general. — Midrash Psalm 9 § 7 (42B): "Two nations שני גוים are in your womb" (Gen 25:23); those hated among the nations שנאיהון דאומיא are in your womb (שְׁנֵי is thus interpreted from שְׂנָא "to hate"): all nations hate Esau (= Rome) and all nations hate Israel. A different explanation. Two nations that hate each other: the one (Rome) is proud of its prosperity, the other (Israel) is proud of its Torah. ‖ Exodus Rabbah 30 (89B): (God says,) "When I (so read instead of אדם) come to consider them (the nations of the world), I will destroy them from the world; but I do not have wrath (cf. Isa 27:4), as they are full of wrath against my children (the Israelites). Yet what will I do to them? 'I will let loose on them, burn them at once' (Isa 27:4)." R. Levi (ca. 300) said, "God says to the nations of the world, 'The Israelites are mine, as it says, "The children of Israel are my servants" (Lev 25:55). And wrath is mine, for it says, "Yahweh is an avenger and mighty in wrath" (Nah 1: 2), and you want to be filled with what is mine (wrath) against what is mine (Israel)?'" ‖ Babylonian Talmud Pesaḥim 49B: Greater is the hate with which the *'amme ha'areṣ* hate the student of the scholars than the hate with which the idolaters (non-Israelites) hate Israel. ‖ Midrash Psalm 109 § 4 (233A): The Israelites say to the nations of the world, "God does all this to you because of us (gives you blessings, sunshine, and rain), and you hate us; as it says, 'For my love they are hostile to me' (Ps 109:4). We offer seventy young bulls on the Feast (of Tabernacles) for the seventy nations, and we pray for them, that showers might fall, thus, 'for my love they are hostile to me and I am prayer' (Ps 109:4)." — On the seventy young bulls at the Feast of Booths, see the excursus "The Feast of Tabernacles," VI, #2, n. *b*. ‖ See further b. Pesaḥ. 87B and Midr. Ps. 9 § 9 (43B) at § Rom 2:19–20, #2, n. *c*, second third. ‖ Haman's accusation against the Jews in Esth 3:8. Babylonian Talmud Megillah. 13B: Raba († 352) said, "There is no one who knows how to slander like Haman. He said to him (the king), 'Come, let us destroy them (Israel)!' He answered him, 'I fear their God; he may do to me as he did to those in earlier times.' He said to him, 'They are far from fulfillments of the commandments (without them)!' He answered him, 'There is a teacher among them.' He said to him, '"They are a single people," and if you should say I would make a bleak spot in your kingdom (by eradicating Israel), they are "scattered among the nations"; and if you should say, "We derive benefit from it," it is "set apart" מפורד like this mule פִּרְדָּה that bears no fruit; and if you should say, "There is a region of them," Scripture teaches: "In all the regions of your kingdom." "And their laws are different from those of every people," for they eat nothing from us and do not marry from us and do not get married to us. "And they do not keep the laws of the king," for all year they keep quiet and wander about (on their Sabbath and feast days, instead of working); "and it is not fitting for the king to accommodate them," for they eat and drink and despise the king: if a fly falls into one of their cups, they throw it out and drink it up; but if my lord king touched one of their cups, they shatter it on the ground and do not drink it.'" — Targum Esther 3:8: "Haman said to king Ahasuerus, 'It is a people dispersed and separated among the people and nations and tongues, and a part of them dwells in all the regions of the kingdom, and the law of their Torah is different from that of every people. They do not eat our bread and our food, they do not drink our wine, they do not keep the birthday festivals among us and they do not keep our law and they do not follow the legal decrees of the king, and the king has no benefit from them; or what advantage does he have from them, if he lets them remain in the land (on the earth)?'" — See further Midr. Esth. 3:8 (95B) below in n. *b* toward the end. ‖ See the edict for the destruction of the Jews by Haman in Midr. Esth. 3:9 at § Rom 2:19–20, #2, n. *f.*

b. Megillah Taʿanit 9: A great king like you should bow before this Jew?! See § Matt 10:5, B, #4, first third. ‖ Jerusalem Talmud Berakot 5.9A.30: You arise before these Jews? See § Acts 6:15. — See the same question in y. Ber. 5.9A.32 at § Rom 2:17 A, n. *b.* ‖ "Your face looks like that of a Jewess," an offense that cannot be atoned for; see Midr. Lam. 1:11 (55A) at § Rom 2:17 A, n. *c.* ‖ Midrash Esther 2:3 (92B): "Let the king appoint officials in all the regions of his kingdom, and let all the virgin girls be gathered ... in the women's house" (Esth 2:3). What was the reason? R. Huna (ca. 350) said, "Because they (the non-Jewish women) snubbed the daughters of Israel as ugly, so that no one bothered with them, so they came into this dubious situation (to put their beauty to the test)." R. Hanina of Shilka (so read!) and R. Joshua of Sikhnin (ca. 330) and R. Levi (ca. 300) said in the name of R. Yohanan († 279), "An Israelite and a *goy* (non-Israelite) dwell in a yard; if the Israelite scrubs (?) his pot and then the *goy* touches it, it is not unclean; but it the *goy* scrubs (?) it and then the Israelite touches it, the former says, "Unclean!" And even if who knows how many abominable and creeping animals fell into it, he would eat from it; but if an Israelite puts in something of his own, he shatters it (so the Jew appears to be contemptible to the non-Jew; as a counterpart to this, see b. Meg. 13B above in β). ‖ Genesis Rabbah 88 (55D): "Save me from all my transgressions, do not make me a disgrace for a fool" (Ps 39:9). R. Hama b. Hanina (ca. 260) and R. Samuel b. Nahman (ca. 260). R. Hama b. Hanina said, "The nations of the world were not destined to have sick and shabby people among them (but rather to enjoy this world in unhindered luxuriousness). And why are there sick and shabby people among them? Lest they (mockingly) slight the Israelites and say to them, 'You are a nation of sick and shabby people!' Therefore: 'Do not make me a disgrace for a fool!'" R. Samuel b. Nahman said, "The nations of the world were not destined to have anyone afflicted with rashes among them; and why are there those afflicted with rashes among them? Lest they (mockingly) slight the Israelites and say to them, 'You are a nation of lepers!' (Probably an allusion to Manetho's opinion that the Israelites originated from leprous Egyptians.) Therefore, 'Do not make me a disgrace for a fool!'" ‖ In 4 Macc 5:5f., king Antiochus mocks the old priest Eleazar with the words, "Before I have them begin to torture you, O old man, I would like to counsel you to save yourself by savoring pork; for I have respect for your age and your gray hair, although you, who already bear it for a long time, do not appear to be a philosopher to me, since you keep the worship of God of the Jews." ‖ On the public mockery of Jews in the theater and circus, see Midr. Lam. Intro. #17 (33B) at § Matt 12:1, #2, end. ‖ Midrash Esther 3:8 (95B): "There is יֶשְׁנוֹ a people" (Esth 3:8). (Haman said to the king,) "Their fences שְׁנֵיהוֹן have gotten large, for they eat and drink and say, 'A feast of the Sabbath, a feast of a festival day!' They decrease the fortune of the world: one of seven days in a Sabbath, one of thirty days is the beginning of a month, in Nisan is the Feast of Passover, in Sivan is the Feast of Weeks, in Tishri the New Yea and the great fast (= the Day of Atonement) and the Feast of Booths (work is cancelled, so they decrease the fortune of the world)." Ahasuerus said to him, "This is what they have been commanded in their Torah." Haman answered, "If they observed their feast days and our feast days, they would act rightly; but they despise your feasts and they do not keep the laws of the king; for they do not observe the calends nor the Saturnalia."

2:16: Killing the hostility.

If ἔχθρα refers to the hostility between God and world, we can compare those passages in which a peace-making significance is attributed to either Israel[a] or the tent of meeting.[b]

a. Genesis Rabbah 66 (42B): R. Samuel b. Tanḥum and R. Hanin said in the name of R. Idi (ca. 310), "'"Shulamite" שׁוּלַמִּית (Song 7:1) is the nation' (God says) 'that has made peace between me and my world (i.e., Shulamite refers to Israel); for if it had not existed (and had not accepted the Torah), I would have destroyed my world.'" — In Midr. Song. 7:1 (125B), where R. Jeremiah (ca. 320) is the author, it explicitly says: "if it had not accepted my Torah."

b. Pesiqta 7A: R. Yohanan († 279) said, "'On the day when Moses ceased' (Num 7:1). On the day when hostility disappeared from the world; for as long as the tent of meeting was not erected (in which the Torah first became legally binding for Israel), hostility, jealousy, disputes, quarreling, and factionalism were in the world. But after the tent of meeting was erected, love, affection, friendship, righteousness, and peace were given in the world. What is the scriptural basis? 'I will hear what God, Yahweh, says' (namely in the tent of meeting between the cherubim, Exod 25:22; Num 7:89); 'he speaks peace to his people and to his pious ones' (Ps 85:9)." ‖ TanḥumaB נשא § 25 (19B): R. Judah b. Simon (ca. 320) said, "On the day when the tent of meeting was erected, Moses went in ... and said, ... 'I will hear what God, Yahweh, says' (Ps 85:9). God said to him, 'Moses, I speak peace. In my heart there is nothing against my children'; for it says, 'He speaks peace to his people and to his pious ones, lest they only return to foolishness!' (Ps 85:9). And then it is written, 'Yes, his salvation is near to those who fear him' (Ps 85:10). When? On the day when the tent of meeting was erected." For R. Joshua (b. Nehemiah, ca. 350) said in the name of R. Eleazar (ca. 270), "Before the tent of meeting was erected, there was conflict between God and Israel; but on the day when the tent of meeting was erected, peace came (see Ps 85:9)." — The same is found in Pesiq. Rab. 5 (22A). — A similar statement is found under the name of R. Judah b. Simon (ca. 320) in Pesiq. Rab. 5 (22A) and Num. Rab. 12 (164D) as well.

2:17: Peace to those far and peace to those near.

See Isa 57:19 in SNum 6:26 § 42 (12B) at § Matt 5:9; Num. Rab. 8 (149D) at § Eph 2:13, n. *a*; b. Ber. 34B at § Matt 4:17, A, #2, paragraph 3. — On τοῖς μακράν and τοῖς ἐγγύς, see § Eph 2:13.

2:20 A: On the foundation of the apostles and prophets.

1. θεμέλιος, θεμέλιον α. = תֵּימֶלְיוֹס[a] "base, foundation"; β. = יְסוֹד,[b] Aram. יְסוֹדָא, "basis, foundation," which is not to be confused with יִסּוּד "stipulation, order." The unvocalized יסוד נביאים could thus mean both "basis of the

prophets" and "order of the prophets"; the context of the relevant passages everywhere speaks in favor of the latter meaning.[c]

a. Genesis Rabbah 3 (3C): R. Judah (ca. 150) said, "Light was created first (before the world). Like a king who wanted to build a palace, and that place was dark. What did he do? He lit lamps and lanterns to know how to lay the foundations תימליוסים. In the same way, light was created first." ‖ Jerusalem Talmud Sanhedrin 10.29A.43: When David wanted to dig the foundations תימליוסים for the sanctuary, he dug 1500 cubits without hitting the primal depths.

b. Midrash Song of Songs 1:1 (78B): His (Solomon's) father built the foundations יְסוֹדוֹת (of the temple) and he (Solomon) built the upper levels.

c. Babylonian Talmud Sukkah 44A: R. Yohanan († 279) and R. Joshua b. Levi (ca. 250). The one said, "The willow (in the temple procession at the Feast of Booths) was an order of the prophets יסוד נביאים (read יִסּוּד)." The other said, "The willow was a custom of the prophets." ‖ Jerusalem Talmud Šebuʿot 1.33B.50: R. Abba b. Zabda (ca. 270) said in the name of R. Hunia of Beth Hauran (ca. 230), "The willow and the water libation (at the Feast of Booths) and the ten plantings (i.e., the ten young trees for which an acre may be plowed up to the beginning of the fallow year, see m. Šeb. 1.6) are among the stipulations of the earlier prophets יִסּוּד נ׳." — The same is found in y. Sukkah 4.54B.35.

2. On the metaphorical use of θεμέλιος in reference to people, see § Matt 16:18, #2 and especially Yelamedenu in Yalquṭ 1 § 766 at § Matt 16:18, #2.

2:20 B: While Jesus Christ himself is the cornerstone.

1. ἀκρογωνιαῖος (sc. λίθος) α. = פִּנָּה (Isa 28:16); LXX: ἰδοὺ, ἐγὼ ἐμβάλλω εἰς τὰ θεμέλια Σιὼν λίθον ..., ἀκρογωνιαῖον = פִּנָּה. — The targum translates without the image: "Behold, I set a king in Zion, a king strong, heroic, and fearsome; I strengthen him and I keep him...." — β. = רֹאשׁ פִּנָּה (Ps 118:22); LXX: κεφαλὴ γωνίας (likewise, Matt 21:42); the targum sidesteps the image here as well: "The youth that the master builders (= the scholars) among the sons[281] of Jesse left behind (passed over), he has obtained to be appointed as king and ruler." — γ. = אֶבֶן פִּנָּה (Job 38:6); LXX: λίθος γωνιαῖος; targum: אֶבֶן זָוִיתָא "stone of the corner." — From ʾAbot R. Nat. 28, we learn that the cornerstone אבן פנה had two smoothed sides. — See also § Matt 21:42, #3.

ʾAbot de Rabbi Nathan 28 (7D): R. Eleazar b. Shammuah (ca. 150) said, "There are three types of students of the scholars: the hewn stone אבן גָּזִית, the cornerstone אבן פנה, and the cubic stone אבן פיספס (read פְּסֵיפַס = ψῆφος). The 'hewn stone,' what is this? This is a student who has studied the midrash (scriptural interpretation). When a student of the scholars comes to him and asks him about the midrash, he answers him. This is the 'hewn stone,' which has only one (smoothed) side. The 'cornerstone,' what is this? This is a student who has studied the midrash and the halakoth (the applicable regulations). When a student of the scholars comes to him and asks him about the midrash, he answers him; when about

281. S-B: Instead of הוה בני בניא, with the deletion of הוה, read: ביני בניא "between the sons."

the halakoth, he answers him. This is the 'cornerstone,' which has two (smoothed) sides. The 'cubic stone,' what is this? This is a student who has studied the midrash and the halakoth and the haggadoth (the nonhalakic interpretations of Scripture) and the Tosafoth (the halakic traditions that go alongside the Mishnah). When a student of the scholars comes to him and asks him about the midrash, he answers him; when about the halakoth, he answers him; when about the Tosafoth, he answers him; when about the haggadoth, he answers him. This is the cubic stone, which has four (smoothed) sides according to its four directions.

2. On the metaphorical use of "cornerstone," see, in addition to the passage just adduced from ʾAbot R. Nat. 28, also § Matt 16:18, #2 and § Matt 21:42.

2:22: Into a dwelling of God.

See b. Taʿan. 11A at § 1 Cor 3:16.

3:10: So that the manifold wisdom of God might now be made known to the authorities and powers in heaven through the church.

We can compare the often-expressed thought that one day the righteous will be nearer to God than the angels, so that the latter will come and ask the righteous: "What has God done?" See Deut. Rab. 1 (196A); y. Šabb. 6.8D.21; Tanḥ. בלק 236A in the excursus "Sheol, Gehenna, and the Garden of Eden," III, #4, n. *m*.

3:14f.: To the Father, from whom all fatherhood in heaven and on earth takes the name ("fatherhood").

πατριά = "fatherhood" is the designation of a family clan whose origin goes back to a common ancestor. Carried over to the angelic world, it signifies a "class of angels." This is similar to the Old Testament and rabbinic term בֵּית אָב (plur. בֵּית אָבוֹת, rabbin. בָּתֵּי אָבוֹת) "house of the father" = "familial dynasty," except that this term is nowhere applied to angels; their "classes" are instead called כִּתּוֹת (also כִּתִּים, sing. כַּת, from כַּנְתְּ ,כְּנָת = everything that bears the same name). By contrast, the rabbis have a different designation also borrowed from the realm of familial relations, a designation that was applied both to the angelic world as well as to Israel, namely פָּמִלְיָא "family" = servants, where, though, God is not viewed in the first place as אָב "father," as in Eph 3:14f. in comparison to the πατριαί, but rather as בַּעַל הַבַּיִת "lord of the house."[a] More precisely, then, the angelic world is called the "upper family" פָּמִלְיָא שֶׁל מַעְלָה and Israel the "lower family"[b] פמליא של מַטָּה.

a. Mishnah ʾAbot 2.15: R. Tarfon (ca. 100) used to say, "The day is short and the work is a lot; the workers are lazy, and the recompense is great, and the Lord of the house בעל הבית (= God) presses hard." ‖ Babylonian Talmud Soṭah 35A: "The men who had gone up with him said, 'We cannot go up to this people; for it is stronger than we are' (Num 13:31)." R. Hanina b. Papa (ca. 300) said, "The scouts said a great word in that hour: 'For it is stronger ממנו.' Do not interpret מִמֶּנּוּ 'than we are,' but rather מִמֶּנּוּ 'than he is.' Even, if one may say so, the lord of the house בעל הבית (= God) cannot remove (get back) his tools from there (which he has put down there as a deposit)."

b. See the following passages at § Matt 16:19 B, #2, n. *c*: b. Sanh. 38B; 98B; 99B. – In SNum 6:26 § 42 (13A), it is asked in a comparison between Job 25:3 and Dan 7:10: Has the upper family been decreased? – The same is found in b. Ḥag. 13B. ‖ Babylonian Talmud Berakot 16B: Rab Safra (ca. 300) said after his prayer (i.e., following the Prayer of Eighteen Benedictions), "May it be your will, Yahweh our God, to fashion peace in the upper family and in the lower family and between the students of the scholars who occupy themselves with your Torah." ‖ Babylonian Talmud Sanhedrin 67B: R. Yohanan († 279) said, "Why is their (sorcerers') name כַּשָּׁפִים? Because they adversely affect מכחישין the upper family (they wreck the decisions of fate made by the upper court)." ‖ Midrash Psalm 11 § 6 (51A): "He who is righteous will see פנימו" (Ps 11:7); it does not say פניו "his face," but rather פנימו, that is, the face of the Shekinah and his family (= angels). —The suffix מו is interpreted as the plural suffix = ימו. ‖ Pesiqta Rabbati 35 (160B): "And I ואני will be for it a fiery wall around it" (Zech 2:9). What does "And I" mean? God meant: I and my whole family (= the angelic world) will be a wall for Jerusalem. (The ו in ואני has an inclusive significance.) ‖ Targum Song of Songs 1:15: "When the children of Israel do the will of their king, he praises them by his Memra (i.e., he himself) before the (upper) family, before the holy angels."

3:18: Rooted and established in love.

For the nations of the world there is no taking root; see Midr. Song. 7:3 (127A) at § Rom 3:9 A, #2, n. *a*.

3:19: The love of Christ which surpasses knowledge.

See the depiction of the love of the Messiah for Israel in Pesiq. Rab. 36 (161A) at § Luke 24:26, I, #4, n. *k* and Pesiq. Rab. 37 (162B) at § Luke 24:26, I, #4, n. *m*.

4:2: With all humility and gentleness, with long-suffering, bearing each other in love.

1. On humility and gentleness, see § Matt 5:3, #3 and 5:5, #1.

2. μακροθυμία = אֲרִיכָה, אֲרִיכוּת פָּנִים.

See Gen. Rab. 70 (44D) at § 1 Cor 16:19, n. *d*. ‖ Midrash Ecclesiastes 7:8 (34B): A Persian came to Rab († 247) and said to him, "Teach me the Torah!" He said to him, "Say, aleph!" He answered him, "Who says that this is an aleph? It could be said that it is not." He said to him, "Say, beth!" He answered him, "Who says that this is a beth?" Then he snapped at him and dismissed him with an expulsion (נְזִיפָה, a type of ban). He went to Samuel († 254) and said to him, "Teach me the Torah!" He said to him, "Say, aleph!" He answered him, "Who says that this is an aleph?" He said to him, "Say, beth!" He answered him, "Who says that this is beth?" Then he grabbed him by his ear so he yelled, "My ear, my ear!" Samuel said to him, "Who says that this is your ear?" He answered him, "All the world knows that this is my ear." He said to him, "Here too all the world knows that this is an aleph and this is a beth." Then the Persian was silent and accepted it. Therefore: Better a long-suffering man אֶרֶךְ רוּחַ than a proud man גְּבַהּ רוּחַ. Better was the long-suffering אֲרִיכָה that Samuel showed to the Persian than the rage הַקְפָּדָה that Rab showed toward him. ‖ See the narrative about Hillel's (ca. 20 BCE) gentleness and long-suffering in b. Šabb. 30B at § Matt 5:5, #1, first third. ‖ Seder Eliyahu Rabbah 24 (135): "If you keep the commandments of Yahweh your God and walk in his ways" (Deut 28:9).... What are God's ways? He is long-suffering אֶרֶךְ אַפַּיִם; he shows his long-suffering מאריך רוחו to the godless and accepted them in repentance. So you too should show long-suffering to one another מאריכין פנים for the good; but you should not show long-suffering to one another for payback. — See further אֶרֶךְ רוּחַ m. ʾAbot 6.2.

3. ἀνεχόμενοι ἀλλήλων, see m. ʾAbot 6.5f. at § Gal 6:2 A.

4:3: To keep the unity of the Spirit in the bond of peace.

See § Matt 5:9, #1; § 1 Cor 11:19; and § Rom 12:18.

4:4–6: One body and one Spirit ... in one hope ..., one Lord, one faith, one baptism, one God and Father of all.

In comparison, the synagogue emphasized in 2 Bar. 48:24: "We all are one people that bears one renowned name, we who received one law from one." — 2 Baruch 85:14: "Therefore, there is one law given by one, one world and for those who are in it, one end for all."

4:7: According to the measure of the gift.

Leviticus Rabbah 15 (115C): "To determine the weight of the wind, and so that he might set the water according to measure" (Job 28:25).... R. Judan b. Simeon (ca. 320) said, "Also the water that falls from above is given only according to measure במדה...." R. Aha (ca. 320) said, "Also the holy spirit that rests on the prophets rests on them only according to weight (according to the measure determined by God): one prophesied one book and another two...." R. Judan b. Ishmael (ca. 300, so read instead of b. Samuel,) "Also the words of the Torah (both the written and the oral), which were given from above, were given only according to measure במדה; and these are: Scripture, the Mishnah, the Talmud, the halakoth, and the haggadoth (the nonhalakic traditions). One attains Scripture, another the Mishnah, another the Talmud, another the haggadah, and some attain them all."

4:8 A: Therefore it says.

On λέγει without a subject, see § Rom 15:10 and § 1 Cor 6:16.

4:8 B: Ascended to the heights, he took captivity captive, he gave gifts to people.

1. Psalm 68:19 according to the base text: "You went up to the heights, you have led captivity (captives) captive, you have received gifts among people, and even rebellious ones (are there) to dwell with Yah, God." — Septuagint: Ἀναβὰς εἰς ὕψος ᾐχμαλώτευσας αἰχμαλωσίαν· ἔλαβες δόματα ἐν ἀνθρώπῳ, καὶ γὰρ ἀπειθοῦντες τοῦ κατασκηνῶσαι.

2. Ancient rabbinic literature consistently interpreted Ps 68:19 with reference to Moses, as he went up to the heights to receive the Torah. Among the relevant passages, there is one that interprets the words "you have received gifts" precisely as the apostle does "you have given gifts."[a] Two other passages explain the words "you have received gifts among people" as "you have received gifts for people," namely to give them to people, and thus they turn out to have the same sense as the reinterpretation found in the apostle.[b] It is therefore quite possible that the apostle's interpretation is based on an older tradition that had become known to him in the Jewish houses of learning. Most passages, though, retain the original sense of the words "you have received gifts," and then interpret this in manifold ways.[c]

a. Targum Psalm 68:19: "'You went up to heaven': this is Moses, the prophet. 'You have led away captivity captive': you have studied the words of the Torah, you have given them to the children of men as gifts (bounties), and the Shekinah of the glory of Yahweh Elohim dwells even with the rebellious if they turn in repentance."

b. ʾAbot de Rabbi Nathan 2 (2A): When Moses went up to the heights to receive the tablets..., the angels of service brought an accusation against Moses and said, "Lord of the world, 'what is man that you think of him ...' (Ps 8:5–9). Then they grumbled about Moses and said, "What is so special with this one born of a woman (see § Gal 4:4 B) that he has gone up to the heights? As it says, 'You went up to the heights, you have led captivity captive, you have received gifts' (the tablets of the law for Israel)." He took then (the two tablets) and went down and rejoiced with great joy. When he then saw the evil deed that they committed by making the calf, he said, "How can I give them the tablets! I would oblige them with commandments that are too heavy and they would declare them guilty of death by God (= eradication) ..." (see the continuation at § 2 Cor 3:7 B, B, n. *dd.* ‖ Midrash Psalm 68 § 11 (160A): "You went up to the heights, you have led captivity captive" (Ps 68:19). This is what Scripture said: "To a city defended by heroes the wise man goes up and makes the rampart in which it trusts fall" (Prov 21:22). This is Moses; as it says, "Moses went up to God" (Exod 19:3). "You have received gifts for people" (so now the Midrash Ps 68:19); this is the Torah which was given freely as a gift[282] to Israel. "Yet the rebellious dwell in arid land" (Ps 68:7); these are the nations of the world who did not want to accept it (the Torah). "But Yah, God, will dwell even with the rebellious" (so the Midrash Ps 68:19); these are the Israelites who were rebellious, and when they accept the Torah, the Shekinah dwells with them.

c. Tractate Soperim16 § 10: R. Joshua b. Levi (ca. 250) said, "In my whole life I have never looked into a book of the haggadah;[283] only once did I look in and found it written, 'The 175 sections in which the word "speak," "say," and "command" is written in the Torah

---

282. S-B: The Torah is described as a gift elsewhere as well; see, e.g., § 2 Cor 3:7, n. *y*.

283. S-B: R. Joshua b. Levi regarded writing down the haggadah (the nonhalakic traditions) as so reprehensible that he declared: Whoever writes down the haggadah has no share in the future world; whoever muses over them burns himself (falls prey to the ban); whoever listens to them receives no recompense for it (y. Šabb. 16.15C.32).

(= Pentateuch) correspond to the years of the life of our father Abraham; for it is written, "You (Moses) went up to the heights, you led captivity captive, you have received gifts because of (by the merit of) the man" (so now the Midrash Ps 68:19); and further it is written, "The great 'man' among the Anakim (giants)" (Josh 14:15; this refers to Abraham; see § 1 Cor 15:45 B, n. *b*; thus, Moses received the Torah by his merit); therefore, he appointed the 175 sections of reading in the Torah for the individual Sabbaths as a constant burnt offering." — Parallels are found in y. Šabb. 16.15C.33; Midr. Ps. 22 § 19 (95A). ‖ Exodus Rabbah 28 (88B): "Moses went up to God" (Exod 19:3). This is what is written, "You went up to the heights, you led captivity captive" (Ps 68:19). What does "You went up" עלית mean? You have been raised נתעלית (exalted to a high worth), you have wrangled with the angels of the upper world. A different explanation. "You went up to the heights": (this means) that no creature has had any authority up there as Moses has had. R. Berekhiah (ca. 340) said, "The tablets (of the law) had a length of six handbreadths; of these, if one may say so כִּבְיָכוֹל, two handbreadths were in the hand of the one who spoke and the world came into being, and two handbreadths were in the hand of Moses, and two handbreadths accounted for the separation from hand to hand. A different explanation. 'You went up to the heights, you led captivity captive.' According to the custom of the world, someone who enters a city receives something that the citizens of the city do not direct their eyes to (= something worthless); yet Moses went up to the heights and received the Torah, which all kept their eyes directed to. Therefore, 'You went up to the heights, you have led captive what is captive (watched and held fast by the eyes).' If he led it (the Torah) captive, did he receive it without recompense (for free)? Scripture teaches: לקחת מתנות באדם 'you have bought gifts by the merit of (because of) the man.' It was given it to him by a purchase לְקִיחָה. So he had to pay him (God) a purchasing price? Scripture teaches: מתנות 'gifts,' as a gift it was given to him. In that hour the angels of service wanted to set themselves on Moses; but God made the facial features of Moses like those of Abraham. Then God said to them, 'Are you not ashamed before him? Is this not the one to whom you descended and in whose house you ate (Gen 18)?' God said to Moses, 'To you the Torah is given only by the merit of Abraham; as it says, "You have received gifts באדם 'because of the man,'" and the "man" who is spoken of here is none other than Abraham; as it says, "The great man about the Anakim (the giants)"' (Josh 14:15)." ‖ Babylonian Talmud Šabbat 88B: R. Joshua b. Levi (ca. 250) said, "When Moses went up to the heights, the angels of service said before God, 'Lord of the world, what does the one born of woman have to look for among us?' He answered them, 'He has come to receive the Torah.' They said before him, 'The well-kept gem that has been kept for you since the six days of creation, 974 generations before the world was created (see § John 1:1–4, #1, notes *a* and *b*), you want to give to a man (literally: flesh and blood)? What is the man that you think of him, and the son of man that you should consider him! Yahweh, our Lord, so glorious is your name on the whole earth, but leave your splendor (= Torah) in heaven!' (so Midr. Ps. 8:5, 2). God said to Moses, 'Give them an answer!' He said before him, 'Lord of the world, I fear that they might burn me with the breath of their mouth!' God said to him, 'Hold fast to the throne of my glory and then give them an answer!' For it says, 'He seized the front of the throne, then he spread his cloud over him' (so Midr. Job 26:9).... Moses said before him, 'Lord of the world, what is written in the Torah that you want to give me?' 'I am Yahweh, your God, who led you out of the land of Egypt, out of the house of slavery' (Exod 20:2). Then he said to the angels, 'Did you go down to Egypt and become subject to pharaoh? What should the Torah be to you! Further, what is written in it? "You shall have no other God except me." Do you dwell among uncircumcised men who commit idolatry?...' Immediately they praised God; as it says, 'Yahweh, our Lord, how glorious is your name on the whole earth!' (Ps 8:2).... Immediately each angel befriended him and gave something to him; as it says, 'You went up to the heights, you led captivity captive, you received gifts באדם,' that is, as a recompense for them (scornfully) calling you 'man,' you received gifts. And even the Angel of Death gave him something (handed a secret over to him); for it says, 'He took the incense and made atonement for the people' (Num 17:12); and further it says, 'He stood between the dead and the living ...' (Num 17:13). If he (the Angel of Death) had not told him, how would he have known?" ‖ Tanḥuma כי תשא 115A: "He gave the two tablets to Moses when he had finished speaking with him" (Exod 31:18). This is what is written: "You went up to the heights, you led שבי captive" (Ps 68:19). According to the custom of the world, one takes silver, gold, and clothes from someone else; can he also take away what is in his heart? But you have led captive the Torah, which was in my heart; therefore, "You have led captive שבי = what was in me (in my heart)." "You have received gifts באדם." R. Zeira (ca. 300) said, "This refers to the halakoth concerning impurity, which are applicable to children of men: 'If any man becomes flowing'; 'If any woman becomes flowing' (Lev 15:2, 19)." (באדם is thus interpreted: "Which concern a person.") — In Midr. Song. 8:11 (133B) a similar exposition is found in the name of R. Aha (ca. 320).

4:9: To the lower parts of the earth.

Among the seven names that gehenna has according to R. Joshua b. Levi (ca. 250), there is also אֶרֶץ הַתַּחְתִּית "lowest earth"; here it is remarked that this is a teaching handed down גְּמָרָא; see b. 'Erub. 19A in the excursus "Sheol, Gehenna, and the Garden of Eden," I, #3, n. *a*.

4:10: So that he might fill everything.

God as the one who fills everything.

See Gen. Rab. 4 (4A) at § Matt 10:5, B, #5, second third; b. Sanh. 39A at § Matt 18:20, middle; Exod. Rab. 2 (68C) at § Acts 7:30 C. ‖ Exodus Rabbah 3 (69D): A matron said to R. Yose (ca. 150), "My God is greater than your God." He said to her, "Why?" She answered him, "When your God revealed himself to Moses in the thorn bush, Moses hid his face (Exod 3:6); but when he saw the snake, which is my God, Moses immediately ran from it" (Exod 4:3; he therefore was more afraid of the snake than of God, a proof that the snake is more powerful than God). He answered her, "May you vanish! When our God revealed himself in the thorn bush, Moses had no place he could flee. Where should he have fled? To heaven or to the sea or onto dry land? What does it say about out God? '"Do I not fill heaven and earth?" says Yahweh' (Jer 23:24). Yet when a person flees two or three steps from the snake, which is your god, he can save himself from it." — The whole is an example of Ophian Gnosticism. ‖

Leviticus Rabbah 4 (107D): Why did David praise God with his "soul" (in, e.g., Ps 104:35)? David meant: The soul fills the body and God fills his world; as it says, "Do I not fill heaven and earth?" (Jer 23:24). So let the soul come, which fills the body, and praise God, who fills the whole world.

4:14: By virtue of human deceit.

κυβία, κυβεία = game of dice, then in general = deceit. The word passed over into the rabbinic writings as well in the form קוּבְיָא, though here it only has the meaning "game of dice."[a] The passage adduced by Schöttgen for the meaning "fraud" is not probative.[b] However, the derivative קוּבְיוּסְטוֹס = κυβευτής "dice player"[c] does appear to exist in rabbinic literature also with the derived meaning "fraud."[d]

a. Mishnah Sanhedrin 3.3: The following are unfit (for the office of judge or witness): The dice player המשחק בקוביא (literally: the one who plays with dice) etc. (see § Matt 5:21 B, #3, B, #3, n. *e*). — Parallels are found in m. Roš Haš. 1.8; t. Sanh. 5.2 (423); also see y. Roš Haš. 1.57C.1; y. Sanh. 3.21A.33; b. ʿErub. 82A and b. Sanh. 24B. ‖ TanḥumaB נה § 20 (24B): Balaam had his beginning with brothels, with the game of dice קוביא, with the (idolatrous hairstyle of the) curl on the top of the head and with sorcery.

b. Mishnah Šabbat 23.2: One may cast the lot with his children and members of his house (on the Sabbath) at the table (for the cooked portions to be distributed); however, one may not purposely make a large portion against a small one (but rather they should as much as possible be equally big), because of playing dice (a game of chance) משום קוביא. — See b. Šabb. 149B: Samuel († 254) said, "A large portion against a small portion is also forbidden with respect to strangers (guests) on a day of the week. What is the reason? משום קוביא." — Here Schöttgen translates: *propter fraudem* "because of fraud," but this cannot possibly be right. For Samuel's words entail that casting lots for unequal portions on a day of the week in the circle of the members of one's own house was not necessarily prohibited. If, however, casting lots for unequal potions would have been evaluated as "fraud," it would have been prohibited in all cases. So משום קוביא can only mean: because of a game of dice or chance. Apportioning unequal portions of food by means of a game of chance should never happen with guests, and at least not on a Sabbath or feast day with the members of one's own house. The reason: To prevent envy and jealousy.

c. Tosefta Baba Batra 4.7 (403): If someone sells his slave to someone else and it becomes apparent that he is a thief or dice player קוביוסטוס, he has acquired him (the sale cannot be reversed). — The same is found in y. B. Bat. 7.15D.11; b. Ketub. 58A; b. Qidd. 11A; b. B. Bat. 92B. ‖ See further Yalquṭ on Deut 7:12 (1 § 847) in Yelamedenu.

d. In b. Bek. 5A, the general Antigonus—so read with the parallel passages—says to Rabban Yohanan b. Zakkai († ca. 80), with reference to Exod 38:26 and 27: "Your teacher Moses was a thief or a קוביוסטוס, or he was not good with calculations. The one half he gave away and the other half he took for himself. Not once did he release the full half!" — There is no good reason to understand why Moses is described specifically as a "dice player"; only if the word קוביוסטוס has the more general meaning "fraud" does it fit in the context. —

The parallels in y. Sanh. 1.19D.2 and Num. Rab. 4 (141D) lack the word קוביוסטוס. – It is similar with b. Ḥul. 91B; see § Luke 2:13 B; here too the translation of the loanword with "fraud" is more appropriate than with "dice player."

4:17: That you not walk as the pagans walk.

The admonition is of a general sort and pertains to the entire moral lifestyle. The rabbinic דַּרְכֵי הָאֱמֹרִי "ways of the Emorite" = דַּרְכֵי הַגּוֹיִם "ways of the gentiles" (see already Jer 10:2) is essentially narrower. This term applies exclusively to superstitious gentile mores and customs.

The main passage in t. Šabb. 6f. (117.3), which in b. Šabb. 67A.35 is named exactly פרק אמוראי "Chapter of the Emorite." A few things may follow here from this: The following are among the ways of the Emorite (= gentile customs): If someone sheers his hair (specifically so that the entire front part of the head is shorn bald and the hair of the back part of the head is tied together in a braid, Rashi), or if someone makes a braid (on top of his head), or if someone sheers his head bald for the god of fortune (?), or if a woman passes her son between the dead, or if someone binds a bead from a trinket around his hips or a red thread on his finger, or if someone casts stones into the sea or into a river while counting. See, these are among the ways of the Emorite. If someone strikes on the shoulder or claps in the hands or jumps in front of a flame, see, these are among the ways of the Emorite. If someone has dropped (according to the reading נפלה) a morsel of bread and he says, "Give it back to me lest my blessing be lost"; ... if sparks have fallen down from it (a light), and he then says, "Today we will have guests." See, these are among the ways of the Emorite. If a raven squawks and someone says to him, "Squawk!"; if a raven squawks and someone says to him, "Turn around!" See, these are among the ways of the Emorite. If someone says, "Eat this bud of lettuce so you may remember me"; Do not eat it because of going blind; "Touch the dead man's coffin so you may see us (at night)"; Do not touch the dead man's coffin, lest you see us at night; "Reverse your shirt so you may dream dreams"; "Do not reverse your shirt, lest you dream dreams"; "Sit on a broom so you may dream dreams"; Do not sit on a broom, lest you dream dreams. See, these are among the ways of the Emorite.... If someone says, "Do not put your hand on your back, lest you hinder us in our work," see, this is among the ways of the Emorite.... If a woman screams into an oven, so that the bread does not drop (from the walls); or if someone puts wood shavings in a pot handle so it does not move and tilt backward, see, these are among the ways of the Emorite.... If someone consults his stick and says, "Should I go?" or "Should I not go?," see, this is among the ways of the Emorite.... If someone says מַרְפֵּא "(to) health!"[284] (after another has sneezed), see, this is among the ways of the Emorite. R. Eleazar b. Zadok (I, ca. 100; II, ca. 150) did not say "Health!" so as not to interrupt the study of the Torah; those from the house of Rabban Gamaliel (ca. 90) did not say "Health!".... If someone says, "No, no" לא לא!, see, this is among the ways of the Emorite; and even if there is no proof for it, it is still a reminder of the following: "They say to God, 'Depart from us (this is the first No!), we do not long to know your ways (this is

284. TN: The German word is *Gesundheit*, which is still used in response to a sneeze.

the second No!)'" (Job 21:14).... If someone says, "Do not pass between us, lest our friendship cease," see, this is among the ways of the Emorite. But if it happens for deference, it is allowed. – Partial parallels are found in y. Šabb. 6.8C.40; b. Šabb. 67A. – From the Mishnah, we can here add m. Šabb. 6.10; also see y. Šabb. 6.8C.37 and b. Šabb. 67A.

4:23: That you be renewed with respect to the spirit of your reason.

At § John 3:3, #2, it was said, "It is particularly noteworthy that, when it comes to the new creation of a person, the rabbinic scholars never have in view a moral renewal in the sense of the rebirth of the New Testament. A person's moral renewal belongs, according to the rabbinic view, only to the future, which alone can bring the promised new spirit or the new heart." This is also right if the older period is in question. Only in the late Midrash Rabbah on Exodus (from the 11th or 12th century[285]) is there a passage that comes close to the Christian view and perhaps can be compared with Eph 4:23.

Exodus Rabbah 15 (76C): The angels are daily renewed מתחדשים and praise God, and then they return to the stream of fire from which they had proceeded. But God renews them מחדשן again and makes them become again as they were in the beginning; as it says, "Those who are renewed every morning" (Lam 3:23). Likewise, the Israelites sink into sinning as a consequence of the evil inclination which is in their body. Yet then they turn in repentance, and God forgives their sins every year (on the Day of Atonement) and renews their heart מחדש לבם to fear him; as it says, "I will give you a new heart ..." (Ezek 36:26).

4:24: To put on the new man.

On ἐνδύσασθαι see § Luke 24:49, #2.

4:25 A: Put aside lies.

We limit ourselves to reproducing some noteworthy sayings about lies and lying.

ʾAbot de Rabbi Nathan 30 (8B): R. Simeon (ca. 150) said, "Such is the punishment of a liar בַּדַּאי, that one does not listen to him, even when he tells the truth. For so we find with the sons of Jacob: when they lied כיזבו to their father originally, he believed them. As it says, 'They slaughtered a billy goat ...' (Gen 37:31); and further it is written, 'He looked at it closely and said, "The robe of my son"' (Gen 37:33). But ultimately, although they spoke the truth before him, he did not believe them; as it says, 'They reported to him, saying, "Joseph is still alive ..., and he did not believe them"' (Gen 45:26)." ‖ Genesis Rabbah 94 (59C): R. Hiyya (ca. 200) taught, "How does it go with a liar בדאי? Even if he speaks words of truth, he is not believed." ‖ Babylonian Talmud Sanhedrin 89B: (Satan tempted Abraham before the offering of Isaac and) said to him, "A word has sneaked out to me. This is what I heard from behind the curtain, 'A lamb for the burnt offering and not Isaac for the burnt offering!'" He answered

285. Strack, *Einleitung in den Talmud und Midraš*, 208.

him, "Such is the punishment of a liar בדאי: even when he speaks the truth, no one listens to him!" ‖ Pesiqta Rabbati 24 (125B): R. Samuel b. Nahman (ca. 260) said, "We find that God created everything in his world, except for the measure (the manner) of the lie שֶׁקֶר, which he did not create and the measure (the manner) of falsehood שָׁוְא, which he did not make. Rather, humans concocted these from their own hearts; as it says, 'Accepting and uttering from the heart words of a lie שָׁקֶר' (Isa 59:13)." ‖ Babylonian Talmud Šabbat 104A: (The two letters Shin ש and Tav ת stand next to each other in the alphabet.) Shin means שֶׁקֶר "lie"; Tav אֱמֶת "truth." Why does the word שֶׁקֶר have its letters close together (in the alphabet in a cluster), while the word אֱמֶת has its letters far apart? (א is the first, מ the absolute middle, and ת the last letter in the alphabet.) A lie is found frequently, but the truth is not found frequently. Why does the word שקר (with each of its letters) stand on one leg? (Incidentally, from this it follows that ש in older time did not, as in the present print, have a broad base, but rather must have petered off in sharp point at the bottom.) And why is the word אמת (with each of its letters at the base) stretched out wide like a brick? The truth endures, but a lie does not. ‖ See the fable poems of R. Levi (ca. 300) about lies and poverty as allies in Midr. Ps. 7 § 11 (34B) at § Matt 19:22, #3, n. *c.* ‖ Babylonian Talmud Soṭah 42A: R. Jeremiah b. Abba (ca. 250) said, "Four classes will not greet the face of the Shekinah (will not see God): the class of mockers and the class of hypocrites and the class of liars שַׁקְרִים (see Ps 101:7) and the class of slanderers. — The same is found in b. Sanh. 103A; anonymously in Midr. Ps. 101 § 3 (214B). ‖ Babylonian Talmud Roš Haššanah 22B: Rab Kahana (ca. 250) said, "… In a matter that is apt to be made known, people usually do not lie." ‖ Babylonian Talmud Taʿanit 9B: Ulla (ca. 280) came to Babylon; he saw bright fleeting clouds (under dark thick clouds) and said, "Remove the implements; for now the rain comes. At last, no rain came." Then he said, "As the Babylonians lie משקרי, so too their rainfall lies (in its signs)." ‖ Babylonian Talmud Sukkah 46B: R. Zeira (ca. 300) said, "Let no one say to a child, 'I will give you something,' and then give him nothing; for thereby he would be taught the lie שִׁקְרָא. As it says, 'They have taught their tongues (become accustomed to) tell lies' (Jer 9:4)." ‖ See further b. Šebu. 30B.

4:25 B: Speak the truth, each one with his neighbor.

The base passage is Zech 8:16: "Speak truth, each one with his neighbor." — The targum translates verbatim: מַלִּילוּ קוּשְׁטָא גְּבַר בְּחַבְרֵיהּ. — Septuagint: λαλεῖτε ἀλήθειαν ἕκαστος πρὸς τὸν πλησίον αὐτοῦ. — Testament of Dan 5 cites the passage according to the LXX in this form: Ἀλήθειαν λαλεῖτε ἕκαστος πρὸς τὸν πλησίον αὐτοῦ and then continues: "So you will not fall into anger and turmoil, but rather will be in peace and have the peace of God τὸν θεὸν τῆς εἰρήνης, and war will not overcome you." — In rabbinic literature the 2nd part of Zech 8:16 is often used as a biblical basis for judicial conciliation between two parties; see as an example t. Sanh. 1.2ff. (415) at § Rom 4:15 A.

4:26: Be angry and do not sin.

1. The base passage is Ps 4:5: רִגְזוּ וְאַל תֶּחֱטָאוּ, which can mean: α. "Quake or fear (God) lest you sin"; β. "Be angry but do not sin." — The first interpretation is adopted by the targum: זעו מניה ולא תחטון "Tremble before

him (Yahweh), so you will not sin"; the second by the LXX and, with it, the apostle: ὀργίζεσθε καὶ μὴ ἁμαρτάνετε. — Most of the time, the rabbinic scholars understood רִגְזוּ transitively = "arouse, provoke, bother" and added as the object the evil inclination or the good inclination.

Babylonian Talmud Berakot 5A: R. Levi b. Lahma (ca. 260, so read instead of b. Hama) said that R. Simeon b. Laqish (ca. 250) said, "Let a person always provoke (bring to anger) the good inclination against the evil inclination; as it says, 'Provoke, lest you sin' (Ps 4:5)." ‖ Midrash Psalm 4 § 9 (23B): R. Aha (ca. 320) said, "Anger ארגיז your (evil) inclination so that he may not mislead you to sin." The rabbis said, "Contradict אכחיש (really: 'make lean') your (evil) inclination so that he may not mislead you to sin, so that you may not come into the power of sin." — Parallels are found in Pesiq. 158A and Midr. Ruth 4:16 (137A). ‖ Differently, see Midr. Ruth 8 at the beginning (137A) at § Matt 1:5 C, #1, n. *b*. — The same is found more briefly and anonymously in Midr. Ps. 4 § 9 (23B): David said to the Israelites, "How long will you sin and get upset and say, 'He is a reprehensible (illegitimate) one, he stems from the Moabite Ruth!' Speak in your heart concerning your own bed and stay quiet! Selah."

2. The following passages deal with anger that is justified in certain circumstances.

Babylonian Talmud Megillah 6B: R. Isaac (ca. 300) said, "When you see that the hour smiles on the godless (instead of לא read: לו), do not get upset (in anger) against him אל תתגרה בו. As it says, 'Do not flare up (in anger) about evildoers' (Ps 37:1)." Yet R. Yohanan († 279) said in the name of R. Simeon b. Yohai (ca. 150), "One may get upset התגרות (in anger) against the godless in this world; as it says, 'Those who forsake the Torah praise the godless, but those who keep the Torah get upset with them!' (Prov 28:4)." Further, it has been taught as a baraita: R. Dosetai (Dustai) b. Judah (ca. 180; so read with Bacher instead of R. Dosetai b. Mathun[286]) said, "It is permitted to get upset (in anger) with the godless in this world; and if someone whispers to you the words, 'Do not flare up over evildoers and do not envy those who act wickedly!' (Ps 37:1), (know:) the one whose heart strikes him (who has a bad conscience) speaks like this. Instead (the words of Ps 37:1 mean): 'Do not flare up over evildoers,' in order for you yourself to be like the evildoers, 'and do not get worked up over those who act wickedly,' in order for you yourself to be like those who act wickedly. Yet it says, 'Let your heart not get worked up over sinners (but rather be in the fear of God at all times)!' (Prov 23:17). There is no contradiction: the one (namely, that one should not get worked up) applies when it is a matter of one's own affairs, and the other when it is a matter of godly things. And if you want, say: In both cases, it is about your own affairs, without there being a contradiction: in the one case (namely that one should not get worked up) it is a matter of a completely righteous person and in the other it is a case of one who is righteous but not completely." For Rab Huna († 297) said, "What does 'Why do you look at the faithless? Why are you silent when the godless consumes the one who is more righteous than he is?' (Hab 1:13) mean? He may consume the one who is more righteous than he is (without getting worked up), but he may not consume

286. Bacher, *Die Agada der Tannaïten*, 2:391.5.

the completely righteous one. And if you want, say: If the hour smiles on him, the situation is different (then one should not get worked up)." — Parallels are found in b. Ber. 7B; in Der. Er. 2 (19A), there is only the saying of R. Dosetai, which is correctly designated as "a baraita of Judah." ‖ See SLev 19:18 (352A) at § Matt 5:43, #2, n. *b*, end; see the passages that deal with permissible hatred at § Matt 5:43, #2, notes *b* and *c*.

4:27: Do not give space to the devil.

τόπον διδόναι α. = נָתַן מָקוֹם "to give occasion, opportunity," see § Luke 14:9 and § Rom 12:19 B; β. = נָתַן פִּתְחוֹן פֶּה לְ "to give to someone an opening of the mouth (i.e., an occasion or opportunity for something)" (on פתחון פה see already Ezek 16:63; 29:21). The expression is used in reference to God,[a] people (heretics)[b] and Satan.[c] It is synonymous with פָּתַח פֶּה לְ "to open the mouth to someone" = to give an opportunity;[d] the opposite is סָתַם פֶּה "to close or block the mouth."[e]

a. Pesiqta 108B: "I am Yahweh, your God" (Exod 20:2). This is what Scripture says, "Listen, my people, and let me speak!" (Ps 50:7). R. Hama b. Hanina (ca. 260) said, "Listen, my people, so I may speak, so there may be an opening of the mouth פתחון פה for me (= so that I may have the opportunity), to indict the ruling angels of the nations." — Something similar is attributed to R. Phineas b. Hama (ca. 360) in TanḥB וארא § 1 (9A). ‖ Midrash Esther 3:9 (96B): (According to R. Isaac [ca. 300], the banquet of Ahasuerus in Esth 1:3 was meant to mislead the Israelites to fornication and to awaken God's wrath against them.) When Mordecai saw this, he arose and made it known to them (Israel) and said to them, "Do not go to eat from the banquet of Ahasuerus; for he has invited you only to make accusations valid against you, so that the divine punitive righteousness may have opportunity פתחון פה to indict you before God." Yet they did not listen to the words of Mordecai and all went to the site of the banquet.

b. Leviticus Rabbah 20 (119D): R. Eleazar of Modiim († ca. 135) said, "Come and see, how costly the death of the sons of Aaron (Lev 16:1) was before God; for everywhere where he (God in Scripture) mentions their death, he also mentioned their sin. Why all this? To make you know that those who come into the world should have no opportunity פתחון פה to say, 'Shameful works were in their hands at Sinai; for this is why they died.'" ‖ In b. Ḥul. 63B, Rabbi († 217?) says, "In order to give the opponent (in a discussion) no opportunity שלא לתן פתחון פה לבעל דין to be of a divided opinion." ‖ Sifra Leviticus 1:2 (13B): R. Yose (ca. 150) said, "Everywhere where it says, 'An offering,' it is said in connection with *yod-he* (i.e., with Yahweh) (thus: 'an offering for Yahweh,' not 'an offering for God'; yet the rule does not apply in view of Lev 23:14), in order to give the sectarians[287] no opportunity שלא ליתן פתחון פה to be mighty (to vaunt; for from קרבן לאלהים they would infer either that they should present offerings to their divinities too, or, more probably, that offerings can conciliate only the harsh and cruel demiurge = אלהים, אל שדי, but not the highest and good God = יהוה)." ‖

287. S-B: The text has the form מאינים for the otherwise common מינין. This passage seems to have escaped Levy's notice when he says that a form of מאני does not appear for מין in the older Midrashim (*Chaldäisches Wörterbuch*, 3:104A). On 4:156f., he actually presents the passage with: מינין.

Genesis Rabbah 8 (6C): R. Simlai (ca. 250) said, "Everywhere where you find an opening of the mouth פתחון פה for the sectarians (where they think they have an opportunity to establish their view from Scripture), you find an answer to it on its (the relevant passage's) page. – For a more detailed exposition of this claim, see the parallel in y. Ber. 9.12A.44 at § Gal 3:11, S-B footnote.

c. Pesiqta 177B: R. Simon (ca. 280) said in the name of R. Joshua (b. Levi, ca. 250), "Why does the high priest not go in with golden garments (on the Day of Atonement into the holy of holies)? Yet an accuser cannot become a defender, so as not to give Satan an opportunity כדי שלא ליתן פתחון פה לשטן to accuse and say, 'Yesterday they made for themselves a god of gold, and today they want to perform the service (of offering) in golden clothes!'" (The golden garments would bring into remembrance the sin with the golden calf and arouse Satan to accuse them, and this is why the high priest cannot conduct Israel's affairs in them as a defender in the holy of holies.) – On the times and situations in which Satan opens his mouth to accuse, see § Matt 4:1 B, #3, B, notes *d* and *e*.

d. See the baraita in b. Ber. 60A at § Matt 4:1 B, #3, B, n. *d*, toward the beginning; b. Ber. 19A at § Matt 7:7 A, #2, n. *p*. – Similarly, b. Ketub. 8B.

e. See Exod. Rab. 13 (75C) at § Rom 9:18.

4:28 A: The one who steals should steal no more.

On the 7th commandment, see § Matt 19:18 A.

4:28 B: Rather, let him work, doing something good with his hands, so that he may have something to share with the one who lacks.

For praise of manual work, see § Mark 6:3 and § Acts 18:3. – For the whole sentence, see Lev. Rab. 3 (106C.42.54): R. Isaac opened his presentation with, "'Better a handful of rest than two fists full of toil and slippery striving' (Eccl 4:6).... Better is the one who goes and works and gives alms from what is his than the one who goes and robs and extorts and gives alms from what belongs to others. In a proverb it says, 'She vies for apples and shares them with the sick. But his wish to be called a benevolent person is slippery striving.'" – The same is found anonymously in Midr. Eccl. 4:6 (23A). – The exposition is based on the general claim that a commandment cannot be considered to have been fulfilled if it was fulfilled with the help of a sin. Such a fulfillment of a commandment was called in brief a מצוה הבאה בעבירה "a fulfillment of a commandment that comes about by a transgression"; see, for example, the baraita in b. Sukkah 43A; m. Sukkah 3.1, 2, 3, 5; Pesiq. 182A; y. Sukkah 3.53C.10 in the excursus "The Feast of Tabernacles," II, A, n. *l*. – See further b. Sukkah 29B; m. Giṭ. 5.5; b. Giṭ. 55B; SLev 1:10 (30A); b. B. Qam. 66B.

4:29: No worthless talk should leave your mouth.

λόγος σαπρός "lazy, worthless, ugly talk" may be collocated with דְּבָרִים בְּטֵלִים "void, useless, worthless, vacuous words"[a] or with דְּבַר נְבָלָה "sword of wickedness" = "ugly word"; for the latter, one can also say נִבּוּל הַפֶּה or נַבְלוּת פֶּה "ugly (lewd, indecent) speech."[b]

a. Babylonian Talmud Šabbat 30B: The Shekinah does not rest (on someone) in indolence, nor in distress, nor in thoughtlessness, nor in twaddle, nor in useless words דברים בטלים, but rather only in a word of joy in a (completed) fulfillment of a commandment; for it says, "Now fetch me a string musician! And it happened that when the string musician played, the hand of Yahweh came upon him" (2 Kgs 3:15). — A similar passage is found in b. Ber. 31A; see also b. Pesaḥ. 117A at § Rom 4:17.

b. Babylonian Talmud Ketubbot 8B: "Therefore, Yahweh will not rejoice in his youths and he will not have mercy on his orphans and widows; for as a whole (the people) are godless and sinful, and every mouth speaks what is shameful דובר נְבָלָה" (Isa 9:16). Rab Hana b. Rabba (ca. 250) said, "All know why a bride enters the bridal chamber; but when someone engages in ugly (indecent) speech הַמְנַבֵּל פִּיו and lets an ugly word leave his mouth ומוציא דְבַר נְבָלָה מפיו, even if his judgment was sealed for 70 years for good, it will be changed for him to evil." ‖ Leviticus Rabbah 24C (123A): "He (God) may see nothing ugly (foul עֶרְוַת דָּבָר) in you" (Deut 23:15), that is, עֶרְוַת דִּבּוּר "shamefulness of speech." R. Samuel b. Nahman (ca. 260) said, "This is ugly talk נבול הפה." ‖ Babylonian Talmud Šabbat 33A: Because of the sin of ugly speech נַבְלוּת פֶּה great (many) hardships and severe disasters are renewed and the youths of those who hate Israel (= of the godless Israelites) perish, orphans and widows cry out and are not heard, as it says in Isa 9:16; see above b. Ketub. 8B. Then follows, as there, the saying of Rab Hanan b. Rabba. At the close it says: Rabbah bar Shela (ca. 325) said that Rab Hisda († 309) said, "Whoever engages in ugly talk המנבל את פיו, for him gehenna is made deep; as it says, 'A deep grave is the mouth of strangers (= adulteresses)' (Prov 22:14)."

4:30: In whom you were sealed.

ἐσφραγίσθητε, see § 2 Cor 1:22 A.

5:1: Be imitators of God, as beloved children.

See § Matt 5:45 A. — On imitating God, see also TanḥB בהקתי § 6 (56A): "For who in the heights of the clouds matches Yahweh, who is like Yahweh among the sons of God?" (Ps 89:7). God said, "Whoever acts according to my works will be like me." ‖ Seder Eliyahu Rabbah 24 (135.16): "If you keep the commandments of Yahweh your God and walk in his ways" (Deut 28:9). In the ways of God; what are the ways of God? He is merciful and has mercy on the godless and accepts them in repentance. So too should you be merciful toward one another. A different explanation. What are the ways of God? He is gracious; he gives gifts freely to those who know him and to those who do not know him. So too should you give gifts to one another. A different explanation. What are the ways of God? He is long-suffering; he shows his long-suffering to the godless and accepts them in repentance. So too should you show long-suffering to one another for good; but you should not show long-suffering to one another for payback. A different explanation. What are the ways of God? He is great in grace; he inclines to the side of grace. So too should you have regard for goodness (should turn to the side of goodness) more than for evil.

5:2: As an odor of pleasure.

ὀσμὴ εὐωδίας = רֵיחַ נִיחוֹחַ, in the OT, this is frequently said of the offering fragrance (e.g., Exod 29:18). The targumim avoid the expression for the offering; they translate, for example, Exod 29:18: "A burnt offering is before Yahweh, to be accepted with pleasure." — See more on εὐωδία at § 2 Cor 2:15 A.

5:3: Greed (see § Luke 12:15 A).

5:4 A: Foolish chatter or frivolous (salacious) talk.

1. μωρολογία "foolish chatter" perhaps = דִּבְרֵי בוֹרוּת[a] "words of foolishness, of ignorance," or = דִּבְרֵי תַפְלוּת[b] "words of absurdity."

a. A baraita in b. Nid. 69B: The people of Alexandria asked R. Joshua b. Hananiah (ca. 90) twelve things: three concerned words of "wisdom" (= the halakah), three words of the haggadah, three words of foolishness דברי בורות, and three words of ordinary life.... (70B:) Three words of foolishness: "The wife of Lot (who was turned into a pillar of salt), does she make unclean (by touching her corpse)?" He answered them, "A dead person makes unclean, but a pillar of salt does not make unclean." — "The son of the Shunammite woman (brought back to life in 2 Kgs 4:35), does he make unclean?" He answered them, "A dead person makes unclean, but one who is living does not make unclean." — "The dead in the future, will they (after the resurrection) need to be sprinkled (with the water of purification) on the 3rd and on the 7th day, or will they not need to be?" He answered them, "When they have become living again, we will find out." Some say (that he answered), "When our teacher Moses comes with them (we will find out)."

b. Sifre Deuteronomy 1:1 § 1 (64B): "Between Tophel and Laban" (Deut 1:1). (The place is called תֹּפֶל in reference to) the words of foolishness דִּבְרֵי תַפְלוּת, which they foolishly spoke about the manna. And so it says, "Our soul has disgust for the wretched food" (Num 21:5). He (God) said to them, "You fools, every royal person selects for himself only light bread, lest they get diarrhea, but you argue with me because of the good I have shown you, and you grumble before me!" ‖ See Num. Rab. 4 (142D) at § 1 Cor 14:16 B, #6, n. *n*, end.

2. εὐτραπελία, frivolous, facetious nature, perhaps = נִבּוּל הַפֶּה, דְּבַר נְבָלָה, and נַבְלוּת פֶּה, see § Eph 4:29, n. *b*.

5:4 B: Which are not fitting.

Numbers Rabbah 10 (160A): When a person has drunk a cup (of wine), which is as much as a quarter of a log, the person loses a quarter of his knowledge (consciousness); when he has drunk two cups, he loses two parts of his knowledge; when he has drunk three cups, he loses three parts of his knowledge, and his heart becomes confused; immediately he begins to say what is not fitting שֶׁלֹּא כְהוֹגֶן (literally: which is not as what is fitting). — The corresponding Aramaic expression is found in b. Taʿan. 22B: When his (King Josiah's) soul entered rest, Jeremiah saw that his lips moved. He said, "Perhaps—God forbid—he will say in his pain a word that is not fitting מִילְּתָא דְּלָא מְהַגְּנָא!" He bowed low and heard how he acknowledged the judgment (the verdict) over himself to be just. He said, "Righteous is he, Yahweh, for I opposed his mouth" (Lam 1:18). Then in that hour Jeremiah raised up concerning him, "The breath of our nose, the anointed of Yahweh" (Lam 4:20).

5:5 A: Greedy person, who is an idolater.

In order to mark the magnitude of a sin, it was common to equate it with a notoriously bad sin. One would say, "Whoever does this or that is like one who plants an *Asherah*; like one who erects a *bamah*; like one who sheds blood; like one who commits incest ...."[a] Here the comparison with an idolater was particularly popular.[b] Likewise, the value of a fulfillment of a commandment was glorified by putting it on the same level as a particularly laudable work. One would declare, for example, "Whoever does this or that, it is as if he has built the (destroyed) altar and presented sacrifices on it."[c] It is possible that the apostle coined his saying about the greedy person in connection with this way of speaking; yet the difference remains that he equates the greedy person not simply with the idolater, but also designates him explicitly as such.

a. See examples in b. Sanh. 7B; y. Ned. 9.41B.45; see also b. Soṭah 4B at § Luke 1:51, n. *c*; b. Yebam. 63B at § John 2:1 A, #1, n. *a* and b. Ber. 35A at § Eph 5:20.

b. Tosefta Pe'ah 4.20 (24): R. Joshua b. Qarha (ca. 150) said, "How do we know that everyone who veils his eyes before good-doing is like an idolater? ..."; see the parallel in SDeut 15:7ff. at § Matt 5:42, #1. — The same is found as a baraita in b. Ketub. 68A and b. B. Bat. 10A. — See t. B. Qam. 9.31 (366) at § Matt 5:22 C, middle. ‖ Tosefta ʿAbodah Zarah 4.5 (466): Whoever leaves the land (of Israel) in times of peace and goes abroad is like one who commits idolatry. ‖ Tosefta ʿAbodah Zarah 6, 16 (471): Just as one who casts a stone on a heap of stones devoted to Mercury is an idolater, behold, so too is the one who honors the godless like one who commits idolatry. ‖ Tosefta ʿAbodah Zarah 6.18 (471): R. Simeon b. Eleazar (ca. 190) said, "Just as the one who casts a stone on a heap of stones devoted to Mercury is an idolater, so too everyone who teaches a godless student is an idolater." — Here the teacher of an unworthy student is designated as an idolater exactly like the greedy person in Eph 5:5. ‖ Babylonian Talmud Pesaḥim 118A: Rab Sheshet (ca. 260) said in the name of R. Eleazar b. Azariah (ca. 100), "Whoever scorns the feasts is like an idolater." — The same is found in b. Mak. 23A. ‖ Jerusalem Talmud Nedarim 9.41B.41: R. Yannai (ca. 225) said, "Whoever listens to his (evil) inclination is like an idolater. What is the scriptural basis? 'You shall not have in you a strange god and not worship a god from outside' (so Ps 81:10 according to the midr.); do not make the stranger within you (= the evil inclination) into a king over you." ‖ See b. Soṭah 4B at § Luke 1:51, n. *c*. ‖ Babylonian Talmud Berakot 31B: Do not look at your servant-girl as a contemptible woman בת בליעל. R. Eleazar (ca. 270) said, "From here it follows that a drunken person who prays is like an idolater." ‖ Babylonian Talmud Sanhedrin 92A: R. Eleazar (ca. 270) said, "Whoever leaves over pieces of bread on his table is like an idolater." R. Eleazar also said, "Whoever speaks ambiguously (in order to deceive) is like an idolater." ‖ Schöttgen adduces the following citation from Exod. Rab. 31: מרבה הונו

בנשך עכ"ום = *qui opes suas multiplicat per foenus, ille est idolatra.*[288] Yet this citation is not found in Exod. Rab. 31.

c. Babylonian Talmud Menaḥot 110A: Resh Laqish (ca. 250) said, "What does 'This is the law for the burnt offering and for the food offering, for the sin offering, and for the guilt offering' (Lev 6:2, 7, 18; 7:1) mean? Whoever occupies himself with the Torah is like one who presents a burnt offering, a food offering, a sin offering, and a guilt offering...." R. Isaac (ca. 300) said, "Whoever occupies himself with the law of the sin offering is like one who presents a sin offering, and whoever occupies himself with the law of the guilt offering is like one who presents a guilt offering." ‖ See b. Ber. 6B at § Matt 9:15 B, n. *a.* ‖ See b. Ber. 14B at § Matt 15:2 B, #2, n. *i.* ‖ See b. Sukkah 45A in the excursus "The Feast of Tabernacles," II, D. ‖ See m. ʾAbot 3.3 at § Luke 10:42 A.

5:5 B: In the reign of Christ.

βασιλεία τοῦ Χριστοῦ = מַלְכוּת הַמָּשִׁיחַ "the kingship, the kingdom of the Messiah."

See 2 Bar. 39:7 at § Matt 1:1 B, #3, n. *c*; see Agad Shir ha-Shirim 6.10 at § Matt 24:27, n. *a*; see Tg. Isa. 53:10 at § Matt 8:17 A; see also Tg. Song. 7:14 at § 2 Cor 2:15 A.

5:6 A: With empty words.

κενὸς λόγος = דָּבָר רֵק, דָּבָר רֵיקָם,[a] or דָּבָר בָּטֵל.[b]

a. Deuteronomy 32:47: "For it is no empty word דבר רק from you (= from which you have nothing), but rather it is your life." — Targum Onkelos: "For it is no empty word פִּתְגָם רֵקָא from you מִנְּכוֹן, for it is your life." — Targum Yerušalmi I: "For there is no empty word פִּתְגָם רֵקָם in the Torah except for those who transgress them, for it is your life." — Septuagint: ὅτι οὐχὶ λόγος κενὸς ουτος ὑμῖν· ὅτι αυτη ἡ ζωὴ ὑμῶν. ‖ See Gen. Rab. 1 (3A) at § Rom 3:1f. D, first third. ‖ See y. Peʾah 1.15B.39 at § Acts 7:38 B. ‖ See further SDeut 11:22 § 48 (84B) and 32:47 § 336 (140B).

b. דבר בטל, see § Eph 4:29, n. *a.*

5:6 B: Children of disobedience (see § Matt 8:12 A).

5:7: Do not be partakers with them.

1. συνμέτοχος = תֻּתָּשׁ "companions, co-owners." — Jerusalem Talmud Sanhedrin 1.19B.16: R. Yohanan b. Zakkai († ca. 80) answered, "The companion תותוש of a robber is like the robber." ‖ Tosefta Ketubbot 9.3 (271): (One makes) a co-owner תותוש (swear) as long as he is a co-owner; when he leaves his partnership, he is like all other people.

2. On the whole sentence, see the saying of R. Aqiba († ca. 135) in ʾAbot R. Nat. 30 (8B): Whoever associates קבדמה with those who commit a transgression receives the same punishment as they (do), even if he does not act according to their works. Whoever associates

288. Schöttgen, *Horae Hebraicae et Talmudicae*, 1:779.

with those who fulfill a commandment receives the same recompense as they (do), even if he does not act according to their works.

5:8 A: You were darkness, but now (you are) light in the Lord.

On the metaphorical usage of darkness and light, see § Rom 13:12 B; § John 3:19 A; 3:19 B.

5:8 B: As children of the light (see § Luke 16:8 B).

5:9: Fruit of the light.

On καρπός see § Matt 7:16 A and § Matt 12:33.

5:11: Works of darkness (see § Rom 13:12 B).

5:12: What happens in secret.

κρυφῆ = בְּצִנְעָה or בַּסֵּתֶר, see § John 7:4.

5:14: Therefore, it says, "Wake up, you who sleep, and rise up from the dead, and Christ will shine on you."

The introductory formula διὸ λέγει marks the following words as a scriptural citation (see § Rom 15:10). In fact, though, they are not here; one thus has to assume a *lapsus memoriae* on the part of the apostle. The sentence "If someone wishes to kill you, preempt him with killing" (b. Ber. 58A; 62B and b. Sanh. 72A) is also similarly cited as a word of the Torah, while according to TanḥB פנחס § 4 it is actually a saying of the scholars (see § Rom 12:14 A). — On the source of the saying in Eph 5:14, see the citations from the church fathers in Schürer.[289] — See further § 1 Tim 2:8 B.

5:16: Redeeming the time.

The words: "You will buy (= gain) time" עדנא אנתון זבנין (Dan 2:8) are rendered in the LXX with: καιρὸν ὑμεῖς ἐξαγοράζετε "you buy up time." Then, the middle τὸν καιρὸν ἐξαγοράζεσθαι means: "to buy up time for oneself," namely to make use of it, thus = to redeem the time.

5:18: Do not get drunk with wine, wherein lies licentiousness (desolateness).

There are innumerable warnings about wine in rabbinic literature; we limit ourselves to reproducing three passages.

Numbers Rabbah 10 (158A): "Do not look at wine, how it appears beautifully red" (Prov 23:31). The holy spirit (which speaks in Scripture) concerning wine that a person should not get drunk יִשְׁתַּכֵּר. Why? Because it is red; for its end is blood, if a person (while intoxicat-

---

289. Schürer, *Geschichte des jüdischen Volkes*, 3:362 and 365f.

ed) commits a sin by which he makes himself guilty of death.... "How it goes down easily" (Prov 23:31). R. Asi (ca. 300) said, "If he (the wine drinker) is a student of the scholars, he will ultimately declare what is clean unclean and what is unclean clean." A different explanation. "How it goes down easily בְּמֵישָׁרִים (in directness, so smoothly, easily)." Ultimately, he (the scholar) declares transgressions to be permitted and makes them an ownerless good (i.e., deregulates them) as one level כְּמִישׁוֹר, chats with a woman on the street, and speaks shameful words in drunkenness without being ashamed. "Ultimately it bites like a snake" (Prov 23:32). Just as the earth was cursed (see Gen 3:17) because of the snake, who misled Eve to drink wine,[290] so too was a third of the world (= humanity) was cursed because of wine; as it says, "Noah awoke from his intoxication from wine.... Then he said, 'Cursed be Canaan!'" (Gen 9:24f.)... As the basilisk separates between life and death, so too wine separates people from the ways of life and onto the ways of death, because wine provokes him to idolatry.... (Then follows in 158B a long exposition of Amos 6:1–7 which says in conclusion:) By wine they were misled to fornicate and therefore they were led into captivity (see Amos 6:7). Here we learn that everywhere (in Scripture) where there is mention of wine, there is fornication. "Give strong drink to the one who is near to perishing, and wine to those who are afflicted in soul" (Prov 31:6). R. Hanan (ca. 300) said, "Wine was created in this world only to give wicked people their recompense in this world, since they perish in the future world, and to comfort mourners." (This saying of R. Hanan is also found in b. ʿErub. 65A and b. Sanh. 70A.) ... (159D:) "In strength and not with drinking" (Eccl 10:17); in the strength of the Torah and not with drinking wine. Therefore, Isaiah said, "The strength of the Torah lies in salvation, but the strength of wine lies in sorrow: Woe to those who are heroes at drinking wine!" (Isa 5:22). Likewise, it says, "To whom is there woe? For whom is there sorrow?... For those who sit late over wine" (Prov 23:29f.)... (160A:) When wine goes in, understanding goes out; everywhere where there is wine, there is no understanding. When wine goes in, a secret goes out: the word יין (wine) has a numerical value of 70, and the word סוד (secret) has a numerical value of 70.... A priest who has drunk a quarter *log* of wine is unfit for service; an Israelite who has drunk a quarter *log* of wine is unfit to judge. This teaches you that nothing good comes from wine. ‖ Babylonian Talmud Sanhedrin 70A: "Noah, the farmer, began and planted a vineyard" (Gen 9:20). Rab Hisda († 309) said that Rab Uqba (I, ca. 220) said—according to others, Mar Uqba (II, ca. 270) said that R. Zakkai (ca. 250) said, "God said to Noah, 'Should you not have learned from the first man, whom only wine caused (to fall into sin and misery)?' He means it as the one who said, 'That tree from which the first man ate was a grapevine'; for in a baraita it has been taught: R. Meir (ca. 150) said, 'That tree from which the first man ate was a grapevine; for you have nothing that brings shame to man except for wine.'" ‖ Babylonian Talmud Yoma 76B: Why is wine called יַיִן (wine) and תִּירוֹשׁ (cider)? It is called יין because it brings shame (lamentation יְלָלָה) into the world (here יין is derived from ינה = אנה "to wail"); it is called תירוש because everyone who flares up in passion because of it is impoverished נַעֲשָׂה רָשׁ.

290. S-B: The tree of knowledge was supposed to be a grapevine; see the next citation from b. Sanh. 70A.

5:19: Speaking to one another in psalms and songs of praise ....

See m. ʾAbot 3.3 at § Luke 10:42 A. ‖ See the baraita in b. Sanh. 101A at § Matt 9:15 B, n. *aa.*

5:20: Giving thanks at all times for everything.

See m. Ber. 9.5 at § Matt 22:37, end. ‖ Mishnah Berakot 9.2f.: Over good messages, one says (as a blessing): "Blessed be the one who is good and who shows good!" Over bad news, though, one says, "Blessed be the true judge!" ... One speaks a blessing over misfortune as over what is good and over what is good as over misfortune. — Examples of this are found in b. Ber. 60A. ‖ See b. Ber. 35A at § Matt 14:19 B, #1, n. *a.*

5:22: Wives (should submit themselves) to their own husbands.

See § 1 Cor 11:10 A.

5:25: You men, love your wives.

The admonition that a man should love and honor his wife is found often among the rabbis.[a] One knows that the wife is the man's happiness and life, his prosperity and his crown;[b] and if she were nothing else for him, it is enough that she raises his children for him.[c] Conversely, it becomes dark around the man whose wife is torn away from him by death; in principle the woman dies only to her husband.[d] Alongside this series of thoughts there is another, which in some ugly words expresses the deep scorn for the female gender.[e]

a. See b. Yebam. 62B at § John 2:1 A, #2, n. *c.* ‖ʾSee Abot R. Nat. 26 (7C) at § Matt 5:43, #1, penultimate paragraph; in this passage, the "neighbor" whom one should love like himself in Lev 19:18 is interpreted to refer to one's own wife. ‖ See b. B. Meṣ. 59A at § Matt 19:22, #4, second third. ‖ Babylonian Talmud Nedarim 50A: (R. Aqiba [† ca. 135] honored his wife before his students with the words,) "What is mine and what is yours is hers" (i.e., what I and you are, we owe to her, who has gone without me for many years, so that I could devote myself to the study of the Torah). — The same is found in b. Ketub. 63A. ‖ Jerusalem Talmud Ketubbot 11.34B.50: R. Jacob b. Aha (ca. 300) said in the name of R. Yohanan († 279) and R. Hela (ca. 310) in the name of R. Eleazar (ca. 270), "Just as a man takes care for the honor of his widow, so too he should take care for the honor of his divorced wife." ‖ Babylonian Talmud Baba Meṣiʿa 59A: Rab († 247) said, "Let a man always be careful not to offend his wife; for because her tears come (easily), the punishment for her offense is near (so according to Rashi)". ‖ Babylonian Talmud Moʿed Qaṭan 26B: One tears his clothing at the death of the father-in-law and the mother-in-law for the honor of the wife.

b. See b. Yebam. 63A at § Matt 19:4, last paragraph. ‖ See b. Yebam. 62B at § John 2:1, A, #1, n. *a.* ‖ Babylonian Talmud Baba Batra 145B: R. Hanina (ca. 225) said, "'All the days of the poor are evil' (Prov 15:15): this is the one who has an evil wife. 'Yet whoever is glad of heart always has a meal of joy' (Prov 15:15): this is the one who has a good wife." ‖ Babylonian Talmud Berakot 8A: "At the time of finding" (Ps 32:6). R. Hanina (ca. 225) said, "At the time of finding": this refers to a wife; for it says, 'When someone finds a wife, he has found something good' (Prov 18:22)." ‖ Babylonian Talmud Yebamot 63B: Raba († 352) said, "Come and see how good a good wife is!... For it is written, 'When someone finds a wife, he has found something good' (Prov 18:22). If the Scripture passage speaks about her herself (thus it should be understood according to the wording about a wife), how good then is a good wife, since Scripture praises her! But if the Scripture passage speaks of the Torah (so it is not in the literal sense about a wife), how good then is a good wife since the Torah is compared with her!" ‖ A baraita in b. Šabb. 25B: Who is rich?... R. Aqiba († ca. 135) said, "Any man who has a wife beautiful in works." ‖ Babylonian Talmud ʿArakin 19A: Hezekiah (ca. 240) said, "People say, 'An old man in the house, nothing (פָּאחָא = lowness) in the house; an old woman in the house, a treasure in the house (since she can be helpful everywhere).'" ‖ Genesis Rabbah 47 (29C): It is written, "A virtuous wife is her husband's crown" (Prov 12:4.) R. Aha (ca. 320) said, "Her husband is adorned (crowned) by her, but she is not adorned by her husband."

c. Babylonian Talmud Yebamot 63A: The wife of R. Hiyya (ca. 200) distressed him (she piqued him a lot). When he found something (where he thought he could make his wife happy), he tied it in his turban and brought it to her. Then (his nephew) Rab († 247) said to him, "Look, she distresses her lord (why then give her a gift)?!" He answered him, "It is enough for us that they raise our children for us and keep us from sin."

d. Babylonian Talmud Sanhedrin 22A: R. Alexandrai (ca. 270) said, "When someone's wife dies in his lifetime, the world becomes dark around him; as it says, 'The light darkens in his tent and his lamp over him goes out' (Job 18:6)." R. Yose b. Hanina (ca. 270) said, "His steps are shortened; as it says, 'His mighty steps become constricted' (Job 18:7)." R. Abbahu (ca. 300) said, "His counsel tumbles (his plans fail); as it says, 'And his own counsel casts him down' (Job 18:7)." ‖ Babylonian Talmud Sanhedrin 22B: In a baraita it has been taught: The man dies only to his wife (see Ruth 1:3) and the wife dies only to her husband; for it says, "When I came from Paddan, Rachel died (of suffering) to me in the land of Canaan." ‖ Babylonian Talmud Sanhedrin 22A: R. Samuel b. Nahman (ca. 260) said, "For everything there is a replacement, except for the wife of one's youth (cf. Isa 54:6)."

e. Tosefta Berakot 7.18 (16): R. Judah (ca. 150) said, "Three blessings must be said every day: Blessed (be God), for he has not created me as a *goy* (non-Israelite)!; Blessed, for he has not created me as a woman!; Blessed, for he has not created me as an ignorant person! Blessed, for he has not created me as a *goy*: 'For all the *goyim* are like nothing before him' (Isa 40:17). Blessed, for he has not created me as a woman; because a woman is not obligated to the fulfillments of the commandments[291] (see § Gal 3:28, #1, B). Blessed, for he has not created me as an ignorant person; for an ignorant person does not shy away from sin." — Parallels are found in y. Ber. 9.13B.48 and b. Menaḥ. 43B; in the latter passage, R. Meir (ca. 150) is the author. ‖ Babylonian Talmud Niddah 31B: R. Isaac (ca. 300) said that R. Ammi (ca. 300) said, "When a male child comes into the world, peace comes into the world.... When a male child comes into the world, his bread comes (with him) in his hand ...; when a female, nothing comes with it...." R. Simeon b. Yohai (ca. 150) said, "... (At the birth of a male child) all feel joy ...; (at that of a female) all feel sorrow." ‖ A baraiata

291. S-B: Krauß rightly says that this implies an unmistakable contempt for women (*Talmudische Archäologie* [Leipzig: Fock, 1910], 2:48). See at § Gal 3:28, #1, B, β, n. *h*.

in b. Qidd. 82B: Rabbi († 217?) said, "... The world cannot exist without male and female children. Happy is the one whose children are male, and woe to the one whose children are female!" – In b. Sanh. 100B the same appears as a saying of the Rabbanan. ‖ Sirach 42:9ff. is cited in b. Sanh. 100B in the following way: "A daughter is a deceptive treasure for her father; due to concern about her he cannot sleep at night: in her childhood she might be seduced; in her youth (from 12–12.5 years old) she might engage in fornication; when she is nubile, she might not get married. If she is married, she might receive no children; when she has grown old, she might become a sorceress." ‖ Babylonian Talmud Šabbat 33B: (R. Simeon b. Yohai [ca. 150] said,) "The mind of women is frivolous." – The same is found in as a baraita from the school of Elijah in b. Qidd. 80B. In S. Eli. Rab., this saying is not found; however, Friedmann in his *Einleitung* (p. 45) refers to the passage that is related in content, S. Eli. Rab. 21 (122), where it says: "A woman gives herself up for a perishable meal and commits a sin and says, 'It does not matter (it is nothing)!' As it says, 'Our skin glows like an oven from the fires of hunger' (Lam 5:10); and further it says, 'Women were sapped in Zion' (Lam 5:11). What do these passages have to do with each other (since one follows the other)? It teaches you that as long as there is hunger in the world, a woman gives herself up and commits a sin and says, 'It does not matter!'" ‖ Babylonian Talmud Soṭah 3.4: R. Joshua (ca. 90) said, "A woman prefers 1 *qab* (a small measure for foodstuff) in unrestrainedness than 9 *qabs* in abstinence." – This Mishnah is cited in b. Ketub. 62B. ‖ Midrash Ecclesiastes 7:26 (38A): "Her (a woman's) hands are chains" (Eccl 7:26). R. Eleazar (ca. 270) said, "If Scripture did not say of her, 'Her hands are chained' (by morals; this is how Eccl 7:26 is now interpreted, by understanding אסורים not as a substantive, but rather as a passive participle), she would seize a man on the street and say, 'Come and sleep with me!'" – A similar text is found anonymously in Num. Rab. 9 (152B). ‖ Babylonian Talmud Ketubbot 65A: It has been taught as a baraita: One cup is fine for a woman, two mean a desecration (for her), with three she invites with her mouth (to fornication), with four she herself requests a donkey on the three without any consideration. ‖ Genesis Rabbah 18 (12B): R. Joshua of Sikhnin (ca. 330) said in the name of R. Levi (ca. 300), "'He built' וַיִּבֶן, it is written (Gen 2:22), that is, he considered הִתְבּוֹנֵן (וַיִּבֶן thus interpreted = וַיָּבִין) from where he should create her. He said, 'I will not create her from the head (of Adam), lest she proudly raise her head; not from his eye, let she gawk all around; nor from his ear, lest she be an eavesdropper; nor from his mouth, lest she be talkative; now from his heart, lest she be envious (jealous); not from his hand, lest she touch everything, and not from his foot, lest she run about. Rather (I will create her) from a place that is hidden in Adam; even if the man is unclothed, that place will remain covered.' And with each single member that he created in her, he always said to her, '"Be a moral woman! Be a moral woman!" Nevertheless, "she disregarded all my counsel" (Prov 1:25). I did not create her from the head, and behold, she raises her head proudly, as it says, "They go about with an out-stretched neck" (Isa 3:16); nor from the eye, and behold, she gawks about, as it says, "And winking with the eyes" (Isa 3:16); nor from the ear, and behold, she is an eavesdropper, as it says, "Sarah eavesdropped at the entrance of the tent" (Gen 18:10); nor from the heart, and behold, she is envious (jealous), as it says, "Then Rachel became jealous of her sister"

(Gen 30:1); nor from the hand, and behold, she touches everything, as it says, "Then Rachel stole the *terafim*" (touching leads to stealing) (Gen 31:19); nor from the foot, and behold, she runs about, as it says, "And Dinah went out" (Gen 34:1).'" — There is a parallel in Deut. Rab. 6 (203C). ‖ Genesis Rabbah 45 (28C): Our teachers said, "Four qualities are stated about women: they are sweet-toothed (greedy eaters), eager to eavesdrop, indolent, and jealous. Sweet-toothed: (this can be seen) from Eve, 'She took from its fruits and ate' (Gen 3:6); eager to eavesdrop: 'And Sarah eavesdropped' (Gen 18:10); indolent: 'Quickly, three *seahs* of zesty flour' (Abraham had to push for a hurry) (Gen 18:6); jealous, for it is written, 'Then Rachel became jealous of her sister' (Gen 30:1)." R. Judah b. Nahman (ca. 280, so read instead of b. Nehemiah) said, "Also defiant and talkative. Defiant: 'Then Sarai said to Abram, "The wrong done to me is your fault"' (Gen 16:5); and talkative: 'And Miriam and Aaron spoke against Moses' (Num 12:1)." R. Levi (ca. 300) said, "Also thieving, as it says, 'Then Rachel stole the *terafim*' (Gen 31:19), and running about: 'And Dinah went out' (Gen 34:1)." — A parallel with a different authorial attribution can be found in Deut. Rab. 6 (203C). ‖ Babylonian Talmud Qiddušin 49B: Ten *qabs* of gossip (talkativeness) came down to the world; women received nine of them and the rest of the world one. — "Women are talkative" is also found in b. Ber. 48B. ‖ Midrash Esther 1:22 (91A): "He sent letters into all the king's territories ..., that every man should be lord in his house" (Esth 1:22). R. Huna (ca. 350) said, "Ahasuerus had a perverse mind. In ordinary life, if a man wants to eat lentils and his wife wants to eat chickpeas, can he force her? Does she not do what she wants?" (so according to Matthenoth Kehunna). ‖ Mishnah ʾAbot 2.7: (Hillel [ca. 20 BCE]) said, "... Many women, much sorcery." — Tractate Sopherim 15 toward the end: R. Simeon b. Yohai (ca. 150) taught: "The most virtuous among women is a sorceress." — The same is found in y. Qidd. 4.66B.32; see also above in n. *e* Sir 42:9ff. according to b. Sanh. 100B.

5:26: So that he might sanctify her, cleansing her by a bath of water.

See the washing and adorning of the bride for her husband at § Matt 9:15 B, n. *c* and n. *i*.

5:27: So that he himself might present the church to himself as a glorious one that has no spots or wrinkles ..., but rather that she may be holy and without blemish.

1. ἔνδοξος "beautiful, glorious." — In a self-praise the community of Israel says of itself in Midr. Song. 1:5 (87B.2, 24): "I am black, but beautiful" (Song 1:5). The community of Israel says, "I am black in my own eyes, but beautiful in the eyes of my creator; as it says, 'Are you not like the sons of the Cushites? But to me you are sons of Israel' (so the midr. interprets Amos 9:7). 'You are like the sons of the Cushites in your own eyes, but to me you are like sons of Israel,' says Yahweh...." R. Levi b. Hayyetah (ca. 350) interpreted (Song 1:5) in a threefold way. "'I (the community of Israel) am black,' namely all days of the week; but I am beautiful on the Sabbath. 'I am black,' namely all days of the year; but I am beautiful on the Day of Atonement.... 'I am black,' namely in this world; but I am beautiful in the future world."

2. ῥυτίς "wrinkle" = קֶמֶט (from קָמַט = to pull together); for an example, see b. B. Meṣ. 87A at § Rom 4:19 B.

3. ἁγία = קְדוֹשָׁה. — The community עֵדָה of Israel bears this epithet in, for example, Exod. Rab. 21 (84A): R. Meir (ca. 150) said, "God said to Moses, 'The Israelites do not need to pray before me. If I created the dry land for the sake of the first man, who was one single person; as it says, "The waters under heaven shall be gathered ..." (Gen 1:9). How much more does this go for the holy community עדה קדושה, which will say before me, "He is my God, in whom I boast!" (Exod 15:2).'" — For a smaller religious community that bore the designation "holy community, see § Matt 16:18, #3, n. *b*.

4. ἄμωμος. — For bodily flaws in a woman that undid an engagement and marriage in certain circumstances, see § John 2:1 A, #3, D, n. *u*.

5:31: On Gen 2:24, see § Matt 19:5 and § 1 Cor 5:1 B, #2, n. *f*.

5:33: Yet the woman, that she fear her husband.

φοβεῖσθαι "to fear" = to have reverence for. Babylonian Talmud Qiddušin 31A: The son of a widow asked R. Eliezer (ca. 90), "If my father says 'Give me water to drink,' and if my mother says 'Give me water to drink,' who takes priority?" He answered him, "Leave reverence כָּבוֹד before your mother and render reverence before your father, for you and your mother are obligated to revere your father." ‖ See b. Ker. 6.9 at § Matt 15:4, first third. ‖ On the love of a woman, see the archetype of the women of the vineyard in Pesiq. 147A: In Zayedan (= Zidon) it happened that someone took a wife, and he waited with her 10 years without her giving birth (this was considered grounds for divorce). They came to R. Simeon b. Yohai (ca. 150) and wanted to get divorced. He (the husband) said to her, "Every article of value that I have in my house, take it and go to the house of your father!" R. Simeon b. Yohai said to them, "Just as you were bound to each other with food and drink (at the wedding banquet), so too you may be divorced from each other with only food and drink." What did she do? She prepared a large meal and gave him more than enough to drink. Then she beckoned to her servant-girls and said to them, "Carry him to the house of my father!" At midnight he woke from his sleep; he said to them, "Where am I?" They said to him, "Did you not say to me, 'Every valuable item you have in my house, take it and remove it and then go to the house of your father?' And so it happened: I have no more beautiful item of value than you!" When Ben Yohai heard this, he prayed for her and she was remembered (with the blessing of children). — There is a parallel in Midr. Song. 1:4 (87A).

6:1: Children, obey your parents in the Lord.

On the question of when a child did not have to obey its parents, see SLev 19:3 (344A) at § Matt 15:4 A, near the end. ‖ Babylonian Talmud Baba Meṣiʿa 2.10: If his father (who is a priest) says to his son, "Make yourself unclean!" or if he says to him, "Do not give back (what you have found)!," he should not obey him. — See the baraita in b. B. Meṣ. 32A: If his father says to him, "Make yourself unclean!" or if he says to him, "Do not give back!," how do we know that he should not obey him? Because it says, "Everyone should nurture reverence for his mother and his father, and you shall keep my Sabbaths, I am Yahweh" (Lev 19:3);

you are all obligated to keep reverence before me (this is why the commandment pertaining to God precedes the commandment about parents).

6:2 A: Honor your father and mother.

On the 4th commandment, see § Matt 15:4–6 and § Matt 22:36, #2, n. *c*. Here we can add a few passages that were not used there.

See Sib. Or. 3:584ff. at § Rom 1:26 A, #2, n. *a*. ‖ Babylonian Talmud Qiddušin 31A: Ulla the elder (ca. 260?) gave a presentation at the entrance to the house of the patriarch: "What does 'All kings of the earth praised you, Yahweh, when they heard the words of your mouth' (Ps 138:4) mean? It does not say 'the word' your mouth, but rather 'the words' (= the ten commandments) of your mouth. When God said, 'I am Yahweh, your God,' and 'You shall have no other God' (Exod 20:2f.), the nations of the world said, 'He does this for his own honor!' Yet when he said, 'Honor your father and your mother' (Exod 20:12), they changed their mind and accepted the earlier words." – Something similar is found in a longer exposition in Exod. Rab. 8 (148D) and Pesiq. Rab. 23/24 (121A). ‖ Seder Eliyahu Rabbah 24 (134): "Remember the day of rest, to sanctify it" (Exod 20:8); "Honor your father and your mother" (Exod 20:12). What does this passage have to do with the other (since they stand alongside each other)? It means to teach you that as long as a person honors his father and his mother, no sin comes over him; for it says, "Blessed is the man who does this ..., who keeps מחללו the Sabbath" (Isa 56:2); do not read מחללו = "not to desecrate it," but rather: מָחַל לוֹ = "who is forgiven." ... A person who honors his father and his mother does not suffer terrible disasters (see Isa 29:13) .... "Honor your father and your mother" (Exod 20:12), and "You shall not murder" (Exod 20:13). Why do these passages stand alongside each other? It means to teach you the following: if a person has a lot of food in his house and he does not give any food to his father and his mother in their old age, it is as if he had been a murderer his whole life, as if he had slaughtered souls before God. Therefore, it says, "Honor your father and your mother" and "You shall not murder."

6:2 B and 6:3: This is the first commandment with a promise: "So it may go well with you and you may live long on earth."

A baraita in b. Qidd. 39B: R. Jacob (ca. 170) said, "You do not have any commandment that is written in the Torah and on its page there is a promise of recompense that is not connected with the resurrection of the dead. In the case of honoring father and mother (i.e., in the 4th commandment) it is written, 'So the days of your life may be long and it may go well for you' (Deut 5:16). In the case of setting free a mother bird it is written ..."; see § Matt 6:27. ‖ Sifre Deuteronomy 32:47 § 336 (141A): "By this word you will live long" (Deut 32:47). This is one of the things, which, if one does them, he enjoys their fruits in this world and length of days in the future world. Clearly it is said here (Deut 32:47) about the study of the Torah. And concerning giving honor to parents, where? Scripture teaches, "Honor your father and your mother, so that the days of your life may be long" (Exod 20:12).... For the whole, see b. Qidd. 40A. ‖ See y. Qidd. 1.61B.58 at § Matt 22:36, #2, n. *c*. ‖ Deuteronomy Rabbah 6 (203A): Scripture says, "Lest you weigh the way of life, her (wisdom's = Torah's) ways are faltering, lest you have insight" (so Prov 5:6 according to the midr.). What does "Lest you weigh the way of life" mean? R. Abba b. Kahana (ca. 310) said, "God says, 'You shall not sit and weigh the commandments of the Torah; as it says, "He weighed the mountains with a scale" (Isa 40:12). You should not say, "Since this commandment is great (important, heavy), I will do it, because its recompense is large; and since that commandment is small (light), I will not do it."' What did God (therefore) do? He did not make known to human beings what the recompense is for each individual commandment, so that they would do all the commandments in simplicity. How do we know this? Because it says, 'Her ways are faltering (uncertain), lest you have insight' .... So too God did not make known the recompense for the commandments, except for two commandments the heaviest among the heavy and the lightest among the light: showing honor to parents is the heaviest among the heavy, and the recompense for it is length of the days of one's life (see Exod 20:12). And the lightest is releasing the mother bird; and what is the recompense for this? Length of the days of one's life (see Deut 22:7)." — Parallels are found in y. Pe'ah 1.15D.9; y. Qidd. 1.61B.41; Tanḥ. עקב 6A; TanḥB עקב § 3 (8B); Pesiq. Rab. 23/24 (121B); Midr. Ps. 9 § 3 (41A). ‖ Seder Eliyahu Rabbah 24 (134): Look, everyone who wishes for days and years and prosperity and fortune and life in this world and long life in the future world, which has no end, let him do the will of his Father in heaven and the will of his father and his mother; as it says, "Honor your father and your mother, so that your days may be long" (Exod 20:12).

6:4 A: Fathers, do not provoke your children.

Babylonian Talmud Šabbat 10B: Rabba b. Mehasia said that Rab Hama b. Guria (ca. 270) said that Rab († 247) said, "Let no one ever distinguish between one son and the other sons (by favoring him more than the others); for it was because of a garment worth two *selas*, which Jacob gave more to Joseph rather than his other sons, that his brothers became jealous of him. And then it ended up that our ancestors went down to Egypt."

6:4 B: But rather raise them in the discipline and correction of the Lord.

Among a father's obligations to his son, there was, among others, the requirement to have him study the Torah; see t. Qidd. 1.11 (336) at § John 2:1 A, #3, n. *c* and b. Qidd. 29A at § Acts 18:3, #1. Women (mothers) were exempt from this duty; see m. Qidd. 1.7 at § Gal 3:28, #1, B, β, n. *i* and b. Qidd. 29B at § 1 Cor 14:35 A toward the end. ‖ Babylonian Talmud Qiddušin 29B: How do we know that he has to teach him Torah? Because it says, "Teach them to your children" (Deut 11:19). ‖ Babylonian Talmud Qiddušin 30A: He has to teach him Scripture, but he does not have to teach him Mishnah (the material of the tradition). And Raba († 352) said, "'Scripture': this is the Torah." — ‖ On the praise of a good upbringing, see b. Yebam. 62B at § John 2:1 A, #2, n. *c*. ‖ Exodus Rabbah 1 (65A): "He who withholds his stick hates his son; but he who loves him visits him with chastisement" (Prov 13:24). ... This is supposed to teach you that anyone who withholds chastisement from his son, so that he ultimately falls into a bad way, hates him. (For examples, the text then names Ishmael, Esau, and Absalom; then follows: Bad upbringing תַּרְבּוּת רָעָה in someone's house is worse than the war of Gog and Magog; see b. Ber. 7B at § Acts 4:25 B.) Yet when someone chastises his son, he increases in love for his father and honors him; as it says, "Chastise your son, and he will refresh you" (Prov 29:17). And it further says, "Chastise your son, for there is (still) hope" (Prov 19:18) … (here vaunting reference is made to the strict chastisement in the house of the patriarchs). — There is a parallel in Tanḥ. שמות toward the beginning.

6:5 A: You servants (slaves).

See the excursus "The Nature of Ancient Jewish Slavery."

6:5 B: As to Christ.

This is similar to the principle in Tanḥ. בשלח 85B: How do we know that reverence before one's teacher is worth just as much as reverence before God? It says, "Then Joshua, the son of Nun, the servant of Moses from his youth, arose and said, 'My lord Moses, restrain them!'" (Num 11:28). He said, "My lord Moses, as God restrains them, so you can restrain them too." ‖ See b. Sanh. 110A at § Matt 10:40 A, #2, end.

6:9 A: Leaving aside threats.

On the treatment of slaves, see the excursus "The Nature of Ancient Jewish Slavery."

6:9 B: There is no respect of the person with him (see § Rom 2:11).

6:11: In order to endure the intrigues of the devil.

1. στῆναι = עָמַד. — Mishnah ʾAbot 5.3: Our father Abraham was tried with ten temptations, and he stood up in them all יָעֲמַד בְּכֻלָּם.

2. Against the intrigues of the devil, see § Matt 4:1 B, #3.

6:12: We do not fight with flesh and blood, but rather against the authorities, against the powers, against the rulers of this darkness, against the spirit of wickedness in the heavenly places.

1. σὰρξ καὶ αἷμα = בָּשָׂר וָדָם, see § Matt 16:17 B.

2. ἀρχαί and ἐξουσίαι are not here, as in Eph 1:21, designations for classes of angels, but rather for classes of demons. On the kingdom of the devil, see § Matt 25:41 B; see also § Matt 12:24, #3. — Martyrdom and Ascension of Isaiah 2:2: "Manasseh served Satan, his angels, and powers." ‖ Jubilees 49:2: "All the forces of Mastema (= Satan) were sent to kill all the firstborn in the land of Egypt." — See further in the excursus "Ancient Jewish Demonology," #3 (Structure of the Demon World).

3. κοσμοκράτορες τοῦ σκότους τούτου. — On the devil as κοσμοκράτωρ, see § John 12:31, #1. — Satan as the angel of death = darkness חֹשֶׁךְ, see Lev. Rab. 18 (118A) at § Matt 4:1 B, #4, n. *a*. — A שׂי החושך "prince of darkness" is mentioned several times in Pesiq. Rab.; yet this does not refer to Satan, but rather to the archangel who is appointed over the darkness. — Pesiqta Rabbati 20 (95A): When God created his world, he said to the prince of darkness,

"Depart from me, for I will create the world in light." — Similarly, Pesiq. Rab. 203A.10. — See further in the excursus "Ancient Jewish Demonology," #5 (Demons of darkness).

4. ἐν τοῖς ἐπουρανίοις, see § Eph 2:2 A.

6:13 A: The armor of God.

Wisdom 5:17–20: "He (God) will take his zeal ζῆλον as armor πανοπλίαν and make the creation into a weapon to repel his enemies. He will put on righteousness δικαιοσύνην as a suit of armor θώρακα and put on candid judgment κρίσιν ἀνυπόκριτον as a helmet κόρυθα. He will take holiness ὁσιότητα as an unconquerable shield ἀσπίδα, and he will sharpen his strict anger ὀργήν into a sword ῥομφαίαν." — See the oldest model in Isa 59:17: "He put on righteousness צְדָקָה like a suit of armor שִׁרְיָן, and the helmet of salvation כּוֹבַע יְשׁוּעָה was on his head, and he put on clothes of vengeance בִּגְדֵי נָקָם as a garment and wrapped zeal קִנְאָה around him as a mantle." — Septuagint: καὶ ἐνεδύσατο δικαιοσύνην ὡς θώρακα καὶ περιέθετο περικεφαλαίαν σωτηρίου ἐπὶ τῆς κεφαλῆς καὶ περιεβάλετο ἱμάτιον ἐκδικήσεως καὶ τὸ περιβόλαιον αὐτοῦ. — The targum has turned the metaphor of armor into nonpictorial language. — In rabbinic literature there is also seldom mention of spiritual armor. It says generally in y. Qidd. 3.63D.41: R. Hanina set up his weapons מתרס כליו against R. Haggai (ca. 330). — Here, the objections or counterarguments to be raised are described as weapons. — Similarly, the scholars are called בעלי תְּרִיסִין "people of the shield" = shielded ones, because the halakic discussions are thought of as מלחמת תורה = "a battle of Torah." Babylonian Talmud Berakot 27B: (Rabban Gamaliel, ca. 90) said to him (a student, ostensibly R. Simeon ben Yohai), "Wait until the shielded ones come into the house of learning. When the shielded ones had come, the questioner arose and asked ...." — See details further below.

6:13 B: On the evil day.

ἡμέρα πονηρά = יוֹם רַע "fatal day" (Amos 6:3), plural יְמֵי רַע (Ps 49:6; 94:13); Aram. יוֹם בִּישׁ "evil day," opposite: יוֹם טָב "good day."[a] — The "fatal days" in Ps 49:6 are once interpreted to refer to the divine judgment in the hereafter,[b] an explanation that is inappropriate for Eph 6:13. With "evil day" the apostle seems to be thinking of a time when the devil will display extraordinary activity to harm believers. In that case, here belong the sayings from rabbinic writings according to which Satan uses times of danger in particular to raise accusations against human beings.[c]

a. Babylonian Talmud Qiddušin 39B: One (= God) prepares for him a good day and an evil day יום טב ויום ביש.

b. Babylonian Talmud ʿAbodah Zarah 18A: R. Simeon b. Laqish (ca. 250) said, "What does '(Why should I fear in the days of evil, when) the sin of my heels surrounds me' (so Ps 49:6 according to the midr.) mean? The sins that a person treads on with his heels (= that he thinks are nothing) will surround him on the day of (divine) judgment."

c. Jerusalem Talmud Šabbat 2.5B.12: R. Hiyya b. Ba (ca. 280) said, "It is written, 'When you move out to camp against your enemies, protect yourself from every evil' (Deut 23:10). If he does not go out, does he not have to protect himself? Rather, it follows from this that Satan accuses only in the hour of danger." R. Ahai b. Jacob (ca. 325) said, "It is written, 'If harm befalls him on the way' (Gen 42:38). Not in the house? Rather, it follows from this that Satan accuses only in the hour of danger." R. Bisna (ca. 340) said in the name of R. Layya (= Hela, ca. 310), "It is written, 'This day is a day of tribulation and chastisement and slander' (Isa 37:3). Not another day? Rather, it follows from this that Satan accuses only in the hour of danger." R. Aibo (Aibu) b. Naggari (ca. 320) said, "It is written, 'If he is judged, let him emerge as wicked' (Ps 109:7). It does not say, 'Let him emerge as "righteous,"' but rather as 'wicked'; it only follows from this that Satan accuses only in the hour of danger." R. Ba b. Bina (ca. 250) said, "It is prohibited to go over a board that is laid from one roof to another, even if it is so wide. Why? Because it follows from this that Satan accuses only in the hour of danger." — The saying of R. Aha b. Jacob is also found in Gen. Rab. 91 (58A), under the name of R. Eliezer b. Jacob (ca. 150), which according to Bacher arose from an erroneous decomposition of the abbreviation רא"בי.[292] — See also § Matt 4:1 B, #3, B, n. *d* and § Eph 4:27.

6:14 A: Having girded your loins with truth.

Babylonian Talmud Berakot 16B (in a prayer): May it be your will that you gird yourself תתאזר with grace. — See the whole passage at § Luke 24:49, #2. ‖ Numbers Rabbah 2 (138A): Immediately (after the sin with the golden calf) Moses girded הגר his loins with prayer. — The whole at § Rom 9:26, #1. — ‖ In his admonition, the apostle might have been thinking of Isa 11:5: Faithfulness will be the girdle for his (the shoot of Jesse) loins. — Septuagint: καὶ ἀληθείᾳ εἰλημένος τὰς πλευράς. — The targum is nonpictorial: "Those who practice faithfulness will be near him."

6:14 B: And having put on the breastplate of righteousness.

Isaiah 59:17: "He put on righteousness as armor." — Wisdom 5:18: ἐνδύσεται θώρακα δικαιοσύνην, see above at § 6:13 A. ‖ Babylonian Talmud Baba Batra 9B: R. Eleazar (ca. 270) said, "What does 'He will put on mercy (so the midr.) as armor' (Isa 59:17) mean? It means: Just as this armor consists of nothing but individual scales that are united to become one great suit of armor, so too benevolence (mercy, צְדָקָה) consists of nothing but individual *perutot* (pennies) that are united to become one great sum."

6:16: Taking up the shield of faith.

In Wis 5:19, ὁσιότης is described as ἀσπίς; see above at § 6:13 A. — In m. ʾAbot 4.11, repentance and good works appear as a shield תְּרִיס = θυρεός against punishments; see the passage at § John 14:16, n. *e*.

6:17 A: Take the helmet of salvation.

Isaiah 59:17: כּוֹבַע יְשׁוּעָה = "helmet of salvation"; LXX: περικεφαλαίαν σωτηρίου. — In Wis 5:18—see above at § 6:13 A—candid judgment is called a κόρυς = helmet. ‖ *Beth ha-Mi-*

292. Bacher, *Die Agada der babylonischen Amoräer*, 138.12.

drash 3.73.17: In that hour God will adorn the Messiah with a crown and put the helmet of salvation כובע ישועה on his head and put splendor and glory on him and adorn him with clothes of glory and set him on a high mountain, to make it known to Israel and to make it heard with his voice: salvation is near קרבה ישועה!

6:17 B: The sword of the Spirit, which is the word of God.

In Wis 5:20—see above at § 6:13 A—wrath ὀργή is called a sword ῥομφαία. – The words of the Torah are compared with a sword in, for example, Tg. Song. 3:8: "The priests and Levites and all the tribes of Israel together held fast (in the days of Solomon) to the words of the Torah, which are like a sword חַרְבָּא, and handled it like heroes who are skilled in battle." ‖ Midrash Psalm 45 § 17 (136A): "Gird your sword around your hips, O hero" (Ps 45:4); this is Moses, who obtained the Torah, which is like a sword חֶרֶב. – See further passages at § Heb 4:12. – The fulfillments of the commandments can also be compared with a sword. Genesis Rabbah 97 (61B): R. Judah (ca. 150) said, "'With my sword and my bow' (Gen 48:22), that is, by fulfillments of the commandments מצות and good works."

6:18: Praying at all times.

See § Luke 18:1.

6:19: With the opening of my mouth.

TanḥumaB תבא § 1 (23A): R. Abbahu (ca. 300) said in the name of R. Yose b. Hanina (ca. 270), "How well it goes and how much opening of the mouth פִּתְחוֹן פֶּה for those who fulfill the commandments (by them being able to bring all their concerns before God with the certainty that they will be heard)!" ‖ Targum 1 Chronicles 17:25: "Therefore your servant found an opening of the mouth פִּתְחָא דְפוּמָא to pray before you." – See further at § Eph 4:27.

The Letter of Paul to the Philippians

1:6 A: He who began a good work in you will bring it to completion.

Genesis Rabbah 60 (37C): "Show grace to my lord Abraham" (Gen 24:12); if you have begun, complete it התחלתה גמור. R. Haggai (ca. 330) said in the name of R. Isaac (ca. 300), "Everyone needs (divine) grace; even Abraham, for whose sake grace prevails in the world, needed grace; as it says, 'Show grace to my lord Abraham' (Gen 24:12). If you have begun it, complete it." – This expression apparently had a proverbial character. ‖ Letter of Aristeas 195: "The king asked (in the table discussions) the next one what would be the highest (good) for his life. And he responded, 'The knowledge that God rules over everything and that in our best actions we do not carry out our decisions, but rather God completes τελειοῖ and guides everything with his power.'" See Let. Aris. 227, 239, 255.

1:6 B: Until the day of Christ Jesus.

The singular יוֹם הַמָּשִׁיחַ "day of the Messiah" is not found in rabbinic literature, though the plural יְמוֹת המ׳ is all the more frequent; examples are found everywhere in the excursus "This World, the Days of the Messiah, and the Future World." Only in the pseudepigrapha do we once find the term: "at the hour of his (the Messiah's) day"; see 4 Ezra 13:52 at § Luke 17:22.

1:11: To the honor and praise of God.

God's honor is the ultimate purpose of creation; see § Luke 2:14 A, as well as § Matt 5:16, #2. – Here reference may also be made to Num. Rab. 8 (148D): "I will honor those who honor me" (1 Sam 2:30). (Scripture) is speaking about proselytes: they honor מכבדים God by leaving their evil works and coming and fleeing under the wings of the Shekinah. It honors God (again) to teach you that everyone who makes his ways straight honors God; as it says, "Whoever presents thanks as an offering honors me rightly; and whoever opens up the path, him I will show the salvation of God with delight" (Ps 50:23). And further it says, "Give honor כָּבוֹד to Yahweh your God before he it makes dark ..."(Jer 13:16).

1:12: For the advancement of the gospel.

προκοπή "thriving, advancement, progress," see § 1 Tim 4:15, n. *a*. In the rabbinic writings פְּרוֹקְפֵּי or פְּרוֹקוֹפֵּי has the significance "distinction, dignity."

Genesis Rabbah 12 toward the end: "When Yahweh-Elohim made earth and heaven" (Gen 2:4; earth is named before heaven). Like a legion that first proclaimed the king as king. The king said, "Since this legion first proclaimed me as king, behold, I will give it a distinction פרוקפי that shall never depart from it." Likewise, God said, "Since the earth first did my will (in the gathering of the waters in Gen 1:9), behold, I will give it a distinction

פרוקפי that will never depart from it; this is what is written, 'He established the earth on its pillars so that it would never falter' (Ps 104:5)." There is a parallel in Midr. Ps. 93 § 2 (207A). – For further examples see Gen. Rab. 48 (30A); 90 (56D); Lev. Rab. 18 (118A); TanḥB ויהי § 10 (109A); Pesiq. Rab. 43 (180A); 14 (59A); 8 (29B).

1:13: In the whole praetorium.

On πραιτώριον see § Matt 27:27; in our passage it refers to the barracks of the imperial praetorian guard in the east of Rome (near the *porta viminalis*).

1:19: That it will turn out for my deliverance.

Job 13:16: הוּא לִי לִישׁוּעָה; targum: הוּא לִי לְפוּרְקָנָא "it will serve for my redemption, release"; LXX: τοῦτό μοι ἀποβήσεται εἰς σωτηρίαν.

1:23 A: To be with Christ (cf. § Luke 23:43).

1:23 B: For it is so much better.

Tobit 3:6: "For it is better for me to die than to live" διότι λυσιτελεῖ μοι ἀποθανεῖν ἢ ζῆν.

1:25: προκοπήν (see above at § Phil 1:12).

2:3: By virtue of humility.

On the praise of humility, see § Matt 5:3, #3 and § Matt 5:5, #1.

2:4: Each one not being mindful of his own affairs, but rather of those of others.

ʾAbot de Rabbi Nathan 17 toward the beginning: R. Yose (ca. 150) said, "Let your neighbor's fortune be as dear to you as your own. How so? If a student of the scholars enters your house, saying, 'Teach me!', teach him, if you have the possibility to teach; but if not, dismiss him immediately and do not accept any money. As it says, 'Do not say to your neighbor, "Go and come back and tomorrow I will give you," while it is with you (to give to him immediately)' (Prov 3:28)." – In later editions, after the first sentence, there is an insertion: As a person regards רואה (= is mindful of) his own fortune, so too he should regard his neighbor's fortune; and just as a person wishes that there be no evil slander expressed about his own fortune, so too he should wish that there be no evil slander expressed about his neighbor's fortune. ‖ Mishnah ʾAbot 5.10 at § Rom 5:6.

2:5: Keep this in your mind, as also (happened) in Christ Jesus.

Babylonian Talmud Soṭah 5A: Rab Joseph († 333) said, "Let a person always learn from the mind of his creator מדעת קונו; for look, God left all the (high) mountains and heights and made his Shekinah (divinity) dwell on Mount Sinai, and he left all fruit trees and made his Shekinah dwell in the thorn bush." (So a person should learn humility from God.)

2:6 A: When he was in the form of God.

The ancient synagogue knew nothing of a preexistent Messiah (see § John 1:1 A).

2:6 B: Did not consider being like God robbery.

The rejected ἁρπαγμός would have happened if Jesus Christ had forcefully snatched the κυριότης intended for him like a robber. See y. Hor. 3.47C.27, where R. Yose b. Bun (ca. 350) infers the following from "Sons of the fourth generation shall sit on the throne of Israel for you (Jehu)" (2 Kgs 10:30): "From then on there were no longer rightful kings in the Northern Kingdom, but rather they usurped dominion like robbers."

2:8: He humbled himself (see § Matt 23:12).

2:9: He gave him the name above every name.

Babylonian Talmud Sanhedrin 38B: (Rab Idit [ca. 325] said about the throne angel Metatron,) "His name is like the name of his Lord; for it says, 'My name is in him' (Exod 23:21)."

2:10f.: So that every knee ... should bow and every tongue confess that Jesus Christ is Lord.

On Isa 45:23, see § Rom 14:11. — The gentiles' falling before the Messiah is spoken about on the basis of Isa 49:23 in Midr. Ps. 2 § 3 (13A); see § Rom 3:9 A, #3, B, n. *h* toward the end.

2:15 A: In the midst of a crooked and twisted generation.

Septuagint Deuteronomy 32:5: γενεὰ σκολιὰ καὶ διεστραμμένη. Base text: דּוֹר עִקֵּשׁ וּפְתַלְתֹּל "a perverse and twisted generation." — Targum Onkelos: "A generation that changed its actions and was (itself) changed." — Targum Yerušalmi I: "A perverse (treacherous) generation that changed its actions and even the right order of the world was changed because of it." — The last words should be understood according to SDeut 32:5 § 308 (133B): "A perverse and twisted generation" (Deut 32:5). Moses said to the Israelites, "With the measure by which you measure," (God says), "I will measure you." And likewise, it says, "To the one who keeps himself pure you keep yourself pure, and to the one who is twisted you let yourself be found perverse" (2 Sam 22:27; Ps 18:27).

2:15 B: As bearers of light in the world.

φωστήρ = נֵר or מָאוֹר, which first denotes a bearer of light and then the light itself.

On נֵר see § Matt 5:14 A. — On מָאוֹר see b. Ḥag. 12A in a baraita: In the light אוֹר that God created on the first day, Adam looked and saw from one end of the world to the other. So R. Jacob (I, ca. 120; II, ca. 170). (This light, the primordial light, God is supposed to have withdrawn and hidden for the future.) Yet the scholars said, "(The light created on the 1st day) is identical with the bodies of light מְאוֹרוֹת (i.e., with the sun and moon), which were created on the 1st day, but which were hung up (fixed in the firmament) only on the 4th day." – However, מָאוֹר = "light" in y. Ḥag. 1.76C.37: "Since they have abandoned my Torah" (Jer 9:12). R. Hiyya b. Abba (ca. 280) said, "'They have abandoned me' (Jer 16:11): this I would have pardoned them for, if they only kept my Torah! For if they had abandoned me but kept my Torah, the light (see § Matt 16:6) that is in it would have brought them close to me again." – On the light of the Torah, see further at § John 1:1–4, #6.

2:16 A: The word of life.

דברות של חיים "words of life" in, for example, Exod. Rab. 29 (89A) at § Matt 7:13f., #2, end. – See also § Rom 3:1f., D.

2:16 B: That I did not run in vain nor toil in vain.

See Gen. Rab. 62 (39A) § Rom 5:1, #2, n. *l*.

2:21: They all search after their own affairs (cf. § 1 Cor 10:24).

2:25 A: Co-worker (see § Rom 16:3).

2:25 B: Your delegates (see § Rom 15:26, #1).

2:29: Hold such people in honor (see § John 12:43, #2).

2:30: Putting his life at risk.

παραβολεύεσθαι τῇ ψυχῇ perhaps = מסר למותא נפשיה, see Tg. Isa. 53:12 at § Matt 8:17, A, paragraph 2, or = מסר (נתן) נפשו, see § John 10:11 B and § Acts 15:26.

3:2: Look out for the dogs!

"Dogs" is used to describe the ignorant, the godless and non-Israelites. See examples at § Matt 15:26, n. *e*. Here we can refer also to the following passages.

a. Dogs = the godless. Targum Psalm 22:17: "For the godless, who are like dogs לְכַלְבַיָּא, have surrounded me."

b. Dogs = non-Israelites. 1 Enoch 90:4: "I looked until those sheep (= Israelites) were eaten by dogs, eagles, and harriers (= non-Israelites)." – Esther calls king Ahasuerus a dog; see b. Meg. 15B at § John 19:24, #3, D, Verse 2.

3:4: Confidence.

πεποίθησις = הַבְטָחָה, see § Rom 4:13 A, #2, n. *a*, paragraph 2.

3:5 A: With respect to circumcision on the eighth day.

ὀκταήμερος, see the excursus "Circumcision," #1.

3:5 B: (From) the tribe of Benjamin.

See § Rom 11:1 B. ‖ In Midr. Esth. 3:4 (94B), Mordecai boasts about his tribe Benjamin with the words, "I am the noblest of God (instead of איסגנטירין read אַוְגְּנִיסְטֵירוֹן = εὐγενέστερον); for all the tribal ancestors were born abroad, but my forefather was born in the land of Israel." — In Midr. Abba Gurion 3.4 the last sentence is missing.

3:5 C: A Hebrew from Hebrews.

Ἑβραῖος ἐξ Ἑβραίων = a Hebrew (Aramaic) speaking Jew from Hebrew (Aramaic) speaking Jews. — On equating Aramaic with Hebrew, see § John 5:2, #2.

3:7: Gain ... loss.

κέρδος — ζημία = שָׂכָר — הֶפְסֵד (Strack: הַפְסֵד), see m. ʾAbot 2.1 at § Matt 16:26 B, end.

3:8 A: Filth.

σκύβαλον perhaps טִנּוֹפֶת "waste, filth"; see also § 1 Cor 4:13. ‖ Numbers Rabbah 4 (141B): Like a king who had many threshing floors, and they were all garbage and טינופות and full of cockle.

3:8 B: So I may gain Christ.

κερδαίνω = הִשְׂתַּכֵּר, see t. Maʿaś. Š. 3.18 (92) at § Matt 10:39.

3:17: Example.

τύπος, perhaps סִימָן, סֵימָנָא, see § Luke 2:34 B and § Rom 5:14 B.

3:19 A: Whose end is destruction.

Numbers Rabbah 20 (189B): The angel of Yahweh said to Balaam, "'Go with your men' (Num 22:35); for your portion will be with them, and your end סופך will be to perish out of the world." ‖ Targum Yerušalmi I Numbers 24:20: "Their end will be that they will fall victim to destruction forever." — Targum Yerušalmi I Numbers 24:24: "They will fall victim to destruction forever." ‖ Targum Psalm 109:13: "His end will be destruction."

3:19 B: Whose god is the stomach.

The "men of God," who worship the true God, are in the Letter of Aristeas 139f. juxtaposed with the "men of food and drink and clothing"; see the passage at § Rom 4:2f., #1, n. *d*, β. — The same people are called בַּעֲלֵי הֲנָאָה "men of indulgence" in rabbinic literature.

Tosefta Soṭah 14.3 (320): Since the men of indulgence have increased, reverence for the Torah has ceased and justice was corrupted. — In b. Sanh. 26B, R. Eleazar (ca. 270) calls Shebna, Hezekiah's palace prefect, a בעל הנאה.

3:19 C: (Whose) honor is in their shame.

αἰσχύνη = קָלוֹן. – Jerusalem Talmud Ḥagigah 2.77C.23: R. Yose b. Hanina (ca. 270) said, "Whoever seeks his honor המתכבד in the disgrace קָלוֹן of his neighbor has no share in the future world."

3:20: Our citizenship is in heaven.

This is comparable to Midr. Ps. 18 § 3 (68B): "For the leader of music, of the servant of Yahweh" (Ps 18:1). Why did David say, "of the servant of Yahweh"? To teach you that God adds honor to everyone who turns from sin.... Likewise, you find it with David: before he had turned from that deed (of adultery), he was not enrolled in the upper host אִיסְטְרַטְיָא שֶׁל מַעְלָה; but after he had repented, he was enrolled in the upper host and called "servant of God."

4:3 A: True Syzygus.

A genuine Syzygus, since his name means what he himself in fact was to the apostle, namely a "yoke-companion," that is, a co-worker. – Similar interpretations of proper names are frequent in rabbinic literature.

In b. Giṭ. 7A Rab Huna († 297) interprets the name of Rab Hisda († 309): "'Grace' (חִיסְדָּא) is your name, and 'lovely' חִסְדָּאִין are your words." ‖ Babylonian Talmud Nedarim 66B: Someone said to his wife, "I pledge that you shall not have any benefit from me until you prove to R. Ishmael b. Yose (ca. 180) (so read instead of R. Simeon b. Yose) that you have something beautiful in you." R. Ishmael b. Yose said to them, "Perhaps her head is beautiful!" It was answered, "It is round. Maybe her hair is beautiful! It is like strands of flax. Maybe her eyes are beautiful! They are narrow (slitted). Maybe her ears are beautiful! They are doubled (very big?). Maybe her nose is beautiful! It is swollen (clogged). Maybe her lips are beautiful! They are thick. Maybe her neck is beautiful! It is sunken. Maybe her stomach is beautiful! It is swollen. Maybe her feet are beautiful! They are wide like those of a goose. Maybe her name is beautiful! 'Likhlukhith' (i.e., dirt) is her name." Then he said, "She has been named 'Likhlukhith' beautifully, because she is soiled with bodily flaws. Then he undid his vow." ‖ See b. Meg. 12B at § Col 4:3.

4:3 B: Whose names are in the book of life (see § Luke 10:20, #1).

4:4: Rejoice in the Lord at all times.

The great weight placed on a joyful disposition comes to expression in the statement that the holy spirit dwells only with a joyful person; see b. Pesaḥ. 117A at § Rom 14:17 and y. Sukkah 5.55A.42 in the excursus "The Feast of Tabernacles," IV, n. *p*.

4:5: Let your gentle nature be recognized by all people.

R. Judah (ca. 150) emphasized about the Messiah particularly that he will be gentle רַךְ with Israel; see SDeut § 1 (65A) at § Matt 1:21 B, #2, n. *b*.

4:6: Do not worry about anything.

On worrying, see § Matt 6:25–34.

4:7: The peace of God, which exceeds all understanding.

Mishnah ʿUqṣin 3.12, which is also the concluding saying of the Mishnah: R. Simeon b. Halapta (ca. 190) said, "God found no other (better) vessel that could hold a blessing for Israel than peace; as it says, 'Yahweh will bestow strength on his people; Yahweh will bless his people with peace' (Ps 29:11)." — On the glorification of peace, see § Matt 5:9, #1 and § Luke 2:14 B.

4:8: If there is any praise.

Mishnah ʾAbot 2.1: Rabbi († 217?) said, "What is the right way to act that a person should select? Any action that is an adornment תִּפְאֶרֶת (honor, praise) for the one who does it, and which is reckoned to him by people as an adornment."

4:9: The God of peace (see § Rom 15:33).

4:15: With respect to a reckoning about giving and receiving.

1. δόσις καὶ λῆμψις = מַתַּת וְלֶקַח (in Sirach) or = מַשָּׂא וּמַתָּן (in rabbinic literature); here, מַתַּת (מִתַּת?) and מַתָּן = δόσις = giving = sale, and לֶקַח or מַשָּׂא = λῆμψις = receiving = purchase; both expressions together, though, paraphrase the concept "trade," "business,"[a] and then in a broader sense also = "association, dealings with people."[b] — The corresponding verbs are נָשָׂא וְנָתַן, Aram. נְסַב וִיהַב or שְׁקַל וּטְרָא = to give and receive = to do business,[c] and in a figurative sense also = "to deal with," for example, in discussions in the house of learning.[d]

a. Sirach 42:7: "Giving and receiving (sale and purchase), let everything happen in writing" מַתַּת וְלֶקַח הַכֹּל בִּכְתָב; the Greek: καὶ δόσις καὶ λῆψις πάντα ἐν γραφῇ. — Greek Sirach 41:19: "(Be ashamed) of a berating fit of anger in receiving and giving (= in business)." This is missing in Hebrew Sirach. ‖ Babylonian Talmud Berakot 17A: (Rab [† 247] said,) "In the future (= transcendent) world ... there is no receiving and giving" משא ומתן = "there is no trade and change." — See the whole passage at § Matt 22:30 A. ‖ In b. Šabb. 89A, God asks the angels, "Is there among you receiving and giving" (= commercial transactions) משא ומתן? ‖ Babylonian Talmud Šabbat 120A: There is no contradiction: the one (that the Jerusalemites were reliable) pertains to the words of the Torah; the other (that they were not reliable) pertains to receiving and giving במשא ובמתן (= trade and change). — The same is found in b. Ḥag. 14A. — For further examples, see b. Pesaḥ. 49B; b. Taʿan. 12B; b. Meg. 6B; b. Qidd. 35A; b. Tem. 116A.

b. Babylonian Talmud Yoma 86A: If someone studies Scripture and the Mishnah and deals subserviently with the scholars, if his dealings משאו ומתנו with people happen in gentleness, what do people say about him? — See the whole passage at § Matt 5:16, #2.

c. Babylonian Talmud Šabbat 31A: Raba († 352) said, "If one (God) brings a person into judgment (in the hereafter), one says to him, 'Did you receive and give (= do business) נשאת ונתת with integrity?'" ‖ Mishnah Pe'ah 8.9: If someone owns 50 *zuz* and conducts business נושא ונותן (receives and gives) with them, he should not receive from the poor box. ‖ Genesis Rabbah 77 (49C): R. Hiyya the elder (ca. 200) and R. Simeon b. Rabbi (ca. 220) received and gave in business נסבין ויהבין בפרגמטיא = they made a business transaction. ‖ Babylonian Talmud Baba Meṣiʿa 64A: What is the case if there is a person who came from somewhere and with whom no one had done any business dealings לא שקיל וטרי (literally: had not received and given)?

d. Babylonian Talmud Ḥagigah 11B: If two (students) sit before their teacher, the one deals with שקיל וטרי (= receives and gives) his teacher, while the other inclines his ear to learn. Yet if there are three, the one deals with שקיל וטרי his teacher, while the other two deal with each other שקלו וטרו, so that they do not know what their teacher said. ‖ Targum 1 Chronicles 4:10: "Jabez prayed to the God of Israel thus, 'If you bless me with sons and make my territory wide with students, and if your hand is with me in dealings (disputing, במשקל ומטרא, in receiving and giving) and you make peers for me ....'"; see b. Tem. 116A. ‖ Midrash Song of Songs 3:6 (105B): R. Huna (ca. 350) said, "In that hour (of wrestling with Jacob) the angel said, 'I will not make known to him whom he is up against נסיב ויהיב (receives and gives).'" — Further examples are found in Tg. Song. 3:8; b. Soṭah 7B.

2. λόγος "reckoning" = חֶשְׁבּוֹן, see § Matt 18:23.

4:17: Yet I wish for the fruit that will become abundant for your account.

On καρπός see § Matt 7:16 A and § Matt 12:33. — The καρπός that the apostle wants to accrue to the account of the Philippians on the receiving end is the recompense of blessing that arises for them from their giving and sacrificing for the sake of the apostle.

4:18: The aroma of a fragrance, a sacrifice, pleasant, pleasing to God.

ὀσμὴ εὐωδίας = רֵיחַ נִיחֹחַ, see § Eph 5:2. — On describing works pleasing to God as "sacrifices," see Heb 13:15, 16.

The Letter of Paul to the Colossians

1:6: Bearing fruit and growing.

καρποφορούμενον καὶ αὐξανόμενον corresponds to the compound פָּרָה וְרָבָה "to be fruitful and multiply." However, in rabbinic literature this is used only in a literal, not a figurative, sense. For the latter meaning, "to bear fruit" is rendered with עָשָׂה פֵּירוֹת.

Babylonian Talmud Qiddušin 40A: A sin that bears fruit שעושה פירות (that has bad consequences, gives occasion for new sins) has fruits (punitive consequences for the perpetrator in this world); but if it does not bear fruit, it has no fruits (it remains unpunished in this world, so that the sinner's punitive capital קֶרֶן may become as large as possible in the next world). — See also the citations at § Matt 7:16 A and § Matt 12:33.

1:12: Share in the inheritance of the saints.

Deuteronomy 10:9 coordinates חֵלֶק וְנַחֲלָה "portion and inheritance" alongside each other. — Septuagint: μερὶς καὶ κλῆρος. — Targum Onkelos and Yerušalmi I: חוּלָק וְאַחְסָנָא "portion and property" (possession).

Daniel 12:13: "Arise for your lot" לגורלך. ‖ 1 Enoch 48:7: "He (the Messiah) preserves the lot of the righteous." ‖ Babylonian Talmud Šabbat 118B: R. Yose (ca. 150) said, "May my portion חלקי (one day) be with those who hold three meals on the Sabbath." R. Yose said, "May my portion be with those who daily say the Hallel in its entirety...." R. Yose said, "May my portion be with those who pray with the coming of the twilight (mornings and evenings)...." R. Yose said, "May my portion be with those who die from an abdominal disease (this disease was thought to have atoning power because of its painfulness)." R. Yose said, "May my portion be with those who die by means of a fulfillment of a commandment." R. Yose said, "May my portion be with those who enter into the Sabbath in Tiberias (here the Sabbath began early), and with those who exit from the Sabbath in Sepphoris (here the Sabbath ended as late as possible)." R. Yose said, "May my portion be with those who cause people to sit (remain) in the house of learning, and not with those who cause people to stand up (go away) in the house of learning." R. Yose said, "May my portion be with those who collect (raise) alms, and not with those who distribute alms (since they easily make mistakes in doing so)." R. Yose said, "May my portion be with the one who is under suspicion while there is nothing (no guilt) in him." ‖ Jerusalem Talmud Berakot 4.7D.57: R. Yohanan († 279) used to pray (after ending the Prayer of Eighteen Benedictions): "May it be your will, Yahweh, our God, ... that we rejoice over our portion בחלקינו in the garden of Eden...." — In the parallel passage in b. Ber. 16B the closing words are: "That you give (us) our portion in the garden of Eden."

1:13: From the power of darkness (cf. § Eph 6:12).

1:15 A: Of the invisible God (see § Rom 1:20 A).

1:15 B: The firstborn before all creation.

1. In rabbinic literature, the following are designated as "firstling" רֵאשִׁית or "firstborn" בְּכוֹר: the Torah, Adam, Jacob, Israel, and the Messiah (see § Rom 8:29 B). — Here we may also add Num. Rab. 4 (141C), where Adam is called the "firstborn of the world"; with respect to the Messiah, we may also refer to Pesiq. Rab. 34 at § Heb 1:6 A.

2. According to the general rule in SDeut 11:10 § 37, as well as according to ʾAg. Ber. 31 and Exod. Rab. 15 (78D)—see the passages at § Rom 8:29 B—the designation "firstborn" expresses the particular love and esteem that God has toward the one in question. This is doubtlessly correct, though it does not touch on the actual meaning of πρωτότοκος πάσης κτίσεως in Col 1:15. What the apostle wants to emphasize with this designation is rather that Christ has temporal priority before every created thing: since he existed before the world was created, he is called in an absolute sense "the firstborn of all creation." The ancient synagogue did not know of a Messiah who in his real preexistence prior to the world possesses a characteristic that distinguishes him from all other people (see § John 1:1 A). The conception that the apostle connects with his πρωτότοκος πάσης κτίσεως in Col 1:15 is also completely distant from the two passages presented from Exod. Rab. 19 (81D) and Pesiq. Rab. 34 (159B) at § Rom 8:29 B, #1, n. *e* and § Heb 1:6 A. However, the apostle's idea can be compared with those conceptions that the ancient synagogue developed about the Torah on the basis of Prov 8:22ff.; it too is regarded as a preexistent firstling by which the world was created (see § John 1:1–4). — The expression that comes closest to the apostle's πρωτότοκος πάσης κτίσεως is the one used of God, קַדְמוֹנוֹ שֶׁל עוֹלָם "the one who was before the world."

Genesis Rabbah 38 (23B): ("It happened, when they went מִקֶּדֶם" [Gen 11:2].) R. Eleazar b. Simeon (ca. 180) said, "They withdrew themselves from the one prior to the world מקדמונו של עולם (= from the one who was before the world); they said, 'We do not want him or his divinity!'"

1:16 A: Because everything was created in him ....

Just as here the creation of the world is attributed to the πρωτότοκος τῆς κτίσεως (see δι᾽ αὐτοῦ at the end of verse 16), so too in rabbinic literature the Torah as the "firstling" appears also as the medium of creation; see § John 1:1–4, #4; see also SDeut 11:22 § 48 (84B) at § Matt 23:8 A.

1:16 B: Whether thrones or dominions ... (see § Eph 1:21).

1:16 C: Everything ... was created for him.

εἰς = לְ. — Babylonian Talmud Sanhedrin 98B: Rab († 247) said, "The world was created only in view of David" לדוד (for David, with reference to David); Samuel († 254) said,

"In view of Moses" למשה; R. Yohanan († 279) said, "In view of the Messiah" למשיח. — The figures named are supposed to represent the purpose and goal of the creation of the world; see the excursus "Signs and Calculations of the Messianic Time."

1:18: So he might be first in everything.

For the Messianic name רִאשׁוֹן "first," see § Matt 1:21 B, #2, n. *c*.

1:20: Making peace.

εἰρηνοποιεῖν = הֵטִיל שָׁלוֹם or עָשָׂה שָׁלוֹם; see examples at § Matt 5:9. — It is often said of God that he makes peace among his creatures; see, for example, b. Ber. 16B at § Matt 6:10 B; see also Midr. Song. 3:11 (108A), where the name Solomon in the Song is interpreted to refer to God as the "king who makes peace among his creatures."

2:1: In Laodicea.

Λαοδικία, in rabbinic literature is most of the time לוֹדִקְיָא, but also לדוקיא (y. ʿAbod. Zar. 3.42C.18) or לודיקיא (b. Menaḥ. 85B). Since there were several other cities that bore this name aside from our Phrygian Laodicea (e.g., in Lycaonia and in Lebanon south of Emesa), it remains uncertain which Laodicea is meant in many rabbinic passages.

The Laodicea mentioned in Col 2:1 may be referred to in m. Kelim 26.1, where, referring to Laodicean sandals סנדל לדיקי, it says that they make unclean. This assumption relies on the idea that the Laodicea in Phrygia had an extensive wool industry.[293] ‖ In b. Moʿed Qaṭ. 26A, the following remark of R. Ammi (ca. 300) comes after the passage adduced at § Acts 2:9, #5, n. *a*: As a result of the (rebels') string music from Mezigath Caesarea (= Mazaca, capital of Cappadocia) the wall of Laodicea burst (so according to Rashi, whom Levy follows[294]). Neubauer considers it certain that this refers to the Phrygian Laodicea;[295] but it is more likely that the Lycaonian Laodicea is in view, which was not half as distant from Mazaca as the Laodicea in Phrygia. — See further § Rev 3:14 A.

2:3: Treasures of wisdom.

Concerning the θησαυροὶ τῆς σοφίας it says in (Greek) Sir 1:22: "A wise saying lies in the treasuries of wisdom."

2:8: Elements of the world (see § Gal 4:3).

2:9: In him dwells the fullness of the divinity in a bodily way.

The ancient synagogue knows only of the Shekinah or the spirit of God resting on a person; see b. Pesaḥ. 117A at § 1 Cor 14:26. ‖ Babylonian Talmud Soṭah 48B: A voice from heaven sounded, which called out, "There is a person among you who would be worthy

---

293. See Schürer, *Geschichte des jüdischen Volkes*, 2:81.

294. Levy, *Chaldäisches Wörterbuch*, 2:477B.

295. Adolf Neubauer, *La Géographie du Talmud* (Paris: Trèves, 1868), 319.

of the Shekinah dwell on him שתשרה שכינה עליו; but his time is not worthy of it." — A few lines later, the same words of a voice from heaven appear again. See the unabbreviated report according to the parallel passage in t. Soṭah 13.3f. (318) at § Matt 3:17 A, #8. Here the voice from heaven cries out: "There is a person here who is worthy of the holy spirit." This shows that the expression about the Shekinah resting on a person is synonymous with the spirit of prophecy or inspiration resting on a person. At the same time, one can recognize how infinitely far the apostle's statement about Christ in Col 2:9 goes beyond the idea of the Shekinah resting on a person. ‖ A baraita in b. Sukkah 28A: Hillel the elder (ca. 20 BCE) had eighty students: thirty of them were worthy to have the Shekinah rest on them like our teacher Moses, and thirty of them were worthy to have the sun stand still for them as for Joshua the son of Nun; twenty of them were mediocre. The greatest among them was Jonathan b. Uzziel (the author of the targum at the Prophets), while the smallest among them was Rabban Yohanan b. Zakkai († ca. 80). ‖ See b. Ned. 38A at § 1 Cor 1:26, #1.

2:11: In putting off the body of flesh.

Philo, *De circumcisione* § 2 (Mangey's ed., 2:211) says of circumcision: "I consider … circumcision also to be a symbol for two completely necessary things. First for cutting away the lusts that beguile the understanding. For since among the temptations by lusts sexual communion of a man with a woman carries off the prize (occupies the first place), it seemed good to the lawgivers to remove the tip from the implement used for intercourse by alluding to it with the cutting away of the greatest lust, not simply one (lust), but rather by the one that is also the most forceful among them all…."

2:13: Dead because of transgressions.

νεκρός as מֵת = spiritually dead, see § Matt 8:22.

2:14 A: Wiping out the chirograph against us.

The certificate of debt was called שְׁטָר = "a piece of writing, register," or more precisely שטר חוֹב or גֵּט חוֹב; מָחַק, Aram. מְחִק served as a verb for "wiping out."

See m. ʾAbot 3.16 at § Matt 10:29 B, #3 toward the beginning. ‖ Tanḥuma צו (140B): Rabbi († 217?) said, "When a person sins, God records death for him; if he repents, the writ is annulled הכתב מתבטל (declared invalid); if he does not repent, what has been recorded remains a true (valid) writ (cf. Dan 10:21)." ‖ On eliminating certificates of debt שְׁטָרִין, שְׁטָרוֹת that God has in his hand against human beings, see y. Peʾah 1.16B.37 at § Rom 2:6. The parallel to this in b. Pesiq. 167A calls the certificate that God snatches away from the weighing pan of transgressions שטר חוב של עוונות "debt certificate of sins." — See another parallel in b. Roš Haš. 17A. ‖ In the prayer Avinu Malkeinu[296] there is a plea that reads as follows: Our father, our king, by your great mercy wipe out מְחוֹק all our certificates of debt כָּל־שִׁטְרֵי

296. S-B: R. ʿAqiba († ca. 135) already cited some statements from this prayer in b. Taʿan. 25B.

חוֹבוֹתֵינוּ! — Burning certificates of debt is also mentioned; see Exod. Rab. 15 (77A). — To speak of exacting payment for a certificate of debt, the verb גָּבָה was used; see Gen. Rab. 23 (15C).

2:14 B: And has himself taken it away from our midst.

See the wording in Tg. 1 Chr. 21:15: "Remove Abishai, their master, from their midst" טול אבישי רבהון מביניהון.

2:15: Stripping the rulers and powers, he boldly made a show of them, triumphing over them in him.

1. See Pesiq. Rab. 36 (161A) at § Luke 24:26, I, #4, n. *k*. 2. ἐν παρρησίᾳ, see § Mark 8:32.

2:16: No one should judge in matters of feasts or new moon- or Sabbath celebrations.

See § Acts 21:21.

2:17: Which is a shadow of the future thing, but the body belongs to Christ.

In Josephus, *J. W.* 2.2.5, Archelaus is accused in the following way: "Now he comes to ask for the shadow σκιάν of dominion from the lord (Caesar), the body σῶμα of which he long ago usurped ἥρπασεν by not making Caesar lord of things τῶν πραγμάτων (= σῶμα), but rather (lord) of names τῶν ὀνομάτων (= σκιά)." — Josephus, *J. W.* 6.3.3: "The troubles that befell them (those besieged in Jerusalem) cannot be depicted. For in every house, as soon as only a shadow of food τροφῆς σκιά appeared to be present, war broke out, and best friends lashed out against each other." ‖ In rabbinic literature, the image of the shadow is rare. — Genesis Rabbah 96 (60C): "When the days came for Israel to die" (Gen 47:29). It is written: "For I am a stranger (guest) with you, a resident alien like all (my ancestors)" (Ps 39:13). "For we are strangers before you and resident aliens like all our ancestors; our days on earth are like a shadow צֵל, without hope" (1 Chr 29:15). If only they were like the shadow of a wall or like the shadow of a tree (which endures as long as the wall or tree exist)! Yet they are like a bird's shadow at the time when it flies, as it is written: "His days are like a passing shadow" (Ps 144:4). — A similar statement is found in a longer explanation in Midr. Eccl. 1:2 (4B).

2:18: In humility and worship of angels.

1. τῶν ἀγγέλων, an objective genitive, coordinated only with θρησκίᾳ. — See warnings about angel cults in t. Ḥul. 2.18 (503) at § 1 Cor 8:1 A; see a parallel in b. ʿAbod. Zar. 42B; see also y. Ber. 9.13A.54 at § Matt 7:7 A, #2 n. *a*.

2. τῶν ἀγγέλων, a subjective genitive, coordinated with ταπεινοφροσύνῃ καὶ θρησκίᾳ. — ʾAbot de Rabbi Nathan 12 (4D): From where can it be proven that they (the angels) have reverence before one another and mutually show each other honor, and that they are humbler than the children of men? In the hour when they open their mouth to sing (God) a song, one says to another, "You go up, for you are greater than I!" And this one answers the other, "You go up, for you are greater than I!" Not as people do, where one says to the other, "I am

greater than you!" And this one answers the other, "I am greater than you!" Some say that this refers to divisions of angels (not individual angels); one division says to another, "You go up, for you are greater than I!" As it says, "One called out to another" (Isa 6:3.)

2:21: Do not touch, do not taste, do not handle!

Mishnah Tamid 1.4: One called out to him (to the priest who removed the ashes from the altar of burnt offering in the morning): Take care that you do not touch תִּגַּע any implement before you have washed your hands and feet from a basin! ‖ Mishnah Makkot 3.7f.: If a Nazirite has drunk wine the whole day, he makes himself guilty only once (of lashing). Yet if one called out to him (whenever he wanted to drink): "Do not drink, do not drink" אַל תִּשְׁתֶּה! and he (nevertheless) drank, he makes himself guilty for every single drink. If he has made himself unclean a whole day with the dead, he makes himself guilty only once (of lashing). Yet if one called out to him, "Do not make yourself unclean, do not make yourself unclean!," and he (nevertheless) made himself unclean, he makes himself guilty for every single case. ‖ On the cry of the leper "Unclean, unclean!," see the excursus "Leprosy and Lepers." — See further Lam 4:15; this passage is used in Midr. Ps. 119 § 20 (248A) at § 1 Cor 3:12, #5, n. *a*.

2:22: According to the commandments and teachings of human beings.

The underlying text is Isa 29:13: וַתְּהִי יִרְאָתָם אֹתִי מִצְוַת אֲנָשִׁים מְלֻמָּדָה "and their fear of me is a commandment of men that is learned." — Targum: "And their fear of me is like a decree of men who teach," that is, like a decree that men have taught. — Septuagint: μάτην δὲ σέβονταί με, διδάσκοντες ἐντάλματα ἀνθρώπων καὶ διδασκαλίας = "In vain (futilely) do they honor me by teaching the commandments and teachings of men." — μάτην σέβονταί με appears to be based on a vocal reading of ותהי as תֹּהוּ: "Their fear of me is vanity." διδάσκοντες, like the מלפין of the targum, gives the impression that one read, instead of מלמדה in the base text, מלמדם = מְלַמְּדִים "by them teaching." Then, the tacked on καὶ διδασκαλίας would be a gloss that ended up in the text of the LXX. — In Matt 15:9, Isa 29:13b is cited closely following the LXX, except (καὶ) διδασκαλίας has been given a different placement and relation in the sentence. In Col 2:22 as well, the words καὶ διδασκαλίας have found a more fitting place before τῶν ἀνθρώπων.

2:23: Not sparing the body.

On the reprehensibility of unauthorized self-mortification, see § 1 Cor 9:25 A, #2, n. *d*; see more in the excursus "Fasting."

3:1: What is above.

ἄνω = מַעְלָה, τὰ ἄνω = מָה לְמַעְלָה "what is above (= in heaven)"; opposite: מָה לְמַטָּה "what is below (= on earth)." — Examples:

See b. Ḥag. 2.1 at § Matt 25:31 B, #2, n. *b*. — See b. Ḥag. 15A at § Rom 3:4 A. — See m. Roš Haš. 3.8 at § Matt 6:4 A, #2, n. *c*, second third. — See also § John 3:31 and § Luke 2:13 A.

3:4: Yet when Christ is revealed.

φανεροῦσθαι = הִתְגַּלָּה, נִגְלָה, Aram. אִתְגְּלִי. — Examples at § Matt 4:17 B, B, #2, n. *c*; see also Pesiq. Rab. 36 at § Matt 24:27, n. *b*.

3:5: Greed, which is idolatry.

πλεονεξία, see § Luke 12:15 A. — ἥτις ἐστὶν εἰδωλολατρεία, see § Eph 5:5 A.

3:11: Barbarian, Scythian.

On βάρβαρος see § Rom 1:14, #2. — Barbarians and Scythians may be named alongside each other in Midr. Ps. 109:3 (not in ed. Buber): "They have fought against me without cause" (Ps 109:3). (The Israelites say,) "If Esau hates Jacob because he took his birthright from him—what has he (Jacob = Israel) done, though, to barbarians and שתותיא?" — Following ʿArukh, Krauß considers this word to be a corruption from שקותיא = Scythians.[297] In the parallel Midr. Ps. 25 § 14 (108A), we find instead ענתיים, and in other manuscripts ענתותים; Yalquṭ reads גונתיים = Goths (?). — On the proverbial ferocity and cruelty of the Scythians, see 2 Macc 4:47; also, 3 Macc 7:5: "(The enemies of the Jews) also led them chained with abuse like slaves, indeed even like traitors, and they tried to kill them without any trial or verdict, having acted with ferocious cruelty, as is the custom of Scythians." ‖ Josephus, *Against Apion* 2.37, calls the Scythians people who rejoice over the murder of people and who are little different from wild animals.

3:12 A: Put on a heart of compassion.

See § Luke 24:49, #2, especially b. Ber. 16B.

3:12 B: As the elect of God, holy and beloved.

1. ἐκλεκτοί. — See § Rom 11:28; see also Tob 8:15. — The righteous are called "the elect" especially frequently in 1 Enoch. 1 Enoch 1:3: "I am speaking now about the elect and I have raised my pronouncements over them." — 1 Enoch 1:8: "He (God) will make peace with the righteous and protect the elect." — 1 Enoch 25:5: "Its fruit (that of the tree of life) will serve as life for the elect." — See further 1 En. 40:5; 41:2; 48:1, 9; 51:5; 56:6, 8; 58:3; 61:4, 12; 62:7, 8, 11; 93:2.

2. ἅγιοι. — See § Acts 9:13.

3. ἠγαπημένοι = חֲבִיבִין, see § Rom 1:7 B.

3:12 C: Goodness, patience, gentleness, long-suffering.

On ταπεινοφροσύνη, see § Matt 5:3, #3; on πραΰτης, see § Matt 5:5, #1; on μακροθυμία, see § Eph 4:2, #2.

---

297. Krauß, *Lehnwörter*, 2:583B.

3:17: Everything that you do ..., everything in the name of the Lord Jesus.

Mishnah ʾAbot 2.12: R. Yose (the priest, ca. 100) said, "... All your actions should happen in the name of God" לְשֵׁם שָׁמַיִם (i.e., with a view to God or for God's sake).

3:19: Do not become bitter toward them.

Babylonian Talmud Baba Meṣiʿa 59A: Rab († 247) said, "A person should always be careful not to offend his wife; for since her tears come (quickly), the punishment for her offense is near...."

4:1: Equality.

ἰσότης "equality"; on the duties of a master toward a Hebrew slave, see the excursus "The Nature of Ancient Jewish Slavery."

4:3: That God might open for us a door for the word.

Genesis Rabbah 91 (57B): He found a door פֶּתַח = opportunity etc.; see § Acts 21:23f. ‖ Babylonian Talmud Megillah 12B: Ben Kish (Esth 2:5) means that he knocked הִקִּישׁ on the gates of mercy, and they were opened ונפתחו for him. ‖ See y. Ḥag. 2.77C.45 at § Matt 5:18 B, #2. ‖ See b. Menaḥ. 29B at § Matt 5:18 B, #2. — There is a parallel in b. Šabb. 104A. ‖ Babylonian Talmud Baba Qamma 80B: A door that has been closed is not so quickly opened, that is, a missed opportunity does not come again so quickly. ‖ See also § Acts 14:27 and § 1 Cor 16:9.

4:6 A: Your word in mercy at all times.

See b. Giṭ. 7A: Mercy חִסְדָּאִין (plural) are your words; see the passage at § Phil 4:3.

4:6 B: Prepared with salt.

On salt, see § Matt 5:13 and § Mark 9:49, 50. ‖ A baraita in b. Ber. 34A: Whoever steps before the lectern for the leader of prayer should refuse (to step forward), and whoever does not refuse to step forward is like food with no salt. If, though, he refuses unduly, he is like food that (too much) salt has destroyed. How should one act? The first time, one should refuse (out of modesty); the second time, one should signal his partial consent; the third time, one should stretch out his feet and walk over there. — We could not find the citation of Wettstein from b. Ber. 34A: *Qui inter orandum vocem quandam omittit, illum oportet a principio inchoare: quod si non facit, similis est cibo cocto, in quo non est sal.* The first sentence, however, is found in b. Ber. 24B, though without the concluding words: *quod si non facit ....*

4:6 C: To know how you have to answer each one (cf. § 1 Pet 3:15 B).

4:16: The letter.

ἐπιστολή = אִגֶּרֶת, plur. אִגְּרוֹת, see Neh 2:7, 8, 9 among many others. For the Aramaic form אִיגְּרָא, det. אִגַּרְתָּא, see some examples at § Acts 9:2 A, #1.

The First Letter of Paul to the Thessalonians

1:4: Your election (cf. § Rom 11:28).

1:6: With the joy of the Holy Spirit (cf. § Phil 4:4).

1:7: An example (see § Phil 3:17).

1:10: From the future wrath (cf. § Matt 3:7 A).

2:9: Working day and night.

On the praise of work, see § Mark 6:3; § Acts 18:3, #1 and #2 and § 2 Thess 3:10.

2:13: The word of the message.

ἀκοή, see § Rom 10:17 A, #1.

2:16 A: By hindering us from preaching to the gentiles so that they might be blessed.

See passages like b. Ber. 7A; Deut. Rab. 1 (196D); 5 (202A) at § Matt 5:43, #1, n. *g*, near beginning; b. Sanh. 58B; Pesiq. 156A; Deut. Rab. 2 (197D) at § Matt 5:43, #1, n. *g*, second third; b. Ḥag. 13A; Midr. Song. 2:7 (99A) at § Matt 7:6 A, #2; SDeut 33:4 § 345 (143B) at § Rom 2:19–20, #2, n. *b*; Mek. Exod. 15:2 (44A) at § Rom 2:19–20, #2, n. *a*.

2:16 B: To fill up their sins.

See examples at § Rom 3:9 A, #1, n. *l*.

2:17: Orphaned by you.

Likewise, יָתוֹם "orphan" can be used in the broader sense of "orphaned" = "abandoned"; see, for example, y. Ḥag. 1.75D.34: No age is orphaned יתום, in which R. Eleazar b. Azariah (ca. 100) lives.

3:5: The tempter (see § Matt 4:1 B, #3).

3:13: With all his saints (see § Matt 25:31 A).

4:3: For this is the will of God, your sanctification, that you keep yourselves from fornication.

Numbers Rabbah 9 (151B): How do we know that the Israelites are called holy if they keep themselves from adultery and fornication? Because it says, "So show yourselves as holy and be holy; for I am Yahweh your God" (Lev 20:7). It follows from this that he is their God at the time when they are holy. What is written after this? "And keep my statutes and do them; for I am Yahweh, who sanctifies you" (Lev 20:8). When does God sanctify Israel? When they keep his statutes. And what are these statutes? Those concerning fornication. ‖ See further at § 1 Thess 4:4 B.

4:4 A: That each one of you know how to acquire his own vessel.

1. σκεῦος = כְּלִי, α. in general, "implement, garment, vessel" (see § Rom 9:21, #2); β. specifically = wife.

Babylonian Talmud Megillah 12B: Raba († 352) said, "The seventh day (Esth 1:10) was a Sabbath; when the Israelites eat and drink, they start with words of the Torah and with words of songs of praise; yet when the idolatrous nations of the world eat and drink, they start only with words of exuberance (absurdities תִּיפְלוֹת). Likewise, at the banquet of that impious one (Ahasuerus) some said, "The women of Media are beautiful." Others said, "The women of Persia are beautiful." Then Ahasuerus said to them, "The vessel כְּלִי I make use of is neither a Median nor a Persian but rather a Chaldean." — The same is found in Midr. Esth. 1:11 (89B) with R. Aibo (Aibu [ca. 320]) as the author. ‖ Pesiqta 94B: When (R. Eleazar b. Simeon [ca. 180]) had died, (Rabbi [† 217?]) sent word and proposed to his wife. However, she sent word to him, "The vessel כלי that has been used by a holy man should be used by a profane man?!" — The same is found in b. B. Meṣ. 84B; Midr. Eccl. 11:2 (51B), y. Šabb. 10.12C.46. ‖ Babylonian Talmud Sanhedrin 22B: R. Samuel b. Onia (if = Samuel b. Inia, then ca. 360) said in the name of Rab († 247), "A woman is an unfinished mass גּוֹלֶם and makes a covenant only with the one who makes her a (finished) vessel כלי; as it says, 'For your husband is your creator, whose name is Yahweh of hosts' (Isa 54:5)." ‖ See also b. Sanh. 99B, where Raba († 352), though using another term, says, "All bodies are containers הָרַפְתְּקֵי; blessed is the one who has become worthy to be a container of the Torah."

2. κτᾶσθαι. — Mishnah Qiddušin 1.1: A wife is acquired נִקְנֵית in a three-fold way ...; see § John 2:1 A, #5, n. *i*.

4:4 B: In sanctification and honor.

Leviticus Rabbah 24 (122D.46): R. Judah b. Pazzi (ca. 320) said, "Why does the section about sins of fornication (Lev 18) stand right alongside the one about sanctification (Lev 19)? To teach you that everywhere where you find a fence against fornication, you also find holiness." This corresponds to the opinion of R. Judah b. Pazzi, who said, "Whoever separates himself from fornication is called holy." — The 1st saying is attributed to R. Joshua b. Levi (ca. 250) in Lev. Rab. 24 (123A). ‖ Babylonian Talmud Šebuʿot. 18B: R. Benjamin b. Pazzi (ca. 320) said that R. Eleazar (ca. 270) said, "Whoever sanctifies himself in the hour of intercourse, on him male children will be bestowed; as it says, 'Show yourselves holy and be holy' (Lev 11:44), and this is connected with 'If a woman gives birth to a male' (Lev 12:2)."

4:6 A: That he not cheat his brother in business.

1. Cheating (= אוֹנָאָה, Aram. אוֹנָאוּתָא, אוֹנָאִיתָא; verb: אִנָּה, הוֹנָה) existed in the business of sale and exchange whenever the stipulated price exceeded

a sixth of the true value. The buyer had the right in this case either to the entire sum paid if the sale was reversed, or to demand back the money overpaid if the sale was not reversed. However, the transaction had to be challenged within a period that was sufficient to inquire with a merchant about the real price range. The seller had the same right in case, in a closed transaction, the selling price was a sixth below the actual value.[a] The recipient could also gain an advantage bordering on cheating if he used coins that were heavily worn. The Mishnah made a regulation in this case too.[b] – The following were named as objects of value where no cheating occurred: slaves, certificates of claims, properties, and what has made holy (i.e., dedicated to God or the temple).[c]

a. Mishnah Baba Meṣiʿa 4.3f.: There is cheating אונאה when there are 4 silver pieces to 1 *sela* out of 24 silver pieces, a sixth of the price. How long is he allowed to reverse the sale? As long as there is enough time for a buyer or his relative to show (the wares). R. Tarfon (ca. 100) once taught in Lydda: "Cheating happens with 8 silver pieces to 1 *sela*, a third of the price." Then the merchants in Lydda rejoiced. Yet when he said to them: "One can withdraw the whole day," they said to him, "Let R. Tarfon leave us in our (earlier) arrangement!" Then they complied again with the words of the (other) scholars. There is cheating for both buyers and sellers. Just as there is cheating for a layman, so too there is for the merchant. R. Judah (ca. 150) said, "For the merchant (so the expert) there is no cheating. The one cheated has the upper hand. If he wants, he says, 'Give me (all) my money!' or 'Give me what you have cheated me of.'"

b. Mishnah Baba Meṣiʿa 4.5f.: How much can be lacking in 1 *sela* without there being any cheating (for the recipient)? R. Meir (ca. 150) said, "4 *issars*, so 1 *issar* to 1 *denar*" (1 *denar* = 24 *issars*). R. Judah (ca. 150) said, "4 *pondions*, at 1 *pondion* to 1 *denar*" (1 *pondion* = 2 *issars*). R. Simeon (ca. 150) said, "8 *pondions*, at 2 *pondions* to 1 *denar*." (The attrition could thus amount to the 24th part of the coins according to R. Meir, the 12th part of the coins according to R. Judah and the 6th part of the coins according to R. Simeon.) For how long can the recipient take back the coins? In the cities, until he can show them to a money changer; in the villages, until the evening before the Sabbath (on which the country people frequently came to the cities and so had the opportunity to consult with a changer). If he (the giver of the worn coin) recognizes it, he will take it back even after 12 months (out of politeness) from him (the recipient); (if he does not do it,) the recipient has no other right except to gossip about him. (Legal action is excluded due to the lapse of the period to lodge a complaint.)

c. Mishnah Baba Meṣiʿa 4.9: With the following things there is no cheating: in the sale of slaves, of certificates of debt, and of properties, and with things made holy.... R. Judah (ca. 150) said, "Even if one sells a Torah scroll or livestock or pearls, there is no cheating here (because with these things, the emotional value comes into consideration)." It was responded to him, "Only the things mentioned above have been determined."

2. See a general admonition to honesty in trade and change in b. Šabb. 31A at § Matt 5:13 A, #4.

4:6 B: For the Lord is an avenger concerning all of this.

See b. Šabb. 31A in the preceding #2. ‖ Mishnah Baba Meṣiʿa 4.2: If a buyer has taken fruits from a seller (and thereby taken them into his possession) without having given him money for them, he cannot withdraw (from the purchase). If he has given him the money, without taking the fruits from him, he can withdraw. Yet it has been said, "The one who punished the generation of the flood and the generation of the dispersion (of the confusion of languages) will also punish the one who does not stand by his word (does not keep a word given in business transactions)." — The same is found in more expansive form in the name of R. Simeon (ca. 150) in t. B. Meṣ. 3.14 (377) and b. B. Meṣ. 48A.

4:9: You yourselves are taught by God.

It was generally assumed that God himself will teach his people in the future; see, aside from § John 6:45 and § Heb 8:8–12, especially the excursus "Sheol, Gehenna, and the Garden of Eden," III, #4, n. *m*.

Genesis Rabbah 95 (60B): God said to Abraham, "You have taught your children Torah in this world, but in the future world I will teach you the Torah in my glory; as it says, 'All your sons will be taught by Yahweh' (Isa 54:13)." ‖ Midrash Psalm 21 § 1 (89A): All Israel will learn the Torah from God.

4:13: Those who have fallen asleep.

κοιμᾶσθαι "to sleep, fallen asleep" = to die, in the LXX this is the rendering of שָׁכַב "to lie, fall asleep," in, for example, 1 Kgs 2:10: וישכב דוד "and David fell asleep," LXX: καὶ ἐκοιμήθη Δαυίδ. Further examples are found in 1 Kgs 11:43; 14:31; 15:8, 24; 16:6; Isa 43:17, among many others — In rabbinic literature the Aramaic equivalent is most often דְּמַךְ; see examples at § Matt 27:45, #1; οἱ κοιμώμενοι then = דַּמְכַיָּיא, in, for example, y. Ber. 2.5A.10: The Rabbanan said, "If the king, the Messiah, is from the living חייא, David is his name; if he is from those who have fallen asleep דמכייא, David is his name."

4:14: God will bring those who have fallen asleep in Jesus with him.

4 Ezra 7:28: "My son, the Christ, will be revealed together with all those who are with him." — This does not refer to the angels (so Gunkel), but rather to the righteous, such as Moses, Ezra, Enoch, who had passed into the hereafter and now would return with the Messiah to earth. — The same idea is present in 1 En. 38:1ff.: "When the community of the righteous appears (from heaven) …, and when the righteous one (= Messiah) appears before the elected righteous ones (on earth) …, where will the dwelling of sinners be? …" — See also the concluding chapter of the Didache.

4:16 A: With the voice (cry) of an archangel and with (the sound) of the trumpet of God.

1. ἀρχάγγελος, according to Dan 12:1 = שַׂר הַגָּדוֹל "great prince," LXX: ἄρχων ὁ μέγας. In rabbinic literature שָׂרִים "princes" is used to designate the ruling angels of the nations (see § Rom 1:23 A, #2, A) and then the

"angels of the face" (= archangels), such as Michael and Gabriel.[a] On the number of the angels of the face, see § Rev 8:2.

a. In b. Ḥag. 12B, Michael is called השר הגדול "the great prince" (see § Jude 9). ‖ Genesis Rabbah 63 (40B) Michael and Gabriel = שרים; Gen. Rab. 78 (49D) Michael and Gabriel = שרים של מעלה "the princes of those above" (of the angel world); see the passages at § Luke 1:19 A, #3, n. *a.* ‖ For Michael and Gabriel as the "kings of the angels," see Pesiq. 45A at § Rom 1:18 A, n. *b.*

2. The voice of an archangel. — It is said of Gabriel's voice קוֹל that it goes from one end of the world to the other; see ʾAbot R. Nat. 2 at § Luke 1:19 B.

3. σάλπιγξ in the LXX is the rendering of both חֲצוֹצְרָה "trumpet" (Num 10:2) and שׁוֹפָר "horn" (trumpet) (Lev 25:9). By analogy with Isa 27:13; Joel 2:1; and Zech 9:14, the σάλπιγξ in our passage should doubtlessly be understood as the שׁוֹפָר. See supporting passages at § Matt 24:31, #2.

4:16 B: The dead in Christ will rise first.

At the beginning of the 3rd century, the view arose in the synagogue that the dead of the land of Israel will "first" rise; see § Rev 20:5. — A different theory is represented by R. Berekhiah (ca. 340) in Midr. Eccl. 1:4 (5B): "A potter lowers (the vessels) into the oven; what he lowers in first will be the last (when taking everything out); but here (in the resurrection of the dead) it is like this: what went first comes back first; what went last comes back last."

4:17 A: We will be carried off in clouds to meet the Lord.

1. The clouds as vehicles for Israel.

TanḥumaB צו § 16 (10B): (In the future Jerusalem will rise to the 7th heaven.) R. Eliezer b. Jacob (II, ca. 150) said, "Until it comes to the throne of glory. And how will they (the Israelites) rise up? God brings clouds, and they let them fly up; as it says, 'Who are these who fly like a cloud?' (Isa 60:8) …" — On this passage and its parallels, see the excursus "Sheol, Gehenna, and the Garden of Eden," III, #4, n. *e.* ‖ Pesiqta Rabbati 1 (2A): "And it will happen, whenever there is a new moon, on that new moon, and whenever the Sabbath comes, on that Sabbath, all flesh will come to worship before my face, says Yahweh" (Isa 66:23). How so? Is it possible that all flesh come to Jerusalem on every new moon and on every Sabbath? R. Levi (ca. 300) said, "One day Jerusalem will be (as big) as the land of Israel and the land of Israel as the whole world; and how will they come (to Jerusalem) at the beginning of a month and on the Sabbath from the end of the world? Clouds will come and bear them and bring them to Jerusalem, and they will worship there early in the morning; and this is what the prophet boasts about in them: 'Who are these who fly like a cloud?' (Isa 60:8)." A different explanation: "And it will happen whenever there is a new moon …" (Isa 66:23). And see, if the beginning of the month falls on a Sabbath and yet Scripture says, "Whenever there is a new moon and whenever the Sabbath comes," how should this be understood? R. Phineas, the priest, b. Hama (ca. 360) said in the name of R. Reuben (ca. 300), "They will come twice, once for the Sabbath and once for the beginning of the month, and the clouds will bear them bright and early and bring them to Jerusalem, and they will pray there early in the morning, and they will bear them (back to their homes) and then bring them again to Jerusalem. 'Who are these who fly like a cloud?' (Isa 60:8): this refers to the morning; 'and like doves to their nests?' (Isa 60:8): this refers to the afternoon (to the second coming)." ‖ See further Midr. Ps 48 § 4 (138A).

2. ἀπάντησις = אַפַּנְטִי ἀπαντή (= ἀπάντησις or ἀπαντίον. — εἰς ἀπάντησιν then = לְאַפַּנְטִי.

TanḥumaB אמור § 30 (51A): The great one of the city began to go to meet the king לאפנטי של מלך (literally: for the encountering of the king). ‖ Jerusalem Talmud ʿAbodah Zarah 2.41B.57: R. Yohanan († 279) went to meet the patriarch R. Judan in Akko (= לאפנטי) לַפַּנְטִי דרבי יודן.

4:17 B: And so we will always be with the Lord.

1 Enoch 62:14: "The Lord of Spirits will dwell over them (the righteous) (after the dawn of the messianic age), and they will eat with that Son of Man (= Messiah), lie down, and rise up forever."

5:2: Like a thief in the night.

On the sudden coming of the Messiah, see b. Sanh. 97A at § Matt 11:12, at the end.

5:13: Keep peace with one another (see § Rom 12:18).

5:14: Be long-suffering toward all (see § Eph 4:2, #2).

5:15: So that no one repays anyone evil for evil (see § Rom 12:17 A).

The proverbial maxim in Lev. Rab. 22 (121B) is different: If you have done good for evil, you have done evil; do not do good for evil, so no evil will befall you. — In Gen. Rab. 22 (15A) there is only the 2nd sentence, in Midr. Eccl. 5:8 (27A) both sentences are found, though in reverse order.

5:17: Pray without ceasing (see § Luke 18:1).

5:22: Keep yourselves from every kind of evil.

The words have often been reinterpreted: Keep yourselves from every appearance of evil. Then reference could be made to b. Beṣah 9A: Rab Judah († 299) said that Rab († 247) said, "Everywhere where the scholars have forbidden something because of (evil) appearance, it is forbidden even in the most hidden chambers." — Similarly, y. ʿErub. 8.25B.45.

5:24: Who will also do it.

Midrash Ruth 4:1 (136A): R. Eliezer (ca. 90) said, "Boaz had done his part, Ruth had done hers, and Naomi had done hers. Then God said, 'I too will do mine.'" ‖ Tanḥuma וירא (27A): Daniel said, "If God has determined about us that we should eat unclean bread, he only wants to try us: we will do our part, and he will do his." ‖ See further Gen. Rab. 23 (15C) and Exod. Rab. 23 (85A).

The Second Letter of Paul to the Thessalonians

1:5: So that you may be worthy (see § Luke 20:35).

1:7: With the angels of his might (see § Matt 25:31 A).

1:8: In flaming fire, when he exacts revenge.

The underlying text is probably Isa 66:15: "For behold, Yahweh will come in fire בָּאֵשׁ ..., to repay (pay out) his anger in fervor and his chastisements in blazing flames בְּלַהֲבֵי אֵשׁ." – Septuagint: ἰδοὺ γὰρ κύριος ὡς πῦρ ἥξει ..., ἀποδοῦναι ἐν θυμῷ ἐκδίκησιν αὐτοῦ καὶ ἀποσκορακισμὸν αὐτοῦ ἐν φλογὶ πυρός.

1:12: So that the name of our Lord Jesus may be glorified.

See § Matt 6:9 C and the notes there at *l*, *m*, and *p*.

2:3 A: If the apostasy has not yet come.

In the view of the ancient synagogue, the time immediately before the days of the Messiah will be a time of complete degeneracy; see the excursus "Signs and Calculation of the Messianic Times." A sign of this degeneracy will be, among others, falling away from God and his Torah.

1 Enoch 93:9: "Then an apostate generation will arise in the seventh week (of the world); its deeds will be numerous and all its deeds will be apostasy." – See 1 Enoch 90:26: "Those blinded sheep (the apostate Israelites) were brought; all were judged, found guilty, and cast into that pool of fire." ‖ Jubilees 23:16ff.: "In this generation children will rebuke their parents and their elders, ... because they forsook the covenant that God had made between them and himself ... For they have forgotten the commandment and covenant and festival and month and Sabbath and Jubilees and every just regulation ...." ‖ See Philo, *Exsecr.* § 6 at § Rom 11:17, #2, n. *b.* ‖ See b. Šabb. 138B at § 1 Cor 1:19 #2; see the continuation of b. Šabb. 138B in a baraita at § Matt 5:6, final paragraph. See also Mek. Exod. 12:26 (16A).

2:3 B: And the man of wickedness has been revealed.

Interpreters unanimously agree that the ἄνθρωπος τῆς ἀνομίας refers to the "antichrist." – ἀντίχριστος α. in general = "opponent, adversary of the Christ"; so the plural ἀντίχριστοι in 1 John 2:18, as well as 1 John 2:22 and 2 John 7; β. specifically = "the anti-Messiah," so one who puts himself in Christ's place; so the singular in 1 John 2:18 and 4:3. According to the description given by the apostle in our passage in verses 4 and 9ff., he too saw in "man of profanity" a character who will appear claiming to be the true Messiah. — Ancient Jewish literature does not have a term that corresponds to ἀντίχριστος;[a] even in content there are practically no points of contact with the New Testament conception of the antichrist. This goes together with the fact that opposition to the synagogue's Messiah lies exclusively on the political plane—most of the time, his adversary is considered to be the last ruler of Rome,[b] and many times also Gog and Magog[c]—whereas a religious anti-Messiah, so the antichrist in the New Testament sense, was completely unknown to the ancient synagogue.[d] Only the posttalmudic period combined the dual conception of the last tyrant of the end time and the antimessianic false prophet in the person of Armilos, who will appear as the last and most dangerous opponent of the Jewish people and its Messiah at the end of days. This Armilos,[e] created from a marble statue of a beautiful virgin in Rome by the peoples of the nations of the world or, according to another tradition, by Satan himself, appears claiming that he is the Christ of the nations of the world. After he is generally recognized as such, he desires the same recognition from the Jews. The Messiah b. Joseph (see § Luke 24:26, II) denies him this and falls in battle against him. Then Armilos moves against Jerusalem to take revenge, but here he meets his end, by the Messiah b. David killing him with the breath of his mouth (Isa 11:4).[f] — The Christ of Christianity thus one day becomes the anti-Messiah defeated by the Jewish Messiah.

a. The term אַנְטִיקְרִישְׁטוֹ = ἀντίχριστος is first found in posttalmudic literature. Othoth ha-Maschiach (*Beth ha-Midrash* 2.60.20): This adversary השמן זה (Armilos), whom the nations call "Antichrist" ....

b. See 2 Bar. 39:7; 40:1f. at § Matt 1:1 B, #3, n. *c.*

c. On Gog and Magog, see § Acts 4:25 B and § Rev 20:8f. — Sometimes a tyrant of the end time is talked about without there being any mention of the Messiah. So As. Mos. 8:1ff.; 4 Ezra 5:6; y. Taʿan. 1.1 (63D); see the last passage at § Matt 4:17 A, #1.

d. The passage Sib. Or. 3:63ff. originates from a Christian hand:[298] "Beliar will then come from the Sebastenes (Sebaste = Samaria) and will make high hills arise, and will make the sea stand still, as well as the fiery great sun and the shining moon, and he will also make the dead rise, and he will do many signs among men. Yet there will not be perfection in him, but rather (only) deception, and so he will deceive many people, both believing and elect Hebrews and other lawless men, who have never heard God's speech." — Whereas here Beliar (= Satan) himself appears as the lying prophet of the end time, according to 2 Thess 2:9, the apostle sees a tool of Satan in the ἄνθρωπος τῆς ἀνομίας; Beliar = Satan also in 2 Cor 6:15. — A Christian interpolation is also found in Sib. Or. 2:165ff.: "The destruction is near when, instead of the prophets, lying deceivers draw near, speaking on

298. See Schürer, *Geschichte des jüdischen Volkes*, 3:579.

the earth. And even Beliar will come and do many wonders for men. Then there will be turmoil for holy men and elect believers, and they and the Hebrews will be plundered."

e. אַרְמִילוֹס, and ארמילאוס[299] (Nistaroth R. Simeon b. Yohai in *Beth ha-Midrash* 3.80.9), were interpreted α. from ἐρημόω and λαός = "destroyer of the people," and here some also found an allusion to Balaam; β. = Ῥωμύλος (Romulus), so that the first king of Rome was thought of as a type for all Roman rulers; γ. = Ἀρειμάνης (Ahriman); δ. = Armillatus, as an allusion to the emperor Gaius Caligula, who occasionally wore bracelets for women (*armillae*); ε. = Ἕρμιλος, Greek proper name that corresponds to the Syriac Armilos. Building on this interpretation, Dalman says: "'Ἕρμιλος ... relates the one with this name to Hermes. The prince of nations bears this name because he was born from a statue (of Hermes)."[300] See, n. *f.*

f. The earliest passage that mentions Armilos is Tg. Isa. 11:4: "He (the Messiah) will judge the wretched (poor) in righteousness and in faithfulness (truthfulness) rebuke those who make the people of the land wretched; he will strike those in the land who are laden with guilt with the word of his mouth, and with the speech of his lips he will kill Armilos, the godless." — Yet אַרְמִילוֹס here is a gloss that later intruded into the text.[301] ‖ Targum Yerušalmi I Deuteronomy 34:3: "(God showed Moses from Nebo the events of the future that will be associated with specific places; here also) the king of Rome, who will band together with the king of the north to destroy the inhabitants of the land (of Israel), ... and the punishment of the godless (ארמלגוס = ארמילוס[302]) and the battle lines of Gog, at the time of this great distress, Michael will arise with his arm as redeemer." ‖ Midrash Vajjoschaᶜ (*Beth ha-Midrash* 1.56.13): After him (Gog) another king will appear, a godless one and with a brazen face (cf. Dan 8:23), and he will wage war with Israel for three months, and his name is Armilos ארמילוס. And these are his identifying features: he will be bald, and one of his eyes is small and the other big; his right arm is one handbreadth long and his left 2.5 cubits. And he will have leprosy on his forehead, and his right ear is deaf (closed) and the other open. If someone comes to say something good to him, he inclines his closed ear to him, and if someone comes to tell him something bad, he inclines his open ear to him (he thus only takes pleasure in evil). And he will go up to Jerusalem and kill the Messiah b. Joseph (see Zech 12:10). Then the Messiah b. David will come; as it says, "Behold, one like a human being came with the clouds of heaven" (Dan 7:13). Then it is written, "And his will be (so Dan 7:14 is cited) power and honor and dominion," and he will kill Armilos, the godless; as it says, "And he will kill the godless (evildoer, רָשָׁע) with the breath of his lips" (Isa 11:4). ‖ Armilos is dealt with in detail in Sepher Zerubbabel (*Beth ha-Midrash* 2.55.11), Othoth ha-Maschiach (*Beth ha-Midrash* 2:60.16), Nistaroth R. Simeon b. Yohai (*Beth ha-Midrash* 3.80.8) and Tephillath R. Simeon b. Yohai (*Beth ha-Midrash* 4.124.25). We will reproduce

299. S-B: In Sepher Elij (*Beth ha-Midrash* 3:65.12 f.) we also find the forms הרמלת and תרמילא.

300. Gustaf Dalman, *Der leidende und der sterbende Messias der Synagoge im ersten nachchristlichen Jahrtausend* (Berlin: Reuther, 1888), 14 n. 1.

301. See Gustaf Dalman, "Aramaische Dialektproben," *Monatsschrift für Geschichte und Wissenschaft des Judentums* 41 (1897): 328.

302. See Samuel Krauß, *Griechische und lateinische Lehnwörter im Talmud, Midrasch und Targum* (Berlin: S. Calvary & Co., 1898), 1:243.

the last passage here: It was said that there is a marble statue אבן של שיש (literally: marble stone) in Rome that has the appearance of a beautiful virgin and has been created since the six days of creation. And good-for-nothing men will come from the nations of the world and sleep with her, and she will become pregnant and at the end of nine months burst open, and there will go forth from her a male in human form;[303] he is 12 cubits long and 2 cubits wide; his eyes are red, treacherous עקומות (in Othoth ha-Maschiach [2:60.22] עמוקות = deep), the hair of his head is red like gold and the steps of his feet are ירוקים (= green or yellow, which is meaningless; perhaps one should read רחוקים = wide), and he will have two partings, and he will be called Armilos. He will go to the Romans (actually: to Edom = Esau = Rome) and say to them, "I am your Messiah, I am your God," and he will deceive them. Immediately they will believe him and make him king; and all the children of Esau (children of Rome = the Christian world) will band together with him and come to him. And he will go and proclaim to all lands and speak to the children of Esau, "Bring me my Torah, which I gave you!" And while the nations of the world are still coming, they will bring the book (in the manuscript there follows an erased word; according to Othoth ha-Maschiach, it should be filled out with: תפליתם = "their absurdity," a designation for the NT). And he will say to them, "This is what I have given you!" And he further says to them, "I am your God and I am your Messiah and your God!" In that hour he will send to Nehemiah (b. Hushiel, a name for the Messiah b. Joseph) and to all Israel and send word to them, "Bring me your Torah and certify for me that I am God!" And straightaway all the Israelites will stumble in wonder and in dread. Yet in that hour Nehemiah and three men with him from the sons of Ephraim will start off, and they will go with him, bringing the book of the Torah with them; and they will read before him, "I am Yahweh your God. You shall not have another God beside me" (Exod 20:2f.). Then he will say to them, "In your Torah there is nothing written about this one, and I will not let you go until you believe that I am God, just as the nations of the world believe in me." Immediately Nehemiah will rise up against him and say to him, "You are not God, but rather Satan!" Then he will say to them, "Why do you lie to me? I will give a command to kill you." And he will say to his servants, "Seize Nehemiah!" Yet immediately he and 30,000 heroes from Israel will arise and fight with him, and he will kill 200,000 from the army of Armilos. Then the wrath of Armilos will burn, and he will gather all the forces of the nations of the world and wage battle with the children of Israel and kill a thousand times a thousand of the Israelites, and he will also kill Nehemiah at midday (see Amos 8:9). (Israel then flees into the wilderness, Armilos moves against Egypt according to Dan 11:42 and then turns against Jerusalem in order to destroy it [Dan 11:45].

---

303. S-B: Othoth ha-Maschiach: There is a marble statue in Rome that looks like a young virgin beautiful in appearance, and it is not made by human hands, but rather God created it by his omnipotence. And the godless from the nations of the world will come, good-for-nothing men, and they will make her come into heat and lie with her, and God will store their sperm-drops in the stone and create in her a new creature and form in her a child, and she will burst open and there will go forth from her one in the form of a human, and his name is Armilos. ‖ Sefer Zerubbabel: Armilos b. Eben, who will proceed from a stone. ‖ Nistaroth R. Simeon b. Yohai: This one (Armilos) is a son of Satan and of stone בריה דסטנא ודאבנא.

Then the Messiah b. David is revealed and God himself fights against Armilos and his host. In this battle, according to the parallels, Armilos is killed.)

2:4 A: The adversary.

In Othoth ha-Maschiach as well, the antichrist Armilos הַשָּׂטָן זֶה is called "this adversary" (see above § 2:3 B, n. *a*).

2:4 B: Who exalts himself over everything that is called God (cf. Dan 11:36f.).

2:4 C: Making himself out to be God.

It is said of Nero in Sib. Or. 5:33f.: "Then he will come again, making himself equal to God ἰσάζων θεῷ αὐτόν. Yet he (God) will convict him that he is not." ‖ Armilos, the antichrist, introduces himself to the nations of the world with the words: "I am your Messiah, I am your God!" See Tephillath R. Simeon b. Yohai above at § 2 Thess 2:3 B, n. *f*. ‖ The ancient synagogue considers Hiram, Nebuchadnezzar, pharaoh, and Joash as representatives of self-divinization; Sisera, Sennacherib, and the prince of Tyre are also often named as examples of blasphemous pride; see TanḥB וארא § 7ff. (11B) at § John 5:18, #1, Lev. Rab. 7 (110B) at § Luke 1:51, n. *p*, and Mek. Exod. 15:11 at § 1 Cor 8:5.

2:6, 7: What is holding back … who is holding back.

Babylonian Talmud Sanhedrin 97B: "If it delays, wait for it" (Hab 2:3). If you should say, "We are waiting, but he (God) does not wait," it says, "Yahweh waits for it" (Isa 30:18). But how so? If we wait (for the arrival of the Messiah) and he (God) waits for it, who is holding it back מִי מְעַכֵּב? The divine righteousness holds it back מעכבת (which does not consider the Israelites worthy of the age because of their sin). — See the whole passage at § Acts 1:7. ‖ Jerusalem Talmud Taʿanit 1.64A.20: "Who is holding back מעכב (the coming of the messianic redemption)?" He answered, "The repentance (that you do not do)"; see the passage at § Matt 11:12, n. *a*. ‖ Pesiqta Rabbati 23/24 (124A): R. Nehuniah (ca. 350) said in the name of R. Tanḥum b. Judan (ca. 320), "Who is holding back איחר (אֵיחֵר) the honor (glorification) of Jacob in this world? The great honor that Esau showed his father (its recompense, which is not yet fully paid by God, requires the ongoing existence of Edom, that is, the Roman Empire; only when Rome falls can Israel's glorification begin)." ‖ Midrash Psalm 14 § 6 (57B): Like a king's son who got engaged to a king's daughter; and they set the appointed time (wedding) for this or that day. The king's son looked forward to his wedding and the king's daughter looked forward to her wedding. Who held it up מעכב (so that the wedding did not occur earlier)? Say: The appointed time held it up מעכב. Likewise, God looks forward (longingly) to the redemption of Israel, and the Israelites wait (with desire) for the salvation of God. And who holds it up מעכב? The time set (see Isa 63:4). ‖ See Midr. Esth. 1:1 (84A) at § Rom 3:9 A, #2, n. *e*. — These passages show how intensively the ancient synagogue was occupied with what "holds up" the coming of the end time.

2:8: The wicked man, whom the Lord Jesus will destroy with the breath of his mouth.

4 Ezra 13:8ff., 37: "Then I looked, behold, all who had gathered for battle against him (the Messiah) fell into great dread yet still dared to battle. Yet when he saw that onslaught of the host that was unleashed upon him, he did not raise a hand, nor did he take a sword or another weapon, but rather I saw only how he let out something like a fiery stream from his mouth, from his lips a flaming breath, and from his tongue he made darting sparks go forth: yet all these mixed together with one another: the fiery stream, the flaming breath, and the violent storm. This fell upon the assaulting host that was ready for battle, and it consumed them all, so that in the same moment there was nothing to see of the innumerable host except for the dust of ashes and the vapor of smoke. When I saw this, I was terrified ... (v. 37:) Yet he, my son (= Messiah), will punish the sins of the nations that have moved against him, which are like air. He will reproach them for their evil attacks and their future torments; they are like fire. Then he will destroy them effortlessly at his behest; this is like flame. — The last sentences are probably a rationalistic interpretation of the preceding older tradition. ‖ See Tg. Isa. 11:4 above at § 2 Thess 2:3, n. *f.* ‖ See TanḥB תרומה § 6 (46B) at § Matt 1:21, n. *a*, middle. ‖ See also the passages at § Rom 3:9 A, #3, B, n. *h.* ‖ See Pesiq. Rab. 37 (163A) at § Luke 24:26, I, #4, n. *o.* ‖ See Midr Vajjoschaʿ (*Beth ha-Midrash* 1.56.13) above at § 2:3, n. *f.*

2:9: In every powerful deed and signs and wonders.

See Sib. Or. 3:63ff. above at § 2 Thess 2:3 B, n. *d.*

3:2: That we may be saved from perverse and evil people.

See a prayer of Rabbi († 217?) for the salvation of evil men in b. Ber. 16B at § Matt 6:13 B.

3:10: If someone does not want to work, he shall also not eat.

On the praise of work, see § Mark 6:3 and § Acts 18:3, #1 and #2; also see Gen. Rab. 13 (9D) and ʾAbot R. Nat. 11 at the beginning. — ‖ ʾAbot de Rabbi Nathan 11 toward the beginning: R. Dustai (b. Yannai? [ca. 180]) said, "How do we know that a person, if he has not worked the whole six days (of the week), will have to work the whole seven days? Look, if someone sat all the days of the week without working and on the day of preparation for the Sabbath he has nothing that he can eat (on the Sabbath), he goes and falls into the hands of non-Jews; they seize him and fasten him in a neck iron, and in it he has to work on the Sabbath; all this, because he did not work the whole six days." R. Simeon b. Eleazar (ca. 190) said, "Even the first man was not allowed to enjoy anything before he had worked; as it says, 'He placed him in the garden of Eden, to cultivate and maintain it' (Gen 2:15); and then it says, 'From all the trees of the garden you may eat' (Gen 2:16)." ‖ Genesis Rabbah 2 (3A): "The earth had become like a waste and empty תהו ובהו" (Gen 1:2).... R. Abbahu (ca. 300) said, "Like a king who acquired two slaves, both by one and the same deed of sale and at one and the same price. Concerning one he commanded that he be fed at the public expense, and concerning the other he commanded that he should work to have something to eat. Then the latter sat down, raved תּוֹהָא (= θύων) and shouted בּוֹהָא (= βοῶν) and said, 'We were both obtained by one and the same deed of sale and for one and the same price, yet that one is fed at the public expense, and I, if I do not work, have nothing to eat!' So the earth sat raving and shouting and said, 'Those above and those below were created at once; those above feast on the splendor of the Shekinah, and those below, if they do not work, have nothing to eat!'" ‖ Genesis Rabbah 14 (10D): "The man became a living being" (Gen 2:7). R. Huna (ca. 350) said, "God made him a slave emancipated עבד מחורר for himself; for if he does not work, he has nothing to eat." — A person is his own slave since he has to work only for his sustenance. This idea becomes sharper with the reading: עבד מכודן = "a slave strained for himself." Parallels are found in Midr. Lam. 1:14 (56A); Midr. Eccl. 2:17 (15A).

3:12: That they eat their own bread.

ʾAbot de Rabbi Nathan 31 toward the beginning: R. Ahai b. Josiah (ca. 180) said, "Whoever buys grain from the market, what is he like? Like a child whose mother died and that is handed around at the doors of the other women who have recently given birth (so that they may suckle it), and it is not satisfied by this. Whoever buys bread from the market, who is he like? He is like someone who digs a grave (= like a mourner). Yet whoever eats from his own (= grain and bread that is self-acquired), he is like a child that grows at its mother's breast." The same man used to say, "If a person eats from his own (now = what he has worked on or earned for himself), his mind finds satisfaction; yet he eats, either from what is his father's or his mother's or his son's, his mind finds no satisfaction, let alone if he eats from what belongs to others."

3:14f.: Yet if someone does not obey ..., take note of him. Do not associate with him ...; do not consider him an enemy, but rather correct him as a brother.

Disobedience to the instructions of the scholars of Scripture entailed the ban. Associating with someone under the ban was to be avoided. However, there was an obligation to challenge the conscience of one under the ban so that he might give up his disobedience. The names of those who were banned were therefore made known to the community. See passages in detail in the excursus "Excommunication from the Synagogue."— Also see § Matt 18:15–18.

3:17: Which is a sign (of authenticity) in every letter.

On the letter signatures, see § Rom 16:22.

The First Letter of Paul to Timothy

1:1 A: Of God our savior (see § 1 Tim 2:3).

1:1 B: Christ Jesus, our hope.

1 Enoch 48:4: "He (the Son of Man-Messiah) will be the light of the nations and the hope of those who are afflicted in their heart."

1:2: Timothy, my true child.

On "child," see § 1 Cor 4:14 and § 1 Cor 4:17 A.

1:10: Robbers of people (Sellers of people).

On interpreting the 7th commandment in Exod 20:15 as referring to stealing human beings, see § Matt 19:18 A, #2.

1:12: That he considered me faithful.

A person's faithfulness is the precondition for his call to leadership; see Exod. Rab. 2 (68B) at § Matt 25:21 A.

1:13: Because I acted in ignorance.

See § Luke 23:34.

1:15: To save sinners (see § Matt 1:21 C.).

1:16: So that Jesus Christ might show his great long-suffering in me as the first.

See SDeut 3:23 § 26 (70B): King David said before God, "The sin that I have committed before you, may it not be written down hereafter." God said to him, "It is worth nothing to you at all that people will say, 'Because he loved him, he forgave him?'" — The greater the human sin is, all the greater must the divine love be that forgives it.[304]

1:17: To the king of the ages.

βασιλεὺς τῶν αἰώνων is not to be paired with the later רִבּוֹן הָעוֹלָמִים "Lord of the worlds," but rather with מֶלֶךְ עוֹלָם "eternal king" (Jer 10:10); see § Rom 16:26. Here reference may also be made to Sir 36:22: So that all on the earth may know that you are the Lord, the God of eternity ὁ θεὸς τῶν αἰώνων. The Hebrew text reads: וידעו כל אפסי ארץ כי אתה אל (עולם).

---

304. See also Kittel, *Sifre zu Deuteronomium*, 37.

1:19: A good conscience (see § Rom 2:15 B).

1:20: Whom I have handed over to Satan (see § 1 Cor 5:5).

2:1: For all people.

Babylonian Talmud Berakot 12B: Rabbah b. Hinenah the elder said in the name of Rab († 247), "Whoever can ask for mercy for his neighbor, and he does not ask for it, he is called a sinner; as it says, 'Even I, far be it from me that I should sin against Yahweh, desisting from prayer for you' (1 Sam 12:23)." ‖ Babylonian Talmud Berakot 34A.27: R. Jacob (ca. 340) said that Rab Hisda († 309) said, "Whoever asks for mercy for his neighbor does not need to mention his name; for it says, 'I beg, heal her!' (Num 12:13). Yet he did not mention Miriam's name here." — See further § Jas 5:16 B.

2:2: For kings and all in a position of authority (see § Rom 13:3 A).

2:3: Before God our savior.

σωτήρ perhaps = גּוֹאֵל. — The 7th benediction of the Prayer of Eighteen Benedictions reads as follows: "See our misery and take up our cause and redeem us גְּאָלֵנוּ quickly for your name's sake; for you are a strong redeemer גּוֹאֵל. Blessed be you, Yahweh, redeemer גּוֹאֵל of Israel!" ‖ In the prayer Geʾullah (closing benediction of the morning Shema) it says, "You are the first and you are the last, and aside from you we have no king, redeemer and helper מֶלֶךְ גּוֹאֵל וּמוֹשִׁיעַ." — See also § Matt 1:21 C, n. *b*.

2:5: There is also one who is mediator.

μεσίτης = סַרְסוֹר, see § Gal 3:19.

2:6: Who gave himself as a ransom.

ἀντίλυτρον α. = כֹּפֶר, Aram. כַּפְרָא, "atonement money"; β. = פִּדְיוֹן "ransom." כַּפָּרָה "atonement" is also used in the sense of "means of atonement."

Mekilta Exodus 21:30 (93A): "'If atonement money כּוֹפֶר is imposed on him, he shall give the ransom פִּדְיוֹן for his life (his soul)' (Exod 21:30), for the life of the one killed." These are the words of R. Ishmael († ca. 135). R. Aqiba († ca. 135) said, "The ransom is for the life of the killer. And so we find that those who have been forfeited to death by the hand of men (by the authority) may not give a ransom פדיון; there is no ransom anywhere for those who are guilty of death by a court; as it says, 'Everything banned that is banned by men (so the midr.) shall not be redeemed; it shall be killed' (Lev 27:29). Yet here (Exod 21:30) it says, 'Let him give the ransom for his life.'" ‖ Babylonian Talmud Baba Qamma 40A: Who is the teacher of the Mishnah who said, "The atonement money is an atonement כֹּפֶר כַּפָּרָה (i.e., that the atonement money is paid to make atonement for the deed of the perpetrator)?…" Rab Hisda († 309) said, "This is R. Ishmael b. Yohanan b. Beroqah (ca. 150); for in a baraita it has been taught: 'Let him give the ransom for his life' (Exod 21:30), the value of what has been damaged (the value that one would pay for the damaged item, if it would be sold, say, as a slave; here the ransom is not viewed as a means of atonement for the sake of the one who has caused the damage, but rather as compensation for the thing damaged)." Yet R. Ishmael b. Yohanan b. Beroqah said, "The value of the one who does the damage (the one who does the damage should pay as much as he himself would be worth as a slave, for the ransom is supposed to be an atonement for him, himself)." Does their difference of opinion not consist in the Rabbanan thinking that the atonement money כּוּפְרָא is (compensatory) money מָמוֹנָא (for the thing damaged), and R. Ishmael b. Yohanan b. Beroqah thinking that the atonement money is an atonement כּוּפְרָא כַּפָּרָה? Rab Papa († 376) said, "No. For the whole world is of the view that the atonement money is an atonement. Where they differ in opinion is that the Rabbanan would think that one assesses (the ransom) according to the value of the thing damaged, while R. Ishmael b. Yohanan b. Beroqah would think that one assesses it according to the value of the one who does the damage." ‖ Mekilta Exodus 21:30 (93B): For the nations there is no ransom פדיון; Scripture teaches, "A man cannot redeem a brother, and he cannot give God his atonement money כפרו: the ransom פדיון for their life (for their soul) is too expensive" (Ps 49:8f.). Beloved are the Israelites; for God gives the nations of the world in their stead תַּחְתֵּיהֶן as an atonement כַּפָּרָה for their souls תחת נפשותיהם; as it says, "I give Egypt as atonement for you כפרך" (Isa 43:3). Why? "Because you are precious in my eyes, you are esteemed and I love you, and I give men in your stead and nations instead of your life" (Isa 43:4). ‖ For כַּפָּרָה = atonement, means of atonement, see examples at § Rom 9:3, #2, n. *a* and § Luke 24:26, I, #2, notes *h* and *m*.

2:7: As a herald.

κήρυξ = כָּרוֹז, כָּרוֹזָא "proclaimer, herald." — See b. Sanh. 43A at § Matt 26:66 B, #5, n. *b*. ‖ Genesis Rabbah 30 (18B): Abba b. Kahana (ca. 310) said, "God had a herald כרוז in the generation of the flood; it was Noah (insofar as he called his contemporaries to repent)."

2:8 A: Raising holy hands.

Babylonian Talmud Soṭah 39A: R. Joshua b. Levi (ca. 250) said, "A priest who has not washed his hands should not raise לא ישא his hands (for the blessing); for it says, 'Lift your hands in holiness and bless Yahweh' (so Ps 134:2 in the sense of the midrash)." ‖ On spreading out and raising the hands as a prayer gesture, see § Luke 22:41 B, #4.

2:8 B: Without anger.

Babylonian Talmud 'Erubin 65A: Rab Hiyya b. Ashi (ca. 270) said that Rab († 247) said, "Whoever does not have a mind at rest should not pray; as it says, 'In distress בצר one should not give thanks (read יודה instead of יורה).'" — Rashi on this: "I have searched all of Scripture, but the passage is not in any of the Scriptures; this may be in the book of Ben Sira." — One would have to think of Sir 7:10: μὴ ὀλιγοψυχήσῃς ἐν τῇ προσευχῇ σου = "Do not be fainthearted in your prayer." The Hebrew text reads: אל תתקצר בתפלה = "Do not be impatient in prayer." — It is striking that even R. Hanina (ca. 225) cites the saying above as a word of Scripture. It further says in b. 'Erub. 65A: R. Hanina did not pray on a day of wrath

ביומא דרתחה (i.e., on a day when he was angry or irascible); he said, "In enmity בצר one should not give thanks," it is written.

2:9: Not with hair done up and gold or pearls.

In Palestine, this is what people would sing about a bride: "Not makeup, not powder, not frilly hair—and yet a chamois full of grace!" See b. Ketub. 16B at § Matt 9:15 B, n. *p.* – On women's hairstyle, see § 1 Cor 11:5 A.

2:10: By good works.

Sarah is praised in Num. Rab. 14 (176C) as follows: Abraham and Sarah, both were full of good works מלאים במעשים טובים ... Abraham made men and Sarah made women proselytes.

2:12 A: I do not permit a woman to teach.

See § 1 Cor 14:34f.

2:12 B: Nor to have authority over a man.

See Midr. Esth. 1:22 (91A) at § Eph 5:25, n. *e*, near end; b. ʿErub. 100B at § 1 Cor 7:3, n. *g*.

2:13: Adam was created first, then Eve.

The underlying thought here is that what is created earlier is more valuable than what is created later; see the general rule in SDeut 11:10 § 37 (76A) at § Rom 8:29 B, first paragraph.

A baraita in b. Sanh. 38A: Adam was created on the day of preparation for the Sabbath (and not, say, on the 1st day of creation), lest the heretics be able to say that he was God's companion (assistant) in the work of creation. A different explanation: So that it can be said to someone when his mind wants to exalt itself (proudly): The mosquito preceded you in the work of creation (and therefore is greater than you; what do you have to be proud of?). ‖ Genesis Rabbah 8 (6A): ("You have formed me behind and in front," so Ps 139:5 according to the midrash.) R. Simeon b. Laqish (ca. 250) said, "After the work of the last day of creation (= behind) and before the work of the first day of creation (= in front) ..."; for Resh Laqish said, "'The spirit of God hovered over the waters' (Gen 1:2): this is the spirit of the first man (so read, see § John 1:1 A, D).... If a person is righteous, it is said to him, 'You preceded (in the creation) the angels of service (your spirit was created before the angels who were created on the 2nd or on the 5th day)'; but if he is not righteous, it is said to him, 'The fly preceded you (in the creation), the mosquito preceded you, the worm preceded you (for you were created as the last work of creation).'" ‖ Exodus Rabbah 21 (83D): When Moses went to split the sea, this one did not accept that it would be split. The sea said to him, "For your sake I will not be split; I am greater than you; for I was created on the 3rd day and you were created on the 6th day." – A similar narrative is found in Midr. Ps. 114 § 9 (238A).

2:14: Adam was not misled, but rather the woman was misled and fell (thereby) into transgression (sin).

1. ἀπατάω deceive, mislead = הִשִּׁיא (see LXX Gen 3:13).

On the abilities of the snake to mislead, see Gen. Rab. 19 (12D) and ʾAbot R. Nat. 1 at § Matt 15:2 A, #4; Pirqe R. El. 13 toward the beginning at § Matt 4:1 B, #2, n. *a.* ‖ Genesis Rabbah 19 (12D): R. Joshua of Sikhnin (ca. 330) said in the name of R. Levi (ca. 300), "(The snake) began to speak slander against her creator. It said, 'From his tree he has eaten and (by virtue of eating) he created the world. And (now) he says to you, "Do not eat from it!" lest you create other worlds; for everyone hates the one who equals him in craft (out of professional jealousy).'" R. Judah b. Simon (ca. 320) said, "Everything that was created after something else rules over (this) other thing (the earlier was created for the sake of the latter and has to serve it, see Gen. Rab. 19 [12D] at § Rom 8:20f., n. *c*).... And you were created after everything, in order to rule over everything. Then preempt him and eat, before he creates other worlds so that they rule over you! This is what is written, 'The woman saw that it was good' (Gen 3:6). She saw the words of the snake (that they were good) ... 'And she took from its fruits and ate' (Gen 3:6)." R. Aibu (Aibo, ca. 320) said, "She crushed grapes and gave it to him (Adam; the underlying assumption is that the tree of knowledge was a grapevine)." R. Simlai (ca. 250) said, "With restful thought (with rational reasons according to a well-thought plan) Eve came over to Adam. She said to him, 'Do you think that if I die, another Eve will be created for you? There is nothing new under the sun! Or that I will die and you will remain unmarried? He did not create it to be a wasteland; he prepared it to be inhabited" (Isa 45:18).'" The Rabbanan said, "She began to yammer loudly before him (cf. Gen 3:17)."

2. παράβασις = עֲבֵירָה, α. "transgression,"[a] β. "sin,"[b] especially "fornication."[c]

a. Babylonian Talmud Sukkah 29B: (A robbed festal bouquet is unfit to fulfill the festal bouquet commandment; see m. Sukkah 3.1.) R. Yohanan († 279) said in the name of R. Simeon b. Yohai (ca. 150), "Since it would be a fulfillment of a commandment that would come about by a transgression (of another commandment) מצוה הבאה בעבירה."

b. Babylonian Talmud Yoma 86B: Sins עֲבֵירוֹת between one person and another; ... sins between a person and God. ‖ Babylonian Talmud Baba Batra 164B: Rab Amram (ca. 260) said that Rab († 247) said, "There are three sins עבירות that one does not remain protected from on any day; (these are:) sinful thoughts הִרְהוּר עֲבֵירָה (thinking of sin, especially unchaste thoughts) and negligence in prayer and an evil tongue (slander)."

c. For example, b. Qidd. 81A.32, 34: R. Meir (ca. 150) scoffed at those who commit a sin of fornication עוברי עבירה. The same is said shortly afterward about R. Aqiba († ca. 135); see the unabbreviated passages at § Rom 2:22 A.

3:2 A: A bishop should be a man of one wife.

1. Polygamy, covered by the example of the fathers (Gen 16:2; 25:6; 29:23, 28; 30:4, 9; 37:2; 46:10; Judg 8:30f.) and approved by several regulations of the Torah (cf. Exod 21:8, 10; Deut 21:15), even required by the law in the case of levirate marriage in certain circumstances (see Deut 25:5ff.),

was legally considered entirely permissible in Jewish thought at the time of Jesus. Josephus describes the simultaneous possession of multiple wives simply as an ancestral custom of his people.[a] The Mishnah in its casuistic discussions constructs a series of cases in which a man has two to five wives;[b] it allows the king to marry eighteen women.[c] The oldest halakic midrash on Deuteronomy applies Deut 21:15 to the case where someone has not only two, but rather many wives.[d] Rabban Gamaliel II (ca. 90) borrows features of bigamy for a parable.[e] One authority, such as Rab († 247), gives the advice not to take two wives alongside each other; however, if a man has two wives, he should for his personal security marry a third one in addition.[f] All this presupposes that polygamy was not a rare occurrence in Israel in the New Testament period. Life with its demands and necessities made sure by itself that this practice did not become the rule. If in principle the claim was postulated that a man could take who knows how many wives, in view of the duty obliging a man to maintain his wives, the qualification was immediately added: he must be able to support her.[g] No less did the thought of domestic peace curb polygamic inclinations.[h] — Historical evidence for the existence of polygamy in the ancient rabbinic period is not all that frequent. Herod the Great had ten wives[i] (see Schürer, *Geschichte des jüdischen Volkes*, 1:406f.). — In Jerusalem there were two priestly families of which it was generally known that they descended from secondary wives, so from marriages where the husband had several wives at his side.[k] — It is reported of R. Yose b. Halapta (ca. 150) that he entered into a levirate marriage with the widow of his brother, in which five sons were born to him; yet it is nowhere evident whether he had previously been otherwise married.[l] — The Jerusalem Talmud recounts that a man married twelve widows of his brothers by levirate marriage.[m] — R. Tarfon (ca. 100) even married 300 women at a time when living costs were high, in order to enable them to enjoy the offering that was allowed to him as a priest.[n] — Two Babylonian authorities—Rab († 247) and Rab Nahman († 320) when they moved from their residence to another location—used to enter into a marriage for the short period of their stay,[o] a procedure that however was an offense against the rather old principle that no one should keep wives in different places.[p] — Only extremely rarely are voices raised that take a position decisively more or less against polygamy.[q] Without doubt, R. Judah b. Batera (ca. 110) did this most ingeniously.[r]

2. The requirement that a bishop should be a man of one wife seems so obvious to us now that it has been reinterpreted to mean that he should be married only once. Yet the issue at the time of the apostle was completely different. Then the requirement meant that the bishop should have only one, not many wives simultaneously, an absolutely new thing, no more and no less than a break with an age-old customary law, by declaring that any

polygamy was incompatible with the spirit of the gospel, even if it occurs in legal form as among the Jewish people. Therefore, it must be absolutely maintained that 1 Tim 3:2 forbids exclusively the simultaneous possession of multiple wives. The case is different with the analogous statement in 1 Tim 5:9: "A widow is taken onto the list if she ... was a woman of one husband." In Israel there was no polyandry in the literal sense of the word, that is, a marriage where a woman simultaneously had several legitimate husbands; the saying in 1 Tim 5:9 cannot refer to such a case. Yet, probably the young church had from its standpoint a good right to assume that there was concealed polyandry in the case when a woman, divorced for the most invalid reasons, though legally from a Jewish perspective, quickly entered a marriage in order, after a short time, to undergo a repeated divorce and remarriage for the second and third and fourth time. It is against this hidden kind of polyandry that the saying in 1 Tim 5:9 is directed. — The idea that μιᾶς γυναικὸς ἄνδρα in 1 Tim 3:2 should be interpreted in the same way as ἑνὸς ἀνδρὸς γυνή in 1 Tim 5:9 would be justified only if the same matrimonial law existed for both genders. The difference in the matrimonial law implies by itself that the formally identical expressions in 1 Tim 3:2 and 5:9 are in fact different in content.

a. Josephus, *Jewish Antiquities* 17.1.2: πάτριον γὰρ ἐν ταὐτῷ (at the same time) πλείοσιν ἡμῖν συνοικεῖν. — *Jewish War* 1.24.2: ὡς ἂν ἐφιεμένου τε πατρίως Ἰουδαίοις γαμεῖν πλείους.

b. Mishnah Yebamot 4.11: If four brothers were married to four women and died childless, the eldest (of the surviving brothers) can, if he wants, marry all these women as their brother-in-law; the right is in his hand. — If someone was married to two women (at the same time) and has died, carrying out levirate marriage or removing the shoe of one of them exempts the secondary wife (i.e., the brother of the man who has died has to marry only one of the two widows). ‖ — Mishnah Yebamot 16.1: If it is reported to a woman whose husband and co-wife traveled to a distant land: "Your husband has died," she may not get married, nor enter into a levirate marriage, until she knows (for certain) whether the co-wife is pregnant (only then does the obligation for levirate marriage no longer apply for her and only then does she acquire the freedom to marry someone else). ‖ Mishnah Ketubbot 10.1: If someone was married to two women (simultaneously) and died, the first takes priority over the second (with her rights of inheritance), and the heirs of the first over the heirs of the second. ‖ Mishnah Ketubbot 10.4: If someone is married to three women and dies, and the marriage settlement of one amounts to 100 *zuz* and that of the other 200 *zuz* and that of the third to 300 *zuz*, and there are still there (in the estate) only 100 *zuz*, they apportion them in equal shares. ‖ Mishnah Ketubbot 10.5: If someone has four wives and dies, the first takes priority over the second (with her legal claims), the second over the third, the third over the fourth.... ‖ Mishnah Ketubbot 10.6: If someone is married to two women and sells his field .... ‖ Mishnah Qiddušin 2.6: If someone has betrothed two women (at the same time) with something that is worth (only) one *prutah* (the smallest coin) ..., the betrothal is invalid. (Simultaneous betrothal to two women is permissible per se, but the value of the item presented for the engagement of each woman has to be worth at least one *prutah*. Since the latter is not so in the given case, the betrothal is declared invalid.) ‖ Mishnah Qiddušin 2.7: It once happened with five women, two of whom were sisters, that someone gathered a basket of figs ... and said, "Look, you all should be engaged to me because of this basket!" One of them accepted the basket for them all (and thereby also the engagement). Then scholars declared, "The sisters are not engaged (because the law forbids simultaneous marriage to two sisters [Lev 18:18]; the engagement to the three other women was legally valid, though)." ‖ See further m. Bek. 8.4 and m. Ker. 3.7. ‖ See the baraita in b. Giṭ. 34B at § Acts 13:9 A, #2.

c. Mishnah Sanhedrin 2.4: "The king should not take many wives" (Deut 17:17), but rather (only) eighteen. See SDeut 17:17 § 159 (105B); t. Sanh. 4.5 (420) and b. Sanh. 21A. In the last passage the king is allowed also 24 and even 48 wives.

d. Sifre Deuteronomy 21:15 § 215 (113A): "If a man has two wives" (Deut 21:15). Here I hear only about two wives; how do we also know if there are many of them? Scripture teaches "wives."

e. See b. ʿAbod. Zar. 55A at § Rom 1:23 A, #2, D, n. *m*, middle.

f. Babylonian Talmud Pesaḥim 113A: Rab († 247) said to Rab Assi, "Do not take for yourself two wives; but if you have taken two, then take three (two can make common cause against you, but the third will safely bring their intrigue to you)." – The counsel of Raba († 352) is different in b. Yebam. 63B: "If a wife is evil and her marriage settlement is high (so that one cannot dismiss her because of this), then a secondary wife at her side! For people say, 'By her companion (co-wife), but not by the thorn bush (is a nasty wife made better).'"

g. Babylonian Talmud Yebamot 65A: Raba († 352) said, "A man may add however many wives to his (first) wife; but only if he is able to support them."

h. Targum Ruth 4:6: "The redeemer said, 'In this way I cannot redeem her for myself. Since I have a wife, it is not allowed to me to add another to her; she might get into a quarrel in my house, and I might destroy my estate. Redeem her for yourself, for you do not have a wife. Therefore, I cannot redeem her.'" – See b. Ber. 32B: Resh Laqish (ca. 250) said, "The community of Israel says before God, 'Lord of the world, if a man adds a wife to his first wife, he remembers the action of the first; but you have left and forgotten me' (see Isa 49:14)."

i. Of his ten wives, Herod had at one point in time nine simultaneously; see Josephus, *Ant.* 17.1.3: Ἡρώδῃ δὲ τῷ βασιλεῖ κατὰ τοῦτον τὸν χρόνον συνῴκουν ἐννέα γυναῖκες.

k. Babylonian Talmud Yebamot 15B: "I (R. Joshua [ca. 90]) testify to you concerning two great families in Jerusalem, concerning the family of the house of Sebaim from the house of Akhmai and concerning the family of the house of Qipai of Ben Meqoshesh, that they were descendants of secondary wives, and that among them there were high priests who carried out the altar service. – The names in the parallel passages t. Yebam. 1.10 and y. Yebam. 1.3A.48 at points are very different.

l. Jerusalem Talmud Yebamot 1.2B.9: R. Yose b. Halapta (ca. 150) had entered into levirate marriage with the wife of his brother: he plowed five ploughings (a metaphorical description for intercourse) and he planted five plantings (= he sired 5 sons). – Parallel passages are found in b. Šabb. 118B; Gen. Rab. 85 (54C).

m. Jerusalem Talmud Yebamot 4.6B.35: There were once thirteen brothers, of whom twelve died without children. They came and requested that he (the surviving brother) would be required to enter levirate marriage before Rabbi (Judah I [† 217?]). Rabbi said to him, "Go, perform the levirate marriage!" He answered him, "I do not have the means to do so." Then they (the widows) declared one after the other, "I will provide food for my month (the one of the 12 months of the year that falls to me)!" He said, "But who will provide food during this month in the leap year?" Rabbi said, "I will provide food in the month of the leap year." Then he prayed for them, and they went from there. After three years they came, carrying 36 children; they came and set themselves before Rabbi's dwelling. Someone went up and reported to him, "Down there a village of children wants to greet you." Rabbi looked out the window and saw them. He said to them, "What is your request?" They said to him, "We ask, give us (food) for this leap month." Then he gave them for this leap month.

n. Tosefta Ketubbot 5.1 (266): R. Menaḥem b. Nappaḥ said in the name of R. Eleazar Haqqappar (ca. 180), "It once happened that R. Tarfon was married to 300 women in years of drought (famine) and he let them eat the offerings because those were the years of drought." — We find a somewhat different text in y. Yebam. 4.6B.51.

o. Yoma 18B = b. Yebam. 37B, see § Rom 2:22 A, middle.

p. Babylonian Talmud Yebamot 37B: R. Eliezer b. Jacob (I., ca. 90) said, "Let a man not marry a woman in this city (or: in this country) and go and marry a woman in another city. Perhaps they (the children who spring from such marriages) might be bound to each other, so that the case will arise that a brother takes his sister for a wife." — The same is found in b. Yoma 18B.

q. Midrash Samuel 1 § 7 (23A): "He had two wives" (1 Sam 1:2).... R. Levi (ca. 300) said in the name of R. Hama b. Hanina (ca. 260), "Scripture begins with his (Elkanah's) praise (namely in 1 Sam 1:1), and then mentions his dishonor (namely, that he had two wives)." — In Pesiq. Rab. 43 (181B), R. Jonah (ca. 350) says this in the name of Rabbi († 217?). ‖ Babylonian Talmud Yebamot 65A: R. Ammi (ca. 300) said, "... I say, 'Whoever adds a wife to his wife, let him dismiss (the first one with a certificate of divorce) and pay the marriage settlement.'"

r. ʾAbot de Rabbi Nathan (ed. Schechter, chapter 2 p. 9): R. Judah b. Batera (ca. 110) said, "Job searched himself: 'What is the portion given by God from above' (with respect to marriage)? (Job 31:2). If the first man should have been given ten women, they would have been given to him (by God). Yet he was given only one woman. So let my wife, who is my portion, be enough for me too!"

3:2 B: A bishop should be blameless ....

On the moral requirements that were set by Jews for community overseers and judges, see § Acts 6:3, #2.

3:7: He should also have a good testimony from those who are outside.

1. μαρτυρία καλή, see § Rom 12:17 B.
2. οἱ ἔξωθεν, see § 1 Cor 5:12.

3:10: And they too should be tested.

Men called to honorary posts were tested specifically with a view to their legitimate lineage (see § Matt 1:1 A, #3).

3:14 A: In the house of God.

See Num 12:7: בְּכָל בֵּיתִי "in my whole house." — Septuagint: ἐν ὅλῳ τῷ οἴκῳ μου. — See a use of Num 12:7 in, for example, Pesiq. Rab. 10 (35B) at § Matt 5:43, #1, n. *g*, middle. — See also § Matt 21:13 A and § Matt 23:38.

3:14 B: Pillar.

στῦλος, see § Gal 2:9.

4:1 A: In the last times some will fall away from the faith.

On ἀποστασία in the end time, see § 2 Thess 2:3 A.

4:1 B: Holding fast to misleading spirits and teachings of demons.

See Sib. Or. 3:63ff. at § 2 Thess 2:3 B, n. *d*.

4:2: Branded in their own conscience.

The term κεκαυστηριασμένοι is derived from the custom of impressing a brand onto a slave as a sign of his bondage.

See t. Mak. 4.15 (443) at § Gal 6:17.

4:3 A: They prevent marrying (and command that people) refrain from food.

Among the Jewish people, efforts of this kind appear as signs of the mourners of the destruction of Jerusalem; see t. Soṭah 15.11ff. (322) at § Rom 14:2 and a baraita in b. B. Bat. 60B at § John 8:33 A.

4:3 B: With thanksgiving (see § Matt 14:19 B and § Eph 5:20).

4:8: Godliness is beneficial in everything, as it has a promise of life in the present and the future.

1. πρὸς πάντα ὠφέλιμος, see m. Qidd. 4.14 at § Matt 6:33, #1; the other passages adduced there also belong here.

2. ἐπαγγελία, see § Rom 4:13 A, #2.

3. ζωὴ ἡ νῦν καὶ ἡ μέλλουσα, see, for example, m. ʾAbot 6.7: Great is the Torah, for it bestows on those who do it life in this and in the future world; see Prov 4:22; 3:8, 18; 1:9; 4:9; 9:11; 3:16; 3:2.

4:12: Let no one despise your youth.

See m. ʾAbot 4.20 at § Matt 9:17; Lev. Rab. 11 (113B) at § 1 Tim 5:17.

4:13: Maintain reading.

On the reading of Holy Scripture in the communal liturgy, see the excursus "The Ancient Jewish Synagogue Service."

4:14: With laying on of hands.

See § Acts 6:6.

4:15: So that your progress may be evident to all.

προκοπή = "progress";[a] this passed into rabbinic literature as פְּרוֹקוֹפֵּי, פְּרוֹקְפֵּי = "distinction, dignity"; see § Phil 1:12.

a. Sirach 51:16f.: "I inclined my ear a little and received (wisdom) and I found much discipline for myself; progress προκοπή was (given) to me in it. To the one who gave me wisdom, I will give honor!" — The Hebrew text reads: "Much wisdom (knowledge) I have found; its yoke עֻלָּהּ became an honor for me, and to the one who taught me, I will give thanks!" — The Greek translator appears to have understood עֻלָּהּ as עָלָה in the sense of "advancement, exaltation" (= עִלּוּי). ‖ Testament of Gad 4: "Hatred works together with jealousy, and against those who are happy in advancement τῇ προκοπῇ, it is weak at all times if it hears or sees this." — See further 2 Maccabees 8:8.

4:16: You will save yourself and those who listen to you.

Deuteronomy Rabbah 11 (206D): Noah said to Moses, "I am greater than you, for I was saved out of the generation of the flood." Moses answered him, "I have been more exalted than you; you saved yourself הצלת את עצמך, but in you there was no power to save your age. Yet I saved myself and saved my age, when they had made themselves guilty of destruction because of the (golden) calf." How do we know this? Because it says, "And Yahweh repented of the calamity he had said he would inflict on his people" (Exod 32:14). What can this be compared with? With two ships on the sea in which there were two helmsmen. The one saved himself but not his ship, and the other saved himself and his ship. Who would have been praised? Is it not the one who saved himself and his ship? So too Noah saved only himself, but Moses saved himself and his age; therefore, "You surpass them all" (Prov 31:29).

5:1: Do not rebuke an older man.

ἐπιπλήσσειν = גָּעַר, Aram. גְּעַר, "to rebuke"; see as an example b. Šabb. 31A at § Matt 23:15 A, n. *w*.

5:4: To make a repayment (compensation) to their forebears.

Similarly to the way the apostle calls what children do for their parents an ἀμοιβή (repayment, compensation) for what the parents have done for their children, R. Abin (ca. 325) calls it a פְּרִיעַת (? פֵּרָעוֹן) חוֹב a "removal of debt"; see y. Qidd. 1.61B.58 at § Matt 22:36, #2, n. *c*.

5:6: But the woman who lives wantonly is dead even while she lives.

1. σπαταλάω "to revel, to be wanton," outside of Jas 5:5, is also found in Sir 21:15: "When an understanding man hears a wise word, he will praise it and heed it; when a wanton man ὁ σπαταλῶν hears it, he does not like it, and he tosses it behind his back." — The Hebrew text is not preserved at this point.

2. τεθνηκέναι = to be dead spiritual; מֵת "dead" is used in the same way in rabbinic literature (see § Matt 8:22). A further example is found in TanḥB יתרו § 1 (35A): "I have seen the godless, who were buried and came" (so Eccl 8:10 according to the midr.). How so? Are there godless people who were buried and came back again, so that Solomon says, "Who were buried and came"? Rather, R. Simon (ca. 280) said, "This refers to the godless, who are buried and dead in their life; as it says, 'All his says the wicked man is pierced מתחולל' (so Job 15:20 according to the midr.)." What does מתחולל mean? That he is dead and pierced. — The same is found in Tanḥ. יתרו at the beginning. — The same idea is found in a more extensive exposition in Tanḥ. הברכה 32B. — Conversely, the pious are called "living" חַיִּים even in death; see § Matt 8:22 and Yalquṭ on 1 Kgs 2:1 (2 § 169). — Passages that claim that the poor, leprous, blind, childless, rebellious, and persecuted should be viewed as dead are of a different sort; see, for example, b. Ned. 64B (at § Matt 19:22, #1); Gen. Rab. 71 (64A); b. ʿAbod. Zar. 5A; Exod. Rab. 5 (70D); Gen. Rab. 32 (19B); 38 (22D); Midr. Ps. 52 § 4 (142B); see also m. ʾAbot 5.21 at § 1 Tim 5:9 A.

5:8: Who has repudiated the faith.

ἀρνεῖσθαι = כָּפַר בְּ; see the 2nd passage from b. ʿArak. 15B at § Matt 5:11 B, #2.

5:9 A: Who is not less than sixty years old.

One started to get old at 60.

Mishnah ʾAbot 5.21: (Judah b. Tema, a Tannaim of uncertain time, said,) "At 5 years the (Holy) Scripture, at 10 years the Mishnah, at 13 years the doing of the commandments, at 15 years the Talmud, at 18 years the wedding canopy, at 20 years hunting (for a livelihood), at 30 years full vigor, at 40 years insight, at 50 years counsel, at 60 years aging, at 70 years old age, at 80 years the fullness of age (cf. Ps 90:10), at 90 years being bent over, at 100 years one is like one dead and gone and out of the world." — Elsewhere this remark is attributed to Samuel the small (ca. 100).[305]

5:9 B: Who was a woman of one husband.

See § 1 Tim 3:2 A, #2.

5:10: If she washed the feet of the saints.

That even women of better position bestowed this service of love on strangers is shown by Abot R. Nat. 16 (6A): R. Eliezer the elder (ca. 90) let the daughter of his sister grow up for 13 years in his house in his bed. When the sign (of puberty) came for her, he said to her,

305. See Bacher, *Die Agada der Tannaïten*, 1:372.5.

"Go and get married to a man!" She answered him, "Can I, your servant, not be a servant girl to wash the feet of your students?" He said to her, "My daughter, I am already too old. Go, and get married to a young man who is fitting for you!" She answered, "I have said to you, 'Can I, your servant, not be a servant girl to wash the feet of your students?'" When he heard her words, he separated himself from her; then he betrothed her and slept with her. — See also § John 13:5 B and SDeut 33:24 § 355 (148A) at § Matt 6:17 A, #1, n. *f.*

5:13: Running about in houses ..., gossipy.

A baraita in b. Soṭah 22A: A praying virgin, a widow running about אַלְמָנָה שׁוֹבָבִית and a boy whose months are not full (= a student who despises his teachers) destroy the world. ‖ Jerusalem Talmud Soṭah 3.19A.37: "A widow running about": by running about חגלה, she earns herself a bad reputation. ‖ Genesis Rabbah 18 (12B)—see the passage at § Eph 5:25, n. *e*, middle—mentions the woman who runs about פַּרְסָנִית and the gossiping woman דַּבְּרָנִית.

5:17: Elders who preside well should be deemed worthy of double honor.

Leviticus Rabbah 11 (113B): R. Yose b. Halapta (ca. 150) said, "Great is the dignity of the elders (the teachers and leaders of Israel): when they are old, they are lovable (venerable); when they are young, their youth is a (beautiful) addition to them." For R. Simeon b. Yohai (ca. 150) taught: "Not in one passage, nor in two passages, do we find that God showed honor to the elders זְקֵנִים, but rather in very many passages. With the thorn bush (see Exod 3:16); in Egypt (see Exod 3:18); on Sinai (see Exod 24:1); in the wilderness (see Num 11:16); with the tent of meeting (see Lev 9:1). Also in the future God will show the elders honor. This is what the following means: 'And the moon will turn red and the sun will fade' (Isa 24:23). Further, it is written, 'And before his elders there is honor' (Isa 24:23)." — According to SNum 11:16 § 92 (25B) only the final sentence comes from R. Simeon b. Yohai, which is then followed by: "See, here the inference from the greater to the lesser is justified: if the one who spoke and the world came into being will one day show honor to the elders, how much more will flesh and blood show honor to the elders!" ‖ Sifre Deuteronomy 1:15 § 15 (68B): "Then I took your tribal heads ... and made them heads over you" (Deut 1:15), so that they should be honored among you.

5:18 A: You shall not bind the mouth of a threshing ox (see § 1 Cor 9:9).

5:18 B: The worker is worth his recompense (see § Matt 10:10 E).

5:19: On the basis of two or three witnesses (see § Matt 18:16).

5:20 A: Rebuke those who sin in the presence of all (cf. § Matt 18:17 A).

5:20 B: So that the others too may fear.

See Deut 17:13 in m. Sanh. 11.4, in the excursus "The Day of Jesus' Death," B, #2, middle.

5:21: Before ... the elect angels.

1 Enoch 39:1: "In these days some of the elect and holy children of the high heaven (= angels) will come down, and their seed will unite with the children of men."

5:22: Do not have fellowship with the sins of others (cf. § 2 Cor 6:14).

5:23: No longer drink (only) water, but also enjoy a little wine because of your stomach and your frequent weaknesses.

1. Drinking water. – Babylonian Talmud Berakot 40A: Rabba b. Samuel (ca. 260) said in the name of R. Hiyya (ca. 200), "After all your eating, eat salt, and after all your drinking, drink water, so you will not suffer any harm." A different baraita: Eat every food, but do not eat salt; drink all drinks, but do not drink water; during the day one would have to be concerned about bad breath and at night one has to be concerned about quinsy. In a baraita: Whoever makes his (consumed) food swim in water will not suffer any abdominal pain. And how much (should one drink)? Rab Hisda († 309) said, "One cup for a piece of bread." ‖ See b. Giṭ. 70A at #2.

2. Drinking wine. – Babylonian Talmud Giṭṭin 70A: There are eight things that are harmful in excess but are good (salutary) in small measure, and there are: going away, intercourse, prosperity, work, wine, sleep, warm water (as a drink and a bath), and bloodletting. ‖ Babylonian Talmud Berakot 35B: Mar Zutra (ca. 400) said, "Wine nurtures but oil does not ... Wine strengthens but oil does not." But does wine strengthen? Raba († 352) used to drink wine on every day of preparation for the Passover, in order to stir up his appetite (literally: heart), so that he could eat a lot of unleavened bread! A lot (of wine) stirs up (the appetite), but a little strengthens. But does it strengthen at all? It says, "Wine makes the heart of a person happy ..., but bread strengthens a person's heart!" (Ps 104:15). It is bread that strengthens; but wine does not strengthen. Rather, two things are true of wine: it strengthens and makes happy; bread, however, strengthens but it does not make happy. ‖ Babylonian Talmud Baba Batra 58B: They (the pagan governing officials) said, "Since he (R. Benaiah [ca. 220]) is very wise, he likes to sit in the gate and administer justice. Then he saw that it was written at the city gate, '... I, blood, stand at the head of all causes of death; I, wine, stand at the head of all life!' (He said to them,) 'So if someone falls from a roof and dies, or if someone falls from a palm tree and dies, did blood kill him!? Furthermore, if someone's way is heading toward death and someone lets him drink wine, will he remain alive? Rather, one should write, "I, blood, stand at the head of all sicknesses; I, wine, stand at the head of all remedies."' Someone then wrote (as an addition to the original inscription) the following: 'Yet the elders of the Jews say, "I, blood, stand at the head of all sicknesses; I, wine, stand at the head of all remedies."' In a place where there is no wine, there medicines are desired." – See also § Eph 5:18 and b. Taʿan. 11A at § 1 Cor 9:25 A, #2, n. *d*.

5:24: They (sins) follow after some.

On ἐπακολουθεῖν, see 4 Ezra 7:35: The recompense follows. — See further at § Rev 14:13 B.

6:1: As many slaves are under the yoke.

ὑπὸ ζυγόν, see t. B. Qam. 7.5 (358) at § 1 Cor 7:23 B.

6:4: Suffering from questions (inquiries) and arguments.

There were the same sort of ζητήσεις and λογομαχίαι in the Jewish houses of learning as well. Babylonian Talmud Sanhedrin 59B: "Rule over the fish of the sea and the birds of heaven ..." (Gen 1:28). Does that not mean (they should serve you) as food? No, also for work. But are fish suited for work? Yes, according to the opinion of Rahba (ca. 300). For Rahba asked, "If someone drives a cart with a goat and a *shibbuṭa* (a type of fish), what is the case (concerning the *kil'ayim* law in Lev 19:19; Deut 22:9ff.)? ‖ See b. Sanh. 59B at § Acts 10:11ff.; b. Nid. 69B at § Eph 5:4 A, #1, n. *a.* ‖ See also b. Šabb. 30B at § Matt 5:5, #1, middle and b. Menaḥ. 37A: If a person has two heads, on which one should he put the tefillin?

6:6: With contentment.

See the citations at § Matt 19:23, #1.

6:7: For we brought nothing into the world, (know) that we can bring nothing out of it.

Mishnah ʾAbot 6.9: (R. Yose b. Qisma [Qosma?, ca. 110] said to someone who requested that he take up residence in his city,) "My son, if you give me all the silver and gold in the world, I will still dwell only in a place of the Torah, because in the house a man departs, neither silver nor gold nor gems nor pearls accompany him, but rather only (the knowledge of) the Torah and good works; as it says, 'In your wandering it will lead you,' in this world; 'in your lying down it will keep watch over you,' in the grave; 'when you wake up (at the resurrection of the dead), it will address you,' in the future world (Prov 6:22)." ‖ Midrash Ecclesiastes 5:14 (29A): "As he came out from his mother's womb, he will go again naked, as he came" (Eccl 5:14). Geniba (ca. 250) said, "Like a fox that found a vineyard that was fenced about on all its sides; yet there was a hole there that he tried to get in through; but he could not. What did he do? He fasted for three days until he was emaciated and frail. Then he went in through that hole and ate until he became fat. He wanted to get out, but he could not (through that hole) at all. Then he fasted again for three more days until he was emaciated and frail, like before; then he went out. When he went out, he turned his face, looked at it and said, 'Vineyard, vineyard, how beautiful you are and how beautiful are those fruits in you, and everything that is in you is beautiful and precious! Yet what good are you? As one goes into you, so one goes out again. It is the same with this world.'" — See the continuation at § Matt 16:26 B.

6:9: Who want to become rich die ... (see § Matt 19:23, #3).

6:10: The love of money is a root of all evils.

On ῥίζα, see Sir 1:18: “The root ῥίζα of wisdom is fearing the Lord.” ‖ Wisdom 15:3: “To know your strength is the root ῥίζα of immortality.”

6:11: Pursue righteousness.

διώκειν δικαιοσύνην = רָדַף צֶדֶק (Isa 51:1) or רֹדֵף צְדָקָה (Prov 15:9).

6:15: Who is the king of those who are kings and the lord of those who are lords.

1. ὁ βασιλεὺς τῶν βασιλευόντων perhaps = מֶלֶךְ מַלְכֵי הַמְּלָכִים (cf. Dan 2:37). See m. ʾAbot 3.1 and 4.22 at § Matt 12:36, #2; m. Sanh. 4.5 at § Acts 17:26; b. Ber. 28B at § Matt 10:28, #1, n. *c.*

2. κύριος τῶν κυριευόντων. — Deuteronomy 10:17: אֲדֹנֵי הָאֲדֹנִים; LXX: κύριος τῶν κυρίων. — Targum Onkelos and Yerušalmi I: מָרֵי מַלְכִין “Lord of kings.” ‖ Psalm 136:3: אדני האדנים; LXX: κύριος τῶν κυρίων. — Targum: מָרֵי מָרַיָּא “Lord of lords.” Levy also offers the manuscript reading: רִבּוֹנֵי רִבּוֹנַיָּא = “Lord of lords.”[306]

6:16 A: Who dwells in inaccessible light.

See 1 En. 14:9ff.; b. Ḥag. 12B at § Matt 25:31 B, #2; see Tanḥ. בהעלותך 204A at § Matt 5:14 A, n. *a.* ‖ Targum Ezekiel 8:2: “I saw, and behold, a form like an appearance of fire, an appearance of the (divine) glory, that no eye could look at, and it was not possible to look at it; and beneath an appearance of fire and an appearance of glory that no eye could look at, and it was not possible to look at it, and above like an appearance of splendor like *chashmal* (of the angels?).” ‖ Midrash Psalm 27 § 1 (111A): “God made a separation between the light and the darkness” (Gen 1:4). R. Judah b. Simon (ca. 320) said, “He separated it (the light) for himself. Like a king who saw a beautiful portion; he said, ‘It belongs to me!’ Likewise, when God created his world, he too created a great light (the primordial light); then he said, ‘Not every creature can make use of this; only I can. Likewise it says, “And light dwells with him” (Dan 2:22).’” — There is a parallel in Gen. Rab. 3 [3D]. On this primordial light, see more at § John 1:1 A, C, #6, second S-B footnote in that section. ‖ Numbers Rabbah 15 (178D): R. Hanina (ca. 225) said, “God said, ‘In the eyes that you have, there is white and black, and you do not see by virtue of the white, but rather by virtue of the black; if you with your eyes, in which there is black and white, see only by virtue of the black, should God, who is entirely light שכולו אורה הוא need your light?!’” ‖ Numbers Rabbah 15 (178D): God is entirely light כולו אורה; as it says, “And light dwells with him” (Dan 2:22) .... Great is the light of God. The sun and the moon illuminate the world, and where do they shine from (receive their light from)? They seize some of the sparks of the upper; as it says, “Your arrows go forth for light, for shining the lightning of your spear” (Hab 3:11). Great is the upper light; for only one-hundredth of it is given to all creatures; as it says, “He knows what is in darkness” (Dan 2:22).

---

306. Levy, *Chaldäisches Wörterbuch*, 2:401A.

6:16 B: Whom no one among humans has seen nor can see (see § Rom 1:20 A).

6:17 A: The rich in this age.

The expression τοῖς πλουσίοις ἐν τῷ νῦν αἰῶνι does not correspond in any way to the expressions adduced by Schöttgen. עֲשִׁירֵי עוֹלָם in Pirqe R. El. 25 (12D) designates the Sodomites as the richest people of the world: The richest people of the world were the Sodomites as a result of their good and fat land in which they lived. —עֲשִׁירוֹ שֶׁל עוֹלָם "Rich one of the world" in Deut. Rab. 2 (197B) is God to whom everything belongs. — עשיר בעלמא "The ordinary rich man" in b. B. Bat. 4A refers to the one who is no more than rich, in distinction from a king who in addition to his fortune also possesses power. — עניי עולם in b. B. Bat. 8B also does not belong here; this refers to the "poor of the land" in contrast to the "poor of a locale" עניי העיר. — However, the following passage from the Alphabet Midrash of R. Aqiba (*Beth ha-Midrash* 3.22.34) is in fact comparable: Whoever is poor in this world will be rich in the future world, as the Israelites, because they occupy themselves with the fulfillments of the commandments. The rich in this world עֲשִׁירִים בְּעוֹלָם הַזֶּה will be poor in the future world, as the nations of the world and the godless (among the Israelites), because they do not occupy themselves with the fulfillments of the commandments, and because God gives the rich in this world their recompense (already) in this world ...

6:17 B: Uncertainty of prosperity.

See Pesiq. 11B. 12A; TanḥB משפטים § 8 (43A); Exod. Rab. 31 (91C); b. Šabb. 151B at § Matt 19:22, #3, n. *a*; see Tanḥ. מטות 244B at § Matt 6:24, #3. ‖ Prosperity as a gift of God. — See Tanḥ. מטות 244B at § Eph 2:8. — Tanḥuma משפטים 96B: God gave him (the rich man) fortune from his (divine) treasure, which is a reliable one, and this one (the rich man) made from it a treasure of deceit; as it says, "You have plowed wickedness, you have harvested villainy, ate the fruit of swindle; for you trusted in your way" (Hos 10:13).

6:18: Doing good ..., generous, sharing.

On the blessings and dangers of prosperity, see § Matt 19:23, #2 and #3.

6:19: Gathering for themselves a good foundation like a treasure.

On ἀποθησαυρίζειν, see § Matt 6:19f. ‖ On the treasury of God and the treasures stored there, see b. Ḥag. 12B: In the (7th heaven) Araboth are the treasures of life גנזי חיים and the treasures of peace and the treasures of blessing. ‖ See Exod. Rab. 45 (101A) at § Rom 9:15. ‖ Babylonian Talmud Šabbat 105B: R. Simeon b. Pazzi (ca. 280) said, that R. Joshua b. Levi (ca. 250) said in the name of Bar Qappara (ca. 220), "Whoever sheds tears over a pious person, his tears are counted by God and deposited in his treasury בבית גנזיו; as it says, 'Put my tears in your bottle! Do you not write them in your book?' (Ps 56:9)." ‖ See also § Luke 23:43, E.

The Second Letter of Paul to Timothy

1:2: My beloved child (see 1 Tim 1:2).

1:18: May the Lord let him find mercy from the Lord.

Similarly, Gen 19:24: "Yahweh made sulfur and fire rain ... from Yahweh." — Septuagint: καὶ κύριος ἔβρεξεν ... παρὰ κυρίου.

2:4: No one who goes to the field gets tangled up in the affairs of subsistence, so that he may please the one who gathers the army.

1. πραγματία = פְּרַגְמַטְיָא or פְּרַקְמַטְיָא "business, trade."

A baraita in b. Roš Hašš.31B: Rabban Yohanan b. Zakkai († ca. 80) lived 120 years: 40 years he occupied himself with trade פרגמטיא, 40 years he studied, and 40 years he taught. ‖ See b. Ber. 34B at § Matt 10:42, #2.

2. On the idea of the whole verse, see Mek. Exod. 16:4 (55B) at § Matt 6:25.

2:6: The farmer who toils should first have a share in the fruits (see § 1 Cor 9:7 B and C).

2:12: We will also reign with him.

See § 1 Cor 4:8 and § 1 Cor 6:2.

2:18: The resurrection has already happened.

This is in line with the saying of Hillel (ca. 300) that the Israelites had already enjoyed the Messiah; see b. Sanh. 99A at § Matt 1:10, #1.

2:19: This seal.

σφραγίς = חוֹתָם, see § John 3:33 and § John 1:14, #2, toward the end.

2:20: Some for honor, others for dishonor.

See § Rom 9:21–23.

2:22: With those who call on the Lord from a pure heart.

Exodus Rabbah 22 (84C): Just as they (the Israelites at the Red Sea) purified טיהרו their heart and then sang a song—for so it is written, "The people feared Yahweh and believed in Yahweh" (Exod 14:31); and then it says, "Then Moses and the children of Israel sang to Yahweh this song" (Exod 15:1)—so too a person must purify his heart צריך אדם לטהר לבו before he prays. So says Job as well: "No injustice is in my hands and my prayer is pure" (Job 16:17). R. Joshua, the priest, b. Nehemiah (ca. 350) said, "Is there than an impure prayer (literally:

a prayer done dully)? Rather: If someone whose hands are stained by robbery calls on God, he does not hear him. Why? Because his prayer happens with sin; as it says, 'Yahweh said to Noah, "The end of all flesh has come before me; for the earth is full of violence because of them. Therefore, I will destroy them together along with the earth" (Gen 6:13).' Yet since Job's toil was not robbery, his prayer was pure. Therefore he says, 'Since no injustice is in my hands; since no dishonesty is in my hands and in my toil, my prayer is pure.'" R. Hama b. Hanina (ca. 260) said, "How do we know that the prayer of someone in whose hands there is robbery is an impure prayer? Because it says, 'If you spread out your hands, ... even if you pray a lot, I will not hear it' (Isa 1:15). Why? 'Because your hands are full of blood' (Isa 1:15). And how do we know that the prayer of someone who refrains from robbery is a pure זכה one? Because it says, 'Whoever has clean hands and a pure heart' (Ps 24:4). What is written after this? 'He will receive blessing from Yahweh ...; this is the generation of those who seek him' (Ps 24:5f.)."

2:23: Foolish ... questions (inquiries) (see § 1 Tim 6:4).

3:1 A: In the last days.

ἐν ἐσχάταις ἡμέραις, Old Testament = בְּאַחֲרִית הַיָּמִים; in the targumim: α. בְּסוֹף יוֹמַיָּא "at the end of days"; so Tg. Onk. Gen. 49:1; Num. 24:14; Yer. I Gen. 49:1; Tg. Isa. 2:2 and Mic. 4:1; β. בְּסוֹף עֲקֵב יוֹמַיָּא "at the last end of days," Tg. Yer. I Num. 24:14. — This was understood to refer to the time of the arrival of the days of the Messiah; see the citations at § Heb 1:1.

3:1 B: Hard times.

See the excursus "Signs and Calculations of the Messianic Time."

3:6: Taking little old ladies captive.

Tanḥuma ויקרא 134A: "A heart that prepares unholy thoughts, feet that quickly run to evil" (Prov 6:18): this refers to Ahab b. Kolaiah and to Zedekiah b. Maaseiah (cf. Jer 29:21ff.), who had sinned in Jerusalem. As if this were not enough, after they were led into exile in Babylon, they continued to sin. What had they done in Jerusalem? They had been lying prophets and did not cease from their craft in Babylon and were brokers for each other in sins. Ahab b. Kolaiah went to the great ones of the kingdom in Babylon and said to them, "God has sent me to say something to your wife." The one addressed said to him, "Look, she is before you." He went to her; and when he was alone with her, he said to her, "God will make prophets arise from you; go and copulate with Zedekiah b. Maaseiah, so he will beget prophets from you." And she listened to him, sent for Zedekiah, and he came and slept with her. And Zedekiah did the same and acted as the broker for Ahab. This was their craft. Come and see, how godless they were to get for themselves in Babylon the reputation that they were great prophets. When a pregnant woman would see one of them and say to him, "If you are a prophet, (tell me) whether I am pregnant with a boy or a girl?"—he would answer her, "With a boy!" Then he went to her neighbor and said to her, "So-and-so will give birth to a girl!" If she gave birth to a boy, she would say, "The words of the prophets have been fulfilled." And if she gave birth to a girl, her neighbor would say, "The prophet told us so; he just did not want to grieve you." So they acted until they came to Semiramis, the wife of Nebuchadnezzar. Zedekiah went to her and said, "God has sent me to you, go and copulate with Ahab, so you will bear prophets." She answered him, "I can do that only with my husband's foreknowledge; so come so that we can tell him so that he may agree!" She went to her husband and said to Nebuchadnezzar, "Send for them!" When both had come, he said to them, "Did you say this to my wife?" They answered, "So it is; for God wants to make prophets arise from her." He said to them, "Have I not heard about your God, though, that he hates fornication, and that because of Zimri, who was decadent in fornication, 24,000 fell? And you say this? Has he changed his mind? Whether you are prophets of a lie or prophets of the truth, I do not know; but I once tested Hananiah, Mishael, and Azariah and heated the oven for them for seven days, and they were cast into it and came out alive and unharmed. But for you I will have the oven heated for only one day and cast you in. If you are saved from it, I will know for certain that you are prophets of the truth. Then we will do everything according to your word, everything that you will say." They answered him, "Hananiah, Mishael, and Azariah were three, and we are two, and the miracle happened because of three." He said to them, "Is there a third here who is like you?" They said, "Joshua, the high priest!" Yet they thought in themselves that they would be saved because of him. The priest Joshua was brought and cast with them into the oven. Both of them were burned, but Joshua, the high priest, was saved; as it says, "Is he (Joshua) not a log, torn from the fire?" (Zech 3:1). "And a curse was taken from Ahab and Zedekiah for the whole captivity of Judah in Babylon, with it being said, 'May God make you like Zedekiah and like Ahab, whom the king of Babylon roasted in the fire!'" (Jer 29:22). — Parallel narratives are found in Pesiq. 164B; TanḥB ויקרא § 10 (4A); b. Sanh. 93A. ‖ In a similar way, the priests of the temple of Isis in Rome misled a noble Roman woman named Paulina, who was the wife of Saturninus, to fornicate with a certain Decius Mundus (see Josephus, *Ant.* 18.3.4). See further Josephus, *Ant.* 18.3.5 at § Rom 2:22, C, #2.

3:8: As Jannes and Jambres resisted Moses.

1. The names of both men are, in the Talmud and sometimes in the midrashic works, יוֹחָנִי or יוֹחָנָא (= John) and מַמְרֵי (= the rebellious); in the targumim, יַנֵּיס and יַמְבְּרֵיס or יַמְרֵיס. — יַמְבְּרֵיס = Ἰαμβρῆς arose from מַמְרֵי, because, under Hellenistic influence for the purpose of easier pronunciation, the first מ in ממרי was softened to י and then a ב was inserted before ר. The same insertion of β between μ and ρ is found with Νέμβροδ in LXX Gen 10:8 and with Μάμβρη in LXX Gen 13:18; 14:13. — In later midrashic works, we also encounter the name forms יוּנּוֹס and יוּמְבְּרוֹס or יָנוֹס and יַמְבְּרִינוּס. See the passages in the following citations.

2. Most of the time in the Jewish tradition, Jannes and Jambres are considered to be sons of Balaam.[a] Together with their father they occupy a privileged position in the court of the Egyptian king.[b] They use their position to propose to pharaoh the plan to cast all Israelite boys into the water.[c] When Moses remains alive, their father counsels the king to have

him eliminated immediately. Yet even this plan fails.[d] Then they consider it advisable to leave Egypt; they go to Ethiopia. Later they return to pharaoh's court[e] and appear now as the sorcerers who with their arts try to thwart the release of Israel.[f] When they nevertheless cannot prevent the exodus, they ostensibly acknowledge Moses' superiority and convert as proselytes to Judaism.[g] In reality, though, they undertake this step only in order to be able to continue to harm Israel. So it is they in the first place who cause the people to demand of Aaron to make the golden calf.[h] As a punishment for this, they perish in the slaughter of Exod 32:27ff.[i] There is another tradition alongside this that claims that they perished with the Egyptians in the sea.[k] These views stand in contradiction, though, with the interpretation of Num 22:22 that holds that they were the two "knaves" or "fellows" who accompanied Balaam on his journey to king Balak.[a] Consequently, they would still have been alive at the end of the forty years of wandering in the wilderness. There was, accordingly, no unified tradition about Jannes and Jambres; all the statements only agree that they oppose Moses at every turn and are filled with a hostile attitude toward Israel.

3. Apart from the entirely incidental mention of Yuhna and Mamre in b. Menaḥ. 85A—see, n. *f*—we hear nothing about the legend of Jannes and Jambres in all of the older rabbinic literature. The later Targum Yerušalmi I and the later midrash work Tanḥuma are the first writings that know about the details of the legend. Nevertheless, in view of 2 Tim 3:8, it cannot be doubted that the kernel of the traditions about Jannes and Jambres, namely their hostility toward Moses, was already generally known in the oldest period. We have here a classic proof for the truth that traditions can be old even if they are encountered literarily only in a later period.

a. Targum Yerušalmi I Numbers 22:22: "(Balaam) rode on his jenny and his two youths עולימוי (boys, knaves) Jannes and Jamres with him." — The tradition then made the two knaves Balaam's sons. Yalquṭ Reubeni (ed. Amsterdam 1700) 148A from a "midrash": Balaam the wicked had his strength from two letters מי; these were his two sons Mamre and Yohani (whose names begin with מ or י); this corresponds in holiness to Moses and Joshua (whose names also begin with מ and י). — The following citations everywhere offer additional supporting texts.

b. Yalquṭ Simeoni on Exodus 2:23; 1 § 168 (55B) from the "Chronicle of Moses": When pharaoh had become king over Egypt, his heart became hard against all the inhabitants of his land, and even the house of Jacob he did not spare, according to the counsel of Balaam, the sorcerer, and his two sons; for they were the king's counselors in those days. ‖ Yalquṭ Reubeni 146C from צִיוּנִי: "His two knaves (youths) were with him" (Num 22:22). Who were they? Our teachers of blessed memory said, "They were Junnos and Jumbros, scribes of pharaoh." Some say, "They were his (Balaam's) sons."

c. Targum Yerušalmi I Exodus 1:15: "When pharaoh slept, he saw in his dream, and lo, the whole land of Egypt was in a pan on a scale and a young lamb was in the other pan on the scale; and the scale tilted to the side of the lamb. Immediately he sent for and called all the sorcerers of Egypt and told them his dream. Immediately Jannes and Jambres, the chiefs of the sorcerers, opened their mouth and said to pharaoh, 'A son will be born in the community of the Israelites, by whom the whole land of Egypt will be destroyed.'" (As a result, the order in Exod 1:15f. is then given.) — The dream is found in a more expansive form also in the Chronicle of Moses (*Beth ha-Midrash* 2.1.2); yet here the interpretation and advice are not given by Jannes and Jambres, but rather by "one of the princes"; see the passage also in Yalquṭ Simeoni on Exodus 1:15, 1 § 164 (53C); here, though, the advice comes from one of the royal eunuchs.

d. Chronicle of Moses (*Beth ha-Midrash* 2.3.21): In the third year of the birth of Moses, pharaoh sat at the table, and his wife sat at his right hand and his daughter Bithiah at his left; yet before him sat his princes (chiefs) and his ministers. And the boy (Moses) sat with Bithiah, the king's daughter; and the boy stretched out his hand and took the crown from the king's head and set it on his own head. And the king was disquieted about this together with his princes, and they marveled among themselves. Then Balaam, the sorcerer, one of the king's princes and counselors, answered and said, "Remember, my lord king, the dream that you dreamed and that your servant interpreted for you! Do you not know that this boy belongs to the children of the Hebrews and that the spirit of God is in him and that he has acted from his wisdom? And he is the one who will destroy Egypt; and now let the king decree immediately that his head be taken off!" And the word was good in the king's eyes and those of his friends. Then God—blessed be He!—sent the angel Gabriel,[307] and he resembled one of the king's princes and his friends (i.e., he had taken on his form and appearance). He said to him, "My lord king, this word is not good to kill a person of innocent blood; for the boy has no thought. And now command that a gem be set before him and a glowing coal. If he stretches out his hand and takes the gem, it is certain that he is a child of thought and of death, and we will carry out the sentence; but if he stretches out his hand and takes the coal, it is certain that there is no thought in him, and let him remain exempt from punishment." And all his wise men saw this and said, "This word is good!" Then a gem and a coal were brought before him; and the boy stretched out his hand to take the stone. Then the angel pushed his hand so that he took the coal, and he led it to his face and touched it with his lips and the tip of his tongue, and (as a result) he had a sluggish mouth and a sluggish tongue, and because of this he was saved. — This legend is also found in Exod. Rab. 1 (67B), except that instead of the angel Gabriel, Jethro is the saving counselor; see the passage at § Luke 1:19 A, #4, n. g, first third. See also Josephus, *Ant.* 2.9.7.

e. Chronicle of Moses (*Beth ha-Midrash* 2.5.22): When Balaam saw that his counsel was not followed and that it did not come about that the children of Israel would be destroyed according to the evil plan that he had thought of, he left Egypt and went to king Niqanos together with his two sons Jannes and Mamres (ממרים); yet it was king Niqanos, king of Edom (which in the wider course of the narrative is identified with Cush, i.e., Ethiopia). — It is then further reported that king Niqanos waged war in the time with the sons of the east and that he entrusted Balaam with administering his country during his absence. Yet the latter lures the Ethiopians to fall away from Niqanos and makes himself

307. S-B: On this task of Gabriel, see § Luke 1:19, #4.

king and proclaims his sons as princes of the land. At his return Niqanos is refused entry into his capital city; so he finds himself forced to besiege it. This has already lasted for nine years when the king dies. In the meantime, Moses enlisted himself in his army. The great popularity that he soon enjoyed with everyone in the company makes him appear to be worthy to succeed Niqanos. So he is chosen as king. His wisdom soon succeeds in conquering the besieged city. Then it says at the conclusion: When Balaam, the son of Beor, saw that the city was taken, he fled from there in the air by all kinds of magical arts, he and his sons, and they fled to Egypt to pharaoh. — The text in Yalquṭ Simeoni 1 § 168 (55B) is taken from a different recension; the king of Ethiopia is here called קוקנוס.

f. Yalquṭ Simeoni on Exodus 5:1, 1 § 176 (57D): "Then Moses and Aaron went" (Exod 5:1). It happened when they came to the gate of the royal palace, behold, there were there two young lions with iron chains put on them, and no one could go out or in before them, except when the king commanded that the guards go out and remove the young lions by their magic spells. Then he was brought in. And Moses quickly swung the staff over the lions and let them loose, and so they came into the royal palace, and the lions went with them with great joy, as a dog rejoices over its master when he comes from the field. When pharaoh saw this, he was astounded and was very afraid of the men, for their appearance was like the appearance of sons of God (cf. Dan 3:25). Then the king said to them, "What do you want?" They answered him, "Yahweh, the God of the Hebrews, has sent us to you to say, 'Let my people go so that they may serve me'" (cf. Exod 5:1). And he was very afraid of them and said to them, "Go for today and come tomorrow!" And they did according to the king's word. When they had gone away, the king called for Balaam, the soothsayer, and his sons Janos and Jambrinos ינוס וימברינוס, the sorcerers. ‖ Targum Yerušalmi I Exodus 7:11: "Then pharaoh called the wise men and the sorcerers. They too, Jannes and Jambres, the sorcerers in Egypt, did the same by the magic spells of their sorcery." ‖ Babylonian Talmud Menaḥot 85A: Yuhna and Mamre said to Moses (when they were just about to turn their staffs into snakes; Exod 7:11f.), "You want to bring straw to Hafaraim?"[308] Moses answered them, "People say, 'To a vegetable city, bring vegetables'" (for in a place that is famous for cultivating vegetables, most of the time people demand vegetables). — In the parallel passage Exod. Rab. 9 (73C), the names of the sorcerers are Yuhani and Mamre. ‖ See further Tanḥ. כי תשא in, n. *h.*

g. Yalquṭ Reubeni on Exodus 7:11 (81B) from Zohar: "When they (the Egyptian sorcerers) saw the signs and wonders that were done by Moses in Egypt, they came later to Moses and wanted to become proselytes. God said to Moses, 'Do not take them!' Yet Moses took them by himself (i.e., unauthorized). (This is referred to by the words:) 'And a large mix went up with them' (Exod 12:38): these were the scribes of the Egyptians, at the head of whom were Junnos and Jumbros יונוס ויומברוס." ‖ See further Yalquṭ Reubeni 106D in, n. *h.*

h. Tanḥuma כי תשא 115B: "When the people saw that Moses delayed in coming down from the mountain" (Exod 32:1). The sixth hour (= 12 noon) had come, and then 4,000 men assembled who had gone up with Israel (from Egypt; this refers to the masses that are called

308. S-B: Aphraim, the Samaritan Ἀφαραίμα, according to Neubauer (155), was renowned because of his flour (see m. Menaḥ. 8.1) and, as the present passage shows, because of his abundance of straw. The proverb in the mouth of the sorcerers means: In Egypt, the home of sorcery, will you come up with magic and impress us?

"large mix" in Exod 12:38 and "mob" in Num 11:4); and among them there were two scribes of Egypt named Junnos and Jumbros, who had performed all those magical arts before pharaoh; as it says, "And they too, the scribes of Egypt, did so by their secret arts" (Exod 7:11). They all gathered around Aaron and said, "Arise, make us a god!" ‖ Yalquṭ Reubeni on Exodus 32:11 (106D) from Tiqqunim: What reason did the godless have to make the calf? Yet in fact these were only pharaoh's sorcerers Junnos and Jumbros, of whom it says, "And they did so too, the scribes, by their secret arts" (Exod 7:11). Yet when they saw that there was nothing actual in them (their magical works), they turned to (?) the people of Moses and accepted the covenant of circumcision. … And when they bore jealousy (hostility) in their heart, they said, "Arise, make us a god that may come before us, as he came before you!"

i. Yalquṭ Reubeni on Exodus 32:28 (108C) from Zohar: "The children of Levi acted according to the word of Moses, and on that day 'about' 3,000 men fell" (Exod 32:28). How so? Is there in a calculation a less (an approximation), as when someone says an "approximate" number? (What is כְּ = "about" or "like" before 3,000 supposed to mean?) This refers only to Junnos and Jumbros, who were tantamount to 3,000 men.

k. Yalquṭ Simeoni on Exodus 14:27, 1 § 235 (73C) from midrash אבכיר: The Egyptians conducted their sorcery and rose from the sea. Then the sea said, "A deposit that God has entrusted to me, how can I let it go?" Immediately the waters ran after every single Egyptian and cast them into the sea.… Yet there were two sorcerers among the Egyptians, Yohani and Mamre. They had by sorcery made themselves wings and flew in the air and hovered in the height of the world. Then (the angel) Gabriel said (before God), "In the fullness of your grandeur you tear down your adversaries" (Exod 15:7). Immediately God said to Michael, "Arise, carry out the judgment against them!" Then Michael seized them by the crest of their head and destroyed them over the water; this is what "You split the sea by your might, you have shattered the heads of the dragons over the water" (Ps 74:13) means. ‖ Yalquṭ Reubeni on Exodus 15:7 (89A) from חכם הרזים: "In the fullness of your grandeur you tear down your adversaries; you send out your blaze, it consumes them like stubble" (Exod 15:7). Yohani and Mamre were two brothers (as sons of Balaam) and they were skilled in sorcery; and they performed magic for themselves and flew in the air. Michael and Gabriel saw them, but they did not have power over them. Immediately they called out and said, "Lord of the world, they are those who have enslaved your children, in a sense you are obliged by what is said, 'In the fullness of your grandeur you tear down your adversaries' (Exod 15:7), and you do not carry out judgment against them!" Immediately God said to the prince of the face (one of the throne angels), "Go down and exact revenge on them!" Then he went down and brought them low; as it says, "You blew with your breath, then the sea covered them" (Exod 15:10). ‖ Midrash Vajjoschaʿ on Exodus 15:10 (*Beth ha-Midrash* 1.52.26): "You blew with your breath" (Exod 15:10). The scholars said, "When the Egyptians perished in the sea, there were among them two sorcerers, whose names were Yohani and Mamre. They said to pharaoh, 'If this happens by the hand of God, we can do nothing against it; but if it happens by the hand of an angel, we will be able to pour them into it' (cf. Exod 14:27). Immediately they performed their sorcery and plunged them (the angels) into the sea. Then the angels said, 'Help us (so the text is cited), God, for the waters come to the soul!' (Ps 69:2). Yet you brought them low by your word in glorious waters. Therefore, it says, 'You blew with your breath: then the sea covered them; they sank like lead in the glorious waters' (Exod 15:10)."

3:15: Since you know the Holy Scriptures, which can make you wise, from your childhood.

1. ἀπὸ βρέφους. – It was among the duties of every father to instruct boys in the Torah;[a] this was supposed to begin preferably when the child was 5 or 6 years old.[b] Introduction to the Torah was very simple because Scripture was the actual book used in school;[c] the first reading exercises occurred with the 3rd book of Moses.[d] Early study of the Torah was extolled in many saying.[e]

a. See passages at § Eph 6:4 B.

b. On the 5th year of life, see m. ᾿Abot 5.21[309] at § 1 Tim 5:9 A. – On the 6th year of life, see b. B. Bat. 20B: (On the sentence from the Mishnah: "One cannot forbid someone from working [in a common yard] and say to him, 'I cannot sleep because of the noise of the hammer or because of the noise of the mill or because of the noise of the children'" [m. B. Bat. 2.3], it is remarked:) Raba († 352) said, "The final words refer to school children (who go to school at the house of a children's teacher who lives in the yard in question), specifically since the decree of Joshua ben Gamela" (ostensibly the high priest ca. 63–65 CE, but this can hardly be correct). For Rab Judah († 299) said that Rab († 247) said, "In truth, let that man be remembered for the good, and Joshua b. Gamela is his name! For if it had not been for him, the Torah would have been forgotten by Israel. For at the beginning, if someone had a father, he taught him Torah, but if he did not have a father, he did not learn the Torah. What scriptural interpretation (was there for this)? 'And you shall teach it (to your children)' (Deut 11:19): you yourselves should teach them. Then it was decreed that one should hire children's teachers in Jerusalem. What scriptural interpretation (was there for this)? 'For from Zion knowledge of the Torah will go forth' (Isa 2:3). Yet still one brought up the one who had a father and had him learn, but the one who did not have a father did not go up and did not learn. Then it was decreed that one should hire (children's teachers) in each individual area and bring (the sons) to them at the age of 16 or 17. But if his teacher got angry with him, he scorned him and went away, until finally Joshua b. Gamela came and decreed that one should hire children's teachers in every province and in every city and bring (the children) to them at the age of 6 or 7." Rab († 247) said to Rab Samuel b. Shilat (ca. 270), "Do not accept him (as a student) until 6 years; from then on, accept him and give to him (as much) as to an ox." ‖ See b. Ketub. 50A at § Luke 2:42, first third. – The time indicator is quite general in Midr. Eccl. 11:9 (52B): "Rejoice, young man, in your childhood יַלְדוּתֶךָ" (Eccl 11:9). R. Judan

309. S-B: This passage is referred to in TanḥB קדושים § 14 (40A): "If you plant all kinds of trees for food, keep their fruit as their foreskin (as unconsecrated)" (Lev 19:23ff.); the words speak (allegorically) of a child. "Three years may they have foreskin for you": for it can neither speak nor talk. "And in the fourth year all their fruit shall be a dedication": for its father dedicates it to the Torah. "For the praise of Yahweh": what does "for the praise" mean? From the time when it praises God. "And in the fifth year you may eat their fruit": from the time when it begins to read in the Torah. "To multiply its produce for you": from here our teachers taught (namely in m. ᾿Abot 5.21): "The five-year-old for Scripture, the ten-year-old for Mishnah …." – There is a parallel in Tanḥ. קדושים 170A.

(ca. 350) and R. Phineas (ca. 360). R. Judan said, "(Rejoice) 'in your childhood,' your Torah that you learned in your childhood. 'And make your heart glad in the days of your youth': this refers to the Mishnah (that is studied in the time of youth). 'And walk in the ways of your heart and according to what your eyes have seen': this refers to the Talmud. 'And know that God will bring you into judgment for all this': this refers to the fulfillment of the commandments and good works (that a person has to perform)." R. Phineas said, "'Rejoice, chosen one (so now בָּחוּר in Eccl 11:9), in your childhood'; who has caused you to be chosen (for a high position) in your old age? The Torah that you learned in your childhood. And if you were chosen in your old age, do not remove yourself (do not go your own ways) in the words of the Torah, but rather 'go in the ways of your heart and in what your eyes have seen,' that is, according to the teaching that you have learned from your teacher. 'And know that God will bring you into judgment for all this': he is obligated to pay you the recompense for the fulfillments of the commandments and good works."

c. It is indicative of the central place that the Torah occupied in the entire course of instruction given in school that the school for children was called in brief בֵּית הַסֵּפֶר, ב׳ סִפְרָא = "house of the book," that is, of the Torah. Genesis Rabbah 48 (30A): R. Jeremiah b. Eleazar (ca. 270) said, "Like two children who had run away from school מבית הספר; one received blows and the other trembled." — Leviticus Rabbah 9 (110D): Once I (a guest in the house of R. Yannai [ca. 225]) passed by a school בית ספרא and heard the voices of the children, how they said, 'Moses laid on us the Torah as an inheritance for the community of Jacob' (Deut 33:4)...." ‖ Deuteronomy Rabbah 8 (205A) is instructive concerning the gradual introduction of the child to Holy Scripture: "How does a person first learn the Torah?" It was answered, "First he reads in a scroll מְגִילָּה (the child did not immediately have the whole Torah put into its hand, but rather first received certain selections that had been written on a special *megillah*); then he reads in the book בַּסֵּפֶר (i.e., in the Torah in the narrower sense = Pentateuch); then in the Prophets; then in the hagiographa כְּתוּבִים. When he has finished Scripture הַמִּקְרָא, he studies the Talmud (the traditional teachings), then the halakic (the individual fixed legal principles), and then the haggadoth (the nonlegal traditional material). ‖ The child and its book (= Torah) in, for example, a baraita in y. Taʿan. 4.69A.11: Rabban Simeon b. Gamaliel (ca. 140) said, "There were 500 schools in Betar, and the smallest among them had no less than 500 children, and they said, 'If the enemies come against us, let us go out with these styluses against them and stick out their eyes.' And as the sins rose, they (the enemies) wrapped each child in its book בספרו and burned it, and from all of them I am the only one remaining; and he applied this Scripture passage to himself, 'My eye hurts my soul because of all the daughters of my city' (Lam 3:51)." — The same is found in Midr. Lam. 3:51 (73A); see also b. Giṭ. 58A. ‖ Tanḥuma וישב 42B: The child takes the book הספר (Torah = Pentateuch) and reads the ten generations from Adam to Noah at once. When it has arrived at the ten generations from Noah to Abraham, it also reads them at once. Yet when it comes to the pearls of Abraham, Isaac, and Jacob, it begins to occupy itself with them (in detail).

d. See Tanḥ. צו 144B at § 2 Cor 5:21 A. Also see ʾAbot R. Nat. 6 (3B).

e. ʾAbot de Rabbi Nathan 23 (6D): The same one (R. Nehorai [ca. 150]) used to say, "He who studies Torah in his childhood בילדותו, what can he be compared with? With a young cow that was tamed (became accustomed to the yoke) when it was still small; as it says,

'Ephraim is a young cow, accustomed to thresh with pleasure' (Hos 10:11). Yet he who studies Torah in his old age is like a cow that has been tamed only in its old age; as it says, 'Israel balks like a refractory cow' (Hos 10:11)." The same used to say, "He who studies Torah in his childhood is like a woman who kneads (the dough) with warm water; but he who studies Torah in his old age, what can he be compared with? With a woman who kneads with cold water." (In the 1st case, success is sure, in the 2nd it is uncertain.) R. Eliezer b. Jacob (ca. 150) said, "He who studies Torah in his childhood is like writing that is written on new paper; he who studies Torah in his old age is like writing that is written on old paper." — See the continuation: Rabban Simeon b. Gamaliel (ca. 140) said …, at § John 2:1 A, #3, D, n. *t.* ‖ See m. ʾAbot 4.20 at § Matt 9:17. ‖ ʾAbot de Rabbi Nathan 24 (7A): (Elisha b. Abbuyah, the apostate [ca. 120]) said, "If someone learns Torah in his childhood, the words of the Torah go into his flesh and blood[310] and come out of his mouth in a clear presentation; but if someone learns Torah in his old age, the words of the Torah do not go into his flesh and blood and do not come out of his mouth in a clear presentation. And likewise, the proverb says, 'If you have not desired (read חפצתם instead of קפצתה) it in your youth, how will you acquire it in your old age?'" (See: Whatever a person wants in his youth he has the fullness of in old age.)

2. ἱερὰ γράμματα. — On the designations for Holy Scripture and its partition, see the excursus "The Old Testament Canon and Its Inspiration."

3:16: All Scripture, inspired by God, is also beneficial … for instruction in righteousness.

1. θεόπνευστος, see the excursus "The Old Testament Canon and Its Inspiration."
2. πρὸς παιδίαν τὴν ἐν δικαιοσύνῃ, see Bar 4:12f.

4:2: At an opportune or an inopportune time.

εὐκαίρως ἀκείρως = בין בזמנו בין שלא בזמנו; see as an example Exod. Rab. 15 (76A) at § Matt 16:19 B, #2, n. *g*, middle.

4:13 A: The coat.

φελόνης (φαιλόνης) = φαινόλης = *paenula*, "a coat made of coarse material, without sleeves, clinging tightly to the body, buttoned up, and clasped lengthwise on the front."[311] The word passed over into rabbinic literature in the form פְּלוֹנָס, which is corrupted in many ways in the prints; see examples in y. Taʿan. 4.69A.51 (Midr. Lam. 2:2) and y. Ned. 10.42B.21.

4:13 B: The parchments (see the excursus "The Institution of the Ancient Jewish Synagogue").

4:21: Before winter.

It was generally judged that the time of year unfit for sea travel began with the Feast of Booths (see § Acts 27:9, #2).

---

310. S-B: נבלעין בדמיו, literally: are consumed, eaten up by his blood.

311. Krauß, *Talmudische Archäologie*, 1:169f.

The Letter of Paul to Titus

1:3: Of God our savior (see § 1 Tim 2:3).

1:6: A man of one wife (see § 1 Tim 3:2 A).

1:7: A bishop should be blameless ... (cf. § 1 Tim 3:2 B).

1:12: One of them, their own prophet.

See the way R. Abina (ca. 325) handles a sectarian in b. Sanh. 39A (see § Rom 2:19–20). — According to S. ʿOlam Rab. 21 and b. B. Bat. 15B, the non-Israelite world had seven prophets (see § Luke 16:28).

1:15: To the pure.

οἱ καθαροί = טְהוֹרִין; see Tanḥ. צו 144B at § 2 Cor 5:21 A, n. *a*.

2:3: Not slanderous.

See Gen. Rab. 18 (12B) and 45 (28C) at § Eph 5:25, n. *e*, middle.

2:5: Domestic.

On the inclination of women to run around from house to house, see Gen. Rab. 18 (12B) and 45 (28C) at § Eph 5:25, n. *e*, middle. — See further Gen. Rab. 8 (6D): A man may compel his wife not to run out on the street; for every wife who runs out on the street will finally stumble. Whence comes this idea? From Dinah (see Gen 34:1, 2). ‖ See t. Soṭah 5.9 (302) at § Matt 1:16, #5.

2:9f.: Slaves should be subject to their masters ....

See the excursus "The Nature of Ancient Jewish Slavery," especially II, #3.

2:12: The worldly lusts.

τὰς κοσμικὰς ἐπιθυμίας. — קוֹזְמִיקוֹן or קוֹסְמִיקוֹן = κοσμικόν, which is sometimes found in rabbinic literature as a loanword, does not mean "worldly" in the ethical sense, but rather is meant spatially = "affecting the whole world."

Jerusalem Talmud Berakot 9.13D.7: R. Judan b. Shalom (ca. 370) said, "... Only the wind of Elijah was such that it affected the whole world קוסמיקון (see 1 Kgs 19:11)." — Parallels are found in Gen. Rab. 24 (16A); Midr. Eccl. 1:6 (7A). — Leviticus Rabbah 15 (115C) avoided the foreign word.

2:14: A people for his possession that is zealous for good works.

Deueronomy Rabbah 1 (195C): R. Judah b. Simon (ca. 320) said in the name of R. Levi (ca. 300), “As the bee heaps up מסגלת (gathers) for its master everything that it heaps up, so the Israelites heap up מסגלין for their Father in heaven everything that they heap up in fulfillments of the commandments and good works.”

3:4: The goodness ... of God (see § Rom 11:22).

3:7: Heirs of eternal life.

See § Matt 19:16 and § Matt 19:29 B.

3:9: Foolish questions (see § 1 Tim 6:4).

The Letter of Paul to Philemon

7: The innards of the saints have been soothed (refreshed).

ἀναπαύεσθαι = נוּחַ; ἀναπαύειν = הֵנִיחַ, see § 1 Cor 16:18.

10: Because of my child.

On τέκνον, see § 1 Cor 4:14 and § 1 Cor 4:17 A.

11 A: The one who was useless ... very useful.

ἄχρηστον ... εὔχρηστον; see a similar common wordplay dealing with the slave trade in Exod. Rab. 43 (99C): R. Judah b. Shalom (ca. 370) said in the name of R. Judah b. Simon (ca. 320) in the name of R. Levi b. Perata (ca. 300), "Like someone who wanted to buy a slave. He said to its master, 'Is this slave, whom you want to sell, of a bad sort קאקוגריסין (= κακὴ αἵρεσις) or of a good sort קלוגריסין (= καλὴ αἵρεσις)?'[312] He answered him, 'He is of a bad sort, and that is why I am selling him'" (See the continuation at § Matt 24:48).

11 B: Whom I am sending back to you.

The law specifies the following about handing over a slave who has escaped: "A slave who delivers himself from his master to you, you shall not hand over to its master. He shall remain with you, in your midst, at the place that he chooses in one of your gates, wherever he pleases. You shall not oppress him" (Deut 23:16f.). — This passage was interpreted in very different ways by the ancient synagogue.

1. The slave in Deut 23:16f. is a non-Israelite who has handed himself over from idolatry to the faith of Israel (עֶבֶד "slave" is interpreted as עוֹבֵד "idolater").

So Tg. Yer. I Deut. 23:16f.: "You shall not hand over into the hand of an idolatrous companion a non-Israelite who has delivered himself to you in order to be under the shade of my Shekinah (divinity); for this is why he fled from his idolatry. He shall remain with you and observe the commandments in your midst. Teach him Torah; set up for him a school in the place where he wishes in one of your cities; occupy yourselves with him in what is good for him; do not oppress him with words." ‖ A baraita in b. Giṭ. 45A.13: "They (the original inhabitants of Canaan) shall not dwell in your land, lest they mislead you to sin against me" (Exod 23:33). The passage may speak of a non-Israelite נָכְרִי who has taken it on himself not

312. S-B: So according to Krauß, *Lehnwörter*, 1:273f.; Krauß, *Talmudische Archäologie*, 2:88. — Dalman, *Wörterbuch*, reads: קַקְפְּרָסִין = κακὴ πρᾶσις "sale without guarantee" and קָאלְפְּרָסִין = καλὴ πρᾶσις "sale with guarantee."

to serve idols (thus of a proselyte)?! Scripture teaches: "A servant (of idols; thus עֶבֶד = עֹיבֵד) who has delivered himself to you from his lord אֲדֹנָיו (= divinity), you shall not hand over to his master (= the earlier divinity)" (Deut 23:16). What is his deliverance? "With you he shall remain, in your midst ..." (Deut 23:17). ‖ A vestige of this interpretation is also found in SDeut 23:16 § 259 (121A): "Who delivers himself from his master to you" (Deut 23:16): this includes the sojourning proselyte (a non-Israelite immigrant who repudiates idolatry). – Against this interpretation of Deut 23:16, it is objected in b. Giṭ. 45A.16 that it then could not say: "who delivers himself from his master to you," but rather, "who delivers himself from his father to you." ("Father" אָב appears as a description of an idol, for example, in the mouth of R. Aqiba [† ca. 135] on the basis of Jer 2:27 in SDeut 21:13 § 213 [113A]; b. Yebam. 48B).

2. The slave in Deut 23:16f. is a slave who is sold by an Israelite to somewhere abroad and therefore has to be emancipated in accordance with the existing regulations.

Sifre Deuteronomy 23:16 § 259 (121A): "You shall not hand over a slave to his master" (Deut 23:16). On the basis of this passage it has been said (namely in m. Giṭ. 4.6): "If someone sells a slave to a non-Israelite or to somewhere abroad, he goes out as an emancipated man." ‖ Babylonian Talmud Giṭṭin 45A.17: R. Josiah (ca. 140) said, "The passage of Scripture ('A slave who delivers himself to you from his master, you shall not hand over to his master' [Deut 23:16]) is speaking of someone who sells his slave to somewhere abroad" (ed. Amsterdam 1644ff.: abroad). – According to this view, Deut 23:16 would entail the admonition to the Jewish authorities not to tolerate handing over a slave sold to somewhere abroad to his foreign purchaser, but rather, in agreement with m. Giṭ. 4.6, to decree the compulsory emancipation of such a slave. – Against this interpretation, in b. Giṭ. 45A.17 the words in Deut 23:16 are made valid: "who delivers himself to you"; in the sense of that interpretation, it would have to say rather: "who is delivered from you."

3. The slave in Deut 23:16f. is a slave who is purchased by an Israelite with the purpose of or under the condition of his subsequent emancipation.

A baraita in b. Giṭ. 45A.19: "You shall not deliver a slave to his master ..." (Deut 23:16). Rabbi († 217?) said, "The passage of Scripture is speaking about someone who buys a slave under the condition of setting him free." What is this case like (how is it to be understood)? Rab Nahman b. Isaac († 356) said, "He declares to him in writing, 'When I purchase you, behold, you acquire yourself from then on'" (i.e., you thereby go out to freedom)! – Parallels are found in b. Yebam. 93B; b. Qidd. 63A. According to this view, the passage Deut 23:16f. would forbid continuing to use as a slave someone who was purchased with the purpose of emancipation.

4. The slave in Deut 23:16f. is, as the wording of the passage requires, a slave who has fled from his master. Here the following cases are to be differentiated depending on the whither and whence of the escape.

a. The whither of the escape remains unspecified in the base text.

Targum Onkelos Deuteronomy 23:16f.: "You shall not deliver a slave from the nations (i.e., according to the otherwise common expression, 'a Canaanite slave') into the hand of his master if he has delivered himself to you from his master. He shall swell with you, in your midst, in a place that is pleasing, in one of your cities, in which he wants to live. You shall not oppress him." ‖ Septuagint Deuteronomy 23:15f.: οὐ παραδώσεις παῖδα (slaves) τῷ κυρίῳ αὐτοῦ, ὅς προστέθειταί σοι (who has joined you) παρὰ τοῦ κυρίου αὐτοῦ· μετὰ σοῦ κατοικήσει, ἐν ὑμῖν κατοικήσει, οὗ ἂν ἀρέσῃ αὐτῷ· οὐ θλίψεις αὐτόν.

b. The escape occurs from abroad to the land of Israel.

Babylonian Talmud Giṭṭin 45A.18: R. Ahai b. Josiah (ca. 180) said, "The passage of Scripture (Deut 23:16f.) is speaking of a slave who has fled from abroad to the land (of Israel)." (According to Deut 23:16f., such a person cannot be handed back to his master).[313] ‖ Babylonian Talmud Giṭṭin 45A.9: A slave had fled from abroad to the land (of Israel). His master pursued him and came before R. Ammi (ca. 300). He said to him, "He (the slave) shall write for you a promissory note in the amount of his worth, and you shall write for him a declaration of emancipation; but if not, I will let him go out before you as a free man according to the opinion of R. Ahai b. Josiah (see above)." ‖ Differently, y. Giṭ. 4.46A.23: If a slave has fled from abroad (to the land of Israel), one may hand him over. (The commentary פני משה squares this decision with the above decision of R. Ahai b. Josiah and R. Ammi so that the Jerusalem Talmud is speaking of a slave who was originally abroad; this one may be given back. Accordingly, Deut 23:16 would have referred only to a slave who had originally been in Palestine, then had gone abroad, and finally from there fled back to the land of Israel: such a slave should not be given back.)

c. The escape happens from the land of Israel to somewhere abroad.

Jerusalem Talmud Giṭṭin 4.46A.24: If the slave had fled from the land (of Israel) to somewhere abroad, it is, as R. Josiah (II, ca. 280) said in the name of R. Hiyya the elder (ca. 200), allowed (to give him back); R. Hoshaiah the elder (ca. 225) said, "It is allowed"; R. Marinos b. Hoshaiah the elder said, "It is prohibited." R. Zeira (ca. 300) said, "They were not of different opinions. The one who said, 'It is allowed,' meant it of one who was accustomed to flee there; and the one who said, 'It is prohibited,' meant it of one who was not accustomed to flee there." R. Yose (ca. 350) said, "They were not of different opinions. The one who said, 'It is allowed,' meant it in the case that one could fetch him from there; and the one who said, 'It is prohibited,' meant it in the case that one could not fetch him from there."

d. The escape happens from somewhere abroad to somewhere abroad.

Babylonian Talmud Giṭṭin 45A.21: A slave fled from Rab Hisda († 309; who lived in Babylonia, and thus abroad) to the Samaritans (thus abroad). He sent word to them, "Extradite him!" They sent word to him, "You shall not hand over a slave to his master ..." (Deut 23:16). He sent word to them, "So you shall do with his donkey and with his garment and likewise with everything your brother has lost, what he has lost and what you find. You cannot refrain (from giving it back to him)" (Deut 22:3). They sent word to him, "Yet it is written, 'You shall not hand over a slave to his master!'" He sent word to them, "This pertains (only) to a slave who fled from abroad to the land (of Israel)" (in all other cases Deut 23:16f. does not apply).

313. S-B: The same regulation existed concerning a slave who had fled from a gentile prison; see b. Giṭ. 38A in the excursus "The Nature of Ancient Jewish Slavery," II, #5.

Since Onesimus' escape to the apostle was an escape from somewhere abroad (Colossae?) to somewhere abroad (Rome or Caesarea),[314] it can be compared only to the escape of the slave of R. Hisda described in the last citation. The apostle would then have followed a similar halakah in handing over Onesimos, which later Rab Hisda asserted.

15: So that you should have him forever.

See the excursus "The Nature of Ancient Jewish Slavery," II, #5, n. *a* and the remark there.

314. S-B: Caesarea was consistently considered to be abroad; see t. Šeb. 4.11 (66); SDeut 11:24 § 51 (85B); y. Šeb. 6.36C.20.

The Letter to the Hebrews

1:1 A: At the end of these days.

ἐπ' ἐσχάτου τῶν ἡμερῶν τούτων is substantively hardly different from the simple ἐπ' ἐσχάτου τῶν ἡμερῶν. The latter in Aram. = בְּסוֹף יוֹמַיָּא[a] "at the end of days," or = בְּסוֹף עֲקֵב יוֹמַיָּא[b] "at the end of the heel of days" = at the very end of days. In substance, this refers to the age of the Messiah.

a. בסוף יומיא corresponds in all the following passages to the phrase found in the base text: בְּאַחֲרִית הַיָּמִים. – Targum Onkelos Genesis 49:1: "Jacob calls his sons and said, 'Assemble, so that I may indicate for you what you will encounter at the end of days'" (Yer. I has the same: בסוף יומיא). ‖ Targum Onkelos Numbers 24:14: "I will show you what this people will do to your people at the end of days" (see Yer. I in n. *b*). ‖ Targum Onkelos Deuteronomy 31:29: "Calamity will befall you at the end of days" (Yer. I: בסוף כל יומיא = "at the end of all days"). ‖ See also Tg. Mic. 4:1 and Isa. 2:2.

b. בסוף עקב יומיא. – Targum Yerušalmi II Genesis 3:15 at the end: "They (people) will make peace with one another at the last end of days, in the days of the king, the Messiah." – Yerušalmi I: "At the end, in the days of the king, the Messiah" בעיקבא ביומי מלכא משיחא. ‖ Targum Yerušalmi I Numbers 24:14: "After this they will rule over your people at the last end of days." ‖ Instead of בסוף עקב יומיא, one can also simply say בסוף בעקב = at the end in the close, so Midr. Song. 1:8 (89B).

1:1 B: In the Son (see § Rom 1:3 A).

1:2 A and B: Through him he also made the world.

A. The ancient synagogue knows the following as the means of creation:
1. The word of God.

Sirach 42:15: ἐν λόγοις κυρίου τὰ ἔργα αὐτοῦ "by the word of the Lord his works (came to be)." – The Hebrew text is uncertain. Strack: באומר אלהים רצ(ו)נו = "by the word of God his will (happens)." Strack adds: *Fortasse* נוצרו *legendum est.* Then it would have to be translated: "By the word of God they (namely his works) were created." In favor of this is the marginal gloss מעשיו = his works. ‖ Wisdom 9:1: ὁ ποιήσας τὰ πάντα ἐν λόγῳ σου. ‖ Genesis Rabbah 4 (4B): "And God made the firmament" (Gen 1:7). This is one of the passages of Scripture by which Ben Zoma (ca. 110) brought the world into turmoil. "And he made" ויעש? Did they (the heavens) not come about by the word בְּמַאֲמָר; as it says, "By the word of Yahweh the heavens were made and by the breath of his mouth all their host" (Ps 33:6)? (The further treatment of the question is not given.) ‖ See further passages at TanḥB בראשית § 11 (4A); m. ʾAbot 5.1: By ten words מַאֲמָרוֹת the world was created. – A parallel passage is found in ʾAbot R. Nat. 31 (8B). – Nine of the ten creative words of God are enumerated in Pirqe R. El. 3, specifically Gen 1:3, 6, 9, 11, 14, 20, 24, 29 and 2:18; in b. Meg. 21B and b. Roš

Haš. 32A, Gen 1:1 is added as the tenth. ‖ Mekilta Exodus 15:17 (51B): When God created the world, he created it only by the word במאמר; see Ps 33:6. ‖ See further the blessing in m. Ber. 6.3: Blessed be the one by whose word דבר everything came to be! ‖ See some of the targum passages that belong here in the excursus "The Memra of Yahweh," #2, n. *b*. — Finally, see the periphrastic designation for God: "The one who spoke and the world came into being"; see the excursus "The Memra of Yahweh," #3, A, n. *l*.

2. The Torah. — See the textual evidence at § Col 1:16 A.

B. οἱ αἰῶνες = עוֹלָמִים, Aramaic עָלְמַיָּא. The plural is found particularly in the common form of address to God: "Lord of the worlds"[a] or "Lord of all worlds."[b] A multiplicity of worlds is mentioned explicitly in Midr. Ps. 18 §15.[c]

a. רִבּוֹן הָעוֹלָמִים. — See y. Taʿan. 2.65D.44 at § Matt 1:6 B, #1, end. ‖ See Pesiq. 131B at § 1 Cor 10:11, n. *e*. ‖ Pesiqta Rabbati 8 (29B): The Israelites said to God, "Lord of the worlds, are these all our advantages, so that it says, 'I will search Jerusalem with lanterns' (Zeph 1:12)?" ‖ See also Midr. Lam. Intro. 24 (38A, B) at § Matt 2:18. — For the singular "Lord of the world," see passages at § Luke 10:21 B.

b. רִבּוֹן כֹּל הָעוֹלָמִים. — See Gen. Rab. 63 (40A) at § Rom 1:27 A, #1, near end. ‖ Genesis Rabbah 63 (39B): R. Hoshaiah (ca. 225) said, "The angels of service said before God, 'Lord of all worlds, woe, for Ahaz has become king!'" ‖ See Gen. Rab. 33 (20A) at § Matt 3:9 A, #3, 3rd paragraph; y. Soṭah 1.4 (16D.56) at § Matt 1:3 B, #2, middle. — The Aramaic רבון כל עלמיא, but not as a form of address to God, is found in Tg. Yer. I Gen. 18:30: "May the wrath of the Lord of all worlds, Yahweh, not become strong now if I (keep) speaking." See Tg. Yer. I Gen. 18:32.

c. Midrash Psalm 18 § 15 (72B): "A passage of Scripture says, 'He soars on the wings of the wind' (Ps 18:11), and another passage of Scripture says, 'He appears on the wings of the wind' (2 Sam 22:11). From this you learn that he has many worlds עולמות הרבה, and he soars on the winds of the cherubs and does so in order to appear in them (the many worlds)." — According to the parallel passage Midr. Song. 1:9 (91A), R. Aha (ca. 320) is the author of this remark.

1:3 A: The reflection of glory.

It says of wisdom in Wis 7:26: "She is a reflection ἀπαύγασμα of the eternal light and an immaculate mirror ἔσοπτρον of God's work and a likeness of his goodness" εἰκὼν τῆς ἀγαθότητος αὐτοῦ. — From rabbinic literature, we can compare this to expressions like זִיו יְקָרָא "splendor of glory,"[a] זִיו אִיקוֹנִין "splendor of likeness, of appearance"[b] and נוֹבֶלֶת = "likeness, reflection, (imperfect) counterpart."[c]

a. See Tg. Onk. Exod. 34:29 at § 2 Cor 3:7 C, #1. ‖ See Tg. Onk. Deut. 34:7 at § 2 Cor 3:7 C, #3.

b. See Tg. Yer. I Exod. 34:29 at § 2 Cor 3:7 C, #1. ‖ Genesis Rabbah 53 (33D): "Sarah ... bore Abraham a son in her old age לִזְקֻנָיו" (Gen 21:2); this shows that the splendor of his (Isaac's) image (appearance) was like his (Abraham's). — The midrash interprets לזקניו as a notarikon = לְזִיו אִיקוֹנָיו = "after (according to) the splendor of his image."

c. Genesis Rabbah 17 (12A): R. Hanina b. Isaac (in the 4th cent.) said, "There are three likenesses נוֹבְלוֹת: The likeness of death is sleep, the likeness of prophecy is a dream, the likeness of the future world is the Sabbath." R. Abin (I, ca. 325; II, ca. 370) added two more,

"The likeness (reflection) of the upper light is the orb of the sun, the likeness (reflection) of the upper wisdom is the Torah." — The same is found in Gen. Rab. 44 (27D).

1:3 B: The imprint (impress) of his being.

χαρακτήρ = קְלַסְטֵר (קְלַסְתֵּר) "imprint, facial features, face."[a]
— χαρακτήριον = כְּלַקְטֵירִין "imprint, image, facial features."[b]

a. Babylonian Talmud Baba Meṣiʿa 87A: (After Isaac's birth, the people said,) "Abraham, the hundred-year-old, is supposed to have begotten? Immediately Isaac's facial expression קלסתר פנים changed so that he was like Abraham." ‖ See b. Ber. 7A at § 2 Cor 3:7 C, #2, n. *e*.

b. Leviticus Rabbah 23 (122B): (The adulterer) does not know that the one who sits in the hidden place of the world, that is, God, forms its (the child's) imprint (facial features כלקטירין; so read instead of כל קטורין) according to his (the adulterer's) likeness, in order to make it known (as a bastard). — The same is found in Pesiq. Rab. 24 (124B); in a broader version in Num. Rab. 9 at the beginning; Tanḥ. נשא 195A; the last two passages replace the foreign word with צוּרָה = form, image.

1:3 C: The one who bears all things by the word of his power.

Genesis Rabbah 22 (15B): "Cain said to Yahweh, 'My guilt is too great to bear'" (Gen 4:13). The ones above and those below you bear אתה סובל, but my sin you do not bear. ‖ Exodus Rabbah 36 (95D): "You would call, and I would answer; you would long for the work of your hands" (Job 14:15). In four pieces God longs for the works of his hands … And these are: God bears סוֹבֵל his world (see Isa 46:4) …, God protects his world …, He illuminates the world. (The 4th piece is missing; yet see the commentaries.) ‖ Leviticus Rabbah 4 (107D): The soul bears the body and God bears סובל his world (see Isa 46:4). So let the soul, which bears the body, come and praise God, who bears his world. ‖ Targum Yerušalmi I Deuteronomy 33:27: "The dwelling (of God) was from the beginning and under the arm of his strength, which bears the סביל world." — See more on this passage the excursus "The Memra of Yahweh," #4, A, n. *c*.

1:3 D: Who sat down at the right hand of the majesty on high.

On the Messiah sitting at the right hand of God, see the excursus "The 110th Psalm in Ancient Jewish Literature."

1:4: Became more excellent than the angels.

1. The righteous are greater and more beloved before God than the angels.

The oldest form of this idea appears in Gen. Rab. 78 (50A); see the passage at § Luke 22:27, #1. — The following sayings come from a later time. Babylonian Talmud Sanhedrin 92B: R. Yohanan († 279) said, "Greater are the righteous than the angels of service; for it says, 'He answered and said, "Behold, I see four men walking around freely in the fire, without getting injured, and the appearance of the fourth (i.e., of the last in rank) is like a son of the gods' (= angels) (Dan 3:25)." — The angel is thus lesser than the three righteous. On this argumentation, see the parallel Pesiq. Rab. 35 (160B). ‖ In Tanḥ. ויקרא 132A, R. Tanḥum

b. Hanilai (ca. 280) represents the idea that the righteous are greater than the angels of service. Parallels are found in Midr. Ps. 103 § 18 (219B) and Lev. Rab. 1 (105A). ‖ Babylonian Talmud Ḥullin 91B: The Israelites are more beloved before God than the angels of service ... (see § Luke 2:13 B). — On the thought that the righteous are greater than the angels, see more at § Eph 3:10.

2. The Messiah is greater than the angels.

See TanḥB תולדות § 20 (70A) at § Matt 8:17, A, 3rd paragraph.

1:5 A: "You are my son; today I have begotten you" (Ps 2:7).

The second psalm was interpreted by the rabbinic scholars as follows:

1. As referring to Aaron.

See Midr. Ps. 2 § 3 (13A) § Rom 13:2.

2. As referring to David.

So above all Rashi, perhaps on the basis of older traditions. He says concerning Ps 2:1: "Our teachers interpreted the passage (i.e., Ps 2) as referring to the king, the Messiah; but according to its wording it would be appropriate if one interprets it as referring to David himself; as it says, 'When, though, the Philistines heard that the Israelites had anointed David as king over themselves, the Philistines assembled their armies and fell into his hand' (cf. 2 Sam 5:17; 1 Chr 14:8). And concerning them it says, 'Why do the *goyim* rage and all gather together?' (Ps 2:1f.)." — We highlight the following from Rashi's explanations of the individual verses. "Verse 6: 'I have appointed you my king': Why do you rage, since I have determined for myself this one (David), to commission him and make him king on my holy Mount Zion? ‖ Verse 7: 'Yahweh said to me': through Nathan and Gad and Samuel. — 'You are my son': the head of the Israelites, who in the Torah are called 'my firstborn son' (see Exod 4:22); and they endure because of you, as it says in the case of Abner, 'So Yahweh has said, "By the hand of my servant David I will save my people Israel" (2 Sam 3:18), and for their sake you (David) are as a son before me, for they all hang on you' (are brought together in you). — 'Today': since I have made you king over them. — 'I have begotten you': in order to be called 'my son' and to be dear to me like a son for their sake, as it says, 'And David knew that Yahweh had confirmed him as king over Israel, and that his army was exalted for the sake of the people of Israel' (1 Chr 14:2). Further, we find with the kings of Israel, who were beloved before him, that they are called 'sons,' as it says of Solomon, 'He shall be a son to me, and I will be a father to him' (so 2 Sam 7:14 is cited). Further, we find of David, 'He will call me:' 'You are my father, my God, and the rock of my salvation' (Ps 89:27)." ‖ "Verse 9: 'With an iron scepter': this refers to the sword." ‖ "Verse 10: 'And now, you kings, be wise.' — The prophets of Israel were men of mercy: they rebuked the idolaters to turn from their wickedness; for God stretches out his hand to the godless and the righteous." ‖ "Verse 11: 'Rejoice with trembling!': when that trembling comes, of which it says, 'Trembling seizes the godless' (Isa 33:14), you will rejoice and be glad if you have served Yahweh." ‖ "Verse 12: נַשְּׁקוּ בַר: spur yourselves on with a pure heart זרזו עצמכם בבר לב."

3. As referring to the people of Israel in the messianic age.

Midrash Psalm 2 § 4 (13A): R. Berekhiah (ca. 340) said in the name of R. Levi (ca. 300), "Cursed be the godless, who contrived a plan (counsel) against Israel .... Gog and Magog will also one day say, 'The earlier ones were foolish, for they were cunning in their plans against the Israelites without considering that they have a protector in heaven. Yet I will not do this; but rather I will deal with their protector first and then I will turn against the Israelites.' This is what 'The kings of the earth arise, and the princes have taken counsel together against Yahweh and his anointed one' (Ps 2:2)[315] means." — Parallels are found in Pesiq. 78B; Lev. Rab. 27 (126A); Tanḥ. אמור 176A; TanḥB אמור § 18 (48A); Midr. Esth. 3:12 (97A); ʾAg. Ber. 2. ‖ Midrash Psalm 2 § 2 (13A): Whoever sets out to harm Israel falls before them ... Nimrod and his peers set out to deal with Abraham and they fell before him (see Gen 14:15); Abimelech (fell) before Isaac; Esau and Laban before Jacob; pharaoh and the Egyptians before Israel and likewise many (others) in the Torah, and (in the same way) Gog and Magog (will fall) in the future before Israel. And David looked at him (Gog and Magog) and called out, "Why do the nations rage?" (Ps 2:1). ‖ Tanḥuma פקודי 128B: R. Hiyya b. Abba (ca. 280) said, "What are idolaters like? A person who hated the king and tried to attack him but could not. What did he do? He went to his statue and tried to topple it. Yet he feared the king, that he might kill him. What did he do? He took an iron spade and put it under it. He said, 'If I make the foundation collapse, the statue will fall.' So idolaters try to attack God, and since they cannot, they come and attack Israel. David said, 'The kings of the earth arise ...' (Ps 2:2). A proverb (says,) 'Whoever cannot hit the donkey hits the saddle.'" — There is a parallel in Exod. Rab. 51 (103C). ‖ In Midr. Song. 7:3 (127A), the words נשקו בר [316] Ps 2:12 are understood to mean: "Kiss the (pure) corn" = pay homage to Israel! — See the passage itself at § Rom 3:9 A, #1, n. *c*. — Parallels are found in Gen. Rab. 83 (53A); Midr. Ps. 2 § 14 (16A). ‖ See Midr. Ps. 2 § 17 (16B) at § Rom 1:3 A, A, #3, α, 2nd third.

4. As referring to the Messiah b. David. — This interpretation is the oldest and most widespread. It is already found in the Psalms of Solomon[a] and certainly contributed considerably to the messianic king being called in brief the "anointed" מָשִׁיחַ and the "son" (of God) (see Ps 2:2 and 7). Psalm 2 is often related to the rebellion of Gog and Magog against God and his Messiah.[b]

a. Psalms of Solomon 17:23f. (= 17:26 in Fritzsche): "In wisdom, in righteousness may he (the Messiah) chase sinners away from the inheritance, may he smash the sinner's arrogance like clay vessels ὡς σκεύη κεραμέως. May he shatter all their being with an iron

---

315. S-B: The anointed king is considered to be the head or representative of the entire people (see Rashi above in #2 on verse 7); therefore, what refers in the first place to the king can also be interpreted in relation to the people.

316. S-B: The בַּר in Ps 2:12 is most of the time interpreted as = "what is pure" (see § Rom 1:3 A, A, #1, β). — Further, Midr. Ps. 2 § 17 (16B): נשקו בר (Ps 2:12). Rab († 247) and R. Hiyya (ca. 200; another reading: R. Aha). Rab said, "Defer to the purity of the Torah ברה של תורה; as it says, 'Come, eat of my bread (= Torah)' (Prov 9:5), before strict justice rises up against you and you forfeit the way of the Torah." R. Hiyya said, "Defer to the purity of repentance ברה של תשיבה, before strict justice rises up against you and you forfeit the way of the Torah." ‖ Babylonian Talmud Sanhedrin 91B: Rab Hana b. Bizna (ca. 260) said that R. Simeon the Pious (ca. 210) said, "Whoever withholds a halakah from the mouth of a student is cursed by even the embryos in their mother's wombs; as it says, 'Whoever holds back what is pure is cursed by the people' (so Midr. Prov. 11:26; it interprets בַּר 'corn, grain' as בַּר 'what is pure' = the Torah). ... And בר (what is pure) means nothing other than the Torah; as it says, 'Defer to what is pure or kiss what is pure (= Torah)' (Ps 2:12)."

rod ἐν ῥάβδῳ σιδηρᾷ συντρίψαι." – These words trace back to LXX[317] Ps 2:9. ‖ Presumably the targum also interpreted Ps 2 messianically; for the later period thought of hardly anything other than the messianic king when it came to the "anointed one" of Yahweh. The targum translation reads: "Why do the peoples rage and the nations contemplate (read מרננין instead of מרגנין) vanity? The kings of the earth rise up, and the armies gather, to rebel before Yahweh and to quarrel against his anointed one (= the Messiah). 'Let us tear apart their bonds and cast from ourselves their chains!' The one who is enthroned in heaven will laugh, the Memra of Yahweh will mock them. Then (read הָיְדֵין instead of הֵידֵין) he will speak to them in his wrath and frighten them in his anger. 'I have consecrated (anointed) my king and appointed him on the mountain of my sanctuary. I will tell of a determination of Yahweh.' He said to me, 'You are precious to me like a son to a father, innocent, as if I had created you today (like a newborn child). Ask of me, and I will give to you the goods (the fortune) of the nations as your possession and as your property the rulers of the ends of the earth. You may shatter them as with an iron rod, shatter them as an earthen vessel!' And now, you kings, be wise; accept chastisement, your princes of the earth! Serve before Yahweh with fear and pray with trembling! Accept teaching, lest he get angry and you perish from the way; for his anger could easily flare up. Blessed are all who hope in his Memra!" ‖ We highlight the following from the great number of messianic interpretations in rabbinic literature. On verse 2. Midrash Psalm 2 § 3 (13A): "The kings of the earth arise, and the princes have taken counsel together against Yahweh and against his Messiah" (Ps 2:2). When they come to God, he will say to them: "אני מנגינתם" (Lam 3:63), that is, "I will smash them." As it says, "Who has given מִגֵּן your adversaries into your hand" (Gen 14:20). (אֲנִי מַנְגִּינָתָם "I am their satirical song" so according to מִגֵּן = מִגַּנְתִּים "I will give them up.") See the continuation of the passage according to the parallel in Midr. Ps. 21 § 3 (90A) at § Rom 3:9 A, #3, B, n. *h*: When it is said to him (the Messiah) .... ‖ On verses 3 and 4. Babylonian Talmud ʿAbodah Zarah 2A: R. Hanina b. Papa (ca. 300)—it has also been said R. Simlai (ca. 250)—said in a public presentation, "One day God will lay the book of the Torah in his lap and say, 'Whoever has devoted himself to the Torah, let him come and receive his recompense!' (Then a long explanation follows about the rebukes that will be given to the nations of the world, because they did not accept the Torah and did not keep the Noachide commandments, see the excursus "Depictions of the Judgment in Ancient Jewish Literature.") Then they will say to him, 'Lord of the world, give it to us anew, so we may do it.' God answers them, 'You biggest fools in the world, whoever has toiled on the day of preparation for the Sabbath (i.e., in this world) will eat on the Sabbath (= in the future world); but whoever has not toiled on the day of preparation for the Sabbath, how will he eat? Yet still, I have a light commandment and "sukkah" is its name, go and observe it! ...' Immediately each one will set off and go and make a sukkah up on his roof. Yet God will make the sun scorching hot over them as at the time of the summer solstice, and everyone will knock down his sukkah and go from there; for it says, 'Let us tear their bonds and cast their chains from us!' (Ps 2:3).... Immediately God will sit down and laugh about them;

317. S-B: It is an open question whether the LXX itself related Ps 2 to the Messiah or to David or to another theocratic king of Israel.

as it says, 'The one who is enthroned in heaven laughs; the Almighty mocks them' (Ps 2:4)." R. Isaac (ca. 300) said, "There is a laughing before God only on that day alone." – Parallel passages are found in Tanḥ. שופטים 15B; TanḥB שופטים § 9 (16A); in Pesiq. 185B, only the beginning; see also Midr. Ps. 2 § 5 (13B). See a further parallel from y. ʿAbod. Zar. 2.40C.19 at § Rom 3:9 A, #3, B, n. *dd.* ‖ On verses 6 and 7, see Midr. Sam. 19 § 1 (51A) and Midr. Ps. 2 § 9 (14B) at § Luke 24:26, I, #4, n. *g.* ‖ On verse 7, see Midr. Ps. 2 § 9 (14B) at § Rom 1:3 A, #3, α, 2nd third; Midr. Ps. 2 § 9 (14B) at § Rom 1:3 A, #3, n. β; Midr. Ps. 2:7 (ed. Warsaw [1875], folio 5A) at § Rom 1:3 B, end. ‖ On verse 8. Midrash Psalm 2 § 10 (15A): "Ask of me, and I will give you the *goyim* for your inheritance and the ends of the earth for your possession" (Ps 2:8). If the *goyim* (are the object of your plea), they have long since been your inheritance (see Ps 72:8), and if the ends of the earth, they have long since been your possession (see Ps 72:8). R. Jonathan (ca. 240, so read instead of R. Yohanan) said, "To three righteous people God said, 'Ask!' These are Solomon (see 1 Kgs 3:5), Ahaz (see Isa 7:11), and the king, the Messiah; for it is written, 'Ask of me …' (Ps 2:8). Likewise, it says, 'He asked you for life; you granted it to him' (Ps 21:5). What did he ask for? He asked that the Israelites might remain alive and endure forever." – There is a parallel in Gen. Rab. 44 (27C). ‖ See b. Sukkah 52A at § Luke 24:26, II, #2, n. *e* and § Rom 1:3 A, A, #3, n. β.

b. See TanḥB נח § 24 (27A) and b. Ber. 7B at § Acts 4:25 B. ‖ See b. Ber. 10A at § Rev 20:8f., #3. ‖ Midrash Psalm 3 § 2 (17A): R. Jacob (probably b. Abbayye [ca. 340?]) said in the name of R. Aha (ca. 320), "Why does the section about Gog and Magog (i.e., Ps 2) stand right alongside the section about Absalom (i.e., Ps 3)? To tell you that a bad son is worse for his father than the wars of Gog and Magog." ‖ Midrash Psalm 2 § 2 (12B): "Why do the gentiles rage?" (Ps 2:1). This is what Scripture said, "He who is enthroned over the vault of the earth, so that its inhabitants (appear) as grasshoppers" (Isa 40:22). What are the godless like? Grasshoppers that are put in an urn: they fidget to rise up, but they fall down (again and again, without knowing that their effort is futile). So too the godless. R. Judah b. Nahmani (ca. 280) said, "According to (the narrative about) the generation of the flood it is written: 'The whole population of the world had one language' (Gen 11:1) (and this was the reason for their rebellion and punishment). Could the later ones not have learned from the earlier ones? (Certainly! But the fact that they as a matter of fact do not learn from the story is their misfortune.) Gog and Magog will also come and fall in the future world, and David saw this and said, 'Why do the gentiles rage? …' (Ps 2:1ff.)." ‖ See Midr. Ps. 118 § 12 (242B) at § Rev 20:8f., #5. ‖ See Midr. Ps. 2 § 4 (13A) and Midr. Ps. 2 § 2 (13A) above at the beginning of #3. ‖ Interpretation of the individual verses of Psalm 2 as referring to Gog and Magog. Verses 1ff.: See b. ʿAbod. Zar. 3B in a baraita at § Matt 23:15 A, n. *r.* – See Midr. Ps. 2 § 5 (13B): "Let us tear their bonds" (Ps 2:3): these are the tefillin on the hand; "and cast their chains from ourselves": these are the tefillin on the head. ‖ Verses 1 and 4. Mekilta Exodus 15:9 (48B): "You have stretched out your right hand" (Exod 15:12). Like a robber who stood there and spewed abuse against the king's palace. He said, "When I meet the king's son, I will seize him and kill him and crucify him and let him die a hard death." So pharaoh stood there and spewed abuse in the land of Egypt, "I pursue, I attain; I distribute the booty!" (Exod 15:9). And the holy spirit (who speaks in Scripture) mocks him and says, "You blew with your breath—then the sea covered them" (Exod 15:10); it further says, "You stretched out your right hand ..." (Exod 15:12). And likewise it says, "Why do the nations rage?" (Ps 2:1); it further says, "He who sits enthroned in heaven laughs" (Ps 2:4). Further, "They salivate with their mouth (delete אחריו) ..." (Ps 59:8). What is written after this? "You, Yahweh, laugh at them" (Ps 59:9). It further says, "And it will happen on that day, on the day when Gog comes against the land of Israel ..." (Ezek 38:18); furthermore: "The fish of the sea will quake before me (so read instead of מפניי)" (Ezek 38:20). See, all those thousands and myriads "sunk like iron in the glorious waters of the sea" (so Exod 15:10 is cited). — See Yalquṭ Simeoni on Ps 2:2 (2 § 620) at § Rom 1:3 A, A, #3, β. ‖ On verses 7f., see b. Sukkah 52A in a baraita at § Luke 24:26, II, #2, n. *e* and § Rom 1:3 A, A, #3, n. β.

5. As referring to the Messiah b. Joseph or b. Ephraim.

See the passages that belong here from Leqach Tob on Num 24:17 (2.129B) at § Luke 24:26, II, #3, n. *b*; Pirqe R. El. 19 (10B) at § Luke 24:26, II, #2, n. *a*; Tg. Yer. I Exod. 40:9–11 at § Luke 24:26, II, #2, n. *c* (however, in the last passage, there is no explicit reference to Ps 2). ‖ Yalquṭ Simeoni on Psalm 2:9 (2 § 621 at the end): "You may smash them with an iron scepter" (Ps 2:9); this refers to the Messiah b. Joseph, who will chastise them with the rod. And likewise, it says, "The scepter will not pass from Judah until Shiloh (= Messiah b. David) comes" (Gen 49:10). (Yet immediately before the coming of the latter, the scepter will rest in the hand of the Messiah who stems from Joseph.)

1:5 B: "I will be a father to him, and he will be a son to me."

We have not encountered in rabbinic literature an interpretation of 2 Sam 7:14 that refers to the Messiah. — See the translation of 2 Sam 7:14 in the targum at § Rom 1:3 A, #1, β.

1:6 A: The firstborn.

See § Rom 8:29 B and § Col 1:15 B. — Also Pesiq. Rab. 34 (159B): By the merit of (because of) the Messiah God will protect them (Israel) and lead them on an even path and redeem them; as it says, "They will come crying and with pleading I will guide them, will lead them to streams of water on an even path on which they will not stumble; for I have become a father to Israel, and Ephraim (in the midrash, a nickname for the Messiah b. David), he is my firstborn" (Jer 31:9). What does Scripture mean to teach with "he" הוּא? He is the one in the days of the Messiah and he is the one in the future world, and there is no one alongside him (the Messiah b. David remains God's firstborn for all eternity). "And I will clothe his enemies with shame" (Ps 132:18); these are those (among the Israelites) who will oppose him; "but over him his crown shall shine" (Ps 132:18), over him and over those who are like him. — The term "firstborn" designates the Messiah as the object of special divine love.

1:6 B: All the angels of God should worship him.

Psalm 97:7 is the base text: "Let all the gods כָּל־אֱלֹהִים bow down before him (worship him)." — Septuagint: προσκυνήσατε αὐτῷ πάντες ἄγγελοι αὐτοῖ "worship him, all his angels!" — Targum: "All the world, the servants (worshipers) of the stars will fall down before him." — The rabbinic scholars did not understand אלהים in Ps 97:7 to refer to the angels, but rather to idols.

See Midr. Ps. 31 § 4 (119B) at § Rom 1:23 A, #2, D, n. *l*; see y. ʿAbod. Zar. 4.44A.47 and Midr. Ps. 31 § 4 (119B) in the excursus "Depictions of the Judgment in Ancient Jewish Literature."

1:7: Who makes his angels winds and his spirits flames of fire.

Psalm 104:4: עֹשֶׂה מַלְאָכָיו רוּחוֹת מְשָׁרְתָיו אֵשׁ לֹהֵט. — Two construals are possible: α. who makes his messengers (angels) winds and his servants flaming fire; β. who makes winds his messengers, flaming fire his servants. — The context in the psalm, which speaks of the ways the powers of nature are used in the service of God, demands the second construal. However, an instinctive feeling for the Hebrew language would have given preference to the first construal. This is indicated not only by the LXX[a] (and the letter to the Hebrews following it), but also by the ancient rabbinic scholars consistently following the formulation in α.[b] The targum of the passage is also no exception in this respect, despite its metaphorical reinterpretation.[c] Only a later period turned to the formulation in β.[d]

a. Septuagint Psalm 104:4: ὁ ποιῶν τοὺς ἀγγέλους αὐτοῦ πνεύματα καὶ τοὺς λειτουργοὺς αὐτοῦ πῦρ φλέγον.

b. Exodus Rabbah 25 (86A): R. Simon (ca. 280) opened his presentation in the name of R. Eleazar (ca. 270) with the following, "'Yahweh, the God of hosts' (Hos 12:6).... 'God of hosts' הצבאות (is what he is called), because he executes his will צביונו through his angels. When he wants, he makes them sit (see Judg 6:11); and sometimes he makes them stand (see Isa 6:2 and Zech 3:7). Sometimes he makes them appear in the form of women (see Zech 5:9), and sometimes in the form of men (see Gen 18:2). Sometimes he makes them winds; as it says, 'Who makes his angels winds' (Ps 104:4). Sometimes he makes them appear as fire; as it says (Ps 104:4), 'And his servants flaming fire.'" ‖ Genesis Rabbah 21 (14C): ("And he made the cherubs and the blaze [the flash] of the turning sword encamp east of the garden of Eden" [Gen 3:24].) "And the blaze," because of "(He makes) his servants flaming fire" (Ps 104:4); "turning," for they (the angels) are transformed sometimes into men and sometimes into women, sometimes into spirits (this is what רוחות means here) and sometimes into angels. ‖ Pesiqta 57A: R. Isaac (ca. 300) said, "It is written, 'My offering, my food for my offering by fire' (Num 28:2). What is this? Is there eating and drinking before the one whose name is to be praised!? And if you should say that there is, learn from his angels and servants who are flaming fire; as it is written, '(Who makes) his servants flaming fire' (Ps 104:4)." — The same is found in Pesiq. Rab. 16 (80A); Num. Rab. 21 (192A). ‖ Yalquṭ Simeoni on Judges 13:17 (2 § 69 at the beginning) from Yelamedenu: ("Manoah said to the angel of Yahweh, 'What is your name?'" [Judg 13:17].) The angel answered him, "I do not know after whose likeness I have been created (in whose likeness I appear); in each hour he (God) changes me. 'Why do you ask for my name, since it is wonderful?' (Judg 13:18). He does wonders upon wonders in me: sometimes I am wind; as it says, 'Who makes his angels winds' (Ps 104:4). Sometimes I am fire, as it says (Ps 104:4), 'And his servants flaming fire.'"

And likewise, you find it with Abraham, to whom they were like men (see Gen 18:2); yet in Sodom they appeared as angels (see Gen 19:1).

c. Targum Psalm 104:4: "Who quickly makes his messengers like wind, his servants forcefully like glowing fire."

d. Rashi on Psalm 104:4: עשה מלאכיו רוחות: (i.e.,) "he makes the winds his messengers" עושה את הרוחות שלוחיו. – The commentary מצודת דוד: "He makes the winds so that they are his messengers" עושה הרוחות להיות שלוחיו. – Here we should probably also list R. Yohanan († 279), who in Midr. Ps. 104 § 7 (221B) explains: "The angels who serve for purposes of sending are made out of wind, and those who are appointed for songs of praise are made of fire."

1:8f. From Ps 45:7f. (almost verbatim according to LXX Ps 45:6f.).

Psalm 45:7f. according to the base text: "Your throne, O God, is forever and ever; a scepter of righteousness (uprightness) is the scepter of your kingship. You have loved righteousness and hated godlessness. Therefore, God, your God, has anointed you with the oil of joy before your companions (= more than your companions)." – In rabbinic literature, Psalm 45 is interpreted to refer to the sons of Korah, to Moses, to Aaron, and to Solomon; see the explanations in Midr. Ps. 45. Alongside this we find the messianic interpretation, which is represented mainly in the targum.

Targum Psalm 45:3ff.: "Your beauty, O king, Messiah, is more excellent than that of the (other) children of men. The spirit of prophecy is laid upon your lips; therefore Yahweh has blessed you forever. Gird your sword about your hips, O hero, to kill kings together with rulers, your majesty and your glory. And your glory will be great; therefore you will have fortune to ride along on royal steeds (another reading: to sit on the royal throne) for the sake of faithfulness and truth and gentleness and righteousness, and Yahweh will teach you, to perform deeds that awaken fear with your right hand. Your projectiles are drawn to kill masses, to topple nations under you and the children of your bow (= your arrows) are sent into the heart of the enemies of the king. The throne of your glory, Yahweh, remains for all eternity. A scepter of righteousness תְּרִיצְתָא (uprightness) is the scepter of your (the Messiah's) kingship. Since you have loved righteousness and hated godlessness, Yahweh, your God, has anointed you with the oil of joy more than your companions. All your garments are fragrant with myrrh, aloe, and cassia; from palaces that are covered with ivory, string music delights you (others: that are covered with ivory from the land of Armenia, you are delighted). The provinces of your kingdom will come to greet your face and to honor you, while the book of the Torah will lie at your right side (read דמעתד instead of דמעתר), which is written with pure gold of Ophir. Hear, community of Israel, the Torah of his mouth and look at this wondrous works and incline your ear to the words of the Torah and do not forget the wicked deeds of the godless of your people and the house of idols which your father's house served. Then the king will long for your beauty, for he is your Lord and you will bow before him. And the inhabitants of the city of Tyre will come with gifts and seek your face, to your sanctuary the richest of the nations will come. Everything beautiful and desirable among the goods of the provinces (and) among the treasures of kings that had been stored up, will be presented to the (Israelite) priests, whose garments are interwoven with pure gold. In embroidered garments they will present their offerings before the eternal king, and the rest of their companions who are dispersed among the nations will be brought to you with joy in Jerusalem. With joy they will be brought and with songs of praise, and they will go up into the temple of the eternal king. In place of your fathers there will be for you the righteous, your sons; you will appoint them as princes in all the earth. In that time you will say, 'We will remember your name from generation to generation. Therefore the nations that have become proselytes will praise your name for all eternity.'" ‖ Genesis Rabbah 99 (63B): "The scepter will not depart from Judah" (Gen 49:10); this refers to the throne of kingship (as it says,) "Your throne, O God, endures forever and ever, a scepter of righteousness is the scepter of your kingship" (Ps 45:7). When? (When the following is fulfilled:) "Nor the ruler's staff from his feet" (Gen 49:10); when that one comes, to whom the kingship is due (i.e., Shiloh = the Messiah), of whom it is written: "The crown of arrogance will be trampled with feet ..." (Isa 28:3). ‖ In the course of R. Eliezer (ca. 90) and his colleagues treating the question whether one will wear weapons in the messianic age, the former had answered the question in the affirmative on the basis that the weapons would then serve as an adornment. Then it says further in b. Šabb. 63A: Abbayye († 338/39) said to Rab Dimi (ca. 320) or, as others say, to Rab Avayya—others say that Rab Joseph († 333) said to Rab Dimi or, as others say, to Rab Avayya—still others say that Abbayye said to Rab Joseph, "What was the scriptural basis for R. Eliezer, so that he said that they (the weapons) would be items of adornment? Because it is written, 'Gird your sword around your hips, O hero, your highness and your glory' (Ps 45:4)." ‖ See b. 'Abod. Zar. 65B (read 65A) at § Rom 1:26 B, #2. This is followed by: Rab Pappi (ca. 360) said, "He should have answered him with this passage of Scripture. 'Daughters of kings are among your honored ladies; your wife stands at your right hand in gold jewelry of Ophir' (Ps 45:10)." — Since the conversation of Bar Shishak with Rab refers to the days of the Messiah, Rab Pappi would also have related Ps 45:10 to this time.

1:10: The heavens are the works of your hands.

If one wants to think of the angels as being included in οὐρανοί, which verse 11 speaks against, though, the following passages could serve as analogies.

Midrash Psalm 148 § 1 (269B): "Hallelujah! Praise Yahweh from the heavens, praise him on high!" (Ps 148:1). This refers to those who are in the heavens. And who are these? The angels of service. ‖ Targum Psalm 50:4: "He calls on the angels up on high (base text: אל השמים מעל = 'to heaven up high') and the righteous of the earth below to propagate judgment over his people." ‖ Targum Psalm 50:6: "The angels on high (base text has simple שמים 'the heavens') proclaim his righteousness; for (or: that) God is the judge forever." ‖ Targum Job 15:15: "The angels on high (base text has simply שמים) are not pure before him."

1:13: Sit at my right hand.

See the excursus "The 110th Psalm in Ancient Jewish Literature."

1:14: Are they not all ministrant spirits ...?

λειτουργικὰ πνεύματα. – This designation comes closest in rabbinic literature to the term מַלְאֲכֵי הַשָּׁרֵת = "angels of service"; see some examples above at § Heb 1:4 and § 1 Cor 10:10. The concept of the angels that guard and accompany human beings also belongs here; see § Matt 4:6; 18:10 B; § Acts 12:15; and § 1 Cor 11:10 B, #2.

See 1 En. 40:1ff. at § Rev 1:4 B. ‖ See T. Levi 3 at § Eph 1:21, #1, n. *a.* ‖ TanḥumaB וישב § 2 (89B): "And Jacob dwelt in the land of his father's peregrination, in the land of Canaan" (Gen 37:1). This is what Scripture says, "Your assembled ones (namely angels, so Isa 57:13 according to the midrash) shall save you at your cry." Who are these? These are the angels who were given to protect him (Jacob) when he went out to go to Mesopotamia. For the angels who serve משמשין in the land do not serve abroad, and those abroad do not serve in the land of Israel. So Jacob saw them going up and others going down (Gen 28:12) to go with him abroad. And when he prepared to return, God summoned those angels who had served משמשין in the land of Israel, and said to them, "Behold, Jacob is returning, so then, we will go to meet him!" ... When Jacob raised his eyes, he saw them, as it says, "And Jacob went his way, and angels of God met him" (Gen 32:2). If Jacob (also) saw them, how do we know that they were those who had served him שהיו משמשין אותו in the land of Israel? Because it says, "Then Jacob said, when he had seen them: This is God's army camp" (Gen 32:3). Therefore it says, "Your assembled ones shall save you at your cry" (Isa 57:13): these are the angels.

2:2: For if that word spoken by angels was firm (see § Gal 3:19 B).

2:5: The future world.

ἡ οἰκουμένη ἡ μέλλουσα = עוֹלָם הַבָּא; see the excursus "This World, the Days of the Messiah, and the Future World."

2:6: "What is man, that you think of him ...!" (Ps 8:5f.)

The words in Ps 8:5 are often put in the mouth of the angels in the midrash, most of the time in a scornful way disparaging humanity. God then has to appear juxtaposed to the angels as the advocate for humanity. – See an interpretation that relates Ps 8:5f. to the three patriarchs in Midr. Ps. 8 § 7 at § Heb 2:7 A, n. *b.*

Pesiqta 34A: You find that when God wanted to created humanity, he took counsel with the angels of service and said to them, "Let us make humanity in our image" (Gen 1:26). They said before him, "What is man, that you think of him!" (Ps 8:5). He answered them, "This man, whom I will create in my world, his wisdom will be greater than yours. What did he do? He brought all the livestock, wild animals, and birds together and made them pass by them." He said to the angels, "What are their names?" And they did not know. When he had created the first human, he brought all the livestock, wild animals, and birds together and made them pass by him. He said to him, "What are their names?" He said, "For this one, it is beautiful to call it 'ox,' for that one it is beautiful to call it 'horse,' for that one 'camel,' for that one 'eagle,' for that one 'lion' and so with all of them." This is what is written: "And the man named the names for all the livestock ..." (Gen 2:20). Then God said to him, "And you, what is your name?" He answered: אָדָם (= human being). He said to him, "And why?" He answered him, "Because I have been created from אֲדָמָה (= earth)." God said to him, "And me, what is my name?" He answered him: אֲדֹנָי (= Lord), because you are Lord אָדוֹן over your creatures. [Immediately God said to the angels, "See how great his wisdom is! And you say, 'What is man, that you think of him?!'"] — Parallels are found in Tanḥ. חקת 224B; Num. Rab. 19 (185D); Midr. Eccl. 7:23 (37A); Gen. Rab. 17 (11D) without reference to Ps 8:5 and with R. Aha (ca. 320) as the author; Midr. Ps. 8 § 2 (37A), with Rabbi (?) as the author, offers as a conclusion the words that are in the brackets above. ‖ In b. Šabb. 88B the angels oppose giving the Torah to Moses by invoking Ps 8:5; see the passage at § Eph 4:8 B, #2, n. *c*. — See also the parallels in Midr. Ps. 8 § 2 (37B) and Pesiq. Rab. 25 (128A). ‖ Babylonian Talmud Sanhedrin 38B: Rab Judah († 299) said that Rab († 247) said, "When God wanted to create humanity, he created a division of the angels of service to whom he said, 'If it pleases you, let us make a human being according to our image.' They said before him, 'Lord of the world, what is his action?' He answered them, 'His action is such and such.' They said before him, 'Lord of the world, "what is man, that you think of him, and the son of man, that you are mindful of him!"' (Ps 8:5). He stretched out his little finger between them and burned them, and the same he did with the second division. The third division said before him, 'Lord of the world, what did it help the earlier ones who spoke before you (trying to dissuade you)?! The whole world is yours! Everything that you want to do in your world, do!' When he came to the people of the generation of the flood and to the people of the generation of the dispersal, whose deeds were evil, they (the angels) said before him, 'Lord of the world, did the earlier ones not speak rightly before you?' He answered them, 'Until old age I am the same and until aged hair I will carry the load; I have done it, and I will bear it, I will carry the load and save' (Isa 46:4)." ‖ See Gen. Rab. 8 (6B) at § Rom 8:20f., n. *b*. ‖ See Tanḥ. וירא 22A at § Heb 6:13 A, n. *b*.

2:7 A: "You have made him a little lower than the angels" (Ps 8:6).

Psalm 8:6 according to the base text: "You made him lack (only) a little in divinity" וַתְּחַסְּרֵהוּ מְּעַט מֵאֱלֹהִים. — Septuagint and targum[a] interpreted אלהים as angels, whereas the rabbinic scholars[b] maintain the meaning "God."

a. Septuagint: ἠλάττωσας αὐτὸν βραχύ τι παρ' ἀγγέλους· ‖ Targum: "You have made him lack (only) a little in comparison with the angels מִמַּלְאֲכַיָּא."

b. Babylonian Talmud Roš Haššanah 21B: "The words of Yahweh are pure words ..., purified seven times שִׁבְעָתָיִם (this is interpreted by the midrash as "seven times seven times," fifty minus one)" (Ps 12:7). Rab († 247) and Samuel († 254). The one said, "Fifty gates of insight (understanding) were created in the world, and all were given to (bestowed on) Moses with the exception of one (so 49 were made accessible to him; therefore purified

שבעתים [Ps 12:7]); as it says, 'You have made him lack one less (= 1 gate of insight) vis-à-vis God.'" (The further bit, which presents a comparison of Ecclesiastes with Moses, does not belong here.) — The same is found in b. Ned. 38A. ‖ Midrash Psalm 8 § 7 (39B): "What is man, that you think of him?" (Ps 8:5). This refers to Abraham; as it says, "God thought of Abraham" (Gen 19:29). "And the son of man, that you remember him?" (Ps 8:5). This refers to Isaac who was born as a result of this "remembering"; as it says, "Yahweh remembered Sarah" (Gen 21:1). "You made him lack only a little in divinity" (Ps 8:6); this refer to Jacob, who determined the small livestock, to cast away striped, speckled, and spotted young ones (Gen 30:39). This teaches that he lacked (in comparison with God) only the ability to put a soul in them.

2:7 B: "You have crowned him with glory and honor" (Ps 8:6).

See TanḥB וארא § 7ff. (11B) at § John 5:18. — It says specifically of the crowning of the Messiah with majesty and glory in Midr. Ps. 104 § 5 (221A): "In majesty and glory you have clothed yourself" (Ps 104:1) … God has two things: majesty and glory … God said, "In the future I will bestow them on the king, the Messiah; as it says, 'You will meet him with blessings of what is good … you put majesty and glory on him' (Ps 21:4, 6)." — See also Pesiq. Rab. 37 (163A) at § Luke 24:26, I, #4, n. *o*.

2:9: So that he might taste death.

On γεύεσθαι θανάτου, see § Matt 16:28; see also § John 8:52.

2:11: He is not ashamed to call them brothers.

Jerusalem Talmud Berakot 9.13A.33: R. Simeon b. Laqish (ca. 250) said, "Flesh and blood (= a human being) has a relative: if he is rich, one acknowledges him; if he is poor, one denies him. Yet it is not so with God: even when the Israelites have entered into the deepest humiliation, he calls them my brothers and my friends; as it says, 'For the sake of my brothers and my friends I will speak, "May peace be in you!"' (Ps 122:8)." R. Abun (probably I, ca. 325) and R. Aha (ca. 320) said in the name of (so read!) R. Simeon b. Laqish, "Flesh and blood has a relative: If he is a philosopher (so a respected man), one says, 'So and so is related to us.' Yet God calls all Israelites 'relatives'; as it says, 'The children of Israel, the people that is related to him' (Ps 148:14)." — The same is found in Midr. Ps. 4 § 3 (21B); in Deut. Rab. 2 (198A) anonymously and with significant differences. — See further at § John 15:14.

2:12: "I will proclaim your name to my brothers" … (Ps 22:23).

The citation is almost verbatim according to LXX Ps 21:23 (Hebrew 22:23). — The paraphrase of the targum is closely connected to the base text, except that instead of שמך we find גבורת שמך "the power of your name." — On the interpretation of Psalm 22, see § John 19:24; we have not found an interpretation of verse 23.

2:13: "I will trust in him.... Behold, I and the children that God has given me" (Isa 8:17f.).

Isaiah 8:17f. is cited only rarely and then is consistently interpreted to the prophet himself; see Midr. Ps. 90 § 4 (194A); y. Sanh. 10.28B.59; Gen. Rab. 42 (25D); Lev. Rab. 11 (113A); Midr. Ruth 1:2 (124A); Midr. Esth. 1:1 (82B); Tg. Isa. 8:17f.

2:14: So that by death he might destroy the one who has the power of death, that is, the devil.

For the equation: Devil = the Angel of Death, see § Matt 4:1 B, #3, C. — On the elimination of the Angel of Death at the giving of the law and in the messianic age, see § Matt 4:1 B, #4 and § 1 Cor 15:54; see also Pesiq. Rab. 36 (161A) at § Luke 24:26, I, #4, n. *k*.

3:1: The apostle and the high priest of our confession, Jesus.

For the high priest as שָׁלִיחַ = envoy, delegate, representative, see, for example, m. Yoma 1.5 at § Rom 1:1 B, #2, n. *d*; see also b. Qidd. 23B at § Rom 1:1 B, #2, n. *e*, γ.

3:2: Who was faithful ... just as Moses was in his whole house.

On Moses' faithfulness and approval according to Num 12:7, see the following:

Sifre Numbers 12:7 § 103 (27B): "In my whole house he is approved"(Num 12:7), besides the angels of service (who were found just as approved as Moses). R. Yose (ca. 150) said, "Even more than the angels of service." ‖ Exodus Rabbah 37 (96A): Like the friend of a king who was the minister of the house קוֹמֵיס (= *comes*) and chief justice רפוסא (corrupted from *praepositus*? Dalman thinks of רופילא = *rufulus*, military tribune). When the king wanted to make someone a general, he let him (his friend) know. He would say to him, "It is your brother." So too God made Moses the minister of his house, as it says, "In my whole house he is approved" (Num 12:7); and likewise chief justice, as it says, "Moses sat down to judge the people" (Exod 18:13). When God wanted to appoint a high priest, he let Moses know. He would say to him, "It is Aaron, your brother" (Exod 28:1). ‖ Yalquṭ Simeoni on Numbers 12:7 (1 § 739) from Midrash אספה: "In my whole house he is approved" (Num 12:7). "I showed him" (God says) "what is above and what is below, what was before and what will be hereafter." What can this be compared with? With a king who had many overseers. Each one was appointed over a specific treasure, but one was appointed over all of them. So there is an angel who is appointed over fire, another who is appointed over hail, another who is appointed over the locusts; but Moses rules over them all. Like a rich man who acquired properties and had bills of sale written in the name of someone else. Then it was said, "Now this one will say they belonged to him." But the rich man responded, "He is approved!" So too God had created the world by means of the Torah and named it after Moses; as it says, "Remember the Torah of Moses, my servant" (Mal 3:22). Then it was said, "Now he will say, 'I too am a joint partner in his world!'" But God responded, "In my whole house he is approved." — See further Pesiq. Rab. 10 (35B) at § Heb 3:5f.

3:5f.: Moses is faithful in his whole house as a servant ..., but Christ as a son over his house.

Moses too is called in the midrash "a son of the house" of God, although only in the sense of the Old Testament בֶּן בַּיִת = caretaker.

See Pesiq. Rab. 10 (35B) at § Matt 5:43, #1, n. g, 3rd paragraph; aside from the parallels listed there, see also Tanḥ. במדבר 186B.

3:7 A: As the Holy Spirit says.

The "holy spirit" is in this connection tantamount to the "spirit of inspiration," who speaks in Scripture and from Scripture. — The introduction of a citation of Scripture with the formula: the holy spirit speaks or calls out or proclaims is frequent in rabbinic literature. See examples at § Luke 2:25 C, #4, n. *b* and in the excursus "The Old Testament Canon and Its Inspiration."

3:7 B: "Today, if you hear his voice" (Ps 95:7).

See b. Sanh. 98A at § Luke 24:26, I, #4, n. *e*. ‖ See y. Taʿan. 1.1 (64A) with parallels at § Matt 4:17 A, #1, 2nd paragraph.

3:8: "As with the bitterness on the day of temptation in the wilderness" (Ps 95:8).

Psalm 95:8 according to the base text: "Do not harden your heart as at Meribah, as on the day of Massah in the wilderness." — Both the LXX[a] (which is followed by the author of the Letter to the Hebrews) and the Targum[b] interpreted the proper names מְרִיבָה (= strife, dispute) and מַסָּה (= temptation) appellatively, a technique that was observed also by, for example, R. Joshua (ca. 90) with the name Rephidim[c] (Exod 17:1).

a. Septuagint Psalm 95:8: μὴ σκληρύνητε τὰς καρδίας ὑμῶν ὡς ἐν τῷ παραπικρασμῷ (at the bitterness) κατὰ τὴν ἡμέραν τοῦ πειρασμοῦ ("on the day of temptation"; another reading: "on the day of bitterness" τοῦ πικρασμοῦ) ἐν τῇ ἐρήμῳ. — Differently, LXX Exodus 17:7: here the names מַסָּה and מְרִיבָה are also translated—the former with Πειρασμός "temptation" and the latter with Λοιδόρησις "revilement, blasphemy"—but even the translated names are meant to be viewed as proper names, not as appellatives.

b. Targum Psalm 95:8: "Do not harden your hearts as at the dispute (discord) בְּמַצּוּתָא, as on the day when you tested (God) in the wilderness." — Yet Targum Onkelos Exodus 17:7 reads: "The place was called נַסֵּיתָא 'temptation' and מַצּוּתָא 'discord, strife.'" — Targum Yerušalmi I Exodus 17:7: "That place was called נִסְיוֹנָא 'temptation' and מַצּוּתָא." Thus, here too the translated terms are proper names.

c. Babylonian Talmud Sanhedrin 106A.37: "And Israel sat in Shittim" (Num 25:1). R. Eliezer (ca. 90) said, "Shittim was the name (of the place)"; R. Joshua (ca. 90) said, "It means that they concerned themselves with foolish things בדברי שְׁטוּת ...." What does the word רְפִידִים (Exod 17:1, 8) mean? R. Eliezer said, "Rephidim was the name (of the place)"; R. Joshua said,

"It means that they loosed themselves ריפו from the words of the Torah; as it says, 'Fathers will not turn to their children due to the slackness רִפְיוֹן of their hands' (Jer 47:3)." — There is a parallel in b. Bek. 6B.

3:9: Where your fathers tested me in a trial.

The probing trial was implied in the question in Exod 17:7: הֲיֵשׁ יהוה בְּקִרְבֵּנוּ אִם אָיִן "Is Yahweh in our midst or not?" — Septuagint: εἰ ἔστι κύριος ἐν ἡμῖν ἢ οὔ; — Targum Onkelos: "Is the Shekinah of Yahweh among us or not?"

Interpretations of this question: Mekilta Exodus 17:7 (60B): R. Joshua (ca. 90) said, "The Israelites said, 'If he is a Lord of everything created, as he is Lord over us, then we know it (that he dwells in our midst); but if not, then we do not know it.'" R. Eliezer (ca. 90) said, "They said, 'If he supplies our needs for us, we will serve him; but if not, we will not serve him.'" ‖ Pesiqta 28A.1: R. Judah (ca. 150) and R. Nehemiah (ca. 150) and the rabbis. R. Judah said, "They said, 'If he is Lord over every created thing, as is he Lord over us, we will serve him; but if not, we will not serve him.'" R. Nehemiah said, "They said, 'If he supplies us with our food, as a king who dwells in a city, so that the city lacks nothing, we will serve him; but if not, we will rise up against him.'" The rabbis said, "They said, 'If we speak in our hearts and he knows what we say (thus, if he is literally inside us), we will serve him; but if not, we will rise up against him.'" — Parallel passages are found in TanḥB תצא § 15 (21B); Pesiq. Rab. 13 (55A) with variations; Exod. Rab. 26 (87B); Tanḥ. יתרו 87A among many others ‖ Pesiqta Rabbati 13 (55A): R. Abbahu (ca. 300) said, "(They said,) 'If we move the words (raise the question) inside ourselves whether he is in our midst, and he knows what we think (move) in ourselves, then we will serve him; but if not, we will not serve him ….' See the foolishness in them! The Shekinah had carried them. They were carried on the clouds of glory and surrounded by them, and a pillar of cloud went before them 'and in the wilderness where you have seen that Yahweh your God carried you'! (Deut 1:31). And they said, 'Is Yahweh in our midst?'" R. Berekhiah (ca. 340), the priest, the son of Rabbi, said, "Like a hero who went on his way, and his son sat on his shoulder, and he carried him to a market. The son saw something that he liked and said to his father, 'Buy it for me!' And he bought it for him; so it happened once, twice, three times; and his son sat on his shoulder. Finally he saw a man and said to him, 'Have you seen my father?' Immediately his father took him and cast him to the earth. He said to him, 'This is the sequence (so is the course of things); I had carried you on my shoulder and now you say, "Have you seen my father?!"' So the Israelites were carried on the clouds of glory 'and in the wilderness where you have seen that Yahweh your God carried you, as when a man carries his son' (Deut 1:31). And then they say, 'Is Yahweh in our midst'? And immediately Amalek came (for punishment, Exod 17:8)." — In the parallel Pesiq. 21B, R. Levi (ca. 300) is the author of the parable instead of his student R. Berekhiah.

3:11: "I swore in my anger: They shall not enter my rest."

The oath in Ps 95:11 was significantly weakened in Num. Rab. 14 (177C): It says, "So that I swore in my anger, 'Truly, they shall not enter my rest!'" (Ps 95:11). Yet when my anger has abated, they shall enter my rest. – See further t. Sanh. 13.10f. at § 1 Cor 10:5; see also § Heb 4:9.

3:13: As long as it is called today.

Mishnah ʾAbot 1.14: (Hillel the elder [ca. 20 BCE]) used to say, "... If not now, when?" ‖ Mishnah ʾAbot 2.4: Hillel (the elder) used to say, "... Do not say, 'When I have leisure, I will study (Torah).' You might not have any leisure!" ‖ See m. ʾAbot 2.10 and b. Šabb. 153A at § Matt 4:17 A, #2. ‖ Targum Isaiah 55:6: "Seek the fear of God as long as you live; ask of him as long as you still exist." ‖ See Sir 5:4–7 at § Heb 6:4–6, #1, n. *a*.

3:16: Were they not all those who went out of Egypt by Moses?

Joshua and Caleb are not in view. – We find an idiosyncratic view about the infinite number of those who did not go out from Egypt with Moses in baraita in b. Sanh. 111A: R. Simai (ca. 210) said, "It says, 'I will take you to myself as a people' (Exod 6:7), and further it says, 'I will bring you into the land (of Israel)' (Exod 6:8). Scripture compares their exodus from Egypt (Exod 6:7) with their coming to the land: as their coming to the land took place (only) with two (Joshua and Caleb) from 60 myriads, so too their exodus from Egypt (only) with two from 60 myriads (i.e., from every 60 myriads of the Israelites in Egypt only two men took part in the exodus)." Raba († 352) said, "And it will be the same in the days of the Messiah; for it says, 'And she will answer there as in the days of her youth and as on the day when she went up out of Egypt' (Hos 2:17)." (Thus, even in the messianic age only 2 from every 600,000 men of the Jewish diaspora will return to Palestine.) ‖ Mekilta Exodus 13:18 (29A): "The children of Israel went out armed חמשים" (Exod 13:18), that is, one in five מחמשה; others say, "One in fifty מחמשים"; others say, "One in five hundred." R. Nehorai (ca. 150) said, "By the temple service! Not even one in five hundred went up; for it says, 'I made you countless like the weeds of the field' (Exod 16:7), and further it is written, 'The children of Israel were fruitful and prevalent, and they increased very greatly and became numerous' (Exod 1:7), for a woman gave birth to six in one pregnancy; and you think that one in five hundred went up? By the temple service! Not even one in five hundred went up! Rather, many of the Israelites had died in Egypt. And when did they die? In the three days of darkness; for it says, 'One did not see another' (Exod 10:23). They buried their dead and thanked and praised God that their enemies did not see (in the darkness) and rejoice over their perishing." – The same is found in Mek. Exod. 12:26 (16B); Pesiq.85B; Tanḥ. ויהי בשלח 78A.

3:17: Their bodies fell in the wilderness.

Traditions specifically about the death of the scouts.

See b. Soṭah 35A at § Acts 12:23, #2; this is then followed by the words: Rab Nahman b. Isaac († 356) said, "They died of quinsy." ‖ Midrash Ecclesiastes 9:12 (44B): "Neither does a man know his time, like the fish that are caught in an evil net" (Eccl 9:12). R. Berekhiah (ca. 340) said, "How so? Is there an evil net and a good net?" Resh Laqish (ca. 250) said, "This refers to fishing hooks; this is what is written, 'The men died who had spread evil רעה slander over the land' (Num 14:37)." How did they suffer death? The rabbis and R. Simeon b. Yohai (ca. 150). The rabbis said, "Quinsy appeared in their throat so that they choked and died." R. Simeon b. Yohai said, "They died by their limbs falling off." (A scriptural proof follows.) The saying of Resh Laqish about fishing hooks is also found in b. Sanh. 81B.

4:1: Since the promise still remains.

On ἐπαγγελία see § Rom 4:13 A, #2.

4:2 A: We too received the good news.

On εὐαγγελίζεσθαι see § Rom 1:1 D, #2.

4:2 B: The word of the promise.

On ἀκοή see § Rom 10:17 A.

4:2 C: Since it was not bound (mingled) with the hearers.

Wettstein does not correctly render the passage he cites from Midr. Song. 4:11 (115B) and Exod. Rab. 41 (97D). The verb ערב, which appears here several times, does not mean "to mingle," but rather "to be pleasant." — However, the following expression can probably be compared: the words of the Torah are swallowed up, absorbed by the blood of the one who studies = pass into his flesh and blood; see ʾAbot R. Nat. 24 (7A) at § 2 Tim 3:15, #1, end.

4:3 A: We who have come to believe enter into the rest.

κατάπαυσις here = ζωὴ αἰώνιος.

See m. Tamid 7.4; b. Roš Haš. 31A in a baraita at § Luke 1:10, final third. ‖ ʾAbot de Rabbi Nathan 1 (1C): "The day of the Sabbath" (Ps 92:1); this is the day that is entirely Sabbath (rest), on which there is no eating and drinking, no buying and no selling; but rather the righteous will sit with crowns on their heads and refresh themselves by the splendor of the Shekinah. ‖ Pirqe Rabbi Eliezer 18 (9D): God created seven eons, and of them all he created only the seventh eon for himself. There are six for (human) going and coming, and one (the seventh) is entirely Sabbath and rest in eternal life. ‖ See Gen. Rab. 17 (12A) at § Heb 1:3 A, n. *c*.

4:3 B: Since the foundation of the world.

See § Matt 25:34 C and § Eph 1:4, #3.

4:4: "God rested on the seventh day from all his works" (Gen 2:2).

See § John 5:17.

4:7: In David.

On this citation formula, see § Mark 12:26 and § Rom 11:2. — See further SDeut 11:13 (80A): And likewise it says in David בדוד: "May my prayer stand before you, the raising of my hands as an evening meal offering" (Ps 141:2). ‖ Tosefta Berakot 3.6 (6): Should one pray all (prayers to be prayed in the course of a day) at once? Scripture declares in David בדוד: "Evening and morning and noon ..." (Ps 55:18).

4:9: So there is still a Sabbath rest for the people of God.

On σαββατισμός see the passages above at § Heb 4:3 A. — The content is comparable with Midr. Eccl. 10:20 (49B): R. Abbahu (ca. 300) said in the name of his father-in-law R. Tahlifa (ca. 270), "It is written, 'To whom I swore in my anger' (Ps 95:11). God said, 'In my anger I have sworn, but I have relented, "Truly, they shall not enter my rest"' (Ps 95:11); to this rest they will not come, but they will come to another rest." R. Bebai (ca. 320) said in the name of R. Joshua b. Levi (ca. 250), "Like a king who became angry with his son and swiftly removed him from his palace and swore that his son not be allowed to come into the palace. (Then the king regretted his oath.) What did he do? Since the palace had been built, he had it (now) torn down; then he built it again and brought his son in. It ended up that he could bring his son in and that he kept his oath. In the same way, God said, 'In my anger I have sworn, but I have relented. "Truly, they shall not enter my rest!" To this rest they will not come, but they will come to another rest (namely to the rest of eternal life).'" — A parallel passage with partially different authorial attribution is found in Lev. Rab. 32 (129D).

4:12: The word of God is ... sharper than any two-edged sword.

See Tg. Song. 3:8 and Midr. Ps. 45 § 6 (136A) at § Eph 6:17 B. ‖ Pesiqta 102B: "A two-edged sword חֶרֶב פִּיפִיּוֹת in their (the pious') hand" (Ps 149:6). R. Judah (ca. 150) ... said, "This refers to the written and the oral Torah." — In Midr. Song. 1:2 (83A), R. Nehemiah (ca. 150) is the author. ‖ Babylonian Talmud Berakot 5A: R. Isaac (ca. 300) said, "He who reads the Shema (of the evening) on his bed is like one who has a sword with two edges חרב של שתי פיפיות in his hand; as it says, 'Raising praises to God in their mouth and a two-edged sword in their hand' (Ps 149:6)." ‖ Midrash Song of Songs 1:2 (83A): R. Samuel (so read!) b. Nahman (ca. 260) said, "The words of the Torah are like a weapon: as a weapon remains (as assistance) for its owner in the hour of the battle, so the words of the Torah remain for the one who occupies himself earnestly with them." R. Hanina b. Aha (ca. 330) proved this from the following, "'Raising praises to God in their mouth and a two-edged sword in their hand' (Ps 149:6). As a sword consumes on two sides, so the Torah gives life in this and in the future world." — The last saying is attributed in Pesiq. 102B to R. Nehemiah (ca. 150). ‖ See further Midr. Ps. 149 § 5 (271A); Gen. Rab. 21 (14C).

4:15: Without sin.

On the sinlessness of the righteous in the days of the Messiah, see § Matt 1:21 D; on the sinlessness of the Messiah himself, see § Matt 1:21 D, particularly Pss. Sol. 17:26ff. in § Matt 1:21 D, A, n. g.

5:4: And no one takes this honor for himself, but rather he who is called by God, just like Aaron.

1. οὐχ ἑαυτῷ τις λαμβάνει τὴν τιμήν; see the citations at § Rom 13:1 B.

2. See specifically on Aaron in Midr. Ps. 2 § 3 (13A) at § Rom 13:2. — Further, Tanḥ. קרח 218A: Like a king who had many slaves; he wanted to emancipate one in order to confer an official office (literally: rulership) on him. Then he made him a counselor. His peers rose up against him. The king said to them, "If he had made himself a freedman, and if he had appropriated this greatness to himself, then it would be right to rise up against him. Yet now, since his lord has conferred it on him, does not anyone who rises up against him rise up against his lord?" So too Moses said (to Korah and his mob), "If my brother Aaron had taken the dignity of the priesthood for himself, you would be right to grumble about him. Yet now, since God, whose is the lordship and the greatness and the power, has given it to him, does not everyone who rises up against my brother Aaron rise up against God? Therefore it says, 'For Aaron, what is he that you grumble against him?' (Num 16:11)." — The same is found in Num. Rab. 18 (183C).

5:5: "You are my son ..." (Ps 2:7, see § Heb 1:5).

5:6: "According to the order of Melchizedek."

See the excursus "The 110th Psalm in Ancient Jewish Literature."

5:7: Petitions and supplicatory prayer ... with loud cries and tears.

1. δεήσεις τε καὶ ἱκετηρίας = תפילות ותחנונים in, for example, Deut. Rab. 11 (207C): What did Moses do in that hour (when he was supposed to die)? He put on a sack and wrapped himself in the sack and rolled himself in ashes and stood in prayer and supplication בתפילה ובתחנונים before God until heaven and earth were shaken....

2. μετὰ κραυγῆς ἰσχυρᾶς καὶ δακρύων, see Yalquṭ Simeoni on Genesis 22:9 (1 § 101) from "midrash": In that hour (when he lay bound on the altar) Isaac opened his mouth with crying בבכיה and cried out with great cries געיה גדולה.

5:9: Author of eternal salvation.

σωτηρία αἰώνιος = תְּשׁוּעַה עוֹלָמִים "eternal salvation, eternal redemption" (Isa 45:17). — Septuagint: σωτηρίαν αἰώνιον. — Targum: פּוּרְקָן עָלְמַיָּא "eternal redemption." ‖ In Tg. Yer. I on Gen 49:18, פּוּרְקָן דְּשָׁעֲתָא "redemption for an hour," that is, for a short time, is juxtaposed with פּוּרְקָן עָלְמִין = eternal redemption. — Targum Yerušalmi II on Genesis 49:18 replaces פורקן דשעתא once with פורקן שעה "redemption for an hour" and then פורקן עבר = "temporary redemption." See both targum passages on Gen 49:18 in the excursus "The Memra of Yahweh," #5, 2nd third.

5:12: You need milk, not solid food.

Philo, *De agricultura* § 2 (Mangey's ed., 1:301): Ἐπεὶ δὲ νηπίοις μέν ἐστι γάλα τροφή, τελείοις δὲ τὰ ἐκ πυρῶν πέμματα (baked goods), καὶ ψυχῆς γαλακτώδεις μὲν ἂν εἶεν τροφαὶ κατὰ τὴν παιδικὴν ἡλικίαν, τὰ τῆς ἐγκυκλίου μουσικῆς προπαιδεύματα· τέλειαι δὲ καὶ ἀνδράσιν εὐπρεπεῖς αἱ διὰ φρονήσεως καὶ σωφροσύνης καὶ ἁπάσης ἀρετῆς ὑφηγήσεις.

6:1: Repentance (conversion) from dead works.

νεκρὰ ἔργα, see *mortalia opera* in 4 Ezra 7:119: "What does it help us that eternity has been promised to us if we have done the works of death?" — See also § 1 Tim 5:6.

6:2: Laying on of hands (see § Acts 6:6).

6:4–6: It is impossible to restore again to repentance those who had once been illumined and had tasted the heavenly gift and had participated in the Holy Spirit and had tasted the good word of God and the powers of the future world, and who (then) fell away.

1. The idea that repentance could become an impossibility in certain circumstances was also common in the ancient synagogue. This was assumed to be the case α. for someone who recklessly sins in the confidence of later repentance;[a] β. for someone who knows God's power and nevertheless rises up against God;[b] γ. for someone who initially stubbornly refuses repentance;[c] δ. for someone who is fully immersed in sin,[d] and ε. for someone who misleads the multitude to sin.[e]

a. See m. Yoma 8.9 at § Matt 4:17 A, #3, n. *e*; see ʾAbot R. Nat. 39. 40 and b. Yoma 86B in a baraita at § Matt 4:17, A, #3, n. *e*. Also see Sir 5:4–7 (Hebrew): "Do not say, 'I have sinned, and what has happened to me?' For God is longsuffering. Do not say, 'Yahweh is merciful, and he will wipe out all my guilt!' Do not trust in forgiveness in order to add guilt upon guilt, so that you say, 'His mercy is great; he will forgive the multitude of my sins.' For mercy and wrath is with him, and his anger rests on the godless. Do not tarry to turn to him, and do not put it off day after day; for suddenly his wrath will go out, and on the day of vengeance you will perish."

b. Jerusalem Talmud Ḥagigah 2.77B.49: (R. Meir [ca. 150] said to his teacher, the apostate R. Elisha b. Abbuyah [ca. 120],) "You possess all this wisdom, and you will not turn (in repentance)?" He answered him, "I cannot!" He said to him, "Why?" He said to him, "Once I rode on my horse on a Day of Atonement, which fell on a Sabbath, past the holy of holies and heard a voice from heaven, which came out from the holy of holies and called out, 'Turn back, children, except for Elisha b. Abbuyah; for he knew my power and rose up against me!'" — The same is found in Midr. Ruth 3:13 (135A); Midr. Eccl. 7:8 (34A).

c. See Exod. Rab. 13 (75C) at § Rom 9:18. ‖ See Exod. Rab. 11 (74C) at § Matt 4:17 A, #3, n. *e*, end. ‖ Exodus Rabbah 11 toward the end: "Yet Yahweh hardened pharaoh's heart" (Exod 9:12). When God saw that he did not go into himself because of the first five plagues, God said, "From this point on, even if he wants to go into himself, I will harden his heart, in order to collect the full penalty from him, 'as Yahweh had spoken to Moses' (Exod 9:12); for so it is written, 'I will harden pharaoh's heart' (so Exod 4:21 is cited)."

d. Midrash Psalm 1 § 22 (12B): R. Phineas (b. Hama, ca. 360) said, "He who has completely fallen victim to sin cannot (penitently) go into himself and there will never be forgiveness for him."

e. See m. ʾAbot 5.18 at § Rom 5:15 A, #3. ‖ Tosefta Yoma 5.11 (191): Whoever misleads the multitude to sin, to him the opportunity is not given (by God) to repent, lest his students go down to Sheol (gehenna), while he obtains the future world; for it says, "A person who is weighed down by human blood (has human souls on his conscience) flees to the grave; he will not be upheld" (Prov 28:17) (namely by heaven, by him being given the opportunity to repent, Rashi on Prov 28:17). — Similar statements are found in ʾAbot R. Nat. 40 (10B) and b. Yoma 87A.23.

2. καλὸν θεοῦ ῥῆμα, see Jer 33:14: "I will establish the good word הַדָּבָר הַטּוֹב that I have spoken to the house of Israel." — In the LXX the whole passage of Jer 33:14–26 is missing.[318] — Targum: פִּתְגָּמָא תָּקְנָא = "the right word."

3. γευσαμένους δυνάμεις μέλλοντος αἰῶνος. — γεύεσθαι corresponds to טָעַם, and in strengthened form: טָעַם טַעַם "to taste a taste"; see § Matt 16:28 and § John 8:52. — So too טָעַם מֵעֵין הָעוֹלָם הַבָּא = to taste something of the future world.[a] — Essentially the same is meant by the expression: to so-and-so a sample דּוּגְמָם, דִּיגְמָא (δεῖγμα) was given, that is, a foretaste of the future world.[b]

a. Babylonian Talmud Baba Batra 15B: What does "The cattle plowed and the jennies pastured alongside them" (Job 1:14) mean? R. Yohanan († 279) said, "This teaches that God let Job taste something of the future world" שהטעימו מעין העולם הבא. (That one has a bit of a field plowed and in the same hour also has it grazed upon does not happen in this age, but in the future age [see Amos 9:13]; therefore, Job in that hour had a foretaste of the future world.) A baraita in b. B. Bat. 16B: God let three people in this world taste something of the future world. These are Abraham (see Gen 24:1), Isaac (see Gen 27:33), Jacob (see Gen 33:11). ("Everything," understood in an absolute sense, includes also the enjoyment of the future world.)

b. Pesiqta 65B: What does "The cattle plowed and the jennies pastured alongside them" (Job 1:14) mean? R. Hama b. Hanina (ca. 260) said, "A sample of the future world was given to him" נעשה לו דוגמא מעין עוה״ב. See b. B. Bat. 15B above in n. *a.* ‖ Pesiqta 107A: (After God had healed all the infirmities in the Israelites before the giving of the law, he said,) "I am performing a renewal of things among you and prepare among you a sort of sample of the future world" ועישה בכם מעין דוגמת העולם הבא. ‖ For further examples, see Gen. Rab. 51 (32D); Midr. Eccl. 9:11 (43B) and Gen. Rab. 73 (47B).

6:7: A land that has drunken the rain that has frequently come upon it and brings forth (bears) plants is beneficial to those for whom it is cultivated, and it receives blessings from God.

In rabbinic literature we encounter the concept that the rain as a male principle and the earth together with its moisture as a female principle have to work together to bring forth growth.

318. See Geiger, *Urschrift und Übersetzungen der Bibel*, 84f.

A baraita in b. Ber. 9.14A.17: R. Simeon b. Eleazar (ca. 190) said, "You have no stretch (of rain) that falls down from above that has not made the earth rise up two stretches (in its ground water). What is the scriptural basis? 'Torrent (from above) calls to torrent (from below) at the roar of your water gushes' (Ps 42:8)." R. Levi (ca. 300) said, "The upper waters are masculine and the lower ones (in the earth) are feminine. What is the scriptural basis? 'The earth opens itself' (Isa 45:8), as a woman opens herself before a man; 'so that salvation sprouts' (Isa 45:8); this refers to procreation (bringing forth growth); 'and let righteousness shoot forth at the same time' (Isa 45:8), this refers to the falling down of the gushes of rain (צדקה is taken as the subject of תצמיח)." – Parallels are found in y. Taʿan. 1.64B.19; Gen. Rab. 13 (10A). The saying of R. Simeon b. Eleazar is found also in b. Taʿan. 25B and t. Taʿan. 1.4 (215); here with the addition: "Why is it (the former rain) called רְבִיעָה? Because it mated with the earth שרובעת את הארץ." According to y. Taʿan. 1.64B.24 and y. Ber. 9.14A.22, this additional saying has Rabban Simeon b. Gamaliel (ca. 140) as its author. ‖ Babylonian Talmud Taʿanit 6B: R. Abbahu (ca. 300) said, "What does רְבִיעָה (= former rain) mean? Something that has mated רובע with the earth. This corresponds to the opinion of Rab Judah († 299). Rab Judah said, 'The rain is the spouse of the earth; for it says, "As the rain and the snow come down from heaven and do not return without saturating the earth and impregnating (fertilizing הילידה) it and making it sprout" (Isa 55:10)....' Rab Judah said, 'Blessed is the year that is widowed (that does not have too much rain)!'" ‖ See further Pirqe R. El. 5 (3C).

6:13 A: Since he could swear by no one greater.

The midrash has God swear countless times by the life of human beings;[a] we also find in God's mouth oaths by the life of the angels and by the life of the temple gates.[b]

a. See Lev. Rab. 34 (132A) at § Matt 5:36 F, n. *m.* ‖ Deuteronomy Rabbah 11 (207B): God said to Moses, "You think you have done something small (by taking Joseph's coffin with you out of Egypt); by your life, this work of love that you have done is great!" ‖ Midrash Song of Songs 1:1 (80A): God said to Solomon, "You have asked for wisdom, and not for prosperity, fortune or the life of your enemies. By your life, may wisdom and insight be given to you!" ‖ See further Deut. Rab. 1 (197A) and Deut. Rab. 11 (207A). ‖ See God swearing by the life of the Messiah in Pesiq. Rab. 36 (161A) at § Luke 24:26, I, #4, n. *k*; see Pesiq. Rab. 36 (162A) at § Luke 24:26, I, #4, n. *l*.

b. Tanḥuma וירא 22A: God said to the angels of service: Come, we will visit the sick man (Abraham after his circumcision). They answered him, "Lord of the world, 'what is man, that you think of him, the son of man, that you are concerned about him?' (Ps 8:5). You want to go to a place of filth, to a place of blood, abomination, and fetidness?" He said to them, "By your life, that blood of circumcision is more pleasant to me than myrrh and incense!" ‖ Tanḥuma בהעלותך 206A: God said to the temple gates, "You have shown me honor (by broadening at the mention of my name, so that the ark of the covenant could make its entry); by your life, when I have my house destroyed, no one shall obtain authority over you!" (As a consequence of this oath, according to the tradition, the temple gates were hidden at the destruction of the sanctuary.)

6:13 B: He swore by himself.

Babylonian Talmud Berakot 32A: "Remember Abraham, Isaac, and Jacob, your servants, to whom you have sworn by yourself" (Exod 32:13). What does "by yourself" mean? R. Eleazar (ca. 270) said, "Moses said before God, 'Lord of the world, if you had sworn to them by heaven and by the earth, I would say, "As heaven and earth pass away, so too your oath passes away"; but now you have sworn to them by your great name (= by yourself). As your great name lives and endures forever and ever, so too your oath endures for all eternity.'" — In Exod. Rab. 44 (100A), Hezekiah (b. Hiyya, ca. 240) is named as the author.

7:1: This Melchizedek, king of Salem, priest of the Most High God.

1. Melchizedek is identified by the haggadah with Shem, the son of Noah; on the basis of Gen 14:18 he then appears as the holder of the high priesthood of God, which he then has to relinquish to Abraham due to a formal error that he had become guilty of in the words of Gen 14:19f. See more detail in the excursus "The 110th Psalm in Ancient Jewish Literature."

2. βασιλεὺς Σαλήμ, see verse 2.

3. ἱερεὺς τοῦ θεοῦ τοῦ ὑψίστου. — According to the haggadah, from Adam until the tribe of Levi arose, the sacrificial service lay in the hand of the firstborn; so in his day also in the hand of Shem-Melchizedek; see Num. Rab. 4 (141C): When Methuselah died, the priestly garments were transferred to Noah; Noah arose and presented an offering (see Gen 8:20). Noah died and handed them over to Shem. Yet how? Was Shem a firstborn? Was not Japheth firstborn; as it says, "To Shem ..., the brother of the older Japheth"? (So the midrash formulates this in agreement with the accents in Gen 10:21.) And why did he give them over to Shem (and not to the older Japheth)? Because Noah saw (in the spirit) the sequence of the fathers that was to arise from him (Shem). You can know that Shem sacrificed; for it says, "And Melchizedek, the king of Salem, brought out bread and wine. He was a priest of the Most High God" (Gen 14:18). Yet had the priesthood been bestowed on him? Was the priesthood not bestowed only after Aaron had arisen? When then does (Scripture) mean when it says, "He was a priest"? (This is said,) because he sacrificed like the priests. Shem died and handed it over to Abraham .... ‖ See further references to Gen 14:18: "He was a priest of the Most High God" in b. Ned. 32B in the excursus "The 110th Psalm in Ancient Jewish Literature"; Tg. Yer. I Gen. 14:18 and Midr. Ps. 76 § 3 (171A) at § Heb 7:2 B and C; also Gen. Rab. 43 (26D): "He brought out bread and wine; he was a priest of the Most High God" (Gen 14:18). R. Samuel (b. Nahman, ca. 260) said, "He (Melchizedek) made known the regulations concerning the high priesthood to him (Abraham); for 'bread' refers to the show bread loaves and 'wine' the drink offerings." The rabbis said, "The Torah made it known to him (for it is compared to bread and wine); as it says, 'Come, eat of my bread and drink of the wine that I have mixed' (Prov 9:5)."

7:2 A: To whom even Abraham gave a tenth of everything (see § Heb 7:4).

7:2 B: Translated in first place as "king of righteousness."

מַלְכִּי־צֶדֶק is interpreted as מֶלֶךְ צֶדֶק = "king of righteousness," that is, righteous king.

Josephus, *Jewish Antiquities* 1.10.2: "There (in the King's Valley [Gen 14:17]) the king of the city of Solyma, Melchizedek, received him (Abraham); yet this means 'righteous king' βασιλεὺς δίκαιος. And according to general opinion he was such that he was also for this reason a priest of God." ‖ See Philo, *Leg.* 3.25 (Mangey's ed., 1:102f.) at § Heb 7:2 C, β. ‖ Targum Yerušalmi I Genesis 14:18: "A righteous king, namely Shem (= Melchizedek), Noah's son, the king of Jerusalem (= Salem), went out, met Abraham and brought out to him bread and wine; for in that time he served (as a priest) before the Most High God." – With the understanding of מַלְכִּי־צֶדֶק as a personal name, alongside it in Gen 14:18 שָׁלֵם also has the character of a proper name; מֶלֶךְ שָׁלֵם thus = "king of Salem" (later Jerusalem).

7:2 C: Then, though, also king of Salem, that is, "king of peace."

Interpretations of Salem.

α. שָׁלֵם is a proper name for the place Salem (= Jerusalem). This is the most common interpretation; see above at 7:2 B at the end.

Genesis Rabbah 43 (26D.18): "Melchizedek, the king of Salem" (Gen 14:18). This place (Salem-Jerusalem) made its inhabitants righteous (therefore Shem was also called Melchizedek = king of righteousness). ‖ See Gen. Rab. 56 (36A) at § Luke 19:42 A. ‖ Genesis Rabbah 56 (36A.44): R. Berekhiah (ca. 340) said in the name of R. Helbo (ca. 300): When it (Jerusalem) was still Salem, God made therefore a booth for himself in which he used to pray; as it says, "His booth was in Salem and his dwelling on Zion" (Ps 76:3). And what did he used to say (in his prayer)? May it be pleasing that I see the construction of my house (soon)! ‖ Midrash Psalm 76 § 3 (171A): "His booth was in Salem and his dwelling on Zion" (Ps 76:3). R. Berekhiah (ca. 340) said, "From the beginning of the creation of the world God made for himself a booth in Jerusalem, in order to, if one may say so, pray in it, 'May it be pleasing that my children do my will, so that I do not have to destroy my house and my sanctuary.' ... And after it was destroyed, he prayed, 'May it be pleasing before me that my children repent, so that I may hasten the construction of my house and my sanctuary.' These are what the words 'His booth was in Salem' (Ps 76:3) mean. You find that the sanctuary is called 'Salem'; for it says, 'Melchizedek, the king of Salem' (Gen 14:18). And he was Shem, the son of Noah; for it says, 'And he was a priest of the Most High God' (Gen 14:18). Further it is written, 'May God give broad space to Japheth, and may he dwell in the tents of Shem' (Gen 9:27); for he (God) made him (Shem) dwell in his tent, because he served him (as a priest), as we interpret the words, 'He was a priest of the Most High God' (Gen 14:18) in the targum: 'And he served (as a priest) before the Most High God ' (see Tg. Onk. Gen. 14:18); he (Melchizedek) was thus Shem." – There then follows a parallel to the citation from Gen. Rab. 56 (36A) adduced at § Luke 19:42 A with small deviations.

β. שָׁלֵם is understood appellatively as שָׁלוֹם, Aram. שְׁלָם "peace"; מלך שלם (Gen 14:18) thus = king of peace.

So Heb 7:2; also Philo, *Leg.* 3.25 (Mangey's ed., 1:102f.): "God made Melchizedek the king of peace, this is what Σαλήμ means, his priest." — Philo immediately then interprets the name Melchizedek as = βασιλεὺς δίκαιος, thus = מֶלֶךְ צֶדֶק.

γ. שָׁלֵם is adjectivally interpreted as שָׁלֵם "perfect."

Genesis Rabbah 43 (26D): מַלְכִּי־צֶדֶק means "Lord of Zedek" (righteousness); yet Zedek is what Jerusalem was called, because it says, "Righteousness dwelt in her" (Isa 1:21). He was called מֶלֶךְ שָׁלֵם (perfect king) because he, as R. Isaac the Babylonian (an Amora of uncertain time) said, has been born circumcised. (A man becomes perfect only by circumcision; see the excursus "Circumcision," #4, n. *n.*)

7:3 A: Without father, without mother, without genealogy.

ἀπάτωρ and ἀμήτωρ can be used to designate α. שאין לו אב ואם, someone who does not have a father or a mother because they have both died;[a] β. שאינו מכיר לא אביו ולא אמו, someone who knows neither his father nor his mother, for example, a foundling;[b] γ. someone whose genealogy is unknown, thus = ἀγενεαλόγητος. This is the sense at least in the present passage, Heb 7:3. According to the regulations pertaining to the Levitical priesthood (see § Matt 1:1 A, #3) Melchizedek as ἀγενεαλόγητος would have been unfit for priestly service.

a. Midrash Esther 2:7 (93B): Rab († 247) said, "Was Esther a foundling, so that it is said of her, 'She had neither father nor mother' (Esth 2:7)? Rather, when her mother became pregnant with her, her father died, and when she was born, her mother died ...." R. Berekhiah (ca. 340) said in the name of R. Levi (ca. 300), "God said to Israel, 'You weep and say, "We have become orphans, fatherless אֵין אָב" (Lam 5:3); by your life, even the redeemer whom I will cause to arise for you one day among the Medes (i.e., Esther) will have neither father nor mother. This is what is written, "(Esther) had neither father nor mother" (Esth 2:7).'"

b. See m. Qidd. 4.1–3 at § Matt 1:1 A, #2, n. *b.*

7:3 B: Having neither beginning of days nor end of life.

This is said because in Scripture neither the birth nor the death of Melchizedek is mentioned. Here the principle applies: *quod non in thora, non in mundo.* Some examples are given here for elucidation.

Babylonian Talmud Baba Meṣiʿa 87A: Up until Abraham there was no aging (זִקְנָה "aging, old age" is first mentioned in Scripture in the case of Abraham; see Gen 18:12; 24:1; from this it is inferred that before Abraham there was no aging yet); whoever wanted to speak with Abraham spoke with Isaac, whoever with Isaac spoke with Abraham (father and son could not be distinguished from each other). Then Abraham came and asked for mercy, and aging came about; as it says, "Abraham became old זקן, came into days" (Gen 24:1). Up until Jacob there was no sickness. Then Jacob came and asked for mercy (that sickness might precede dying as a preparation for death), and sickness arose; as it says, "After these events it was said to Joseph, 'Behold, your father is sick'" (Gen 48:1). Up until Elisha came, there was no one who was sick and recovered (again). Then Elisha came, asked for mercy and recovered (again); as it says, "Elisha was afflicted with his sickness, from which he was going to die" (2 Kgs 13:14). It follows from this that he (already earlier) was afflicted with another sickness. — There is a parallel in b. Sanh. 107B. ‖ Genesis Rabbah 65 (41A): R. Judah b. Simon (ca. 320, so read!) said, "Abraham wished for old age. He said before him, 'Lord of the worlds, a man and his son go to the market, and no one knows to whom he should show honor (because both are completely like each other); yet if you crown him (the father) with old age, one will know to whom he must show honor.' God said to him, 'By your life, you have wished for something good, and it (aging) shall begin with you!' From the beginning of the book (of the Torah) until here (Gen 24:1) the word 'aging' is not written; but when Abraham arose, God bestowed on him old age: 'And Abraham became old, came into days' (Gen 24:1). Isaac wished for sufferings. He said before him, 'Lord of all worlds, a man dies without sufferings and the measure of strict (divine) righteousness is stretched out against him (applies to him); but if you (beforehand) bring sufferings (with their purifying power) upon him, the measure of strict righteousness is not stretched out against him.' God said to him, 'By your life, you have wished for something good, and I will make the beginning of it with you!' From the beginning of the book until here (Gen 27:1) 'sufferings' is not written; but when Isaac arose, he bestowed sufferings on him: 'And it happened, when Isaac had become old and his eyes cloudy' (Gen 27:1). Jacob wished for sickness. He said before him, 'Lord of the worlds, a man dies without (preceding) sickness and he cannot (beforehand) arrange anything among his children; but if he is sick for two or three days, he can arrange (what is necessary) among his children.' God said to him, 'By your life, you have wished for something good and (sickness) shall begin with you': 'And it was said to Joseph, "Behold, your father is sick"' (Gen 48:1)." R. Levi (ca. 300) said, "Abraham introduced old age, Isaac sufferings, Jacob sickness, and Hezekiah curable sickness as something new. He (Hezekiah) said to him (God), 'You have preserved him (the human being) until the day of his death; but if a person gets sick and rises up again (in recovery), gets sick and rises up again, he will repent.' God said to him, 'By your life, you have wished for something good, and I will make the beginning of it with you!' This is what is written: 'The memoir of Hezekiah, the king of Judah, when he had gotten sick and recovered from his sickness' (Isa 38:9)." ‖ Genesis Rabbah 60 (38A): "Her (Rebekah's) brother and her mother said, 'Let the girl remain a few (more) days with us'" (Gen 24:55). Where was Bethuel (her father)? He sought to prevent (the marriage) and was struck in the night (by Yahweh) (he had died). — Since Bethuel is not mentioned again, it is inferred that he is no longer present, that is, had died. ‖ TanḥumaB לך לך § 7 (32B): "Their sword will piece their own heart" (Ps 37:15): this refers to the four kings, Amraphel and his companions (Gen 14), for until now there had not been any war in the world, and they came and made a beginning with the sword; as it says, "And it happened in the days of Amraphel when they began to wage war" (so Gen 14:1, 2 is cited). God said to them, "You godless, you have made a beginning with the sword; the sword shall pierce the heart of these men (i.e., your heart), as it says, 'Their sword will piece their own heart' (Ps 37:15)." Immediately Abraham rose up against them and killed them, as it says, "And he split up against them in the night" (Gen 14:15). — Since there is no mention of military battles before Gen 14 in Scripture, it is inferred that the battle mentioned in Gen 14 was the first war that raged on the earth. ‖ For further examples, see TanḥB נח § 20 (23B); חיי שרה § 5 (59B).

7:3 C: He remains a priest forever.

The אַתָּה כֹהֵן לְעוֹלָם "you are a priest forever" (Ps 110:4), which applies to the king, is transferred without hesitation to the archetype and model of Melchizedek. It is a גְּזֵרָה שָׁוָה inference (conclusion by analogy).[319]

7:4: To whom even Abraham gave a tithe.

Genesis Rabbah 43 (26D): "He (Abram) gave him (Melchizedek) a tenth of everything" (Gen 14:20). R. Judah b. Simon (ca. 320) said, "From the power of that blessing the three great stakes יְתֵידוֹת (mighty ones) of the world lived, Abraham, Isaac, and Jacob. Of Abraham it says, 'Yahweh blessed Abraham with "everything"' (Gen 24:1), because he gave him a tenth of 'everything.' Of Isaac it says, 'I ate of "everything"' (Gen 27:33), because he gave him a tenth of 'everything.' Of Jacob it says, 'God was gracious to me, and I have "everything"' (Gen 33:11), because he gave him a tenth of 'everything.'" ‖ See further Gen. Rab. 44 (27B).

7:7: Without question, though, the lesser is blessed by the greater.

This statement is not in line with the Jewish view.

Babylonian Talmud Megillah 15A: R. Eleazar (ca. 270) said that R. Hanina (ca. 225) said, "Never let the blessing of an ordinary person הֶדְיוֹט (= ἰδιώτης) be small in your eyes; for see, two ordinary people blessed two greats of the generation (of the age), and it was fulfilled in them. And these (the greats) were David and Daniel. David: Araunah blessed him, as it is written, 'Araunah said to the king, "May Yahweh, your God, be gracious to you!"' (2 Sam 24:23). Daniel: Darius blessed him, as it is written, 'May your God, whom you consistently worship, save you!' (Dan 6:17)."

7:8: Someone who has the testimony that he lives.

See § Heb 7:3 B.

7:20ff.: And just as it did not happen without an oath ... just so has Jesus too become the guarantor of a superior covenant.

1. In the same way, in ʾAbot R. Nat. 34 (9A), the inference is drawn from God's oath in Ps 110:4 that the Messiah will one day be more beloved (precious) before God than the high priest of the eschaton. The passage reads:

"These are the two sons of oil who stand by the Lord of the whole earth" (Zech 4:14). This is Aaron (= the high priest) and the Messiah. I do not know, though, which of them is more beloved חָבִיב. Since it says, "Yahweh has sworn and will not relent, 'You are a priest

---

319. See Strack, *Einleitung in den Talmud und Midraš*, 97 #2.

forever'" (Ps 110:4), know that the king, the Messiah, will be more beloved than the priest of righteousness כֹּהֵן צֶדֶק (a designation for the eschatological high priest).

2. διαθήκης ἔγγυος. — For the idea of the guarantor of a covenant, see Midr. Song. 1:4 (85B) at § Matt 21:16. The connection of the explanation with Song 1:4 shows that the verb משכני "draw me" (Song 1:4) was connected with מִשְׁכֵּן "to take as a pledge": "take me as a pledge, we will run after you." — The expression עָרְבָיךְ עָרְבָא צָרִיךְ "your guarantor (itself) needs a guarantor," which is used several times there, has a proverbial character; in Aramaic in b. Sukkah 26A.43 it is as follows in the mouth of Rab Mesharshia (ca. 350): ערביך ערבא צרוך. — We should add Midr. Prov. 6 § 2 (27A) to the parallels given at § Matt 21:16.

7:26: Set apart from sinners.

The halakah also knows of a "setting apart" of the high priest.

Mishnah Yoma 1.1: Seven days before the Day of Atonement the high priest is set apart מַפְרִישִׁין from his house to the hall of the presider (see § Matt 26:57, #1, final paragraph). Furthermore, another priest is appointed for him in his place, in case something that would make him unfitting should befall him. ‖ Babylonian Talmud Yoma 6A: (Why is he set apart from his house?) In a baraita: R. Judah b. Batera (ca. 110) said, "His wife might be in a state of uncertainty concerning the onset of menstruation and he might have intercourse with her. Yet do we have anything to do with the wicked (who purposely flout the regulation not to have intercourse with a woman in such a state)? Rather, he might have intercourse with his wife and (then) a doubt about the onset of menstruation that has already happened beforehand might arise (whereby he would be unclean for seven days and prevented from entering the temple) …." Babylonian Talmud Yoma 6B: Instead of having him be set apart due to the uncleanness of his house (= his wife), have him (rather) be set apart due to the (possible) defilement by a dead person. — See also m. Parah 3.1: Seven days before the burning of the red heifer the priest who shall burn the heifer is set apart from his house to the hall that lies at the front of the temple in the northeast, which is called "the stone space."

7:27: Who does not need, as does the high priest, first to present offerings daily for his own sins, and then for those of the people.

1. The following were presented daily as offerings: α. for the high priest as a continuous meal offering, מִנְחָה תָּמִיד, the plate meal offering, which is mentioned in Lev 6:12–16, and which in rabbinic literature (cf. though already 1 Chr 9:31) is most of the time called חֲבִיתִּין; β. for the people as a continuous burnt offering, עֹלַת תָּמִיד or עֹלָה תָּמִיד, the daily burnt offering (Exod 29:38–42; Num 28:3–8), which in rabbinic literature (cf. but also already Dan 8:11–13; 11:31; 12:11) is called in short תָּמִיד or הַתָּמִיד; see m. Pesaḥ. 5.1, 3, 4; m. Yoma 2.5; 7.3; m. Taʿan. 4.6; plural הַתְּמִידִין in m. Menaḥ. 4.4. — Since the daily meal offering of the high priest should, according to Lev 6:13, be offered half in the morning and half in the evening and since the Tamid offering had to be presented, according to Exod 29:38ff. and Num 28:3ff., also daily as a morning and evening sacrifice, the sacrificial rite

of the ancient synagogue had brought the two offerings into the closest connection: after initially six priests had presented on the altar of burnt offering the individual parts of the offering and then a seventh presented the meal offering that belonged with the Tamid offering (see Exod 29:40; Num 28:5, 8), an eighth priest offered in connection with this the high priestly חֲבִיתִּין; a ninth priest finally concluded the whole business of offering with the libation offering prescribed for the Tamid offering in Exod 29:40f. and Num 28:7, 8. The high priestly meal offering was thus presented between the meal offering and the drink offering, which belonged with the Tamid offering, and thus in a certain way constituted an integral component of the Tamid offering itself.[a] It therefore comes as no surprise if it is sometimes said that nine priests were necessary for the presentation of the Tamid offering,[b] although strictly speaking only eight took part in it, since the ninth priest was needed only for the חביתין. Yet we can see from this how much the view of the ancient synagogue had gradually become accustomed to view of the high priestly meal offering simply as an addition to the Tamid offering.

2. We may assume that with his words in 7:27, the author of the Letter to the Hebrews had in view both of these offerings, the meal offering for the high priest and the Tamid offering for the community. This is not undermined by the term θυσία used by him, for θυσία denotes not only the bloody sacrifice, but also the bloodless Mincha offering; precisely in the section that deals with the high priestly meal offering (Lev 6:12ff.; according to the numbering in the LXX 6:19ff.), the LXX rendered מִנְחָה תָּמִיד "continuous meal offering" with θυσία διαπαντός, as well as מִנְחַת פִּתִּים "meal offering of morsels" with θυσία ἐκ κλασμάτων and מִנְחַת כֹּהֵן "meal offering of the priest" with θυσία ἱερέως. — This is also not undermined by the fact that in Heb 7:27 θυσίαι doubtlessly refers to an offering with an atoning character. For in the view of the ancient synagogue, this character was not lacking in the communal Tamid offering nor in the high priestly חֲבִיתִּין. The Tamid offering was among the burnt offerings and these are explicitly ascribed atoning power in Lev 1:4 (cf. Job 1:5; 42:8); in the rabbinic view they were to serve as an atonement for sinful thoughts.[c] In the same way, atoning power is attributed to meal offerings generally (not simply to the meal offerings that represent the sin offering according to Lev 5:11ff.) in Lev. Rab. 3;[d] so it was specifically assumed that the daily high priestly meal offering would atone for Aaron's action in making the golden calf.[e] — This is also not undermined by the fact that in Heb 7:27 ostensibly the high priest himself appears as the one who presents the offerings in question, while, in the presentation of the Mishnah, the Tamid offering and the high priestly חביתין were normally presented by other priests.[f] One must maintain that the high priest had the right to carry out every sacrifice himself in the first

place.[h] Therefore, he can be spoken of as presenting the sacrifices, even if he in fact had others perform the sacrifice in his name. So Philo has no qualms to say occasionally of the high priest generally (*Spec.* 1 § 23, Mangey's ed., 2:321) that he presents prayers and offerings every day εὐχὰς δὲ καὶ θυσίας τελῶν καθ' ἑκάστην ἡμέραν, although it was certainly not unknown to him that the high priest only rarely performed the sacrificial service. According to Josephus, the high priest regularly participated in the altar service on Sabbath and feast days.[g] According to the Mishnah, he was supposed to actively participate in the temple service especially during the last seven days before the Day of Atonement.[h] — Yet a truly serious difficulty arising from the reference of our passage to the meal offering of the high priest and the Tamid offering of the community lies in the specific claim of Heb 7:27 that the high priest has to first present an offering for his own sins and then for those of the people. In contrast to this, the offering practice of the ancient synagogue leaves no doubt that rather, conversely, first the Tamid offering was presented for the people and then the meal offering for the high priest.[a] This difference is so significant that in our view one cannot maintain any reference by Heb 7:27 to the high priestly meal offering and the communal Tamid offering. One has to get along with not pressing the καθ' ἡμέραν in Heb 7:27, but rather to understand it in a looser sense = "every day when he had to offer." Then this would refer primarily to the Day of Atonement, on which, according to Lev 16:6ff, 15ff., it was literally correct that the high priest first had to present certain offerings for his own sins and then for those of the people.[i]

a. Mishnah Yoma 2.3: The 2nd drawing (for official priestly matters in the temple comprised of 13 services for which 13 priests had to be appointed): (1–4) he who slaughters (the Tamid lamb), he who sprinkles the blood (on the altar), he who cleanses the inner altar (i.e., the incense altar in the holy place) of ash, he who cleanses the lampstand (in the holy place). (The other 9 services concerned bringing the pieces of meat from the Tamid lamb, the communal meal offering, the high priestly meal offering and the libation for the Tamid offering onto the ramp of the altar of burnt offering.) He who brings the limbs (of the Tamid offering) onto the ramp, namely 1. the head and the right hind foot, 2. the two front feet, 3. the tail and the left hind foot, 4. the breast and the neck, 5. the two side pieces, 6. the entrails. (Furthermore, he who brings them onto the ramp) 7. the fine-grained flour (for the communal or Tamid meal offering), 8. the חֲבִיתִּים (the high priestly plate meal offering), and 9. the wine (for the Tamid drink offering). — Parallels are found in m. Tamid 3.1; t. Yoma 1.13 (181). ‖ Mishnah Yoma 2.4f.: The 3rd drawing (concerns the presentation of the offering of incense). The 4th drawing: ... He who should bring the limbs of the Tamid lamb etc. (to be burnt) from the ramp onto the altar. The Tamid offering is presented by nine (priests). — A more detailed explanation is not given; we therefore have to assume that the Tamid offering and the high priestly meal offering were brought up onto the altar in precisely the same sequence as they were brought up to the altar ramp in the previous citation in m. Yoma 2.2. Then the high priestly *ḥabittin* were offered between the Tamid meal offering and the Tamid drink offering. This is explicitly said in b. Yoma 33A; see the passage at § Heb 9:2 B, #3, n. *h.* — Mishnah Tamid 7.3 depicts more precisely how the high priest himself used to perform the presentation of the Tamid offering; see the passage at § Luke 1:10, middle; yet this report ultimately closes very summarily, so that neither the Tamid meal offering nor the high priestly meal offering is mentioned. — See the description of the Tamid offering in Sir 50 at § Luke 1:10, beginning.

b. See m. Yoma 2.4f. above in n. *a.*

c. Leviticus Rabbah 7 (110A.21): R. Simeon b. Yohai (ca. 150) said, "A burnt offering עולה is always presented only because of sinful thoughts of the heart." R. Levi (ca. 300) said, "There is a whole passage of Scripture for this: 'And the burnt offering for your interior, so that nothing come from this' (so Midr. Ezek 20:32). From whom can you learn this? From the sons of Job. First 'his sons went and prepared a meal' (Job 1:4) ..., and then it says, 'Job would get up early and present burnt offerings ...; for Job said, "Perhaps my children have sinned and departed from God in the hearts"' (Job 1:5). This proves that a burnt offering is presented only because of evil thoughts of the heart." ‖ Jerusalem Talmud Yoma 8.45B.51: The burnt offering makes atonement for evil thoughts of the heart. What is the scriptural basis? See Ezek 20:32 and Job 1:5 (as before). — The same is found in y. Šebu. 1.33B.43. ‖ Tanḥuma צו 140B: You find that all the offerings were presented for transgressions: if someone presented a guilt offering, it was presented because of a transgression; as it says, "And they all gave their hands in pledge to dismiss their wives, and they each atoned for the guilt with a ram" (Ezra 10:19). And a sin offering was presented for unintentional sins; as it says, "And their sin offering before Yahweh for their error" (Num 15:25). A burnt offering was presented for sinful thoughts of the heart; as it says, "(Job) got up early and presented burnt offerings ..., for Job said, 'Perhaps my children have sinned and departed from God in their hearts'" (Job 1:5). Yet when a thank offering was presented, it was presented without a (particular) reason. God said, "It is beloved by me before all (other) offerings!" — A parallel passage is found in TanḥB צו § 9 (9A).

d. Leviticus Rabbah 3 (106D): The rabbis and R. Simeon b. Yohai (ca. 150). The rabbis said, "God showed all the atoning sacrifices to our father Abraham, peace be upon him! (namely in Gen 15:9f.), except for the tenth of an *ephah* (for the atoning sin offering, Lev 5:11)." R. Simeon b. Yohai said, "God also showed the tenth of the *ephah* to our father Abraham; for it says here (Lev 2:8) אלה 'these,' and it says there (Gen 15:10) אלה 'these.' Just as the אלה 'these' spoken of here (Lev 2:8) refers to the tenth of the *ephah*, so too the אלה 'these' spoken of there (Gen 15:10) refers to the tenth of the *ephah*." — One should note that R. Simeon does not demonstrate that Abraham was instructed about the atoning meal offering by appealing to Lev 5:11, but rather by appealing to Lev 2:8, a proof that R. Simeon attributed atoning power even to each meal offering. In the parallel in Gen. Rab. 44 (27D), the views are reversed, with R. Simeon's opinion being represented by the rabbis and with their opinion being represented by R. Simeon.

e. Leqach Tob Leviticus 6:13: "This (זה) is the (high priestly meal) offering of Aaron" (Lev 6:13); let this (זה) come and make atonement for this (זה) calf; and it says, "This (זה) (the molten calf) is your God, who led you up out of Egypt" (Neh 9:18).

f. See m. Yoma 2.3, 4f. above in n. *a.*

g. Josephus, *Jewish War* 5.5.7: "Those of the priests who were without bodily flaw would go up to the altar and the temple .... The high priest would go up with them, though not always; but on the Sabbaths and the days of the new moon and when a national feast or a year festival of the entire people happened."

h. Mishnah Yoma 1.2: The whole seven days (before the Day of Atonement) the high priest sprinkles the blood (from the morning and evening Tamid offering on that altar), presents the incense offering (in the holy place), prepares the lamps (of the holy lampstand in the holy place) and presents the head and the right hind foot (of the lamb of the Tamid offering on the altar of burnt offering). On all other days he may sacrifice when he wants to sacrifice; for the high priest may (at any time) sacrifice a portion first and first take for himself a portion (from the offering portions that are due to the officiating priests).

i. Of the three confessions of sin that the high priest had to say on the Day of Atonement, the first concerned himself and his house, the second the rest of the priesthood, and the third and last the people. — α. See the first confession of sin in m. Yoma 3.8 at § Matt 3:6 B, n. *a* and see also the excursus "The Memra of Yahweh," #3, B, β. — β. The second confession of sin. Mishnah Yoma 4.2: (After the lottery for the two goats [Lev 16:5ff.]) the high priest a second time approached his young bull and lifted both his hands onto it and confessed (the confession of sin), and he used to say the following, "Alas, O God, I have erred, been wicked and sinned before you; I and my house and the sons of Aaron, your holy people. Alas, O God, forgive the failings and wickedness and sins that I have erred in, acted wickedly in, and sinned with before you, I and my house and the sons of Aaron, your holy people, as it is written in the Torah of Moses, your servant, 'For on this day atonement will be made for you ...' (Lev 16:30)." — This second confession of sin is found in briefer form also in SLev 16:11 (312A). — Concerning the difference between the first and the second confession of sin, it says in b. Yoma 43B: What sort of difference is it that he did not say in the first confession: "And the sons of Aaron, your holy people"? And what sort of difference is it that he said in the second confession: "And the sons of Aaron, your holy people"? In the school of R. Ishmael († ca. 135) it has been taught: "So there is logical thinking here: It is more correct that the innocent come and make atonement for the guilty than that the guilty come and make atonement for the guilty." (Let the high priest seek forgiveness for himself first and then let him seek it for the entire priesthood.) — γ. The third confession of sin. See m. Yoma 6.2 at § Matt 6:13 C, #1.

In the same way, the high priest on the Day of Atonement first presented the atoning blood of his own bull of the sin offering and then that of the goat of the sin offering for the people in the holy of holies; see m. Yoma 5.3f. at § Rom 3:25 A, #6, n. *c.*

7:28: The word of the oath.

On the weight of the oath in Ps 110:4, see ʾAbot R. Nat. 34 (9A) at § Heb 7:20ff., #1.

8:2: A priestly servant of the holy place and of the true tent that God, not a human being, has made.

The idea of a heavenly sanctuary is old and generally widespread and acknowledged in the post-Christian period. The earliest pieces of evidence for this may be T. Levi 5 and Wis 9:8. In the following we give a few of the most noteworthy from the great number of passages that belong here.

Testament of Levi 5: "The angels opened the gates of heaven for me, and I saw the holy temple τὸν ναὸν τὸν ἅγιον and on the throne of glory the Most High." — Wisdom 9:8: "You commanded a temple be built on your holy mountain and an altar in the city of your dwelling, a likeness of the holy tent that you prepared beforehand from the beginning μίμημα σκηνῆς ἁγίας ἣν προητοίμασας ἀπ' ἀρχῆς." ‖ The heavenly sanctuary is among the things that were created before the world; see § Matt 25:31 B, #1 and § John 1:1 A, B, n. *a*. The text most often used as a proof is Jer 17:12. ‖ Babylonian Talmud Ḥagigah 12B: (In the fourth heaven, called זְבוּל) there is Jerusalem and the sanctuary and the altar erected, and Michael, the great prince, stands there and presents an offering on it. ‖ Babylonian Talmud Menaḥot 110A: ("You who stand in the house of the Lord at night" [Ps 134:1]). Rab Giddel (ca. 270) said that Rab († 247) said, "This refers to the altar built (in heaven), and Michael, the great prince, stands there and presents an offering on it." — The same is found in Midr. Ps. 134 § 1 (259B). ‖ Babylonian Talmud Zebaḥim 62A: How did they (those who exulted at their return to Jerusalem) know the site of the altar? R. Eleazar (ca. 270) said, "They saw the altar built (in heaven) and Michael, the great prince, stood there and offered on it (and precisely juxtaposed to this heavenly altar was the place of the altar below; see the following citations)." ‖ Genesis Rabbah 55 (35B): ("Go to the land of Moriah" [Gen 22:2]). R. Simeon b. Yohai (ca. 150) said, "To the place that is chosen to lie juxtaposed to the upper sanctuary." — Parallel passages are found in TanḥB וירא § 45 (56B); Pesiq. R 40 (170A); Tanḥ. פקודי 126A. ‖ Genesis Rabbah 69 (44C): R. Simeon b. Yohai said, "The upper sanctuary is only 18 *mils* above the lower sanctuary. What is the scriptural basis? 'And this וזה is the gate of heaven' (Gen 28:17); the numerical value of וזה is 18." ‖ Tanḥuma ויקהל 124A: R. Nathan (ca. 160) said, "Beloved (before God) is the work of the ark of the covenant as the throne of glory above; for it says, 'Precisely juxtaposed to your dwelling, Yahweh, you have prepared the sanctuary that your hands, Almighty, have made' (Exod 15:17, so the midrash; see further); for the upper sanctuary lies precisely juxtaposed to the lower sanctuary, and the ark of the covenant precisely juxtaposed to the throne of glory above; as it says, 'The throne of glory on high is from the very beginning the site of our sanctuary' (Jer 17:12, so the midrash). And on which site was the site of our sanctuary? Say: 'Precisely juxtaposed to your dwelling, Yahweh, you have prepared the sanctuary that your hands, Almighty, have made' (Exod 15:17); do not read מָכוֹן (site, Exod 15:17), but rather מְכוּוָּן, that is, 'precisely juxtaposed to' the throne of glory, which is made by him above." — A parallel passage is found in Num. Rab. 4 (142B). ‖ Mekilta Exodus 15:17 (51A): The throne from below (i.e., the ark of the covenant) is precisely juxtaposed to the throne above. ‖ Tanḥuma פקודי 127A: God created the sanctuary above; for it says, "Precisely juxtaposed to your dwelling, Yahweh, you have prepared the sanctuary" (Exod 15:17); do not read מָכוֹן, but rather מְכוּוָּן, that is, "precisely juxtaposed" to your dwelling, juxtaposed to the throne of glory. ‖ Concerning the statement that the one who prays should direct his heart to the holy of holies in the temple, it is asked in y. Ber. 4.8C.14: "To which holy of holies?" R. Hiyya, the elder (ca. 200), said, "To the holy of holies above"; R. Simeon b. Halapta (ca. 190) said, "To the holy of holies below". R. Phineas (b. Hama [ca. 360]) said, "They were not of differing opinions: the holy of holies above lies precisely juxtaposed to the holy of holies below." The same is found in Midr. Song. 4:4 (112B). — This saying of R. Phineas is attributed in Midr. Ps. 30 § 1 (117A) in a garbled remark to R. Hisda († 309): see Buber on the passage. — Without naming an author, Midr. Song. 3:10 (108A) says, "The holy of holies above lies precisely juxtaposed to the holy of holies below; see Exod 15:17. ‖ Pesiqta Rabbati 5 (22B): "And it happened at the time when Moses had finished erecting the dwelling" (Num 7:1). R. Simon (ca. 280) said, "When God commanded the Israelites to erect the dwelling, he indicated that when the dwelling below is erected, (also) the dwelling above is erected; for it says, 'And it happened at the time when Moses had finished erecting the dwelling את המשכן' (Num 7:1); המשכן is not written here, but rather את המשכן; this refers to the upper dwelling." (The את indicates that at the same time "with" the lower dwelling, another dwelling was erected, namely the dwelling above). — Parallel passages are found in Tanḥ. נשא 199B; Num. Rab. 12 (167A); in the last passage there is the addition: And this (the upper dwelling) is the dwelling in which the youth whose name is Metatron presents the souls of the righteous, to make atonement for Israel in the days of their exile. And therefore את המשכן is written, because another dwelling was erected at the same time "with" it; and likewise it says, "Precisely juxtaposed to your dwelling, Yahweh, you have prepared the sanctuary that your hands, Almighty, have made" (Exod 15:17). ‖ Jerusalem Talmud Yoma 7.44B.37: Why did the high priest on the Day of Atonement perform the service in white garments (cf. Lev 16:4)? R. Hiyya b. Abba (ca. 280) said, "As the service above (in the upper sanctuary), so the service below; as above "one was among them clothed in linen" (Ezek 9:2), so too should be below "put on a holy white undergarment" (Lev 16:4). ‖ TanḥumaB בראשית § 13 (5A): Job said, "O that I would find him, that I could come to the place of his dwelling!" (Job 23:3). R. Abba b. Kahana (ca. 310) said, "If he is in the upper temple, I will go to the place of his dwelling, and if he is in the lower temple, I will go to the place of his dwelling." ‖ Pesiqta Rabbati 20 (98A): When Moses ascended on high, God opened the seven heavens and showed him the upper sanctuary and the four colors from which he had made the dwelling; for it says, "Erect the dwelling according to its regulation which is shown to you on the mountain" (Exod 26:30). ‖ Tanḥuma נשא 197B: "Come and see!" When God said to Moses that he should say to the Israelites that they should make him a dwelling, God said to Moses, "Moses, behold, my sanctuary is built above; as it says, 'The throne of glory on high since the very beginning' (Jer 17:12). And there is the temple; as it says, 'Yahweh is in his holy temple—let all the earth be still before him!' (Hab 2:20). And there the throne of his glory is erected, as it says; 'Yahweh has prepared his throne in heaven' (Ps 103:19). And likewise, Isaiah says, 'I saw Yahweh sitting on a high and exalted throne, and his hems filled the temple' (Isa 6:1)." "Yet because of my love for you," God said, "I will leave the upper sanctuary that was made before the world was created and I will come down and dwell in your midst; as it says, 'I will dwell in the midst of the children of Israel' (Exod 29:45);

and furthermore, it says, 'They shall make me a sanctuary, so that I may dwell in their midst' (Exod 25:8)." — See also § Gal 4:26 A.

8:5 A: A likeness and shadow of the heavenly one.

On likeness, see also § Heb 1:3 A, n. *c*. — On shadow, see § Col 2:17.

8:5 B: According to the pattern that was shown to you on the mountain (see Exod 25:9, 40; 26:30; 27:8).

A baraita in b. Menaḥ. 29A: R. Yose b. Judah (ca. 180) said, "An ark of fire, a table of fire, and a lampstand of fire (fire is everywhere the heavenly construction material) came down from heaven, and Moses saw them and fashioned in their likeness; as it says, 'Behold and make them according to their design, which was shown to you on the mountain' (Exod 25:40)...." R. Hiyya bar Abba (ca. 280) said that R. Yohanan († 279) said, "(The angel) Gabriel was girded with a type of girdle and showed to Moses the work of the lampstand; as it says, 'And this was the work of the lampstand' (Num 8:4)." In the school of R. Ishmael († ca. 135) it has been taught, "Three things were too difficult for Moses until God showed them to him with his finger: the lampstand, the beginning of the month (new moon), and the creeping creatures. The lampstand, as it says, 'This is the work of the lampstand' (Num 8:4); the beginning of the month, as it says, 'Let this month be for you the first month' (Exod 12:2); the creeping creatures, as it says, 'This is the unclean thing for you among the swarm' (Lev 11:29)." (The demonstrative זה common to all three passages indicates that God indicated the three things in question alike with his finger). — This tradition from the school of R. Ishmael is attributed to R. Aqiba († ca. 135) in Mek. Exod. 12:2 (3A) and SNum 8:4 § 61 (16A); to R. Simeon b. Yohai (ca. 150) in Pesiq. 54B and Pesiq. Rab. 15 (78B); it is anonymous in Exod. Rab. 15 (79A) with the addition that the holy anointing oil in Exod 30:31 was also among the things that God showed to Moses with his finger. ‖ Tanḥuma שמיני 149A: Three things were too difficult for Moses, and God showed them to him with his finger, namely the making of the lampstand, (the beginning of) the month, and the abominable creatures. How is it with the making of the lampstand? When Moses ascended, God showed him on the mountain how he should make the dwelling. When God showed him the work of the lampstand, it was too difficult for Moses. God said to him, "Behold, I will make it before your eyes." What did God do? He showed him white fire, red fire, black fire, and greenish-yellow fire (fire is thought of as the heavenly building material), and from this he made the lampstand, its chalices, its knobs, its flowers, and the six ducts. He said to him, "Make it thus and so!" As it says, "This is the work of the lampstand" (Num 8:4). This teaches that God showed him the lampstand with his finger. Nevertheless, it was still too difficult for Moses to fashion it. What did God do? He drew it for Moses on his palms and said to him, "Look and 'make it according to its model' (Exod 25:40), as I have drawn it on your palms." Nevertheless, it was still too difficult for Moses, and he said: מקשה תיעשה המנורה (Exod 25:31; in the sense of the base text: "with driven work the lampstand shall be made"), that is, how difficult מה קשה it is to make the lampstand! God answered him, "Cast the gold into the fire, and the lampstand will come about by itself"; as it says: תיעשה המנורה "the lampstand will come about"; it will come about by itself (interpretation of the passive תיעשה).... Parallels are found in TanḥB שמיני § 11 (14B); Num. Rab. 15 (178C); Tanḥ. בהעלותך 203B. ‖ Tanḥuma בהעלותך 204B: R. Levi (ca. 300) said, "A pure lampstand came down from heaven; for God had said to Moses, 'Make a lampstand of pure gold' (Exod 25:31)." Moses said to God, "How should it be made?" God answered, "As driven work" (Exod 25:31). Nevertheless, it was too difficult for Moses, and he forgot how to make it. He went up and said, "Lord of the world, I have forgotten its production!" Then God showed it to Moses; yet it was still too difficult for him. God said to him, "See and do!" Finally God took a model מַטְבֵּעַ from fire and showed him its making. Nevertheless, it was too difficult for Moses. Then God said to him, "Go to Bezalel; he will make it." Moses went down and told this to Bezalel. Immediately he made it. At once Moses arose to marvel at it and said, "How often God showed it to me, and it was too difficult for me to make it, and you have made it from your insight, without having seen it! In the shade of God בצל אל (hence the name בְּצַלְאֵל) you stood, when God showed me its making." — The same is found in TanḥB בהעלתך § 11 (25A); Num. Rab. 15 (178D). ‖ Pesiqta Rabbati 20 (98A): When Moses ascended on high, God opened the seven heavens for him and showed him the upper sanctuary and the four colors, in which he should make his dwelling; as it says, "Erect the tent of meeting according to its regulation, which was shown to you on the mountain" (Exod 26:30). Moses said, "Lord of the world, I do not know the appearance of the four colors." God answered him, "Turn to your right!" He turned and saw a host of angels that was clothed with a garment that was like the sea. God said to him, "This is the violet purple תְּכֵלֶת. Then he said to him, "Turn to your left!" He turned and saw men who were clothed with a red garment. God said to him, "What do you see?" He answered, "Men who are clothed with a red garment." God said to him, "This is the red purple אַרְגָּמָן." Then he turned to the back and saw a host that was clothed with garments that were neither red nor greenish-yellow. God said to him, "This is crimson תּוֹלַעַת שָׁנִי." He turned to the front and saw before him hosts that were clothed with a white garment. "This is (God said) twined byssus שֵׁשׁ מָשְׁזָר." ‖ Pesiqta 4B: R. Joshua (so read instead of R. Simeon) of Sikhnin (ca. 330) said in the name of R. Levi (ca. 300), "When God said to Moses, 'Make me a dwelling,' he could have brought him four poles and stretched out the dwelling over them (but God did not do this); rather this teaches that God showed Moses red and greenish yellow and black and white fire and said to him, 'Make me a dwelling!' Moses said to God, 'Lord of the worlds, where should I get red and greenish yellow and black and white fire from?' God answered him, 'According to its pattern, which was shown to you on the mountain' (Exod 25:40)." R. Berekhiah (ca. 340) said in the name of R. Levi, "Like a king who showed himself to his steward in a frock that was completely אולו (= ὅλος) made of pearls. He said to him, 'Make me something exactly like this!' He answered him, 'My lord king, where should I get a frock from that is completely made of pearls?!' The king said to him, 'You with your colors (read with the parallels בסממניך instead of בסימנך) and I with my glory!' So too God said to Moses, 'When you make below what is above, I will leave my council above and come down and narrow my Shekinah (which otherwise fills the whole world) among you. As the seraphim stand above, so too below planks of acacia wood (Exod 26:15) will stand upright below; as the stars are above, so too are hooks below (Exod 26:6, 11, 33; 35:11).'" R. Hiyya b. Abba (ca. 280; so read instead of R. Abba, see Buber on the passage) said, "This teaches that the golden hooks appeared in the dwelling like the stars that are seen in the firmament." — Parallels are found in Midr. Song. 3:11 (108B); Num. Rab. 12 (166C); Exod. Rab. 35 (95B).

8:8–12 (according to Jer 31:30–33).

The prophet's word about the "new covenant" (Jer 31:30–33) is cited relatively rarely in the older midrash.

See LXX and Tg. Jer 31:32, as well as Midr. Eccl. 2:1 (12B) at § Rom 2:15 A, n. *a.* ‖ Pesiqta 107A: It does not say: "on that day" (Exod 19:1), but rather "on this day." "In this world (God says) I have given you the Torah, and individuals occupy themselves with it; but in the future I will teach every Israelite, and they will learn it and not forget it; as it says, 'This is the covenant that I will make with the children of Israel after these days, says Yahweh, I will put my Torah in their heart and write it on their heart, and I will be their God, and they will be my people' (Jer 31:32)." (The passage is not cited precisely in the midrash.) — The same is found in TanḥB יתרו § 13 (38B). ‖ Yalquṭ Simeoni on Jeremiah 31:33 (2 § 317) from Yelamedenu: "No longer will each one teach his neighbor and his brother ..." (Jer 31:33); and it further says, "All your sons will be taught by Yahweh" (Isa 54:13). In this world Israel learns the Torah from flesh and blood; this is why they forget that which was given by Moses, who was flesh and blood. Just as flesh and blood pass away, so too what is learned from it passes away; as it says, "You let your eyes fall upon it, it is not there anymore" (Prov 23:5). But in the future the Israelites will learn only from God's mouth; and just as God lives and exists forever, so too that which is taught by him. What the Israelites learn from him they will never forget. ‖ Midrash Song of Songs 1:2 (82B): R. Judah (ca. 150) said, "When the Israelites (at the giving of the law) heard 'I am Yahweh your God' (Exod 20:2), the teaching of the Torah sank into their heart, they learned it, and did not forget. Then they came to Moses and said, 'Moses, our teacher, be a mediator (the task of a delegate) between us (and God); as it says, "You, speak with us and we will hear" (Exod 20:19). And now, why should we die, and what benefit is there in our perishing?' Again they learned, but they forgot. They said, 'As Moses is perishable flesh and blood, so too is his teaching perishable.' Immediately they came again to Moses and said to him, 'Moses, our teacher, may he (God) reveal himself a second time to us, may "he kiss me with the kisses of his mouth" (Song 1:2), may the teaching of the Torah sink into our heart as before!' He answered them, 'This cannot happen now, but in the future (in the messianic age) it will happen; as it says, "I will put my Torah within them ..."' (Jer 31:32)." — See also § John 6:45; § 1 Thess 4:9; and in the excursus "Sheol, Gehenna, and the Garden of Eden," III, #4, n. *m.*

9:1: The worldly (earthly) sanctuary (see § Tit 2:12).

9:2: A booth (tent) was erected, the anterior one, in which there was the lampstand and the table and the presentation of the loaves, which is called the "holy place."

A. τὰ ἅγια, as well as in the singular τὸ ἅγιον, the "holy place," a designation for the anterior (eastern) section of the actual temple building. The corresponding Hebrew הַקֹּדֶשׁ "the holy place" is found in the same sense already in the OT.[a] In rabbinic literature the "holy place" in the temple is frequently called הֵיכָל[b] (= palace, temple). — In contrast to ἅγια (ἅγιον), τὰ ἅγια (τὸ ἅγιον) τῶν ἁγίων (cf. Heb 9:3) designates the "holy of holies," the smaller western section of the temple building. So too קֹדֶשׁ הַקֳּדָשִׁים in the OT.[a] A further Old Testament name for the "holy of holies" is דְּבִיר. Both designations are common in rabbinic literature as well;[c] additionally, we find, though rarely, also לִפְנַי וְלִפְנִים = in "the innermost place."[d] — On the lack of the altar of the incense offering alongside the lampstand and the table for the show bread in the holy place, see verse 4.

a. Exodus 26:33: "Let the curtain divide for you between the holy place and the holy of holies" בֵּין הַקֹּדֶשׁ וּבֵין קֹדֶשׁ הַקֳּדָשִׁים. — Septuagint: ἀναμέσον τοῦ ἁγίου καὶ ἀναμέσον τοῦ ἁγίου τῶν ἁγίων. — Targum Onkelos: בֵּין קוּדְשָׁא וּבֵין קֹדֶשׁ קוּדְשַׁיָּא. — Targum Yerušalmi I: בֵּינֵי קוּדְשָׁא וּבֵינֵי קוֹדֶשׁ קוּדְשָׁא.

b. הֵיכָל specifically designates the "holy place" of the temple house already in 1 Kgs 6:5; 7:50. ‖ See m. Yoma 5.1 in n. *c.* ‖ Mishnah Yoma 5.4: The high priest went out (from the holy of holies) and set the bowl with the (leftover) blood on a golden stand that was in the holy place הֵיכָל. ‖ See b. Zebaḥ. 57B in n. *d.*

c. קֹדֶשׁ and קֹדֶשׁ הַקֳּדָשִׁים. — Mishnah Yoma 5.1: The high priest (on the Day of Atonement) walked through the holy place הֵיכָל until he came to the two curtains that divided between the holy place and the holy of holies בין הקדש ובין קדש הקדשים. ‖ Babylonian Talmud Yoma 77B: R. Phineas (ca. 360) said in the name of R. Huna of Sepphoris (ca. 300), "The fount that will go out from the site of the holy of holies מבית קדשי הקדשים (see Ezek 47:1ff.) will in the beginning be like the horns of grasshoppers…." — דְּבִיר, in the OT in, for example, 1 Kgs 6:5. — The Septuagint retains the word in the form δαβίρ. — Targum replaces this with בֵּית כַּפּוֹרֵי "place of atonement" = holiest place in the temple. ‖ Jerusalem Talmud Berakot 4.8C.21: (The holy of holies was called) דְּבִיר. R. Hiyya (ca. 200) and R. Yannai (ca. 225). The one said, "Because the plague דֶּבֶר goes out from there into the world." And the other said, "Because from there the words דִּבְרוֹת (דַּבְּרוֹת of God) will go out into the world." — Parallels are found in Gen. Rab. 55 (35B); Midr. Song. 4:4 (112B).

d. Babylonian Talmud Zebaḥim 41A: The bull of the Day of Atonement and the goat of the Day of Atonement …, the blood of both comes into the holy of holies לפניי ולפנים. ‖ Babylonian Talmud Zebaḥim 57B: As (the high priest on the Day of Atonement) in the holy of holies לפני ולפנים sprinkles once above and seven times below from the blood of the bull, just so he sprinkles in the holy place הֵיכָל, and just as he in the holy of holies לפניי ולפנים sprinkles once above and seven times below from the blood of the goat, just so he sprinkles in the holy place היכל. — Just as the holy of holies is called the "innermost place," so the holy place can correspondingly also be designated as the "outer house" בַּיִת הַחִיצוֹן. Mishnah Yoma 5.1: (After the high priest on the Day of Atonement had filled the holy of holies with a cloud of smoke from the incense,) he went back out again the same way that he had come in by and prayed a short prayer in the outer house בבית החיצון (= in the holy place).

B. The lampstand, λυχνία, Hebrew מְנוֹרָה, Aram. מְנָרְתָא; Josephus, *Ant.* 3.8.3; 14.4.4 also ἡ ἱερὰ λυχνία "the holy lampstand."

1. The description of the seven-armed lampstand of the tent of meeting is found in Exod 25:31–40; 37:17–24; Num 8:4. The description that Josephus gave departs from this concerning the adornment of the lampstand. Scripture knows as the only kind of embellishment on the shaft and on the side arms of the lampstand the גְּבִעִים "calyxes," which it then has consisting more precisely of two parts: of the כַּפְתּוֹר "knob" at the base of the calyx and of the פֶּרַח "flower," the calyx formed by the actual flower petals. Yet Josephus speaks of four different embellishments. He calls them α. σφαιρία, small oblate spheres; they correspond to the כַּפְתּוֹרִים in the base text, Exod 25:31ff.; β. κρίνα, lilies, corresponding to the גְּבִעִים; γ. ῥοΐσκοι, pomegranates, not indicated in Scripture; δ. κρατηρίδια, bowls of flowers, corresponding to the פְּרָחִים. The total number of these adornments on the lampstand he states to be 70.[a] These four different embellishments, though, are also shown on the seven-armed lampstand on the arch of Titus in Rome.[b] We may assume, then, that the lampstand that was in the Herodian temple at the time of Josephus and that served for the Roman artist as the basis for the depiction on the arch of Titus was in fact furnished with those four adornments which Josephus mentions in the case of the lampstand in the tent of meeting. Josephus, who as a priest could himself have seen the lampstand of the Herodian sanctuary, would have transferred the adornments on this lampstand in an unhistorical manner to the lampstand of the Mosaic sanctuary. Unfortunately, the descriptions that we have about the golden lampstand in rabbinic literature provide no further clarity in this regard. Instead, they are closely connected to Exod 25:31ff., though against the view of the base text they interpret the גבעים and כפתורים and פרחים as three independent adornments to be distinguished from one another. The גבעים "chalices" would have been similar to Alexandrian cups, the כפתורים "knobs" to the Cretan apples and the פרחים "calyxes" to the flower-shaped *capitula* on the pillars. In total, the count on the lampstand was 22 גבעים, 11 כפתורים, and 9 פרחים, thus together 42 adornments, whereas Josephus, as already said above, gives their total as 70.[c] Although the rabbinic descriptions on the whole are simply a repetition of the statements in Exod 25:31ff., they still offer some very noteworthy new bits of information about the lampstand of the Herodian temple, which cannot automatically be dismissed as unhistorical. We summarize the most important of these traditions here. α. The total height of the lampstand was 18 handbreadths (= 3 cubits = approximately 1.32 meters); exactly in the middle of it, thus at a height of 9 handbreadths, there was the fork of the two lowest or outermost side arms; then every 2 handbreadths going up there was a fork for the two other (inner) pairs of side arms.[d] — β. The tops of the six side arms lay at the same height as the middle one or main shaft, so that the lamps set on top formed a straight line.[e] The entirely singular tradition that

the height of the middle shaft protruded above the other six arms cannot be determined more specifically as to its date.[f] — γ. Concerning the pedestal יָרֵךְ of the lampstand, Exod 25:31ff. with parallels does not contain any more specific stipulation. Targum Onkelos translates יָרֵךְ, which actually means "hip" and which in Exod 25:31 denotes the "foot" of the lampstand, in a completely nondescript way with שִׁדָּא "shaft" (LXX: χαυλός = shaft end); Targum Yerušalmi I is more specific with בָּסִיס = βάσις "base frame." According to Rashi on Exod 25:31 the pedestal was shaped like a "box" תֵּיבָה, which rested on three feet. Additionally, the "feet" רַגְלַיִם of the lampstand are mentioned in b. Menaḥ. 28B and in the "Baraita about the construction of the tent of meeting"; in these passages too, one should think of three feet.

a. Josephus, *Jewish Antiquities* 3.6.7: "Opposite the table (in the holy place), near to the wall on the south side, stood the lampstand made of gold.... It was made of small spheres (σφαιρία) and lilies (κρίνα) with pomegranates (ῥοΐσκοι) and small flower bowls (flower chalices, κρατηρίδια); in total there were 70. It was fashioned out of them from its base (βάσις, pedestal) to its height by being constructed in seven limbs (arms), whose total corresponded to the planets and the sun. It went out, though, in seven tips that stood alongside each other in a line. On these, seven lamps were set, one each (on each arm), in imitation of the number of the (seven) planets; yet they looked both to the east and to the south, with the lampstand standing diagonally (in a south-east orientation)." (On the positioning of the lampstand, see #2.)

b. See the depiction of the lampstand in Riehm, *Handwörterbuch*, 1:902.

c. The main passage, aside from Tg. Onk. and Yer. I on Exod 25:31–37, is b. Menaḥ. 28B: Samuel († 254) said in the name of an elder, "The height of the lampstand was 18 handbreadths." (There then follows the calculation of the height and the count of the 42 adornments in detail.) Then it says: Rab († 247) said, "The height of the lampstand was 9 handbreadths." Rab Shimi b. Hiyya (ca. 250) raised the objection against Rab: "There was a stone before the lampstand which had three levels and on which the priest stood when he cleaned the lampstand (how, then, can the lampstand have been only 9 handbreadths high; see further below)!" He answered him, "Are you really Shimi?! I mean this about the edge of the branches and upward" (i.e., from the branching of the lowest side arms up to the top the height was 9 handbreadths; the root of the side arms thus began at exactly half the height of the lampstand). — Parallels are found in the baraita about the construction of the tent of meeting (*Beth ha-Midrash* 3.151.10) and Leqach Tob on Exod 25:32ff.

d. See b. Menaḥ. 28B in n. *c*.

e. See Josephus, *Ant.* 3.6.7 in n. *a*, b. Menaḥ. 28B in n. *c*.

f. Midrash Aggad on Numbers 8:2 (ed. Buber 2:92): The actual lampstand גופה של מנורה (i.e., the middle shaft of the lampstand) was higher than the branches (i.e., the side arms).

2. Position and orientation of the lampstand in the holy place.

According to Exod 26:35 and 40:24, the table for the show bread was supposed to stand on the north side of "the holy place" (to the right of the one entering) and the lampstand on the south side (to the left of the one entering).[a] More precisely, the tradition says that both, the table and lampstand, were pulled forward 2.5 cubits from the wall[b] and would have been a little closer to the curtain in front of the holy of holies than to the temple entrance on the east side.[c] There is less agreement in the views about the orientation in which the lampstand stood in its place. Here we encounter three opinions. α: The lampstand stood with its broad side (the line of lamps) in an east-west orientation, running parallel to the southern wall of the holy place. This may have been the predominant view; this corresponded above all to the canon[d] that, apart from the ark of the covenant, all the items in the temple were positioned with their length axis in the orientation of the temple building itself, that is, from east to west. The arrangement of the seven lamps on the lampstand in this case would have been the same, so that the three located east of the middle shaft pointed west and the three located west of the middle shaft pointed east, with all being directed to the middle lamp, while the latter, directed to the north, let its light fall forward, and so toward the table for the show bread.[e] — β: The lampstand stood with its broad wide (line of lamps) perpendicular to the south wall of the holy place, and thus parallel to the curtain of the holy of holies in a south-north orientation. The lamps in this case would have been so arranged that the three located south of the middle shaft pointed north and the three located north of the middle shaft pointed south, with all being directed to the middle lamp, while the latter, directed to the west, let its light fall forward, that is, toward the holy of holies.[f] — γ: The lampstand stood diagonally in a south-east orientation; so Josephus.[g] — The orientation of the lampstand comes into consideration with the question of what is referred to by the so-called "western" lamp נֵר מַעֲרָבִי. This lamp, glorified in tales of miracles,[h] was understood by representatives of the first view (α, orientation of the lampstand from east to west) to be the "second" lamp, that is, the one next to the easternmost or first one, and, precisely since it was more to the west than the first (easternmost), it was the "western one," and since it was closer to the holy of holies than the first (easternmost), it was called the lamp "before Yahweh."[i] However, the representatives of the second view (β, orientation of the lampstand from south to north) claimed that the lamp on the middle or main shaft was the western lamp;[k] it was the only one that cast its light to the west, toward the holy of holies, and hence its name was the "western" lamp. — A third view was represented by Rabbi († 217?): by assuming that the orientation of the lampstand was oriented from east to west, he understood the "western" lamp to refer to the one that was "before Yahweh," that is, closest to the holy of holies, and so the western one in the literal sense of the word; see b. Menaḥ. 98B and Rashi on the passage.

a. Babylonian Talmud Menaḥot 86B: The table (for the show bread) stood in the north and the lampstand in the south. ‖ See Tg. Song. 4:16 at § Luke 1:11 B. ‖ See b. B. Bat. 25B at § Matt 19:22, #4, 2nd third. A similar statement is found also in b. Yoma 21B.32.

b. See b. Yoma 33B at § Luke 1:11 B.

c. Sifra Leviticus 24:3 (419A): "'Outside the curtain of witness in the tent of revelation, Aaron shall put them (the lamps) on' (Lev 24:3). What does Scripture mean to teach with this? Since it is said 'He placed the lampstand in the tent of revelation opposite the table (for show bread) (on the south side of the holy place)' (Exod 40:24), I do not know whether it was closer to the curtain (before the holy of holies) or whether it was nearer to the entrance (into the holy place in the east) since it says, 'Outside the curtain of witness in the tent of revelation' (Lev 24:3), this teaches that it (the lampstand) was closer to the curtain than to the entrance." — The same is found with small deviations in Leqach Tob on Lev 24:3 (2.67B).

d. See m. Menaḥ. 11.6 and the baraita in b. Menaḥ. 98A at § Rom 3:25 A, #3, n. *d.* ‖ Leqach Tob on Exodus 26:35 (92B): "Set the table outside the curtain and the lampstand opposite the table" (Exod 26:35). They shall be situated lengthwise in the lengthwise orientation of the dwelling. (Then follows the baraita in b. Menaḥ. 98A just mentioned.)

e. Sifre Numbers 8:1 § 59 (15B): "Why has this section (Num 8:1–4) been said? If it says, 'Its lamps shall be put on it, and they shall cast light on what lies opposite it' (Exod 25:37), I take from this that all the lamps should shine to the front side of the whole lampstand. Then Scripture teaches, 'They shall cast light toward the lamp shaft (middle shaft)' (so Num 8:2 is formulated); the lamps are supposed to be turned toward מקבלים (perhaps = מכוונין) the lamp shaft and the latter toward the lamps. How so? Three (lamps directed) toward the east and three toward the west and one in the middle; so all will be found to be turned toward the middle one." From this R. Nathan (ca. 160) has said, "The middle one is the honored one" (proverbially: everything in the middle is usually the most valuable and esteemed). (We have to think of the lamps as oblong bowls that were furnished in front with a little mouth for a wick. Their wick or light side was to be turned toward the lamp shaft (the middle shaft), while the latter let its light fall forward from its lamp, that is, onto the show bread table on the north side of the holy place). — This view is represented in b. Menaḥ. 98B by Rabbi († 217?). ‖ Rashi remarks on Num 8:2: אל מול פני המנורה (= "to the front side of the lampstand") means "toward the lamp in the very middle" אל מול נר האמצעי, that was not on the branches (the side arms), but rather on the lampstand itself (on the lamp shaft). "The seven lamps shall cast their light" (Num 8:2): of the six lamps on the six branches, the three eastern ones directed the wicks that were in them toward the lamp in the very middle, and likewise, the three western ones directed the tips of the wicks toward the lamp in the very middle. And why? Lest it be said, "He (God) needs light!" (Such idle talk was excluded by the six lamps letting their light fall not to the west onto the holy of holies, where God is enthroned, but rather to the lamp in the very middle, which cast its own light to the north, onto the show bread table.) — This tradition is also found in Tg. Yer. I Num. 8:2; Leqach Tob on Num 8:2 (96A) and Midr. Aggad on Num 8:2 (93.4). ‖ The arrangement of the lamps in the direction of the lampstand from east to west is thought of differently in Midr. Aggad on Num 8:2 (92.26): "To the front side of the lampstand" (Num 8:2), that is, toward the table (of show bread) in the north,[320] as when, according to the custom of the world, a person arranges his table and the lampstand opposite it.

f. Babylonian Talmud Menaḥot 98B: R. Eleazar b. Simeon (ca. 180) would have said to you, "The lampstand itself stood in a north-south orientation" (and not in an east-west orientation, as Rabbi thought, see n. *e*)! (Rashi: "If the lampstand stood from north to south, only one lamp was directed westward, namely the one in the very middle [on the actual shaft of the lampstand], and the little mouth for its wick was directed to the west [which is why the lamp in the very middle was also called the western one], while the little mouths of the other wicks were turned sideward toward the lamp in the very middle, and those that were on the north side were turned to the south and those on the south side were turned to the north.") ‖ Babylonian Talmud Megillah 21B: In a baraita we have learned: "'אל מול פני המנורה ("To the front side of the lampstand") the seven lamps shall cast their light' (Num 8:2). This teaches that their front side (= their little mouth) was turned sideward toward the 'western' lamp (which was on the actual shaft of the lampstand, so that the little mouth of the three south lamps was directed toward the north and that of the three northern lamps was directed toward the south), while the 'western' lamp (the one on the middle shaft of the lampstand) was directed toward the Shekinah (i.e., toward the holy of holies or toward the west)." R. Yohanan († 279, read: R. Jonathan = R. Nathan, ca. 160) said, "From here it results that the middle one is the honored one." — The orientation of the lampstand is in this passage naturally from south to north. ‖ See further Leqach Tob Exod 25:37 (91B).

g. See Josephus, *Ant.* 3.6.7 above at #1, n. *a.*

h. Tosefta Sukkah 13.7 (319): As long as Simeon the Righteous (II, ca. 200 BCE) lived, the western lamp was constantly (burning). After he had died, one went and found it extinguished. From then on, (in the morning) it was sometimes extinguished, sometimes burning. — Parallels are found in y. Yoma 6.43C.48; b. Yoma 39A. — This saying is alluded to in b. Menaḥ. 86B: "Outside the curtain of witness in the tent of revelation, Aaron shall fix them" (Lev 24:3); it (the lamp that always burns) shall be a witness for all who come into the world that the Shekinah dwells in Israel ... What does "witness" refer to? Raba († 352) said, "This refers to the 'western' lamp, into which just as much oil was put as into the others, and by which (the others) were lit and with which (in the evening) the cleaning was finished (since it used to burn constantly, while the others were out)." — In b. Šabb. 22B instead of Raba, Rab († 247) is named as the author. — The following saying in Tanḥ. תצוה 104A refers not to the "western" lamp, but rather to all the lamps of the lampstand: R. Hanina (Hananiah), the head of the priests (ca. 70), said, "I served in the sanctuary, and a miracle happened with the lampstand: when one lit it at the beginning of the year, it did not go out until the next year." Once the olives did not produce any oil; then the priests began to weep (so according to the reading לבכות). R. Hanina (Hananiah), the head of the priests, said, "I was in the sanctuary and found the lampstand burning more (more brightly) than it burned from olives; he saw a miracle every day of the year."

---

320. S-B: This explanation of the words in Num 8:2 corresponds to the sense of the base text.

i. Mishnah Tamid 6.1: He who had obtained (by lot) the cleaning of the lampstand, went in (to the holy place); if he found the two eastern lamps burning, he would clean the "eastern" one (so the first) and let the "western" one (i.e., the second) burn. — Here it is assumed that the orientation of the lampstand is from east to west; then the second lamp is called the "western" one because it was the one that was west of the two eastern ones. ‖ Tosafot on b. Menaḥ. 98B מדכתיב: Of the "western" lamp, it is written "before Yahweh" (Lev 24:3); the second lamp of the two eastern ones is called the "western" one; see also Rashi on b. Šabb. 22B. ‖ Bertinoro on m. Tamid 3.9: The second lamp is called the "western" one; for if he (the priest who had to clean the lampstand) entered the holy place (of the temple), he came upon it first; and one does not pass by commandments[321] (but rather begins carrying them out and fulfilling them immediately where the first opportunity offers itself); with the first (eastern) lamp, though, it was not possible because "before Yahweh" is written (Lev 24:3); this refers to the lamp that stood toward the Shekinah, that is, toward the west. — The second lamp is thus the "western" one, because it among the two eastern lamps stood "before Yahweh," that is, most to the west. — See also Malbim on SLev 24:2 (419A § 212): The second lamp on the eastern side was said to be "before Yahweh" because it was closer to the היכל than the eastern one that lay before it.

k. See the citations in n. *f.*

3. The servicing of the lampstand.

The OT does not specifically answer the question of whether the lamps of the golden lampstand burned day and night. When it says in Exod 27:20 and Lev 24:2: "To constantly תָּמִיד put the lamps (נֵר collectively = נֵרוֹת) on," it appears to speak in favor of the idea that the lamps burned also during the day. But then when it immediately says after this (Exod 27:21; Lev 24:3) that the lamps should be trimmed (to burn) from evening until morning, only the night is thought of as the time that the lamps would burn. The same view may be present in 1 Sam 3:3, where the expression: "the lamp of God was still not out" is supposed to express that the morning had not yet dawned. The specification of the time could happen, though, only if the lamp of God regularly went out in the morning and did not continue burning during the day. Also according to Philo the lamps burned only from evening until morning.[a] However, Josephus asserts that three lamps also burned during the day, while the others were lit only in the evening.[b] The testimony of (Pseudo-)Hecataeus in Josephus, *Against Apion* 1.22, is ambiguous in its details, though it very specifically presupposes a permanent illumination of the holy place day and night.[c] This view is represented by the rabbinic scholars as well. They unanimously declare that all seven lamps burned only at night, though by day one, the "perpetual lamp" נֵר תָּמִיד, burned, which was the "western" lamp,[d] that is, according to what is said above in #2, either the second (counted from the east) or the one that was on the

321. S-B: This was a principle of Resh Laqish (ca. 250); see, e.g., b. Yoma 33A.35; 58B.27.

middle shaft of the lampstand. — There are detailed regulations in rabbinic literature concerning the cleaning and preparation of the lamps for use; yet at the level of detail, these contradict one another—in particular concerning the question of whether the tasks for the lampstand had to be completed after the blood of the Tamid offering was sprinkled or only after the presentation of the morning incense offering—in such a way that we cannot come to a secure judgment about the actual course of these tasks. In what comes below, we follow Bertinoro († 1510) and limit ourselves to giving mostly only the sources on the contradictory views. — In accordance with this, the handling of the lampstand proceeded specifically in the following way. Still before the morning Tamid lamb was slaughtered, the priest whom the lot had tasked with attending to the lampstand[e] came with a golden jug כוז, which was designed to take the waste from the lamps, into the "holy place" of the temple in order to begin here on the spot for his task with the lamps.[f] For these could not be prepared for use anywhere outside the temple building, but rather all the tasks with them had to be carried out at the lampstand itself.[g] Furthermore, these tasks then were carried out in two acts separated from each other in time. The first part of the task, the preparation of the five western lamps, came before the slaughtering of the Tamid lamb and before the sprinkling of its blood; the second part, the preparation of the two eastern[322] lamps, was completed only after the sprinkling of blood (or, as an opposing view has it, only after the presentation of the morning incense offering).[h] The first part of the task, that is, the preparation of the five western lamps, proceeded differently, depending on whether the priest found the two eastern lamps burning or extinguished when he entered into the holy place. — α. If he came upon them still burning, he let them continue to burn in their place untouched, in order to immediately turn to his task with the five western lamps. Since the lampstand (without lamps) had a height of 18 handbreadths (see #1) and therefore would have reached approximately the shoulder height of a medium-sized man, a large three-leveled stone had been set before the lampstand, in order to make it possible for the priest on duty to handle the lamps comfortably and safely. The priest stepped onto the stone,[i] took away the five lamps one by one, removed the remnants of their wick and oil, cleaned them of ash and with a sponge wiped them clean of the settled soot from the oil.[k] All waste and refuse went into the available golden jug. After the priest then had furnished the five lamps with a new wick and the best olive oil (one calculated for each lamp .5 *log* = 0.27356 liter of oil),[l] he set them again on the lampstand in their earlier position; here he was

322. S-B: The designation "western" and "eastern" lamps presuppose that the lampstand stood in an east-west orientation. The five "western" lamps were then those that were nearest the curtain in front of the holy of holies.

supposed to use neither little pieces of wood nor small stones to support them or fix them in the flower studs on top of the arms of the lampstand.[m] — β. If when he entered the holy place the priest came upon the two eastern lamps already having gone out (which was viewed as the rule since the death of Simeon the Righteous, see #2, n. *h*), his task pertained first to these two lamps. He cleaned them of ash and then lit them again (without, however, putting new oil or a new wick in them),[323] either with one of the still burning five western lamps or, in case these had gone out, with fire that was taken from the altar of burnt offering. Then he turned to the five other lamps and prepared them for use in the evening in the same way as stated above. Thereby the first part of the tasks with the lampstand was completed. The priest set the jug with the waste on the second level of the stone before the lampstand and removed himself.[n] This is where the tasks with the lampstand were interrupted,[o] which, as already mentioned above, was occasioned by the slaughtering of the Tamid lamb and the presentation of its blood. Only after the sprinkling of blood (or as an opposing view would have it, only after the presentation of the morning incense offering) the priest returned to the holy place to take up the second part of his tasks, the preparation of the two eastern lamps. Here too the execution of his tasks was different, depending on whether at his return he found the two lamps burning or extinguished. α. If he came upon them still burning, he put out the first or eastern one and prepared it by cleaning it and providing it with new oil and a new wick for the evening, without lighting it again at the moment. The second, though, he left burning (after adding oil), in order to light the other lamps with it in the evening. β. Yet if at his return he found this second lamp extinguished, he cleaned it too, furnished it with new oil and a wick and lit it again with fire from the altar of burnt offering; for this was the lamp that was supposed to burn perpetually, and thus also during the day. Thereby the whole task to be carried out with the lampstand in the morning was complete. The priest took the golden jug with the waste, prostrated in worship, and went out.[p] — Only in the afternoon after the presentation of the evening incense offering[q] did the priest[r] have to again service the lampstand. Now all the lamps had to be set aflame for the night. The priest would light the six lamps that did not burn by day with the perpetually burning one, the so-called "western" lamp (see #2), and prepared them for the night by cleaning them, furnishing them with new oil and wicks and finally lighting them again with the lamps already burning;[s] hence the saying that with the "western" or perpetually burning lamp, the lighting (of the morning) began and (of the evening) ended.[t]

---

323. S-B: This preparation of the two eastern lamps was of only a preliminary sort.

a. Philo, *De vict offer* § 7 (Mangey's ed., 2:256): "He further arranged that from evening until early in the morning the lamps should burn on the holy lampstand within the curtain (= in the holy place)."

b. Josephus, *Jewish Antiquities* 3.8.3: "Among them (the lamps), three on the holy lampstand of God had to shine the whole day, while the others were lit in the evening."

c. Josephus, *Against Apion* 1.22: "(Near the altar of burnt offering) there was a great building in which there was an altar (βωμός) and a lampstand, both of gold, weighing two talents. On these there was light (φῶς) that went out neither at night nor by day."

d. Sifra Leviticus 24:2 (419A): "To keep a lamp on constantly" (Lev 24:2), that is, so that the "western" lamp (the second, counted from the east) should burn perpetually, for with it he should begin (with the lighting) and by it he should complete (it). ‖ Sifre Numbers 8:2 § 59 (16A): "The seven lamps shall cast light" (Num 8:2). Here I hear that they should burn perpetually. Scripture teaches: "From evening until morning" (Lev 24:3). If from evening until morning, should he put them out (at morning)? Scripture teaches: "The seven lamps shall cast light" (Num 8:2). How so? The seven lamps shall cast light "from evening until morning," which are constantly "before Yahweh" (Lev 24:3); the "western" lamp (the second, counted from the east = "which is before Yahweh") shall be perpetual, for by it he lights the lampstand between the evenings. — See also Leqach Tob on Lev 24:2 (67B.20).

e. See m. Yoma 2.3 at § Luke 1:5 A, #1, n. *e*; a parallel passage is found in m. Tamid 3.1.

f. See m. Tamid 3.6 at § Luke 1:9, #1.

g. Sifra Leviticus 24:4 (420A): "On the clean lampstand he shall prepare the lamps continually before Yahweh" (Lev 24:4); he shall not prepare them outside (outside the temple building) and (then) bring them in. — The same is found in Leqach Tob on Lev 24:4 (67B.34).

h. Concerning the sequence of the individual services carried out in the temple, it says in b. Yoma 33A: Abbayye († 338/39) said in a presentation about the sequences (of the services) in the name of teaching passed down and in the spirit of Abba Saul (ca. 150): "The large woodpile (for burning the Tamid offering) takes priority over the second woodpile (for burning) the incense (in the holy place), the second woodpile for incense takes priority over stacking the two wood logs (see Lev 6:6), the stacking of the two wood logs takes priority over removing the ashes (cleaning) of the inner altar, the removal of ashes takes priority over the cleaning (preparation) of the five (western) lamps, the cleaning of the five lamps takes priority over the blood (the sprinkling of the blood) of the Tamid lamb, the blood of the Tamid lamb takes priority over cleaning the two (eastern) lamps, the cleaning of the two lamps takes priority over the incense offering, the incense offering takes priority over the burning of the pieces of the Tamid offering, the pieces of the Tamid offering over the meal offering (associated with them), the meal offering over the high priestly plate meal offering (see § Heb 7:27, #2), the high priestly plate meal offering over the (Tamid) drink offering, the drink offering over the additional offerings (on the Sabbath), the additional offerings over the bowls (with incense for the show bread loaves [Lev 24:5ff.]) and the bowls over the Tamid offering between the evenings." — For the different view that the preparation of the two eastern lamps occurred only after the presentation of the incense offering, see b. Yoma 14B; 15A; b. Pesaḥ. 59A.

i. Mishnah Tamid 3.9 at the end: A stone was before the lampstand, and it had three levels; on it the priest stood when he cleaned (prepared הֵטִיב) the lamps. – This Mishnah is cited in, for example, SNum 8:3 § 60 (16A); b. Menaḥ. 29A. – The biblical basis is given by SNum 8:2 § 59 (16A) in the words: "When you put on בהעלותך the lamps" (Num 8:2); this entails: make levels מעלות for them. – A similar statement is also in SNum 8:3 § 60 (16A).

k. The cleaning of the lamps is described as follows in b. Menaḥ. 88B: R. Yohanan († 279) said that Rabbi († 217?) said, "If a lamp went out, the oil had become ash and the wick had become ash. How did he (the priest) proceed? He cleaned it and put oil in it מטיבה ונותן בה שמן" (Rashi: "He threw away everything that was in the lamp and put different oil and a different wick in it"). – A few lines later it says: "How did he (the priest) proceed? He removed[324] מסלקן them (the lamps) off and put them down in the tent and wiped them off with a sponge and put oil in them." – In wiping off the lamps, one had to pay special attention to removing the soot from the oil; see b. Menaḥ. 88B toward the end: The little mouth of the lamps becomes black פי נרות אשחורי משחר, namely from the soot from the oil. Ordinarily, one used a small copper hook צִנּוֹרָא to remove it; see b. Šabb. 90A and b. Menaḥ. 107A.

l. Fibers of flax and tow weaved together were used as a wick פְּתִילָה; see m. Šabb. 2.3 and t. Šabb. 9.5 (121). – Yet m. Šabb. 2.1 shows that other material (bast fiber, silk, nettles, etc.) were used as a wick. – The best olive oil was used as oil שֶׁמֶן. Mishnah Menaḥot 8.4, 5: There are three types of olives (= seasons of olives, vintages of olives) and each of these in turn makes three kinds of oil. The first olive: the berries are picked at the top of the olive tree, crushed and put in a basket (vat). R. Judah (ca. 150) said, "Around the sides of the basket." This (oil that flows out automatically from the basket) was the first (most excellent). Then they were pressed with a clamp. R. Judah said, "With stones." This was the second (in quality). Then they were crushed and pressed again; this was the third. The first for the lampstand and the rest for the meal offering. The second olive: the olives are left to dry (shrivel) on a roof, they are crushed and put in a basket (vat). R. Judah said, "Around the sides of the basket." This (oil that flows out automatically from the basket) is the first. They were pressed with a clamp. R. Judah said, "With stones." This is the second. Then they are crushed and pressed again; this is the third. The first for the lampstand and the rest for the meal offering. The third olive: the olives were piled up in the house (another reading: in the pressing house) until they became crumbly (putrid); then they were taken onto a roof and left there to dry. They were crushed and put into a basket (vat). R. Judah said, "Around the sides of the basket." This was the first. They were pressed with a clamp. R. Judah said, "With stones." This was the second. Then they were crushed and pressed again; this was the third. The first for the lampstand and the rest for the meal offering. This first with the first (olive): beyond this there was none (it was the very best oil). The second with the first and the first with the second were of equal value. The third with the first and the second with the second and the first with the third were of equal value. The third with the second and the second with the third were of equal value. The third with the third: below this there was none (it was the least valuable). – Parallels with differences are found in SLev 24:2 (418A); Tanḥ.

324. S-B: Another opinion was that the lamps could not be removed; for a discussion on this, see b. Menaḥ 88B.

תצוה 105A. ‖ Sifra Leviticus 24:2 (418A): "Olive oil" שֶׁמֶן זַיִת (Lev 24:2), and not sesame oil or nut oil or radish oil ... "Pure" זָךְ (Lev 24:2): it should be pure; "pounded" כָּתִית. R. Judah (ca. 150) said, "'Pounded' means nothing other than 'crushed' כָּתוּשׁ." ‖ See further TanḥB תצוה § 3 49A; Tanḥ. תצוה 105A; Lev. Rab. 31 (129B); TanḥB תצוה § 6 (50A); Tanḥ. תצוה 105B. Each lamp required .5 *log* of oil. Mishnah Menaḥot 9.3: 3.5 *logs* (of oil) for the (entire) lampstand, .5 *log* for each lamp. ‖ See further t. Menaḥ. 10.3 (527); SNum 8:3 § 60 (16A); b. Menaḥ. 89A.

m. Sifra Leviticus 24:4 (420A): "On a clean lampstand" (Lev 24:4), that is, upon cleaning the lampstand: he should not support them (the lamps) with little pieces of wood or tiny stones. — In b. Menaḥ. 29A.21, the term "clean lampstand" is explained as follows: R. Samuel b. Nahman (ca. 260) said that R. Jonathan (ca. 220) said, "What does 'On a clean lampstand' (Lev 24:4) mean? That its (the lampstand's) work came down from a pure place (= heaven). — See b. Menaḥ. 29A; Tanḥ. שמיני 149A; בהעלותך 204B at § Heb 8:5 B.

n. Mishnah Tamid 3.9: The (priest) who had obtained the cleaning דִּשּׁוּן (= removing the ashes) of the lampstand (by lot) went in (to the holy place). If he found the two eastern lamps burning, he cleaned מדשן the other (five) and left them burning in their place. If he found them, that they had gone out, he cleaned them (first) (Bertinoro: He removed the ash from the top of the old wick ..., without putting new oil and a new wick in them) and lit them from those (still) burning (Bertinoro: And if not from the burning lamps, he lit them from the altar of burnt offering). Then he cleaned the rest. And there was a stone in front of the lampstand and it had three levels; on it the priest stood when he prepared (cleaned מֵטִיב) the lamps. And he set the jug on the second level and went out.

o. The partition of the task into two acts separated from each other in time is grounded exegetically in the twice-occurring בַּבֹּקֶר in Exod 30:7. Here R. Yohanan († 279) found the instruction: "Apportion it (the preparation of the lamps) to two times in the morning." Yet Resh Laqish (ca. 250) said, "Why did they prepare (the lamps) and then do it again (so in two acts)? So that the whole atrium noticed it,"[325] b. Yoma 33B. In the parallel passage in y. Yoma 2.39D.21, where the author names are switched, instead of: "So that the whole atrium noticed it," we find the more descriptive, "to make a public spectacle פּוֹמְפֵּי (= πομπή, *pompa*) of the matter." — On the further question of why five lamps were prepared in the first part of the tasks and two lamps in the second part, see b. Yoma 33B.

p. Mishnah Tamid 6.1: The (priest) who had acquired the cleaning of the lampstand (by lot) went in (to the holy place after the sprinkling of the blood of the morning Tamid). If he found the two eastern lamps burning, he cleaned the eastern one (= the foremost or first) and left the "western" one (= the second) burning, for by it he lit the lampstand between the evenings. If he found it (the second or "western" lamp), that it had gone out, he cleaned it (Bertinoro: put new oil and a new wick in it) and lit it from the altar of burnt offering. Then he took the jug (with the waste) from the second level (of the stone in front of the lampstand) and prostrated in worship and went out (to shake out the waste from the lamps onto the place for ashes east of the ramp of the altar of burnt offering). — There is a parallel in SLev 24:2 (419A).

---

325. S-B: הִרְגִּישׁ, probably with respect to רָגֶשׁ Ps 55:15.

q. A baraita in b. Pesaḥ. 58B: The (evening) incense offering takes priority over the lamps. — A baraita in b. Pesaḥ. 59A: The (evening) Tamid offering takes priority over the (evening) incense offering, and this one over the lamps. — According to both these passages, the lighting of the lampstand in the evening occurred only after the presentation of the evening incense offering.

r. The question of whether a different priest was appointed by lot for the evening servicing of the lampstand, or whether the same priest who had carried out the task in the morning was obliged to do it, was disputed; see y. Yoma 2.39D.48; b. Yoma 26A; and the Tosafot on b. Yoma 26A אלא.

s. So the sequence of the individual actions according to the Tosafot on b. Šabb. 22B ובה and according to Bertinoro on m. Tamid 3.9. — According to Rashi on b. Šabb. 22B ובה היה מסיים, the priest would have first prepared the perpetually burning lamp and lit it again with its old, still burning wick, and only then would the other lamps have been set aflame by the former.

t. Sifra Leviticus 24:2 (419A): "To put on (light) a lamp" (so the midrash by emphasizing the singular נֵר in Lev 24:2); the "western" (= second of the two eastern ones) shall perpetually burn, for with it he shall begin (with the lighting in the morning, in case it has gone out; see above n. *n*) and with it he shall complete it. ‖ Babylonian Talmud Šabbat 22B: By it (the "western" = second lamp) he lit (the others) and with it he ceased (with the lighting). — The same is found in b. Menaḥ. 86B. — In SNum 8:2 § 59 (16A): "Constantly before Yahweh" (Lev 24:3); the "western" (= second) lamp shall perpetually burn; for by it he lights the lampstand between the evenings.

4. The significance of the seven-armed lampstand and the recompense for its accurate servicing.

Philo and Josephus saw in the seven-armed lampstand a symbol for the seven planets.[a] This idea, in connection with the thought that the seven-armed lampstand corresponded to the seven days of the week, is encountered also in rabbinic literature,[b] though here the view prevails that in the lampstand, and particularly in the perpetually burning "western" lamp Israel possesses a pledge of the divine presence in its midst.[c] — The blessings that God bound to the conscientious servicing of the lampstand were glorified in many ways. The citations below give detailed information on this.[d]

a. Philo, *De vita Mosis* 3 § 9 (Mangey's ed., 2:150f.): "(The lawgiver set up) the lampstand λυχνίαν in the south (of the foretemple = the holy place), because he signifies by it the movements of the light-bearing heavenly bodies. For the sun and the moon and the other (heavenly bodies), which are far removed from the northern regions, complete their rotations in the south. Therefore, six arms κλάδοι (literally: branches) went forth, three on each side of the middle lampstand (the middle shaft), thus (with this one) forming the number seven. On all (the arms), though, there were (altogether) seven lamps and lights (wicks), symbols σύμβολα of the planets, so-called among those skilled in nature. For the sun, which has its place in the middle of the (other) six, just like the middle shaft of the lampstand, bestows light in its fourth position on the three heavenly bodies above it and for the same number of heavenly bodies below it, harmoniously uniting the artistic and truly divine work (of creation). — See Josephus, *Ant.* 3.6.7 above in #1, n. *a*; *J. W.* 5.5.5: The seven lamps signify the planets.

b. Numbers Rabbah 15 (178C): "The seven lamps shall cast their light on the lampstand" (so Num 8:2 according to the midr.). Hence: "For who scorns the day of small things, while these seven joyfully look at the plumb line in the hand of Zerubbabel?" (Zech 4:10). "These": this refers to the lampstand; "seven": this refers to the seven lamps, which correspond to the seven stars, "which roam over the whole earth" (Zech 4:10). These (seven lamps) are just as honored, so that you not to despise them. Therefore it is said, "On the lampstand the seven lamps shall cast their light." ‖ Yalquṭ on Numbers 8:2 (1 § 719): "When you put on the lamps ..." (Num 8:2). Why seven lamps? With a view to the seven planets, sun, Venus, Mercury, moon, Saturn, Jupiter, Mars.[326] A different explanation is as follows: With a view to the seven days of creation. — The same is found in Jellinek, *Beth ha-Midrash* 6.89.6 from Yelamedenu. ‖ Leqach Tob on Exodus 25:37 (91B.18): "Make its lamps seven" (Exod 25:37), corresponding to the seven days of creation. — This is dealt with in detail in *Beth ha-Midrash* 6.88.13 (from Yelamedenu = Yalquṭ on Numbers 8 toward the beginning).

c. Sifra Leviticus 24:3 (419A): "Outside of the curtain of witness ... Aaron shall prepare them (the lamps)" (Lev 24:3), as a testimony for all who come into the world that the Shekinah dwells in Israel. A similar statement is found in b. Šabb. 22B and Tg. Yer. I Lev. 24:3. See further b. Menaḥ. 86B and b. Šabb. 22B above in #2, n. *h.*

d. Numbers Rabbah 15 (178B): "When you put on the lamps" (Num 8:2). We find in many places that God gave a command concerning the lamps and their lighting with olive oil; so Exod 27:20, as well as Lev 24:4 and Num 8:2. This is what Scripture says, "It pleased Yahweh, so that he could declare it righteous to make the Torah great and glorious" (so Midr. Isa. 42:21, by interpreting צִדְקוֹ as a *piel* infinitive = צַדְּקוֹ).[327] God said to Moses, "Not because I need the lamps have I admonished (warned) you concerning the lamps, but rather to let you acquire merits (to declare you righteous)." — R. Aha (ca. 320) says something similar several times in Lev. Rab. 31 (129B); see also TanḥB בהעלתך § 2 (23B). ‖ Numbers Rabbah 15 (178C): God said to Moses, "If you are diligent before me with the lighting (of the lamps), I will keep your souls from all evil; for souls are compared with a light, as it says, 'A light of Yahweh is a person's soul' (Prov 20:27)." — A parallel passage is found in Tanḥ. אמור 177B. ‖ TanḥumaB בהעלתך § 5 (24A): "When you put on the lamps" (Num 8:2). This is what Scripture says, "You make my light bright" (Ps 18:29). The Israelites said before God, "Lord of the world, you say that we should kindle a light before you; but you are the light of the world and light dwells with you (see Dan 2:22), and you say, 'They shall cast light on the front of the lampstand' (Num 8:2)! Rather, thus: You make my light bright!" God said, "Not that I need your light, but rather you shall shine for me, as I have

---

326. S-B: On the sequence of the planets, see § John 2:4 C, penultimate paragraph.

327. S-B: This interpretation of Isa 42:21 is found already with R. Hananiah b. Aqashia (ca. 150); see m. Mak. 3.16; ʾAbot R. Nat. 41 at the end; it is also found in Tg. Isa. 42:21; Exod. Rab. 9 (73B.37); Tanḥ וארא 71A.13; TanḥB וארא § 11 (14A.3).

shone for you, to exalt you before all nations, so that they say, 'See how the Israelites shine for the one who illumines all things!'" — Parallels are found in Exod. Rab. 36 (95C); Num. Rab. 15 (178C). ‖ TanḥumaB בהעלתך § 2 (23B): "If you are diligent" (God says) "to light the lamps for my name, I too will make a great line shine for you in the future (= in the messianic age); as it says, 'Arise, become light, for your light comes ... And the nations will stream to your light and kings to the rising of your shining' (Isa 60:1, 3)." — The same is found in Num. Rab. 15 (178B). ‖ Tanḥuma תצוה 105B: God said to Moses, "Say to the Israelites, 'My children, in this world you were obligated to the light of the sanctuary and you lit the lamps in it. Yet in the future world I will bring to you by the merit of those lamps the king, the Messiah, who is compared with a light; as it says, "There I will make a horn sprout for David. I have prepared a light for my Messiah"' (Ps 132:17)." ‖ Leviticus Rabbah 31 (129C): "Outside the curtain of witness ... Aaron shall prepare them (for burning)" (Lev 24:3). R. Eleazar b. Shammuah (ca. 150) said, "By the merit of the 'he shall prepare' יערך, you will be guarded from the: 'a site of abomination has been prepared ערוך long ago' (in the sense of the midrash = gehenna)." R. Hanin (ca. 300) said, "By the merit of putting on the continual lamp you will be worthy to greet the light of the king, the Messiah. What is the scriptural basis? 'There I will make a horn sprout for David—I have prepared a light for my Messiah' (Ps 132:17). It further says, 'I rejoiced when it was said to me: Let us go to the house of Yahweh!' (Ps 122:1)."

5. Traditions of different content.

The lampstand made by Moses was preserved for continued use in Solomon's temple; see t. Soṭah 13.1 at § Rom 3:25, A, #8, n. *d*, S-B footnote. — Before the destruction of the first sanctuary, it was hidden along with other items of the temple; see Tanḥ. בהעלותך 205A at § Rom 3:25 A, #8, n. *c*, end. The same view is probably also represented in 2 Bar. 6:4ff. (see § Rom 3:25, A #8, n. *c*, beginning), when it says that all the holy vessels (items) of the tent were handed over to the earth for safe-keeping. — The lampstand of the Herodian sanctuary was moved by Titus to Rome; see b. Giṭ. 56A at § Matt 24:2, #2, middle and toward the end of ʾAbot R. Nat. 41 at § Rom 3:25, A, #8, n. *c*, middle. — Lastly, we may refer to the regulation that replicas of the seven-armed lampstand for private use were forbidden.

A baraita in b. Menaḥ. 28B: A house may not be built according to the model of the temple, nor any atrium corresponding to the atrium of the temple, nor any court corresponding to the forecourt (of the temple), nor any table corresponding to the table (for show bread), nor any lampstand corresponding to the (holy) lampstand; however, such an item may be made with five or six or eight arms, yet not with seven arms, not even with another type of metal (as from gold). — There is a parallel in b. Roš Haš. 24A.

C. The table, ἡ τράπεζα, Hebrew שֻׁלְחָן in Exod 25:23 (LXX: τράπεζα χρυσῆ, Tg. Onk. and Yer. I: פָּתוֹרָא = table); more precisely הַשֻּׁלְחָן הַטָּהֹר "the pure table," because it was coated with pure gold (Lev 24:6; LXX: ἡ τράπεζα ἡ καθαρά, Tg. Onk.: פתורא דַכְיָא = "pure table," differently, Tg. Yer. I); שֻׁלְחַן הַפָּנִים "the table of the face," because it stands before God (Num 4:7; LXX:

ἡ τράπεζα ἡ προκειμένη, Tg. Onk.: פתורא דִלְחֵם אַפַּיָא = "table for the show bread loaves," which is replaced in Tg. Yer. I by: (פתור לחים אפיא); שֻׁלְחַן הַמַּעֲרֶכֶת "the table of the stacking (of bread)" (2 Chr 29:18; LXX: ἡ τράπεζα τῆς προθέσεως, targum: פתורא דְסִידוּרָא "table of the lining up [of bread]"). — 1 Maccabees 1:22: ἡ τράπεζα τῆς προθέσεως "table of the presentation (of bread)"; in Josephus, it is, concisely, τράπεζα (*Ant.* 3.6.6; *J. W.* 5.5.5); more fully: χρυσῆ τράπεζα "golden table" (*J. W.* 7.5.5) or also ἡ ἱερὰ τράπεζα "the holy table" (*Ant.* 3.10.7). — A description of the show bread table is found in Exod 25:23ff. and 37:10ff.; it remains uncertain whether here two golden wreaths or only one is mentioned, as well as whether the ledge מִסְגֶּרֶת, near which the rings for the carrying rods were (Exod 25:25, 27), should be mounted immediately under the tabletop or in the middle of the four feet of the table. In both cases, the first assumption seems to be right. The table stood on the north side of the "holy place" (to the right of the entrant) opposite the seven-armed lampstand, pulled forward from the wall 2.5 cubits, a bit nearer to the curtain in front of the holy of holies than to the entrance on the east side of the "holy place," specifically with its long axis in line with the length axis of the temple building, that is, from east to west; see the supporting passages above at B, #2, notes *a–d*. — According to the tradition, which is not indicated by the wording of Scripture, though, there was a particular trestle or scaffold connected to the show bread table, which served to receive or support the show bread loaves; see in the following section D. — After the destruction of the temple by Titus, the golden table was brought to Rome.

Josephus, *Jewish War* 7.5.5: "Other items of booty were (in the triumphal procession in Rome) brought along en masse. Yet outstanding before all (others) were those items that had been plundered in the sanctuary in Jerusalem: the golden table, which weighed several talents, and the lampstand, which was similar fashioned out of gold." — See further toward the end of 'Abot R. Nat. 41 at § Rom 3:25 A, #8, n. *c*, middle.

D. The presentation of the loaves ἡ πρόθεσις τῶν ἄρτων = the presented loaves, that is, the "show bread loaves." — The show bread loaves are called by the following terms: α. לֶחֶם פָּנִים "bread of the face," because they lay in the face of Yahweh on his table, Exod 25:30 (LXX: ἄρτοι ἐνώπιοι). — β. לֶחֶם הַפָּנִים, Exod 35:13 (lacking in the LXX); 39:36 (LXX: οἱ ἄρτοι οἱ προκείμενοι; another reading: τῆς προθέσεως). — γ. לֶחֶם הַתָּמִיד "the constant bread," Num 4:7 (LXX: οἱ ἄρτοι οἱ διαπαντός). — δ. לֶחֶם הַמַּעֲרֶכֶת "bread of the layering," 1 Chr 9:32 (LXX: ἄρτοι τῆς προθέσεως); Neh 10:34 (LXX: ἄρτοι τοῦ προσώπου = ἄρτοι ἐνώπιοι above). — ε. לֶחֶם קֹדֶשׁ "holy bread," 1 Sam 21:5 (LXX: ἄρτοι ἅγιοι). — In Aramaic, for לֶחֶם פָּנִים in Exod 25:30, we read לְחֵם אַפַּיָא in Tg. Onk.; yet, in Tg. Yer. I, we read: לַחְמָא גַוָּאָה "the inner (located inside the sanctuary) bread," פָּנִים is interpreted as פְּנִים "inner." — For לֶחֶם הַפָּנִים in Exod 35:13 and 39:36, we read לְחֵם אַפַּיָא in Tg. Onk.; in Tg. Yer. I:

לְחֵם דְּאַפַּיָא, or לְחֵם אַפַּיָא. — For לֶחֶם הַתָּמִיד in Num 4:7: לְחֵם תְּדִירָא = "constant bread," Tg. Onk. and Yer. I. — For לֶחֶם הַמַּעֲרֶכֶת in 1 Chr 9:32: לְחֵם סִדּוּרָא "bread of lining up (layering)," so the targum the passage. — For לֶחֶם קֹדֶשׁ in 1 Sam 21:5: לַחְמָא דְקוּדְשָׁא "holy bread," so the targum of the passage. — The LXX also knows the designation ἄρτοι τῆς προσφορᾶς "loaves of the presentation" (1 Kgs 7:48); Josephus also uses the expression ἄρτοι τοῦ θεοῦ "loaves of God" (*Ant.* 8.3.7), whereas Philo concisely says ἄρτοι "loaves"; see, for example, *Mos.* 3.3 (Mangey's ed., 2:151); *De victim* § 3 (Mangey's ed., 2:239).

1. In the last period before the destruction of the temple, the preparation of the show bread loaves was in the hands of the (priestly) family Garmu. They alone knew the secret to keeping the loaves from becoming moldy, but their craft was also paid for at great expense.[a] The show bread loaves were prepared from fine wheat flour,[b] without adding leaven,[c] although the latter was not explicitly forbidden in the Torah. According to Lev 24:5, each loaf contained two tenths of an *ephah*,[d] that is, 7.88 liters of flour. The show bread loaves were baked in a hall that was in the northwest corner of the temple area.[e] The dough could be kneaded and formed outside the sanctuary; however, opinions on this point were divided.[f] Here the rule was that not the whole mass of dough at once, but rather each loaf should be kneaded by itself.[g] Only thus, it was thought, could one be assured that each individual loaf really contained the amount of flour specified by the Torah; for each loaf that did not correspond to this measurement, which exceeded the other loaves in size or was left behind them, was considered to be unusable.[h] In order to give all the loaves the same size and shape, particular molds were used in producing them.[i] In the first the mass of dough received its shape; in a second, probably a bit larger, the dough was baked, and the loaves went into the oven two at a time;[k] after the baking, they were finally laid individually in a type of lid pan, so that they would not be damaged in transport to the site determined for them.

a. Mishnah Yoma 3.11: The following are remembered dishonorably: the family Garmu, who was not willing to teach (anyone else) how to make the show bread loaves; the family of Abtina, which was not willing to teach (anyone else) how to make the incense; the Levite Hygras, who knew how to modulate[328] (?) in singing and who was not willing to teach (anyone else); Ben Qamsar, who was not willing to teach (anyone else) writing[329] .... Of these it was said, "May the name of the wicked rot!" (Prov 10:7). ‖ Mishnah Šeqalim 5.1: The family Garmu was appointed over the making of the show bread loaves. ‖ Tosefta Yoma 2.5 (183): the family Garmu was experienced in making the show bread loaves, but

328. S-B: פֶּרֶק, literally the "taking off." "When he let his voice resound in melodiousness, he put his thumb into his mouth and his index finger onto the fold in the middle of the upper lip" (a baraita in b. Yoma 38B).

329. S-B: "He took four writing reeds in his fingers, and if there was a word of four letters, he wrote it at one time" (a baraita in b. Yoma 38B).

they were not willing to teach anyone else. The scholars had skilled people come from Alexandria; they baked just as well as those people, but they were not as experienced as they were in removing them from the oven. The family Garmu heated the oven from outside, while the bread was baked and pushed off inside. The people from Alexandria did not proceed in this way. Some say, "Their bread became moldy." When the scholars learned of this, they said, "God created the world only for his honor; as it says, 'Whoever calls himself by my name, which I have created for my honor' (Isa 43:7, so the midrash)." They sent to them (the member of the family Garmu); but they were not willing to come until their pay was doubled: (earlier) they had daily received 12 *minas* (1 *mina* = 65 German Marks), then they received 24 *minas*. R. Judah (ca. 150) said, "(Earlier) they had received 24 *minas*, then they received 48 *minas*. It was said to them, 'Why are you not willing to teach (others)?' They answered, 'Our father's house knew that the sanctuary will one day be destroyed, and they were not willing to teach (anyone), lest these be baked for an idol in the same way as for God.' Yet for the following reason one remembers them to their praise: a white (literally: pure) loaf was never found in the hand of their sons and daughters, lest the Israelites say, 'They are eating from the show bread loaves,' in order to fulfill what is said, 'You shall be pure before Yahweh and before Israel' (Num 32:22)." — In the parallel passages in y. Yoma 3.41A.35; y. Šeqal. 5.48D.55 and b. Yoma 38A, there are some differences.

b. Mishnah Menaḥot 6.6: With the show bread loaves 24 tenths of an *ephah* (of flour) were gained from 24 *seahs* (of wheat) (thus 2 tenths of an *ephah* of flour went into 1 loaf of show bread). — See b. Menaḥ. 76B: 1 tenth of an *ephah* of first-rate wheat flour was acquired from 1 *seah* of wheat. ‖ Mishnah Menaḥot 6.7: The flour of the meal offering of the *omer* (Lev 23:13) was sifted in 13 sieves (and each was finer than the other); the flour for the two (first fruit) loaves (Lev 23:17) in 12 sieves and the flour for the show bread loaves in 11 sieves. R. Simeon (ca. 150) said, "There was no fixed rule about this, but rather the fine flour was brought that had been sufficiently sifted (as often as it was necessary); as it says, 'Take fine flour and bake it for 12 cakes' (Lev 24:5), that is, after it is adequately sifted." — On the last sentence, see b. Menaḥ. 76B in a baraita: "Take fine flour and bake it" (Lev 24:5); this teaches that fine flour was taken. How do we know that ordinary wheat flour may also be taken? Scripture teaches, "Take" (generally, without qualification). Perhaps as also with the other meal offerings? Scripture teaches, "And bake it (this and not another)" (Lev 24:5), out of consideration for frugality. R. Eleazar (ca. 270) said, "What does 'out of consideration for frugality' mean?" R. Eleazar said, "The Torah deals sparingly with Israel's money (by not absolutely demanding the most expensive flour for the show bread loaves, as with the other meal offerings)." — This baraita is found in SLev 24:5 (420A).

c. Josephus, *Jewish Antiquities* 3.6.6: Ἐπὶ ταύτης (sc. show bread table) ... διετίθεσαν ἄρτων τε δώδεκα ἀζύμους κατὰ ἓξ ἀπαλλήλους κειμένους, καθαροῦ πάνυ τοῦ ἀλεύρου ἐκ δύο ἀσσαρώνων. — See *Ant.* 3.10.7 in n. *k.* ‖ Mishnah Menaḥot 5.1: All the meal offerings (among which the Mishnah consistently counts the show bread loaves) are prepared without leaven, except for the leaven in the thank offering and the two loaves of the first fruits, which are leavened. ‖ Sifra Leviticus 2:11 (51A): "No meal offering that you present to Yahweh shall be prepared with leaven" (Lev 2:11). R. Yose the Galilean (ca. 110) said, "This includes the show bread loaves."

d. See m. Menaḥ. 6.6 in n. *b*; Josephus, *Ant.* 3.6.6 in n. *c*; SLev 24:5 (420A) in notes *g* and *h*.

e. Mishnah Tamid 3.3: There were four halls there (in the northwest corner of the forecourt): one for the lambs (for the Tamid offering), one for the seals (markings on which the drink offerings appointed for the individual types of offerings were administered by those bringing offerings, m. Šeqal. 5.3); one for the site of burning (on which fire was constantly maintained for the use of the altar) and one in which the show bread loaves were prepared. ‖ Mishnah Middot 1.6: There were four halls in the house of burning, like small rooms that open onto a dining room; two of them were in the holy area and two of them in the profane space (outside the inner forecourt; cf. #5, n. *g*), and the tips of the ledges (beams) formed the division between the holy and profane place. What were they used for? The southwest hall was for the offering lambs; the southeast was the hall for the show bread loaves (these two halls were in the holy area). In the northeastern one, the Hasmoneans had hidden the altar stones that the Greek (i.e., Syrian) kings had desecrated; in the northwestern one, one descended into the immersion bath. See also t. Menaḥ. 11.1 (529).

f. Mishnah Menaḥot 11.2: Both the two loaves of the first fruits and the show bread loaves may be kneaded and prepared (rolling and opening the dough) outside (the sanctuary); yet they have to bake inside (the sanctuary). These tasks do not supersede the Sabbath (i.e., they may not be done on the Sabbath). R. Judah (ca. 150) said, "All the preparations for the show bread loaves occur within (the sanctuary)." R. Simeon (ca. 150) said, "Always be accustomed to say, 'The two loaves of the first fruits and the show bread loaves are fitting (valid), whether they are made in the forecourt or in Bethphage.'" — Somewhat broader is t. Menaḥ. 11.1 (529).

g. Mishnah Menaḥot 11.1: The two loaves of the first fruits are kneaded individually and baked individually; the show bread loaves are kneaded individually and baked two at a time. ‖ Sifra Leviticus 24:5 (420A): "There shall be two tenths (of an *ephah*) for each cake" (Lev 24:5) ...; each one should be kneaded and prepared by itself.... And how do we know that they should be put into the oven two at a time? Scripture teaches, "You shall put them (plural, so at least two)" (Lev 24:6). — The same is found as a baraita in b. Menaḥ. 94A.

h. Tosefta Menaḥot 8.2 (523): If the show bread loaves ... are bigger than the measure fixed for the cakes (2 tenths of an *ephah*), or if they fall short of this measure, if the measure of one loaf is bigger than that of the other or smaller than that of the other, they are (ritually) unsuitable. — See the general norm in b. Menaḥ. 76B.18. ‖ Sifra Leviticus 24:5 (420A.22): "Bake it into twelve cakes" (Lev 24:5), that is, they should be the same. "Each cake shall be two tenths (of an *ephah*)" (Lev 24:5), that is, they should be the same.

i. Mishnah Menaḥot 11.1: The show bread loaves were prepared in a mold, and when they were pushed off from the oven, they were put in a mold, so that they would not be damaged. — Sifra Leviticus 24:6 (421A) is more precise: "You shall put" (Lev 24:6), namely in a mold. There were three molds there. They were put in a mold when they were dough; in the oven there was a (further) mold for them, and when they had been pushed off in the oven, they were put in a (third) mold, so that they would not be damaged. — Similarly, in t. Menaḥ. 11.3 (529): here the third mold is described as אִלְפָּס (= λοπάς) "pan" (with a cover?). — The same is found in Num. Rab. 4 (142C).

k. See the citations above in n. g. — Josephus, *Jewish Antiquities* 3.10.7: "From the public means (of the temple) the show bread loaves σῖτος were baked without leaven, and 24 tenths (of an *ephah* of flour) were consumed. They were always baked two at a time on the day before the Sabbath."

2. A reliable picture of the shape of the show bread loaves, which are called "cakes" חַלּוֹת already in Lev 24:5, cannot be obtained from the contradictory traditions. A vague note indicates that the loaves were one handbreadth thick.[a] According to more precise reports, their length was 10 and their width 5 handbreadths. Aside from this, we hear that their four corners went out in horns or tips, which had a length of 7 fingerbreadths. Since according to Lev 24:6, the loaves had to be stacked in two columns next to each other on the show bread table and the tabletop itself (at least according to one view) was exactly the same size as one show bread loaf (10 handbreadths long, 5 handbreadths wide), 2 columns of loaves could be accommodated alongside each other on the table only if the loaves were laid lengthwise across the narrow side of the table. Two loaves next to each other then exactly matched with their widths the length of the table, but extended with their length beyond the front and back edge of the table by 2.5 handbreadths on each side, if one does not first consider their corner horns. To prevent these protruding parts from breaking off, one bent the 2.5 handbreadths with their corner horns first upward and then again specifically the corner horns inward.[b] So each loaf with its base surface formed a square, with each of its 4 sides being 5 handbreadths long, and as a whole took on a form that was thought to be comparable to a broken box,[c] that is, with a box that lacked a top in part and the two panels on the opposite sides (right and left) completely. — This basic form of the show bread loaves was maintained also by the older Jewish authorities that assumed the measure of the top surface of the show bread table to be somewhat bigger, namely 12 handbreadths long and 6 handbreadths wide (so in particular R. Meir [ca. 150] whose view was later received by the halakah). In this case the loaves no longer extended 2.5, but rather only 2 handbreadths in front and in back beyond the narrow side of the table, so that correspondingly only 2 handbreadths of bread in front and in back had to be turned upward. Furthermore, now the base surface of the bread had a length of 6 handbreadths and a breadth of 5 handbreadths, and thus lost its earlier square form, and finally, there was between the two columns of bread on the table a gap of 2 handbreadths, while in the case of the

measurements first mentioned above, there was no such gap between the two layers of bread at all.[d] – These are the oldest traditions present in the Mishnah that have come to us about the shape of the show bread loaves.

We obtain a completely different picture of the show bread loaves from the Tosefta and some passages in the Babylonian Talmud. Here it says that the loaves were like a ship. According to this view, from their center line outward—as it were, the keel of the emerging bread ship—the rolled-out mass of dough would have been diagonally folded upward right and left and then pressed together in front and behind, in order to let it here run out into two tips. Thus it could take a form that could be compared with a ship. This tradition, presented anonymously in the Tosefta,[e] later found a representative in R. Yohanan († 279)[f] and Rab Judah († 297).[g] – The ambivalence of the traditions above shows that Jewish scholars already in the 2nd century—strikingly enough—had no certain knowledge about the shape of the show bread loaves.

a. Babylonian Talmud Pesaḥim 37A: How thick is a thick loaf? Rab Huna († 297) said, "One hand wide. This is how we find it with the show bread loaves: one hand wide (thick)."

b. On folding the bread ends and their horns, see, aside from n. *d*, especially b. Menaḥ. 96A in #3, n. *g*.

c. For the comparison with a broken box, see b. Menaḥ. 94A in n. *f*; b. Menaḥ. 94B in #3, n. *e*; b. Menaḥ. 94B in #3, n. *h*; b. Menaḥ. 94B in #3, notes *i, m*.

d. Mishnah Menaḥot 11.4f.: The length of the two loaves of the first fruits was 7 and their width 4 handbreadths, and their horns had a length of 4 fingerbreadths. The length of the show bread loaves was 10 and their width 5 handbreadths, and their horns had a length of 7 fingerbreadths. R. Judah (ca. 150) said, "Lest you err, (remember): זד״ד יה״ז." (These are numeric formulas; the loaves of the first fruits is referred to by: זד״ד = 7 + 4 + 4; the show bread loaves by: יה״ז = 10 + 5 + 7.) .... "The length of the (show bread) table was 10 and its width 5 handbreadths. The length of a show bread loaf was 10 and its width 5 handbreadths. Its (the loaf's) length is laid across the width of the table and (from its protruding length) 2.5 handbreadths on this side and 2.5 handbreadths on that side are folded (upward); the result is that its length (5 handbreadths after the folded parts of the bread are discounted) fills out the whole width of the table." (The same goes for the second layer of bread on the table, so that between the two layers of bread there remains no gap.) These are the words of R. Judah. R. Meir (ca. 150) said, "The length of the table was 12 and its width 6 handbreadths. The length of one show bread loaf was 10 and its width 5 handbreadths. Its length is laid across the width of the table and (from its protruding length) 2 handbreadths on this side and 2 handbreadths on that side are folded (upward); then 2 handbreadths of a gap in the middle (of the two layers of bread), so that air can pass between them."

e. Tosefta Menaḥot 11.6 (529): The show bread loaves were like a ship. – See the whole passage in #3, n. *k*. – Likewise anonymous, Num. Rab. 4 (142C): The cake (= show bread) was made like a rocking ship, pointed below and folded out upward and broad. – Also, b. Menaḥ. 94B in #3, *e*; b. Menaḥ. 94B in #3, notes *h, i, k, m* and Num. Rab. 4 in #3, n. *l*.

f. Babylonian Talmud Menaḥot 94A: It has been said, "How were the show bread loaves made? R. Hanina (ca. 225) said, 'Like a broken box.' R. Yohanan said, 'Like a ship that rocks.'"

g. See b. Menaḥ. 94B.19 in #3, n. *k*.

3. The arrangement of the loaves on the show bread table. — According to Lev 24:5, twelve loaves should always lie on the show bread table before Yahweh. Here the number twelve was certainly determined by the number of the tribes of Israel.[a] Interpretations of the twelve loaves as referring to the twelve months of the year to the twelve signs of the zodiac, as Philo and Josephus are familiar with,[b] are not found in the rabbinic writings. What concerns the arrangement of the twelve loaves on the table itself is that they were stacked alongside each other in two piles, so that in each pile six loaves lay on top of one another. A different arrangement was not allowed.[c] To mitigate the pressure of the loaves on each other, as well as to facilitate air getting to the individual loaves, golden rods were laid between the layers of bread, which were cut into pieces according to their length: the first and lowest loaf of the pile lay immediately above the golden tabletop; on the first up until the fourth loaf, one laid three such half rods on each of them from front to back (from south to north): the fifth loaf, since it had to bear the weight of only one (the sixth or uppermost) load, received two rods. So for each pile of loaves, 4 × 3 + 2 = 14 rods were needed, and 28 rods for both piles.[d] — Another device was supposed to prevent the parts of the bread folded above in front and in back from crumbling (see above in #2) and also to give the rods just named a firm support and thereby a certain stability. To this end, a golden stand סָנִיף (thus altogether, four stands סְנִיפִין) was attached in front of and behind each pile of loaves, presumably a bar (slat) or pillar that, resting on the floor,[i] rose up to the highest layer of bread and was firmly fit to the folded parts of the bread by its inner side, that is, the side turned toward the table, holding and supporting them.[e] In all the sources it says that the *seniphin* were "split" מוּפְצָלִים in their upper part, that is, the part extending beyond the tabletop. The ancient Jewish interpreters (see, e.g., Rashi and the Tosafists in n. *f*) understood this in various ways so that the sides of the stands facing the loaves were furnished with grooves (incisions, notches), into which the ends of the rods that lay between the layers of bread were inserted so that here they could have a firm support point for themselves. Yet since the three rods between the individual loaves did not lie right on top of each other, but rather lay as far as possible from each other, the stands, if their grooves were to serve as deposit points for the rods, must have been almost as wide as the loaves themselves, a consequence that the Tosafists commenting on b. Menaḥ. 94B דסמכי in fact accepted.[f] In this case we would have to think of the stands as wide boards that more or less covered the entire front and back side of the table from the ground up to the very last layer of bread;

and since the whole structure extended upward beyond the table by at least twelve handbreadths,[g] the show bread table thus would have taken on the appearance of a misshapen box, completely ignoring the fact that the loaves would have completely disappeared behind the stands. One should perhaps therefore better understand סניפין מופצלים to designate "forked stands," that is, bars or posts that were furnished with pronged or branch-like fixings onto which the ends of the rods were placed (cf. the term דוּקְרָן "forked pointed post" further below). — The description of the boards is given by those rabbis who compared the shape of the show bread loaves with a "broken box" (see above in #2). — Those Jewish authorities who attributed to the show bread loaves the shape of a "ship" (see #2), assumed also that there were (28) rods as an underlay between the individual loaves; yet it remains unclear how they conceived of the arrangement of these rods and their position in more detail.[h] However, they compare the "split stands," which are supposed to have stood not on the floor, but rather on the table itself in front of and behind each stack of bread,[i] with a "forked pointed- or supporting post" דוּקְרָן = δίκρανον.[330] Accordingly, we would have to think of the stands as posts (bars) with branch-like fixings, yet with these it remains uncertain whether they were also supposed to serve as a support for the rods or rather simply for the loaves.[k] In favor of the latter, there is a passage in the late midrash work Num. Rab., where, due to a misunderstanding, דוקרן is changed into קרנין = "horns," and where it says about these horns that they supported the lowest loaf of both stacks. Here the "horns" appear to be conceived as crescent-shaped clamps that were attached to the inner side of the post (or bar) facing the table and which were placed around the front or back edge of the ship of bread.[l] However, b. Menaḥ. 94B suggests that in the stands themselves there were half-circle cavities, into which the ship-shaped bread that extended in front and in back diagonally and pointedly was inserted.[m] — In view of these traditions which appear so early and are so specific, one cannot consider the stands at the show bread table to be simply a figment of the imagination that rabbinic erudition fashioned on the basis of some misinterpreted passage of Scripture. To be sure, a scriptural proof was sought for these stands; yet the attempt arises only in the 2nd half of the 3rd century,[n] so that traditions already belonging to the 2nd century about the *seniphin* cannot have been influenced by this. It must therefore be all the more surprising, though, when an authority such as R. Yose b. Halapta (ca. 150) declares with all certainty that there were no stands, but rather that a border extended around the table that supported the loaves.[o]

---

330. See Krauß, *Lehnwörter*, 2:193f.

a. Targum Yerušalmi I Leviticus 24:5: "Take fine flour and bake it into twelve bread cakes like the twelve tribes" (read לתריסר instead of לתליסר).

b. Philo, *De profug* § 33 (Mangey's ed., 1:573): Τέλειος δ' ἀριθμὸς ὁ δώδεκα, μάρτυς δὲ ὁ ζωδιακὸς ἐν οὐρανῷ κύκλος.... Μάρτυς καὶ ἡ ἡλίου περίοδος· μησὶ γὰρ δώδεκα τὸν ἑαυτοῦ περατοῖ κύκλον.... Μωϋσῆς δ' οὐκ ἐν ὀλίγοις ὑμνεῖ τὸν ἀριθμὸν, δώδεκα φυλὰς τοῦ ἔφνους ἀναγράφων, ἄρτους δώδεκα τῆς προθέσεως νομοθετῶν.... — Philo, *De victim* § 3 (Mangey's ed., 2:239): Ἄρτοι δὲ προτίθενται ταῖς ἑβδόμαις ἐπὶ τῆς ἱερᾶς τραπέζης ἰσάριθμοι τοῖς μησὶ τοῦ ἐνιαυτοῦ.... ‖ Josephus, *Jewish War* 5.5.5: ἐνέφαινον δὲ οἱ μὲν ἑπτὰ λύχνοι τοὺς πλανήτας ... οἱ δὲ ἐπὶ τῆς τραπέζης ἄρτοι δώδεκα τόν τε ζωδιακὸν κύκλον καὶ τὸν ἐνιαυτόν.

c. Tosefta Menaḥot 11.14 (530): How are the show bread loaves arranged (on the table)? Six cakes חַלּוֹת are laid in one column and six in the other column. If eight cakes have been put in one column and four cakes in the other column, or if three columns of four cakes each have been laid, nothing has been done (the whole presentation of the bread is invalid). If two columns of 14 loaves have been made, then according to Rabbi († 217?) the two upper ones are viewed as if they were not present, and the (twelve) below are valid. — The same is found in b. Menaḥ. 98A; Num. Rab. 4 (142C); Rabbi's saying is also found in y. Pesaḥ. 7.34A.39. ‖ Similarly, SLev 24:6 (421A) and b. Menaḥ. 98A.

d. Mishnah Menaḥot 11.6: There were 28 rods there, like the halves of a hollow reed: 14 for the one and 14 for the other column of bread. — The same is found in SLev 24:6 (421A). ‖ Tosefta Menaḥot 11.7 (530): There were 28 golden rods which were split (lengthwise) and made one unclean. — Tosefta Menaḥot 11.16 (530): How were the rods arranged? After the Sabbath (on which new loaves were put on the table), one went in (to the holy place), raised one end of the cake and put a rod under it; then one raised the other (של should be deleted) end and put a (second) rod under it and one (the third rod) in the middle. There were three rods under each cake and two under the uppermost, because no weight rested on it (on the pressure of the weight, see also b. Menaḥ. 94B in the following n. *e*); yet the lowest cake was laid on the pure table. — Parallels are found in b. Menaḥ. 97A; Num. Rab. 4 (142C). — Tosefta Menaḥot 11.15 (530): If there was something separating between the (lowest) bread and the table, they (the loaves) were unsuitable (the presentation of the loaves was invalid). — The same is found in Num. Rab. 4 (142C), yet here instead of פטורין one should read פסולין. ‖ Numbers Rabbah 4 (142C.26): Why were rods placed between them? So that air could have free access to them (literally: reign over them) and so that the bread would not get moldy. And why were the rods made like the halves of a hollow reed? So that they would not be too heavy on the bread. — See b. Menaḥ. 97A: What was the reason (for putting the rods under the loaves)? So that the bread would not get moldy.

e. Mishnah Menaḥot 11.6: There were four golden stands סְנִיפִין there that were split מוּפְצָלִין in their upper parts (those extending beyond the table), with which the loaves were supported: two for one column of bread and two for the other. — The same is found in SLev 24:6 (421A). ‖ Babylonian Talmud Menaḥot 94B: In support of someone who says that the show bread loaves were like a rocking ship is the fact that they needed a stand (as a support); yet according to the one who says that they were like a broken box, what were the stands for? Due to the weights of the loaves, they could break. – On the stands, see further in notes *i, k, l, m, n*.

f. Tosafot on b. Menaḥ. 94B דסמכי: "It appears as if the stands were 5 handbreadths wide, corresponding to the width of the loaf, and in their upper parts they were notched (this is probably what מפוצלין means); for in the commentary (Rashi on b. Menaḥ. 94B) it says that the ends of the rods of each loaf rested in those notches פיצולין (clefts)."

g. Babylonian Talmud Menaḥot 96A: R. Yohanan († 279) said, "According to the words of the one who says, '2.5 handbreadths are folded' (upward in front and in back of the loaves), (such as R. Judah, see #2), one finds that the table sanctifies 15 handbreadths upward (beyond the tabletop); according to the words of the one who says, '2 handbreadths are folded' (such as R. Meir, see #2), one finds that the table sanctifies 12 handbreadths high. (The setup of the bread on the table thus had a height of at least 12 handbreadths.) Yet the rods were there (which must have made the setup rise even higher)! They were pressed (into the loaves, so that they did not bear them up higher). Why (was there an underlay of rods)? So that the bread would not get moldy. Yet ultimately (if the rods were completely pressed into the loaves) the bread would have gotten moldy! The rods raised the bread a little (so that the air had access, and thus were not fully pressed into the bread). Yet then there was this little bit (which, repeated five times, must have made the setup higher)! Since (together) they did not constitute a handbreadth, it was not included in the calculation (in the statements made above about the height). Yet the incense bowls were there (which, according to the view of those who had the 2.5 handbreadths at the ends of the bread folded upward, stood on both stacks of bread and so made the setup higher)! (According to the view of those who had only 2 handbreadths folded), they were set between the two columns of bread, and they stood right next to the loaves. Yet there were the horns (on the 4 corners of the loaves)! The horns of the loaves were folded inward so that the loaves rested on them."

h. Babylonian Talmud Menaḥot 94B: In favor of the one who said that the show bread loaves were like a broken box is the fact that the rods lay on them; yet according to the one who said that they were like a rocking ship, how could the rods lie on them (they could not have served as an underlay for a ship-shaped loaf)?! A tip was made for the loaves (from the dough, right and left, on both ends, and the rods were put over this, so according to Rashi).

i. Babylonian Talmud Menaḥot 94B: In favor of the one who said that the show bread loaves were like a rocking ship is the fact that the stands rested on the table; yet according to the one who said that they were like a broken box, where were the stands placed? They were placed on the floor. Yes, so it is; for R. Abba b. Memel (Mammel? [ca. 300]) said, "According to the words of the one who says that the show bread loaves were like a rocking ship, the stands stood on the table; according to the words of the one who says that they were like a broken box, the stands stood on the floor."

k. Tosefta Menaḥot 11.6 (529): There were four stands of gold that were like forked supporting posts דקרנין; with these the cake was supported, because it was like a ship, so that it would not rock. – The same is found as a baraita in b. Menaḥ. 95A. ‖ Babylonian Talmud Menaḥot 94B: With whose opinion did what Rab Judah († 299) said comply: "The loaves held the stands and the stands held the loaves"? With the opinion of the one who said that the show bread loaves were like a rocking ship.

l. Numbers Rabbah 4 (142C): "Four stands of gold were like it, and its horns"[331] were there, for with them the lowest loaf was supported, two (of the stands) for this column (of bread) and two for that column, because the loaves were like a ship, so that they did not rock. And the stands were before (opposite) the bread, so that the stands would not raise the bread from the table. And what does "the bowls 'of the covering'" (so the midrash interprets הנסך in Num 4:7) mean? For they (the stands = bowls of the covering) also held up the ends of the of the lowest loaves, which (namely, the ends) did not touch the table, and (thus) covered the table. Yet the middle of the lowest loaf (the keel of the ship-shaped bread) touched the table, because the bread was made like a rocking ship, with a point below and folded out above and wide. — According to this explanation, the stands would have served as a support only for the two lowest loaves.

m. Babylonian Talmud Menaḥot 94B: In favor of the one who said that the show bread loaves were like a broken box is the fact that the stands supported the loaves (by being attached in front and behind to the folded sides of the loaves); yet according to the one who said that they were like a rocking ship, how could the stands support the loaves (which came to a point in front and in back)? They (the stands) were made (hollowed out) in half-circle shapes.

n. Babylonian Talmud Menaḥot 97A: There were four stands of gold. How do we know this? Rab Qattina (ca. 270) said, "Scripture says, 'And make its bowls קערתיו and its pans וכפתיו and its jugs וקשותיו and its basins ומנקיתיו' (Exod 25:29). קערתיו: these are the molds (in which the loaves were shaped and baked); כפתיו: these are the basins (for the incense); קשותיו: these are the stands; and מנקיתיו: these are the rods. 'With which it was covered' (so the midrash understands יֻסַּךְ in Lev 25:29); for with them (the rods) the loaves were covered מסככין." — A similar scriptural proof, though anonymous and more expansive, is also found in Num. Rab. 4 (142C.2–39). — See also Tg. Yer. I Exod. 37:16, where קסויתא דמחפין בהון presumably is supposed to designate the rods with which (the loaves) were covered. Differently, Tg. Yer. I Exod. 25:29 and Num 4:7.

o. Tosefta Menaḥot 11.6 (529): R. Yose (ca. 150) said, "There were no stands, but rather there was a ridge at the table that was one handbreadth high; as it says, 'You shall make a bar around it that is one handbreadth' (Exod 25:25). He was answered, 'Was the bar not simply at the feet (of the table)?'" ‖ Babylonian Talmud Menaḥot 96B: According to the one who said, "Its (the table's) bar was above," it rose diagonally outward and the bread lay on the table (not on the bar), as it says in a baraita: R. Yose (ca. 150) said, "There were no stands, but rather the bar of the table held the bread." He was answered, "Its bar was below."

4. The incense offering. — According to Lev 24:7, pure incense had to be placed on each column (stack) of bread. From the Jewish tradition we hear that the incense reached the show bread table in two bowls (בָּזִיךְ).[a] According to the practice of the temple, which is attested to by Josephus,

331. S-B: דומין לו וקרניו, these words are misunderstood from t. Menaḥ. 11.6 (see n. *k*): דומין לדקרנין = "they were like forked supporting posts."

the bowls stood with the incense on top of the loaves.[b] The rabbinic scholars disputed about the placement of the incense: some shared the view of Josephus, others represented the opinion that the two bowls with the incense were placed on the table itself in the gap between the two stacks of bread (see above #2, n. *d*).[c] The latter opinion was (according to Maimonides) recognized as halakah, presumably on the basis of the authority of Rabbi († 217?).[d] Aside from incense, salt was also placed on the show bread loaves, according to LXX Lev 24:7. Philo's view, which accords with this, is probably simply derived from the LXX, without presenting an independent tradition.[e] Rabbinic literature knows only that salt was mixed in as an ingredient with the incense of the show bread loaves; see b. Menaḥ. 20A at § Mark 9:49 B, n. *c*; a parallel is found in SLev 2:13 (53B). The incense was renewed every Saturday at the same time as the show bread loaves. Then the old incense arrived at the altar of burnt offering as a part of the fragrance אַזְכָּרָה in the morning Tamid offering on the Sabbath.[f]

a. Sifra Leviticus 24:7 (421A): "'Put it on the column' (Lev 24:7); (only) on one column? Look, I infer: It says here, 'the column' and it says there (Lev 24:6): six 'the column.' As the column that is spoken of there comprises two columns, so the column that is spoken of here comprises two columns. 'Pure incense' (Lev 24:7); it should be the choicest. 'It shall serve for the bread' (Lev 24:7); it is obligatory for the bread. 'It shall serve for the bread': this teaches that it impedes the bread, makes it objectionable and unsuitable (incense that is presented at the wrong time or in the wrong place or in the wrong way makes the presentation of the show bread loaves invalid). 'It shall serve for the bread': it shall not lie (directly) on the bread, but rather it shall be put in two bowls בזיכים that have a bottom rim (for stability), and they shall be placed on the table (in accordance with the later halakah, see notes *b, c, d*), so that they do not make the bread crumble. 'It shall serve for the bread as a component of the fragrance' (Lev 24:7)." R. Simeon (ca. 150) said, "It says here 'component of the fragrance' and it says there (Lev 5:12) 'component of the fragrance.' Just as the component of the fragrance that is mentioned there is a handful (as much as can be grasped with the three middle fingers), so too here a handful. This teaches that it (the component of the fragrance) must contain two handfuls, one handful for this column of bread and one handful for that column of bread." ‖ Tosefta Menaḥot 11.12 (530): Two handfuls of incense are put (in the two bowls). All the bowls in the sanctuary did not have a bottom rim, except for these, which had one.

b. Josephus, *Jewish Antiquities* 3.6.6: "Two golden bowls full of incense were placed on the loaves." – *Antiquities* 3.10.7: "Early on the Sabbath (the show bread loaves) were brought and placed on the holy table, six opposite each other. After two golden bowls full of incense were placed on them, these remained until the next Sabbath. Then others are brought to replace them, but the old ones are given as food to the priests, while the incense went up in some over the holy fire, on which they also burnt the whole burnt offering. Yet this incense was replaced with other incense on the loaves." – See also LXX Lev 24:7 in n. *e*.

c. Tosefta Menaḥot 11.15 (530): How were the bowls (with the incense) arranged? One bowl was placed on top of one column of bread and the other bowl on top of the other column of bread. If the bowls were placed without incense or the incense was set down without bowls, or if there was something separating the bowls and the loaves or the loaves and the table, behold, they were invalid. Abba Saul (ca. 150) said, "Two bowls were placed in the gap that was two handbreadths wide between the two columns of bread (see R. Meir above in #2, *d*). Yet how do I maintain the following, 'You shall put pure incense on על the column' (Lev 24:7)? It should lie right nearby the column." — The same is found in Num. Rab. 4 (142C). ‖ Mishnah Menaḥot 11.5: Abba Saul (ca. 150) said, "There (in the gap between the two columns of bread) the two bowls were set down with the incense for the show bread loaves." He was told, "Was it not said long ago, 'You shall put pure incense on על the column' (Lev 24:7)?" He answered them, "Was it not said long ago, 'And alongside (beside) it ועלוו the tribe of Manasseh' (Num 2:20)?" (Thus על does not necessarily mean "on"). — See another parallel in y. Pesaḥ. 7.34A.37; also see b. Menaḥ. 96A above in #3, n. *g*.

d. A baraita in b. Menaḥ. 98A: Rabbi († 217?) said, "'You shall lay pure incense על המערכת' (Lev 24:7); על means 'close to.' You say, 'על means "close to"; does it not rather mean "on" in the literal sense? Since it says, "Cover the curtain in front of על the ark" (Exod 40:3), say: על means "close by."'"

e. Septuagint Leviticus 24:7: καὶ ἐπιθήσετε ἐπὶ τὸ θέμα (= on the column of bread) λίβανον καθαρὸν καὶ ἅλα. ‖ Philo, *De vita Mosis* 3 § 10 (Mangey's ed., 2:151): Ἡ δὲ τράπεζα τίθεται πρὸς τοῖς βορείοις, ἐφ ᾗς ἄρτοι καὶ ἅλες. — *De victim* § 3 (Mangey's ed., 2:239): Συνεπιτίθεται δὲ τοῖς ἄρτοις λιβανωτὸς καὶ ἅλες.

f. See Josephus, *Ant.* 3.10.7 above in n. *b*. ‖ Tosefta Menaḥot 11.12 (530): On the morning (of the Sabbath), after the blood of the Tamid offering was sprinkled, two priests took two bowls and put in them two handfuls of incense (to bring this to the show bread table). ‖ Tosefta Menaḥot 11.13 (530): Both those priests in whose hands were the two bowls with the old (cleaned away) incense of the show bread loaves, brought this together with the parts (offering pieces) of the Tamid lamb onto the altar. — See further SLev 24:8 in #5, n. *a*; m. Menaḥ. 11.7 in #5, notes *c*, *e*; t. Menaḥ. 11.13 (530) in #5, n. *e*.

5. The weekly renewal of the show bread loaves and their distribution to the priesthood. — The show bread loaves were always out for eight days, from one Sabbath to the next.[a] In the morning hours of the Sabbath, four priests appeared in the holy place of the temple building in order to clean away the old and put out the new show bread loaves with a certain formality and solemnity. The preparatory and closing tasks, which involved replacing the loaves, were carried out on the day before (Friday) and the day after (Sunday).[b] The incense was replaced at the same time as the loaves; here as well four priests were active.[c] The old loaves which were cleared away were then set on the golden table in the temple forehall אוּלָם.[d] Then, after the old incense, which had also been removed, had been burned in the presentation of the morning Tamid offering as a component of the fragrance for the show bread loaves, the latter were distributed

to the priesthood; those priests who were departing from the weekly service on the Sabbath in question and those who were newly taking it up each received six loaves;[e] for festivals, there were special regulations.[f] The weekly division of priests themselves distributed the loaves to the individual priests, the departing on the south side, and the newly arriving on the north side of the altar of burnt offering.[e] The loaves could be eaten only by the priests, and only in a holy place, that is, probably in the inner forecourt.[g] Legend asserts that by a miracle the loaves were just as fresh when they were removed (and therefore just as tasty) as when they were set out.[h] Then again, though, it is also lamented that the loaves had lost their nourishing power since the death of Simeon the Righteous (II, ca. 200 BCE).[i]

a. See Josephus, *Ant.* 3.10.7 in #4, n. *b.* ‖ Sifra Leviticus 24:8 (421A): "On the Sabbath day" (Lev 24:8); on the Sabbath day the new (loaves) are stacked and on the Sabbath the old (incense) is presented as incense.

b. Mishnah Menaḥot 11.6: Neither arranging the rods (between the individual loaves) nor removing them supersedes the Sabbath (thus, these tasks may not be performed on a Sabbath). Rather, one goes in on the day of preparation for the Sabbath and removes them and sets them in the length orientation of the table (in an east-west orientation). All the implements in the sanctuary were oriented with their long axis oriented to the length orientation of the temple (except for the ark of the covenant). In SLev 24:8 (422A), the following words come next: And after the Sabbath one went in and arranged three (rods) under each loaf and two under the uppermost, because there was no weight on it. — See the parallel to the last sentence in t. Menaḥ. 11.16 (530) in #3, n. *d*; elements of this are also found as a baraita in b. Menaḥ. 99A. ‖ Tosefta Menaḥot 11.12 (530): How were the show bread loaves brought in (to the holy place of the temple)? On the day of preparation for the Sabbath they were taken out of the old and placed on the table that was located in the forehall of the temple near the entrance to the sanctuary. (On this table, see in the next n. *c.*)

c. Mishnah Menaḥot 11.7: There were two tables inside the forehall אוּלָם near the entrance to the sanctuary: one of marble and one of gold. On the one of marble, the show bread loaves were placed on the one of marble when they were brought in (see the last citation in n. *b*), and on the one of gold when they were brought out; for one makes them rise in holiness, but not sink. There is a table of gold (in the holy place) on which there are constantly show bread loaves. Four priests go in (on the Sabbath): two hold the two columns of bread in their hands, and two hold the two bowls of incense in their hands. Four (priests) went in before them, two to remove the two (old) columns of bread, and two to remove the two (old) bowls of incense. Those who carry them in place them on the north side (of the table) with their face to the south; those carrying them out place them on the south side (of the table) with their face to the north. The latter remove (the old loaves) and set the former (the new loaves) down, and the handbreadth of the latter (at which the bread is removed by the one) exactly matches the handbreadth of the former (at which the bread is placed by the other); for it says, "Lay show bread constantly on the table before me" (Exod 25:30) (thus, the table cannot be without the show bread loaves for a moment). R. Yose (ca. 150) said, "Even if they (first) remove (everything) and others (then) put down the new, the 'constant' is still preserved." — The same with variations in t. Menaḥ. 11.12 (530).

d. Mishnah Menaḥot 11.7 (Continuation of the citation in n. *c*): Then the priests went out (from the holy place with the old loaves) and set them down on the golden table in the forehall (see n. *c*). ‖ Tosefta Menaḥot 11.9ff. (530): Solomon had ten tables made (see 2 Chr 4:8); yet loaves were placed only on the table of Moses (see 1 Kgs 7:48) .... R. Yose b. Judah (ca. 180) said, "Loaves were placed on all the tables; for it says, 'The tables with the show bread on them' (2 Chr 4:19) ...." In the name of R. Eleazar b. Shammuah (ca. 150) it has been said, "What does Scripture mean to teach with 'The tables with the show bread on them' (2 Chr 4:19)? This refers to the golden table in the inner place of the temple and the table that stood in the forehall near the entrance to the sanctuary, on which the old show bread loaves were placed."

e. Mishnah Menaḥot 11.7: (After the old show bread loaves were placed on the golden table in the forehall of the temple,) the (two) bowls (of incense) were presented as an incense offering; however, the cakes (show bread loaves) were distributed. If the Day of Atonement fell on a Sabbath, the cakes were distributed (only) in the evening (so that the priests would not be tempted to eat them on the Day of Atonement itself, which was a great fasting day). ‖ Tosefta Menaḥot 11.13 (530): Those two priests in whose hands were the two bowls with the incense for the old show bread loaves brought these together with the limbs (offering pieces) of the Tamid lamb onto the altar. After the two bowls (of incense) were presented as incense offerings, half of the loaves were given to each division of priests (the departing and the newly arriving), and they distribute them among themselves. R. Judah (ca. 150) said, "The one who distributed the show bread loaves stood on the stone floor in the forehall of the temple, broke (the loaves), set them down, and each (priest) came and took his portion; yet those among the priests afflicted with blemishes had their portion brought out to them, because they could not come between the forehall and the altar of burnt offering." ‖ Mishnah Sukkah 5.8: On the other (Sabbath) days of the year (that did not coincide with a festival) the newly arriving division of priests received six loaves and the departing also received six loaves. R. Judah (ca. 150) said, "The arriving received seven and the departing five. The arriving distributed in the north (of the altar of burnt offering), the separating in the south. The class of Bilgah always distributed in the south. (See § Luke 1:5, A, #5, n. *d*; parallels to be added to those at § Luke 1:5 are found in t. Sukkah 4.28 [200.15] and y. Sukkah 5.55D.33.) ‖ Sifra Leviticus 24:9 (422A): "It shall belong to Aaron and to his sons ...; it belongs to him (Aaron) as sacrosanct" (Lev 24:9). "It belongs to him" (Aaron); to him alone? Scripture teaches, "And to his sons." If to his sons, then to his sons and not to him? Scripture teaches, "To Aaron." How then? To Aaron without division and to his sons by division; as Aaron as high priest may eat without division, so too his sons who are high priests may eat without division. (The high priests may take from it as they please, without being bound to the measure of the rule of division.)

f. Mishnah Sukkah 5.7f.: At three times in the year, all the divisions of the priests participated equally in the offering pieces of the festal offerings and in the division of the show bread loaves. (The three times were the three great feasts, at which all the divisions of priests were present to serve in Jerusalem.) At the feast of weeks (if it fell on a Sabbath) he (the priest) was told, "Here you have something unleavened (i.e., from the show bread loaves; see #1, n. *c*)! Here you have something leavened (i.e., from the two first fruits loaves, Lev 23:17) ...." If a feast day was right alongside the Sabbath, whether before or after, all the divisions of priests were equal in the division of the show bread loaves (since all had to be present in Jerusalem on the Sabbath in question on which the division of the show bread occurred). Yet if a day fell between them (so that the priests who helped could depart already before the Sabbath or would have had to come only after the Sabbath), the divisions of priests who just had their appointed time of service received ten loaves (so the departing weekly division five and the newly arriving also received five); yet those who tarried longer received two loaves. (The explanation for the last sentence is controversial.)

g. Sifra Leviticus 24:9 (422A): "It shall belong to Aaron and to his sons, and they shall eat it in a holy place" (Lev 24:9); this teaches that the eating should occur in a holy place. – See SLev 6:9 (137A): "It shall be eaten in a holy place" (Lev 6:9). Perhaps in the camp of the Levites (= in the outer forecourt)?[332] Scripture teaches: "In the forecourt of the tent of revelation they shall eat it" (Lev 6:9). Here I hear only about the forecourt of the tent of revelation; how do we know that this includes the halls that are erected in the profane area (the outer forecourt), but stand open in the holy place (have their exits to the inner forecourt)? Scripture teaches, "In a holy place." – These passages together with SNum 5:3 § 1 (see S-B footnote) make it virtually certain that the inner forecourt was understood as the holy place where the show bread loaves should be eaten. ‖ Mishnah Menaḥot 11.9: The show bread loaves were never eaten before the 9th nor after the 11th day (from when they were made). How so? They were baked on the day of preparation for the Sabbath (= Friday) and eaten on the Sabbath (the next week), so on the 9th day. If a feast day fell on the day of preparation for the Sabbath (so that they had to be baked already on Thursday), they were eaten on the 10th day. If the two feast days of the New Year fell on the days before the Sabbath (so that the loaves had to be baked already on Wednesday), the loaves were eaten on the 11th day, since it (the baking) supersedes neither the Sabbath nor a feast day. Rabban Simeon b. Gamaliel (ca. 140) said in the name of R. Simeon, the son of the chief of the priests, "It supersedes the feast day, but not the day of fasting (i.e., the Day of Atonement)."

h. Babylonian Talmud Menaḥot 29A: Resh Laqish (ca. 250) said, "... The show bread table was raised high for the festival pilgrims and the show bread loaves were shown to them and they were told, 'See your love (i.e., how you are beloved) before God!' What does 'your love' mean? It is as R. Joshua b. Levi (ca. 250) said. For R. Joshua b. Levi said, 'A great miracle (regularly) occurred with the show bread loaves: their removal as well as

---

332. S-B: Sifre Numbers 5:3 § 1 (1B): "Lest they make their camp unclean" (Num 5:3). From this it has been said, "There are three camps: the camp of the Israelites and the camp of the Levites, and the camp of the Shekinah (divinity). From the entrance of Jerusalem to the temple mountain is the camp of the Israelites; from the entrance of the temple mountain to the (inner) forecourt is the camp of the Levites; from the entrance of the (inner) forecourt and beyond is the camp of the Shekinah."

their stacking (as they were layered, they were also taken away); as it says, "By placing the bread warm on the day when it was removed (from the show bread table)" (so Midr. 1 Sam. 21:7).'" — God's love for Israel was revealed in that, as a result of a divine miracle, the show bread loaves were just as warm (and tasty) when they were removed as on the day they were set out. — Parallels are found in b. Menaḥ. 96B; b. Ḥag. 26B; b. Yoma 21A.

i. A baraita in b. Yoma 39A: (Until the death of Simeon the Righteous) a blessing was put into the sheaf (for the first fruits, Lev 23:10ff.) and into the two loaves (of the first fruits, Lev 23:17f.) and into the show bread loaves; and each priest, who acquired even as much as the size of an olive from this, ate and was satisfied, and another ate and had some left over. From then on, a curse was put into the sheaf (for the first fruits) and into the two loaves (of the first fruits) and into the show bread loaves; and each priest received as much as the size of a bean: the modest withdrew their hands from this, and the greedy took and ate (without being satisfied). It happened that one took his portion and the portion of his companion; then he was called until the day of his death בן הַמְּצָן (maybe: "son of greed"). — Levy vocalizes it as הִמְּצָן "one who often eats chickpeas,"[333] because he had snatched his portion and the portion of his companion, which was as big as a chickpea. In favor of this explanation there is particularly the parallel in y. Yoma 6.43C.54, where instead of בן המצן we read בֶּן הָאָפוֹן "son of a chickpea." — A partial parallel is found in b. Qidd. 53A as well.

9:3 A: Behind the second curtain.

"The second curtain" τὸ δεύτερον καταπέτασμα, a designation for the curtain in front of the holy of holies; opposite: "the first curtain," that is, the curtain in front of the entrance to the holy place. Philo, *De vita Mosis* 3 § 9 (Mangey's ed., 2:150) distinguishes between the two curtains linguistically so that he calls the one in front of the holy of holies καταπέτασμα and the one in front of the holy place κάλυμμα "cover, veil." — On the two curtains, see § Matt 27:51 A, #2 and #3. In § Matt 27:51 A, #3, a passage from m. Yoma 5.1 is adduced, which depicted the curtain in front of the holy of holies as a double curtain, which consisted of two curtains, between which there was a space of one cubit. We did not go into this question in more detail at § Matt 27:51. Mr. D. Heinrich Laible has very kindly provided us with an essay in which this question is thoroughly dealt with. We gladly provide the essay here in the following, even if we cannot follow the views of the author.

Supplement on Matthew 27:51

There was one curtain that separated the holy of holies from the holy place says some sources; others say two. Among the first is the priest Josephus (born 37), who saw the temple for 33 years. He writes in his *Jewish War* 5.5.5: "The innermost division of the temple

333. Levy, *Chaldäisches Wörterbuch*, 2:74B.

(the holy of holies) was divided from the outer ('the outer house,' as the holy place is called in m. Yoma 5.1) in the same way by a curtain (καταπετάσματι, sg.)," in the same way namely as the holy place was from the forecourt. The singularity of the curtain hanging in front of the holy of holies could not be expressed more clearly. The older Tannaim, who still saw the temple or were students of eyewitnesses, are in agreement with Josephus. Rabbi Simon, son of the (last) chief priest, says in m. Šeqal. 8.5: "The thickness of the curtain (singular!) was 1 handbreadth, its length 40 cubits, its width 20 cubits, and two were made every year." To clarify the last passage, the Tosefta on it adduces a saying of R. Hananiah ben Antigonos, who, according to t. ʿArak. 1 toward the end, witnessed the temple service: "There were two curtains there, one raised and the other a battered one. If the raised one became (Levitically) unclean, the battered one was hung up. On the day of preparation for the Day of Atonement the new one was brought in and the old one was carried out." A dispute between R. Judah ben Ilai and R. Nehemiah about this curtain (singular) that was carried out is reported in t. Šeqal. 3.13ff. The teacher of Judah was R. Tarfon, who still witnessed the temple service in his youth (see y. Yoma 40.62). This R. Judah claims: "It was hung up outside in front of the temple entrance," against which R. Nehemiah says, "in the upper holy of holies juxtaposed to the lower one." Neither of the disputants knows anything about the two curtains. Another student of R. Tarfon, R. Yose ben Halapta, uses a scriptural proof to reject (m. Yoma 5.1) the claim of his colleagues that the high priest went through two curtains into the holy of holies: "The curtain (singular!) shall make for you a division between the holy place and the holy of holies." Why does R. Yose not use a שמעתי ("I have heard") to invoke the authority of his teacher Tarfon? Precisely because he, in not giving the contrary "two," never had reason to explicitly assert the singularity of the curtain. — A third student of Tarfon is R. Yose the Galilean, "very valued by Tarfon as a sole worthy opponent to Aqiba."[334] We encounter him in a baraita (b. Yoma 58B, cf. m. Yoma 5.5 and t. Yoma 4 [3] 1), which deals with the question: with which horn did the high priest coming out from the holy of holies begin atoning for the altar of the incense offering? We read: "Where did he make a beginning? (Answer:) 'On the southeast horn, then followed the southwest, the northwest, the northeast.' These are the words of R. Aqiba. R. Yose the Galilean says, 'At the northeast, then followed the northwest, the southwest, the southeast.'" Thus the baraita. Thus, according to R. Aqiba, the high priest who began with the southeast horn had come out from the holy of holies in the south, that is, at the south end of the outer curtain. He thus presupposes two curtains. However, R. Yose the Galilean, who has the high priest come out at the north end of the curtain at the actual entrance to the holy of holies and therefore starts with the northeast horn, knows of only one curtain. — Yet we also encounter another baraita in b. Yoma 51B in which R. Judah ben Ilai, the first among the three students of Tarfon named above, no longer as there asserts a singularity, but rather a duality of curtains. The baraita reads: "'He (the high priest who goes through the holy place to the entrance of the holy of holies) stepped between the altar of the incense offering and the lampstand.' These are the words of R. Judah. Yet R. Meir says, 'Between

334. Bacher, *Die Agada der Tannaïten*, 1:359.

the altar and the show bread table.'" If R. Judah has the high priest take a path past the lampstand, he has him go to the southern entrance, and thus to the southern end of the outer curtain. Thereby he presupposes two curtains. Yet R. Meir, who has the high priest pass by the show bread table, which was near the northern entrance, knows of only one curtain. R. Judah thus later gave up his earlier view that he represented in that controversy with R. Nehemiah, and adopted the teaching of Aqiba, his other teacher, who, as we saw above (b. Yoma 58B), represented the duality of the curtains. Elsewhere the rabbis withdraw earlier views (הזר בו).

Thus far the incontestable witnesses are for the singularity of the curtain. Opposed to them stands R. Aqiba, as we just saw above, and t. Yoma 3 (2).4, 5. Here we read: "He (the high priest) went barefoot (on the Day of Atonement) through the holy place until he reached the place between the two curtains, which separated the holy place and the holy of holies, and between them there was a distance of one cubit. – R. Yose ben Halapta says, 'There was only one curtain there; for it says, "The curtain shall make for you a division between the holy place and the holy of holies" (Exod 26:33).' – The outer one was affixed on the south side, the inner one on the north side. Between the two he stepped barefoot until he reached the north side. Having reached the north side (and having gone into the holy of holies), he turned his face to the south and stepped barefoot on the curtain to the left until he reached the ark. Having reached the ark, he pressed the curtain back with his hips and put down his pan between the two poles, piled the incense on the coals, and the house was filled with the smoke. Then he went out, going in the same way as he had gone in, and he prayed in the outer house a short prayer. He did not do it long, lest he scare the Israelites." Here, the Tosefta contains the same text that we find verbatim in the parallel in m. Yoma 5.1. It is a striking double! Can, one asks, the Tosefta, whose purpose is to provide a complementary or corrective marginal gloss to the text of the Mishnah, have made a marginal gloss that is completely identical with the Mishnah and of such significant extent? One has to remember that the Mishnah redactor Judah I made the Mishnah of R. Meir the basis for his work.[335] In R. Meir's Mishnah, though, nothing was written other than what we read in the baraita in b. Yoma 51B, namely that R. Meir said, "between the altar and the show bread table" (the high priest went to the north end of the curtain). This text of Meir's Mishnah was furnished with a corrective gloss by the Tosefta scribe. And this Tosefta scholion, which also agreed with the Mishnah of Aqiba (cf. the baraita above in b. Yoma 58B), was adopted by the Mishnah redactor in its current place, after he deleted the passage of Meir's Mishnah. Mishnah Yoma 5.1 is among the Tosefta texts worked into the Mishnah, which are dealt with in the 4th chapter of A. Spanier's *Die Toseftaperiode in der tannaitischen Literatur*: "The scholia as a source of the last Mishnah redactor."[336]

The Tosefta scribe, of course, did not by himself make up his scholion about the two curtains. What he wrote was an old school tradition from the period when the temple existed, which cannot have been unknown to those witnesses known to us by name, who saw the

335. See Strack, *Einleitung in den Talmud und Midraš*, 18.

336. A. Spanier, *Die Toseftaperiode in der tannaitischen Literatur* (Berlin: C. A. Schwetschke, 1922).

temple. However, these, since they knew "the" curtain as eyewitnesses, must understand the tradition differently than the Tosefta scribe. For them, the tradition was about an exceptional case that appeared once, which was of a peculiar sort, so that it could not be forgotten but rather lived on in the tradition. Once, at the time when the temple stood, there was the extraordinary case that the high priest on the Day of Atonement went into the holy of holies through two curtains, first through an outer one whose entrance was in the south, and then through the inner one, whose entrance was in the north. Something had happened that had made it necessary to veil the inner curtain by means of an outer curtain hung up in front of it. The tradition is silent about the latter. It must have been of an embarrassing nature. Yet light comes into darkness with Matt 27:51: "The curtain of the temple was torn in two pieces, from top to bottom." It was in the hour of Jesus' death when this tear occurred by an invisible hand, at the same time as the collapse of the lintel of the temple entrance reported by the Gospel of the Hebrews, a consequence of the severe earthquake that accompanied the death of Jesus. It is understandable that there was reluctance about immediately removing the curtain that had been torn asunder in such an uncanny way and to replace it with a reserve curtain; and in any case there was also a concern about showing the torn curtain to the people, which would have been unavoidable if it had been carried out. So, it was left hanging as it hung, and in front of it, at a distance of a cubit (called a cubit *traxin* or *trixin*), a second curtain (probably the reserve curtain) was hung up, whereby the opened holy of holies was closed again and the torn curtain removed from view. About all this, the Jewish tradition is understandably silent. Yet it retained the memory of the Day of Atonement that followed this Passover, where the high priest, which had never happened before, went through two curtains. (Whether the inner one was still the torn one on this Day of Atonement and whether simply the outer one had been replaced on the day of preparation cannot be determined.) This event must have been something jarring even for the Sadducee Caiaphas. For the two curtains vividly reminded him of the prodigious occurrence from the previous Passover, which in a brief time had been connected with further prodigious events pointing to the destruction of the temple, especially that the call of spirits that was heard at night on Pentecost by the priests in the forecourt, stronger than a human voice: "Arise! Let us go away from here!," accompanied by a din of invisible armies moving out. (These prodigious occurrences do not fall in the last times of the temple, as is often supposed; for Josephus narrates them in *Jewish War* 5.5.3 not as an eyewitness, but rather as one who has taken them from the records of eyewitnesses who lived before him.[337]) Therefore, the tradition (t. Yoma 3 [2].5) of the anonymous high priest, who on the Day of Atonement after coming out from the holy of holies gave expression about his serious concerns about the endurance of the sanctuary in a rather long prayer for the preservation of the temple, fits no high priest so well as the one who had experienced those prodigious events and for whom they were still fresh in mind, namely Caiaphas. — Whether the high priest passing through the two curtains was repeated in the next year may be doubted. After the exceptional case of the year 30, which had been brought about by necessity, the normal setup

337. Cf. Theodore Zahn, "Der zerrissene Tempelvorhang," *NZK* 13 (1902): 743f.

returned, so that one curtain divided the holy of holies from the holy place and so that the high priest entered into the holy of holies through its northern end. The witnesses adduced at the beginning for the singular had this normal setup in view.

The preceding is a (partly filled out) excerpt from my essay which appeared as Heinrich Laible, "Der zerrissene Tempelvorhang und die eingestürzte Oberschwelle des Tempeleingangs von Talmud bezeugt."[338]

Heinrich Laible.

9:3 B: Which is called the holy of holies.

On ἅγια ἁγίων, see § Heb 9:2, A.

9:4: Containing the golden incense altar and the ark of the covenant covered everywhere with gold, in which the golden small jug with the manna and the staff of Aaron, which had sprouted, and the tablets of the covenant were located.

1. θυμιατήριον can signify α. the incense pan. The word is used in this sense in LXX Ezek 8:11; 2 Chr 26:19; and Josephus, *Ant.* 4.2.4; 8.3.8. In Heb 9:4, then, θυμιατήριον would refer to that pan מַחְתָּה, on whose glowing coals the high priest on the Day of Atonement poured the incense before Yahweh in the holy of holies[a] (Lev 16:12f.). Yet the Jewish tradition never names this coal pan among the implements that were stored in the holy of holies. However, it does tell of a ladle (spoon) כַּף that went together with that pan, in which the high priest on the Day of Atonement held the incense until he put it on the fire of the coal pan in the holy of holies (see m. Yoma 5.1ff. at § Rom 3:25), so that it was brought to the high priest from the hall of implements;[b] this would have also been the storage place for the coal pan, which on the Day of Atonement served as the θυμιατήριον. — θυμιατήριον can also mean β. the golden incense altar in the holy place of the temple; so in Philo, *Mos.* 3 § 7, 9 and Josephus, *Ant.* 3.6.8. This is the meaning that θυμιατήριον has in Heb 9:4, since the enumeration of the things that were in the tent or the temple building could not possibly pass over the altar of incense. However, against this is the difficulty that in Heb 9:4 the incense altar would have had its place in the holy of holies, while in fact it stood in the holy place between the lampstand and the show bread table.[c] This difficulty can be removed only by assuming an oversight on the part of the author of the Letter to the Hebrews.

a. This pan is discussed in b. Yoma 4.3f. and t. Yoma 3.3 (185).

b. Babylonian Talmud Yoma 47A in a baraita.

c. Babylonian Talmud Yoma 33A: Resh Laqish (ca. 250) said, "One does not pass by obligatory commandments (a person shall carry out first that which first encounters him).

338. Heinrich Laible, "Der zerrissene Tempelvorhang und die eingestürzte Oberschwelle des Tempeleingangs von Talmud bezeugt," *NZK* 35 (1924): 287ff.

When one entered into the holy place הֵיכָל, he first came upon the altar (of incense). For in a baraita it has been taught: The show bread table stood in the north, pulled forward from the wall 2.5 cubits, and the lampstand stood in the south, pulled forward from the wall 2.5 cubits. The altar (of incense), which was in between them, stood in the middle and was pulled forward a little to the outside" (i.e., to the east, to the side of the entrance of the holy place, Rashi). — A parallel is found in t. Yoma 3.4 (185): The (show bread) table was located in the north of the third part of the space toward the inside, pulled forward from the wall 2.5 cubits. The lampstand was located opposite it in the south of the third part of the space toward the inside, pulled forward from the wall 2.5 cubits. The golden altar (of the incense offering) stood between both of them opposite the two carrying rods of the ark of the covenant (so precisely on the west-east midline of the holy place), pulled forward toward the east. Yet they all were located from the half of the space toward the inside. — Delitzsch, in Riehm, *Handwörterbuch*, 1390A: "The table on which the show bread was placed in two layers every Sabbath stood in the holy place on the north side opposite the lampstand (Exod 26:35); between the two, more toward the *parocheth* (the curtain of the holy of holies), was the place of the incense altar." Similarly, Hermann L. Strack writes (on Lev 24:1ff.): "The table stood in the holy place on the north side (Exod 25:36), the lampstand on the south side, the incense altar between the two, but somewhat closer to the holy of holies."[339]

2. τὴν κιβωτὸν τῆς διαθήκης = אֲרוֹן הַבְּרִית. — On the ark of the covenant, see § Rom 3:25 A. — According to 1 Kgs 8:9 the ark of the covenant contained only the two stone tablets that Moses had laid in it on Horeb.[340] Ancient Jewish tradition goes somewhat further: it assumes that aside from the tablets of the law, two silver posts that went with them, as well as the broken pieces of the first tablets, a Torah exemplar and the names of God were also received in the ark of the covenant.[a] However, we do not find in ancient Jewish literature the tradition represented by Heb 9:4 that aside from the two tablets of the law there also lay in the ark of the covenant a golden jug with manna and the sprouting staff of Aaron. Ancient Jewish literature assumes rather that the flask with the manna, as well as Aaron's staff with its flowers and almonds and finally the box with gifts that had been sent by the Philistines (1 Sam 6:8), was indeed found in the holy of holies, but not in the ark of the covenant, but rather alongside it.[b] There they remained until King Josiah had them hidden at the same time with the ark of the covenant;[c] but the prophet Elijah will bring them back in the future.[d]

a. Babylonian Talmud Baba Batra 14A: "The ark that Moses made was 2.5 cubits long [and 1.5 cubits wide] and 1.5 cubits high with one cubit consisting of 6 handbreadths (according to the opinion of R. Meir [ca. 150]); the tablets of the law, though, were 6 (hand-

339. Hermann L. Strack, *Die Bücher Genesis, Exodus, Leviticus und Numeri Erste Abteilung*, Kurzgefasster Kommentar zu den heiligen Schriften des Alten und Neuen Testament (Munich: Beck, 1894), 356.

340. S-B: When Josephus, *Ant.* 3.6.5 says that Moses laid the two tablets of the law in the ark, it does not follow that in his opinion only these and no other items were placed there.

breadths) long and 6 wide and 3 thick and lay in the length orientation of the ark (on its floor alongside each other). How much space did the tablets take up in the ark? 12 handbreadths; there remained 3 handbreadths left (2.5 cubits = 15 handbreadths - 12 handbreadths = 3 handbreadths); take 1 handbreadth away, namely half a handbreath for this wall (of the ark) and half for that wall, and there were 2 handbreadths left, in which the book of the Torah lay;[341] as it says, 'In the ark there was nothing except the two stone tablets (of the law) that Moses had deposited there' (1 Kgs 8:9). What does 'in the ark there was nothing except' mean? This is an exclusion (qualification) after an exclusion, and an exclusion after an exclusion intends merely to include something, namely the book of the Torah, which lay in the ark. You have accommodated (taken care of = calculated) the ark according to its length; go and accommodate the ark according to its width. How much space did the tablets take up in the ark? 6 handbreadths; 3 handbreadths were left (the width of the ark was 1.5 cubits = 9 handbreadths - 6 handbreadths for the width of the tablets = 3 handbreadths of empty area); take away 1 handbreadth, specifically half a handbreath for this wall (of the ark) and half for that wall; 2 handbreadths are left, lest the book of the Torah be laid in it pressed (crammed) and need to be taken out." These are the words of R. Meir (ca. 150). R. Judah (ca. 150) said, "(The measurements of the ark: 2.5 cubits long and 1.5 cubits wide,) one cubit consisting of 5 handbreadths, and the tablets hand a length of 6 handbreadths and a width of 6 and a thickness of 3 and lay in the length orientation of the ark (on the bottom alongside each other). How much of the ark did the tablets take up? 12 handbreadths; half a handbreadth was left (2.5 cubits now = 12.5 handbreadths - 12 handbreadths = half a handbreadth of empty area), specifically 1 fingerbreadth for this wall (of the ark) and 1 fingerbreadth for that wall (1 handbreadth = 4 fingerbreadths, half a handbreadth = 2 fingerbreadths). You have accommodated the ark according to its length; go and accommodate the ark according to its width! How much of the ark did the tablets take up? 6 handbreadths; 1.5 handbreadths were left (1.5 cubits now = 7.5 handbreadths - 6 handbreadths = 1.5 handbreadths); take away half a handbreadth, specifically 1.5[342] fingerbreadths for this wall and 1.5 fingerbreadths for that wall; 1 handbreadth was left in which the posts (for the tablets of the law) stood; as it says, 'King Solomon made himself a glorious sedan from the wood of Lebanon. He made its posts silver, its backrest golden, its seat of purple' (Song 3:9f.); and the box in which the Philistines sent gifts to the God of Israel (1 Sam 6:8) stood at its side (that of the ark of the covenant), as it says, 'And the golden implements that you have replaced as an atoning gift, put in a box at its side ...' (1 Sam 6:8); and on it lay the book of the Torah, as it says, 'Take this book of the Torah and put it at the side of the ark of the covenant of Yahweh' (Deut 31:26), at the side (thus of the ark) it lay and not in it. How do I maintain though (the words that include something else): 'There was nothing in the ark except' (1 Kgs 8:9)? This means to include the broken pieces of the (first) tablets which lay in the ark ....." (14B:) Yet where did the book of the Torah lay according to R. Judah, as long as there was no box (of the Philistines)? A board

341. S-B: One should note that the presence of the Torah exemplar in the ark of the covenant is so taken for granted that nothing further is said about it.

342. S-B: Read: 1 fingerbreadth, as in what precedes.

went out from the ark, and on it lay the book of the Torah. And what does R. Meir do with the following: "Lay it at the side of the ark of the covenant" (Deut 31:26)? He would have needed to say that the book of the Torah was laid at the side, and not that it was laid between the tablets! Always inside sideways. And where were the posts according to R. Meir? Outside. And where does R. Meir deduce the idea that the broken pieces of the (first) tablets lay in the ark? From what Rab Huna († 297) said. For he said, "What does 'Which was called by the name, the name of Yahweh Sabaoth, who is enthroned above the cherubs' (2 Sam 6:2) mean? This teaches (namely the twofold 'by the name') that the (second) tablets and the broken pieces of the tablets lay in the ark." And the former (how does he interpret 2 Sam 6:2)? He could have interpreted it following R. Yohanan († 279). For Yohanan said that R. Simeon b. Yohai (ca. 150) said, "This teaches that the name (of Yahweh) and all his other names lay in the ark. Yet the others also need it for this!" Yet if also thus (in this sense), where did he get the idea from that the broken pieces of the (first) tablets lay in the ark? From what Rab Joseph († 333) taught as a tannaitic tradition. For Rab Joseph taught as a tannaitic tradition: "'Which you broke, and shall lay them' (so the Midrash Deut 10:2); this teaches that the (second) tablets and the broken pieces of the (first) tablets lay in the ark." — Parallels are found in y. Šeqal. 6.49D.10; y. Soṭah 8.22C.44. — On the tablets in the ark, see also b. Ber. 8B: R. Joshua b. Levi (ca. 250) said to his sons, "... Be careful with an elder who has forgotten what he has learned by compulsion (of sickness or the like) (lest you encounter him irreverently); for we said, 'The tablets and the broken pieces of the tablets lay in the ark' (the latter were thus deemed worthy of the honor of the first ones)." — A different tradition about the broken tablets is found in y. Soṭah 8.22B.57 in a baraita: R. Judah b. Laqish (ca. 180) said, "Two arks went with Israel in the wilderness: one in which the Torah (i.e., the second tablets and the book of the Torah) lay, and one in which the broken pieces of the (first) tablets lay. The one in which the Torah lay was located in the tent of meeting; this is what is written, 'The ark of the covenant, though, and Moses did not depart from the camp' (Num 14:44). And the one in which the broken pieces of the tablets lay went with them in and out." — See further t. Šeqal. 2.18 (177) § Rom 3:25, A, #8, n. *a*. — On the names of God in in the ark, see y. Soṭah 8.22B.46: "To help you" (these closing words in the address of the priest of the battlefield in Deut 20:4) ... refer to the name (of God), which lay in the ark. — The words at the end in m. Soṭah 8.1 ("But it is not so with you, for Yahweh your God goes with you to fight for you" [Deut 20:4]) are commented on in b. Soṭah 42B as follows: And why all this? Because the name (of God) and all his other names lay in the ark (which went with Israel to the battlefield).

b. Tosefta Yoma 3.7 (186): The little basket (?) צִנְצֶנֶת with manna and the flask with the oil of anointing and Aaron's staff, its almonds, and its flowers, and the box in which the Philistines had sent a gift to Yahweh the God of Israel (1 Sam 6:8); they were all deposited in the holy of holies. ‖ Targum Onkelos Exodus 16:33f.: "Moses said to Aaron, 'Take a flask צְלוֹחִית and put in it an *omer* full of manna and store it before Yahweh for safe-keeping for your generations.' Just as Yahweh had assigned Moses, Aaron stored it in front of the testimony (= in front of the ark of the covenant with the tablets of the law) for safe-keeping." — Almost verbatim the same in Tg. Yer. I. ‖ Targum Onkelos Numbers 17:25: "Yahweh said to Moses, 'Bring Aaron's staff back in front of the testimony (= in front of the ark with the tablets of the law) for safe-keeping, as a sign for the rebellious people.'" — Similarly, Tg. Yer. I. — See a divergent tradition about the safe-keeping of Aaron's staff in #4, n. *c*.

c. Tosefta Yoma 3.7 (186): When the ark was hidden, they (the things enumerated in n. *b* at the beginning) were hidden with it. ‖ Jerusalem Talmud Soṭah 8.22C.6: When the ark was hidden, the little basket with manna and the flask with the oil of anointing and Aaron's staff with its flowers and almonds and the box that the Philistines had replaced as an atoning gift for the God of Israel were hidden with it (1 Sam 6:8). And who hid them? (See the continuation with parallels at § Rom 3:25 A, #8, n. *b*). — Also cf. ʾAbot R. Nat. 41 at § Rom 3:25 A, #8, n. *c*.

d. Mekilta Exodus 16:33 (59B): This (the container with the manna) is one of the three things that Elijah will one day restore to the Israelites: the flask צְלוֹחִית with the manna and the flask with the water of purification (Num 19:9) and the flask with the oil of anointing. Some also add Aaron's staff with its almonds and flowers; as it says, "Bring back Aaron's staff" (Num 17:10). — The same is found in Tanḥ. בשלח 84A. — On Aaron's staff, see also Num. Rab. 18 (185B) in #4, n. *c*.

3. στάμνος χρυσῆ. — στάμνος "jug" the word used in the LXX in Exod 16:33 to render צִנְצֶנֶת. The designation of the jug as a "golden" one also originates from the LXX. — In rabbinic literature צנצנת is almost as a rule replaced by צְלוֹחִית = flask,[a] and since this צלוחית is also said to have been "earthen" (from clay or mud),[b] the rabbinic scholars also would have thought of the צנצנת above all as a jug-like vessel.

a. See Tg. Onk. on Exod 16:33f. above in #2, n. *b*; Mek. Exod. 16:33 (59B) in #2, n. *d*; Tg. Yer. I on Exod 16:33 in n. *b*.

b. Mekilta Exodus 16:33 (59B): "'Moses said to Aaron, "Take a צִנְצֶנֶת"' (Exod 16:33). I do not know what this was made of, whether it was made of silver or of iron or of lead or of copper or of tin. Scripture teaches: a צנצנת. By this I only understand something that imbibes מציץ some more than another vessel; here you will not find anything other than an earthen vessel כְּלִי חֶרֶס." — The same is found in Tanḥ. בשלח 84A; see also Leqach Tob on Exod 16:33 (57B). — Targum Yerušalmi I Exodus 16:33: "Take a flask צלוחית from a potter ...." — Midrash Aggad (ed. Buber) on Exodus 16:33 (148): Take a צנצנת. This was an earthen vessel, and why was it called צנצנת? Because it kept מצננת the manna cool. — See also ʾAbot R. Nat. 41 (10D.10) on earthen vessels.

4. ἡ ῥάβδος Ααρών = מַטֵּה אַהֲרֹן or מַקְלוֹ שֶׁל אַהֲרוֹן. — Aaron's staff was reckoned to be among the things that were created on the evening before the entrance of the Sabbath of creation.[a] Most of the time it was assumed that it was stored in the holy of holies.[b] A different tradition about it is presented in Num. Rab. 18.[c]

a. Mekilta Exodus 16:32 (59B): This (the manna) is one of the ten things that was created on the day of preparation for the Sabbath (of creation) between the evenings (= in the twilight): The rainbow, the manna, the staff (of Moses), Scripture, the *shamir*, the tablets of the law, the opening of the mouth of the earth to consume the godless, the opening of the mouth of (Balaam's) jenny, Moses' grave, and the cavern in which Moses and Elijah stood. Some say, "Also the clothes of the first man and Aaron's staff with its almonds and its flowers." — See the parallels at § 1 Cor 10:4 B, middle.

b. See supporting passages above in #2, n. *b*.

c. Numbers Rabbah 18 (185B): "Aaron's staff" (Num 17:13). Some say, "This was the staff that was in Judah's hand" (see Gen 38:18). Others say, "This was the staff that was in Moses' hand, and it blossomed by itself; as it says, 'Behold, Aaron's staff had brought forth flowers' (Num 17:8)." Others say, "Moses took a beam and cut it in 12 slats and said to them, 'You are all from one beam, accept your staff!'" Why did he do this? "It is an honor for a man to stay far from strife; but every fool vehemently breaks forth" (Prov 20:3). They should not say, "His staff was fresh and therefore it bloomed!" Yet God determined about the staff, and the name of Yahweh was found on it, which was on the high priestly brow leaf צִיץ; as it says, "It had brought forth blossoms and produced flowers צִיץ" (Num 17:8), and it produced blossoms at night and bore fruit and "produced ripe almonds" וַיִּגְמֹל שְׁקֵדִים (Num 17:23), that is, it repaid גָּמַל everyone who watched over שׁוֹקֵד the tribe of Levi. And why almonds and not pomegranates or nuts? Because the Israelites are compared with these. And that staff was in the hand of every king until the sanctuary was destroyed, and then it was hidden. And that staff will one day be in the hand of the king, the Messiah—may he come soon in our days—as it says, "Yahweh stretches out the staff of your might from Zion; rule in the midst of your enemies!" (Ps 110:2).

5. αἱ πλάκες τῆς διαθήκης = לוּחֹת הַבְּרִית Deut 9:9. — On the tablets of the covenant, see § 2 Cor 3:7 B.

9:5: Above this the cherubs of glory, which overshadowed the atoning cover.

On Χερουβείν, see § Rom 3:25, A, #2, n. *f*. — On ἱλαστήριον, see § Rom 3:25 A, #1.

9:7 A: Once a year.

"Once a year," namely on the Day of Atonement; but several times on this day; according to m. Yoma 5.1–4, three times: a. with the incense (Lev 16:12); b. with the blood of the young bull (Lev 16:4) and c. with the blood of the goat (Lev 16:15); see m. Yoma 5.1ff. at § Rom 3:25, A, #3, n. *h*. — Yet, strikingly, it says in Num. Rab. 7 (148A): The high priest entered into the holy of holies four times on the Day of Atonement.

9:7 B: Not without blood, which he presents for himself and for the unconscious sins of the people.

See § Rom 3:25 particularly A, #6, notes *c* and *e*.

9:12: An eternal redemption.

αἰωνία λύτρωσις = גְּאוּלַּת עוֹלָם[a] (cf. Isa 45:17: תְּשׁוּעַת עוֹלָמִים "eternal salvation"); Aramaic: פּוּרְקַן עָלְמִין,[b] פּוּרְקַן עָלְמַיָּא.[c]

a. Midrash Psalm 31 § 2 (119A): The Israelites said before God, "Lord of the world, as long as we are enslaved, we are in dishonor and shame; redeem us, so we will have no shame, for your redemption is an eternal redemption גאולת עולם...." God said to them, "Since your redemption happened (earlier) by flesh and blood ..., your redemption was a redemption for a fleeting hour גְּאוּלַּת שָׁעָה, but in the future I myself will redeem you, for I live and abide forever; then your redemption will be a redemption that endures forever."

b. See Tg. Yer. I Gen. 49:18 in the excursus "The Memra of Yahweh," #5.

c. Targum Isaiah 45:17 renders תְּשׁוּעַת עוֹלָמִים with פורקן עלמיא.

9:13: The ashes of the cow.

On the burning of the red heifer, and on the preservation of its ashes, see m. Parah 3.6f., 11; t. Parah 3.14 at § Matt 21:1 B; m. Parah 3.5 at § Matt 26:3 B, n. *b*; m. Parah 3.9 at § Mark 13:3; m. Parah 3.2, 3 at § John 2:6 A, #2; t. Parah 3.2ff. at § John 2:6 A, #2. Also see Pesiq. 40A at § Matt 21:24; a parallel, in addition to the passages adduced at § Matt 21:24, is Num. Rab. 19 (186B).

9:16: A testament (cf. § Gal 3:15).

9:19 A: After each commandment was proclaimed to the people.

This statement is underlain by a tradition that was later represented by Rabbi († 217?).

Mekilta Exodus 19:10 (71B): "He took the book of the covenant and read it before the ears of the people" (Exod 24:7). We do not hear from where he read before their ears. R. Yose b. Assi[343] (ca. 200?) said, "From the beginning of Genesis up to here (Exod 23)." Rabbi said, "The commandment that was required of the first man, the commandments that were required of the Noachides, the commandments that were required in Egypt and in Marah and all the other commandments (he read out)." R. Ishmael († ca. 135) said, "What does it say at the beginning of the process (Lev 25:1)? 'The land shall keep a period of rest for Yahweh ...' (Lev 25:2f.). These are the fallow year and the jubilee year, the blessings and the curses. What does it say at the close of the process? 'These are the statutes and the regulations and the laws ...' (Lev 26:46)." — According to R. Ishmael, Moses therefore read Lev 25:2–26, 46. This opinion coheres with R. Ishmael's theory, shared in b. Soṭah 37B.6, that on Sinai only the general laws were given, while the specific statutes were proclaimed only in the tent of revelation, and so after the covenant was made. — In Leqach Tob on Exod 24:7 (87B), R. Ishmael's view is given as follows: "The blessings and the curses (he read out); as it says, 'These are the words of the covenant ...' (Deut 29:1)."

---

343. S-B: In Leqach Tob on Exodus 24:7 (87B) R. Jose b. Judah (ca. 180) and in Yalquṭ on Exodus 19:10 (1 § 279) R. Ishmael b. Yose (ca. 180) is the author.

9:19 B: With water, scarlet wool, and hyssop, and sprinkled … the whole people.

The tossing זרק of the blood on the people in Exod 24:8 was reinterpreted by Tg. Onk. and Yer. I into a tilting out of the blood over the altar for the people, that is, for the atonement of the people. The verb זרק would have been the occasion for this. Others maintained that according to Exod 24:8 the blood was put on the people itself and therefore converted the tilting out זרק into a sprinkling הַזָּאָה,[a] the execution of which was conceived on the analogy of Lev 14:5–7, 49–52 with the application of water, crimson wool, and hyssop.

a. Babylonian Talmud Keritot 81A: "Moses took half of the blood and tossed it on the people" (Exod 24:8), and there is no sprinkling הזאה without an immersion bath. ‖ Leqach Tob on Exodus 24:8 (87B): Moses took the blood and tossed it on the people; this refers to a sprinkling הזאה. — Rashi on Exodus 24:8: "He tossed" (Exod 24:8) signifies a sprinkling הזאה.

9:22: Without the pouring out of blood, forgiveness is not brought about.

Babylonian Talmud Yoma 5A.5, 13: There is no atonement except by blood. — The same is found in b. Menaḥ. 93B; b. Zebaḥ. 6A.

9:24: Not into the holy of holies made with hands (see § Heb 8:2).

9:26: Ends of the ages (see § 1 Cor 10:11).

10:1: Shadows of the future goods (see § Col 2:17).

10:5: "Sacrifice and offering you have not desired, but the body you have prepare for me" (Ps 40:7).

σῶμα, according to LXX Ps 40:6, whereas the base text, Ps 40:7, has אָזְנַיִם "ears." Presumably, σῶμα in the LXX is simply a corruption from ὠτία "ears."

10:7: "Behold, I come (it is written about me in the scroll), to do your will, O God" (Ps 40:8f.).

Midrash Ruth 4:15 (137B): R. Isaac (ca. 300) opened his presentation with: "'Then אָז I (David) said, "Behold, I have come" (Ps 40:8); I had to sing a song that I have come (namely into the community of Israel, which was originally denied to me as a descendant of the Moabite Ruth); and אז (= then) means nothing but "song"; as it says, "Then אז Moses and the children of Israel sang this song" (Exod 15:1). While I was subject to the rule, "Shall not come" (Deut 23:4), I (still) came. "In the scroll of the book it is decreed for me" (Ps 40:8); in the scroll: "*goyim* come …, whom you commanded not to come into your community" (Lam 1:10); in the book, "An Ammonite or a Moabite shall not come into the community of Yahweh" (Deut 23:4). And it is not enough that I have come; it is also written about me in a scroll and in a book; in a scroll, "Perez, Hezron, Ram, Aminadab, Nahshon, Boaz, Obed, Jesse, David" (Ruth 4:18ff.); in a book, "Yahweh said to Samuel, 'Arise and anoint him (David); for he is the one'" (1 Sam 16:12).'" ‖ See b. Yebam. 77A at § Matt 1:5 B, #1, n. *b*, end. ‖ Babylonian Talmud Yebamot 77A: Raba († 352) publicly said in a presentation, "What does 'Then I said, "Behold, I have come; in the scroll of the book it is written about me"' (Ps 40:8) mean? David said, 'I meant that now (that I have been anointed as king) I have come (been found by God and determined as worthy to be king), and I did not know that (long ago) it was written about me in a book scroll. There it is written (of the daughters of Lot), "Who are with you" (Gen 19:15), and here it is written, "I have found David, my servant, anointed him with holy oil" (Ps 89:21).'"

10:13: "Until his enemies are placed as a footstool for his feet" (Ps 110:1).

See the excursus "The 110th Psalm in Ancient Jewish Literature."

10:25: By not leaving our gathering, as some are accustomed to.

Mishnah ʾAbot 2.4: Hillel (ca. 20 BCE) said, "Do not separate yourself from the community." ‖ See b. Taʿan. 11A and b. Roš Haš. 17A at § Matt 16:18, #3, n. *c*; b. Taʿan. 11A at § Luke 12:19. ‖ A baraita in b. Sukkah 53A: (Hillel the elder [ca. 20 BCE]) used to say, "My feet bring me to the place that I love. 'If you come into my house' (God says), 'I will come into your house; if you do not come into my house, I will not come into your house; as it says, "In every place where I will bring about a memory of my name, I will come to you and bless you."'" — In Mek. Exod. 20:24 (80B), this appears as a saying of R. Eliezer b. Jacob (I, ca. 70; II, ca. 150). ‖ Babylonian Talmud Berakot 8A: R. Levi (ca. 300) said, "Whoever has a synagogue in his city and does not go for prayer is called an evil neighbor; as it says, 'So Yahweh says about all the evil neighbors who touch his property (interpreted to mean synagogue), which I have given to my people Israel as their own' (Jer 12:14). Not only this but he also brings exile upon himself and his children; as it says, 'Behold, I will tear them out from their soil and the house of Judah I will tear out of their midst' (Jer 12:14)." ‖ Babylonian Talmud Berakot 6B: Rabin b. Ad(d)a said that R. Isaac (ca. 300) said, "If someone usually goes to the synagogue and one day does not go, God asks about him; as it says, 'Where is the one who used to be among you, who feared Yahweh and listened to the voice of his servant? If he has secretly gone away, no light will shine for him' (so the Midrash Isa 50:10): if he has gone away because of something commanded, light will shine for him, but if he has gone away because of some voluntary thing, no light will shine for him; 'he should have trusted in the name of Yahweh' (Isa 50:10). Since he should have trusted in the name of Yahweh and he did not trust in it."

10:26: There is no further offering for sins.

One can here think of the regulation that the presentation of an offering was denied for the Jewish apostate.

Sifra Leviticus 1:2 (11A): "If a person אדם from you מכם wants to present an offering" (Lev 1:2). "From you": this means to exclude the apostates מומרים (for they no longer belong to the community of Israel). Why do you say this? Say (rather): "A person" (in general): this means to include apostates; "from you": this means to exclude the proselytes .... Scripture teaches: "Say to the children of Israel" (Lev 1:2); as the children of Israel are those who have accepted the covenant, so too are the proselytes those who have accepted the covenant. Here the apostates are excluded, who have not accepted the covenant. — This passage is referred to in y. Šeqal. 1.46B.10. ‖ Leviticus Rabbah 2 (in the supplements to folio 134B): It was said, "All kinds of offerings are accepted from the godless among the Israelites, in order to bring them under the wings of the Shekinah, except for the apostates and whoever presents wine as a libation (for idols) and whoever desecrates the Sabbaths."

10:37: For there is a little more, and the one who shall come will come and not delay.

Targum Habakkuk 2:3: "For the prophecy is determined for the appointed time and the end date is firmly set; it will not be annulled. If the saying undergoes a delay, hope in it; for at his time he will come and will not be restrained." — On the interpretation of Hab 2:3 in b. Sanh. 97B, see the excursus "Signs and Calculations of the Messianic Times."

10:38: "My righteous one will live by faith" (cf. § Gal 3:11).

11:4: By God giving testimony about his gifts.

Rashi on Genesis 4:4 (probably based on older traditions): "Fire came from heaven and consumed his (Abel's) offering."

11:5: Enoch was carried away.

The pre-Christian synagogue represented the view that Enoch was transported to heaven without having tasted death.[a] The earliest post-Christian synagogue also maintained this view.[b] Only when Enoch was celebrated as a prototype of the exalted Christ in Christian circles did the synagogue change its position: it was declared not only that Enoch died as all other men,[c] but there were also no qualms about disparaging Enoch's moral standing.[d]

a. So the whole book of 1 Enoch with 2 Enoch. — See further Jub. 4:23: "And he (Enoch) was removed from among the children of men, and we (angels) led him to the garden of Eden in majesty and honor and behold, there he writes the judgment and the verdict over the world and all the evils of the children of men." — Enoch appears as the heavenly scribe also in 1 En. 12:3f.; 15:1; 2 En. 22:11; 23:4ff.; 40:13; 53:2; 64:5; see Jub. 10:17; see also Tg. Yer. I in n. *b.* ‖ Sirach 44:16 (Hebrew): "Enoch was found to be blameless תמים and walked with Yahweh and was taken away נלקח as a sign of the recognition (of God) for all generations." — The Greek text: "Enoch pleased the Lord and was removed μετετέθη, an example of repentance for (future) generations." ‖ Septuagint Genesis 5:24: "Enoch pleased God and was found no more; for God had moved μετέθηκεν him." ‖ Sirach 49:14 (Hebrew): "Hardly was anyone on earth created like Enoch and he too was taken away into (heaven) נלקח פנים." – The Greek text: "No one was created on earth like Enoch, for he was taken up ἀνελήφθη from the earth."

b. Josephus, *Jewish Antiquities* 1.3.4: "After this one (Enoch) had lives 365 years, he was taken away ἀνεχώρησε to God. Therefore, his death was not recorded." ‖ Targum Yerušalmi I Genesis 5:24: "Enoch served Yahweh in uprightness, and he was no longer among the inhabitants of the earth, for he was removed אִתְנְגִיד and rose up to heaven by the word before Yahweh (by virtue of the divine command), and he named him 'Metatron, the great scribe.'"

c. Targum Onkelos Genesis 5:24: "Enoch walked in the fear of Yahweh, and he was no more, for Yahweh made him die אמית." – The bracketed לָא "no" before אמית is probably a later addition to correct the אמית. ‖ Genesis Rabbah 25 (16B): The sectarians (Jewish Christians) asked R. Abbahu (ca. 300) and said to him, "We do not find any dying concerning Enoch (mentioned in Scripture)." He answered them, "Why?" They said to him, "Here (Gen 5:24) it mentions a removal and there (2 Kgs 2:3) it is said, 'Do you know that today Yahweh will "remove" your lord (the prophet Elijah) from your head?'" (Just as here it refers to an exaltation to heaven, so to there.) He answered them, "If you explain the 'removal,' here a removal is mentioned and there (Ezek 24:16) it is said, 'See, I will "remove" from you the delight of your eyes by sudden death'" (thus the removal does not consistently exclude dying). R. Tanḥuma (ca. 380) said, "R. Abbahu answered them beautifully!" A matron asked R. Yose (ca. 150) and said to him, "We find no dying in the case of Enoch." He answered her, "If it (Gen 5:24) were said, 'Enoch walked with God' and nothing else, then I would say as you say. Since it says, though: 'He was no more, for God had taken him away,' (this means:) he was no longer in this world (no longer alive), for God had taken him away (by death)."

d. Genesis Rabbah 25 (16B): "Enoch walked with God and was no more; for God had taken him away" (Gen 5:24). R. Hama b. Hoshaiah (if the son of the elder Hoshaiah, then ca. 260) said, "He was not written down in the register of the righteous, but rather in the register of the godless." R. Aibbu (Aibo [ca. 320]) said, "Enoch was a hypocrite, sometimes righteous, sometimes godless. God said, 'While he is in his righteousness, I will take him away.'" R. Aibbu (Aibo) said, "On New Year's Day he judged him in the hour when he judges all who come into the world."

11:9: By faith he (Abraham) resettled in the land of the promise …, dwelling in huts with Isaac and Jacob, the coheirs of the same promise.

On Abraham's life of faith, see § Rom 4:2f., n. *d.* – Babylonian Talmud Sanhedrin 111A: (God said,) "I said to Abraham, 'Arise, go around in the land according to its length and width; for I will give it to you' (Gen 13:17). And when he then sought a site to bury Sarah, he found none, until he bought one for 400 *shekels* of silver. And yet he did not think anything bad about the way I proceeded. I said to Isaac, 'Remain in this land, and I will be with you and bless you' (Gen 26:3). Then when his servants searched for water to drink, they found none, until a conflict about it arose; as it says, 'Then the shepherds of Gerar disputed with the shepherds of Isaac, saying, "The water belongs to us"' (Gen 26:20). And yet he did not think anything bad about the way I proceeded. I said to Jacob, 'The land on which you are lying I will give to you' (Gen 28:13). Then when he searched for a place to pitch his tent, he found none, until he bought one for 100 *qesitahs* (Gen 33:19). And yet he did not think anything bad about the way I proceeded."

11:11: By faith Sarah herself also received power for the establishment of a seed, even in the face of the time of her age.

See § Rom 4:20 A, #2 and § Rom 4:19 B.

11:12 A: By one ... with a dead body (see § Rom 4:19 A).

11:12 B: Like the stars of heaven (see § Rom 4:18).

11:12 C: Like the sand on the shore of the sea.

See Num. Rab. 2 (137D) and Gen. Rab. 100 (64B) at § Rom 4:18, #2, n. *a*. – See further Gen. Rab. 69 (44C); Midr. Aggad Gen 22:17 (ed. Buber p. 54).

11:16: He prepared for them a city.

On the heavenly Jerusalem, see § Gal 4:26 A.

11:19 A: God is powerful even to raise from the dead (see § Rom 4:17 B).

11:19 B: Therefore he received him as a parable.

A later tradition in fact has Isaac killed in his sacrifice and then raised again.

Pirqe Rabbi Eliezer 31 (16B): R. Judah (ca. 150, the name should be viewed as pseudepigraphal, though) said, "When the knife touched Isaac's throat, his soul fled and departed. Yet when he (God) made his voice heard between the two cherubs and said, 'Do not stretch out your hand against the boy' (Gen 22:12), the soul returned to his body, and he untied him and Isaac stood up on his feet. Then Isaac knew the resurrection of the dead on the basis of the Torah, namely that one day all the dead will come alive again. In that hour he arose and said, 'Blessed be you, Yahweh, who make the dead alive'" (closing of the 2nd benediction of the Prayer of Eighteen Benedictions).

11:21: Jacob ... worshiped over the tip of his staff.

So following LXX Gen 47:31; here the מִטָּה "bed" in the base text has been interpreted as מַטֶּה "staff." – The haggadah incidentally had a number of things to recount about Jacob's staff (Gen 32:11).

Pirqe Rabbi Eliezer 40 (22C): The staff, which was created in the twilight (before the arrival of the Sabbath of creation; see Mek. Exod. 16:32 at § Heb 9:4, #4, n. *a*), was given to the first man in paradise. Adam gave it to Enoch, he to Noah, he to Shem, he to Abraham, he to Isaac, and he to Jacob. Jacob took it with him to Egypt and gave it to his son Joseph.

When Joseph died, his whole house was plundered, and so (the staff) was taken to pharaoh's palace. And Jethro (so read with Yalquṭ on Exodus 4:17, 1 § 173 instead of "pharaoh") was one of the scribes of the land of Egypt, and he saw the staff and the letters on it and longed for it in his heart. He took it with him and planted it in the garden of his house, and he saw the staff, how no one could approach it anymore. Then when Moses came into his house, he went into the garden of Jethro's house and saw the staff and read the letters on it and stretched out his hand and took it. Jethro saw Moses and said, "This one will redeem the Israelites out of Egypt." Therefore he gave him his daughter Zipporah for a wife (see Exod 2:21). — The letters on the staff specified the ten plagues of the land of Egypt by way of notarikon; so Exod. Rab. 5 (70D); 8 (73B). — For more about this staff, see Yalquṭ on Ps 110:2 § 869 from Yelamedenu and Num. Rab. 18 (185B).

11:22: Joseph ... gave an order concerning his bones (see § Acts 7:16 A, #1, notes *b* and *c*, #2, n. *a*).

11:24: Moses refused to be called a son of pharaoh's daughter.

Tanḥuma תזריע 155A: Moses had grown up in pharaoh's house and was considered to be a son of his house (i.e., one of his family members).

11:25: In that he preferred to suffer with God's people than to have the fleeting enjoyment of sin.

Babylonian Talmud Sanhedrin 99B: She (Timna, Lotan's sister in Gen 36:22) wanted to convert to Judaism. She came to Abraham, Isaac, and Jacob, but they were not willing to accept her. Then she went and became the concubine of Eliphaz, the son of Esau. She said, "It is better to be a servant girl for this nation than to be a mistress for another nation." From her Amalek came forth, who oppressed the Israelites. Why? Because they (the fathers) should not have kept Timna at a distance (when she desired to become a Jew). — See Gen. Rab. 45 (28B) at § Gal 4:24 C.

11:28: The destroyer.

ὁ ὀλοθρεύων, see § 1 Cor 10:10, #2.

11:31: Rahab.

See traditions about Rahab at § Matt 1:5 A. — Concerning her endowment with the holy spirit, that is, the spirit of prophecy, see also SDeut 1:24 § 22 (69B).

11:37: (Others) were sawed apart.

So according to the tradition, particularly the prophet Isaiah.

Jerusalem Talmud Sanhedrin 10.28C.37: Manasseh ran after Isaiah and wanted to kill him; but he fled before him. He fled to a cedar that swallowed him up with the exception of the tassels of his overcoat. Then someone came and reported it to Manasseh. He said to them, "Go and saw apart the cedar!" They sawed the cedar apart and blood was seen flowing. And Yahweh was not willing to forgive this, and so Manasseh has no share in the future (= in the future world). — See further legendary material in Mart. Isa. 5:2–14; b. Yebam. 49B. ‖ Babylonian Talmud Yebamot 49B and Sanhedrin 103B are also general: Manasseh killed Isaiah.

11:38: The world was not worthy of them.

ἄν οὐκ ἦν ἄξιος ὁ κόσμος, similar to שאין דורו זכאי לכך = his age is not worthy of him, does not deserve it; see t. Soṭah 13.3f. at § Matt 3:17 A, #8.

12:5f.: Do not disregard the Lord's chastisement.... For the Lord chastises the one he loves.

On the whole thought in Heb 12:5ff., see § Luke 13:2; 24:26, I, #2; § 1 Cor 11:32 and b. ʿArak. 16B at § Rom 8:18, #2, n. *b.* ‖ Mekilta Exodus 20:23 (79B): R. Eliezer b. Jacob (II, ca. 150) said, "See it says, 'Do not despise the chastisement of Yahweh, my son' (Prov 3:11). Why? 'For he whom Yahweh loves, he punishes' (Prov 3:12). Come and see: what causes (makes it possible for) a son to conciliate his father? Say: The chastisements." — Parallels are found in SDeut 6:5 § 32 (73B); Tanḥ. כי תצא 19B; Midr. Ps. 94 § 2 (209B).

12:9: To the Father of spirits.

One of the most common designations of God in the Similitudes of 1 Enoch is "the Lord of Spirits," perhaps = אֱלֹהֵי הָרוּחוֹת. This entails that God is the one who creates[a] and knows[b] the spirit of the human being.

a. Targum Yerušalmi I Numbers 16:22: "God, who puts the spirit of the soul in human bodies and by whom spirit is given to all flesh." — Targum Yerušalmi I Numbers 27:16: "May the Memra of Yahweh, who rules over the human soul and by whom the spirit of the soul is given to all flesh, appoint a reliable man over the whole community." — In both passages the targum uses a paraphrase to rewrite the phrase we find in the base text: אלהי הרוחות. ‖ Babylonian Talmud Niddah 31A: Three work together in the origin of the human being: God, his father, and his mother. His father gives the white seed, from which the bones, sinews, nails, the brain in the head, the white in the eye arise. The woman gives the red seed, from which the skin, the flesh, the hair, and the black in the eye originate. God adds the spirit, the soul, the facial expression, the sight of the eye, the hearing of the ear, the speaking of the mouth, the walking of the feet, insight and understanding. (See the continuation at § Matt 5:13 A, #4.)

b. Numbers Rabbah 18 (184A): "They fell on their face and said, 'God, God of the spirits of all flesh, is it the case that one man sins and you get angry with the whole community?'" (Num 16:22). They said before him, "Lord of the world, if one city (province) rebels against a king of flesh and blood, and one kicks and curses the king or his emissaries, whether there be ten or twenty of them, he sends his legions there and commits a massacre among them and kills the good with the bad, because he does not know who among them rebelled and who did not, who honored the king and who cursed him. Yet you know the thoughts of a human being and what counsel the hearts and the kidneys give, and you understand the inclinations of your creatures and you know who has sinned and who has not, who has rebelled and who has not, you know the spirit (mind) of each one of them. Therefore it says, 'God of the spirits of all flesh ...' (Num 16:22)." — The same is found in Tanḥ. קרח 219A; TanḥB קרח § 19 (46A). — See also Tanḥ. פנחס 240A with parallels TanḥB פנחס § 1 (75B); Num. Rab. 21 (192A).

12:11: Afterward it (chastisement) produces a peaceful fruit of righteousness.

This can be compared to passages like Gen. Rab. 9 (7A) at § Matt 5:20 B, #3; Pesiq. 151B, 179B at § Luke 24:26, I, #2, n. *d*; Gen. Rab. 92 at the beginning also belongs here.

12:14: Pursue peace with all.

See the citations at § Matt 5:9, #1, middle starting with m. ʾAbot 1.12; see also § Rom 12:18. — Leviticus Rabbah 9 (111B): Hezekiah (ca. 240) said, "Great is peace; for in all the commandments it is written, 'When you see' (cf. Exod 23:5), 'when you encounter' (Exod 23:4), 'when you meet' (Deut 22:6); thus, when the opportunity for a commandment offers itself to you, you are obligated to carry it out; but if not, you are not obligated to carry it out. Yet here (with peace) it says, 'Seek peace and pursue it!' (Ps 34:15); 'seek it' concerning your place 'and pursue it' concerning another place." — See 1 Pet 3:11.

12:16 A: Lest anyone be a fornicator or unholy one (= despiser of God) like Esau.

Concerning Esau's wicked deeds, it says generally in Tanḥ. תולדות 33A: You find that all the sins that God hates were together in Esau. — In the tradition he lived on specifically as a fornicating[a] and impious man who lacked any sense of the eternal and divine.[b] Otherwise he was also accused of idolatry, deceit, hypocrisy, shedding blood, and thievery.[c]

a. Genesis Rabbah 65 (40D.44. 50): R. Phineas (ca. 360) said in the name of R. Simon (ca. 280): "... For the whole (first) 40 years (of his life) Esau trapped married women and raped them." ‖ Genesis Rabbah 63 (40A): R. Hiyya (ca. 280) said, "Esau exposed himself like the field. The Israelites said before God, 'Lord of all worlds, is it not enough that we are enslaved by the 70 nations, but also by this one whom men sleep with as with women?'" — See further b. B. Bat. 16B and parallels in n. *b*.

b. Genesis Rabbah 65 (41D): When Jacob said, "Since Yahweh your God let it meet me" (Gen 27:20), Isaac thought, "I know that Esau does not mention the name of God, and this one mentions him. This one is not Esau, but rather Jacob." ‖ Genesis Rabbah 63 (40A): "Once Jacob cooked a dish" (Gen 25:29). Esau said to him, "What is the case with this dish?" He answered him, "(I have prepared it) because that old man (Abraham) has died." (The meal of mourning was a lentil dish according to Jewish custom.) Esau said, "So divine righteousness has struck even that old man!" He answered him, "Yes!" Then Esau said, "If this is so, then there is no recompense (repayment) and no the resurrection of the dead." See Gen. Rab. 63

(40B) and Tg. Yer. I Gen. 25:32, 34 at § Heb 12:16 B. ‖ Babylonian Talmud Baba Batra 16B: R. Yohanan († 279) said, "That wicked man (Esau) committed five transgressions on that day (when Abraham died): he had intercourse with an engaged virgin, he killed a man, he denied God (ולמה זה לי in Gen 25:32 is interpreted as: What should this one, namely God, be to me?!), he denied the resurrection of the dead, and he despised primogeniture." — Parallels are found in Midr. Ps. 9 § 7 (42A); Tanḥ. שמות 59B; Tg. Yer. I Gen. 25:29.

c. Genesis Rabbah 63 (40A); 63 (39D); Lev. Rab. 4 (107D); Tg. Yer. I Gen. 25, 27; Gen. Rab. 63 (39D); Pesiq. 22B; Tanḥ. כי תצא 20A; TanḥB תצא § 4 (17B); Gen. Rab. 63 (40A).

12:16 B: Who gave up his birthright for a meal.

Genesis Rabbah 63 (40B): He despised primogeniture את הבכורה (Gen 25:34). And what did he despise it with? (The *nota accusativi* את has an inclusive character.) R. Levi (ca. 300) said, "He despised the resurrection of the dead with it." ‖ Targum Yerušalmi I Genesis 25:32, 34: "Esau said, 'Behold, I am going to die, and I will not live again in another world. What should the birthright and the share in the future world, of which you (Jacob) speak, be to me!...' And Jacob gave Esau bread and the lentil dish, and he ate and drank and stood up and went away from there. And so Esau despised the birthright and the share in the future world."

12:17: He found no space for repentance.

See § Matt 4:17 A, #3, n. *e* and § Heb 6:4.

12:22: The heavenly Jerusalem (cf. § Gal 4:26 A).

12:24: Which speaks more powerfully than Abel.

See a parable about the voice of Abel's blood in Gen 4:10 at § 1 Cor 9:25 A, #1, n. *b*.

12:26: "Again I will shake not only earth but also heaven" (Hag 2:6 according to the LXX).

Haggai 2:6 in rabbinic literature.

Babylonian Talmud Sanhedrin 97B: And (the messianic period has) not (arrived), as R. Aqiba († ca. 135) supposed; for he said in a presentation: "Once more, a little bit, then I will shake heaven and earth" (Hag 2:6). — Unfortunately, it is not stated in what way R. Aqiba thought he could calculate from these words the arrival of the messianic kingdom; see the excursus "Signs and Calculations of the Messianic Times." ‖ Exodus Rabbah 18 (81A): Why is the night called a "night of observations"? (so the midrash interprets Exod 12:42). Since he (God) did a great thing for the righteous on it, as for the Israelites in Egypt. On it he saved (King) Hezekiah, on it he saved Daniel from the lion's den, and on it the Messiah and Elijah will one day become great; as it says, "The watcher said, 'Morning is coming and also (simultaneously) night'" (Isa 21:12). Like a woman who waited for her husband who had gone into a distant land, he had said to her, "Let this sign be in your hand. At the time when you see this sign, know that I am coming and I am close to coming." So too the

Israelites wait since Edom (Rome) arose. God said, "Let this sign be in your hand: On the day when I fashioned help for you (in Egypt), in the same night (= Passover night) you shall know that I will redeem you (hence this night is a 'night of observations,' that is, a night which one looks to, in which one waits). And if (it has) not (arrived up until now), do not think that the time is not near; for it says, 'I Yahweh will hasten it at its time' (Isa 60:22), and further it says, 'There is still a time, a short time, then I will shake heaven and earth ...' (Hag 2:6)." ‖ Deuteronomy Rabbah 1 (196D): "Long protracted waiting makes the heart sick" (Prov 13:12). R. Azariah (ca. 380) said, "This is talking about the help that is due to come. How? When the prophet says to Israel, 'Once more, a little, then I will shake heaven and earth' (Hag 2:6), behold, here it says, 'Long protracted waiting makes the heart sick.' Yet when he said to them, 'Behold, your help comes' (Isa 62:11), here they said, 'A wish fulfilled is a tree of life' (Prov 13:12)." ‖ TanḥumaB דברים § 1 at the beginning.: Blessed be his (God's) name and his memory be glorified! For all the signs that he did for Israel in the wilderness, he will likewise do for them in Zion (in the messianic age). About the wilderness it is written, "These are the words" (Deut 1:1), and about Zion, see Isa 42:16; about the wilderness it is written, "The whole people heard the voices" (Exod 20:18), and about Zion, see Jer 7:34; about the wilderness it is written, "Then the earth quaked" (Ps 68:9), and about Zion it is written, "I will make heaven and earth quake" (Hag 2:6); about the wilderness, see Exod 13:21; and about Zion, see Isa 52:12.

12:27: The reversal of what is shaken as created (because it is a creature).

Genesis Rabbah 42 (26A): (R. Samuel b. Nahman [ca. 260] said,) "Everything that was created on the first day (of creation) will one day become brittle (pass away); as it says, 'For the heavens will disperse like smoke ... (Isa 51:6)." – The same is found in Lev. Rab. 11 (113B); Midr. Esth. Intro. 82B; Midr. Ruth 1:1 (124B) among many others.

12:29: "Our God is a consuming fire" (Deut 4:24).

See b. ʿAbod. Zar. 54B; 55A at § Rom 1:23 A, #2, D, n. *m*, end.

13:2 A: Do not forget hospitality.

See § Rom 12:13 B.

13:2 B: For by it some have harbored angels without knowing it.

See b. Qidd. 32B at § Matt 20:26; also see Philo, *Abr.* § 23.

13:8: Jesus Christ is the same yesterday and today and forever.

See the interpretation of the name of Yahweh in Exod. Rab. 3 (69C): R. Isaac (ca. 300) said, "God said to Moses, 'Say to them, "I am who I was, and I am now the same, and I will be the same in the future"' (cf. Exod 3:14f.)."

13:15: Through him let us present the offering of praise at all times to God.

See Pesiq. 79A at § Matt 5:18 B, #1, 2nd third.

13:16: For such offerings please God.

On the merit and recompense of beneficence, see the excursus "Ancient Jewish Private Charity."

13:20: The God of peace (see § Rom 15:33).

The Letter of James

1:2: Consider it pure joy when you fall into all kinds of temptations.

See Exod. Rab. 31 (91C) at § Matt 19:22, #3, n. *d.* – See in more detail about temptations at § Matt 4:1 A; § Matt 4:1 B, #3, A; § Matt 6:13 A.

1:8: A man with two souls.

Psalm 12:3: "With smooth lips they speak from two hearts בְּלֵב וָלֵב." ‖ Sirach (Greek) 1:25: "Do not be disobedient to the fear of the Lord and do not approach him with a divided heart ἐν καρδίᾳ δισσῇ." ‖ Tanḥuma כי תבא 23B: "So keep and do them (the statutes) with all your heart" (Deut 26:16). Scripture warns the Israelites and says to them: "When you pray before God, you shall not have two hearts שתי לבבות: one before God and one for something else." – The same is found in TanḥB תבא § 3 (23B). ‖ Tanḥuma כי תבא 24A: "With all your heart" (Deut 26:16). R. Eliezer b. Jacob (I, ca. 70; II, ca. 150) said, "Scripture intends to warn the priests lest they have two hearts when they perform the priestly service: one before God and one for something else."

1:10f.: Like a flower of the grass ....

See b. ʿErub. 54A and Sir 14:11ff. at § 1 Cor 9:25 A, #2, n. *d.*

1:12 A: Blessed is the man who bears up in temptation (affliction).

The citation from Exod. Rab. 31 (91C) begins exactly the same at § Matt 19:22, #3, n. *d*: אשרי אדם שהוא עומד בנסיונו, blessed is the man who endures in his temptation!

1:12 B: The crown of life (see § 1 Cor 9:25 B).

1:12 C: Which he has promised.

God frequently remains unnamed as subject or otherwise in rabbinic literature; see, for example, Midr. Song. 1:2 (82B) at § Heb 8:8ff.; Exod. Rab. 18 (81A) and TanḥB דברים § 1 at § Heb 12:26; m. ʾAbot 5.2, 3 at § Matt 3:9 A, #1; Gen. Rab. 8 (6C) at § John 3:31; Deut. Rab. 11 at § Matt 4:1 B, #3, C, 1st third; b. Ḥag. 14A at § John 1:1 A, B n. *b*, γ; b. Yebam. 63B in a baraita at § John 2:1 A, #1, n. *a*; Deut. Rab. 6 (203B) at § Luke 12:24 B. See further Kittel, *Sifre*, 91.2. Even Josephus occasionally observed this custom; see *J. W.* 4.8.2 at § Luke 10:30 A, #1. The reason lay in the effort to say God's name as rarely as possible; one simply left it out where there was no reason to be wary of misunderstanding.

1:13: He himself tempts no one.

Babylonian Talmud Menaḥot 99B: Hezekiah (ca. 240) said, "What does 'And he entices you too from the jaws of distress to a wide plane where there is no constriction' (Job 36:16) mean? Come and see that God's way is not like man's way. With men, it is the case that one entices another from the ways of life to the ways of death; but God lures a man away from the ways of death to the ways of life; as it says, 'He entices you too from the jaws of narrowness, that is, from gehenna, whose jaw is narrow, lest its smoke be accumulated in him....' And if you should say that this is the only recompense (for someone following God's leading); it says, 'The setting of your table is rich in fat' (Job 36:16)."

1:14: Each one is tempted when he is drawn and lured by his own desire.

Apocalypse of Moses 19: "It (the snake) put the poison of its evil, that is, its desire in the fruit that it gave to me (Eve) to eat; for desire is the beginning of all sin." — See further in the excursus "The Good and the Evil Inclination," #5 and #8.

1:17 A: The purely good gift and purely perfect gift comes down from above.

Genesis Rabbah 51 (32C): R. Hanina (b. Pazzi [ca. 300]) said, "Nothing evil comes down from above!" He was responded to: "Yet it is written, 'Fire and hail, snow and smoke (fog)' (Ps 148:8)!" He answered them, "This is the tempest, which accomplishes his word (Ps 148:8)." A saying of R. Simeon b. Laqish (ca. 250) deviates from what R. Hanina b. Pazzi said (namely): "'Yahweh will open up his good treasure to you' (Deut 28:12); from this it follows that he has other (bad) treasures." (The saying of R. Simeon b. Laqish drawn upon here is found in Pesiq. 100A; TanḥB ראה § 17.) — Presumably in order to harmonize the saying of R. Hanina b. Pazzi with that of Resh Laqish, it was given the following formulation in TanḥB וירא § 18 (48A): R. Hanina b. Pazzi said, "God does not make anything evil come down from above, except for rain that becomes sulfur." ‖ Another saying lies on the same level with the saying of R. Hanina b. Pazzi, namely: "Nothing impure comes down from heaven"; see b. Sanh. 59B at § Acts 10:11ff. ‖ The following sayings are different: Tanḥuma ראה 9A: "Do not evil and good proceed from the mouth of the Most High?" (Lam 3:38). R. Abin (ca. 325) said, "This verse arouses astonishment. (It means, though:) From the mouth of the Most High no evil comes for the righteous and no good for the godless." See Midr. Lam. 3:38 (72A) and Deut. Rab. 4 (201D). ‖ Babylonian Talmud Šabbat 59B: R. Aha b. Hanina (ca. 300) said, "Never has a decision for good come out of God's mouth that God then reversed for evil, except in the case of Ezek 9:4ff. (first the cross in verse 4 for good and still at the close of verse 6: 'With my sanctified one'—so the midrash interprets the wording—'you shall make a beginning')."

1:17 B: From the father of lights.

If one relates τῶν φωτῶν to τοῦ πατρός (which is in any case the most obvious), it can be compared with Apoc. Mos. 35f.: (Eve sees how the heavenly beings pray for Adam who has died. She makes her son Seth aware of it and says to him,) "'Who might the two

Ethiopians be who stand by your father in prayer?' Then Seth says to his mother, 'These are the sun and moon; they too fall down and pray for my father Adam.' Eve says to him, 'Where did their light (go)? And why do they look black?' And Seth says to her, 'They have not lost their light; but they cannot shine in the face of the light of all, the Father of lights, because of whom the light from them hid.'" — Apoc. Mos. 38: "The archangel Michael asked the Father of lights to tend to (Adam's) remains."

1:18: He has given birth to us by the word of truth.

Philo once says in *Leg.* 3 § 77 at the end: "The Lord sired Isaac; for he himself is the Father of perfect nature who scatters seed in souls."

1:19 A: Let everyone be quick to listen, slow to speak.

Sirach 5:11 (Hebrew): "Be quick to listen, but with patience give a word in response." — Sirach 5:11 (Greek): "Be quick in (with) your listening and in patience (with thoughtfulness) speak an answer." ‖ Mishnah ʾAbot 1.15: Shammai (ca. 30 BCE) said, "Speak little and do much!" ‖ Mishnah ʾAbot 1.17: Simeon (probably b. Gamaliel II [ca. 140]) said, "My whole life I grew up among the scholars and found that there is nothing better for a man than to be silent ...; and whoever makes many words brings about sin (cf. Prov 10:19)." — A parallel, extended with an addition, is found in ʾAbot R. Nat. 22 (6D). ‖ Mishnah ʾAbot 3.13: R. Aqiba († ca. 135) said, "A fence for wisdom is silence." ‖ Babylonian Talmud Pesaḥim 99A: The scholars said, "Silence is beautiful for scholars, how much more for fools; as it says, 'Even a fool, if he remains silent, is considered wise.'" ‖ Jerusalem Talmud Berakot 9.12D.40: Jacob of Neburaya (ca. 350) gave an interpretation of the following in Tyre: "'For you silence is a song of praise, O God on Zion' (so Midr. Ps. 65:2); the main thing above all is silence. Like a pearl that is invaluable; whoever praises it does it harm." — The same is found in Midr. Ps. 19 § 2 (86B). In b. Meg. 18A it is found with a different authorial attribution and without the parable, but with the addition: When Rab Dimi (ca. 320) came, he said, "In the west, one says, 'Speaking is worth one *sela*, but silence two.'" — In Lev. Rab. 16 (116C) the author of the addition is R. Joshua b. Levi (ca. 250) in Midr. Eccl. 5:5 (25B), Joshua (b. Hananiah, ca. 90); here it is followed by: Rabbi († 217?) said, "The spice of speech is silence." ‖ ʾAbot de Rabbi Nathan 1 (1A): Be cautious (deliberate) in judgment (an admonition that according to m. ʾAbot 1.1 should be said by the men of the great synagogue). How? It teaches that a person should wait patiently with his words and not be quick with his words. For whoever is quick with his words forgets his words. (Moses serves as an example on the basis of Num 31:14, 21; cf. SNum 31:21 § 157 folio 60A and b. Pesaḥ. 66B.23).... Ben Azzai (ca. 110) said, "Guard yourself in your words from useless chatter." — See also Eccl 5:1.

1:19 B: Slow to anger.

See m. ʾAbot 2.10; 5.11 at § Matt 5:22, C.

1:20: A man's anger does not work the righteousness that counts before God.

On the harmfulness and reprehensibility of anger, see § Matt 5:22, C.

1:22: Be doers of the word and not only hearers.

See § Rom 2:13. ‖ Babylonian Talmud Šabbat 88A: R. Eleazar (ca. 270) said, "When the Israelites made 'we will do' come before 'we will hear' (Exod 24:7), a voice from heaven went out that said, 'Who revealed this secret to my children, which angels of service use? For it says, "Praise Yahweh, you his angels, you strong heroes who do his word, to hear the voice of his word" (so Ps 103:20 according to the midr.).' First 'do,' then 'hear.'" R. Hama b. Hanina (ca. 260) said, "What does 'Like an apple tree among the trees of the wood' (Song 2:3) mean? Why are the Israelites compared with the apple tree? To tell you: as with the apple tree the fruit precedes the leaves, so too the Israelites made 'we will do' precede 'we will hear.'" ‖ Mishnah ʾAbot 6.7: Great is the Torah; for it bestows on its doer life in this and in the future world, see Prov 4:22; 3:8, 18; 1:9; 4:9; 9:11; 3:16, 2.

1:23: In a mirror (cf. § 1 Cor 13:12).

1:25 A: In a perfect law, that of freedom.

Torah and freedom; see Tanḥ. כי תשא 115A with parallels at § 2 Cor 3:7 B, B, n. *w*, as well as m. ʾAbot 6.2 and b. B. Meṣ. 85B at § John 8:32.

1:25 B: A hearer of forgetfulness.

Mishnah ʾAbot 3.8: R. Dustai b. Yannai (ca. 180) said in the name of R. Meir (ca. 150), "Whoever forgets a word from his study material, to him one (God) counts it as if he became guilty with respect to his soul; as it says, 'Yet watch yourself and guard your soul greatly, lest you forget the words (so the midrash) that your eyes have seen' (Deut 4:9). Even if his study material was too difficult for him? Scripture teaches, 'Lest they depart from your heart your whole life long' (Deut 4:9). Consequently, he becomes guilty with respect to his soul only when he sits down and removes them from his heart." — See a parallel in a different form with Rab Nahman b. Isaac († 356) as the second author in b. Menaḥ. 99B. ‖ ʾAbot de Rabbi Nathan 23 (6D): Whoever studies and forgets is like a woman who bears children and buries them. ‖ Mishnah ʾAbot 5.12: There are four kinds of students: he who understands quickly and forgets quickly, his gain comes undone in his disadvantage; he who understands with difficulty and forgets with difficulty, his disadvantage comes undone in his gain; he who understands quickly and forgets with difficulty is a wise man; he who understands with difficulty and forgets quickly, this is a bad lot.

1:25 C: He will be blessed in his doing.

Mishnah ʾAbot 5.14: There are four types among those who go into the house of learning. He who goes but does not do (what he has heard) receives the recompense for going; he who does but does not go receives the recompense for doing; he who goes and does is a pious man; he who does not go and does not do is a godless man.

1:26: Not reining in his tongue.

On the "evil tongue" = slander, see § Matt 5:11 B.

1:27 A: Orphans.

See Midr. Esth. 2:5 (93A) at § Matt 2:4 #2, n. *b*.

1:27 B: A pure and unblemished worship of God.

Targum Yerušalmi I Deuteronomy 6:5 once mentions a "true, right" worship of God פּוּלְחָנָא קְשִׁיטָא; see § Matt 22:37. — On "rational" worship, see § Rom 12:1.

2:1–4: ... Not so that you respect the person....

See b. Šebu. 31A: How can we prove that if two appear before a court, one of whom is clothed in rags and the other in a garment that costs 100 *minas*, one says to the latter, "Clothe yourself like him or clothe him like you?" It says, "Keep far from a false case!" (Exod 23:7)! (Any court action, though, can easily turn into a false case when outward circumstances begin to influence the judge.) When such men came before Rabbah (read רבה) b. Huna († 322), he said to them, "Remove your fine shows and then come before the court!" — See further b. Šebu. 30B at § John 7:49, #8, n. *d*.

2:5: Rich in faith.

πλούσιοι ἐν πίστει. In rabbinic literature, similar expressions include: עשיר בנכסים "rich in goods," עשיר בדעת "rich in good will"; see § Matt 5:3, #1, B; as well as עשיר בתורה "rich in knowledge of the Torah"; opposite: רש בתורה or אביון בת׳ "poor in knowledge of the Torah," in, for example, Lev. Rab. 34 (131A); Midr. Ps. 49 § 2 (139B).

2:7: The good name that was named over you.

Just as proclaiming the name of Yahweh over Israel declares them to be the possession of Yahweh (see Deut 28:10; Isa 63:19; Jer 14:9; 15:16; cf. Amos 9:12), so too Christians are marked as belonging to Jesus by Jesus' name being named over them. See § 3 John 7.

2:8: You shall love your neighbor as yourself (see § Matt 5:43).

2:10: Whoever keeps the whole law yet offends against one commandment has become guilty of all.

The same idea is present specifically in application to Exod 22:24: "You shall not be as a usurer to him (the impoverished Israelite)." Exodus Rabbah 31 (92C): "Come and see. Whoever loans at interest transgresses all transgressions that are in the Torah, and finds none (among the angels) who claim merit for him; as it says, 'He has loaned with interest and taken interest and he should live? He will not remain alive' (Ezek 18:13)." — The converse of the idea is encountered more frequently: "Whoever keeps a commandment is like one who has kept the whole Torah." So Midr. Prov. 1:10 (22B). R. Aqiba († ca. 135) thoroughly emphasized this principle before Rabban Gamaliel (ca. 90) in Midr. Ps. 15 § 7 (60A); see the excursus "Preliminary Remarks on the Sermon on the Mount," toward the end. – Special applications of this principle to those who observe the Sabbath commandment and the prohibition of interest are found in Exod. Rab. 25 (87B); 31 (91C.54; 92C.20, 46).

2:13: The judgment will be without mercy for the one who has not shown mercy.

On κρίσις ἀνέλεος see m. Ketub. 9.2, where R. Aqiba († ca. 135) says, "In court one has no pity" אֵין מְרַחֲמִין בַּדִּין, that is, in a judicial proceeding, one cannot plead for pity. – On the whole maxim, see § Matt 5:7.

2:23 A: "Abraham believed God" ... Gen 15:6 (see § Rom 4:2f., #1, n. *d*, σ).

2:23 B: He was called "friend of God."

Abraham is called "my (God's) friend" אֹהֲבִי in Isa 41:8; targum: רְחִימִי "my beloved" or "my friend"; LXX actively: ὃν ἠγάπησα. – On the basis of Isa 41:8, Abraham is called "your (God's) friend" אֹהַבְךָ also in 2 Chr 20:7; targum: רְחֵמָךְ; LXX: τῷ ἠγαπημένῳ σου.

Babylonian Talmud Soṭah 31A: R. Meir (ca. 150) said, "It says of Job, 'He was god-fearing' (Job 1:1), and likewise of Abraham (see Gen 22:12). As the fear of God in Abraham's case arose from love, so too the fear of God in Job's case. How do we know this about Abraham? Because it says, 'The seed of Abraham, my friend' (אהבי in Isa 41:8 is interpreted as 'who loved me')." ‖ Genesis Rabbah 41 (25C): "Whoever loves purity of heart, whosever lips are gracefulness, his friend is the king" (Prov 22:11): this refers to Abraham, who was flawless and pure of heart and became a friend of God אוהבו של מקום (see Isa 41:8). – In Lev. Rab. 6 (109A)—see § Luke 2:25 C, #4, n. *d*—God is called "the friend of Abraham" on the basis of Prov 27:10. – The following are designated generally as "friends of God" by the following authors: the prophets by Philo, *Mos.* 1 § 28 (Mangey's ed., 2:105, toward the end); all who occupy themselves with the Torah for its own sake, by R. Meir (ca. 150) in m. ʾAbot 6.1; and on the basis of Ps 122:8, the Israelites by R. Hiyya b. Abba (ca. 280) in Deut. Rab. 3 (200D).

2:25: Rahab the prostitute.

On Rahab's life and recompense, see § Matt 1:5 A.

3:1: Not many of you should become teachers.

The sentence from b. Taʿan. 30B adduced by Schöttgen, which is general sounding—"Rabban Simeon b. Gamaliel (ca. 140) said, 'Let everyone always make himself like a student of the scholars'"—has an entirely specific relationship to the 9th of Ab (the day of the destruction of Jerusalem): just as every scholar had to be solemn and fast on this day, so everyone should in this respect make himself like a student of the scholars and let all work cease. The passage has nothing to do with the ambition to become a teacher. However, see SDeut 11:22 § 48 (84B); b. Ned. 62A and SDeut 11:13 § 41 (79B) at § Matt 23:8 A, end.

3:2: If anyone does not fall short in word (speech), he is a perfect man.

See Prov 10:19. – See m. ʾAbot 1.17 at § Jas 1:19 A.

3:5: The tongue is a small member and boasts of great things.

See Midr. Ps. 39 § 2 (128A) at § 1 Cor 12:12ff.

3:6 A: The tongue is a fire.[344]

Leviticus Rabbah 16 (116C): R. Eleazar (ca. 270) said in the name of R. Yose b. Zimra (ca. 220), "There are 248 members in a person; one of them is found in a lying position, others in an upright one. Yet the tongue is fixed between the two jaws and a water channel (saliva) flows under it, and it is furnished with who knows how many doublings (enclosed by two lips, two jaws, two rows of teeth). Come and see, how many fires it lights! How much more (would it do this) if it stood upright." – See a different version of the saying in b. ʿArak. 15B in the following section § Jas 3:6 B and at § Jas 3:8 A. ‖ Sirach 28:22f.: "It (the tongue) will not become lord over the pious and will not burn them with its flame; but those who abandon the Lord fall prey to it, and among them it burns, an unquenchable fire."

3:6 B: The tongue is as a world of unrighteousness among our members.

In Ps 120:2, 3, the tongue is called "a tongue, which is deception." See a use of this psalm passage in ʿArak. 15B § Matt 5:11 B, #2.

3:6 C: It both sets the wheel of existence (life) on fire.

1. φλογίζουσα, see § 3:6 A. 2. τὸν τροχὸν τῆς γενέσεως, for the image of the wheel, see TanḥB משפטים § 8 (43A); Exod. Rab. 31 (91C); b. Šabb. 151B at § Matt 19:22, #3, n. *b*.

3:6 D: And is set on fire by hell.

See b. ʿArak. 15B at § Matt 15:11 B, #4; TanḥB מצורע § 5 at § 1 Pet 3:10–12, #2.

3:8 A: No one among men can tame the tongue.

Midrash Psalm 52 § 6 (143B): R. Yose b. Zimra (ca. 220) said, "Come and see how bad the wicked tongue is! There are 248 members in a person, some of which stand upright, others are stretched out, and others stand; yet the tongue is laid in a prison, and the jaws and the teeth surrounded it and how many artful contraptions there are against it, and yet no one endures against it, so how much less if it were upright!" – See also § Jas 3:9 A.

---

344. S-B: Connect in verse 6: ἡ γλῶσσα πῦρ.

3:8 B: Full of deadly poison.

See b. ʿArak. 15B and Pesiq. 32A at § Matt 5:11 B, #3; Lev. Rab. 33 at the beginning at § 1 Cor 16:19, n. g; Midr. Ps. 39 § 2 (128A) at § 1 Cor 12:12ff.

3:9 A: With it we praise ..., with it we curse ....

Tanḥuma תולדות 34A: You find that God created three members that are in the person's power, and three that are not in his power. The following are in his power: The hands, the mouth (tongue), and the feet. The mouth: if one is willing to occupy himself with the Torah, and to speak good (about his neighbor), extol, praise, pray, sing, the mouth does it. If one wants to speak evil (about his neighbor), revile, slander, swear falsely, the mouth does it ... The following are not in his power: the eyes, the ears, and the nose (smell) .... According to the parallels in Gen. Rab. 67 (42D.12) and TanḥB תולדות § 21 (70B), this saying is associated with R. Levi (ca. 300).

3:9 B: Who are created according to God's likeness (image).

See SLev 19:18 and Gen. Rab. 24 (16B) at § Matt 5:43, #1, n. *f.*

3:10: From one and the same mouth come blessing and cursing.

Leviticus Rabbah 33 (130B): (The slave Tebi of R. Simeon b. Gamaliel [ca. 140] says to him,) "From it (the tongue) comes good and from it comes bad. If it is good, there is nothing better than it, and if it is bad, there is nothing worse than it."

3:17: Wisdom from above.

"The Torah is the reflection of the wisdom above חָכְמָה שֶׁל מַעְלָה"; see Gen. Rab. 17 (12A) § Heb 1:3 A, n. *c*.

4:3: Because you ask wickedly.

On evil, conceited, inappropriate prayers, see m. Ber. 9.3 at § Matt 7:7 A, #2, n. *i*; b. Roš Haš. 18A at § Matt 7:7 A, #2, n. *m*; b. Taʿan. 4A at § Matt 20:22 A. ‖ Babylonian Talmud Sanhedrin 106B: (Raba [† 352] said,) "We cry out and there is no one who asks about us (heeds us). Yet God wants the heart, for it is written, 'Yahweh looks at the heart' (1 Sam 16:7)."

4:5: "The spirit that dwells in us longs jealously for us."

It also happens in rabbinic writings that citations appear as quotations of Scripture when in fact they are not (see § Rom 12:14 A; § 1 Cor 2:9; and § Eph 5:14).

4:6: "God resists the proud, but he gives grace to the humble."

Citation of Prov 3:34 following the LXX. — The rabbinic scholars follow the wording of the base text. Therefore, they do not apply Prov 3:34 in combatting pride (see § Matt 5:6 and § 1 Pet 5:5). — For the condemnation of pride, see § Luke 1:51; for the praise of humility, see § Matt 5:3, #3.

4:7: Resist the devil and he will flee from you.

Testament of Simeon 3: "If one takes his refuge to the Lord, the evil spirit runs away from him." – Testament of Naphtali 8: "If you do good ..., the devil will flee from you ὁ διάβολος φεύξεται ἀφ' ὑμῶν." – Testament of Benjamin 5: "If you do good, the unclean spirits will flee from you."

4:11: Whoever speaks wickedly about a brother or judges his brother speaks wickedly about the law and judges the law.

See the second passage from b. ʿArak. 15B at § Matt 5:11 B, #2; there is a parallel in Deut. Rab. 6 (203D). – On calumnies, see § Matt 5:11 B; on uncharitable judgment, see § Matt 7:1 and 7:2 A.

4:12: One is ... judge, who can save and destroy.

Psalm 75:8: "God is judge, he humbles one and exalts another." – This psalm passage is cited in Exod. Rab. 31 (91C.34).

4:13f.: You say, "Today or tomorrow we will go ...," you who do not know what will be tomorrow ....

See Deut. Rab. 9 (205C) at § Matt 4:1 B, #3, C, last paragraph; b. Giṭ. 68A in the excursus "Ancient Jewish Demonology," #3, n. *b* (Ashmedai laughs about a man who orders seven years of boots for himself and does not have seven more days to live). – On ἀτμίς see 2 Bar. 82:2ff. at § Rom 3:9 A, #2, n. *c*.

4:15: Instead, say: If the Lord wills and we live.

Following the procedure of others, Schöttgen, *Horae*, 1030f., brings forth the following passage: *In Proverbiis Ben Sirae* (this must mean: in the alphabet of Ben Sira) *hoc etiam legitur: Sponsa ascendit in cubiculum, nec novit, quid sibi eventurum sit. Ad quae verba anonymus quidam Judaeus sic commentatur: Nunquam homo dicat, se aliquid acturum, sine hac conditione: Si Deus voluerit. Erat quidam, qui dixit: Cras sedebo cum sponsa mea in cubiculo eique adhaerebo. Dixerunt ipsi: Dic, si Deus decreverit vel voluerit. Ille vero responsit: Sive Deus velit, sive minus, cras sedebo cum sponsa in cubiculo. Fecit ita, intravit cum sponsa in cubiculum ibique per totum diem cum illa sedit. Nocte ambo lectum iverunt, sed ambo mortui sunt, antequam illam cognosceret.* – This citation from the Alphabet of Ben Sira is also partly adduced by Friedmann, *Einleitung*, 29 for Seder Eliyahu Rabbah. Then Friedmann provides the following narration (also from the Alphabet of Ben Sira): "It once happened with a man who was a rich noble that he possessed many estates without having enough oxen to plow them. What did that man do? He took a bag of money with 100 *denars* and went to a city to buy oxen and cows to plow his estates. On the way he met Elijah of blessed remembrance. He said to him, 'Where are you going?' He answered, 'To a village with oxen (or, if a proper name: to Oxenville), to buy oxen or cows.' Elijah said to him, 'Say, "If God wills" אם יגזור השם!' He answered, 'Whether he wills or not, look, my money is in my hand and I will do what I need.'" – The man then loses his money, turns back, and fetches fresh money;

he again meets Elijah; then the same dealing between the two men follows with the same result. The man loses his money a second time. He turns back, fetches fresh money, and meets Elijah again. The latter says to him, "Where are you going?" The former answered, "To buy oxen, if God wills אם יגזור השם." Then Elijah said to him, "Go in peace with good success!" — Then he gets back his lost money and is richly blessed. Conclusion: Therefore, everyone who wants to do anything must say, "If God wills."

4:17: Whoever knows how to do good and does not do it, for him it is a sin.

See the saying of R. Tanḥum b. Hiyya (tradent R. Aha) in Lev. Rab. 25 (123A) at § Gal 3:10, #2.

5:4: The recompense of the workers ..., which is withheld by you.

On paying wages, see § Matt 20:8.

5:7: Until it receives the early and late rains (or the early and late fruit).

1. If by πρόϊμον and ὄψιμον one understands the early and late rains, we can compare what is said about their starting time in t. Taʿan. 1.3 (214) and b. Taʿan. 6A at § Luke 2:8 B, n. *a*, S-B footnote. — Parallel passages are found in SDeut 11:14 § 42 (80A) and Tg. Yer. I Deut. 11:14; 28:12. — The early rain fell as a rule in three outpourings that lay a few days apart. Here it was assumed that the later outpouring always exceeded the pervious rains in productivity. Tosefta Taʿanit 1.4 (215): R. Judah (ca. 150) said, "The first early rain (penetrates) one handbreadth (into the earth), the second two handbreadths, and the third three handbreadths."

2. If one relates πρόϊμον and ὀψιμον to the preceding καρπόν, so that the adjectives refer to the early and late fruits, the following passages serve to clarify. Mishnah Terumot 4.6: One assesses the fruit basket at three different times (for the purpose of setting apart the tithes etc.): with early fruits בְּכּוּרוֹת, with late fruits סְיָיפוֹת, and in the middle of the summer (for the fruits do not have the same value at all times). — The same temporal specification is also found in t. Ter. 9.2 (42). ‖ Mishnah Bikkurim 3.1: In what way does one set apart the first fruits? If a person goes through his field and sees a fig that is ripening early, a grape that is ripening early, a pomegranate that is ripening early, he binds them (to mark them) with bast fiber and says, "Behold, these shall be first fruits!" — Parallels are found in t. Bik. 2.8 (101); SDeut 26:10 § 301 (128A). ‖ The early fruits were particular esteemed. Babylonian Talmud Sanhedrin 91A: Like a king of flesh and blood who had a beautiful arboretum in which there were beautiful early fruits ...; see the whole passage at § Matt 10:28, #1, n. *c*. — Genesis Rabbah 22 (14D): "Cain brought a gift from the fruits of the soil to Yahweh" (Gen 4:3), from the unusable (bad) ones. Like a bad tenant who had eaten the early fruits himself and honored the king with the late fruits הסייפות.

5:12 A: Do not swear, neither by heaven, nor by the earth.

On oaths, see § Matt 5:33; for the admonition itself, see § Matt 5:34 and § Matt 5:34–36.

5:12 B: Let your Yes be Yes and your No be No.

See § Matt 5:37.

5:14 A: If someone among you is sick, let him call the elders of the community, and they shall pray about him.

See b. B. Bat. 116A at § Matt 8:5. — On visiting the sick, see the relevant section in the excursus "Works of Love," II, E.

5:14 B: Anointing with oil in the name of the Lord.

Midrash Ecclesiastes 1:8 (9A): Hananiah, the son of the brother of R. Joshua (ca. 110), had gone to Kefar-Nahum (Capernaum). The sectarians (Jewish Christians) did something to him (by magical arts) and brought him in (to the city), with him riding on a donkey on a Sabbath (a sign of apostasy from Judaism). When he came to his uncle Joshua, he put oil on him (anointed him with oil), whereby he was healed.[345] — On the use of oil as a remedy, see § Matt 6:17 A, #2; § Mark 6:13; also see the excursus "Sheol, Gehenna, and the Garden of Eden," III, #2, A, n. *q*, specifically the passages that depict the tree of life as an olive tree whose oil heals all sicknesses.

5:16 A: Confess your sins to one another.

On the confession of sin of the sick person, see the excursus "Works of Love," II, E.

5:16 B: Pray for one another.

The obligation to intercede for another person is given as a charge in b. Ber. 12B; see § 1 Tim 2:1. — The leprous man is supposed to call out, "Unclean, unclean!" (Lev 13:45), so that all who hear it may plead for mercy for him; see b. Moʿed Qaṭ. 5A in the excursus "Leprosy and Lepers," #2 n. *n*. — Mourners and people on whom the ban was imposed had to walk through the forecourt in a different direction than all the others so that one might remember them in intercessory sympathy; see in the excursus "Excommunication from the Synagogue," II, A, #4, n. *m*. — Even a sick tree was supposed to be outwardly recognizable "so that the people might see it and plead for mercy for it" (b. Šabb. 67A.33). — On intercession for the sick in particular, see b. Ned. 40A, b. Šabb. 12A and b. Ned. 39B in the excursus "Works of Love," II, E." See also § 2 Cor 1:11.

345. Adolf Schlatter, *Die Kirche Jerusalems vom Jahr 70–130* (Gütersloh: C. Bertelsmann, 1898), 10f.

5:16 C: The prayer of a righteous man.

Mekilta Exodus 15:25 (53A): "(Moses) cried out to Yahweh, and Yahweh pointed out to him a piece of wood" (Exod 15:25). From here it follows that it is not difficult for the righteous to accept (what is requested). Incidentally, you learn that the prayer of the righteous is short. — God longs for the prayers of the righteous; see b. Yebam. 64A at § Matt 7:7 A, #2, n. *d*. — The prayer of the righteous turns God's thoughts from severity to mercy; see b. Sukkah 14A at § Matt 7:7 A, #2, n. *g*. — On the relation between the power of repentance and the power of prayer, see Lev. Rab. 10 (111D) at § Matt 4:17 A, #2, middle of 3rd paragraph; see also § Matt 7:7 A, #2.

5:17: Three years and six months.

In 1 Kgs 17:1, it says generally: "Neither dew nor rain shall come 'these years.'" 1 Kings 18:1 is somewhat more specific: "And it happened 'after many days' that the word of Yahweh came to Elijah 'in the third year' and said, 'Go and appear to Ahab, so that I may make it rain some upon the earth.'" — The targum sticks closely to the wording of the base text. Yet the chronologist of the ancient synagogue says in S. ʿOlam Rab. 17: In the 3rd year of Ahab, there was a great famine in Samaria for three years. Later, R. Yohanan († 279), assumes that the drought lasted 18 months; according to another tradition, 14 months.

Leviticus Rabbah 19 (118D): "It happened after many days ..." (1 Kgs 18:1). R. Berekhiah (ca. 340) and R. Helbo (ca. 300) said in the name of R. Yohanan: 3 months in the 1st year and 3 months in that last (= 3rd year) and 12 in the middle (in the 2nd year); see, these are 18 months. Yet were those "many days"? Yet they were days of hardship, so (Scripture) calls them "many." — The parallel in Midr. Esth. 1:4 (86A) replaces "three months" in the 1st and 3rd year with "one month" and so comes to a total of 14 months as the length of the dry period.

Both traditions (18 months and 14 months) alongside each other show that the numbers should not be pressed, but rather are understood according to the rule according to which a part of a day, a month, or a year should be calculated as a full day, a full month, or a full year (see § Matt 12:40 and b. Roš Haš. 2A); the 18 or 14 months of R. Yohanan thus ultimately mean the same thing that the 3 years of S. ʿOlam Rab. mean, except that they more precisely express that those 3 years amounted to at least 18 or 14 months. — In Ratner's edition of S. ʿOlam Rab., there is a statement that goes one step further, explaining that the Oxford manuscript in chapter 17 does not read "three years," but rather "three and a half years." Here we encounter the same tradition in Jewish circles that meets us in the NT in the "three years and six months" in Luke 4:25 and Jas 5:17. Yet one must be cautious of finding here a view expressed that opposes the passages above. The temporal specification "three and a half years" is found in rabbinic literature so frequently and in such different contexts[a] that it can hardly be taken literally, but rather should be seen simply as a popular replacement for the general expression "for some time," that is, the number three and a half as half of seven became a round number, like the number seven itself. So too the three years and six months in Luke 4:25 and Jas 5:17 is merely a different expression for "for some time," corresponding exactly to the "many days" in 1 Kgs 18:1.

a. Dalman and Kittel have referred to the following passages:[346] Midrash Lamentations 1:1: An Athenian came to Jerusalem and spent 3.5 years there in order to study the language of wisdom. — Jerusalem Talmud Šabbat 7.9B.67: R. Yohanan († 279) and R. Simeon b. Laqish (ca. 250) spent 3.5 years studying one paragraph. — Midrash Song of Songs 2:16 (103A): R. Yohanan was beset by pain and suffered 3.5 years from shivers (Dalman: "from a bladder stone"). — Midrash Lamentations Introduction 30 (40A): Nebuchadnezzar sent Nebuzaradan to destroy Jerusalem, and he spent 3.5 years there ... and he was unable to conquer it. — Midrash Lamentations 2:2 (63A): Emperor Hadrian besieged Betar for 3.5 years. ‖ Midrash Psalm 93 § 6 (208A): Emperor Hadrian wanted to fathom the depth of the Adriatic Sea. He took ropes and let (them) down for 3.5 years. Then he heard a voice from heaven, which called out, "Let off, Hadrian!" ‖ Midrash Lamentations Introduction #25 (39A): R. Jonathan (ca. 220) said, "For 3.5 years the Shekinah lingered on the Mount of Olives in the hope that the Israelites would repent." ‖ Midrash Lamentations 1:5 (51B): For 3.5 years Vespasian besieged Jerusalem. ‖ Seder ʿOlam Rabbah 30: The battles of Ben Kozeba lasted 3.5 years (so read instead of 2.5 years).

5:19: If anyone has strayed from the truth and someone brings him back.

On the duty to bring back an erring person to the right way, see § Matt 18:15.

5:20 A: Whoever has brought back a sinner from the error of his way will save his (own) soul from death.

See m. ʿAbot 5.18 at § Rom 5:15 A, #3; see t. Yoma 5.11 (191) (b. Yoma 87A.23) at § Heb 6:4–6, #1, n. *e*.

5:20 B: To cover a multitude of sins.

See § 1 Pet 4:8.

346. Gustaf Dalman, *Jesus-Jeschua: Die Drei Sprachen Jesu; Jesus in der Synagoge, auf dem Berge, Neim Passahmahl, am Kreuz* (Leipzig: J. C. Hinrich, 1922), 48; Gerhard Kittel, *Rabbinica: Paulus im Talmud; Die "Macht" auf dem Haupte; Runde Zahlen* (Leipzig: J. C. Hinrich, 1920), 33f.

The First Letter of Peter

1:2: May (your) peace be increased!

On the greeting formula in letters: "May your peace be (or become) great" שלמכון יסגר, see t. Sanh. 2.6 (416) with parallels at § Matt 4:12, #2.

1:3: To a living hope.

4 Ezra 7:120 mentions an everlasting (= imperishable) hope *spes perennis*: "(What does it help us) that an everlasting hope is promised to us if we have so woefully fallen prey to vanity?"

1:4: That is preserved in heaven.

τετηρημένος = הַמְשׁוּמָּר, Aram. דְּאִצְטְנַע; this is said of the wine that is preserved in its grapes since the days of creation for the meal of the righteous; see b. Sanh. 99A and b. Ber. 34B § Matt 26:29; and Tg. Song. 8:2 at § Matt 25:34 B, penultimate paragraph.

1:5: In the last time (see § Heb 1:1).

1:10: Concerning this salvation, prophets searched and looked.

Targum Ecclesiastes 1:8: "The earlier prophets toiled away at all the things that should happen in the world, and they were not able to find the end of them."

1:11: The sufferings affecting Christ.

See the rabbinic passages that deal with the sufferings of the Messiah at § Luke 24:26, I, #4.

1:12: Into which angels long to take a look.

Also in the Greek fragments of Syncellus from 1 Enoch, παρακύπτειν is predicated of the angels; see the passage at § Rev 8:2, n. *b*.

1:15: To the holy one who has called you.

ὁ ἅγιος "the holy one" appears as a designation for God only here in the NT. In the OT קָדוֹשׁ we find it in the same sense in Isa 40:25; Hab 3:3; Job 6:10 (cf. also קְדוֹשׁ יִשְׂרָאֵל "the holy one of Israel" in Isa 1:4; 5:19, 24; 10:20; 12:6, among many others). — "The holy one" is found more often as a designation for God in the apocrypha and pseudepigrapha. Sirach 4:14: "Those who serve her (namely wisdom) serve the holy one ἁγίῳ." — The Hebrew text reads: "The servants of the holy one are her servants משרתי קדש משרתיה." — Sirach 23:9:

"Do not become accustomed to naming the holy one τοῦ ἁγίου." The passage is missing in the Hebrew text. — Sirach 43:10: "According to the words of the holy one ἐν λόγοις ἁγίου (Hebrew: בדבר אל = according to the word of God) they (the stars) stand in their order." — Sirach 47:8: "In all his works he offered thanks to the holy one ἁγίῳ." — Sirach 48:20: "The holy one ὁ ἅγιος exalted them up to heaven." — In the last two passages the Hebrew text does not have a word corresponding to ἅγιος. ‖ See further Bar 4:22, 37; 5:5; Tob 12:12, 15. ‖ 1 Enoch 1:3: "The great holy one will go out from his dwelling." — 1 Enoch 93:11: "Who is there among all the children of men who could hear the voice of the holy one and would not be shaken?" — See further 1 En. 10:1; 12:3; 14:1; 25:3; 84:1; 92:2; 97:6; 98:6; 104:9. — In rabbinic literature the simple קָדוֹשׁ "the holy one" is found only rarely as a replacement for God's name; see, for example, b. Sanh. 92A at § 1 Cor 15:51, n. *a*. However, the fuller "the holy one—blessed be He!" הַקָּדוֹשׁ בָּרוּךְ הוּא became the most common designation for God, which can be found on every page. This corresponds to the Aramaic expression קֻדְשָׁא בְּרִיךְ הוּא "the holiness, blessed may it be!," see the excursus "The Memra of Yahweh," #3, A, n. *k*. Yet the simple "the holiness" הַקֹּדֶשׁ, Aram. קוּדְשָׁא is also used as a designation for God. Sifre Numbers 15:31 § 112 (33A): If someone says, "He (Moses) said the whole Torah from a mouth of holiness מפי הקודש, but this (one) word Moses said from his own mouth," then this is true of such a person: "He has despised the word of Yahweh" (Num 15:31). ‖ Targum Lamentations 3:8: "If he (God) wants to enact something good in the world, it goes forth from the mouth of holiness מִן פּוּם קוּדְשָׁא (while calamity is proclaimed by a *bath qol*).

1:16: You shall be holy, for I am holy.

See SLev 19:2 (342A) at § Matt 6:9 C, n. *d*.

1:17: Who judges without respect of the person (see § Rom 2:11).

1:18: From your idle walking handed down by your fathers.

That which is handed down by the fathers is seen as a ground to excuse those who come later. Babylonian Talmud Ḥullin 13B: Hiyya b. Abba (ca. 280) said that R. Yohanan († 279) said, "The non-Israelites outside the land (Israel) are not idolaters (by their free self-decision), but rather they (simply) maintain the custom of their fathers." ‖ Midrash Esther 1:3 (85B): R. Hiyya b. Abba (ca. 280) said, "The kings of Media were blameless, and God had nothing against them, apart from idolatry, which their fathers had handed down to them." — Parallels are found in TanḥB חקת § 27 (60A); Pesiq. 40B (here instead of R. Judah b. Abba, one should read: R. Hiyya b. Abba) and Pesiq. Rab. 14 (65A), without authorial attribution.

1:20: Known before the creation of the world.

On the preexistence of the Messiah, see § John 1:1 A. — πρὸ καταβολῆς κόσμου, see § Eph 1:4 and § Heb 4:3 B.

1:23: Born again … by … the word of God (see § Jas 1:18).

1:25: The word of the Lord remains forever.

On the eternal existence of the Torah, see § Matt 5:18 B, #1.

2:2: Like newborn babes.

It was said of a proselyte that he was like a newborn child; see b. Yebam. 48B and 62A at § John 3:3, #3.

2:4 (see on Ps 118:22f. at § Matt 21:42, #1).

2:6–10.

On the citations from Isa 28:16; 8:14; and Hos 2:23, see § Rom 9:33 and § Rom 9:25, 26. — On "cornerstone," see § Eph 2:20 B; on βασίλειον ἱεράτευμα, see § Rev 1:6.

2:12: So that they ... might praise God ... on the basis of the good works.

See § Matt 5:16, #2 and § Rom 2:24, #2.

2:13f. (see § Rom 13:1–5).

2:17: Honor everyone!

Derek Ereṣ Zuṭa 1 (20B): Love people and honor them! — See further at § John 12:43, #2.

2:18: You servants, be subject to your masters in all fear.

See the excursus "The Nature of Ancient Jewish Slavery."

2:19: If someone endures pain while suffering unjustly.

See § Matt 5:10, #1; see 2 En. 50:3; 51:3 at § Rom 4:2f., #1, η.

2:23 A: Who when reviled did not revile in turn.

See b. Šabb. 88B = Yoma 23A at § Matt 5:11 A; Der. Er. Zut. 1; Sanh. 7A; Midr. Ps. 16 § 11; Midr. Ps. 86 § 1 at § Matt 5:11 B, #7.

2:23 B: He entrusted himself to the one who judges justly.

Appealing to God is not without danger (see § Rom 12:19 C, #2).

3:1: So that they might be won by their wives' behavior without words.

See the citations at § 1 Cor 7:16.

3:3: The external kind with the braiding of the hair.

On women's hairstyles, see § 1 Cor 11:5, 4th paragraph.

3:6: As Sarah obeyed Abraham, calling him "lord."

Tanḥuma חיי שרה 29A: Abraham's wife honored him and called him "lord"; as it says, "Since my lord is old" (Gen 18:12).

3:7 A: The weaker vessel.

On σκεῦος in general, see § Rom 9:21 #2; on σκεῦος specifically concerning women, see § 1 Thess 4:4 A.

3:7 B: Showing honor (see § Eph 5:25).

3:7 C: Lest your prayers be hindered (made fruitless).

This can be compared with the expression תְּפִלָּה עֲקוּרָה "an uprooted, unfruitful, failed prayer"; see b. Bek. 44B at § Matt 7:7 A, #2, n. *n*.

3:9 A: Do not repay evil for evil (see § Rom 12:17 A).

3:9 B: Rather, bless (cf. § Rom 12:14 A).

3:10–12 (following Ps 34:13–17).

1. Psalm 34:13–17 according to the base text: "Who is the man who desires life, loves length of life, that he may see good? Keep your tongue from evil and guard your lips lest they speak deceit. Renounce evil and do good, seek peace and pursue it. The eyes of Yahweh (pay heed) to the righteous and his ears to their cry. The face of Yahweh (is) against those who do evil."

2. ὁ γὰρ θέλων ζωὴν ἀγαπᾶν etc.; see Lev. Rab. 16 (116B) at § 2 Cor 2:16; and b. ʿAbod. Zar. 19B.25 at § Matt 19:17 A. ‖ Sifre Deuteronomy 11:26 § 54 (86B): Likewise, it says (literally: you say = you read): "Death and life is in the hand of the tongue, and whoever loves it enjoys its fruit" (Prov 18:21). Whoever loves good enjoys the fruits; whoever loves evil enjoys fruits (thus the good and wicked man are equal concerning success and recompense!). R. Eliezer b. Yose the Galilean (ca. 150) said, "Who whispered (this) to you? The Torah (= Holy Scripture) says, 'Keep your tongue from evil and guard your lips lest they speak deceit'" (thus there is a difference between the good and the evil!). ‖ TanḥumaB מצורע § 5 (23A): "Death and life are in the hand of the tongue" (Prov 18:21). Wicked is the evil tongue (= slander); for no one lets it go forth from his mouth until he denies God (= before he does not deny God); as it says, "Those who say, 'We will make our tongues mighty, our lips are with us, who is our Lord?!'" (Ps 12:5). God calls out, so to speak, against those who speak slanders: "Who rises up for me against the wicked, who steps up for me against evildoers?" (Ps 94:16). Will someone be able to resist them and will gehenna be able to resist them? And gehenna cries out, "I too cannot resist them!" Then God said, "I speak from above and you from below. I hurl arrows at them from above, and you toss glowing coals on them from below; as it says, 'The hero's arrows, sharpened, along with broom coals' (Ps 120:4)." (Broom coals are supposed to have embers for a long time, so they are used by gehenna as fuel; see excursus

"Sheol, Gehenna, and the Garden of Eden," II.) God said to them, "If you wish to be kept safe from gehenna, then keep far from slander, and you will obtain this and the future world; as it says, 'Who is the man who desires life, loves length of life, that he may see good?' (Ps 34:13). 'Who desires life' in this world, 'loves length of life' in the future world. Therefore it says, 'Keep your tongue from evil ...' (Ps 34:14)." ‖ See b. Ber. 17A at § Matt 5:39 A, TanḥB מצורע § 4 (23A) at § Luke 2:25 C, #4, n. *c*.

3. On the power of the tongue, see § Jas 3:5ff.

4. ζητησάτω εἰρήνην καὶ διωξάτω αὐτήν; see the passages at § Rom 12:18; and § Heb 12:14. – Notably, Aaron was celebrated as the man of peace and the peacemaker (see § Matt 5:9, #1, middle). ‖ See Lev. Rab. 21 (120B) at § 1 Cor 1:10 B, middle.

5. ὀφθαλμοὶ κυρίου ... καὶ ὦτα αὐτοῦ; see m. ʾAbot 2.1 at § Luke 10:20, #2, n. *a*.

3:14: If you suffer for the sake of righteousness, (you are) blessed! (cf. § Matt 5:10).

3:15 A: Hallow the Lord Christ in your hearts.

ἁγιάσατε; see Isa 8:13: אֶת־יהוה ... אֹתוֹ תַקְדִּישׁוּ "Yahweh ..., hallow him." ‖ See SLev 19:2 (342A) at § Matt 6:9 C, n. *d*. ‖ Exodus Rabbah 15 (78C): God said, "... Behold, I hallow Israel, and they shall hallow me" והן מקדשין אותי!

3:15 B: Always be ready to answer everyone who demands an account of you concerning the hope in you, but with gentleness and timidity.

Mishnah ʾAbot 2.14: R. Eleazar (b. ʿArakh [ca. 90]) said, "Be keen to study the Torah and know what you may answer to the freethinkers." – The same is found as a baraita in b. Sanh. 38B with the addition: R. Yohanan († 279) said, "This has been taught only concerning a non-Jewish freethinker; but an Israelite freethinker will only further degenerate in this way (he should not be given any answer at all)." ‖ Sifre Numbers 18:20 § 119 (39B): "'Keep me that I may be freed' (Ps 119:117) .... They might ask me from the nations of the earth and from the families of the earth, and I might not know how to answer them and would be found ashamed in their eyes; and so it says, 'I will speak of your testimonies before kings and will not be put to shame' (Ps 119:46)." ‖ Sifre Deuteronomy 6:7 § 34 (74A): "Inculcate them in your children" (Deut 6:7); so that they (the words of the Torah) may be well-ordered in your mouth; for if someone asks you about something, you should not answer stammering (uncertainly), but rather tell him immediately (clearly and certainly). – The same is found as a baraita in b. Qidd. 30A. ‖ Leviticus Rabbah 3 (supplement 134D): Blessed is the man who has the words of the Torah as his own and in whose hand they are kept safe, and who knows how to give a complete answer with them in the right place! About such a man Scripture says, "The counsel of a man's heart is deep water" (Prov 20:5). ‖ Babylonian Talmud Sanhedrin 38B: Rab Nahman (b. Jacob? [† 320]; according to Bacher, Ben Isaac [† 356] is meant)[347] said, "Whoever knows how to answer the sectarians like Rab Idit (2nd half of

---

347. Bacher, *Die Agada der palästinensischen Amoräer*, 3:708.

the 3rd century) may answer; but if not, he should not answer." That sectarian said to Rab Idit, "It is written, 'He (God) said to Moses, "Go up to Yahweh"' (Exod 24:1); 'go up to "me"' it should say!" (The sectarian means to infer a plurality in God on the basis of the juxtaposition of "God" and "Yahweh.") He answered him, "This refers to Metatron (the highest angel of the throne), whose name is like the name of his Lord; as it is written, 'My name is in him' (Exod 23:21)." "If this is so" (answered the sectarian), "one should worship him!" "It is written, 'Do not exchange him' (so Rab Idit interprets Exod 23:21): do not confuse me (God) with him!" (So he cannot be worshiped.) "Yet if this is so" (responded the sectarian), "what should I make of this: 'For he will not forgive your misdeed' (Exod 23:21)?" (For if he is not a God worthy of worship, then it is obvious that he cannot forgive sin!) He said to him, "We have the conviction that we have not assumed him to be a envoy;[348] for it is written, 'He (Moses) said to him (God), "If you do not go (with us) in person, do not lead us up from here"' (Exod 33:15)."

3:19: To the spirits in prison.

On gehenna as a dungeon, see the excursus "Sheol, Gehenna, and the Garden of Eden," II, #5, n. *w*.

3:20: Who were once disobedient ....

On the generation of the flood, see § Matt 24:38, 39. — On God's longsuffering in the days of Noah, see m. ʾAbot 5.2: There were ten generations from Adam to Noah to make known how great longsuffering אֶרֶךְ אַפַּיִם is before him (God); for all the generations had caused wrath to arise before him, until he brought the waters of the flood over them.

3:22: Angels and dominions and powers (see § Eph 1:21).

4:8: Love covers a multitude of sins.

Proverbs 10:12: "Love covers תְּכַסֶּה אַהֲבָה all misdeeds"; the targum replaces the Hebrew for "love covers" with מְכַסָּא רַחֲמוּתָא. — Proverbs 10:12 is rarely cited in rabbinic literature. Midrash Psalm 1 § 18 (9A): R. Hiyya (ca. 280) said, "As the waters cover the nakedness of the sea, as it says, 'Like the waters that cover the sea' (Isa 11:9), so the words of the Torah cover the nakedness of Israel, for it says, 'Love covers all misdeeds' (Prov 10:12)" (here, following Buber on the passage, "love" = "Torah" on the basis of Prov 5:19). ‖ Leviticus Rabbah 7 (109D): "Hate arouses disputes" (Prov 10:12). The hate that the Israelites brought forth between themselves and their Father in heaven (by the golden calf) aroused many judgments for them.... Yet "love covers all misdeeds" (Prov 10:12), for God loved the Israelites; as it says, "I have loved you, says Yahweh" (Mal 1:2). A different explanation. "Hate arouses disputes." The hate that Aaron called forth between the Israelites and their Father in heaven (by the golden calf) aroused many judgments for them.... Yet "love covers all misdeeds," that is,

348. S-B: On פַּרְוַנְקָא "messenger, envoy," see Nöldeke in Richard Adelbert Lipsius, *Die Apokryphen Apostelgeschichten und Apostellegenden* (Braunschweig: C. A. Schwetschke und Sohn, 1883), 1:299.

the prayer that Moses prayed for him (Aaron).... ‖ Rashi explains Prov 10:12B as follows: "If people adapt their works well, God covers their misdeeds."

4:9: Hospitality (see § Rom 12:13 B).

4:12: Happening to test you (cf. § Matt 4:1 A).

4:14: If you are reviled because of Christ's name, blessed are you! (cf. § Matt 5:11 A).

4:15: Like one who gets mixed up in the affairs of others.

ἀλλοτριεπίσκοπος (so Gebhardt 1881) perhaps = הנכנס בתחום שאינו שלו "whoever intrudes on a prayer that is not his," or שנכנס בתחומו של חבירו "whoever intrudes on the prayer of another."

Numbers Rabah 7 (147D): (That leprosy comes as a punishment) for someone intruding on a prayer that is not his is shown by Uzziah, who tried to intrude on the prayer of the priesthood. What is written of him? "Leprosy broke out on his forehead" (2 Chr 26:19). — See also the citations at § Rom 8:20f., n. *p*. The last passage adduced in that section (Gen. Rab. 6 folio 5A) is followed by the words: If Scripture so belittled the one who intruded with (divine) permission, how much more does this go for the one who (intrudes) without permission.

4:17 A: So that judgment may begin with the house of God.

1. On the expression, see Midr. Eccl. 9:15 (45A): (Noah's contemporaries said to him,) "Where will the punishment begin מְשָׁרְיָא? With the house מן בייתיה of this man (i.e., with your house) it will begin!" When Methuselah died (before the flood), they said to Noah, "Did his (God's) punishment not begin with the house of this man?"

2. On the maxim, see T. Benj. 10: "The Lord will judge Israel first because of the godlessness against him.... And then he will judge all the gentiles." ‖ Babylonian Talmud Baba Qamma 60A: R. Samuel b. Nahman (ca. 260) said that R. Jonathan (ca. 220) said, "A judgment of God comes only when the godless are in the world, but it begins מתחלת only with the righteous at first; as it says, 'If fire breaks out and finds thorns' (Exod 22:5). When does fire break out? When there are thorns for it. Yet it begins only with the righteous at first; for it says, 'And a heap of grain was consumed' (Exod 22:5). It does not say, 'and it (the fire) consumes a heap of grain,' but rather 'A heap of grain was consumed,' for it was already consumed (before the fire caught the thorns)." Rab Joseph († 333) taught as a tannaitic tradition: "What does 'Among you no one shall go out from the door of his house until morning' (Exod 12:22) mean? If authority was given to the destroyer (see § 1 Cor 10:10), he makes no difference between the righteous and the godless, and not only this but also he begins first with the righteous; as it says, 'I will root out from you the righteous as well as the evildoer' (Ezek 21:9) (the righteous man is named first)." Then Rab Joseph wept (and said), "Even they are all considered as nothing!" Abbayye († 338/39) said to him, "This is a

happiness for them; for it is written, 'The righteous is taken away before misfortune' (Isa 57:1)." ‖ Babylonian Talmud Roš Haššanah 8B: A different baraita: "'For this is a statute for Israel' (Ps 81:5; to be judged on New Year's Day). Here I hear only about Israel. What about the nations of the world? Scripture teaches, 'A law of the God of Jacob' (Ps 81:5). If this is so, what does Scripture mean to teach with 'For this is a statute for Israel'? It teaches that the Israelites first come into judgment. This corresponds to the view of Rab Hisda († 309), for Rab Hisda said, 'If king and community, the king comes into judgment first; as it says, "To do justice with his servant (the king) and justice with his people Israel" (1 Kgs 8:59) (the king is mentioned first).'" ‖ See b. Šabb. 55A at § Matt 19:20 A, 1st third.

4:17 B: Yet if first with us, what will the end of the disobedient be?

Midrash Psalm 3 § 1 (17A): "You are fearsome, O God, from your sanctuary ממקדשיך" (Ps 68:36). R. Yohanan († 279) said, "Because of what they (the enemies) did to the sanctuary (מן in ממקדשיך is not local, but rather causal, understood to mean 'due to'). If he took no consideration for his house and his sanctuary, how much less will he take consideration for others when he exacts punishment from the others!" — Parallels are found in Midr. Ps. 9 § 12 (44B); 99 § 1 (212A). The idea is applied differently in b. Zebaḥ. 115B. ‖ Exodus Rabbah 29 (88D): (The prophet Jeremiah said,) "I called God 'king of the nations' (see Jer 10:7), in order to say, 'If he has not spared his children and the members of his house, should he spare others? For it says, "You are fearsome, O God, because of your sanctuary" (Ps 69:35).'"

4:19: The faithful creator.

On the faithfulness of God, see § 1 Cor 1:9.

5:2 A: Shepherd the herd of God (cf. § John 21:15, 16).

5:2 B: Not by compulsion, but rather willingly.

The citation from Num. Rab. 11 (163D) adduced by Wettstein does not belong here. Correctly translated, the passage reads: "God said to the priests, 'Not because I told you that you should bless the Israelites may you bless them in a hurry (literally: with an introduction) and hastiness, but rather you shall bless them with attentiveness (reverence) of heart.'"

5:4: The unfading crown of glory.

Testament of Benjamin 4: "Imitate his (Joseph's) mercy with a good disposition so that you too may bear crowns of glory στεφάνους δόξης."

5:5: God resists the proud, but he gives grace to the humble.

Proverbs 3:34 according to the base text: "With the scoffers, he (God) scoffs; but he gives grace to the humble." — Septuagint: Κύριος ὑπερηφάνοις ἀντιτάσσεται, ταπεινοῖς δὲ δίδωσι χάριν. — Targum: "He topples scoffers, but he gives grace to the humble." — See rabbinic passages that cite Prov 3:34 at § Matt 5:6, penultimate paragraph beginning with Mek. Exod. 15:26 (53B). ‖ Numbers Rabbah 4 (142D): "Do not gloat before the king and do not step into the place of the great" (Prov 25:6). If a person has to make an effort at humility before a king of flesh and blood, how much more before God! Further, we have learned (see m. ʾAbot 5.20): "Be firm (courageous) like the leopard and light like the eagle and quick like the stag and strong like the lion to do the will of your Father in heaven!" (The author of this saying is Judah b. Tema, a Tannaim of an uncertain time.) This intends to teach that pride (arrogance) is not valid before God. — For the condemnation of pride and for the praise of humility, see § Luke 1:51 and § Matt 5:3, #3. — See further § Jas 4:6.

5:7: Casting all your cares on him, because he cares for you.

Psalm 55:23 according to the base text: "Cast your burden (יְהָבְךָ according to the Aram. יְהָבָא = burden) on Yahweh, and he will uphold you." — Septuagint: ἐπίρριψον ἐπὶ κύριον τὴν μέριμνάν σου, καὶ αὐτός σε διαθρέψει. — Targum: "Cast your hope on Yahweh, and he will nourish you." ‖ Genesis Rabbah 79 (51A): R. Hiyya the elder (ca. 200) and R. Simeon, the son of Rabbi, and R. Simeon b. Halapta had forgotten some expressions from an Arabic targum. They came to an Arab merchant to learn them from there. Then they heard his voice, how he said to someone else: "Hoist this burden יְהָבָא on me!" From this they heard that יהבא = מַשּׂוֹי "burden," as it says, "Cast your burden on Yahweh, and he will uphold you" (Ps 55:23). — Similar material is found in b. Roš Haš. 26B.17 and b. Meg. 18A.36. — On cares, see further § Matt 6:25 and 26.

5:8: Your adversary, the devil.

On διάβολος, see § Matt 4:1 B, #1 and #2; on ἀντίδικος, § Matt 4:1 B, #3, B. — The devil is explicitly designated as "adversary" in LAE 10, 17, and 33.

5:9: Resist him (see § Jas 4:7).

5:13: The elect in Babylon.

If "Babylon" refers to Rome, the passages at § Rev 14:8 should be compared.

The Second Letter of Peter

1:1: Simeon Peter.

On the form Simeon, see § Matt 10:2 B.

1:5–7 (for this inference chain, see § Rom 5:3 B).

1:13: In this dwelling (see § 2 Cor 5:1).

1:21 A: Prophecy was never issued by the will of man.

Sifre Deuteronomy 1:6 § 5 (66B): "Yahweh our God spoke to us on Horeb, saying" (Deut 1:6). He (Moses) said to them, "I do not speak to you from myself, but rather from the mouth of God I speak to you." — The same is also found in § 9 (67A.13); § 12 (67B.14); § 19 (69A.36). ‖ A baraita in b. Sanh. 99A: "He has despised the word of Yahweh" (Num 15:31).... Even if someone says, "The whole Torah originates from God with the exception of this verse, which is not God, but rather Moses spoke from his own mouth, he is like one to whom it applies, "He has despised the word of Yahweh." ‖ Midrash Song of Songs 1:1 (79A): "And furthermore, since Ecclesiastes was a wise man" (Eccl 12:9). If someone else had said them (the words of Ecclesiastes), you would have had to incline your ears to hear these words, and furthermore (= and this is all the more the case) since Solomon said them; and if he had said them according to his opinion (according to his own discretion), you would have had to incline your ears and listen to them, and furthermore since he said them in the holy spirit (by the power of inspiration). — See further passages in the excursus "The Old Testament Canon and Its Inspiration," II, n. 17.

1:21 B: Driven by the Holy Spirit, men spoke from God.

See on this the excursus "The Old Testament Canon and Its Inspiration," II, notes 16ff.; see also § 2 Pet 1:21 A.

2:4 (see § Jude 6).

2:5 A: Noah, a herald of righteousness.

Noah appears as κῆρυξ = כָּרוֹז "herald" also in Gen. Rab. 30 (18B): R. Abba b. Kahana (ca. 310) said, "There arose a herald for God in the generation of the flood; this was Noah."

2:5 B: While he brought about a flood over a world of godless people.

See § Matt 24:39 A.

2:6 A: And the cities of Sodom and Gomorrah he condemned to destruction by burning them.

See § Matt 10:15 and § Jude 7.

2:6 B: As an example.

On ὑπόδειγμα, see δεῖγμα at § Jude 7 B.

2:7 A: The righteous Lot.

The judgment of the ancient synagogue about the moral stance of Lot was essentially different: only in a relative sense could he be called a righteous man, namely if he was compared with his wicked contemporaries. Yet, measured by the absolute measure of the law, he was a godless man.[a] He was specifically branded as a despiser of God[b] and fornicator.[c] It therefore is not surprising when even Abraham's connection with him is rebuked several times.[d] See a judgment about Lot that corresponds to that of the apostle in b. Ber. 54B at § Luke 17:32.

a. Genesis Rabbah 50 (32B): "Escape to the mountain, lest you be carried off" (Gen 19:17), by the merit of Abraham, who is called "mountain" (see Song 2:8 and Mic 6:2). "I cannot escape to the mountain" (Gen 19:19).... R. Berekhiah (ca. 340) and R. Levi (ca. 300) said in the name of R. Hama b. Hanina (ca. 260): "... Lot said, 'Before I came to Abraham, God saw my works and the works of the people of my city, and I was a righteous man in their midst. Now when I go to Abraham (= to the mountain), whose works are greater than mine, I cannot exist in his portion.'" — The same is found anonymously in Pesiq. Rab. 3 (10A); ʾAg. Ber. 25 (21B). ‖ Pesiqta Rabbati 3 (9B): If a person is righteous, so too the members of his house and anyone who is associated with him are righteous like him himself. And if someone is godless, so too the members of his house are godless like him himself. — This statement is then explained with the shepherds of Abraham and Lot: the former drove out the livestock with a bound mouth, lest they pasture on the lands of others; the latter let the livestock go about on the property of others with an unbound mouth, not worried about the fact that in this way they robbed others of their possessions and goods. Here Lot is reckoned among the godless; for as the master, so the servant, and as the servant, so the master. — According to Gen. Rab. 41 (25B), this explanation comes from R. Judah b. Simon (ca. 320). ‖ Pesiqta Rabbati 3 (10A): R. Eleazar b. Pedat (ca. 270) said in the name of R. Yose b. Zimra (ca. 220), "See how Lot, the wicked רָשָׁע, cut Abraham, the righteous, out of the divine speech with him! For as long as Lot was associated with him, God did not speak with Abraham; but when Lot separated from him, the (divine) speech rushed to speak to Abraham; as it says, 'And Yahweh said to Abram, after Lot had separated from him' (Gen 13:14)." — The same is found in Tanḥ. ויצא 37B; TanḥB ויצא § 21 (79B).

b. Genesis Rabbah 41 (25C): "Lot went eastward מקדם" (Gen 13:11); he withdrew from the primordial one of the world מקדמונו של עולם (i.e., God). He said, "I like neither Abraham nor his God!"

c. Targum Yerušalmi I Genesis 13:10: "Lot raised his eyes for fornication." ‖ Pesiqta Rabbati 3 (10A): "Lot raised his eyes" (Gen 13:10), for he directed his eyes to fornication; as it says, "The wife of Joseph's master raised her eyes to him" (Gen 39:7). (Proof by word analogy between וישא and ותשא in Gen 13:10 and 39:7.) "And he saw the whole circle כִּכָּר" (Gen 13:10); as it says, "Since for a prostitute one comes down to a loaf כִּכָּר of bread" (Prov 6:26). "So that it was a completely soaked land מַשְׁקֶה" (Gen 13:10); for they (the women there) were all whores and deserved to be tested like women suspected of adultery (by the drink of the water of jealousy מַשְׁקֶה). So R. Simeon b. Yohai (ca. 150) propounded. — In b. Naz. 23A and b. Hor. 10B, R. Yohanan († 279) is the author; in Gen. Rab. 41 (25B), R. Yose b. Hanina (ca. 270) is the author. ‖ Genesis Rabbah 41 (25C): "Lot chose for himself the whole ring of the Jordan" (Gen 13:11). R. Yose b. Zimra (ca. 220) said, "Like someone who chooses the place of his mother's fornication."[349] ‖ Genesis Rabbah 41 (25B): Rab Nahman b. Hanin (an Amora of an uncertain time) said, "Whoever burns לָהוּט (a play on the name לוט) with a ravenous hunger for fornication, one (= God) has him ultimately eaten by his own flesh" (see the deed of Lot and his daughters in Gen 19:30ff.). — The same is found in Gen. Rab. 51 (32D).

d. Genesis Rabbah 41 (25C): "Yahweh said to Abram, after Lot had separated from him" (Gen 13:14). R. Judah (ca. 150) said, "It vexed our father Abraham when Lot, the son of his brother, separated from him. God said, 'He knows how to associate himself with each one and he does not know how to associate himself with Lot, the son of his brother!'" R. Nehemiah (ca. 150) said, "It vexed God when Lot went with our father Abraham. God said, 'I told him, "To your seed I will give this land"' (Gen 12:7), and he associates himself with Lot, the son of his brother, so that he will be his heir. He might as well go and fetch two scroungers from the street and make them his heirs, just as he wants to with the son of his brother!" ‖ Genesis Rabbah 44 (27C): "And behold, the word of Yahweh came to him, saying 'This one will not be your heir'" (Gen 15:4). (This passage, as the previous material shows, was interpreted by R. Eleazar [ca. 270] to refer to Lot.) R. Judan (ca. 350) and R. Eleazar (ca. 270) said in the name of R. Yose b. Zimra (ca. 220): "'Yahweh to him,' 'the word of Yahweh to him,' 'and behold, the word of Yahweh to him,' one angel after the other, one word after the other. I and three angels (God said) will be revealed to you and say, 'Lot, the cursed one (לוט ליטא, wordplay interpreting Lot's name), shall not be Abraham's heir!'" ‖ See Pesiq. Rab. 3 (10A) in n. *a*.

2:7 B: Who was tormented by the way of the wicked in licentiousness.

What Lot heard and saw of scandalous deeds in Sodom is shown by the citations at § Matt 10:15 and § Jude 7. — Persecutions to which Lot himself

349. So Levy, *Chaldäisches Wörterbuch*, 4:18A. The commentary Matt. Keh. is different.

was exposed in Sodom are not mentioned in rabbinic literature; at the most, one could draw on the offensive words in Gen 19:9 here.

Genesis Rabbah 50 (32A): On that day (in Gen 19:1), Lot was appointed chief justice.... When he said to them words that pleased them, they said to him, "Come closer (so the midr interprets גש הלאה in Gen 19:9), move up!" Yet when he said words that did not please them, they said to him, "This one has come to reside here as an alien, and he always wants to play the judge?!" (Gen 19:9).

2:11 (cf. § Jude 9).

2:12: To be caught and destroyed.

Babylonian Talmud Berakot 17A: R. Yohanan († 279) said, "When R. Meir (ca. 150)[350] had finished the book of Job, he would say, 'The end of the human being is to die and the end of cattle is slaughter שְׁחִיטָה.'" ‖ Babylonian Talmud Baba Meṣiʿa 85A: Once a calf was led to slaughter שחיטה; it came and laid its head on the tail of Rabbi's († 217?) cloak and wailed. He said to him, "Go to what you were created for לכך נוצרת!" It has been recounted: Since he had no pity, sufferings came upon him (13 years of tooth pain). — There is a parallel in Gen. Rab. 33 (20B).

2:15: Balaam ..., who loved the recompense of unrighteousness.

See b. Sanh. 106A at § 1 Cor 10:8; see a parallel in Num. Rab. 20 (109A.50); 22 (192D.44); also b. Sanh. 106A at § Rev 2:14, #2. — Balaam is accused several times of greed. Numbers Rabbah 20 (188D): Balaam had three characteristics: an envious eye, a proud (arrogant) mind, and a greedy soul נֶפֶשׁ רחָבָה (so read instead of נ' קצרה). An envious eye, for it is written: "Balaam raised his eyes and saw Israel, how it was encamped according to its tribes" (Num 24:2). A proud (arrogant) mind, for it is written: "For Yahweh refused to let me go with you" (Num 22:13). A greedy soul, for it is written: "If Balak gives me the fullness of his house in silver and gold ..." (Num 22:18). — The same is found in Tanḥ. בלק 232B. ‖ Numbers Rabbah 20 (189B): Balak said, "I will honor you greatly" (Num 22:17); and when he (Balaam) came, he sent him only a steer and a sheep. Then Balaam began to gnash against him with his teeth, for his soul was greedy. — See also m. ʾAbot 5.19 at § Matt 5:3, #2, penultimate paragraph.

2:16: A speechless beast of burden, speaking with the mouth of a human, opposed the foolishness of the prophet.

The conversation between the jenny and Balaam in Num 22:30 is explained in b. Sanh. 105B = b. ʿAbod. Zar. 4B in the following way: What is the case with the understanding of his animal? Balaam was told, "Why do you not ride on a horse?" He answered them, "I sent them (the horses) to fresh grass." The jenny said to him, "Am I not your jenny?" (Balaam,) "Simply to carry burdens." (Jenny,) "On which you have ridden?" (Balaam,) "Only occasion-

350. So read with Bacher, *Die Agada der Tannaïten*, 2:13.1.

ally." (Jenny,) "As long as you have lived up until this day; and not only this but I also perform the work of the wife at night (serve you for intercourse)." ‖ TanḥumaB בלק § 13 (69B): "Yahweh opened the mouth of the jenny"[351] (Num 22:28), to make it known to you that the mouth and the tongue are in his (God's) power, that, when he (Balaam) wanted to curse, his mouth was in (God's) power. "And it (the jenny) said to Balaam, 'What have I done to you that you have hit me now three times שלש רגלים?'" (Num 22:28). Thereby she indicated to him, "You want to eradicate a nation that celebrates three festivals a year?" (שלש רְגָלִים "three meals" = ש' רְגָלִים "three festivals.") Balaam answered the jenny, "Because you have acted wantonly with me" (Num 22:29). Although he was an idolater, he still spoke in the holy language. The language of an idolater, (though,) is indecent (foul; התעלל is an obscene term). "If only there were a sword in my hand, I would have killed you!" (Num 22:29). Like a doctor who went to heal with his tongue (by talking) someone who while traveling had been bitten by a snake. He saw a lizard on the way and began to make the attempt to kill it with a stick. Then he was told, "You cannot kill this. How will you heal with your tongue someone who has been bitten by a snake!" So the jenny said to Balaam, "You cannot kill me unless a sword is in your hand. How will you eradicate a whole nation?" Then he fell silent and found no answer. The princes of Moab, though, began to marvel, for they saw a miracle that had no equal in the world. Some say that he said to them, "It (the jenny) is not mine (this is why it does not follow my leading)." But it answered him, "Am I not your jenny, on which you have ridden as long as you have lived up until this day?" (Num 22:30). You learn that he was not an old man, for it was older than he. "Have I ever had the habit of acting this way with you?" (Num 22:30). When it had spoken, it dies, lest the people say, "This is the one that spoke," and lest they make it a divinity. A different explanation: God spared the honor of that wicked man, lest it be said, "This is the one that Balaam killed." — Parallels are found in Tanḥ. בלק 233B; Num. Rab. 20 (189A). ‖ Targum Yerušalmi I Numbers 22:28ff.: "In that hour the Memra of Yahweh (i.e., God) opened its mouth, and speech came into it, and it said to Balaam, 'What have I done to you that you have hit me now three times?' Balaam said to the jenny, 'Because you have acted faithlessly toward me. If a sword were in my hand, I would have killed you now!' The jenny said to Balaam, 'Woe to you, Balaam, you lack insight! For I am an unclean animal that dies in this world and does not come into the future world, and you are not able to curse me. How much less then the sons of Abraham, Isaac, and Jacob, for whose sake the world was created! And you are going to curse them? Truly, you have deluded the sense of these people and said, "This jenny is not mine. It is loaned into my hand and my horse has been sent into fresh grass (to pasture)." Am I not your jenny, on which you have ridden from your youth until this day? Behold, I have had pleasure from you in intercourse, and I have not intended to act this way with you.' Then he said nothing."

2:19: He is a slave to the one to whom he is subject (cf. § John 8:34).

351. S-B: The mouth of the jenny in Num 22:28 is among the ten things that were created shortly before the start of the Sabbath of creation (see m. ʾAbot 5.6 at § 1 Cor 10:4 B).

2:21 (cf. t. Šabb. 13.5 at § Matt 5:43, #3, end).

2:22 A: A dog that returns to its vomit.

See the baraita in b. Yoma 86B at § Matt 4:17 A, #3, n. *a.* — Babylonian Talmud Yoma 53B: Like a student who has departed from his teacher; if he immediately returns again, he is like "a dog that returns to its vomit" (Prov 26:11). ‖ Leviticus Rabbah 16 (116D): R. Abba b. Kahana (ca. 310) said, "The filthy (profligate) man turns back to his filth; as it says, 'Like a dog that turns back to its vomit' (Prov 26:11)." R. Joshua b. Levi (ca. 250) said, "The fool returns to the way of his foolishness; as it says, 'A fool that returns with his foolishness' (Prov 26:11)."

2:22 B: A pig, washed, to wallow in the mud (cf. b. Ber. 43B at § Matt 7:6 C, #1).

3:7: Saved for fire.

The destruction of heaven and earth by a world fire is represented especially by the Sibylline Oracles;[a] in the other pseudepigrapha this idea is rare.[b] However, rabbinic literature sometimes also mentions a "flood of fire" that God will bring about; yet this serves not to destroy heavens and earth, but rather to punish godless humanity.[c]

a. Sibylline Oracles 3:81ff.: "God who dwells in the ether rolls up the heaven as when a scroll is rolled up, and the whole multifarious vault of heaven will fall to the noble earth and into the sea, and a torrent of mighty fire will flow unremittingly, burning the earth, burning the sea, and the vault of heaven and the days (?) and the creation itself will melt together into one.... And then the judgment of the great God will appear." — Sibylline Oracles 4:170ff.: "Yet if you of evil mind should not obey me ..., fire will come upon the world.... It will burn the whole earth and destroy the whole race of men and all cities, the rivers too and the sea; everything will burn to sooty dust." — See further Sib. Or. 2:196ff.; 4:160; 5:155ff., 274ff., 530f.

b. 1 Enoch 1:6f.: "The high mountains will be shaken, fall, and dissolve; the towering walls will sink and melt in flame like wax before the fire." ‖ Life of Adam and Eve 49: "Because of your transgressions our Lord will bring his wrathful judgment upon your descendants, first with water (in the flood), and a second time (at the end) with fire."

c. Mekilta Exodus 18:1 (64B): R. Eleazar of Modiim († ca. 135) said, "... When Israel was given the Torah ..., all the kings of the world assembled with Balaam, the wicked. They said to him, 'Balaam, maybe he (God) will do to us the same thing that he did to the generation of the flood!...' He answered them, 'You biggest fools in the world; long ago God swore to Noah that he would not bring a flood into the world (see Isa 54:9).' They answered him, 'He may not bring a flood of water, but a flood of fire מַבּוּל שֶׁל אֵשׁ he will bring!' He said to them, 'Neither a flood of fire nor a flood of fire will he bring (now); rather, he is giving the Torah to his people ....'" — There is a parallel in b. Zebaḥ. 116A at § John 1:1–4, n. *a*, near the beginning. ‖ Genesis Rabbah 49 (31C): ("Far be it from you to do this" [Gen 18:25].) R. Aha (ca. 320) said, "(Abraham said to God,) 'You have sworn that you will not bring any more flood into the world. Will you act cunningly against the oath? Will you not bring a flood of water, but a flood of fire? In this case you would not have fulfilled the oath!'" — There is a parallel in Gen. Rab. 39 (23D); Pesiq. 139A. — See also t. Ta'an. 3.1 (218.22); b. Sanh. 108B.

3:8: One day with the Lord is like a thousand years and a thousand years are like one day.

Genesis Rabbah 19 (13A): (Interpretations of Gen 3:8:) They heard the voice of angels who said, "Yahweh Elohim is going to those in the garden (i.e., to Adam and Eve)." R. Levi (ca. 300) and R. Isaac (ca. 300). R. Levi said, "(The voice of the angels said, 'Yahweh Elohim,) the one in the garden is dead (מִתְהַלֵּךְ = he has passed away).'" R. Isaac said, "(The voice of the angels asked, 'Yahweh Elohim,) is he dead, passed away?' (מתהלך as a notarikon = מֵת הָלַךְ לוֹ?). God answered them, 'לְרוּחַ הַיּוֹם' (Gen 3:8), that is, 'with increase of day' לריוח היום; 'behold, I am leaving him alive this day. So I have said to him, "On the day when you eat of it, you will surely die" (Gen 2:17). Yet you do not know whether I mean a day among mine or a day among yours. But behold, I give him a day among mine, which is 1,000 years, and he shall live 930 years and leave 70 years to his descendants; as it says, "Our lifespan—it encompasses 70 years' (Ps 90:10)." ‖ Pesiqta Rabbati 1 (4A): R. Eliezer b. Yose the Galilean (ca. 150) said, "(The days of the Messiah last) 1,000 years; as it says, 'For 1,000 years in your eyes are like yesterday' (Ps 90:4). And it further says, 'The day (singular = a day) of vengeance is in my heart' (Isa 63:4), and a day of God lasts 1,000 years." R. Joshua (ca. 90) said, "2,000 years; for it says, 'Make us glad according to the length of days that you have stricken us' (Ps 90:15), and 'days' (plural) are not less than two days, and one day of God is 1,000 years (so two days = 2,000 years)." R. Abbahu (ca. 300) said, "7,000 years; for it says, 'As a groom has his delight in his bride' (Isa 62:5). How long does the groom's delight in the bride last? Seven (wedding) days, and one day of God is 1,000 years." — The saying of R. Joshua is also found in Midr. Ps. 90 § 17 (197A). ‖ See Gen. Rab. 8 (6A) with parallels at § John 1:1–4, #1, n. *b.* ‖ Genesis Rabbah 22 (14C): "Remember your mercies, Yahweh, and your graces; for they are from eternity" (Ps 25:6): not from now on, but rather they are from eternity. R. Joshua b. Nehemiah (ca. 350) said, "For you bestowed them on the first man; for you said this to him, 'On the day when you eat of it, you will die of death' (Gen 2:17); and if you had not granted him one day among yours, which is 1,000 years, how would he have managed to have progeny?" — In Midr. Ps. 25 § 8 (107A), R. Joshua b. Levi (ca. 250) is the author.

3:9 A: The Lord does not tarry.

Sirach 35:22 (Hebrew): "Even God will not tarry לֹא יִתְמַהְמַהּ and, like a hero, will not restrain himself until he crushes the loins of the unmerciful and exacts revenge on the gentiles לגוים" (perhaps we should read לְגֵאִים "the arrogant"). — The Greek text in Sir 32:18 (according to the numbering in Fritzsche): "The Lord will not tarry ὁ κύριος οὐ μὴ βραδύνῃ, nor show long-suffering to them until he ...." ‖ 2 Baruch 48:39: "The judge will come and not tarry." ‖ See b. Sanh. 97B at § Acts 1:7.

3:9 B: Since he does not want them to perish, but rather for them all to come to repentance.

1. Sifre Numbers 6:26 § 42 (12B): One passage of Scripture reads, "I do not desire the death of anyone who dies" (Ezek 18:32); and another passage reads, "Yahweh desired to kill them" (1 Sam 2:25). How can the two passages be maintained (alongside each other)? Before the judgment is sealed, this applies, "I do not desire ..."; but after the judgment is sealed, this applies, "Yahweh desired ...." There is a parallel in Tanḥ. צו 140B. ‖ A baraita in b. Nid. 69B: The people of Alexandria asked R. Joshua b. Hananiah (ca. 90) twelve things.... One passage of Scripture reads, "I do not desire ..." (Ezek 18:32); another reads, "Yahweh desired ..." (1 Sam 2:25). In the one case (Ezek 18) it deals with those who repent; in the other case with those who do not repent. ‖ Midrash Ecclesiastes 7:15 (36B): R. Josiah (II, ca. 280) said, "God has patience with the godless in this world, in case they might repent or do good deeds, for which he could give them their recompense in this world, or in case righteous children might issue from them." ‖ Tanḥuma וירא 24A: R. Phineas b. Hama (ca. 360) said, "God takes no pleasure in declaring anyone guilty; for it says, 'I do not desire the death of anyone who dies' (Ezek 18:32); likewise it says, 'You are not a God who takes pleasure in evil' (Ps 5:5), and furthermore, 'As surely as I live, says Yahweh Elohim, I never desire the death of the godless' (Ezek 33:11). What does he take pleasure in? Declaring his creatures righteous; as it says, 'Yahweh was pleased to make the Torah great and glorious so that he could declare righteous' (so Midr. Isa. 42:21). You can know this by the following: when people sin and incense him and he is angry with them, what does God do? He goes about and looks for an intercessor for them who can claim a merit for them, and prepares the way before the intercessor. So you find in the days of Jeremiah when he said, 'Roam ... and search ..., whether you find a man ..., who does what is right ..., so I might forgive' (Jer 5:1). And likewise, when the Sodomites sinned, he revealed to Abraham that he might claim merit for them; as it says, 'Yahweh said, "Shall I conceal from Abraham ...?"' (Gen 18:17). Immediately Abraham began to make intercession for them." — Parallels are found in Midr. Ps. 5 § 7 (27A); TanḥB וארא § 11 (13B); Exod. Rab. 9 (73B). — See in TanḥB תזריע § 11 (20A) for a similar explanation that uses Adam to explain the sentence: "God does not take pleasure in declaring a person guilty." ‖ Numbers Rabbah 20 (189A): "If the men have come to call you (Balaam), arise! Go with them!" (Num 22:20). From here you learn that one (= God) lets him go on the way a person wishes to go. For first it says, "You shall not go" (Num 22:12). Yet since he insolently became set on going, he went; for so it is written, "The wrath of God burned because he went" (Num 22:22). God said to him, "O godless man, I take no pleasure in the perdition of the godless, but since you want to go to disappear out of the world, arise, go!" ‖ See Mek. Exod. 15:1 (41B) at § Luke 15:7 A; a similar explanation is found in b. Meg. 10B.35. ‖ See m. Sanh. 6.5 at § 2 Cor 1:3 A.

2. See the essentially different judgment in SNum 18:8 § 117 (37A) and SDeut 32:36 § 326 (139A) at § Luke 15:7 A. — See also b. Sanh. 113B in a baraita: When a godless person perishes from the world, happiness comes into the world; for it says, "When the godless perish, rejoicing reigns" (Prov 11:10). — See also § 2 Cor 2:15 B.

3:10: The earth and the works (creatures) in it will burn (see § 3:7 above).

3:13: New heavens and a new earth (see § Rev 21:1).

3:16: Consider the longsuffering of our Lord to be salvation.

On God's longsuffering, see § Rom 2:4 A; also see b. Sanh. 111A in a baraita at § Matt 5:45, end; m. ʾAbot 5.2 at § 1 Pet 3:20. ‖ Jerusalem Talmud Šeqalim 5.48D.31: R. Hanina (ca. 225) said, "Whoever says, 'The merciful one is lenient וַתְּרָן (forgoes punishment),' may his bowels become unfastened (get diarrhea יִתְוַותְּרוּן, wordplay on ותרן)! Rather, he is longsuffering; but he exacts what is his (when his time comes)." — The same is found in y. Taʿan. 2.65B.42; Gen. Rab. 67 (42D); Pesiq. 161B; in a different version in b. B. Qam. 50A. — In Mek. Exod. 15:6 (46A.23), God's patience is proven in the way he acted with the generation of the flood, the generation of the dispersion, the people of Sodom ….

3:17: Lest you lose your firm standing.

On στηριγμός, see Philo, *Exsecr.* § 6 at § Rom 11:17, #2, n. *b* and 4 Maccabees 17:5 at § Eph 2:6.

The First Letter of John

1:4: So that our joy may be complete (see § John 3:29 B and § John 16:24).

1:5: God is light and there is no darkness in him.

On light and darkness, see § John 3:19 A and B; also see § Matt 5:14 A, n. *a* and § 1 Tim 6:16; see also Wis 7:26.

1:8: If we say that we have no sin … (see § Rom 3:9 B and § Matt 19:20 A).

1:9: If we confess our sins … (see § Matt 4:17 A, #2 and #3).

TanḥumaB חקת § 46 (63B): Then the people came to Moses and said, "We have sinned, for we have spoken against Yahweh and against you. Pray to Yahweh, that he might remove the snakes from us." And Moses prayed for the people (Num 21:7). This makes known to you the kindness of Moses, for he did not hesitate to ask for mercy for them; and this makes known to you the power of repentance. When they said, "We have sinned," they were immediately forgiven. — The same is found in Tanḥ. חקת 229A and Num. Rab. 19 (187B).

2:1: We have an intercessor before the Father.

On παράκλητος, see § John 14:16. — Philo, *De vita Mosis* 3.14 (Mangey's ed., 2:155): "The priest of the Father of the world (i.e., the Jewish high priest) necessarily had to make use of the virtue of the most perfect son (i.e., the Logos) as an intercessor for the forgiveness of sins and the administering of the richest blessings." ‖ Schöttgen adduces the following passage from Gen. Rab. 60: *Et introduxit eam Isaac in tentorium Sarae matris suae: Intelligitur Rex Messiah, qui fuit in generatione malorum et reprobavit eos, elegit autem Deum* S. B. *et nomen sanctum eius, totamque mentem eo direxit,* לבקש רחמים *ut misericordiam impetraret Israelitis proque ipsis ieiunaret ac se humiliaret,* q. d. Isa 53:5: *Vulneratus est propter peccata nostra. Et quando Israelitae peccant, ipse pro illis intercedit,* q. d. Isa 53:6: *Et in livore eius sanati sumus.* — This passage is not in Genesis Rabbah.

2:3ff.: By this we know that we have known him, if we keep his commandments ….

Knowing God puts one in communion with God by driving one to fulfill his will. This idea is also found in the following:

Sifre Deuteronomy 11:22 § 49 (85A): The allegorists said, "Do you want to know תכיר the one who spoke and the world came into being, then study the haggadah (the nonhalakic interpretation of Scripture). By this you know אתה מכיר God and hang on his ways (= imitate his action)." — Also see SDeut 6:6 § 33 at § 1 John 5:3 A.

2:11: He walks in darkness and does not know where he is going (see § John 12:35).

2:13: Because you have overcome the evil one (= the devil).

On πονηρός, see § Matt 6:13 B; also see Midr. Ps. 21 § 3 (90A) at § Rom 3:9 A, #3, B, n. *h*.

2:16: The desire of the flesh and the desire of the eyes and the arrogance of life is not from the Father, but rather from the world.

תַּאֲוָה = ἐπιθυμία is listed among the things that bring people out of the world; see m. ʾAbot 4.21 at § Rom 7:7, n. *d*. — On "desire" in general, see § Rom 7:7.

ʾAbot de Rabbi Nathan 28 (7D): R. Judah, the prince († 217?), said, "Whoever takes upon himself (= selects) the delights of this world is denied the delights of the future world (by God); and whoever does not take upon himself the delights of this world is granted the delights of the future world."

2:18: The antichrist ..., many antichrists (see § 2 Thess 2:3).

2:19 A: They went out from us.

See Pesiq. 126B at § Luke 2:25 B: "From you came the one who plotted evil against Yahweh" (Nah 1:11). ‖ See b. Ber. 17A at § Luke 23:2 A; m. Sanh. 10.4 at § Acts 12:2.

2:19 B: Yet they were not from us.

ʾAggadat Berešit 27 (23A): The one who said this word ("The appearance of the fourth is like that of a son of the gods" [Dan 3:25]), was not from you לא מכם היה. Nebuchadnezzar was not from you. He was a Babylonian.

2:20: And you have the anointing from the holy one.

Wettstein cites the expression *unctus in lege* from Tg. Yer. I Num. 21:27, 28, 29. However, the text should not read מְשִׁיחִין באורייתא = who are anointed by the Torah, but rather מְשַׁחִין בא׳ = those who speak about the Torah.

2:28: So that we may have boldness.

On פַּרְהֶסְיָא = παῤῥησία, see § Mark 8:32 and § John 7:4.

3:1: See what a love the Father has bestowed on us that we may be called children of God!

On the whole statement, see m. ʾAbot 3.14 at § Matt 5:9, #2, middle. — On the designation "children of God," see § Matt 5:9, #2; § Matt 5:45 A; and § John 1:12.

3:2 A: That we will be like him.

See Deut. Rab. 1 (196A) at § Rom 1:21 B and the citation that follows immediately there from y. ʿAbod. Zar. 4.44A.44. ‖ Pesiqta Rabbati 11 (46B): In this world the Israelites clung to God; as it says, "You who have clung to Yahweh your God" (Deut 4:4); but in the future they will be and be like דּוֹמִים (God). As God is a consuming fire, as it is written, "For Yahweh your God is a consuming fire" (Deut 4:24), so too they will be a consuming fire, as it is written, "The light of Israel will become a fire and its holy one a flame" (Isa 10:17).

3:2 B: Because we will see him as he is.

See Midr. Ps. 149 § 1 (270A) at § Matt 5:8 B, #2, n. *c*, near the end.

3:5 A: So that he may take away sins.

On αἴρειν τὰς ἁμαρτίας, see § John 1:29.

3:5 B: And sin is not in him (cf. § Matt 1:21 D, A, n. *g*).

3:9: Everyone who is born from God does not do sin (cf. § Matt 19:20 A).

3:15: Everyone who hates his brother is a murderer.

See Der. Er. (closing chapter) at § Matt 5:43, #2, n. *a*, end; also see SDeut 19:11 § 186f. (108B) at § Matt 5:43, #2, n. *a*, middle — On hate in general, see § Matt 5:43, #2.

3:16: We too should give up life for the brothers.

See SLev 19:16 (352A) and SLev 25:36 at § Matt 5:43, #1, last paragraph in that section.

3:21: We have boldness with God.

See παῤῥησία = פַּרְהֶסְיָא above at § 2:28. — This word appears with the meaning "boldness" also in T. Reu. 4; see § Rom 2:15 B, #2, end.

4:1: Many false prophets.

On ψευδοπροφῆται, see § Matt 7:15 A and § Matt 24:11.

4:8: God is love.

TanḥumaB וירא § 1 (42A): R. Simlai (ca. 250) said, "Do you want to know that all the ways (= every action) of God are love חסד (Ps 25:10)? In the beginning of the Torah he adorned a bride (see Gen 2:22); at its end, love, for he buried a dead man (see Deut 34:6); and in its middle he visited a sick person (see Gen 18:1). — Parallels are found in b. Soṭah 14A; Gen. Rab. 8 toward the end; Midr. Ps. 25 § 11 (107A); in Midr. Eccl. 7:2 (32A), R. Berekhiah (ca. 340) is the author.

4:12: No one has ever seen God.

See § Matt 5:8 B; § Matt 18:10 C; § John 1:18 A; and § Rom 1:20 A.

4:17: As that one is, so too we are in this world.

See the citations at § Matt 5:45 A, n. *b*.

4:18: There is no fear in love.

See SDeut 6:5 § 32 (73A) at § Luke 1:74.

5:3 A: This is love for God, that we keep his commandments.

See Wis 6:18f. at § Rom 2:13, #2, n. *a*. ‖ Sifre Deuteronomy 6:6 § 33 (74A): "These words, which I command you today, shall be on your heart" (Deut 6:6). Why is this said? Because it says, "You shall love Yahweh your God with your whole heart" (Deut 6:4). Yet I do not know how one loves God. Scripture teaches here, "And these words, which I command you today, shall be on your heart"; take these words to heart, for by them you know God and cling to his ways (follow his example, and this is love for God).

5:3 B: And his commandments are not burdensome (cf. § Matt 22:36, #2).

5:14: And this is the confidence that we have toward him, that if we ask anything in accordance with his will, he hears us.

On the hearing of prayers, see § Matt 7:7 A, #2.

5:16: Sin unto death.

ἁμαρτία πρὸς θάνατον = עֲוֹן מִיתָה.

Babylonian Talmud Soṭah 48A: (Yohanan the high priest = John Hyrcanus [135–104 BCE]) said to them, "My children, come, I will tell you something. As with the great heave offering (to the priesthood, about 2 percent of the harvest) there is a sin unto death עון מיתה, so too with the heave offering of the tithe (which the Levite had to render to the priesthood from the so-called first tithe) and with the fruits not yet tithed there is a sin unto death."

5:19: The whole world lies in evil.

On πονηρός = devil, see above at § 2:13. — On the entire thought, see b. B. Bat. 16A: "In everything Job did not sin with his lips" (Job 2:10). Raba († 352) said, "With his lips he did not sin, but in his heart he sinned. What did he say? 'The earth is surrendered into the hand of the wicked רָשָׁע, he (God) veils the face of its judges; if not (he, God), then who?' (Job 9:24)." Raba said, "Job wanted to turn the bowl over on its mouth (to completely tidy up with belief in God's righteous rule over the world)." Then Abbayye († 338/39) said to him, "Job said this (that the earth is given into the hand of the wicked) only concerning Satan (who is called רָשָׁע)." This corresponds to the opinion of the Tannaites. "The earth is surrendered into the hand of the wicked." R. Eliezer (ca. 90) said, "Job wanted to turn the bowl over on its mouth." Then R. Joshua (ca. 90) said to him, "Job said this only concerning Satan." — Differently, Exodus 32:22: "Aaron answered, … 'You know the people, that it lies in evil בְרָע (i.e., in turpitude and wickedness).'" — Targum Yerušalmi I: "You know the people, that they are sons of the righteous; but it is the evil inclination that misleads them." ‖ See further at § John 12:31.

The Second Letter of John

Verse 8: That you may receive a full recompense.

Targum Ruth 2:12: "Your recompense will be complete אַגְרִיךְ שְׁלֵימָא in the future world." ‖ Targum Ecclesiastes 1:3: "In order to receive a full recompense אגיר שלים in the future world before the Lord of the world." — Similarly in Tg. Eccl. 2:10, 11; 5:18.

The Third Letter of John

Verse 7: They went out for the name.

As in rabbinic literature הַשֵּׁם "the name" is said for "God" or "Yahweh" — see the excursus "The Memra of Yahweh," #3, B, n. *e*. — so here τὸ ὄνομα replaces Ἰησοῦς.

Verse 13: With ink and a writing reed.

See μέλαν and κάλαμος at § 2 Cor 3:3 A, n. *a*.

The Letter of Jude

Verse 2: May it be increased (see § 1 Pet 1:2).

Verse 4: Who were written down long ago for this judgment.

See § Luke 10:20, #3, especially Midr. Esth. Intro. (82A).

Verse 6 A: Angels who did not keep to their dominion, but rather left their own dwelling....

The words have in view the fall of the angels, to which the oldest period in general saw a reference in Gen 6:2ff. Only the understanding of the LXX remains uncertain.[a] Yet Philo[b] in all probability and Josephus[c] with certainty understood the sons of God in Gen 6:2 to refer to angels; likewise, 1 Enoch[d] and 2 Enoch[e] and the Book of Jubilees.[f] Only in the circle of the rabbinic scholars does any wavering appear: while some interpreted Gen 6:2 to refer to angels,[g] others considered the "sons of God" to be the sons of the great and noble men of the earth.[h]

a. Septuagint Genesis 6:2: Ἰδόντες δὲ υἱοὶ τοῦ θεοῦ τὰς θυγατέρας τῶν ἀνθρώπων, ὅτι καλαί εἰσιν, ἔλαβον ἑαυτοῖς γυναῖκας ἀπὸ πασῶν, ὧν ἐξελέξαντο. — What the LXX understood the υἱοὶ τοῦ θεοῦ to be is not indicated in any way.

b. Philo, *De gigantibus* § 2 at the beginning (Mangey's ed., 1:263): "When the angels of God οἱ ἄγγελοι τοῦ θεοῦ saw the daughters of humanity, that they were beautiful, they took for themselves wives from all who pleased them." — In the following, though, the ἄγγελοι are identified with (human) souls ψυχαί.

c. Josephus, *Jewish Antiquities* 1.3.1: "Many angels of God, mingling with women, sired wicked sons and despisers of everything good because of confidence in their power."

d. 1 Enoch 6f.: "After the children of men had increased, in those days (Gen 6:1ff.) beautiful and lovely daughters were born to them. However, when the angels, the sons of heaven (= sons of God) saw them, they lusted after them, and they said among themselves, 'Come, let us choose for ourselves wives among the daughters of men and beget children for ourselves!' Yet Semyaza (= שְׁמְחֲזַי, see further below), their head, said to them, 'I fear that you will not be willing to carry out this deed, so that I alone will have to suffer for a great sin.' Then all answered and said, 'Let us all swear an oath and obligate ourselves to one another by curses not to give up on this plan, but rather to carry out this intended work.' Then all swore together and obligated themselves to one another with curses. There were 200 of them in all who descended in the days of Jared to the top of Mount Hermon. Yet they called the Mount 'Hermon,' because on it they swore and had obligated themselves to one another with curses. (חֶרְמוֹן thus = site where one became obligated by a curse of the ban חֵרֶם) ....

This one and all the others with them took wives for themselves, each of them chose one for himself, and they began to go into them and to defile themselves with them. They taught them magical cures, incantations, and the cutting of roots and revealed to them the (medicinal) plants. Yet they became pregnant and bore giants 3,000 cubits long who drained the earnings of humanity. Yet when humanity could no longer give anything, the giants turned against them and ate them up. And humanity began to sin with the birds, animals, reptiles, and fish (by eating them), to eat the flesh of one another, and drink blood. Then the earth wailed about the unrighteous." ‖ 1 Enoch 9:ff.: "The archangels said to the Lord, '... You have seen what Azazel (= עֲזָאזֵל Lev 16:8ff., one of the fallen angels) has done, how he has taught every kind of unrighteousness on earth and revealed the heavenly secrets of primordial time, which humanity has taken an interest in learning. Semyaza, to whom you gave authority to execute dominion over his peers (so he was the prince of his division of angels) taught incantations. They went to the daughters of men on the earth, slept with them, and defiled themselves with women and revealed to them all sins. Yet the women bore giants, and thereby the whole earth became full of blood and unrighteousness.'" ‖ 1 Enoch 69:4f.: "The name of the first (angel) is Yeqon (this is probably a variant tradition). This is the one who misled all the children of the angels (= בני האלהים, with אלהים being understood as 'angels'), brought them down onto the land, and misled them by the daughters of men. The second is called Asb'el. He gave the children of the angels evil counsels to corrupt their bodies by the daughters of men." ‖ 1 Enoch 12:4: "(The angels said to Enoch,) 'Enoch, scribe of righteousness, go, proclaim to the Watchers of heaven (= עִירִין Dan 4:10, 14, 20, Ἐγρήγοροι "Watchers"), who have left the high heaven, the holy eternal place, corrupted themselves with women, acted like the children of men act, taken wives for themselves and have plunged themselves into great corruption on earth: They will find no peace or forgiveness.'" ‖ 1 Enoch 15:3: "(Enoch is supposed to tell the fallen angels,) 'Why did you leave the high, holy, and eternal heaven, sleep with women, defile yourselves with the daughters of men, take wives for yourselves, and act like the children of earth and beget sons of giants?... Earlier, you were eternally living spirits who were supposed to be immortal throughout all generations of the world. Therefore, I created no wives for you, for the spirits of heaven have their dwelling in heaven.'" ‖ See further 1 En. 10:11ff. at § Jude verse 6, B, n. *a*.

e. 2 Enoch 18:f.: "From them (the class of angels of the Ἐγρήγοροι) three (1 En. 6f. in n. *d* has the number 200) came down to the earth from the throne of the Lord at the place Hermon. They agreed to a vow on the top of Mount Hermon (cf. 1 En. 6f. above in n. *d*). And they saw the daughters of men, that they were good, and took for themselves wives and defiled the earth with their works .... And giants and monsters and great evildoing were born."

f. Jubilees 4:15: "In his (Jared's, Gen 5:15ff.) days, the angels of God, which are called the 'Watchers,' descended to the earth to teach the children of men to do justice and righteousness on earth." – Jubilees 5:6: "And he (God) became mightily angry with the angels whom he had sent to the earth (after they had sinned with the daughters of men). And he commanded to uproot them from their entire dominion." (One should note the different tradition here: the angels do not leave their heavenly region unauthorized, but rather go down to earth with God's consent and at God's behest. The result, though, is the same: they defile themselves with the daughters of men. This mitigating tradition is also found in rabbinic literature; see Midrash Shemhazai in n. *g*.) ‖ Jubilees 5:1ff.: "And it happened when the children of men began to increase on the face of the earth, and daughters were born to them that the angels of God saw ... that they were beautiful to look at, and they took wives for themselves from them, whom they chose, and they bore them children, and these were the giants. And violence increased on the earth, and all flesh corrupted its way, from humans to livestock and to the animals (of the field) and to the birds and to everything that walks on the earth. They all corrupted their way and their morals and began to mutually swallow one another up, and violence increased on the earth, and all the thoughts of the knowledge of all people were evil every day." ‖ Jubilees 4:22: "And he (Methuselah) testified of the 'Watchers,' who sinned with the daughters of men; for they began to have intercourse with the daughters of men so that they polluted themselves."

g. Midrash Shemhazai (*Beth ha-Midrash* 4.127.2): Rab Joseph's († 333) students asked him, "What is the deal with Azazel (Lev 16:8ff.)?" He answered them, "When the generation of the flood began to commit idolatry, God became angry." Immediately two angels, Shemhazai and Azael (so now!), came and said before him, "Lord of the world, when you created your world, did we not say before you (warning you about the creation of humanity): 'What is man that you think of him!?' (Ps 8:5)." He said to them, "And what should become of the world (without humanity)?" They said to him, "Lord of the world, let us suffice for her (?)!" He said to them, "It is revealed and known before me that if you resided on earth, the evil inclination would rule over you, and you would be worse than the children of men." They said to him, "Give us permission and we will dwell with men and you will see how we will sanctify your name!" He said to them, "Go down and dwell with them!" Immediately they sinned with the daughters of men, for they were beautiful, and they were not able to tame their (evil) inclination. – Shemhazai, so the narrative continues, then casts his eye on a girl named Istehar אִיסְטְהַר. Yet she explains that he will have his way with her only if he teaches her the inexpressible name of Yahweh. After fulfilling this word, she raises herself to heaven by the power of the name of Yahweh and here at God's command she is transposed as a star into the Pleiades כִּימָה as a recompense for her virtue. Shemhazai and Azael continue to work on earth until Metatron (an angel of God's throne) presents to them the message about the coming judgment of the flood. Then it says at the close: "Shemhazai turned in repentance and suspended himself between the heavens with his head at the bottom and his feet at the top, and he still hangs in penance between earth and heaven. Azael did not turn in repentance, and still persists in his corruption to mislead the sons of men to sin (fornication) by means of the various colors (for makeup) of women.[352] Therefore the Israelites presented as an offering on the Day of Atonement a goat for Yahweh, to make atonement for the children of Israel, and a goat for Azael, so that he carry away יסבול Israel's sins, and this is the Azazel of the Torah" (see Lev 16:8ff.). – The portion of Scripture for the Mincha service on the Day of Atonement was Lev 18 (laws about marriage and chastity); it is very

352. S-B: In an earlier passage it says, "Azael was appointed over the various kinds of colors and over the various kinds of jewelry for women, which misled the sons of men to sinful thoughts." – This tradition is also in 1 En. 8:1.

probable that the above tradition about Azael as the one who misleads to unchastity was a deciding factor in the choice of precisely this pericope. ‖ Deuteronomy Rabbah 11 (208B): (When Moses neared the hour of his death,) his soul said before God, "Lord of the world, from your Shekinah two angels descended from on high (to earth), Azza and Azael, and they longed for the daughters of the lands, and they corrupted their way on earth, until you suspended them between earth and heaven. Yet the son of Amram has not gone to his wife since the day you appeared to him in the thorn bush …." ‖ Babylonian Talmud Yoma 67B: In the school of R. Ishmael († ca. 135) it has been taught, "Azazel (receives the goat in Lev 16), because it makes atonement for the deed of Uza (so!) and Azael." (Rashi: "These were angels of destruction, who in the days of Naamah, the sister of Tubal-cain (Gen 4:22), came down to earth; and about them it says, 'The sons of God saw the daughters of men' [Gen 6:2]. So here too Azazel makes atonement for sins of fornication.) ‖ Pesiqta Rabbati 34 (159A): "Therefore, wait for me, says Yahweh, for the day I will arise as a witness" (so Midr. Zeph. 3:8); on the day when I arise to witness about the Messiah, that his merit counterbalances that of my (whole) family (the whole people of Israel). How so? There are all those measures (of my action in Zeph 3:5–7) before me, and you will not wait for me? They (the mourners of Zion) say before him, "Lord of the world, you have given us a heart of stone, and this has led us astray, and if Azza and Azael, whose body is made of fire, sinned when they descended to earth, will that not be all the more true of us?" ‖ Pirqe Rabbi Eliezer 22 (11C): Rabbi († 217?, yet the authorial attributions in Pirqe R. El. are completely unreliable) said, "The angels, who had fallen from heaven from their holy place, saw the daughters of Cain, who went about with exposed shame and put makeup on their eyes like prostitutes, and they went astray after them and took from them for their wives; as it says, 'The sons of God saw the daughters of men …' (Gen 6:2)." R. Joshua b. Qarha (ca. 150) said, "The angels are flames of fire, as it says, 'Your servants are flaming fire' (Ps 104:4); and the fire would have slept with flesh and blood without burning the body? Yet in the hour when they fell from heaven from their holy place, their power and form became like that of the children of men, and their clothing was the grime of the dust of the earth; as it says, 'His body was clothed with vermin and the grime of the dust of the earth' (so Job 7:5 is cited)." R. Zadok (I, ca. 70; II, ca. 130) said, "The giants עֲנָאקִם were sired by them, who went about in exalted form and put their hands to every kind of robbery and violence and bloodshed (see Num 13:33: 'There we saw the giants נְפִילִים, the sons of Anak'); and further it says, 'And the giants נפילים were on earth' (Gen 6:4)."

h. Genesis Rabbah 26 (16D): "The sons of God saw" (Gen 6:2). R. Simeon b. Yohai (ca. 150) called them "sons of judges" (people in authority). R. Simeon b. Yohai cursed everyone who called them "sons of God" (= angels) …. And why does (Scripture) call them "sons of God"? R. Hanina (ca. 225) and R. Simeon b. Laqish (ca. 250) both said, "Because they led a long life without distress and suffering." (Thus "sons of God" may = God's spoilt children.) ‖ Targum Onkelos Genesis 6:2ff.: "The sons of the great בְּנֵי רַבְרְבַיָּא saw the daughters of men, that they were beautiful, and they took for themselves wives from all who pleased them …." (Verse 4:) "Heroes were on the earth in those days and also afterward; for the sons of the great went into the daughters of men, and they gave birth to them. These are the heroes of ancient time, men of name." ‖ Targum Yerušalmi I Genesis 6:2, 4: "The sons of the great saw the daughters of men, that they were beautiful. They put makeup on and combed themselves (dressed their hair) and went about in nakedness of flesh and planned on fornication. And they took wives for themselves from all who pleased them ...." (Verse 4:) "Shemhazai and Uzziel (so!), these are those who fell from heaven נְפִיִין (interpretation of נפילים in Gen 6:4), and they were on the earth in those days and also afterward; for the sons of the great went into the daughters of men, and they gave birth to them; and they are called heroes of ancient time and men of name." — One should note that here the "sons of God" are understood to be the sons of great men, although in verse 4 the fall of the angels is mentioned. ‖ Genesis Rabbah 26 (16D): ("The sons of God, that is, after the preceding discussion, the sons of judges, so the great and noble, saw) that the daughters of men (the little people) were beautiful" (Gen 6:2). R. Judan (ca. 350) said, "טבת (not טוֹבוֹת) is written (in Gen 6:2; i.e., טבת should be interpreted as a singular): when they had adorned מטיבין a woman (a virgin bride) for her husband (on the wedding day), a great man would come and sleep with her first. This is what is written, 'that they were beautiful (= adorned as a bride)' (Gen 6:2): this refers to the virgins. 'And they took for themselves wives': this refers to the married women. 'From all who pleased them': this refers to men and livestock (for fornication contrary to nature)."

Verse 6 B: He detained in eternal fetters under darkness for the judgment of the great day.

1. The punishment of the fallen angels is twofold: a preliminary one, which consists in the angels being held in storage in the darkness of the earth embedded between sharp stones,[a] and then the ultimate one, which will be carried out with them at the time of the last judgment amidst pillars of fire crashing down in a vast pool of fire.[b] (This pool of fire is different from that of gehenna, which is made for godless humans, cf. 1 En. 90:24f. with 1 En. 90:26.) One reads different traditions about the punishment of the angels in 2 En. 7:1ff.; 18:1ff.; and 1 En. 67:4ff.

a. 1 Enoch 10:4ff.: "To Raphael the Lord said, 'Shackle Azazel, hands and feet and cast him into the darkness. Make a hole in the wilderness in Dudael and cast him into it. Put under him sharp and pointed stones and cover him with darkness. He shall dwell there forever (until the day of judgment), and cover his face so that he may not see light. Yet on the day of the great judgment he shall be cast into the pool of fire (for the ultimate punishment)." — Note: in m. Yoma 6.8, the place that is 3 *mils* from Jerusalem and to which the goat that was sent away into the wilderness on the Day of Atonement is called בֵּית הַדּוּדוּ "site of sharp or pointed stones"; the Mishnah of the Babylonian Talmud has the same (Munich manuscript, though בית הדורי); the Mishnah of the Jerusalem Talmud has בית הורון, which is certainly wrong, since Beth-Horon was much farther than 3 *mils* from Jerusalem. Targum Yerušalmi I Leviticus 16:21, 22 reads בית חרורי = בֵּית חֲרוֹרֵי "site of steep rocks." One may assume that the words of the passage from 1 Enoch, "in Dudael" = בְּדוּדָא אֵל = "in the cauldron[353] of God,"

353. S-B: Following b. Yoma 69B (= b. Sanh. 64A)—see the passage at § Rom 2:22 B, #2, n. *b*—the evil inclination to idolatry was closed up in a lead cauldron בְּדוּדָא דאברא and thereby made harmless for Israel.

are somehow connected with בֵּית הַדּוּדוֹ. Then, during his preliminary punishment, Asasel (= Azazel in Lev 16), bound underground at the site of the sharp stones and covered with eternal darkness, regularly receives a goat on the Day of Atonement to atone for certain sins of Israel. ‖ 1 Enoch 10:11ff.: "To Michael the Lord said, 'Go, bind Semyaza (= Shemhazai) and his other companions, who mingled with women, to defile themselves with them in their uncleanness. When their sons (the giants in Gen 6:4) have been slaughtered among themselves and when they (the fathers) have seen the destruction of their beloved (sons), bring them for 70 generations under the hills of the earth until the day of their (final) judgment and their consummation, until the eternal judgment is carried out. In those days they will be led away into the abyss of fire, and they will be enclosed in torment and prison forever. Whoever is condemned and destroyed together with them from now on will be bound (held) until the end of all generations. Destroy all the spirits of the repressible and the sons of the Watchers because they have mistreated humanity.'" ‖ 1 Enoch 14:5f.: (After Enoch has told the fallen angels that their plea for pardon has been rejected, he continues:) "Henceforth you will never rise up to heaven, and it is commanded that you be bound with chains on earth for all generations of the world. Beforehand, though, you shall see the destruction of your beloved sons. None of them will be left, but rather they will fall before you by the sword." ‖ Jubilees 5:6ff.: "And he became mightily angry with the angels whom he had sent to earth (cf. § Jude verse 6, A, n. *f*). And he commanded to root them out from their whole dominion. He said to us (the angels) that we should bind them in the depths of the earth; and behold, they are bound in the middle of it and (held) alone. And over their children the word from his face was issued that he wanted to pierce them with the sword and disperse them under heaven.... And he sent his sword among them, so that one might kill another; and they began to kill one another until they had all fallen by the sword and were destroyed from the earth. Yet their fathers saw, and then they were bound in the depths of the earth forever until the day of the great judgment, when a judgment will take place over all who corrupted their way and their works before God."

b. See 1 En. 10:4ff.; 10:11ff. in n. *a*. ‖ 1 Enoch 18:11–19:3: "I (Enoch) saw a deep abyss with pillars of heavenly fire, and I saw under them pillars of fire falling down. They could be measured neither in depth nor height. Behind this abyss I saw a place where there was neither solid heaven above nor firm earth beneath nor water under it, nor (were there) birds (there), but rather it was a place desolate and ghastly.... Then Uriel said to me, 'Here the angels who mingled with women will stand ... on the day (so following Dillmann) of the great judgment, when they will be judged unto their complete destruction. Yet the wives of the fallen angels will become sirens.'" ‖ 1 Enoch 21:7ff.: "From there I (Enoch) went to another place.... I saw (there) something terrifying: a great fire was there, which blazed and flamed. The place had clefts to the abyss (and was) completely full of large pillars of fire falling down. I could not see its extent and breadth, nor was I able to calculate it. Then I said, 'How terrifying is this place and (how) terrible to look at!' Then Uriel, one of the holy angels who was with me, answered me, and said to me, 'Enoch, why are you afraid and what terrifies you?' I answered, 'Because of this terrifying place and because of this dreadful sight.' Then he said to me, 'This place is the prison of the angels, and here they will be kept imprisoned for eternity.'" ‖ 1 Enoch 54:4ff.: "I (Enoch) asked the angel of peace, who accompanied me, saying, 'For whom are these instruments of torture prepared?' He said to me, 'These are prepared for the hosts of Azazel, to seize them and to cast them into the abyss of complete damnation. They will cover their jaws with coarse stones, just as the Lord of Spirits has commanded (concerning their preliminary punishment). Michael, Gabriel, Raphael, and Phanuel will seize them on that great day (of the final judgment and) on that day cast them into the burning furnace, so that the Lord of Spirits may exact revenge for their unrighteousness, because they were subject to Satan and misled the inhabitants of the earth.'"

2. κρίσις μεγάλης ἡμέρας. On the "great day," see 1 En. 54:4ff. above in #1, n. *b* at the end. ‖ 2 Enoch 18:6: "(The fallen angels) are treated ignominiously on the great day of the Lord (i.e., on the day of the great final judgment)." – See synonymous expressions in the excursus "Sheol, Gehenna, and the Garden of Eden," II, #10, n. *b*.

Verse 7 A: As Sodom and Gomorrah and the cities around them that had fornicated in the same way as these (the fallen angels in verse 6) and went after different flesh.

The people of Sodom are accused in ancient Jewish traditions of the following: Mercilessness toward the poor, cruelty to strangers, and bending justice; see supporting passages at § Matt 10:15. – The true vice of Sodom was considered to be fornication, specifically pederasty,[a] which is intended wherever Sodomitic sins or the sin of Sodom is mentioned.[b] "Going after different flesh" in Jude 7 targets this specific sin, not unnatural fornication with animals. This vice (in connection with pederasty) was rather considered to be the characteristic feature of the people of the generation of the flood.[c]

a. Josephus, *Jewish Antiquities* 1.11.1: "The Sodomites, having become cocky because of prosperity and the greatness of their fortune, were violent toward people, and godless concerning divinity, so that they were no longer mindful of the blessings that they had received from the divinity and they hated strangers and gave themselves over to pederasty." ‖ See Gen. Rab. 50 (32A) and Gen. Rab. 26 (16D) at § Rom 1:27 A, A, #l. Parallels to the last passage are found in Gen. Rab. 50 (32A.29) and Lev. Rab. 23 (122B). ‖ TanḥumaB וירא § 22 (49B): They called Lot and said to him, "... Lead them out to us so that we may know them (Gen 19:5); they wanted to rape them." R. Hiyya b. Abba (ca. 280) said, "From here you learn that they (the people of Sodom) were completely given over to fornication." ‖ Targum Yerušalmi I Genesis 19:5: "Lead them out to us so that we may have intercourse with them." – Targum Onkelos retains the word in the text, ידע.

b. 2 Enoch 10:4ff.: "And I (Enoch) said, 'Woe, woe! what an exceedingly terrifying place this is (namely hell)!' And those men (= angels) said to me, 'This place, O Enoch, is prepared for those who dishonor God, who commit (do) unnatural fornication on earth, which is pederasty in the hind passage quarters sodomitically....'" ("Sodomitically" is thus a short way to designate pederastic fornication.) ‖ Jubilees 16:5f.: "In this month (Tammuz) God carried out the judgment on Sodom and Gomorrah and Zeboim and the whole land of Jordan and burned them with fire and sulfur and destroyed them up to this day, as I (an angel) made known their action to you (Moses), how they were unrighteous and very sinful and defiled themselves and committed fornication with their body and did impure things on earth. And likewise God will carry out the judgment in places where they have acted according to the impurity of Sodom, according to the judgment on Sodom." ‖ Jubilees 20:5: "(Abraham) recounted (to his sons and grandchildren) the judgment on the giants (Gen 6:4) and the judgment on the Sodomites, how they were judged for their wickedness and for their fornication and impurity and died because of their mutual sexually immoral corruption." ‖ See T. Naph. 4 and T. Benj. 9 at § Rom 1:27 A, B, #1.

c. See Gen. Rab. 26 (16D); Sanh. 108A; 2 En. 34:2 at § Rom 1:27 A, A, #1.

Verse 7 B: Existing as an example.

δεῖγμα = דּוּגְמָא or דִּיגְמָא. — Mishnah Šabbat 10.1: If someone has stored up (grain) for sowing, as a sample דוגמא or for medicinal purposes and carries some of it out on the Sabbath, he is guilty (of desecrating the Sabbath), however little it may have been. ‖ Tanḥuma קדושים 119A: They punched (a Jew who had wanted to honor the emperor Hadrian with a basket of fruit) in the face and undressed him until he was naked … and made him an example דוגמא. — The same is found in TanḥB קדושים § 8 (38B).

Verse 9 A: Michael, the archangel.

In Dan 10:13, Michael is called אַחַד הַשָּׂרִים הָרִאשֹׁנִים "one of the first (angel) princes"; Dan 12:1 הַשַּׂר הַגָּדוֹל "the great prince"; therefore, in rabbinic literature שַׂר הַגָּדוֹל perhaps = ἀρχάγγελος. — See b. Ḥag. 12B and b. Menaḥ. 110A at § Heb 8:2. — See more about the angel Michael at § Rev 12:7.

Verse 9 B: When he talked with the devil about the body of Moses, he did not dare to pass a cursing judgment, but rather said, "The Lord rebuke you!"

1. On the background of this saying from the Assumption of Moses, see Schürer, *Geschichte des jüdischen Volkes* (3:294, 298, 303). There is nothing that corresponds to this in ancient rabbinic literature. However, once we find a narrative about a dialogue between Michael and Satan about Moses' soul shortly before his death. Here, though, Michael has no qualms about passing a cursing judgment on the devil, but rather calls him in short wicked רָשָׁע.

Deuteronomy Rabbah 11 (207C): The angel Sammael (= Satan), the wicked, the head of all satans, had calculated every hour up until the death of Moses and said, "When will the appointed time or moment come when Moses will die, so that I may go down and take his soul from him?" Concerning him David said, "The wicked waylays the righteous and seeks to kill him" (Ps 37:32). Among all the satans, there is none as wicked as Sammael and among all the prophets there is none as righteous as Moses; as it says, "No longer did any prophet arise in Israel like Moses, whom Yahweh knew face to face" (Deut 34:10). What can this be compared with? Like a person who was invited to a wedding. We waited and said, "When will the joyful feast come so that I may rejoice in it?!" So too Sammael the wicked waited for Moses' soul and said, "When will Michael (as the patron of Israel) weep and my mouth be full of laughing?," until Michael said to him, "What, you wicked רשע! I weep and you laugh? 'Do not rejoice, my enemy, because of me. If I have fallen, I will rise up again; and if I sit in darkness, Yahweh is my light' (Mic 7:8)." "If I have fallen" as a result of Moses' demise, "I will rise up again" as a result of Joshua's leadership when he brings down the 31 kings (of Canaan). "If I sit in darkness" during the destruction of the first and second temple, "Yahweh is my light" in the days of the Messiah (see the continuation see at § Matt 4:1 B, #3, C, middle). — There is a parallel in the midrash about the demise of Moses (*Beth ha-Midrash* 1.125.19).

2. The words: "The Lord rebuke you!" stem from Zech 3:2; Satan demands their application to him, so to speak, as his right in b. Qidd. 81A: see § Matt 4:1 B, #3, A.

Verse 11: They have given themselves.

ἐκχεῖσθαι "to give oneself," "to throw oneself into" may = שָׁטַף "to pour out"; from this comes שָׁטוּף = one who surrenders himself to something, plunges into something. Midrash Ecclesiastes 1:13 (11A): שטופין בגזל "given to robbery"; Num. Rab. 9 (151B): שטופין בזנות "given to fornication." Also see, for example, Num. Rab. 20 (190B.46); b. Šabb. 152A.32.

Verse 13: Roaming stars, for whom the gloom of darkness is reserved for eternity.

1 Enoch 18:13ff.: "I (Enoch) saw there (see 1 En. 18:11ff. above in § verse 6 B, #1, n. *b*) seven stars like great burning mountains. When I asked about this, the angel said, 'This is the place where heaven and earth come to an end. This is a prison for the stars and for the host of heaven. The stars that roll along over the fire are those that transgressed the command of God at the beginning of their arising; for they did not come forth at their time. Then he became angry with them and bound them for 10,000 years until the time when their sin is completed.'" — 1 Enoch 21:1–6: "I (Enoch) went around until I came to a place where there was nothing. There I saw something terrifying: I saw no heaven above and no firmly established land (below), but rather a bleak and ghastly place. There I saw seven stars of heaven bound and thrust into it like great mountains and burning in fire. Then I said, 'For what sin are they bound and why are they cast out here?' Then Uriel spoke to me ... and said, 'Enoch, why do you ask and you are you fervently concerned to learn the truth? These are those stars of heaven that transgressed the command of God, and they are bound here until 10,000 years, the time of their sin, is completed.'"

Verse 14 A: The seventh from Adam, Enoch.

1 Enoch 93:3: "Enoch began to narrate from the books and said, 'I was born as the seventh in the first week (one week = 7 generations).'" ‖ 1 Enoch 60:8: "Where (in the garden of

Paradise) the elect and the righteous dwell, to where my (Noah's) grandfather (i.e., Enoch) was taken up, the seventh from Adam, the first man that the Lord of Spirits had created." ‖ Leviticus Rabbah 29 (127C): All sevens (i.e., every seventh thing in a category) are loved (beloved) forever. (So the 7th heaven, the 7th name for "earth," namely תֵּבֵל). Among the generations the seventh is loved: Adam, Seth, Enosh, Kenan, Mahalalel, Jered, Enoch; and it says, "Enoch walked with God" (Gen 5:24). (The following are given as further examples: Moses, the 7th among the fathers; David, the 7th among the sons of Jesse; Asa, the 7th among the kings; the fallow year, the 7th among the years; the Jubilee year, the 7th among the fallow years; the Sabbath, the 7th among the days; Tishri, the 7th among the months.)

Verse 14 B: Prophesied, saying: "Behold, the Lord came with his holy myriads" ....

This prophecy is found in 1 En. 1:9: "And behold, he (God) comes with myriads of holy ones to execute judgment on all, and he will destroy all the godless and rebuke all flesh for all their godless works that the godless sinners committed, and for all the violent speech that they spoke, and for every evil thing they have said about him." — In Pseudo-Cyprian (Fabricius, *Codex Pseudepigraphus Veteris Testamenti*, 160): *Ecce venit cum multis millibus nunciorum suorum facere judicium de omnibus et perdere omnes impios et arguere omnem carnem de omnibus factis impiorum, quae fecerunt impie.*

Verse 15: Godless sinners.

This description is also found in 1 En. 1:9 (see § Jude verse 14 B).

Verse 16: While they flatter people (honor them in a biased way) for their (own) benefit.

On θαυμάζειν πρόσωπον, see § Rom 2:11, #1; also see there Pss. Sol. 2:18.

The Revelation of John

1:4 A: From the one who is and who was and who is coming.

For this interpretation of the divine name יהוה, see Exod. Rab. 3 (69C) at § Heb 13:8. — Targum Yerušalmi I Exodus 3:14: "You shall say to the children of Israel, 'It is I am, I who was and will be, who sent me to you.'" ‖ Targum Yerušalmi I Deuteronomy 32:39: "I am who is and who was and I am who will be, and there is no other God aside from me."

1:4 B: From the seven spirits that (are) before his throne.

These seven spirits do not refer to the seven angels of God's throne. Against this is their designation once as πνεύματα instead of as ἄγγελοι, as in Rev 8:2, and also their position between God and Jesus Christ (verse 5). See more detail on these seven, or four angels of the throne at § Rev 8:2; see there also 1 En. 40:1ff. — Rather, the seven spirits before God's throne are identical with the one Spirit of God, in that seven, as elsewhere, comes into view merely as the number of limited and complete unity. — On the words "that are before his throne," see § Luke 1:19 B; see the passage adduced there, Pesiq. Rab. 46 (188A), at § Rev 8:2, n. *b*.

1:5: The prince of the kings of the earth.

See § Rom 3:9 A, #3.

1:6: He has made us a kingdom, priests for his God and Father.

The abstract βασιλεία "kingdom" stands for the concrete βασιλεῖς "kings." This is not in the base passage Exod 19:6,[a] but this is the interpretation in the ancient synagogue.[b]

a. Exodus 19:6: "You shall be for me a kingdom of priests (i.e., a kingdom whose subjects and members are priests) and a holy people."

b. Septuagint Exodus 19:6: ὑμεῖς δὲ ἔσεσθέ μοι βασίλειον ἱεράτευμα (= a royal priesthood, i.e., a priesthood, that is clothed with royal dignity) καὶ ἔθνος ἅγιον. — A similar idea can be found in 2 Maccabees 2:17, though the interpretation of the passage is controversial. ‖ Targum Onkelos and Yerušalmi II: "You shall be before me kings, priests, and a holy people." ‖ Targum Yerušalmi I: "You shall be before me kings, adorned with a crown, and serving priests, and a holy people." ‖ Mekilta Exodus 19:6 (71A): "You shall be for me" (Exod 19:6). I do not appoint, as it were, and make others rulers over you, but rather only I (am your ruler) Likewise it says, "See, the protector of Israel does not sleep or slumber" (Ps 121:4). "A kingdom" (Exod 19:6): I do not make kings of the nations of the world, but rather of you. Likewise it says, "One who is my dove, my unscathed one" (Song 6:9). R. Eliezer b. Yose (the Galilean [ca. 150]) said, "How can you say that each one of the Israelites will one day (in the messianic age) have as many children (sons) as went out of Egypt (i.e., 600,000)? Because it says, 'In place of your fathers your sons will be for you' (Ps 45:17). If sons, will they perhaps be poor and tormented? Scripture teaches, 'You will make them princes on all the earth' (Ps 45:17). If princes, maybe princes of trade? Scripture teaches, 'Kingship' (Exod 19:6). If a king, will he suppress again? Scripture teaches, 'Priests' (Exod 19:6). [Priests who wander? Scripture teaches: 'Kingdom' (Exod 19:6), that is, councilors, as it says, 'And the sons of David were princes' (so the midrash takes כֹּהֲנִים in 2 Sam 8:18).] ... 'A holy people,' holy and sanctified, set apart from the nations of the world and from their abominations." — The statement in square brackets follows the text in Yalquṭ on Ps 45:17 (2 § 750 at the end). — Parallels to the saying of R. Eliezer b. Yose the Galilean are found in Tanḥ. תולדות 33B and Midr. Ps. 44 § 7 (136A).

1:7 A: Behold, he comes with the clouds (see § Matt 24:30 B, #1).

1:7 B: Who have pierced him (see § John 19:37 B).

1:7 C: All the tribes of the earth will mourn him.

On the lament of Zech 12:12, see § Luke 24:26, II, #3, n. *c*; also see b. Sukkah 51B at § Rom 3:19 A, #1.

1:8 A: I am the Alpha and the Omega.

Likewise, in rabbinic literature, *aleph* א features as the beginning letter in the alphabet = the first, most excellent, etc., and *tav* ת as the final letter in the alphabet = the last. Hence, from *aleph* to *tav* = from beginning to the end.

Genesis Rabbah 81 (52A): What is the seal of God? ... R. Bebai (ca. 320, so read instead of רבינו) said in the name of R. Reuben (ca. 300), "'Truth' אֱמֶת. What is the deal with אמת? Resh Laqish (ca. 250) said, '*Aleph* stands at the head of the letters (in the alphabet), *mem* in the middle, and *tav* at the end. Therefore, it says, "I am the first and I am the last and aside from me there is no God" (Isa 44:6).'" — Parallels are found at § John 1:14, #2, final paragraph. ‖ For א = the most excellent, see m. Menaḥ. 8.1 at § John 11:54; t. Menaḥ. 9.5 (526) at § Matt 4:12, #2, penultimate paragraph; m. Menaḥ. 8.6 at § Acts 9:35, #1. ‖ See "from א to ת" at § Rom 3:9 B, n. *e*. See also Tanḥ. ראה 9B; b. B. Bat. 88B.25.

1:8 B: The Almighty.

ὁ παντοκράτωρ = שַׁדַּי or אֵל שַׁדַּי. — Haggadically, it was customary to explain שַׁדַּי from דַּי (= enough).

Genesis Rabbah 46 (29A): R. Nathan (ca. 350) said in the name (so read!) of R. Aha (ca. 320) and R. Berekhiah (ca. 340) in the name of R. Isaac (ca. 300), "'I am the almighty God' אל שדי (Gen 17:1): I am the one who said to my world, to heaven and to earth, 'Enough' דַּי! For if I had not said to them, 'Enough!', they would have continued to stretch out until today."

In a baraita it has been taught in the name of R. Eliezer b. Jacob (I, ca. 90; II, ca. 150), "I am the one of whose divinity the world and its fullness is not worthy כְּדַי (or for whose divinity the world and its fullness is not sufficient כְּדַי)." Aquila (see § 1 Cor 16:19, n. g) translated: ואקנוס[354] אכסיוס = ἄξιος and ἱκανός "worthy and sufficient."

1:10: On the day of the Lord.

See designations for Sunday at § Matt 28:1 B.

1:16: As when the sun shines in its power.

In rabbinic literature the comparison is made most of the time on the basis of Judg 5:31: "As the rising of the sun in its power."

Sifre Deuteronomy 11:21 § 47 (83A): "As the days of heaven over the earth" (Deut 11:21); for the faces of the righteous will be like the sun כיום. And likewise it says, "Those who love him are like the rising of the sun in its power" (Judg 5:31). — See the continuation of the passage, where the comparison from Judg 5:31 appears once, at § Matt 5:8, #2, n. *b.* ‖ See b. Šabbat 88B at § Matt 5:11 A; Gen. Rab. 12 (9A) at § Matt 1:3 D; Midr. Eccl. 1:7 (8A) at § Matt 13:43. ‖ Midrash Psalm 49 § 1 (139A): R. Isaac (ca. 300) said, "How sweet is the light of the future world! Blessed is the man who has good works, so that he can see the light; as it says, 'Those who love him are like the rising of the sun in its power' (Judg 5:31)." — See also § Matt 17:2 A and Pirqe R. El. 4 at § Rev 4:6 B, #1.

1:17: I am the first and the last.

Isaiah 44:6 is related to God in Gen. Rab. 81 (52A); see the passage at § Rev 1:8 A; see Exod. Rab. 29 (88D) at § John 10:33 B; see Num. Rab. 2 (138C) at § Rom 9:25, #2. — The Messiah is called "first" רִאשׁוֹן, specifically on the basis of Isa 41:27, in b. Pesaḥ. 5A and Gen. Rab. 63 (39D); see § Matt 1:21 B, #2, n. *c*; there is a parallel to Gen. Rab. 63 from Pesiq 185A in volume II, excursus "The Feast of Tabernacles," II, D.

1:18 A: I live forever.

חֵי הָעוֹלָמִין (cf. חֵי הָעוֹלָם, Dan 12:7, Aram. חַי עָלְמָא, Dan 4:31) "the one who lives forever" is found in rabbinic literature quite often as a designation for God; so several times in Mek. Exod. 13:19 (29A); see § Acts 7:16, #1, n. *a*.

1:18 B: I have the keys of death and the underworld.

On the key metaphor, see § Matt 16:19 A. ‖ Doorkeepers and guards of the gates of Hades are mentioned in 2 Enoch 42:1; recension B speaks of the guards of the "key of Hades"; a doorkeeper of gehenna is also mentioned once in b. Ḥag. 15B; see the passages in the excursus "Sheol, Gehenna, and the Garden of Eden," II, #9, n. *i*.

---

354. S-B: So read instead of ואנשוס.

1:20: The seven stars are the angels of the seven churches.

The ἄγγελοι τῶν ἐκκλησιῶν could by themselves be angelic beings who as heavenly patrons keep watch and guide the doings of the churches on earth that were under their custody; then they would constitute a counterpart to the oft named angel princes of the nations of the world.[355] Yet this explanation is untenable, since according to Rev 2:1–3, 22, the letters are written to the angels of the churches. This presupposes that they dwelt on earth, just like the churches assigned to them. Therefore, one should understand the ἄγγελοι to denote people who are called the ἄγγελοι τῶν ἐκκλησιῶν because they served in the communities as God's emissaries, agents, appointees, that is, men who occupied a position of leadership in the churches. Similarly, in Hag 1:13, the prophet and, in Mal 2:7, the priest is called a מַלְאַךְ יהוה, a messenger of God[356] (LXX: ἄγγελος κυρίου), and in rabbinic literature not only the priests appear as God's שְׁלוּחִים (= ἄγγελοι, ἀπόστολοι), that is, as God's messengers and agents, but also anyone who acted in any divine mission could be described as God's שָׁלִיחַ (= ἄγγελος, ἀπόστολος); see supporting passages on this at § Rom 1:1 B, #2, n. *e*. Due to the Jewish linguistic usage of מַלְאָךְ and שָׁלִיחַ, there is nothing striking about the designation of the church leaders in Rev 1:20 as ἄγγελοι. — As is well known, in rabbinic literature there is a much used term that precisely overlaps with ἄγγελος τῆς ἐκκλησίας, namely שְׁלִיחַ צִבּוּר = "emissary, agent, appointee of the community." This was the designation for the leader of prayer in the community who in the liturgical gatherings brought the concerns of the community before God in prayer as an appointee and representative of the community. Perhaps the generally known and used שליח צבור somehow contributed to the designation of the church leaders in Rev 1:20 as ἄγγελοι τῶν ἐκκλησιῶν; however, one must be cautious about inferring a material equivalence in the offices from the formal equivalence. In fact, they had nothing in common with each other: the שליח צבור was summoned for his office temporarily, and on the next day someone else could be summoned to it; for anyone who was qualified could serve the community as its leader of prayer. Above all, the leader

355. S-B: On these angel princes of the nations of the world, see § Rom 1:23 A, #2, A.

356. S-B: Just how broadly the concept מַלְאָךְ could be understood is shown by Midr. Eccl. 5:5 (25B): "Do not let your mouth bring your body into punishment" (Eccl 5:5). R. Joshua b. Levi (ca. 250) interpreted the passage as referring to those who pledge publicly (in the synagogues) to give alms and afterward do not give them. "And do not say before (God's) messenger" מַלְאָךְ (Eccl 5:5); this refers to the overseer of the synagogue חַזָּן. — One sees here that even the one who was invested with an office of only little authority, namely the overseer of the synagogue (see the excursus The Institution of the Ancient Jewish Synagogue), was viewed as a representative of God for the service of the community, i.e., as a מַלְאָךְ or ἄγγελος. It is all the less strange if in Rev 1:20 men in a leading position are designated as ἄγγελοι. — The parallel in Midr. Ps. 52 § 1 (141A) does not read חַזָּן, but rather שְׁלִיחַ צִבּוּר = "leader of prayer"; this goes together with the fact that in a later period the overseer of the synagogue was also often the leader of prayer.

of prayer did not have anything to do with leading the community. This was rather in the hands of the community overseer (see the excursus "The Institution of the Ancient Jewish Synagogue"). Yet, according to Rev 2 and 3, the ἄγγελοι τῶν ἐκκλησιῶν were men in a position of leadership who were permanently entrusted with their office. Furthermore, the שְׁכִיח צבור was one appointed by the community to his office, while the ἄγγελοι τῶν ἐκκλησιῶν in Rev 2 and 3 feature completely as God's appointees.

2:5: Remember … the first works.

Mishnah Baba Meṣiʿa 4.10: If someone is a penitent, one should not say to him, "Remember your earlier deeds" זְכוֹר מַעֲשֶׂיךָ הָרִאשׁוֹנִים.

2:7 A: Whoever has an ear, let him hear (cf. § Matt 11:15).

2:7 B: From the wood of life that is in the paradise of God.

1. ξύλον τῆς ζωῆς = עֵץ הַחַיִּים (Gen 2:9); so in the literal sense also in our verse. — עֵץ חַיִּים in the metaphorical sense according to Prov 3:18; 11:30; 13:12; 15:4 = wisdom = Torah; see the reference at § Rom 3:1f., D, toward the end; also, Lev. Rab. 35 (132C) at § Rom 3:1f., D, middle, and the citations at § John 6:35 A, n. *a*. — ξύλα τῆς ζωῆς = pious ones; see Pss. Sol. 14:2: The paradise of the Lord, the trees of life, are his pious ones.

2. παράδεισος = פַּרְדֵּס and גַּן עֵדֶן; on these three names, see the excursus "Sheol, Gehenna, and the Garden of Eden," III, #1.

3. The ancient synagogue knows of a threefold paradise.

a. The paradise of Adam in Gen 2:8ff. In the middle of it stood the tree of life, whose height and circumference were immeasurable and whose aroma far exceeded all other fragrances. Its leaves and blossoms never wilted, and its fruits were like the grapes of the palm tree. This tree of life is repeatedly depicted as an oil tree. After the fall, the paradise of Adam together with the tree of life were withdrawn somewhere in hiddenness. See more detail on this in the excursus "Sheol, Gehenna, and the Garden of Eden," III, #2.

b. The paradise of the souls in heaven, which serves as an abode for the righteous who have died during the intermediate state. This heavenly paradise also has a tree of life in the middle of it: planted in the area of the righteous, it spreads its branches over every table of every righteous person. It bears produce of all fruits, and the righteous come and eat of it continually; see the excursus "Sheol, Gehenna, and the Garden of Eden," III, #3; see also the brief remarks at § Luke 23:43, #2.

c. The eschatological paradise, which is given to the righteous in the blessed age of perfection. Smaller, spiritually oriented circles (namely 2 Enoch and 2 Baruch) assumed that the absolute eschatological perfection will have its place in heaven; they therefore identified the eschatological paradise (c) with the heavenly paradise of souls (b). However, rabbinic Judaism represented the view that the blessed eschatological perfection in the *ʿolam ha-ba* will occur on earth; then the lost paradise of Adam will also be revealed again to the righteous and the tree of life will give its fruits to all the holy ones. The site of paradise, though, will be the immediate surroundings of Jerusalem, directly beside gehenna. The eschatological paradise thus is the paradise of Adam made accessible again; see the excursus "Sheol, Gehenna, and the Garden of Eden," III, #4; here one can also read about the stance of 4 Ezra on our question.

2:9: Who say they are Jews.

For "Jew" as a name of honor, see § Rom 2:17 A.

2:11: Second death (see § Rev 20:6).

2:14: Bileam, who taught Balak to place an offense (a snare) before the children of Israel, to eat idol sacrifices and to fornicate.

1. Balaam's name. — Babylonian Talmud Sanhedrin 105A: Balaam (means:) "without people" בְּלֹא עַם. A different explanation is the following: (He was called) Balaam because he chafed against the people בִּלָּה עַם (according to a different reading: because he consumed the people בָּלַע עַם).

2. Balaam's counsel to destroy Israel. — Babylonian Talmud Sanhedrin 106A: (Balaam) said to them (to Balak and his people), "The God of these (Israelites) hates fornication, and they desire linen garments. Come, I will give you counsel. Make tents for them and put an old woman outside and a young woman inside, so that they may sell them linen garments. He made them tents from Har-sheleg (Snow Mountain) to Beth Hajeshimoth (Num 33:49; the text has Beth Hajeshimon) and put whores in them, an old one outside and young one inside. When the Israelites had eaten and drunk and were playful and stepped outside to go for a walk on the street (market), the old woman would say to them, 'Would you like linen?' The old woman named the right price for it, but the young woman named a lower price. This happened two or three times, Then, though, she said to him, 'See, you are like a child of the house, sit down and choose something for yourself!' At the other side, though, there was a jug with Ammonite wine, and there at that time the wine of the Ammonites and the wine of non-Israelites (*goyim*) was not yet forbidden. And she said to him, 'Would you like to drink a cup of wine?' When he had drunken, it burned in him; he said to her, 'Do what I want!' Then she drew her idol from her breast and said to him, 'Worship this!' He answered her, 'Am I not a Jew?' What does that matter? (she would respond,) we want you only to discharge פְּיעוֹר (the customary worship of Baal Peor). Moreover, I will not let you go until you deny the Torah of your teacher Moses!' For it says, 'Yet they went to Baal Peor and devoted themselves to shame and became beasts like their beloved' (Hos 9:10)." — A starkly divergent parallel is found in Num. Rab. 20 (190C) and Tanḥ. בלק 237B. — See further § 1 Cor 10:8 and § 2 Pet 2:15.

2:17 A: To the one who overcomes I will give to him from the hidden manna.

1. For the glorification of the manna given during the wilderness wandering, see § John 6:31, #2.

2. In the messianic age, the Messiah will make manna come down from heaven; see § John 6:31, #1.

3. In the future world עולם הבא, that is, in the hereafter, in the heavenly world of souls, manna is the food of the righteous.[a] It is prepared in the third heaven, which is called שְׁחָקִים;[b] here, שחקים is interpreted according to שָׁחַק "to crush, grind."

a. TanḥumaB בשלח § 21 (33B): Zabdai b. Levi (ca. 240) said, "Food for 2,000 years (so read with Buber on Midr. Ps. 78 § 3, note ט) came down daily as manna (in the wilderness) and lasted until the 4th hour (= 10 in the morning). Yet when the sun shone on it, it melted and became pure streams and drained off. And for whom is it now determined (or: for whom is it now prepared)? For the righteous in the *'olam ha-ba* (in the hereafter). Whoever is devout מאמין will be worthy to eat of it; but whoever is not devout 'cannot see his desire in rivers, stream-like rivers of honey and cream' (Job 20:17)." — The statement of time is completely nonspecific in Mek. Exod. 16:25 (58B): "Today you will not find it (the manna) on the field" (Exod 16:25). ... R. Eleazar (ben) Hasama (ca. 110) said, "In this world (= today) you will not find it, but in the future world עולם הבא you will find it." — *'Olam ha-ba* can refer to the beyond (the world of souls), but also the messianic age and finally also the future world in the narrower sense, that is, the time of the eschatological consummation after the course of the days of the Messiah.

b. See b. Ḥag. 12B at § 2 Cor 12:2 C, n. *c*.

4. The μάννα κεκρυμμένον is reminiscent of the original light that God hid גָּנַז for the righteous in the garden of Eden; see § John 1:1 A, C, #6, second S-B footnote in that section.

2:17 B: A new name written on the stone.

1. ψῆφος. — In b. Sukkah 53A a (white) shard הַסְּפָא serves to write down God's name: When David dug the *shith* (a cavity in the earth at the southwest corner of the altar of burnt offering to receive the wine of the drink offering flowing down), the primordial depth rose and wanted to sweep the world away. Then David said, "Is there anyone who knows whether it is allowed to write the name of God (Yahweh) on a shard and to cast it into the primordial depth to calm it?" (Ahithophel declares it to be allowed.) Then he wrote the name on a shard and cast it into the primordial depth, and it delved.... Parallel passages are found in b. Mak. 11A; y. Sanh. 10.29A.42.

2. ὄνομα καινόν. — This can be compared with Midr. Ps. 18 § 3 (68B): "Of the servant of Yahweh, of David" (Ps 18:1). Why did David say, "Of the servant of Yahweh"? To teach you that God adds honor to everyone who penitently renounces his sin, and calls him by a precious (beloved) name. Come and see this with the sons of Korah. Before they repented, they were not called "lilies," but when they despaired of the deed of their father and repent-

ed, they were called "lilies" (see Ps 45:1). And likewise you find it with David. Before he repented because of that deed (with Bathsheba), he was not enlisted in the upper army (in God's service); but after he repented, he was enlisted in the upper army and called "servant of Yahweh."

2:22: I cast her onto a bed and those who commit adultery with her into great affliction.

Babylonian Talmud Šabbat 33A.26: R. Hoshaiah (ca. 225) said, "Whoever surrenders himself completely to fornication, wounds and sores emerge on him; as it says, 'Sores and wounds (come), you surrender yourself completely to evil' (so Prov 20:30 according to the midr.). And not only this, he is also punished with dropsy: 'And blows (plagues) in the innermost place of the stomach' (Prov 20:30)." — Plagues of leprosy were particularly viewed as punishment for sins of fornication; see Tanḥ. מצורע 159B and b. ʿArak. 16A at § Luke 13:2, n. *d*, end.

2:27: He will shepherd them.

תְּרֹעֵם "you will smash them" (Ps 2:9), interpreted according to the approach taken by the LXX (ποιμανεῖς αὐτούς) = תִּרְעֵם "you will shepherd them."

3:1: That you have a name.

See Josephus, *J. W.* 2.2.5 at § Col 2:17.

3:4 A: Who have not stained their clothes.

See b. Šabb. 153A and Midr. Eccl. 9:8 (42A) at § Matt 22:2–14; see b. Šabb. 152B in the excursus "Sheol, Gehenna, and the Garden of Eden," II, #4 toward the beginning. ‖ Midrash Ecclesiastes 9:8 (42A): Bar Qappara (ca. 220) and R. Isaac (ca. 300) said, "Like the wife of a court courier who preened herself before her female neighbors. Her female neighbors said to her, 'Your husband is not here; for whom are you preening yourself?' She answered them, 'My husband is at sea (literally: a seaman). If the sea joins him a little, he will soon be here and stand before me. Is it not better if he sees me when I preen myself in my finery than in my ugliness?' 'So let your clothes be white at all times' (Eccl 9:8), that is, pure of sins, and 'let there be no lack of oil for your head' (Eccl 9:8), that is, may there be no lack of the fulfillments of the commandments and good works." ‖ Babylonian Talmud Šabbat 153A: "Let your clothes be white at every time" (Eccl 9:8): this refers to the show threads (tzitzit); "and let there be no lack of oil for your head" (Eccl 9:8): this refers to the tefillin (prayer straps). ‖ Targum Ecclesiastes 9:8: "At every time may your garments be white from every impurity of sin and acquire a good name, which is like the oil of anointing, so that blessings may come on your head and there be no lack of good for you."

3:4 B: They will walk with me in white clothes because they are worthy (of this).

Concerning the angels, Enoch says: "Their clothes were white and their garment and face luminous like snow" (1 En. 71:1). ‖ Jerusalem Talmud Kil'ayim 9.32B.4: R. Yohanan († 279) decreed, "Clothe me (after my death) with a garment[357] that is neither white nor black. If I stand among the righteous, I will not have to be ashamed (for my clothing is not black), and if I stand among the wicked, I will not have to be ashamed (for my clothing is not white)." R. Josiah (II, ca. 280) decreed, "Clothe me with a white garment with sleeves." He was told, "Are you better than your teacher (the previously named R. Yohanan)?" He answered them, "Must I be ashamed of my works?" (See the continuation at § Luke 12:40 A). — Parallels are found in y. Ketub. 12.35A.13; Gen. Rab. 96 (60D); 100 (63D); Tanḥ. ויחי 55A; TanḥB ויחי § 6 (108A). ‖ See b. Šabbat 114A at § Matt 9:15 B, n. *a*.

3:5: I will not erase his name from the book of life (see § Luke 10:20, #1).

3:7: Who has the key of David, who opens and no one will shut.

See § Matt 16:19 A and § Matt 16:19 B, #1, n. *c*.

3:8: An opened door.

See § 1 Cor 16:9 and § Col 4:3.

3:12 A: Pillar (see § Gal 2:9).

3:12 B: The name of the city of my God, the new Jerusalem.

1. The new name of Jerusalem. Genesis Rabbah 49 (31A): R. Phineas (ca. 360) said in the name of R. Samuel (ca. 260), "Abraham also knew the name by which God will one day call Jerusalem; as it says, 'At that time Jerusalem will be called "Yahweh's throne"' (Jer 3:17)." ‖ Babylonian Talmud Baba Batra 75B: Rabbah († 331) said that R. Yohanan († 279) said, "One day the righteous will be called by God's name; for it says, 'All who are called by my name and whom I have created for my honor' (Isa 43:7)." Furthermore, Samuel b. Nahman (ca. 260) said that R. Jonathan (ca. 220, so read instead of R. Yohanan) said, "Three will be called by God's name, and these are: The righteous and the Messiah and Jerusalem. The righteous, as we (just) said (thus on the basis of Isa 43:7). The Messiah, for it is written, 'And this is his name by which he will be called: "Yahweh our righteousness"' (Jer 23:6). Jerusalem, for it is written, 'And the name of the city is from the same day "Yahweh"' שמה (Ezek 48:35); do not read שָׁמָּה 'there,' but rather שְׁמָהּ 'its name' (so 'Yahweh' will be its name)." ‖ Midrash Lamentations 1:16 (58B): R. Levi (ca. 300) said, "Blessed is the city whose name is like that

---

357. S-B: The word in the text for garment is בירדיקא; according to Krauß, it is כירדיקא, which is corrupted from Atrebatica "Atrebatic garments," named after the Gallic people of the Atrebates (*Lehnwörter*, 2:144). According to Michael Sachs (*Beiträge zur Sprach- und Alterthumsforschung: aus jüdischen Quellen* [Berlin: Veit, 1852], 1:135), who is followed by Levy (*Chaldäisches Wörterbuch*, 1:203), the word means *bardaici cuculli* "coats with covers." Dalman (*Wörterbuch*, 61A) has בּוּרְדִּיקָא (*bardaicus*), Bardaic (Illyric) hoods. However, Dalman inserts a question mark here.

of its king and the name of its king like that of its God! Blessed is the city whose name is like that of its king (see Ezek 48:35, as in the preceding citation), and the name of its king like that of its God (see Jer 23:6, as in the preceding citation)." — The same is found in Midr. Ps. 21 § 2 (89B). ‖ See Pesiq. 148A at § 3:12 D.

2. καινὴ Ἱερουσαλήμ. — Testament of Dan 5: "The holy ones will rest in Eden (= paradise) and the righteous will rejoice over the new Jerusalem ἐπὶ τῆς νέας Ἱερουσαλήμ."

3:12 C: Which descends from heaven from my God.

Jerusalem descending from heaven is rarely mentioned in the pseudepigrapha,[a] and not at all in the older rabbinic literature and only a few times in the later small midrashim.[b] — On the heavenly Jerusalem, see § Heb 12:22.

a. 4 Ezra 7:26: "Behold, the days are coming when the signs that I told you earlier will arrive, when the invisible city (i.e., the heavenly Jerusalem) will appear." ‖ 4 Ezra 13:36: "Zion will appear (from heaven) and be revealed to all, completely built." ‖ In the face of Zion's lament and glory, 4 Ezra 10:54 says: "No human structure may exist where the city of the Most High shall be revealed (from heaven)." — 1 Enoch 90:29 and 2 Baruch 4:3ff. do not belong here. In the first passage, the "new house," that is, the new Jerusalem, is a structure that originates from God, but nothing indicates that the new house was previously in heaven, and from the heavenly city of the second passage it cannot at all be assumed that it is destined for the earth, since according to 2 Baruch, the site of the blessed eschatological consummation will not be earth, but rather heaven.

b. Midrash Vajjoscha[c] (*Beth ha-Midrash* 1.55.23): When Moses saw God's love with which he loved Israel, he said before him, "Lord of the world, bring them (Israel) in and plant them there (in the holy land), and may it be a planting that will never be uprooted. Let Jerusalem come down from heaven and never destroy it. Gather the dispersed of Israel there so that they may dwell there in security." ‖ Apocalypse of Elijah (*Beth ha-Midrash* 3.67.29): Elijah said, "I saw a beautiful and great city coming down from heaven, completely built." ‖ Nistaroth R. Simeon b. Yohai (*Beth ha-Midrash* 3.80.25): (After the gathering of the diaspora) fire will fall from heaven and consume Jerusalem (which was built again in the days of the Messiah b. Joseph) ... and eliminate the foreigners and the uncircumcised and the impure from its midst. Then Jerusalem, completely built, will descend from heaven with 72 pearls that shine from one end of the world to the other ... And the temple,[358] built, will also come down from heaven, which is in Zebul (the 4th heaven). ‖ Ma[c]aśe Daniel (*Beth ha-Midrash* 5.128.11): In place of the destroyed Jerusalem, the Jerusalem that is built will come down from heaven, and the sprout from the stump of Jesse, the Messiah b. David, will appear.

---

358. S-B: The temple descending from heaven is also mentioned in *Beth ha-Midrash* 1.56.27 and 1.64.15 (in the midrash on the Ten Commandments).

3:12 D: My new name.

Pesiqta 148A: R. Levi (ca. 300) said, "God will one day renew six things in the future. These are heaven, earth, the heart, the spirit, the name of the Messiah, and the name of Jerusalem. Heaven and earth, how do we know this? 'For, look, I will create a new heaven and a new earth' (Isa 65:17). Heart and spirit, how do we know this? 'And I will give you a new heart, and I will put a new spirit in you' (Ezek 36:26). The name of the Messiah, how do we know this? 'May his name remain forever! Before the sun (before the sun was created) his name was Yinnon' (so Ps 72:17 according to the midr., Yinnon is thus the new name of the Messiah; see § Matt 1:21 B, #2, n. *f*). The name of Jerusalem, how do we know this? 'You will be called by a new name, which Yahweh's mouth will designate' (Isa 62:2)."

3:14 A: In Laodicea.

Λαοδίκια or Λαοδίκεια = לוֹדִקְיָא. — The Laodicea mentioned in SDeut 33:24 § 355 (148A) was the one in Syria; see the passage at § Matt 6:17 A, #1, n. *f*. However, the Phrygian Laodicea could be intended in b. Šabb. 119A; see § Matt 19:22, #4, 2nd third. Also see § Col 2:1.

3:14 B: The basis of the creation of God.

ἡ ἀρχὴ τῆς κτίσεως not in the sense in which God says of Adam in Tanḥ. נח 7B: The first man was the beginning of my creatures תְּחִלַּת בְּרִיּוֹתַי, or in which the light of the beginning of his (God's) creation is called תְּחִילַּת בְּרִיָּיתוֹ in b. Pesaḥ. 53B. Instead, it is a statement of the causal relationship in which Christ stands to the creation of God: he is the basis, the *principium activum* of creation.

3:16: Because you are lukewarm.

χλιαρός maybe = the nonmetaphorical בֵּינוֹנִי, the middle, mediocre, half; see b. Roš Haš. 16B at § Matt 1:19, #1, n. *a*; y. Roš Haš. 1.57A.49 at § Luke 10:20, #1, n. *b*, last paragraph; ʾAbot R. Nat. 32 (8C) at § Rom 2:15 B, #3, n. *k*.

3:17: Rich ... poor.

עָשִׁיר and אֶבְיוֹן in Ps 49:3 are also understood by the targum in the metaphorical sense = righteous and unrighteous: Both the sons of the first man and the sons of Jacob, at the same time the righteous and the guilty זַכָּאָה וְהַיָּבָא.

3:18: Ointment.

κολλύριον, in rabbinic literature: קְלוֹר, קְלוֹרִין, קְלוֹרִית, קְלוֹרִיתָא "ointment, particularly eye ointment."

Jerusalem Talmud Šabbat 1.3D.64: One may put ointment קילורית on the eye on the day of preparation for the Sabbath so that it may be gradually healed. ‖ Babylonian Talmud Šabbat 108B: Mar Uqba (II, ca. 270) said that Samuel († 254) said, "One may soften ointment קילורין on the day of preparation for the Sabbath and put it on the eye on the Sabbath ...."

Samuel said, "Better is a drop of cold water in the morning and washing the hands and feet with warm water in the evening than all the eye ointment קילורין in the world." ‖ Leviticus Rabbah 12 (113D): Hezekiah (ca. 240) taught as a tannaitic tradition, "The words of the Torah are a crown for the head (see Prov 1:9), a necklace for the neck (see Prov 1:9), a refreshment for the heart (see Ps 19:9), an ointment קילורית for the eyes— as it says, 'The commands of Yahweh ... illuminating the eyes' (Ps 19:9)—and a wholesome cup for the bowels (see Prov 3:8)." — Parallels are found in Midr. Ps. 19 § 15 (86A); Deut. Rab. 8 (205B) with R. Hiyya, the father of R. Hezekiah, as the author.

3:19: Those I love I rebuke and chastise.

"Chastisements out of love," see § Luke 13:2; also see b. Ber. 5A at § Luke 24:26, I, #2, beginning. ‖ Sifre Deuteronomy 6:5 § 32 (73B): Let a man rejoice over sufferings ייסורין (chastisements) more than over good; for if a person sat in fortune (in good) his whole life, the sin that he has is not (thereby) forgiven. And by what is it forgiven? By sufferings it is forgiven him. R. Eliezer b. Jacob (II, ca. 150) said, "Look, it says, 'The one Yahweh loves he corrects יוכיח (he punishes), as a father atones for the son' (so Prov 3:12 according to the midr.). Who brings it about for the son that he is reconciled with his father? Say: It is sufferings (chastisements)." — See further § Heb 12:5f.

3:20: I stand before the door and knock.

κρούειν = דָּפַק or טְרַף, though other expressions were also in use (see § Matt 7:7 C). Sudden entry into a house was frowned upon.[a] Propriety absolutely required that one knock[b] or otherwise make oneself audible,[c] for example, by calling out (cf. φωνή, Rev 3:20). Incidentally, doorbells were familiar.[d]

a. Leviticus Rabbah 21 (120C): R. Simeon b. Yohai (ca. 150) said, "Four things God hates, and I too do not love them .... (The fourth:) whoever suddenly פִּתְאוֹם enters the (i.e., his own) house, and all the more the house of someone else." Rab († 247) said, "... Do not enter a house suddenly!" — There is a parallel in b. Nid. 16B; see § Matt 7:7 C.

b. Mishnah Tamid 1.2: When the supervisor (of the morning) came (into the temple), he would knock דּוֹפֵק at their quarter (those keeping watch), and they would open פָּתְחוּ to him. ‖ See Lev. Rab. 5 (108D) at § Matt 7:7 C; there are also other examples there; also see SDeut 33:2 § 343 (142B) at § Rom 1:20 E, n. *d*, 1st third.

c. See b. Qidd. 81A at § Matt 4:1 D, #3, A; see b. Šabb. 30B at § Matt 5:5, #1, 3rd paragraph. ‖ Leviticus Rabbah 21 (120C): When R. Yohanan († 279) would go up to greet R. Hanina (ca. 225), he used to make a noise הוה מְבַעְבַּע (at the door) so that his voice would be heard.

d. Tosefta Kelim Baba Meṣiʿa 1.13 (579): The doorbell זוּג שֶׁל דֶּלֶת is clean (does not make unclean). — Here there are several other similar regulations. See a parallel at b. Šabb. 58B.

4:2: A throne.

The throne of glory is among the creations made before the world; see § Matt 25:31 B, #1; at § Matt 25:31 B, #2, there are some descriptions of the throne; here reference may also be made to Pirqe R. El. 4.

4:4 A: On the thrones 24 elders.

On the honoring of elders on the part of God, see SNum 11:16 (25B) at § 1 Tim 5:17. See parallels to this in Lev. Rab. 11 (113B); Tanḥ. שמות 67A; שמיני 152A.

4:4 B: On their heads, golden garlands.

On the garlands or crowns כְּתָרִים, עֲטָרוֹת on the heads of the righteous in the next world, see Rab's († 247) saying in b. Ber. 17A at § Matt 5:8 B, #2, n. *b*, 1st third, as well as the citations at § 1 Cor 9:25 B, #2.

4:6 A: Before the throne like a glassy sea.

Apparently, "the waters above the firmament" (Gen 1:7) played a certain role in the theosophical speculations of the Jewish scholars for quite some time; see t. Ḥag. 2.5 (234) and parallels at § Matt 3:16, n. *b*. ‖ A baraita in b. Ḥag. 14B: Four have gone into paradise (have delved into speculations about the heavenly dwelling of God), and these are Ben Azzai and Ben Zoma (both ca. 110), Aher (the apostate Elisha b. Abbuyah [ca. 120]), and R. Aqiba († ca. 135). R. Aqiba said to them, "When you come to the pure alabaster stones אַבְנֵי שַׁיִשׁ טָהוֹר (before God's throne), do not say, 'Water! Water!' because it says, 'Whoever speaks lies does not endure before my eyes' (Ps 101:7)." ‖ Also see the heavenly water in the description of God's throne in 1 En. 14:9ff. at § Matt 25:31 B, #2, n. *a* and the sayings about the upper waters in Pirqe R. El. 4 at § Rev 4:6 B and 4:7ff.

4:6 B and 4:7ff.: Around the throne four living beings, full of eyes in front and in back. And the first living being is like a lion ....

1. For the four ζῷα = חַיּוֹת, see Ezek 1:5ff. and 10:10ff.

Midrash Song of Songs 3:10 (108A): R. Berekhiah (ca. 340) and R. Bun (I, ca. 325) said in the name of R. Abbahu (ca. 300), "There are four mighty (exalted) ones. The mighty one among the birds is the eagle, the mighty one among the domestic animals is the bull, the mighty one among the wild animals is the lion, the mightiest of all is the human being. God took them all and fixed them to his throne." — Parallels are found in Midr. Ps. 103 § 16 (219A); TanḥB בשלח § 14 (31A); Exod. Rab. 23 (85C). — Underlying this explanation is a saying of R. Simeon b. Laqish (ca. 250) which does not, however, refer explicitly to the *chayyoth* at the divine throne chariot; see b. Ḥag. 13B.23 and Rashi on the passage. ‖ Pirqe Rabbi Eliezer 4: What kind of firmament did God create on the second day? R. Eliezer (ca. 90, though the authorial attributions of Pirqe R. El. have no historical value) said, "The firmament that is above the heads of the four living beings (*chayyoth*); as it says, 'An appearance was above the heads of the *chayyoth* like a firmament, which looked like fine crystal' (Ezek 1:22). What does 'like fine crystal' mean? Like gems and pearls, and it (the firmament) shone over the whole heaven, like a lamp that is in the house, and like the sun when it shines in its full strength at midday .... If this firmament did not exist, the world would have been swallowed up by the waters that are above and beneath it; but this firmament forms a division between the waters (Gen 1:6) .... The appearance of his throne is like that of sapphire with four feet, and four holy living beings each have their fixed place at a foot. Each of them has four faces and four wings (Ezek 1:6), and they are identical with the cherubs (cf. Ezek 10:20). When he (God) speaks toward the east, he speaks forth between the two cherubs with the human faces (the two cherubs on the east side at the corners of the throne chariot thus turn their human face toward the east). When he speaks toward the south, he speaks forth between the two cherubs with the face of a lion. When he speaks toward the west, he speaks forth between the two cherubs with the face of a bull. And when he speaks toward the north, he speaks forth between the two cherubs with the face of an eagle.... The living beings do not know the place of his glory,[359] and they stand there in awe and fear, in trembling and quaking, and from the perspiration of their wings a stream of fire proceeds,[360] which goes out before him (Dan 7:10). Two seraphim are there, one at God's right hand and the other at his left. Each of them has six wings: with two he covers his face so as not to look at the face of the Shekinah; with two they cover their feet, lest they see the face of the Shekinah, in order to bring into oblivion the standing there of the feet of the (golden) calf (here it is presupposed that the seraphim have calf feet, as also the *chayyoth* do in Ezek 1:7); and with two they fly and show (God) reverence, by sanctifying the great name (of Yahweh). The one answers when the other raises his voice, saying, 'Holy, holy, holy is Yahweh Sabaoth; all lands are full of his honor!' And the living beings that stand near his glory, without knowing the place of his glory, answer and say, 'In every place where his glory (always) resides, may the glory of Yahweh be praised from its place (cf. Ezek 3:12)!' And Israel, the only people on earth that evermore day by day proclaims the unity of his name, answers and says, 'Hear, Israel, Yahweh our God is one Yahweh' (Deut 6:4). And he answers his people Israel, 'I, Yahweh, am your God who saves you from all distress.'"

2. γέμοντα ὀφθαλμῶν; see Ezek 10:12. — See b. ʿAbod. Zar. 20B at § Matt 4:1 B, #3, C.

4:9: When they give honor, praise, and thanks.

1. δόξαν διδόναι = נתן (יהב, שים) כָּבוֹד, see § Luke 17:18 and § John 9:24. ‖ 2. τιμὴν διδόναι = נתן שֶׁבַח. — Pirqe Rabbi Eliezer 4 (3A): The angels of the wheel and the cherubs and the living beings give praise before him. ‖ 3. εὐχαριστίαν διδόναι = נתן הוֹדָיָה. — Mishnah Berakot 4.2: R. Nehuniah b. Haqqanneh (ca. 70) said, "... When I go out (from the house of learning) I give thanks for my portion (lot) (which has come to me)."

4:10: They cast down their crowns.

On this act of homage, see Yalquṭ Simeoni on Exodus 7:9 (1 § 181): When the kings of the east and west saw them (Moses and Aaron during their audience before pharaoh), all fear of them fell on them, and trembling and quaking and agitation seized pharaoh and all who sat before him, and they removed their crowns והסירו כתריהם from their heads ands and bowed down before them.

359. S-B: See the citations at § Matt 18:10 C.

360. S-B: See Gen. Rab. 78 (49D) at § Matt 25:31 B, #2, n. *a*, toward the end.

5:1 A: A little book.

On the heavenly books, see § Luke 10:20, particularly #4.

5:1 B: Sealed with seven seals.

1. One has to distinguish between sealing at the bottom and sealing the whole: the former makes a decision of God unalterable. As long as the sealing has not yet occurred, it can still be changed and lifted.[a] The latter removes the thing in question from the knowledge of humans and from misuse by any unauthorized party.[b]

a. See SNum 6:26 § 42 (12B) at § Rom 2:11 and § 2 Pet 3:9 B. ‖ Babylonian Talmud Sanhedrin 108A: R. Yohanan († 279) said, "Come and see, how great the power of violence is! For behold, the generation of the flood had committed all transgressions, and yet the judgment decreed over them was only sealed (made unchangeable) when they stretched out their hands to robbery; as it says, 'The earth is full of violence, which proceeds from them; so I will destroy them together with the earth' (Gen 6:13)." — Yet the remark connected to a baraita from the school of R. Ishmael († ca. 135) counts as an exception: Even over Noah God's decree of judgment was sealed, though he "found grace in Yahweh's eyes" (Gen 6:8) (so that the decree was lifted).

b. Here, Dan 12:4, 9 above all should be named. ‖ In b. Ḥul. 105B, a demon says, "From everything that is wrapped, sealed חֲתִים, measured, and counted, we have no authority to take anything." ‖ Babylonian Talmud Niddah 17A: Even if they (certain peeled foods) are lying in a basket tied up and sealed חתימו, a harmful (evil) spirit rests on them. ‖ See 1 En. 90:20 at § Rev 6:1.

2. A counterpart to the "seven seals" in rabbinic literature is the seven years that precede the arrival of the Messiah; see b. Sanh. 97A.5 in a baraita in the excursus "Signs and Calculations of the Messianic Times," I, n. *a.* "Second," λ. — However, 2 Bar. 25:1–29:2 separates the premessianic period of woe into 12 sections; see the excursus Signs and Calculations of the Messianic Times," I, n. *a.* "First," ζ.

5:2: Who is worthy to open the little book?

On "opening" a book, see § Rev 6:1.

5:5 A: The lion from the tribe of Judah.

Yalquṭ Simeoni on Genesis 49:9 (1 § 160): "Judah is a young lion" (Gen 49:9); this is the Messiah b. David, who will go forth from two tribes. His father is from Judah and his mother from Dan, and both (tribes) are called "lion"; as it says, "Judah is a young lion." It says further, "Dan is a young lion" (Deut 33:22).

5:5 B: The root of David.

Targum Isaiah 11:10: "It will happen at that time when a descendant of Jesse will come as a sign (banner) for the nations. Kings will submit to him and the place of his dwelling will be in glory." ‖ TanḥumaB ויחי § 12 (110A): Why will your brothers praise you (Judah)? (see Gen 49:8).... Because the Messiah will go out from you who will redeem Israel; as it says, "A rod will arise from the stump of Jesse ..." (Isa 11:1). — Also see § Matt 1:6 A.

5:6: With seven horns.

On the horn of the Messiah, see the passages at § Matt 1:1 B, #2 on Ps 132:17 and on 1 Sam 2:10; see also § Luke 1:69.

5:8: They had golden bowls full of incense, which are the prayers of the saints (see § Rev 8:3, 4).

5:9 A: They sang a new song.

Israel will sing a new song only in the days of the Messiah as a song of praise for the wonders of his redemption.

Targum Song of Songs 1:1 enumerates ten songs of Israel, among which the tenth and last is the song that "the sons of the exile will say at the time when they will go up from the exile" (to Jerusalem, so in the days of the Messiah). ‖ Targum Isaiah 26:1: "In that time a new song of praise will be sung in the land of the house of Judah: 'We have a city of strength, salvation (redemption) is set on its walls and mercy.'" ‖ Exodus Rabbah 23 (85B): All songs that are sung (by Israel) in the world were feminine in gender (i.e., they were called שירה and not שיר). This means: As a woman becomes pregnant and gives birth and gives birth again and again, so too the afflictions that came (ever anew) over the Israelites, and they sang songs that were feminine in gender. So Babylon, Media, Greece, and Edom (= Rome) rose up and enslaved Israel. Yet in the future (= the days of the Messiah) no more afflictions will come over them; as it says, "The former afflictions are forgotten" (Isa 65:16). Furthermore, it says, "They will obtain delight and joy" (Isa 35:10). In that hour they will sing a song masculine in gender (שִׁיר); as it says, "Sing to Yahweh a new song שִׁיר חָדָשׁ, for he has done wonders!" (Ps 98:1). — According to Midr. Song. 1:5 (87B), where Isa 26:1 is cited as a supporting passage instead of Ps 98:1, R. Joshua b. Levi (ca. 250) is the author. ‖ Midrash Song of Songs 1:5 (87B.34): R. Berekhiah (ca. 340) said in the name of R. Samuel b. Nahman (ca. 260), "Israel is like a female person. Just as such a one receives a tenth portion of the paternal fortune (as an inheritance) and is compensated with it,[361] so too Israel (in Canaan) inherited (took into possession) the land of seven nations, the tenth portion of the seventy nations, and since Israel inherited as a female person, they sang a song feminine in gender; as it says, 'Then Moses and the children of Israel sang to Yahweh this song הַשִּׁירָה הַזֹּאת (feminine form).' Yet in the future (= the days of the Messiah) they will inherit like a male person, who inherits the whole paternal fortune. This means, 'From the east side to the west side, Judah one, Dan one, Asher one' (Ezek 48:1ff.), and so all. Then they will sing a song masculine in gender; as it says, 'Sing to Yahweh a new song!' (Ps 96:1). It does not say here, 'a new שִׁירָה,' but rather, 'a new שִׁיר.'" ‖ Midrash Psalm 98 § 1 (211B): "Sing to Yahweh

361. S-B: So according to Rabbi († 217?); see b. Ketub. 68A at § Gal 3:15, #2, n. *k*.

a new song!" (Ps 98:1). This is what Scripture said, "Sing to Yahweh a new song, his praise from the end of the earth" (Isa 42:10); for a song will be sung because of the redemption of Israel. ‖ See further Midr. Ps. 18 § 5 (68B) at § Matt 1:1 B, #2, 5th paragraph, and Exod. Rab. 23 (85A) at § Rom 4:2f., #1, n. *d*, σ, middle.

5:9 B: From every family (tribe) and tongue and nation and people.

Targum Esther 1:22; 3:8; 7:8 and 8:15 alongside each other: Peoples, nations, and tongues עַמְמַיָא אוּמַיָא וְלִשָׁנַיָא, probably following Dan 3:4, 7, 8; 5:19.

6:1: Opened one of the seven seals.

The opening of a sealed or stored book expresses that the fullness of time for what is written down in it has come. The base passage is Dan 7:10.

1 Enoch 47:2ff.: "In these days the holy ones who dwell in the heavens above will intercede in agreement ... because of the blood of the righteous and because of the prayer of the righteous, that it may not be futile before the Lord of Spirits, that the judgment for them be carried out and it may not be delayed for them forever. In those days I saw how the ancient one (God) sat on the throne of his glory and the books of the living were opened before him.... The hearts of the holy ones were filled with joy because the number of righteous drew near, the prayer of the righteous was heard and the blood of the righteous was avenged before the Lord of Spirits." — From the opening of the books, the conclusion is here directly drawn that it is the hour of vengeance. ‖ 1 Enoch 90:20: "I saw until a throne was erected in the lovely land (Palestine) and the Lord of the sheep sat on it, and the other (Michael?) took the sealed books and opened those books before the Lord of the sheep". (Then, as is further detailed in what follows, the judgment immediately began over the stars, the 70 angel princes of the nations, and the apostate Israelites.) ‖ See 4 Ezra 6:20ff. at § Luke 10:20, #4, n. *a*.

6:2: A white horse (see § Rev 6:4).

6:4: A red horse.

Babylonian Talmud Sanhedrin 93A: R. Yohanan († 279) said, "What does 'I saw in the night, and behold, a man riding on a red steed who stopped between the myrtle trees that are in the deep ground' (Zech 1:8) mean? What does 'I saw in the night' mean? God wanted to change the whole world into night. 'And behold, a man, riding'; 'man' refers to God (see Exod 15:3). 'On a red steed': God wanted to change the whole world into blood. Yet when he saw Hananiah, Mishael, and Azariah, his mind calmed down; as it says, 'who stopped between the myrtle trees that are in the ground' 'Myrtle trees' refer to the righteous, as it says, 'Who had reared the hadassa (= myrtles, i.e., the righteous Esther)' (Esth 2:9). 'Deep ground' means nothing but Babylon (see Isa 44:27). Immediately the (steeds) filled with anger became auburn and the red became white (see Zech 1:8)." Rab Papa († 376) said, "Take from this that a white steed designates something good in a dream." — Here we have a historical interpretation of Zech 1:8. An eschatological interpretation is found in ʾAg. Ber. 56 toward the beginning: R. Berekhiah (ca. 340) said, "The cruelest (among the enemies of Israel) is the angel prince of Edom (= Rome); for so Zechariah saw him. It says, 'I saw in the night, and behold, a man riding on a red steed who stopped between the myrtle trees that are in the deep ground' (Zech 1:8). He wished to equate himself with those[362] who are called 'myrtles,' the Israelites, who are found in the depth (of exile), and he wanted to equate himself with those who are called 'stars,' the Israelites. As it says, 'Count the stars ..., so your seed will be' (Gen 15:5). It says further, 'If your nest sat among the stars, I will cast you down from there' (Obad 4). 'And behind him red, auburn, and white steeds' (Zech 1:8). This refers to the kings (emperors) that arose from Rome: ('red,') for they love gold; 'auburn' שרוקים, for they comb מסרקים (with iron combs) the flesh of the body of the Israelites[363] and take away their wealth; 'white,' so that they might atone for (make white) the sins of the Israelites (by their distress)."

6:9: Under the altar the souls of the slaughtered (martyrs).

The souls of the martyrs are in the most immediate nearness to God; see b. Pesaḥ. 50A and Midr. Eccl. 9:10 (42B) at § Matt 5:10, #3. Their *mechiza* surround the throne of God in a circle. Inside of their *mechiza*, so even nearer to God's throne than they are, no one dwells. — Rabbinic literature never mentions the site of the heavenly altar as the abode of the departed souls, though it does mention the place under God's throne rather frequently (see § Luke 23:43, #3, D). — It is once mentioned hypothetically that being buried beneath the altar of the Jerusalem temple is tantamount to being buried under the throne of glory.

ʾAbot de Rabbi Nathan 26 (7C): R. Aqiba († ca. 135) said, "Whoever is buried in the other lands (outside of Babylonia and Palestine), it is as if he were buried in Babylon. Whoever is buried in Babylon, it is as if he were buried in the land of Israel. Whoever is buried in the land of Israel, it is as if he were buried under the altar, because the whole land of Israel is suited for the altar. Whoever is buried under the altar, it is as if he were buried under the throne of glory (see Jer 17:12): The throne of glory, exalted from the beginning, the site of our sanctuary (the heavenly throne of God is situated exactly juxtaposed to the earthly sanctuary)." — See b. Ketub. 111A: Rab Anan (ca. 280) said, "Whoever is buried in the land of Israel is like someone who is buried under the altar. It says here, 'You shall make an altar of earth for me' (Exod 20:24), and it says there, 'Its earth makes atonement for his people'" (so Deut 32:43 according to the midr.; sense: just as the earth of the altar makes atonement, so the earth of the land of Israel in general; so whoever rests in it rests like one under the altar).

6:10: When will you judge and avenge our blood?

See 1 En. 47:2ff. at § Rev 6:1.

---

362. S-B: We follow the text in Bacher, *Die Agada der palästinensischen Amoräer*, 3:361.

363. S-B: See b. Ber. 61B at § Matt 5:10, #3.

6:11: Until their coservants and their brothers have been completed.

If one is guided by the pseudepigraphic parallels, πληρώσωσιν should be filled out with the object τὸν ἀριθμόν: until they have completed the number (of martyrs) determined by God.

See 1 En. 47:2ff. at § Rev 6:1. Here "the number of righteousness" means the number of the righteous or martyrs fixed by God. — Also, 4 Ezra 4:35f.: "This question of yours ('how long until the end comes?') has already been asked by the souls of the righteous in their chambers. They said, 'How long shall we remain here? When will the fruit finally appear on the threshing floor of our recompense?' Yet the archangel Jeremiel answered them and said, 'When the number of those like you is complete.'" ‖ See also 2 Bar. 23:4f.: "When Adam had sinned, ... the great number of those who were to be born was numbered. ... Yet now the previously mentioned number is becoming full: so the creature does not live (any longer and the end is near)." — See further at § John 1:1 C, #5.

6:12: There was a great earthquake, and the sun went black like sackcloth made of hair and the entire moon became as blood.

1. σεισμός; see 2 Bar. 70, 2ff. and Pesiq. Rab. 1 (4B) in the excursus Signs and Calculation of the Messianic Times," I, n. *a*, "Second." On the signs in the sun and moon see § Matt 24:29 A.

6:13: The stars of heaven fell to the earth.

Sibylline Oracles 5:528ff.: "Heaven itself rose until it shook the fighters (the stars fighting with one another); enraged it cast them forward to the earth. Easily hurled down to the bath of Oceanus they set the whole earth on fire. The ether remained starless."

6:14: As when a book is rolled up (cf. Isa 34:4).

Sibylline Oracles 3:80ff.: "All the elements of the world will be abandoned when the God who dwells in the ether rolls up heaven, as when a scroll is wound up."

6:17: The great day of his wrath.

1. ἡ ἡμέρα ἡ μεγάλη. — 1 Enoch 54:6: "Michael, Gabriel, Raphael, and Phanuel will seize them (the hosts of Asasel) on that great day and on that day cast them into the burning furnace." See further 1 En. 22:11; 2 En. 18:6.

2. ἡ ἡμέρα τῆς ὀργῆς. — Jubilees 24:28, 30: "Isaac cursed the Philistines and said, 'Cursed be the Philistines until the day of wrath and anger.... And no remnant shall be left for them and no one who will be saved on the day of the wrath of judgment.'"

7:5–8: 12,000 sealed from the tribe of Judah ....

In the enumeration, the tribe of Dan is missing and Manasseh is named instead. In rabbinic literature, the tribe of Dan does not enjoy any special esteem, and most of the time is accused of idolatry.

Sifre Deuteronomy 34:1 § 357 (149A): "Yahweh made Moses look upon the whole land from Gilead to Dan" (Deut 34:1). This teaches that he made him look upon the descendants of Dan who were idolaters (see Judg 18:30). ‖ Genesis Rabbah 98 (62B): "Dan will do justice for his people as one of the tribes" (Gen 49:16); as the most outstanding of the tribes (i.e., Judah). R. Joshua b. Nehemiah (ca. 350) said, "If he had not associated with the most outstanding among the tribes, he himself would not have appointed the one judge that he appointed. Who was this? It was Samson, the son of Manoah." See Num. Rab. 14 (175D.4). — Numbers Rabbah 14 (175D.8): The blessing of Jacob (Gen 49:16) was bestowed on Dan only because of Samson. — In SDeut 33:22 § 355 (147B), Moses' blessing over Dan is written off with two brief geographical remarks. ‖ Targum Yerušalmi I Exodus 17:8: "Amalek came and waged war with the Israelites in Rephidim and took and killed men from those of the house of Dan who had not accepted the cloud (of glory) because of the foreign cult (= idolatry) that ruled among them." — The ejection of the tribe of Dan from the cloud of glory because of idolatry is also found in Tg. Yer. 1 Num. 22:41 and 23:1; Deut 25:18; Tg. Song. 2:15. ‖ Genesis Rabbah 43 (26C): "Abraham pursued until Dan" (Gen 14:14); idolatry was there, and he damaged it before and after. He damaged it before, for it says, "He pursued until Dan" (he was prevented from pursuing beyond this point because of the idolatry that would appear there later). And he damaged after, for it says, "From Dan one hears the snorting of his steeds" (Jer 8:16). ‖ Numbers Rabbah 2 (137B): Darkness goes out from the north into the world, and correspondingly the tribe of Dan (camped in the north, Num 2:25), because he brought darkness into the world by idolatry. For Jeroboam had made two golden calves, and idolatry is darkness (see Isa 29:15). And Jeroboam went around among all the Israelites, but only the tribe of Dan accepted it from him (see 1 Kgs 12:28f.). — The same is found in Pesiq. Rab. 46 (188A, B). ‖ See further unfavorable judgments about the tribe of Dan in Pesiq. 99A; Tg. Yer. I Num. 11:1; Tg. Jer. 8:16.

7:9 A: A great multitude that no one could count.

Sifre Deuteronomy 11:21 § 47 (83A): "Those who brought many to righteousness (are) like the stars forever" (Dan 12:3).… As the stars are hosts upon hosts, for which there is no number, so the righteous are hosts upon hosts, for which there is no number.

7:9 B: Palms in their hands.

The palm is a sign of victory; see Lev. Rab. 30 in the excursus "The Feast of Tabernacles," II, C, #1.

7:15: Will dwell over them.

σκηνώσει ἐπ' αὐτούς, see Ezek 37:27: והיה מִשְׁכָּנִי עליהם "My dwelling will be over them." — In rabbinic literature it is said: שרתה שכינה על "the Shekinah dwelt (rested) upon" so and so, see b. Soṭah 48B at § Col 2:9; הקב"ה משרה שכינתו על "God makes his Shekinah dwell (rest) upon" (b. Šabb. 139A).

7:17 A: Fonts of waters of life.

See § Luke 16:24 C. ‖ 1 Enoch 48:1: "At that place (paradise) I saw a fount of righteousness that was inexhaustible. Many founts of wisdom surrounded it. All who were thirsty drank from it and became full of wisdom, and they had their dwellings with the righteous, holy, and elect." ‖ See Exod. Rab. 15 (77D) at § Rom 8:20f., n. *s*.

7:17 B: God will wipe away every tear from their eyes.

Mishnah Moʿed Qaṭan 3.9: Of the future it says, "He will swallow up death forever," and "Yahweh Elohim will wipe away the tears from every face" (Isa 25:8).

8:2: The seven angels who stand before God.

These angels are probably identical with the angels of the throne, which the ancient synagogue sometimes enumerated as seven[a] (six), sometimes as four.[b]

a. Seven throne angels. — Tobit 12:15 (1st recension): "I am Raphael, one of the seven holy angels who carry up the prayers of the holy ones and go before the glory of the holy one." — (2nd recension:) "I am Raphael, one of the seven angels who stand and go before the glory of the Lord." — (3rd recension:) "I am Raphael, one of those who stand before God." ‖ 1 Enoch 20:1ff.: "These are the names of the holy angels, who keep watch: Uriel, one of the holy angels, who (is appointed) over the host (of angels) and Tartarus. Raphael, one of the holy angels, who (is appointed) over the spirits of human beings. Raguel (רעואל), one of the holy angels, who exacts revenge on the world of lights. Michael, one of the holy angels, appointed over the best portion of human beings, over the people of Israel. Sariel one of the holy angels, who (is appointed) over the spirits who sin against (?) the spirit. Gabriel, one of the holy angels, who (is appointed) over paradise, snakes, and the cherubs." — While here only six archangels are named, the Greek text, Recension G,[364] adds Remiel as the seventh, who is one of the holy angels, whom God has appointed ἐπὶ τῶν δηισταμένων. — Friedrich Spitta replaces δηισταμένων with ἀνισταμένων, according to which Remiel would be the angel of the resurrection.[365] This would fit well with the fact that in 4 Ezra 4:36 (see above at § 6:11) Jeremiel features as the protector of the souls of the righteous during the intermediate phase.[366] ‖ 1 Enoch 90:21f.: "The Lord called those seven first white ones (so the archangels are called; here too the manuscripts vacillate between the numbers six and seven) and commanded them to come before him ... all the (fallen) stars.... He said to

---

364. S-B: Alexander Kohut points out that the number of the *ameshaṣpentas* also vacillates between six and seven (*Über die jüdische Angelologie und Dämonologie in ihrer Abhängigkeit vom Parsismus* [Leipzig: Brockhaus, 1866], 3 n. 9).

365. Friedrich Spitta, *Zur Geschichte und Literatur des Urchristentums* (Göttingen: Vandenhoeck & Ruprecht, 361AD), 2:361.

366. S-B: In the Apocalypse of Elijah 10:8 an angel named Eremiel says, "I am the great angel Eremiel, the one who down there is over the abyss and Hades, the one in whose hand all souls are enclosed from the end of the flood that was on the earth, until this day" (Georg Steindorff, trans., *Die Apokalypse des Elias* [Leipzig: J. C. Hinrichs, 1899], 51). — A different sphere of activity is attributed to an angel called Ramael in 2 Bar. 55:3. Here it says, "When I (Baruch) considered this and the like, behold, the angel Ramael, who presides over the true visions, was sent to me."

that man who wrote before him (= Michael), who was one of the seven white ones, and said to him, 'Take these 70 shepherds (the ruling angels of the 70 nations) ....'" ‖ Targum Yerušalmi I Genesis 11:7: "Yahweh said to the seven angels who stand before him, 'Come now, so that we may go down and confuse their language!'" — However, Tg. Yer. I Deut. 34:6 mentions only six angels by name; yet it is entirely questionable whether here the text is talking only about throne angels; see the passage at § Luke 1:19 A, #3, n. *c.* ‖ For Pirqe R. El. 4, see n. *b* at the end.

b. Four angels of the throne. — 1 Enoch 40:1ff.: "Then I saw thousands of thousands and myriads of myriads, an innumerable and incalculable multitude standing before the Lord of Spirits. I saw and caught sight of four spirits at the four sides of the Lord of Spirits (these are the מַלְאֲכֵי הַפָּנִים 'the angels of the face,' cf. Isa 63:9), who are different from those who never sleep. I learned their names.... I heard the voice of those four angels of the face, how they sang praise before the Lord of glory. The first voice praises the Lord of Spirits forever. The second voice I heard praising the elect one (= Messiah) and the elect who are stored safely with the Lord of Spirits. The third voice I heard pleading and praying for the inhabitants of the dry land and interceding in the name of the Lord of Spirits. The fourth voice I heard, how it repelled the satans and did not allow them to come before the Lord of Spirits to accuse the inhabitants of the dry land. Then I asked the angel, who accompanied me (about those four angels) .... He said to me, 'The first is the merciful and long-suffering Michael; the second, who is appointed over all sicknesses and over all the wounds of the children of men, is Raphael (from רָפָא "to heal"); the third, who is over all powers, is Gabriel (from גָּבַר "to be strong"); and the fourth, who is appointed over the repentance and the hope of those who inherit eternal life, is called Phanuel (from פָּנָה "to turn oneself" = to turn in repentance).' These are the four angels of the Lord of Spirits, and the four voices I heard in those days." — These four archangels are also named alongside each other in 1 En. 54:6; 71:8, 13. — Most of the time, their four names are Michael, Gabriel, Uriel, and Raphael. So in 1 En. 9:1, according to the Greek fragments in Syncellus,[367] we read: καὶ ἀκούσαντες οἱ τέσσαρες μεγάλοι ἀρχάγγελοι Μιχαὴλ καὶ Οὐριὴλ καὶ Ραφαὴλ καὶ Γαβριὴλ παρέκυψαν (cf. 1 Pet 1:12) ἐπὶ τὴν γῆν ἐκ τῶν ἁγίων τοῦ οὐρανοῦ. — Also, 1 En. 10:1, 4, 9, 11 in Syncellus (Dillmann, *Das Buch Henoch*, 84f.), while another recension of the fragments reads "Arsyalalyur" instead of "Uriel."[368] ‖ Pesiqta Rabbati 46 (188A): "By wisdom Yahweh founded the earth, established the heavens by insight" (Prov 3:19). As God created four heavenly regions, so he surrounded his throne with four angels. And these are: Michael, Gabriel, Uriel, and Raphael. Likewise, he (according to the camping arrangement in Num 2) erected four banners דגלים. Michael at his right hand (= south side) corresponding to Reuben with the banners (see Num 2:10). Dan to the north (Num 2:25); Judah to the east (Num 2:3); Ephraim toward the sea (= west side) (Num 2:18). Why is his name called Michael מיכאל? Because he (Moses) arose and said in the hour when the

---

367. S-B: See August Dillmann, *Das Buch Henoch* (Leipzig: F. C. W. Vogel, 1853), 83. The Ethiopic text reads: Michael, Gabriel, Surian (Surel), and Urian.

368. See Beer in Kautzsch, *Apokryphen und Pseudepigraphen*, 1:241 n. ee.

Israelites went through the sea:[369] "Who מי is like you among the gods, Yahweh?" (Exod 15:11). When the Torah was complete, he said, "No one is like the God כאל of Jeshurun" (Deut 33:26). Who מי is like you? and no one is like God כאל, see, this sis מיכאל ("who is like God?"). Uriel at the left, corresponding to Dan, who is in darkness (see above § Rev 7:5–8). And why is his name called Uriel אוריאל? Because of (the truth) of the Torah, the Prophets, and the hagiographa, for God makes atonement for him (Dan) and illuminates the Israelites; as it says, "If I walk in darkness, Yahweh is my light אוֹר" (so Mic 7:18 is cited. — Uriel thus = light of God). Gabriel corresponds to Moses and Aaron and to the kingdom of the house of David (cf. Num 2:3; 3:38). And why is his name called Gabriel גבריאל? Because it is written of Judah: "Judah was strong גָּבַר among his brothers" (1 Chr 5:2); it further says, "His name is wonderful, counselor, god, hero אל גבור" (Isa 9:5) (Gabriel thus is "the strong one or God's hero"). Raphael behind (= west side). And why is his name called Raphael רפאל? To heal the breach of Jeroboam who proceeded from Ephraim, which camped in the west (Num 2:18); as it says, "O God אל, heal רפא them!" (Num 12:13; Raphael thus = "God heals"). — See the parallel in Num. Rab. 2 (137C) at § Luke 1:19 B. ‖ In Pirqe R. El. 4 (3A.18. 27), the two traditions of the four and the seven angels of the throne were connected with each other: Four hosts of angels of service offer praise before God. The first encampment Michael is at God's right hand; the second encampment Gabriel at his left; the third encampment Uriel in front of him; the fourth encampment Raphael behind him (their arrangement around God's throne is here different than in the last citation). And the Shekinah of God in the middle, and he sits on a high and exalted throne.... And a curtain is spread out before him, and his seven angels, who were created at the beginning, serve before him inside the curtain, and this is called פַּרְגּוֹד (curtain, veil = παραγαύδιον). — Accordingly, then, the four angels of the throne serve outside the throne curtain and the seven angels serve inside it, a harmonistic construction of a later time, of which the earlier period knew nothing.

8:3: Much incense was given to him.

Incense = prayer in Rev 5:8. — Numbers Rabbah 13 (171B): In that time (when Joseph was sold) Reuben was penitent and put on sackcloth and fasted and prayed before God that he might forgive him the sin because of his act with Bilhah. And the prayer is compared with incense; as it says, "May my prayer stand before you as an incense offering" (Ps 141:2).

8:4: The smoke of the incense rose up from the hand of the angel before God.

The angels appear as bearers of the human prayers in, for example, 3 Bar. 11: "A violent noise arose like thunder. I (Baruch) said, 'O, Lord, what sort of noise is this?' And he said to me, 'At this very moment the angel prince Michael is going down to receive the prayers of human beings.'" ‖ See Tob 12:15 at § Rev 8:2, n. *a.* ‖ 1 Enoch 99:3: "In those days (before the end time) prepare yourselves, you righteous, to raise your prayers of remembrance, and you will present them to the angels as testimony, so that they may present the misdeed of

369. S-B: Instead of שעבדו read שעברו.

the sinners to the Most High as a remembrance." ‖ See b. Šabb. 12B = b. Soṭah 33A at § 1 Cor 13:1 A, n. *d.* ‖ Exodus Rabbah 21 (83C): R. Phineas (ca. 360) said in the name of R. Meir (ca. 150) and R. Jeremiah (ca. 325) in the name of R. Hiyya b. Abba (ca. 280), "In the hour that the Israelites pray, you do not find that they all pray at once, but rather each synagogue prays for itself in particular: the one synagogue first and then another. When all the synagogues have completed all the prayers, though, the angel who is appointed over prayers takes all the prayers that they have prayed in all the synagogues, and makes from them crowns and set them on God's head; as it says, 'You who hear prayer, your adornment' (so Midr. Ps. 65:3). And עדיך (in the base text = 'to you') means nothing but 'crown'; as it says, 'You will put them all on like a jewel (crown)' (Isa 49:18). Likewise it says, 'Israel, by which I am adorned' (Isa 49:3). For God is crowned with the prayers of Israel, as it says, 'A splendid crown on your head' (Ezek 16:12)." — Parallels are found in Midr. Ps. 19 § 7 (84A); 88 § 2 (190B).

8:7 A: Hail and fire mixed with blood.

On the mix of hail and fire, see Exod 9:24: "There was hail and fire clustered together in the midst of the hail." — Septuagint: "There was hail and flaming fire in the hail." — Targum Onkelos: "There was hail and burning fire in the midst of the hail." — Targum Yerušalmi I: "There was hail and fire that went into the middle of the hail." — More precisely, Exod. Rab. 12 (75B): "There was hail and fire clustered together in the middle of the hail" (Exod 9:24); this was a miracle in a miracle. R. Judah and R. Nehemiah (both ca. 150). The one said, "Like the peel of a pomegranate, out of which (= through which) its core is seen (the fire is the outer peel and the hail is the core)." The other said, "Like a lantern in which water and oil were mixed together, and from its middle the light burns (the hail the outer, the fire the inner). A parable. What can the matter be compared with? With two ferocious legions that fought against each other. After some days the time came when the king had to wage war. Then the king made peace between the two of them and they carried out the king's order together. So fire and hail fight against each other. But when the time of the war against the Egyptians came, God made peace between them so that they might strike Egypt (together). This is what the words 'There was hail and fire in aggregate form מתלקחת' (Exod 9:24) mean." (A different explanation:) What does מתלקחת mean? This means (as a notarikon): מת לקחת = "seizing the dead": after the hail had hit him, the fire seized him and burned him. — Parallels are found in Pesiq. 3B: R. Judah said, "A flask made out of hail, filled with fire." R. Nehemiah said, "Fire and hail blended together." — The comparison with the pomegranate and the lantern is then presented by R. Hanin (ca. 300). Starkly different versions are found in Midr. Song. 3:11 (108B); Tanḥ. וארא 72A; TanḥB וארא § 22 (18B).

8:7 B: A third part of the earth was burned ....

According to b. B. Meṣ. 59A, a third of the olives, a third of the wheat, and a third of the barley were struck on the day when the scholars imposed the ban on R. Eliezer (ca. 90); see the passage in the excursus "Excommunication from the Synagogue."

8:10: A great star fell from heaven ....

See Sib. Or. 5:158ff.: "A great star will come down from heaven into the terrible flood of salt and will burn the deep sea and Babylon (= Rome) itself and the land of Italy."

8:12: A third of the sun was struck ....

ἐπλήγη = לָקָה; the latter is the ordinary term for being struck, that is, the stars being made dark.

See b. Sukkah 29A in a baraita at § Matt 27:45, #2. ‖ Genesis Rabbah 11 (8A): R. Simeon b. Judah of Kefar-Akko (ca. 180) said in the name of R. Simeon (ca. 150), "Although the heavenly lights were cursed on the day of preparation for the Sabbath (of creation, because of Adam's sin), they were struck לקו (diminished in their luminous power) only after the exit of the Sabbath (= on Sunday, for the sake of the honor of the Sabbath)." — The same is found in Gen. Rab. 12 (9A) in the name of R. Meir (ca. 150).

9:1: The mouth of the abyss.

1. ἄβυσσος α. = שְׁאוֹל, so here; β. = תְּהוֹם "deep"; see § Rom 10:6–8, #4.

2. φρέαρ τῆς ἀβύσσου denotes the mouth or the entrance to the abyss. According to the rabbis, the entrance to gehenna פִּי גֵיהִנֹּם was narrow at the top and wide at the bottom; see the excursus "Sheol, Gehenna, and the Garden of Eden," II, #9 and the citation at § Rev 9:2.

9:2: Smoke from the mouth.

Smoke is connected with the entrance to gehenna in b. Menaḥ. 99B: Hezekiah (ca. 240) said, "... God beckons the person from the ways of death to the ways of life; as it says, 'He has also beckoned you away from the opening of the straits' (Job 36:16), that is, from gehenna, whose entrance is narrow, because its smoke עָשָׁן is heaped up in it" ("so that the godless may be judged in fire and smoke," Rashi).

9:5 A: Five months.

On the number five, see § 1 Cor 14:19.

9:5 B: Like the anguish by a scorpion when it stings a person.

παίειν = הִכָּה to strike, hit, wound, here by stinging, thus = to sting. In rabbinic literature a scorpion is said both to sting[a] and to bite.[b] The danger of the scorpion more than the snake was said to consist in the fact that it did not wound only once but rather several times, one immediately after the other.[c]

a. Mishnah ʾAbot 2.10: Their (the scholars') sting is like the sting of a scorpion עֲקִיצַת עַקְרָב. ‖ Numbers Rabbah 10 (160A): As the scorpion stings מכה (strikes, wounds) with its stinger, so ultimately wine stings too (see Prov 23:32).

b. Leviticus Rabbah 22 (121A): A cry of woe was heard in the city. A scorpion has bitten נשכו so and so, and he died.

c. Jerusalem Talmud Berakot 5.9A.44: "Even if a snake has wounded him (one praying) on his heel, it (his prayer) should not cut off" (m. Ber. 5.1). R. Huna (ca. 350) said in the name of R. Yose (= Rab Joseph [† 333]), "It was only taught 'a snake,' but if a scorpion, he may cut off. Why? Because it wounds (stings) מהיוא again and again." — In b. Ber. 33A, where Rab Sheshet (ca. 260) is the author, the last sentence is missing.

9:11 A: Angels of the abyss.

In 1 En. 20:2 it says that the angel Uriel is appointed over Tartarus; see § Rev 8:2, n. *a*; also, in the S-B footnote in that section, the angel Eremiel is said to preside over the abyss and Hades. — In the rabbinic writings, a "prince of gehenna" is שַׂר שֶׁל גֵּיהִנֹּם mentioned occasionally (b. Sanh. 52A; b. Šabb. 104A; b. ʿArak. 15B) without his name being given; see the passages in the excursus "Sheol, Gehenna, and the Garden of Eden," II, #9. The prince of gehenna should not be confused with the "prince of spirits" שר של רוחות, who is appointed over the souls of those who have died and whose name was "Duma"; see about him the excursus "Sheol, Gehenna, and the Garden of Eden," II, #9.

9:11 B: His name is Abaddon.

In rabbinic literature אֲבַדּוֹן means α. as an appellative "demise, destruction,"[a] and denotes β. as a *nomen proprium* the place of damnation = gehenna.[b] It does not appear to be present in ancient Jewish writings as a name for the prince of Abaddon, as in Rev 9:11.

a. Sifra Leviticus 23:30 (412A): When it says "I will destroy והאבדתי (this soul from the midst of its people)" (Lev 23:30), this intends to teach concerning eradication (see Lev 23:29) that it signifies nothing other than destruction אֲבַדָּן.

b. In b. ʿErub. 19A R. Joshua b. Levi (ca. 250) names "Abaddon" among the seven names that gehenna bears; see the passage in the excursus "Sheol, Gehenna, and the Garden of Eden," I, #3 n. *a.* ‖ Babylonian Talmud Šabbat 89A: R. Joshua b. Levi (ca. 250) said, "When Moses came down from God, Satan came before God and said, 'Lord of the world, where is the Torah?' He answered him, 'I have given it to the earth.' He went to the earth and said to her, 'Where is the Torah?' She answered him, 'God knows the way to her, and he knows her place' (Job 28:23). Then he went to the sea; it said to him, 'It is not in me'; to Tehom (the deep, abyss), it said, 'It is not in me' (see Job 28:14). Abaddon and the kingdom of the dead אבדון ומות said, 'With our ears we heard a rumor about her' (Job 28:22). He returned and said before him, 'Lord of the world, I have searched on the whole earth and not found it'! He said to him, 'Go to the son of Amram!' He went to Moses and said to him, 'The Torah that God gave you, where is it?' He answered him, 'What is this? What am I that God would have given me the Torah!' Then God said to Moses, 'Moses, are you a liar?' He said before him, 'Lord of the world, you have a well-kept gem in which you delight day after day. Should I myself be granted anything of it?' God said to Moses, 'Since you have considered yourself humbly, it shall be called by your name; as it says, "Remember the Torah of Moses, my servant" (Mal 4:5).'" ‖ Midrash Ecclesiastes 5:8 (26B): The soul of (the emperor) Titus fled to Abaddon for eternal abomination (for eternal damnation) לְדִרְאוֹן עוֹלָם (cf. Dan 12:2). ‖ Tanḥuma ויקרא at the end: "He makes nations great and destroys them ויאבדם" (Job 12:23), he cast them down into Abaddon.

9:12 A: The first woe has passed.

οὐαί corresponds to וָאי = *vae!*, which appears to feature only as an interjection in rabbinic literature. However, בִּיָא, בִּיָה is used both as an interjection = woe![a] and as a substantive = the woe.[b]

a. Leviticus Rabbah 17 (117B): "And behold, north of the altar gate there was the same image at the entrance בַּבִּאָה" (Ezek 8:5). What does בביאה mean? R. Aha (ca. 320) said, "Woe, woe בייה בייה! The residence (of the idols) supplants the Lord of the house."

b. Genesis Rabbah 93 (58D): "Please בִּי, my lord!" (Gen 44:18); you are bringing a woe בִּיָּיה upon us, my lord.

9:12 B: Behold, there are two more woes after this.

R. Yohanan († 279) says about the time immediately before the arrival of the Messiah in b. Sanh. 97A: "Many hardships and severe disasters burst forth again and again; while the earlier one is still enacted (in power), the second comes quickly." — The same is found as a saying of the Rabbanan in Midr. Song. 2:13 (101A).

11:2: 42 months.

On the 3.5 years in rabbinic eschatology, see the excursus "Signs and Calculations of the Messianic Times," II; see also § Jas 5:17.

11:3: My two witnesses.

Baruch is kept (alive in the next world) in order to give testimony at the end of time against the gentile nations; see 2 Bar. 13:1–12 at § Rom 3:9 A, #3, B, n. *d.*

11:4: These are the two oil trees ... that stand before the Lord of the earth.

Zechariah 4:14 in rabbinic literature. The two olive trees are understood to refer to the following:

1. Moses and Aaron. — Exodus Rabbah 15 (76B): "These are the two sons of oil who stand by the Lord of the whole earth" (Zech 4:14). R. Levi (ca. 300) said, "This teaches that God searched again and again for some reason he could redeem the Israelites. Yet he found nothing until he found the merit of Moses and Aaron, and this assisted them; this is what is written, 'These are the two sons of oil' (Zech 4:14)."

2. Aaron and David. — Numbers Rabbah 18 (184B): R. Levi (ca. 300) said, "Why did Korah rebel against Moses?" He said, "I am a son of oil, the son of Izhar (Exod 6:21), and Izhar means oil (see Deut 7:13); and with all liquids into which oil is put, the latter is found

as the uppermost. And not only this but also it is written, 'These are the two sons of oil who stand by the Lord of the whole earth' (Zech 4:14). Yet does oil have sons? This refers to Aaron and David who were anointed with the oil of anointing. Aaron received the priesthood and David the kingdom. Korah said, 'If these, who were anointed only with oil, received the priesthood and the kingdom, should I who am (as ben Izhar) a son of oil, not be anointed and become priest and king?' Immediately he rebelled against Moses." ‖ Sifra Leviticus 7:35 (172A): This is the anointing of Aaron and the anointing of his sons (so Midr. Lev. 7:35, by interpreting משחה = "anointing") ... R. Judah (ca. 150) said, "Do Aaron and his sons need the oil of anointing also in the future (or are all Aaron's successors anointed in Aaron at the same time)? Scripture teaches, 'This is the anointing of Aaron and the anointing of his sons' (Lev 7:35; i.e., in Aaron all his successors are anointed for all times). Yet how do I then maintain, 'These are the two sons of oil who stand by the Lord of the whole earth' (Zech 4:14)?" (From the passage it appears to follow that each particular high priest and king had to be anointed!) This refers to Aaron and David (as representatives of the priesthood and kingdom). ‖ Midrash Lamentations 1:16 (58A): "Over this אלה I weep" (Lam 1:16). R. Nehemiah (ca. 150) said, "Over the ceasing of the priesthood and the kingdom. This is what 'These אלה are the two sons of oil who stand by the Lord of the whole earth' (Zech 4:14) means. These are Aaron and David: Aaron pleads concerning his priesthood, and David pleads concerning his kingdom."

3. Zerubbabel and Joshua. — Targum Zechariah 4:14: "These (Zerubbabel and Joshua) are the two sons (descendants) of the princes who stand before the Lord of the whole earth." — The "princes" are David and Aaron, who are called "oil" יצהר because they were anointed with the holy oil of anointing. Their "sons" are Zerubbabel and Joshua as the holders of the kingdom and priesthood at the time.

4. The righteous and the scholars. — Jerusalem Talmud Maʿaśer Šeni 5.56C.46: It is written, "These are the two sons of oil who stand by the Lord of the whole earth" (Zech 4:14). R. Abbahu (ca. 300) said, "R. Yohanan († 279) and R. Simeon b. Laqish (ca. 250) were of different opinions about this. The one said, 'This refers to those who come before God forcefully (insisting on their right).' And the other said, 'This refers to those who come before God in the power of the fulfillments of the commandments and good works.'" — The reason for this interpretation appears to have been given by the expression עמד על, which was understood according to the rabbinic עמד על רגליו = "to tread firmly." ‖ Babylonian Talmud Sanhedrin 24A: "The two sons of oil" (Zech 4:14). R. Isaac (ca. 300) said, "These are the students of the scholars in the land of Israel, who are smooth like olive oil toward each other in the halakah. 'And two olive trees above' (Zech 4:3): these are the students of the scholars in Babylon, who are bitter (sharp) like an olive leaf toward each other in the halakah."

5. The Messiah and the high priest of the messianic age. — See ʾAbot R. Nat. 34 (9A) at § Heb 7:20ff., #1.

6. The Messiah b. David and the Messiah b. Ephraim. — See Pesiq. Rab. 8 (30A) at § Luke 24:26, II, 1, n. *d*.

11:5: Fire goes out from their mouth.

The same is said about the Messiah; see 4 Ezra 13:8ff., 37 at § 2 Thess 2:8. — See also b. Ḥul. 137B: (R. Yohanan [† 279] asked Isi b. Hini, when he came from Babylonia to Palestine,) "Who is the head of the house of learning in Babylon?" He answered him, "Abba Arikha" (this is [Rab, † 247], who bore the epithet Arikha = "the long one" because of his size). He said, "You call him Abba Arikha" (and not by his name of honor "Rab")? I remember when I sat 17 rows behind him (in the house of learning) and Rab before Rabbi († 217?), sparks of fire went out from the mouth of Rab to the mouth of Rabbi and from the mouth of Rabbi to the mouth of Rab, and I did not understand what they were saying. And yet you call him Abba Arikha?!"

11:8: Which spiritually ... is called Egypt.

Egypt appears as the prototypical name of the anti-theocratic empires in Gen. Rab. 16 (11C): R. Huna (ca. 350) said in the name of R. Aha (ca. 320), "All kingdoms are called by the name Assur אשור because they enrich themselves מתעשרות by Israel." R. Yose b. Hanina (ca. 270) said, "All kingdoms are called by the name Nineveh נינוה, because they beautify themselves מתנאות by Israel." R. Yose b. Halapta (ca. 150) said, "All kingdoms are called by the name Egypt מצרים, because they oppress מצרות Israel." — In the parallel in Lev. Rab. 13 (114C), the sentence about Nineveh is missing and the one about Egypt is attributed to R. Yose b. Hanina. — The saying of R. Yose b. Halapta is also found in Mek. Exod. 14:25 (39A) in a different and more expansive version.

11:15: The kingship over the world has become that of our Lord and of his Christ.

The ancient synagogue expected the fulfillment of Obad 21: "The kingship will fall to Yahweh" to occur simultaneously with the fall of Rome; see Lev. Rab. 13 (114C) at § Matt 7:6 C, #2.

12:1: A woman wrapped with the sun ....

On the allegorical presentation of Zion as a woman, see above all 4 Ezra 9:38–10, 55; also Pesiq. Rab. 26 (131B) at § Gal 4:26 C, n. *c*.

12:3: A dragon ... with seven heads.

Such a figure is mentioned in b. Qidd. 29B; see the excursus "Ancient Jewish Demonology," #7, n. *h*.

12:6: The woman fled into the wilderness.

The flight of the community of Israel into the wilderness immediately before the dawn of the final redemption is among the fixed traits in the depictions of the future eschaton; see Tanḥ. עקב 7B and Pesiq. 49B at § Luke 24:26, I, #4, n. *a*, as well as Leqach Tob Num 24:17 (2.129B) at § Luke 24:26, II, #3, n. *b*.

12:7 A: Michael and his angels.

1. Michael. – See ample material about the archangel Michael in W. Lueken, *Michael*.[370] – On the name מיכאל see Num. Rab. 2 (137C) at § Luke 1:19 B; Pesiq. Rab. 46 (188A) at § Rev 8:2, n. *b*. – In rank Michael was the highest among the angels, the actual representative of God (= the angel of Yahweh).[a] Therefore Israel is entrusted especially to his care[c] (partly sharing this care with the angel Gabriel).[b] As the patron of Israel, he defends them against all accusations of Satan[d] and will one day join in helping to bring about the ultimate redemption of Israel.[e]

a. See b. Yoma 37A and Gen. Rab. 48 (30B) at § Luke 1:19 A, #3, n. *e*. ‖ Exodus Rabbah 2 (68C): "The angel of Yahweh appeared to him" (Exod 3:2). R. Yohanan († 279) said, "It was Michael"; R. Hanina (ca. 225) said, "It was Gabriel…." Everywhere where Michael appeared, the glory of the Shekinah (divinity) was there.

b. See Exod. Rab. 18 (80C) at § Luke 1:19 A, #4, n. *f*.

c. Daniel 10:13, 21; 12:1. ‖ See 1 En. 20:1ff. at § Rev 8:2, n. *a*. ‖ In b. Yoma 77A God says to Michael, "Michael, your nation (= Israel) has sinned." ‖ See Tg. Pss. 137:7 at § Luke 1:19 A, #4, n. *e*. ‖ In ספר חנוך (*Beth ha-Midrash* 5.187.1) Michael is called in brief שרם של ישראל "the (angel) prince of Israel."

d. Exodus Rabbah 18 (80C): R. Yose (ca. 150? 350?) said, "Who are Michael and Sammael (= Satan) like? The defender and the accuser who stand before the court: the one speaks and the other speaks. If this one has ended his words and that defender notices that he has overcome, then he begins to praise the judge that he renders the verdict. If then that accuser tries to add (another) word, the defender says to him, 'Be silent so that we may hear the judge!' So Michael and Sammael stand before the Shekinah: Satan sues and Michael asserts the merit of Israel; if then Satan (still) wishes to speak, Michael tells him to be silent; for it says, 'I want to hear what God Yahweh will speak (as judge), for he speaks peace to his people' (Ps 85:9)." ‖ Pesiqta Rabbati 44 (185A): "Turn, Israel; Yahweh is witness" (so Hos 14:2 according to the midr.). The Israelites said to him, "Lord of the world, if we repent, who will be a witness that you have accepted us?" He said to them, "Your defender, that is, Michael; as it says, 'And at that time Michael will arise, the great prince, who stands by the sons of your people' (Dan 12:1)." (At Israel's pleading, God declares himself ready to be willing to be a witness for them himself.)

e. See § Matt 1:21 D, A, n. *h*. ‖ Exodus Rabbah 18 (80C.37): As God carried out his deeds in this world through Michael and Gabriel, so too he will carry them out through them in the future (= in the messianic age); for it says, "Liberators will go up onto Mount Zion to judge the mountain of Esau (= Rome)" (Obad 21). These are Michael and Gabriel. Our holy teacher (= Rabbi [† 217?]) said, "This is Michael all by himself; for it says, 'In that time Michael will arise …' (Dan 12:1; see above). He arises for the needs of Israel and speaks for them; as it says, 'Then the angel of Yahweh (= Michael) responded and said, "Yahweh Sabaoth, how long

---

370. W. Lueken, *Michael: Eine Darstellung und Vergleichung der judischen und der morgenländisch-christlichen Tradition vom Erzengel Michael* (Göttingen: Vandenhoeck & Ruprecht, 1898).

will you not have mercy on Jerusalem?" (Zech 1:12), and furthermore, "There is no one who assists me against them, as Michael, your prince" (Dan 10:21).'"

2. Michael and his angels. — This corresponds in the mouth of R. Levi (ca. 300) to מִיכָאֵל וְדִגְלוֹ "Michael and his host (his banner)" in Midr. Song. 2:4 (97A); see also 6:10 (124B.2).

12:7 B: The dragon and his angels.

See the expression "devil and his angels" at § Matt 25:41 B. — In Pirqe R. El. 13, 14, 27 the expression is סמאל וכת שלו "Sammael and his horde (host)"; see the passages at § Matt 4:1 B, #2, n. *a*, § Rom 8:20f., n. *g*; and § Matt 4:1 B, #2, n. *g*.

12:7 C: Michael and his angels fought with the dragon.

There is an echo of this battle, which is otherwise not mentioned explicitly in rabbinic literature, in Pirqe R. El. 27; see § Matt 4:1 B, #2, n. *g*.

12:9 A: The great dragon, the old snake, called devil and Satan, was cast to the earth.

1. ὁ ὄφις ὁ ἀρχαῖος = Satan; see § Matt 4:1 B, #2, n. *e*. — Tanḥuma מצורע 159A: Likewise you find it with the old snake נחש הקדמוני: since it spoke slanders against its creator, it became leprous (hence the spots on a snakeskin); see Tanḥ. חקת 228B; TanḥB מצורע § 7 (24A).

2. ἐβλήθη εἰς τὴν γῆν; see § Luke 10:18.

12:9 B: Who misleads the whole world.

See § Matt 4:1 B, #3, A.

12:10: The accuser ... who accuses before God.

See § Matt 4:1 B, #3, B. — Here reference may also be made to Exod. Rab. 31 (91C): Like a person who had a legal matter before the king, but also intercessors who put in a word for him. So it is also with a person who keeps the commandments and is a son of the Torah and completes works of love. When Satan comes and accuses him, then his intercessors confront the latter and assert his merit; as it says, "A person's gift (= alms) makes space for him" (Prov 18:16). What he does toward the poor stands by him. Therefore, it is said, "Blessed is the one who acts properly toward the wretched" (Ps 41:2). — See Exod. Rab. 18 at Rev § 12:7 A, n. *d*.

12:11: And have not loved their soul to the point of death.

See 1 En. 108:10 at § 1 Cor 15:15.

12:15: The snake cast from its mouth ... water like a stream.

For the whole idea, see b. B. Bat. 74A.28: R. Yohanan († 279) narrated, "We once went on a ship and saw a fish that stretched its head out of the water and its eyes were like two moons, and water was cast out from its two nostrils like the two rivers of Sura."

13:1 A: I saw a beast rising from the sea.

In 4 Ezra 11:1ff., the eagle, which symbolizes the Roman Empire, arises from the sea with twelve feathered wings and three heads, while the Messiah who destroys the empire comes forth as a lion from the woods (4 Ezra 11:37). ‖ Leviticus Rabbah 13 (114C): "I looked in my vision during the night, and behold, the four winds broke forth against the great sea, and four great beasts rose up from the sea" (Dan 7:2f). If you have merits, from the sea, but if not, from the woods. When a water animal rises up from the sea, it is powerless; but when an animal comes up out of the woods, it is not powerless. Likewise, it says, "The pig from the forest מִיָּעַר strips it bear (the vine)" (Ps 80:14). The ע hovers: if you have merit (the word is read): מִן הַיְאוֹר "from the river," but if not: מִן הַיַּעַר "from the woods." If an animal rises up from a stream, it is powerless; if it comes out of the woods, it is not powerless. — According to Midr. Song. 3:4, R. Yohanan († 279) appears to be the author of this remark; here we find the clarifying parenthesis: If you have merits, no nation will rule over you. — Additional parallels are found in Midr. Ps. 80 § 6 (182A); ʾAbot R. Nat. 34 (9A.3). Also see b. Ḥul. 127A.16 and Midr. Ps. 104 § 20 (223A).

13:1 B: Names of blasphemy.

Blasphemies are a characteristic of the Roman Empire.

See Lev. Rab. 13 (114C) at § Matt 7:6 C, #2; b. Giṭ. 56B at § Matt 3:17 A, n. *h*, #4; in ʾAbot R. Nat. 1 (1B), Titus strikes at the altar in Jerusalem with the words "Wolf, wolf (see b. Sukkah 56B at § Luke 1:5 A, #5, n. *d*), you are a king and I am a king, come and wage war with me!" ‖ Sifre Deuteronomy 32:38 § 328 (139B) at § Matt 24:2, #2, paragraph 4.

13:8: In the book of life (see § Luke 10:20).

13:10: He who (leads) into captivity will go away into captivity ....

On the principle "measure for measure," see § Matt 5:38 and § Matt 7:2 B; also see § Luke 13:2.

13:15: It was granted to him to put spirit in the image of the beast so that the image of the beast spoke too.

See § Rom 1:23 A, #2, D, n. *l*.

14:1: Who bore his name and the name of his father written on his forehead.

The name on the forehead is a sign of belonging; see the brands of the owner on the neck or on the clothing of his slaves in the excursus "The Nature of Ancient Jewish Slavery," B, #1 notes *c* and *e*.

14:6–9.

In 14:6, 8, and 9, three angels appear for three different messages. Grotius: *Quot res nuntiandae, totidem nuntii.* This corresponds to the rabbinic theory that an angel can go always only with one mission.

Genesis Rabbah 50 (31D.40): In a baraita it has been taught: One angel cannot accomplish two missions (orders) and two angels cannot accomplish one mission. — For illumination, we may look to Tg. Yer. I Gen. 18:2: "(Abraham) raised his eyes, and behold, three angels stood before him in the form of men who were sent in three matters. For it is not possible that one angel of service be sent in more than one matter. The one came to bring him the message that Sarah would bear a son; the other came to save Lot; and the third came to destroy Sodom and Gomorrah." — Underlying these claims is the view that the angels are embodiments of divine commands. So R. Samuel b. Nahman (ca. 260) says in the name of R. Jonathan (ca. 220) in b. Ḥag. 14A: "From each word that goes from God's mouth, an angel is created; for it says, 'By the word of Yahweh the heavens were made and by the breath of his mouth all their host (= angels)' (Ps 33:6)." — Since every divine command constitutes a whole in itself, neither can one command be embodied in two angels, nor can two commands be embodied in one angel. The ultimate consequence of this theory was naturally that the angels receded again into nothingness with the execution of their order. — This conclusion was also drawn in Gen. Rab. 78 (49D); see the passage at § Luke 1:19 A, #3, n. *a.*

14:6: In the middle of heaven.

ἐν μεσουρανήματι = צְאֶמְצַע הָרָקִיעַ. — Tanḥuma שופטים 15B: R. Hanina (the Bible Reader [ca. 225]) said, "One day God will make his glory visible to all who come into the world, and will lower his throne in the middle of heaven ..." (see the whole passage in the excursus "Ancient Jewish Depictions of the Judgment").

14:8: The great Babylon.

1. Babylon as a code name for Rome. — Sibylline Oracles 5:158: "A great star will come down from heaven into the terrible flood of salt and will burn the deep sea and Babylon itself and the land of Italy, because of whom many holy and devout ones of the Hebrews and the true temple ναὸς ἀληθής (it is probably more correct to read with Blaß in Kautzsch λαὸς ἀληθής 'the true people'[371]) perished." — Alongside "the land of Italy," "Babylon" can hardly be anything other than Rome. ‖ Midrash Song of Songs 1:6 (89A): R. Levi (ca. 300) said, "... On the day when Jeroboam b. Nebat set up two golden calves, two bulrush huts were constructed in Rome, and when they had been built, they collapsed. They were built again, and they collapsed. There was an old man there by the name of Abba Qolon. He said to them, "If you do not take water from the river Euphrates and mix it with this clay and build those (huts), they will not be able to last." It was said to him, "Who can do such a thing!" He said to them, "I will do it myself." He went as a wine merchant from city to city, from province to province until he came there (to the Euphrates). When he had ar-

371. Kautzsch, *Apokryphen und Pseudepigraphen*, vol. 1.

rived, he went and took water from the Euphrates, and it was mixed with clay and those (huts) were built and they stayed standing. Since that time one used to say, "A city (built) without Abba Qolon is not called a city, and (therefore) Rome was called 'Babylon' בָּבְלוֹן." — In the parallel passages that deal with the founding of Rome—y. ʿAbod. Zar. 1.39C.33; b. Šabb. 56B; b. Sanh. 21B; SDeut 11:25 § 52 (86A); Midr. Esth. 1:9 (88B); Midr. Ps. 10 § 6 (48A)—we find neither the explanation about Abba Qolon nor the remark about Babylon as a name for Rome. ‖ TanḥumaB תזריע § 16 (21B): God will say (to the wicked Roman Empire), "By your life, I will sit in judgment over you and judge you and declare you guilty; as it says, 'Go down and sit in the dust, you virgin daughter Babylon; sit down on the earth without a throne, you daughter of the Chaldeans!' (Isa 47:1)." He calls Edom (= Rome) "daughter Babylon" and "daughter of the Chaldeans." What does "daughter Babylon" mean? Twin sister of Babylon: as Babylon destroyed my house, so too did this one destroy my house. Therefore, daughter of Babylon, "sit down on the earth without a throne".... — In Tanḥ. תזריע 157A, we do not find the interpretation of Isa 47:1. — On Assur, Nineveh, and Egypt as prototypical names for world powers hostile to God, see Gen. Rab. 16 (11C) at § Rev 11:8.

2. Βαβυλὼν ἡ μεγάλη = בָּבֶל רַבְּתָא (Dan 4:27). — In rabbinic literature Rome is several times called either briefly כְּרַךְ גָּדוֹל "the great city"[a] or more fully כְּרַךְ גָּדוֹל שֶׁבְּרוֹמֵי "the great city in Rome"[b] (i.e., in the Roman Empire).

a. In Pesiq. Rab. 14 (65B) it says in an allegorical interpretation of Num 19:2ff.: One day God will drive out the angel prince "of the great city" from his (heavenly) division. — So according to the reading in Yalquṭ on Num 19:2. See the whole passage according to the parallel in Pesiq. 40B at § 1 Cor 9:9, #2, C, beginning of 2nd third.

b. Babylonian Talmud Pesaḥim 118B: There are 365 markets (streets) in the great city in the Roman Empire.... ‖ Jerusalem Talmud ʿAbodah Zarah 1.39C.33: R. Levi (ca. 300) said, "On the day when Solomon became related by marriage to pharaoh Neccho, the king of Egypt, Michael went down and thrust a reed into the sea and made a sand bank appear (read שִׂרְטוֹן = σύρτις instead of the incomprehensible שלעטיט), and a great thicket arose, and this is the great city in the Roman Empire." — See the parallels at § Luke 1:19 A, #4, n. *i*. — For further examples see b. Pesaḥ. 118B; b. Sanh. 21B; y. ʿAbod. Zar. 3 at the beginning; y. Taʿan. 1.64A.12 and Midr. Eccl. 5:7 (26A). — In Lev. Rab. 6 (109D.12) we read the connection כְּרַךְ גדוֹל שֶׁל רוֹמֵי.

14:10: Fire and sulfur.

Fire and sulfur are among the means of punishment in gehenna, see the excursus "Sheol, Gehenna, and the Garden of Eden," II.

14:11: The smoke (cf. § Rev 9:2).

14:13 A: Yes, says the Spirit, for they will rest from their labors.

1. λέγει τὸ πνεῦμα see § Heb 3:7 A and § Luke 2:25 C, #4, especially notes *b* and *c*.

2. ἵνα ἀναπαήσονται ἐκ τῶν κόπων αὐτῶν. — Genesis Rabbah 9 (7A): R. Yohanan († 279) said, "... Why is death imposed on the righteous? As long as the righteous live, they fight with their (evil) inclination. When they have died, they rest נחין. This is what is

written: 'There those who have toiled with strength rest' (so the midrash: ינוחו יגיעי כח, Job 3:17), we have enough of what we have toiled with מה שיגענו."

14:13 B: Their works follow them.

Mishnah ʾAbot 6.9: R. Yose b. Qisma (ca. 110) said, "… In the hour that a person dies, neither silver nor gold nor gems accompany him מְלַוִּין אותו, but rather only knowledge of the Torah and good words." – See the whole passage at § 1 Tim 6:7. ‖ Midrash Ecclesiastes 5:17 (29A): Is there an eating or drinking that accompanies מלוין a person into the grave? And what accompanies him מלוהו? Knowledge of the Torah and good words. – Parallels are found in Midr. Eccl. 2:24 (15B); 3:12 (20A); 8:15 (40B). – Most of the time, it is said that the words of a person go before him in death. Babylonian Talmud Soṭah 3B: R. Samuel b. Nahman (ca. 260) said that R. Jonathan (ca. 220) said, "Whoever carries out a commandment in this world, it hurries before him and goes ahead of him in the future world (= the beyond); as it says, 'Your righteousness will go before you' (Isa 58:8). And whoever commits a transgression in this world, it ensnares around him and goes before him on the day of judgment; as it says, 'They are ensnared (לפת is interpreted as לפף) on the paths of their change, they rise up into a wasteland and perish' (Job 6:18)." R. Eleazar (ca. 270) said, "It (the transgression) is bound to him like a dog (which follows its master everywhere)." – The same is found in b. ʿAbod. Zar. 5A; in a different form anonymously in Tanḥ. וישב 46A. ‖ See b. Taʿan. 11A at § Matt 12:36, #1; SDeut 32:4 § 307 (133A) at § Luke 10:20, #2, n. *a*. ‖ Pirqe Rabbi Eliezer 34 (18B): (In a person's dying hour, his good works say to him,) "Go to peace! Before you go there, we have gone before you מקדימים אותך; as it says, 'Your beneficence (so the midrash) will go before you and the glory of Yahweh will go behind you' (Isa 58:8)."

14:14: A sickle in his hand (see b. Sanh. 95B at § Luke 1:19 A, #4, n. *i*).

14:15: The harvest of the earth has become ripe.

For the harvest image, see 4 Ezra 4:28ff.

14:20: Blood flowed from the winepress up to the reins of the horses, 1,600 *stadia* wide.

1 Enoch 100:2f.: "(In those days before the last judgment) sinners will massacre one another from dawn until dusk. A steed will wade up to its chest in the blood of sinners and a cart will sink into it up to its height." ‖ Jerusalem Talmud Taʿanit 4.69A.7: They committed murder among them (the people of Betar) again and again until a steed sank up to its nostrils in blood. And the blood would roll away boulders weighing 40 *seahs*, until the blood poured 4 *mils* into the sea (this is as far as the stream of blood was recognizable in the sea). If you should think, though, that Betar lay near the sea, was it not 40 *mils* from the sea? – The same is found in Midr. Lam. 2:2 (63A), except the distance of Betar from the sea is stated as 4 *mils*. ‖ Babylonian Talmud Giṭṭin 57A: When (the Romans) had taken Betar, they killed men, women, and children in it, until their blood flowed further and further and poured into the great sea. If you should think, though, that it lay near it, it was rather one *mil* מִיל (almost 1.5 kilometers) from it. – Presumably, here the number before מיל has gotten lost.

15:4: All the nations will come and worship before you (see § Rom 3:9 A, #3).

16:1ff.

The bowl plagues are partly reminiscent of the Egyptian plagues. For the boils in verse 2, see Exod 9:9ff.; for the blood in verses 3f., see Exod 7:17ff.; for the darkness in verse 10, see Exod 10:21ff.; for the hail in verse 21, see Exod 9:18ff. — It was a common idea for the rabbinic scholars that the plagues imposed on Egypt at the time will come again before the arrival of the days of the Messiah also on the last (Roman) world empire.

Exodus Rabbah 9 (74A): R. Eleazar b. Pedat (ca. 270) said, "What God brought upon the Egyptians is what he will one day bring upon this wicked (= Roman) empire; for it says, 'As with the news of Egypt, so they will quake at the news about צֹר' (Isa 23:5)." R. Eleazar said, "When צֹר is written defectively in Scripture, Scripture is speaking about the wicked (Roman) empire, and when צוֹר is written fully, Scripture is speaking about the city of Tyre." — צֹר is accordingly interpreted as צר "enemy"; yet the enemy is plainly Rome. Parallels are found in Tanḥ. וארא 71B; בא 74B; TanḥB וארא § 15 (15B); בא § 6 (22A); in Pesiq. Rab. 17 (89B) the interpretation of Isa 23:5 is associated with R. Berekhiah (ca. 340). The rule about צר and צור is also found in Gen. Rab. 61 (38D). ‖ Pesiqta 67B: R. Levi (ca. 300) said in the name of R. Hama b. Hanina (ca. 260), "The one who took revenge on the first (earlier) ones will also take revenge on the last. As Egypt (was punished) with blood, so too (one day) Edom (= Rome); as it says, 'I will give miraculous signs in heaven and on earth: blood, fire, and pillars of smoke' (Joel 3:3). As Egypt with frogs, so too Edom; see Isa 66:6: 'Reverberating noise (from frogs, so in the sense of the midrash) from the city (= Rome).' As Egypt with mosquitoes, so too Edom; see Isa 34:9: 'Then her streams will turn into pitch and her dust into sulfur,' as it says, 'Strike the dust of the earth and it shall become mosquitoes' (Exod 8:12). As Egypt by all kinds of animals ערוב, so too Edom; see Isa 34:11: 'And the pelican and the hedgehog will take possession of it ....' As Egypt with pestilence, so too Edom; see Ezek 38:22: 'I will judge him with pestilence and blood.' As Egypt with boils, so too Edom; see Zech 14:12: 'He makes his flesh rot.'[372] As Egypt with hail stones, so too Edom (so according to Buber's emendation); see Ezek 38:22B: 'I will make ... torrential rains and hail stones ... rain on him.' As Egypt with locusts (winged things), so too Edom; see Ezek 39:17f.: 'And you son of man, so says Yahweh Elohim, Say to the birds, to everything that has wings ..., "You shall eat the flesh of heroes."' And further it is written, 'You shall eat fat till you are satisfied' (Ezek 39:19). As Egypt with darkness, so too Edom; see Isa 34:11: 'He will stretch over it the line of chaos תהו and the plumb line of emptiness בהו.' And as in Egypt he removed the greatest (noblest?) among them and killed them, so too in Edom; for it says, 'Buffaloes רְאֵמִים must go down with them' (Isa 34:7)." R. Meir (ca. 150) said, "The Romans רוֹמִים must go down with them." — Parallels are found in Pesiq. Rab. 17 (90A); Tanḥ. בא 74B; TanḥB בא § 6 (22B).

372. S-B: So according to Pesiqta Rabbati; the text inappropriately cites Ezek 38:22B.

16:5: I heard the angel of the waters saying.

Angels of the elements or nature are mentioned quite frequently in ancient Jewish writings. This is hardly astonishing, since in Midr. Ps. 104 § 3 (220B) the following claim is set out in a completely general way: You find that over each thing an angel is appointed. — We limit ourselves here to ancient rabbinic literature and provide only the most important sources from the pseudepigrapha. These are Jub. 2:2; 1 En. 60:12–22; 66:2; 69:22; 75:3 (cf. also 20:1–7; 40:9); 2 En. 4–6; 11:4f.; 19:1–4; 3 Bar. 6, 7, 8, 9. — In rabbinic literature the following in particular are named:

1. The (angel) prince of the world שר העולם, but not in the sense of the ἄρχων τοῦ κόσμου in John 12:31; 14:30; 16:11, but rather as the angel who is appointed over natural life as a whole. — Babylonian Talmud Yebamot 16B: R. Samuel b. Nahman (ca. 260) said that R. Jonathan (ca. 220) said, "This verse—'I was young, but have also gotten old' (Ps 37:25)—was spoken by the angel prince of the world. Who (else) should have said it? God? Is there aging before him? Or would David have said it? Yet did he really get that old? Rather, I conclude from this that the angel prince of the world said it." ‖ See b. Sanh. 94A at § Matt 1:10, #1. ‖ Midrash Psalm 104 § 24 (224A): R. Berekhiah (ca. 340) said in the name of R. Levi (ca. 300), "When God created the world, how is it written there? 'God saw everything that he had made, and behold, it was very good' (Gen 1:31). Then the angel prince of the world arose and said, 'May the glory of Yahweh exist forever!' (Ps 104:31). All creatures arose and said, 'Let Yahweh rejoice in his works!' (Ps 104:31)." ‖ Babylonian Talmud Ḥullin 60A: R. Hanina b. Papa (ca. 300) publicly said in a presentation, "The verse—'May the glory of Yahweh exist forever! Let Yahweh rejoice in his works!' (Ps 104:31)—was spoken by the angel prince of the world. When God said, 'According to their kind' (Gen 1:11), the herbage drew a conclusion from the greater to the lesser from the trees pertaining to themselves: if God had pleasure in mixings, why would he have said in the case of the trees, 'According to their kind'?! And further it should be inferred from the greater to the lesser: if in the case of the trees, whose manner it is not to grow wildly in a confused way, God said, 'According to their kind,' how much more does that go for us! Immediately each thing went up according to its kind. Then the angel prince of the world arose and said, 'May the glory of Yahweh exist forever ...' (Ps 104:31)." ‖ Exodus Rabbah 17 (80A): "Yahweh will pass through to strike Egypt" (Exod 12:23). This is what "What would I do if God arose; and if he examined, what would resist him?" (Job 31:14) means. Who said this verse? The angel prince of the world said it (namely when God struck the firstborn in Egypt).

2. The (angel) prince of the sea שר של ים. — See b. Pesaḥ. 118B at § 2 Cor 1:22 B; b. ʿArak. 15A at § 1 Cor 10:9 A. ‖ Genesis Rabbah 10 (7D): When Titus (after the destruction of Jerusalem) had gone by ship, a violent storm (read נחשלא instead of שילא) met him on the sea. He said, "It appears as if the power of God of this (Jewish) nation is only in the water. The generation of Enosh and the flood, as well as pharaoh and his host he punished only with water. He could not stand against me even when I was in his house and sphere of power. This is why he preempts me now, thinking that he will kill me by water." Then God said to him, "You wicked man, by your life, I will punish this wicked man by the smallest creature

among all the creatures that I created in the six days of creation!" (An allusion to the legend that Titus was killed by a mosquito that penetrated into his brain.) Immediately God beckoned the angel prince of the sea, that he refrain from his storms. — The parallel passage in b. Giṭ. 56B does not mention the angel prince of the sea. ‖ Babylonian Talmud Baba Batra 74B: Rab Judah († 299) said that Rab († 247) said, "When God wished to create the world, he said to the angel prince of the sea, 'Open your mouth and swallow up all the waters in the world!' He answered him, 'Lord of the world, it is enough that I exist in my own area (the water of the sea, without swallowing up the other bodies of water on earth)!' Immediately he struck him and killed him; see Job 26:12: 'By his power he agitates the sea and by his insight he shatters Rahab.'" R. Isaac (ca. 300) said, "From here one may conclude that the name of the angel princes of the sea is Rahab. And if the water did not cover him, no person could endure because of his odor; see Isa 11:9: 'As the waters that cover the sea.' Do not read, 'that cover the "sea,"' but rather 'that cover the "angel prince of the sea."'" — The text is somewhat different in Num. Rab. 18 (185A). ‖ See y. Sanh. 7.25D.18 at § John 6:1. ‖ See also y. Sanh. 7.25D.28, 43 and Exod. Rab. 24 (85D).

3. The (angel) prince of darkness שר החושך. — See Pesiq. Rab. 20 (95A) at § Eph 6:12, #3.

4. רְדִיָא, the angel of rain. — Babylonian Talmud Taʿanit 25B: Rabbah († 331) said, "Ridya appeared to me. He is like a three-year-old (?) calf and his lips were split. He stood between the water depths below and above (= the heavenly ocean). He cried out to the water depths above, 'Spread your water!' He cried out to the water depths below, 'Let your water bubble (shoot up)!'" (Rashi: "The angel that is appointed over rain showers is called Ridya.") ‖ A baraita in b. Yoma 20B: Three voices go from one end of the world to the other: the voice of the wheel of the sun, the voice of the tumult of Rome, and the voice of the soul when it parts from the body.... Some say: "Also that of Ridya."[373]

5. יוּרְקְמִי, the (angel) prince of hail שר הברד. — Midrash Psalm 117 § 3 (240B): When Hananiah, Mishael, and Azariah were thrown into the furnace, Yurqami, the angel prince of hail, came before God and said before him, "Lord of the world, I am the prince of hail. I will go down and put out the fire of the oven." Gabriel responded to him, "I am the angel prince of fire שר של אש. I will go and make it glowing outside and cool it inside and so do a miracle in a miracle." God said to him, "Go down!" He went down and saved them. — In b. Pesaḥ. 118A, R. Simeon the Shilonite (when?) is the author. — For Gabriel as שר של אש, see 1 En. 40:9: "The one who presides over all powers is Gabriel." — 1 Enoch 20:7: "Gabriel ... who is appointed over paradise, snakes, and the cherubs." See also the next section.

6. Gabriel, the angel who is appointed over the ripening of fruits. — See b. Sanh. 95B at § Luke 1:19 A, #4, n. *i.*

7. לַיְלָה, the angel of conception. — See b. Nid. 16B at § Rom 9:11 B; Tanḥ. פקודי 127A at § John 1:1 A, C, #3, beginning of 2nd third.

8. Various angels of the elements alongside one another. — Midrash Lamentations 2:2 (65A): Jeremiah said to the Israelites, "Repent, lest you have to go into exile." They answered him, "If the enemies come, what can they do to us?!" The one said, "I will surround it

---

373. See Kohut, *Angelologie und Dämonologie*, 45ff.; Bacher, *Die Agada der babylonischen Amoräer*, 101.13.

(the city) with a wall of water!" And the other said, "I will surround it with a wall of fire!" And the third said, "I will surround it with a wall of iron!" Then God said to them, "You want to help yourself to what is mine (= the angels)?" Then God arose and changed the names (and thereby also the tasks) of the angels: the one over water he made into the one over fire and the one over fire he made into the one over iron. When they mentioned (called upon) their names from below, they did not answer them. Is this not what is written: "I desecrated holy (angel) princes?" (Isa 43:28). ‖ See the angels of wind, earthquakes, and fire alongside one another in Tg. 1 Kgs. 19:11f. at § Luke 2:13 B. ‖ Yalquṭ Simeoni on Numbers 12:7 (1 § 739): There is an angel that is appointed ממונה over fire, another angel is appointed over hail, another over locusts.

16:8: It was granted (to the sun) to scorch people with fire.

On the sun that burns everything as the executor of the divine last judgment on humanity, see the excursus "Sheol, Gehenna, and the Garden of Eden," II, #10, n. *k*.

16:14: To gather them for the slaughter of the great day of Almighty God.

In 1 En. 56:5ff., it is the angels who incite the kings of the east to the last move against Jerusalem: "In those (last) days the angels will gather and turn to the east, to the Parthians and the Medes, to incite their kings so that a spirit of unrest comes over them, and they bolt from their thrones, so that they break forth like lions from their lairs and like hungry wolves among their packs. They will go up and tread the land of his elect. And the land of his elect will be before them like a threshing floor and a (trodden down) path. Yet the city of my righteous ones will be a hindrance for their horses. They will begin to murder one another, and their right hand will gain strength against them themselves. A man will not know his brother, nor a son his father or his mother, until their corpses have become innumerable by their murdering, and their judgment will not be in vain. In those days Sheol will open wide its jaws. They will sink down and their demise will come to an end. Sheol will swallow up the sinners before the face of the elect."

16:15: Blessed is the one who ... preserves his clothes (cf. § Rev 3:4 A).

16:16: In Hebrew Armagedon.

See § John 5:2 #5. — Apart from the places where it is mentioned in the OT, Megiddo is mentioned in the targumim also in Tg. Lam. 1:18: "King Josiah went and drew the sword against pharaoh, the lame, in the valley of Megiddo, which he had not been commanded to do. And he had not requested any instruction from Yahweh (by the Urim and Thummim). Therefore, the shooters cast arrows at King Josiah, and he died there."

16:21: Great hail.

Exodus Rabbah 12 (75A): "Behold, I will make it rain a very heavy hail at this time tomorrow, the likes of which were not in Egypt since the day of its founding up until now" (Exod 9:18). This intends to teach that the likes of it had not been in the world nor in Egypt.

It does not say, "nor will be," but rather "the likes of which were not," in order to say: "In the past there was not such hail, but in the future there will be such." When? In the days of Gog and Magog; as it says, "Have you seen the stocks of hail that I have saved up for the time of distress, for slaughter, and the day of war?" (Job 38:22f.). It further says, "I will make ... torrential rains and hail stones ... rain on him" (Ezek 38:22). — The text is found in a shorter form in Tanḥ. וארא 73A and TanḥB וארא § 20 (18A); in the last passage, R. Hanina (b. Papa? [ca. 300]) is the author. ‖ See Exod. Rab. 9 (74A) at § Rev 16:1ff.

17:15: The waters ... are nations.

"Waters" as an image for nations can be found in, for example, Num. Rab. 2 (138B): R. Samuel b. Nahman (ca. 260) said, "If all the nations of the world came together to remove the love between him (God) and Israel, they would not be able to do it; for it says, 'Great waters cannot extinguish love and streams do not overrun it' (Song 8:7). 'Great waters' means nothing but the nations of the world (see Isa 17:12). 'And streams do not overrun it': this refers to their kings and princes (see Isa 8:7)." — The same is found anonymously in Midr. Song. 8:7 and Tg. Song. 8:7. ‖ Midrash Psalm 93 § 4 (207B): R. Simeon b. Laqish (so read, ca. 250) said, "When the Philistines led the ark of the covenant away captive, they began to gloat and said, 'We led away captive not only the ark of the covenant, but also the God who is in the ark of the covenant.' This is what 'Streams, Yahweh, raise ... their roaring' (Ps 93:3) means. And 'streams' should be understood to refer to the Philistines (see Isa 8:7)." ‖ Isaiah 8:7. מי הנהר "Waters of the stream" is rendered by the targum with: "the army camp of the nations." — מים רבים "Great waters" (Ps 18:17) in the targum: "many (mighty) nations"; similarly, Tg. Ps. 32:6 and 144:7.

17:18: The great city (see § Rev 14:8, #2).

18:20: Rejoice ...; for God has carried out your judgment on her.

See 1 En. 47:2ff. at § Rev 6:1.

18:23: The voice of a groom and of a bride shall not be heard in you.

"May the voice of the bridegroom and of the bride ... not be heard in the cities of Judah and in the alleys of Jerusalem ...!," a prayer request in the blessing over the bridal couple at the wedding celebration; see b. Ketub. 7B at § Matt 9:15 B, n. *u*. ‖ See further Deut. Rab. 7 (204A).

19:1: Hallelujah!

1. Ἀλληλούϊα = הַלְלוּ יָהּ, in the NT it appears only in the closing sections of Revelation 19:1, 3, 4, 6. Also see b. Ber. 9B at § Acts 13:33, #1 and Midr. Ps. 104 § 27 (224B) at § 2 Cor 2:15 B.

2. Opinions differed about the way to write the word: some wrote הללו יה, others (e.g., R. Meir) הללויה. The latter thus viewed the word as an interjection. The manner of writing was of practical significance for the

question of whether one was permitted to erase the word or not. Those who wrote הללו יה as separate words answered the question in the negative, since for them יָהּ counted as God's name. Those who considered the word an interjection answered the question in the affirmative.

Jerusalem Talmud Sukkah 3.53D.59: Rab († 247) and Samuel († 254). The one (Samuel) said הללויה; the other said הללו יה. According to the one who said הללו יה, it may be written as separate words but not erased. According to the one who said הללויה, it may be erased but not written as separate words. It was unknown, though, who said the latter and who the former. Yet from the fact that Rab said, "I heard from my uncle (i.e., R. Hiyya [ca. 200]), 'If someone gave me a book of psalms that belonged to R. Meir (ca. 150), I would erase all the Hallelujahs in it, because he did not intend to view them as holy,' infer who said הללויה (namely Samuel)." — The same is found in y. Meg. 1.72A.4. — See b. Pesaḥ. 117A: Rab († 247) said, "I saw the psalms of my uncle's (R. Hiyya's) house of learning, how in them הללו was written on one side and יה on the other side." (R. Hiyya separated the word because he viewed יה as a designation for God.)

3. For the esteem in which Hallelujah was held, see b. Pesaḥ. 117A: R. Joshua b. Levi (ca. 250) said, "The Book of Psalms was said (authored) with ten expressions for praise.... The greatest of all is Hallelujah, because it comprises simultaneously the name (of God) and the praise." — Parallels are found in y. Sukkah 3.54A.1; y. Meg. 1.72A.9; Midr. Ps. 1 § 6 (4B). — Also in b. Pesaḥ. 117A we find the interpretation of the word as follows: R. Joshua b. Levi (ca. 250) said, "What does Hallelujah mean? Praise Yahweh with many songs of praise בהילולים הרבה!"

19:7: The marriage of the lamb was come, and his wife has been prepared.

1. Israel as a bride. — See Tg. Song. 4:9 at § 2 Cor 3:3 B. — Midrash Song of Songs 4:10 (115A): R. Berekhiah (ca. 340) and R. Helbo (ca. 300) said in the name of R. Samuel b. Nahman (ca. 260), "In ten passages (of Scripture) the Israelites are called 'bride': six times here (in Song 4:8, 9, 10, 11, 12; 5:1) and four times in the Prophets (Jer 7:34; Isa 61:10; 49:18; 62:5). And accordingly God puts on ten garments (see § Rev 19:13)." — Parallels are found in Deut. Rab. 2 (199D) with R. Berekhiah as the author; Pesiq. 147B is anonymous. ‖ Mekilta Exodus 19:17 at § Matt 25:1. ‖ Pirqe Rabbi Eliezer 41 at § Matt 25:6.

2. The days of the Messiah feature as the time of the wedding celebration (see § Matt 9:15 C).

3. For the adorning of the bride for the bridegroom, see § Matt 9:15 A, n. *h*; there in ʾAbot R. Nat. 4 we also find the term "to prepare" תִּקֵּן for adorning the bride; also § Matt 9:15 B, n. *c*. — See also Midr. Eccl. 9:8 (42A) at § Rev 3:4 A.

19:9: Blessed are those who are called to the marriage feast of the lamb.

See the passages in which blessedness is spoken about with the image of a meal in the excursus "Sheol, Gehenna, and the Garden of Eden," III, #4, n. *o*.

19:10: The spirit of prophecy (see § Luke 2:25 C, #3).

19:13: Clothed with a garment dipped all around in blood.

Midrash Song of Songs 4:10 (115A): (R. Samuel b. Nahman [ca. 260] said, "Corresponding to the tenfold designation of Israel as a bride [see above at Rev § 19:7]) God put on ten garments: 'Yahweh mustered his kingdom, put on grandeur; Yahweh put on strength, girded himself' (Ps 93:1; = three garments). 'He put on righteousness like armor, he put on clothes of vengeance, garb, he wrapped zeal around him like a mantle' (Isa 59:17; 4th–7th garments). 'The one who is regal in his garment; why is there red on your garment?' (Isa 63:1; 8th and 9th garment). 'In majesty and glory you have clothed yourself' (Ps 104:1; 10th garment), to take revenge on the nations who have hindered the Israelites from observing the ten commandments, around which they clustered like a bride (to adorn themselves with them)." — Similarly in Deut. Rab. 2 (199D). ‖ Pesiqta 147B: The 1st garment that God donned on the day of the creation of the world was of majesty and glory (Ps 104:1); the 2nd garment that God donned, in order to take vengeance on the generation of the flood, was of grandeur (Ps 93:1); the 3rd garment, in order to give the Torah to Israel, was of strength (Ps 93:1); the 4th garment, in order to take vengeance on the kingdom of Babylon, was white (Dan 7:9); the 5th and 6th garment, in order to take vengeance on the kingdom of Media, was of vengeance (Isa 59:17); the 7th and 8th garment, in order to take vengeance on the Greek kingdom, was of righteousness (Isa 59:17); the 9th garment God will don, in order to take vengeance on the kingdom of Edom (= Rome), is red, as it says, "Why is there red on your garment?" (Isa 63:2); the 10th garment, in order to take vengeance on Gog and Magog, will be majesty (Isa 63:1). — Other lists name only 7 garments. Among these, the "red" one in Isa 63:2 is regularly interpreted to refer to Rome; see Pesiq. 149A; Pesiq. Rab. 37 (163B); Midr. Ps. 93 § 1 (207A).

19:20: Sea of fire burning with sulfur.

See fire and sulfur as a means of punishment in gehenna in the excursus "Sheol, Gehenna, and the Garden of Eden," II, #8, notes *b, d, f, h, i, l*. — The term "pool of fire" = λίμνη τοῦ πυρός (Rev 19:20; 20:10, 14, 15; 21:8) is also found in 1 En. 90:26f.; see the excursus "Sheol, Gehenna, and the Garden of Eden," II, #8, n. *b*. — On "sulfur" see also Sib. Or. 3:60f.: "(The day) will come when the smell of sulfur will penetrate all people."

20:1: A great chain.

Chains feature as instruments of torture for Asasel's droves in 1 En. 54:3ff.: "There my (Enoch's) eyes saw how they made iron chains of immeasurable weight (as torture) instruments for them.... These were prepared for the droves of Azazel, to seize them and cast them into the abyss of complete damnation."

20:2: And bound him.

On "binding" evil spirits, see 1 En. 10:4ff., 11ff.; 13:1, 5; 18:16; 21:6; 69:28; 90:23. ‖ See T. Levi 18 at § Luke 10:18, #3, n. *c*.

20:4 A: Of those put to death.

πεπελεκισμένοι, specifically those put to death by the axe. — On the execution of decapitation, see m. Sanh. 7.3 at § Matt 5:21 B, #3, B, #5, n. *b*.

20:4 B: They ruled with Christ for a thousand years.

The pre-Christian synagogue made the time of the absolute eschatological consummation begin with the appearance of the Messiah; for it, then, the reign of the Messiah had to last forever. Only the post-Christian synagogue differentiates between the days of the Messiah and of the eschatological consummation in the *ʿolam ha-ba*, that is, in the future world: the former are temporally limited, and only the *ʿolam ha-ba* lasts forever. From the beginning, opinions differed widely about the length of the messianic period. The various traditions on this may be gathered here first.

1. The length of the days of the Messiah.

A. The Palestinian traditions.

a. Tanḥuma עקב 7B: How long do the days of the Messiah last? R. Aqiba († ca. 135) said, "40 years. Just as the Israelites spent 40 years in the wilderness, so he (the Messiah) will haul them out into the wilderness and make them eat tumbleweed and gorse[374] (see Job 30:4)." — R. Eliezer (presumably the son of R. Yose the Galilean [ca. 150]) said, "100 years." — R. Berekhiah (ca. 340) said in the name of R. Dosa (ca. 180?), "600 years." — Rabbi († 217?) said, "400 years.[375] As it says, 'As in the days when you went out from the land of Egypt, I will display miracles' (Mic 7:15). As (the stay) in Egypt lasted 400 years, so too the days of the Messiah will last 400 years." — R. Eliezer (presumably b. Hyrcanus [ca. 90]) said, "1,000 years. As it says, 'Make us rejoice according to the length of days that you have chastened us, according to the length of years we have seen evil' (Ps 90:15)."[376] — R. Abbahu (ca. 300) said, "7,000 years. As it says, 'As a bridegroom delights in his bride, so will your God delight in you' (Isa 62:5). As the days of the wedding celebration amount to 7 days, so too the days of the Messiah will be 7,000 years (for 1 day of God = 1,000 years; see Ps 90:4)." — The Rabbanan said, "2,000 years. As it says, 'The day of vengeance (= 1,000 years) is in my heart and my year of redemption (= 1,000 years) has come'" (Isa 63:4; presumably another supporting passage belongs here).

b. Pesiqta Rabbati 1 (4A): How long will the days of the Messiah last? R. Aqiba said, "40 years; see Deut 8:3: 'He chastened you and made you hunger' (40 years during the

---

374. S-B: R. Aqiba, who acknowledged Bar Kokhba as Messiah, considered the messianic time to be merely a turbulent transitional period to the *ʿolam ha-ba*, just as Israel's 40 years in the wilderness constitute the transitional stage to the possession of the promised land. Hence his 40 years.

375. S-B: The days of the Messiah will last for 400 years also according to 4 Ezra 7:28; see the passage at § 1 Cor 15:51, n. *b*.

376. S-B: If one counts together the 400 years of the stay in Egypt, the 111 years of foreign rule in the time of the judges (see Judg 3:8, 14; 4:3; 6:1; 10:6; 13:1) and the 490 years that the official chronology of the ancient synagogue assumes from the Babylonian exile until the destruction of Jerusalem by the Romans, one acquires the sum of 1,001 years or, rounded, the 1,000 years of R. Eliezer.

wilderness wandering). It says further: 'Make us rejoice according to the length of days that you have chastened us' (Ps 90:15). As the chastening there lasted 40 years, so too the chastening that is spoken of here."[377] R. Abin (I, ca. 325; II, ca. 370) said, "What was R. Aqiba's scriptural basis? 'As in the days when you went out from the land of Egypt, I will display miracles' (Mic 7:15)." (As the miracles after the exodus from Egypt lasted in the wilderness for 40 years, so too the miracles in the messianic age.) — R. Eliezer (ben Hyrcanus [ca. 90] is meant) said, "400 years; see Gen 15:13: 'They will serve them and they will oppress them for 400 years.' And in Ps 90:15 it says, 'Make us rejoice according to the length of days that you have chastened us.'" — R. Berekhiah said in the name of R. Dosa the elder, "600 years; see Isa 65:22: 'The days of my people will be as the days (duration) of trees.' Which tree is meant? The sycamore tree (so according to Gen. Rab. 12 [9B] and according to Num. Rab. 13 [170A]), which stands for 600 years." — R. Eliezer b. Yose the Galilean (ca. 150) said, "1,000 years; see Ps 90:4: '1,000 years are in your eyes like yesterday.' See also Isa 63:4: 'The day of vengeance is in my heart and my year of redemption has come.' And 1 day of God lasts 1,000 years." — R. Joshua (ca. 90) said, "2,000 years; see Ps 90:15: 'Make us rejoice according to the length of days that you have chastened us.' "Days" (plural) are not fewer than 2 days, and 1 day of God lasts 1,000 years." — R. Abbahu said, "7,000 years; see Isa 62:5: 'As a bridegroom delights ...'" (see above in *a*). — Rabbi († 217?) said, "One cannot calculate (the beginning of the messianic period); for it says, 'The day of vengeance is in my heart'" (Isa 63:4; thus, he will make it known to no one; see Midr. Ps. 9 § 2; Midr. Eccl. 12:9 and b. Sanh. 99A). And how long do the days of the Messiah last? The days of the Messiah last for 365,000 years. (Isa 63:4 speaks of a "year of redemption"; 1 year = 365 days, 1 day of God = 1,000 years, so one year of God = 365,000 years.)

c. Midrash Psalm 90 § 17 (197A): How long will the days of the Messiah last? R. Eliezer (ca. 90) said, "1,000 years; see Ps 90:4: '1,000 years are in your eyes like yesterday.'" — R. Joshua (ca. 90) said, "2,000 years; see Ps 90:15: 'Make us rejoice according to the length of days that you have chastened us.' 'Days,' that is, 2 days, and 1 day of God lasts 1,000 years; see Ps 90:4." — R. Berekhiah and R. Dosa the elder said, "600 years; see Isa 65:22: 'The days of my people will be as the days of trees.' And a sycamore tree stands for 600 years in the earth." — R. Yose (the Galilean [ca. 110]) said, "60 years; see Ps 72:5: 'So they will fear you (the Messiah) ... generation, generations.' A generation is 20 years, generations (at least two) are 40 years, that is, altogether, 60 years." — R. Aqiba († ca. 135) said, "40 years, corresponding to the days that you chastened us in the 40 years that the Israelites spent in the wilderness; see Deut 8:3: 'He chastened you and made you hunger.'" —The rabbis said, "354 years, corresponding to the number of days of a lunar year, according to which the Israelites reckon; for it says, 'My year of redemption (= 354 days) has come'" (so according to older editions and manuscripts, while the Buber edition reads: "Our teachers said, '4,000 years; see Isa 63:4." Yet this passage leaves the 4,000

377. S-B: Here too for R. Aqiba the messianic period is nothing other than a period of turbulence and compulsion.

years unexplained). – R. Abbahu said, "7,000 years, corresponding to the days of the bridegroom in his in his wedding chamber; see Isa 62:5" (as above in *a* and *b*).

d. Pesiqta 29A: "Yahweh has war against Amalek from generation to generation" (Exod 17:16).... R. Yose the Galilean (ca. 110) said, "From the generation of Mordecai and Esther until the generation of the Messiah, which will last for 3 generations. How do we know that the generation of the Messiah will last for 3 generations? Because it says, 'They will fear you ... generation, generations'" (Ps 72:5; see above in *c*). – Likewise, Tanḥ. כי תצא 23A and TanḥB תצא § 18 (22B), except that here the epithet "the Galilean" is missing. In Mek. Exod. 17:16 (64B), this saying is attributed to R. Eliezer (b. Hyrcanus [ca. 90]), certainly incorrectly, because this scholar immediately before interpreted the words "from generation to generation" in the sense of "always." – In SDeut 32:7 § 310 (134A) too, which is anonymous, we find the conclusion from Ps 72:5 that the time of the Messiah lasts 3 generations.

B. The Babylonian traditions.

a. Babylonian Talmud Sanhedrin 99A (1st baraita): R. Eliezer (ca. 90) said, "The days of the Messiah will last 40 years; see Ps 95:10: 'Forty years I am disgusted with the generation.'" – R. Eleazar b. Azariah (ca. 100) said, "70 years; see Isa 23:15: 'It will happen on that day that Tyre will be a forgotten place for 70 years, like the days of a king.' Who is this only king? It is the Messiah." – Rabbi († 217?) said, "3 generations; see Ps 72:5: 'They will fear you ... generation, generations'" (that is, 3 generations).

b. Babylonian Talmud Sanhedrin 99A (2nd baraita): R. Eliezer (ca. 90) said, "The days of the Messiah will last 40 years. Here it says, 'He chastened you and made you hunger' (namely for 40 years in the wilderness; Deut 8:3), and there it says, 'Make us rejoice according to the length of days that you have chastened us ...' (Ps 90:15)." – R. Dosa said, "400 years. It says here, 'They will serve them and they will oppress them for 400 years' (Gen 15:13), and there it says, 'Make us rejoice according to the length of days that you have chastened us' (Ps 90:15)." – Rabbi († 217?) said, "365 years, corresponding to the number of days in a solar year; see Isa 63:4: 'The day of vengeance is in my heart ....'" – Abimi b. Abbahu (ca. 330) taught as a tannaitic tradition, "The days of the Messiah will last for Israel for 7,000 years; see Isa 62:5: 'As a bridegroom delights ....'" – Rab Judah († 299) said that Samuel († 254) said, "The days of the Messiah will last as long as from the days of the creation of the world until now; see Deut 11:21: 'So that your days and the days of your children may be as long ... as the duration of heaven over the earth.'" – Rab Nahman b. Isaac († 356) said, "As long as from the days of Noah until now; see Isa 54:9: 'As long as it has been since the days of Noah, this is valid for me (this is how long the oath will last) ... no longer to be angry against you.'" (The midrash reads כי מי נח as כימי נח.)

c. Babylonian Talmud Sanhedrin 97A: In the school of Elijah it has been taught: "The world will exist for 6,000 years: 2,000 years of which are for the Tohu (time without Torah), 2,000 years for (the rule of) the Torah, and 2,000 years for the days of the Messiah; and because of our sins, which are great, what has passed of the latter (which should have dawned in the year 4,000 after the creation of the world, i.e., 240 CE) has passed." – The same is found in b. ʿAbod. Zar. 9A; S. Eli. Rab. 2 toward the beginning.

2. With careful deliberation over all the aspects that come into consideration, we believe that we may apportion the various opinions in the following way among the individual rabbinic scholars:

a. R. Eliezer b. Hyrcanus (ca. 90) estimates the reign of the Messiah on the basis of Ps 90:15 to be 1,000 years.

b. R. Joshua (ca. 90) on the basis of Ps 90:15, 2,000 years.

c. R. Eleazar b. Azariah (ca. 100) on the basis of Isa 23:15, 70 years.

d. R. Aqiba († ca. 135) on the basis of Deut 8:3 and Ps 90:15 or on the basis of Mic 7:15 and Ps 95:10, 40 years.

e. R. Yose the Galilean (ca. 110) on the basis of Ps 72:5, 3 generations = 60 years.

f. R. Dosa (ca. 180?) on the basis of Isa 65:22, 600 years.

g. R. Eliezer b. Yose the Galilean (ca. 150) on the basis of Gen 15:13 and Ps 90:15, 400 years; likewise, 4 Ezra 7:28.

h. R. Eliezer, without being able to be more specific as to who this is, 100 years.

i. Rabbi († 217?) on the basis of Isa 63:4, 365 years (in a later period, using Ps 90:4, lengthened to 365,000 years).

k. A majority of rabbis, presumably at the time of R. Joshua (ca. 90), on the basis of Isa 63:4, 2,000 years.

l. A majority of rabbis, presumably at the time of Rabbi († 217?), 354 years.

m. A baraita from the school of Elijah, 2,000 years.

n. A baraita (later R. Abbahu) on the basis of Isa 62:5, 7,000 years.

o. Samuel († 254) makes the duration of the messianic period equal to the period of time since the creation of the world to the present, which is about 4,000 years, specifically on the basis of Deut 11:21. The number 4,000 follows a reading in Midr. Ps. is also accepted by a majority of rabbis.

p. R. Abbahu (ca. 300) on the basis of Isa 62:5, 7,000 years.

q. Rab Nahman b. Isaac († 356) reckons to the messianic period as many years as have elapsed since Noah until his time, specifically on the basis of Isa 54:9. Since Noah's birth to 356 CE would be 3,060 years and since the flood, 2,460 years.

3. The calculation of the length of the messianic period is made:

a. on the basis of the scheme of the week of the world, according to which the world period without the Torah is 2,000 years, the time of the reign of the Torah is 2,000 years (from the 53rd year of Abraham's life until 240 CE), the days of the Messiah are 2,000 years (which would have needed to arise in the year 240 CE) and the Sabbath for world is 1,000 years. – So R. Joshua, a rather large number of the scholars, who presumably were his contemporaries, and the baraita from the school of Elijah;

b. on the basis of attempts to flesh out the second or messianic redemption according to the example of the first redemption from Egypt. Here belong the 40 years of R. Aqiba, corresponding to the 40 years of wilderness wandering, and the 400 years of R. Eliezer b. Yose the Galilean and of 4 Ezra, corresponding to the 400 years of slavery in Egypt. Psalm

95:10 and Micah 7:15 serve as scriptural proof for the 40 years, though particularly Deut 8:3 is used in connection with Ps 90:15; Gen 15:13 and Ps 90:15 are used for the 400 years;

c. on the basis of various passages of Scripture. So R. Eliezer, R. Eleazar b. Azariah, R. Yose the Galilean, R. Dosa, Rabbi, Samuel, R. Abbahu, and Rab Nahman b. Isaac.

4. R. Eliezer b. Hyrcanus (ca. 90) is the oldest rabbinic authority that represents the 1,000-year duration for the reign of the Messiah. From this it does not follow, though, that he was the actual originator of this view. R. Eliezer was considered by his contemporaries as the most tenacious representative of older observances and traditions; he himself could say of himself, "I have never offered any saying that I did not hear from the mouth of my teacher" (b. Sukkah 28A). So it is completely probable that the 1,000-year duration of the messianic period was already taught in Jewish schools before R. Eliezer. The possibility that the author of Revelation formulated the 1,000-year kingship of the returning Christ in dependence on the Jewish tradition about the 1,000-year messianic kingdom can therefore not be disputed on chronological grounds.

20:5: The rest of the dead were not living (resurrected) until the end of the 1,000 years. This is the first resurrection.

As long as the ancient synagogue expected the fruition of absolute salvation from the arrival of the Messiah, it assumed that the resurrection of the dead would happen soon after his appearance.[a] In the 1st post-Christian century, a distinction began to be made between the days of the Messiah and the time of the absolute consummation of salvation: the former, so it was thought, were supposed to bring Israel sovereignty over the nations of the world.[b] Yet the actual eschatological consummation, arising with the resurrection of the dead and the destruction of all the godless in the world judgment, would happen only after the close of the messianic period in the *ʿolam ha-ba*, that is, in the future world. In this way the resurrection of the dead was detached from the days of the Messiah and connected with the *ʿolam ha-ba* and the general world judgment. This remained the dominant view during the entire Mishnaic period (until around 200 CE).[c] At the beginning of the 3rd century, a new direction took shape. Now it was assumed that already in the messianic age first the dead of the land of Israel would resurrect. After them the righteous, who were buried outside the holy land, would be rolled through subterranean caverns until they reached the land of Israel and would here participate in the resurrection.[d] The general resurrection of the dead did not come into consideration here. It remained attached to the world judgment, as it had been before. In this conceptual combination, it was first a matter merely of the dead who rested in the ground of the land of Israel, and second the righteous who were buried abroad. The whole, though, was aimed at glorifying the motherly soil of the land of Israel: its dead, insofar as they belong to Israel, arise already in the days of the Messiah, first before all others. The righteous abroad, though, also take part in the resurrection during the messianic period, though only from the earth of the holy land. Hence the painful subterranean rolling of the dead until they reach the womb of the home soil. In substance, the synagogue also knew of a double resurrection: the first in the days of the Messiah in the land of Israel, and the second, the general one, at the time of the world judgment. Yet the terms "first" or "second resurrection" are not found in rabbinic literature.

a. Daniel 12:1–3. — 1 Enoch 51:1f.: "In those days (after the appearance of the Messiah) the earth will give back those who have accumulated in her, and Sheol will also give back what she has received, and Abaddon (cf. § Rev 9:11 B) will pay what he owes. He (Messiah) will elect the righteous and holy among them (the resurrected), for the day of their redemption is near." ‖ 1 Enoch 61:5: "These measures (in the hands of the angels) will reveal all the secrets in the depths of the earth and those who perished in the wilderness or were swallowed up by the fish of the sea or by animals, so that they might return (at the resurrection) and might lean on the day of the elect one (= the Messiah); for no one will perish before the Lord of Spirits." — Also see 1 En. 90:33; 91:10. ‖ Testament of Judah 25: "Those who died in sadness will rise in joy (in the messianic age) ..., and those who died for the Lord's sake will awake in life.... Yet the godless will mourn, and the sinners will moan, and all the nations will praise the Lord forever." — See further T. Sim. 6; T. Zeb. 10; T. Benj. 10; Sib. Or. 4:178ff.

b. Passages at § Rom 3:9 A, #3.

c. The main passage is m. Sanh. 10: All Israel has a share in the future world. — From beginning to end, this chapter relies on the presupposition that the *ʿolam ha-ba* begins with the resurrection of the dead and the general world judgment.

d. Jerusalem Talmud Ketubbot 12.35B.5: "You shall take me out of Egypt and bury me (in the land of Israel) in their (the fathers') grave" (Gen 47:30). If Jacob had been buried wherever he was, what sort of disadvantage would he have suffered? R. Eleazar (ca. 270) said, "Therein lies something (special) דברים בגב." R. Joshua b. Levi (ca. 250) said, "Therein lies something." R. Hanina (ca. 225) said, "Therein lies something." What does "Therein lies something" mean? R. Simeon b. Laqish (ca. 250) said, "'I will walk before Yahweh in the lands of life (the living)' (Ps 116:9). Are not the lands of life only Tyre and Caesarea and their neighboring area? Everything is there, abundance is there!" R. Simeon b. Laqish said in the name of Bar Qappara (ca. 220), "This refers to the land whose dead will first become living (resurrect) in the days of the Messiah. What is the scriptural basis? 'He gives the soul back to the people that (dwells) on it (the land of Israel)' (Isa 42:5). Yet our teachers in Babylon would be at a disadvantage (if only the inhabitants of the land of Israel should resurrect in the days of the Messiah)!" R. Simai (ca. 210) said, "God will hollow out (read מחליד) the earth before them and they will be rolled מתגלגלין like pipes, and when they have come to the land of Israel, their souls will be united with them. What is the scriptural basis? 'I will bring you to your land and will put my spirit in you so that you will live' (so Ezek 37:14 is cited)." R. Berekhiah (ca. 340) asked R. Helbo (ca. 300), and he asked R. Ammi (ca. 300), and he asked R. Eleazar (ca. 270), and he asked R. Hanina (ca. 225) and he asked, as some say, R. Joshua (b. Levi [ca. 250]), "Even Jeroboam and his companions (are to resurrect in the land of Israel in the messianic age)?" He answered him, "Sulfur and salt, his whole land burned out" (Deut 29:22)! R. Berekhiah said, "What does that have to do with the matter everyone asked about? We hear nothing at all about the issue! When the land of Israel was burned, the judgment was carried out on them" (Jeroboam and his companions, so they too will rise in the days of the Messiah). — Parallels are found in y. Kil. 9.32C.1; Gen. Rab. 96 (60D); Tanḥ. ויחי 54B; TanḥB ויחי § 6 (107B); Gen. Rab. 74 at the beginning.; TanḥB ויצא § 23 (80B); Pesiq. Rab. 1 (2B); here the following words come at the close: Here you learn that the dead of the land of Israel are destined for life (for resurrection) in the days of the Messiah and the righteous abroad are destined to reach the land of Israel (by subterranean caverns) to become living there. If this is the case, will even the nations of the world that are buried (read: שקבורים) in the land (of Israel) become living again? No! Isaiah said, "No sojourner (so the midrash) should say, 'I have gotten sick! The people that dwells in it is forgiven their guilt!'" (Isa 33:24). Sojourners should not say, "We too have been entangled in the suffering (of Israel), so we too will become living with them." Rather the one who belongs to the people that lives in it whose guilt is forgiven. Which people is it whose guilt is forgiven? It is those of whom it says, "Who is a God like you, who forgives guilt and passes over sin for the remnant of his inheritance" (Mic 7:18). — On the subterranean caverns, see also Pesiq. Rab. 31 (147A): God will make for them (the dead abroad) pure caverns below, and they will be rolled in them (so read) until they come below the Mount of Olives at Jerusalem. And God will stand on it, and it will be split before them and they will rise up out of the middle of it; see Zech 14:4. — See further b. Ketub. 111A.34. ‖ It is instructive to compare m. ʾAbot 6.9 with SDeut 6:7 § 34 (74B). In the first passage it says: R. Yose b. Qisma (ca. 110) said, "'... In your walking she (wisdom = Torah) will guide you, in your lying down she will keep watch over you, and when you have woken up, she will speak to you' (Prov 6:22). 'In your walking she will guide you,' in this world; 'in your lying down she will keep watch over you,' in the grave; 'when you have woken up, she will speak to you,' in the future world לעולם הבא." — Here the resurrection is bound to the future world, entirely in line with the sense of m. Sanh. 10; similarly in the parallels in SLev 18:4 (338A); b. Soṭah 21A; TanḥB ויצא § 2 (73A); ʾAg. Ber. 45 § 2 (33A). However, in the Sifre passage named above it says: "In your walking she will guide you," in this world; "in your lying down she will keep watch over you," in the hour (time) of death; "when you have woken up" (= resurrected), in the days of the Messiah; "she will speak to you," in the *ʿolam ha-ba*. — Here, in the spirit of the 3rd century, the resurrection is detached from the *ʿolam ha-ba* and relocated to the days of the Messiah. ‖ Exodus Rabbah 32 (93B): "I will give you a delightful land" (Jer 3:19). Why is it called a delightful חמדה (desirable) land?... The rabbis said, "A land that the fathers of the world longed for שנתחמדו...." And why did they long for it? R. Simeon b. Laqish (ca. 250) said, "Because they (the inhabitants of the land) will first become living (resurrect) in the days of the Messiah." — The following passages also know of a resurrection in the days of the

Messiah: see y. Kil. 9.32B.7 at § Luke 12:40 A; see Midr. Ps. 93:2 at § Matt 1:21 B, #2, n. *f*; Midr. Ps. 18 § 11 (71A); b. Sanh. 92A.42; S. Eli. Rab. 29 (164, 24); Leqach Tob Num. 24:17 (2, 129B.32); Midr. Eccl. 1:7 (7B); Tg. Hos. 14:8.

20:6: Over these the second death has no power.

1. ὁ δεύτερος θάνατος = מָוֶת שֵׁנִי, Aram. מוֹתָא תִנְיָנָא. The Hebrew expression appears only in the late Pirqe R. El., the Aramaic term only in the targumim. Yet the rabbinic scholars also know of the "second death," albeit the content and not the expression. This idea was understood to refer to α. exclusion from the resurrection, remaining in the grave,[a] and β. being consigned to eternal damnation.[b]

Comment: Wettstein's assumption at Rev 2:11 that the rabbinic term מִיתָה מְשׁוּנָּה denotes the "second death" is wrong. That expression, which appears frequently (see, e.g., b. Taʿan. 11A.4; b. Soṭah 35A.28; b. Šabb. 156B.25; b. B. Bat. 10A.37; Midr. Prov. 10 § 1) means "unusual, violent death."

a. Genesis Rabbah 96 (60D): R. Hama b. Hanina (so read, ca. 260) said, "Whoever dies abroad and is buried there suffers a twofold death שתי מיתות (two deaths); for so it is written, 'Yet you Pashhur and all the inhabitants of your house, you will go away to captivity, and to Babylon you will come and die there and there be buried' (Jer 20:6). Thus he suffered a twofold death (see further). Therefore Jacob said to Joseph, 'Do not bury me in Egypt' (Gen 47:29)." R. Simon (ca. 280) said, "If this is the case then the righteous who are buried abroad suffer a loss! Rather, what will God do for them? He makes for them caverns in the earth and makes them as it were into pipes (read כנודות instead of כמערות), and they are rolled until they come to the land of Israel. Then God puts the spirit in them and they rise (from the dead); see Ezek 37:12" (and § Rev 20:5, n. *d*). — For R. Hama b. Hanina, the two claims "You will die there" and "there you will be buried" seemed striking alongside each other. Therefore in the second he finds the meaning: "'There you will remain buried forever.' This, the exclusion of the righteous buried abroad from the resurrection, counts for him as a second death." This is made even clearer by some parallels. In y. Ketub. 12.35B.21 it says: Whoever dies there (in Babylonia) and is buried there suffers two things (death in the hour of death and remaining in the grave). Whoever dies there and is buried here (in Palestine) suffers one thing (death in the hour of death, but not remaining in the grave; for the dead of the land of Israel rise in the days of the Messiah). In Pesiq. Rab. 1 (3A.14), where R. Helbo (ca. 300) represents the view of R. Hama b. Hanina, the introductory words read: "Whoever dies abroad and is buried abroad suffers two kinds of hardships: the hardships of dying and the hardships of being buried (proof: Pashhur's fate in Jer 20:6)." Then we read this saying of R. Hama b. Hanina: "If someone who died abroad is moved from abroad and buried in the land (of Israel), he suffers only one death" (for he is spared the other death, exclusion from the resurrection). — This whole idea is underlaid by the assumption that there will be a resurrection of the dead only in the land of Israel. Additional parallels are found in Tanḥ. ויחי 54B; TanḥB ויחי § 6 (107B) and y. Kil. 9.32C.18. ‖ Pirqe Rabbi Eliezer 34 (18A): (God says,) "If a non-Israelite says that there is a second God, I will kill him (make him die) by the second death במות שני, and here there is no revivification. Yet if a non-Israelite says there is no second God, I will raise him to life in the future world in the future." ‖ Targum Jeremiah 51:39. "They will die the second death מותא תנינא and not become living in the future world, says Yahweh." — Targum Jeremiah 51:57: "They will die the second death so that they will not come (by the resurrection) into the future world."

b. Jerusalem Talmud Pe'ah 1.15B.53: (The proselyte Monobazus—see t. Pe'ah 4.18 at § Matt 6:19f., #1, 2nd paragraph—said,) "My fathers gathered treasures in this world, and I have gathered for the future world; as it says, 'Alms rescue from death' (so Prov 10:2 according to the midr.). Yet does he (the alms giver) not die? It means that he will not die the death in the future (i.e., that he will not fall victim to damnation)." ‖ Midrash Psalm 15 § 6 (59B): "Whoever does this will never stumble" (Ps 15:5). R. Samuel (b. Ammi [ca. 325]) said, "I do not know what this 'stumbling' means. Then Solomon came and explained it: 'Save those who are dragged to death, and hold back those who are stumbling to slaughter!' (Prov 24:11). Accordingly, say, ('He will not stumble' means) 'He will not die in the future world' (not be consigned to damnation)." The following parallels are different: t. B. Meṣ. 6.18 (385); y. B. Meṣ. 5.10D.15; b. B. Meṣ. 71A.13. ‖ Babylonian Talmud Sanhedrin 92A.11: Raba († 352) said, "How can the resurrection be proven from the Torah? It says, 'May Reuben live and not die!' (Deut 33:6). 'May Reuben live,' in this world; 'and not die,' in the future world." — On this, Tg. Yer. I Deut. 33:6: "May Reuben live in this world and not die in the death in which the godless die in the future world." — Targum Onkelos reads: "May Reuben live in eternal life and not die the second death מותא תנינא." Targum Yerušalmi II: "May Reuben live in this world and not die in the second death in which the godless die in the future world." ‖ TanḥumaB ויגש § 10 (105A): "In sorrow I will go down into the underworld to my son" (Gen 37:25). What does "In grief into the underworld" mean? Jacob said, "Perhaps I will die the death of the godless in this and in the future world; for God had assured me that he would give me 12 tribes, and now one of them has died. Perhaps I was not worthy of them and have to die in both worlds. Therefore he said, 'In sorrow I will go down into the underworld to my son.' From here you can know this: when Jacob saw that he (Joseph) lived, what did he say? 'Then Israel said to Joseph, "I will die once"' (so Gen 46:30 according to the midr.). Why did he say, 'I will die once'? He said, 'When they came and said to me that Joseph had died, I thought that I would have to die in both worlds. Now, since I see that you are alive, the good news has come to me that I will die only once. Therefore it says, "I will die once."'" — The death of the godless in the future world = eternal damnation. There is a parallel in Tanḥ. ויגש 53A.27. ‖ Midrash Psalm 70 § 2 (161B): Woe to the godless who die (= are damned) in the future world only because of envy and anger! As it says, "Anger kills fools and envy makes the simple die" (Job 5:2). ‖ Targum Yerušalmi I Numbers 31:50: "So that we may not die the death that the godless will die in the future world." ‖ Targum Isaiah 22:14: "This guilt will never be remitted for you until you die the second death מותא תנינא." — Targum Isaiah 65:6: "Behold, it is written down before me. I will not give them length of life, but rather I will bring the punishment for their sins upon them and surrender their body to the second death." — Targum Isaiah 65:15: "You will leave behind your names as an oath for my elect and Yahweh Elohim will make you die the second death (fall victim to damnation)."

2. οὐκ ἔχει ἐξουσίαν. — In Jewish circles too it would have been assumed that those who resurrected in the days of the Messiah (see above at § Rev 20:5) would not die again. Seder Eliyahu Rabbah 29 (164): All who resurrect in the days of the Messiah will go to the land of Israel; yet they will not become dust a second time; see Isa 4:3 and b. Sanh. 92A at § 1 Cor 15:51, n. *a*.

20:8 and 9: Gog and Magog (Ezek 38 and 39).

1. The names.

גּוֹג in Ezek 38 and 39 is a personal name, as is מָגוֹג in Gen 10:2. — In SDeut 32:8 § 311 (134A), מָגוֹג is certainly also used as the name of a country.[378] Yet in Ezek 38:1 and 39:6 it seems to be the name of the people. — In Γὼγ βασιλεία (LXX Num 24:7) and in χώρα Γὼγ ἠδὲ Μαγώγ (Sib. Or. 3:319), the meaning of the names remains uncertain. According to their form, they could be either nominative or genitive: in the former case, they would be names of countries, and in the latter names of persons or peoples. — Most of the time the rabbinic scholars probably would have meant the names as names of nations, as presumably also the author of Revelation does in our passage. — In rabbinic literature both names appear frequently alongside each other as גּוֹג וּמָגוֹג. (See examples everywhere in the following citations.) So also in the compounds: "the war of Gog and Magog" מלחמת גוג ומגוג (b. Šabb. 118A.30); "the days of Gog and Magog" ימי ג׳ ומ׳ (b. Meg. 11A.19); "the forces of Gog and Magog" (Aramaic:) חֵילָוָתֵיהָ דְּגוֹג וּמָגוֹג (Tg. Song. 8:4). — Yet גּוֹג often appears alone, as in, for example, Exod. Rab. 30 (90C): pharaoh was not comforted about all his swarm until he saw Gog (cf. Ezek 32, 31). So in particular in compounds such as: "the day of Gog" יומו של גוג (Mek. Exod. 16:29 [59A]); "the days of Gog" ימי ג׳ (SLev 26:44 [459A]); "the kingdom of Gog" מלכותו של ג׳ (Pesiq. Rab. 31 [146A]); "the war of Gog" מלחמת (sic!) של ג׳ (t. Ber. 1.11 [2.22]); "the battle lines of Gog" סדרי קרבא דג׳ (Tg. Yer. I Deut. 34:3); "the camps of Gog" מַשִׁירְיָיתֵיהּ דגוג (Tg. Yer. I Num. 24:17); "the camp of Gog" משרית גוג (Tg. Isa. 33:22); "Gog and his horde" גוג וְסִיעֲתֵיהּ; "Gog and his camp" גוג ומשיריתיה (Tg. Yer. I Deut. 32:39). — Magog, however, is rarely mentioned alone; for example, Tg. 1 Sam 2:10: "Magog and the camp of the nations"; Tg. Yer. I Num. 11:26: אֲרְעָא דְמָגוֹג "the land of Magog." — The following is striking in the mouth of Rab († 247): "They will one day come עם גוג מגוג with Gog from Gog (?)" (b. Sanh. 95B.23). There is a mistake in the text and we should read, with Tg. Isa. 10:32, עם גוג ומגוג.

2. The time of Gog's appearance.

Revelation sets the campaign of Gog and Magog after the course of the 1,000-year messianic kingdom and immediately before the general world judgment. This scheme is also found in rabbinic literature, alongside others as well.

a. Gog at the time of the Messiah b. Joseph, that is, before the days of the Messiah.

---

378. S-B: The passage reads as follows: God sent the sons of Gomer to Gomer and the sons of Magog to Magog.

See Tg. Yer. I Exod. 40:9–11 at § Luke 24:26, II, #2, n. *c.* – See Leqach Tob Num 24:17 (2.129B) at § Luke 24:26, II, #3, n. *b.*

b. Gog before the days of the Messiah.

Midrash Psalm 17 § 9 (66B): R. Phineas (ca. 360) said in the name of R. Hoshaiah (ca. 225), "Five times David commanded God 'Arise!' in the (first) book of Psalms (this refers to Ps 3:8; 7:7; 9:20; 10:12; 17:13). Four of these correspond to the four world empires; for in the holy spirit (in the spirit of prophecy) he saw how they would one day subjugate Israel, and he summoned God to rise up against each one. The fifth time, when he saw that the kingdom of God and Magog would come upon Israel with power, he said to God, 'Arise, Yahweh, God, lift up your hand!' (Ps 10:12). We have no ruler who could set on him except for you alone." – The statement "We have no ruler" proves that Gog was expected in the premessianic period. Parallels with differences can be found in the following: Midr. Ps. 3 § 7 (20A); Pesiq. Rab. 31 (146A); here Ps 17:13 is interpreted to refer to Gog. ‖ Targum Song of Songs 8:8: "In that time (of the appearance of Gog) the angels will say among themselves, 'We have one nation on earth whose merits are little, and she has neither kings nor rulers who could go out to fight with the forces of Gog. What shall we do for our sister on the day when the nations think of going up למסק against her for war?' Then Michael, the angel prince of Israel, will say, 'If she stands firm like a wall among the nations and gives away silver in order to make the oneness of the name of the Lord of the world her own (in order to hold fast to the monotheistic confession of God), we, I and you, together with her teachers will coddle her like silver plates, and the nations will not have power to harm her, just as no worm has power to harm silver. And even if she is poor in the fulfillments of the commandments, we will plead for mercy for her before Yahweh, so that he might remember for her the merit of the Torah with which the young men occupy themselves, which is written on the tablet of the heart. Then she will stand firm against the nations like a cedar.'" ‖ Midrash Vajjoscha' (*Beth ha-Midrash* 1.56.1): When the days of the Messiah draw near, Gog and Magog will go up יעלה against the land of Israel, because he will hear that Israel is without a king and dwells in security. ‖ Sifre Deuteronomy 33:2 § 343 (143A): "Shining forth" is spoken of four times (in Scripture): The 1st time in Egypt (see Ps 80:2); the 2nd time at the giving of the law (see Deut 33:2). The 3rd time in the days of Gog and Magog; as it says, "Shine forth as the God of vengeance, Yahweh, as the God of vengeance!" (Ps 94:1). The 4th time in the days of the Messiah; as it says, "From Zion, the fullness of beauty, let God shine forth" (Ps 50:2). – The parallel in Leqach Tob Deut 33:2 (2.62B.18) diverges. ‖ See b. Sanh. 97B at § Matt 10:34, #2. ‖ See Lev. Rab. 11 (112C) and y. Šeb. 4.35C.25 at § Matt 9:15 C.

c. Gog at the time of the Messiah b. David.

Targum Yerušalmi II Numbers 11:26: "At the end of days Gog and Magog and its hosts will go up סלקין against Jerusalem and fall into the hands of the king, the Messiah." ‖ Targum Yerušalmi I Numbers 24:17: "I see him, though he does not exist yet. I perceive him, although he is not yet near: when the king becomes a mighty king from the house of Jacob and the Messiah becomes great and a scepter becomes mighty from Israel, he will kill the great ones of the Moabites and eliminate all the sons of Seth, the military camps of Gog, which will arrange the battle lines in Israel and their bodies will all fall before him (read קדמוי)." ‖ Targum 1 Samuel 2:10: "Yahweh will shatter the opponents who rise up to do evil to his people; from heaven with lifted voice he will strike יַשְׁקֵף them. Yahweh will exact punishment from Magog and from the army camps of the thieving nations who come with him from the ends of the earth, and he will bestow power on his king and make the sovereignty of the Messiah great." ‖ Targum Song of Songs 8:4: "The king, the Messiah, will say (to Israel), 'I implore you, my people, house of Israel, why do you wish to get upset against the nations of the earth to go out of exile, and why do you wish to rise up against the forces of Gog and Magog? Hold back a little bit longer until the nations are destroyed who have come to fight against Jerusalem; then the Lord of the world will remember for you the love of the righteous, and it will be pleasing before him to redeem you." ‖ See Pesiq. 78B at #3 below.

d. Gog after the messianic age but before the world judgment.

See b. 'Abod. Zar. 3B at § Matt 23:15 A, n. *r.* ‖ See y. Ber. 2.4D.52 at § Matt 21:9 A, #1, n. *b*, end. ‖ See Pesiq. 147B at § Rev 19:13. ‖ Genesis Rabbah 88 (56A): R. Joshua b. Levi (ca. 250) said, "In accordance with the four cups of trembling that God will make the nations of the world drink (see Jer 25:15; 51:7; Ps 75:9—so according to the parallels—and Ps 11:6), God will in the future make Israel drink four cups of help (salvation); see Ps 16:5: 'Yahweh is my possession and my cup'; Ps 116:13: 'I will raise the cup of helps (salvific acts)'; Ps 23:5: 'My cup has an overflow.' (This would be only three cups! Yet it says,) 'Cup of helps' (Ps 116:13), not 'Cup of help'—(that is, two because of the plural): the one in the days of the Messiah and the other in the days of Gog." — See parallels at § Acts 2:25, n. *b.* ‖ Babylonian Talmud Megillah 11A: Samuel († 254) said, "'I will not reject them' (Lev 26:44), in the days of the Greeks; 'I will not abhor them' (Lev 26:44), in the days of Nebuchadnezzar; 'so that I would wear them down' (Lev 26:44), in the days of Haman; 'would break my covenant with them' (Lev 26:44), in the days of the Persians (= Romans); 'for I am Yahweh, their God' (Lev 26:44), in the days of Gog and Magog." — The Romans are the opponents of the Messiah, then Gog and Magog after the messianic period are the opponents of God. — Parallels with divergences can be found in SLev 26:44 (459A); Midr. Esth. 1:1 (81A); b. Meg. 11A; Tg. Yer. I Lev. 26:44. ‖ Sifre Numbers 10:9 § 76 (19B): "Against the oppressors who oppress you" (Num 10:9). The passage is talking about the war of Gog and Magog. You say, "The passage is talking about the war of Gog and Magog; not rather about all the wars that are mentioned in the Torah?" It says, "You will be saved from your enemies" (Num 10:9). Go out and see which war it is in which Israel is saved and after which no oppression follows! Then you will find only the war of Gog and Magog. (This war is thus the last, since the final judgment follows it.) — Here belong presumably also t. Ber. 1.11 (parallels are found in y. Ber. 1.3D.47; 4A.11; Mek. Exod. 13:2 [23A]; 13:3 [23B]); Pesiq. Rab. 37 (163A); Exod. Rab. 23 (85A); Midr. Ps. 17 § 10 (67A); see below #7, *c.*

e. Gog's time as not more precisely specifiable:

See Gen. Rab. 98 (61B); Tg. Isa. 10, 32; Tg. Yer. I Num. 11:26; Mek. Exod. 16:29 (59A) with parallels: Mek. Exod. 16:25 (58B); b. Šabb. 118A. Also ʾAbot R. Nat. 34 (9A); b. Ber. 7B; TanḥB נח § 24; see the last two passages at § Acts 4:25 B; see Midr. Ps. 18 § 18 (74A) below at #8, *d.*

3. Gog's motives.

According to Ezek 38:4; 39:2, the actual initiator of the last onslaught of the nations under Gog is God (cf. Midr. Ps. 118 § 12 at #5); the human motive on the part of Gog is presented as greed (Ezek 38:10ff.). — In 1 En. 56:5ff., it is the angels who instead of Gog and Magog incite the Parthians and the Medes for the last move against Jerusalem (see the passage at § Rev 16:14). — Revelation traces Gog's move back to satanic influences (see 20:7f.).[379] — In rabbinic literature, it is specifically the spirit of rebellion and of pride that incites Gog to his undertaking.

Babylonian Talmud Berakot 10A: A sectarian said to R. Abbahu (ca. 300), "It is written, 'A song of David, when he fled from his son Absalom' (Ps 3:1). Furthermore, it is written, 'A song of David, when he fled from Saul ...' (Ps 57:1). Which event was first? Since the one with Saul was first, he (God) should (also) have written it first (Ps 3 should come after Ps 57)!" He answered him, "For you who do not interpret the sequence (of the sections of Scripture), it is difficult, for us who do interpret the sequence, it is not difficult.... Why does the section about Absalom (Ps 3) follow the section about Gog and Magog (= Ps 2)? If a person should say to you, 'Is there a servant who rises up against his master (like Gog against God according to Ps 2),' say to him, 'Is there a son who rises up against his father (like Absalom according to Ps 3)?' Yet as it was here the case (with Absalom), so it will be the case there (with Gog)." — Psalms 2 and 3 thus stand next to each other because of the relationship of their content. Therefore, the chronological relationship between Ps 3 and 57 in the arrangement of the psalms remained overlooked. ‖ See Midr. Ps. 2 § 4 (13A) at § Heb 1:5 A, #3. ‖ Pesiqta 78B: R. Levi (ca. 300) said, "Woe to the godless who consider themselves wise in wicked assaults against Israel! Each one of them thought, 'My plan is more correct than your plan.'" (Then follows an explanation about how Esau considered himself to be more clever than Cain, pharaoh than Esau, Haman than pharaoh.) Then follows: R. Levi said, "Even Gog and Magog will also say in the future, 'The earlier ones were foolish who appeared with bad plans against Israel without considering that they have a protector in heaven. I will not act that way, but rather I will first set myself upon their protector and then I will set myself upon them; as it says, "The kings of the earth draw up and the princes sit together against Yahweh and his Messiah" (so Ps 2:2 according to the midr.).' God answered him, 'You wicked one, you will set yourself against me? By your life, I will wage war with you!' As it says, 'Yahweh will go out and fight with these gentiles' (Zech 14:3). It further says, 'Yahweh steps forth like a fighter, like a warrior he stirs up zeal ...' (Isa 42:13)." — The same is found in Lev. Rab. 27 (126A); Midr. Esth. 3:12 (97A); Tanḥ. אמור 176A; TanḥB אמור § 18 (48A); Midr. Ps. 2 § 4 (13A); anonymous in a changed form in ʾAg. Ber. 2 (5B); see also Midrash Vajjoschaʿ (*Beth ha-Midrash* 1.56.3). ‖ See further #8, *c*.

379. S-B: See Mordecai's dream vision in Add Esth 1:4–6: "Behold, roaring and noise, thunder and earthquakes, terror on earth. And behold, two violent dragons burst forth, ready to fight with each other. And their roaring became great. And by their roaring all the nations were incited to fight so that they fought against the people of the righteous (= Israel)."

4. Gog's masses for war.

Babylonian Talmud Sanhedrin 95B: Rab Judah († 299) said that Rab († 247) said, "Sennacherib, the wicked, came upon them with 45,000 royal princes who sat in golden chariots and they brought with themselves concubines and prostitutes, and 80,000 heroes of war who were clothed with scale armor, with 60,000 armed with swords who went before him, and the rest consisted of riders. Likewise they came upon Abraham;[380] and likewise one day they will come with Gog (and) Magog." — The same is found in Tg. Isa. 10:32. ‖ Midrash Vajjoscha' (*Beth ha-Midrash* 1.56.3): Immediately (Gog) took with himself 71 nations and went up to Jerusalem. — See Tanḥ. חקת at the end: Gog and Magog, in its numerical worth, signifies 70 nations. (גוג = 12 + ו = 6 + מגוג = 52, together 70).

5. The duration of Gog's campaign.

According to R. Hama b. Hanina (ca. 260), R. Abba b. Jeremiah (ca. 270), and R. Abba b. Kahana (ca. 310), the "years of Gog" are supposed to be seven years; see Lev. Rab. 11 (112C) and y. Šeb. 4.35C.25 at § Matt 9:15 C. Yet the passages do not allow us to know whether those entire seven years will be years of war, or whether they are supposed to indicate the time in which the repercussions of the war will have an impact. The proof text adduced, Ezek 39:9, speaks in favor of the latter. A longer duration of the war is presupposed by the passages that speak about a threefold campaign by Gog against the land of Israel.

Midrash Psalm 119 § 2 (244B): R. Tanḥuma (ca. 380) said, "So it has been taught: R. Judah, the Levite, bar Shalom (ca. 370) and R. Phineas, the Priest (ca. 360), and R. Huna (ca. 350), all three, said that Gog and Magog will gather three times against Israel in the future. The third time they will come and go up to Jerusalem. Then they will go to the Judeans and undertake an enlistment among them because there will be mighty men; as it says, 'I make them strong in Yahweh' (Zech 10:12)." (See the continuation of the passage at #8, *e*.) ‖ Midrash Psalm 118 § 12 (242B): "All the gentiles surrounded me. In the name of Yahweh, in truth I will cut them off (destroy them)!" (Ps 118:10). Three times Gog and Magog will come upon Israel and go up against Jerusalem, just as Sennacherib went up three times to the land of Israel and just as Nebuchadnezzar went up three times to Jerusalem. The first time, it says, "All the gentiles surrounded me" (Ps 118:10). For he (God) will one day gather all the nations and lead them up to Jerusalem; see, "Now many nations will gather together against you" (Mic 4:11) and the whole subsequent section. And will they not be wiped out? (Surely, they will be.) Therefore it says, "In the name of Yahweh, in truth I will cut them off (destroy them)." The second time, it says, "They surrounded, yes surrounded me" (Ps 118:11). For he will one day make all the nations of the world rage and lead them up to Jerusalem; see Ps 2:1, "Why do the nations rage?" and the whole subsequent song. And will they not be wiped out? (Certainly.) Therefore it says the second time, "In the name of Yahweh, in truth I will cut them off." The third time, it says, "They surrounded me like bees" (Ps 118:12). For he will one day issue orders (read דיטגמיות = διατάγματα instead of ריש גמיות) to the countries, which

380. S-B: According to Tg. Isa. 10:32, when he was thrown into the furnace; according to Rashi sometimes, the campaign in Gen 14.

will be proclaimed by heralds, which is written, "Call this out among the nations, 'Sanctify a war'" (Joel 3:9) and so on until the end of the section. Will they not be wiped out? (Certainly.) Therefore it says for a third time, "In the name of Yahweh, in truth I will cut them off" (Ps 118:12). — A different explanation. "All the gentiles surrounded me" (Ps 118:10). For he will gather all the nations and lead them up to Jerusalem, and the Israelites will be afraid at that time. Yet God will say to them, "Do not fear!" See Isa 41:14: "Do not fear, you little worm Jacob ..." until the end of the section. Will they not be wiped out? (Certainly.) Therefore it says, "In the name of Yahweh, in truth I will cut them off" (Ps 118:10). "They surrounded, yes surrounded me" (Ps 118:11). For the tribe of Judah will be seized and bound and each one of them will be given up to his enemies, as one will think. (One will compel the Judeans to assault Jerusalem, so that the Israelites will mutually destroy themselves.) Yet they (the Judeans) will say, "May our brothers (the Jerusalemites) come and become our master, and may our enemies not become our master!" See Zech 12:5: "The rulers of Judah will say in their hearts, 'May the inhabitants of Jerusalem be strength toward me through Yahweh Sabaoth, their God!'" (so the midrash). And God will do miracles for them and make their enemies fall before them; see, "On the same day I will make the rulers of Judah like a brazier in the middle of the wood and like a burning torch in a sheaf, and on the right and on the left they will consume all the nations about them" (Zech 12:6). Will they not be wiped out? (Certainly.) Therefore it says, "In truth I will cut them off" (Ps 118:11). "They surrounded me like bees" (Ps 118:12). As the bee gathers honey for their owner, so God will gather all the nations of the world and make them go up to Jerusalem; see, "Behold, a day is coming for Yahweh when your spoil will be divided in your midst" (Zech 14:1). Will there be anything actual (abiding) in them (the nations)? It says, "They are extinguished like a fire by thorns" (Ps 118:12). Like a king into whose house thieves broke in. The king was clever. The king said, "If I go against them immediately, they will say, 'What have you found in our hands in the break-in?!' But I know that they will come three times. Then I will meet them and kill them." So too here: the king is God and the thieves are the nations; see, "I will gather all the gentiles against Jerusalem for a fight" (Zech 14:2). The place of the break-in is the city of Jerusalem; see, "The city will be conquered and the houses will be plundered" (Zech 14:2). This is the spoil; "the women will be violated" (Zech 14:2); these are the sins of fornication; "half of the city will go into exile" (Zech 14:2); this is captivity; and God will go out and fight with them; see, "Yahweh will go out and fight with these gentiles" (Zech 14:3). Then God will send a plague upon them; see, "This will be the plague with which Yahweh will strike all the nations" (Zech 14:12) and so on until the end of the section. Will they not be wiped out? (Certainly.) Therefore it says, "In truth I will cut them off" (Ps 118:12).

6. The site of Gog's defeat.

a. Jerusalem. — Sibylline Oracles 3:663ff.: "Yet again the kings of the nations make an assault together against this land (Palestine), bringing death to themselves. For they will wish to destroy the temple of the great God and the most splendid men. When they have come into the land, the shameful kings will each erect his throne around the city (Jerusalem; cf. Jer 1:15), having his disobedient (?) nation with him." — Jerusalem is also the site of the destruction of the mass of Parthians and Medes in 1 En. 56:5ff. (see the passage at § Rev 16:14).

– The same view is present in Rev 20:9, where "the beloved city" is also Jerusalem. – In rabbinic literature Gog always meets its end in Jerusalem, where Ezek 38f. is combined with Zech 12 and 14. So Leqach Tob Num 24:17 (2.129B) at § Luke 24:26, II, #3, n. *b*; Midr. Ps. 119 § 2 (244B) and 118 § 12 (242B) above in #5; SNum 10:9 § 76 in #2, n. *d*; Pesiq. 78B in #3. See further Tg. Song. 8:4 and Tg. Yer. II Num 11:26 in #2, n. *c*; ʾAbot R. Nat. 34 (9A) also belongs here.

b. The plane of Jericho. – Mekilta Exodus 17:14 (63B): How do we know that God made Moses see Gog and all his swarm? Because it says, "Yahweh made him look at the plain of Jericho" (Deut 34:1ff.). From here we learn that Gog and all his swarm will one day go up and fall in the plain of Jericho. – The same is found in SDeut 34:3 § 357 (149B).

c. The mountains of the land of Israel (according to Ezek 39:4). – So Tg. Yer. I Num. 11:26; see #8, n. *a*.

d. The south. – Leviticus Rabbah 9 (111A): R. Eleazar (ca. 270) said, "... When Gog is aroused, which is located in the north, it will come and fall in the south; see Ezek 39:2." – The same is found in Num. Rab. 13 (168B); Midr. Song. 4:16 (117B).

7. The destroyer of Gog. – The following appear in this role:

a. The Messiah b. Joseph. – See Tg. Yer. I Exod. 40:9–11 at § Luke 24:26, II, #2, n. *c*.

b. The Messiah b. David. – See Tg. Yer. II Num. 11:26; Tg. Yer. I Num. 24:17, see #2, n. *c*.

c. God. – So most of the time; see, for example, Midr. Ps. 17 § 9 and SDeut 33:2 § 343 in #2, n. *b*; Tg. 1 Sam. 2:10 in #2, n. *c*; SNum 10:9 § 76 in #2, n. *d*; Pesiq. 78B in #3; Midr. Ps. 118 § 12 in #5; Tg. Yer. I Num. 11:26 in #8, n. *a*; Pesiq. 147B at § Rev 19:13; ʾAbot R. Nat. 34 (9A). – Here we may also add Midr. Ps. 17 § 10 (67A): R. Joshua of Sikhnin (ca. 330) said in the name of R. Levi (ca. 300), "God says, 'Twice I have said with an oath by myself that I will bring the end (קֵץ = messianic redemption) and redeem you from your servitude to the kingdoms of the world. Even if Gog and Magog come in the future, I will fight with him'; see Zech 14:3." – In the parallel Pesiq. Rab. 31 (146B), the sentence about Gog and Magog is missing.

d. Michael. – Targum Yerušalmi I Deuteronomy 34:3: "(On Mount Nebo the Memra of Yahweh made Moses) see the battle of Gog, and in the time of this great distress Michael will arise with a strong arm as redeemer" (cf. Dan 12:1).

8. The means of fighting against Gog.

Ezekiel 38:19ff. names earthquakes and mutual murder, plague and blood, downpours and hail stones, fire and sulfur; 39:3 adds that God will make Gog helpless. – Revelation 20:9 highlights only the fire that falls from heaven and consumes Gog's hordes. – The most detail is given in Sib. Or. 3:669–692, with constant reliance on Ezek 38:19ff. concerning the destructive means in the "immortal hand." – 1 Enoch 56:7 (the campaign of the Parthians and Medes against Jerusalem) limits itself to the depiction of mutual slaughter; see the passage at § Rev 16:14. – In rabbinic literature, by analogy with the ten Egyptian plagues, ten punishments are enumerated that will come upon Gog. "As I plagued Egypt with ten plagues in this world," said God, "so I will punish Gog in the future world in the same way"; see Ezek 38:22; TanḥB וארא § 10 (13B); Tanḥ. וארא 71A. The following individually are highlighted in particular among the means of punishment:

a. Fire. – Midrash Psalm 11 § 5 (50B): God says, "Whoever exalts himself will ultimately be judged (punished) by fire. The people of the generation of the flood (see Job 6:17); the people who built the tower (see Job 22:20); the people of Sodom (see Gen 19:24); pharaoh (see Exod 9:24); Sennacherib (see Isa 10:16); ... Sisera (see Judg 5:20); Nebuchadnezzar (see Dan 3:22); Edom (= Rome; see Dan 7:11); Gog and Magog (see Ezek 39:6: 'I will send fire over Magog [land and people]'); the other nations (see Isa 66:16); Hiram (see Ezek 28:18)." – The same is found in a broader version, though without mentioning Gog in TanḥB צו § 3 and 4; Tanḥ. צו 139A; Lev. Rab. 7 (110B); see § Luke 1:51, n. *p.* ‖ Tanḥuma ראה 11A: The Egyptians all died by a breath; as it says, "You blew with your breath, and then the sea covered them" (Exod 15:10). Likewise, one day Gog and Magog will gather against Israel, and they too will all be burnt by a fire; see Ezek 38:22. ‖ Targum Yerušalmi I Numbers 11:26: "Two men remained in the camp; the name of one was Eldad and that of the other was Medad.... Both prophesied together and said,[381] 'Behold, a king will go up at the end of days from the land of Magog and gather kings who are adorned with crowns, and eparchs who are clothed with armor; and all the nations will obey him and wage war against the sons of the exile (i.e., against those who returned from the exile, cf. Ezek 38:8–14) in the land of Israel. Yet the Lord (read: קירים = κύριος) will stand by for them in the hour of need and kill them by burning their souls with a flame of fire[382] that will go out from under the throne of glory, and their corpses will fall on the mountains of the land of Israel, and all the wild animals and the birds of heaven will come and eat their bodies. Then all the dead of Israel will resurrect and be refreshed with the good (read טובא instead of טורא) that has been stored up for them from the beginning, and receive the recompense for their deeds (works).'"

b. Hail. – See Exod. Rab. 12 (75A) at § Rev 16:21. ‖ TanḥumaB וארא § 22 (19A): "Then thunder and hail ceased, and rain did not pour to the earth" (Exod 9:34). Where did it stay then? Our teachers said, "It hovers in the air until Gog and Magog comes; see Ezek 38:22." – Parallels can be found in Tanḥ. וארא 73A; Exod. Rab. 12 (75B). – On אבני אלגביש = "hail stones" (Ezek 38:22), see b. Ber. 54B.8: What does "hail stones" mean? Stones that stood "because of a man" על גב איש (see Exod 9:34), and came down because of a man (see Josh 10:11).

c. Leprosy. – TanḥumaB חזריע § 16 (21B): "Gog too" (God says), "who proudly exalted himself in this world, I will strike with leprosy"; see Zech 14:12 (further below). – The same is found in Tanḥ. מצורע 157B. ‖ ʾAggadat Berešit 2 (6A): What will they do (Gog and his allies)? They will defiantly plant themselves on their feet and look up against God and say, "We will exterminate them (Israel) so that they will no longer be a people and the God שֵׁם of Israel will no longer be remembered!" (so Ps 83:5 according to the midr.). What does "שם of Israel" mean? They mean: We will exterminate the one of whom it says, "Blessed be Yahweh, the God of Israel!" (Ps 41:1–4). (שֵׁם "name" thus interpreted = God.) What will God do to them from on high? While they (impudently) plant themselves on their feet, he will punish them; as it says, "This will be the plague ...: he will make his flesh rot while he stands

381. S-B: R. Nehemiah (ca. 150) first said that Eldad and Medad prophesied about Gog (see b. Sanh 17A.28).

382. S-B: A flame of fire consumes the interior of a person without showing traces of this externally on the body.

on his feet" (Zech 14:12). Concerning those feet that rushed to stand against God, it says, "He will make his flesh rot while he stands on his feet"; concerning those eyes that looked up, it says, "His eyes shall decay in their eye sockets" (Zech 14:12); and concerning that tongue that spoke against Yahweh, it says, "Their tongue shall decay in their mouth" (Zech 14:12).

d. General confusion. — Midrash Psalm 18 § 18 (74A): There are three wars of confusion according to Exod 23:27 and Deut 7:23 or according to Josh 10:10; Judg 4:15 and 1 Sam 7:10.... R. Simon (ca. 280) said, "There are two more; see Ps 18:15 and Zech 14:13: 'The confusion of Yahweh will be powerful among them.'" R. Simon said in the name of R. Abba (ca. 290, perhaps the names should be transposed), "Of these, the one (confusion) pertains to the past and came upon pharaoh (cf. Exod 14:24), and the other will come upon Gog and Magog in in the future" (see Zech 14:13, as above). — The parallel in Midr. Sam. 13 § 3 (42B) names R. Abba b. Kahana (ca. 310) as the author.

e. The victorious action of the Judeans. — Midrash Psalm 119 § 2 (245A): (When Gog and Magog have gone up to Jerusalem with the Judeans conscripted by force—see #5) what will they do? They will join to each of the Israelites two strong men so that they may not flee. When the heroes of Judah have gone up and reached Jerusalem, they will pray in their heart (so, quietly) and say, "May we fall into their (the Jerusalemites') hand and not they into our hand!" Why do they pray in their heart? Because they will be afraid of making their voice heard; as it says, "The rulers of Judah will say in their heart" (Zech 12:5). Yet God will say to them, "In purity you have come; by your life, I will repay you for the purity; as it says, 'The purity of the upright guides them' (Prov 11:3)." In that hour God will bestow heroic power on Judah, and they will draw their weapons and strike at those men on their right and left and kill them. — Elements of this can be found also in Tg. Zech. 12:2, 5.

9. The judgment on Gog.

ʾAggadat Berešit 2 (6A; see the beginning at #8, n. *c*): God will say to them, "Originally you (nations) had no peace among yourselves; as it says, 'There is no peace, says Yahweh, for the godless' (Isa 48:22). Yet now you have made peace with one another to move against me[383] (see Ps 83:6–8). You all have made peace to move against me. I too will do this: 'But you, O son of man, ... say to the birds and to all the wild animals of the field, "Flock together ...; you shall eat the flesh of heroes and drink the blood of princes of the earth ..."' (Ezek 39:17f.). Just as you have no peace among yourselves but have made peace to move against me, so I will summon the birds and the wild animals who had no peace among them, and I make peace for them with one another so that they may come upon you. And since you have said, 'The name of Israel will no longer be remembered' (Ps 83:5)—by your life!—you shall die and they will bury you and receive a name in the world. As it says, 'The whole people of the land will bury and it will give them a name (= fame)' (Ezek 39:13)." ‖ Midrash Psalm 150 § 1 (271A): The holy spirit said through Ezekiel, "I will make my holy name known ... and the gentiles shall know that I, Yahweh, am holy in Israel" (Ezek 39:7). When will the gentiles know that I am holy? When I carry out in them what is written earlier: "You shall eat the flesh of heroes ..." (Ezek 39:1–3 and 39:18f.). Ezekiel, though,

---

383. S-B: The discontinuance of all mutual enmity in order to make common cause against Israel at the end of days is also emphasized in 4 Ezra 13.

did not clearly state how long the wild animals and the birds will consume the corpses of Gog. Here Isaiah comes and clearly states this; as it says, "The vulture will summer on them (on the slaughtered), and every beast of the field will winter on them" (Isa 18:6). Behold, for 12 months he (God) will carry it out against Gog: one summer and one fall (= winter) are 12 months. When will God show himself holy in his world? When he exacts punishment from the godless. ‖ Mishnah ʿEduyyot 2.10: R. Aqiba († ca. 135) said, "There are five things that last 12 months: the judgment on the generation of the flood, on Job, on Egypt, on Gog and Magog in the future, and the judgment on the godless in gehenna (see Isa 66:23)." — This Mishnah is found also in Midr. Lam. 1:12 (55A). — In S. ʿOlam Rab. 3, it says about Gog: The judgment on Gog in the future will last 12 months; see Isa 18:6 (as above in Midr. Ps. 150 § 1).

10. Gog's grave.

Sibylline Oracles 3:682f.: "Foggy gorges in the high mountains will be full of corpses." ‖ Targum Ezekiel 39:11: "It will happen at this time that I will give Gog a place that is suitable for a grave in Israel, in the valley of narrow passes east of the Sea of Gennesaret, a gorge between two mountains. There they shall bury Gog and all his swarm, and it will be called the valley of Gog's swarm."

11. Miscellanea.

a. ἐν ταῖς τέσσαρσιν γωνίαις τῆς γῆς (Rev 20:8); see Tg. 1 Sam. 2:10 at #2, n. *c*.

b. ἀνέβησαν (Rev 20:9) should be understood, as elsewhere, to refer to going up to the land of Israel; see Tg. Song. 8:8 and Midr Vajjoschaʿ in #2, n. *b*; Tg. Yer. II Num. 11:26 in #2, n. *c*; Midr. Ps. 119 § 2 and 118 § 12 in #5; Mek. Exod. 17:14 (63B) in #6, n. *b*; see also § Luke 18:10 A.

20:12 A: The dead, great and small.

See the excursus "General or Partial Resurrection of the Dead?" — Specifically for the participation of children in the future world, see § Matt 18:14 B.

20:12 B: Books were opened up ....

On the heavenly books, see § Luke 10:20. — Here a few other passages may be added. Books of life: 1 En. 103:2; Jub. 36:10; Pesiq. 157B.13; b. Roš Haš. 32B (see § 2 Cor 11:22 B, n. *b*); Tg. Isa. 49:3 (see § Luke 2:25B); Tg. Ezek. 13:9. — Books of guilt (or debt): 1 En. 97:6; 98:7f.; 2 En. 19:5; 50:1; 53:2; 2 Bar. 24:1; see 1 En. 89:61ff., 70f., 76f.; 90:17, 20; Midr. Lam. 1:14 (55B); Midr. Esth. 1:1 (84A); Midr. Ps. 149 § 6 (271A). — Angels as scribes: 1 En. 89:61ff.; 90:14, 22; see 100:10.

20:13: The sea ... and death and the underworld gave (back) the dead in them.

1. ἡ θάλασσα. — Targum Psalm 68:23: "The righteous who died and were consumed by the animals of the field, says Yahweh, I will bring back; I will bring back the righteous who drowned in the depths of the sea." ‖ See 1 En. 61:5 at § Rev 20:5, n. *a*.

2. ὁ θάνατος καὶ ὁ ᾅδης. — See 1 En. 51:1f. at § Rev 20:5, n. *a*. ‖ 4 Ezra 7:32: The earth will give back those who rest in her, the dust will release those who sleep in it, the chambers

(in Sheol) will restore the souls that have been entrusted to them. — On Sheol as the storage place of the dead, see the excursus "Sheol, Gehenna, and the Garden of Eden," I.

21:1 A: I saw a new heaven and a new earth; for the first heaven and the first earth have passed away.

The end and renewal of the world.

A. The pseudepigraphic literature.

There are two different views in the pseudepigrapha about the end of the world. Representatives of the first view deny the end of the world in the literal sense of the word.[a] They understand it to refer simply the destruction of life on earth, which is the result of human sin and by which the whole creation is shaken.[b] Correspondingly, the renewal of the world means a revival of the old world to new life, a transfiguring transformation of the old world that presupposes the purification of the world from all sin.[c] The expression "new creation" in Jub. 1:29; 4:26[c] is then tantamount to transformed = transfigured creation and the expression "new world" in 2 Bar. 44:12[d] tantamount to transformed = transfigured world, unless one prefers (probably more correctly) to understand the "new world" to refer to the new eon = the *ʿolam ha-ba.*

Representatives of the other view acknowledge an end of the world in the literal sense of the word and understand it to refer either to the world sinking back into the primordial silence of the chaos of creation, whether for a shorter or longer time,[e] or a complete destruction of the world that is brought about by a violent world conflagration.[f] In this view, the renewal of the world signifies either the transformation of the chaotic mass of the old world into a new world[g] or the complete new creation of a new heaven and a new earth. So "new creation" in 1 En. 72:1 = a creation called into being completely anew and "new heaven" in 1 En. 91:16 = a heaven created completely anew.[h]

a. 2 Baruch 3:7–4:1: "Shall the structure of the world return to its (original chaotic) nature? And shall the world again fall to the silence that originally (ruled)? And shall the (great) mass of living beings be eradicated and there be no more mention of human nature? ... And the Lord said to me (Baruch), '... The world does not pass away.'"

b. Jubilees 23:18: "Behold, the earth will perish because of all their (humanity's) action, and there will be no (longer) seed of wine or oil; for their action is sheer unfaithfulness, and they will all perish together, (wild) animals and (tame) livestock and birds and all the fish of the sea because of the children of men." ‖ 2 Baruch 31:5–32:1, 6: "Behold, days are coming when everything that has come into being will be surrendered to destruction, and it will be as if nothing had been. Yet if you prepare your hearts by sowing the fruits of the law in them, this will shelter you in that time when the Almighty shakes the entire creation.... Yet greater ... will be the fight when the Almighty renews his creation (i.e., summons it to new life)." — See 1 En. 10:2, where it says about the flood: "The whole earth will perish, and a flood is about to come upon the whole earth, and everything on it will perish."

c. 2 Baruch 57:2: "Belief in the future judgment was born then (in Abraham's days), and the hope that the world will be renewed (through the resurrection of the dead) was then constructed, and the promise of life to come was then planted." ‖ See 2 Bar. 31:5–32:1, 6 in n. *b.* ‖ 1 Enoch 45:4ff.: "On that day I will make my elect one (= the Messiah) dwell in their midst (that of the elect), and I will transform (= transfigure) heaven and make it into an eternal blessing and light. I will transform (= transfigure) the earth, make it into a new blessing and make my elect dwell on it. But those who commit sin and wrongdoing shall not tread it.... For the sinners, the judgment is imminent to wipe them from the face of the earth." ‖ Jubilees 1:29: "From the day of the new creation, when heaven and earth and all their creatures are renewed (to new life), both the power of heaven and all the creatures of the earth, until the sanctuary of God in Jerusalem is created on Mount Zion, and all the lights are renewed (transformed, transfigured) for salvation and peace and blessing for all the elect of Israel." ‖ Jubilees 4:26: "Four places on earth belong to God: the garden of Eden and the Mount of the East and this mountain on which you are today, Mount Sinai, and Mount Zion. It will be sanctified in the new (transformed, transfigured) creation for the sanctification of the earth. Therefore, the earth will be sanctified from all sin and from all their filth among the generations of eternity." ‖ 2 Baruch 49:2f.: "In what form will those who are alive in your day (continue to) live?... Or will you transform those who were in the world (will you give them a new transfigured body), just as also the world (itself)?"

d. 2 Baruch 44:11f.: "There is a time that does not pass away; and the period is coming that will abide forever, and the new world that does not make those decay who pass away (to blessedness as) at the beginning, and that has no mercy with those who pass away to torment and those who live in it do not go to ruin...." (Verse 15:) "For the world will be given to those who come there" (i.e., the *'olam ha-ba*, probably = "new world" above).

e. 4 Ezra 7:29ff.: "After these (400) years (of the messianic period) my son, the Christ, will die and all that have the breath of humanity. Then the world will turn to the primordial silence (cf. 2 Bar. 3:7ff. in n. *a*) for seven days, as at the very beginning, so that no one will remain. After seven days, though, the new age that now sleeps (i.e., the *'olam ha-ba*) will awake and perishability will itself pass away." (Then follows the resurrection of the dead and the last judgment, when simultaneously gehenna and the garden of Eden appear, probably on the new earth transfigured from the chaos.) ‖ Sibylline Oracles 5:476ff.: "The terrible generation will moan unspeakably much when at the end the sun goes down so as not to come up again .... For it has seen the unholy wicked deeds of many people. Yet there will be moonless darkness in the great heaven itself, and not a little darkness will shroud the realm of the stars for a second time" (as the first time in Gen 1:2). ‖ 2 Enoch 33:1f. has the world Sabbath last 1,000 years: "I appoint the eighth day (= the first day after the week of creation) so that the eighth day itself will be the first created over my works, and so that they will be found as an image of the seventh thousand, so that the eighth thousand may be the beginning of the time of innumerability and so that it may be infinite: neither years nor months nor weeks nor days nor hours." (The present age, which = *'olam ha-zeh*, comprises

6,000 years, and then follows as the end a 7th millennium in which the world returns to the primordial silence. Then the future world, the *ʿolam ha-ba*, begins; cf. b. Sanh. 97A, B at B, n. *b* below.) ‖ Just how the world sinking back into the chaos of creation was imagined is shown in 1 En. 83:3f.: "I (Enoch) looked in the vision, how heaven collapsed, disappeared and fell to the earth. Yet when it crashed to the earth, I saw how the earth was swallowed up in a great abyss, mountains fell down on mountains, hills sank down on hills, high trees were torn from (the roots of) their trunks, swirled down, and sank in the deep."

f. See passages at § 2 Pet 3:7, notes *a* and *b*.

g. 4 Ezra 7:75: "If I (Ezra) have found favor before you, Lord, show your servant this too: whether after our death, when we have to give back our soul, we will be temporarily kept in peace until those times come when you will renew the creation (to new life from the chaos), or whether we will immediately fall prey to torment?" — See 4 Ezra 5:45: "I (Ezra) said, 'How does this cohere with the word that you have just said to your servant, that one day you would awaken the whole creation to life all at once?'"

h. 1 Enoch 72:1: "(The angel Uriel) showed me (Enoch) how it is with all their (the heavenly lights') laws, with all the years of the world until eternity, until the new, eternally abiding creation is created." ‖ 1 Enoch 91:14, 16: "In the ninth week (of the world) ... the world will be written down for ruin.... (In the tenth week) the first heaven will disappear and pass away; a new heaven will appear, and all the powers of heaven will shine sevenfold forever."

B. Rabbinic literature.

The situation is the same in rabbinic literature. Some teachers deny an end of the world. They understand the renewal of the world to refer to a making new, a restoration of the world so that it returns to its original condition when it was clean of sin and evil.[a] However, others speak of the destruction of the world and here think of the earth lying waste, being deserted of all life, as well as sinking back into its original chaos.[b] For them the renewal of the world is the world being brought out from the state of destruction to a pure new existence. Still others suppose an actual passing away of the world and see in the new heaven and in the new earth works of a new divine creation.[c]

a. Targum Yerušalmi I Deuteronomy 32:1: "When the end of Moses, the prophet, came so that he should depart (be gathered) from the world, he said in his heart, 'I will not take as witnesses against this people witnesses who will taste death in this world; behold, I will take as witnesses against them witnesses who will not taste death in this world, but rather whose end will be to be renewed in the future world.'" — He is referring of course to heaven and earth (Deut 32:1). There is no demise pending for them, but rather a renewal or restoration that transfigures them at the dawn of the *ʿolam ha-ba*. See, however, Tg. Yer. II Deut. 32:1 in n. *c*. ‖ Midrash Ecclesiastes 1:4 (6A): "One generation goes and one generation comes, but the earth endures forever" (Eccl 1:4). R. Joshua b. Qarha (ca. 150) said, "Should Scripture not rather have said, 'The one earth goes and the other earth comes, but the (human) race endures forever?' For who was created for whose sake? Was the earth created for the sake of the (human) race or was the (human) race created for the sake of the earth? Indeed the earth for the sake of the (human) race! (Therefore, the human race shall remain eternally as the true purpose (of creation) and therefore the more important and the earth shall pass away as the means to an end and therefore the less important.) Yet since the (human) race did not remain in the statutes of God, it will fade away, and since the earth remained in the statues of God, it will not fade away." — The same is found in a different form in SDeut 11:21 § 47 (83B). ‖ Genesis Rabbah 12 (9C): "When Yahweh Elohim made earth and heaven" (Gen 2:4). (The mention of the earth before heaven should be interpreted.) Like a legion that first proclaimed a king as king. The king said, "Since this legion has proclaimed me first as king, I will bestow a distinction (προκοπή) on it that shall never depart from it." So too God said, "Since this earth has done my will first (Pseudo-Rashi refers to Gen 1:11), I will bestow a distinction that shall never depart from it; as it says, 'He established the earth on its foundations so that it would never falter' (Ps 104:5)." ‖ See further Tg. Jer. 31:35f.; 33:20f., 25. — When the end of the world was denied, a renewal of the world could naturally only be understood to refer to a making new or a restoration of the world. For this attenuated meaning of the verb "renew," see Midr. Ps. 96 § 1 (211A): R. Abbahu (ca. 300) said, "… In the morning the Israelites praised God that he each day regularly renews מחדש the work of creation." — See on this the Prayer of Joṣer ʿOr at § Matt 6:5 A, n. *b*. — Also b. Ḥag. 12B: The heaven called "Velon" (the lowest of the 7 heavens) serves for nothing other than that it comes in the morning (to cover the stars) and goes in the evening (to let the stars become visible), and so each day it renews the work of creation. — Here the following passages may also be added. Midrash Psalm 104 § 24 (224A): "You let out your breath, they are created (= the dead arise)" (Ps 104:30). When? When you renew the face of the earth. ‖ Kaddish de Rabbanan: Glorified and sanctified be his great name that will renew the world דְּעָתִיד לְחַדָּתָא עָלְמָא and awaken the dead. ‖ Targum Onkelos Deuteronomy 32:12: "Yahweh alone will make them dwell in the world that will be renewed." ‖ Targum Jeremiah 23:23: "I, God, created the world from the beginning; I, God, will one day renew the world for the righteous." ‖ Targum Micah 7:14: "Guide your people by your Memra, the people of your possession, in the world that will one day be renewed." ‖ Targum Habakkuk 3:2: "You will make known your power in the years when you have promised to renew the world to take vengeance on the godless who have transgressed your word; yet in mercy you will remember the righteous who do your will." ‖ New Pesiqtha (*Beth ha-Midrash* 6.42.21): I am the one who spoke and the world came into being, and who guides the order of creation, and I will one day complete and renew it. ‖ See Tg. Yer. I Deut. 32:1 at the beginning. — In this attenuated sense, the new heaven and the new earth in Isa 66:22 can also be a renewed heaven and a renewed earth, that is, a heaven and an earth without deficiency or lack. So Lev. Rab. 29 (127C): R. Tahlifa of Caesarea (ca. 270) said, "With all the supplemental offerings it is written, 'You shall present,' and here it says, 'You shall prepare' (Num 29:2). How should this be understood? God said to Israel, 'My children, I reckon it to you as if you had been prepared (made) by me today, as if I had created you today (on New Year's Day) as a new creature. This is what is written, 'As the new heaven and the new earth that I prepare will endure before me …' (Isa 66:22)." — As Israel is considered to be a new creature because it is forgiven its sin on New Year's Day, so the new heaven and the new earth are as it were a newly created world, because they will be without deficiency or lack. ‖ We may also adduce Deut. Rab. 11 (207C.5) here.

b. Babylonian Talmud Sanhedrin 97A, B: Rab Qattina (ca. 270) said, "The world will exist for 6,000 years and it will be destroyed חריב for 1,000 years; for it says, 'Yahweh alone will be exalted on that day' (Isa 2:11; and 1 day of God is, according to Ps 90:4, 1,000 years)." Abbayye († 338/39) said, "It will be destroyed for 2,000 years; for it says, 'He will make us live after two days' (Hos 6:2; and 2 days of God are 2,000 years)." A baraita corresponds to the view of Rab Qattina: As the seventh year is a fallow year, one year in seven years, so too the world will lie idle משמט for 1,000 years in 7,000 years; see Isa 2:11 (as above). It says further, "A song for the Sabbath day" (Ps 92:1), on the day that is entirely Sabbath (rest). It says further, "A thousand years before you are as one day" (Ps 90:4). (Thus the "Sabbath day" in Ps 92:1[384] is the great world pause of 1,000 years when the earth lies fallow, is robbed of all life.) ... (97B.7:) Rab Ḥanan b. Tahlifa sent word to Rab Joseph († 333), "I met someone in whose hand there was a scroll that was written in Assyrian (= in square script) and in the holy language. I said to him, 'Where did you get this?' He answered me, 'I served among the troops of Rome and found it in a Roman archive.' In it was written, 'After 4,291 years since the creation of the world (i.e., from the year 531 CE) the world will be deserted יתום. A part of them (namely the closing part of the 4,291 years) are comprised by the wars of the sea monsters (the world empires), another part the wars of Gog and Magog, and the rest are constituted by the days of the Messiah. Yet God will renew מחדש his world only after 7,000 years.'" (Here the renewal of the world = restoration from the state of destruction.) – The saying of Rab Qattina and Abbayye is also found in b. Roš Haš. 31A.20. ‖ Seder Eliyahu Rabbah 2 (6.31): "In your book were written all that days that were formed (predestined)" (Ps 139:16). This refers to the seventh day (= 7th millennium) of the world. For this world exists for 6,000 years: 2,000 of these the Tohu (i.e., the time without the Torah) reigns, 2,000 the Torah, and 2,000 the Messiah.... And as we keep a fallow year in seven years, so too will God prepare for the world a fallow year, one day long, which is 1,000 years (see Ps 90:4 as above). It further says, "There will be a day that is known to Yahweh, neither day nor night (thus darkness as in the very beginning)" (Zech 14:7). This is the seventh day of the world (the great world Sabbath). "Yet it will happen at the time of the evening (of this 7th day) that there will be light" (Zech 14:7); this is the future world (the *ʿolam ha-ba*, which begins after the course of the 7th millennium); as it says, "Immediately the Sabbath will come, and on that Sabbath (= *ʿolam ha-ba*) all flesh will come to worship" (Isa 66:23; the passage is thus not interpreted to refer to the days of the Messiah, but rather to the *ʿolam ha-ba*). And further it says, "A Song for the Sabbath day" (Ps 92:1) (= *ʿolam ha-ba*), that is, for the age that is entirely Sabbath. – The same is found with an expanded scriptural proof in the manuscript in Buber, Midr. Ps. 90 § 17 note 95. ‖ Midrash Psalm 50 § 1 (140A): Starting from where did God create his world? From Zion, as it says, "From Zion he completed the

384. S-B: This interpretation of Ps 92:1 is also found in S. Eli. Rab. 2 (7.9); otherwise, the psalm passage is related to the "*ʿolam ha-ba*, which is very long"; this is done by R. Aqiba († ca. 135) in b. Roš Haš. 31A at the beginning; anonymously in m. Tamid 7.4; Midr. Song. 4:4 (111B); ʾAbot R. Nat. 1 (1C); see also the next citation above, S. Eli. Rab. 2 (6).

beauty" (so Midr. Ps. 50:2), namely the beauty of the world. What does "He made it shine" (Ps 50:2) mean? He made the light shine (namely from Zion during the creation of the world).... And when he destroys (סתר) the world, he starts with Zion; see Jer 9:10, "I make Jerusalem a heap of rubble"; and then, "The whole earth will become a wasteland" (Jer 4:27), and furthermore, "The earth will become a wasteland because of its inhabitants" (Mic 7:13). Yet when God renews יחדש his world, he will renew it starting from Zion; as it says, "The mountain of the house of Yahweh will be established first among the mountains" (so Midr. Isa. 2:2). ‖ Genesis Rabbah 2 at the beginning (3B): "The earth had become as a waste and void" (Gen 1:2). R. Berekhiah (ca. 340) opened his presentation with the following, "'Even a boy is known by his deeds' (Prov 20:11)." R. Berekhiah said, "When the briar is still soft it (already) brings forth thorns. What is the prophet supposed to have prophesied about it (the earth) last? 'I saw the earth. Behold, it was a waste and void' (Isa 4:6)." – The end returns to the beginning, to chaos. ‖ See b. Sanh. 92A at § 1 Cor 15:51, n. *a*, end. ‖ Midrash Psalm 23 § 7 (101B.9. 18): Our teachers interpreted the passage (namely Ps 23:2–6) to refer to Israel.... "You anoint my head with oil" refers to the king, the Messiah, who is anointed with the oil of anointing. "My cup overflows": this is the cup of salvation, which is a cup of comforts. "Truly, goodness and grace will follow me all the days of my life": this refers to the 1,000 years (of the destruction of the world), when God will renew his world (from the chaos). "I will dwell in the house of Yahweh," in the sanctuary—may it be built soon in our days—Amen and (again) Amen! "Throughout the length of days": this refers to the world that is really long, to the life of the future world (*'olam ha-ba*). ‖ Midrash Psalm 46 § 2 (136B): "Therefore, we will not fear at the changes of the earth" (Ps 46:3). The sons of Korah (as authors of the 46th psalm) said, "Do not fear on the day when God shakes the world; as it says, 'To measure the borders of the earth so that the godless may be shaken off of it' (Job 38:13). It further says, 'Behold, I will create a new heaven and a new earth' (Isa 65:17). And where will the righteous stand in that hour (when God shakes the earth to create it anew)? They will cling to the throne of glory under the wings of the Shekinah; as it says, 'You, you who cling to Yahweh your God, will all remain alive on that day' (so Deut 4:4 according to the midr.)." – Here too what is in view is not a completely new creation of heaven and earth, but rather a renewal of the old world by which all evil is eliminated.

c. Sifre Deuteronomy 32:1 § 306 (130B): One day the community of Israel will say before God, "Lord of the world, behold, my witnesses are still alive; as it says, 'I call upon heaven and earth today as witnesses against you' (Deut 30:19). Then he will answer them, "I will make them pass away מעבירן (i.e., I will eliminate them); as it says, 'Behold, I will create a new heaven and a new earth' (Isa 65:17)." ‖ Exodus Rabbah 44 (100B): What does "To them (the patriarchs) you swore by yourself" (Exod 32:13) mean? ... Hezekiah (b. Hiyya [ca. 240]) said, "Moses said (to God), 'If you had sworn to the fathers by heaven and by the earth, you would act rightly against them if you destroyed their children; for just as heaven and earth cease בטלים (pass away), so too the oath made by them would pass away עוברת (vanish). Yet Lord of the world, you did not swear it in this way to their fathers that you would not destroy their children! Did you not say to Abraham, "By myself I swear" (Gen 22:16)? What does "By myself I swear" mean? God said to Abraham, "As I live and abide forever, so my oath shall abide for all eternity!"'" — Similarly, R. Eleazar (ca. 270) in b. Ber. 32A. ‖ Genesis Rabbah 42 (26A): R. Samuel b. Nahman (ca. 260, when someone challenged his exegetical rule that ויהי in Scripture refers to distress and והיה to joy by pointing to Gen 1:5, "And it was ויהי evening and it was morning, a first day") said, "Even this was not a complete joy; for everything that was created on the first day, will one day be worn out בלות (= vanish); as it says, 'The heavens will scatter like smoke and the earth will be ground תבלה (become frail) like a garment.'" — Parallels are found in Lev. Rab. 11 (113B), where instead of R. Ishmael we should read R. Samuel; Num. Rab. 13 (169B); Midr. Esth. 1:1 (82B); Midr. Ruth 1:2 (124B); Tanḥ. שמיני 151B, here with the omission of the author's name, mixed with a saying of R. Yohanan († 279); in Pesiq. Rab. 5 (19B) our sentence is missing. ‖ Genesis Rabbah 34 (21B): "From now on for all the days of the earth seed and harvest will no longer cease ..." (Gen 8:22). R. Judan (ca. 350) said in the name of R. Samuel b. Nahman (ca. 260), "How so? Do the sons of Noah (= non-Israelites) think that the covenant that was made with them (Gen 8:22) will endure forever? Rather, as long as heaven and earth abide, the covenant with them will abide. When, however, that day comes of which it is written, 'The heavens will scatter like smoke ...' (Isa 51:6), on that day it will be broken (destroyed)." — See further Midr. Eccl. 1:2 (4B). — From the targumim, reference may also be made to Isa 51:6: "As smoke, which passes away, so the heavens will pass away, and the earth will become brittle (ground) like a garment that becomes brittle." ‖ Targum Yerušalmi II Deuteronomy 32:1: "When the end of Moses approached so that he should depart from the world, he said, 'What shall I take as witnesses against the people? Behold, the things that will not taste death I will take as witnesses against them, heaven and earth, which will not cease כלין in this world, but rather which will cease סופהון דכליין only in the future world; for so it says clearly in a passage of Scripture, "Raise your eyes to heaven and call as a witness the earth below; for the heavens will disappear like smoke and the earth will become brittle like a garment" (Isa 51:6). Yet I will create a new heaven and a new earth (Isa 65:17).'" — See, though, Tg. Yer. I Deut. 32:1 above in n. *a*. ‖ Targum Psalm 102:27: "They (heaven and earth) will perish יהובדון, but you remain. They all will become brittle like a cloak; like a garment you will change them, and they are subject to change (pass away)." — We have not found in rabbinic literature the view that the end of the world is accomplished by a world conflagration; see § 2 Pet 3:7. ‖ The new heaven and the new earth are mentioned in TanḥB בראשית § 20 (8A): A matron asked R. Yose (ca. 150) and said, "It says, 'So that your life and the life of your children may be long on the soil, which Yahweh swore to your fathers to give you, as the duration of heaven above the earth' (Deut 11:21). You will thus abide only as long as heaven and earth will abide, and heaven and earth will one day pass away; see Isa 40:26 and 51:6." He answered her, "From the same prophet from which you have adduced the proof to me, I will give you the answer. It says, 'Just as the new heaven and the new earth that I prepare will endure before me, says Yahweh, thus your seed and your name will continue to exist' (Isa 66:22)." ‖ Genesis Rabbah 1 (3A): R. Huna (ca. 350) said in the name of R. Eliezer b. Yose the Galilean (ca. 150), "Even those of whom it is written, 'Behold, I will create a new heaven and a new earth' (Isa 65:17) were created long ago, since the six days of creation; this is what 'Just as the new heaven and the new earth ...' (Isa 66:22) means. It does not say here 'as "a new earth,"' but rather 'as "the new earth."'" — The definite article indicates a new earth that already exists. — The same is found in another form in TanḥB בראשית § 9 (3B). ‖ Sifre Deuteronomy 11:21 § 47 (83A): "As the duration of heaven over the earth" (Deut 11:21). (This means) that they (Israel) will live and endure for all eternity. Likewise, it says, "As the new heaven and the new earth that I prepare will endure before me …" (Isa 66:22). Here the inference from the lesser to the greater applies: If heaven and earth, which were created only for Israel's honor, live and endure for all eternity, how much more does this go for the righteous, for whose sake the world was created! ‖ Seder Eliyahu Rabbah 17 (86): As they (humanity) returned to dust, they will not return (= resurrect) with the exception of Israel alone. As a consequence of the love with which he (God) loves them, and as a consequence of the joy in which he rejoices over them, he will place them on their feet from the dust and set them between his knees and hug them and press them and kiss them and bring them into the life of the future world; as it says, "As the new heaven and the new earth that I prepare will endure before me …" (Isa 66:22). — See further Midr. Ps. 46 § 2 above in B, n. *b*; SDeut 32:1 § 306 and Tg. Yer. II Deut 32:1 in B, n. *c*; Pesiq. 148A at § Rev 3:12 D.

Comment. As in 2 Bar. 44:12 (above in A, n. *d*), the expression "new world" עוֹלָם חָדָשׁ is also found in rabbinic literature. Here it means in the idiom "to see a new world" essentially "to enter into new relations, experience changed circumstances"; so Gen. Rab. 30 (18B.47, 50–55); Midr. Esth. 2:5 (93A.35–93B.1); Tanḥ. שמות 63A; TanḥB שמות § 11 (4A); Yalquṭ Simeoni on Job at the beginning. The expression is found once, though, also in an eschatological context. In Mek. Exod. 16:25 (58B) R. Eleazar of Modiim († ca. 135) says the following with reference to the "six days" in Exod 16:25: "If you are so happy to observe the Sabbath, God will give you six good gifts: the land of Israel, the future world עולם הבא, the new world עולם חדש, the kingdom of the house of David, the priesthood, and the Levitehood." — The same is found with a different connecting point and with a differing sequence of the six goods also in Mek. Exod. 18:9 (66B); lastly, these six gifts are briefly referred to in Mek. 59A. עולם הבא in this context would have been understood to refer to the heavenly world of souls = the garden of Eden, and עולם חדש to refer to the new age that appears after the days of the Messiah, so that עולם חָדָשׁ would be identical with the eschatological future world. So too Weiß on Mek. 58B and Bacher.[385]

21:1 B: The sea is no more.

The disappearance of the sea in the eschaton also appears in the pseudepigrapha.

See Sib. Or. 3:81ff.; 4:170ff. at § 2 Pet 3:7, n. *a*. ‖ Sibylline Oracles 5:158f.: "Yet a great star will come down from heaven into the terrible salt flood and will burn the deep sea and Babylon itself (Rome) and the land of Italy." — Sibylline Oracles 5:447: "Once in the last time the sea will be dry." See T. Levi 4: "And now know that the Lord will hold judgment over the children of men, when the rocks rupture and the sun goes out and the waters dry up and the fire is frozen and every creature is moved and the invisible spirits melt." — Assumption

385. Bacher, *Die Agada der Tannaïten*, 1:195.2.

of Moses 10:6: "The sea will recede to the abyss, and the springs will fail to appear and the rivers congeal." — Incidentally, Rashi once remarks on b. Šabb. 104A, presumably on the basis of older traditions: גיהנם קרוי ים "gehenna means sea." — See the passage b. Šabb. 104A in the excursus "Sheol, Gehenna, and the Garden of Eden," II, #7, n. *m*.

21:2 A: I saw the new Jerusalem coming down from heaven.

1. Ἰερουσαλὴμ καινή; see § Rev 3:12 B, #2.
2. καταβαίνουσαν ἐκ τοῦ οὐρανοῦ; see § Rev 3:12 C.

21:2 B: As a bride adorned for her husband (see § Rev 19:7, #1–3).

The earthly Jerusalem is similarly once compared with a bridegroom. Targum Psalm 48:3: "(Jerusalem) beautiful like a bridegroom, the joy of all who dwell on earth."

21:3: He will dwell with them, and they will be his people, and he, God, will be with them.

On the intimate communion of God with the righteous in the future world, see the excursus "Sheol, Gehenna, and the Garden of Eden," III, #4, n. *m* and *n*. — On the whole verse, see b. Qidd. 70B: R. Hama b. Hanina (ca. 260) said, "When God (one day) makes his Shekinah rest (on Israel), he will make it rest only on the legitimate families in Israel; for it says, 'At that time, says Yahweh, I will be God to all the families of Israel' (Jer 49:30). It does not say here 'to all Israelites,' but rather 'to all the families.' 'And they shall be my people' (Jer 49:30)." Rabbah bar Rab Huna (ca. 300) said, "This is Israel's great advantage over proselytes: while in the case of the Israelites it says (unconditionally on the basis of their natural descent from Abraham), 'I will be their God and they shall be my people' (Jer 31:32), it says in the case of proselytes (in a conditional way only on the basis of being explicitly joined to God), 'Whoever pledges his heart to draw near to me, says Yahweh—they shall be my people and I will be their God' (so Jer 30:21f. is interpreted)."

21:4 A: He will wipe away every tear from their eyes.

See Gen. Rab. 26 at § 1 Cor 15:54, #2; also see § Rev 7:17 B.

21:4 B: Death will be no more, nor lament, nor cries.

1. θάνατος οὐκ ἔσται; see § 1 Cor 15:54, #2. ‖ See Exod. Rab. 15 (77D) at § Rom 8:20f., n. *s*.
2. οὔτε πένθος οὔτε κραυγή; see Exod. Rab. 15 (77D) at § Rom 8:20f., n. *s*.

21:6: From the fount of the water of life freely.

1. πηγὴ τοῦ ὕδατος τῆς ζωῆς; see § Rev 7:17 A.
2. δωρεάν, see § Matt 10:8 B, n. *b*.

21:11: It had the glory of God, and its light was like the most precious stone.

Pesiqta 143B: R. Yose b. Jeremiah (so read with the parallels) and R. Dustai (both in the 4th cent.) said in the name of R. Levi (ca. 300), "Up until now you still do not know the (whole) praise of Jerusalem (see Pesiq. 143A at § Rev 21:16). But from its saying, 'I will be for her, says the Lord, a fiery wall all around, and I will be the glory inside her' (Zech 2:9)—you know the (whole) praise of Jerusalem." — See parallels at § Rev 21:16 to Pesiq. 143A. ‖ Exodus Rabbah 15 (77D): He will build Jerusalem with sapphires (see Isa 54:11f.), and those stones will shine like the sun and the nations of the world will come to see the glory of Israel (see Isa 60:3). — See the whole passage at § Rom 8:20f., n. *s*.

21:12: It has twelve gates, ... and names are written on them, which are those of the twelve tribes of Israel.

Midrash Psalm 48 § 4 (138B): How many gates will there be there (in the future Jerusalem)? 144; 12 for each tribe. — In b. B. Bat. 75B and Midr. Ps. 48 § 4 (138A) there are different details; see the passages at § Rev 21:17.

21:15: The one who spoke with me had a golden measuring rod.

See b. B. Bat. 75B at § Rev 21:16. ‖ μέτρον κάλαμον = קְנֵה הַמִּדָּה (Ezek 40:3, 5); likewise, m. Miqw. 2.10.

21:16: The city is a square, and its length is the same as its width. And he measured the city ... at 12,000 *stadia* (= 300 miles): its length and width and height are the same (each 3,000 *stadia*).

Babylonian Talmud Baba Batra 75B: R. Hanina b. Papa (ca. 300) said, "God wanted to give Jerusalem a certain measure; as it says, 'I said (to the man with the measure), "Where are you going?" He said to me, "To measure Jerusalem to see how great its width and how great its length is"' (Zech 2:6). Then the angels of service said to God, 'Lord of the world, you created many great cities in your world for the nations of the world without fixing the measure of their length and their width, and for Jerusalem, where your name, your sanctuary, righteous ones are, you want to fix a measure?' Immediately it says, 'He said to him, "Hurry and say this to that young man, 'Jerusalem shall lie open because of the multitude of people and livestock in it'"' (Zech 2:8)." ‖ Pesiqta 143A: Once R. Eleazar b. Azariah (ca. 100) and R. Eleazar of Modiim († ca. 135) sat and busied themselves with this passage of Scripture: "At that time Jerusalem will be called 'Yahweh's throne,' and all the gentiles will be gathered to her" (Jer 3:17). R. Eleazar b. Azariah said to R. Eleazar of Modiim, "Will Jerusalem be able to encompass (them all)?" He answered him, "God will say to Jerusalem, 'Elongate yourself, widen yourself, accept your hosts! Widen the space of your tent' (Isa 54:2), and all the gentiles will be gathered to her. Jerusalem will extend to the gate of Damascus. What is the scriptural basis? 'An oracle, a word of Yahweh is in the land of Hadrach and Damascus is its resting place' (so Zech 9:1 according to the midr.)." What does חַדְרָךְ mean? R. Judah (ca. 150) and R. Nehemiah (ca. 150). R. Judah said, "Hadrach means only the king, the Messiah, who will be sharp חַד against the nations of the world and mild רַךְ toward Israel." R. Nehemiah said, "The place is called Hadrach." R. Jose, the son of the Damascene (ca. 120), said, "By the temple service! I am from Damascus, and there is a place there that is called Hadrach." R. Judah said to him, "How then do you understand 'Damascus its resting place'?" (Does the Shekinah then rest in Damascus?!) (Answer:) "As a fig tree is narrow at the bottom but wide at the top, so too Jerusalem will widen itself, and those who went into exile will go up and come and camp in it to fulfill what is said: 'Damascus its resting place.' 'Resting place,' though, means only Jerusalem. As it says, 'This (Zion) is my resting place forever' (Ps 132:14)." (Jerusalem thus = Damascus, because the former will extend to the latter.) R. Judah said to him, "How then do you understand 'The city will be built on its hill' (Jer 30:18)?" He answered, "It will not be moved from its place (it will remain on its hill), but it will be broadened and be raised on all sides, and the exiles will come and camp in it, to fulfill what it said: 'You will break out (broaden yourself) to the right and left' (Isa 54:3). Thus into the width (from north to south). Into the length (from east to west); how do we know this? 'From the Tower of Hananel to the vats of the king' (Zech 14:10)." R. Berekhiah (ca. 340) said, "To the ocean (the Mediterranean Sea)." R. Zakkai the elder (ca. 250) said, "To the cisterns of Joppa." And these are not in conflict with each other. Whoever says, "To the ocean," means the vats that the king of all kings, God, laid out; and whoever says, "To the cisterns of Joppa," means the vats that king Solomon laid out (cf. 2 Chr 2:15). Thus into the length and into the width; into the height; how do we know this? "And it broadened and went upward more and more" (Ezek 41:7). It has been taught that R. Eliezer b. Jacob (I, ca. 90; II, ca. 150) said, "Jerusalem will one day be raised and ascend until it comes to the throne of glory, and it will say to God, 'The space is too narrow for me, make room for me so that I may dwell here!' (Isa 49:20)." — Parallels to the whole section or to individual parts are found in SDeut 1:1 § 1 (65A); Midr. Song. 7:5 (127B); Tanḥ. צו 142A; TanḥB יתרו § 14 (39A); צו § 16 (10B); Pesiq. 108A; Pesiq. Rab. 21 (103B); see also Pesiq. Rab. 41 (172B); Gen. Rab. 5 (4D); Lev. Rab. 10 (112C). ‖ Babylonian Talmud Baba Batra 75B: Rabbah († 331) said that R. Yohanan († 279) said, "One day God will make Jerusalem three *parasangs* high (about 17 kilometers); for it says, 'It will soar and its lower part will lie there' (Zech 14:10), that is, 'as its lower part'" (as its extent below = three *parasangs*, so too its extent on high). And how do we know that its lower part is three *parasangs*? Rabbah said, "An old man said to me, 'I saw the earlier Jerusalem, and it was as big as three *parasangs*.' Yet if you should say that the going up takes a lot of effort, Scripture teaches, 'Who are these who fly like a cloud, and like doves with their flapping?'"[386] (Isa 60:8). Rab Papa († 376) said, "Take from this that a cloud is raised three *parasangs* high.... 'And the chambers, chamber on chamber, three or thirty times'" (so Ezek 41:6 according to the midr.). What does "three or thirty times" mean? R. Abba b. Pappi (ca. 350) said in the name of R. Joshua of Sikhnin (ca. 330) that R. Levi (ca. 300, so read) said, "If there are three Jerusalems (i.e., if the future Jerusalem is three times as big as the earlier one), each (house) in it will have thirty floors on top of one another. Yet if there are thirty Jerusalems, each (house) in it will have three floors on top of one another." ‖ Babylonian Talmud Pesaḥim 50A: "On that day it will be holy to Yahweh, as long as a

---

386. S-B: On the service of the clouds in the future Jerusalem, cf. Midr. Ps. 48 § 4 (138A): Rab Nahman (ca. 400) said, "'What has been will be' (Eccl 1:9). As God took Israel into the glory of the clouds and enclosed them and carried them; as it says, 'I carried you on eagle's wings' (Exod 19:4)—so he will do for them one day as well; as it says, 'Who are these who fly like a cloud?' (Isa 60:8)." ‖ See TanḥB צו § 16 (10B) and Pesiq. Rab. 1 (2A) at § 1 Thess 4:17 A. — See also Tanḥ צו 142A.

horse casts shadows" (so Zech 14:20 according to the midr.). What does על מצילות הסוס mean? R. Joshua b. Levi (ca. 250) said, "One day God will add to the area of Jerusalem, as far as a horse runs and casts shadows" (i.e., as far as a horse can run from morning until noon; for at noon the shadow falls under the animal itself. Here מצילות is interpreted as a denominative of צֵל "shadow"). — The same is found in a somewhat different form in y. Pesaḥ. 3.30B.49. ‖ Pesiqta 137B: The area of Jerusalem = twelve square *mils*; see § Rev 21:21 B. ‖ Pesiqta 144B: R. Phineas (ca. 360) said in the name of R. Reuben (ca. 300), "One day God will fetch Sinai and Tabor and Carmel and build the sanctuary on their summits. And what is the scriptural basis? 'It will happen at the end of days, when the mountain of the house of Yahweh will be situated at the tops of the mountains' (Isa 2:2)." — Parallels are found in Midr. Ps. 36 § 6 (126A); 87 § 3 (189B).

21:17: Their walls are 144 cubits.

On the wall of the future Jerusalem, see b. B. Bat. 75B: Resh Laqish (ca. 250) said, "One day God will add to Jerusalem (specifically to its walls) 1,000 sides with cornerstones, 1,000 double towers, 1,000 castles connected to one another, and 1,000 overhanging gates with four colonnades. Each (of these installations) will be as large as Sepphoris in the time of its prosperity." In a baraita: R. Yose (ca. 150) said, "I saw Sepphoris in its prosperity, and there were in it 180,000 markets (outlets?) of people who sold spices for food." — The interpretation of the individual terms at the beginning of the passage is, incidentally, uncertain. — The parallel in Midr. Ps. 48 § 4 (138A) reads: How many corners (pillars?) will there be in (the future) Jerusalem? 1,184. How many towers will be in it? 1,485. How many gates with four colonnades? 1,496. How many running sources (νυμφαῖον)? 1,876.

21:18: The city is of pure gold, like pure glass.

See Exod. Rab. 15 (77D) at § Rev 21:11.

21:19: The foundation stones of the walls ... are decorated with all kinds of precious stones.

The following passages do not deal with the foundation stones but rather with the battlements of the walls. Babylonian Talmud Baba Batra 75A: "I will make the battlements of your walls out of כַּדְכֹּד (ruby?)" (Isa 54:12). R. Samuel b. Nahman (ca. 260) said, "Two angels in heaven, Gabriel and Michael, had different opinions about this. Others say, 'Two Amoraim in the West.' And who were they? Judah and Hezekiah, the sons of R. Hiyya (both ca. 240). The one said, '(*kadkod*) is *shoham*' (cf. Gen 2:12), and the other said, 'It is jasper.' God said to them, 'May it be like the latter and the former כְּדֵין וּכְדֵין' (interpretation of כַּדְכֹּד)." — In Midr. Ps. 87 § 2, R. Abba b. Kahana (ca. 310) is the author. ‖ Pesiqta 135B: "I will make the battlements of your walls out of *kadkod*" (Isa 54:12). R. Abba b. Kahana (ca. 310) said, "Like the latter and the former" (see the previous citation). R. Levi (ca. 300) said, "It is carbuncle" (read כַּרְכְּדוֹנִין = καρχηδόνιος). R. Joshua b. Levi (ca. 250) said, "They are carbuncle stones" (read כרכדוניא). R. Joshua (b. Levi) longed to see those carbuncle stones. Elijah of blessed remembrance came to him. He said to Elijah, "Will my lord show me those carbuncle stones?"

He answered him, "Yes!" And he showed them to him by a miracle. It happened namely that a ship went out into the great sea, which was full of *goyim* (non-Israelites), and there was only one Jewish child on it. A great storm arose against it in the sea; yet Elijah appeared to that child and said to him, "If you go to R. Joshua b. Levi and show him these carbuncle stones, I will save this ship for your sake." The child answered, "R. Joshua b. Levi is a great man of the age, and he will not believe me." He said to him, "He is gentle and will believe you; and when you show him them, do not show them to him in the presence of anyone, but rather lead him to a cavern that is three *mils* from Lud (Lydda), and show them to him there." Immediately a miracle happened (by the sudden landing of the ship), and the child came from there safely. He went to R. Joshua b. Levi and met him, as he sat in the great academy of Lud. He said to him, "My lord, I have something to tell you." R. Joshua b. Levi arose. Here one sees the gentleness (humility) of R. Joshua b. Levi; for he went a distance of three *mils* behind the child without saying to him, "What do you want from me?" When they came to his cavern, the child said to him, "My lord, these are those carbuncle stones of which the scholars have spoken." Yet when he saw them, all Lud became ablaze from their light. Then the child let them fall to the earth, and they were hidden. — The same is found in Pesiq. Rab. 32 (148B).

21:21 A: Each one of the gates consisted of one pearl.

Babylonian Talmud Baba Batra 75A: "And your gates out of carbuncle stones" (Isa 54:12). The following accords with this. R. Yohanan († 279) sat and gave a presentation: "One day God will provide gems and pearls that are 30 square cubits in size; and he will make an opening in them 10 cubits (wide) and 20 cubits (high) and then set them as gates of Jerusalem." Then a certain student laughed at him, "Now you do not find any as big as a pigeon's egg, so how should one find such as these?!" After a few days a ship went to sea. Then he saw angels of service, as they sat there and saw gems and pearled that were 30 square cubits in size, and there was an opening hollowed out in them 10 cubits (wide) and 20 cubits (high). He said to them, "For whom are these?" They answered him, "God will one day set them as the gates of Jerusalem." He came to R. Yohanan and said to him, "Give a presentation, Rabbi. Presenting suits you. As you said, so I have seen!" He answered him, "You fool ריקא (= ῥαχά Matt 5:22), if you had not seen, you would have not believed. You want to laugh about the words of the scholars?" Then he directed his eyes to him, and he became a heap of bones. It was objected (against what was said about the size of the gates of Jerusalem): "I make you go about upright קוממיות" (Lev 26:13). R. Meir (ca. 150) said, "In a size of 200 cubits, as much as two heights (קוממיות = שתי קומית) of the first man" (Adam was supposed to have been 100 cubits tall). R. Judah (ca. 150) said, "100 cubits, corresponding to the temple and its walls; as it says, 'Our sons shot up in their youth like plants, our daughters like beautifully hewn corner pillars, the reflection of the temple' (Ps 144:12)." (If this is the future size of human beings, how can we speak of gates that are supposed to be only 20 cubits high!) As R. Yohanan said, "It refers to the holes" (in the gates[?], not to the gates themselves). — Parallels are found in b. Sanh. 100A; Midr. Ps. 87 § 2 (189A); there are differences in Pesiq. 136B and Pesiq. Rab. 32 (149A); here R. Yohanan does not speak about the gates of Jerusalem, but rather about the east gate of the temple with its two small portals; see m. Šeqal. 6.3 and Pesiq. 136B and 137A at § Rev 21:22.

21:21 B: The street of the city is pure gold.

Pesiqta 137A: "And your whole border (your whole area) gems" (Isa 54:12). R. Benjamin b. Levi (ca. 325) said, "One day the borders of Jerusalem will be full of gems and pearls and the Israelites will come and take from them as they please (חפציהן expounds on the word in the base text, אבני חפץ, 'stones in which one takes pleasure'). Whereas in this world the boundaries (of pieces of land) are set with stones and *chaṣuba* herb (the roots of which are hard to remove), in the (messianic) future the borders will be fixed with gems and pearls. This is what is written, 'And your whole border gems.'" (137B:) R. Levi (ca. 300) said, "One day the borders of Jerusalem will be 12 square *mils* full of gems and pearls ..." (see the continuation at § Matt 5:25 B, where instead of "4 square *mils*," we should read "12 square *mils*"; there one also finds the parallel passages).

21:22: I did not see a temple in it.

The future Jerusalem without a temple was an unthinkable thought for the ancient synagogue. The construction of the sanctuary was the most taken for granted element in ancient Jewish hope about the future.

ʿAbodah, the 16th (17th) benediction of the Prayer of Eighteen Benedictions: Take pleasure, Yahweh our God, in your people Israel and in their prayer. And bring back the sacrificial service to the holy of holies of your house. And accept in love the fire sacrifices of Israel and their prayer with pleasure. And may the daily offering of Israel your people be pleasing. May our eyes see your return to Zion in mercy. Blessed be you, Yahweh, who makes his Shekinah return to Zion! ‖ Habinenu Prayer (Palestinian recension): May all who trust in you rejoice over the construction of your city and over the renewal (= restoration) of your sanctuary. — Babylonian recension: Over the construction of your city and the preparation of your temple. ‖ Kaddish de-Rabbanan: May his great name be glorified and sanctified, which will one day renew the world ... and build the city of Jerusalem and complete the holy and glorious temple. ‖ Pesiqta 136B: R. Jeremiah (ca. 325) said in the name of R. Samuel b. Isaac (ca. 300), "One day God will make the eastern gate of the sanctuary, it itself and its two small portals, out of a pearl." — In Midr. Ps. 87 § 2 (189A), R. Judah (ca. 320) is the tradent; it is anonymous in Pesiq. Rab. 32 (149A). ‖ Pesiqta 137A: Once a pious man strolled on the rocky cliff of the sea of Hefa. He thought in his heart and said, "Will God one day make the east gate of the sanctuary and the two small portals out of a pearl?" Immediately a voice from heaven went out, which said to him, "If you were not a completely pious man, the punitive righteousness would have struck this man (= you). He created the whole world in only six days (see Exod 31:17), and he should not be able to make the east gate of the sanctuary, it itself and its two small portals, out of a pearl?" Immediately he pled for mercy for himself and said to God, "Lord of the worlds, if I have pondered (in doubt) in my heart, I did not express it with my lips." At once a miracle happened for him: the sea was split before him, and he saw angels of service, as they chiseled at it (the pearl) and engraved it and added wickerwork to it (as an adornment). They said to him, "This is the east gate of the sanctuary, it itself and its two small portals, made out of a pearl!" – The same is found more briefly with the authorial name of R. Phineas b. Hama (ca. 360) in Midr. Ps. 87 § 2 (189A). ‖ See b. B. Bat. 75B and Pesiq. 144B at § Rev 21:16.

21:23: The city will not need the sun or the moon to illumine it, for the glory of God illumines it.

Pesiqta 145A: R. Samuel b. Nahman (ca. 260) said, "In this world they (the Israelites) walk in the light of the sun by day and in the light of the moon at night. But in the future they will walk neither in the light of the sun by day nor in the light of the moon at night; for it says, 'No longer will the sun serve as light for you by day, and the moon will not shine as brightness for you' (Isa 60:19). And in whose light will they walk? In the light of God; as it says, 'Yahweh will be your eternal light, and the days of your mourning will be completed' (Isa 60:20)." – The same is found in Midr. Ps. 36 § 6 (126A); see § Matt 4:16, middle. ‖ Exodus Rabbah 15 (77D): God will renew ten things in the future. First, he will illuminate the world (see Isa 60:19, 20, as above). Yet can a person look at God (if he himself is supposed to be the light of the world)? What will God do with the sun? He will make its light shine forty-nine times as strong; as it says, "The light of the moon will be like the sunlight and the light of the sun will be seven times sevenfold" (so Midr. Isa. 30:26). God will also command the sun to heal a sick person; as it says, "The sun of mercy will rise for you, who fear my name, with healing under its wings" (Mal 3:20). (See the whole passage at § Rom 8:20f., n. *s*.) ‖ Sibylline Oracles 3:787: "In your (Zion's) midst he (God) will dwell; you will have immortal light." ‖ In Amos 5:18, the day of Yahweh is described as a day "that is darkness and not light." – Also, 4 Ezra 7:39ff.: "That day is such that it will not have sun or moon or stars; no clouds nor thunder nor lightning; no wind nor rain nor fog; neither darkness nor evening nor morning; no summer nor spring nor heat; no winter nor ice nor frost; no hail nor storm nor dew; no midday nor night nor dusk; no splendor nor shining, but rather all alone the splendor of the glory of the Most High by which all will be able to see what is destined for them. See also Sib. Or. 3:88ff.

21:24 A: The nations will walk in its light.

Pesiqta 144B: R. Hoshaiah (ca. 225) said in the name of R. Aphes (Ephes [ca. 210]), "One day Jerusalem will be a light קסילפנס (= ξυλοφανός?[387]) for the nations of the world, in whose light they will walk; as it says, 'Nations will flow to your light and kings to the rising of your shining' (Isa 60:3)." ‖ Babylonian Talmud Baba Batra 75A: R. Yohanan († 279) said, "One day God will make for the righteous a tabernacle from the skin of Leviathan; as it says, 'You will fill it with tabernacles (שוכות interpreted as סוכות) from its skin' (so Job 40:31 according to the midr.).… The rest (of its skin) God will spread over the walls of Jerusalem, and its splendor will shine from one end of the world to the other; as it says, 'Nations will flow …' (Isa 60:3, as above)." ‖ TanḥumaB בהעלתך § 2 (23B): (God said to Israel,) "If you

387. Krauß, *Lehnwörter*, vol. 1; Levy, *Chaldäisches Wörterbuch*, 4:346.

are careful to light lamps for my name, I too will make a great light shine for you in the future; as it says, 'Arise, become light; for your light comes.... And nations will flow to your light ...' (Isa 60:1, 3)." ‖ See also § Rom 3:9 A, #3, B, n. *n*; § Luke 2:32; see Midr. Ps. 36 § 6 (125B) at § Matt 4:16, middle; Exod. Rab. 15 at § Rev 21:11. ‖ Jerusalem as the world capital. ʾAbot de Rabbi Nathan 35 at the end: R. Simeon b. Gamaliel (ca. 140) said, "One day Jerusalem will be where all the nations and kingdoms gather; as it says, 'All the nations will gather to the name of Yahweh in Jerusalem' (Jer 3:17)." ‖ Midrash Song of Songs 1:5 (87B): R. Yohanan († 279) said, "One day Jerusalem become a metropolis for all lands." – Parallels are found in Exod. Rab. 23 (85B); TanḥB supplements to דברים § 3 (2B). ‖ See Pesiq. 143A at § Rev 21:16.

21:24 B: The kings of the earth will bring their glory into it.

See supporting texts at § Matt 2:11. – Also, Pss. Sol. 17:31: "That nations will come from the end of the earth to see his (the Messiah's) glory, bringing as a gift their (the Israelites') exhausted sons." ‖ Midrash Song of Songs 4:8 (114A): R. Judah (ca. 320) said, "... The nations of the world will one day present themselves (namely the Jews living in the diaspora) to the king, the Messiah, as a gift; for it says, 'They will bring all your brothers from all the nations as a votive offering for Yahweh ...' (Isa 66:20)...." R. Aha (ca. 320) said, "It does not say, 'You nations, bring Yahweh the generations (of Israel, so the midrash)' (Ps 96:7), but rather, 'Bring the generations (of Israel) in honor and glory' (so the midrash), that is, when you bring them, you shall not bring them in a scornful way, but rather in honor and glory." – There is a parallel in Midr. Ps. 87 § 6 (189B).

21:25 A: Its gates will not be closed by day.

See Isa 60:11. – See b. B. Bat. 75B at § Rev 21:16.

21:25 B: There will be no night there.

Exodus Rabbah 18 (81A): In this world (God) did a miracle for the Israelites at night (reference: killing the Egyptian firstborn), for it was a passing miracle. Yet in the future night will become day; as it says, "The light of the moon will be like the sunlight ..." (Isa 30:26).

21:27: No common thing may enter it ....

Psalms of Solomon 17:30: "He (the Messiah) will make Jerusalem pure and holy, as it was at the beginning." ‖ See b. B. Bat. 75B at § Rom 1:6.

22:1: He showed me a stream of living water ..., which proceeded from the throne of God.

Tosefta Sukkah 3.3–10 (195f.): Why is it (the one gate on the southside of the inner forecourt) called "water gate"?... R. Eliezer b. Jacob (I, ca. 90; II, ca. 150) said, "In it 'the waters will trickle forth' מפכין (cf. Ezek 47:2). This teaches that they will trickle forth and rise up as high as the mouth of a flask פַּךְ (an interpretation of מפכין), but 'they will come forth below the threshold of the house' (Ezek 47:1). And so it says further, 'When the man went out to the east with the measure in his hand, he measured 1,000 cubits. Then he made me go through the water, water up to the ankles' (Ezek 47:3). This teaches that a person will go through the water up to his ankles. 'Then he measured (another) 1,000 and made me go through the water, water up to the knee' (Ezek 47:4). This teaches that a person will go through the water up to his knee.... 'Then he measured (another) 1,000 and made me go through the water, water up to the hips' (Ezek 47:4). This teaches that a person will go through the water up to his hips. 'Then he measured (another) 1,000 and made me go through (so the midrash cites the text); (it was) a stream that I could not go through' (Ezek 47:5). Perhaps he could not pass over by foot, but by swimming (read בְּסָחוֹ instead of בסוכי), (or) perhaps he could have gone over on a small boat?! Scripture teaches, 'For the waters went high מי סחו' (Ezek 47:5), that is, they went too high for someone to swim (מי סחו read as one word = מִסָּחוֹ). Perhaps he could not go over in a small boat, but in a large ship? Scripture teaches, 'A boat with oars will not go upon it' (Isa 33:21). Perhaps he could not go over in a large ship, but in a large, fast glider? Scripture teaches, 'A mighty war ship will not cross over it' (Isa 33:21). It further says, 'It will happen on that day that living waters will go out from Jerusalem, half to the anterior sea and half to the hinter-sea, in summer and in winter they will be' (Zech 14:8). Maybe other sources will mix with it! Scripture teaches, 'On that day a wellspring will be opened for the house of David and for the inhabitants of Jerusalem against sin and impurity' (Zech 13:1). And where will they flow? Into the Great Sea (= the Mediterranean Sea) and into the Sea of Tiberias and into the Sea of Sodom (= Dead Sea), to heal its waters; as it says, 'And he said to me, "These waters stream out to the east area,"' that is, the Sea of Sodom, 'and drain off to the lowlands,' that is, the Sea of Tiberias, 'and come (here a textual corruption), and the waters will be healed' (Ezek 47:8), that is, the Great Sea. 'And it will happen ...' (Ezek 47:9–11)." — This is the oldest passage that deals with waters that will one day proceed from the sanctuary. The next oldest is found in y. Šeqal. 6.50A.3: It is written, "It will happen on that day that living waters will proceed from Jerusalem" (Zech 14:8). In a baraita it has been taught: From the holy of holies to the curtain (the waters will be as miniscule) as the antennae of a crab (?) or of turtles (?); from the curtain to the golden altar as the antennae of locusts; from the golden altar to the threshold of the house (we have transposed the sentences, as the context demands) as the threads of the hoist; from the threshold of the house to the forecourts (temple halls) like the threads of the woof; from there on like the outflow from the opening of a flask; (as it says,) "And behold, the waters trickled forth מפכים (as from a flask פַּךְ) from the right wing of the house" (Ezek 47:2). Further, it is written, "When the man went out to the east with the measure in his hand, he measured 1,000 cubits and made me go through the water, water אפסים" (Ezek 47:3), that is, water up to the ankles. "And he measured (another) 1,000 and made me go through the water, water of the knee" (Ezek 47:4), that is, water up to the knee. "And he measured (another) 1,000 and made me go through the water, water of the hips" (Ezek 47:4), that is, water up to the hips. From there on "he measured 1,000, a stream through which I could not go" (Ezek 47:5); even a large, fast glider could not cross it. What is the scriptural basis? "A mighty war ship could not cross it" (Isa 33:21). Why? "For the waters went high מי שחו" (Ezek 47:5). What does מי שחו mean? "So that no one could swim through them" מלשוט (see above in t. Sukkah).... (Line 19:) It is written, "He said to me, 'These waters stream out to the east area'" (Ezek 47:8), that is, the Sea of Samekho (= Hule- or Semekhonite Sea; see § Matt 3:5, #2, S-B footnote); "and they drain off to the lowlands" (Ezek 47:8), that is, the Sea of Tiberias; "and come (lead) to the Sea" (Ezek 47:8), that is, the Salt Sea (= Dead Sea); "into the sea from which waters are emitted" (so the midrash interprets המוצאים in Ezek 47:8), that is, the Great Sea (the Mediterranean Sea). And why is its name called "from which waters are emitted"? In view of the two times that it went out: once in the time of Enosh and once in the time of the diaspora (the confusion of languages).... (Line 26:) ("So that the stream from the sanctuary should heal the waters,") pertains to the Great Sea and the Salt Sea, namely to make them fresh. But (it pertains) also to the Sea of Tiberias and to the Sea of Samekho (even though their water is sweet), namely to multiply their fish: "According to their kind their fish will be there" (Ezek 47:10), that is, their fish will be of all possible kinds. It has been taught: Rabban Simeon b. Gamaliel (ca. 140) recounted the following: "Once I traveled to Sidon, and they brought before me more than 300 kinds of fish in a bowl. 'And the waters will be healed' (Ezek 47:8). 'Its swamps and its marshes will not be healed וְלֹא יֵרָפְאוּ; they are determined for salt' (Ezek 47:11). It is written, 'And the waters will be healed' (Ezek 47:8). Then you say (in verse 11), 'The waters will not be healed'? Perhaps this is a place (in verse 11) that is named Lo-Yerafu." (Verse 11 should thus be translated: "Its swamps and its marshes and Lo-Yerafu are determined for salt.") — See shorter parallels in b. Yoma 77B; Pesiq. Rab. 33 (156B); Pesiq. 125A; Midr. Lam. 2:13 (67B). ‖ In Pirqe R. El. 51 (30C), the stream that proceeds from the sanctuary appears to be identified with the spring of Miriam, which guided Israel in the wilderness wandering. It separates into twelve streams corresponding to the twelve tribes of Israel. ‖ See Exod. Rab. 15 (77D) at § Rom 8:20f., n. s.

22:2: On both sides (of the stream) are trees of life, which yield fruit twelve times. They yield their fruit every month, and the leaves of the trees serve for the healing of the nations.

Jerusalem Talmud Šeqalim 6.50A.31: "At the river shores on both sides there will be all kinds of trees with edible fruit growing. Its leaves will not wither and its fruits will not wear out. Every month לְחֳדָשָׁיו they will bear fresh fruits; for their waters—they go out from the sanctuary—and their fruits serve as food and their leaves as medicine" (Ezek 47:12). In a baraita it has been taught: R. Judah (ca. 150) said, "In this world grain needs 6 months and the tree fruit 12 months (to grow and ripen). But in the future the grain will need 1 month and tree fruit 2 months; for it says, 'In their months (plural = in 2 months) they will produce fresh fruit' (Ezek 47:12; while the grain needs half the time, so 1 month)." R. Yose (ca. 150) said, "In this world, grain needs 6 months and tree fruit 12 months. In the future, the grain will need 15 days and tree fruit 1 month. For thus we find that the grain in Joel's days needed 15 days until the offering of the firstling sheaf from it; for it says, 'You children of Zion, rejoice and be glad in Yahweh, your God.... He makes the early rain and the late rain come down on you on the first (of Nisan)' (Joel 2:23)." (On the 1st of Nisan, there will be the early rain and the late rain and sowing. On the 16th of Nisan, rejoicing at the presentation of the firstling sheaf. Hence, from sowing until harvest, 15 days. Tree fruit needs twice the time, so 1 month.) Yet how does R. Yose maintain the words "In their months they will produce fresh fruits" (Ezek 47:12)? He explains it as follows: "In each month they will produce fresh fruits." — The same is found in y. Taʿan. 1.64A.48. ‖ Numbers Rabbah 21 (192B): What does "They bring forth early fruits every month" (Ezek 47:12) mean? Every tree will bring forth different early fruits each month, and the early fruits of one month will not be like those of another month. ‖ Babylonian Talmud Šabbat 30B: Rabban Gamaliel (ca. 90) sat and gave a presentation: "One day (in the messianic age) the trees will bring forth fruits daily; for it says, 'It will prepare branches and bring forth fruit' (Ezek 17:23); just as branches daily, so too fruits daily." Then that one (a certain) student[388] laughed at him and said, "It is written, 'There is nothing new under the sun' (Eccl 1:9)!" He said to him, "Come, I will show you an example of this in this world!" He went out and showed him a caper shrub. ‖ See Exod. Rab. 15 (77D) at § Rom 8:20f., n. s. ‖ Jerusalem Talmud Šeqalim 6.50A.41: "Their leaves will serve as medicine" (Ezek 47:12). R. Yohanan († 297) said, "As a means of healing תְּרַפְיָה (= θεραπεία); one will look at them, and eating them is healing." Rab († 247) and Samuel († 254). The one said, "To loosen the mouth above" (i.e., their leaves serve to give the mute speech). The other said, "To loosen the mouth below" (to open the cervix of barren women). R. Hanina (ca. 225) and R. Joshua b. Levi (ca. 250). The one said, "To loosen the mouth of the barren"; and the other said, "To loosen the mouth of the mute." — In b. Sanh. 100A, the view of Rab and Samuel is represented by Rab Isaac b. Abdimi (ca. 300) and Rab Hisda († 309) and the view of Hanina and Joshua b. Levi by Hezekiah (ca. 240) and Bar Qappara (ca. 220). Then follows: R. Yohanan († 279) said, "As medicine in the literal sense. What does 'as medicine' mean?" R. Samuel b. Nahman (ca. 260) said, "To beautify the face of those who occupy themselves with the mouth (i.e., the scholars)." — Further parallels with differences can be found in the following: b. Menaḥ. 98A; Midr. Song. 4:13 (116B); Deut. Rab. 1 (195A); Midr. Ps. 23 § 7 (101B). ‖ Pirqe Rabbi Eliezer 51 (30D): There on the shore of the stream all kinds of trees will grow, producing every fruit according to its kind (see Ezek 47:12). And every month they will bring forth ripe fruits (see Ezek 47:12); while one is eaten, the other will grow; for it says, "Their waters—they will go out from the sanctuary, and their fruits will serve as food and their leaves as medicine" (Ezek 47:12). Everyone who is sick who bathes in those waters will be healed; as it says, "Everyone will live, wherever the stream comes" (Ezek 47:9). Everyone who has a wound will take from their leaves and be healed; for it says, "Their leaves as medicine." R. Yohanan said, "(The leaves serve) as a means of healing: one will look at their leaves, and eating them is healing" (read ותרף מזונה instead of ושרף מזונה).

22:4: They will see his face (see § Matt 5:8 B, #2).

22:5: There will be no more night, and they will not need ... the light of the sun (see § Rev 21:23, 25).

22:11: Whoever acts unjustly, let him act unjustly ....

There are echoes of this in b. Yoma 38B; see the passage at § Matt 15:11, #3.

388. S-B: If this referred to the apostle Paul, there would of course be a confusion of Gamaliel II with his grandfather Gamaliel I.

22:15 A: Outside are the dogs.

See § Matt 15:26 notes *e* and *f* and § Phil 3:2. — Here reference may also be made to b. Beṣah 20B: The school of Hillel said, "... What do the words 'This day shall be a day of remembrance for you' (Exod 12:14) mean? For you, and not for the Samaritans; for you, and not for the dogs (= non-Israelites)."

22:15 B: Whoever does and loves a lie.

Targum Psalm 5:6: "I hate all who practice lies and deceit."

22:16: I am ... the bright morning star.

Mordecai is once compared with the morning star. See Tg. Esth. 10:3: "Mordecai was like the morning star כּוֹכַב נוּגְהָא (really 'star of splendor' = Venus), which shines among the stars, and the dawn that comes up at the time of morning."

22:17: Water of life ... freely (see § Rev 21:6).

22:18f.: If anyone adds to them ..., and if anyone takes away.

See b. Meg. 14A and Midr. Ruth 2:4 (130B) at § Matt 11:13, #1.

22:20: Yes, I am coming quickly. Amen! Come, Lord Jesus!

The Amen! in the mouth of the hearer accepts with desire and affirmation the assurance he hears: "I am coming quickly," and it means, "Yes, let it be so! Come, Lord Jesus!"

So, for example, Num. Rab. 20 at the end: God said, "In this world they (the Israelites) are numbered because of sin, but in the future (the messianic age), then 'the number of the children of Israel will be like the sand of the sea, which cannot be measured and cannot be counted' (Hos 2:1). Quickly, Amen! May it be his will (so be it)!"

Bibliography

Bacher, Wilhelm. *Die Agada der babylonischen Amoräer: Ein Beitrag zur Geschichte der Agada und zur Einleitung in den babylonischen Talmud.* Straßburg: Trübner, 1878.

———. *Die Agada der palästinensischen Amoräer.* Vol. 1. Straßburg: Trübner, 1892.

———. *Die Agada der palästinensischen Amoräer.* Vol. 3. Straßburg: Trübner, 1899.

———. *Die Agada der Tannaïten.* 2nd ed. Vol. 1. Strassburg: Trübner, 1902.

———. *Die Agada der Tannaïten.* 2nd ed. Vol. 2. Strassburg: Trübner, 1902.

Bertholdt, Leonhard. *Christologia Judaeorum Jesu apostolorumque aetate.* Erlangae: Palm, 1811.

Bousset, Wilhelm. *Die Religion des Judentums im neutestamentlichen Zeitalter.* 3rd ed. Berlin: Reuther & Reichard, 1903.

Christian Fabricius, Johann. *Codex Pseudepigraphus Veteris Testamenti.* Vol. 1. Hamburg & Leipzig: Liebezeit, 1713.

Cremer, Hermann. *Biblisch-theologisches Wörterbuch des neutestamentlichen Griechisch.* 11th ed. Stuttgart: Perthes, 1923.

Dalman, G. *Die Worte Jesu: Mit Berücksichtigung des nachkanonischen jüdischen Schriftums and der aramäischen Sprache erörtert.* 2nd ed. Vol. 1. Leipzig: Hinrichs, 1930.

Dalman, Gustaf. "Aramaische Dialektproben." *Monatsschrift für Geschichte und Wissenschaft des Judentums* 41 (1897).

———. *Der leidende und der sterbende Messias der Synagoge im ersten nachchristlichen Jahrtausend.* Berlin: Reuther, 1888.

———. *Jesus-Jeschua: Die Drei Sprachen Jesu; Jesus in der Synagoge, auf dem Berge, Neim Passahmahl, am Kreuz.* Leipzig: Hinrich, 1922.

Delitzsch, Franz. "Horae Hebraicae et Talmudicae: Ergänzungen zu Lightfoot und Schöttgen." *Zeitschrift für die gesammte lutherische Theologie und Kirche* 38 (1877).

———. "Horae Hebraicae et Talmudicae: VIII. Zweiter Brief an die Korinther." *Zeitschrift für die gesammte lutherische Theologie und Kirche* (1877): 450–54.

Dillmann, August. *Das Buch Henoch.* Leipzig: Vogel, 1853.

Friedländer, Moriz. *Der vorchristliche jüdische Gnosticismus.* Göttingen: Vandenhoeck & Ruprecht, 1898.

Fritzsche, Otto F. *Kurzgefasstes Exegetisches Handbuch zu den Apokryphen des Alten Testamentes: Die Weisheit Jesus-Sirach's.* Vol. 5. Leipzig: Hirzel, 1859.

Geiger, Abraham. *Urschrift und Übersetzungen der Bibel: In ihrer Abhängigkeit von der innern Entwicklung des Judentums.* Breslau: Hainauer, 1857.

Grätz, Heinrich. *Geschichte der Juden von den ältesten Zeiten bis auf die Gegenwart.* 2nd ed. Vol. 4. Leipzig: Leiner, 1900.

Horowitz, Chaim Meir. *Sammlung kleiner Midraschim.* Berlin: Itzkowski, 1881.

Kautzsch, E., ed. *Die Apokryphen und Pseudepigraphen des Alten Testaments.* Vol. 1. Freiburg im Breisgau & Leipzig: Mohr (Siebeck), 1900.

Kittel, Gerhard. "Die Fünfzahl Als Geläufige Zahl Und Als Stilistisches Motiv." *Arbeiten Zur Religionsgeschichte Des Urchristentums* 1.3 (1920).

———. "Die 'Macht' auf dem Haupte 1 Cor 11, 10." *Arbeiten für Religionsgeschichte des Urchristentums* 1.3 (1920).

———. *Rabbinica: Paulus im Talmud; Die "Macht" auf dem Haupte; Runde Zahlen.* Leipzig: Hinrich, 1920.

———. *Sifre zu Deuteronomium: Übersetzt und erläutert.* Stuttgart: Kohlhammer, 1922.

Klostermann, August. *Probleme im Aposteltexte neu erörtert.* Gotha: Perthes, 1883.

Kohut, Alexander. *Über die jüdische Angelologie und Dämonologie in ihrer Abhängigkeit vom Parsismus.* Leipzig: Brockhaus, 1866.

Krauß, Samuel. *Griechische und lateinische Lehnwörter im Talmud, Midrasch und Targum.* Vol. 1. Berlin: S. Calvary & Co., 1898.

———. *Griechische und lateinische Lehnwörter im Talmud, Midrasch und Targum.* Vol. 2. Berlin: S. Calvary & Co., 1898.

———. *Talmudische Archäologie.* Vol. 1. Leipzig: Fock, 1910.

———. *Talmudische Archäologie.* Vol. 2. Leipzig: Fock, 1910.

Laible, Heinrich. "Der zerrissene Tempelvorhang und die eingestürzte Oberschwelle des Tempeleingangs von Talmud bezeugt." *NZK* 35 (1924).

Levy, J. *Neuhebräisches und Chaldäisches Wörterbuch über die Talmudim und Midraschim.* Vol. 1. Leipzig: Brockhaus, 1876.

———. *Neuhebräisches und Chaldäisches Wörterbuch über die Talmudim und Midraschim.* Vol. 2. Leipzig: Brockhaus, 1876.

———. *Neuhebräisches und Chaldäisches Wörterbuch über die Talmudim und Midraschim.* Vol. 3. Leipzig: Brockhaus, 1883.

———. *Neuhebräisches und Chaldäisches Wörterbuch über die Talmudim und Midraschim*. Vol. 4. Leipzig: Brockhaus, 1889.

Lipsius, Richard Adelbert. *Die Apokryphen Apostelgeschichten und Apostellegenden*. Vol. 1. Braunschweig: Schwetschke & Sohn, 1883.

Lueken, W. *Michael: Eine Darstellung und Vergleichung der judischen und der morgenländisch-christlichen Tradition vom Erzengel Michael*. Göttingen: Vandenhoeck & Ruprecht, 1898.

Némethy, Geyza. *Euhemeri reliquiae: Collegit, Prolegomenis et Adnotationibus Instruxit*. Budapest: Kiadja a Magyar Tud. Akadémia, 1889.

Neubauer, Adolf. *La Géographie du Talmud*. Paris: Trèves, 1868.

Philo. *Philōnos tou Ioudaiou Ta Heuriskomena hapanta: Philonis Iudaei Opera quae reperiri potuerunt omnia*. Edited by Thomas Mangey. London: Innys, 1742.

Riehm, E. *Handwörterbuch des Biblischen Altertums für gebildete Bibelleser*. Leipzig: Velhagen & Klasing, 1884.

Sachs, Michael. *Beiträge zur Sprach- und Alterthumsforschung: aus jüdischen Quellen*. Vol. 1. Berlin: Veit, 1852.

Schlatter, Adolf. *Die Kirche Jerusalems vom years 70–130*. Gütersloh: Bertelsmann, 1898.

Schöttgen, Christian. *Horae Hebraicae et Talmudicae in universum Novum Testamentum*. Vol. 1. Leipzig: Christoph. Hekelii B. Filium, 1733.

———. *Horae Hebraicae et Talmudicae in universum Novum Testamentum*. Vol. 2. Leipzig: Christoph. Hekelii B. Filium, 1742.

Schürer, Emil. *Geschichte des jüdischen Volkes im Zeitalter Jesu Christi*. 4th ed. Vol. 1. Leipzig: Hinrichs, 1901.

———. *Geschichte des jüdischen Volkes im Zeitalter Jesu Christi*. 4th ed. Vol. 2. Leipzig: Hinrichs, 1907.

———. *Geschichte des jüdischen Volkes im Zeitalter Jesu Christi*. 4th ed. Vol. 3. Leipzig: Hinrichs, 1909.

Siegfried, Carl. *Philo von Alexandria als Ausleger des alten Testaments: An sich selbst und nach seinem geschichtlichen Einfluss betracht*. Jena: Dufft, 1875.

Singer, W. *Das Buch der Jubiläen oder die Leptogenesis*. Stuhlweissenburg, Hungary: Singer, 1898.

Spanier, A. *Die Toseftaperiode in der tannaitischen Literatur*. Berlin: Schwetschke, 1922.

Spitta, Friedrich. *Zur Geschichte und Literatur des Urchristentums*. Vol. 2. Göttingen: Vandenhoeck & Ruprecht, 361AD.

Steindorff, Georg, trans. *Die Apokalypse des Elias*. Leipzig: Hinrichs, 1899.

Strack, Hermann L. *Die Bücher Genesis, Exodus, Leviticus und Numeri Erste Abteilung*. Kurzgefasster Kommentar zu den heiligen Schriften des Alten und Neuen Testament. Munich: Beck, 1894.

———. *Einleitung in das Alte Testament einschliesslich Apokryphen und Pseudepigrapha*. 6th ed. Munich: Beck, 1906.

———. *Einleitung in den Talmud und Midraš*. 5th ed. Munich: Beck, 1921.

———. *Jesus, die Häretiker und die Christen: nach den ältesten jüdischen Angaben: Texte, Übersetzung und Erläuterungen*. Leipzig: Hinrichs, 19s10.

———. *Sanhedrin-Makkoth. "Gerichtshof, Geißelstrafe."* Munich: Hinrich, 1910.

Volz, Paul. *Jüdische Eschatologie von Daniel bis Akiba*. Tübingen: Mohr, 1903.

Wagenseil, Johann Christoph. *Sota*. Altdorf: Endter, 1674.

Winer, Georg Benedict. *Biblisches Reallexikon*. 3rd ed. Vol. 2. Leipzig: Reclam, 1847.

Zahn, Theodore. "Der zerrissene Tempelvorhang." *NZK* 13 (1902).